Fiske and Fisk family : being the record of the descendants of Symond Fiske, lord of the manor of Stadhaugh, Suffolk County, England, from the time of Henry IV to date, including all the American members of the family

Frederick Clifton Pierce 1855-1904

Charolette -1831-1890
Nathan Fisk -1791-1857
Experience Fisk -1751-1825
Nathan Fisk -1727-1788
William " -1678-1750
Lt Nathan Fisk -1643-1694
Nathan Fisk -1615-1696
Nathaniel " -1594-1675
Nathaniel " -1574-
William Fiske -1550-1620
Sir Robert Fiske -1521-1600
Richard Fiske -1493-1536
Geoffrey Fiske -1462-1538
Geoffrey Fiske -1427-1504
Lord Symond Fiske -1399-1464

FISKE AND FISK FAMILY

BEING THE RECORD OF THE

Descendants of Symond Fiske, Lord of the Manor of Stad-
haugh, Suffolk County, England, from the time of
Henry IV. to Date, including all the American
Members of the Family.

BY

FREDERICK CLIFTON PIERCE,

AUTHOR OF THE

Histories of Grafton and Barre, Mass., and Gibson, Harwood, Pierce,
Peirce, Pearce, Forbes, Forbush, and Whitney Genealogies.

Ffische, Fisc, Fiske, Fisk (spell it either way)
Meant true knighthood, freedom, faith, good qualities that stay.
Brethren, let the ancient name mean just the same for aye:
" Forward, every youth!   To seek the higher good " today!

REV. PERRIN B. FISKE, Lyndon, Vt.

PUBLISHED BY THE AUTHOR

1896
PRESS OF W. B. CONKEY COMPANY
CHICAGO, ILL.

To Flora,

MY ANCESTOR, THIS VOLUME IS MOS
RESPECTFULLY DEDICATED BY

The Author.

ANCESTRAL WORSHIP.

EGYPTIAN mappage or the Grecian urn
    Did once perpetuate a father's clay;
    Preserving through slow centuries and gray
The human remnant for the hope eterne.
And what the fires of funerals could not burn,
    Nor Time's insidious tooth gnaw quite away,
    Became a shrine of virtues, where might pray
The latest sons, and of their fathers learn.

But we, grown wiser, plant a family tree,
    And 'neath its broadening branches sit us down,
Content to trace a noble pedigree
    Unapt to urn a rich and high renown;
Content to dream of knights armed *cap-a-pie*,
    Yet hoping from the sky to see a crown.

HORACE SPENCER FISKE.

CHICAGO, May 6, 1896.

TABLE OF CONTENTS.

LIST OF ILLUSTRATIONS.

AUTHOR'S PREFACE.

I VENTURE the assertion that thus far no antidote has been discovered for the cure of the so-called "genealogical fever." My friends tell me I have it in an aggravated form and it would seem so. Last year I published the Whitney Genealogy, a volume of 700 pages, and now present "The Fiske Family." I have been greatly assisted in my work by Bond's Watertown and the volume compiled by Rev. Albert A. Fiske of Austin, Ill., on the Amherst, N. H., Fiskes. The family is noted for its strong religious proclivities inherited from its English ancestors, who on account of their Puritanic belief, were obliged to flee from their native land or be beheaded or burnt at the stake at the pleasure of their fanatical associates. One of the emigrant ancestors—a graduate of Immanuel College and an eminent divine—was secreted in a wood-pile for nearly a year and finally escaped to America in disguise, here to become one of the ablest preachers; and as Cotton Mather said, "Did he shine in the golden candlestick of Chelmsford, a plain, but an able, powerful and useful preacher of the Gospel." But few of the early New England families can boast of as many descendants who were in the various professions as the Fiske family.

Until this publication the many emigrant ancestors of the Fiskes have not been connected in any one publication. The matter has been arranged in the same manner as my previous publications, like the Register issued by the New England Historic-Genealogical Society. It is the simplest, most comprehensive and the best of any plan yet devised.

A number of abbreviations will be found in the book of which the following are explanations: ae., aged; abt., about; dau., daughter; dec'd, deceased; res., resides or resided, residence; w., wife; wid., widow and widower; yr., year; n. f. k., nothing further known; s. p., sine prole (without issue). There are a number of other abbreviations of such common use that their meaning will be readily understood. A name in parenthesis thus: Anna Fisk, dau. of Robert and Sybil (Gould) Fiske, indicates the maiden name of the mother. An interrogation point implies doubt or want of absolute certainty. Birthplaces of the children are not always given, but can be ascertained by reference to the residence of the parents which is always given. I wish to return thanks to all those who so generously furnished the requested information. If all had responded a number of the lines would be more complete. Thanks are especially due, Mrs. Silas A. Pierce, Grafton, Mass.; Miss Lou M. Pierce, Worcester, Mass.; F. L. Ora of Chicago, Ill.; Prof. John Fiske, Cambridge, Mass.; Col. Francis S. Fiske of Boston; Hon. Joseph Fiske of Wellesley Farms, Mass.; Rev. A. A. Fiske and others who rendered valuable aid and assistance.

It is the sincere wish of the writer that the descendants of the Fiskes will take as much pleasure in perusing these pages as I did in compiling them.

Very truly,

Frank C. Pierce

Chicago, July 30, 1896.

THE FIRST FISK.

The family of Fiske flourished for a very long period in England, in the County of Suffolk. So early as the eighth year of the reign of King John, A. D. 1208, we find the name of Daniel Fisc of Laxfield appended to a document issued by the King, confirming a grant of land in Digneveton Park, made by the Duke of Loraine to the men of Laxfield. The original is in the Public Record office in London and is dated May 1, 1208. The following is a copy:

ROTULI CHARTARUM, VOL. I, PART 1, PAGE 177.

Public Record Office, London.

Confirmation by King John, May 1, 1208, to the men of Laxfield of land in the Park of Digneveton, granted by the Duke of Loraine. The following are the names of those to whom the grant was made:

Robert Garenoise, Eustice Percario, Henry de la Hose, Walter de Holoc, William son of Robert, William Daniel, Jeffrey Daniel and Daniel their brother, Daniel Cuppario, Brithmaro, son of Brithwalden, Stephen Proest, Stephen Archer, Eustace son of Phillip, Melvine wife of Roger Gadermod, Picot son of William, Bernard son of Roger, Edmund son of Robert, Jordan son of Robert, William son of Gilbert, Robert son of Brithmar, Simon son of Edric, William Odonis, Godfrey and Herbert, Robert son of Jeffrey, Osbert a clerk, Ralph a clerk, Hadebrand Haiward, Robert son of William, Simon son of Turstan, Brithmar son of Godwin, Roger Haiward, Richard Haddoc, Reignald son of Godwin, and Robert and Daniel his brothers, John Emelin, Johnson of Roger, William Wudewell, Roger Crespig, Henry son of Ade, Roger Hunne, Matilda wife of Gilbert, Ernest de Radbrooke, and Robert his brother, Gerald son of Adwin and DANIEL FISC.

ORIGIN OF THE NAME FISKE.

The name Fisk is simply an older form of Fish. In Anglo-Saxon times the termination sh was regularly sounded hard, like sk. The breakfasting Engliscman of those days ate his fisc from a disc. The name is one of a large class of appellatives taken from the animal world, such as Herring, Salmon, Pike, Crabb, Tench, Spratt, Peacock, Swan, Drake, Crane, Hawke, Bird, Lyon, Hart, Fox, Bull, Lamb, Kidd, Cheever (goat), Todd (fox), Purcell (piggy), Hare, Colt, Palfrey, etc.

The origin of this class of surnames is not perfectly clear. The largest and most familiar groups of surnames are either (1) patronymics, such as Johnson, Jones, Wilson, etc.; or (2) names of villages and estates, such as Washington, Frothingham (a corruption of Fotheringham), Greenough (green field), Holmes (meadow), Stanley (stony pasture), etc.: or (3) names descriptive of occupation or social position, such as Mason, Carpenter, Franklin (country squire), Baker and its feminine Baxter, Thatcher and Thaxter, Weaver and Webster, Draper, Smith, Fletcher (arrow-maker), Chapman (merchant), Cooper, Butler, Cartwright, Sargent, Waterman, Sawyer, Chandler, Bishop, Abbot, Clark, Constable, Spencer (steward) Grosvenor (chief huntsman), Woodward (forest-keeper), Youmans (yeoman), etc.

The earliest use of family names in England was about the beginning of the eleventh century. Long before that time, indeed, clan names were common, and such were always patronymics, e. g., Fotherings, the descendants of Fother; Beormings, the descendants of Beorm; Icklings, the descendants of Ickel. At the time of the Anglo-Saxon conquest of Britain (fifth and sixth centuries) it was customary for a clan to settle in a stockaded village by itself, and all English towns whose names end in ham or ton, preceded by ing, were originally the abodes of single clans; e. g., Birmingham, home of the children of Beorm; Icklington, town of the children of Ickel. Besides these general clan names no others were in use except individual names, such as Alfred or Edith.

The use of family names, beginning in the eleventh century, increased slowly. It was not until the fifteenth century that such names became nearly universal, and also stationary. At first they were shifting in usage. Thus, the same man might be called Henry Wilson, because his father was named William, or Henry Frothingham, because he lived at the village of Fotheringham, or Henry Draper, because of his occupation. If the son of this Henry were named Robert, and were any kind of a worker in metals, from an armourer to a blacksmith, he might be known as Robert Harrison or Robert Smith. Surnames had not ceased to fluctuate in this way until the fifteenth century, and it was not until late in the sixteenth that more importance began to be attached to the family surname than to the individual baptismal name. It appears, therefore, that in tracing back the Fiske genealogy into the fourteenth century, we are approaching the time at which difficulty must arise from fluctuations of surname. Thus the paternal grandfather of David Fiske might have been called David Johnson, if John were his father's name, or David Franklin, if he were a country squire. In the thirteenth century we should be quite likely to encounter such confusion and to find the helpfulness of surnames in tracing genealogies vastly diminished.

Surnames derived from estates or localities seem to have been the first to become stationary, and next after them the surnames derived from trade or office, since sons have so commonly followed their fathers in business. The class of names to which Fiske belongs is certainly quite different in origin from the three great classes above mentioned. What, then, was its origin? Why should a man be called Wolf, or Heron, or Pike?

We are at first struck with the fact that barbarians commonly use such names, both for individuals and for clans. Such individual names as Grey Wolf or Yellow Raccoon often owe their origin to some personal peculiarity or to some irrecoverable incident. Among American Indians, and in general among barbarians all over the world, the clans are apt to have such names as Wolf, Eagle, Salmon, Turtle, etc.; the totem, or symbol of the Wolf clan, the idol or image of its tutelar deity, is likely to be a rude image of a wolf or wolf's head; and in many cases the clan is supposed to have had a wolf for its first ancestor.

Shall we say, then, that animal surnames in modern English are survivals of ancient heathen clan-names? Are Fiskes descended from a Fish clan among the East Angles? To this view there seems to be a serious objection. The conversion of our English forefathers from heathenism to Christianity was completed in the seventh century, at least four hundred years before the earliest use of surnames in England. The old clan system, moreover, had crumbled to pieces long before the Norman Conquest. It is not likely, therefore, that habits of naming characteristic of the old heathen clans could have persisted long enough to give rise to a whole class of surnames so late as the eleventh and twelfth centuries.

Between the ancient systems of totem devices and the heraldry of the Middle Ages there were many analogies and doubtless some points of connection; though, on the whole, the former must be regarded as the predecessor of the latter, not as its ancestor. The mediaeval heraldry was growing up in England during the eleventh and twelfth centuries, and it made an extensive use of conventionalized heads of familiar animals, not merely lions, wolves, and bulls, but many kinds of bird and fish, as well as such imaginary creatures as dragons, griffins, and cockatrices. For example, Lucy is the heraldic name for pike, and the shield of the De Lucy family bears on a field gules three lucies or. From this emblem the family surname is likely to have arisen, just as Geoffrey Plantagenet was so called from the sprig of broom or genesta plant worn in his helmet. The familiar name of Pike, as well as that of the Puritan magistrate, Sir Thomas Lucy, who arrested Shakespeare for poaching, has probably come from the heraldic use of pikes or lucies.

The explanation which serves for one of this class of animal surnames might perhaps serve for all; but there is another point to be considered. Heraldic devices were used not only upon banners and coats-of-arms, but also upon signboards, not merely of inns but of other places of business. In days when reading and writing were not common accomplishments, such devices were in general use, and they survived down to a recent time. For tavern signs they are not yet extinct. In old times, as often at the present day in Europe, the shop and the homestead were usually contained in the same building. Thus in the seventeenth century the father of John Milton, who was a solicitor, notary public, and law-stationer, had his office and his home in a certain house known as the Spread Eagle, in Bread Street, Cheapside. Over the front door was the figure of an eagle with outstretched wings. For four or five centuries before Milton's time, in going through any town, you would have passed by a succession of such signs of hawks, cranes, dolphins, salmon, lambs, and bulls, thus finding your way to the particular shop and homestead of which you were in quest. The principle upon which the signs were chosen is not always obvious. Sometimes a family name may have suggested the sign, as if a man named Crow were to paint a black crow over his door; but in early times the sign undoubtedly preceded and suggested the name. The family which dwelt at the sign of the crow came to be called Crow, in the same way that a family which dwelt at a country house called Greenough or Greenhalge (green field) came to be called by the name of the house.

There is nothing in the Fiske coat-of-arms, as used in the last three or four centuries, to suggest fishes or any occupation associated therewith. But if the name goes back into the twelfth century, as quite possibly it may, there is a chance that it may have been connected with some heraldic fish emblem since disused. It is quite as likely to have its origin in a sign. As I said above, it is difficult to determine with confidence the precise origin of names of this class.

The reader may be interested in the coincidence that Laxfield, the name of the parish where our Fiske forefathers dwelt for at least three centuries, means "salmon field." I think the name has been applied to the place for more than a thousand years, but I have no theory as to its origin. The name Stadhaugh (sometimes incorrectly written Stradhaugh) is compounded of stead and haugh. The former means station or home, so that the word "homestead" is a case of tautology. A haugh was a cleared field in the days when much of England was covered with virgin forest. Stadhaugh is thus equivalent to "home in a cleared field."

John Fiske

What Prof. Rasmus B. Anderson says:

Prof. Rasmus B. Anderson of Madison, Wis., ex-minister to Denmark, in writing sends the following:

Madison, Sept. 19, 1896.

Col. Fred Pierce, Chicago, Ill.

My Dear Sir:—I have your favor of the 13th inst., in regard to the name of "Fisk." Fisk means in Norwegian "fish" and of course the name may be of Scandinavian origin. I am pretty familiar with Scandinavian nomenclature, but I cannot recall any Dane, Swede or Norwegian by that name."

Dr. Henry Mortimer Fiske, a native of Sturbridge, residing in San Francisco, writing in September, 1895, says: "The name for long centuries back was Fiske. It is a Scandinavian name and is as common in Denmark and Sweden as Smith is here. The meaning of the name is 'fish' and all Scandinavians call a fish, fiske. The Danes have in Greenland a harbor called Fiskenares, and also one in the island of St. Thomas, one of the West Indies, of the same name Fiskenares, meaning in English fish harbor. I have also an old book published in London in 1760, called the young man's book of knowledge, which is dedicated to the Rev. James Fiske, a rector of the church of England.' In an old book, a history of one of the counties of England, speaking of one of the civil wars there the name of lord or viscount Fiske is there mentioned as one of the civil magistrates. The book is one of the first printed and is nearly 300 years old. In both Sweden and Denmark the name is always spelt Fiske. I have satisfied myself the name was introduced into England at the time of the Danish invasion. I am further satisfied that the 'e' was left off in England more for the convenience of spelling on the part of our forefathers than any other cause, as those old fellows, even the most learned, had a habit of phonetic spelling in many instances a desire to cut things short."

The late Miss Fidelia Fisk of Ooroomeyah, Persia, a veteran missionary, informed the writer of this sketch that "there seemed to be some connection between the name and the word 'fiscal.' Somewhere she had been told that, before the appearance of the family name, 'the fisk' was one of the appointed public officers. Much of the revenue of those days was collected in dried fish, and Fisk, or Fiske, is the plural of fish in the Danish language. Quintals of fish were at that time used as currency even.

"A ministerial crank, whom I came upon once in traveling, claimed that 'there were few of the family names in N. E. that could not be traced back to the Greek!' Whereupon I replied, 'Let me hear you take my name over that course.' Without hesitation he replied, 'Your name came by way of Denmark, did it not? It is probably all one with Fish. Now, in the Greek, fish is ichtheus. Prefix the digamma and you have Fichtheus. Drop the termination, and you have Fich, or Fisch, or Fische, which would very soon be worn down to Fish, or Fiske-Fisk.'"

In reading a valuable article from Rev. Wm. H. Griffis, on the "Influence of the Netherlands upon the N. E. Emigrants," I found a statement to the effect that "many of the emigrants from Suffolk County, England, to Holland, in returning to England, or coming over to America, were found to have shortened their names to a monosyllable. Fisher thus became Fish."

This led to a brief correspondence, in the beginning of which that stalwart defender of the rights and honors of the Dutch expressed his confidence, that "the name of Fiske-Fisk was among those mentioned in the early literature of the Netherlands." Search, however, only discovered a "Fisker" in Holland, who came from and returned to England, but neither in England nor America was the name of Fisker found thereafter, but the name of Fiske-Fisk is there among the emigrants before 1640.

It only adds to the plausibility of this theory to remember that almost every one of the emigrant Fiske-Fisk name had a trade which must have been originally learned in Holland—weaver, tanner, spinner, dyer, etc.

Webster's Dictionary has this to say of the name: Fisk (fisk) verb irrelevant (ch. Swedish fjeska, to bustle about), to run about; to frisk; to whisk. "He fisks abroad and stirreth up erroneous opinions."—Latimer.

Fisk, fisc, fiskin, fysk (Swedish fjeska). "What frek of thy folde fisketh thus aboute?"—Piers Plowman, c. x. 153.

Scots Law: The right of the crown to the movable estate of a rebel. (Encyclopedic Dictionary.)

Fish, fis, fisc, fisch, fiss, fisshe, fyche, fysch, fysshe, s. (Anglo-Saxon, fisc; cognate with Dutch, visch; Icelandic, fisky; Danish, fisk; German, fisch; Swedish, fisk; Goth., fisks; O. Fris., fisk; Welsh, pysg; Irish and Gaelic, iasg; Latin, piscis. (Under head Fish, Encyclopedic Dictionary.)

LORD OF THE MANOR OF STADHAUGH.

Symond Fiske, Lord of the Manor of Stadhaugh, held lands in Laxfield Parish, and was probably grandson * of Daniel Fisc, before mentioned. He bore for his arms, chequey, argent and gules, upon a pale, sable, three mullets pierced, or. These arms, with a crest added, were confined to Prof. Nicholas Fiske, professor in Physic, of Stadhaugh, in Laxfield.

In 1633 a charter of confirmation was issued from Herald's College. It acknowledges the use of the arms by an ancestor to all the emigrants.

To all and singular persons to whom these presents shall come, Wm. Segar, Knight, Garter Principall, King of Arms of Englishmen, sendeth his due commendations and greeting in our Lord God everlasting. Know yea that anciently

----

* According to Herald's Visitations.

Motto: Macte virtute sic itur ad astra.

"So to the stars we go
For doing as we ought below."

Arms of Symond Fiske of Stadbaugh.

from the beginning it hath been a custome in all countries and common wealths well governed, that the bearing of certain signes in shields (commonlie called arms) hath been and are the only markes and demonstrations either of prowess, virtue and valour in times of war or peace, and of good life and conversation for learning, magistracy and civil government in times of peace diversley distributed according to the qualities and deserts of the persons demeriting the same, which order, as it was most prudentlie devised in the beginning, to stirr and kindle the hearts of men to the imitation of virtue and nobleness; even so hath the same been and yet is continually observed to the end that such as have done commendable service to Prince and country either in war or peace may receive due honor in their lives, and also devise after their deathes successively to their posterity. Amongst the which number I find Nicholas Fiske of Studhaw in the parish of Laxfield, in the county of Suffolk, Professor in Phisick, son of Nathan Fiske of the same son of William, son of Thomas, son of William Fiske of Studhaw aforesaid that lived in the raignes of King Henry the sixt, Edward the III, Richard the third and King Henry the seventh, who beared for their coats armor, as followeth viz, checkey argent and gules, upon a pale sable, three mullets or, pearced and wanting further for an ornament onto his said coate of Armes, as diverse auntient coates are found to want, a convenient creaste or cognizence fitt for him the said Nicholas to beare, who hath requested me the saide Garter to assign him such a one as he may lawfullie use without wrong doing or prejudice to any person or persons whatsoever which according to his due request I have accomplished and granted in manner and forme followeth (that is to say), on a healme a torse argent and gules a triangle, argent, above the upper angle an estoile, or, mantelled gules, doubled argent, as more plainly appeareth depicted in the margent hereof. All which armes and creaste I the said Garter King of Armes by power and authoritie of my office, under the great seal of England, due appoint, give, grant, ratifie and confirme onto the said Nicholas Fiske and to his posteritie forever, and that it shall be lawfull for him and them to use and show forth the same in signet, shield, ensigne, or coate armor or otherwise at his or their pleasure, at all times, and in all places, according to the ancient laws or arms and laudable custome of England, without let or mollestation. In witness whereof, I the saide Garter have hereonto set my hand and seale of office, the 16th day of November, A. D. 1633, and in the 9th yeare of the raigne of our Souveraigne Lord Charles by the Grace of God, King of England, Scotland, France and Ireland, defender of the Faith, etc.

This motto is evidently taken from Virgil's Aeneid, the ninth book. In the 640th and 641st lines of this book you will find: "Atque his victorem affatur Iulum: Macte nova virtute, puer: sic itur ad astra."

Another authority describes the arms as follows: Fisk Armes: Checkie, Argent and Gules, on pale sable 1.88 by .43 inches, check ¼ inch Gules right hand upper corner alternate Argent, Form. Top & side 5 checks right lined and right angled; bottom, spade shaped, three Mullets, or, pierced. Crest: Torse 1.03 by .1 inch Argent & Gules, Triange equilateral, .65 inch, above upper angle an Estoile, or, mantled Gules, doubled Argent, .1 inch.

The said arms and crest are registered in the Heraldry book of Middlesex, made by Sir Henry, signed George Knight Richmond. Hen: Lily, Rouge, Rose.

Heraldry, a relic of the feudal ages, took its rise in the crusades, and was employed to denote the manly virtues. Since then armorial bearings have served very much the same purpose of the modern diploma, and have been cherished because deemed the patent or respectability. Esteemed at first by the landed gentry at pleasure, they afterwards came under the regulation of law. The Herald's College was established, and a general registration took place in the sixteenth century, when pedigrees were accepted and registered, the disorder or irregularity or fraudulent bought rectified.

FROM BOHN'S ENCYCLOPEDIA OF HERALDRY.

Fiske Harrison—see Harrison—Harrison, as borne by Fiske Goodeve. Fiske Harrison, of Copford Hall, County Essex, Esquire, who assumed his additional name and arms of Fiske, on succeeding to the family estate of his mother, Sarah Thomas, only child of Rev. John Fiske, of Thorp, Moriaux County Suffold, by his wife the daughter and heir of the late Samuel Thomas, of Lavenham, Esquire. Arms—Quarterly, first and fourth, az. two bars, one between six estoiles, three, two and one. er. second and third and three crescents bareg under az. and gu. Crest—A Stork, wings expanded ar. beaked and membered or. Motto—Ferendo et Feriendo.

FISKE WILLS IN SUFFOLK COUNTY, ENGLAND.

In 1854 Col. Francis S. Fiske, of Keene, N. H., now a resident of Boston, Mass., and United States Commissioner, employed the well known American genealogist and antiquarian, Horatio G. Somerby, then residing in Camden Square, London, to thoroughly inspect and copy from the records in the various parishes in Suffolk County, England. He found a mass of very valuable data relating to the English ancestors of the American Fiskes from 1462 to 1635.

Mr. Somerby first visited the several Suffolk parishes where he knew the Fiskes had resided and made extracts from the parish registers which were of sufficient antiquity to suit his purpose. The registers of South Elmham and Weybread, however, in one of which he expected to find the baptism of one of the American emigrants, did not date back far enough to give it. He next consulted some of the wills of the early Fiskes and found sufficient to justify him in the belief that Nathan Fiske, of Watertown, Massachusetts Colony, was the eighth in descent from the first Simon of Laxfield, through Robert, of St. James, South Elmham, who was his great-grandfather. Simon was Lord of the Manor of Stadhaugh, in Laxfield, Suffolk County, England, in the time of Henry the Sixth.

Between the years 1462 and 1635 he found some fifty wills of Fiskes proved in Suffolk County, all of the same family, abstracts of which were furnished and are inserted in their proper places, others of this family are as follows:

WILLIAM FISKE, OF RENDHAM. Will presented July 17, 1472. Mentions his sons, William, Robert, Thomas and John and Walter Fiske, of Peasenhall. Wife Margaret.

THOMAS FISKE, OF BADENHAM. Will dated Sept. 13, 1488. Wife Agnes. Sons, William and John.

JOHN FISKE OF DISS CO., NORFOLK. Will dated in 1488. Speaks of his wife, Elizabeth. and Mr. John Fiske, clerk.

WILLIAM FISKE, OF BEEDES. Will dated 1505. Wife, Jane. Witnessed by John Fiske and others.

NICHOLAS FISKE, OF EAST DEREHAM, E. NORFOLK. Will dated Apr. 8, 1529. Wife, Elizabeth. Sons, William, Thomas, John and Ambrose. Daughters, Cicily and Wyborough.

JOHN FISKE, OF LAXFIELD. Will dated Oct. 2, 1535; proved 1535. Desires to be buried near his mother. Bequeaths legacies to John Fiske, of East Dereham; William Fiske, of East Dereham; Thomas Fiske, of Lowstoft, and to John, son of Simon Fiske. Appoints Jeffrey Fiske, the elder, and his son, John, executors.

JOHN FISKE, THE ELDER, OF WENHASTON. Will dated May 4, 1558; proved Jan. 6, 1558-9. Wife, Marion. Son, John. Daughters, Agnes and Susan; daughter Joan Barfot.

THOMAS FISKE, OF NORTHALL. Will dated May 16, 1557; proved May 27, 1557. Desires to be buried at Southrow. Wife, Agnes. Sons, John and William. Daughter, Margaret. Godson, Christopher Fiske.

MARIAN FISKE, OF WENHASTON, widow. Will dated Jan 30, 1558; proved July 31, 1559. Son, John. Daughter, Agnes; daughter, Joan Barfot.

WILLIAM FISKE OF SOUTH COVE. Will dated Mar. 13, 1576; proved Dec. 5, 1581. Wife, Elizabeth. Late daughter, Alice, wife of Richard House. Grandchildren, Judith and Dorothy Fiske. Legacy to Robert Pease and his children.

WILLIAM FISKE, OF ALDBOROUGH. Will dated Sept. 3, 1584; proved Oct. 6, 1584-5. Wife, Margaret. Sons, Francis, Thomas, John and William. Daughter, Margaret. Brothers, John and George.

WILLIAM FISKE OF RENDON. Will dated June 20, 1572. Wife, Isabel.

GEORGE FISKE, OF ALDBURGH. Will dated Jan. 25, 1584-5; proved Feb. 26, 1584-5. Wife, Joan. Brother, John. Mentions William Fiske and his son, Thomas.

RICHARD FISKE, OF SHOTLEY. Will dated Apr. 6, 1589. Wife, Ursula. Son, Jonas.

WILLIAM FISKE, OF LAXFIELD. Will dated Dec. 29, 1590; proved Jan. 22, 1591. To his wife, Jane, a tenement at Stradbrook. Brothers, John and Jeremy. Brothers-in-law, John Punchyard and Thomas Bowett.

JOAN FISKE, OF IPSWICH. Will dated May 22, 1562. Desires to be buried in the churchyard of St. Mary-at-Elms, in Ipswich.

ROBERT FISKE, OF GREAT LINSTED, single man, nuncupative will, dated Mar. 18, 1601-2. Father and mother, Thomas and Alice Fiske, of Great Crattfield. Brothers, William and John. Sister Alice Sparham and sister, Joan.

ROBERT FISKE, OF ST. JAMES, SOUTH ELMHAM. Will dated Apr. 10, 1592; proved July 28, 1602. Eldest son, William; son, Eleazer, and his wife, Elizabeth; son, Thomas. Daughter, wife of Robert Barnard. Appoints his sons, Jaffrey and Eleazer executors.

WILLIAM FISKE, OF MIDDLETON. Will dated Mar. 18, 1611-12, proved Apr. 22, 1612. Wife, Joan. Sons, Nicholas, William, John and Thomas, all under 22. Daughters, Frances and Margaret, not 21.

WILLIAM FISKE, OF RENDHAM. Will dated Oct. 20, 1603; proved Nov. 17, 1604. Son, Thomas. Daughter, Frances, wife of Anthony Cressye, of Dennington.

ARTHUR FISKE, OF BULCHAM HAMLET, IN BLITHEBOROUGH. Will dated Dec. 20, 1610; proved Jan. 9, 1610. Wife, Mary. Mentions Agnes, daughter of his brother Samuel, and John Fiske, his apprentice.

JOHN FISKE, THE ELDER, OF ALDBURGH, WOOLEN DRAPER. Will dated Mar. 31, 1617; proved May 18, 1617. Wife, Katherine. Sons, John and Thomas. Daughter, Anne; daughter, Emma Bawkey, wife of Edward Bawkey; daughter, Dorothy. Sister, Margery Palmer. Cousin, Thomas Fiske and his children.

THOMAS FISKE, OF MARLFORD. Will dated Sept. 18, 1617; proved Nov. 24, 1617. Mentions his grandchild, Thomas, son of his son-in-law, Ralph Everard; William, son of his sister, Amy Richardson, deceased. Uncles, Robert and John Godfrey. Cousin, Reynolds, of Baddingham; cousin, Blith, of Halesworth; cousin, Goodall, of Parham; wife's sister, Margary French. Father-in-law, Whight.

ANNE FISKE. Will dated Jan. 6, 1619. Sons, Thomas and Robert. Sisters, Hudson and Palmer.

WILLIAM FISKE, OF SPEXHALL. Will dated Mar. 29, 1618; proved May 2, 1618. Gives to the poor of Hedingham Co., Norfolk. Wife, Elizabeth. Son, William, and his son, William; son, Edward, and his son, William. Daughters, Mary and Marian; and son-in-law, Robert Balls.

ROBERT FISKE, OF REEDHAM. Will dated Feb. 16, 1609-10; proved Nov. 18, 1610. Wife, Elizabeth. Son, Robert, not 21. Daughters, Elizabeth, Mary and Joan. To son, Richard, "who, whether he be living or dead, I know not," forty shillings, to be paid to him within one year after his return to England.

THOMAS FISKE, OF WENHASTON. Will dated Mar. 16, 1602-3; proved June 5, 1604. Wife, Alice. Legacies to his sister, Knight, and William Fiske, residing with him. Makes William, son of William Fiske, of Hockingham, to Norfolk, his principal heir.

MARY FISKE, OF WEST ORETHAM CO., NORFOLK, widow. Will dated Aug. 21, 1623; proved Feb. 26, 1624. Eldest son, Christopher. Grandchil-

dren, Robert, William and Edmund.   Son-in-law, Edward Page.   Mentions
Robert, son of Robert Fiske.
  HENRY FISKE, OF WENHASTON. Will dated Apr. 15, 1628; proved
July 9, 1628. Wife, Margaret. Son, Henry. Daughters, Rose, Margaret and
Prudence.
  SIMON FISKE, OF ELMSWELL. Will dated Mar. 15, 1615. Wife, Elizabeth.
  EMME FISKE, OF ELMSWELL, widow. Will dated Feb. 17, 1625;
proved Nov. 27, 1626. Son. Robert and his daughter, Margaret; son Edward and
his daughter, Elizabeth. Grandchild, Mary Palmer. Daughter, Elizabeth Martin;
daughter, Frances, wife of Roger Bardwell.
  JOHN FISKE, OF ELMSWELL. Will dated Sept. 4, 1616; proved Oct.
14, 1616. Brothers, Robert, Simon and Edward. Brother-in-law, Thomas Palmer;
brother-in-law, Thomas Bardwell; brother-in-law, Thomas Martin. Appoints his
mother, Emme Fiske, executrix.
  MARGARET FISKE, OF SWIFTING, widow. Will dated Apr. 19, 1636.
To her son, Nathan, one-third of all her goods, and the residue to her daughters,
Mary, Margaret and Sarah. Appoints her son, Nathan, executor.
  JOHN FISKE, THE ELDER, OF WENHASTON. Will dated May 6,
1636; proved Apr. 21, 1640. To his daughter, Susan Fiske, £40. Appoints his son,
John, executor.
  AMOS FISKE, OF DENNINGTON, singleman. Will dated Jan. 8, 1641-2;
proved Apr. 21, 1642. Sister Frances, wife of John Russell; sister Margaret Fiske.
Father-in-law, William Fiske. Mother, Margaret. Directs that his brothers,
John and William, the younger, be bound apprentices; brother, William, the elder,
residuary legatee.
  ZACHARY FISKE, OF WETHERSDEN. Will dated Feb. 18, 1646-7;
proved Jan. 27, 1647-8. Wife, Mary. Mentions William Fiske, eldest son of John
Fiske, of Ruttlesden, Gent. and Zachary Fiske, son of Robert Fiske, of Norton,
Gent.
  THOMAS FISKE, OF SANDCROFT, IN SOUTH ELMHAM. Will dated
1661. Mentions his brother, James and Samuel Fiske, Weybred.
  THOMAS FISKE, THE ELDER, OF ALDBOROUGH. Will dated Aug.
9, 1623; proved July 9, 1633. Wife, Emme. Sons, Francis, Thomas and William.
Daughters, Emme and Elizabeth. Grandson, John.
  FRANCIS FISKE, OF ALDBOROUGH. Will dated Mar. 31, 1634; proved
Nov. 27, 1634. Mother, Emma Fiske. Son, John. Appoints his wife, Anne, exec-
utrix.
  JOHN FISKE, OF SOUTHWOLD. Will dated Apr. 20, 1648. Bequeathes
to his wife, Mary, lands in Wenhaston. Sons, John, Sturgeon and Anthony, all
under 21. Daughter, Margaret, wife of Gilbert Hopkin. Daughter, Susan Fiske.

RECOLLECTIONS OF A VISIT TO LAXFIELD.

(By Isabella H. Fiske, of Wellesley Farms, Mass.)
  To the member of the family who is interested in its early history, and is
taking a trip in England there will be hardly anything more fruitful of enjoyment
than turning aside a little from the beaten track and visiting his ancestral home
of Laxfield, in Suffolk, from which the American branch of the Fiskes emigrated.
  The town and its vicinity make an interesting study. The nearest railroad
town, and one with which the Fiskes themselves were early identified, is Framlingham, some eight miles distant, and with twenty-five hundred inhabitants. The
town itself claims through tradition to date from the time of Redwald, king of the
East Angles. It is certainly as early as the Norman period, as the structure of its
castle shows.
  This is a fine old ruin, one of the largest in England, covering over an acre
of ground, with its thick walls, arched gateway, and rising towers. It has a most
interesting history, having been held since the earliest records till through the
thirteenth century by the baronial family of the Bigods, these being bestowed by
Edward I. upon his son Thomas, of Brotherton, and still later coming into the
hands of the Mowbrays and Howards; families later represented by the earls and

dukes of Norfolk. It was at one time surrendered into the hands of John, and again, much later, was seized by the crown and became the residence of Queen Mary of England, being afterwards restored to the Howards by James I. Coming, in the seventeenth century, through purchase, into the hands of Sir Robert Hitcham, it was considerably dismantled, and was finally, on the hard terms of its entire demolishment given over by his will into the possession of Pembroke College, Cambridge.

There is also in Framlingham, the fine old church of St. Michael's, dating in part from the thirteenth century, and harboring as its chief treasure the altar tombs of the Howards; the most noted among whom are the two earls of Surrey, one victor of Flodden field, the other, the gifted poet of the Tudor era, and a victim of Henry VII.

Modern Framlingham is quiet enough, boasting as its chief interest, the Albert Memorial College, a large school for boys. It still keeps its antiquarian interest as central, however.

The name of Fiske is by no means an unknown one here. It may be found upon the stones in St. Michael's churchyard, which is comparatively recent, occurring about half a dozen times. It is to be seen in the town records also, and over shop doors and the like, occasionally. In one instance, however, the proprietor—whose name was Fisk—of one of the stores there, on being interviewed in regard to his family was unfortunately unable to trace back his lineage even so far as his own grandfather. But we may feel ourselves quite justified in identifying the early history of the family with that of the town in all the stirring scenes that were witnessed there.

In Framlingham we have a strong recollection of the past. In Laxfield we have the past itself, as something still present, not yet outgrown. It is all delightfully typical of England. In the first place, we have the real English country. We have behind us all thought of time and press of circumstances, and stroll leisurely along the winding lanes, shut in by green hedgerows from the sloping hillsides where the sheep and cattle graze peacefully. We have the country life of centuries ago, too. It is all just as it was when, as an old play tells us: "Prince Charlie came riding down to hunt the deer at Laxfield with his men," or when Cromwell and his men came riding along that way on their destructive mission.

Come they did, most probably along this route, for the little church at Laxfield bears traces of vandal hands, which marked the overzeal of the Roundheads. As we enter the little town, of about five hundred inhabitants, the whole atmosphere is delightful, this stepping out of the whirl of traffic, the rush of modern life, and breathing this quieter air, with its suggestions of lavender and musk, its folds and creases of the past still lingering. The great charm is the quaint unconsciousness of it all. The centuries have slipped by unnoted, and the old church still waits for the awakening touch that seems as far away as ever. The handful of houses grouped around it are true English country homes. The rectory one would wish particularly to visit; a charming little place, which, with its bower of green and rosevines and suggestions of perpetual summer, has all the romance and quaintness of the setting of the "Vicar of Wakefield." The rector seems the Vicar himself, gray and gentle as he is; a most hospitable man, who keeps up from his little retreat with the movement of the world's forces, yet with a contemplative, rather than an active interest.

We have a strong sense of ownership in this ancestral home of ours as we linger along its shaded street, on our way to the churchyard. This grows upon us as we find upon the mossgrown stones half obliterated epitaphs, containing the familiar family name. It is something set off from the thoroughfare of the ceaseless throng of tourists; a little by-way in which we can take an especial pride, and something as deserving of study as many a better known object of attention.

As we enter the exquisite little church, we note the rich, time-darkened carving, the finely executed stone-work of the fourteenth century, and the later Jacobin influence in the work. It is all genuine from the quaint baptismal font within, to the square tower without, rising amid the trees.

In the parish register, which is hardly ever opened, the records begin with the sixteenth century and the name of an Elizabeth Fisk is found to be one of the first entries, in 1519. Thus the old register bears witness that the Fiskes were identified with the town at the earliest account, and suggests a far-stretching past as a fertile field for the imagination.

The feeling of ownership culminates, of course, in visiting the old homestead, Stadhaugh perhaps a mile distant. It is a fine old estate, with its hundreds of acres still kept up and well stocked with sheep and cattle, and its traces of manor-house dignity. Its quaintly arranged chambers, its rambling roominess, and low-reaching rafters make an effective background for the bright laughter and merry sport of the rosy cheeked English children in the family now occupying it. We may look back here in imagination upon the environments of the Stadhaugh Fiskes in the old days of Henry IV. and Henry VI., when they were persecuted for their loyalty, and picture the lives of our own ancestors there to whose deeds of highmindedness Cotton Mather has made stirring allusion, naming this very estate of Stadhaugh as the scene of the events he has narrated to us. Surely the old homestead, arousing as it does our pride and patriotism, is a fitting link in the past and present of the family history.

Typical as Laxfield and its environs are, it is hard to describe even in detail without seeming to generalize. The associations are of course of more immediate interest than the objects themselves. Yet one gets a great deal of satisfaction, in this particular instance at least, by going back to the haunts of his family's childhood. If you can not do this in person, take down your Oliver Goldsmith and read over again some of the descriptions of Wakefield and its vicar You will hardly be far from the truth. If you can go, do. You will see no reason, if you are a lover of freshness in quaintness, of the historic past, and of rural England of today to regret having visited your family's early home, Laxfield.

Isabella Flow Fiske

THE MANOR OF STADHAUGH.

(Rev. Franklin Woodbury Fisk.)

Extracts from my notebook of travel, describing a visit made in July, 1872, to the Manor of Stadhaugh, town of Laxfield, county of Suffolk, England, for several generations in the possession of the Fisk family:

July 23, 1872, Laxfield, at "The Royal Oak" hotel.—Leaving Cambridge at 10 o'clock yesterday morning, I came by rail to Framlingham, the nearest station to Laxfield, six miles distant. Calling on two brothers, Henry and George Fisk, the first a glazier, and the other a shop-keeper, to see if I could learn anything respecting their ancestry. I found that I could learn absolutely nothing except that their father, many years before, came from the neighborhood of Laxfield. I ordered dinner at "The Crown" hotel, at 5 o'clock, and meanwhile visited the old castle, now in ruins, to which Queen Mary fled when Lady Jane Grey was placed upon the throne. It must have been a very strong castle in its day. I also visited the ancient church in which is the tomb of the celebrated poet, Henry Howard, Earl of Surrey, beheaded by Henry VIII. After dinner I started off at 6 o'clock to walk to Laxfield. It was a sweltering day, and I had a hard walk, though in many respects a pleasant one, reaching Laxfield about 8 o'clock. I called at once on the rector of the church, Rev. John Dallas, a gentleman of some 60 years of age, who has been pastor of the church here twenty years. He received me very courteously, and kindly offered to go with me in the morning to the old church and inspect the records of the baptisms, marriages and deaths of persons who had lived in the parish since the time of Queen Elizabeth, as the records did not extend back of that date. After engaging lodgings at "The Royal Oak," I called, at the suggestion of the rector, on an aged gentleman (Mr. Brightly), who for many years has been an officer in the church, and has known the inhabitants of the town for sixty years. He kindly gave me all the information about the Fisk family he possessed, and said that there had been no one of that name living in the town for the last twenty years.

Woodbridge, July 24.—After breakfast yesterday morning, I accompanied Rev. Mr. Dallas and his accomplished daughter to the venerable church edifice, with its ancient Norman tower. We opened the rusty iron chest, took from it the old records, and pored over them for hours, till 12 o'clock, trying to decipher the almost hieroglyphic characters of the writing. We turned first to the records of baptisms, which we found did not extend back of 1579, and these records, as nearly as we could make them out, were as follows. (There is copied into my notebook a list of twenty-seven baptisms extending from the year 1579 to the year 1651, which was as far as I copied.) The name Fisk stands the second one of the names on these records, and is almost uniformly spelled for some years, "Ffyske," but when a new minister or clerk came to enter the name, he spelled it differently, and often without the final "e." Indeed, in one or two instances the name seemed to have been spelled differently in the same entry of a baptism, thus: "Mary Ffyske, daughter of Nicholas Ffysk, was baptized the 8th day of Nov., 1581." After the entry in the year 1514, the "y" in the name becomes changed into "i," thus: Ffiske or Ffisk.

I noticed this record of a marriage: "Married, Henry Ffiske and Margarette Smith, the 20th day of Sept., 1590."

I find that the "Studhaw" estate (or as it is indifferently spelled, "Studhaw," "Sudhaw," "Stadhaugh"), was in the possession of a Mr. John Smith, and I suspect that he came into its possession through the marriage connection of the Fisks and Smiths referred to above. This Mr. Smith appears to have been a man of intelligent and benevolent views, as he willed the whole estate, consisting of about 112 acres of excellent land, with good buildings, to the town of Laxfield intrust, the income of which should be forever appropriated to the support of a school for the training in the common branches of an English education, of forty poor orphan boys of the town of Laxfield, or if necessary, of the county of Suffolk, after which these boys were to be taught some useful trade. The bequest was made, I think, in 1718, and ever since the school has been doing this noble work. It is under the care of seven trustees, of whom the Rev. John Dallas is chairman. I visited the school and was much pleased with it.

I walked out with Mr. Dallas to the estate, lying about half a mile from the village, and was politely received and hospitably entertained by the tenants, Mr. Thomas Reed and wife, who showed me through the house, which must have been quite a grand one in its day, though changed from age to age, not always, as I think, for the better. In the garret of the house I saw fine old oak wainscoting that generations ago adorned the lower rooms of the manor house. The building is of stone, of very ample dimensions on the ground, and has a very large kitchen, and butter and cheese rooms, and has commodious outbuildings. The rent of the estate is £170 a year. Mr. Reed's father and grandfather lived as tenants on the estate, in all for ninety years. After spending a very pleasant hour at this delightful house of my ancestors for several generations, I returned to the quaint little village of Laxfield, and bidding "good-bye" to my kind friend, Mr. Dallas, walked back to Framlingham, and taking a railway train to this place (Woodbridge), stopped here over night to call on Mr. Samuel Fisk and his two sons, whom I found to be prosperous business men. The father had left Laxfield forty years ago, and had established himself in Woodbridge, in the cabinet-making business, in which he had been very successful.

VISIT TO FRAMLINGHAM, DENNINGTON AND LAXFIELD.

(By Prof. John Fiske, of Cambridge.)

With regard to an article on the English Fiskes, I hardly think I know anything which you do not know already, but with regard to the Manor House, I can tell you briefly of a visit which I made there in June, 1880. I had been giving some lectures in London, and was going thence to Edinburgh to give a course of lectures there. I stopped at Ipswich and passed a night at the Great White Horse Inn, immortalized in "Pickwick Papers." Took the train next morning for the quaint old market town of Framlingham. The English, by the way, do not pronounce that "l", and I suppose that our Framingham was named after it. At

Framlingham, my wife and I took a dog cart and drove through Dennington, where Nicholas Fiske lived in the days of "Bloody Mary," to Laxfield, which is nine miles from Framlingham, and almost within the salt smell of the German Ocean. I felt very doubtful whether there would be anything to see at Laxfield more than a meadow or potato patch, but it would be something to see even the site which one's forefathers left when they came to New England. I inquired of a man working on the road, and learned that the Manor House of Stadhaugh was still standing, and that information on local history might be obtained from Mr. Aldrich, the parish clerk. After a pleasant call at the house of this gentleman, I continued on my way until at the end of a very long hedgerow I saw the quaint farmhouse known as Stadhaugh Manor. The present occupant, Mr. Thomas Read, was standing at the gate. On my mentioning my name, he invited us into the dining-room, a long, low-studded room with large fire-place, tall clock well stocked bookshelves, plants in the window, and all the appearance of comfort. I learned from Mr. Read that the house was built in the time of Henry VIII., apparently at a season when window taxes were high. Fiskes had lived on the spot since the time of Richard II., and how much earlier I do not know. They came to America in such numbers that the name became nearly extinct in Suffolk. The last Fiske of Stadhaugh died about 1675. The estate then passed into the hands of John Smith, Esq., who died in 1715, leaving the Manor House and farm of about three hundred acres to the Parish of Laxfield with a provision that the income should be devoted to preparing poor boys for the University at Cambridge. The place was leased by the parish to a family named Read on a ninety-nine year lease, and at the expiration of that period, the lease was renewed for another century.

My entertainer belonged to the sixth generation of Reads who had lived in that house. He was a fine, tall, stately man, quick in mind and well informed, very like the best type of New England deacon. He seemed interested in seeing a descendant of the ancient Fiskes, and said that it was not often that he had such visitors.

We called upon the vicar, Rev. William Mothersole, who said that we would find on the floor of the parish church the names of some Fiske ancestors buried beneath. The little parish church was built about the time of King Alfred, 1,000 years ago. The floor was covered with strips of a kind of hemp carpet, and on raising them, there was a good deal of dust to be cleared away, and as my time was limited, I gave up the search for Fiske graves. I, however, saw that of "John Smith, Armiger."

The vicar's son, a bright boy of twelve, who was much interested in the proceedings, took me to the village green where the one martyr of Laxfield was burned in the evil days of Mary Tudor. This victim was the Rev. John Noyes, and Fox, in his "Book of Martyrs," tells how his brother-in-law, Nicholas Fiske, of Dennington, visited him the evening before his execution.

I believe there is nothing more of interest to be said about my visit. The country at Laxfield and all about it has that finished, pastoral beauty so characteristic of the English landscape.

ANCESTRAL AND HISTORICAL.

(By Rev. Albert A. Fiske.)

The Fiskes in America are descended from an ancient family of that name, which for centuries and until a recent period, had its seat and manorial lands in Laxfield, in the county of Suffolk, England. As early as 1422, one Symond Fiske resided there as Lord of the Manor of Stadhaugh, and entitled by grant to coat armour. Several of his descendants appear to have justly gained repute for piety and education, both among churchmen and non-conformists, and numbers of them during the protracted struggle of the Reformation, and especially in the days of Queen Mary, endured severe persecutions on account of their staunch adherence to Evangelical principles.

Robert Fiske, of Laxfield, son of Simon, and fourth in descent from Symond Fiske, of the same, married Sibyl Gold, and had sons, William, Jeffrey, Thomas and Eliezer. These parents were the progenitors of all the Fiskes that settled in New England, so far as known, before 1640. In considering their posterity here, we must trace them as descended from two distinct groups, coming over about the same time (1637), one group settling in Wenham, and the other in Watertown, Mass. William Fiske, eldest son of Robert, married Ann Anstye, and had children, John, Nathaniel (who died young), Eunice and Hannah, the last of whom married William Candler, and was the mother of Rev. Matthias Candler, whose manuscripts, now on file in the British Museum, furnish the records from which the early history of the Fiskes in England have been compiled. John Fiske, the eldest son of William, above, and grandson of Robert and Sibyl Fiske, married Ann, a daughter of Robert Lantersee, and had children, John, William, Anne and Martha, all of whom, with their mother, embarked for America in 1637. Their father had died previously (in 1633), and during the passage the mother died also. The two brothers, having married in England, settled with their families in Wenham, then a village of Salem, Mass., about 1640. John, who had been already ordained in the English Church, became a noted and influential minister in the colony, and was settled as the first minister of the church in Wenham. Cotton Mather, in that quaint volume entitled "Magnalia," makes honorable allusion to him, both as scholar and preacher, and said that "like the beloved Luke, his praise was in all the churches." His brother, William, became also a man of mark, filled various public offices, was representative to the general court of Massachusetts, but died in the prime of his powers and usefulness, under 40 years of age. Both were able and useful men, were zealous Puritans in religion, and left descendants who perpetuated their good name for several generations.

About the same time that Rev. John and his brother established themselves in Wenham, several of their relations became also emigrants to the colony. David Fiske, of Watertown, who settled there with his son, David, and nephews, John and Nathan; and Phinehas Fiske, of Wenham, who brought with him sons, James (afterwards of Haverhill), John and Thomas—these two separate groups of families were respectively descended from Jeffrey Fiske and Thomas Fiske, the third sons of Robert and Sibyl, previously mentioned; their cousins, Rev. John and William, being descended, as we have already shown, from William Fiske, the first son of the same. From these brothers and cousins, eight in all, who were thus early colonized in the commonwealth, have sprung a numerous, widely scattered, and very respectable posterity. Over one hundred and sixty of their number, bearing the family name, are on the roll of college graduates, while very many of them have variously attained distinction as divines, authors, scholars, and public men, two having been prominent candidates for the Presidency of the United States. There is not a university or collegiate institution in this land, which has not had at some period a Fiske filling a prominent chair on its board of faculty, while four of them have been elected to the presidency of such corporations. And as to ministers and deacons of churches, their number is almost beyond enumeration.

We will now consider more particularly the Wenham group of Fiskes. Rev. John Fiske and family arrived in Cambridge, Mass., in 1637. There he engaged for awhile in teaching school, and afterwards in Salem, where he conducted the first grammar school with remarkable success, his pupils being able, it is said, to compose readily in Latin, verse or prose. In 1643 he removed to Wenham (adjoining Salem), gathered a church, and became its first pastor, in 1644, and continued such for more than twelve years. In 1655 he removed to the pastorate of the church in Chelmsford, in which he continued till 1677, when he died at the age of 76, leaving a family. Rev. John Fiske was twice married. His first wife, after living with him about thirty-seven years, died in 1771. Such was her remarkable knowledge of Scripture that she was called her husband's concordance. She was the mother of his children.

Moses, only son of Rev. John Fiske that arrived to maturity, graduated at Harvard College in 1662—the first of the Fiske alumni in this country; was licensed to preach in 1671, and ordained and settled over the church in Braintree (now Quincy), Mass., the following year. He was a preacher of considerable power and animation. Several of his sermons were published, and may be found in the archives of the Massachusetts Historical Society. Rev. Moses Fiske was twice married. His first wife was Sarah, a daughter of William Symmes, of Charleston, whom he married in 1671. Of his fourteen children those that lived were named as follows: Mary, Sarah, Ann, Elizabeth, Moses, John, William, Samuel. Mrs. Sarah, wife of Rev. Moses Fiske, died in 1692. In 1700, Jan. 7, he married Mrs. Quincey, a daughter of the distinguished Rev. Thomas Shepard. By her he had, Shepard Fiske, born April 19, 1703; Margaret Fiske, born Dec. 15, 1705. Shepard Fiske, youngest son of Rev. Moses Fiske, graduated at Harvard College in 1721, and died a physician at Bridgewater, Mass., in 1779. Mr. Fiske's daughters, except the last, all married clergymen. Two of his sons also, John and William, were clergymen. But the subsequent history of their brothers, Moses and William, is not definitely known.

John Fiske, second son of Rev. Moses Fiske, of Braintree (Quincy), graduated at Harvard College in 1702, preached awhile in Braintree Church, and was ordained pastor of a church in Killingly, Conn., October 19, 1715; his brother-in-law, Rev. Joseph Baxter, of Medfield, preaching the sermon. Here he remained until 1741, when disaffection arising in the church, he was dismissed and retired upon his large landed estate in Killingly, where he died in 1773, in the 89th year of his age. He is reported to have been a good scholar, an able preacher, and wise counselor. His wife was Abigail, a daughter of Rev. Nehemiah Hobart, of Newton, Mass. Of his five children only one was a son, and he died in infancy.

Samuel Fiske, youngest son of Rev. Moses Fiske, of Braintree, graduated at Harvard College in 1708—where his name appears on the roll without the vowel termination—and was ordained minister of the First Church, in Salem, Mass., in October, 1708. Says Bentley, in his memorial sermon: "Rev. Samuel Fiske was a man of eminent talents in the pulpit, of firm and persevering mind, and held in high esteem until disaffection sprang up in his church from the ill-defined discipline then existing in our churches. He was a preacher of real abilities, but his high notions of church authority were repugnant to many persons, and interfered with his usefulness. He was dismissed from the First Church, in 1735, and accepted the charge of a new society established by his friends. He preached the first centenary lecture of the First Church, August 6, 1729. The election sermon delivered by him before the Governor and Legislature, in 1731, may be reckoned as among the best. It was published and a copy is preserved among the state archives. He was dismissed from the Third Church in 1745, when he retired from the ministry. By wife, Anna Gerrish, he had five children, but only one of his sons reached maturity, John, born May 6, 1744. Rev. Samuel Fiske died in Salem, in 1770, at quite an advanced age.

John Fiske, only surviving son of Rev. Samuel Fiske, of Salem, engaged in commercial pursuits and acquired property. At the time of the Revolution he commanded the first vessel of war commissioned in the service. At the close of the war, he was commissioned a Colonel, then a Brigadier, and finally a Major General in the State Militia, which position he held until his death, in 1797. He was a man of princely hospitality, of enterprising spirit, and of benevolent impulses. He took great interest in the various religious and charitable movements of the day, and contributed freely to their support. He was thrice married, but left no male issue.

Peter Fiske, a grandson of Rev. Moses, of Quincy, married Sarah Perry, of Grafton, Mass., November 15, 1758. Four of their children were there born, Moses, Nathaniel, Peter, Sarah, John. Of these the eldest, Moses, graduated at Dartmouth College, in 1786; was licensed and preached awhile, but never ordained to the pastorate. He was a tutor in Dartmouth College from 1788 to 1795, when he removed to Helham, Tenn., and died there about 1842. He remained single until 50 years of age, and then reared a family of nine children. He ever manifested a strong disapprobation of negro slavery, although living in the midst of slavery all his days in the south. He was the author of several published works on slavery. John Fiske, brother of above, graduated at Dartmouth College, in 1791, studied theology with Rev. Dr. Lyman, of Hatfield, and was ordained to the ministry at Hadley, Mass., in May, 1794. Preaching for awhile as an evangelist, he accepted a call to the church in New Braintree, and was installed pastor, in August, 1796. In 1809 he enjoyed with his church a remarkable revival, which was repeated in 1818, 1819, 1826, 1831 and 1842. The fruits of these awakenings were numerous additions to the church. He preached his half century discourse October 26, 1846, which was published. He took a deep interest in the cause of education; was one of the efficient helpers in the building up of Amherst College, and received the degree of D. D. from that institution in 1844. He continued to preach with the assistance of a colleague, until October, 1854. In March following, he died in great peace, after a ministry of sixty-one years with the same people. He made a fine figure in the pulpit, being tall, dignified, of serene and intelligent countenance. He possessed a clear and well balanced mind, and a general completeness of character seldom found. His pulpit efforts were marked by eminent good sense and great appropriateness, especially in prayer. Several of his discourses were published. Mr. Fiske married, in 1796, Elizabeth Mellen, of Milford. They had children: John M., Mary W., William, Sarah, Abby and James. The youngest daughter married George Merriam, one of the publishers of Webster's Dictionary. William Fiske, son of Rev. Dr. John, was ordained to the ministry in 1865, and for years did good and efficient service among the Freedmen.

William Fiske, Esq., who emigrated to America in 1637, in company with his brother, Rev. John Fiske, was born in England, about 1614, and was there married to Bridget Musket, by whom he had several children. He was admitted Freeman (at Wenham), in 1643, and chosen town clerk of the same during the following year. He was elected Representative to the General Court of the Commonwealth in 1647, and continued in that office by annual election until 1652. He appears to have enjoyed to a large extent the confidence and respect of his townsmen, but was cut short in his career by death, in 1654, in the prime of his life, under 40 years of age; having during the eleven years of his residence in Wenham, repeatedly served in all the positions of trust within the gift of the people. He died intestate, and therefore most probably of some sudden and acute disease. Letters of administration were granted to his widow, in July, 1654, by which provision was made for the following children, therein named: William, Samuel, Joseph, Benjamin, and Martha. William, the eldest, was born 1642. Other children may have been born previously, but must have died young. The above named were evidently the only living heirs at the time of their father's decease. No records of births, marriages or deaths were kept on the town books of Wenham before 1686, when Capt. Thomas Fiske was instructed to commence their registration . Consequently the facts respecting the early generations are derivable only where private sources are wanting, from the public records of the land and probate offices. These records, for the entire counties of Essex and Middlesex, and covering a period of over two hundred years, in connection with various town records, have been carefully examined, and the results of the investigation, after much study, have been compiled in the following pages.

William Fiske, Jr., the eldest son of William Fiske, the emigrant, born in 1642, was married to Sarah Kilham, of Wenham, Jan. 15, 1662, and by her had several children, the record of whose names and births was found among the private papers of his grandson, William Fiske, Sr., of Amherst, N. H.

Mr. Fiske, by occupation a weaver, was admitted a Freeman in 1670; was chosen deacon of the Congregational Church, of which his uncle, Rev. John Fiske, was first pastor, in 1679. He also held various public offices, such as clerk, moderator of the town for many years. He also represented the town of Wenham for eleven different sessions in the General Court of Massachusetts. Indeed, he and others of the family, for fifty years consecutively, were the sole representatives of the town in that body, and until 1720. He inherited to a large extent his father's ability and worthy character, being deacon of Wenham Church for above forty years, and died at a good old age, in his 86th year. In his will, dated 1725, and proved 1728, all of his children are mentioned as legatees, except those who had died previously. But to his sixth son, Ebenezer, who was principal heir and legatee, and also his immediate successor in the deacon's office, was bequeathed "the original homestead," which property became by inheritance the residence also of his grandson, William Fiske, fourth son of Dea. Ebenezer, and remained in the family until March, 1773, when, upon the removal of said William Fiske to Amherst, N. H., it was sold to one Wm. Webber. Nothing now remains to mark the spot but a heap of stones, and the family name becoming extinct in Wenham, only the venerable slabs in the cemetery are left to bear witness to the fact that here was the ancestral seat of an ancient and honorable family, whose descendants, widely scattered but still maintaining the high character of their lineage, constitute today the main body of the Fiskes in America. To this source may be traced five distinct branches, which in this work are classified as the Amherst, Upton, Shelburne, Rhode Island and Connecticut lines.

William Fiske, fourth son of Dea. Ebenezer, of Wenham, principal heir of his estate and sole executor of his will, resided at the ancient homestead in Wenham, where probably his father, himself and his own children were all born, until the decease or removal of his own immediate relatives. Of himself personally little is known, except that in his character and principles he was a staunch Puritan. And considering that the characteristics of race and parentage stamp the individual, it would be strange were the case otherwise. His ancestors from a remote period were Puritans or Reformers, a lineage illustrious for their piety and inflexible virtues. His father and grandfather were successively deacons in the original Wenham church, for upwards of seventy years; the same ancient church of which the Rev. John Fiske himself, was the original pastor. More remotely still the family had been identified with that great reformatory struggle in England, from which were gathered the rich fruits of a purer faith and constitutional liberty. Such were the forefathers of William Fiske, and such the ancestral virtues, a goodly measure of which he inherited with his patrimony. That he was a man of strong religious convictions and most exemplary life is manifest from the admirable parental discipline by which his children were trained to become excellent citizens, godly men and women, and enabled to exert a wide and beneficent influence in their day and generation. And in this respect they but bear emphatic testimony, alike with other collateral branches, to the strength of that moral principle which, taking root with the parental stock in Wenham, over two centuries ago, has marvelously spread and diffused itself, like a spiritual leaven, through the various descendant and divergent lines, to this day. Mr. Fiske—to resume the thread of family history—having been appointed sole executor of Dea. Ebenezer's will, remained in Wenham long enough to settle the estate and dispose of the homestead, and various tracts of land, when (in 1773) he removed to Amherst, N. H., with his wife Susanna, and nine children, and two daughters-in-law, Mary Bragg, the wife of their son, Jonathan, and Eunice Nourse, wife of their son, William. The father, William, Sr., purchased a tract of land on the south side of Walnut Hill, and there the original homestead of the Amherst Fiskes was established. Having lived to see his country proclaimed free and independent, and his family settled in comparative comfort, he died in 1777, in the 52d year of his age.

Of their sons and daughters, all, except Anna, married, and she and two others excepted, William and David, remained in Amherst; all eventually removed and settled elsewhere. Some of them raised large families, and all more or less prospered in circumstances, and the good esteem of their fellow citizens. Of them all, it is believed, it may be truly said that their lives were blameless before God, and their end calm and full of peace. Among the descendants of William Fiske, Sr., of Amherst, may be mentioned Judge Jonathan Fiske, his son, Hon. Jonathan Fiske, Hon. William Fiske, Hon. Francis N. Fiske, Rev. Dr. Franklin W. Fiske, Rev. Dr. L. R. Fiske, Rev. Dr. William Allen Fiske, Rev. A. A. Fiske, and a long roll of deacons and other church officers.

COLLEGE GRADUATES BY NAME OF FISKE.

Below will be found a list of persons by the name of Fiske and Fisk, who have graduated at the various colleges in this country:

HARVARD UNIVERSITY, CAMBRIDGE, MASS.—the following is a list of graduates of Harvard College by the name of Fisk—Fiske. The date at the left denotes the year of graduation, the letters l and m signify Law and Medical Schools.

FISKE GENEALOGY.

Graduates not preceded by a star are supposed to be living at the present time:

FISK.—RESIDENCE.

*1708 Samuel.
*1721 Shepard.
*1759 Samuel.
*1772 William.
*1805 Charles.
*1824 Benjamin Franklin.
*1843 l Stuart Wilkins.
*1846 l Robert Farris.
*1864 Albert Levi.
1873 Lyman Beecher, C a m b r i d g e, Mass.
1880 m Samuel Augustus, 37 18th Ave., Denver, Colo.
*1885 James Lyman.
1886 Frederic Daniell, 32 Quincy St., Cambridge, Mass.
1889 m Arthur Lyman, 13 West 50th St., New York City.
*1894 l Arthur Gilman.

FISKE.

*1662 Moses.
*1702 John.
*1754 Nathan.
*1774 Abel.
*1785 Thaddeus.
*1787 Oliver.
*1793 Samuel.
*1798 Isaac.
*1801 Timothy.
*1815 John Minot.
*1816 Luke.
*1818 Robert Treat Paine.
*1819 Thomas.
*1825 Augustus Henry.
*1829 m Calvin Park.
1846 l Francis Skinner, 98 Federal Bldg., Boston, Mass.

FISKE.—RESIDENCE.

1849 Charles Carroll, 149 E. 46th St., New York City.
1853 Cornelius, 120 Broadway (Room 20), New York City.
*1853 Edward.
1860 Charles Henry, 60 Congress St., Boston, Mass.
1861 Joseph Emery, Wellesley Hills, Mass.
1862 George Alfred, Jr., Lombard St., Dorchester, Mass.
1863 John, Prof., 22 Berkeley St., Cambridge, Mass.
*1863 m Eugene Rufus.
1866 Amos K i d d e r, "New York Times" Office, New York City.
*1868 J. McK. Campbell.
1869 Arthur Irving, 17 Montrose St., Roxbury, Mass.
1872 George, Room 5, 60 Congress St., Boston, Mass.
1875 Andrew, 10 Tremont St., Boston, Mass.
1881 Fred. Aug. Parker, 44 Cherry St., Somerville, Mass.
*1882 William Boyd.
*1882 l John Winthrop.
1886 m Eustace Lincoln, 22 Pritchard St., Fitchburg, Mass.
1887 Edward, Lincoln, Mass.
1887 Robert Francis, Milton, Mass.
1890 Winthrop Edwards, 465 Beacon St., Lowell, Mass.
1891 George Stanley, 261 Clarendon St., Boston, Mass.
1893 Charles Henry, Weston, Mass.
1894 George Converse, Lombard St., Dorchester, Mass.

YALE COLLEGE, NEW HAVEN, CONN.—The list of graduates by the name of Fisk and Fiske from this institution is as follows:

FISK.

1743 Samuel, Haddam, Conn.; d. 1749.
1747 Benjamin, Portland, Conn.; d. 1802.
1770 Ichabod E., Georgia; d. 1810 (Rev.).
1817 Ezra, honorary degree (Williams College, 1809).
1826 Charles B., Staunton, Va.; d. 1866.
1829 William L., New Haven, Conn.; d. 1834 (M. D.).
1840 Stuart W., Natchez, Miss.; d. 1862.
1844 Robert F., St. Paul, Minn.; d. 1863.
1844 Samuel A., Northampton, Mass.; d. 1884.
1849 Franklin W., Chicago (D. D.).
1863 Marcus B., m.

FISK.

1877 Samuel A., Denver, Colo. (M. D.).
1881 Pliny B., d., Ree Heights, So. Dak. (Rev.).
1883 Arthur L., New York City (M. D.).
1883 Henry E., Chicago.
1892 Otis H., Covington, Ky.

FISKE.

1704 Phinehas, Haddam, Conn.; d. 1738.
1793 Moses, honorary degree (Dartmouth College, 1786).
1856 John M., Boston, Mass.
1863 John S., Alassio, Italy.
1883 Elisha S., d., Waitsfield, Vt. (Rev.).
1883 George F., m., Chicago (M. D.).

BROWN UNIVERSITY, PROVIDENCE, R. I.—Below will be found all graduates of the name of Fisk or Fiske. In regard to the abbreviations at the end of each notice: Nec. stands for Brown University Necrology. P. stands for Personal. Harvard stands for Harvard University General Catalogue. Newton stands for Newton Theological Institute General Catalogue. And. stands for Andover Theological Seminary General Catalogue. The rest explain themselves. The degree given is that of Bachelor of Arts unless otherwise marked.

1826—CALVIN PARKE FISKE, M. D., Harvard, 1829. From Sturbridge, Mass.; d. 1874.

1825—DAVID WOODWARD FISKE. Principal Framingham Academy, 1825-26; lawyer, Wrentham, Mass., 1831-36; merchant, Detroit, Mich., 1836-55; Greenfield, Mich., 1855-71; alderman, Detroit. Born Sturbridge, Mass., Nov. 2, 1801; died Detroit, Mich., July 12, 1871.　　　　　　　Nec. 1872

1844—EUGENE RUFUS FISKE; M. D., Harvard University, 1863. Physician, Scottsburg, Ore., 1849-64; Salem, Ore., 1864-77; one of the founders, Medical Department, Willamette University; professor Theory and Practice of Medicine eight years; one of the founders Oregon Medical Society. Editor "Surgical and Medical Reporter," Oregon. Born Cambridgeport, Mass., June 4, 1817; died Salem, Ore., Aug. 27, 1877.　　　　　　　Harv., Nec. 1878

1825—GEORGE FISKE. Theological student, Cambridge, Mass., 1825-26; in business, Lowell, Mass., 1826-30; teacher, Oswego, N. Y., 1830-32; ordained Episcopal, 1832; pastor, Oriskany, N. Y., and Rome, N. Y., 1832-37; home missionary, Richmond, Ind., 1837-44; pastor St. Paul's Church, Richmond, 1844-55; farmer and preacher, Richmond, 1855-60. Born Lincoln, Mass., 1804; died Richmond, Ind., Feb. 24, 1860.　　　　　　　Nec. 1862

1812—ISAAC FISKE. From Weston, Mass.; died 1813.

1808—JOSIAH JONES FISKE, A. M. From Sturbridge, Mass.; died 1838.

1840—OLIVER FISKE. Graduated Newton Theological Institution, 1843; not ordained; resident, Tewksbury, Mass.　　　　　　　Newt.

1837—OLIVER JOHNSON FISKE. Student Newton Theological Institution, 1833-35; ordained Baptist, 1837; pastor, Limerock, R. I., 1838-39; teacher, Stewart's Creek, Tenn.; Robertson County, Tenn.; Nashville, Tenn., two years; president, Eno College, Gallatin, Tenn., until 1849; pastor various churches, Ill., until 1873. Born Nashville, Tenn., Jan. 24, 1809; died Crawfordsville, Ind., Jan. 8, 1886.　　　　　　　Nec. 1886, Newt.

1803—PHILIP MANCHESTER FISKE. From Scituate, R. I.; died 1828.

1805—AMASA FISK. Lawyer, Dover, Vt. From Upton, Mass.; died Dover, Vt., Mar. 23, 1847.　　　　　　　Nec. 1847

1824—CHARLES ROBINSON FISK, A. M. Graduated Andover Theological Seminary, 1828; ordained Congregational, 1828; home missionary, 1828-31; pastor, Holden, Me., 1831-33; Poland, Me., 1834-35; Presbyterian Church, Logan, Ohio, 1836-?; editor, Galesburg, Ill., 1849?-51; pastor, Mendota, Ill., 1853-55; resident, Mendota, 1862-?; editor, Delavan, Ill. Born Wrentham, Mass., Oct. 27, 1804; died Delavan, Ill., Dec. 28, 1869.　　　　　　　And.

1869, Ph. B.—DANIEL MOSES FISK, A. M., 1876; Ph. D., Finlay College, Ohio, 1890. Professor Biology, Hillsdale College, 14 years; pastor First Congregational Church, Jackson, Mich., five years; First Church, Toledo, Ohio. Address, 2024 Robinwood Ave., Toledo, Ohio.　　　　　　　P.

1818—ELIAS FISKE. Student Andover Theological Seminary one year, with class of 1821; not ordained. From Upton, Mass. Born May 24, 1790; died 1854.　　　　　　　And.

1795—ELISHA FISK, A. M. Tutor, 1796-99; pastor Congregational Church, Wrentham, Mass., 1800-51. Born 1770; died Wrentham, Mass., Jan. 11, 1851.　　　　　　　Nec. 1851

1815—WILBUR FISK, A. M.; D. D., 1835; Augusta College, Kentucky, 1829. Law student, 1815-17; teacher, near Baltimore, Md., 1816-17; Methodist preacher, Craftsbury Circuit, Vt., 1818; Charlestown, Mass., 1819-20; presiding elder, Vermont district, 1823-27; delegate Methodist General Conference, 1824, '28, '32; chaplain Vermont Legislature, 1826; principal Wesleyan Academy, Wilbraham, Mass., 1826-31; president Wesleyan University, 1831-39; visitor U. S. Military Academy, West Point, N. Y., 1832; chaplain Middletown Artillery, 1832-39; delegate Wesleyan Conference, England, and in Europe, 1835-36; member Connecticut Board of

Education, 1839. Author "Future Rewards and Punishments," 1823; "Sermon on Spirituality and Truth of Divine Worship," 1824; Introductory Address, Wesleyan Academy," 1825; "Discourse Before the Legislature of Vermont, General Election," 1826; "Report of Committee on Education, General Conference," 1828; "Two Discourses on Universal Salvation," 1829; "Sermon, Mass., General Election," 1829; "Discourse on Predestination and Election," 1831; "Science of Education, Inaugural Address, Wesleyan University, 1831," 1832; "Substance of a Discourse on Death of Rev. Edward Hyde, 1832," 1833; "Address on Traffic in Ardent Spirits," 1833; "Substance of an Address Before Middletown Colonization Society," 1835; "Calvinistic Controversy," 1835; "Travels on the Continent of Europe," 1838; "Reply to Pierpont on the Atonement," 18—. See "Life by J. Holdich," 1842. Born Brattleboro, Vt., Aug. 31, 1792; died Middletown, Conn., Feb. 22, 1839.

Wesl., Allibone

1829—ALBERT WILLIAM FISKE. Graduated Andover Theological Seminary, 1832; ordained Congregational, 1833; pastor, Alfred, Me., 1832-44; Scarboro, Me., 1844-48; Houlton, Me., 1848; Upton, Mass., 1849; Kittery, Me., 1850-57; Fisherville, now Penacook, N. H., 1857-63; acting pastor, Center Harbor, N. H., 1864; Boscawen, N. H., 1865; Warner, N. H., 1865; Barnstead, N. H., 1866-68; Groton, N. H., 1869-71; resident, Penacook, 1863-92. Author of "A New Year Offering." Born Upton, Mass., Jan. 16, 1802; died Penacook, N. H., Dec. 7, 1892.

Cong. yr. bk., Nec. 1893

1821—HON. CALEB FISKE, M. D. Surgeon Continental Army; physician, Scituate, R. I.; Justice Court Common Pleas; original member R. I. Medical Society; president, 1823-24. Born Scituate, R. I., 1753; died Scituate, Sept., 1835. R. I. cyc.

AMHERST COLLEGE, AMHERST, MASS.—Following is the list of Fisks and Fiskes graduated here. Information up to 1871 about those marked * will be found in Montague's Biographical Record of Amherst Alumni, 1 vol., 800.

*Rev. Asa S. Fiske, class of 1855; present address, Ithaca, N. Y.

*Pliny Fisk, class of 1840; died in 1872.

*Samuel Fisk, class of 1848; died in 1864.

Frederick A. Fiske, class of 1836; died in 1878.

Warren C. Fiske, class of 1840; died in 1887.

Warren Cooley Fiske, the son of Stephen and Lucina (Thompson) Fiske, was born at Wales, Mass., Sept. 21, 1816, and was fitted for college at Monson Academy. He was graduated at East Windsor (now Hartford) Theological Seminary, 1845; was ordained at East Haddam, Conn., May 19, 1847, and was a home missionary in Wisconsin until 1850, when he became pastor in Marlboro, Conn. After eight years there he was pastor at Canton Centre, Conn., 1858-61; and afterward was acting pastor one year at Barkhamstead and at Wolcott, Conn., from 1869 to 1872. His health failing, he moved to a farm in Charlton, Mass., in May, 1872, and from there to Southington, Conn., Sept. 20, 1884, where he died of consumption, Apr. 17, 1887. Mr. Fiske was married May 19, 1847, to Harriet M., daughter of Rev. Isaac Parsons, of East Haddam, Conn. Four children.

*Rev. Daniel T. Fiske, class of 1842; present address, 273 High Street, Newburyport, Mass.

John Winthrop Fiske. From Bath, Me. Class of 1876; present address, 170 Broadway, New York City.

Arthur W. Fiske. From Granby, Mass. Class of 1880; present address, Granby, Mass.

Arthur S. Fiske. Class of 1884; died 1891.

George F. Fiske. From Hyde Park, Mass. Class of 1894; present address, 75 Milton Avenue, Hyde Park, Mass.

George W. Fiske. From Holliston, Mass. Class of 1895; present address, Theological Seminary, Hartford, Conn.

WILLIAMS COLLEGE, WILLIAMSTOWN, MASS.

FISK, EZRA, M. A. (also Yale, 1817; D. D. Hamilton, 1825), graduated 1809; born at Shelburne, Mass., 1784; lived at Goshen, N. Y., 1813-1833; died at Philadelphia, Dec. 5, 1833.

FISKE, FREDERICK WILLIAM, M. A., graduated 1872; then lived at Southbridge, Mass., but before 1871 at Hammonton, N. J.; now at 849 Grand Ave., St. Paul, Minn.

FISKE, CHARLES ALBERT, graduated 1879; res. then Southbridge, Mass.; now a teacher at St. Paul, Minn.

STUDENTS WHO DID NOT GRADUATE.

FISK, EPHRAIM, class 1827 (graduated at Union College, 1827; died at Schenectady, N. Y., 1827).

FISK, RICHMOND, JR., class 1858; in college from 1853 to 1855 or 1855; res. at that time, Hoosick Falls, N. Y.

FISK, ELBRIDGE N., class 1869; in college from 1865 to 1866 or 1867; res. at that time, New York City.

FISKE, ARTHUR WILMOT, class 1880; in college from 1876 to 1877; res. at that time, Granby, Mass.

FISKE, ELISHA SMITH, class 1882; in college from 1878 to 1879; res. at that time, Shelburne, Mass.

DARTMOUTH COLLEGE, HANOVER, N. H.

The list of graduates by the names of Fiske and Fisk from this college are as follows:

FISK, ALLEN, graduated 1814.

FISK, CYRUS M., HON., graduated 1870; res. Lowell, Mass.

FISK, GEO. A., MED., graduated 1860; res. Jesup, Ia.

FISK, JOHN B., graduated 1798.

FISK, MARTIN H., graduated 1852; res. Temple, N. H.

FISK, MOSES M., graduated 1802.

FISKE, CHARLES A., graduated 1861; res. Greenwich, Conn.

FISKE, FRANCIS S., graduated 1843; res. Boston, Mass., No. 94 P. O. Bldg.

FISKE, JOHN, graduated 1791.

FISKE, MOSES, graduated 1786.

FISKE, NATHAN W., graduated 1817.

ANN ARBOR UNIVERSITY, ANN ARBOR, MICH.

The graduates are as follows in the several departments.

LITERARY DEPARTMENT.

LEWIS RANSOM FISKE, A. B., 1850; A. M., 1853; LL. D., 1879; president of Albion College, Albion, Mich.

EDWARD DANIEL FISKE. A. B., 1860; A. M., 1863; died at Detroit, Mich., June 7, 1873.

JOSEPH HENRY FISKE (son of L. R. Fiske), A. B., 1877; res. Leadville, Colo. (1890).

HORACE SPENCER FISKE. A. M., 1885; A. B. (Beloit College), 1882. Chicago. Ill. (Chicago University extension lecturer).

GEORGE MYGATT FISK, A. B., 1890; Ashtabula, O.

MEDICAL DEPARTMENT.

JOEL H. FISK, M. D., 1857; registered from Oberlin, O.

MELANCTHON H. FISK, M. D., 1866; Wauwatosa, Wis.

LAW DEPARTMENT.

LEONARD FISKE. LL. B., 1894; Burlington, Vt. (1894).

NON-GRADUATES.

LEWIS ROSS FISKE (son of L. R. Fiske), 1870-73 (Literary); died Sept. 8, 1895.

ORLANDO PORTER FISK, 1863-64 (Law); registered from Rochester, N. Y.

ROBERT WASHINGTON FISK, 1882-83 (Law); registered from Melrose, Ill.

WILBUR WASHINGTON FISK, 1882-83 (Law); registered from Greencastle, Ind.

JOSEPH BAKER FISK, JR., 1894-95 (Literary); registered from Toledo, O.

PHILLIPS ACADEMY, ANDOVER. MASS.

JOSIAH FISK, aged 17, entered the academy in 1778, the first year of the institution, hailing from Andover. As a matter of fact, I find by the manuscript register that he entered on the very first day of the school. He remained in the school until 1780. He is registered as having died in 1781.

ELBRIDGE FISK entered the school in 1811, aged 12, from Beverly, Mass., and left it in 1812. He was a merchant in Beverly and died in 1846. I found the notice of his death in the Salem Register of Dec. 14, 1846, where he is given the title of "Esq.," and is registered as 47 years old.

AUGUSTUS HENRY FISKE entered in 1821, at the age of 15, to complete his preparation for college, being from Weston, Mass. He graduated at Harvard in 1825. He studied law with Hon. Benjamin Rand, Boston, and at Harvard Law School; was a lawyer of extensive practice in Boston. From 1848 he resided in Weston. He was son of Isaac Fiske, Register of Probate in Middlesex County, and Sukey Hobbs.

JOHN LANDON FISKE left middle class June '90 (at P. A. year); res. 139 Oxford St., North Cambridge, Mass.

HENRY FREEMAN FISKE left middle class in '87 (at P. A. four years). Cliftondale, Mass.

WESLEYAN UNIVERSITY, MIDDLETOWN, CONN.

This is the list of Wesleyan graduates (including one non-graduate) of the name of Fisk. There were none named Fiske:

FISK, EVERETT OLIN, 1873; 4 Ashburton Place, Boston, Mass.

FISK, HERBERT FRANKLIN, 1860; Evanston, Ill.

FISK, SEWALL H., 1840 (non-graduate; died Sept. 18, 1862, in hospital, at Savannah, Ga.

CORNELL UNIVERSITY, ITHACA, N. Y.

No one name Fisk or Fiske has thus far graduated at Cornell University, though several persons of that name have matriculated at the university and have pursued studies there. Below are the names of all these persons, with their home address at the time of their attendance in the university:

EPHRAIM JOHN FISKE, of Lebanon, N. Y.; student in Cornell University 1878-79.

FERDINAND COMSTOCK FISKE, of Maquoketa, Ia.; student in Cornell University 1878-79.

CHRISTABEL FORSYTHE FISKE, of Ithaca, N. Y.; student in Cornell University 1894-96.

JOSEPH BAKER FISK, JR., of Toledo, O.; student in Cornell University 1895-96.

COLLEGE OF NEW JERSEY, PRINCETON, N. J.

The following is a list of all of the names of Fiske given in our Alumni Catalogues.

FISK, HARVEY, graduate from Hamilton College, 1826; received a degree here in 1830.

FISK, E. W., graduated in 1849; present add. Greencastle, Ind.

FISK, H. E., graduated in 1877; present add. 28 Nassau St., New York City.

FISK, P., graduated in 1881; present add. 28 Nassau St., New York City.

FISK, W. C., graduated in 1890.

FISK, C. L., graduated in 1895; home add. Wallingford, Conn.

BELOIT COLLEGE, BELOIT, WIS.

The following is a list of the graduates from this institution:

1876—FRANKLIN L. FISK, M. A., clergyman, Elkader, Ia.

1878—FRANKLIN P. FISK, prin. N. W. Div. H. School, Chicago, Ill.

1880—JOHN P. FISK, JR., real estate dealer, Redlands, Cal.

1881—EDWARD O. FISK, M. A., insurance, Minneapolis, Minn.

1882—HORACE S. FISKE, M. A., Lect. Univ. Exten., Univ. Chicago, Ill.

1885—GEORGE F. FISKE, Sec. Mfg. Co., Chicago, Ill.

BOWDOIN COLLEGE, BRUNSWICK, ME.—The only graduate of the name of Fiske (or Fisk) was Rev. John Orr Fiske, D. D., class of 1837: b. July 13, 1819, Bangor, Me. Pastor at Bath, Me., where he died Dec. 18, 1893.

UNIVERSITY OF MINNESOTA, MINNEAPOLIS, MINN.—The only graduate from this college is Douglas Andrus Fiske, Bachelor of Laws, 1891; res. Minneapolis, Minn.

TUFTS COLLEGE, ANDOVER, MASS.—Warren Herbert Fiske, 1891; res. 1189 Madison St., Brooklyn, N. Y.

KNOX COLLEGE, GALESBURG, ILL.—Sarah R. Fisk, gr. 1851; Mrs. Dunn; died 1861.

NORTHWESTERN UNIVERSITY, EVANSTON, ILL.—The only graduate of Northwestern named Fisk is Mrs. Aurora Fisk Zeublin, '90, now abroad. Her father is Dr. H. F. Fisk, principal of the Academy of N. W. U., Evanston, Ill.

DE PAUW COLLEGE, DE PAUW, IND.—The only graduate is Wilbur A. Fisk, class of 1889, from Richmond, Ind.

PHILLIPS EXETER ACADEMY, EXETER, N. H.

The graduates are as follows:

ABEL FISK, 1797, ae. 13, Wilton, N. H.

ROBT. T. P. FISKE, 1813, ae. 14, Worcester, Mass.; H. U., 1818, A. M., M. D.

SAMUEL PHILLIPS FISK, 1817, ae. 16, Claremont, N. H.; merchant.

ROBT. FARRIS FISK, 1839, ae. 19, Cambridge, Mass.; Yale College, 1844, A. M., LL. B.; merchant.

SAMUEL AUGUSTUS FISK, 1839, ae. 17, Cambridge; Yale College, 1844, A. M., M. D.; physician.

CORNELIUS FISKE, 1849, ae. 19, Lincoln, Mass.; H. U., 1853; lawyer in New York.

ARTHUR IRVING FISKE, 1862, ae. 14, Holliston, Mass.; H. U., 1869, A. M ; teacher in Boston.

FRANK WALKER FISKE, 1867, ae. 16, Concord, N. H.; business, Kansas City, Mo.

FRANK WINSLOW FISKE, 1868, ae. 19, Peterboro, N. H.

LEWELLYN EUGENE FISKE, 1869, ae. 16, Peterboro.

ANDREW FISKE, 1869, ae. 15, Boston; H. U., 1875, LL. B.; lawyer, Weston.

JOHN WINTHROP FISKE, 1872, ae. 15, Bath, Me.; Amh. Coll., 1876; lawyer.

GEORGE MYGATT FISK, 1886; Ashtabula, O.

IRVING LESTER FISK, 1893; Hoosick Falls, N. Y.

CHARLES NORMAN FISKE, 1894; Upton, Mass.

FISKES AND FISKS IN THE REVOLUTIONARY WAR.

During the past few years it has been quite the fad to look up one's Revolutionary ancestors and at once make application for membership in one of patriotic hereditary societies. Following I give a list of all persons by this name who actively participated in the struggle for American independence. Three of this name were killed at the battle of Bunker Hill; another was the Surgeon who attended the wounded at Lexington.

SOLDIERS FROM MASSACHUSETTS.

Aaron Fisk, private.

Abel Fisk, first lieutenant, Hopkinton.

Abel Fisk, chaplain, Pepperell.

Abel Fisk, first lieutenant, Sherborn.

Abel Fisk, New Salem.

Abijah Fisk, sergeant.

Abijah Fisk, private, Waltham.

Abner Fisk, private, Wells, Me.

Abner Fisk, private, Holliston.

Abraham Fisk, private.

Adam Fisk, lieutenant.

Alpheus Fisk, private, Sturbridge.

Amos Fisk, private, Waltham.

Asa Fisk, private, Holliston.

Benjamin Fisk, private, Hadley.

Benjamin Fisk, corporal, Upton.

Benjamin Fisk, private, Cambridge.

Benjamin Fisk, private, Tewksbury.

Benjamin Fisk, private, Andover.

Benjamin Fisk, private, Southborough.

Benjamin Fisk, private, Lexington.

Benjamin Fisk, private, Groton.

Charles Fisk, private, Hull.

Charles Fisk, private.

Daniel Fisk, Upton.

Daniel Fisk, private, Deerfield.

Daniel Fisk, private, Waltham.

Daniel Fisk (and e), surgeon, Oxford.

Daniel Fisk, private, Pepperell.

Daniel Fisk, second lieutenant.

David Fisk, private.

David Fisk, fifer.

David Fisk (Dr.), private, Lexington.

David Fisk, drummer.

David Fisk, private, Holden.

David Fisk, private, Andover.

David Fisk, private, Concord.

David Fisk, drummer, Pepperell.

David Fisk, sergeant, Lincoln.

David Fisk, Jr., Worcester County.

Ebenezer Fisk, private, Deerfield.

Ebenezer Fisk, lieutenant.

Eleazer Fisk, private, Dunstable.

Elijah Fisk, corporal, Natick.

Elisha Fisk, private, Hampshire County.

Enoch Fisk, private, Needham.

Experience Fisk, corporal, Partridgefield (Peru).

Halloway Fisk, private, Mendon.
Henry Fisk, private.
Hezekiah Fisk, private, Brimfield.
J. Fisk, captain.
Jacob Fisk, private.
James Fisk, sergeant.
James Fisk, Greenwich.
James Fisk, private, Holden, N. H.
James Fisk, sergeant, Worcester.
Jonathan Fisk, sergeant, Holden.
Joseph Fisk (and e), surgeon's mate,
    later surgeon.
Joseph Fisk (Dr.), (possibly same as
    above), Lexington.
Joseph Fisk, first lieutenant.
Joseph Fisk, sergeant, Ipswich.
Joseph Fisk, private.
Joshua Fisk, private, Providence.
Joshua Fisk, captain, Natick.
Josiah Fisk, private, Hollis, N. H.
Josiah Fisk, private.
Jason Fisk, private, Barre.
Jeremiah Fisk, lieutenant.
John Fisk (and e), superintendent of
    sloop "Tyiannieide;" later com-
    mander of Brig. "Massachusetts."
John Fisk, private, Wells, Me.
John Fisk, seaman on "Winthrop."
John Fisk, private, Danvers.
John Fisk, corporal, Groton.
John Fisk, private, Littleton or West-
    ford.
John Fisk (and e), captain, Framing-
    ham.
John Fisk. Sherborn.
Jonas Fisk, private, Sherborn.
Jonathan Fisk, Billercia.
Jonathan Fisk, lieutenant. Weston.
Jonathan Fisk, captain, Weston.
Jonathan Fisk, private, Tewksbury.
Jonathan Fisk, Brimfield.
Jonathan Fisk, corporal, Wenham.
Jonathan Fisk, gunner.
Jonathan Fisk, on board sloop "Provi-
    dence."
Levi (or y) Fisk, private.
Luther Fiske, private.
Moses Fisk, private, Needham.

Moses Fisk, second lieutenant.
Moses Fisk, corporal, Framingham.
Nathan Fisk, private, Holliston.
Nathan Fisk, private, Northfield.
Nathan Fisk, Gageborough or Par-
    tridgefield.
Nathan Fisk, private, Sturbridge.
Nathaniel Fisk, Uxbridge.
Nathaniel Fisk, private, Topsfield.
Olivier Fisk, private.
Patrick Fisk, private, Falmouth.
Peter Fisk, private, Groton.
Peter Fisk, private, Westford.
Peter Fisk, corporal.
Pomp (y) Fisk, private, Lexington.
Reuben Fisk, private, Groton.
Richard Fisk, captain, Framingham.
Robert Fisk, private, Woburn.
Robert Fisk, private, Lexington.
Robert Fisk (and e), sergeant.
Rufus Fisk, private. Stafford, Conn.
Samuel Fisk, sergeant, Weston.
Samuel Fisk, sergeant, Templeton.
Samuel Fisk, private, Rutland.
Samuel Fisk, private, Topsfield.
Samuel Fisk (and e), private, Swanzey.
Samuel Fisk, Jr., private, Shelburne.
Seth Fisk, Abington.
Simeon Fisk (and e), private, Shirley.
Simeon Fisk, private, Sturbridge.
Stephen Fisk (and e), private, Green-
    wich.
Sylvanus Fisk. Partridgefield.
Thaddeus Fisk, private, Pembroke.
Thomas Fisk, private, Newton.
Thomas Fisk (and e), private. Par-
    tridgefield.
Thomas Fisk, corporal, Pepperell.
Wainwright Fisk, Pepperell.
William Fisk. Greenwich.
William Fisk, second lieutenant.
William Fisk, first lieutenant.
William Fisk, Upton.
Zedekiah Fisk, corporal, Shutesbury.
Zadoc Fisk. Shutesbury.
    Also the name is given under the
Fisks of Daniel Fisket, private. Nana-
guagus.

RECORD OF CONNECTICUT MEN IN THE WAR OF THE REVOLU-TION.

Page 26, Jonathan Fisk, 10 days, town of Windham, Windham County.
Page 26, David Fisk, 18 days, town of Windham, Windham County.
Page 26, David Fisk, Jr., 17 days, town of Windham, Windham County.
Page 617, David Fisk, private in Capt. Wale's Co.: Col. Jeremiah Mason's Regt.
    of militia.
Page 663, Eunice Fisk, census of pensions. 1840.
Page 284, Isaac Fisk, Sergeant Major. Southington; appointed Sergeant Apr. 20,
    1777; promoted to Sergeant Major in 1780.
Page 631, Isaac Fisk, Sergeant Major. Lamb's Continental Artillery; promoted
    Lieutenant, Jan. 26, 1781.
Page 40, John Fisk, private Third Co.. First Regt. (Gen. Wooster's), 1775; en-
    listed May 14, 1775; discharged Dec. 10. 1775.

Page 115, John Fisk, Ensign; appointed Apr. 15, 1776; resigned Oct. 2, 1776; Capt. Parmelee's Co.

Page 222, John Fisk, private, Warner's Co.; enlisted Apr. 15, 1777; discharged Oct. 23, 1777.

Page 100, Rufus Fisk, private; Revolutionary rolls, Pension Office; Capt. Gallup's Co., Parson's Regt., Nov. 6, 1776.

Page 504, Rufus Fisk, Corporal, Capt. Hewitt's Co., Col. Latimer's Regt., militia at Saratoga, 1776; paid from Aug. 24, to Nov. 7, 1777.

Page 210, Samuel Fisk, private, Kirtland's Co.; enlisted May 8, 1777; deserted July 1, 1780; Sixth Regt. Connecticut Line; paid to 1780.

Page 534, Samuel Fisk, Corporal, Capt. Wheeler's Co., Col. Chapman's Regt., 1778; entered service, Aug. 3; discharged Sept. 12.

NEW YORK LINE. NEW YORK STATE ARCHIVES.

Page 245, Fisk, Isaac, Sergeant in Capt. John Brown's Co.; enlisted in spring of 1777; appointed Sergeant Major, 1779; Second Lieutenant, June 29, 1781; resigned for family reasons, July 14, 1782; A. P. 21-153; Southington, Hartford Co., Conn.

Page 372, Fisk, Abraham, private, Yates' Regt., Hadlock's Co.

Page 372, Fisk, Joseph, private, Van Renssalaer's Regt., Turner's Co.

Page 372, Fisk, William, private, Van Renssalaer's Regt., Turner's Co.

Page 372, Fisk, Wm., private, Graham's Regt., Lansing's Co.

RHODE ISLAND IN 1776. 352 PAGES.

Page 23, Fisk, Squire, Ensign of Sixth Co. (Capt. Barton's), Col. Richmond's Regt., Oct., 1775.

Page 24, Fisk, Squire, Lieutenant.

Page 36, Fisk, Benjamin, private in Capt. Martin's Co., Col. Lippel's Regt., Sept., 1776.

NEW HAMPSHIRE REVOLUTIONARY ROLLS. VOL. I.

Page 564, Fisk, Cato, private; enlisted from Epping in Capt. Rowel's Co., Fourth Militia Regt., 1777.

Page 301, Fisk, David, private in Capt. Timothy Clement's Co., Col. David Gilman's Regt., Apr. 15, 1776; paid £2, 0, 0, Apr. 9, 1776.

Page 391, Fisk, David, private; mustered in Sept. 19, 1776; same company and regiment as above.

Page 487, Fisk, David, private; pay 40 shillings, commenced Dec. 7, 1776; same company and regiment as above.

Page 509, Fisk, David, private; paid £2, 0, 0, Jan. 14, 1777; same company and regiment as above.

Page 513, Fisk, David, private; paid £2, 0, 0, from Jan. 7, to Feb. 7, 1777; same company and regiment as above.

Page 304, Fisk, Ephraim, private in Capt. Joshua Abbott's Co., Fifth Regt., Apr., 1776 Report.

Page 306, Fisk, Ephraim, private in Capt. Joshua Abbott's Co.; paid Feb. and Mar., 1776; signed by mark.

Page 465, Fisk, Eprafaim, private in Capt. Joshua Abbott's Co.; paid Nov. 5, for Oct., 1776.

Page 33, Fisk, James, private in Capt. Reuben Pow's Co. of Minute Men who marched from Holles, Apr. 19, 1775.

Page 33, Fisk, Josiah, private in Capt. Reuben Pow's Co. of Minute Men who marched from Holles, Apr. 19, 1775.

Page 346, Fisk, Josiah, fifer in Capt. Daniel Emerson's Co., Col. Wingate's Regt., July, 1776; paid $10, 6, 0.

Page 25, Fisk, Jonathan, private in Capt. Marston's Co., at Crown Point, Sept. 30, 1762.

Page 6, Fisk, Mashon, private in Col. Sir Charles Hobby's Regt., Oct. 10, 1710, to Oct. 10, 1711.

Page 566, Fisk, Solomon, private in Capt. Livermore's Co., Col. Thomas Stickney's Regt., 1777.

Page 630, Fiske, Cato, private from Epping, in Capt. Wm. Rowell's Co., Col. Nathan Hale's Regt., Mar. 4; paid £26, 0, 0, Mar. 4, 1778.

Page 244, Fiske, David, private in Capt Taylor's Militia Co., Dec. 8, 1775.

Page 653, Fiske, Solomon, private, Mar., 1777; muster roll of Capt. Daniel Livermore's Co., Col. Alexander Scammel's Regt.

VOLUME 2.

Page 224, Fisk, Aron, private; discharged Sept. 23, 1777; paid £15, 6, 0; pay roll of Capt. Kimball Carlton's Co., Col. Moses Nichol's Regt.

Page 451, Cato X Fisk, private, Col. Folsom's Battalions; from Eppin, Feb. 26, his mark. 1778.

Page 725, Fisk, Cato, private Eighth Co., Second Regt., commanded by Col. Geo. Reid.

Page 207, Fisk, Ebenezer, private in Capt. James Ford's Co., Col. Moses Nichol's Regt.; discharged Sept. 19, 1777.

Page 664, Eleazer X Fisk, Jr., private; mustered July 27, 1779, in Col. Nichol's his mark. Regt.; enlisted from Dunstable.

Page 671, Fisk, Eleazer, Jr., private; mustered July 27, 1779, in Col. Nichol's Regt.; enlisted from Dunstable.

Page 186, Fisk, Ephraim, private in Capt. Peter Kimball's Co., Col. Thos. Stickney's Regt.; discharged Sept. 25, 1777.

Page 671, Fisk, Ephraim, Jr., private in Capt. Peter Kimball's Co., Col. Thos. Stickney's Regt.; discharged Sept. 25, 1777.

Page 129, Fisk, Ephraim, Jr., private; discharged July 12, 1777; paid £1, 18, 4, Col. Thos. Stickney's Regt.

Page 743-4, Fisk, James, private in Capt. Reuben Dow's Co., Col. Wm. Prescott's Regt.; died of disease at Cambridge, May 29, 1775.

Page 87, Fisk, Josiah, private; discharged July 14, 1777, in Capt. Dan. Emerson's Co., Col. Nichol's Regt.

Page 510, Fisk, Josiah, private; discharged Aug. 28, 1778, in Capt. Dan. Emerson's Co., Col. Nichol's Regt.

Page 743, Fisk, Josiah, private in Capt. Reuben Dow's Co., Col. Wm. Prescott's Regt.

Page 211, Fisk, Simeon, private; discharged Sept. 28, 1777, in Capt. John Goss' Co., Captain (¾) Nichol's Regt.; paid £12, 7, 9.

Page 609, Fisk, Solomon, private, enlisted for nine months in Capt. Livermore's Co., Col. Thomas Stickney's Regt.

Page 677, Fiske, Eleazer, private; discharged Jan. 13, 1780, in Major Dan Reynold's Co., Col. Hercules Mooney's Regt.

Page 729, Fiske, Solomon, private Fourth Co., Third Regt., commanded by Col. Alexander Scammel.

VOLUME 3.

Page 539, Fisk, Amos, private; an account for supplies, £11, 15, 4.

Page 207, Fisk, Cato, private Eighth Co., Second Regt., commanded by Col. Geo. Reid, for 1780, from Epping.

Page 227, Fisk, Cato, private Third Co. (Capt. Wm. Rowell's Co.), Second Regt., commanded by Col. Geo. Reid, for 1781.

Page 275, Fisk, Cato, private Eighth Co., Second Regt., commanded by Col. Geo. Reid, for 1781.

Page 505, Fisk, Cato, private from Epping; from record of town returns.

Page 644-5, Fisk, Cato, private from Epping; from record of town returns.

Page 113, Fisk, Eleazer, private; enlisted July 9, 1780, in Capt. James Aiken's Co., Col. Thos. Bartlett's Regt.

Page 635, Fisk, Eleazer, private; Aug. 31, 1779, paid £39, 0, 0; Dunstable town records.

Page 105, Fisk, Epheram, private, Capt. Kinsman's return, Concord, July 11, 1780.

Page 148, Fisk, Ephraim, private; discharged Oct. 25, 1780, in Capt. Webster's Co., Col. Nichol's Regt.

Page 479, Fisk, Dr. Joseph, Surgeon.

Page 84, Fisk, Nathan, private; discharged Dec. 13, 1780; Dunstable; from pay roll for recruits, etc.

Page 91, Fisk, Nathan, private, aged 16. (Probably in 1780.)

Page 31, Fisk, Solomon, private; enlisted Mar. 22, 1777, in Capt. Daniel Livver-
         more's Co.; died Aug. 10, 1778.
Page 33, Fisk, Solomon, private; enlisted Mar. 22, 1777, in Capt. Daniel Livver-
         more's Co.; died Aug. 10, 1778.
Page 59, Fisk, Solomon, private; paid $6.60; original of this item in possession
         of Wm. P. Fiske, of Concord, N. H., 1887.

VOLUME 4.

Page 339, Fisk, Eleazer, Jr., private; enlisted from Dunstable, July 27, 1779, in
         Fifth Regt.
Page 312, Lieutenant Fisk, mentioned in letter of Col. Bedel to Gen. Gates, dated
         Haverhill, Jan. 13, 1778.

WORCESTER COUNTY HISTORY, MASS. Volume 2.

Page 114, Town of Sturbridge, Simeon Fiske, Nathan Fiske and Joshua Fiske.
Page 904, Upton, Wm. Fisk, a selectman and treasurer in 1779.
·Page 909, Upton, Wm. Fisk, First Lieutenant, Company of Capt. Robert Taft.
         Regt. of Col. Silas Wheelock.
Page 909, Upton, Daniel Fisk, private Company of Capt. Robert Taft, Regt. of
         Col. Silas Wheelock.
Page 910, Upton, Daniel Fisk, private Company of Capt. Robert Taft, in 1777.
Page 910, Upton, Nathaniel Fisk, private Company of Capt. Thomas Marshal
         Baker, 1779; service at Hudson River; Regt. of Col. James Denney.
Page 911, Upton, Jacob Fisk, in July, 1780, at R. I., Capt. Thos. Marshal Baker's
         Co., Col. Nathan Tyler's Regt.
Page 1202, Rutland furnished 103 men. among them is a Jacob Fisk.
Page 1391, Holden. David Fiske, an assessor in 1777-78 and '80.
    Essex County History, 2 vols., of over 1,900 pages, found not a single item in re-
gard to a Fisk or Fiske.
    Plymouth County History, 2 vols., of over 1,200 pages, not a single item found
concerning a Fisk or Fiske.

NORFOLK CO. HISTORY (1884).

Page 524, Needham, June 6, 1780, Moses Fisk one of a committee on legislative
         business.
Page 855, Brookline, Thomas Fisk (of Newtown), private in Capt. Timothy
         Corey's Co., Col. Baldwin's Regt., Aug. 1, 1775.
Page 856, Brookline, Enoch Fisk, private in Capt. Thos. White's Co., Col. Will-
         iam Heath's Regt., Apr. 19, to May 12, 1775 or 6.
    Bristol County History (1883-6), over 800 pages, no mention of any Fisk or
Fiske.
    Berkshire County History (1885), 2 vols., of over 1,400 pages.
Page 188, Adams, Ebenezer Fisk.
Page 196, Lanesborough. Isaac Fisk.
Page 201, Peru, Experians Fisk, Sylvanus Fisk, Thomas Fisk.
    No companies, regiments or service is given of the Berkshire Co. Rev. soldiers,
their names are merely copied from the records at Boston, Mass.

HISTORY OF CONNECTICUT VALLEY (1879).

Page 69, William Fisk, of Greenwich, Hampshire Co., a minute man in a company
         commanded by Second Lieutenant Thomas Weekes, Col. Elijah Por-
         ter's Regt.
Page 658, Vol. 2, Nathan Fisk. of Northfield, Franklin Co., minute man at Lex-
         ington, in Capt. Eldad Wright's Co.
Page 749, Jonathan Fisk, of Coleraine, Franklin Co., at Lexington, in Capt. Hugh
         McLellan's Co., Col. Sam. William's Regt.
Page 783, Zedekiah Fisk, recorded with six other men as Revolutionary soldiers
         from Wendall, Franklin Co., Mass.
Page 1003, Jonathan Fisk, a resident of Broomfield, Hampden Co.
Page 1073, Asa Fisk, of Wales, Hampden Co., was one of a committee to inspect,
         was probably a minute man; an Asa Fisk of this town was a Captain
         in the Shay Rebellion.

FROM THE HISTORY OF MIDDLESEX CO., MASS. 3 Vols. (1890).

Vol. 2, Page 621. David Fiske. of Lincoln (a minute man in 1775), was Sergeant
         in Capt. William Smith's Co., Col. Abijah Pierce's Regt.

Vol. 3, Page 229, Wainwright Fisk, of Pepperell, was at Concord; he was a private in Capt. Nutting's Co., Col. Wm. Prescott's Regt.

Vol. 3, Page 233, Wainwright Fisk, of Pepperell, killed at Bunker Hill, aged 24 years.

Vol. 3, Page 297, Jonathan Fisk, of Tewksbury, was a Revolutionary soldier.

Vol. 3, Page 297, Benjamin Fisk, of Tewksbury, was a Revolutionary soldier.

Vol. 3, Page 721, Abijah Fisk, in Waltham's Co. of minute men, Apr., 1775; also in Capt. Abraham Pierce's Co., Col. Thos. Gardner's Regt.

Vol. 3, Page 721, Amos Fisk, in Waltham's Co. of minute men, Apr., 1775.

Vol. 3, Page 721, Also both names in muster roll of (Oct. 6, 1775,) Capt. Abijah Child's Thirty-seventh Regt. of Foot, commanded by Lieutenant Colonel William Bond.

Also same names, in 1778, in the "Eight Months' Company."

Vol. 3, Page 784, Abner Fisk, a selectman of Hopkinton, in 1782; Lieutenant Abel Fisk a selectman in 1784.

FROM RHODE ISLAND IN 1776. A volume of 352 pages.

Page 23, Ensign Squire Fisk, October, 1775, Sixth Co. (Capt. Barton's), Col. Richmond's Regt.

Page 24, Lieutenant Squire Fisk, in Continental pay.

Page 36, Private Benjamin Fisk, September, 1776, Capt. Martin's Co., Col. Lippel's Regt.

FROM "NEW YORK STATE ARCHIVES. NEW YORK IN THE REVOLUTION." 638 pages.

Page 245, Fisk, Isaac, Sergeant, Capt. John Brown; enlisted spring of 1777; appointed Sergeant Major, 1779; Second Lieutenant, June 29, 1781; resigned for family reasons, July 14, 1782. A. P. 21-153, Southington, Hartford County, Conn.

Page 372, Fisk, Abraham, private Yates' Regt., Hadlock's Co.

Page 372, Fisk. Joseph, private Van Renssalaer's Regt., Turner's Co.

Page 372, Fisk, William, private Van Renssalaer's Regt., Turner's Co.

Page 372, Fisk, Wm., private Graham's Regt., Lansing's Co.

FROM HEITMAN'S HIST. REGISTER OF OFFICERS OF THE CONTINENTAL ARMY, 1775-1783.

Page 176, Fisk, Joseph (Mass.), Second Lieutenant, Twelfth Continental Infantry, Jan. 1, to Dec. 31, 1776; Surgeon's mate, First Massachusetts. Jan. 1. 1777; Surgeon, Apr. 17, 1779, and served to close of war. (Died Sept. 25, 1827.)

Page 176, Fisk, Squire (R. I.), Ensign of Richmond's R. I. State Regiment, Nov. 1, 1775, to Apr., 1776.

Page 176, Fisk, Thomas (Mass.), Second Lieutenant of Learned's Massachusetts Regiment. May. 1775——.

Page 176, Fisk, William (R. I.). Lieutenant of Elliott's Regiment. R. I. State Artillery. Dec. 12. 1776. to June. 1777.

Page 176, Fiske, Daniel (R. I.). Ensign of Tollman's R. I. State Regiment, Dec. 12, 1776. to June, 1777.

"The Official Register of the Officers and Men of New Jersey in the Revolutionary War." By Adjt. Gen. Wm. S. Stryker, 1872. 878 pages.

"Saffel's Records of the Revolutionary War," 555 pages; 1894 edition. page 419, Fisk, Joseph. Surgeon. Massachusetts.

An alphabetical list of all Revolutionary War pensioners of the name of Fisk or Fiske that could be found in the lists of 1820 and 1835; the Census Report of 1840, and the "Rejected and Suspended Claims," of 1850:

Abijah Fisk, Middlesex Co.. Mass.: died March 14 1833.

Abner Fisk, York Co.. Me.; 79 years old in 1835.

Abner Fisk, Oneida Co.. N. Y.: 79 years old in 1835.

Abner Fisk, Westport. Essex Co.. N. Y.: 81 years old in 1840.

Abner Fisk, Lee, Oneida Co.. N. Y.; 86 years old in 1840.

Mrs. Abigail F., Sturbridge, Worcester Co., Mass.; from rejected and suspended claims, 1850. Widow.

Amey Fisk, Cumberland. Providence Co.. R. I.: 79 years old in 1840.

Artemas Fisk, Newport Co.. R. I.: 74 years old in 1835.

Mrs. Betsey Fisk, Framingham, Middlesex Co., Mass., 81 years old in 1840. Widow.

Cato Fisk, Rockingham Co., N. H.; 64 years old in 1835.

Daniel Fisk, Worcester Co., Mass.; 78 years old in 1835.

David Fisk, Hillsborough Co., N. H.; 70 years old in 1835.

David Fisk, Amherst, Hillsborough Co., N. H.; 83 years old in 1840.

David Fisk, Middlesex Co., Mass.

David Fiske, private and drummer, Middlesex Co., Mass., 73 years old in 1835.

Ephraim Fisk, Merrimack Co., N. H.; 70 years old in 1835.

Ephraim Fisk, Hopkinton, Merrimack Co., N. H.; 81 years old in 1840.

Mrs. Eunice F. Chaplain, Windham Co., Conn.; 86 years old in 1840. Widow.

Experians Fisk, Orleans Co., Vt.; died June 2, 1825.

Jacob Fisk, Worcester Co., Mass.; 71 years old in 1835.

Jacob Fisk, Windsor, Berkshire Co., Mass.; 77 years old in 1840.

James Fisk, Franklin Co., Vt.; 70 years old in 1835.

James Fiske, Swanton, Franklin Co., Vt.; 77 years old in 1840.

John Fisk, private and seaman, Worcester Co., Mass.; 73 years old in 1835.

John Fisk, Genesee Co., N. Y.; 71 years old in 1835.

John Fisk, Attica, Genesee Co., N. Y.; 79 years old in 1840.

Jonathan Fisk, Otsego Co., N. Y.; 77 years old in 1835.

Jonathan Fisk, Warren Co., N. Y.; 77 years old in 1835.

Mrs. Johanna F., Brookfield, Madison Co., N. Y.; from rejected and suspended claims, 1850. Widow of John Fisk.

Joseph Fisk, Surgeon, Middlesex Co., Mass.

Joseph Fisk, Sergeant, Massachusetts.

Mrs. Mehitable Fisk, Freedom, Cattaraugus Co., N. Y.; from rejected and suspended claims, 1850. Widow of Jonathan Fisk.

Nathan Fiske, Middlesex Co., Mass.; 74 years old in 1835.

Nathan Fisk, Dunstable, Hillsborough Co., N. H.; did not serve six months; from rejected and suspended claims.

Noah Fisk, Providence Co., R. I.; 81 years old in 1835.

Mrs. Ruth Fiske, Brookfield, Orange Co., Vt.; 89 years old in 1840. Widow.

Samuel Fisk, Ostego, Ostego Co., N. Y.; a deserter; from rejected and suspended claims, 1850.

Seberry Fisk, Hampden Co., Mass.; 74 years old in 1835.

Stephen Fisk, private and Sergeant, Windsor Co., Vt.; 75 years old in 1835.

Stephen Fisk, Royalton, Orange Co., Vt.; 82 years old in 1840.

Thomas Fisk, Sergeant, Genesee Co., N. Y.; died Nov. 19, 1828.

William Fisk, Windsor Co., Vt.

Zedekiah Fisk, Wendall, Franklin Co., Mass.; 76 years old in 1840.

A List of Revolutionary Pensioners. Collected from Various Government Publications.

FIRST.

A LIST OF PENSIONS GRANTED TO REVOLUTIONARY SOLDIERS. PRINTED IN 1835.

NAME.	COUNTY.	RANK.	DESCRIPTION OF SERVICE.	WHEN PLACED ON PENSION ROLL.	COMMENCEMENT OF PENSION.	AGE.	ANNUAL ALLOWANCE.	SUMS RECEIVED.	REMARKS.
Maine State Rec., p. 150.									
Abner Fisk....York	Priv. and Serg.		Massachusetts militia	Aug. 1, 1833.	Mar. 4, 1851.	79	$41.66.	$124.98.	
New Hampshire Rec., p. 48.									
David Fisk....Hillsborough	Private		N. H. Continental Line.	Nov. 29, 1819.	Apr. 18, 1818.	76	96.00.	1,526.13.	
New Hampshire Rec., p. 56.									
Ephraim Fisk..Merrimack	Private		N. H. Continental Line.	July 15, 1819.	Mar. 16,1823.	70	96.00.	1,524.80.	
New Hampshire Rec., p. 62.									
Cato Fisk....Rockingham	Private		N. H. Continental Line.	Jan. 14, 1819.	Apr. 6, 1818.	64	96.00.	567.46.	
Mass. Rec., p. 120.									
Zedekiah Fisk..Franklin	Private		Mass. Continental Line.	Oct. 18, 1818.	Sept.15,1818.	—	96.00.	121.06.	Pens'n suspended
Zedekiah Fisk..Franklin	Private		Mass. Continental Line.	Sept. 24, 1832.	Mch. 4,1831.	71	80.00.	240.00.	Act of May 1, 1820, renewed June 7, 1832.
Mass. Rec., p. 140.									
Seberry Fisk...Hampden	Private		N. Y. Continental Line.	Nov. 2, 1832.	Mar. 4, 1831.	74	80.00.	240.00.	
Mass. Rec., p. 167.									
Abijah Fisk...Middlesex	Seaman		Naval service.	Mch. 7, 1833,	Jan. 1, 1825.		72.00.	590.80.	Died Mar. 14, '33.
Mass. Rec., p. 177.									
David Fiske...Middlesex	Musician		Mass. Line.	Apr. 5, 1819.	June 3, 1818.		96.00.	158.26.	Pen. susp'd act of May 1, 1820.
Mass. Rec., p. 178.									
Joseph Fisk...Middlesex	Surgeon		Mass. Line.	June 26, 1819.	May 9, 1818.		240.00.	436.66.	Pen. susp'd act of May 1, 1820.
Mass. Rec., p. 194.									
Nathan Fiske..Middlesex	Private		Mass. Militia.	May 8, 1833.	Mar. 4, 1831.	74	31.33.	78.33.	
Mass. Rec., p. 194.									
David Fiske...Middlesex	Prv. & Drum'r		Mass. Militia.	July 29, 1833.	Mar. 4, 1831.	73	34.00.	102.33.	
Mass. Rec., p. 316.									
Daniel Fisk...Worcester	Private		Mass. Militia.	Nov. 5, 1832.	Mar. 4, 1831.	78	32.70.	98.10.	
Mass. Rec., p. 316.									
Jacob Fisk....Worcester	Private		Mass. State troops.	Nov. 12, 1832.	Mar. 4, 1831.	71	46.66.	139.98.	
Mass. Rec., p. 318.									
John Fisk....Worcester	Pvr. & Seaman		U. S. N., R. I. State troops and militia.	Feb. 22, 1833.	Mar. 4, 1831.	73	66.66.	199.38.	

Mass. Rec., p. 339.

NAME.	COUNTY.	RANK.	ANNUAL ALLOWANCE.	SUMS RECEIVED.	DESCRIPTION OF SERVICE.	WHEN PLACED ON PENSION ROLL.	COMMENCEMENT OF PENSION.	AGE.	REMARKS.
Joseph Fiske	Middlesex	Surgeon	4,800.00	4,320.00	1st Regt. Mass. Line.				
Rhode Island Rec., p. 28.									
Attamas Fiske	Newport	Private	60.00	150.00	R. I. Mil. & State troops.	Feb. 26, 1833.	Mar. 4, 1831.	74	
Rhode Island Rec., p. 34.									
Noah Fisk	Providence	Private	40.00	120.00	R.I. Con'l Mil.York State.	Oct. 23, 1832.	Mar. 4, 1831.	81	
Vermont Rec., p. 9.									
Experians Fisk, Jr.	Orleans	Private	$96.00	$1,064.53	31st Regt. U. S. Infantry.	June 9, 1819.	Apr. 30, 1814.	—	Died June 2, 1825.
Vermont Rec., p. 11.									
William Fisk	Windsor	Private	64.00	1,202.88	25th Regt, U. S. Infantry.	Aug. 10, 1817.	May 18, 1815.	—	
Vermont Rec., p. 105.									
James Fisk	Franklin	Private	70.66	211.98	Mass. Continental Line.	May 30, 1833.	Mar. 4, 1831.	70	
Vermont Rec., p. 147.									
Stephen Fisk	Windsor	Priv. and Sergt.	96.00	183.60	Mass. Continental Line.	May 23, 1820.	Apr. 6, 1818.	75	Dropped under Act March 1, '26.
Stephen Fisk	Windsor	Priv. and Sergt.	90.00	270.00	Mass. Continental Line.	Dec. 20, 1832.	Mar. 4, 1831.	—	Pensioned again June 7, 1832.
New York State Rec., p. 148.									
Thomas Fisk	Genesee	Sergeant	96.00	902.39	Massachusetts Line	Nov. 26, 1819.	June 26, 1819.	70	Died Nov.19,1828.
New York Rec., p. 213.									
Jonathan Fisk	Otsego	Private	96.00	1,478.39	Connecticut Line.	Mar. 11, 1820.	Apr. 11, 1818.	77	
New York Rec., p. 252.									
Jonathan Fisk	Warren	Private	96.00	1,522.09	Massachusetts Line	Oct. 13, 1818.	Apr. 27, 1818.	77	
New York Rec., p. 312.									
John Fisk	Genesee	Private	40.00	100.00	Vermont Militia.	Oct. 5, 1733.	Mar. 4, 1831.	71	
New York Rec., p. 360.									
Abner Fiske	Oneida	Private	26.66		Mass. Continental Line.	May 2, 1833.	Mar. 4, 1831.	79	

SECOND.

SUSPENDED AND REJECTED CLAIMS, 1850.

NAME.	TOWN.	COUNTY.	REMARKS.

N. H. Rec., p. 16.

Nathan Fiske..............Dunstable ..Hillsborough .Did not serve six months.

Mass. Rec., p. 61.

Abigail Fiske, wid. of Nathan
Fiske ....Sturbridge..Worcester....Did not serve six months.

N. Y. Rec., p. 96.

Samuel Fisk................Otsego......Ostego .

N. Y. Rec., p. 156.

Mehitable Fisk, wid. of Jona-
than Fisk...............Freedom ...Cattaraugus ..Married long after service;
not a widow July 7, 1838,

N. Y. Rec., p. 162.   and died before August
Joanna Fisk, widow of John   16, 1842.
Fisk ....Brookfield..Madison .....Suspended for proof of serv-
ice from N. H. Rec.

THIRD.

FROM THE CENSUS OF PENSIONERS, 1840, PRINTED IN 1841.

NAME.	AGE.	TOWN.	COUNTY.	Name of head of family where pensioner resided June 1, '40.	REMARKS.

N. H. Rec., p. 18.

Ephraim Fisk........81..Hopkinton.

N. H. Rec., p. 18.

Ephraim Fisk.......81..Hopkinton...Merrimack Ephraim Fisk, jr.

P. 20.

David Fisk..........83..Amherst.....Hillsboro'gDavid Fisk, 3d.

P. 26.

William Fisk.........52..Dalton.......Coos ......William Fisk .He must be a son
Mass. Rec., p. 33.   of a Rev. soldier.

Jacob Fisk ....77..Windsor ....Berkshire..Jacob Fisk.

P. 34.

Zedekiah Fisk........76..Wendal.....Franklin...Zedekiah Fisk.

P. 36.

Seberry Fisk..........79..W. Hampton.Hampshire.

Mass. Rec., p. 38,

David Young.........84..Athol ....Worcester.Moses Fisk.   A. Fisk in 2d
P. 41.   column.

Betsey Fisk ....81..Framingham.Middlesex.Joseph Ballard.

P. 44.

Lucy Stodder.........82..Fifth ward...Boston ....Susan Fisk.   Fisk name in
R. I. Rec., p. 46.   last column.

Amey Fisk...........79..Cumberland.ProvidenceAmey Fisk.

Con. Rec., p. 57.

Eunice Fisk.........86..Chaplain ....Windham .Eunice Fisk.

Vt. Rec., p. 52.

James Fiske..........97..Swanton.....Franklin ..James Fisk.

P. 63.

Ebenezer Fisk........53..Groton ......Caledonia..Ebenezer Fisk. Must be a son
P. 65   of a Rev. soldier.

Ruth Fiske..........87..Brookfield...Orange....Artemas Fiske.

P. 70.

Stephen Fisk.........82..Royalton ....Orange....Stephen Fisk.

N. Y. Rec., p. 76.

Fisk Durand........74..Westfield ...Chatauqua.Fisk Durand. Prob. immedi-
P. 80.   ate desc. of Fisk.

Abner Fisk..........81..Westport....Essex .....Ashael Havens.

P. 82.

John Fisk ....79..Attica ....Genesee...John Fisk.

P. 89.

Abner Fisk..........86..Lee ....Oneida....Alvin Walker.

The following copy from the Pension Office at Washington, shows how the records are kept:

O. W. & N. Division.

DEPARTMENT OF THE INTERIOR,

F. S.   BUREAU OF PENSIONS,   M. E. C.

WASHINGTON, D. C., March 26, 1894.

......*Madam :—*
   In reply to your request for a statement of the military history of Zedekiah Fisk, a soldier of the Revolutionary war, you will please find below the desired information as contained in his (or his widow's) application for pension on file in this Bureau.

Dates of Enlistment or Appointment.	Length of Service.	Rank.	Officers Under Whom Service Was Rendered.		State.
			Captain.	Colonel.	
June, 1780...	6 months.	Pvt.	Josiah Smith.	Marshall.	Mass.
August, 1781	2 months.	Pvt.	Conant.	Sears.	Mass.
May, 1782...	1 year.	Pvt.	Burnham.	Jackson.	Mass.
June, 1783 ..	1 year.	Pvt.	Potter.	American Regiment.	......
....	....	....	....	....	......
....	....	....	....	....	......

Battles engaged in.   None mentioned.
Residence of soldier at enlistment.   Town not stated.
Date of application for pension.   September 15, 1818.
Residence at date of application.   Wendell, Massachusetts.
Age at date of application.   Fifty-five years.
   Remarks:

Very respectfully,

WM. LOCHREN, Commisioner.

SOMETHING OF THE ENGLISH
AND AMERICAN FISKES.

(By Rev. Thaddeus Fiske, of North Cambridge, Mass.)

The most remote ancestors of the Fiske family that have come to our knowledge lived in a village or parish of St. James, in the County of Suffolk, England, in the reign of Queen Mary, in the sixteenth century.

There were six brothers, three were Papists and three were Protestants. Their ancestors, parents, grandparents, and great-grandparents, as far as history gives an account, are said to have been eminently pious and religious people. Those of Protestant religion were grievously persecuted. One of them, to avoid being burned at the stake, was hid many months in a wood-pile, and afterward half a year in a cellar where he worked by candle light at manufactures and remained undiscovered. But his many hardships shortened his life. In 1637 four of his children, two sons and two daughters, in consequence of the persecuting spirit of that day, left their home and came over to New England and took up their abode in Salem. John was the eldest of the four, and his father at his death committed to him the charge of his mother, two sisters and youngest brother. John had been educated at Immanuel College, England, and became a preacher of the Gospel, but on account of his non-conformity, being advised by his friends, he relinquished the ministry and turned his attention to the study of medicine, and obtained license for public practice as a physician. On arriving at Salem, however, he recommenced the work of the ministry, his favorite pursuit. He was both a preacher of the Gospel and tutor and instructor to divers young men in Salem, and was also employed as a physician whenever he would consent. Their mother died before they arrived in New England. They came well provided with servants and all sorts of tools for husbandry and carpentry, and with provisions for their support for three years, out of which they helped others, whom they found in want and distress. They remained together at Salem about three years. John then went to a new village in Salem, called Wenham, where he gathered a church and congregation, and continued their pastor about fourteen years. About the end of the year 1655 he removed to a town called Chelmsford, where he lived the greater part of his days. He died Jan. 14, 1676, aged seventy-five. He left four children, two sons and two daughters. John lived with his father in Chelmsford and was a very useful and respected citizen. Moses was brought up at school, graduated at Harvard University in 1662; was settled in the ministry at Braintree. On the 14th of February, 1671, the wife of Rev. John Fiske died, which was the greatest of all his trials and afflictions. She was endeared to him by forty-three years of mutual care and toil, affection and piety. By her incomparable knowledge of the Scriptures she became his concordance of the Bible and he needed no other. She could refer him to any passage of the Scripture that he wished to find. The youngest brother of John Fiske who came over with him settled in Watertown and was mechanic or farmer. His name probably was Nathan, for mention is made in Watertown records of Nathan Fiske there in 1664 and of Nathan Fiske, Jr., in 1728, who was representative of the town. Nathan, the son of the above named Nathan Fiske, went from Watertown and settled at Weston. He was the grandfather of Rev. Thaddeus Fiske, of West Cambridge. On Oct. 9 he married Anna Warren, by whom he had three children: Anna, Nathan and Sarah. Having lost his wife he married, Feb. 21, 1738, for his second wife widow Mary Fiske, of Sudbury, by whom he had seven children, namely: Jonathan, Ezra, Samuel, Thaddeus, Mary, Hepzibeth and Nathan, the eldest, who graduated at Harvard in 1754 and was settled in the ministry in Brookfield. It appears that the name of Nathan was uniformly given to the firstborn son, a practice transmitted from generation to generation. Jonathan married Abigal Fiske, of Waltham, Mar. 10, 1760, by whom he had nine children: Nathan, Thaddeus, Micah, Ebenezer, Abigal, Jonathan (who died in infancy), Jonathan, Abigal and Isaac. Among the descendants of Nathan there are eight who have received collegiate educations, seven Hummis of Harvard University, one of Dartmouth

EIGHT MANOR HOUSE, STALBRIDGE, ENGLAND

College, namely, 1st, Nathan Fiske, D. D., his eldest son, minister of Brookfield, graduated 1754; 2d, Thaddeus Fiske, his grandson, son of Jonathan Fiske, minister of West Cambridge, graduated 1785; 3d, Oliver, M. D., his grandson, son of Nathan Fiske, D. D., physician of Worcester, graduated 1787; 4th, Samuel, A. M., his grandson, son of Nathan Fiske, D. D., trader in Claremont, N. H., and alternately senator and representative to the general court, graduated 1793; Isaac, A. M., his grandson, son of Jonathan, register of probate court in the county of Middlesex, graduated 1798; 6th, Nathan W. Fiske, A. M., his grandson, son of Nathan, son of Jonathan, professor of intellectual and moral philosophy in Amherst College, graduated at Dartmouth College 1817; 7th, Robert Treat Paine Fiske, M. D., son of Oliver Fiske, M. D., son of Nathan Fiske, D. D., physician in Hingham, graduated 1818; 8th, Augustus Henry Fiske, son of Isaac Fiske, son of Jonathan, attorney-at-law in Boston, graduated 1825. Such are the ancestors and some of the descendants of the Fiske family to which I, Rev. Thaddeus Fiske, of Cambridge, am more immediately related. There are other branches from the same stock, which are spread out in various directions over the United States.

NAMED FOR FISKES.

There are a number of places in the United States named Fisk and quite a number of postoffices of this name. In all cases the names were given in honor of a person by this name. Below will be found a few illustrations:

FISK, VT.—In the years 1765 and 1766 a French general from Canada named Lamathe built a large fort and had it garrisoned with soldiers and implements of war in what is now called the town of Isle La Mott, which is an island surrounded by the waters of Lake Champlain, containing 4,883½ acres by the original survey, and was named in part after the said French general Lamathe, they changed Lamathe to La Mott for some reason not now known. The town being an island, hence it was called Isle La Mott. There were enlightened, educated French officers occupying said fort from 1766 to some time unknown at this time. when it was evacuated for at least fifty-seven years before a blow had been struck elsewhere within the present domain of the state of Vermont by civilized man. I do not know as you care to have an account of the war for which this fort was built and I have not time to give it. In 1802 Samuel Fisk, Esq., representing said Isle La Mott in the legislature of Vermont, had the name changed from Isle La Mott to Vineyard. In 1830 it was changed back to Isle La Mott. The present postoffice is Fisk, named in honor of Hon. Nelson W. Fisk, lieutenant-governor of Vermont.

FISKDALE, MASS.—Chase's History gives the following account of Fiskdale, which is a village in the town of Sturbridge: "Two brothers, Henry and Josiah J. Fiske, sons of David, of Fiske hill, and grandsons of Henry, bought Moses Allers' farm, erected the first factory and laid the foundation of the village that bears their name. Moses Allen's farm was deeded to them in 1826." Frederick D. Fiske. office 87 Milk Street, Boston, is at present at the head of the business.

FISK, MO.—Fisk, Mo., Sept. 4, 1895. Dear Sir: Your letter of 28th addressed to town clerk is handed me for a reply. The postoffice here was given the name of "Fisk" for the reason it was a short name, and as a compliment to me, having done quite a mill business here for several years, and am now the postmaster here. I came to this place twelve years ago from Kalamazoo, Mich., or near there, in Van Buren County. My parents originally came from Rhode Island. I was born in Vermont in 1831. My father's name was Samuel B. Fisk. Am cousin to James Fisk, Jr., who was shot by Stokes some years ago. I suppose I have a cousin living in Chicago by name of C. W. Fisk. If I can be of any help to you in compiling your work shall be glad to do what I can.

Very truly,

S. W. FISK.

OUR ENGLISH ANCESTORS.

1. LORD SYMOND FISKE, grandson of Daniel, was Lord of the Manor of Stadhaugh, Parish of Laxfield, County of Suffolk, England, lived in the reigns of Henry IV. and VI. (1399-1422), he m. Susannah Smyth; she d. and he m. 2d Katherine ———. Simon Fiske, of Laxfield, will dated Dec. 22, 1463, proved at Norwich, England, Feb. 26, 1463-4. Bequeaths his soul to God, the Virgin Mary and all the Saints in Heaven. Bequeaths to each of his sons, William, Jeffrey, John and Edmund, 20 pounds. Mentions his dau. Margaret Dowsing. Appoints his wife, Katherine, son John and Nichols Noloch executors. He d. in Feb., 1464; res. Stadhaugh, Laxfield, Suffolk Co., England.

    2.   i.   WILLIAM, b. in England; m. Joan Lynne.
    3.   ii.   JEFFREY, b. in England; m. Margaret ———.
    4.   iii.   JOHN, b. in England; m. ——— ———.
    5.   iv.   EDMUND, b. in England; m. Margery ———.
    6.   v.   MARGARET, b. in England; m. Dowsing or Dowling.

2. WILLIAM FISKE (Symond), b. Stadhaugh, County Suffolk, England; m. Joan Lynne, of Norfolk. He was of Stadhaugh and lived during the reigns of Henry VI., Edward IV., Richard III. and Henry VII. He d. before his wife, for Joan Fiske, late wife of William, of Laxfield, made her will July 15, 1504, which was proved Feb. 28, 1505. Mentions her sons John, Augustine and Simon, son's wife Anne and daus. Margery and Margaret. Appoints Sir John Fiske, son of John Fiske, and her son Simon executors. He d. about 1504. Res. Laxfield, Eng.

    7.   i.   THOMAS, b. in England; m. Anne ———.
    8.   ii.   WILLIAM, b. in England, m. Joan ———.
    9.   iii.   AUGUSTINE, b. in England; m. Joan ———.
    10.   iv.   SIMON, b. in England; m. Elizabeth ———.
    11.   v.   ROBERT, b. in England; m. ——— ——— and Joan ———.
    12.   vi.   JOHN, b. in England; m. ——— ———.
    13.   vii. MARGERY, b. in England.
    14.   viii. MARGARET, b. in England.

3. JEFFREY FISKE (Symond), b. Laxfield, Eng., ———; m. Margaret ———, d. 1504. His will is dated May 3, 1504, and proved May 13, 1504. Mentions sons Jeffrey, John and Simon, and daus. Joan and Margery.
His wife made her will the following day, May 4, and it was proved the 13th. Mentions John and Jeffrey Fiske, brothers, and appoints Rev. John Fiske executor. He d. May, 1504; res. Laxfield, Eng.

    15.   i.   JEFFREY, b. in England; m. ——— ———.
    16.   ii.   JOHN, b. in England.
    17.   iii.   SIMON, b. in England.
    18.   iv.   JOAN, b. in England.
    19.   v.   MARGERY, b. in England.

4. REV. JOHN FISKE (Symond), b. Laxfield, Eng., ———; m. there ———. His will is dated Jan. 18, 1507, and was proved Feb. 5, 1512. Mentions son Sir John Fiske, Chaplain, and son Robert Fiske, Canon of Leyston. To Jane, dau. of Robert, he gives six and eight pence. He d. in 1512. Res. Laxfield, Eng.

    20.   i.   JOHN, b. in England; m. Phillis ———.
    21.   ii.   ROBERT, b. in England; m. ——— ———.

5. EDMUND FISKE (Symond), b. Laxfield, Eng., ———; m. Margery
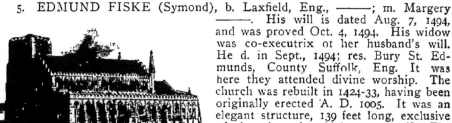
———. His will is dated Aug. 7, 1494, and was proved Oct. 4, 1494. His widow was co-executrix oī her husband's will. He d. in Sept., 1494; res. Bury St. Edmunds, County Suffolk, Eng. It was here they attended divine worship. The church was rebuilt in 1424-33, having been originally erected A. D. 1005. It was an elegant structure, 139 feet long, exclusive of the chancel, which was 74x68. The roof of the nave, which was framed in Caen, Normandy, is admired for its lightness and elegance.

ST. MARY'S CHURCH, BURY ST. EDMUNDS, ENG.

7. LORD THOMAS FISKE (William, Symond), b.———; m. Annc ———. Thomas Fiske, the elder, of Laxfield, was Lord of the Manor of Stadhaugh, made his will Oct. 27, 1525. It was proved Dec. 10, 1525. In the document he refers to his wife, but does not mention name; sons William, Thomas and Henry; dau. Agnes and brother Simon. Mentions his lands in Fressingfield. Appoints his sons Henry and Thomas executors. He d. Dec., 1525; res. Stadhaugh, Eng.

 22. i. WILLIAM, b. in England; m. Margaret Ball.
 23. ii. THOMAS, b. in England; m. ——— ———.
 24. iii. HENRY, b. in England; m. ——— ———.
 25. iv. AGNES, b. in England.

8. WILLIAM FISKE (William, Symond), b. Laxfield, Eng.; m. Joan ———. He was of Halesworth, made his will Jan. 31, 1512-13, proved May 12, 1513. Mentions wife Joan, son Thomas, and brothers Simon and Thomas. He d. in 1513; res. Halesworth, Eng.

 26. i. THOMAS, b. in England.

9. AUGUSTINE FISKE (William, Symond), b. Laxfield, Eng., ———; m. Joan ———. He was of Laxfield; his will is dated Mar. 15, 1507-08, and was proved Apr. 11, 1508. His wife was Joan, son Thomas, and brothers Simon and Thomas. He d. 1508; res. Laxfield, Eng.

 27. i. THOMAS, b. in England.

10. SIMON FISKE (William, Symond), b. Laxfield, Eng., ———; m. Elizabeth ———. She d. in Halesworth in June, 1558. He resided in Laxfield and made his will July 10, 1536. It was proved July 13, 1538. He desires to be buried at the chancel end of the Church of All Saints, in Laxfield, next his father, son Robert, son William, and wife Elizabeth, son Jeffrey, daus. Joan Iverton, Gelyne Warner, Agnes Fiske, son Simon. John Fiske of Holton was supervisor. He d. in June, 1538; res. Laxfield, Eng.

 28. i. SIMON, b. in England; m. ——— ———.
 29. ii. WILLIAM, b. in England.
 30. iii. ROBERT, b. in England; m. Alice ———.
 31. iv. JOAN, b. in England; m. ——— Iverton.
 32. v. JEFFREY, b. in England.
 33. vi. GELYNE, b. in England; m. ——— Warner.
 34. vii. AGNES, b. in England.
 35. viii. THOMAS, b. in England.
 36. ix. ELIZABETH, b. in England.
 37. x. JOHN, b. in England.

11. ROBERT FISKE (William, Symond), b. Rendham, ———; m. ——— ——— and Joan ———. He was a clothmaker by trade; will dated Feb. 15, 1563. He desired to be buried in the parish of St. Mary's at Elms in Ipswich, where his former wife is buried. John Cole, of Ipswich, was executor. He d. 1563; res. Ipswich, Eng.

 38. i. MARGARET, b. in England.

JOHN FISKE (William, Symond), b. Laxfield, Eng., ———; m. ——— His wife d. before he did. His will is dated Nov. 23, 1550, and proved

July 2, 1562. Desires to be buried in the churchyard in Holton near his children.
He d. 1562; res. Laxfield and Holton, Eng.

    39. i.   WILLIAM, b. in England.
    40. ii.   FRANCIS, b. in England.
    41. iii. JANE, b. in England; m. ——— Keene.

    15. JEFFREY FISKE (Jeffrey, Symond), b. in England, ———; m. ———
———. He was a cooper. He d. Apr. 29, 1591; res. Laxfield, Eng.

    20. SIR JOHN FISKE, Chaplain, (John, Symond), b. Laxfield, Eng.,
———; m. Phillis ———. John Fiske, of Halesworth, Mercer, will dated Oct. 5,
1530, proved Apr. 21, 1531, wife Phillis; brother Robert. John Fiske, of Holton,
was executor. He d. s. p. 1531; res. Halesworth, Eng.

    21. ROBERT FISKE (John, Symond), b. Laxfield, Eng., ———; m. ———
———. He was Canon of Leyston; res. Leyston, Eng.

    42. i.   JANE, b. ———. Mentioned in her grandfather's will.

    22. WILLIAM FISKE (Thomas, William, Symond),b. Stadhaugh, Eng.,
———; m. Margaret Ball. William Fyske, of Stadhaugh, in Laxfield, County
Suffolk, diocese of Norwich, will dated Oct. 15, 1558, proved May 4, 1559. Mentions wife Margaret, son John, son Rauf, daus. Alice, Meriam, Jane and Margaret;
William Fíyske, son of brother Henry, dec., my daus. Faith and Katherine; executors to be my wife and brother-in-law Robert Ball and Roger Wade of Bermond-
sey. He d. 1559; res. Stadhaugh, Eng.

    43. i.   MATHEW, b. in England; m. Elizabeth Jordain, Margaret Hay-
                wood and Anne Haggune.
    44. ii.   FRANCIS, b. in England.
    45. iii. JOHN, b. in England; m. Joan Couper.
    46. iv. RALPH, b. in England; d. s. p.
    47. v.   ALICE, b. in England; m. ——— Meriam.
    48. vi. JANE, b. in England.
    49. vii. MARGARET, b. in England.
    49¼.viii. FAITH, b. in England.
    49½.ix. KATHERINE, b. in England.

    23. THOMAS FISKE (Thomas, William, Symond), b. in England, ———;
m. ——— ———. His will is dated Jan. 20, 1559. No sons mentioned. He d.
Jan., 1559; res. Stadbrook, Eng.

    50. i.   CHRISTIAN, b. in England; m. Edward Sewell.
    51. ii.   MARGARET, b. in England; m. Alan Barrett.
    52. iii. ALICE, b. in England.
    53. iv. DOROTHY, b. in England.
    54. v.   JOAN, b. in England.

    24. HENRY FISKE (Thomas, William, Symond), b. Stadhaugh, Eng.,
———; m. ——— ———. Henry Fiske, of Cratfield, made his will Aug. 19, 1558,
and it was proved Sept. 16, 1558. He bequeaths to his son William all his lands
in Frissingfield, called Gooches, son Thomas, and his dau. Mary, son Jeffrey,
godson Francis Fiske. Appoints his brother Thomas Fiske, of Stadbrook, and
his son William executors. He d. 1558; res. Cratfield, Eng.

    55. i.   WILLIAM, b. in England; m. ——— ———.
    56. ii.   JEFFREY, b. in England.
    57. iii. THOMAS, b. in England; m. Alice ———.

    28. SIMON FISKE (Simon, William, Symond), b. Laxfield, Eng., ———;
m. ——— ———. His will is dated Jan. 25, 1505. He gave legacies to his children
who were all young and a bequest to his brother, Master John Fiske, ten marks,
to sing for his soul one year. He d. 1505; res. Laxfield, Eng.

    58. i.   ROBERT, b. in England; m. Mrs. Sybil (Gould) Barber.
    59. ii.   JOHN, b. in England; m. Thomasine Pinchard.
    60. iii. GEORGE, b. in England; m. Anne ———.
    61. iv. NICHOLAS, b. in England; m. Joan Crispe.
    62. v.   JEFFREY, b. in England.
    63. vi. JEREMY, b. in England; m. ——— ———.
    64. vii. WILLIAM, b. in England; m. ——— ———.
    65. viii. RICHARD, b. in England; m. Agnes Crispe.

66. ix.   JOAN, b. in England.
67. x.   GELYNE, b. in England.
68. xi.   AGNES, b. in England.

30. ROBERT FISKE (Simon, William, Symond), b. Laxfield, Eng., ———;
m. Alice ———. His will is dated Mar. 6, 1549, proved Apr. 5, 1551. His children were all under twenty-one years of age. Appoints his wife, John Jacob of
Forncett and Edmund Crispe of Laxfield executors. He d. 1551; res. Laxfield,
Eng.

69. i.   NICHOLAS, b. in England.
70. ii.   ANNE, b. in England.
71. iii. CHRISTIAN, b. in England.

43. MATHEW FISKE (William, Thomas, William, Symond), b. Stadhaugh, Eng., ———; m. Elizabeth Jordain, dau. of Wm. She d. Jan. 6, 1592; m.
2d, Oct. 24, 1592, Margaret Hayward, d. Sept. 13, 1611; m. 3d, Jan. 30, 1612, Anne
Huggune. Res. Laxfield, Eng. He d. Nov. 5, 1627. He was a yeoman and
resided in Laxfield, but d. in Ubbeston. His will is dated June 11, 1627, and was
proved Jan. 13, 1628. Mentions wife Anne, son Nicholas, son John and his son
John, dau. Elizabeth, wife of Edmund Stannard.

72. i.   WILLIAM, bap. in England; d. June 23, 1579.
73. ii.   ELIZABETH, bap. Feb. 12, 1580; m., July 25, 1604, Edmund
            Stannard; res. Laxfield.
74. iii. NICHOLAS, b. in England; m. Judith Reade.
75. iv.   JOHN, b. in England; m. Elizabeth Button.

45. JOHN FISKE (William, Thomas, William, Symond), b. Stadhaugh,
Eng., ———; m. Joan Couper, dau. of William of Suffolk. He d. ———; res.
Studhaugh and Cratfield, Eng.

76. i.   WILLIAM, b. in England; m. Arone Hart.
77. ii.   JOHN, b. in England.

55. WILLIAM FISKE (Henry, Thomas, William, Symond), b. Stadhaugh,
Eng., ———; m. ——— ———. William Fiske, the elder, of Cratfield, made his
will Mar. 27, 1607. It was proved Apr. 14, 1608. Mentions sons William, John,
Gregory and Henry and brother Thomas. He d. 1608; res. Cratfield, Eng.

The Fiske Family.—In editing the transcript of the Parish papers of Cratfield,
Suffolk, England, made by the late Rev. W. Holland, M. A., Rector of Hunting-
field, it became necessary to examine the original documents. Among them I
found an indenture of the register for the year 1565 containing among entries of
the Plimpton, Mills, Baker, Grimsby-Newson, Gilberde, Brokbanke, Saunders,
Button, Curdie and Long families, "William Fyske, sonne of Jefrey Fyske and
of Christian his wyfe, was bap. the last daye of Sept. In 1566 William Fyske and
Jefrey Fyske were contributors, respectively, toward the enfranchisement of the
parish lands.

78. i.   HENRY, b. in England; m. Margaret Gibson.
79. ii.   JOHN, b. in England.
80. iii. GREGORY, b. in England.
81. iv.   WILLIAM, b. in England; m. Mrs. Elizabeth ———.

57. THOMAS FISKE (Henry, Thomas, William, Symond), b. in England,
———; m. Alice ———. He d. s. p. His will is dated Mar. 16, 1603, and was
proved June 5, 1604. His wife was Alice. He gave legacies to his sister Knight,
and William Fiske residing with him. He makes William, son of William Fiske
of Hockingham to Norfolk his principal heir. He d. in 1604; res. Wenhaston, Eng.

58. ROBERT FISKE (Simon, Simon, William, Symond), b. Stadhaugh,
Eng., about 1525; m. Mrs. Sybil (Gould) Barber. For some time he was of the
Parish of St. James, South Elmham, Eng. Sybil, the wife of Robert, was in great
danger in the time of the religious persecution, 1553-58, as was her sister Isabella,
originally Gould, who was confined in the castle of Norwich, and escaped death
only by the power of her brothers, who were men of great influence in the
county. Robert fled for religion's sake in the days of Queen Mary to Geneva,
but returned later, and died at St. James. His will is dated Apr. 10, 1590, and
proved July 28, 1590. Robert Fiske had by Sybil Gould, his wife, four sons and
one daughter. The sons were William, Jeffrey, Thomas and Eleazer. Eleazer had

no issue, but the progeny of William, Jeffrey and Thomas in whole or in part settled in New England. About this time was a season of great religious persecution. From the "Magna Brittannica" we learn that Waybred is a town in Suffolk County, England.

John Noyes, of Laxfield, Suffolk County, shoemaker, was burned at Laxfield Sept. 21, 1557. Vol. V., p. 303.

John Alcock was taken for heresy at Headley Church, imprisoned, and died in prison, and buried in a dunghill. P. 305.

William Brown, a minister, was a long time in trouble for charges of heresy, his living taken from him, and died in poverty. P. 305.

Oliver Cromwell was of Suffolk County. P. 175.

Res. Broad Gates, Laxfield, near Framlingham, and St. James, South Elmham, Suffolk County, Eng. He d. in 1600.

82. i. WILLIAM, b. in 1566; m. Anna Anstye and Alice ———.
83. ii. JEFFREY, b. in England; m. Sarah Cooke.
84. iii. THOMAS, b. in England; m. Margery ———.
85. iv. ELEAZER, b. in England; m. Elizabeth ———. He d. s. p. in Metfield, England, in July, 1615. His will is dated June 3, 1613, and was proved July 4, 1615. To his wife Elizabeth he gave lands, etc., in the parish of St. James, South Elmham, during her life. Gave property to nephews Nathaniel and David, sons of brothers William and Jeffrey, and legacies to the other children of said brothers, and to the children of his brother Thomas. The widow d. in 1629. Her will is dated Jan. 9, 1629. Made bequest to Elizabeth, dau. of Samuel Fiske, ten shillings. Her will was witnessed by Nicholas Bancroft and others.
86 v. ELIZABETH, b. in England; m. Robert Bernard. It will be remembered that Robert and Sybil Fiske, of whom their descendants were accustomed to speak with respect as Protestant confessors in the reign of Queen Mary, had beside the four sons a daughter Elizabeth, who married Robert Bernard, who was a farmer of the estate of Custrick Hall, in Wecky, County Essex, which he held of Sir Edward Coke, the lord chief justice. And, having mentioned this marriage, Candler brings before us a genealogical fact of great curiosity and importance. It is that a daughter of this Bernard married a Locke, and was the mother of John Locke, who writing about 1660, he describes simply as "John Locke, M. A." Very little is known of Locke's father, but, any one who has written on his life has not had the slightest knowledge of the mother to whom we owe this eminent man. The mother of Locke was brought up among the more zealous Puritans of the Counties of Essex and Suffolk, and heard from her infancy stories of religious persecutions. She must have seen near connections of her family leaving their native homes to find, as they supposed, security and peace in a distant land, and the feeling thus engendered in her mind we may easily believe to have been communicated to her son, who in due time became the great defender of the principles of the utmost tolerance in dealing with men in force of conscience and religious opinion. This is a digression, but perhaps it will not be unacceptable to see the name of so illustrious a person now for the first time placed in public in family connection with so many of the ——; Puritan settlers in New England. Bernard stood in the relation of great-uncle to Candler, who records the facts which I have now brought from their hiding place, and to all the Fiskes who laid the foundation of the families of that name in the New England states. John Locke (grandson of Robert Fiske), English philosopher, was born at Wrington, Somersetshire, Aug. 29, 1632, died at Oates, a country seat in Essex, Oct 28, 1704. The moderate inheritance of his family was considerably reduced during the civil wars, in which his father was

a parliamentary captain.   Under the brief political ascendancy of the Puritans he imbibed the religious principle and spirit of liberty which actuated that body of men.   His education began at Westminster school, from which he was elected in 1651 to Christ Church College, Oxford, where he graduated bachelor of arts in 1655 and master in 1658, continuing to reside in that city till 1664.   In after life he regretted that he had spent so much of his time in the university, chiefly from his contempt of the scholastic philosophy and methods which were there upheld; yet he applied himself diligently to the classics, read in private the works of Bacon and Descartes, and enjoyed the friendship of persons whose society and conversation first suggested the idea of his greatest work.   His companions were chosen rather from among the lively and agreeable than the studious and learned, and his early correspondence often displays wit and irony.   The precise and scientific method of Descartes seems to have given the first impulse to his speculations, but Bacon exerted a more permanent and congenial influence, and he may be called the metaphysician of the Baconian philosophy.   After receiving his degrees he devoted himself principally to medicine, which occupied much of his attention through life, and his eminent proficiency in which is attested by Dr. Sudenham, the greatest authority of his time. In 1664 he accepted the post of secretary in a diplomatic mission to the court of Brandenburg, and, returning to Oxford within a year, was in doubt whether to begin the practice of medicine as a profession, to continue in diplomatic employment, offers of which both in Spain and Germany were made to him, or to enter the church, a considerable preferment in which was promised through the duke of Orleans, lord lieutenant of Ireland.   He was engaged in studies of experimental philosophy, when in 1666 he became acquainted with Lord Ashley, afterward earl of Shaftesbury, who was then suffering from an abscess in the chest.   Locke divined the nature of the disorder, which no one else had been able to discover; the life of the nobleman was believed to have been saved by a surgical operation which the philosopher advised; and the result was a close and permanent friendship between them.   Locke accompanied him to London, and in his house enjoyed the society of the duke of Buckingham, the earl of Northumberland, Lord Halifax, and others of the most distinguished characters of the time.   Ashley united engaging manners with distinguished ability, and was an admirable talker; and Locke, whose esteem for conversational capacity led him to assign it a first place in the formation of a man's mind, was probably attached in this instance very much by his quality.   While residing with him, he superintended the education of his son, and subsequently of his grandson, the third earl of Shaftesbury, the elegant philosophical writer of Queen Anne's reign. In 1668 he accompanied the earl and countess of Northumberland on a tour in France, and after his return was employed by Ashley to draw up the fundamental laws of Carolina, which province had been granted to him and seven others.   The scheme of government which was prepared, aristocratic and conformed to monarchy, yet tolerant of all religions, indicates the cautious and practical tendencies of his mind, since, though a lover of freedom, he proposed to establish it in a new country only in so far as it had been realized in England.   In 1670 he made the first sketch of his "Essay concerning Human Understanding," which was finished in 1687 and published in 1690.   In a discussion with five or six friends at his chambers in Oxford, he suggested that the dispute and perplexity could only be solved by a preliminary examination of our own abili-

ties, and of what subjects our understandings are or are not
fitted to deal with. He set down several thoughts on the subject previous to their next meeting, and the work thus begun
was often resumed and often neglected during his various avo-
cations, and was ultimately completed in retirement and leisure. While Shaftesbury was lord chancellor, Locke held the
appointment of secretary for the presentation of beneficies, and
afterward of secretary to the board of trade. In 1675 he went
to France for the benefit of his health, residing at Montpellier,
where he became acquainted with Mr. Herbert, afterward earl
of Pembroke, to whom his "Essay" is dedicated, and in Paris,
where his conversation was welcomed by the most eminent
literary and scientific men. He was recalled to England when
Shaftesbury regained power for a brief season in 1679; and
when that nobleman charged with high treason had taken
refuge in Holland, he followed him thither in 1683. He continued to reside there after the death of Shaftesbury, having
incurred the hostility of the court by his connection with him.
At Amsterdam he kept aloof from the British exiles who were
plotting the rebellion of Monmouth, auguring their ill success,
and joined with Limborch, Le Clerc, and others, in the formation of a philosophical society for the weekly discussion of important business. Spies were set about him to suggest irri-
tating topics, and to report his words to his ruin, but they
were foiled by his steady silence concerning the politics of the
day. The court therefore resolved to punish him in the only
point where he was vulnerable, and ejected him from his stu-
dentship in Christchurch College. Still he refused to take part
in the schemes of invasion, and concealed himself at Utrecht,
where he was employed in writing his letter "On Toleration."
In the Bibliotheque universalle et historique of Le Clerc he
published in French in 1686 a "New Method of a Commonplace Book," in 1687 an abridgement of his "Essay on the
Human Understanding," which was published in England in
the same year, and in Latin at Gouda in 1689. Its liberal views
were attacked by an Oxford theologian, and were defended by
Locke in two additional letters. Adopting the theory of a
compact, he maintained that the state relates only to civil interests, has nothing to do with matters in the world to come,
and should therefore tolerate all modes of worship not im-
moral in their nature or involving doctrines inimical to good
government. Conscious of no crime, he refused to accept a
pardon which William Penn promised to obtain for him from
James II., but returned to England after the revolution of
1688 in the same fleet which brought the Princess of Orange,
and obtained through Lord Mordaunt the office of commissioner of appeals. In 1690 appeared his "Essay concerning
Human Understanding," the first work which attracted attention in England to metaphysical speculations, except on the
part of merely studious men, and one of the greatest contributions in modern times to the philosophy of the human mind.
The celebrity of the author as a friend of religious liberty, the
attacks upon it, and the attempts made at Oxford to prevent
the students from reading it, were among the secondary
causes of its success. Six editions appeared within fourteen
years, and through translations into Latin and French the
fame of the author was made European. He published in
1690 two "Treatises on Civil Government," written to support
the principles of the revolution by establishing the title of
King William upon the consent of the people as the only
title of lawful government. In 1693 his "Thoughts Concerning Education," in which his object is to fashion a gentleman
rather than a scholar, and therefore he lays less stress on

learning than on virtue, breeding and practical wisdom; and in 1695 "The Reasonableness of Christianity," the object of which was to determine what points of belief were common to all the Christian sects, in order to facilitate a plan of the king for the reconciliation and union of them all. He published a vindication of this work against the charge of Socinianism, and conducted a controversy with Stillingfleet, who in his work on the Trinity denounced some of the principles of the "Essay" as opposed to fundamental Christian doctrines. In 1700 he resigned his commissionership in consequence of his failing health, and, declining a pension offered him by the king in a personal interview, returned to the mansion of his friend Sir Francis Masham at Oates, in Essex, where he devoted the remainder of his life to the study of the Scriptures. Among the fruits of his later labors were a "Discourse on the Miracles," "Paraphrases, with Notes, of the Epistles of St. Paul," and an "Examination of Father Malebranche's Opinion of Seeing all Things in God," which were published posthumously. His excellent treatise on the "Conduct of the Understanding," which may be regarded as the ethical application of his "Essay," being a scheme of the education which an adult person should give himself, also appeared after his death. He received during his last years, while suffering under an incurable asthma, the affectionate attentions of Lady Masham, a daughter of Ralph Cudworth, and died ultimately in his chair, from the natural decay of a constitution originally weak, while she was reading the Psalms to him. The course and circumstances of Locke's life were in every respect favorable to the production of such work as the "Essay" Concerning Human Understanding." Early imbued with zeal for liberty and with the principles of a severe morality, l s whole life was a warfare against the enemies of freedom i speculation, freedom in worship, and freedom from ever unnecessary political restraint. Acquainted by his studies both with scholastic subtleties and the physical sciences, he was in mature age admitted to the society of wits and politicians, and became a man of business and of the world. The "Essay" was the product of meditation continued through many years, was composed at intervals, and is in a studied colloquial and rather racy style, which, however attractive to the reader, is too figurative, ambiguous, various, and even contradictory, for the purposes of philosophy. The essential character and tendency of his system has therefore always been a matter of dispute between metaphysicians of different schools, and different passages suggest very opposite conclusions. His object was to inquire into the origin, certainty, and extent of human knowledge, and his method was purely psychological, by the patient and tentative observation of the phenomena of consciousness. In the first book he confutes the Cartesian doctrine of innate principles or axioms, which would conflict with his whole theory of the empirical origin of our ideas. This theory is fully developed in the second book, in which he shows that our natural faculties are capable of forming every notion that we possess, that the action of these faculties takes its rise from experience, and that the mind may therefore be compared to a sheet of white paper void of all characters till the events of time inscribe them. Having thus stated the principle that all the materials of our knowledge come from experience, he explains it more particularly by making a distinction between sensation and reflection as sources of ideas. The former is observation of the external world, the latter of our own mental operations. Though he uses the term reflection in a wavering and indefinite sense, it does not plainly appear that he ascribed to it any other power than that of a mere formal and logical mechanism, to act upon, to combine and compare, and to extensively modify the materials primarily afforded by the senses. In long and acute processes of reasoning he aims to bring the ideas of space, time, infinity, causality, personal identity, substance, and good and evil within the limits of experience. The third book is a treatise on the nature, use and abuse of language. In the fourth book he passes from ideas to knowledge, from psychology to onthology, treating the question as to the adequacy of our ideas and the reality of our knowledge. He held a representative theory of perception, maintaining that the mind does not know things immediately, but by the intervention of ideas; that knowledge is real only in so far as there is conformity between our ideas and the reality of things; and that ideas may be entirely inadequate, however distinct they are, thus rejecting the criterion of Descartes. This theory contains the germ of utter skepticism, and was the ground on which Berkeley denied the existence of the material world, and Hume involved all human knowledge in doubt. The distinction established by Kant between the cause and the occasion of our conceptions, making the former to exist in the original constitution of the mind, and the latter in the circumstances of experience, would have removed the fundamental error involved, perhaps without design, in the system of Locke. There are indications in many passages of his work that he was not satisfied with that tendency to sensationalism, which when rigidly developed bore fruits of utilitarianism in morals, materialism in metaphysics, and skepticism in religion. A biography of Locke was published in 1829 by Lord King, a lineal descendant of his sister, and added to Bohn's "Standard Library" in 1858. The best complete edition of his works is in 10 vols. (London, 1823). His philosophical works have been published by J. A. St. John (2d ed., 2 vols., London, 1854). A new biography by H. R. Fox Bourne was announced in 1874. Another daughter of Elizabeth (Fisk) Bernard married Thomasine, and brother-in-law, John Pinchard of Bedingfield. He d. s. p. 1607; res. Twitshall, St. Mary, England.

59.   JOHN FISKE (Simon, Simon, William, Symond), b. in Laxfield, Eng., ———; m. Thomasine Pinchard.   His will is dated Oct. 1, 1607, mentions his wife, Thomasine, and brother-in-law, John Pinchard of Bedingfield. He d. s. p. 1607; res. Twitshall, St. Mary, England.

60.   GEORGE FISKE (Simon, Simon, William, Symond), b. Laxfield, Eng., ———; m. Anne ———.   His will is dated Jan. 6, 1591, and proved Apr. 7, 1593. His widow was living in 1613. He d. March, 1593; res. Westhall, Eng.
 87. i. GEORGE, b. in England; m. Margery Simonds.
 88. ii. THOMAS, b. in England. He was of Westhall; made his will
      Apr. 15, 1613, which was proved Aug. 28, 1613. Mentions his
      mother Anne Fiske, brother George, sister Margaret Whit-
      tingham, brother Jeffery and his four children Gelyon, Eliza-
      beth, Anne and Milicent. Appoints his brother George and
      Thomas Fiske of Westhall executors.
 89. iii. MARGARET, b. in England; m. Jeffrey Whittingham. Ch.:
      Gelyon, Elizabeth, Anne and Milicent.
 89½.iv. JEFFREY, b. England.

61.   NICHOLAS FISKE (Simon, Simon, William, Symond), b. Laxfield, Eng., ———; m. Joan Crispe, dau. of William of Laxfield. His will is dated Aug. 20, 1569; proved Sept. 28, 1569. Witnessed by John Fiske. Fox in his "Book of Martyrs" in relating the account of the burning of John Noyes refers to Nicholas Fiske as Noyes' brother-in-law. He d. Sept., 1569; res. Dennington, Eng.
 90. i. WILLIAM, b. in England; m. Helen ———.

91. ii. AMOS, b. in England; m. Mary ———.
92. iii. RACHEL, b. in England.
93. iv. ESTHER, b. in England.
94. v.   MARY, b. in England.

63. JEREMY FISKE (Simon, Simon, William, Symond), b. in England, ———; m. ——— ———. She d. Nov. 15, 1624. He resided in Laxfield. His will is dated Aug. 22, 1630, and was proved Sept. 16, 1630. Made bequests to his son-in-law Peter Cook and his son John, of a house and land in Tittleshall, County Norfolk. He d. Sept., 1630; res. Laxfield, Eng.

95. i. ALICE, bap. Dec. 22, 1588; d. Apr. 7, 1593.
96. ii. ANNE, bap. Mar. 12, 1591; m. Peter Cook. They had a son John.

64. WILLIAM FISKE (Simon, Simon, William, Symond), b. Laxfield, Eng., ———; m. ——— ———. She d. before 1575. He resided in South Elmham and fled for religion's sake in the time of Queen Mary. His will is dated Oct. 10, 1575, and proved Jan. 30, 1578. Witnessed by Robert and Jeffrey Fiske and William Ryarde; res. St. Michaels, South Elmham, Eng.

97. i.   GELYON, b. in England; m. ——— Aldus.
98. ii. MARGARET, b. in England; m. ——— Bancroft.
99. iii. AGNES, b. in England; m. ——— Borough.
100. iv. MARY, b. in England; unm., 1575.
101. v. JOSEPH, b. in England.

65. RICHARD FISKE (Simon, Simon, William, Symond), b. Stadhaugh, Suffolk County, Eng., about 1510; m. Agnes Crispe, dau. of Edmund. According to Cotton Mather he lived in the reign of Queen Mary and endured grievous persecution. There were several branches of Fiskes in the southern parts of the County of Suffolk, England, all springing from a Richard Fiske, who lived at Broad Gates, in Laxfield, a rural village north of Framlingham, where the inhabitants were so zealous for the reformation that one of them, John Noyes, was most barbarously put to death in the reign of Queen Mary. Fox, in his account of the burning of Noyes, speaks of Nicholas Fiske, who was one of the sons of Richard. Two other of his sons, Robert and William, fled in the time of that terrible persecution. It does not appear that Nicholas had any issue. William who had fled was the subject of a parricide, for which his son, Joseph Fiske, suffered the penalty of death at Bury St. Edmunds. Of this branch of the family nothing more need be said, or of the descendants of other sons of Richard, than Robert, from whom sprang all of the name who were in the early emigration. He resided in Laxfield and made his will Sept. 7, 1572, which was proved Nov. 5, 1572. His wife was Agnes, son Elias, daus. Mary, Margaret, Anne, Elizabeth and father-in-law Edmund Crispe. Appoints his brother Robert Fiske supervisor. Witnessed by John, Jeffrey and Nathaniel Fiske. He d. in 1572; res. Laxfield, Suffolk County, Eng.

102. i.   ELIAS, b. in England; m. Alice ———.
103. ii. MARY, b. in England.
104. iii. MARGARET, b. in England.
105. iv. ANNE, b. in England.
106. v.   ELIZABETH, b. in England.

74. PROF. NICHOLAS FISKE (Mathew, William, Thomas, William, Symond), b. Stadhaugh, Eng., ———; m. Judith Reade, dau. of William Reade, of Colchester, Parson of Trinity Church and of St. Martin's Lane. He was born on the old place in Stadhaugh, Parish of Laxfield, Suffolk County, Eng. He received an excellent education, studied medicine, and practiced until his death. On Nov. 9, 1633, he was granted the right to use the Fiske Coat of Arms by the Herald's College. At that time he was professor of physics. He d. ———; res. Stadhaugh, in Laxfield, Middlesex, Eng.

107. i.   JOHN, b. in England; m. ——— Heigham.
108. ii. MATHEW, b. in England; d. s. p.
109. iii. MARY, b. in England; m. John Stanard.
110. iv. ELIZABETH, b. in England.
111. v.   CATHERINE, b. in England.

75. JOHN FISKE (Mathew, William, Thomas, William, Symond), b. in Laxfield, Eng., ———; m., May 5, 1600, Elizabeth Button. He was a weaver by trade. His will is dated Dec. 24, 1639, and was proved July 4, 1640. He bequeathed to his wife Elizabeth a house in the hamlet of Chepenlake in Fressingfield, which he had of his uncle John Fiske of Cratfield. The will also mentions brother-in-law Richard Spalding and John Tillott. He d. in 1640; res. Laxfield and Mendham, Eng.

 112. i. JOHN, bap. Jan. 8, 1603. He d. Nov. 7, 1628. He resided in Stadhaugh, in Laxfield. His will is dated Feb. 22, 1628; was proved Dec. 4, 1628. Mentions his uncle Matthew and his son Nicholas, John son of John son of said Matthew, brother William and his son John, nephew Samuel Cook, brother-in-law Erasmus Cook, clerk, dec'd.

 113. ii. WILLIAM, bap. Feb. 23, 1605; m. ——— ———.

 114. iii. ELIZABETH, bap. Feb. 26, 1608; m. Erasmus Cook. He was a clerk; d. before 1628, leaving son Samuel.

 115. iv. MATTHEW, bap. Mar. 12, 1614.

76. WILLIAM FISKE (John, William, Thomas, William, Symond), b. Stadhaugh, Eng., ———; m. Arone Hart, dau. of William. He d. ———; res. Hardings, in Norton, County Suffolk, Eng.

 116. i. JOHN, b. in England; m. Alice Hart.

 117. ii. THOMAS, b. in England.

 118. iii. SAMUEL, b. in England; m. ——— ———.

78. HENRY FISKE (William, Henry, Thomas, William, Symond), b. in England ———; m. Margaret Gibson. He resided in Cratfield. His will is dated Mar. 6, 1627, and was proved Nov. 22, 1628. His wife was Margaret, father William Fiske dec'd, sons William, John and Henry, dau. Margaret wife of John Barrett, dau. Mary, kinsman Wolfram and Christopher Smith, brother Henry Gibson. He d. in 1628; res. Cratfield, Eng.

 119. i. WILLIAM, b. in England.

 120. ii. JOHN, b. in England.

 121. iii. HENRY, b. in England.

 122. iv. MARGARET, b. in England; m. John Barrett.

 123. v. MARY, b. in England.

81. WILLIAM FISKE (William, Henry, Thomas, William, Symond), b. in England ———; m. Mrs. Elizabeth ———. In his will he is referred to as William Fiske, the elder, of Cratfield, Gentleman. The instrument is dated Nov. 5, 1636, and was proved May 29, 1640. His wife was Elizabeth, son William, wife's dau. Frances Meene, nephew William Sandcroft. Appoints his son William executor and his nephew Francis Sandcroft supervisor. He d. 1640; res. Cratfield, Eng.

 124. i. WILLIAM, b. in England; res. Cratfield.

82. WILLIAM FISKE (Robert, Simon, Simon, William, Symond), b. Laxfield, Eng., 1566; m. Anna Anstye, dau. of Walter, of Tibbenham, Long Row, in Norfolk. She d., and he m. 2d, Alice ———. William is described as of St. James in South Elmham, and it is said of him that he fled with his father for religion's sake. His wife was Anne, dau. of Walter Anstye, of Tibbenham, Long Row in Norfolk. They had John, Nathaniel and Eleazer, Eunice, Hannah and Esther. Eunice died unmarried. Esther married John Challie, or Chalke, of Road Hall, and Hannah, William Candler, and was the mother of the genealogist, the compiler of the Candler manuscript in the British Museum. Of the sons, Eleazer settled at Norwich and had female issue only. Nathaniel was of Waybred, and had children who appear to have remained in England; but of the children of John all that lived to grow up, four in number, transferred those to the new country. An old record says: "William fyske has livery of the manor and advowson of Hekingham, in County Norfolk, lately belonging to Robert Fyske, his father." His will is dated Nov. 25, 1616, and was proved May 17, 1623. He was of Ditchingham, County Norfolk. The instrument mentions now wife Alice, To the poor of Ditchingham and Bungay. To his eldest son John, lands in St. James, South Elmham; grandchildren Matthias, John and Mary Candler; grandchildren John, Anne, Martha, Nathaniel and Eleazer Fiske, all under twenty-one;

dau. Anne Candler. To son John lands in Metfield, he paying to his brothers Nathaniel and Eleazer and sister Hester six score pounds. Appoints his son John executor. He d. in 1623; res. St. James, South Elmham, and Ditchingham, Norfolk, Eng.

125. i. JOHN, b. South Elmham, Eng.; m. Anne Lantersee.
126. ii. NATHANIEL, b. South Elmham, Eng.; m. Mrs. Alice (Hend) Leman.
127. iii. ELEAZER, b. South Elmham, Eng.; m. and settled in Norwich; had female issue only.
128. iv. EUNICE, b. South Elmham, Eng.; d. unm.
129. v. HANNAH, b. South Elmham, Eng.; m. May 4, 1603, William Candler. He was school master at Tofford. Their son, Rev. Mathias Candler, was the author of the celebrated Candler manuscript on file in the British Museum. Other children were John and Mary Candler.
130. vi. HESTER, b. South Elmham, Eng.; m. John Chalke, of Rednall, Eng.
131. vii. MARY, b. South Elmham, Eng.; m. Anthony Fisher, proprietor of Wignotte, County Suffolk, Eng. He d. Apr. 11, 1640, a son Anthony, Jr., bap. at Syleham, Eng., Apr. 23, 1591; m. in England, Mary ———. He d. in America in Dedham or Dorchester Apr. 18, 1671. His son Anthony, Jr., b. at Syleham, Eng., m. in Dorchester, Mass., Sept. 7, 1647, Joanna Faxon. He d. in Dorchester, Feb. 13, 1670. She was b. in England in 1626, and d. Oct. 16, 1694. His son Eleazer, b. Sept. 18, 1669, m. Oct. 13, 1698, Mary Avery, b. Aug. 21, 1674, d. Mar. 25, 1749. He d. Feb. 6, 1722. His son Benjamin, b. May, 1721, at Dedham, Mass., m. Aug. 11, 1742, Sarah Everett, b. June 7, 1718, d. Aug. 2, 1795. He d. Jan. 18, 1777. His son Aaron, b. Jan. 16, 1758, m. Betty Moore, of Bolton. He was sergt. in Rev. army, and d. Oct. 10, 1843. His son Aaron, b. Aug. 30, 1783, m. Hepzibah Walker, d. 1858. His son Rev. Otis, b. June 16, 1808, m. Oct. 13, 1844, Harriet Newell Day, b. Mar. 31, 1816, d. Aug. 1, 1890. He d. Sept. 17, 1880. His son Albert Judson, b. Feb. 27, 1851, m. July 12, 1893, Ada Ashard; res. Chicago, Ill., with Capt. S. E. Gross, Masonic Temple. Two others of the early settlers from Suffolk County, England, were related to the Fiskes. These were Joshua and Anthony Fisher, who took their freedom, Joshua in 1640 and Anthony, Jr., in 1646. They were brothers, sons of Anthony Fisher, of Syleham, by his wife Mary, who was another dau. of William and Anne Fiske, of South Elmham; but this is another instance in which we have to regret that Candler in his manuscript did not draw his pedigrees with more precision. Candler does not give us any further information respecting them, but we may form some idea of the class of society from which they sprang from the notice which he takes of two of their brothers who appear to have remained in England: Cornelius, who was M. A. and taught the school at East Bergholt, and Amos who farmed an estate called Custridge Hall in the Parish of Wesley, which is in the hundred of Tendring between Colchester and the sea. Cornelius left no issue, and his widow remained with George Smith who was one of the ministers at Dedham, a famous city of Puritan piety. Amos married Anne Morice, the relict of Daniel Locke, and had several children, settled in those parts of Essex, of whom it is not known that any of them followed in the steps of their two uncles.

83. JEFFREY FISKE (Robert, Simon, Simon, William, Symond), b. at Laxfield, Eng., ———; m. Sarah Cooke. Jeffrey was another son of Robert Fiske and Sibil his wife. The account of his family is not so clearly given in the Candler manuscript in the British museum as to remove all doubt respecting the true descent as Mr. Candler understood it; but it appears that Jeffrey had a son David Fiske (see will of his uncle Eleazer) of this branch of the family, who emi-

grated, whose wife was Sarah Smith, a dau. of Edmund Smith, of Mentham. He took his freedom in 1638, and possibly again in 1647. ("David, 1647, was no doubt son of the freemen of 1638-39.") He d. 1628. His will is dated Oct., 1628; proved Nov. 25, 1628; res. Metfield, Eng.

    132. i.   ELEAZER, b. in England.
    133. ii.   DAU., b. in England; m. John Sawyer.
    134. iii. DAVID, b. in England; m. Sarah Smith.

    84. THOMAS FISKE (Robert, Simon, Simon, William, Symond), b. Laxfield, Eng., ———; m. Margery ———. His will is dated Feb. 20, 1610, proved Feb. 28, 1610. His son Thomas was executor. He d. Feb., 1610; res. Fressingfield, Eng.

    135. i.   THOMAS, b. in England, of Medfield.
    136. ii.   JAMES, b. in England.
    137. iii. PHINEHAS, b. in 1610; m. Sarah ——— and Elizabeth Easterick.
    138. iv. ELIZABETH, b. in England.
    139. v.   MARY, b. in England.

    87. GEORGE FISKE (George, Simon, Simon, William, Symond), b. in England ———; m. Margery Simonds. He resided in Westhall and his will was dated March 28, 1622, proved May 25, 1622. His wife was Margery, daus. Alice and Margery, dau. Anne, wife of Robert Porter. Brother-in-law Hugh Simonds. He d. 1622; res. Westhall, Eng.

    140. i.   ALICE, b. in England.
    141. ii.   MARGERY, b. in England.
    142. iii. ANNE, b. in England; m. Robert Porter.

    90. WILLIAM FISKE (Nicholas, Simon, Simon, William, Symond), b. in England ———; m. ——— Helen ———. He made his will Aug. 13, 1580, proved Nov. 22, 1580. His wife was Helen, son Nicholas, not 21, daus. Anne, Rachel and Elizabeth. Late father was Nicholas Fiske, brother Amos Fiske. He d. 1580; res. Dennington, Eng.

    143. i.   NICHOLAS, b. in England; m. Rebecca ———.
    144. ii.   ANNE, b. in England.
    145. iii. RACHEL, b. in England.
    146. iv. ELIZABETH, b. in England.

    91. AMOS FISKE (Nicholas, Simon, Simon, William, Symond), b. Dennington, Eng. ———; m. there Mary ———. He resided in Dennington. His will is dated May 28, 1612, and proved June 17, 1612. He d. 1612; res. Dennington, Eng.

    147. i.   AMOS, b. in England.
    148. ii.   WILLIAM, b. in England.
    149. iii. JOAN, b. in England.

    102. ELIAS FISKE (Richard, Simon, Simon, William, Symond), b. in Laxfield, Eng., ———; m. Alice ———. He was of Laxfield a yeoman. His will was dated May 2, 1601. Mentions his wife Alice, son Henry, not 24, daus. Sarah, Mary and Margaret, and refers to late father, Richard Fiske. He d. Sept. 2, 1601; res. Laxfield, Eng.

    150. i.   SARAH, bap. May 25, 1589.
    151. ii.   HENRY, bap. May 24, 1590.
    152. iii. MARY, bap. April 16, 1593.
    153. iv. MARGARET, bap. Nov. 15, 1596.

    107. JOHN FISKE (Nicholas, Mathew, William, Thomas, William, Symond), b. Stadhaugh, Eng., ———; m. ——— Heigham; res. ———, Eng.

    154. i.   JOHN, b. in England.
    155. ii.   WILLIAM, b. in England.
    156. iii. JUDITH, b. in England.

    113. WILLIAM FISKE (John, Mathew, William, Thomas, William, Symond), bap. Feb. 23, 1605, in Laxfield, Eng.; m. ——— ———. "Wills & Inventories from the Registers of the Commissary, of Bury St. Edmunds, and the Arch Deacon of Sudbury." N. E. His. Gen. Society, Pub. England 1850, p. 207, &c.,&c.:

William Fiske, of Packenham, gent., 1648. Will date 20th March, 1648. First to eldest son, John, large amount of Real & P. estate in Framlingham. Item to my son Thomas. Item to Martha Bright, my eldest daughter (naming son-in-law Henry Bright). Item to Mary Fiske, and Margaret Meadows, my two youngest daughters. Proved Jan. 7-9, 1649. 1 doz. bread Weekly. "Whereas, in anno 1630 I beganne a gift of a dozen of bread weekley to be given to the poore of the town of Norton in Suff., my mynd and desire is that the same gift may continue to the world's end," and provides a fund for that purpose. He d. 1648; res. Packenham, Eng.

157.   i.   JOHN, bap. ———; res. Framlingham.
158.   ii. THOMAS, b. ———.
159.   iii. MARTHA, b. ———; m. June 28, 1626, Henry Bright. He was bap. at Bury St. Edmunds, Eng., Oct. 14, 1593. They had one dau. Katherine. Henry Bright was son of Robert and on

his death he made his son Henry his principal heir, giving him the Packenham and Thurston estates. Henry was also executor of his father's will.

This engraving represents the estate as it was when occupied by Henry and Martha (Fiske) Bright. In Thurston church there are monumental slabs with arms and inscriptions beautifully sculptured to the memory of the Brights.

The children of Henry and Martha (Fiske) Bright, of Netherhall, were Robert Bright, of Ipswich, grocer. His will dated May 29, 1668, and proved on July 3, 1668, gives to his brother-in-law, Francis Woodward, £50; to his bro. John Bright, £250; to his sis. Martha Bright, £50; to his bro., William Bright, £3, to buy him a gold ring; to his co-partner, Wm. Sayer, £50; to his mother, Mrs. Martha Bright, £10; to the poor of the Parish of St. Lawrence, 40s.; to the poor of the Parish of Pakenham, 40s.; to Mrs. Elizabeth Sayer, his partner's mother, £3, to buy a gold

BRIGHT COAT OF ARMS.

NETHERHALL, THURSTON, ENGLAND.

ring; to his bro., Henry Bright, £100; to his bro., Thomas Bright, £100. Appoints his bros. Henry and Thomas executors. This latter, Thomas, was quite wealthy and d. in June, 1698.

160.   iv. MARY, b. ———.
161.   v.   MARGARET, b. ———; m. ——— Meadows.

116. JOHN FISKE (William, John, William, Thomas, William, Symond), b. in England, ———; m. Alice Hart, dau. of William, of Beeston, County Norfolk, Eng.; res. ———, Eng.

118. SAMUEL FISKE (William, John, William, Thomas, William, Symond), b. in England; m. ——— ———; res. England.
162.   i.   ELIZABETH, b. in England. On the death of Mrs. Elizabeth Fiske, of Sandcroft, widow of Eleazar, of Metfield, she gave Elizabeth, dau. of Samuel, ten shillings.

125. JOHN FISKE (William, Robert, Simon, Simon, William, Symond), b. St. James, Eng., ———; m. Anne Lantersee, dau. of Robert Lantersee; d. on

board ship in 1637, bound for New England. John Fiske, the father, died in 1633. His wife was Anne, daughter of Robert Lantersee. These are the four persons of one family, two brothers and two sisters, all married, and who Mather speaks of in the Magnalia, part 3, page 141, and what had not been related, corresponds with what he says of this family being descended of prosecuted ancestors. The two brothers were. John and William. He d. in 1633; res. St. James, So. Elmham, Eng.

163. i.   JOHN, b. in So. Elmham, 1601; m. Ann Gipps and Mrs. Elizabeth Henchman.

164. ii.   WILLIAM, b. in England; m. Bridgett Muskett.

165. iii. ANNE, b. in England; m. Francis Chickering. The same, who came to America in 1637 and who was made freeman May 13, 1640. Who this Francis Chickering was I know not, further than is to be found in the Candler manuscript in the British Museum, which gives no description of him; but in Savage's Winthrop, note to Vol. 1, page 84, the Rev. Mr. Chickering, minister of Woburn, is mentioned, who might be supposed to be a relative. ·Candler, in his manuscript, speaks of another Chickering, whose Christian name was unknown, to whom he married the widow of a first cousin of Candler's father, Benjamin Smith, farmer of Northall, in Wrentham. (Our Henry Chickering, of Dedham, was probably a brother of Francis.) This Mr. Chickering, he further says, went to New England after the death of his wife. Benjamin Smith was brother to Sarah, wife of David Fiske, emigrant. They res. in Dedham. He belonged to an artillery company in 1643 and later was Ensign. He was representative in 1644 and 1653. Their ch. were: Ann and Mary, b. in England; Elizabeth, b. Aug. 26, 1638, d. young; Bertha, b. Dec. 23, 1640; Esther, b. Nov. 4, 1643; John, b. April 19, 1646, d. young; Mercy, b. April 10, 1648.

Anne, the wife, died before 1650, for he then married, June 16, 1650, Mrs. Sarah Libby.

166. iv.   MARTHA, b. in England; m. in England Capt. Edmund Thompson, a son of John Thompson, of Holkham, in Norfolk, by Anne, his wife, dau. of John Hastings of that place. They had four ch. born in New England: Martha, Edmund, Thomas, bap. Feb. 12, 1643; and Hannah, bap. July 4, 1647. They returned to England and resided at Yarmouth, where they had three ch. born to them: John, Esther and John, who all d. in infancy. Candler informs us that Captain Thompson, who was a sea captain, served the States of Holland after the death of King Charles the First. He first resided in Salem, Mass., in 1637. Dec. 29, 1639, he was admitted to the church.

167. v.   NATHAN, b. in England; d. in infancy.

168. vi.   ELEAZER, b. So. Elmham, Eng. He was mentioned in his grandfather's will.

126. NATHANIEL FISKE (William, Robert, Simon, Simon, William, Symond), b. in England ———; m. Mrs. Alice (Henel) Leman. He is named in the wills of his father, Uncle Eleazer and Cousin Eleazer; res. Weybred, Eng.

169. i.   NATHANIEL, b. in Weybred, Eng.; m. Dorothy Symonds.

170. ii.   SARAH, b. in Weybred, Eng.; m. Robert Rogers.

134. DAVID FISKE (Jeffrey, Robert, Simon, Simon, William, Symond), He was of Watertown, was admitted a freeman of the colony in Mar., 1637-8. He had come to America, probably the preceding year, as he was not a proprietor until Feb., 1637. Before 1644 he was a grantee of one lot and a purchaser of six other lots. His homestall of twenty-two acres was granted to John Kingsbury, of whom he had purchased it just prior to his removal to Dedham. This latter property was bounded on the north by the Cambridge line and the property of J. Coolidge; south by the highway (Pond Road); west by land of J. Coolidge, and east by that of B. Bullard. The total amount of his real estate was 227 acres. He was a man of standing in the community and early held office. In 1639 he was elected a

member of the Board of Selectmen, and again in 1642. Was a juror in 1652-4-5-7. His will is dated Sept. 10, 1660, and was proved in January following. The instrument does not mention the name of his wife, but one daughter, Fitch, and one son, David, who was sole executor and residuary legatee, giving him his "houses, lands, cattle and chattels." Signed the mark of David Fiske and seal. (So signed probably on account of age and infirmity.) Inventory Jan. 10, 1661, £78-9-1. Aug. 6, 1673, the son sold his homestall and two other lots of his land in Watertown to John Coolidge. His wife was Sarah Smith, dau. of Edmund Smith, of Wrentham, Co. Suffolk, Eng.

Middlesex, Probate Records, "Wills & Inventories," P. 7, Vol. 2. David Fiske, of Watertown. Will date Sept. 10, 1660. I, David Fiske, of Watertown, in the County of Middlesex, in New Engl.: being sicke in body, but of perfect memory," &c. * * * "& having given a writing under my hand to my sonne in law Fitch, of some L tices (articles) that he is to have after my decease, as my best bed & a bolster & 2 coverlets & a pot & a kettle, and these ytices being taken out, I do dispose of the rest of my goods as followeth: I give & bequeath to my grand-children to be divided amongst them, all my wealth by equall and portions. It. I give and bequeath unto my daughter Fitch five pounds, to be paid her within a year after my decease. And all the rest of my estate that is not in this my will disposed off, as Houses, lands, cattle, chattels, I do give & bequeath to my sonne David Fiske, & do make him my sole exectutor, he to pay all my debts, &c., &c.   THE MARKE OF DAVID FISKE. X
Witness Jn. Coolidge: Thomas Hastings.

    Appr. 22:11:1661.

    He d. in 1660; res. Watertown, Mass.

171. i.   MARTHA, b. in England; m. Thomas Fitch, of Watertown. He was a cordwainer and resided in Boston. Was one of the merchants and traders of that city who petitioned for a bankrupt law in June, 1701. He was a freeman in 1666. He d. in 1678. Ch.: (1) Martha, b. Nov. 9, 1656; (2) Mary, b. Feb. 17, 1659; (3) Sarah, b. June 14, 1661; (4) Elizabeth, b. Aug. 2 (bap. in the First ch. Sept. 4, 1664. The father was then of Watertown); (5) Thomas, b. Feb. 5, 1669.

172. ii.   DAVID, b. in England 1624; m. Lydia Cooper and Seaborn Wilson.

    137. CAPT. PHINEHAS FISKE (Thomas, Robert, Simon, Simon, William, Symond), b. England, in Laxfield; m. there in 1638 Sarah ———; d. Sept. 10, 1659; m. 2d in Wenham, June 4, 1660, Elizabeth Easterick. Phineas Fiske, a freeman in Wenham, 1642, one of the first settlers, and until his death a leading citizen of that town, was the youngest son of Thomas Fiske, of England, and a grandson of Robert and Sybil (Gould) Fiske, of Laxfield, County of Suffolk. He was a captain of the militia in Wenham, and constable in 1644; Representative to the General Court in 1653; appointed "Commissioner to end small causes"—probably a Justice—in 1654; and his estate was settled upon his decease in 1673. Phineas Fiske (sometimes spelled Phinehas) was twice married. His first wife, Sarah, and mother of his children, died in 1659; and in 1660 he married Elizabeth Easterick. His will—the first of the Fiskes found on the records—was made in March and proved in June of 1673, in which mention is made of sons James, John and Thomas Fiske, but not of wife (perhaps deceased) or daughters. Among his legatees were "nephews Samuel, who was to have his great Bible, and Mark Fiske." All of the foregoing were evidently born in England some years before emigration, for son James was freeman same year with his father (1642), and Thomas, the youngest, according to a certain deposition, was at that time about twelve years old. The family most probably came out in company with their relatives, Rev. John and William Fiske, as their names appear simultaneously (in 1641) on the records of Salem Church.

Wenham, Massachusetts, where he resided, was the last of the seven towns in Essex County that was set off from Salem, and is situated about twenty-two miles northeast of Boston. The general surface of the country is level, the soil fruitful, well watered and productive. In olden times the village of Wenham was recorded as remarkable for its quiet arcadian beauty, and its principal lake has obtained celebrity for the purity of its waters. The town was incorporated in 1643. Its settlers and principal inhabitants, like those of the most of the older towns, were Puritans, taken from the great middle class of Englishmen who have always been the backbone of the nation. Intelligent, religious, hardy and industrious, they were undoubtedly the best as to character of any emigrants ever brought to this country. Their influence in shaping the destiny of the nation is apparent in the high rank Massachusetts has always taken among her sister states. From the Wenham town records it is learned that "Phineas Fisk was the first constable, and he, with Charles Gott and John Fisk, constituted the first board of selectmen; Wm. Fisk was town clerk." Capt. Phinehas was representative to the general court in 1653. His will was proved June 26, 1673. One witness was Samuel Fisk. Legatees son James to have one-half the house and land, sons John and Thomas to have the remainder, nephew Samuel to have his great Bible, and Mark Fisk some articles of bedding (above from Salem court records). He d. June 7, 1673; res. England, Salem and Wenham, Mass.

     173.   i.   JAMES, b. in England; m. Anna ——— and Hannah Pike.
     174.   ii.   JOHN, b. in England; m. Remember ———.
     175.   iii.   THOMAS, b. in England, 1632; m. Peggy ———.

143. NICHOLAS FISKE (William, Nicholas, Simon, Simon, William, Symond), b. in Laxfield, Eng., ———; m. Rebecca ———; d. at Laxfield, Jan. 16, 1623-4. He d. ———; res. Laxfield, Eng.

     176.   i.   ANNE, bap. July 1, 1579.
     177.   ii.   MARY, bap. Nov. 12, 1581.
     178.   iii.   REBECCA, bap. July 26, 1584.
     179.   iv.   JOHN, bap. at Laxfield, Eng.; m. Mary Bade.

163. REV. JOHN FISKE (John, William, Robert, Simon, Simon, William, Symond), b. St. James Parish, South Elmham, Suffolk County, Eng., 1601; m. 1629, Ann Gipps, of Frinshall, in Norfolk, England; d. in Chelmsford Feb. 14, 1672; m. 2d, Aug. 1, 1672, Mrs. Elizabeth Henchman, widow of Edmund.

The earliest of the Wenham town records extant is a grant of twenty acres of land to the town, one-half of it by Mr. Smith, on one side of the meeting house, and the other half by Mr. John Fisk, on the other side of it. This grant, which was made March 2, 1642, appears to have been divided into two-acre lots, which were given to actual settlers on condition of building upon them dwellings for themselves and their families. But in case that any such should wish to remove from the village they were required to offer their places for sale first to "the Plantation." The object of this arrangement was to encourage actual settlers, and also to form a village about the middle of the town. From these votes it appears that a meeting house, at least a temporary one, had already been built. It is supposed to have stood on or near the spot occupied by that built in 1664, viz., upon the eminence near the house at one time belonging to Mr. Henry Tarr.

There cannot be a doubt that John is the "Mr. John Fiske" who was made a freeman at a court held in March, 1637-8 (Savage's Winthrop, Vol. 2, p. 367). Mather says that he was "the elder brother," and that he died Jan. 14, 1676. His wife was Ann Gipps, of Frinshall, in Norfolk. They had a child, who was born at Frinshall, but died in infancy. A son, Nathaniel, died an infant. Three other children, John, Sarah and Moses, were born in New England, and here Candler's account in his manuscript in the British Museum of this branch of family ends.

Rev. John Fiske (by Cotton Mather). Among the writers of the Gospel with which the primitive church was blessed was "Luke, the beloved Physician," of whom Jerom elegantly says that as the Apostles from fishers of fish became fishers of men; so from a physician of bodies Luke was made a physician of souls; and as his book is read in the church his medicine will not cease. So among the first preachers who rendered the primitive times of New England happy, there was one who might likewise be called a "beloved physician," one to whom there might also be given the eulogy which the ancients think was given to Luke, a brother whose praise was the gospel throughout all the churches. This was Mr. John Fiske. Mr. Fiske was born in the Parish of St. James, in the County of Suffolk, England, about the year 1601, of pious parents. His grandparents and great-grandparents were eminently zealous in the true religion. In the reign of Queen Mary, of six brothers of this name, three were Papists and three were Protestants. Two of the latter were grievously persecuted. The one from whom

John, the subject of this memoir, descended, was, to avoid burning, hid many months in a wood pile and afterward half a year in a cellar, where he wrought by candle light at manufactures and remained undiscovered. But his many hardships brought on excessive bleeding, which shortened his days and added to "the cry of the souls under the altar." John was the eldest of four children, who all came with him to New England and left posterity with whom God established His Holy Covenant. His parents having devoted him to the Lord Jesus Christ, sent him first to a grammar school at a distance of two miles from their abode. Being there fitted for the university, he was sent to Immanuel College, Cambridge, where he resided until he took his first degree. Having spent some considerable time in preparatory studies he entered upon the work to which he had been devoted and which was his favorite object, the preaching of the Gospel. In this pursuit he would have continued had not Satan hindered him. The conformity act was odious to him. Its friends and supporters "breathed out slanders and the silencers pressed so hard upon him for his non-conformity, that upon the advice of his friends he relinquished the ministry and turned his attention to the study of physics. After a thorough examination he obtained license for public practice. At the age of 28 years he married a virtuous and amiable woman, who did him good and not evil all her days. She was the sharer and soother of all his tribulations until about three years before his death, when she left him to go to be with Christ. In 1633 his father died and left him in charge of his mother, two sisters and younger brother. This event dissolved the strongest ties that bound him to his native soil and removed every obstruction that seemed to be in the way to the engagement of his favorite pursuit. He resolved on going to New England, where he saw an opportunity for the quiet exercise of his ministry. He went on board a ship in disguise to avoid the fury of his persecutors. After they had passed the land's end, he entertained the passengers with two sermons a day, besides other agreeable discourses and devotional exercises, which filled the voyage with so much religion that one of the passengers being examined about his trying to divert himself with a hook and line on the Lord's day, protested that he did not know when the Lord's day was; he thought every day was a Sabbath day, for they did nothing but pray and preach all the week long. Mr. Fiske arrived in New England in the year 1637. His aged mother died quickly after he came on board, and his only infant quickly after he came on shore. He came well stocked with servants and all sorts of tools for husbandry and carpentry, and with provisions to support his family in a wilderness three years; out of which he charitably let a considerable quantity to the country, which he then found in the distresses of a war with the Pequot Indians.

The most prominent name among the first settlers of the town of Wenham was that of Fisk. Rev. John Fisk, who came from the County of Suffolk, in England, was the first minister of the place. As the parish of Wenham, in England, lies in the same county, it is not unlikely that the name of the town was taken from the original residence of this family. Rev. Mr. Fisk, after a residence of twelve years in Wenham, removed to Chelmsford, where he died. Besides him, three others of the name of Fisk were among the original settlers, and did not leave with the colony that removed to Chelmsford. They appear to have been men of property, and acted an important part in the infant settlement. Capt. Phineas and John Fisk were two of the first board of selectmen, and Hon. Wm. Fisk was the first town clerk. From the frequency with which the name occurs in the early records of baptisms, the descendants of the family appear to have been numerous, and for an hundred years or more they acted a prominent part in town affairs. Three of them, at different periods, held the office of deacon of the church. Out of thirty-five times that the town sent a deputy to the General Court, before 1720, it was represented twenty times by some one of this name. The first schoolmaster and the first commander of the militia, appointed in Wenham, was Capt. Thomas Fisk, who, for a period of twenty or thirty years, appears to have been the most important man in the town. As early as 1655 he was appointed town clerk, and two-pence granted to him for every order he should record. The first book of the town records is mostly in his hand-writing, which is not quite as legible as that of the best writing masters. He was a prominent actor in the series of measures which resulted in the division of the common lands. There continued to be several of the name in the place until the latter part of the last century, when it was reduced to a single family. Several farms have been at different times in possession of the family. The place, however, where they lived longest, and which is the most identified with their name, was on a lane leading from the Ober place (so-called) towards Wenham causeway. An old cellar alone remains to mark the spot, where generations lived, labored, and passed away.

The next year, Mr. John Fisk, who had taught the first grammar school established in Salem, and while thus engaged had occasionally assisted Mr. Peters in his ministerial labors, removed to Wenham, and through his efforts a church was regularly organized on the 8th of October, 1644. He at once became its pastor, and continued his labors in the town till 1656, apparently much to the satisfaction of the people. To the duties of the pastor he added those of physician, so that Cotton Mather remarks concerning him: "Among the most famous preachers and writers of the gospel, with whom the primitive church was blessed, there was Luke, the beloved physician, the blessed scholar and colleague of the Apostle Paul."

This appears like high eulogy, but for the times in which he lived, Mr. Fisk was evidently a superior man. He was descended from pious ancestry, and was early devoted to the service of Christ and the church. His parents, after carefully instructing him at home, sent him to the grammar school and afterwards to the university. He graduated at Immanuel College, Cambridge, and after studying theology was engaged for several years in the work of the ministry. In consequence, however, of the persecution then carried on against the Puritans and the difficulties and annoyances in the way of preaching, in accordance with the advice of his friends, he turned his attention to medicine, and obtained the usual license to practice as a physician. Yet he was still so desirous to resume the labors of the ministry that he determined to remove to America. He had previously married a lady of high rank and uncommon worth. To her parents his purpose to come to America was so disagreeable that they resolved to deprive him of several hundred pounds, which were the just share of his wife in her father's estate. At the call of duty, however, he did not hesitate to sacrifice property and all the endearments of home and kindred. Disguising himself to escape the fury of his persecutors, he embarked, in company with the Rev. John Allen, afterwards the first minister of Dedham.

After arriving in this country, Mr. Fisk appears to have taught some years in Cambridge, and afterwards in Salem. Of his services in the latter city, the Mayor of Salem, in a public address in 1842 says: "We may all be proud of the honest fame of the first teacher of our grammar school. He was, by the concurrent testimony of the most learned and honored of his day and generation, ranked high in the list of able, useful and devoted ministers of the gospel. One of his scholars was Sir George Downing, who was a member of the first class that graduated at Harvard College, and who was afterwards minister for Cromwell and Charles II. at The Hague." His pupils, it is said, were fitted "to read any classical authors into English, and readily make and speak true Latin, and write it in verse as well as prose, and perfectly to decline the paradigms of nouns and verbs in the Greek tongue."

Preferring, however, the work of the ministry to the labors of the teacher, he gave up his school in 1643, and, removing to Wenham, joined his fortunes to those of the infant plantation. Upon what salary he was settled we have no means of ascertaining. A piece of land appears to have been granted to him, and in addition to this, he had probably such contributions as the people were able to raise. It is stated that "he drew largely upon his own estate for the benefit of the new plantation." (In 1643 he gave ten acres of land for the benefit of the church and society). In 1654 it was voted by the town that "the yearly maintenance of our minister shall bee fortie pounds a year, whether Mr. Fisk stay among us, or we procure another;" and again, that "Mr. Gott, James Moulton and John Fisk are chosen to go to Mr. Miller, to give him a call in case Mr. Fisk leaveth us." December, 1655, it was ordered "that in case Mr. Brock be secured to stay amongst us, whatsoever the town hath engaged, or shall be levied on any land, shall be paid, two-thirds part in wheat, barley or peas, butter or pork, and the other third part in Indian corn." In consequence of the extreme scarcity of money, taxes and contributions were very generally paid in produce. According to the expenses of living and the means of the people, £40 a year would seem to be full as large a salary as is now usually paid in country towns.

From the previous votes, it appears that Mr. Fisk had already formed the purpose of leaving Wenham. He remained. however, till 1656, when, with a majority of the church, he removed to Chelmsford, where he lived for twenty years, discharging the duties at once of the minister and the physician. "For twenty years," says Cotton Mather, "did he shine in the golden candlestick of Chelmsford, a plain, but an able, powerful and useful preacher of the gospel, rarely, if ever, by sickness hindered from the exercise of his ministry." He died in his new field of labor in 1676, at the advanced age of 75.

Rev. W. Allen, in his history of Chelmsford, has given high testimony to the value of Mr. Fisk's labors in that town. The trials and hardships which he was there called to endure, might have disheartened youthful vigor, but were borne with fortitude and even cheerfulness. For the use of his flock, he wrote a catechism entitled, "Watering of the Olive Plants in Christ's Garden." This little work is moderate in doctrine, catholic in spirit, and admirably designed." His epitaph in Latin is as follows: "vixi et quem dederas cursum mihi Christe peregi, pertaesus vitae, suaviter opto mori." (I have lived and finished the work which Thou, Saviour, didst give me; weary of life, I long to depart in peace.)

.Rev. John Fiske, of Chelmsford, made his will June 18, 1674, which was proved by Samuel Foster, Sr. and Jr., Feb. 22, 1676. The other witness was Edward Spalding. The inventory of the estate was taken 2, 11, 1676 by Samuel Adams, Samuel Foster, Sr., and Abraham Parker. £703-3-10, made oath to by his son Moses, the executor, April 4, 1677. Items, homestead, including a sheep pasture on each side of the brook, meadow on Beaver Brooke; thirty-four acres on great brooke; six acres on Merrimack river; upland on Great Tadnicte meadow at son's place; twenty acres at great pine playne, a part of Mr. John Fiske, Jr.'s, homestead, on which his father, the testator, had built a house for him; meadow purchased of Capt. James Parker; library, which was valued at £60; a still; gally patts; scales and wts., writing his will with his own hand. Legatees, wife Elizabeth brought when married to him household goods, also "bees." He gave to son John, who was the eldest son, and at that time had wife Lydia had a certain legacy which if they deceased leaving no children, one-half of it was to go to son Moses and one-half to daughters Sarah Martha Burton and Anne Thompson, who were then of Salem, and each a legacy. from Mr. John Evered, alias Web, deceased. She was the youngest daughter, also unmarried, and Moses, her brother, was to be her guardian.

Daughter Sarah was then the wife of John Farwell, of Concord, but at that time, it seems, had no children.

Brother William, late of Wenham, deceased, left William for his eldest son and other children, who had legacies.

Sister Rix, of Salem, who was called mother to said children, of brother William.

Sister Martha Thompson, formerly of Salem, deceased, had left daughters Martha Burton and Anne Thompson, who were then of Salem, and each a legacy.

Son Moses, the testator's youngest son, to be executor and have the residue, including the homestead, and he was to put up a stone monument where the widow should be buried.

Rev. John Fiske's bounds, etc., according to the evidence of Samuel Moulton. then Dec. 1, 1698, "of ye town of Rehoboth, formerly of Wenham, being fifty-seven years of age or thereabouts, & "ye bounds between ye lands of Mr. John Fiske & James Moulton senr., both of them formerly of Wenham now deceased which bounds are as followeth & lands in the possession of Samuel Kemball & John Porter is a rock now placed near ye house which was formerly ye said Deponents from thence northward to a red oake which was formerly ye said Deponents from thence northward to a red oake which was ye bounds between ye lands of Mr. John Fiske & James Moulton * * * * * as ye line runs between ye land of said Shipleys & Mr. John Fiske farme to Pleasant Ponde which was in the possession of Samuel Kemball & John Porter when I came from Wenham * * * * in 1652—this was dated as above.

He d. Jan. 14, 1676-7; res. Cambridge, Salem and Chelmsford, Mass.

180. i.   JOHN, b. Frinshall, Aug. 29, 1638; d. infancy ae. 9.

181. ii. NATHANIEL, b. in England; d. infancy; "d. in 1637, quickly
           after he came ashore." [Mather.]

182. iii. JOHN, b. in England; m. 1666 Lydia Fletcher. He d. s. p. in 1700, leaving his estate to his brother Moses, of Braintree.

183. iv. SARAH, bap. July 26, 1640; m. John Farwell, of Concord.

184. v. MOSES, b. April 12, 1642; m. Sarah Symmes and Mrs. Ann Quincy.

185. vi. ANN, b. Jan. 15, 1646; m. Capt. John Brown, of Reading. She d. May 30, 1681. They res. in Reading. She had one child, Ann, b. in 1678. After his wife's death Capt. Brown m. the widow of Rev. Joseph Emerson, of Mendon, South Reading, Mass., Burial Inscription.— "Here lyes the body of Anna Fiske, first wife of Capt. John Brown, Esquire, who dyed May 30, 1681, in her 36th year." Note.—She was the daughter of Rev. John Fiske, the first minister of Wenham and of Chelmsford. She was the great-great-grandmother of Rev. Reuben Emerson, and great-great-great-grandmother of Rev. Alfred Emerson, at one time the Associate Pastors of the 1st Parish in South Reading.

His will is dated June 18, 1674, and was proved Feb. 22, 1676. It occupies twelve pages in the probate records.

186. vii. ELIEZUR, bap. Feb. 14, 1647; d. young.

164. HON. WILLIAM FISKE (John, William, Robert, Simon, Simon, William, Symond), b. England, about 1613; m. at Salem, 1643, Bridgett Muskett of Pelham, England. After his death she m. 2d, Nov. 3, 1661, Thomas Rix of Salem, surgeon. They had one child, Theophilus, b. Aug. 20, 1665. "William, the other son of John senior, and brother of John junior, who emigrated, is probably the William Fiske, who, in 1642, was admitted a freeman." (Candler's Manuscript in the British Museum.) I shall now forbear special reference to Mr. Savage's volume of these admissions. William died in New England in 1654. He married Bridgett Muskett of Pelham, by whom he had William, Samuel, Joseph, Benjamin and Martha. William Fiske was of Salem in 1637, which year he arrived from England and was brother of Rev. John, with whom he came over. He had a grant of land that year and was made freeman May 18, 1642, and member of the Salem church July 2, 1641. Soon after he removed to Wenham, where he was the first town clerk or clerk of the writs, from 1643 to 1660. In the Colonial Record is a settlement of rights between William and his brother John, by which it seems he was under 24 years of age in Sept., 1638. Endicott, Hathorne, and two others of the men of Salem made the terms of agreement. He was elected representative to the General Court of the Commonwealth in 1647 and continued in that office until the year 1652, being annually re-elected. He enjoyed to a large extent the esteem and confidence of his fellow citizens. He died quite suddenly in 1654, having served his townsmen in all the offices in the town. He died intestate, probably his death was caused by some disease. Letters of administration were granted by the court to "Widow Bridget Fiske July 16, 1654, and provision made for the children, viz.: Wm., Samuel, Joseph, Benjamin and Martha. There are no records of births in Wenham prior to 1686.

In 1643, according to the Wenham town records, Wm. Fisk received liberty from the General Court to keep an ordinary (public house), and in 1646 was licensed "to sell wine and strong water;" which privileges were a few years later transferred to Phineas Fisk. One of the appraisers of his property was Phinehas Fisk and one of the items was a "sign with the sign post."

Abstracts from Essex County Judicial Court records: Wm. Fiske, Plt. against Wm. Pester, Deft. of case, court ordered Mr. Pester to pay 20s. upon Mr. Fiske his oath, 31st, 10th mo. 1639. (Vol. I., p. 29.)

Wm. Fiske Plt. against Mathew Water, Deft. of case. Jury find for ye Plt. for the house he hired twentie shillings. Three shillings witnesses & fyve shillings coste and to finish the house within 14 days or elce be liable to all damages & the ——— of the ——— to answer Mr. Fiske servant (Joseph Haungton). Loss of tyme going so farr further to work ye he needed to have done. 30, 1st mo. 1641. (Vol. I., p. 51.)

COUNTY COURT RECORD, SALEM.

Wm. Fiske chosen clerk of the market for the town of Wenham, 7th mo., 1649, and was to hold the office until another was chosen.

Wm. Fiske of Wenham on gury of tryal 25, 10 m., 1649 & 24th, 4, 1651.

The following is a copy of the first town records of Wenham and shows the important part the Fiskes took in the proceedings:

The first entry on record (date worn off but probably 1642 or 3 as the next date was 1643 when Esdras Rread (Read prob.) had a grant of land dated 1643), was the following, viz.: "There is given unto Wenham twenty acres of ground being laid out of eyther side of ye meetinghouse ten acres given by Mr. Smith out of his farme and laid out by him beginning wth ye bounds at ye upper end of Phineas Fisk's Lott & soe to ye swamp and the other ten acres given by Mr. John Fiske being laid out joyning to it on ye sd. of ye meetinghouse.

1644, Dec. 4. Wm. Fiske chosen clerk of the writs and Phineas for constable. And same year Wm. Fisk was one of a committee to lay out a High Drift Way.

1645. Wm. Fisk was made choise of for grand jury.

1654. John Fiske chosen to join with the celect men to make the countery Ratte. Thos. Fiske chosen clerk of the writts. John Fisk chosen constable, & Jan. 1, 1654, Phineas was chosen commissioner to end small causes. Thos. chosen surveyor of the Pound—to have "four pence for every time unpounding." John Fisk chosen clerk of the market 6th, 12th mo., 1654. Ordered that the minister have fortie pounds a year whether Mr. Fiske stays & settle amongst us or we ———— another. "Mr. Gott, James Moulton & John Fiske."

"The widdow of William Fiske of Wenham presented an inventory to this court of her husband's estate amounting to the some of 141£ 12s. 0d., dyeing intest & leaving five children. This court directs administration unto the widow Bridgett Fiske she giving security by her owne hand & by her house & land for the payment of ten pounds to the eldest sonne 5£ to Sam'l the next & 3£ a pece to the rest of the children when they come to age she to Injoy the whole Estate." 26th, 7th mo., 1654. (Court Records at Ipswich.)

He d. Sept., 1654; res. Wenham. Mass.

187. i. WILLIAM, bap. June 4. 1642-3; m. Sarah Kilham.
188. ii. SAMUEL. b. in Wenham; m. Phebe Bragg and Mrs. Hannah Allen.
189. iii. JOSEPH. b. in Wenham; m. Elizabeth Haman.
190. iv. BENJAMIN, b. in Wenham; m. Bethusha Morse.
191. v. MARTHA, b. in Wenham.

169. NATHANIEL FISKE (Nathaniel. William, Robert, Simon, Simon, William, Symond) b. Weybred, Suffolk Co., Eng.; m. Dorothy Symonds of Wendham, dau. of John. There is a tradition in the family that he died on the passage to New England; res. Weybred, Eng.

192. i. JOHN, b. about 1619; m. Sarah Wyeth.
193. ii. NATHAN, b. in England; m. Susanna ————.
194. iii. ESTHER, b. in England.
195. iv. MARTHA. b. in England; m. Martin Underwood. Candler says in his manuscript: A Martha Fiske, another descendant, married an Underwood, and emigrated to America. whose husband was probably the Martin Underwood who had his freedom in 1634. Indeed it is uncertain whether Candler did not mean to say that Jeffrey Fiske himself emigrated.

He was b. 1596 and with his wife, who he had married in England, embarked in April, 1634 at Ipswich. for New England. He settled in Wat. and was admitted freeman Sept. 3, 1634. He was a cloth manufacturer or weaver. He d. s. p. Nov. 17, 1672. By his will. dated Aug. 23, 1663, proved Dec. 10, 1672, he gave the use of his estate to his wife and after her decease gave it all to his cousin (nephew), Nathan Fiske. Jr., and after his death to his brother, John Fiske. To his sister's children, if they come over from England. 20s. each. After his decease, his widow lived with her brother, Nathan Fiske, Sr. She d. May 6, 1684 ae. 82.

√   172. LIEUT. DAVID FISKE, ESQ. (David, Jeffrey, Robert, Simon, Simon, William, Symond). b. in England in 1624. He was "a planter" and was admitted a freeman of the Colony May 26, 1647. He settled in Cambridge at first, or soon after in Cambridge Farms (Lexington). He m. 1646 Lydia Cooper, sister of Dea. John Cooper, with whom he came over, and step-daughter of Dea. Gregory Stone, by whom he had three ch.; she d. Nov. 29, 1654; m. 2d, Sept. 6, 1655, Seaborn Wilson, of Ipswich, dau. of Theophilus Wilson. Wilson—Theophilus, of Ipswich, made his will Oct. 3, 1690, which was proved March 31, 1691. Inv. Jan. 28, 1690. He mentioned son Thomas, grandchild Elizth. Lovel, granddau. Elizth. Russell, grandchild Thomas Pinder, "and I do make my son John Pinder and my son David Fiske my executors." Cousin Nathl. Tredwell was overseer of the will.

Seaborn Fiske, of Lexington, Middlesex Co., Mass., for £8 in money sold to Alexander Lovell, cordwainer, and Thos. Lovell, currier, both of Ipswich, her undivided common right in Ipswich the "said right of land being left to me ye sd. Fiske by my Honored father, Theophilus Wilson, of Ipswich, deceased, for part of portion ye above granted premisses together with ye ways, uses," &c., making her marke March 3, 1717.

Seaborn Fiske, only surviving daughter and heir of Mr. Theophilus Wilson, late of Ipswich, decd., conveying to her kinsmen, Thomas and Alexander Lovell's, of Ipswich. &c., see above ack. before Jono. Tyng, of Middlex Co., July 3, 1719. She d. in Woburn Jan. 12, 1721. His will was dated June 23, 1708, and is proved Dec. 20, 1711. It mentions his wife, Seaborn; son Nicholas Wyeth, his dau. being dead; children David, Elizabeth, Anna, and Abigail; cousin Samuel, son of Dea. Samuel Stone. Inventory Feb. 14, 1710, £405-17-6. Oct. 16, 1676, he his wife Seaborn sold to Samuel Page 149 acres of land in Watertown, granted to his father. Oct. 6, 1663, the court allowed him 10s. each for seven wolf's whelps heads.

David, says Paige, in his History of Cambridge, rem. from Watertown to Camb. about 1646, and res. on the northerly side of Linnaean street, near the Botanic Garden, which estate he sold to Joseph Daniel 13 Dec. 1660, and prob. rem. to the Farms (Lex.) about the same time. He was a wheelwright, but much employed in public service, especially as a surveyor of lands. He was Selectman 1688, and Representative in the critical period of 1689. He was one of the most prominent men in the settlement at the Farms; precinct clerk and assessor; the first subscriber for erecting a meeting house there, and the first named member of the Church. In 1675 the work of settlement at Worcester was prosecuted with vigor, about the middle of April surveys were made of the lands by David Fiske, of Cambridge. Partial surveys were made in May, 1685 (at Worcester), a lot was laid out for Gookin of 100 acres on the east side of Pakachoag Hill and another lot of 80 acres on Raccoon Plain. There were present at this time David Fiske, the surveyor, and others. [History of Worcester.]

"David Fiske," says Hudson, in his Hist. of Lex., "was not only one of the first settlers, but became one of the most prominent and useful men in the precinct. He headed the subscription for a meeting house in 1692, and on the organization of the parish the year after, he was chosen clerk, and one of the selectmen or assessors. He was also chosen chairman of a committee to purchase of the town of Camb. a lot of land for the support of the ministry. These and other similar offices he frequently held under the Parish. He was also a member of the church organized in 1696, and his wife immediately after removed her relation from the church in Camb. to the church gathered in the precinct. He not only served his fellow-citizens in a civil and religious, but also in a military capacity, as appears by the prefix Lieut., which is often in the records connected with his name. He was often employed by the colony as a surveyor. He resided on Hancock St." A handsome monument was erected in 1856 by Benj. Fiske, Esq., with this inscription:

In memory of David Fiske, who died Feb. 14, 1710, and his descendants.

Feb. 3, 1720, an agreement was filed in the Midddlesex probate court. It was between the children of the late Lieut. David Fiske, of Lexington, deceased, viz., John and Elizabeth Russell, Henry and Abigail Baldwin, children of the late Lieut. David Fiske, of Lexington, deceased, and Timothy Carter, of Charlestown, to the office of attorney and trustee for Timothy Carter, of Woburn, his father, and the children of said Timothy Carter, descendants from the said David Fiske deceased, and between David Fiske, of Lexington, only son of the Sd. deceased, in order to a final settlement. We have hereunto set our hands and seals the day and year first above ritten and Timothy Carter, of Woburn above mentioned, who married Anna Fiske, daughter of said Lt. Fisk, being present at this agreement fully concord in the settlement, etc., David Fisk and seal.

John Russell, Henry Baldwin, Timothy Carter, Elizabeth Russell, Abigail Baldwin, Timothy Carter, Jr.

He d. Feb. 14, 1710; res. Watertown, Mass.

196. i. SARAH, b. May 8, 1646-7; d. in Boston, Nov. 8, 1647.

197. ii. LYDIA, b. in Boston Sept. 29, 1647-8; m. Sept. 6, 1681, Nicholas Wyeth, Jr., of Cambridge, afterwards of Watertown. He was the son of Nicholas and Mrs. Rebecca Andrews, his second wife, by whom he had five ch. born between 1650-59: Lydia d. s. p. in Watertown March 10, 1697. Nicholas, Jr., then m. 2d, June 30, 1698, Deborah Parker. They were town charges in 1716 and for some years before. Deborah was a widow in 1723.

198. ii½. DAVID, b. in Boston Sept. 1, 1648; d. Sept 20, 1649.

199. iii. DAVID, b. April 15, 1650; m. Sarah Day. / .↑   ) .↑

200. iv. SEABORN, b. ——; d. s. p.

201. v. ELIZABETH, bap. ——; m. John Russell, of Cambridge.

202. vi. ANNAH (Hannah), bap. Nov. 27, 1659; m. May 3, 1680, Timothy Carter, son of Rev. Thomas Carter, of Watertown and Woburn. Hannah d. Jan. 27, 1715. The father was an inhabitant in New England as early as 1635. He was one of the elders of the Watertown church and ordained the first pastor at Woburn in 1642. The ch. of Timothy and Ann were: David, b. Oct. 17, 1681; Timothy, b. July 12, 1683, d. soon; Ann, b. July 17, 1684; Timothy, b. Oct. 19, 1686; Theophilus, b. Oct. 20, 1688; Thomas, b. Aug. 17, 1690; Abigail, b. March 18, 1692, Sarah, b. Nov. 24, 1694; Eliza, b. Aug. 27, 1696; Benjamin, b. March 22, 1699, d. soon; Mary, b. Jan. 23, 1700; Martha, b. July 22, 1702; Benjamin, b. Nov. 8, 1704, d. July 8, 1727.

203. vii. ABIGAIL, b. Feb. 1, 1674; m. May 4, 1692, Henry Baldwin, of Woburn. Ch.: Henry, b. Jan. 12, 1693; David, b. April 9, 1696. His son William was graduated at Harvard in 1748 and Samuel graduated there in 1752; William, b. Feb. 20, 1700; Abigail, b. Feb. 13, 1702, d. soon; James, b. July 11, 1705, d. 1709; Abigail, b. Nov. 19, 1707; m. John Converse, a son was Robert Converse; James, b. Oct. 17, 1710; Samuel, b. Aug. 31, 1717.

204. viii. EPHRAIM, b. July 13, 1653; d. Sept. 14, 1653.

173. SERGT. JAMES FISKE (Phinehas, Thomas, Robert, Simon, Simon, William, Symond), b. Suffolk Co., England, ——; m. Anna ——; m. 2d Hannah Pike. James Fiske, Sr., eldest son of Phineas, was born in England, emigrated in 1637, joined Salem Church 1642, was same year freeman, and shortly after the family were established in Wenham, he removed to Haverhill, Mass., where he had several grants of land, the first being in 1646. He was a number of times a Selectman in Haverhill.

In the general division of lands, in 1661, James Fiske does not appear among the grantees; had probably then removed, as in 1669 he was one of a committee in Chelmsford appointed "to lay the land northerly of Groton," in which latter place he died. In his will in the Middlesex probate office dated June 14, 1689, proved July 26, 1689, all of the above children, save Ann and James, are mentioned as legatees, but other parties were executors. James Fiske, and Samuel Fiske, who appear on Groton records as heads of families—the first in 1690, the latter in 1704—were sons of the above. Among the descendants of Samuel, in the third and fourth generations, may be mentioned Hon. Levi Fiske, of Jaffrey, and Hon. Thomas Fiske, of Dublin, N. H., the former a State Senator, 1835-6; the latter, 1859-60.

The following data relative to James Fiske while residing in Haverhill is taken from the town records: Attending town meetings was evidently considered by our ancestors as a duty each voter owed to the community in which he lived, and for the neglect of which he deserved punishment. They even considered tardiness in attending as meriting rebuke, as we find by the record of Feb. 13, 1647, that John Ayer, Sr., and James Fiske were fined "for not attending the town meeting in season."

Considerable land was this year granted to individuals west of Little River, on the Merrimack, and among others James Fiske had liberty to lay down his land in the plain, "and have it laid out over Little River, Westward."

It was voted this year by the town "that all the meadows shall be laid out by the 12th of June next, to each man his proportion according to his house lot." At the same meeting it was "ordered that a committee, of which James Fiske was one, shall view the upland that is fit to plough, by the last of March or the tenth of April next, and that they bring in their intelligence to the town by that time." It was also ordered "that all the undivided land, after all the meadows and second division of plough land is laid out, shall remain to the same inhabitants the proprietors of the three hundred and six acres, to every one according to honest and true meaning, all commons remaining in general to them."

James Fiske and Anne, his wyfe, of Haverhill, for 100 pounds, sold to Rev. John Ward, of Haverhill, Nov. 22, 1659, a Dwelling house and house lot of nine acres in Haverhill, bounded by land of Richard Littlehale on the west, by Mr. Ward's on the east and south, by Michael Emerson on the north, etc., also five acres of planting land in the Playne, bounded on the south by Merrimack river and north by the common, etc., two acres of east meadow, bounded on the east by a river; two acres of west meadow, with commonages, etc.

Following are the names of those who received a share in this division: "The lots or draughts for the second division of plough land, with the number of each man's accommodation: John Fiske, four acres.

Among the noteworthy incidents may be mentioned the case of Robert Pike, of Salisbury. The court had prohibited Joseph Peasley and Thomas Macy, of Salisbury, from exhorting the people on the Sabbath, in the absence of a minister. Pike declared that "such persons as did act in making that law, did break their oath to the country, for it is against the liberty of the country, both civil and ecclesiastical." For expressing himself in this manner, he was disfranchised by the General Court, and heavily fined. At the next May Court, a petition was presented from a large number of the inhabitants of Hampton, Salisbury, Newbury, Haverhill and Andover, praying that Pike's sentence might be revoked. Among the names of the Haverhill signers, as copied from the original petition in the State Archives, is that of James Fiske.

The lots in the fifth division of land were drawn Nov. 20, 1721, and it shows who, or rather whose representatives, were the commoners at this time. James Fisk is the forty-second in the list of fifty. They were the heirs and assigns of the original purchasers, and were at this time considered to be the proprietors of the undivided lands in the town. (P. 257, Hist. of Haverhill.)

From the Groton records are found the following entries:

Due to James ffisk & Joh. Nuttin twenty shillings for laying out the hie-way to Chelmsford when they haue perfeted the work wh. they promise to doe as soone as they can.

James Parker William Lakin James ffisk William Martin & Richard Blood are chosen Select men this yeare.

James Fisk, the second town clerk, was an original proprietor of Groton, and the owner of a twenty-acre right. He wrote a good hand, and held the office during one year.

At a town meeting held 6th May, 1667. The towne hauing another meeting about a mill it was agreed & by vote Declared the lands & meadows granted to John Prescott: for to build the towne a mill; namely the 500 acres of vpland and twenty of meadow together with the mill should be freed from all towns charges whatsoeuer for the space of twenty years: and this was the vaote of the major part of the town that was present at this meeting: fouer men manifested their Descent at y time one of whom was James Fisk.

Att a General Town meeting held 31th 10 May 1666 ffor better pceeding in settling seates for the women as well as the men. It was agreed & by vote Declared that the front Gallery on the north side of the meeting house should be divided in the midle; and the mens that shall be placed there; and their wiues are to be placed by their husbands as they are below.

Same meeting theise men gaue vnto Robert parish sum small grants of vp-land as followeth:—James Fiske.

At a meting of the Select men the 27th Dec. 1669, it is ordered that all and euery inhabitant of the Towne shall bring in a tru invoyce of their pticuler estat to any one of the select men whensoeuer it is called for or else it must be left to the discretion of the select men or to a town meeting deputed for that end en-depted to the towne from James Ffisk Thirteen shillings sixpence.

And further these persons here set downe doe promise and Ingage to git Mr. Willard hay mowing making and fetching home for eight shilling pr. load at a seasonable time namely; in the middle of July. James ffisk.

At a general towne meeting held Janevary 13, 1672, this day agreed vpon and by vot declared that there shalbe a commit choosen for to seat the persons in the meeting house according to their best discretion and at the sam time a committee chosen and their names are thess, James fiske.

At a General Town Meeting December 10, 1673 Graunted vnto Alexander Rousse by the Towne ten acres of vpland.

At a general Towne Meeting December 10, 1673 ffor constable William Long-ley Seni. For Select men Serg. ffisk.

At a General Towne Meeting helde December 11, 1674 William Longley sene chusen constable for the year ensueing. Capt. Parker, serge ffisk serge knop ensine Lawrence Matthias ffarnworth serge Lakin John Morsse chussen for sellect men. John Morsse chussen Towne Clark.

He d. July 4, 1689; res. Wenham, Haverhill and Groton, Mass.

205. i.   JAMES, b. Aug. 8, 1649; m. Tabitha Butterick.
206. ii. JOHN, b. Dec. 10, 1651. There is a tradition that he was killed in the Indian wars.
207. iii. ANN, b. May 31, 1654; d. May 31, 1654.
208. iv. THOMAS, b. Jan. 23, 1655. Probably killed in the Indian wars.
209. v.   ANN, b. Feb. 11, 1656; probably d. young, as she is not mentioned in her father's will.
210. vi. SAMUEL, b. Nov. 1, 1658; m. Susanna ———.
211. vii. HANNAH, b. ———. She was given her father's new house in his will in 1689.

174. HON. JOHN FISKE (Phinehas, Thomas, Robert, Simon, Simon, Will-iam, Symond), b. in England, ———; m. Dec. 10, 1651, Remember ———. She m. 2d in 1689 Dea. William Goodhue, of Ipswich. She was his fourth wife, and d. Feb 16, 1702. Goodhue d. in 1699, ae. 86. He was selectman, deacon and repre-sentative. John Fiske, Sr., second son of Phineas Fiske, of Wenham, was a free-man in 1649, constable in 1654, and a representative in 1669 and 1681. He d. intes-tate in 1683. His property, valued at 372 pounds, was by decree of court divided among the following: Widow Remember, and children John, Samuel, Noah, Waite, Elizabeth and Remember. He was familiarly known as "John, the Con-stable," to distinguish him from another of the same name. John Fiske was wit-ness to the will of Thomas Payne in 1638. He was witness to the will of John Fairfield in 1646, also to will of Christ. Yongs in 1647, and in 1679 a John Fiske was in account with the estate of Edward Waldern. John Fisk died about one month previous to the 27th of the ninth month (November), 1683. Widow Remember and eldest son petitioned for letters of administration at the time of above date. Court ordered divided as above stated. Samuel having had con-siderable in father's life time. Son Samuel testifies he is about twenty-four years of age, had received twenty acres of land upon his marriage with Eliz., daughter of Lieut. Whipple, of Ipswich. Deed twenty acres says "John Fisk, carpenter, & wfe Rem'ber, &c., & dated Nov. 10, 1682. Witnessed by Thomas Fisk. Ipswich records show widow Remember's daughter. Remember mar. Nehe-miah Abbott in 1690. Her son Sam'l by wife Eliz. had son Increase born 1700 after his decease." John Fiske of Wenham was in the company commanded by Capt William Turner, Apr. 6, 1676, and in the Falls fight he was left wounded by Capt. Lathroppe.

May 18. "This day that happened which is worthy to be remembered. For at North Hampton, Hadly, and the Towns thereabouts, two English Captives, efcaping from the Enemy, informed that a confiderable body of Indians had (30) feated themfelves not far from Pacomtuck, and that they were very fecure: fo that fhould Forces be fent forth against them, many of the Enemy would (in probability) be cut off, without any difficulty. Hereupon the Spirits of Men in thofe Towns were raifed with an earneft defire to fee and to try what might be done. They fent to their neighbors in Conn. for a fupply of men, but none coming, they raifed about an hundred and four fcore out of their onw towns, who arrived at the Indian Wigwams betimes in the morning, finding them fecure indeed, yea all afleep without having any Scouts abroad, fo that our Souldiers came and put their Guns into their Wigwams, before the Indians were aware of them, and made a great and notable flaughter amongft them. Some of the souldiers affirm, that they numbred above one hundred that lay dead upon the ground, and befides thofe, others told about an hundred and thirty, who were driven into the River, and there perifhed, being carried down the Falls. The River Kifhon swept them away, that ancient river, the river Kifhon, O my foul thou haft troden down ftrength. And all this while but one Englifh-man killed, and two wounded. But God faw that if 'things had ended thus, another and not Chrift would have had the Glory of this Victory, and therefore in his wife providence, he fo difpofed, as that there was at laft fomewhat a tragical iffue of this expedition. For an Englifh Captive Lad who was found in the wigwams fpake as if Philip were coming with a thoufand Indians which falfe report being famed (Fama bella ftant) among the Souldiers, a pannick terror fell upon many of them, and they hafted homewards in a confufed rout: In the mean while a party of Indians from an Ifland (whole coming on fhore might eafily have been prevented, and the souldiers before they fet out from Hadly were earneftly admonifhed to take care about that matter) affaulted our men; yea, to the great difhonor of the Englifh, a few Indians purfued our Souldiers four or five miles, who were in number near twice as many as the Enemy. In this diforder, he that was at this time the chief Captain, whofe name was Turner, loft his life, he was purfued through a River, received his fatal ftroke as he paffed through that which is called the Green River, etc. as he came out of the Water he fell into the hands of the Uncircumcifed, who ftripped him (as fome who faw it affirm) and rode away upon his horfe; and between thirty and forty more were loft in this Retreat.

Thefe Falls we once fuggefted fhould have been named Maflacre Falls: but in all recent geographies and hiftories they are known as Turner's Falls, and we heartily acquiefce in thus defignating them, as it commemorates a brave and excellent man. I do not remember to have met with an Indian name for Thefe Falls. In early accounts they are called fimply The Falls, the Falls in the Conn, etc. They were by fome called Miller's Falls, as they were not far from Miller's river; they have alfo been called Deerfield Falls."

The power of the Indians was broken in this battle, but the war still continued in a desultory manner for two years. In these contests the people of Wenham bore their part in contributions of man as well as of money. The manner in which the state used to pay the services of its old and faithful soldiers may be seen from the following order of the General Court, Mar. 18, 1684: "In answer to the petition of John Fisk, of Wenham, a sore wounded soldier in the late Indian war, and thereby incapacitated to get his living, humbly desiring the favor of this honored General Court (having the approbation of the selectmen of said Wenham), to grant him a license to keep a public house of entertainment, therewith freedom from county rates, and also to sell drink free from imposts and excises." Consent was given.

John Fiske of Wenham, assignee of the committee of Salem, for the building the meeting house, plt. agst Christopher Babag Deft., attachment, 23rd, 9th m., 1675. Babbage, the constable, appealed to high court 21st, 10 m., 75. Ipswich Court Records.

John Fiske carpenter of Wenham & Remember his wife sendeth greeting Know yee that upon contract of marriage between my son Sam'l Fiske and Elizabeth Whipple of Ipswich I doe give grant enfoffe alienate and sett over a parcell of land containing about nyne ares being more or less at it lyeth within the limmetts of Wenham aforesayd bounded by our brother Thomas Fiske his land eastward and the brooke wch runneth out of the great Pond southward and by Mr. Smiths farme & that land called Goodman Bachelers pasture Northward & Westward by the devisionall lyne between our late fathers lott and Richard Goldsmith late deceased together with all the rest of our meadow lyeing att the lower or south end of our land formerly our ffathers as also a convenient high way crose the end of the said Prcell of land to our brother Thomas Fiske class or Prcell of Meadow To Have" &c. Nov. 10, 1682.

Witnessed by Thos. Fiske.

I Remember Goodhue being very weak of body aprehensive of not Continue-ing long in this world yet blessed be god, of perfect understanding & disposing mind do therefore humbly Recomend my spirit to God in faith and hope of a Blessed Resurrection to life againe & body to a decent buriall; and after my funerall Charges are Defrayed and due debts paid, to prevent any Disturbance among my children, do dispose of my few worldly goods in manner following Upon ye good consideration of my Daughter Elizabeth ffisk being in needfull circumstances and not having had her proportion wth ye rest of my children formerly—I do therefore will and bequeath unto my said Daughter Elizabeth all my goods that shall remaine after my funerall is Discharged, all my household goods, books, and wearing apparrell, and all my debts that do or may in any wise appertaine and belong to mee and do make her my Sole Executrix of this my last will and Testament Desiring my well Loved friend Mr. Daniel Rogers and my Son Joseph Ayre to have ye Inspection & Ordering of my funerall & ye Concerns thereof. I acquit the rest of my children from any debts that might be demanded Except my book at my son Abbots. In Testimony that this is my last will & Tes-tament I have hereunto sett my hand & seal this fourteenth day of ffebruary Anno. Signed Sealed & Delivered & Declared as my last will   Mark

in ye presence of witnesses Daniel Rogers, John   Remember X Goodhue Sparkes, Joseph Ayres.

The above will of "Remember Goodhue late of Ipswich widow dec'd was proved Mar. 31, 1702, and adm'n of the same committed to the Ext.

He d. Oct. 27, 1682-83; res. Wenham, Mass.

212. i.   JOHN, b. Dec. 12, 1654; m., Hannah Baldwin.
213. ii.   SAMUEL, b. ——, 1660; m. Elizabeth Whipple.
214. iii. NOAH, b. Nov. 14, 1662; m., June 16, 1686, Marcy Goold; res. Chelmsford, Mass., and elsewhere. He had in 1675 20 pounds out of the estate of Capt. Thomas Lathrop of Beverly. He was "brought up from a little one" and called relation to either Lathrop or his wife who was Bethiah. At a meeting of the selectmen of Wenham, June 2, 1696, "Then that whereas in the year 1694 Lt. Charles Gott did receive into his house or family & entertain his kinswoman Mercy Fiske the widow and relict of Noah Fiske dec'd without the leave of the selectmen & con-trary to the town order & now by the providence of God she being visited with sickness" &c selectmen agree to pay Dr. Ed-ward Wells of Salem provided &c. Noah Fiske died shortly after marriage and I think childless, judging from the above. Lt. Wm. and Lt. Tho. Fiske with Ensign Porter were a com-mittee selected by the town of Wenham to settle with Dr. Wells about ye cost which ne demands & has recovered judgement for her having bin expended about Mercy Fiske while she ley sick & lame &c & Lt Tho. Fiske was on the com. to sell land to pay the above also to pay widow Small for nursing sd. Mercy Fiske while at her house.
215. iv.   ELIZABETH, b. Mar. 8, 1673.
216. v.   REMEMBER, b. ——; m. Jan. 21, 1690, Nehemiah Abbott. He res. in Topsfield, Mass., where he d. in 1736. His wife d. July 12, 1703. Ch.: John, b. Apr. 4, 1691; Nehemiah, b. Oct. 19, 1692; Sarah; Mary; Mehitable, b. Oct. 17, 1700.
217. vi.   WAITE, b. ——; living in 1683 was given part of he. father's estate, 372 pounds, 11 shillings.
218. vii. JONATHAN, b. Dec. 12, 1688; probably d. young; not men-tioned in division of estate. (See Wenham records returned to court.)

NOTE—Massachusetts was divided into four counties in 1643, viz.: Essex, Middlesex, Suffolk and Norfolk. The last named, included all the towns north of Merrimack River, in Massachusetts, and New Hampshire as far as Ports-mouth at first; but after the line between Massachusetts and New Hampshire was

established what was left in Massachusetts was annexed to Essex County. Some
years later when more counties were made outside of Middlesex and Suffolk one
was named Norfolk. (See map of Massachusetts.) At first records were kept at
Ipswich and at Salem, but now all records of the county are at Salem.

175. CAPT. THOMAS FISKE (Phinehas, Thomas, Robert, Simon, Simon,
William, Symond), b. England in 1632; m. Peggy ———. She d., and he m. 2d,
in Boston, by Rev. Charles Morton, of Charlestown, May 14, 1695, Martha Fitch,
of Boston. "Thomas Fiske, youngest son of Phineas Fiske, of Wenham, was
born in England in 1630, was a freeman in 1661, and for above forty years afterward a citizen of great influence in Wenham. He participated very largely in
public affairs, was repeatedly a representative to the General Court, and died in
1705, 'the Patriarch of the town,' as he was called, being in his seventy-sixth
year. By wife Peggy, he had eight children. All the sons died while young,
except the first, Thomas." From the Judicial Court records of Essex County
it is stated that, "The wife of Thomas Fiske was presented for wearing a tiffany
hoode," and was sentenced to pay 10 shillings fine and two shillings six pence
fees to the court in Oct., 1652. Verily the court must have had a royalty on
another make of "hoodes." He came with his father from England, in his early
youth. He was one of the prominent men of the town of Wenham. Was representative 1671-72 and often after, especially in the revolutionary times of 1689-91.
Was captain of the Colony forces. Was foreman of the jury in that sad case
of Rebecca Nurse, when after a verdict of not guilty had been given was prevailed
on to convict by the wonderful perversity and extraordinary ignorance of the
court. His shocking confession against himself and the judges is in Hutch, II., 52,
Until 1719 one public school sufficed for the inhabitants of Wenham, which for
many years was put under the charge of Capt. Thomas Fiske. For the better
protection of the community "a trained band" was organized. Thomas Fiske was
captain, and William Fiske, lieutenant. The emolument to military position in
those days far exceeded the modern estimate, for in seating the congregation (the
pew system being not yet introduced) the officers of the military next to the deacons always had precedence. In 1686 the town of Wenham instructed Capt.
Thomas Fiske to keep a record of births, marriages and deaths, and he began
this registration.

In 1695 Capt. Thomas Fisk was paid "for going representative, for service
as an assessor, and a day going to Ipswich, £2 9s., by the town of
Wenham. He held every office in the gift of his fellow citizens. Represented
the town in the Great and General Court, 1671-72-78-79-80-86-94-97. Was moderator of the town meetings, 1700-04 and 1705; town clerk from 1661 to 1694, over
thirty-three years. His age is determined from a deposition in regard to Joseph
Axey willing property to Joseph Fisk in 1670. He then calls himself about forty
years of age. As stated above Capt. Fiske was foreman of the jury that tried
Mrs. Rebecca Nurse, a respectable old lady in Salem, on the absurd charge of
being a witch. He subsequently made a confession, of which the following is a
copy:

July 4th, 1692.—I Thomas Fisk the subscriber hereof, being one of them that
were of the jury the last week at Salem Court, upon the trial of Rebekah Nurse,
etc., being desired, by some of the relations to give a reason why the jury brought
her in guilty, after the verdict not guilty; I do hereby give my reasons to be as
follows, viz.: When the verdict, not guilty, was given, the honoured court was
pleased to object against it, saying to them, that they think they let slip the
words which the prisoner at the bar spake against herself, which were spoken
in reply to Goodwife Hobbs and her dau. who had been faulty in setting their
hands to the Devil's book, as they had confessed formerly; the words were,
"What do these people give in evidence against me now? They used to come
among us?" After the honoured court had manifested their dissatisfaction of the
verdict, several jury declared themselves desirous to go out again, and thereupon
the honoured court gave leave; but when we came to consider the case, I could
tell how to take her words as an evidence against her, till she had a further opportunity to put her sense upon them, if he would take; and then going into court,
I mentioned the words aforesaid, which by one of the court were affirmed to have
been spoken by her, she being then at the bar, but made no reply nor interpreta-
tion of them; whereupon these words were to me a principal evidence against her.

THOMAS FISKE.

Mrs. Nurse, being informed of the use which had been made of her words, gave in a declaration to the court, that "when she said Hobbs and her daughter were of her company, she meant no more than that they were prisoners as well as herself; and that, being hard of hearing, she did not know what the foreman of the jury said." But her declaration had no effect.

The minister of Salem, Mr. (Nicholas) Noyes, was over zealous in these prosecutions. He excommunicated this honest old woman after her condemnation. One part of the form seems to have been unnecessary; delivering her over to Satan. He supposed she had delivered herself up to him long before. But her life and conversation had been such of which many testimonies were given, that the remembrance of it, as soon as the people returned to the use of their reason, must have wiped off all the reproach which had been occasioned by the manner of her death.

County Court records, Salem. "Thos. Fiske is sworne clerke of ye writts for Wenham as also clerk of ye band to ye company there." 28-9th mo., 1654.

Court of Sessions. Mr. Thomas Jr. Licensed Retailer but not to sell after the manner of an Innholder. June 25, 1695. Thomas Fisk of Wenham had his license renewed June 30, 1696. Capt. Tho. Fiske aged about 63 years June 26, 1694. Tho. Kellum, Daniel Kellum, Richard Hatton, Tho. Nowlton, Jona Hobbs & Sam'l Lumus all personally appeared in upper court & presented their written evidence which they made oath to relating to bounds betwixt the land of Comtt Sallowstell & the land of Capt. Epes dec'd or late his Lyeing nigh Wenham which evidences are filed up with this county Records.

June Session, 1694. Capt. Tho. Fiske testified in relation to what transpired "about twenty years ago"—the land was north of the brook that runeth out of Pleasant Poond & Goodman Edward Lummus was the first one who lived on Col. Saltonstalls farm.

Capt. Thomas Fiske of Wenham made his will Apr. 24, 1705, which was proved Sept. 1, 1707, by all three of the witnesses, viz.: Jacob, James, Jr., and Hannah Brown, all of Ipswich, legatees. Wife Martha was to have by contract when he married her one hundred pounds in money in one year after his decease; to have her wood from his land joining Pleasure Pond, &c. Son Thomas Fiske had already received his double portion. The church in Boston to which he belonged was to have five pounds in money. Son-in-law John Perkins for his children should have two parcels in great meadow that he already occupied, estimated to be about six acres. To Ann Perkins five pounds. Grandson Andrew Dodge to have twenty pounds when he became of age. Son-in-law John Dodge's four children, which he had by the testator's daughter, viz., Phineas, Amos, Martha and Elizabeth, three pounds each. Daughters Sarah Dodge and Elizabeth Browne to have the residue according to the appraisal of three disinterested men chosen by sons-in-law Josiah Dodge and Nathaniel Browne. The executors of the will were Thomas Fiske and son-in-law Nathaniel Browne.

He d. Aug. 15, 1707; res. Wenham, Mass.

219. i. THOMAS, b. ———, 1656; m. Rebecca Perkins.
220. ii. JOSIAH, b. Nov. 4, 1657; d. Apr. 30, 1662.
221. iii. AMOS, b. Feb. 1, 1660; d. May 12, 1662.
222. iv. ELEAZER, b. Dec. 22, 1664; d. Sept. 25, 1668.
223. v. MARTHA, b. Feb. 27, 1667; m. John, son of John and Sarah Dodge, who was b. Apr. 15, 1662, and d. Jan. 18, 1703 or 1704. She d. Dec. 29, 1697. Ch.: Phineas, b. May 23, 1688; d. July 19, 1759; m. 1st, Martha Edwards, and 2d, Sarah Whipple. Amos, b. about 1690; d. Mar. 28, 1705 or 1706; m. Mary Webb. Martha. Elizabeth, b. Aug. 15, 1695.
224. vi. SARAH, b. Jan. 14, 1672; m. Josiah Dodge. Lydia Fiske m. Dec. 18, 1690, Josiah, son of John and Sarah Dodge, who was b. June 4, 1665, and d. Jan. 19, 1714 or 1715. After her death he m. a Sarah Fiske, who d. Mar. 17, 1729 or 1730, in her sixtieth year. Josiah Dodge had eleven children by his two wives.
225. vii. HANNAH, b. July 25, 1674; m. Andrew, son of John and Sarah Dodge, probably May 26, 1696. He was b. Oct. 29, 1676, and d. Feb. 17, 1747 or 1748. She d. Dec. 2, 1703, in her thirtieth year. Ch.: Hannah, b. July 7, 1699; d. Apr. 19, 1704. An-

5

drew, b. Nov. 26, 1703; d. Mar., 1741. Andrew joined an expedition against the Spanish possessions and was killed in the
attack on Cartagena in Mar., 1741.

226. viii.   ELIZABETH, b. Feb. 13, 1677; m. Nathaniel Browne.
227. ix.   ELEAZER, b. May 3, 1670.

179. JOHN FISKE (Nicholas, William, Nicholas, Simon, Simon, William,
Symond), bap. in Laxfield, England, ———; m. Sept. 23, 1600, Mary Bade. Res.
Laxfield, and at Banyard Green, England.

228. i.   ANNE, bap. May 17, 1601.
229. ii.   MARY, bap. Jan. 27, 1604.
230. iii.   ELIZABETH, bap. Feb. 19, 1607.
231. iv.   MARGARET, bap. Feb. 2, 1613.

184. REV. MOSES FISKE, M. A. (John, John, William, Robert, Simon,
Simon, William, Symond), b. Wenham, Mass., Apr. 12, 1642; m. Sept. 9, 1671, by
Capt. Daniel Gookin, assistant. Sarah Symmes, dau. of William of Charlestown
and Woburn; d. Dec. 2, 1692: m. 2d, Jan. 7, 1701, Mrs. Ann (Shepard) Quincy,
widow of Daniel of Boston, and dau. of the distinguished Rev. Thomas Shepard
of Charlestown; d. July 28, 1708. Sarah Symmes was the daughter of William,
Jr., b. Jan. 10, 1627, and his first wife, as his servant, John Warner, testified that
his master was a widower when this daughter married in 1671. Of William's
mother Capt. Johnson says: "Among all the Godly women that came through
the perilous seas to war their warfare, the wife of this zealous teacher shall not be
omitted." He was b. in Wenham, a village in Salem, Mass., and baptized at the
latter place in June, 1642. He was son of John Fiske, who was born in the Parish of
St. James in South Elmham, a subdivision of the Hundred of Wangford in the
County of Suffolk; came to Boston in disguise in 1637 with his wife (Ann Gipps)
and children, sat down, first at Cambridge. Removed the same year to Salem,
was ordained Oct. 8, 1644, as minister of Wenham, and in 1655 became minister at
Chelmsford, where he died Jan. 14, 1677. The son's charges in college, extending
from 3-7-58 to 3-7-59 are for tuition, gallery, detriment and sizing, and he is
credited by 59 pounds of butter and 5 sheep. His part on taking his second
degree at commencement in 1665, has been noticed elsewhere. Not long afterward he was at Dover, N. H., perhaps as a preacher. In 1666 he was made freeman. From 1668 to 1671 he officiated as Pastor at Woronoco, now Westfield,
Mass. After the death of the Reverend William Thompson, in the part of Braintree now Quincy, the church there was so divided that the people could not effect
a settlement for a successor. Accordingly, "at a County Court held at Boston
by the adjournment the 23d of Nov., 1671, the court having taken into consideration the many means that have been used with the Church of Braintree, and hitherto nothing done to effect, as to the obtaining the ordinances of Christ amongst
them, this Court therefore orders and desires Mr. Moses Fiske to improve his
labors in preaching the word of Braintree until the church there agree and obtain
supply for the work of the ministry, or this court take further order." In the
Braintree records, as stated by Lunt, Fiske writes: "Being ordered by the court
and advised by the Reverend Elders and other friends, I went up from the honored Mr. Edw'd Tyng's with two of the brethren of this church, sent to accompany me (2, 10 mo., 1671), being the Saturday, to preach God's word unto them."

"3, 10, 71 (Dec. 3, 1671). After evening exercises was ended I apologized as
to my coming, etc.

"4, 10, 71. About twenty of the brethren came to visit at Mr. Flynt's, manifesting (in the name of the church) their ready acceptance of what the Honored
Court had done (having received and perused their order, with letters sent to their
Townsmen respecting their duty toward their minister) and thanking me for my
complience therewith.

"24, 12, 71. The church by their messengers (Capt. Brackett, Lieut. Quin-
sey, Deacon Bass, John Doscet, sen., Gregory Belchar, Will Veazy, sen., Saml.
Tompson) did jointly and unanimously desire my settlement amongst them, and
that in order to office.

"14, 2, 72. Having advised, I gave the church, after evening exercise was finished (being often urged thereto), an answer of acceptance through God's assistance, understanding the concurrence of the neighbors which was partly expressed,
and part tacit.

"5, 3, 72. The church passed a vote of election (3 or 4 suspending who, after acceptance, etc., manifested their hearty concurrence).'

June 18, 1672, the town voted to give me £60 in money as by a town rate, and he to make provision for himself as housing or else to live in a town house provided for the ministry. And the house and land bought by the town of brother Samuel Tompson, being about five acres and a half or six acres, to be fences and housing set in good repair.

Aug. 18, 1672, having obtained letters of recommendation and dismission from the church at Chelmsford, he joined the church in Braintree and gave his "answer of aceptance to their call to office, the Rev. Elders and others advising and often renewing their request to that end." He was ordained Sept. 11, 1672. "Mr. Eliot prayed and gave the charge; Mr. Oxenbridge and the Deacons joined in laying on hands; Mr. Thatcher gave the right hand of fellowship. Dep. Gov. Leveret, Mr. Danforth, Mr. Tynge and Mr. Stoughton were present." Probably, according to the custom of the day, he preached his own ordination sermon. Oct. 26, 1674, the majority at a public town meeting voted that he "should have £80 for the year—74, in wood part and corn, at the country rate price, which was barley 4s., pease 4s., Indian 3s., malt 4s." Aug. 7, 1704, it was "90 pounds in or as money" (he finding himself with wood), to be annually paid to him, or his assigns, during his performing ye work of the ministry in the town, from the first of Mar., 1704." During the last years of Fiske's ministry his comfort was disturbed by a controversy between two sections of Braintree. The population had outgrown the capacity of the meeting house, and the southern portion, for many years, had petitioned without success for a larger one to be situated near to them. The distance for them to travel was long, the roads bad, particularly in winter, and the Lord's day became one of labour instead of rest. The population of the two sections was nearly equal. The northern section vigourously opposed the project and the other began to build for themselves, promising to be at the whole cost of the meeting house and to maintain their own minister. This, and propositions to pay 10 pounds and afterward 20 pounds of the 90 pounds of Fiske's salary, were declined. Particulars may be found in Adams, Lunt, Marshall, and Pattee, and, according to depositions of parties interested there were questionable measures resorted to. "After long and serious differences the members of the first parish were compelled to yield to a division," and then there was a litigation respecting Fiske's salary. About one-half of the parishioners and supporters were withdrawn on forming the south precinct, where Hugh Adams, H. U., 1697, was settled at the gathering of a church, Sept. 10, 1707, at Monotoquod, now Braintree. During Fiske's ministry there were 147 persons admitted to his church and 799 baptized. From a diary in the library of the Massachusetts Historical Society which was kept by John Marshall, a mason, though formerly thought to be one Fairchild, it appears that Fiske "continued till his dying day, a dilligent, faithful Labourer in the harvest of Jesus Christ. Studious in the holy scriptures, having an extraordinary Gift in prayer, above many good men and in preaching equall to the most; inferior to few, zealously dilligent for God and the good of men, one who thought no Labour, Cost of Suffering too dear a Price for the good of his people; his publick preaching was attended with Convinceing Light and clearness and powerful affectionate aplication, and his private oversight was performed with impartiality, humility and unwearied diligence; he lived till he was near 65 years of age, beloved and honored of the most that knew him; on the 18th of July, being the Lord's day, he preached all day in publick. But he was not well. Going home from his publick Labors he went ill to bed. The distemper, Continued proved a malignant feaver. So that Litel hopes of recovery apearing his church assembled together and earnestly besought the Great Shepherd of the sheep, that they might not be deprived of him. But heaven had otherwise determined for, on Tuesday, Aug. 10 (1708), he dyed about one afternoon." He was m. Sept. 9, 1671, by Capt. Gookin, assistant, to Sarah, dau. of William Symmes, of Charlestown or Woburn. She d. Dec. 2, 1692. They had fourteen children, of whom six died in infancy. Mary, the eldest child, b. Aug. 25, 1673, m. Sept. 16, 1697, Joseph Baxter, of Medfield, H. U., 1693; Sarah, Sept. 22, 1674, m., in 1698, Thos. Ruggles, of New Guilford, Conn., H. U., 1690; Ann, Oct. 29, 1678, m., June 30, 1709, Joseph Marsh, H. U., 1709, her father's successor; Moses, July 19, 1682; John, Nov. 26, 1684, H. U., 1702, of Killingly, Conn.; William, Aug. 2, 1684, and Samuel, Apr. 6, 1689, H. U., 1708. Jan. 7, 1700-1, Samuel Sewall, H. U., 1671, m. 2d, to Anna, b. Sept. 13, 1663, widow of Daniel Quincy and dau. of Thomas Shepard, H. U., 1653. She d. July 24, 1708, less than three weeks before her husband, having had Shepard, H. U., 1721, a physician at Killingly, Conn., and at Bridgewater, Mass., who d. June 14, 1779, and Margaret, b. Dec. 16, 1705, who m., Jan. 23, 1727-28, Rev. Nathan Bucknam, of Medway, H U,, 1721.

Mr. Fiske was placed in the tomb where lie his two wives and his successor, Joseph Marsh, H. U., 1705, besides others. On his tombstone is this inscription:

"Braintree! They prophet's gone, this tomb inters
The Rev. Moses Fisk his sacred herse,
Adore heaven's praiseful art, that formed the man,
Who souls not to himself, but Christ oft won;
Sail'd through the straits with Peter's family,
Renown'd and Gaius hospitality,
Paul's patience, James prudence, John's sweet love,
Is lauded enter'd clear'd and crown'd above."

In the library of the Massachusetts Historical Society a manuscript sermon delivered before the Ancient and Honorable Artillery Company in 1694. The text is taken from Eph: vi., 14. "Stand them therefore so." It is noticeable that one item in the inventory of Fiske's is "His Armour."

Authorities. T. Alden's Collection of American Epitaphs, lii., 24. W. Allen, History of Chelmsford, 125, 126. American Register, viii., 44-53. J. Farmer, Memorial (22). Harvard College Stewards' Account Books, I, 369, 370. J. G. Holland, History of West Massachusetts, 1, 66, 11, 142. W. P. Lunt, Two Hundredth Anniversary Digressions, 44, 102, 114. J. Marshal, Manuscript Diary in the library of the Massachusetts Historical Society. Massachusetts Historical Society Collections, vi. 240; ix., 193; xxx., 157. C. Mather Magnalia, iii., 141. New England Historical and Genealogical Register, ix., 151; xi., 71. W. S. Pattee, History of Quincy, 204. J. Savage, Genealogical Dictionary, ii., 166. W. B. Sprague, Annals of the American Pulpit, i., 107. G. Whitney, History of Quincy, 34.

The ministerial tomb was erected by the Rev. Moses Fiske, the third minister of the first church, in which he and his two wives were buried. After his death this tomb was selected as the ministerial sepulcher in which all the ministers of the first church have been interred with the exception of Mr. Thompson and Mr. Flint. Over the grave of the latter was placed a large flat stone, as was then the custom, to prevent the wild beasts from removing the remains of the dead from their last resting place. Not long before the decease of the Rev. Peter Whitney the monument over the tomb was renewed by the ladies of Quincy, with granite, and the freestone tablet that surmounted it was preserved."

He d. Aug. 10, 1708; res. Dover, Braintree, and Quincy, Mass.

232. i.   MARY, b. Aug. 25, 1673; m. Sept. 16, 1697, Joseph Baxter, of Medfield, Gr. H. U., 1693.
233. ii. SARAH, b. Sept. 22, 1674; m., 1698, Rev. Thomas Ruggles, of New Guilford, Conn., Gr. H. U., 1690.
234. iii. ANN, b. Oct. 29, 1678; m. June 30, 1709, Rev. Joseph Marsh. He was the successor of his father-in-law as minister of Braintree and was ordained pastor May 18, 1709. He was graduated at Harvard College in the class of 1705. He d. Mar. 8, 1725, and was buried in the same tomb with Rev. Mr. Fiske.
235. iv. MOSES, b. July 19, 1682.
236. v.   JOHN, b. Nov. 26, 1684; m. Abigail Hobart.
237. vi. WILLIAM, b. Aug. 2, 1685.
238. vii. SAMUEL, b. Apr. 6, 1689; m. Anna Gerrish.
239. viii. SHEPARD, b. Apr. 19, 1704; m. Alice Alger.
240. ix. MARGARET, b. Dec. 16, 1705; m. Jan. 23, 1727, Rev. Nathan Bucknam.
241. x.   JOHN, b. May 29, 1681; d. Aug. 5, 1681.
242. xi. SAMUEL, b. Feb. 19, 1687; d. Mar. 4, 1687.
243. xii. EDWARD, b. Oct. 20, 1692; d. Oct. 25, 1692.
244. xiii. ELIZABETH, b. Oct. 9, 1679; m. Jan. 28, 1703, Eliezer Foster.
245. xiv. MARTHA, b. Nov. 25, 1675; d. Nov. 28, 1675.
246. xv. ANNA, b. Aug. 17, 1677; d. June 9, 1678.
247. xvi. RUTH, b. Mar. 24, 1692; d. June 6, 1692.

187. DEA. WILLIAM FISKE (William, John, William, Robert, Simon, Simon, William, Symond), bap. Wenham, Mass., June 4, 1642-43; m. there, Jan. 15, 1662, Sarah Kilham, b. 1649; d. Jan. 26, 1737. Austin Kilham, with his brother Daniel, emigrated from the Parish of Kilham, Yorkshire, England, the same year, and probably in company with the Fiskes. Both settled and were freemen in Wenham before 1645, and are presumed to be the ancestors of all New England families of that name. Austin, by wife Alice, had Lot, born Sept. 11, 1640, who settled and died in Enfield; and Sarah, born Jan. 24, 1642, who married Deacon William Fiske, and died Jan. 26, 1737 (as the record says), "aged 98." Her father, and probably his brother, followed Rev. John Fiske to Chelmsford, 1657. Her cousin, Daniel Kilham, Jr., figured conspicuously in town affairs for many years, and his son, Hon. Daniel Kilham (a democrat), was the formidable antagonist of Hon. Timothy Pickering in many a hotly contested campaign in Essex politics.

Killim Austin made his will 2d 4 mo 1667 which was proved Sept 24 1667 Inv of his estate taken 11th 4 mo 1667 and Allace widow of Austin Killum made her will July 3, 1667. In his will is mentioned sons Lott & John—She in her will mentions son Daniel—dau. Elizth Hutten who then had a daughter named Elizth —Daughter Sarah Fisk Daughters Mary & Ruth—Daniel's wife—granddaughter Mary Killum & son Lott.

He was a weaver by trade. He held a number of town offices; was representative in 1701-04-11-13 and 1714; was moderator in 1702-03, 1712-13 and 1714. He was also called lieutenant. He was elected deacon of the Congregational church in 1679. They were the parents of fourteen children, ten of whom grew up and had families. Of these seven were sons. He died universally esteemed and lamented. His son Ebenezer was executor of his will.

Lt William Fiske of Wenham weaver bought of John Newman of Wenham Physition and wife Ruth for 100 pounds 60 acres of upland swamp in Wenham "bounded as followeth Southwardly by ye land of said Wm Fiske Theophilus Rix & Saml Fiske senr, Westwardly by ye land of Wm Fairfield and Northwardly by said Wm Fiske own land in part & by ye great swamp in part according to ye bound markers on that side being from ye Northeasterly corner of Wm Fairfields Land to a white Oake tree standing on a point of upland adjoining to a small parcell of meadow of said Wm Fiskes and so Northeasterly including a parcell of meadow Commonly called Kemps meadow till it comes to ye Northwestwardly corner bounds of John Batchelders Land & Eastwardly by said Batchelders Land and Also ten acres of meadow more or less situated in Wenham great meadow called Mr. Newman's ten acres lot bounded by the meadow John Robinson lot & Jas & Sam Moulton M E Parker John Perkins and by ye great swamp Jan 18 1695-6

Lt Wm Fiske of Wenham had released to him by John Newman of Glocester Treader 70 acres of land in Wenham which tract of land was bought by ye said Wm Fiske of my hond father John Newman Esq &c as bounded in sd William Fisk's deed bearing date Jan ye 18 1695-6 witnessed by The. Rix & Daniel Fisk Feb. 23, 1720-1.

He d. Feb. 5, 1728; res. Wenham, Mass.

248. i.   WILLIAM, b. Jan. 30, 1663; m. Marah ———.
249. ii.   SAMUEL, b. Feb. 16, 1670; m. Elizabeth Browne.
250. iii. JOSEPH, b. Apr. 14, 1672; m. Susan Warner and Mrs. Elizabeth Fuller.
251. iv.   BENJAMIN, b. Apr. 6, 1674; m. Mary Quarles.
252. v.   THEOPHILUS, b. July 28, 1676; m. Phebe Lampson and Mehitable Wilkins.
253. vi.   EBENEZER, b. Mar. 22, 1679; m. Elizabeth Fuller and Mrs. Martha Kimball.
254. vii. JONATHAN, b. July 22, 1681; d. Feb. 14, 1705.
255. viii. SARAH, b. Feb. 5, 1664; m. Sept. 14, 1688, John Cook; was a legatee in her father's will. They moved to Windsor, Conn., and had John, b. 1692.
256. ix.   RUTH, b. Mar. 2, 1666; m., and d. before 1725, leaving heirs.
257. x.   SAMUEL, b. Mar. 2, 1667; d. young.
258. xi.   MARTHA, b. May 5, 1668, a legatee in her father's will.
259. xii. JOSEPH, b. Feb. 10, 1669; d. young.
260. xiii. EBENEZER, b. Feb. 10, 1677; d. June 7, 1678.

261. xiv. ELIZABETH, b. Dec. 12, 1684. She was legatee in her father's will.

188 SAMUEL FISKE (William, John, William, Robert, Simon, Simon, William, Symond,) b. in Wenham, Mass., ——; m. Nov. 6, 1679, Phebe Bragg; d. in Wenham Oct. 1, 1696; m. 2d, May 24, 1697, Mrs. Hannah Allen of Manchester; d. Jan. 30, 1722. She was b. 1662. William Allen of Manchester. Inv. of his estate was taken Dec. 29, 1696, and Hannah Allen, his widow was appointed administrator Jan. 4, 1696; account rendered by the administrator, Hannah Allen alias Fiske, Dec. 13, 1696. Fiske resided in Wenham, where he was born and was made a freeman there March 25, 1685. On the land records he is referred to as Samuel Senr, and his occupation is mentioned as a tailor. He was frequently elected to offices of selectman, tythingman, constable, etc., and he acquired a large estate. Before his death he made a distribution of his property by deed to his five sons.

From Wenham Town Records: 1699. "Sam'l Fiske, Jr., is accepted as a commoner in the right of his brother Joseph Fiske who was accepted and is removed to Ipswich." Same time: "Benj. Fiske is accepted as comon'r in o'r town."

1699. Sam'l Fisk Jr. and Sam'l Fisk Sen'r granted pine & hemlock timber for shingles, &c. Sam'l F. sen'r and jr., juror.

Sam'l Fiske of Wenham Taylor John Stiles Thomas Cummings and David Peabody all of Boxford husbandmen owned a tract of land in Boxford containing 800 acres more or less as it is bounded which was land that old Mr. Zacheus Gould formerly gave to his 4 daughters this land lyeth on ye south side of ye brooke called ye Fishing brook "bounded by stakes & stones" to Andover line & running Northwestwardly on Andover line till it come to ye Fishing brook & so bounded by ye channel till it come to ye first mentioned bounds & they made a division of it Mar. 29, 1708 & acknowledged Mar. 15, 1710-11 in the description is mentioned the names of Long meadow Reddington's meadow brook & eight mile meadow swamp.

Sam'l Fiske of Wenham yeoman gives by deed to two sons Daniel & Benj. Fiske all his real Estate & Personal Estate including House barn land &c in Wenham, to be divided equally at his decease the Grantor "having disposed of all my Estate in Boxford & Rowley Village to my three sons, viz.: Sam'l & John & Wm Fiske as may appear by Deeds under my hand and seal Signed Sept. 18 1716 in presence of Tho Fiske Thos How & Wm Rogers ack'd same time.

Sam'l Fiske of Wenham Taylor bought of John Staniford of Ipswich cordwainer with consent of his wife Margaret upland 47 acres bounded by ye common beginning at a white Oake marked and running Northerly seventy five rods to a white Oake thence running easterly 84 poles to a Black ash bounded by James Bailey & Ezekial Northend & Thence Southerly fifty three Rods by said Northend to an elm & thence southwest fifty eight rods by a piece of meadow &c situated in Rowley July 10 1707. Witnessed by a Wm Fiske.

Samuel Fiske Taylor of Wenham received a quit claim of his part of the 800 acres on south side of ye Fishing brook in Boxford viz the land Old Mr. Zac. Gould gave to his four daughters & which Fisk T Cummings John Steles & David Peabody had a right to, see above. "The bounds of the whole piece is in a deed which Capt. John Gould gave to Mr. Newmarch of Ipswich which deed Thomas Comings of Boxford hath" by Andover line Reddings meadow Fishing brook Eame's meadow & Works meadow &c. Dated Mar 29 1708 acknowledged by them Mar. 15, 1710-11.

Samuel Fiske Jr Wenham weaver & wife Eliz'th sold to Wm Fairfield of Wenham husbandman his dwelling house barn with the 40 acres of lam in several lotts some of it was bounded by said Fairfield Theophilus Fiske swamp called Sam'l Fiskes some of great meadow bounded by Caleb Kimball by the land Capt Fiske bought of Mr Newman by the land the grantor bought of Capt Fiske by land Capt Fiske sold to Tho Tarbox one piece bounded by land Capt Fiske Jr sold to Theophilus Fiske & westerly upon ye meadow of Benj Fiske sold him by Nath'l Brown & northerly upon meadow land of Dea Fiske partly & partly upon meadow said Sam'l Fiske & Joseph Fiske purchased of Nath'l Stone. He d. Oct. 31, 1716; res. Wenham, Mass.

262. i. SAMUEL, b. ——; m. Sarah Reddington.
263. ii. JOHN, b. ——; m. Abigail Poor.

264. iii. WILLIAM, b. June 10, 1687; m. Rebecca Reddington, Lydia Thurston and Bethiah Goodrich.
265. iv. DANIEL, b. ———; m. Sarah Fuller. ✓
266. v. BENJAMIN, b. ———; d. unm. Sept. 16, 1719.
267. vi. HANNAH, b. Jan. 7, 1698; d. Feb. 3, 1699.

189. JOSEPH FISKE (William, John, William, Robert, Simon, Simon, William, Symond), b. Wenham, Mass., about 1650; m. in Lynn, May 22, 1677, Elizabeth Haman. He was born in Wenham, but early removed to Lynn, where he married his wife. Later he moved to Ipswich, where he afterwards resided and later to Swansey, where he died. Joseph Fiske of Lynn was in account with the estate of Wm. Barber in 1677. Mar. 24, 1689, he was "39 years of age or thereabouts" at the time he testified in regard to the will of Edward Richards. Joseph Fiske was a legatee in the will of James Axey with whom he had served. And he was executor of the will of said Axcy's widow in 1670. In 1699 he was residing in Ipswich. He immigrated to Rehoboth and followed the Indian trail to the Pawtucket river through the unbroken wilderness, not iar from 1700. His children were probably born elsewhere, but are recorded in Swansey. He d. ———; res. Lynn, Ipswich, Swansey, Mass.
268. i. JOSEPH, b. July, 1678; in Ipswich; d. there May 24, 1731.
269. ii. SAMUEL, b. July 5, 1680; rec. in Swansey; m. Mehitable Wheaton and Elizabeth ———.
270. iii. MARY, b. Apr. 19, 1684; rec. in Swansey; m. Jan. 9, 1723, Isaac Mason, Jr.

190. BENJAMIN FISKE (William, John, William, Robert, Simon, Simon, William, Symond), b. Wenham, Mass.; m. Nov. 6, 1674, Bethusha Morse, dau. of Dea. Morse; res. Medfield, Mass.
271. i. LYDIA, b. Sept. 18, 1675.
272. ii. MARY, b. July 22, 1677.
273. iii. BETHIA, b. June 25, 1683.
274. iv. BENJAMIN, b. Apr. 25, 1684.
275. v. MARTHA, b. Jan. 14, 1685.
He had probably other children and moved away.

192. JOHN FISKE (Nathaniel, Nathaniel, William, Robert, Simon, Simon, William, Symond), b. England, about 1619; m. Dec. 11, 1651, Sarah Wyeth, eldest and only child of Nicholas by his first wife b. and bap. in England (see Cambridge Church Gathering, p. 58). John Fiske was born in England and came to America with his brother Nathan and father Nathaniel. The mother had probably died in England. The father died on the passage over. John took the oath of fidelity in 1652. In Watertown he purchased the west end of six acres of the Henry Dow lot, next south of Dea. T. Hastings and this was his first homestall which he sold Mar. 15, 1648 to Charles Stearns. The inventory of his estate was made Nov. 28, 1684, and amounted to £94-10-0. His daughters, Sarah, Margaret and Mary received at the age of 18 from Philip Smith, surviving executor of their uncle, John Clarke, late of Newport, R. I., physician, deceased, legacies out of land on the Island of Canonicut, June 2, 1684, George and Martha (Fiske) Adams received a similar legacy, each £3-14 (see Mid. Deeds, Vol. IX., p. 42-45). The inventory of his estate was made by John Warren, Jonathan Smith and John Nevenson. He d. Oct. 28, 1684, ae. 65; res. Watertown, Mass..
276. i. SARAH, b. Feb. 1, 1652.
277. ii. JOHN, b. Nov. 7, 1654; d. Feb. 1655.
278. iii. JOHN, b. Nov. 20, 1655; m. Abigail Parks and Hannah Richards.
279. iv. MARGARET, b. Nov. 28, 1658; d. unm. ae. 91, Jan. 15, 1750.
280. v. MARY, b. July 5, 1661; m. Feb. 5, 1684, Joseph Mason. She d. Jan. 6, 1723. He was a tanner. The inventory of his estate is dated Aug. 11, 1702, £195-7-0; res. Watertown. Ch.: 1 Mary, b. May 2, 1685; m. Thomas Learned, an inholder of Wat. 2. Hester, b. July 8, 1686; m. Nov. 10, 1737, Capt. Joseph Coolidge. He d. 1749, and she m. Edward Johnson of Woburn. 3. Joseph, b. Oct. 2, 1688; m. Mary Monk. 4. Sarah, b. Nov. 17, 1691; m. Thomas Chamberlin of Newton. He d. and she m. 2d, John Bond of Wat.

281. vi. WILLIAM, b. Feb. 23, 1663; m. Hannah Smith.
282. vii. MARTHA, b. Dec. 15, 1666; m. Jan. 20, 1683, George Adams
          of Lex. He was the son of George Adams of Wat., glover,
          and was b. in 1647. He was bap. by Rev. Mr. Angier and
          owned the covenant June 19, 1698. He was assessor in 1702
          and constable 1715. She was bap. in Wat. by Rev. Mr. Bailey,
          Nov. 21, 1686. He d. Jan. 27, 1732; res. Lexington. Ch.:
          George, b. Apr. 28, 1685. He was a physician, "a bonesetter
          and chirurgeon"; m. Judith ——; res. Wat. and Wal.
          Martha, b. Jan. 10, 1686. John, b. Sept. 2, 1688; m. Oct. 27,
          1714, Mary Flagg. She was a daughter of Lt. Gershom and
          Hannah (Leffingwell) Flagg; said Lt. was killed in action
          with the Indians, July 6, 1690, at Wheelwright's pond. The
          descendants of George Adams, Jr., and Martha (Fiske) Adams
          are very numerous. Among the descendants of said George
          and Martha F. Adams living in the region of Chicago are
          Andrews T. Merriman of 1208 Judson Ave. and Richard K.
          Adams of 1242 Judson Ave., Evanston, Ill. The former was
          one of the earlier settlers of Chicago. Nathaniel, bap. June 12,
          1698; m. Eunice Stearns; res. Grafton (see Hist. of G. by Fred
          C. Pierce). Sarah, b. June 12, 1698. Benjamin, b. Dec. 20,
          1701; m. Eunice ——. Abigail, b. ——; m. May 30, 1727,
          Ebenezer Brown. Anna, b. ——; m. Dec. 7, 1727, Isaac
          Child.
283. viii. ELIZABETH, b. May 11, 1669; m. in Sherburne, Dec. 27, 1688,
          Simon Mellen, Jr., of Fram. He was b. Sept. 25, 1665, in
          Winesimet. Ch.: Simon, b. May 16, 1690. Mary, b. June
          4, 1695; d. Apr. 30, 1711. James, b. Mar. 8, 1698. Simon, the
          father, was constable in 1700, tythingman 1703 and selectman
          in 1704. He d. Aug. 30, 1717, ae. 52. His funeral was preached
          by Rev. Mr. Swift. His inventory amounted to £629.
284. ix. NATHANIEL, b. Sept. 11, 1672.
285. x.   ABIGAIL, b. Oct. 8, 1675; m. July 14, 1699, Dea. Jonathan San-
          derson; res. Wat. He was assessor and selectman. She d.
          Apr. 29, 1759, ae. 84. Ch.: Jonathan, b. July 26, 1700; Dea.;
          res. Wal.; selectman 7 years; m. Grace Barnard. Abigail, b.
          Oct. 23, 1702; m. James Mellen of Fram. Margaret, b. Sept.
          9, 1704; m. Benjamin Whitney of Fram. (see Whitney Gene-
          alogy by Fred C. Pierce). Eunice, b. July 1, 1707; m. Isaac
          Pierce (see Pierce Genealogy by Fred C. Pierce). Thomas,
          b. June 18, 1710; res. Wal.; m. Rebecca Fiske, wid. of David
          Fiske, Jr., and 2d, Anna Dix. Nathaniel, b. May 30, 1713; d.
          Sept. 7, 1774; lived in Framingham and Petersham; m. Oct.
          4, 1739, Mary, dau. of John and Susanna (Goddard) Drury, b.
          Mar. 21, 1721; d. Sept. 8, 1805. Their eldest child was: Jon-
          athan Sanderson, b. Sept. 1740; d. ——, 1832; lived in Peters-
          ham; m. Mary Curtis. One of their children was: Curtis
          Sanderson, b. Feb. 12, 1779; d. Aug. 22, 1849. He m. Eunice
          Spooner. David, b. June 4, 1715; m. Abigail Jones, Deacon;
          res. Petersham.

193. NATHAN FISKE (Nathaniel, Nathaniel, William, Robert, Simon,
Simon, William, Symond), b. in England about 1615; m. Susanna ——. He
settled in Watertown as early as 1642, but his name does not appear on the list
of proprietors of that year. He was admitted freeman, May 10, 1643, and was
selectman in 1673. His will attested by Joseph Tainter and William Bond, was
dated June 19, and he died June 21, 1676. His sister, Martha Underwood, testified
that he "was very crazy in his memory" before he died. In 1644 he was proprietor of
one lot of nine acres. This lot, his homestall, was the lot in the Town Plot granted to R. Frake on the north side of the Sudbury road, opposite to A. Browne,
Nathan Fiske, Sen'r of Watertown, Vol. 4, P. 269, Mid. Prob. Rec. Will date
June 19, 1676 Bequests—Sonne Nathan, 30s "he being already thorow the mercy of
God well provided for with my help formerly. 2nd sonne John Fiske—dwelling
house barne &c 4 a of upland upon the little playne & 10 ac of Meadow in the

meadow comonly called Thatcher's Meadow," &c. 3—To my sonne David & Nathaniel Fiske 13 a of my land lying in the further playne, to be equally divided between them. 4 Daughter Sarah Gale. 5 My two eldest sons, Nathan & John Exrs. (P. 270 "a true Inventory of Nathan Fiske, who died the 21 of June 1676.") He d. June 21, 1676; res. Watertown, Mass.

   286. i.   NATHAN, b. Oct. 17, 1642; m. Elizabeth Fry.

   287. ii.   JOHN, b. Aug. 25, 1647. He was living in 1670 and was executor of his father's will. He was a witness in court June 11, 1679, was then ae. 30.

   288. iii.   DAVID, b. Apr. 29, 1650; m. Elizabeth Reed.

   289. iv.   NATHANIEL, b. July 12, 1653; m. Mrs. Mary (Warren) Child.

   290. v.   SARAH, b. 1656; m. Sept. 3, 1673, Abraham Gale. He was a son of Richard Gale, who came from England and settled in Watertown before 1640. Abraham was admr. freeman Oct. 11, 1682. She d. May 14, 1728. Ch.: Abraham, b. 1674. He was a Selectman, Watertown; m. Dec. 6, 1699, Rachel, dau. of John and Abigail (Garfield) Parkhurst, b. Dec. 30, 1678; d. Jan. 30, 1767. One of their children was: Abraham Gale, b. Nov. 28, 1700; d. Sept. 30, 1779. He was a blacksmith, Weston, Mass.; m. Esther, dau. of John Cunningham; she d. July 16, 1782. One of their children was: Daniel Gale, b. June 17, 1721. His final residence was in Warwick, Mass; m. Sept. 8, 1743, Sarah, dau. of John and Abigail Lamson, b. Nov. 29, 1721. One of their children was: Daniel Gale, b. Nov. 18, 1753; lived in Petersham, was a soldier in the Revolution; m. Esther, dau. of Comfort and Martha (Norris) Rice, b. Dec. 29, 1755; d. ——, 1858. Four of their children were: Martha Gale, b. Mar. 31, 1779; d. ——. She m. Philip Spooner. Luther Gale, b. Mar. 31, 1779; d. Mar. 18, 1864; m. Sarah Spooner. He m. 2d, Nancy Spooner. Daniel Gale, b. Mar. 27, 1783; d. Feb. 14, 1867; m. Betsey Holland. Nahum Gale, b. Mar. 17, 1789; d. June 16, 1854; m. Emily Holland. Sarah, b. Feb. 15, 1675; d. young. Richard, b. Sept. 25, 1677. Hopestill, b. and d. Dec, 1678. Mary, b. Mar. 27, 1680; d. young. Abigail, b. Mar. 12, 1681; d. Nov. 21, 1696. Mary, b. Sept. 12, 1683; m. Samuel Sanderson. Ebenezer, b. Apr. 30, 1686; m. Elizabeth Green. John, b. Apr. 23, 1687; m. Lydia ——. Mary, bap. Apr. 1689; m. Michael Pratt of Oxford. Sarah, b. Aug. 29, 1694. Jonas, bap. Nov. 14, 1697; d. Mar. 17, 1717. Elizabeth, b. July 9, 1699. Lydia, b. July 9, 1699. Abigail, b. ——; m. 1720, Edward Jackson, Jr., of Newton. Copy of a portion of Will of Abraham Gale of Watertown: "I give and bequeath to Sarah, my well beloved wife, all my Personal estate within doors for her comfort & support during the time she Remains my widow; and further my will is that my wife shall have a comfortable Room in my mansion house, and to be constantly Provided with sufficient fire wood laid at the door fit for fire, and also to have Ten pounds annually pd. her in corn & meat & other Provisions by my two youngest sons, namely John & Joshua Gael. But in case my wife shall see cause to marry againe, my will is she shall be pd. the sum of Twenty pounds by my two above sons out of my Personal estate and no more, and the annual Rent to sese.".

   199. DAVID FISKE (David, David, Jeffrey, Robert, Simon, Simon, William, Symond), b. Watertown April 15, 1650; m. at Ipswich June 17, 1674, Sarah Day, of that town; b. ——, 1654; d. April 22, 1729. Her father was a bricklayer in Ipswich, "being aged" made his will Aug. 11, 1683 which was proved Sept. 25 1683 in which he mentions sons John—son Thomas—son James Daughter Hannah Lord & daughter Sarah Fiske. v. 4 p. 31. Day James made his will Mar. 16 1690-1 which was proved Mar 31 1691 son Robert to be brought up by the testator's brother Robert Lord, Marshall & Tho Day but if Robert the child shou decease before coming to the age of 21 the estate was to be equally divided between bro.

Tho Day & two sisters Rob Lord senr wife & ye wife of David Fisk." V. 4 p. 276.

David, like his father, was a subscriber to the first meetinghouse in 1692 and, like his father, was ready to sustain the institution of religion, and was elected to the dignified office of tythingman.

Middlesex Probate Records, Vol. 23, page 173. Mch. 18, 1712. David Fisk of Cambridge Husbandman with Sarah "my now married wife, sell to John Munroe. Swamp land in Cambridge towards Concord.

Presence of Jonathan Fisk, David Russell & Thos Merriam.

He d. Oct. 23, 1729; res. Lexington, Mass.

291. i.   DAVID, b. Jan. 5, 1676; m. Elizabeth ———; where did they go?
292. ii.   JONATHAN, b. May 19, 1679; m. Abigail Reed.
293. iii. ANNA, b. April 2, 1683.
294. iv.   ROBERT, b. May 8, 1681; m. Mary Stimpson.
295. viii. EBENEZER, b. Sept. 16, 1692; m. Grace Harrington and Bethia Muzzy.
296. v.   LYDIA, b. May 14, 1685; m. Dea. Joseph Loring, Jr., b. Sept. 26, 1684; d. July 4, 1746. She d. Oct. 4, 1758. He went from Hingham to Lex. abt. 1706. He purchased 90 acres of land in Camb. Farms (Lex.) in 1706 of John Poulter. The deed designates him of Hingham. In 1711 he was one of the subscribers for the purchase of the common. He and his wife Lydia were ad. to the church July 4, 1708, and of course they were m. bef. that time. He was chosen one of the Deacons in 1743. He was a valuable citizen; was constable in 1714 and town treasurer in 1725 and 6. Res. Lex. Ch.: Lydia, bap. June 21, 1711, m. 1731, John Mason; Joseph, bap. Aug. 21, 1713, m. Kezia Gove; was Dea. in 1756. His house was pillaged and destroyed by the British April 19, 1775; res. Lex. Sarah, bap. July 13, 1715, m. Capt. Thaddeus Bowman, res. Lex.; John, bap. Aug. 11, 1717, d. Dec. 13, 1717; Hannah, bap. Sept. 20, 1719, m. Samuel Winship, res. Lex.; Abigail, bap. Jan. 7, 1722; Mary, bap. Jan. 7, 1722, m. Samuel Allen.
297. vi.   SARAH, b. June 16, 1687.
298. vii. ABIGAIL, b. May 20, 1689; d. Aug. 13, 1691.

205. JAMES FISKE (James, Phinehas, Thomas, Robert, Simon, Simon, William, Symond), b. Haverhill, Mass., Aug. 8, 1649; m. per Middlesex Co. Records, Feb. 2, 1686, Tabitha Butterick. He was not mentioned in his father's will. James Fiske and Samuel Fiske were among the early settlers of Groton, Mass., and are supposed to have been brothers. But little is known of their history. It is not definitely known where they originated, nor what became of them. No record or monument of their deaths or emigration has been found. The same is true of their immediate descendants, with one, or at most, two, exceptions. It is believed, however, that James and Samuel Fiske were sons of James Fiske, of Haverhill, Mass., who was the grandson of Thomas, the third son of Robert and Sibyl (Gould) Fiske, of England. Some of the considerations that have lead to this belief are as follows: It has been ascertained that James, of Haverhill, had two sons named James and Samuel; that James was born in 1649 and Samuel in 1658, but all trace of them appears to have been lost, unless James and Samuel of Groton are the same, and if the same, James would have been 41 years old when his first child was born in Groton and 56 when his last. Samuel would have been 46 when his eldest, and 62 when his youngest child was born. This is not improbable. They may have married late in life, or may have had children before coming to Groton. The circumstance that two persons should disappear from one section of the country, and that two about the same time should appear in another section not very remote, bearing the same names and of similar ages, is pretty strong evidence that they are identical, and further the name Samuel seems not to have been very common in the early history of the Fiskes in this country, and if the two above mentioned are identical, the lineage of all, or nearly all, bearing that name can be traced. There were subsequently other families of Fiskes in Groton, but with a single exception it is not known that they were connected with those of James and Samuel. In the history of Groton, the name Fiske is uniformly

spelt with an e, while in the history of Pepperell, by the same author, the name is as uniformly spelt without an e, though the latter were descendants of the former. Res. Groton, Mass.

299. i. MARY, b. Sept. 11, 1690; m. March 2, 1708, Abraham Byam, of Chelmsford.
300. ii. JAMES, b. Feb. 11, 1694; m. Lydia Bennett
301. iii. SAMUEL, b. July 10, 1696; m. ——— ———.
302. iv. JOHN, b. Dec. 10, 1699.
303. v. ANN, b. April 16, 1702.
304. vi. JONATHAN, b. Sept. 10, 1705; m. Mary ———, Sarah Wheeler and Dorcas Fletcher.

210. SAMUEL FISKE (James, Phinehas, Thomas, Robert, Simon, Simon, William, Symond), b. Nov. 1, 1658; m. Susanna ———; d. in 1759. He died in 1728 and his real estate settlement occurred Jan. 29, 1728. One-third was given to the widow Susanna and the remainder to his sons Samuel and Thomas. June 9, 1729, Susanna was appointed guardian to Thomas, in his 17th year. Middlesex Records, Vol. 17, P. 294, June 24, 1725. Samuel Fiske of Groton decas (about 2 y. since) Adm gr to his wid Susanna. After his death the widow moved to Pepperill, where she died in 1759. Her will is dated Sept. 7, 1759, and proved Feb. 11, 1760. "Being indisposed in body, but" To my beloved son Samuel, daughter Susanna Brigham, daughter Experience Fisk, gr. dau. Susanna, gr. dau. Mary Elliot, gr. dau. Sarah Fiske, dau. of my Son Samuel, to gr. children heirs of my son Thomas deceased, viz Thomas, Mary, John, Sarah and Wainwright Fisk, Remainder to be equally divided between my said Samuel and two daughters, provided Experience shall live to receive it, but if not to be equally divided between my said son Samuel and daughter Susanna excepting to my son Samuel four shillings.

Samuel Fisk of Groton admn granted to his widow Susannah June 24 1725 which was about two years after his decease at which time the Inv was exhibited to the Court Item Homestead land at Badcock Pond—at Old Mill—Cow Pond Meadow and in the west side of Burnt Meadow. Division of the estate among the heirs Jan. 29 1728-9 some of the land being (as described then) at Browne Loaf Plaine and some on the west side of Nashua river had been bought of the original owner viz a serjt James Fisk. Children when the division was made were Samuel the eldest son Thomas the other son & was in his 17th year when Susannah his mother was appointed his guardian June 9 1729. Susannah a daughter who then (1728) was about 23 years old, Experience then about 21 years of age and Miriam then about 9 years old—Acct of the admx was presented to court June 24, 1725, when she charges for paying out money to a John Fiske and for her "subsisting the deceased's young children to this day.

He d. in 1728; res. Groton, Mass.

305. i. SAMUEL, b. Mar. 5, 1704; m. Elizabeth Parker.
306. ii. SUSANNA, b. Feb. 8, 1706; m. ——— Brigham. She d. abt. 1760, leaving heirs.
307. iii. EXPERIENCE, b. April 29, 1708; living and unm. in 1761.
308. iv. THOMAS, b. Feb 21, 1712; m. Mary Parker.
309. v. MERIAM, b. April 18, 1716; d. March 26, 1718.
310. vi. MERIAM, b. July 3, 1720; d. young.

212. DR. JOHN FISKE (John, Phinehas, Thomas, Robert, Simon, Simon, William, Symond), b. in Wenham, Mass., Dec. 12, 1654; m. Jan. 17, 1682, Hannah Baldwin, dau. of John of Milford, Conn., and wife Mary Bowen, b. Nov. 20, 1663. John Fiske was made freeman in 1685; he practiced physic and surgery in Wenham, and also in Milford, Conn., to which place he removed with his family in 1694, when he was admitted to the church. Sons born in Wenham were Phineas, Ebenezer, John and Benjamin—all born in Wenham. Dr. John Fiske was a physician of some prominence in his day, and his children inherited from him or acquired large landed property. He disposed of his estate in Wenham Nov. 15, 1693. In proof of his identity Remember Goodhue, formerly Remember Fiske, certifies that she was the natural mother of the said John, that the property belonged to him, the same being inherited. [Essex Co. Reg. Deeds.]

"John Fisk, of Wenham, Physician" sold to Tobias Trow about 18 ac.

"bounded &c &c" signed Nov. 15, 1693. Same day acknowledged before Thos Wade J. P. by him & wife Hannah.

"Remember Goodhue" widow of "Ensign John Fisk" decd of Wenham, being adminx of est. of said Jno F. deed, by virtue of settlement of Salem Court upon said estate, I did set over &c, unto my son John F. all part of said estate as mentioned in above des. premises &c" Various other deeds on record in substance as above, confirm relationship Ensign Jno & Dr Jno. Various sales made 1686 to 1691 on record by Dr John. Probably sale in 1693 was the last, & establishes date his removal to Milford in 1694, for in 1695 a letter of recommendation was sent him by Rev. Jos Gerrish & others.

John Fiske of Wenham "Phisitian doe with the consent and aprobation of my wife Hannah" sold to Tobias Trow of Beverly cordwainer 10 acrs land & a dwelling house &c in Wenham bounded easterly by ye highway: Southward & Northward by the lands of John Porter & westerly by the land of Ens. John Batchiller signed sealed Nov. 15 1693 and one of the witnesses was a Tho Fisk Jr.

Doctor John Fisk appeared & owned the above written instrument to be his act and deed Nov. 20 1693 before Tho Wade Just peace.

I Remember Goodhue some time wid & Relict of Ensigne John Fisk of Wenham deceased being admx of the estate of the said deceased by vertue of the settlement of Salem Court upon said estate I did in the year one thousand six hundred eighty and four set over Deliver and conferme unto my SON John Fisk all the every part of what house and land is mentioned in the above premises as his part Portion" &c I Thomas Fisk senr of Wenham having formerly been owner of some part of the above said land did about thirty years since sell it to my brother John Fisk of Wenham deceased & father of John Fisk the subscriber to ye above premises Nov 20 1693.

Doctor Fiske was a physician of respectability and was accounted skillful in the arts of physick and chirurgery while in Wenham, as appears from the subjoined certificates of commendation copied from the original papers preserved among the state papers of Connecticut at Hartford. We also have his own petition to the General Court for a license, which was granted after his removal to Milford. His professional reputation gave him an elevated position among his medical brethren in his new field of labor. His widow Hannah and second son Ebenezer administered on his estate.

To Mr. John Fiske Doctor; in Milford.

Yours I received bearing date Jan. 29th, 1695. Glad to hear of your welfare and have according to your desire obtained as in the enclosed the hands of as many as may be needful for the end designed, hope it will come to your hands & serve you. The subscribers of Ipswich are Collonell Appleton, the 2 ministers, Major Eps, Deacon Goodhue & Mr. Everson minister att Gloster. And of Wenham myself the deacon, and the selectman, I suppose I might have obtained as many as I would have asked, none refusing who were desired, we wish you all prosperity in temporals & spirituals, a blessing on your family and on your calling, etc. Your good mother hath been sick & weeke most part of this winter desires to hear from you, as doth the deacon, etc. We have nothing new. Indians have not appeared this winter; we are expecting we shal hear of them ere long. You have heard of the killing of 4 & our taking 3 principal leaders of ym the Lord prepare us for trouble, the fruits of our evil ways.

So not to trouble you more at present, but rest your friend to serve you. Mar. 12, 1695, Joseph Gerrish.

These may certify all whom it may concern, that Mr. John Fiske, late of Wenham, in the County of Essex in N. E.; hath for many years with good success, practiced in the arts of physick and chirurgery & hath made many notable cures among us & hath generally been accounted one of good skill & understanding in many maladies & their remedies of which some of us have had experience (& others) credible information & doe therefore hereunto subscribe our names this 21st of Feb., 1695. William Fiske, Samuel Appleton and ten others.

My opinion is of small weight, but being desired I can say that I have so much acquaintance with Mr. Fiske that makes me desire that he may have a license to practice in physic & chirurgic, in the Colony, which I hope may be for the good of many. Apr. 4, 1695, I also am of the same mind, Samuel Mather and two others.

According to the Connecticut Colonial records of May, 1695, John Fisk was granted liberty to practice phissick and chirurgery. A note states Mr. John Fisk had practiced medicine several years in Wenham, Mass., but has now settled in Milford.

At the general assembly session of Oct., 1702, "Mr. John Fisk informs this court that he had received a considerable wound in the former Indian wares, therefore requested this court release him from the payment of the country rates for the future, it is therefore ordered that said John Fisk be freed from paying Countrey rates for the future, viz., during his natural life."

He d. about 1715-18; res. Milford, Conn.

<ul>
<li>311. i. BENJAMIN, b. 1683; bap. Mar. 29, 1696; m. Abigail Bowen.</li>
<li>312. ii. EBENEZER, b. in 1689; m. Mehitable ——— and Rebecca Trowbridge.</li>
<li>313. iii. JOHN, b. in 1693; m. Hannah ——— and Sarah ———.</li>
<li>314. iv. PHINEHAS, b. Dec. 4, 1682; m. Lydia Pratt.</li>
<li>315. v. HANNAH, b. ———; m. Aug. 20, 1713, Jeremiah Peck, son of Joseph, b. 1687. Ch.: Hannah, b. May 6, 1716; m. David Clark. John (4), b. Dec. 9, 1718; m. Sarah Platt, Feb. 15, 1750-51. Jeremiah (4), Jr., b. Jan. 12, 1720-21; m. Frances Platt, Oct. 26, 1743. Phineas (4), b. Apr. 10, 1723; m. Deborah Clark, Feb. 18, 1745-46. Sarah, b. May 25, 1726. Sibella, b. June 24, 1728; m. Jirah Bull. Lucy, b. Oct. 23, 1730. Comfort and Content, twins, b. Apr. 1, 1734. Jeremah's will is on record at New Haven, B. 10, p. 491, dated Oct. 5, 1765. Jeremiah (4) settled first at Milford, Conn., but from there removed to Watertown, Conn., about 1752. He m. Frances Platt, dau. of Josiah Platt. Isaac (5) Peck, b. Feb. 9, 1748-49, son of Jeremah (4), enlisted in the army of the Revolution and was drowned while in the service. Benjamin (5), b. in 1750, son of Jeremah (4), also entered the army and died of the camp distemper. Phineas (4) Peck, son of Jeremiah (3), settled in Amity, now Woodbridge, Conn. He left Milford about 1776. He was deacon of the first church of Woodbridge. Phineas (5) Peck, son of Phineas (4), settled in Woodbridge, Conn. He entered the service in the war of the Revolution; was taken prisoner and confined in the Old Sugar House in New York, where so many perished through the inhumanity of the British. He was reduced to a mere skeleton, but finally released, and brought home by men upon a hand litter from New York. He died soon after. I think he was lieutenant. John (4) resided in Milford, where he died. His son John enlisted in the army in the Revolutionary War and served through that struggle for independence. He m. Mary Camp, and res. in Litchfield, Conn., where he d. Dec., 1831.</li>
</ul>

213. SAMUEL FISKE (John, Phinehas, Thomas, Robert, Simon, Simon, William, Symond), b. Wenham, Mass., (by court records) 1660; m. Elizabeth Whipple, dau. of Lieut. Whipple, of Ipswich. He was made freeman in 1680 and in March, 1694, res. elsewhere. Mr. Samuel Fiske dismissed from church at Wenham and accepted at Milford, Feb. 6, 1703. His father, Ensign John, left no will, but in the papers left at his death in 1683, son Samuel, who was aged about 24 years, had about 20 acres of land promised to him where his house stood; at the time he promised to marry his wife; who was Elizh., daughter of Lt. Whipple. He d. about 1699; res. Wenham and Ipswich, Mass.

<ul>
<li>316. i. INCREASE, b. Jan. 18, 1700 (posthumous).</li>
</ul>

219. CAPT. THOMAS FISKE (Thomas, Phinehas, Thomas, Robert, Simon, Simon, William, Symond), b. Wenham, Mass., 1656; m. Nov. 3, 1678, Rebecca Perkins, youngest child of Rev. Wm. Perkins, of Roxbury. She was b. May 4, 1662, in Topsfield. He was made freeman in 1690. His wife, Rebecca, was the daughter of Rev. William Perkins, "one of the most accomplished divines of his day." Both Capt. Thomas, Sr., and Jr., were wealthy proprietors in Wenham, were liberal patrons of Harvard College and the Christian Church, and bore the rank of "gentlemen" and title of "captain"—terms indicating, in those days, the highest social position; and probably no other family were more prominently identified with the early history of the town than they. Capt. Thomas Fiske, Jr., was frequently in town office, was moderator of the town meetings 1710-11-20; was town clerk, 1702-3-5 and 8, and in 1715 elected Representative to General Court. He died in 1723, mentioning in his will several married daughters and grandchildren, but no sons.

Thomas Fiske, of Wenham, bought of Rev. Joseph Gervith, of Wanham, & Ann his wife a house & about 5 acres of land in Wenham near the meeting house bounded on the east by the farm called Smiths farm Southerly by the lands of Alexander Maxey & John Fiske Westerly by ye common road Northerly by ye common—witness by Tho Fiske sen & Wm Fiske May 26 1693.

Thomas Fiske of Wenham yeoman bought of Saml Gott of Beverly & wife Margaret 7 acres in the field in Wenham called the plains bounded Southwardly by the county road leading to Ipswich, Westwardly partly by ye land of Charles Gott Jr. & partly by land of John Newman   Northwardly by the land of Capt Thomas Fiske   Eastwardly by the land of Wm Rogers   Witnessed by Tho Fiske John Gott & Saml Fiske July 31 1702.

Thomas Fiske of Wenham Gentleman bought of Tobias Trow of Wenham 4 acres in Wenham bounded westwardly upon the country road Northwardly by land of said Fiske Eastwardly by land of widow Maxey & partly upon land of John Edwards & Southwardly by land of sd John Edwards To Have &c Nov. 7, 1709.

Thomas Fiske of Wenham gentleman bought of Zacheus Goldsmith of Wenham husbandman for 2-8 if the div. on ye east side of the highway in the great swamp to be made over & conjoined with s'z &c & 40 shilling in money.—Seven acres of upland & swamp land in Wanham bound Southerly by land of Sam'l Kimball Westwardly by land of E Fiskes Northerly by ye country road & the training place as ye fence now standeth till it comes to Joseph Dodges corner Eastwardly by swamp land of the said Goldsmith from said Dodges corner to the said Kimball corner next to them swamp Feb 22 1709.

Thomas Fiske (Capt.) & wife Rebecca of Wenham sold to Thomas Tarbox of Wenham housewright "A certain House barn & 22 acres of land in Wenham bounded eastwardly upon land of Wm Fairfield   Southerly on land of John Gott Westwardly on land of above named Tho Fiske running from John Gotts Norwest corner of land at a stake & heep of stones formerly Wm Fiske bound so running Northwesterly about one hundred poles to a black Ooak marked and so straight to the meadow northerly bounding upon the Meadow till it cometh to Sam'l Fiskes land so taking said Sam'l Fiske's line to ye said Wm Fairfield's land To Hold" &c reserving a right to pass over the land &c   Feb 11 1711-12.

Thomas Fiske & Wm Rogers of Wenham exchange 108 poles of land in Wenham May 25 1722.

Thomas Fiske, of Wenham, made his will Sept. 27, 1720, which was proved March 4, 1723, by Nathaniel Sparhawk and Nathaniel Knowlton (the other witness being Elizabeth Sparhawk). Legatees, Church of Christ in Wenham, which had £10. Wife Rebecca Fiske, executrix. Eliza Studley, of Ipswich, to have money. Mary ye daughter of Thomas Baker late of Ipswich deceased under 21 years and unmarried. Fineas Dodge of Wenham and Andrew Dodge of Beverly each to have £5. Rebecca Howe of Marlboro wife of Thomas Howe Jr. all his real estate after the decease of his wife, who was to have the use of all as long as she lived. Thomas, son of Thomas and Rebecca, to have testator's gun. Receipts received by Rebecca the admr. in Jan. 1724 she and her husband were called uncle by Benjamin & Elizabeth Studley, Andrew Dodge and Phinehas Dodge.

His gravestone reads as follows: Capt. Thomas Fiske, died Feb. 5, 1723, in the 70th year of his age. The Rightcous shall be had in everlasting Remembrance.

Rebecca Fiske of Wenham wid & ex'x of the will of Capt Tho Fiske of Wenham decd sold to Tho How Jr of Marlborough Middlesex Co a farm in Wenham that Capt Fiske purchased of Mr John Newman bounded on the great meadow Northerly * * * * The one third part of which said Farm belongs unto the said How by a Deed of Gift from said Capt Thomas Fiske & is in common with the other 2-3 undivided to him the sd Tho How" * * * which 4 acres above said shall be added to & laid out with his third part &c Dec 16 1724.

He d. Feb. 5, 1723: res. Wenham, Mass.

    316½. i. REBECCA, b. ———; m. Thomas Howe, Jr., of Marlboro.

236. REV. JOHN FISKE (Moses, John, John, William, Robert, Simon, Simon, William, Symond), b. Braintree, Mass., Nov. 26, 1684; m. Nov. 26, 1717, Abigail Hobart, dau. of Rev. Nehemiah Hobart, of Newton, Mass. He was born in that part of Quincy subsequently incorporated as Braintree, educated at the public schools and by his father and graduated at Harvard in 1702. After his father's death he preached in the Braintree church and was ordained pastor of the church in Killingly, Conn., Oct. 19, 1715, his brother-in-law, Rev. Joseph Baxter, of Medfield, preaching the sermon. There remained until 1741, when disaffection arose in the church. He was dismissed by council and subsequently retired upon his large landed estate in Killingly, where he died.

July 16, 1711, the town of Killingly agreed to give Mr. Fiske three hundred and fifty acres of land for his encouragement to settle in the work of the ministry. James Leavens and Sampson Howe were appointed a committee to lay out the land; Eleazer Bateman and Ephraim Warren to survey it. Two hundred acres were laid out to him on French River, beyond the bounds of Killingly as it afterwards proved. Seventy-five acres for the homestead were selected on the eastern slope of Killingly Hill, and seventy-five on Assawaga or Five-Mile River. Stated religious services were probably held after this date by Mr. Fiske, though some years passed before his settlement.

In the summer of 1714 the meeting-house was raised and covered. Its site was east of the Plainfield road, about one-fourth of a mile south of the present East Putnam meeting-house. Nothing is known of its size and appearance, or of the circumstances of its building. In the ensuing summer it was made ready for occupation and preparations made for church organization. Sept. 15, 1715, was observed in Killingly as a day of solemn fasting and prayer, preparatory to the gathering of a church and the ordination of a pastor.

"October 19, 1715, a church was publicly gathered in Killingly and John Fiske ordained the pastor of it." Mr. Dwight, of Woodstock, opened the service with prayer. Reverend Mr. Baxter, of Medfield, preached from Romans i: 16. Rev. Mr. Thatcher, of Milton, gave the charge to the minister and made the preceding and subsequent prayers. The first marriage recorded by the young minister was that of William Larned to Hannah, the first of the seven notable daughters of Simon Bryant. Mr. Fiske was himself married to Abigail, daughter of Rev. Nehemiah Hobart, of Newton, Mass., and sister of Mr. Samuel Estabrook, of Canterbury. The only incident of his domestic life that has come down to us, is the burning of his house and all its contents one Sabbath, when the family were attending public worship. The ministry of Mr. Fiske was acceptable and prosperous, and large numbers were added to the church. His pastoral charge comprehended also the inhabitants north of Killingly, who were allowed to pay church rates, if not other town charges. Mr. Fiske was remarkably minute and methodical in the registry of church records, keeping separate lists of those uniting with the church by profession and by letter and of those owning the covenant. Very full lists of marriages and baptisms were preserved by him, which acquired additional value from the total lack of town records during the greater part of his ministry. Of the salary and settlement allowed to him nothing further is known, save that the hundred acres of land given by Capt. Chandler to the first settled minister of Killingly, "which land by the ordering of Divine Providence appertains to John Fiske"—were laid out to him in 1721, west of Five-Mile River, a half mile east of the meeting-house.

Killingly's persistent attempts to secure possession of this land occasioned much trouble and confusion. Two hundred acres promised by the town to the Rev. Mr. Fiske, were laid out in Thompson's land, and Hascall and Spalding were encouraged in their unlawful appropriations of Cotton's and Collin's grants. In 1721 the selectmen of Killingly without permission from Government proceeded to lay out this colony land and apportion it among her own inhabitants and its consenting residents. The Mass. Government wrote to Conn. in behalf of Cotton and Collins and received assurance that their claims should be made up to them in the ungranted land near Woodstock. In 1726 Paul and William Dudley, Josiah Wolcott and Samuel Morris represented to the General Court, "that Killingly, by what right they knew not, had laid out large quantities of land north of her prescribed bound, which was unjust and destructive of their rights," and begged relief. Joseph Leavens and Joseph Cady were summoned to answer in behalf of Killingly proprietors, and insisted that the land thus laid out was included within their patent. The court pronounced their plea sufficient, but ordered patents to be granted and executed to such grantees "as shall show grants and surveys made by Mass." Though this decision admitted Killingly's claim to Connecticut's share of this colony land, she was still dissatisfied, and persisted in her efforts to recover the tracts to Massachusetts' grantees.

The various public enterprises in which Killingly engaged, and her expensive controversy with Thompson and Massachusetts proprietors, absorbed much of her income, and she often found it difficult to meet her ordinary expenses. In 1734 the town voted "If any person or persons shall have money sufficient to pro-cure a book for ye record of deeds of the town, they shall have ye same refunded, and repaid them again." Shepherd Fisk and Jacob Dresser were able to advance the requisite sum, which was repaid them after a long interval. Simon Bryant, chosen in 1731 "to wait on the Rev. John Fiske in case he goes to Hartford, and to assist him and to represent him in his absence in case the said Mr. Fiske cannot go." after ten years' delay was reimbursed the four pounds expended in that service.

The ministry to Mr. Fiske was acceptable and profitable to his people until a rupture occurred, from some cause not now manifest. "At a regular meeting of the first church of Killingly, July 8, 1741, after the meeting was opened by prayer, Mr. Fiske upon the advice of neighboring ministers, moved to the church to dismiss him from his pastoral relations." His request was granted by a clear majority. The Windham County association was called, "To consider and deter-mine the differences and difficulties between Rev. Fisk and the church, arising from several scandalous reports spread abroad concerning Mr. Fiske." Deacon Bateman, Justice Leavens, Samuel Danielson, Ebenezer Knight and Gideon Draper were appointed a committee to represent the church and provide for the council. No record of the result is given, but it probably confirmed the dis-missal of Mr. Fiske. The nature of the charges against him is not declared, but a succeeding pastor, with opportunity of judgment, was of opinion that they were not of any immorality. The church, at this date, numbered over four hundred members. Mr. Fiske, during his ministry, performed 763 baptisms, admitted 254 into full communion, and 148 to the half-way covenant. Aug., 1741, the com-mittee of the church applied to the Association for a minister, and were rec-ommended to several candidates, but did not succeed in securing one.

The loss of the minister was soon followed by a protracted and violent con-troversy respecting a meeting-house. The rude church edifice of 1715 was quite inadequate for the populous and thriving township of 1741, and the inhabitants of the south society were called together, Sept. 13, to see if they would vote to build a new meeting-house.

Mr. Fiske, the former pastor, was one of the new pastor's constant hearers, having built himself a pew in the new meeting-house and bearing his part in all society charges.

He d. May 18, 1773; res. Killingly, Conn.

  317. i. JOHN, b. ———; d. infancy.
  318. ii. FOUR DAUGHTERS, 2 m. clergymen.

  238. REV. SAMUEL FISKE (Moses, John, John, William, Robert, Si-mon, Simon, William, Symond), b. Braintree, April 6, 1689; m. Anna Gerrish. He was the youngest son of Rev. Moses Fiske, of Braintree, educated at the public schools and was graduated at Harvard College in 1708, where his name ap-pears on the roll without the e. He was ordained minister of the first church in Salem in Oct., 1718. Says Bentley, in his Memorial Sermon: Rev. Samuel Fiske was a man of eminent talents in the pulpit, of a firm and persevering mind, and held in high esteem till dissensions sprang up in the society from the ill-defined discipline then existing in our churches. He was a preacher of real abilities, but his high notions of church authority were repugnant to many persons and pre-vented his usefulness. He was dismissed from the First Church in 1735 and ac-cepted the charge of a new society established by his friends. He preached the first centenary lecture of the First Church Aug. 6, 1729. The election sermon delivered by him before the Governor and Legislature in 1731 may be ranked among the best. It was published and a copy of it is preserved among the State archives. Rev. Mr. Fiske was dismissed from the Third Church in 1745, when he retired from the public ministry. He was connected by marriage with one of the most flourishing families in Salem.

Rev. Samuel Fiske of Salem clerk bought of Rev John Emerson & wife Mary of Portsmouth N. H. for 250 pounds current money of New England "our messuage & tenement which I bought of Majr Stephen Sewall situate lying and being in Salem * * * containing a dwellinghouse & about twenty six rods or pole of land being same more or less bounded southerly with ye street easterly with land of Capt Benj Pickman late of Salem aforesaid deceased westerly with ye land of Timothy Orne & northerly with land lately belonged to ye Rev. Nicholas Noyes deceased now in ye possession of Mr Sam'l Fiske or however ye same is bounded * * * with ye commonages" &c Sept. 21 1719. V. 36, p. 165.

Rev. Samuel Fiske of Salem clerk bought of Sam'l Phillips of Salem goldsmith & wife Mrs Sarah Phillips a common right in Salem for the garden behind the meetinghouse of 1st parish of Salem bought of Maj Walter Price where was a dwelling house &c. Dated May 18, 1722.

Rev. Sam'l Fiske of Salem Clerk bought of John Slapp of Salem Clothier for £2 10s the common right in Salem June 24 1721 Capt Thomas Fiske of Wenham in Essex co the agreement made Mar 23, 1715 Capt Thomas How of Marlborough heirs in Middlesex co.

Witnesseth "that whereas there is an intended marriage betwixt Thos How son of sd Thos mentioned and Rebeca Parkins a relative of 3d Capt Fiske & brought up by him that if it shall so please god that they Intermarry upon their marriage the said Capt How Covenanteth & promiss to settle so much Real Estate upon his said son as shall Equallize anny of my Oll sons for Quantity and Quality and so Capt. Fiske Covenanth & promiseth to & with the s'd Capt. How that he will give & endow the said Rebeca Perkins & her beloved when said marriage is compleated one third part of all his real estate that he is now possessed of." * * if s'd Tho die before Rebecca she shall have the mpovement during her life & if they have children they to have it forever &c. who died previous to Jan. 18, 1720-1, according to the evidence of John Fiske one of the witnesses.

Rev. Sam'l Fiske of Salem bought of Deacon John Marston & wife Mary of Salem Carpenter one acre in south field Salem by the mill pond Northwesterly and by land of Jona. Archer Henry West Capt Wm Bowditch June 25 1722 V 43 p 36. Saml Fiske clerk also bought of Wm Porter & wife Edith of Salem a common right given to P by his father—Dated June 22 1722.

Rev Saml Fiske of Salem bought of John Abbott of Salem shoreman a common right in the common rights of Salem in the great pasture they belong to the houses where dm it & his son Robert Abbott then lived May 11, 1728. V 46-2201. Rev Saml Fiske of Salem sold to Saml Field of Salem shipwright a house lot of 36 poles in Salem bound by Toun house st Oct 15 1728 Acknowlege Feb. 10 1728-9.

Rev Samuel Fiske of Salem bought of wid Elizth Lowther Benj Allen joiner Abigail Allen alias Dicta, Abigail Lowther daughter of sd. Elizh Lowther & Paul Kimball carrier and Martha Kimball alias Marther Lowther dau of sd E. L. all of Salem, One Common Right in Salem &c July 28 1726. Rev. S. Fiske receives a quit claim from James Ross of Salem wife Martha cordwainer of the common Right he sold to John Slap of Salem, Clothier, about the year 1719 or 20 which was lost.

Rev. Samuel Fisk, of Salem, admn. was granted to his son John Fisk May 11 1770. Inv. of the Est. May 26, 1770. Homestead of house & 20 poles of land & about 4 acres in the South Fields —Books.

a complete sett of Henry's annotations on the Bible, 6 vols	£3-00-00
Pool's Synopsis, 5 vols	0- 6-00
Willard's Body of Divinity	0- 8-00
Collection of Voyages & Travels, 2 vols	0- 6-00
An Exposition on the Epistle of Hebrews, 2 vols	0- 8-00
Ditto on John, 1 vol	0- 3-00
Bishop Hopkins's Works	0- 4-00
A large collection of very old books & Pamphlets &c	3- 6-08
One Small Bible with Silver Clasps	0- 6-00

Whole amt. of Inventory was..........................£126-14-04

The Estate rendered Insolvent Nov. 5, 1770. Acct. of admn. rendered Oct. 21, 1771.

He d. April 7, 1770; res. Salem, Mass.

319. i.   SAMUEL, bap. Oct. 5, 1740; d. young.
320. ii.   SARAH, bap. Oct. 24, 1742.
321. iii. JOHN, b. May 6, 1744; m. Lydia Phippen, Mrs. Martha Hibbert and Mrs. Sarah Gerry.
322. iv.   JOSEPH, bap. July 17, 1748; d. young.
323. v.   ELIZABETH, bap. July 17, 1748; d. young.

239. DR. SHEPERD FISKE (Moses, John, John, William, Robert, Simon, Simon, William, Symond), b. Braintree, Mass., Apr. 19, 1704; m. in Bridgewater in 1732, Alice Alger, dau. of Israel J., and Alice (Hayward) Alger. He was born in Braintree, educated at the public schools, fitted for college and was graduated at Harvard in the class of 1721. He studied medicine afterwards, practiced in Bridgewater, Mass., and died there. But very little was known of him, for in 1803 Mr. William Winthrop, of Cambridge, who, for some time past, had been engaged in a pursuit rather extraordinary, knew nothing of him. Winthrop investigated the following particulars of every one who has received a degree at Harvard College, from the first foundation of that University in 1648 to the present time; viz., the origination or where born, his professional business or employment, his place of residence, time of his death and age; also anything remarkable in their lives and characters; where such matters can be ascertained. At this time, also, Winthrop did not know anything of Dr. Fiske.

He d. June 14, 1779; res. Killingly, Conn., Bridgewater, Mass.

248. WILLIAM FISKE (William, William, John, William, Robert, Simon, Simon, William, Symond), b. Wenham, Mass., Jan. 31, 1663; m. Marah or Mary ———. He was the eldest son of Dea. William, was born in Wenham and resided there until 1710, when he moved to Andover, Mass., where he died in 1745.

William Fiske of Andover husbandman gives to his son Ebenr Fiske "All my housing & lands & meadow lying being in the Township of Andover aforesaid excepting of that such I have given my son Wm Fiske a deed on before the one half of all my housing & land now & meadow in fea and the other half at my decease on condition" first that my son Eben Fiske doe fourthwith pay to my son Joseph Fiske * * * secondly that he pay to Hon'd Father Wm Fiske of Wenham Thirdly that he pay to my son Jonathan Fisk when his time comes out or his prentisship shall come out in possable money * * * Fourthly that he pay to my daughter Sarah ten pounds when she is married or when she cometh of age * * * Fifthly pay my daughter Ruth * * when she is married or comes of age Sixthly pay my daughter Lydia * * when she is married or cometh of age * * * Seventhly that he shall let Mary my wife &c. May 13, 1726. "before I sighn this I doo oblige my said son to pay to my daughter Mary Johnson twenty shillings which is in full of her portion" &c Ack May 16 1726.

Wm. Fiske of Andover husbandman to his eldest son Wm. Fisk of Andover gave land & meadow containing by estimation twenty three acres or be the same more or less Lying & being in the township of Andover aforesaid the twenty acres of land lying on the west end of my farm where my sd sons Dwelling house stands on part of it. Bounded or however Reputed to be bounded viz: on the Northwest corner on a walnut tree stump which is Moses Tiler's bounds then running South Westerly joyning sd Tyler's land & to Thos. Johnson's land; and Ephraim Farnoms ten acre meadow to a red Oak marked on an island, the easterly joyning to Francis Ingalls's land to a stake & stones. Then Northwardly across my farm to a stake & stones then westerly joyning to my said son's meadow which he bought of Mr. Martyn to the first bounds mentioned * * * and the three acres of meadow lieth joyning to the Northwesterly end of my long Meadow * * * lieth Cedar swamp &c Apr 7, 1726 Ack 27 same month

Wm Fisk & wife Mary of Andover husbandman sold to his son Ebenr Fisk of it husbandman ½ of his house barn and land adjoining containing in the whole 60 acres situated in Andover bounded Easterly by land of Daniel Kimball Southerly by Francis Ingalls Westerly partly by Eben'r & partly by Wm Fisk Jr & northerly by some lotts of meadow &c   May 6, 1734.

He d. Dec. 10, 1745; res. Wenham and Andover. Mass.

324. i.   WILLIAM, b. Nov. 30, 1695; m. Mary Kinney and Mrs. Sarah (Buck) Fish (not Fisk).
325. ii.   JOSEPH, b. Sept. 6, 1701; res. Andover.

326. iii. EBENEZER, b. Aug. 15, 1703; m. Susanna Buck.
327. iv. JONATHAN, b. ———.
328. v. SARAH, b. June 5, 1707; d. June 14, 1707.
329. vi. RUTH, b. Feb. 15, 1697; d. April 14, 1704.
330. vii. LYDIA, b. ———.
331. viii. MARY, b. Oct. 2, 1699; d. April 14, 1704.
332. ix. RUTH, b. Oct. 18, 1709; m. May 7, 1728, Richard Easti, of
       Topsfield.

249. SAMUEL FISKE (William, William, John, William, Robert, Simon,
Simon, William, Symond), b. Wenham, Mass., Feb. 16, 1670; m. Dec. 5, 1699,
Elizabeth Browne, of Reading. He was born in Wenham, married in Reading
and in 1710 moved to Rehoboth, where he was living in 1728, as he was a legatee
in his father's will.
Samuel Fiske of Wenham House wright and Eliz'th his wife sold to John
Porter of Wenham yeoman all that his dwelling house barne & about sixteen
acres of upland & meadow * * * in Wenham bounded as followeth eastwardly by ye land of Freeborn Balch Southwardly by ye Brooke that runneth
out of ye Pond called Wenham Pond westwardly and northwardly partly by ye
countrey road & partly by ye land of Isaac Hall sen'r John Edwards Jr. & Joseph
Fowler. Witnessed by Tho Fiske & Wm. Fiske.
Res. Wenham, Reading and Rehoboth, Mass.
333. i. ELIZABETH, b. Dec. 8, 1700.
334. ii. JOSIAH, b. July 7, 1702; m. Sarah Bishop.
335. iii. PHINEHAS, b. May 5, 1705.
336. iv. JONATHAN, b. Jan. 10, 1706.
337. v. SAMUEL, b. Sept. 22, 1708.
338. vi. LOIS, b. Oct. 1, 1710.
339. vii. ANNA, b. Oct. 1, 1710.

250. JOSEPH FISKE (William, William, John, William, Robert, Simon,
Simon, William, Symond), b. Wenham, Mass., April 14, 1672; m. Susannah or
Susan Warner, of Ipswich, d. July, 1742; m. 2d, Jan. 7, 1743, Mrs. Elizabeth Fuller.
She d. Oct. 30, 1755.
Joseph Fiske of Ipswich yeoman & wife Susannah sold to Ammi R. Wise of
Ips shopkeeper ¼ of a right in the 8th div. 5 acres in the Right Feb 1 1723-4.
Joseph & Susanah also sold to Ammi some of great meadow in the West
End of Wenham 5 acres bounded southwesterly on land of Theophilus Fiske &
Northwesterly by Ebenr Fiske Feb 1 1723-4.
Joseph Fiske & wife (no name given) of Ipswich yeoman sold to Mr.
Perley of Boxford 1½ acre upland in Rowley ¼ lot on the Range know by the
letter C bound westerly & southerly by s'd Perley's land meadow easterly &
northerly by sd Fiskes land Feb 7 1726-7.
Joseph Fisk of Ipswich, yeoman, made his will May 1, 1745, which was
proved same month in 1745 on the 13th, by Capt. Samuel Waite, Daniel Chapman
and Daniel Chapman, Jr.
Wife Elizth "all ye household goods she brought to me at marriage," &c.,
among other things the executor "shall carry her to meeting on a good horse
on Sabbath day & Lecture days when she shall desire it." Daughter Susanna
Kilborne. Daughter Ruth Easty. Grandson Mark Platts to have four pounds
old tenor "his mother having had considerable of me before." Son Mark Fisk
to be Exr & have the residue.
He d. May 2, 1745; res. Ipswich, Mass.
340. i. JOSEPH, b. Oct. 20, 1713; d. May 24, 1731.
341. ii. MARK, b. Nov. 20, 1716; m. Lydia Smith.
342. iii. SUSANNA, b. March 18, 1700; m. March 22, 1723, Jedediah Kil-
       burn.
343. iv. SARAH, b. June 19, 1702; d. Aug. 7, 1720.
344. v. ELIZABETH, b. Sept. 15, 1704; m. Dec. 10, 1724, Michael Dwi-
       nell. She d. in Topsfield Dec. 26, 1729. Ch.: Benjamin, b.
       Nov. 10, 1726; Thomas, b. Aug. 26, 1729. Dwinell had seven
       wives.
345. vi. RUTH, b. Aug. 20, 1707; m. March 6, 1731, David Kilburn, of
       Rowley; m. 2d, ——— Esty.
       Richard

346. vii. ABIGAIL, b. Aug. 8, 1711; d. June 29, 1729.
347. viii. JOHN, b. Oct. 13, 1719; d. Dec. 21, 1725.
347½.ix. JOSEPH, b. Jan. 4, 1695; d. Dec. 5, 1698.
347¾.x.   HANNAH, b. Dec. 21, 1697; m. Oct. 29, 1720, James Platts, of
          Rowley.

251. BENJAMIN FISKE (William, William, John, William, Robert, Simon, Simon, William, Symond), b. Wenham, Mass., April 6, 1674; m. March 7, 1699, Mary Quarles, of Ipswich; b. 1678, d. Jan. 11, 1744-5. He held many town offices, was a man of considerable property and a liberal patron of the Wenham church. He left a wife, Mary, but no heirs at his death.

Benj Fisk & wif Mary & Jona Moulton both of Wenham yeoman sold to Benj Cleeves of Beverly taylor 12 acres in Wenham being their "right in the sixth division of common lands at ye east end of our town" bounded east on Manchester line 11 poles & Southerly by the lott laid out to ye heirs of John Dodge decd & westerly upon highway 11 poles Nov 24 1710 and acknowledged by Benj and w Mary May 4 1728 and at court June 1728 Sam'l Herrick made oath that he saw Jona Moulton dec'd sign also Benj Fisk at same time made oath that he saw Moulton sign the deed, &c.

Mary Fisk widow spinster of Wenham sold to Sam'l Batcheller of Salem husbandman ½ of all the housing & land which I ye said Mary Fisk do now possess. That is to say, The one half of the land which may hereafter be described the which my late Husband Benj Fisk settled on me in his Last will dated Jan. the ifth one thousand seven hundred & Forty one—two estimated 17 acres consisting of several parcels of land in Wenham & Ipswich as herein is butted and bounded or described to be bounded in the several instruments wherein they were conveyed to my said husband, viz: in a Deed of gift from Wm Fisk Dated the 20th of Aug. 1703 and in a deed from Simon Epes Dated Oct 22, 1715, & in a deed from Nathl Browne dated Mar 28 1708 and in a deed from Wm Rogers Dated Mar 3 1708 and ye Remainder of ye said lands lying in Wenham great swamp stand bounded in Wenham Town Book of Records all which above" &c. Wit. by Ebenr Fisk and Benj Fairfield Apr 11, 1743.

Mary, widow of Benjamin Fisk, of Wenham, made her will when residing in Ipswich, Dec. 29, 1744, which was proved April 15, 1745, by Rev. Samuel Wigglesworth, Sam'l Dodge, Jr., & Isaac Giddings. Inv. May 13, 1745. Acct. of Exec'r Apr. 20, 1747. a Jacob Fisk was in acct. with the Estate. Samuel Marsters & Jemima Brown May 10, 1745, gave recpts to the Ex'r Nath'l Pollard Legatee's sister Jemima Brown Kinsman Nath'l Pollard who was Exr. Sam'l Marsters Kinsman N. Pollards young son Nath'l Jemima wife of Kinsman Polard and a residue was given to "my six kinsmen & kinswomen, viz., Mercy wife of John Patch, Francis Quarles, Anne wife of Jacob & Jemima Polard above.

He d. s. p. June 6, 1742; res. Wenham, Mass.

252. THEOPHILUS FISKE (William, William, John, William, Robert, Simon, William, Symond), b. Wenham, Mass., July 28, 1676; m. July 18, -- --, of Ipswich, dau. of John and Martha (Perkins) Lamson; . 2d, July 26, 1756, Mehitable Wilkins, of Topsfield. She m. 2d, -- -- Rust, of Ipswich. He was son of Dea. William. He settled in Wenham, where he made his will June 8, 1757. His estate was settled by his brother, Dea. Ebenezer. Of his real estate in the inventory, besides his homestead, was 24 acres of meadow in Wenham, two acres salt marsh in Ipswich, and three lots in Wenham Swamp. His homestead adjoined that of Thomas Fiske.

Theophilus Fiske of Wenham husbandman bought of Symonds Epes of Ipswich & wife Mary 3 acres of marsh in Ipswich bounding as followeth Southerly upon a great Creek westerly upon marsh land of Ebenr. Fiske northerly upon said Epes' own marsh land.

Theophilus Fisk of Wenham, husbandman, made his will June 8, 1757, which was proved Sept. 24, 1759, by Anthony and Elizabeth Wood and the other witness was Elizabeth Bickford. admr. of the intestate part of the estate was granted to his brother, Ebenezer Fiske, Oct. 8, 1759, and same time inventory was dated. Among his lands besides the homestead were 24 acres of meadow in Wenham, 2 acres Salt marsh in Ipswich, two lotts in the west division of Wenham, Swamp

& one lot in East div. of sd swamp. Legatees wife Mehitable who was to have all those household goods he rec'd with her at their marriage &c.

Son Theophilus. Daughter Phebe Manor or Mainer, Daughter Martha Dodge. Daughter Mary Perkins. Daughter Jerusha Moulton.

Son Thomas had recd "Five hundred pounds old tenor equivalent to sixty pounds thirteen shillings & four pence lawful money" for his share of the Estate.

BrotherEbenr Fisk was appointed Exr of the will & he gave acct. of his Exrship & admn. Mar. 17, 1760. A Wm. Fiske was in acct. with the estate.

Committee to set off the wid's part returned their report to the Court June 2, 1760, which homestead part was bounded by Thomas Fisk, John Friend, Josiah Fairfield & some of Great Swamp, some in Great meadow bounded by Abram Kimball, Benj. Fairfield, some meadow bounded by Thos. Tarbox, Abraham & Edmund Kimball.

He d. Sept. 6, 1759; res. Ipswich, Mass.

348. i. PHEBE, b. Jan. 4, 1701; m. Sept. 27, 1737, Jesse Maynard, of Westboro. She received her share of her father's estate in 1700.

349. ii. JERUSHA, b. Oct. 23, 1704; m. Nov. 8, 1734, Caleb Moulton, of Ipswich. Ch.: Jerusha, b. Aug. 1, 1735.

350. iii. THEOPHILUS, b. May 31, 1709; m. Jemima Goldsmith.

351. iv. MARTHA, b. Oct. 25, 1711; m. July 13, 1743, George Dodge, of Ipswich, son of Jonathan and Jerusha (Woodbury) Dodge, who was born May 5, 1709, and died in 1793. Ch.: Daughter m. —— Porter; Jonathan, b. 1744, d. Feb. 9, 1822, m. Mary Brown (was grandfather of Mary Abigail Dodge, whose nom de plume was Gail Hamilton. She was a celebrated American authoress and was born about 1830. She wrote a number of works on "Country Living and Country Thinking," "Gala Days," "Woman's Wrongs," "Twelve miles from a Lemon," "Nursery Musings," and other works besides contributing largely to periodical literature). George, b. 1749, d. May 12, 1827,m. Mary Cleaves (was grandfather of Col. Theodore Ayrault Dodge); Martha m. Joseph Trow; Jerusha, m. Samuel Quarles; Phebe, m. Nathaniel Raymond.

GAIL HAMILTON.

352. v. MARY, b. Sept. 29, 1713; m. Feb. 20, 1750, John Perkins,of Topsfield.

353. vi. THOMAS, b. Aug. 24, 1707; m. —— —— and —— ——.

354. vii. BENJAMIN, b. ——; d. Aug. 25, 1731.

253. DEA. EBENEZER FISKE (William, William, John, William, Robert, Simon, Simon, William, Symond), b. Wenham, Mass., March 22, 1679; m. there May 24, 1710, Elizabeth Fuller, dau. of Jacob Fuller, of Salem, among whose posterity was the celebrated Margaret Fuller. She was b. 1686; d. Aug. 25, 1732; m. 2d, Dec. 1, 1733, Mrs. Martha Kimball; d. Mar. 28, 1764.

Ebenezer Fiske, sixth son of Dea William, of Wenham, Executor of his will, and principal heir of his estate. was married to Elizabeth Fuller, of Salem, and they had a family of nine children. Deacon Ebenezer Fiske was a substantial farmer in Wenham, and was frequently honored by his townsmen by election to various local offices, but appears to have lived a generally quiet life, principally occupied by his private affairs, or those of the church in which he was a Deacon, from his election May 16, 1739, until his resignation "by reason of age," in 1758.

Ebenezer Fiske of Wenham husbandman bought of Thomas Kimball of Marblehead Taylor & wife Hannah for 100 pounds a certain dwelling house & barn and ten acres of land by measure and two acres of meadow and two rights in ye great swamp on the east side of ye highway all situated lying and being within ye bounds of Wenham, bounded as followeth viz: ye house and barn & ten acres of land bounds Eastwardly and Northwardly upon land of Thomas Kimball sen'r and westwardly upon land of John Batchelder and southwardly upon ye highway & ye said meadow is bounded eastwardly upon meadow of Wm. Roger & northwardly upon Meadow of John Gotts & westwardly upon meadow of said Fiske and Southwardly upon meadow of Saml Kimball, ye said two right in ye great Swamp is ye one eight part of ye 7th division and ye one eight part of ye 8th division both division on ye east side of ye highway in ye great swamp as they are entered in Wenham town Books To have &c. Dec. 13 1720. Acknowleged Jan, 11 1720-1.

Ebenezer Fiske of Wenham, husbandman, made his will July 18, 1764, which was proved Oct. 28, 1771. Inventory taken Oct. 31, 1771. Legatees son Ebenezer Fiske, son Jacob Fiske, granddaughter Sarah, dau. of dau. Sarah Moulton, decd., to have among other things all the household goods that was my first wife's, Daughters Elizabeth Bradstreet. Mary Law, Mercy Perkins, Lucy White. Son Wm. Fiske to have the homestead, Bible, etc., and to be executor.

He d. Sept. 30, 1771, ae. 93; res. Wenham, Mass.

355. i.   SARAH, b. July 15, 1711; m. Feb. 23, 1733, Samuel Moulton, of Ipswich. Ch.: Abel, b. Aug. 28, 1741. She d. before her father was deceased in 1771.
356. ii. JONATHAN, b. Dec. 11, 1713; d. unm. Sept. 22, 1737.
357. iii. EBENEZER, b. July 2, 1716; m. Dorcas Tyler.
358. iv. ELIZABETH, b. Oct. 12, 1718; m. Dec. 23, 1742, John Bradstreet, of Topsfield. He was son of Simon and Elizabeth (Capen) Bradstreet and grandson of John Bradstreet, youngest son of the Governor. Simon was b. April 14, 1682. Elizabeth Capen, whom he married Nov. 12, 1711, was daughter of Rev. Joseph Capen. John (2), b. July 22, 1653; m. June 11, 1677, Sarah Perkins. He d. in Topsfield Jan. 11, 1718. The Governor, Simon Bradstreet, b. Lincoln, Eng., March, 1603, Sec. of Mass. Colony 1630-43; assistant, 1630-78; Deputy, Gov., 1678-79; Governor, 1679-86 and 1689-92; d. Salem March, 1697. John and Elizabeth had Priscilla, who m. John Killam, of Topsfield.
359. v.   JACOB, b. Dec. 26, 1721; m. Elizabeth Lampson.
360. vi. MARY, b. Jan. 27, 1723; m. March 9, 1742, Nathaniel Lowe, of Wenham.
361. vii. WILLIAM, b. Nov. 30, 1726; m. Susannah Batchelder.
362. viii. MERCY, b. March 9, 1728; m. March 10, 1752, David Perkins, of Topsfield.
363. ix. LUCY, b. April 22, 1732; m. Jan. 4, 1757, Thomas White, of Wenham.

262. SAMUEL FISKE (Samuel, William, John, William, Robert, Simon, Simon, William, Symond), b. Wenham, Mass.; m. Sarah Reddington; d. Oct. 6, 1748. He was b. in Wenham, but located in Boxford in 1705 on property inherited by him.

At a meeting of the proprietors of the common lands in Boxford Sept. 18, 1710, it was voted: "whear as Richard Kimbol Eapharam dorman and Sammeueal fisk doe appear to Seat vp a Saw-mill vpon the fishing broock with ouer Consent and incorigment wee the—propriatoers doe freely consent that thes thre men shall seat vp a sawmill vpon the foels by Josaph Bixbes houes also wee doe freely give them the veas of as much of our land as they need for flowing and a yeard to lay thair louges and bordes and timber vpon for the ves above so long as thay or thair heaiers or Sucksessors shal keep vp a going mill and for the trew performenc of what is promised on our sied wee doe biend our selves heariers and sucksseaers to the above mentioned Kimbol dorman and fisck and thair lawful sucksessaers that thay shal peassabelly in Joye the ves of the land above said with out anney molistation from vs or anney from by or vnder us." He was selectman in 1709 and 1710.

Samuel Fiske and wife Sarah and Thomas Reddington of Boxford Sold to John Howe of same town 7 acres of meadow "lying partly in Salem and partly in Andover, bounded as followeth at ye Northeast corner with a great Rock with a heep of stones at it easterly to a Maple tree mar keed with stones at it so by fullers Swamp to a white Oak markeed with stones at it by upland in Andover bounds to ye great rock first mentioned this seven acres abovesaid be it more or less it lyes partly in Salem an partly in Andover" May 17, 1715 V 36 p. 101.

Sam'l Fiske of Wenham yeoman sold to his son Sam'l Fiske "all ye one half of all my houseing & lands lying within ye bounds of Boxford the grantor mentions son John who was to share equally in other estate with this son Sam'l Dated May 9 1716.

Samuel Fiske husbandmen and Margaret Reddington Singlewoman both of Boxford Sold to Joseph & Nathl Symonds both of Boxford husbandmen 40 acres in Boxford bounded at the western Corner a white oak tree * * * Northerly by the meadow of Capt John Peabody to a red oak tree * * * Easterly by the land of Thos Cummins to a stake & heepit stones Southerly by the Land of Nath' Symonds Thos Gould * * Westerly by the land of Thos Reddington & a piece of Reddington's meadow of Tho Symonds Dec 20 1717. Margaret Reddington was alive Apr 20 1723 Court Session.

Samuel Fiske of Boxford, admr., was granted to his brother John Fiske and brother-in-law Thomas Reddington Sept. 29, 1719. Inventory of his estate taken Oct. 5, 1719. House, barn, orchard and about 50 acres of land and 100 acres of wood land, tobacco, bees, hemp, books, etc., amount £184 10s. 3d. Made oath to by Thomas Reddington, one of the admrs., Oct. 19, 1719. Samuel's estate was divided into five parts and the return to court was made Oct. 14, 1728. It was done by Samuel Foster, Jere, Perley, Nathan Peabody and John Stiles committee. Viz to son Samuel who had two shares or 5th parts which was bounded—"Beginning at a stake & stones near the Fishing Brook running southerly by land formerly John Fisk's decd to a stake & stones near the house. Then westwardly about a rod & half to a stake & stones, then southerly by land of said John Fisk deceased to a stake & stones near the Hills, then more westerly to a stake & stones near the strippet then Northwesterly to a walnut tree. Then southwesterly over the strippet to a stake & stones more southerly to a white oak tree marked & so on to Redingtons meadow this line being bounded all the way back by land of the said John Fisk deceased then turning south easterly by the meadow as it goes to Ford-way * * * running by John Stiles's land * * * by land laid out to Sarah * * to the fishing brook, then northerly by the brook & land improved by Jona. Byxby to the first mentioned stake & stones the house & barn being within the above said bounds. Likewise was laid out to said Sam'l a wood lot lying between Redingtons meadow & Andover line containing about 2½ acres bounded south by John Stiles's meadow, by land of Elias Smith & the heirs of John Fiske deceased.

To Sarah Fisk a daughter had a lot next to Samls by Fishing brook John Stiles land by Saml between Reddington meadow & Andover line a wood lot near Timothy Stiles's house bounded by Fishing brook &c, 4¼ acres in Long meadow bounded by meadows of Thos. Redington, John Stiles & upland. To Mary another daughter a house lot on Northerly side of Fishing brook bounded— running by an Old Cellar, & by John Buswell's land and a wood lot between Reddings meadow & Andover line also her fathers Right in 18 acres owned by her father & Richard Kimball in two pieces one laying between Lord & Asslebee meadows, and the other between Andover line & Rock Brook, also she had two acres in Dirty meadow bounded by John Buswell s meadow & meadow of Richd Kimball.

To Hannah another daughter who had a house lot on Fishing Brook by Mary's land, land of John Buswell & Tho Redington, ¼ of a wood lot of 22 acres behind the meetinghouse which her father owned in partnership with Thos. Redington, and 1-3 of a wood lot of 30 acres on the Norwesterly side of Cold water meadow lying in partnership with Thos. Redington also ¼ part of a wood lot of 22 acres in Wade's Neck owned also with Tho. Redington, also a Right left in a lot between Pickard's & Maple meadow & Dea. Timothy Foster's land, she also had 2½ acres in Dirty meadow bounded by upland Richard Kimball's meadow Mary's meadow & George Byxby, also all her father had in Rowley marsh. Acct. of the Admr June 10, 1728 rendered to Court.

Childrens guardians were for Mary aged about 18 years & Sarah aged about 16 years. When appointed Oct. 28, 1728, was Wm Fisk of Boxford to whom Mary gives a receipt Apr. 24, 1732, signed by herself Mary Stickney and Jonathan Stickney of "our portion of our fathers estate," & for Samuel aged abt 13. When appointed same time Oct. 28, 1728 was Thomas Reddington of Boxford who rendered his account of guardianship Aug. 3, 1733 Says he "paid to widow Martha Gould £3 to make good ye title to ye said child" and in his stead Wm. Fisk of Rowley was appointed guardian of him with Jonathan Stickney for bondsman.

Samuel Fiske of Boxford deceased husbandman, his admr, was Thomas Reddington of Boxford husbandman. Especially in consideration that Wm. Fiske of Rowley husbandmen & Abigail Fiske widow & relict of John Fiske late of said Boxford died as admrs on said John Fiske estate have before the ensealing hereof signed an instrument whereby they have in the behalf of ye heirs of ye said John Fiske acquitted their right to the respective parcels of land as is therein described. Have given, granted, released and confirmed all my right, title property claim, challenge, pretence and demand which I ye said Thomas Reddington or ye heirs of Samuel Fiske aforesaid have or may have unto ye lands and Housen hereafter described lying & being in ye township of Boxford aforesaid containing by estimation about three acres in the whole being the one half of what ye said Sam'l & John Fisk had given them by their father Samuel Fisk late of Wenham deceased by Deed and which deed ye above said grantor did Improve & authorize the admr of his said sons to divide the above said premises when ever desired and we being now sensable of ye necessity of a division proceed accordingly in behalf of ye aforesaid heirs and that which fell to ye heirs of ye said John Fisk and hereby aquitted is butted & bounded as followeth Beginning at a stake & stones at the fishing Brook running Southerly to a stake & stones near the house wherein ye above said Sam'l Fisk dwelt Then Westerly about a Rod & half to another stake & stones. Then Southerly to another stake & stones near ye edge of ye plain by the Hills, then a little more westerly to a stake & stones then norwesterly to a little walnut &c. Furthermore I ye said Tho. Redington in ye above said Capacity do give liberty to ye said Wm & Abigail Fisk & ye heirs of John Fsk aforesaid to pass over ye lands belonging to ye Heirs of Sam'l Fsk aforesaid &c Witnessed by Amos Jewett & Cahran Stevart Oct 19 1727.

He d. in 1719; res. Boxford, Mass.

364. i.   MARY, b. 1710; m. Jan. 30, 1731, Jonathan Stickney.
365. ii.   SARAH, b. 1713; m. Dec. 19, 1741, Charles Stewart, of Rowley.
366. iii. HANNAH, b. June 6, 1707.
367. iv.   SAMUEL, b. Apr. 10, 1716; m. Judith Noyes.

263. JOHN FISKE (Samuel, William, John, William, Robert, Simon, Simon, William, Symond), b. ———; m. (int.) Dec. 22, 1710, Abigail Poor. She m. 2d, Oct. 15, 1727, Thomas Holt, of Andover. Soon after his marriage, in 1711, he located on land inherited by him in Boxford, where he d. He was a husbandman. His estate was admr. upon Feb. 10, 1725.

Wm Fisk of Rowley & Abigail Fisk widow of John Fisk late of Boxford as Admrs of the est of John Fisk aforesaid acting as such but especially in consideration that Thomas Reddington of Boxford admr of the est. of Saml Fisk late of Boxford decd hath signed an instrument where of he in the behalf of the heirs of Sam'l Fisk aforesaid hath aquitted their right to * * land as is there in described * * being in the township of Boxford containing in the whole about three hundred acres * * being the one half of that the said Saml & John Fisk had given them by their father Sam'l Fisk late of Wenham deceased by deed in which Deed ye above said grantor did Impower & authorize the admrs of his said sons to divide ye above said premises whensoever desired & we being now sensible of the necessity of a division proceed accordingly in behalf of the aforesaid heirs and that which fell to the heirs of said Sam'l Fisk and is hereby aquitted is butted & bounded by Andover line Fishing brook Reddings Meadow &c &c Oct. 19 1727.

Sam'l Fiske & ac of Wenham recieved a deed of Martha Gould of Stonham wid. of John Gould late of Charlestown in consideration of ye sum of fifty pounds formerly Paid by Sam'l Fisk of Wenham to her sd husband * * also of 9 pounds

paid by Wm Fisk & Thos Redington guardians for the children of Sam'l Fisk &
John Fisk late of Boxford—She confirms &c unto Saml & Sarah Fisk ye children
of sd Sam'l Fisk decd & unto John Fisk & Phebe Fisk children of said John Fisk
decd all her right &c land in Boxford 100 acres it being ½ of ¼ part of land
formerly given to the grantor's father John Reddington by Zacheus Gould of
Topsfield the whole tract bounded by Andover line Long Meadow Fishing brook
&c Aug. 17 1731.

The inventory of his estate was taken Feb. 10, 1725, about 100 acres of land,
with housing on it, etc., made oath to by Wm. Fiske, the admr., Mar. 29, 1725,
John Fiske and Phebe Fiske about fifteen years of age. She made choice of
Wm. Fiske to be her guardian, Nov. 6, 1727. At this time he was also appointed
guardian of John. The daughter Phebe gives a receipt to her guardian, Wm.
Fiske, of Rowley, signed Phebe Abbott, with John Abbott, Jr., and they say that
they had received in full of "our portion of our father John Fiske's estate."

He d. Dec. 24, 1724; res. Andover and Boxford, Mass.

  368. i.   PHEBE, b. ——; m. Sept. 20, 1732, John Abbott, Jr., of An-
             dover.
  369. ii.   JOHN, b. Dec. 30, 1715; m. Mary Bridges.

  264. DEA. WILLIAM FISKE (Samuel, William, John, William, Robert,
Simon, Simon, William, Symond), b. Wenham, Mass., ——; m. in Boxford
Dec. 4, 1711, Rebecca Reddington, of Boxford; d. July 24, 1743; m. 2d, Jan. 6, 1744,
Lydia Thurston, of Rowley, b. 1699; d. July 25, 1753; m. 3d, Dec 19 1753 Bethiah
Goodrich, of Newbury.

He was born in Wenham, but settled on property in Rowley left him by his
father. He was Deacon in the Congregational church there and a man of influence
and standing in the community. He had three wives and several children, but did
not leave any male heirs among them, as appears by will dated 1765. Among his
numerous legatees were the sons of Daniel, of Upton, deceased. He joined the
Rowley church Oct. 4, 1732. His wife was admitted Dec. 4, 1732, from the church
in Byfield parish. He was treasurer of the church in 1750.

Wm. Fiske of Rowley bought of Isaac Hardy yeoman and wife Esther of
Bradford, 1¼ acres of Salt meadow on Cow bridge Creek in Rowley bounded
by James Todd land formerly John Stickney of Rowley which meadow come by
ye said Esther and was formerly her father Barker's. May 10, 1721.

Wm. Fiske of Rowley bought two acres marsh of John Boynton of Newbury
which was B.s father and given to granter by dec'd June 1713 bounded by Bs
meadow and on Falls River. Mar. 22, 1722.

Dea. William Fiske, of Rowley, yeoman, "being advanced in old age," made
his will May 23, 1764, which was proved Feb. 14, 1765, by Mary Clarke, Elizabeth
Clarke and Daniel Clarke. The inventory of the estate was taken May 14, 1765,
by Jere Searl, Jere Jewett and Jere Poor, and made oath to by Samul Keezer.
Real Estate homestead, woodlots, salt marsh in Rowley and Newbury. Wife
Bethiah was to have "all the goods and estate I had with her that were hers afore
I married her, etc." He gave to Sarah, widow of Charles Stewart, late of Lan-
caster, decd. To the two daughters of Samuel Fisk late of Boxford, decd. .To
Abigail Goodridge, his daughter-in-law to be paid after her mother's decease.
To the children of Jonathan Stickney, of Rowley, decd., two lots of land ex-
cepting some fenced in to the homestead, one purchased of Thomas Lambert, Esq.,
and the other of Capt. John Northand. To Phebe Abbott, of Andover. To John
Fiske of Andover. To Joseph Stickney of Boxford. To Hannah wife of John
Todd. To Hannah wife of Zacheus Boynton, of Lancaster. To the sons of
Daniel Fiske, late of Upton, decd. To Samuel Kezar, of Rowley, the residue of
his estate and he to be executor of the will.

He d. about 1765; res. Rowley, Mass.

  265. DANIEL FISKE (Samuel, William, John, William, Robert, Simon,
Simon, William, Symond), b. ——; m. in Beverly July 2, 1717, Sarah Fuller, of
Salem.

In 1638, Thomas Fuller, who belonged to a family of high social standing in
England, came over to this country on a tour of observation, not intending to
stay. While in Cambridge he became a convert to Puritanism, under the eloquent
preaching of Rev. Thomas Shepard, a famous Colonial divine, and at once resolved to cast in his lot with his brethren of that faith in the New World. He

purchased a large tract of land in New Salem (afterward Middleton) and having married Elizabeth Tidd, of Woburn, he settled upon his handsome estate and died in 1698, leaving sons Thomas, Benjamin and Jacob, and several daughters. His youngest son, Jacob Fuller, born in 1655, married Mary Bacon and settled on the paternal homestead. Their five children were named Mary, Elizabeth, Edward, Sarah and Jacob. Two of these, Elizabeth and Sarah, married Fiskes (Ebenezer and Daniel, of Wenham). Their uncle, Benjamin Fuller, was the father of Rev. Daniel Fuller, of Gloucester, and also of Col. Archelaus Fuller, who commanded a section of the American forces at the battle of Bennington.

Fiske was born in Wenham, where he continued to reside until 1748, when he moved to Upton, Worcester Co., where he was an early settler. His children were all born in Wenham. He made his will Feb. 6, 1754, probated in 1761, mentions wife Sarah and all his living children.

Daniel Fiske of Wenham husbandman & Theophs Rix of W Taylor had released & quit claimed to them by John Newman of Glocester trader a certain tract of land in Wenham containing 20 acres "which land was bought by one Sam'l Fiske Theophilus Rix of my hond father John Newman Esq. in his life time To have & to hold ye said tract of land as butted & bounded in their ye said Saml Fiske's and Theophilus Rix's Deed bearing Dates June ye 16 1692, to them ye said Theophilus Rix and Daniel Fiske their heirs &c. Witnessed by Wm. & Benj Fisk Feb 24 1720-1.

He d. 1761; res. Wenham and Upton, Mass.

370.   i.   SAMUEL, b. Feb. 14, 1728; m. Sarah Partridge.
371.   ii.   DANIEL, b. June 17, 1718; m. Zilpah Tyler.
372.   iii.   HANNAH, b. May 16, 1721; m. in Wenham July 6, 1742, Ebenezer Ober.
373.   iv.   BENJAMIN, b. May 7, 1724; m. Rebecca —— and Keziah
374.   v.   SARAH, b. March 20. 1730; m. Dec. 17, 1755, in Upton, Ebenezer Walker, of Upton.
375.   vi.   WILLIAM, b. April 14, 1733; m. Jemima Adams.
376.   vii.   JOSIAH, b. Feb. 2, 1734; m. Sarah Barber, Lydia Daniels and Elizabeth Gore.
377.   viii. MARTHA, b. April 8, 1738; m. April 24, 1760, in Upton, Perin Batchelder.
378.   ix.   SARAH, b. Dec. 6, 1719; d. Feb. 1, 1720.
379.   x.   PHEBE, b. Oct. 5, 1726; d. Nov. 18, 1726.
380.   xi.   SARAH, b. March 5, 1722; d. March 31, 1723.

269. SAMUEL FISKE (Joseph, William, John, William, Robert, Simon, Simon, William, Symond), b. Swanzey, Mass., July 5, 1680; m. in Rehoboth, March 16, 1704, Mehitable Wheaton. She d. before 1716, for at that time he had married again, and his wife's name was Elizabeth ——. He was born in Swanzey. Later he moved to Rehoboth and finally located in Johnstown, R. I., where he died. He was possessed of quite a large property at his death. He generally was called "Yeoman," but once or twice in deeds is called "Cordwainer." 1703, Dec. 18, He bought land in Providence of Ephraim Pierce, of Swanzey, Mass. 1709. Sept. 8, he bought land of Zuriel Hall. 1744, Oct. 13, he deeded land to son Joseph for love and affection. 1756, May 9, he sold to Joseph Fiske for £2,000 homestead farm of 55 acres in Providence and two lots of land in Scituate containing 34 acres, and ⅛ of certain undivided land. The homestead was in that part of Providence that subsequently (1759) was set off as town of Johnston. 1757, he took administration of the estate of his son Ezekiel Fiske. He was undoubtedly the father also of Phineas Fiske, who married Mary Colwell in Providence 1729, Jan. 19. [The above Samuel Fiske was probably a brother of Benjamin Fiske, who early settled in Scituate. R. I., and had wife Abigail, daughter Elizabeth, born 1709. sons Hezekiah, Benjamin Jr., Noah, Daniel, Job, John, (and other daughters Mary, Freelove and Abigail, besides Elizabeth, first referred to.] J. O. Austin, Prov. R. I. This is not so; see elsewhere.

He d. after 1757 and before 1763; res. Swanzey, Mass., Providence and Johnstown, R. I.

381.   iv.   DANIEL, b. May 10, 1710; m. Mercy Stone and Sarah Stewart.
382.   iii.   JOSEPH, b. June 8, 1708; m. Freelove Fiske.
383.   ii.   PATIENCE, b. March 28, 1706.

384. v.   EZEKIEL, b. ——. He died Dec. 28, 1757, and the administration of his estate was granted to his father Samuel.

385. i.   PHINEHAS, b. ——; m. Mary Colwell.

278. JOHN FISKE (John, Nathaniel, William, Robert, Simon, Simon,
William, Symond), b. Watertown, Nov. 20, 1655; m. Dec. 9, 1679, Abigail Parks,
dau. of Thomas and Abigail (Dix); b. March 3, 1658; m. 2d, Jan. 7, 1699, Hannah
Richards; d. 1714.

He was a husbandman. May 23, 1697. John and wife Abigail for £10-10-0
sold to John Ward of Newton, turner, 13½ acres in Newton, probably inherited
from her father. Gravestone inscription in Waltham grave yard: Here lyes
the Body of Mr. John Fiske Who Dec'd Jan ye 6th 1718 in ye 63rd year of His age."

He was made a freeman April 18, 1690. His will is dated June 6, 1709, and
proved June 23, 1718. His son John was sole executor and he gave all his real
estate to his wife Hannah. He was a husbandman. He d. Jan. 6, 1718; res.
Watertown and Waltham, Mass.

386. i.   ABIGAIL, b. June 12, 1684; m. Feb. 24, 1701, John Stearns.
He was of Wat. Settled on his father's homestead, where he
was b. June 24, 1677. Inventory of his estate, administrator
his widow Abigail, in 1735 £952-3-10. In the settlement of the
estate mention is made of the heirs of Peter and James. Ch.:
John, b. Nov. 18, 1702, m. Anna Coolidge, res. Wat. and West-
minster; Josiah, b. Oct. 14, 1704, m. Susanna Ball, Dorothy
Prentice and Mary Bowman, res. Wat.; Joseph, b. July, 1706,
d. unm. insane April 11, 1756; Abigail, b. June 3, 1708, m.
Col. Benjamin Bellows, res. Lunenburg and Walpole, N. H.;
David, b. Dec. 24, 1709, m. Ruth Hubbard. He gr. Harvard
Coll. 1728, was a minister in Lunenburg. After his death
she m. Nov. 9, 1768, Rev. Aaron Whitney, of Petersham, gr.
Harvard Coll. 1737. They d. in Keene, N. H.; Thomas, b.
Oct. 8, 1711, m. Hannah Clarke, of Newton, res. Westminster,
and m. 2d, Lydia Hilton. He was a Deacon and d. s. p.;
James, b. 1713, d. 1713; Hannah, b. Dec. 20, 1713, m. Dea.
Samuel Johnson, of Lunenburg; Benjamin, b. ——, m.
Anna Taylor, res. Lunenburg; Peter, m. and left des.; William,
b. Mar. 11, 1717, m. Elizabeth Johnson, was a Deacon, res.
Lunenburg; Lydia, b. Oct. 7, 1719, m. Joshua Goodrich, of
Lunenburg; James, b. July 9, 1721, d. young; Lois, b. Jan. 18,
1722, m. Jonas White; Abijah, b. Dec. 19, 1724, m. Sarah Hey-
wood, was a Colonel; res. Lunenburg and d. s. p. 1783.

387. ii.   ELIZABETH, b. Jan. 20, 1685; m. Mar. 1, 1709, Benjamin Whitney.
He was b. Jan. 31, 1864. His will is dated June 14, and was
proved Nov. 8, 1736. He d. Oct., 1736; res. Watertown, Mass.
Ch.: Joseph, b. Dec. 3, 1710, m. Mary Child; Benjamin, b.
Sept. 14, 1712, m. —— ——; Samuel, b. Nov. 22, 1715, m.
Mary Clark; Elizabeth, b. Mar. 9, 1718, m. Nov. 26, 1747, William McCune, of Weston. Ch.: Lydia, b. Oct., 1748; Isaac,
b. May 31, 1750. She prob. m. 2d, ——; child. (See her
bro. Samuel's will.)

388. iii.   JOHN, b. May 15, 1687; m. Mary Whitney and Elizabeth Chinery.

389. iv.   JONATHAN, bap. Nov. 25, 1688; d. in infancy.

390. v.   JONATHAN, bap. Dec. 8, 1689; m. Lydia Bemis.

391. vi.   HEPZIBAH, b Jan. 13, 1693; m. Dec. 8, 1715, George Harring-
ton. He was b. Aug. 31, 1695. She d. Mar. 26, 1736; res.
Wat. Hannah, b. July 31, 1716, m. William Whitney, Jr., of
Weston; Elisha, b. Aug. 27, 1717, d. 1719; Abigail, b. Oct. 4,
1718; John, b. Dec. 14, 1719, m. Sarah Barnard; Lydia, b.
Feb. 12, 1720; Elisha, b. Nov. 19, 1722; Seth, b. June 22, 1724;
Benjamin, b. Sept. 29, 1725, m. Elizabeth Pierce; Sarah, b.
Oct. 21, 1727; Seth, b. Sept. 25, 1728; Mercy, b. Feb. 7, 1730;
Eunice, b. Oct. 30, 1733; Susana, b. Jan. 9, 1735.

392. vii.   DAUGHTER, b. Nov. 19, 1695; d. Nov. 20, 1695.

393. viii. DAVID, b. April 13, 1697; m. Elizabeth Durkee.
394. ix. HANNAH, bap. Oct. 8, 1704; d. July 21, 1714.

281. WILLIAM FISKE (John, Nathaniel, William, Robert, Simon, Simon, William, Symond), b. Wat. Feb. 23, 1663; m. Oct. 25, 1693, Hannah Smith, of Cambridge, dau. of John and Mary (Beers), b. Dec. 27, 1672; d. Dec. 7, 1728. He was selectman in 1717. His will is dated Feb. 18, 1734; proved Mar. 29, 1742. He was yeoman. His son Samuel was executor and had most of the property, as the other children had already received most of their portions. He d. in 1742; res. Watertown, Mass.
   395. i.   WILLIAM, b. Aug. 24, 1694; d. Dec. 13, 1702.
   396. ii. HANNAH, b. Oct. 13, 1696.
   397. iii. MARY, b. Jan. 16, 1698; d. Dec. 13, 1702.
   398. iv. THOMAS, b. Sept. 12, 1701; m. Mary Pierce.
   399. v.   WILLIAM, b. Mar. 13, 1703; m. Mary Sanderson.
   400. vi   JOHN, b. Aug. 24, 1706; m. Sarah Child.
   401. vii. SAMUEL, b. Jan. 4, 1709; m. Anna Bemis.

286. LIEUT. NATHAN FISKE (Nathan, Nathaniel, William, Robert, Simon, Simon, William, Symond), b. Watertown Oct. 17, 1642; m. Elizabeth Fry; d. May 15, 1696. Oct. 1, 1673, he purchased of Thomas Underwood and wife Magdalen 220 acres of farm lands in Weston for £10. His inventory was £151. He was selectman 1684-88-91. Admr. was granted to his widow Elizabeth Dec. 10, 1694. Inventory by Wm. Bond, Senr., Samuel Jennison, Senr., and Nathaniel Barsham, dated Nov. 27, 1694. House and 22 acres on both sides of the highway £45, 6 acres in Newton £9, 12 acres about Prospect Hill £6, 7 acres in Thatchers Meadow £5, about 250 acres farm land £15. The 220 acres were purchased as stated above of Thos. Underwood and bounded by property of Anthony Pierce, and others. An agreement of his children dated Nov. 23, 1696, was signed by Nathan Fiske; David, the guardian of William; James Ball for Elizabeth, his wife; Edward Park for his wife; John Mixer for his wife and Susanna Fiske.
   Lt. Nathan Fisk of Watertown Oct. 1694 admn granted to Elizabeth Fiske his widow Dec. 10 1694 the inv of the Estate having been taken Nov. 27 1694 Items Homestead some land about Prospect Hill A division of the Estate was divided among the heirs Feb 21 1694-5 Viz Elizth the widow who deceased previous to June 2 1696 when her thirds was divided Children Nathan—Elizth who was then wife of James Ball—Martha then unmarried but had previous to June 2 1696 married Edward Park—Susan who not married before June 1696—Abigail then unmarried but previous to June 2 1696 had married John Mixer—William who was alive in June 1696 and his uncle David Fiske whom he had appointed when he was 16 years old for his guardian Dec. 10, 1694 was also alive at that time.
   He d. Oct. 11, 1694; res. Watertown, Mass.
   402. i. NATHAN, b. Feb. 9, 1665; d. Oct. 9, 1668.
   403. ii. ELIZABETH, b. Jan. 19, 1667; m. Jan. 16, 1693, James Ball, b. Mar. 7, 1670; was a weaver. He d. Feb. 22, 1729. His will is dated Feb. 21 of this year. John Ball, a Concord freeman, brought with him from England, where he lived in Wiltshire, his two sons, Nathaniel and John. He died in Concord, Oct. 1, 1655. John Ball married Elizabeth Pierce, of Watertown, Mass., and had five children. By a second marriage with Elizabeth Fox he had one child. He (John Ball) was killed by Indians at Lancaster, Mass., Sept. 10, 1675. John Ball, born 1644, and married Sarah Bullard, a dau. of Geo. Bullard, of Watertown. They had seven children. He was by trade a weaver, and died May 8, 1722. James Ball, born in Watertown, 1670. He m. Elizabeth Fisk. Ch.: James, b. Feb. 2, 1694; m. Sarah ———; res. Ball Hill, Northboro, Mass. Nathan, b. Feb. 28, 1695; d. Northboro, 1768. John, b. July 22, 1697; m. Abigail Harrington and Lydia Perry; res. Worcester, and he d. there 1756. Elizabeth, b. Apr. 2, 1699; d. 1703. Sarah, b. Sept 21, 1700; m. Aug. 5, 1724, Daniel Hastings; ch. Sarah, Stephen, Hannah, Daniel, Elizabeth, John, Elizabeth, John, David, Hannah. Daniel Hastings m. Priscilla Keyes, Aug. 16, 1753. Their children were Ruth, Elizabeth, Daniel, Henry;

Henry Hastings, b. Sept. 3, 1758, m. Abigail Hawes, July 15, 1785. Their children were Amherst, Daniel, Lois, Elizabeth; Lois Hastings, b. May 29, 1796, m. Asaph Browning, Apr. 9, 1816. Their children were Louise, Silas, Abigail, Clara, Asaph, Mary Louise; Abigail Hastings, b. Feb. 19, 1824, m. Henry Endicott. Their children died in infancy except Emma Endicott, who was b. Jan. 20, 1854; m. Joseph Mason Marean, Jan. 20, 1876, and whose children are Edith, Henry Endicott, Parker Endicott, Mason Browning, and Endicott; res. 46 Brewster street, Cambridge, Mass. Abigail, b. June 5, 1702; m. Dea. Jonathan Livermore. Elizabeth, b. Apr. 9, 1705; m. Thomas Fuller; res. Newton. Susanna, b. Mar. 16, 1707; m. Josiah Stearns. She d. 1740.

404. iii. MARTHA, b. Jan. 12, 1670; m. Mar. 13, 1694, Edward Park, b. Apr. 8, 1661, son of Thomas and grandson of Richard of Camb., the emigrant; res. Newton; ch., Edward, bap. July 8, 1744.

405. iv. NATHAN, b. Jan. 3, 1672; m. Sarah Coolidge and Mrs. Hannah Smith.

406. v. SUSANNA, b. Apr. 7, 1674; d. unm. Will dated Shrewsbury, Feb. 19, 1745; proved June 29, 1752; d. in Shrewsbury, Apr. 28, 1752. Probably living with her niece, Grace Goddard. Susan Fiske then in Shrewsbury Worcester Co residing, spinster "being aged" made her will Feb 19 1745-6 which was proved June 20 1752 when it was said that she was late of Watertown & the two witnesses at that time present were Simon & Susannah Goddard She mentions that her brother Nathan Fisk late of Watertown deceased left 5 sons & 2 daughters and they appear to have received the whole of her estate Among them were mentioned the names of the daughters viz Grace Goddard of Shrewsbury & Hannah Fisk of Watertown and her (the testator's) cousin Nathan Fiske of Watertown who was executor of the will.

407. vi. ABIGAIL, b. Feb. 18, 1675; m. Aug. 15, 1695, John Mixer. He was b. Mar. 5, 1668, son of Isaac, Jr., whose father came from Ipswich, Eng., in 1634. John was a tanner and res. in Wat. and Hampshire Co. Ch.: Abigail, b. June 26, 1696; John, b. Jan. 22, 1698; Elizabeth, b. Dec. 30, 1702; George, b. Dec. 27, 1704; Ann, m. 1738, John Jones, Jr., of Weston.

408. vii. WILLIAM, b. Dec. 5, 1677; d. 1677.

409. viii. WILLIAM, b. Nov. 10, 1678; m. Eunice Jennings.

410. ix. ANNA, b. ———; d. July 13, 1683.

288. DAVID FISKE (Nathan, Nathaniel, William, Robert, Simon, Simon, William, Symond), b. Wat., Apr. 29, 1650; m. Dec. 15, 1675, Elizabeth Reed, b. July 26, 1653, dau. of Dea. George of Woburn. She d. Mar. 21, 1717. Elizabeth dau. of Geo. and Elizabeth of Woburn, and granddau. of William and Maybel, b. July 26, 1653, m. David Fiske, of Watertown. Mr. Fiske was a land surveyor, and did much in laying out townships, etc. He was of the Lexington stock of Fiskes, who were relatives of Rev. John Fiske of Chelmsford. George, as above July 26, 1653, dau. of Dea. George of Woburn, and granddau. of William and Mayson of William & Maybel, born in England, 1629 bought a farm in Woburn of Rebecca Terrace, Nov. 7 1651. Married Elizabeth Gennings, or Gennison of Watertown Aug. 4, 1651; bought land in Weymouth. April 16, 1665 Cambridge, Mass. Probate, Middlesex Co. Will of George Reed, Sen. of Wooburne Yeoman proved 1706 wife Hannah. Ch.: John Timothy, Thomas, Samuel, George, William; daus. Mary Johnson, Hannah Elson, Elizabeth Fisk receives 5 £, Sarah Robason etc etc.

Admr. was granted to widow Elizabeth Dec. 10, 1694. He was a surveyor. He d. 1694; res. Watertown, Mass.

411. i. NATHAN, b. ———; living 1694.

412. ii. DAVID, b. Dec. 11, 1678; m. Rebecca ———.

289. NATHANIEL FISKE (Nathan, Nathaniel, William, Robert, Simon, Simon, William, Symond), b. Watertown, July 12, 1653; m. Apr. 13, 1677, Mrs.

Mary (Warren) Child, b. Nov. 29, 1651, dau. of Daniel Warren, of Watertown, and wid. of John Child, of Watertown, b. 1636, d. Oct. 15, 1676. Inventory £142. She d. May 12, 1734. He was a weaver. His will is dated June 10 and proved Oct. 3, 1735. Vol. 20 Mid Prob. Rec. p. 210. Will. Nathaniel of Watertown weaver dte June 10 1735 appr Dec 22 1735 1st to children of my son Nathaniel decea'd & to children of son John equally amongst them money from Debts due to be divided in 5 equal sharees. To 3 daughters, Hannah Biglow, Sarah Hastings & Elizabeth Flagg, to each one share. to children of daughter Lydia Harrington had by her former husband John Warren one share to children of daughter Abigail Flagg deceased One share— To children of daughter Mary Knapp deceas'd —nothing considering what I did for their mother in her life time. To My daughter in Law Mary Child——"as a requital for her care & good service" &c. He d. Sept., 1735; res. Watertown, Mass.

413. i.   NATHANIEL, b. June 9, 1678; m. Hannah Adams.
414. ii. HANNAH, b. Aug. 29, 1680; m. Oct. 17, 1701, Joshua Bigelow, Jr., b. Nov. 25, 1677. His father was wounded in King Philip's war and was granted land in Worcester, but later went to Westminster. Joshua, Jr., res. in Weston. Ch.: Joshua, b. Feb. 5, 1701. Hannah, b. Mar. 6, 1703; m. —— Cheney; res. Mendon. Nathaniel, b. Jan. 17, 1706; m. Hannah Robinson; res. Fram. Lydia, b. Mar. 8, 1708; m. Isaac Parkhurst. Elizabeth, b. Dec. 2, 1711; m. David Wilson; res. Lancaster. John, b. June 24, 1715; m. Grace Allen; res. Weston. Abigail, b. Oct. 7, 1719. Mary, b. Mar. 18, 1721.
415. iii. JOHN, b. Mar. 17, 1682; m. Lydia Adams.
416. iv. SARAH, b. July 4, 1684; m. Jan. 8, 1706, John Hastings, Jr. (John, Thomas), bap. Dec. 4, 1687. He d. before 1747; res. Watertown and rev. to Lunenburg. Ch.: Sarah, b. Nov. 8, 1707. Susanna, b. Apr. 4, 1710. John, b. Feb. 4, 1711. Na-

Ida Tucker Morris

thaniel, b. June 9, 1714; m. Esther Perry; res. Shrewsbury.
Hannah, b. Jan. 24, 1716; m. Aug. 15, 1735, Lieut. David
Farnsworth (Samuel, Matthais.) He was one of the orig-
inal settlers in Charlestown, N. H., and later removed to
Hollis, N. H. They had a daughter Relief Farnsworth
who married June 4, 1771, Reuben Tucker (Moses, Joseph,
Morris); ch. Charles Tucker m. 1804 Wealthy Ruggles;
their ch. Gilbert Ruggles Tucker m. August 20, 1831.
Evelina Christina Snyder; their child Wm. Stringham
Snyder Tucker (7) m. May 4, 1865, Martha Ann Nesbitt;
their dau. Ida Nesbitt Tucker (8) m. Jan 18, 1888, Tyler
Seymour Morris (Joseph, Ephraim, Isaac, Edward, Ed-
ward, Edward) their son Seymour Tucker Morris, born
Nov. 28, 1890 in Chicago.

Eunice, b. Sept. 3, 1722; Enoch, bap. Oct. 1724; Elisha, bap. Jan. 15, 1726;
Elizabeth, b. 1732.

417. v.   LYDIA, b. Dec. 2, 1687; m. May 14, 1711, John Warren, son of
John Warren, b. May 21, 1678. His wid. admr. on his estate
July 29, 1726. Inventory £391. She m. 2d, June 17, 1730, Benjamin Harrington, b. Oct. 2, 1685, d. 1768. She d. Aug. 21,
1761; res. Weston. Ch. by 1st wife: John, b. Apr. 3, 1701;
res. Marlboro. Sarah, b. Sept. 20, 1702; m. Samuel Harrington. Samuel, b. Mar. 18, 1703; m. Tabitha Stone. Thomas,
b. Mar. 11, 1705; m. Lydia Mixer. David, b. June 22, 1708; m.
Martha Coolidge, "Jr." Ch. by Lydia: Benjamin, b. Apr. 4,
1715. David, b. Jan. 8, 1716. Abigail, b. Oct. 28, 1719. Lucy,
b. Oct. 26, 1721. William, b. Oct. 21, 1723; d. 1739. John,
bap. 1725.

418. vi.   MARY, bap. Apr. 20, 1690; m. in Wat. Oct. 30, 1716, James
Knapp, b. Feb. 4, 1690; res. Wat. and Worcester. Ch.: James,
bap. Nov. 24, 1723; Elizabeth, b. May 15, 1729; John, b. Oct.
31, 1731.

419. vii. ELIZABETH, b. June 24, 1692; m. Jan. 25, 1715, Capt. Benjamin Flagg, Jr., Esq., of Wat. and Worcester. He was b. in
Wat. Aug. 25, 1691, d. in Worcester, June 12, 1751. She d.
there Nov. 30, 1760, ae. 77. He settled in Worcester, where
he acquired much respect and influence. He was selectman
1725 and 1726, and was the schoolmaster in 1729. Inventory
£259. Ch.: Elizabeth, b. May 24, 1717; m. Absolem Rice.
Abigail, b. ———; m. Samuel Hubbard. Benjamin, bap. Aug.
26, 1723; m. Abigail ———; res. Worcester; was on important
committees during the French and Revolutionary wars; was
captain before the Revolutionary war, and in 1777 was lieutenant-colonel. William. Asa, bap. July 21, 1721; an Ensign in
1757. Mary, unm., in 1751.

420. viii. ABIGAIL, b. Aug. 28, 1698; m. Apr. 10, 1717, Allen Flagg, Jr.,
b. Feb. 9, 1690. She d. Mar., 1729; res. Weston. Ch.: Ebenezer, b. Jan. 2, 1718. Abigail, b. July 15, 1719. Josiah, b.
June 9, 1722. Abijah, b. Aug. 29, 1724; m. Mary Stone, of Sudbury. Three other children by second wife.

292. DEA. JONATHAN FISKE (David, David, David, Jeffrey, Robert,
Simon, Simon, William, Symond), b. at Lexington, May 19, 1679; m. Abigail
Reed, dau. of Capt. William of Lexington, b. May 29, 1687. His name first appears
upon the Lex. parish records in 1707, when Corpl. Jonathan Fiske was chosen one
of the assessors. He was also a subscriber for the purchase of the common in
1711, though the church records show that his dau. Abigail was bap. in 1704, when
he owned the covenant. He and his wife united with the church in 1708. He had
a family of fourteen children, five of whom were b. in Lex., and the rest in
Sudbury, to which place he moved about 1713, where he was a deacon. He and
his wife were dismissed to the Sudbury church in 1718. His will, dated Nov. 13,
1740, mentions wife Abigail, five sons and seven daus., two of his children having
died before that period.

Will of Jonathan Fiske of Sudbury gentleman   Being weak in Body etc.   To wife Abigail he gave one third and to sons Bezaleel and David all my lands and rights in Holden in the County of Worcester etc. To my son William all my lands in Sutton. To my son Samuel a tract of land in Sudbury on the east side of the river Called the neck containing about twenty-six acres; To my son Benjamin £25 to be paid him when he shall arrive at the age of twenty-one, Have given to my daughters Abigail Parris, Kezia Noyes, Lydia Patterson Mary Fisk, Beulah Stone Wife Abigail in consideration etc to pay "my daughter Hepzibath Fisk, and my daughter Sarah Fisk and daughter Anna. My two youngest sons David and Benjamin live with their mother until they arrive at twenty-one years of age. My wife Abigal with son in law Samuel Parris executors.

Connecting Jonathan with the Lexington line is the following Worcester Co. Deeds Vol 21 page 100 Jonathan Fisk of Sudbury & Abegail, wife Joseph Manor of Lexington & Elizabeth, wife Edward Johnson of Woburn & Rebechah, wife John Stone, Jr. of Lexington, Mary, wife sell to brother, William Reed of Lexington all rights in estate of father William Reed of Lexington, dec. date Sept 10 1718.

Jonathan Fisk bought land in Sudbury Nov. 25 1711 he was then "of Cambridge."

The town record of Sudbury gives baptism & marriage (Jonathan, May 19 1679. Abegail Reed— also Samuel, May 3 1717 m. Abegail Rice—).

Jonathan Fiske of Sudbury Inv. of his estate Mar. 28 1743 made oath to by an Abigail Fiske (not said whether widow or not) & Sam'l Parris Apr 4, 1743 He owned land in Sudbury also in Holden & Worcester in Worcester County—and in all about 700 acres of land.

William Reed father of Elizabeth was son of George & Elizabeth, and grandson of William & Maybel born Sept 22 1662 m. Abegail Kendall, his fathers cousin, May 24 1686 She had an unusual number of fingers and toes Ch. Abegail born May 29 1687, m. Deacon Jonathan Fisk & moved to Sudbury.

He d. Dec. 27, 1740; res. Lexington and Sudbury, Mass.

421. i.   ABIGAIL, bap. July 23, 1704; m. in Sudbury, Nov. 28, 1760, Dea. Samuel Parris, b. Jan. 9, 1701. He was the son of Rev. Samuel Parris and grandson of Thomas, merchant of London.

422. ii.   JONATHAN, bap. June 9, 1706; m. Jemima Foster.

423. iii. KEZIA, bap. Aug. 8, 1708; m. Nov. 12, 1741, Peter Noyes, of Sudbury.

424. iv. LYDIA, bap. Apr. 16, 1710; m. Oct. 14, 1730, James Patterson. He res. in Watertown, Petersham and Princeton, where he d. May 4, 1766, and left wid. Lydia, who d. in 1776, ae. 66. Ch.: Jonathan, b. Nov. 30, 1735, killed by the Indians in the French war July 20, 1758. David, b. May 11, 1739. Andrew, b. Apr. 14, 1742; m. Oct. 21, 1761, Elizabeth Bond, of Worcester, and had, Sarah, b. 1764; Jonas, b. 1768.

425. v.   MARY, bap. June 30, 1712; m. Nathan Fiske, of Weston (See).

426. vi. HEPZIBAH, b. Oct. 30, 1713; m. May 14, 1747, Joseph Livermore, of Sudbury.

427. vii. BEZALEEL, b. Aug. 24, 1715; m. Beulah Frost, Tabitha Hyns and Rebeckah Rand.

428. viii. SAMUEL, b. May 3, 1717; m. Abigail Rice.

429. ix. BEULAH, b. Nov. 1, 1718; m. in Sudbury, 1737, Benjamin Stone. He was b. Feb. 20, 1717-8; d. 1745, leaving Benjamin, Lucy, Sarah. The wid. m. 2d, Dec. 23, 1747, Benjamin Eaton, of Framingham.

430. x.   WILLIAM, b. Sept. 4, 1720; m. Sarah Cutting.

431. xi. SARAH, b. Dec. 6, 1722; m. Apr. 9, 1746, Richard Heard, of Sudbury.

432. xii. ANNA, b. 1724; m. June 9, 1747, Henry Smith, of Sudbury.

433. xiii. DAVID, b. Sept. 4, 1726; m. Ruth Noyes.

434. xiv. BENJAMIN, b. Mar. 28, 1730; m. Abigail Maynard.

294. DR. ROBERT FISKE (David, David, Jeffrey, Robert, Simon, Simon, William, Symond), b. Watertown, Mar. 8, 1689; m. May 26, 1718, Mary Stimpson, of Reading, b. ———; d. Feb. 11, 1757. In 1711 he was a subscriber for the purchase of the common. He was ad. to the church in 1736. His residence was on Hancock street, where his father David had resided, and was one of the first settled places in the township. The present, which is probably the second house on

that spot, was erected in 1732. Robert Fiske was a physician, and probably the first of the profession in that place. His wife survived him but a few years.

The inventory of his estate sheds light upon the manners and customs of the age. Among other things, we find the following: Hat and wig 100s; Arms—yellow stock gun, 8£ 10s; little gun 5£; carbine 50s; brass pistols 50s; rapier and belt 12s; three staves 20s; two cans and two piggens 15s; one loom, quill wheel and warping bars, 50s; two pairs snow shoes 30s. Books—General Practice of Physic, 30s; English Dispensatory or Synopsis of Medicine 30s. The Structure and Condition of Bones 15s. By these items, it will be seen that the doctor was quite as well armed for the art of war as for the art of healing.

In the distribution of the estate of Dr. Robert Fiske, all of the real estate went to the older brothers of John, so that no deed from him appears to have been thereafter needed and in fact has not been found. 25 April, 1757, Robert Fiske of Woburn, Physician, gave to Joseph Fiske of Lexington, Physician and Jonas Parker of Lexington, laborer, a bond for £27, conditioned that David Fiske on coming of age would convey to Jonas Parker and Joseph Fiske his share in that one third of the estate of Robert Fiske, Physician of Lexington, deceased, which had been set off to his mother, Mary Fiske, widow of the said Robert. The sureties were John Fiske of Lexington, Dr. Jonathan and David Fiske of Woburn, John Buckman of Lexington and Mary his wife, and Lydia Wilson, widow of Lexington. These sureties were evidently the brothers and sisters of Robert, Joseph and David Fiske, mentioned in the body of the bond. 5 December, 1757. John Buckman of Lexington, filed his bond as administrator of that part of the estate of Dr. Robert Fiske, left unadministered by his widow, Mary, the sureties on the bond being John Fiske, Physician, of Lexington and John Fiske of Woburn, yeoman. He died Apr. 18, 1753; res. Lexington, Mass.

435. i. MARY, b. Feb. 8, 1718; d. Feb., 1719.
436. ii. MARY, b. Mar. 16, 1719; m. John Buckman, of Lexington. He d. Feb. 17. 1768, ae. 51. She d. Feb. 10, 1768, ae. 50. Ch.: Mary, b. Dec. 27, 1740; m. Feb. 16, 1766, Francis Brown, of Lex. John, b. Apr. 2, 1745; m. July 21, 1768, Ruth Stone, of Lex. He was an innkeeper and it was at his house that Capt. Parker and his patriotic men assembled on the evening of Apr. 18, 1775, and from this house they issued on the approach of the British the next morning. Shots were fired from this house upon the red coats after they had attacked the Americans upon the common, and some of the clapboards to this day give evidence that the fire was returned. Hist. Lex. 426. Sarah, b. Jan. 3, 1747; m. June 12, 1760, Jonas Stone, Jr., of Lex. Elizabeth, b. Jan. 11, 1753. Ruth, b. Dec. 30, 1755.
437. iii. ROBERT, b. Jan. 12, 1721; m. Mrs. Abigail Grover and Betty ——.
438. iv. SARAH, b. Sept. 26, 1723; d. young.
439. v. LYDIA, b. June 23, 1724; m. James Wilson, of Bedford.
[440. vi. JOSEPH, b. Oct. 13, 1726; m. Hepzibah Raymond.
441. vii. RUTH, b. Mar. 26, 1729; m. —— Farmer. She d. before 1755.
442. viii. JOHN, b. Nov. 8, 1731; m. Mary Ingalls.
443. ix. JONATHAN, b. Mar. 20, 1734; m. Abigail Locke.
444. x. DAVID, b. Mar. 8, 1737; m. Elizabeth Blodgett.

OLD BUCKMAN TAVERN.

295. LIEUT. EBENEZER FISKE (David, David, David, Jeffrey, Robert, Simon, Simon, William, Symond), b. Lex., Sept. 12, 1692; m. Dec. 4, 1718, Grace Harrington, of Wat., dau. of Samuel and Grace (Livermore), b. Aug. 26, 1694, d. Aug. 29, 1721; m. 2d, Bethia Muzzy, b. 1700, d. Nov. 19, 1774. His first wife died four days after the birth of their first child. The monumental stone in the old

burying ground at Lex. has the honorable prefix of Lieut. to his name. He appears to have been popular in his day, having been called to fill many offices in the town. He was selectman ten years, between 1739 and 1758. He resided on the road to Concord, a little more than a mile from the common, at the easterly side of a large swell of land, which from his residence and ownership has taken the name of "Fiske Hill." It was at this house that the gallant Hayward of Acton met a British soldier coming from the well, between whom shots were exchanged, with fatal effect on both sides. Benjamin, my son, "was to have my negro boy Pompee or it sd. do not survive me £30 in lieu thereof." He d. Dec. 19, 1775; res. Lexington, Mass.

445.   i.   GRACE, b. 1721; d. Aug. 25, 1721.
446.   i½.   EBENEZER, b. Mar. 5, 1725; m. Elizabeth Cotton.
447.   i¾.   BETHIA, b. Aug. 1. 1729; m. ———— Oliver, of Boston.
448.   ii.   ELIZABETH, b. May 7, 1731; m. Sept. 3, 1751, Rev. Robert
              Cutler. He was graduated at Harvard College, and was pastor
              in Greenwich, Mass., from 1755 until his death. His son Will-
              iam, b. Dec. 23, 1753, was a doctor in western Massachusetts
              until 1795; was also postmaster and justice of the peace.
449.   iii. JANE, b. Mar. 21, 1733; m. Oct. 28, 1752, Josiah Hadley.
450.   iv.   ANNA, b. July 30, 1735; m. Oct. 24, 1754, Oliver Barrett, of
              Concord. He was a grandson of the emigrant Humphrey
              Barrett. who came from England and settled in Concord in
              1640. Oliver settled in Chelmsford.
451.   v.   BENJAMIN, b. Mar. 24, 1737; d. young.
452.   vi.   SAMUEL, b. Oct. 15, 1739; m. ———— ————.
453.   vii. BENJAMIN, b. Aug. 10, 1742; m. Rebecca Howe.
454.   viii. SARAH, bap. Nov. 24, 1723; m. ———— Alless.

300. JAMES FISKE (James, James, Phinehas, Thomas, Robert, Simon, Si-
mon, William, Symond), b. Groton, Mass., Feb. 11, 1694; m. Mar. 23, 1736,
Lydia Bennett. James Fiske, of Groton, made his will on August 10, 1767, proved
April 13, 1771, in which he speaks of his eldest son James, second son Peter,
daughters Lydia and Mary, and youngest son John, wife Lydia. He d. 1767; res.
Groton, Mass.

455.   i.   JAMES, b. June 28, 1738.
456.   ii.   LYDIA, b. Feb. 20, 1740.
457.   iii. PETER. b. Mar. 16, 1743; m. Oct. 3, 1769, Rachel Kemp. He
              was born in Groton, and at the breaking out of the Revolu-
              tionary War enlisted in Capt. Parker's Company in Col. Pres-
              cott's Regiment from Groton. He was in the battle of Bun-
              ker Hill and killed in that engagement.
458.   iv.   MARY, b. June 9, 1746.
459.   v.   JOHN, b. Mar. 30, 1749; m. Anna Blood and d. July 12, 1821.
              Ch.: John, b. Nov. 15, 1776; d. Apr., 1811. Anna, b. June 3,
              1778. Molly, b. Feb. 20, 1780; d. Feb. 23, 1783. Nathaniel,
              b. Feb. 15. 1782; d. Mar. 16. 1783. Mary, b. Mar. 24, 1784.
              Lydia, b. ————. Anne, b. May 9, 1786. Nathaniel, b. Feb.
              7, 1788. Nabby, b. Oct. 22, 1789. Abel, b. Dec. 10 1791.
              James, b. Feb. 16, 1794; Sarah, b. Aug. 8, 1796; m. Nathan
              Gallott. and Feb. 23, 1857. resided in Groton. At that time
              she had one brother and three sisters living, but her grand-
              father's (James Fiske, Jr.) family were all dead, one of whom
              was killed in the battle of Bunker Hill.

301. SAMUEL FISKE (James, James, Phinehas, Thomas, Robert, Simon,
Simon, William, Symond), b. Groton, Mass., July 10, 1696; m. ———— ————.
Samuel Fisk, late of Newtown, yeoman, will dated June 14. 1769. proved Aug. 1,
1770, "Being advanced in age, but" Bequeaths to son Samuel and heirs, daughter
Lucy Whitin and heirs, dau. Abigail Parrish. wife of Samuel Parrish, dau. Mary
Hammond, wife of Samuel Hammond, to dau. Ann Fisk, to my gr. dau. Rebecca
Mills, to gr. son Elisha Mills, to my two sons, viz., Thomas & Aaron, all lands
and buildings. Aaron & Thomas were executors. He d. 1769; res. Newton, Mass.

460.   i.   SAMUEL. b. ————: m. ———— ————.
461.   ii.   LUCY. b. ———— ————; m. ———— Whitin.

462. iii. ANN, b. —— ——.
463. iv. MARY, b. —— ——; m. Mar. 13, 1755, Samuel Hammond, of Newton.
464. v. AARON, b. about 1763; m. Abigail ——.
465. vi. THOMAS, b. —— ——; was ex. of his father's will.
466. vii. ABIGAIL, b. —— ——; m. Samuel Parrish, son of Dea. Samuel Parrish.

304. JONATHAN FISKE (James, James, Phinehas, Thomas. Robert, Simon, Simon, Simon, William, Symond), b. Groton, Mass., Sept. 10, 1705; m. about 1731, Mary ——, d. May 11, 1742; m. 2d, Mar. 5, 1744, Sarah Wheeler, of Concord, d. May 11, 1762; m. 3d, May 18, 1763, Dorcas Fletcher, d. May 8, 1786. He was of Concord, a saddler by trade. His will was approved Mar. 13, 1783. He gave to his wife Dorcas all his estate in Reading and Pepperell, she to pay the debts, etc. To son Samuel Fisk, of Warren, R. I., to dau. Mary Davis, of Portsmouth, N. H.

The widow Dorcas, of Concord, made her will May 8, 1783; it was probated May 28, 1787; gave to William Fletcher of Norridgewock, Me., my only son; to Amos Fletcher son of William; to Dorcas Davis dau. of Zachariah Davis of Mason N. H; to dau. Mary Bond wife of Henry Bond of Royalston the remainder of the Estate to Henry Bond executor. He d. Feb. 22, 1783; res. Concord, Mass.

467. i. JONATHAN, b. Apr. 8, 1732.
468. ii. MARY, b. June 19, 1734; d. young.
469. iii. ELIZABETH, b. Feb. 14, 1735.
470. iv. MARY, b. Jan. 25, 1738; m. Zachariah Davis, of Portsmouth, N. H.
471. v. SAMUEL, b. May 22, 1740; m. Judith Rowell.
472. vi. SARAH, b. June 18, 1746; m. Apr. 19, 1764, William Fletcher, of Concord.
473. vii. PHINEHAS, b. Feb. 23, 1747; d. Mar. 12, 1747.

305. SAMUEL FISKE (Samuel, James, Phinehas, Thomas, Robert, Simon, Simon, William, Symond), b. in Groton, Mass., Mar. 5, 1704; m. Jan. 12, 1726, Elizabeth Parker; res. Groton, Mass.

474. i. ELIZABETH, b. Aug. 13, 1727; m. Mar. 3, 1746, Zachariah Shattuck.
475. ii. SAMUEL, b. Oct. 12, 1729.
476. iii. ELEAZER, b. Nov. 23, 1731; m. Esther ——; res. Dunstable, N. H. He d. June 21, 1803, leaving a large family.
477. iv. SUSANNA, b. Sept. 29, 1734.
478. v. MARY, b. Oct. 4, 1736; m. —— Elliot.
479. vi. JOSIAH, b. Sept. 27, 1739; d. Aug. 2, 1742.
480. vii. SARAH, b. Nov. 1, 1742.

308. THOMAS FISKE (Samuel, James, Phinehas, Thomas, Robert, Simon, Simon, William, Symond), b. Groton, Mass., Feb. 21, 1712; m. in Groton, Mass., —— 11, 1741, Mary Parker; b. Apr. 7, 1722; d. Mar. 30, 1791; dau. of John and Mary (Bradstreet) Parker. He was born in Groton, Mass., and always resided there. Pepperell was incorporated as a town in 1753, having been set off from Groton. It is said Thomas' farm was in that part of old Groton which was incorporated in the new town. After his death his widow married Robert Blood, by whom she had two children, Abigail, b. Nov. 23, 1758, d. Apr., 1855, and Robert, b. Dec. 14, 1760.

Thomas Fisk of Pepperell adm'n granted to Mary Fisk of said town his widow May 13 1754 Guardian app'd May 23 1760 over Thomas & Mary the children when they were over 14 years of age. Division of the Real Estate made May 29 1768 when the widow was wife of a Blood Thomas the eldest son had two thirds of the estate by paying out to his the other heirs viz his sister Mary dec'd bro John brother Wainwright Fisk who then had a guardian and to the heirs of his sister Sarah dec'd The house stood on the road leading from Townsend to Pepperell Meetinghouse and by land of Rev Joseph Emerson Acc't of Mary the adm'x given Jan. 3 1757 wherein she charges for "nursing the youngest child that died" & for Lying in &c.

He d. in P. Apr. 23, 1754; res. Groton and Pepperell, Mass.

481.   i.   MARY, b. Oct. 18, 1743. She d. unm. 1765. Middlesex Probate
Record, Vol. 29 p 157 Will dated May 3, 1765, proved Oct 29,
1765. Mary Fiske, of the district of Pepperell To Mary, wife
of Robert Blood "My kind & beloved mother," the whole of
estate, all, & both out of estate of my hon'd father Thomas
Fiske, late of Pepperell decs'd & also out of estate of my
grandmother Fiske deceas'd. (Eph'm Lawrence physician
Pepp. Ex'r.)

482.   ii.   THOMAS, b. Mar. 12, 1746; m. Sarah Shipley.

483.   iii.   JOHN, b. July 23, 1748; m. Anna Blood.

484.   iv.   WAINWRIGHT, b. Mar. 7, 1752; d. killed at the battle of Bunker Hill June 17, 1775; was a member of Capt. Nutting's Co.
of Pepperell, in Col. Prescott's regiment.

485.   v.   SARAH, b. Apr. 27, 1750. She d. unm.

311. BENJAMIN FISKE (John, John, Phinehas, Thomas, Robert, Simon,
Simon, William, Symond), b. 1683; bap. Milford, Conn., Mar., 1696; m. July 24,
1701, Abigail Bowen, of Rehoboth, dau. of Obadiah and Abigail (Bullock) Bowen
of Rehoboth. Two branches of Fiskes settled in Rhode Island as early as 1725,
respectively descended from Benj. and Samuel Fiske, who, according to tradition,
were brothers; they resided first in Rehoboth, but moved to Swanzey in 1711.
After Benjamin's removal to Rhode Island he was justice of the peace at Scituate for years.

He d. Feb. 14, 1765; res. Rehoboth and Swanzey, Mass., and Scituate, R. I.

486.   i.   MARY, b. Apr. 28, 1702; m. ———— Pierce.

487.   ii.   HEZEKIAH, b. June 11, 1704; m. ———— ———— and res. in
Scituate, R. I. He had a son Asa and prob. other ch.; he
died, Aug. 20, 1776.

488.   iii.   BENJAMIN, b. Mar. 8, 1706; m. Susannah Briggs.

489.   iv.   ELIZABETH, b. May 9, 1708; d. May 1, 1731, in Scituate.

490.   v.   DANIEL, b. Dec. 16, 1709; m. Freelove Williams.

491.   vi.   JOHN, b. Jan. 11, 1713; m. Elizabeth Williams.

492.   vii.   FREELOVE, b. Mar. 29, 1716; m. Joseph Fiske.

493.   viii.   JOB, b. 1711; m. Mary Whitman.

494.   ix.   NOAH, b. 1722; m. ———— ————.

495.   x.   ABIGAIL, b. ————; m. ———— Kimball.

312. EBENEZER FISKE (John, John, Phinehas, Thomas, Robert, Simon,
Simon, William, Symond), b. Wenham, Mass., in 1689; m. at Milford, Conn., in
1719, Mehitable ————; b. 1694; d. at New Milford Feb. 11, 1737; m. 2d, Nov. 11,
1741, Rebecca Trowbridge. Ebenezer Fiske, second son of Dr. John Fiske, of Milford, and executor of his will, was born in Wenham, settled in Milford upon the
paternal estate, where were born to him a family; but died at the residence of his
son, Ebenezer, in New Milford, same state.

May 21, 1709, John Fisk of Milford deed to his son Ebenezar Fisk one half
right in certain lands in New Milford. After May 19, 1737, Ebenezar Fisk is recorded of New Milford.

We find the following under the heading of "Sketches of Prominent Men"
in the history of New Milford: "Ebenezer Fisk, Sen., came from Milford in 1737,
and settled on Second hill, or on the west side of Town hill. His father, Doct.
John Fisk of Milford, bought a Right of land in New Milford, in 1709, and gave
half of it to his son Ebenezer, the same year, but the latter did not settle here
until 1737. Ebenezer, Sen., had a son Ebenezer Jr. who married and had a son
Ichabod, born in 1747, and apparently removed from the town not many years
after.

Inscriptions from stones in Cemetery: "Here lies the body of Mr. Ebenezer
Fisk. He died Oct. 4, 1747, in the 59th year of his age." "Here lies the body of
Mrs. Mehetabell Fisk, wife of Mr. Ebenezer Fisk, dec'd Feb. 11, 1737, in the 44th
year of her age."

He d. Oct. 4, 1747; res. Milford and New Milford, Conn.

496.   ii.   EBENEZER. b. Dec. 13, 1719; m. Sarah Hart and Sarah Newel.

497.   i.   MEHITABLE, bap. Aug. 10, 1718; m. Mar. 1, 1737, Richard
Platt, Jr., of Milford. She d. Apr. 8, 1775.

498. iii. HANNAH, b. Dec. 27, 1723; m. Oct. 22, 1741, Benijah Bostwick. In settlement of estate of 1st Ebenezar, records show Ebenezar (2d or Capt so called) bought out the interest of above two sisters at New Milford. Eb. 1st bot property in N. M. 1st in 1709, many deeds recorded there before his removal there, subsequently.

499. iv. ANN, b. May 23, 1725; m. Mar. 28, 1748, Samuel Bostwick (son of Major John Bostwick); was born at New Milford, Conn., Aug. 3, 1823. He married Anna Fiske, daughter of Ebenezer Fiske, March 28, 1748. S. B. died Sep. 23, 1789, and his wife Sep. 21, 1783. Their children were: Elisha, b. Dec. 17, 1784; Jared, b. Aug. 9, 1751; Samuel, Jr., b. Jan. 19, 1755. Elisha Bostwick was prominent in his town, holding such local offices as justice of the peace, town clerk, etc. The latter office he held for fifty-five years, resigning in his eighty-fourth year. He was in the Revolutionary war, serving as a lieutenant in the same regiment as Nathan Hale; was Lieut. Colonel of militia 1793, and Representative to the Assembly for fourteen terms. He died Dec. 11, 1834. He married May 14, 1786, Miss Betty Ferriss. She died July 13, 1834. Their children were: Jared, b. May 24, 1787; Betsey Ann, b. July 11, 1792; Samuel Randolph, b. 1799. Jared second son of Sam'l B. was a graduate of Yale, but died soon after. Samuel Bostwick Jr. (third son of Sam'l B. Sr.) married Polypheme Ruggles May 14, 1786. He was a graduate of Yale and attorney at law. Member of State Assembly one term. Ch.: Ann Fiske Bostwick, m. Jos. A. Bostwick: Hannah Lorain Bostwick, m. Hon. S. Sherwood, of Delhi, N. Y., 1814, a son is Samuel Sherwood, of 80 Washington Square, N. Y. city.

500. v. BENJAMIN, b. Jan., 1730; d. Feb. 5, 1730.

313. CAPT. JOHN FISKE (John, John, Phinehas, Thomas, Robert, Simon, Simon, William, Symond), b. Wenham, Mass., 1693; m. in Haddam, Conn., May 10, 1716, Hannah ———; d. Dec. 17, 1723; m. 2d, in Haddam, Oct. 2, 1724, Sarah ———. John Fiske, third son of Dr. John Fiske, was born in Wenham in 1693; settled in Haddam. He was captain in 1735; representative from Haddam in 1742; moved from Milford to Haddam before 1715, and thence to Middletown before 1749. He had two wives. Among his sons was Benjamin, who was a graduate of Yale College, 1747. A citizen of high respectability in Haddam, he was styled Capt. John Fiske. His children were all born in Haddam, Conn., but his residence at the time of his decease was that part of Middletown now known as Portland; here his son Benjamin was born. At the time of the proving of his will he was styled Captain, and in the inventory of his estate may be found mentioned his sword. We also find in the inventory a negro slave, appraised at £35. His wardrobe, included a wig which indicated respectability. He d. in 1761; res. Haddam and Portland, Conn.

501. i. JOHN, b. June 3, 1718; m. Ann Tyler.
502. ii. PHINEHAS, b. Nov. 12, 1734; said to have d. young.
503. iii. BENJAMIN, b. Haddam, Conn., Dec. 17, 1723; m. ——— ———.
504. iv. HANAH, b. Nov. 30, 1719.
505. v. MARTHA, b. Feb. 4, 1721.
506. vi. SARAH, b. May 9, 1727.

One dau. m. Rev. Goodrich, of Chatham, Conn.: another dau. m. Thomas Kilborn, of East Hartford, Conn., and the other m. Phinehas White, of Middletown, Conn.

314. REV. PHINEHAS FISKE (John, John, Phinehas, Thomas, Robert, Simon, Simon, William, Symond), b. Wenham, Mass., Dec. 2, 1682; m. in Saybrook, Conn., July 27, 1710, Lydia Pratt, dau. of John of Essex. Phineas, eldest son of Dr. John Fiske (born in Wenham, in 1682), graduated at Yale College in 1704, was a tutor there, and for some years acting president, before the institution was removed from Saybrook, in which position he acquired a high reputation as an instructor, and also rendered great service to the churches of the colony, by thoroughly fitting numbers of young men for the Gospel ministry. He received his

ordination at Haddam, Conn., in 1714, where he became the colleague and successor of Rev. Jer. Hobart, and died there, after a very successful pastorate of twenty-four years. Rev. Dr. D. D. Field, in his biographies of the early Connecticut clergy, speaks of him in high praise. "He was a man of piety and wisdom, sound in the faith, pleasant in intercourse, plain in reproof. His talents were solid, rather than brilliant; his sermons better calculated to inform the understanding than to remove the passions. A man of scientific attainments, of good literary abilities, and of true Christian deportment, his name was long remembered with sincere respects, in Haddam." Rev. Phinehas Fiske was married in Saybrook, and had three daughters who married clergymen. He d. Oct. 14, 1738; res. Haddam, Conn.

507.　i.　ABIGAIL, b. Aug. 14, 1718; m. 1st, Rev. Chilab Brainard. William Brainard, son of Deacon Daniel and Mrs. Hannah (Spencer) Brainard, was born in 1674. Settled on Haddam Neck. Father of Rev. Chilab Brainard, first ordained Minister of Eastbury Parish in Glastonbury, Conn. He married Abigail Fiske, daughter of Rev. Phineas Fiske, second minister of Haddam, Conn. Rev. Chilab Brainard died Jan. 1, 1739. After his death she was married to Rev. Noah Merrick, minister of Wilbraham, Mass., one of the ancestors of Hon. George Merrick, of Glastonbury, Conn. She died in 1807, aged 89 years.

508.　ii.　LYDIA, b. ———; m. Rev. Moses Bartlett, of Chatham, Conn.

509.　iii.　ELIZABETH, b. June 10, 1720; m. Rev. Nehemiah Brainard, of Eastbury.

510.　iv.　SAMUEL, b. Oct. 9, 1724. He was graduated at Yale in 1743, was subsequently a tutor there, and a licentiate, but was never ordained, being suddenly cut off by death, in his 26th year July 13, 1749.

511.　v.　ANNE, b. July 17, 1716; d. Feb. 6, 1731.

512.　vi.　JEMIMA, b. Oct. 25, 1722; d. Nov. 25, 1724.

513.　vii.　MARY, b. ———; m. Col. Hezekiah Brainard, of Haddam, Conn. He was a member of Congress from Connecticut.

321.　GEN. JOHN FISKE (Samuel, Moses, John, John, William, Robert, Simon, Simon, William, Symond), b. Salem, Mass., May 6, 1744 (memorial sermon says Apr. 10, 1744); m. there June 12, 1766, Lydia, dau. of Deacon Phippen; d. Oct. 13, 1782; m. 2d., Feb. 11, 1783, Mrs. Martha Hibbert, dau. of Col. John Lee of Manchester; d. Nov. 30, 1785; m. 3d., June 18, 1786, Mrs. Sarah Gerry of Marblehead, dau. of Major John and Elizabeth (Quincy) Wendell of Boston and wid. of John Gerry of Marblehead. She d. Feb. 12, 1804. Sarah Wendell was first married to John Gerry, who died in 1785 ae. 45. Her father, John Wendell, was son of John and Elizabeth (Staats) Wendell and grandson of Evart Jansen and ——— Wendell, who came from Embden, Prussia in 1645 and settled in Albany. Sarah's mother, Elizabeth Quincy, was daughter of Hon. Edmund and Dorothy (Flint) Quincy of Braintree, who died in London in 1737; and granddaughter of Col. Edmund and Elizabeth Gookin (Elliot) Quincy. Her daughter Sarah Gerry m. in 1785 Azor Orne, b. Mar. 1, 1762; d. Apr. 17, 1795. She d. Nov. 11, 1846. He was son of Col. Azor Orne of Marblehead. She was gr. dau. of Thomas and Elizabeth Gerry, who was father of Hon. Elbridge Gerry, at one time vice president of the United States. Gen. John Fiske was born in Salem, April 10th, 1744; was son of the Rev. Samuel Fiske, who was ord. at Salem, 8 Oct. 1718, when his was the only Church within the limits of the town. He died April 7th, 1770, ae. 81. The venerable Nathan Bucknam of Medway, who died Feb., 1795, ae. 92, was uncle to Gen. Fiske, whom he baptized at Salem, 6 May (1744). Gen Fiske "early engaged in the business of the Sea." In 1775 he was a master mariner and became captain of the "Tyrannicide," the first war-vessel commissioned by the state of Massachusetts, 8 July, 1776. He made many successful cruises in her, and was engaged in several sanguinary combats. On 10 Dec., 1777 he took command of the state ship "Massachusetts," a larger and a better vessel. After the Rev. war he engaged in commercial pursuits and acquired property. At the commencement of the American Revolution, his knowledge of the sea and personal intrepidity brought him into notice, and he was commissioned the first commander of a vessel of war by the government. At the close of the war, upon the reorganization of the State militia, he was commissioned a Colonel, then a Brigadier, and finally, in 1792, a Major General, which position he held until his death, in September, 1797.

He was a man of princely hospitality, of enterprising spirit, and benevolent impulses. He took a great interest in the various religious and charitable movements of his day, and contributed freely to their support.

There are more transfers of property on the Salem records of deeds from Gen. John Fiske than any other one of this name, and in ten volumes of the records he is about the only Fiske mentioned. He was a very large property owner and was continually buying and selling real estate. I give these few transfers to show something of his purchases:

John Fisk of Salem Gent. bought of David Ropes Jr of Salem Inholder 43½ poles of land & buildings thereon on the back st leading to the Training field in Salem bounded by Geo William, Thomas Pointon &c May 4 1778 John Fisk of Salem Esq bought of Sarah Lemmon widow of Salem Ferry Lane Salem 8 poles square bounded by heirs of David Northey on her other land & easterly on Skerrys lane so called Jan. 15 1779.

John Fisk of Salem Merchant bought of David Ropes of Salem yeoman & wife Priscilla a pew in the East parish meetinghouse Salem where Rev James Dimon officiated then Dec 7 1782 this being one that formerly was Thomas Frye's & mortgaged to Jona Glover.

John Fisk of Salem Merchant bought of John Prince of Halifax Co of Halifax Nova Scotia Merchant Lot No 8 Union Wharf Salem with store & wharf on said lot bounded &c June 7 1785 He also bought of Eben'r Phippen of Salem cabinet maker 12 3-10 poles of land with building, on Loder lane 2 poles 16 links &c July 9 1785 He bought of wid Sarah Lemmon of Salem on southerly side of his other land & bounded by Skerry's lane Mar 10 1786. He bought of Sarah Kimball of Salem widow 7¾ poles southerly on said Fisk's land 64 feet easterly on Sam'l Carleton Sept 1. 1785 He bought of Tim. Fitch of Boston & wife Eunice 1½ share in Long Wharf or Union Wharfes Salem with buildings thereon which estate was assigned to the aforenamed Eunice in the division of the estate of Mary Sherburne late of Boston dec'd—Oct 28, 1786 John Fisk of Salem & wife Martha sold to their kinswomen Fanny Glover Hannah Hibbert & Betty Johnson one third part of 2-3 of Dwellinghouse with land adjoining situate in the town of Manchester &c &c witnessed by Mary Orne & Anna Fisk Oct. 5 1785.

John Fisk Esq. of Salem [son of Rev Sam'l of Salem] Merchant Adm'n of his Estate was granted to Mrs Sarah Fisk his widow Nov 9 1779. and after her decease adm'n De Bonis Non was granted to John Watson Apr 16 1804 Inv. of his Estate was taken Nov 28 1790 and an additional one taken May 3 1804 whole amt about $65,000.00. Widows thirds set off May 6. 1799. Division of the Estate made among the children Apr. 27, 1800, at that time 3 children were living viz: Nancy wife of Edward Allen, Eliz'th wife of Eben Putnam & John Fisk. John the son died previous to Aug 2. 1800, when Benj Pickman. Esq. his guardian app'd Nov. 9, 1797 when he was over 17 years of age received a receipt from Edward Allen & Eben'r Putnam who married his sisters of his Estate received by them. Accts. of the Adm'x & of the Adm'r (De Bonis Non) June 25, 1799.

Mrs. Sarah, [widow of] John Fisk of Salem made her will Jan 18, 1804 which was proved Apr 16, 1804, by Hannah Batchelder Henry Osborn & Tabitha Glover. Legatees Sister Dorothy Skinner & Catherine Davis each had $100, and the use of a part of her homestead during their lives Grandaughter Sally Wendal Orne, Grandsons, John Orne, Gerry Orne Henry Orne. Mrs. Anna Allen wife of Capt Edward Allen of Salem Mrs Eliz'th Putnam wife of Eben'r Putnam, Widow Sarah Stevens, Humane Charitable Society of Salem. Daughter Sarah Orne widow & John Watson gentleman of Salem.

A Funeral Discourse was delivered in the East Meeting house, Salem, on the Sunday after the death of Major General Fiske, who died Sept. 28, 1797, ae. 53. By William Bentley. A. M. Pastor of the Second Congregational Church in Salem. Boston: 1797." 8vo. pp. 37.

He died of apoplexy Sept. 28, 1797; res. Salem, Mass.

514. i.   ANNA. b. 1770: m. Capt. Edward Allen of Salem. Mass.
515. ii. ELIZABETH, b. July 19. 1778; m. Nov. 13. 1796, Ebenezer Putnam, M. A. Among the Graduates of Harvard originating from Salem was Ebenezer Putnam, son of Dr. Ebenezer Putnam (H. U. 1739): he lived, for the most part, without pro-

fession, in Salem; m. (1 & 2) Sally and Elizabeth, daughters of Gen. John Fiske. He d. Feb. 25, 1826. Ebenezer, b. Sept. 6, 1797. Harriet, b. and d. May, 1799. John Fiske, b. May 25, 1800. Charles Fiske, b. Oct. 19, 1802. George, b. Jan. 10, 1804; d. unm. Dec. 4, 1860. He was a well known druggist in Salem, and a great lover of flowers and fruits which he cultivated with great success. Edward, b. Jan. 23, 1806. Francis, b. Jan. 3, 1808. ·

516. iii. JOHN, b. 1779; d. young.

517. iv. SALLY, b. June 30, 1772; m. May 22, 1791, Ebenezer Putnam, M. · A. Sally died Jan. 7, 1795; Elizabeth d. Mar. 1808. Ch.: Ebenezer, b. Aug. 27, 1792; d. July 5, 1796. Harriet, b. Feb. 5, 1794; d. Nov. 22, 1794.

517½.v. LYDIA, b. 1768.

517¾.vi. MARY, b. 1774.

For ages of his children see appointment of his guardian of his children, July 11, 1783.

324. WILLIAM FISKE (William, William, John, William, Robert, Simon, Simon, William, Symond), b. Wenham, Mass., 1695; m. in Nov., 1723, Mary Kinney, of Salem, who d. Mar. 15, 1725; m. 2d, May 22, 1729, Mrs. Sarah (Buck, town records say Sarah Fish (not Fisk) of Woburn.

William Fiske of Andover carpenter bought of Saml Smith of Andover 2 acres of meadow in andover eastwardly of said Smith house mar 4 1719-20.

William Fisk of Andover had then, viz., Jan. 22, 1732, for his wife Sarah, who had been the wife of an Ebenezer Fish (not Fisk), who had remained a widow three years before she married this Wm. Fiske. In Jan., 1732, Ebenezer Fish, her son by her former husband, chose his father-in-law (as he called him), Wm. Fiske, to be his guardian, at which time he is in his fifteenth year of age. His guardian in 1742 was Ephraim Buck. Res. Andover, Mass.

518. i. MARY, b. Sept. 19, 1724; d. Jan. 26, 1726.

519. ii. WILLIAM, b. Apr. 1, 1731.

520. iii. ASA, b. Feb. 28, 1739; d. Mar. 23, 1739.

521. iv. MARY, b. Apr. 28, 1730.

522. v. RACHEL, b. Dec. 7, 1733.

522½.vi. SON, b. Jan. 9, 1736.

326. EBENEZER FISKE (William, William, William, John, William, Robert, Simon, Simon, William, Symond), b. Wenham, Mass., 1703; m. Jan., 1730, Susanna Buck, of Woburn. She d. in Tewksbury, May 28, 1754. Ebenezer Fiske, of Andover, County of Essex, was appointed guardian of Benjamin in his seventh year and Jonathan in his fifteenth year, children of Ebenezer, of Reading, Mar. 20, 1737.

May 29, 1738, an additional account was filed of Sarah Fiske, widow of Ebenezer Fiske, late of Reading, and administratrix on the estate. William Fiske, husband of the said administratrix, who made the payments and performed the services, presents the foregoing and made oath, etc. Res. Andover, Mass., and Tewksbury, Mass.

523. i. EBENEZER, b. 1730; Elizabeth Richardson.

524. ii. EPHRAIM, b. ———; m. Mehitable Frost.

525. iii. BENJAMIN, b. ———. Date of his birth torn off of old Andover record book.

526. iv. JONATHAN, b. ———. Date of his birth torn off of old Andover record book.

526¼.v. CHILD, b. Apr. 14, 1731; d. same day.

526½.vi. DAUGHTER, b. May, 1741; d. same day.

334. JOSIAH FISK (Samuel, William, William, John, William, Robert, Simon, Simon, William, Symond), b. July 7, 1702; m., Rehoboth, June 20, 1723, Sarah Bishop, both of Rehoboth. He died intestate, and his son John was appointed administrator as per records in the Cumberland town clerk's office at Valley Falls, R. I. Josiah Fiske removed to Rehoboth, where he remained a few years, and then removed to Cumberland, R. I., and purchased a farm and remained there until his death. His son John inherited the homestead. He d. Jan. 27, 1773; res. Rehoboth, Mass., and Cumberland, R. I.

527. i.   ESTHER, b. May 4, 1725.
528. ii.   SAMUEL, b. Rehoboth Mar. 23, 1727.
529. iii.   JOHN, b. Cumberland Feb. 20, 1729; m. Mary Bartlett.
530. iv.   RACHEL, b. July 1, 1730; m. in Cumberland Aug. 20, 1749, Benoni Studley; res. Cumberland.
531. v.   JOYCE (dau.), b. Feb. 24, 1732.
532. vi.   SARAH, b. Sept. 5, 1733.
533. vii.   JONATHAN, b. Aug. 13, 1739; m. Hannah ———.
534. viii. MARTHA, b. May 10, 1741.
535. ix.   MARY, b. Apr. 12, 1743.

341. MARK FISKE (Joseph, William, William, John, William, Robert, Simon, Simon, William, Symond), b. Ipswich, Mass., Nov. 20, 1716; m. Sept. 5, 1738, Lydia Smith. He was executor of his father's will. She owned the covenant in 1749, and d. Sept. 21, 1761; m. 2d, Mar. 12, 1762, Mrs. Eleanor Abbott. She d. Apr., 1766. Res. Ipswich, Mass., and Wells and Kennebunk, Me.

536. i.   LYDIA, b. Dec. 23, 1739; d. Sept. 27, 1759.
537. ii.   JOSEPH, b. Jan. 31, 1741; m. Eleanor Abbott and Margaret Hobbs.
538. iii.   MARK, b. Feb. 12, 1743; n. f. k.
539. iv.   JOHN, b. Mar. 30, 1746; d. young.
540. v.   SUSANNA, b. Apr. 10, 1748.
541. vi   JOHN, b. 1755; m. ——— Wakefield and Comfort Stover.
542. vii.   ABNER, bap. Jan. 26, 1755. He served in the Revolutionary Army from Massachusetts as private, and later as sergeant. He was pensioned Mar. 4, 1834, when he was 78 years of age, and at that time resided in York County, Maine.
542¼.viii. ELIZABETH, bap. Mar. 25, 1750; m. Oct. 1, 1772, John Abbott.
542½.ix.   SARAH, bap. Apr. 5, 1752.
542¾.x.   RUTH, bap. Mar. 27, 1757; d. Mar. 17, 1759.

350. THEOPHILUS FISKE (Theophilus, William, William, John, William, Robert, Simon, Simon, William, Symond), b. Ipswich, Mass., May 31, 1709; m. Jan. 11, 1737, Jemima Goldsmith, b. 1715; d. Jan. 23, 1784. She was admitted to full communion with the church in Wenham in Aug., 1737. She died in Topsfield. Their first two children were born in Wenham, but in 1742 and 1750 when he purchased lands of his father, his residence was in the northern part of Salem, now Danvers. He was there as late as 1765, and in 1771 was in Topsfield, a short distance from the borders of Danvers and Wenham, where he was when he made his will, Nov. 4, 1775, which was proved Mar. 5, 1781, the day after an inventory of his estate was taken. The real estate consisted of homestead ninety acres, land in Boxford eight and one-half acres, and salt marsh in Ipswich four acres. Whole amount of inventory £1.058 4s. 4d., $1.481 of old Continental money, valued £5 18s. 5d., and a four dollar bill, new money valued at 12s. 10d.

Theophilus Fisk of Topsfield yeoman made his will Nov 4, 1775, which was proved Mar 5, 1781. Inv. of the Estate was taken Mar 4 1781 90 acres land in the homestead, 8⅛ acres wood land in Boxford 4 acres Salt Marsh in Ipswich. Old Continental Money $1481.00—£5.-18-5 whole amt. of Inv. £1085-4-4 Jemima Fisk the wid. gives a receipt to son Saml the Executor Apr 2, 1781 that she had recd the household furniture willed by her husband. Legatees—wife Jemima. Daughter Tabitha & Jemima unmarried Son Nath'l & Son Benjamin, the deceased had a daughter Sarah Fisk under 21 years Son Samuel to have the residue & be Executor of the will.

He d. Mar., 1781; res. Ipswich, Mass.

543. i.   BENJAMIN, b. Oct. 30, 1738; m. Sarah Towne.
544. ii.   NATHANIEL, b. Mar. 1, 1740; m. Lydia Gould.
545. iii.   SAMUEL, b. 1748; m. Sarah Perkins.
546. iv.   JEMIMA, b. 1749; admitted to the church July 2, 1786; d. unm., Mar. 2, 1795.
547. v.   SARAH, b. ———.
548. vi.   TABITHA, b. 1744; was admitted to the Topsfield church, July 3, 1785; d. unm., Oct. 22, 1823.

351. THOMAS FISKE (Theophilus, William, William, John, William, Robert, Simon, Simon, William, Symond), bap. Ipswich, Mass., Aug. 24, 1707; m.

———— ————; m. 2d, ———— ————. He received his share of his father's estate prior to his death, by deed, Apr. 2, 1757, half of the homestead and the westerly. half of the house. He d. s. p.; res. Ipswich, Mass.

357. EBENEZER FISK (Ebenezer, William, William, John, William, Robert, Simon, Simon, William, Symond), b. in Wenham, Mass., July 2, 1716; m. in Upton, Jan. 28, 1739, Dorcas Tyler, an aunt of President John Tyler.

The original Indian name of the territory, embraced in the town of Shelburne, was "Quabbin." On the 30th of June, 1732, the General Court granted seven townships of land, six miles square each, to the descendants of the soldiers who destroyed the Narraganset fort, on the 19th of Dec., 1675. The number of soldiers was 840. This gave a township of six miles square to each 120 soldiers. These townships were granted on condition that each township should settle at least 60 families on its territory within seven years after the grant, settle a learned Orthodox minister, and lay out a lot of land for him and one for the school. If these conditions were not complied with the grant was to be void. On the 6th of June, 1733, the proprietors met on Boston Common, at 2 o'clock in the afternoon, when they voted that the grantees should be divided into seven societies, one township to be given to each society. Narraganset township No. 4 was first laid out in New Hampshire, but the committee reported that it was not fit for a settlement. Accordingly, on the 14th of Jan., 1737, the General Court granted to the proprietors of No. 4 the territory of Quabbin in exchange for the New Hampshire township. After surveying Quabbin, it was found to contain considerably less than six miles square. So the Court granted a tract of land lying west of, and adjoining to, Hatfield, sufficient to make up the full amount of territory to which the grantees were entitled. This tract is now embraced within the boundaries of Chesterfield. The territory of Shelburne was originally included in Deerfield, and was at first called "The Deerfield Pasture," and afterward "Deerfield North West." It began to be settled not far from 1756. The first two settlements were made near Shelburne Falls, by families from Deerfield. The early settlers were soon obliged to retire, on account of the French and Indian war. The first permanent settlements are supposed to have been made about 1760. Among the first settlers was Ebenezer Fisk. The town was incorporated June 21, 1768, and was named after Lord Shelburne of England, who, according to the usual tradition, gave the town a bell which, as usual, was lost after it had arrived at Boston. The first town meeting was held Oct. 31, 1768, at the house of Daniel Nims. Capt. John Wells, from Deerfield, was the first town clerk; Ebenezer Fiske, constable. Among the descendants of Ebenezer and Dorcas were seven who entered the Christian ministry, inclusive of Rev. Pliny Fiske, of the Syrian mission, Rev. Dr. Ezra Fiske, of Goshen, N. Y., and Rev. Dr. D. T. Fiske, of Newburyport, Mass.

A valuable cane, supposed to have been brought from England and willed by the Deacon to his second son, has been inherited by a male in this family in every generation since, the last possessor being Ebenezer Fiske of Adrian, Mich. Ebenezer and Dorcas resided in Upton, later moving to Grafton, thence to Hardwick, and finally locating in Shelburne, where he died.

He d. 1804; res. in Grafton, Hardwick and Shelburne, Mass.

549.   i.   JOHN, b. Sept. 27, 1757, in Grafton; m. Anna Leland.
550.   ii.   SIMEON, b. July 15, 1762, in Hardwick; m. Dinah Whitcomb.
551.   iii. DORCAS, b. Oct. 17, 1740.
552.   iv.   ELIZABETH, b. Jan. 28, 1743.
553.   v.   JONATHAN, b. Sept. 17, 1746; m. Hannah Rice.
554.   vi.   EBENEZER, b. Sept. 9, 1749; m. Sarah Barnard.
555.   vii. LEVI, b. Dec. 16, 1751. He served through the Revolutionary War. He d. s. p.
556.   viii. ABIGAIL, b. Oct. 7, 1755; m. Samuel Barnard, of Shelburne, Mass., Nov. 26, 1782, and removed to Waitsfield, Vt., in 1793. Their son Ebenezer was born Nov. 30, 1783, and married to Experience Barnard, of Deerfield, Mass., Jan. 19, 1808. He d. Feb. 21, 1862. Joanna, their daughter, was b. Oct. 12, 1810, married to Anson Fisk Nov. 24, 1835 (see).
557.   ix.   MOSES, b. Sept. 13, 1764; m. Hannah Batchelor.

359. JACOB FISKE (Ebenezer, William, William, John, William, Robert, Simon, Simon, William, Symond), b. Wenham, Mass., Dec. 26, 1721; m. (Int), Nov. 5, 1743. Elizabeth Lampson, of Ipswich; res Wenham and Hardwick, Mass.

 558. i.   ELIZABETH, b. Mar. 4, 1745; m. Nov. 12, 1761, David Allen, b. Aug. 18, 1738; d Aug. 5, 1799. He was Selectman and Assessor, Hardwick. She d. Oct. 22, 1791; m. 2d, Jan. 22, 1794, Lydia Woods. One of his children by his first wife was David Allen, b. May 12, 1771; d. Jan. 20, 1835, Hardwick; m. Apr. 27, 1794, Ruth, dau. of Job and Mercy (Hinckley) Dexter b. Mar. 20, 1773; d. Mar. 26, 1847. Two of their children were Clarissa Allen, b. Oct. 7, 1796; d. Mar., 1852. She m. Amaziah Spooner. Willard Allen, b. Feb. 8, 1801; d. Sept. 24, 1852. He m. Mercy P. Ruggles. Another was Lydia, who m. David Fisk.

 559. ii.   JONATHAN, b. May 17, 1747, in Wenham; d. May 22, 1747.
 560. iii.   ABIGAIL, b. Aug. 17, 1750.
 561. iv.   SARAH, b. Dec. 28, 1752.
 562. v.   DAU., b. Sept. 24, 1758.

361. WILLIAM FISKE (Ebenezer. William. William. John, William. Robert, Simon, Simon, William, Symond), b. Wenham, Mass., Nov. 30, 1720: · 25, 1749, Susannah Batchelder, of Wenham. She m. 2d, Benjamin Davis. She was b. 1731; d. 1810.

Joseph Bachelder, the first representative from Wenham (1644), emigrated in 1638, in company with his brothers, Henry and Joshua, who went to Ipswich, and John, who settled with him at Salem. Joseph soon after removed to Wenham, and, according to Dr. Allen, his descendants continue there to this day. Among his children (probably) were Joseph, Mark, David, John and Ebenezer. Ebenezer was constable in 1714. and Mark was one of the five drafted in King Philip's war and perished in the fierce assault upon the fort of the Narragansetts, 1675. David Bachelder, a grandson of Joseph, Sen., by wife Susanna, had sons David, Joseph, Amos, Nehemiah and Abraham. and daughters Mary and Susanna. The latter married William Fiske, Sen.. of Amherst. Her brothers Joseph, Amos, and cousins Israel, Josiah and Ebenezer, were Revolutionary soldiers. The name on the records is frequently spelled Batcheller and Bachelor.

David Batchelder made his will Aug. 25, 1759. which was proved Mar. 11, 1766. Wife Susannah to have the Easterly end of the house &c, son David, son Joseph, son Nehemiah—son Abraham—Daughter Mary to have ten shillings &c— Daughter Susannah to have ten shillings to be paid at the end of one year after my decease also my largest Brass Kettle—son Amos to have the whole estate excepting the above legacy, to be executor.

Wm resided in Wenham, Mass., and in 1774 removed to Amherst, N. H., where they settled on a tract of land on the south side of Walnut Hill. He was the executor of his father's will. He was the founder of the Amherst. N. H., branch. He resided at the ancient homestead in Wenham, where probably his father, himself and his own children were all born, after the decease or removal of his parents and immediate relatives. Of himself personally, little is known, except that in his character and principles he was a stanch Puritan. His father and grandfather were successively deacons in the original Wenham church for upwards of seventy years; the same ancient church of which Rev. John Fiske himself was the original pastor. More remotely still the family had been identified with that great reformatory struggle in England. from which were fathered the rich fruits for a purer faith and constitutional liberty.

Having been appointed sole executor of his will and principal heir by Deacon Ebenezer Fiske, William Fiske remained in Wenham long enough to settle the estate and dispose of the homestead and various tracts of land, when (in 1773 or 4) he removed to Amherst, N. H., with his wife Susanna. nine children and two daughters-in-law, Mary Bragg, the wife of their son Jonathan and Eunice Nourse, wife of their son William. The father. William, Sen.. purchased a tract of land in Amherst. The situation was cozy. well sheltered and watered. but the country then was mostly a wilderness and the land rough. rocky and heavily timbered, requiring immense labor and sturdy courage to clear it off. The fatigue and exposure incidental to establishing the new home under such straitened circumstances. doubtless bore hard on all the members of the family. and must have contributed directly to the father's death, as he lived but a few years after. But they were glad to get away from the disturbances then thickening along the sea-board, and in hopes that the distance from the seat of impending (British) war, would in a measure secure them from its horrors that are attended with every war, its privations and hardships.

Mr. Fiske lived to see his country proclaimed free and independent and his family settled in comparative comfort, and died in 1777, in the 82d year of his age. His widow Susanna was appointed administratrix of his estate June 10, 1777. His widow, surviving many years, married again and died about 1810 at quite an advanced age. Of their sons and daughters all except Anne married, and she and two others excepted William and David remained in Amherst, and settled elsewhere. Some of them raised large families and all more or less prospered in circumstances and the good esteem of their fellow-citizens. Of them all it is believed that it may be truly said that their lives were blameless and their end calm and full of peace.

He d. in June, 1777; res. Wenham, Mass., and Amherst, N. H.

563. i.   JONATHAN, b. May 1, 1751; m. Mrs. Mary Bragg.

564. ii. ELIZABETH, b. June 27, 1753; m. Oliver Roby, of Merrimack, N. H. She d. s. p.

565. iii. WILLIAM, b. Apr. 20, 1755; m. Eunice Nourse and Hannah Walker.

566. iv. DAVID, b. June 25, 1757; m. Edith Tay.

567. v. MARY, b. Oct. 21, 1759; m. Nov. 10, 1785, Dr. Samuel Lolley, a physician of Francistown, N. H. She d. in the prime of life, leaving ch.: 1 Paulina, m. Samuel Stevens; he d. 1851; she d. Jan., 1862. 2 Minerva, m. Charles Wells, of Francistown.

568. vi. EBENEZER, b. Feb. 11, 1762; m. Abigail Woodbury.

569. vii. JOHN, b. Apr. 11, 1764; m. Miss Varnum, of Mt. Vernon, N. H. He was a blacksmith; res. Mt. Vernon, Williamstown and Berlin, Vt. He d. s. p.

570. viii. SUSANNAH, b. Oct. 2, 1766; m. William Bennett, of Lunenburgh, Mass.; res. near Babboosack Pond, Merrimack. N. H., and Washington, where he died leav'ng: 1 William, 2 Thomas, 3 Oliver, 4 John, 5 Susan, 6 Eliza. She moved to Gennesee Co., N. Y., and to Western Reserve, Ohio.

571. ix. ANNE, b. Aug. 22, 1771; d. unm. in Amherst.

367. SAMUEL FISKE (Samuel, Samuel, William, John, William, Robert, Simon, Simon, William, Symond), b. Boxford, Mass., 1716; m. Feb. 1, 1738, pub. Dec. 11, 1737, Judith Noyes, of Newbury.

During the French and Indian conflict we find the names of some of the Boxford men who were in the service. They were in the company of Capt. Joseph Frye, of Andover, doing service at Scarborough. The time of service of Samuel Fiske was from April 27, 1748, to May 1, 1749. His wife was sick while he was serving as soldier in the French and Indian war. Mrs. Fiske had probably gone to the fort to help take care of the sick, and fell a victim to the disorder. The winter was close upon them, and considerable snow having already fallen, the soldiers proceeded to Ticonderoga, where they encamped over night and hurried on their homeward way next morning. They marched in as direct a line as possible, through Vermont and New Hampshire, and reached home just before the first of December.

Samuel Fisk of Boxford yeoman & wife Judith sold to Jona. Bixby of same town yeoman 70 acres in Boxford with house & barn thereon near the house of said Sam'l Fisk bounded "Beginning at a stake & stones by ye Fishing brook running southerly to a stake & stones near ye house of s'd Samuel Fisk then turning Westerly about a rod & half to another stake & stones then running southerly to a stake & stones near ye edge of ye plain by ye Hills, then running a little more Westerly to a stake & stones near ye stripet then running N. Westerly to a little Walnut tree market with stones about it then running S. Westerly over ye stripet to a stake & stones * * more westerly * * near ye upper corner of Redington's meadow which line from ye Fishing brook to Redington's meadow is a parting line between s'd Sam'l Fisk & John Fisks land so on to ye meadow then running &c &c by John Stiles John Emerson so on to Andover line southerly by Mary Stickney stiles again * * & on s'd Fishing brook to bounds first mention also 2 acres in Reddingtons meadow bounded by Elias Smith John Fisk & John Stiles May 23 1746 & ack'd July 14, 1747.

Samuel Fisk of Boxford hus'man bought of Jona. Bixby of Boxford yeoman several parcels in Boxford Viz: 21 acres with a house & part of a barn bounded beginning at a stake & stones near the fishing brook by land of John Fisk running Northerly to an Elm tree standing on the edge of said brook then running south-casterly 22 poles & 2 foot to a stake & stones then running southwesterly to a stake & stones near the hills then running southeasterly 9 poles & ten feet to a stake and stones by land of John Stiles then running westerly by land of said Stiles to a stake & stones over the first stripet by land of the said Bixby then running northwesterly to a little swamp Oak marked with stones about it so on to a stake & stones by land of s'd John Fisk then running Northeasterly by land of said Fisk over the stripett to a Walnut tree market with stones about it and on all other parts bounded on land of the above named John Fisk Also Another piece viz Wood land * * 3 acres * * by land of John Fisk above * * by the path called "Reddington's Meadow Path" Mar 1 1748-9 ack'd Sept 28 1756.

Samuel Fisk of Boxford adm'n was granted to Judith his widow Apr. 6, 1761. Inv. of the Estate taken May 17, 1761. 20 acres in the homestead 2 acres wood land. Addes, Broadaxe, Augers, saw &c wid. Judith presented her acct. of adm'n to the Court May 9, 1763 in which she says she paid the town of Boxford for their Expence on Jonathan Peabody's child'n & due from said Fisk by ye acct. of adm'n, on said Peabody's estate this day. Samuel Fisk above was admt. of the estate of Jonas Peabody and after his decease Judith his widow rendered an account of admn. of this estate.

Samuel Fisk & wife Judith of Boxford Husbandman sold to Thomas Perkins of Topsfield blacksmith 24 acres & 132 poles of land in Boxford bounded by Andover line, Eame's meadow, Elias Smith & Reddingtons meadow &c Dec. 15, 1741 ack'd by him & wife Sept. 24, 1742.

He d. 1761; res. Boxford, Mass.

    572. i.   SARAH, b. Dec. 13, 1738; m. Sept. 16, 1772, Oliver Towne, of
                 Topsfield.
    573. ii.   MARY, b. Feb. 20, 1740.
    574. iii. JUDITH, b. June 17, 1743.

    369. JOHN FISKE (John, Samuel, William, John, William, Robert, Simon, Simon, William, Symond), b. Dec. 30, 1715; m. May 31, 1750, Mary Bridges. She d. Apr. 13, 1763. He joined the church by profession in May, 1763.

John Fisk of Andover new parish labourer bought of John Abbot Jr of same parish yeoman & his wife Phebe all their right title & interest in ye lands buildings & meadows hereafter named excepting our right in our mother Abigail holt her thirds in said lands buildings & meadows lying in Boxford * * and is part of ye living or estate of our father John Fisk late of Boxford aforesaid dec'd which right of ours hereby conveyed is ye one third of two third parts of said premises the first & principal piece containing in ye whole about seventy acres be ye same more or less together with a dwellinghouse & barn thereon * * bounded "beginning at a rock at ye fishing brook running southerly by Tho Cummings's land * * N westerly by Cummings's * to a small brook, thence southerly by other land which was our s'd father's to Redington's meadow to a white oak * * & on all other parts bounded by ye land of Sam'l Fisk & ye Fishing brook And also one piece of meadow lying in Redington's meadow * * 2¼ acres * * And one piece of Dirty meadow containing 2 acres more or less together with our right in ye salt marsh which was our s'd fathers lying in Rowley containing in the whole 2 acres more or less * * and also a lott of wood land * by ye Fishing brook above the Sawmill * * 40 acres * bounded by J Cummings, by "land above mentioned which was our fathers to where a brook runs out of Redingtons meadow" * * by Elias Smith, & Sarah Fisk's land. Also 2 acres of "Eight mile meadow" also another piece of 1½ acres on Fishing brook called "ye works pond" bounded by John Stiles, John Peabody and "by a gutter runing out of ye Ironworks swamp" To Have &c   Oct. 11, 1738.

John Fiske of Andover, "being far advanced in years, as renders it evident, I am near the period of my life. I have therefore thought it best to discharge my mind so far as the social duties of life will admit of to the end I may spend the remainder of my days in preparation for that future state, into which I am hastening." Made his will Apr. 25, 1800, which was proved Sept. 2, 1811. His real estate con-

sisted of homestead of 35 acres, 40 acres near Joel Jenkins two lots in Falls woods
& meadow 11 acres 4 acres on Salem road below Peter Holt's, 15 acres of pasture
near Peter Holt's, Saw mill pasture of 20 acres, wood lot Farmer meadow 20 acres
Pine Hill lot and meadow 10 acres, 20 acres on the plain whole amt. $3,000. Leg-
atees in will were daughter Mary Fisk to have the use of ½ the estate, great gnd
child daughter of gndson Abbott and the testators grand daughter Hepzibeth,
his wife lately deceased to have $500. Daughter-in-law Hepzibeth Burnet, family
wife of son John Fisk deceased to have $50. Gndson Isaac Abbott Jr. to have all
the buildings. He was executor. .

He d. Aug. 14, 1811, ae. 96; res. Andover and South Andover, Mass.

    574¼. i.   JOHN, b. July 15, 1751; m. Hebzibeth ———.
    574½. ii.   MARY, b. Jan. 5, 1753; d. unm. June 29, 1810.
    574¾. iii.   JOSIAH, b. abt. 1760; d. Apr. 23, 1781.

    370. SAMUEL FISKE (Daniel, Samuel, William, John, William, Robert,
Simon, Simon, William, Symond), b. Wenham, Mass., Feb. 14, 1728; m. in Upton,
Mass., by Rev. Elisha Fish, Mar. 24, 1756, Sarah Partridge, of Medway. Samuel
Fiske, third son of Daniel and Sarah (Fuller) Fiske, was married to Sarah Partridge, of Medway, and settled first in Upton, and subsequently in Shelburne. In
the former place were born to him Comfort, Samuel, Sarah and Daniel. The
latter married his cousin, Huldah Fiske, who lived to be over 95 years, a widow,
and the mother of twelve children, all deceased but one. The eldest son, Samuel
Fiske, married also his cousin, Rebecca Fiske, a daughter of Benjamin. Of their
ten children, six died young. He d. Sept. 25, 1797; res. Upton and Shelburne,
Mass.

    575. i.   COMFORT, b. Dec. 13, 1756.
    576. ii.   SAMUEL, b. Apr. 14, 1759; m. Rebecca Fiske, his cousin.
    577. iii.   SARAH, b. in Upton Oct. 14, 1761.
    578. iv.   DANIEL, b. May 16, 1765; m. Polly Crosby, and Huldah Fiske,
        his cousin.
    579. v.   DAVID, b. ———; d., ae. 17.
    580. vi.   SETH, b. ———; d., ae. 8.

    371. DANIEL FISKE (Daniel, Samuel, William, John, William, Robert,
Simon, Simon, William, Symond), b. Wenham, Mass., June 17, 1718; m. Zilpha
Tyler. After his death she married a man by the name of Aldrich. He d. in Rev.
Army; res. Holliston and Upton, Mass.

    581. i.   ROBERT, b. Feb. 24, 1746; m. Mary Hall.
    582. ii.   ZILPHA, b. Apr. 16, 1753; m. Jan. 26, 1792, in Upton, Peter For-
        bush, of that town (Samuel, Thomas, Thomas, Daniel), b. Up-
        ton, Mass., Feb. 16, 1754. He was in the Rev. War; res. Upton,
        Mass. Ch.: Elijah, b. Mar. 12, 1778; m. Anna Nelson. Patty,
        b. Feb. 15, 1780; d. Oct. 9, 1780. Aaron, b. June 11, 1782.
        Esther, b. Oct. 5, 1783.
    583. iii.   HANNAH, b. Upton Mar. 28, 1756; m. in Upton by Rev. Elisha
        Fish Jan. 27, 1778, Isaac Nelson, of U.
    584. iv.   DANIEL, b. 1759; m. Hannah Rockwood and Hannah Palmer.
    585. v.   SUBMIT, b. Oct. 27, 1758; m. in Upton by Rev. Elisha Fish,
        June 25, 1778, William Putnam, of Upton. Had Lydia Putnam,
        b. Mar. 4, 1779; Hannah Putnam, b. June 14, 1781; Elisha
        Putnam, b. May 18, 1786; Wm. Putnam, Jr., b. Mar. 15, 1788;
        Zilpha Putnam, b. Apr. 15, 1789; Daniel Putnam, b. Feb. 29, 1790
        Sarah Putnam, b. Feb. 6, 1792; Abner Putnam, b. July 28, 1794;
        Submit Putnam, b. July 11, 1797. Wm. Putnam, Jr., b. Mar.
        15, 1788; d. Sept. 30, 1865. His wife (Lurany Shepard) d. Oct.
        4, 1875. They had Lexana Lurany Putnam, b. Apr. 13, 1830;
        m. Apr. 10, 1851, Wm. H. Stetson, b. Aug. 31, 1828. They had
        Idella Lurany Stetson, b. Apr. 4, 1852; m. ——— Edward Field
        Doane. She had Karl Wallen Doane, b. Dec. 20, 1880, and she
        m. 2d, Dec. 26, 1886, Levi T. Coats. Mrs. Wm. H. Stetson, of
        Buckland, Mass., is a descendant.

        Submit Fisk (Daniel, wife Zilpha Tyler; Daniel, wife Sarah
        Fuller; Samuel, wife Phebe Bragg; William, wife Bridget Mas-
        kett) married William Putnam, son of (William, son of Elisha,

son of Elisha, son of Edward, son of Thomas, son of John.
See p. 275, "Putnam History") Dea. William Putnam and
Lurany Shepard. Lurany Shepard was dau. of Isaac Shep-
ard, Jr., and Sarah (6) Leonard. This Sarah Leonard's husband's
father was first deacon, husband second deacon, son Isaac
third deacon in the church at "Baptist Corner," in Ashfield,
Lyon. Sarah Leonard (dau. (5) wife Mary, Joseph (4) wife
Lyon. Sarah (6) Leonard (dau. (5) wife Mary, Joseph (4) wife
Mary, Joseph (3) wife Martha, Jacob (2) wife Phebe, Solo-
mon (1)) m. Isaac, Jr., son of Isaac and Jemima (4) Smith
(Chileab (3) Preserved (2), Rev. Henry (1)).

373. BENJAMIN FISKE (Daniel, Samuel, William, John, William, Robert, Simon, Simon, William, Symond), b. Upton, Mass., May 7, 1724; m. Rebecca
———; m. 2d, Keziah ———. His will is dated Aug., 1805. Witnesses, Josiah
and Abijah Fisk and Seth Hastings. He d. Aug. 10, 1805; res. Upton, Mass.

    586. i.   BENJAMIN, b. May 1, 1749; m. Jemima Holbrook and Margery
                  Wood.
    587. ii.   MARY, b. Nov. 4, 1750; d. Nov. 26, 1750.
    588. iii. DANIEL, b. Jan. 24, 1758.
    589. iv. ICHABOD, b. June 18, 1761; d. before 1805.
    590. v.   REBECCA, b. Jan. 8, 1764; m. Jan. 23, 1784, in Upton, by Rev.
                  Elisha Fish, her cousin, Samuel Fiske, of Shelburne.
    591. vi. MARY, b. ———.
    592. vii. OBADIAH, b. ———.
    593. viii. ELIZABETH, b. ———.
    594. ix. REBECCA, b. ———; d. in infancy.

375. LIEUT. WILLIAM FISK (Daniel, Samuel, William, John, William,
Robert, Simon, Simon, William, Symond), b. Wenham, Mass., Apr. 14, 1733; m.
1757, Jemima Adams, dau. of Obadiah of Mendon. She d. in Upton, Oct. 3, 1813.
He was born in Wenham, Mass., in the town where his ancestors settled on coming to this country from England. On moving to Upton he was united in marriage and ever after resided there. The births of his children are recorded in
Grafton also. During the Revolutionary War he was lieutenant in the Upton
company. He served the town in various public offices of trust and honor; was
a member of the Congregational church, and highly respected in the community.

A descendant in writing from Grafton says: On his Gravestone is inscribed
"In Memory of Lieut William Fisk who died March 9, 1818 Aged 85 years" He
served in the Revolutionary War was with Washington when a part of the British
Army was captured at Trenton New Jersey was Town Treasurer many year, Select
and Tithing-man often. He worked on his Farm & in his cooper shop. He had
a meat Tub which was made in England & brought to America by one of his
Ancestors which is still in use at the old Homestead has never been repaired but
appears to be sound & in order for future use.

The old inhabitents of Upton (Those who descended from the first setlers
do not increase & multiply very fast from Four to Ten was the number of children in families formerly—in Ben Fisks family seventeen was numbered two are
omitted in the Book.

Now only from one to five children are counted & one perhaps one family in
six has none. the size of the Fisks is less now than formerly Five feet ten
inches was the common height & from 160 to 190 pounds the common weight.
Now the common height is less than five feet eight inches & the weight less than
160 pounds."

He d. Mar. 9, 1818; res. Upton and Grafton, Mass.

    595. i.   JEMIMA, b. Mar. 19, 1758; m. in Upton, June 4, 1778, Enoch
                  Batcheller. Ch. b. Upton: Sarah, b. Dec. 28, 1781; Mary, b.
                  Feb. 10, 1784; Adams, b. Feb. 28, 1787; Enoch, b. Sept. 11,
                  1789; David, b. May 25, 1792; Huldah, b. Feb. 21, 1796; Levi,
                  b. Aug. 11, 1798; Jemima, b. Feb. 17, 1801; Susanna, b. May 1,
                  1804. The mother d. Aug. 29, 1846.
    596. ix. LYDIA, b. ———; m. in Upton, June 18, 1781, Josiah Torrey,
                  of Upton; went to N. H.

597. iii.   MARY, b. Apr. 29, 1770; m. Reuben Lewis. Had seven children born in Chesterfield, N. H. She d. in Shelburne, ae. 83.
598. vii.   RHODAH, b. ———; m. in Upton, by Rev. Elisha Fish, May 14, 1789, Silas Forbush. He was b. in Grafton, Mass., May 19, 1766, the son of David and Anna (Whitney) Forbush. [See History of Grafton by Fred C. Pierce; Forbes Forbush Genealogy by Fred C. Pierce; and Whitney Genealogy by Fred C. Pierce.]

They were the great-grandparents of the author of this work. Their daughter Nancy married Nathaniel Smith; their daughter Maria N. married Silas A. Pierce; their son is Frederick C.
599. viii. LEVI, b. Upton, Mass., Jan. 21, 1765; m. Aug. 27, 1789, Elizabeth Jane Tait. He d. in Upton, Mass.
600. v.   ELISHA, b. Nov. 4, 1774; m. Betsey Forbush.
601. iv.   HULDAH, b. Nov. 6, 1772; m. Daniel Fiske, of Shelburne. He was a farmer and cooper. She d. in 1866.
602. vi.   DAVID, b. Sept. 6, 1780; m. Sally Stowe and Lydia Allen.
603. ii.   Elisha, b. Aug. 18, 1760; d. young.

SILAS FORBUSH.

376. JOSIAH FISKE (Daniel, Samuel, William, John, William, Robert, Simon, Simon, William, Symond), b. Wenham, Mass., Feb. 2, 1735; m. Jan. 20, 1762, Sarah Barber. She d. June 2, 1771; m. 2d, in Upton, June 10, 1772, Lydia Daniels; m. 3d, Nov. 16, 1783, Elizabeth Gore. He d. in Upton; res. Upton, Mass.
604. i.   JACOB, b. Nov. 22, 1762.
605. ii.   JOSIAH, b. Oct. 20, 1764; m. Kezia Wood.
606. iii.   ABIJAH, b. Dec. 8, 1766; m. Betsey ———.
607. iv.   MARY, b. Nov. 7, 1768.
608. v.   SARAH, b. Mar. 10, 1771; d. Mar. 11, 1771.
609. vi.   ASA, b. Oct. 23, 1773.
610. vii.   SARAH, b. July 22, 1776.

381. DANIEL FISKE (Samuel, Joseph, William, John, William, Robert, Simon, Simon, William, Symond), b. Swanzey, Mass., May 10, 1710; m. Mercy Stone; m. 2d, Sarah Stewart. He was a cooper. He d. in Swanzey in 1764; res. Johnston, R. I.
611. ii.   AMOS, b. ———; m. Mary Wilbour.
612. i.   SAMUEL, b. ———; m., and res. in Rhode Island, and had Rufus, Amos, Daniel.
613. iii.   CALEB, b. ———.
614. iv.   WILLIAM, b. ———.
615. v.   JOSEPH, b. ———.
616. vi.   REUBEN, b. ———.
617. vii.   DANIEL, b. ———.
618. viii. MARY, b. ———.
619. ix.   MERCY, b. ———.
620. x.   MEHITABLE, b. ———.
621. xi.   ABIGAIL, b. ———.

382. JOSEPH FISKE (Samuel, Joseph, William, John, William, Robert, Simon, Simon, William, Symond), b. Scituate, R. I., June 8, 1708; m. Freelove Fiske, dau. of Benjamin of Scituate. He was born in Scituate, R. I., where he resided, finally moving to Providence, and later to Johnston, R. I., where he died. He was possessed of a comfortable estate at his death. Called "yeoman," also "cooper." 1735 Scituate R. I. He was living in Scituate this year and

his two first children's births were recorded in that town. (Scituate was set off from Providence in 1731.) 1744 Providence. He had returned to Providence at this date. 1759 Mar 6 Johnston was set off from town of Providence, and was henceforward his home, though his residence did not change. (That is to say the change in town lines carried him into another town.) 1774 His household consisted of 4 males above 16 and 2 females. (Probably himself, wife, 1 daughter and 2 youngest sons and a hired man.) His son Ephraim at this date had 8 in his family. 1784 Oct 4 Will probated (Made in 1762 July 3). Executors wife Freelove and son Ephraim. To wife the improvement of land north side of Plainfield Road till son Isaac is 14, for the support of children. To son Ephraim a lot in Cranston and £100. To daughter Lois Fiske 2 beds and £20. To daughter Sarah Fiske 2 beds and £20. To son Joseph the house and barn where his grandfather Samuel Fiske lived. To son Isaac the house and barn where I now dwell. To 2 sons Joseph and Isaac remainder of real estate. To 7 children Patience Tracy, Elizabeth Kimball, Ephraim, Lois, Sarah, Joseph, and Isaac Fiske, all movable estate, with a double portion to Ephraim. (This was because he was the oldest son). Inventory £90, 12s. 5d. viz. 1 blue broad cloth great coat, blue straight bodiced serge coat, a snuff colored serge jacket, blue broad cloth straight bodiced coat and breeches, &c, a castor hat, tobacco pouch, pair of braided garters, old warming pan, pewter plates, platters, basin &c, lignum vitae salt mortar, 5 beds, clock, quilt wheel, linen wheel, woolen wheel, 8 weavers sleighs, cedar cheese tub, cedar churn, 16 chairs, large bible, 4 tables, &c.

He d. Aug. 27, 1784; res. Providence, Scituate and Johnston, R. I.

622. i. EPHRAIM, b. ———; m. Lydia Mattewson.
623. ii. JOSEPH, b. ———; m. ——— Knight, and rev. to northern New York.
624. iii. ISAAC, b. June 15, 1757; m. Mercy Fenner.
625. iv. PATIENCE, b. Apr. 12, 1735; m. Prince Tracy.
626. v. ELIZABETH, b. Feb. 20, 1736; m. ——— Kimball.
627. vi. SARAH, b. ———; m. Abner Burlingame.
628. vii. LOIS, b. ———; m. ——— Hammond and Robert Potter.

385. PHINEHAS FISK (Samuel, Joseph, William, John, William, Robert, Simon, Simon, William, Symond), b. ———; m. in Providence, Jan. 19, 1728, Mary Colwell. He d. before 1784; res. Providence, R. I.

629. v. FISHER, b. Sept. 29, 1742; m. June 20, 1784, Hannah Dyer, dau. of Samuel; res. No. Providence, R. I.
630. i. JOHN, b. Aug. 1, 1729.
631. ii. PHINEAS, b. Apr. 8, 1731.
632. iii. AMEY, b. Oct. 14, 1733; m. Samuel Fenner, in Cranston, Sept. 6, 1764.
633. iv. JONATHAN, b. May 24, 1735.

388. LIEUT. JOHN FISKE (John, John, Nathaniel, William, Robert, Simon, Simon, William, Symond), b. Wat. (West precinct, Waltham), May 15, 1687; m. June 7, 1711, Mary Whitney, dau. of Samuel and Mary (Bemis), b. Sept. 30, 1689, d. Feb. 27, 1726; m. 2d, Dec. 14, 1727, Elizabeth Chinery, dau. of John, b. Jan. 27, 1690, d. 1768. His will was proved in the Worcester Probate office Nov. 21, 1758. He d. Nov. 2, 1756; res. Waltham and Worcester, Mass.

634. i. MARY, b. Dec. 28, 1711; m. Nov. 25, 1735, Samuel Hagar. He was the son of Samuel, b. Sept. 1, 1698. By his first wife he had four ch., and by Mary ten ch.: Samuel, b. Sept. 9, 1736; m. Mary Boyington; res. Wal. Moses, b. Sept. 27, 1737; Mary, bap. Dec. 3, 1738; Jonathan, b. Mar. 18, 1741; Abigail, bap. Jan. 20, 1743; Sarah, bap. Aug. 26, 1744; John, bap. Dec. 8, 1745; Susan, b. Oct. 26, 1746; Elijah, b. Oct. 13, 1744; Lucy, bap. Jan. 29, 1748.
635. ii. ABIGAIL, b. Nov. 11, 1714; m. June 5, 1734, Stephen Sawin. He was b. Sept. 17, 1712, the son of John and Elizabeth (Coolidge); res. Wat. Ch.: Jonathan, b. Jan. 2, 1734; Samuel, b. Feb. 17, 1737; Benjamin, b. Feb. 12, 1739; John, b. Nov. 22, 1742; David, b. Mar. 1, 1744.
636. iii. JOHN, b. June 10, 1716; m. Azubah Moore.
637. iv. SARAH, b. May 14, 1718. At her father's death she was unm.

638. v.   JONATHAN, b. June 27, 1729; m. Abigail ———.
639. vi.   DAVID, b. June 16, 1734. He d. Nov. 23, 1777. His will is
             dated Nov. 13, 1777. In it, on record in the Worcester Pro-
             bate office, is mentioned his brother John, sister Abigail, sister
             Mary Hager, sister Sarah and brother Jonathan.
639½.vii.   DANIEL, b. about 1730; m. Sarah Kendall.

390. JONATHAN FISKE (John, John, Nathaniel, William, Robert, Simon,
Simon, William, Symond), bap. Wat. Dec. 8, 1689; m. Apr. 10, 1716, Lydia Bemis,
dau. of John, b. about 1692. He settled in Newton, near Judge Fullers; res.
Newton, Mass.
      640. i.   LYDIA, b. July 21, 1717; m. Nov. 24, 1737, James Cooke, of
                   Wat. He was b. Mar. 3, 1713. She d., and he m. 2d, 1759,
                   Mary Foster, who d. 1770; res. Newton and Framingham. Ch.:
                   Jonathan, b. Dec. 3, 1738; m. Lydia Bacon; 7 ch. Lydia, b.
                   Jan. 22, 1739. Stephen, b. June 24, 1741; m. Mary Miller.
                   Mary, b. Newton; d. 1750. Enoch, b. Jan., 1744; m. Mary
                   Foster. Zebiah Fiske, b. Feb. 26, 1746. Elizabeth, b. July 8,
                   1748. Rebecca, b. June 18, 1753. Esther, b. May 4, 1755.
                   James, b. Jan. 8, 1758.
      641. ii.   ZEBULON, b. Apr. 30, 1719.

393. DAVID FISKE (John, John, Nathaniel, William, Robert, Simon, Simon, William, Symond), b. Watertown, Mass., Apr. 13, 1697; m. in Windham,
Conn,. Dec. 25, 1723, Elizabeth Durkee.
      He was born in Watertown, Mass., and while a young man emigrated to the
colony of Connecticut and located in Windham, one of the oldest places in that
state, where he ever after resided. Eli C. Fisk, of Havanna, Ill., in writing in relation to his ancestor said: "Our ancestor dropped the final e from the family
name and settled first in Mass., and when Hooker went to Conn. in 1636 he accompanied him. Many of his descendants still remain in Conn., but in the early
days some went into Rhode Island. Hence the early Conn. and R. I. Fisks dropped
the final vowel from their names. In the fall of 1867 or spring of 1868 James
Fisk (one of my father's brothers) of Omro, Wis., paid me a visit; he also told me
the same story in respect to our ancestors being one of Hooker's party and that
he was the person that dropped the final e of the family name. Also my father
told me the same, and it came in this way. I received a letter from Stephen Fisk
(another brother of my father) of Wales, Mass., who lived on the old homestead
there that signed the letter e to his son's name. Both of my parents said it did
not belong there, and that the Fisk that emigrated to Windham, Conn., with
Hooker dropped it, and none of the family had ever assumed it since. Now you
have my authority for my statement."
      He was a farmer. He d. Mar. 25, 1748; res. Windham, Conn.
      642. i.   DAVID, b. Nov. 3, 1724; d. Nov. 24, 1724.
      643. ii.   DAVID, b. Dec. 17, 1726; m. Sarah Farnam.
      644. iii.   JOHN, b. Aug. 27, 1729; d. Mar. 3, 1735.
      645. iv.   JONATHAN, b. July 4, 1731; m. Elizabeth Scott and Sarah
                   Leach.
      646. v.   ASA, b. May 26, 1733; m. Elizabeth Knight.
      647. vi.   ELIZABETH, b. Mar. 6, 1736; m. May 14, 1752, Samuel Webb.
                   He was b. in Braintree, Mass., May 14, 1690, and died in Rock-
                   ingham, Vt., Mar. 16, 1779, ae. 89. His first wife was Hannah
                   Ripley, dau. of Joshua and Hannah (Bradford) Ripley. Eliz-
                   abeth d. s. p. By his first wife he had four ch. Res. Wind-
                   ham, Conn., and Rockingham, Vt.
      648. vii.   JOHN, b. Apr. 17, 1738; d. May 31, 1742.
      649. viii. AMAZIAH, b. Feb. 15, 1742; d. Aug. 19, 1745.

398. THOMAS FISKE (William, John, Nathaniel, William, Robert, Simon,
Simon, William, Symond), b. Wat. Sept. 12, 1701; m. June 24, 1725, Mary Pierce,
dau. of Joseph and Hannah (Monroe); b. Mar. 28, 1705. He d. Sept. 28, 1778;
res. Watertown, Mass.
      650. i.   HANNAH, b. Sept. 29, 1727; m. May 1, 1746, Nathan Perry, b.
                   May 2, 1718; res. Wat.; ch.: 1 Hannah, b. July 24, 1747, d.
                   Jan., 1748; 2 Hanah, b. June 1, 1749; 3 Nathan, b. Mar. 30, 1751.

651. ii.   JOHN, b. Apr. 24, 1728; m. Elizabeth Harrington.
652. iii. ABIJAH, b. Mar. 12, 1729; m. Elizabeth Upham.
653. iv.   DAVID, b. Oct. 8, 1731; m. Elizabeth Mansfield and Rebecca
           Garfield.
654. v.   MARY, b. May 20, 1733.
655. vi.   JONATHAN, b. May 14, 1735; m. Abigail Lawrence.
656. vii. LYDIA, b. May 2, 1737; m. Dec. 9, 1756, Jonathan Wellington,
           Jr., b. June 5, 1736. Ch.: Elisha, b. July 20, 1758; m. Lucy
           Cutter. He was of Lexington.
657. viii. ABIGAIL, b. Aug. 16, 1739; m. Apr. 30, 1760, Jonathan Fiske,
           of Weston. (See.)
658. ix.   LOIS, b. Oct. 16, 1741; m. May 3, 1764, Joseph Hagar, Jr., of
           Waltham, b. Dec. 31, 1736; d. Oct. 1, 1776; res. Waltham.
           Ch.: Joseph, b. Feb. 16, 1765; m. Abigail Flagg. Lois, b. Mar.
           30, 1767; m. Jacob Gale. Susanna, b. Apr. 20, 1769; m. Joseph
           Garfield. Miriam, b. Feb. 26, 1772; m. Thomas Bigelow.
           Grace, b. May 10, 1774; m. Abraham Fiske. Anna, b. June 9,
           1775. Uriah, b. Aug 26, 1776; gr. Harvard College, 1798;
           M. D., 1816; Selectman, 1805-6-8-9-14-15; d. Apr. 1, 1841.
659. x.   EUNICE, b. Dec. 4, 1743; m. July 2, 1761, Daniel Mansfield, b.
           Oct. 8, 1740, son of Samuel and Elizabeth (Benjamin). Res.
           Wat. Ch.: Jacob, bap. Nov. 14, 1773.
660. xi.   SARAH, b. Sept. 19, 1745; m. Apr. 16, 1765, John Lawrence, of
           Wal., son of John and Mary (Hammond), b. Nov. 30, 1740.
           She was dismissed to the Concord church Jan. 17, 1803. Ch.:
           Amos, b. Nov. 1, 1766. John, b. Oct. 28, 1769; d. July 26,
           1776. Joshua, b. Nov. 6, 1770. Sarah, b. July 13, 1772. Mary,
           bap. July 10, 1774. Anos, bap. Nov. 10, 1776. Abigail, bap.
           Feb. 21, 1779.

399. WILLIAM FISKE (William, John, Nathaniel, William, Robert, Simon, Simon, William, Symond), b. Wat. Mar. 13, 1703; m. Nov. 14, 1733, Mary
Sanderson, dau. of Edward and Mary (Parkhurst), b. Apr. 18, 1710. She d. in
childbed, July 8, 1734. The real estate of William Fiske was assigned to Mary
Bridge, wife of Nathaniel and only child of William. William Fisk of Waltham
adm'n granted to Nath'l Bridge of said town yeoman Apr 21 1760 Mary the wife
of Nath'l Bridge who was the daughter & only child had the estate there was of
the real estate over 100 acres & bounded by a Sam'l Fisk. He d. Mar. 28, 1760;
res. Waltham, Mass.
661. i.   MARY, b. July 1, 1734; m. Apr. 5, 1753, Cornet Nathaniel
           Bridge; res.. Camb. and Waltham. He was Selectman 1767-77.
           Ch.: William, b. Mar. 2, 1754; m. Elizabeth ———. Mary, b.
           June 11, 1756; m. William Coolidge and Dea. Matthias Brut
           of Fram. Abigail, b. July 24, 1758; m. Nathaniel Bemis of
           Wat. Nathaniel, b. Sept. 24, 1760; m. Nancy ———; gr. Har-
           vard College, 1782, a teacher. Matthew, b. Aug., 1763; d.
           Sept., 1763. Anna, b. Aug. 3, 1765; m. Isaac Sanderson.
           Sarah, b. June 14, 1768; m. Solomon Flagg.

400. JOHN FISKE (William, John, Nathaniel, William, Robert, Simon,
Simon, William, Symond), b. Wat. Aug. 24, 1706; m. June 13, 1734, Sarah Child,
dau. of Daniel and Beriah (Bemis), b. Sept. 14, 1702. Res. Waltham, Mass.
662. i.   DAVID, bap. Oct. 12, 1735.
663. ii.   ABIGAIL, bap. Sept. 4, 1737.
664. iii. JOHN, bap. Mar. 25, 1739.
665. iv.   BULAH, bap. July 25, 1742; m. Apr. 16, 1767, Jonathan Wheeler.

401. DEA. SAMUEL FISKE (William, John, Nathaniel, William, Robert,
Simon, Simon, William, Symond), b. Wat. Jan. 4, 1709; m. Feb. 26, 1734, Anna
Bemis, b. Apr. 29, 1714. After his death she m. Apr. 26, 1763, Hopestill Bent, of
E. Sudbury, b. Nov. 4, 1708, d. 1772. She d. in Walth., a wid., Jan. 7, 1793, ae. 80,
s. p. by second husband. Samuel of Waltham Inv. of his estate
May 18 1761 sworn to by the executors viz Jonas Dix and Mrs Anna Fisk
Apr 26 1762 Guardian to son William app'd Apr 25 1763 when he was under 14
years of age & again a guardian when he was in his 15th year viz in July 1768 Acct

of adm'n made Apr 26 1762 they charge Paid legacys to Sam'l Gale & wife **Anna** to Eliphalet Hastings & wife Susannah to Flagg & wife and to Hobbs & wife **Lucy** His clothing was given by him to his two sons.

Division of his real estate Oct. 11 1762 some of it was by Great Pond by land of a John Fisk by Horse Shoe Meadow and at Prospect Hill the agreement was signed by Anna & Sam'l Fisk—sons Sam'l & Wm had each a third & the widow had the other third.

He d. Mar. 29, 1761; res. Watertown, Mass.

    666. i.   ANNA, b. Jan. 14, 1735; m. July 17, 1755, Samuel Gale. He was b. May 6, 1726; d. May 6, 1793. She d. June 2, 1800. Ch.: Samuel, b. Sept. 11, 1756; d. in the Rev. Army, unm., in the autumn of 1776. Jacob, b. Apr. 14, 1758; m. Lois Hagar. Anne, b. Feb. 28, 1759; m. John Cutting. Alpheus, b. 1761; m. Lydia Hammond. A son of his, Wm., was gr. at Harvard. 1810; d. 1839.

    667. ii.   ELIZABETH, bap. Aug. 28, 1737; m. May 6, 1756, Nathan Hobbs, of Weston, b. there in 1731. They had ten children, four sons and six daus.; three daus. d. young. Ch.: Betsey, m. Amos Pierce, of Waltham. Lydia, m. Ebenezer Ballard, of Weston. Lucinda, m. 1802, her second cousin, Gardner Watkins, of Sturbridge. William, b. 1761; m. Matilda Child. Nathan, b. 1765; m. Lydia Child. John, b. 1771; d. unm., Nov., 1802. Amos, b. 1774; m. Sally Gould.

    668. iii.   GRACE, b. Nov. 7, 1739; m. May 6, 1756, Samuel Flagg, b. June 18, 1733. They res. in Wat. and Spencer. Ch.: Susanna, b. Nov. 7, 1760; m. Solomon Cook; res. Charlton. Sarah, b. Mar. 17, 1763; m. John Guilford. Samuel, b. July 24, 1765. Hannah, b. Sept. 19, 1767; m. Elias Adams. Esther, b. ———; m. Apr. 26, 1791, James Adams. Polly, m. July 5, 1796, John Bemis. Josiah, m. Dec. 29, 1797, Mary Adams.

    669. iv.   SAMUEL, b. Nov. 2, 1741; m. Abigail White.

    670. v.   SUSANNA, b. Oct. 6, 1743; m. Aug. 20, 1760, Eliphalet Hastings, son of Eliphalet; res. Walth. Ch.: Lucy, b. Sept. 30, 1761. Elias, b. Feb. 13, 1763; m. Lucretia Whitney. Susanna, bap. Feb. 17, 1765; d. Sept. 8, 1775. Louisa Ann, b. Apr. 19, 1767; d. Aug. 31, 1775. Wm., bap. Sept. 17, 1769; m. Betsey Abbott.

    671. vi.   LUCY, b. Nov. 21, 1746; m. May 10, 1764, Enoch Hammond, of Newton. He was b. in Waltham Oct. 29, 1734. They res. in Petersham, Mass., and both died there.

    672. vii.   WILLIAM, b. Dec. 28, 1753; m. Hannah Cook and Ruth Smith.

405. DEA. NATHAN FISKE (Nathan, Nathan, Nathaniel, William, Robert, Simon, Simon, William, Symond), b. Wat. Jan. 3, 1672; m. Oct. 14, 1696, Sarah Coolidge, b. about 1678, dau. of Ensign John of Wat., d. Nov. 27, 1723; m. 2d, May 22, 1729, Mrs. Hannah (Coolidge) Smith, b. Dec. 7, 1671, dau. of Simon and wid. of Daniel Smith, Jr., b. Mar. 15, 1668, d. May 14, 1718. She d. Oct. 4, 1750. He was born in Watertown and often held office; was Representative 1727-28-29-32, and much confided in by his townsmen. He was Selectman 1711-14-17-19-20-22-23-24-26-27; Town Treasurer, 1720-22-23; Town Clerk, 1724-28-39; was elected Deacon as early as 1717. His estate was administered upon by his son Samuel. The will of his widow Hannah, dated Sept. 12 and proved Oct. 22, 1750, mentions three ch. of her brother Joseph; ch. of brother Obadiah, d.; ch. of cousin (nephew) Obadiah Coolidge, d.; ch. of kinsman Joshua Grant; ch. of eldest sister Mary, and ch. of her sister Sarah. He d. Jan. 26, 1741; res. Watertown, Mass.

    673. i.   SARAH, b. 1697; bap. Dec. 4, 1698; d. Nov., 1713.

    674. i½.   ELIZABETH, d., ae. 7 years.

    675. ii.   NATHAN, b. Feb. 25, 1701; m. Anne Warren and Mary Fiske, of Sudbury.

    676. iii.   JOSIAH, b. Oct. 10, 1704; m. Sarah Lawrence.

    677. iv.   HENRY, b. Jan. 24, 1706; m. Mary Stone.

    678. v.   DANIEL, b. Aug. 19, 1709; m. Deliverance Brown and Jemima Shaw.

    679. vi.   SAMUEL, b. Feb. 16, 1711; m. Lydia Bond.

680. vii. GRACE G., b. May 9, 1714; m. Sept. 25, 1733, Benjamin Goddard of Shrewsbury. She d. in Hopkinton Oct. 28, 1803, ae. 90. He was b. Aug. 15, 1704; d. Jan. 28, 1754, esteemed for his usefulness and piety. Res. Shrewsbury. Ch.: Grace, b. Jan. 1, 1736; m. Jasper Stone. Benjamin, b. Feb. 19, 1738; d. Sept. 23, 1740. Sarah, b. Jan. 8, 1740; m. Joseph Nichols. Benjamin, b. Mar. 29, 1742, deacon and farmer, m. Hannah Williams, Lucy ——— and Betsey Russell. Susanna, b. Aug. 4, 1744; m. Rev. Isaac Stone of Douglass. Nathan, b. Aug. 4, 1746; gr. Harvard College, 1770, a lawyer; m. Martha Nichols of Fram. Lydia, b. Aug. 2, 1748; d. unm. Hannah, b. Oct. 10, 1750; m. Silas Heywood of Royalston. Submit, b. Aug. 4, 1754; m. James Puffer of Sud.

681. viii. HANNAH P., b. May 19, 1719; m. Feb. 15, 1743, William Smith, Jr., of Weston, b. May 23, 1721. She d. Sept. 2, 1813, ae. 94; res. Wat. Ch.: George, b. Sept. 20, 1745; William, b. Feb. 14, 1748; Mary, b. Oct. 18, 1750; Lydia, b. Apr. 24, 1754; David, b May 6, 1756; Hannah, b. June 27, 1758.

409. WILLIAM FISKE (Nathan, Nathan, Nathaniel, William, Robert, Simon, Simon, William, Symond), b. Wat. Nov. 10, 1678; m. Nov. 3, 1708, Eunice Jennings of Fram., b. 1686, dau. of Stephen, who settled in Framingham, Mass., in 1690, and who m. Jan. 1, 1685, in Sudbury, Hannah Stanhope. After William's death his widow m. Jan. 3, 1754, William Johnson. He d. Mar. 16, 1759; res. Willington, Conn. Ch.: Lydia, b. Feb. 14, 1755; Sarah, b. July 19, 1757; Benjamin, b. Dec. 12, 1758; Abigail, b. May 12, 1760; Eunice, b. May 8, 1762; Mehitable, b. June 3, 1764. Wm. was b. in Watertown and m. his wife in Framingham. During the year 1715 he removed to Connecticut and settled in Ashford. May, 1716, he sold to Thomas Orcutt, "the land where the house he now occupies is situated." In the town records of Ashford, which by the way are in a very bad condition, his wife Eunice is called "Unis." He d. Nov. 8, 1750; res. Watertown, Mass., and Willington, Conn.

682. i. WILLIAM, b. Apr. 20, 1709; bap. Apr. 17, 1715; m. Mary Blaucher and Eunice Whitney.

683. ii. STEPHEN, b. Sept. 14, 1714; bap. Apr. 17, 1715; m. Prudence Farley and Mrs. Ann (Bradish) Green.

684. iii. HANNAH, b. Apr. 20, 1712; m. July 14, 1730, Jeremiah Powers; res. Willington, Conn. Ch.: Hannah, b. Apr. 14, 1731; Jeremiah, b. Feb. 25, 1733.

685. iv. NATHAN, b. Feb. 13, 1722; m. Eleanor Whitney.

412. DAVID FISKE (David, Nathan, Nathaniel, William, Robert, Simon, Simon, William, Symond), b. Wat. Dec. 11, 1678; m. Rebecca ———. After his death she m., Nov. 18, 1725, Thomas Sanderson of Waltham. She d. before 1737, for he then m. his third wife. David Fisk Jr of Watertown adm'n granted to his wid. Rebecca Fiske June 16 1724 Inv taken Mar. 30, 1724 Items Trooping arms &c— New end of his house stood on his father's land—acct of Rebecca the adm'x June 16 1724 Thankfull daughter of David Fisk Jr of Watertown was in the 9th year of her age when her guardian viz: John Cutting was appointed Apr 17, 1732. He d. Mar. 5, 1723; res. Watertown, Mass.

686. i. ELIZABETH, b. May 6, 1722; d. in infancy.

687. ii. THANKFUL, b. Jan. 19, 1724 (posthumous); m. Dec. 24, 1741, Jonas Smith of Waltham. He was b. June 17, 1719, son of Zechariah, d. Nov. 4, 1801. She d. Sept. 18, 1775. Ch.: Anne, b. June 17, 1742. Lydia, b. Feb. 23, 1744. Eunice, b. Nov. 4, 1745; m. Benj. Green. Jonas, b. Nov. 21, 1747; m. Molly ——— and Mary How. Zechariah, b. Aug. 22, 1749; m. Sarah Bemis. David, b. July 9, 1752; m. Martha Green. Jonathan, b. Nov. 24, 1755; m. Ruth Cutler. Nathan, b. Mar. 16, 1758; m. Susanna Bemis. Elijah, b. Jan. 30, 1760; m. Lydia Flagg and Anna Whitney. Amos, b. Feb. 26, 1762; m. Rhoda Whitney. Sarah, b. Feb. 21, 1765; d. Sept. 27, 1775.

413. NATHANIEL FISKE (Nathaniel, Nathan, Nathaniel, William, Robert, Simon, Simon, William, Symond), b. Wat. June 9, 1678; m. in Sherburne,

Jan. 16, 1705-6, Hannah Adams, d. July 21, 1718. He was b. in Watertown, **Mass.,** where he remained until he had nearly attained his majority, when he settled in Sherburne. There he was married and there he ever after resided. He was prominent in church and town affairs. He d. Aug. 24, 1719; res. Sherburne, **Mass.**

    688. i.   NATHANIEL, b. Nov. 11, 1706; did he die at Lake **George** Oct. 5, 1756, as per town record?

    689. ii.   ASA, b. Feb. 27, 1708; m. Lois Leland.

    690. iii. HANNAH, b. Sept. 9, 1710; m. Dec., 1732, Jonathan Carver of Natick. Had several daus.

    691. iv. MOSES, b. Jan. 29, 1713; m. Mehitable Broad.

    692. v.   LYDIA, b. Apr. 24 1715; d. Aug. 19, 1717, in S.

    693. vi. LYDIA, b. Oct. 5, 1718.

    415. JOHN FISKE (Nathaniel, Nathan, Nathaniel, William, Robert, Simon, Simon, William, Symond), b. Wat. Mar. 17, 1682; m. in Sherburne, July 31, 1706, Lydia Adams, b. Feb. 2, 1684, dau. of Moses and Lydia (Whitney) Adams of Sherburne. He was born in Watertown, Mass., where he resided until nearly twenty-one years of age, when in company with his brother Nathaniel he located in Sherburne, where he ever after resided. His wife and brothers were relatives. He was a weaver by trade and the admn. of his estate was granted to his widow July 13, 1730. Inventory was taken July 3, 1730, acct. of Lydia the admr., Sept. 13, 1731, in which she charges for "supporting the deceased four youngest children sixteen months," and paying a Mrs. Hannah Fiske for nursing. He d. May 8, 1730; res. Sherburne, Mass.

    695. i.   JOHN, b. May 8, 1709; m. Abigail (Leland) Babcock.

    696. ii.   LYDIA, b. Jan. 14, 1712; d. May 17, 1715, in Sherburne.

    697. iii. ISAAC, b. Aug. 24, 1714; m. Hannah Haven.

    698. iv. DANIEL, b. Apr. 7, 1716.

    699. v.   LYDIA, b. Aug. 4, 1720; d. young.

    700. vi. PETER, b. Mar. 12, 1722-3; m. Sarah Perry.

    701. vii. ABIGAIL, b. July 24, 1727; d. Aug. 9, 1727, in S.

    702. viii. NATHANIEL, b. Mar. 31, 1730. He d. 1756; was a laborer. His estate admr. upon by his brother Isaac, Dec. 8, 1756; wages were due him from the province.

    422. JONATHAN FISKE (Jonathan, David, David, Robert, Simon, Simon, William, Symond), b. Watertown; m. at Lunenburg, July 28, 1738, Jemima Foster of L. Oct. 29, 1753, administration of his estate was granted by the Middlesex Probate Court to his widow, Jemima. She m. 2d, in 1754, a Cragan, for Feb. 4 of that year she returned her inventory of Jonathan's estate and her name was Cragan. He d. 1753; res. Lunenburg and Groton, Mass.

    703. i.   JEMIMA, b. Feb. 8, 1739.

    704. ii. BENJAMIN, b. Nov. 4, 1744.

    427. SERGT. BEZALEEL FISKE (Jonathan, David, David, David, Robert, Simon, Simon, William, Symond), b. Sudbury, Mass., Aug. 24, 1715; m. there Nov. 11, 1742, Beulah Frost of Framingham; d. Apr. 20, 1744; m. 2d, Aug. 7, 1744, Tabitha Hyns, b. 1724, d. Jan. 27, 1752; m. 3d, in Sudbury, Apr. 11, 1754, Rebeckah Rand of Sudbury. He was born in Sudbury where his father was a prominent citizen. Soon after his first marriage he moved to Holden, where he was an early resident. In the early records of the town, constant references appear relating to militia affairs. The citizens were often called to make practical exhibitions of their patriotism and bravery in their country's service. The town, May 4, 1744, "Voted the sum of £30 to provide powder and bullets, and flints for town-stock." Bezaleel Fiske was sergeant of the company. He was prominent in all the affairs of town and church, was selectman 1759-60, assessor the same years, and town treasurer 1760-61. Res. Holden, Mass.

    705. i.   AMASA, b. Nov. 27, 1745.

    706. ii.   LUTHER, b. Aug. 10, 1758.

    707. iii. EUNICE, b. Oct. 5, 1760.

    708. iv. ASA, b. Oct. 7, 1764; m. Dolly Warren.

    709. v.   NAHUM, b. May 11, 1762; m. Sally Gay.

    428. SAMUEL FISK (Jonathan, David, David, David, Robert, Simon, Simon, William, Symond), b. in Watertown, Mass., May 3, 1717; m. in Sudbury, June 14, 1753, Abigail Rice, b. in Sudbury, Apr. 17, 1723, d. 1798. She

was daughter of Jason and Abigail (Clark) Rice, and was born in Sudbury. The father died there Feb. 19, 1729, ae. 38. The widow then married Dec. 7, 1741, Nathaniel Haven of Framingham. Soon after the death of Jason, the widow was appointed guardian of the three children. Nov. 23, 1741, Abigail, with the other two children, chose Jason Gleason in her stead. Jason Rice was the son of Dea. Edmund and Joyce (Russell) Rice of Cambridge. When the father died the other heirs deeded the Sudbury property to Jason, upon which he subsequently resided, and where he died. Nathaniel Haven was a member of the Framingham church when constituted; was constable in 1707; selectman in 1706. He d. July 20, 1746. Samuel was born nine years after the marriage of his parents; he was the third and youngest child, the other two being Jason and Hepzibath. He was b. Feb. 8, 1762, and went from Sherburne to Barre with his parents when he was about nine years old, and died there in 1832. His father Samuel, and son Samuel are also buried in Barre, I believe. He d. in Barre, Mass.; res. Sudbury, Sherburne and Barre, Mass.

By the will of his father, Johnathan, who died in 1740, he was given "26 acres of land in Sudbury on the east side of the river called the Neck." He moved to Sudbury and was married there, and soon afterward sold his 26 acres and moved to Sherborn, moving later to Barre, Mass., where he died.

Middles'x Co. Deed—At Cambridge.

Vol. 89 page 283—Samuel Fisk of Sudbury, Husbandman, for 100 Lbs sells 26 acres of land at Sudbury to Richard Heard.

Signed Ap. 29 1755   Samuel Fisk
Abegail Fisk, wife.

In March 12 1781   Worcester

Personally appeared the above named Samuel Fisk of Barre & acknowledged the above instrument

Recorded at Cambridge Aug. 22 1785.

Worcester Co Deeds Vol 105 page 212

Jan 7 1788.

Samuel Fisk of Barre for 200 £ sells to Samuel Fisk Jr of Barre (brother of Jason & Hepzibah) yeoman, 48 acres of land in Barre also ½ of barn & my house where I now dwell (the west room excepted) which I reserve for my daughter Hepzibah Fisk during the time she remains single"

Signed   Samuel Fisk.
Abegail Fisk.

Vol. 105 page 213

Jan. 3 1788—Samuel Fisk of Barre for 200 £ sells to Jason Fisk 48 acres & the house where the said Jason Fisk now dwells & ½ of barn.

Signed   Samuel Fisk.
Abegail Fisk.

Vol. 72 page 372   Aug 9 1773.

William Smith of Oakburn for 200 £ sells to Samuel Fisk of Rutland in Rutland District part of Great Farm No 2 100 acres with a house & barn—[Rutland District was finally called Barre, after being named Hutchinson. M. D. C.].

He d. in Barre, Mass.; res. Sudbury, Sherborne and Barre, Mass.

710. i.   SAMUEL, b. Feb. 8, 1762; m. Dolly Gleason and Mrs. Lydia (Brooks) Stowe.

711. ii.   JASON, b. Sept. 1, 1754; m. Elizabeth ———.

712. iv.   HEPZIBAH, b. Mar. 18, 1766; d. unm., Apr. 3, 1839. Worcester Co. Probate Records Dec 1839 Will of Hepzibah Fisk of Barre mentions children of my nephew Sewall Fisk children of my nephew Harvey Fisk children of my nephew Samuel Fisk, Jr. Brother Samuel Fisk, brother Jason Fisk nephews & nieces John Joel Hannah, Levi—Roxanna Sally—children of my brothers Samuel & Jason Executor, Sewall Fisk of Boston.

713. iii.   HEPZIBAH, b. Jan. 24, 1757, in Sudbury; d. young.

430. WILLIAM FISK (Jonathan, David, David, David, Jeffrey, Robert, Simon, Simon, William, Symond), b. Sudbury, Mass., Sept. 4, 1720; m. Nov. 13, 1740, Sarah Cutting. After his death she m. Sept. 18, 1754, Samuel Buckpen. of Sutton. By the will of his father he was given lands in Sutton, to which place he went to reside probably soon after his marriage. He d. intestate about Dec.,

1752, for June 4 of the following year an inventory of his estate was taken which is on file in the Worcester Probate office. He d. Dec., 1752; res. Sutton, Mass.

714. i.   JONATHAN, b. Feb. 3, 1743.
715. ii.   DAVID, b. May 27, 1746; m. Jan. 24, 1769, Sarah Goodale of Sutton.
716. iii. SARAH, b. Sept. 14, 1749; m. Oct. 30, 1766, John Barnard of Sutton.

433. DEA. DAVID FISKE (Jonathan, David, David, David, Jeffrey, Robert, Simon, Simon, William, Symond), b. Sudbury, Mass., Sept. 4, 1726; m. in Sudbury, Dec. 5, 1750, Ruth Noyes. He was a native of Sudbury, but early was a resident of Holden. He was one of the prominent men in the town and for years, from Mar. 31, 1762, was deacon of the church. Among papers belonging to the Rev. Mr. Avery, pastor of the church, I have found a small memorandum book, which contains some entries of peculiar interest. The book bears date 1782. That was a period of great distress among the people. The war had been long. Money was scarce, and it was with some difficulty that Mr. Avery received his annual salary. His parishioners, however, were disposed to share with their pastor, the good things of life. "Memorandum of gifts received." "Of Deacon Hubbard, a piece of beef; a pail of soap; a loaf of bread; a few candles; two quarts of milk; a cheese, and four pounds of butter." "Of Mr. Abbott, a piece of beef and of pork; also a spare-rib; three candles; some malt and a piece of bread, also two wash tubs and thirty nails, and a few hops." "Of Lieut. Hubbard, a piece of beef, a cheese and some malt." "Of Mr. Ebn. Estabrook, a leg of pork." "Of Deacon Fiske, a piece of beef, Jan. 5th."

The ladies of that day were equally thoughtful in regard to the wants of the Parish Priest. "Of Mrs. Benj. Flagg, a cheese." "Of Mrs. Fiske, a lb. of combed flax." "Of Mrs. Elisha Hubbard, some flax."

David Fiske was town clerk 1783-6-8-9; selectman, 1761-2-9-71-77-78-83; assessor, 1767-9-71-7-8-83-5-7-8. When the census of the town was taken in 1773 his family consisted of eight persons. He served in the local militia company as private before and during the Revolutionary War.

He d. ———; res. Sudbury and Holden, Mass.

717. ii.   RUTH, b. Holden, June 30, 1754.
718. iii. DAVID, b. July 19, 1761; m. Naomi Winch.
719. iv.   SAMUEL, b. Oct. 1, 1764.
720. v.   LEMUEL, b. Nov. 8, 1767; m. Eunice ———. A son David d. in H., June 11, 1801.
721. i.   ANNA, b. in Sudbury, Aug. 22, 1751; m. Jan. 31, 1775, Moses Wheeler of Holden.

434. BENJAMIN FISK (Jonathan, David, David, David, Jeffrey, Robert, Simon, Simon, William, Symond), b. Sudbury, Mar. 28, 1730; m. there 1752. Abigail Maynard. He moved to Worcester about the fall of 1755, and moved elsewhere after 1767. Res. Sudbury and Worcester, Mass.

722. i.   WILLIAM, b. Apr. 3 1753, .
723. ii.   MOSES, b. Sudbury, Apr. 18, 1755; d. in Worcester, Sept. 20, 1756.
724. iii. ABIGAIL, b. May 27, 1761.
725. iv.   BENJAMIN, b. Apr. 9, 1759.'
726. v.   JOHN, b. Apr. 9, 1764.
727. vi.   LOIS, b. Sept. 18, 1767.
728. vii. MOSES, b. June 7, 1757.

437. DR. ROBERT FISKE (Robert, David, David, David, Jeffrey, Robert, Simon, Simon, William, Symond), b. Lexington Jan. 12, 1721; m. Mrs. Abigail Grover, m. 2d, Betty ———, d. Dec. 14, 1770. There is no record of his death. He was in Lex. in 1764, and she was a widow in 1767; he must have died between these periods. In 1767 Wid. Betty Fiske bought eighty acres of land in Lex. bounded easterly on the Woburn line and westerly by land of Lemuel Simonds. Her will, dated Dec. 4, 1770, and proved in 1771, mentions sons Robert, John and David and daus. Betty and Ruth. The record of this family is quite defective. Like his father, he was a physician by profession, and appears to have resided in many places. In 1760 he was in the French and Indian war. In 1757 in Woburn, and in 1764 he ret. to Lex.

Middlesex Probate Records Vol 52 405 Dec 4 1770 appr Sept 17 1771 Betty
Fisk of Lexington wid. Will "Being sick & weak in body". & To Son Robert
Fisk—John &c when they arrives at age of 21 also suitable food & raiment until
he (John) arrives to 14—to dr Betty &c when she shall arrive at age of 18 1 dr
Ruth when 18 & food &c till 14—to son David, whom I constitute & ordain sole
Ex'r & all residue of estate. P. 408 Sept 17. David Fisk Ex'r exhibited Inven-
tory.

He d. about 1765; res. Woburn and Lexington, Mass.

729.   i.   RUTH, b. Apr. 10, 1746; m. Feb. 13, 1766, Jonathan Harrington.
            His second wife. He was b. Mar. 21, 1722. By his first wife
            he had seven children, and by Ruth one, Jonathan, b. Oct. 25,
            1766.
730. ii.   ROBERT, b. in 1758; m. Elizabeth ———.
731. iii.   DAVID, b. Nov. 23, 1760; m. Abigail Harrington.
732. iv.   RUTH, b. Oct. 30, 1765.
733.   v.   JOHN, b. ———.
734. vi.   BETTY, b. ———.

440. DR. JOSEPH FISKE (Robert, David, David, David, Jeffrey, Robert,
Simon, Simon, William, Symond), b. Lexington, Oct. 13, 1726; m. Dec. 13, 1751,
Hepzibah Raymond, b. 1729; d. Oct. 9, 1820. He died at the advanced age of eighty-
one years, and his wife aged ninety-one. He was a physician and the successor
to his father who died about the time he began practice. He admr. on his father's
estate, and resided in the same house. He had other children probably besides
those mentioned below, as the imperfect records speak of the death of at least one
of his infant children. He d. Jan. 8, 1808; res. Lexington, Mass.

735.   i.   JOSEPH, b. Dec. 25, 1752; m. Elizabeth Stone.
736. ii.   RUTH, b. Apr. 20, 1758; m. May 7, 1795, John ———.
737. iii.   HEPZIBAH, b. June 22, 1765; m. John Le Baron; res. Little-
            ton.

442. LIEUT. JOHN FISKE (Robert, David, David, David, Jeffrey, Robert,
Simon, Simon, William Symond), b. Lexington, Mass., Nov. 18, 1731; m. July 9,
1755, Mary Ingalls, b. Nov. 6, 1735, dau. of John and Mary (Willis) Ingalls of
Pomfret. He was born in Lexington. He studied medicine, but did not practice
to any great extent. There is not any record of his marriage on the Lexington
records. He was in Lex. in 1752 and later as one of the heirs—"Dr. John Fiske"—
he sold land to Jonas Parker. In 1754 he was in the French and Indian war, and
it is said later he was of Pomfret, town, a housewright and bought in 1753 of
Nathaniel Abbott of Pomfret land lying partly in Pomfret and partly in Ashford.
In 1756 he sold to William Legg of Mendon 30½ acres in Mendon North Purchase,
now Milford.

John Fiske, carpenter, first appears on Pomfret records 21 January, 1753, when
for £1450 bills of public credit, he bought of Nathan Abbott of Pomfret, 54¾ acres
of land lying partly in Pomfret and partly in Ashford. Fiske sold this land the
following year to Jonathan Lyon of Pomfret for £1660, old tennor, buying of
Lyon at the same time for £1700, 35 acres in Pomfret. John Fiske married 9 Jan.,
1755, Mary b. at Pomfret 6 Nov., 1735, daughter of John and Mary (Willis) Ingalls. On Pomfret records Fiske is frequently called Lieutenant. He died at Pomfret 6 Aug., 1790. His will (original on file at Pomfret), dated 28 July, 1790,
mentions wife Mary for whom a provision was made during her natural life and
gives one half of the residue of the estate to son Daniel, dividing the other half
between his three daughters, Mary, Sarah and Alice: Sarah's share was to be deb-
ited with £20 already advanced her. Wife Mary and son Daniel Exrs. Will proved 7
Sept. 1790. The inventory taken 3 Sept. 1790, by Lemuel Ingalls and Daniel
Goodell, amounted to about £300 of which £190 was real estate. He d. Aug. 6,
1790; res. Pomfret, Conn.

738.   i.   MOLLY (Mary) b. Oct. 25, 1755 (No record of her marriage).
            In 1795 she was living unmarried at Pomfret, but had removed
            to Otsego Co., N. Y., prior to 7 Jan., 1796, when she sold to
            William Field a piece of land in Pomfret given her by her
            father's will.
739. ii.   JOHN WILLYS b. 16 Jan., 1758. d. 14 Sep., 1776.

740. iii. SARAH, b. 3 Apr. 1761; m. (date not learned) Solomon son of Lemuel Eldredge of Pomfret and removed with her husband to Springfield, Otsego Co., N. Y., prior to 31 Jan., 1792. The date of death of neither has been learned. Issue: Rosena, who m. Seldon Rathbone and died about 1812. Sarah, b. 13 Nov., 1787 m. 14 Dec., 1806, Bailey Crandall, and d. at Cazenovia, N. Y., 18 April, 1857. Mary, who m. Sheldon Norton of Hudson, Ohio, and died about 1860. Harvey, who m. at Springfield, N. Y., Sarah, b. 25 Feby., 1795, dau. of Samuel and Sarah (Vibber) Way and removed to Findley, Ohio, of which place he was a prominent citizen. Willis, who d. unmarried at De Ruyter, N. Y., Oct., 1858. Evander, b. at Springfield, N. Y., 10 Nov., 1798; m. (date not learned) Betsey Olivia, b. at Springfield, 8 June, 1801, dau. of Samuel and Sarah (Vibber) Way. They removed to Hudson, Ohio, where he died 29 Nov., 1827. His widow returned to Springfield, N Y., where she died 28 Aug., 1829, leaving an only child, Harriet Louise, who was b. at Hudson, Ohio, 11 July, 1824. This child m. at De Ruyter, N. Y., 30 Oct.,1849, Paul King Randall and Frank E. Randall 45 Broadway, N. Y., is the only issue of that marriage. Amelia, who m. ——— Barnes and lived in Ohio. Celestia, b. April, 1805; m. Stephen G. Sears and d. at De Ruyter, N. Y., 23 Aug., 1829.

741. iv. ALICE, born 15 Apr., 1763, m. between the 6th and 11th of Feby., 1793, Sylvanus Eldredge, brother of the above Solomon Eldredge.

742. v. DANIEL, b. 28 Sept., 1766. In 1796 he was living at Springfield, Otsego Co., N. Y.

443. DR. JONATHAN FISKE (Robert, David, David, David, Jeffrey, Robert, Simon, Simon, William, Symond), b. Lexington, May 20. 1734; m. in Woburn, Sept. 4, 1755, Abigail Locke, dau. of Wm. and Jemima (Russell) of Woburn. Her parents resided near the Lex. line in Woburn. In 1752 he was in Lex. where for a consideration he relinquished his rights to his mother's thirds; res. Lex. and Woburn and elsewhere.

444. DAVID FISKE (Robert, David, David, David, Jeffrey, Robert, Simon, Simon, William, Symond), b. Lex., Mar. 8, 1737; m. June 22, 1760, Elizabeth Blodgett. He was a weaver and to distinguish him from others of the same name, he was called "Weaver David." He was famous as a hunter. Though the wild game was not very plenty in his day, he contributed greatly to thin off the deer, bears, etc. He ran down and killed a stately buck on the hill over which the Burlingame road ran, and hence it has taken the name of "Buck's Hill." There is no record of his family. He d. July 20, 1815; res. Lexington, Mass.

743. i. DAVID, b. Nov. 23, 1760; m. Sarah Hadley and Mrs. Ruth Trask.

744. ii. BENJAMIN, b. ———.

745. iii. BETSEY, b. ———; m. Apr. 14, 1788, Joseph Webber. Res. Lex. Ch.: Joseph, b. Feb. 19, 1789; Susanna, b. July 9, 1791. They then moved to Bedford.

446. DR. EBENEZER FISKE (Ebenezer, David, David, David, Jeffrey, Robert, Simon, Simon, William, Symond), b. Lex., Mar. 5, 1725; m. Elizabeth Cotton of Boston. b. Aug. 24, 1727. Her father, Rev. Ward Cotton, married Joanna Rand of Boston. Their children, as far as we have ascertained, were: Isabella, b. 1735, d. July 31, 1752; Elizabeth; Sarah Cotton, b. Oct. 19, 1739. After Mr. Cotton's dismission he removed to Plymouth, Mass., where he d. Nov. 27, 1768, ae. 57 years. Mrs. Cotton survived him, and was married to Mr. Jonathan Gilman of Exeter.

To show how little one knows of their ancestors I give this. A great-grandson of Dr. Fiske in writing to the compiler in 1896 says: "Our branch of the Fisk family, unfortunately, I have been unable to trace back beyond the landing in New York about 1781. My great-grandfather was a physician, evidently from a prominent English family. The place from which, and the date of his departure from England, we cannot discover, nor do we know his name, as he died on the passage over. He was a widower with three small children, but his mother attended him on the passage. The names of the three orphan children who landed in New York about 1781, under the care of their grandmother, were: Ebenezer Fisk, Isabella Fisk and Cotton Fisk. The evidence that our great-grandfather came from a wealthy family in England is supposed from the fact that among his effects, landing in New York, which my grandfather had, was a great chest containing a costly wardrobe, a number of velvet suits, etc., a tortoise shell jewel box with many jewels, and his medical and surgical instruments. This jewel case is now in the possession of Cotton N. Fisk, at Abbotsford, P. Q., Canada."

He d. 1781; res. Epping, N. H.

746. i.   EBENEZER, b. ——; m. —— —— and Azuba Hoyt.
747. ii.   ISABELLA, b. ——; m., and res. in United States.
748. iii. COTTON, b. Aug. 8, 1779; m. Sarah Fifield.

452. REV. SAMUEL FISKE (Ebenezer, David, David, David, Jeffrey, Robert, Simon, Simon, William, Symond), b. Lex., Oct. 5, 1739; m. —— ——. He was gr. H. C., 1759; was an Epis. clergyman in South Carolina. He d. in 1777; res. South Carolina.

453. BENJAMIN FISKE (Ebenezer, David, David, David, Jeffrey, Robert, Simon, Simon, William, Symond), b. Lex., Aug. 10, 1742; m. May 14, 1767, Rebecca Howe, of Concord. After his death she m. 2d, Mar. 28, 1786, Lieut. William Merriam of Bedford. His estate was appraised Apr. 11, 1785, and divided Mar. 27, 1786. He d. Feb. 1, 1785; res. Lexington, Mass.

749. i.   BENJAMIN, b. Aug. 20, 1774; m. Elizabeth Bridge and Nancy
            Adams.
750. ii.   ELIZABETH, b. Apr. 7, 1783; m. May 29, 1802, William Whit-
            ney of Shirley, son of Rev. Phinehas, b. Oct. 3, 1778, d. Jan.
            29, 1837; res. Shirley, Winchendon and Boston, Mass. She d.
            Feb. 24, 1810. Ch.: William F., b. May 19, 1803; m. Frances
            Ann Rice of Boston, Mass. George H., b. May 24, 1809; m.
            Elizabeth B. White.

464. AARON FISK (Samuel, James, James, Phinehas, Thomas, Robert, Simon, Simon, William, Symond), b. Newton, Mass., about 1736; m. Abigail ——. After his death she m. 2d, at Petersham, Mar. 10, 1802, Ebenezer Lock of Wendall. The inventory of his estate was taken Feb. 25, 1790. In the Worcester County Probate Court, Apr. 5, 1791, John Fisk was appointed administrator of the estate of Aaron Fisk, late of Petersham. Abigail was the widow. They were appointed guardians to Samuel, Thomas and Anna. He d. in 1790; res. Newton, Mass., and Petersham, Mass.

751. i.   SAMUEL, b. Nov. 19, 1766; m. Frances Swan.
752. ii.   JOHN, b. ——; m., and res. Petersham.
753. iii. THOMAS, b. ——.
754. iv.   ANNA, b. ——.
755. v.   BETSEY, b. ——.

471. SAMUEL FISK (Jonathan, James, James, Phinehas, Thomas, Robert, Simon, Simon, William, Symond), b. Concord, Mass., May 22, 1740; m. at Nottingham, N. H., Mar. 6, 1764, Judeth Rowell of Nottingham. He was born in Concord, Mass., and during his early manhood worked on a farm in Nottingham, N. H. He was united in marriage at Nottingham by Rev. Benjamin Butler, and soon after moved to Warren, R. I., where several of his children were born. Res. Nottingham, N. H., and Warren, R. I.

756. i.   SARAH, b. Mar. 9, 1765.
757. ii.   JONATHAN, b. Nov. 20, 1766.
758. iii. SAMUEL, b. May 1, 1769; d. Sept. 26, 1769.
759. iv.   MARY, b. June 26, 1774.
760. v.   RICE ROWELL, b. Jan. 11, 1776.

482. THOMAS FISK (Thomas, Samuel, James, Phinehas, Thomas, Robert, Simon, Simon, William, Symond), b. Pepperell, Mass., Mar. 12, 1746; m. Mar. 17, 1768, Sarah Shipley, b. Dec. 25, 1748, d. Feb. 18, 1831, dau. of John and Elizabeth (Boyden) Shipley. He was born in Pepperell, Mass., and continued to reside there until 1780, when he moved to Jaffrey, N. H. His last two children were born there. He was a farmer and respected in the community where he resided.

Mr. Fisk was a soldier of the Revolution and served in several campaigns. He lost his property by the depreciation of the continental money. He moved with his family to Jaffrey, N. H., in 1780, where he died. He d. Mar. 15, 1818; res. Pepperell, Mass., and Jaffrey, N. H.

761. i.   SAMUEL, b. Nov. 28, 1768; m. Mary Twitchell.
762. ii. ASA, b. July 1, 1771; m. Cynthia Mann.
763. iii. LEVI, b. Feb. 16, 1775; m. Hannah Mellen.
764. iv. SARAH, b. Mar. 22, 1779; m. Phinehas Spaulding of Jaffrey, where she d. Apr. 21, 1844. After the death of his wife, Mr. S. removed to Medina, Lenawee Co., Mich., where he died. Ch.: Lyman, b. Aug. 27, 1803; m. Sept. 18, 1831, Susan Marshall, b. in Jaffrey, Dec. 16, 1808. After the birth of their children they removed from Jaffrey, N. H., to Medina, Lenawee Co., Mich. Ch.: 1, Oliver L., b. Aug. 2, 1833. He graduated at Oberlin College in 1855, taught in the academy at Medina one year, and settled in St. Johns, Clinton Co., Mich., in 1857, where he studied and practiced law, till he went into the army, Aug., 1862. For two years he was in command of the 23d Michigan Infantry, the first year as lieutenant-colonel, the last as colonel. m. May 29, 1856, M. Jennie Mead, b. in Lockport, N. Y., Dec. 11, 1830, and d. at St. Johns, Nov. 9, 1857; m. 2d, May, 1859, Martha M. Mead, who d. Nov. 25, 1861, leaving a son, Frank M., b. Nov. 4, 1861. For 3d wife he m. Aug. 12, 1862, M. Cecelia Swegles, b. Mar. 24, 1844. 2, Eliza S., b. Aug. 30, 1835; m. Dec. 16, 1855, Franklin Gallup, b. Sept. 24, 1829. Ch.: Frank J., b. May 8, 1860; Arietta P., b. Jan. 13, 1862. 3, Susan M., b. Oct. 28, 1837. 4, Thomas H., b. Jan. 26, 1840; d. Jan. 11, 1861. 5, Edward M., b. May 5, 1842; d. in the army at Bowling Green, Ky., Feb. 10, 1863. 6, Hattie J., b. Apr. 1, 1844; d. Apr. 25, 1847. Sarah E. Spaulding [42-2], b. Sept. 16, 1817; m. Thomas A. Stearns, and resided in Jaffrey till her death, Feb. 26, 1855. Ch.: 1, Susanna E., b. May 28, 1839, d. Oct. 27, 1839. 2, Harriet E., b. Jan. 7, 1844. 3, Henry M., b. Mar. 4, 1848.
765. v.   POLLY, b. Nov. 3, 1782; d. June 14, 1804.
766. vi. JOEL, b. Jan. 14, 1787; m. Sally Pierce. He settled on the homestead of his father, where he d. Feb. 19, 1823, s. p. She afterward married a Mr. Bridges, and died in Wilton, N. H.

483. JOHN FISK (Thomas, Samuel, James, Phinehas, Thomas, Robert, Simon, Simon, William, Symond), b. Groton, Mass., July 23, 1748; m. Anna Blood. He was a soldier in the Revolution, and was severely wounded in battle by a musket ball which passed through his head. He, however, recovered from his wounds so far as to be able to report for duty, but was soon after taken sick of a fever of which he died. He d. 1781; res. Groton, Mass.

767. i.   JOHN, b. Mar. 9, 1779; m. ——— ———.

488. BENJAMIN FISKE (Benjamin, John, John, Phinehas, Thomas, Robert, Simon, Simon, William, Symond), b. Swanzey, Mass., Mar. 8, 1706; m. Susannah Briggs, dau. of James and Sarah of Kingston, Providence and Cranston, R. I. He d. Sept. 13, 1771; res. Swanzey, Mass., and Scituate, R. I.

768. i.   BENJAMIN, b. ———; m. Hannah Hammond.
769. ii. MARY, b. May 1, 1729.
770. iii. ELIZABETH, b. June 3, 1731.
771. iv. NATHAN, b. Dec. 2, 1732; d. Dec. 3, 1732.
772. v.   NATHANIEL, b. about 1735; m. Anna ———, Lois Rowley, Sylvia ——— and Sarah Arnold.

490. DANIEL FISKE (Benjamin, John, John, Phinehas, Thomas, Robert, Simon, Simon, William, Symond), b. Rehoboth, Mass., Dec. 16, 1709; m. Dec. 24, 1732, Freelove Williams, dau. of Peleg and Elizabeth (Carpenter) Williams, granddaughter of Daniel and great-granddaughter of Rev. Roger Williams. At the time of the marriage he was of Scituate. She was b. Nov. 13, 1713; d. Apr. 20, 1791. He left papers and after his death on examination among them was found the statement "that some of the Swanzey Fiskes mooved from there to quebec

Canada and corrisponded with their friends a few years later & then spelled their name Fiskque." Mrs. Fiske's grandfather was murdered by the Indians. "He was hoeing corn in the field, his wife waching him from their Cabin door when an Indian stealthely crept up Behind him, threw his tomahawk with unering speed and drove the cruel instrument in to his skul. He then tore off his scalp and with his trophy departed leaving a corpes and widow, who dare not utte a shriek for fear the wanton savage would enter her dwelling & she with her helpless Children must then share the father & husband fate." He d. June 27, 1804; res. Scituate, R. I.

773. i. EUNICE, b. Apr. 5, 1736; m. Sept. 30, 1762, William Ashton, Jr., of Scituate, and Providence. She d. Jan. 21, 1814.
774. ii. JOSEPH, b. Apr. 23, 1738; m. ———, and d. s. p. June 18, 1793.
775. iii. WAITE, b. Feb. 23, 1740. She d. Apr. 28, 1807.
776. iv. RHODA, b. Jan. 16, 1751; d. Aug. 5, 1772.
777. v. DANIEL, b. Apr. 28, 1753; m. Freelove Knight.

491. JOHN FISKE (Benjamin, John, John, Phinehas Thomas, Robert, Simon, Simon, William, Symond), b. Swanzey, Mass., Jan. 11, 1713; m. Elizabeth Williams, dau. of Peleg and Elizabeth, granddaughter of Daniel and Rebecca, and great-granddaughter of Rev. Roger Williams. She d. Sept. 24, 1766. She descended in a direct line from Roger Williams. [Alden's Epitaphs.]

He was a justice of the peace for years and was called Esquire. He d. Dec. 5, 1798; res. Scituate, R. I.

778. i. JONATHAN, b. 1738; m. Barbara Brown.
779. ii. PELEG, b. Jan. 24, 1740; m. Lydia Sheldon.
780. iv. CALEB, b. Jan. 24, 1753; m. Mary Manchester.
781. iii. DORCAS, b. Dec. 19, 1741; m. Jan. 18, 1759, Benjamin Knight of Scituate.

493. JOB FISKE (Benjamin, John, John, Phinehas, Thomas, Robert, Simon, Simon, William, Symond), b. Scituate, R. I., 1711; m. Mary Whitman. Daniel Fiske's mother used to speak of the Burial service of Job that aged and honorable man. When the Neighbours had assembled and the house was quiet at the appointed hour the minister arose and with Puritanic dignity and solemnity and a few prefatory remarkes uttered this appropriate piece of holy writ for his text, "so Job died being old and full of days." He d. June 15, 1798; res. Scituate, R. I.

782. i. JOB, b. July 29, 1747; m. ——— ———.
783. ii. THOMAS, b. Feb. 2, 1748.
784. iii. JAMES, b. ———.
785. iv. JEREMIAH, b. in 1731; m. Rebekah Pierce.
786. v. RHODA, b. May 17, 1743.
787. vi. PHEBE, b. Dec. 19, 1741.
788. vii ABIGAIL, b. June 3, 1744.
789. viii. LYDIA, b. Aug. 1, 1745.

494. NOAH FISKE (Benjamin, John, John, Phinehas, Thomas, Robert, Simon, Simon, William, Symond), b. Swanzey, Mass., 1722; m. ——— ———. He d. May 11, 1747; res. Scituate, R. I.

790. i. NOAH, b. 1743; m. ——— ———.
791. ii. MOSES, b. ———; m. Huldah ———.
792. iii. AARON, b. ———; m. ——— ———.
793. iv. PHINEHAS, b. ———.

496. CAPT. EBENEZER FISKE (Ebenezer, John, John, Phinehas, Thomas, Robert, Simon, Simon, William, Symond), b. Milford, Conn., Dec. 13, 1719; m. 1746, Sarah Hart of Southington, dau. of Samuel. She d. same year; m. 2d, at Wallingford, Jan. 4, 1747, Sarah Newel, dau. of Samuel Newel and his wife Sarah Norton, and was b. in Farmington, Conn., July 6, 1713. The father early settled in Southington at the south part of the town, about one-half a mile north of where Fisk settled, and was living there when Sarah was married. He was born on the paternal estate in Milford, Conn., and removed thence to Wallingford, and subsequently to Southington, Conn., where he died. On the records he is styled a captain, and was the possessor of a large landed estate.

From New Milford Church Record. "March 5, 1748-9 Sarah ye wife of Ebenezer Fisk was admited to chh. fellowship by a letter of recom: from ye Chh of X in Southington.

Jeremiah Curtis Pastor."

Capt Ebenezar born 1720 sold the last of his property in New Milford, except two small tracts, in 1750, & his 1st purchase at Southington, dated May 1, 1750, covering 233 acres with 3 dwellings for 5,300 pounds old tenor, seems to show date of his removal. He lived on the same place till his death. His will gives to sons property in Bark, Victory, Grand Isle, & Montgomery Towns, in Vermont, & land in Southington. Also to daughters various items of personal property.

Mr. Ebenezer Fisk attended the Connecticut General Assembly in March, May and August, in 1745, as a Representative for New Milford, Conn.

At the session of the Connecticut General Assembly held 5th to 27th of Jan., 1769, "This assembly do establish Mr. Ebenezer Fisk to be captain of the second company or train hand in the Parish of Southington. At the session of the Connecticut assembly in May, 1760, Ebenezer Fisk's dwelling and land connected, lying between the boundary lines of Wallingford and Farmington, was annexed and made a part of Farmington township and Southington Parish.

May, 1719, Connecticut General Assembly records. Liberty granted to Ebenezer Fiske of Millford administrator of the Estate of Doctor John Fiske to sell lands to pay debts.

Vermont Historical Gazeteer Vol 1 pp 1045 Town of Victory containing 23,040 acres was granted Nov 6, 1780 and chartered Sept 6, 1781 to Capt. Ebenezer Fisk and sixty-four others.

His will is as follows:

In the Name of God Amen — — —

I Ebenezar Fisk of the Southington in the County of Flarllan and State of Connecticut Being advanced in Years & exoused with increasing Infirmity though of sound Mind and Memory considering my Mortality & not knowing the Day of My Death think it my Duty to make & Do accordingly make this my last Will & Testament for the disposition of my worthey Estate: commending myself to God & my Body to Christian Burial at the Discretion of my Executor in manner following, that is to say—

Itemp's,, I give and devise to my four Grand Sons Saml, Ira, Ebenezar, & Solomon the sons of my eldest son Ichabod Ebenezar Fisk. To each of the two first a Right of land in the Town of Victory in the state of Vermont & to each of the others a Right of land in the Town of Bark in S'd State to them and their heirs for ever.

Item—I give and devise unto John Dean the only son of my son John Fisk my Right of land in the Grand Isle socalled in said State of Vermont to him and his heirs forever.

Items,, I give and devise unto my son Isaac Fisk two rights of Land in the town of Montgomery in S'd State also one Right of Land in the Gore so called on Connecticut River & all the lands I own in Company with John Nickerbocker to him the said Isaac Fisk forever.

Item,, I give and Bequeath unto my Two Daughters Sarah Rogers & Ruth Fisk the whole of my Household Goods & Furniture to be Divided between them in such manner as thair Portions Considering what has he advanced to S'd Sarah Shall be equal to them & their Heirs forever.

Item,, I devise and Bequeath unto my Son Solomon Fisk & His Heirs forever all the right and residue of my Estate both real and Personal of every description he paying all my Debts & Funeral Charges of Settling Estate whom also I do hereby constitute & appoint to be sole Executor this my last Will and Testament. In Witness whereoff I have hereunto set my hand & seal this 9th Day of March 1790 Signed Sealed Published Pronounced by the Testator to be his last Will & testament in Presents of us.

John Treadwell
John Roys
Sibel Hunt
Witnesses.

Ebenezer Fisk [Seal].

He d. May 31, 1790; res. New Milford, Wallingford and Southington, Conn.

794. i.   ICHABOD EBENEZER, b. Oct. 19, 1747; m. Eleanor Roberts.
795. ii. SAMUEL, b. Feb. 1. 1750. He was corporal in a Connecticut regiment during the Rev. War, and died at Ticonderoga.
796. iii. SOLOMON, b. Apr. 21, 1751; d. Oct. 31, 1757.
797. iv. JOHN, b. Sept. 24, 1752; m. Lavinia Dean.

798. v. SARAH, b. May 23, 1754; m. Capt. James Rogers of Waterford, Conn., and d. s. p.
799. vi. ISAAC, b. Feb. 26, 1756; m. Lucy ———.
800. vii. SOLOMON, b. Dec. 26, 1757; m. Mary Harris.
801. viii. RUTH, b. Nov. 19, 1759. She was married, but d. s. p.
802. ix. HANNAH (twin of Ann), b. ———; d. young.
803. x. ANN (twin of Hannah), b. ———; d. young.

501. JOHN FISK (John, John, John, Phinehas, Thomas, Robert, Simon, Simon, William, Symond), b. Haddam, Conn., June 3, 1718; m. ——— ——— and Ann Tyler. John settled in Middlesex County, where a son and grandson (John) held the offices of town clerk and clerk of the Supreme Court, in the city of Middletown, for upward of one hundred years. The latter died in 1847. Res. Middletown, Middlesex County and Chatham, Conn.
804. i. JOHN, b. about 1740; m. ——— ———.
805. iii. HANNAH, b. Feb. 11, 1747; m. Reuben Shailer.
806. iv. DORCAS, b. Feb. 7, 1749; m. Solomon Tyler of Branford, Conn.
807. ii. BEZALEEL, b. 1743; m. Margaret Rockwell and Abigail Dobson.
808. v. ANN, b. ———; m. Thomas Shailer.
809. vi. MARY, b. ———; m. Abisha Smith. A son was Bezaleel Fiske Smith of Essex, Conn., b. Jan., 1799.

503. BENJAMIN FISK (John, John, John, Phinehas, Thomas, Robert, Simon, Simon, William, Symond), b. Haddam, Conn., Dec. 17, 1723; m. ——— ———. He gr. at Yale in 1747. Res. Chatham, Conn.
810. i. JOHN, b. ———. He res. in Middletown, Conn., and d. before 1818.
811. ii. SAMUEL, b. ———. He d. unm.; was a tutor at Yale, where he was graduated, and died from overwork.

523. EBENEZER FISKE (Ebenezer, William, William, William, John, William, Robert, Simon, Simon, William, Symond), b. Andover, Mass., 1730; m. Elizabeth Richardson. Ebenezer Fisk (1730-1784) was a farmer, a confessed Christian, and had eleven children. He was in the Continental army for some time. A brief biographical sketch (in Ms.) is in the hands of Rev. D. M. Fisk, written by Oliver Blake Fisk. The powder-horn carried by Ebenezer Fisk at Bunker Hill, and preserved by his son Isaac, was given by the grandson Walter W. [youngest child, deceased 1872] to [Rev.] Daniel Moses Fisk, and is in his possession at the present time, Sept., 1895. He d. Mar., 1784, in Boscowan, N. H.; res. Tewksbury, Mass.
812. i. WILLIAM, b. Mar. 24, 1754; m. Rachel ———.
813. ii. ELIZABETH, b. Aug. 13, 1756-7; d. Oct. 23, 1756-7.
814. iii. ABIGAIL, b. June 23, 1758.
815. iv. JONATHAN, b. Nov. 13, 1759. He was a soldier in the Revolutionary Army, and was killed at the battle of Bunker Hill.
816. v. BENJAMIN, b. Jan. 2, 1762; m. Lydia Kitteridge.
817. vi. RUTH, b. July 14, 1764.
818. vii. SAMUEL, b. June 4, 1767; m. ——— ———.
819. viii. ISAAC, b. Aug. 27, 1769; m. Molly Severance.
820. ix. DAVID, b. Mar. 1, 1772; m. Lydia Morse.
821. x. EPHRAIM, b. Apr. 19, 1774; m. Sally Morse.
822. xi. HANNAH, b. Mar. 13, 1779.
823. xii. EBENEZER, b. ———; m. ———. He died of poison in the war of 1812, at the hands of a woman while on a scout.

524. EPHRAIM FISKE (Ebenezer, William, William, William, John, William, Robert, Simon, Simon, William, Symond), b. about 1732; m. Mehitable Frost, b. 1744. Ephraim Fiske came from Tewksbury, Mass., A. D. 1772, or 1773, and settled in the northwesterly part of Concord, N. H., near the Hopkinton line. He had been married to Mehitable Frost. When her son Ephraim was born she was thirteen and a half years old. She used to ask her mother to tend her baby while she went out with the children to play. A person asked her how old she was when her first child was born? She replied: "Thirteen and a half years old and what is that to you?" Mr. Fiske and his son Ephraim were soldiers in the Rev-

olutionary War. Both were in the battle of Bennington. Ephraim, Sr., signed the following with others at Concord, N. H., in 1775: "We, the Subscribers, do hereby solemnly engage and promise that we will, to the utmost of our Power, at the Risque of our lives and Fortunes, with Arms, oppose the Hostile Proceedings of the British Fleets and Armies against the United American Colonies." He d. about 1825; res. Tewksbury, Mass., and Concord, N. H.

    824. i.   EPHRAIM, b. T., Aug. 27, 1758; m. Martha Sawyer.
    825. ii.   SOLOMON, b. ———; d. young.
    826. iii. MEHITABLE, b. ———.
    827. iv. EBENEZER, b. Jan. 26, 1766; m. Sarah Blanchard.
    828. v.   SARAH, b. ———.
    829. vi. LYDIA, b. ———.
    830. vii. DANIEL, b. ———.
    831. viii. SOLOMON, b. ———.
    832. ix. JONATHAN, b. ———.
    833. x.   BETSEY, b. ———.
    834. xi. REBECCA, b. ———.
    835. xii. JOSEPH, b. ———.

529. MAJOR JOHN FISKE (Josiah, Samuel, William, William, John, William, Robert, Simon, Simon, William, Symond), b. Cumberland, R. I., Feb. 20, 1729; m. in C. May 5, 1755, Mary Bartlett. He was appointed administrator of his father's estate in 1773. He d. Feb. 12, 1789; res. Cumberland, R. I.

    836. i.   SQUIRE, b. Jan. 10, 1756; m. Amey Lapham.
    837. ii.   POLLY, b. June 24, 1758; m. in C., Oct. 12, 1775, William Whitaker of C.
    838. iii. JOHN, b. Oct. 24, 1760; m. Abigail Ballou.
    839. iv. CHLOE, b. Feb. 18, 1763.
    840. v.   FREELOVE, b. Feb. 18, 1766.
    841. vi. DARIUS, b. May 7, 1768; m. Patty Darling.
    842. vii. LUCENA, b. July 21, 1770; m. Jan. 6, 1791, in C., John Hill.

533. JONATHAN FISK (Josiah, Samuel, William, William, John, William, Robert, Simon, Simon, William, Symond), b. Aug. 13, 1739, Rhode Island; m. Hannah ———, b. Nov. 18, 1743, d. Sept. 17, 1814. Jonathan Fisk, the oldest Fisk of this branch, lived three miles from Schuylerville on the Hudson, Saratoga County, New York, in a log house. He was born in Rhode Island, but whether all his children were born there it cannot be ascertained. It has been stated that all of this family of twelve children except one lived over 70 years, and that the exception was not a natural death. During the Revolutionary War he served in the Connecticut line. Soon after the war he moved to New York State with his family. On Mar. 11, 1820, the government granted him a pension, and he was 77 years of age. This would make his birth in 1743. He d. Dec. 22, 1816; res. Rhode Island and Schuylerville, N. Y.

    843. i.   JONATHAN, b. Feb. 12, 1760; m. Mercy Robinson.
    844. ii.   HANNAH, b. May 4, 1762.
    845. iii. HULDAH, b. July 19, 1765.
    846. iv. MARTHA, b. Aug. 13, 1767.
    847. v.   DAVID, b. June 17, 1769; m. Mary Green.
    848. vi. DOSHE, b. July 20, 1771.
    849. vii. CLOAH, b. Apr. 13, 1774.
    850. viii. LYDIA, b. May 19, 1776.
    851. ix. EZRA, b. Apr. 26, 1778; m. Lydia Hannibal.
    852. x.   ABIGAIL, b. May 3, 1780.
    853. xi. STEPHEN, b. May 1, 1782; m. Hannah Curry.
    854. xii. BENJAMIN, b. July 5, 1788; m. Rebecca ———. They settled in Arcadia, Wayne Co., N. Y., and both died there. They had only two children, and both died in infancy.

537. JOSEPH FISKE (Mark, Joseph, William, William, John, William, Robert, Simon, William, Symond), b. Ipswich, Mass., 1741; m. Jan. 29, 1763. Eleanor Abbott; m. 2d, Jan. 9, 1767, Margaret Hobbs (on church and town records it is Sarah Hobbs). Res. Ipswich, Mass., and New Ipswich, N. H.

Mark Fisk & wife Eleanor, of Ipswich yeoman mortgaged to Benj Dutch of Ips yeoman 30 acres of his homestead land in Ips with his dwelling house &c

bounded by land of Dan'l Chapman county road Joseph Metcalf & Fs 'other land
May 7 1763.

Mark Fisk & wife Eleanor of Ipswich yeoman Sold to John Colef of Ipswich
a certain farm, house & barn, lying in Line brook parish Ips'h bounded by Joseph
Metcalf Meadow of Capt Stamford & Daniel Rendge Wm Hobson, Dan'l Chapman
& county road 70 acres more or less Oct 28 1763.

   855. i.   ELEANOR, b. Oct. 28, 1764; m. Aug. 1, 1783, Joshua Jackson
              of Rowley.
   856. ii.   JOSEPH, b. Sept. 5, 1767; m. Margaret Clark.
   857. iii. BENJAMIN, b. Nov. 15, 1768; m. ———— ————.
   858. iv. SARAH, b. Jan. 18, 1770; m. Feb. 7, 1800, John Hutchins of
              Londonderry.
   859. v.   LYDIA, b. Feb. 29, 1776.
   860. vi. ELIZABETH, b. Jan. 9, 1772.
   861. vii. MARK, b. June 21, 1778; m. Eleanor Wilson and Mrs. Elizabeth
              (Stark) Kidder.

     541. JOHN FISK (Mark, Joseph, William, William, John, William, Robert,
Simon, Simon, William, Symond), b. Kennebunk, Me., 1755; m. there———Wakefield, she d. in Kennebunk; m. 2d there Comfort Stover. She was b. 1752; d. at
Waterboro, Mar. 16, 1824. He was born in Kennebunk, Me., where he resided
and was married. In 1801 he sold his farm and the following year moved to
Waterboro, where he afterwards resided and where he died. He d. Apr. 26, 1825;
res. Kennebunk and Waterboro, Me.

   862. i.   JOHN, b. Apr. 28, 1786; m. Sarah Coffin and Nancy Davis.
   863. ii.   MARK, b. ————; died in infancy.
   864. iii. MARK, b. ————.
   865. iv. POLLY, b. ————; m. John Sharples of Kennebunk, Me.
              They resided there; he went to Norfolk, Va., and never re-
              turned. Ch.: Mary, m. Caleb Kimball of Lyman, Me. She
              d. in Somerville, Mass., and was buried at Lyman. Abigail
              m. Moses Gowen and Daniel Walker. She d. in Boston.
              Charles. He was born in Kennebunk, Me. Went to Norfolk,
              Va., to find his father and never heard from again.
   866. v.   BETSEY, b. ————; m. John Simpson of Kennebunk, Me., and
              res. there. She m. 2d, David Davis of Alfred, Me.; m. 3d,
              Nathan Ramond. He d. s. p. Ch. George. He died unm. on
              board ship while en route from the West Indies to Boston of
              yellow fever. John. He was with his brother George and died
              about the same time of the same disease. Samuel Davis, died
              in Alfred, Me. Betsey, m. Col. Elisha Littlefield of Alfred.
              She d. in Lyman.
   867. vi. ABIGAIL, b. ————; m. John Kimball of Kennebunk, Me.; res.
              Denmark, Me. Ch.: Nathaniel, d. in Denmark. John, d. in
              Denmark. William, drowned while skating on the ice in Den-
              mark. Abram, d. in Denmark. Charles, d. in Denmark.
   868. vii. LUCY, b. ————; m. Richard Bean. Ch.. Mary, m. Oliver
              Hanson; res. Waterboro and Gorham, Me. Sally, m. John
              Thwing of Waterboro. John, m. Abigail White; res. Port-
              land, Me. Joseph, m. Julia Cook; res. Waterboro. Brad-
              ford, m. Louisy Coffin; res. Waterboro. Susan, m. ————
              Kimball and Seth Scribner; res. Waterboro.
   869. viii. SALLY, b. ————; m. Moody Pike; res. Great Falls, N. H.
              Lizzie, b. Waterboro, Me. Sinthy, m. Albert Haggett of Low-
              ell; had one son Albert. Julia, m. twice; her second husband
              was a ———— Perry of Lowell. Jane, m. Freeman Brigham;
              had one ch. and res. in Lowell, Mass. Alpheus, d. unm. in
              Great Falls. Sarah, d. in Dover. Charles, d. in Dover, N. H.

     543. BENJAMIN FISKE (Theophilus, Theophilus, William, William, John,
William, Robert, Simon, Simon, William, Symond), b. Ipswich, Mass., Oct. 30,
1738; m. Nov. 19, 1769, Sarah Towne of Topsfield, dau. of Joshua. She was b. 1747,
d. Dec. 27, 1831. He died soon after his marriage, and his widow lived 59 years
after his decease. She was a cloth weaver, leaving a web in her loom unfinished at

9

her death. It is said that those who chanced to pass her residence, early or late, always heard her weaving and singing. Estate of Benjamin Fiske of Topsfield admn. was granted to Sarah Fiske June 1, 1772. Inventory of his estate taken July 4, 1772. Five acres of land with the house and barn, 15 acres of meadow in Wenham, four acres of woodland in Boxford, etc.; made oath to by Mrs. Sarah Fisk, the admr., July 2, 1772. He d. May 1, 1772; res. Ipswich, Mass.

    870. i. SARAH, b. ———; d. May 15, 1770.
    871. ii. SARAH, bap. Nov. 7, 1773; m. Sept. 20, 1792, John Conant, Jr., and died Feb. 25, 1830. He then m. Rebecca Baker, and d. Apr., 1859. ae. 87. Ch.: John, b. Oct. 5, 1793, d. Jan. 16, 1867, leaving six children. Sally, b. Oct. 5, 1796; m. James G. Raymond; res. No. Beverly; her son, John, was colonel in the Civil War. Harriett, m. Benjamin Kent of Danvers. Benjamin F., d. s. p. Irene d. young.

    544. NATHANIEL FISKE (Theophilus, Theophilus, William, William, John, William, Robert, Simon, Simon, William, Symond), b. Wenham, Mass., Mar., 1741; m. in Danvers, Feb. 27, 1764, Lydia Gould, dau. of Solomon and Elizabeth (Robinson) Gould, b. June 11, 1743, d. Apr. 25, 1809. Nathaniel Fiske, son of Theophilus, Jr., married Lydia Gould. He was a soldier during the Revolutionary War, was in the battle at Bunker Hill, and was with Washington at Valley Forge. He had six sons. He resided at Danvers and Topsfield, and died, leaving considerable property. His son and executor was Nathaniel. Lydia Gould of Topsfield had a brother, John Gould, who lived in that town. Nathaniel and wife owned the covenant of the church in Topsfield, where most of their children's baptisms are recorded; but the births of Ruth, John, and first Lydia are recorded on the records of Danvers. They finally settled in Topsfield, about half a mile from Wenham line, the house being the first after crossing the causeway from Wenham. He died, and was buried by the side of this wife in Topsfield.

Nathaniel Fisk of Topsfield yeoman made his will Nov. 27, 1813, which was proved Apr. 17. 1815. Son Benj. had already received a part of his portion. Son Moses had rec'd most of his portion, Son Ebenezer Son John deceased left a son Elbridge, Daughter Ruth was then wife of Elijah Perkins Son David (perhaps the youngest son) & Son Nath'l had a residue & were Executors Inv. of the Estate June 7. 1815. Homestead about 30 acres, meadow & woodland in Danvers about 12 acres & 272 acres in Boxford amt $3695.66.

An acct. of Executor N & Eb Fisk July 2, 1816. Bal $976.03.

He d. Apr. 9, 1815; res. Danvers and Topsfield, Mass.

    872. i. NATHANIEL, b. in Wenham, Dec. 2, 1764; m. Mehitable Balch.
    873. ii. JOHN, b. Aug. 18, 1769; m. Huldah Woodbury.
    874. iii. BENJAMIN, b. Aug. 17, 1774; m. Lydia Hobbs.
    875. iv. MOSES, b. Aug. 20, 1777; m. Sukey Platts.
    876. v. EBENEZER, b. 1775; d. Dec. 27, 1849; m. in 1805, Mary Cleaves Dodge, dau. of George and Mary (Cleaves) Dodge, and granddau. of George and Martha (Fiske) Dodge, who was b. May 16, 1781, and d. Mar. 27, 1852. No children. Was a trader in Beverly, Mass., and New York City. They are both deceased, he suddenly in the western part of the state of New York while they were there on business; and they had no issue.
    877. vi. DAVID, b. Nov. 24, 1783; m. Nancy Baker.
    878. vii. RUTH, b. May 10, 1767, and bap. fourteen days after; m. Nov. 20, 1794, Elijah Perkins; settled in that part of Topsfield called the "Perkins district," which is near Hamilton; and had Dudley, who m. a Sally Perkins, and had children 1, Lydia, who m. first, John Ray, and second, a William Perkins, and had children by both husbands. 2, Daniel, who m. first, Rosamond, a sister to Lydia's husband, and second, Charlotte Towne, and one of his children is Elijah Perkins, the artist of Salem. 3, Huldah, who m. Thomas Ferguson, of Topsfield, and had children; and 4, Abigail, who m. Ebenezer Peabody, of Topsfield, by whom she had children.
    879. viii. LYDIA, bap. Mar. 1, 1772; d. May 16, 1777.
    880. ix. LYDIA, b. Feb. 26; bap. Apr. 23, 1780; d. young.

545. SAMUEL FISKE (Theophilus, Theophilus, William, William, John, William, Robert, Simon, Simon. William, Symond), b. Ipswich, Mass., 1748; m. Mar. 8, 1772, Sarah Perkins. She d. 1810. Samuel, son of Theophilus, Jr., and Jemima Fiske, married Sarah Perkins, of Topsfield. He was executor of his father's will and residuary legatee; had the homestead, where he resided many years, and sold out to Jacob Towne. His son, Waldo G. Towne, occupied the place. He died in that town. He d. Apr. 15, 1826; res. Ipswich, Mass.

    881. i. SAMUEL, b. May 7, 1773; m. Sarah Patch.
    882. ii. EZRA, b. Jan. 7. 1776; m. Polly Lakeman.
    883. iii. SARAH, b. May 3, 1785; m. Nov. 20, 1805, Samuel Fornace. She was b. June 9, 1781; d. Jan. 14, 1865. He was a native of Beverly, a seaman, who d. Apr., 1815, and she remained a widow in that town. Her children were Samuel. who was a seaman, unm. Charles, also a seaman, b. Aug. 3, 1810, who m., but his wife d. without issue. Eleanor H., who d. about 1855, was b. Oct. 23, 1812; m. Oliver O. Brown, who resided in Beverly, by whom she had Benjamin, a clerk in a store in Boston (where the other sons were employed), b. about 1831; Ellen, who m. Augustus Cheever; Charles, Joseph, and George, who was b. about 1850. Sarah, b. Oct. 21, 1814, who resided in Beverly, m. Thomas Welch about 1860, who d. in the army in 1863; she had no children.

549. JOHN FISKE (Ebenezer, Ebenezer, William, William, John, William, Robert, Simon, Simon, William, Symond), b. in Grafton, Sept. 27, 1757; m. Anna Leland. Res. ———.

    884. i. HORACE, b. ———; d. unm., in Phil.

550. SIMEON FISKE (Ebenezer, Ebenezer, William, William, John, William, Robert, Simon, Simon, William, Symond), b. Hardwick, Mass., July 15, 1762; m. Jan. 20, 1784, Dinah Whitcomb, b. 1761. She d. in Goshen, N. Y., 1845. He d. 1838; res. Shelburne, Mass., and Goshen, N. Y.

    885. i. EZRA, b. Jan. 10, 1785; m. ——— Cummins; graduated at Williams College in 1809; studied theology under Rev. Dr. Packard, of Shelburne, and was ordained as an Evangelist in 1810. He preached as a missionary in Georgia for two or three years, and there he married a daughter of the venerable Dr. Francis Cummins. In 1813 he was permanently settled in the ministry at Goshen, N. Y., where he sustained a beloved pastoral relation with his people for upward of twenty years, when he was compelled, by an affection of the lungs, to intermit his labors, and seek relief by a winter's residence at the South. During his absence he was appointed to but declined the office of General Agent of and elected Professor of Ecclesiastical History and Church Government, in the Western Theological Seminary in Pennsylvania, which position, upon his return north, he accepted. On the 4th of November, 1833, while on the way to his new field of labor, he was taken suddenly and fatally ill, at Philadelphia, just after the close of an impressive discourse, Sabbath evening, from the text (Col. i. 12) "Giving thanks," etc. Dr. Ezra Fiske was moderator of the Presbyterian General Assembly, in 1833; was long a director of Princeton Theological Seminary, and from 1823 to 1833 was a trustee of Williams College. He received his doctorate from Hamilton College, and was highly esteemed for his ripe scholarship, for the acumen and strength of his mind, and for his Christian integrity. He was the author of several published sermons and a valuable series of essays on Mental Science. Few men were better read in the Hebrew and Classics, and in the realm of Mental Philosophy he had no superiors in his church. As a preacher he was always master of his theme and audience. His style was logical, polished, always forcible, and at times impassioned; his eloquence, the rich overflow of a well-stored mind sanctified by grace. He labored to win souls, not to himself but to Christ, and not many have had more seals to

their ministry. Nearly six hundred sound and permanent conversions were the fruits of his devoted labors. In his discourses he was accustomed to address both the understanding and the feelings, the reason and the passions of men. To a personal dignity and nobleness of manner, he added a purity of purpose, sweetness of temper and benignity of heart irresistibly fascinating. No one ever doubted his piety, his sincerity or devotion; and he lived in Goshen twenty years without making a personal enemy, and departed thence universally regretted and beloved. He d. in 1833, leaving no children behind him.

886. ii. PETER, b. Feb. 15, 1787. He was a physician in Montague, Mass., and d. unm.

887. iii. SIMEON, b. July 2, 1788. He was a merchant in Western Georgia, and d. unm.

888. iv. JONATHAN, b. Oct. 18, 1790; m. Susanna Williams, Mrs. Maria Roberts and Releafy Blood.

889. v. HARRIETT, b. ———; m. ——— Gillespie.

553. JONATHAN FISKE (Ebenezer, Ebenezer, William, William, John, William, Robert, Simon, Simon, William, Symond), b. Shelburne, Mass., Sept. 9, 1746; m. Jan. 18, 1770, Hannah Rice of Hardwick, Mass., b. July 26, 1747, dau. of Phinehas and Hannah Cummins. He was in the Rev. War. (See Rev. record.) Res. Shelburne, Mass.

890. i. JONATHAN, b. Sept. 27, 1775.
891. ii. ASA, b. July 13, 1771.
892. iii. SOLOMON, b. May 2, 1773.

554. EBENEZER FISKE (Ebenezer, Ebenezer, William, William, John, William, Robert, Simon, Simon, William, Symond), b. Shelburne, Mass., Sept. 9, 1749; m. Sarah Barnard, b. July, 1754, d. Apr. 15, 1816. A pious and worthy couple they were greatly blessed and honored in their children. He d. June 9. 1841, ae. 92; res. Shelburne, Mass.

893. i. RUFUS. b. Mar. 22, 1781; m. Hannah Woodward.
894. ii. SARAH, b. May 17, 1784; m. Mar. 13, 1814, Abijah Forbush (Samuel, Samuel, Thomas, Thomas, Daniel), b. Upton, May 11, 1779; d. June 27, 1845. She d. Feb. 3, 1854. Res. Shelburne, Mass. Ch.: Catherine, b. Apr. 24, 1815; d. May 11, 1843. Sarah Barnard, b. Oct. 20, 1816; d. May 17, 1858. Lucy Whitney, b. May 2, 1818; m. 1840, Edmund Skinner, d. 1842. Rufus, b. Oct. 1, 1820; m. 1841; d. 1846. Alfred, b. Dec. 19, 1822; d. Mar. 11, 1825; Jane, b. Sept. 12, 1826; d. Apr. 2, 1842.

895. iii. EBENEZER, b. Apr. 18, 1785; m. Hannah Terrill.

896. iv. LOVINA, b. July 8, 1787; descendant is Mrs. Elizabeth Beals, Batavia, N. Y.

897. v. LEVI, b. Feb. 21, 1790; m. Cynthia Coleman.

898. vi. PLINY, b. June 24, 1792. Pliny Fisk, missionary, was born in Shelburne, Mass., and died in Beyrut, Syria, Oct. 23, 1825. He was graduated at Middlebury College in 1814, and at Andover Theological Seminary in 1818. He was appointed, with Levi Parsons, by the American board, to the Palestine Mission, in 1818, and sailed from Boston for Smyrna, Nov. 3, 1819. On his arrival in Smyrna, he spent some time in perfecting his knowledge of the oriental languages, and then traveled through Egypt, Arabia, Palestine and Syria, preaching, holding conference meetings and distributing copies of the Bible. He resided at various times in Jerusalem, Damascus, Antioch, Alexandria and Beyrut where he died. After traveling extensively in Greece. Egypt, Palestine and Syria, he joined, in May, 1825, the mission already established at Beyrut, and died there of fever in the following October. Mr. Fisk was eminently fitted to be a missionary in the east, as he preached in Italian, French, Greek and Arabic. On the day of his death, he completed an "English and Arabic dictionary," and wrote numerous papers for the "Missionary Herald." A life of Pliny Fisk was published by Alvin Bond (Boston, 1828).

899. vii. JOHN, b. May 2, 1795; d. Apr. 18, 1819.

900. viii. RUTH, b. July 19, 1797. Descendants are Mrs. Lucy Graves and Mrs. Sarah Barnard, Shelburne, Mass.

557. DEA. MOSES FISKE (Ebenezer, Ebenezer, William, William, John, William, Robert, Simon. Simon, William, Symond), b. Shelburne, Mass., Sept. 13, 1764; m. June 2, 1789. Hannah Batchelor, b. Upton, May 14, 1770; d. Waitsfield, Vt., in 1854. Moses Fiske, youngest son of Ebenezer and Dorcas Fiske, of Shelburne, married Hannah Batchelor, and settled in Waitsfield, Vt., where he and wife were among the original members of the Congregational Church, of which he was also a deacon for forty-five years. To them were born twelve children, the eldest dying young. He d. Feb. 5, 1847; res. Waitsfield, Vt.

901. i. JOEL, b. July 16, 1790; d. July 18, 1795.
902. ii. PERRIN B., b. July 6, 1792; m. Azubah Blaisdell.
903. iii. MOSES, b. July 25, 1794; m. ———— ———— and Rebecca Ferrin.
904. iv. JOEL (2d), b. Oct. 26, 1790; m. Clarinda Chapman.
905. v. HARVEY, b. Apr. 12, 1799; m. Anna Mary Plumb.
906. vi. LYMAN, b. Oct. 15, 1801; m. Mary Spofford.
907. vii. BETSEY, b. May 8, 1804; m. 1847, Phinehas Bailey. She d. Feb. 23, 1847. Ch.: One child died young. Arabella Paulina, b. 1842; d. 1852. Louisa Marietta, b. 1844; m. Rev. Joel F. Whitney (see). Abbot Fisk, b. 1847; d. 1847.
908. viii. ANSON, b. Oct. 31, 1806; m. Joanna Barnard.
909. ix. JONATHAN, b. May 6, 1809; m. Mary A. Imlay.
910. x. ELVIRA ELIZA, b. Aug. 20, 1811; m. at Waitsfield, Vt., Mar. 3, 1840, Dea. John Russell Whitney, b. Wadham's Mills, N. Y., Apr. 18, 1813. She d. Apr. 22, 1892. John R. Whitney was born on the farm, owned and occupied by him till his death, about one mile north of Wadham's Mills. His father, John Whitney, was one of the pioneers who settled that region early in the present century, coming about 1808. Among these settlers were Benjamin Whitney and Daniel Safford, who married Sally Whitney. John was a shoemaker by trade. He was one of the pioneers in the temperance cause, and his house, still standing, was the first building in that region raised without intoxicating liquor (1829). He, with others, responded to the call for the militia in 1812-14, but arrived at Plattsburg too late to participate in the fight. Taken away in the prime of life, 1834, he left an honored name to his family. After the death of his father, John Russell Whitney was obliged to assume the care of the home, and lived with his widowed mother several years. He was married, Mar. 3, 1840, to Elmina E. Fisk, daughter of Dea. Moses Fisk, of Waitsfield, Vt. Having been deprived of educational privileges in his younger days, he was determined to give his family every possible advantage, often making great sacrifices to secure school privileges to his children; for several winters he had a family school. He was deeply interested in the Congregational church at Wadham's Mills, of which he became a member at the early age of fourteen. He was elected deacon about 1863, to fill a vacancy caused by the death of the senior deacon, and held this office till his death in 1880. He was especially active in all church affairs, and did much for the maintenance of public service. Enjoying the advantages provided for them, his children sought to improve themselves, and have all honored the name and memory of their parents. Dea. Whitney passed away after a severe and painful illness of heart disease. He d. July 23, 1880; res. Wadham's Mills, N. Y. Ch.: 1, Elizabeth Hannah, b. Jan. 11, 1841; d. Mar. 11, 1865. 2, Marietta Thankful, b. Feb. 2, 1842; m. Oct. 3, 1866, Rev. A. T. Clarke; res. Shelby, Ala.; ch., Almon Taylor, b. Oct. 7, 1867; m. Elizabeth Perry; res. Parishville, N. Y.; Susan Elmira, b. Dec. 17, 1872; Maud Elizabeth, b. Nov. 10, 1875; John Paul, b. Oct. 17, 1880; Harvey Fisk, b. May 13, 1883; Lena M., b. Mar. 1, 1886. 3, Joel Fisk, b. Mar. 30, 1843; m. Louisa M. Bailey; clergyman; res. Coventryville, N. Y. 4,

Sarah L., b. Sept. 4, 1844; m. Sept. 4, 1873, Edward D. Sturtevant, and d. s. p. Apr. 1, 1874. 5, John R., b. July 29, 1847; m.
Lena Groll; res. Garnett, Kan. 6, Moses Fisk, b. Apr. 18,
1849; m. Ella Burt; res. Walpole, Mass. 7, Lemuel, b. Dec. 12,
1850; res. Wadham's Mills, N. Y. 8, Rosabelle, b. May 15, 1853;
m. Oct. 6, 1877, Rev. Wm. H. Wolcott; res. Moreno, Cal.; ch.,
Lucy, b. 1878; Sarah A., b. 1881; Vernon H., b. 1882. 9, Elmina Eliza, b. Sept. 7, 1855; res. Wadham's Mills. (See
Whitney Genealogy by Fred C. Pierce.)

911. xi.   HORACE ALONZO, b. Aug. 20, 1811; m. and d. Aug. 29, 1851,
            s. p. at Waterville, Vt.

912. xii.   EMILY, b. Jan. 12, 1817; d., unm., May 25, 1891.

563. JUDGE JONATHAN FISKE (William, Ebenezer, William, William,
John, Wilham, Robert, Simon, Simon, William, Symond), b. Wenham, Mass., May
1, 1751; m. Nov. 26, 1772, Mrs. Mary Bragg, b. 1752, d. 1826. Jonathan Fiske, the
eldest son of William Fiske, Sr., of Amherst, established himself in the northwest
parish of that town, since known as Mt. Vernon. After a few years he removed
thence to Francestown, N. H., where he resided several years, and where his
younger children were born. In 1790 he was chosen deacon of the Congregational
church in Francestown and officiated in that capacity until 1794, when in September
he removed to Williamstown, Vt., where he seems to have in time acquired popularity and social influence, to have been again elected deacon and to various other
offices, which he filled to the general satisfaction of his constituents.

A correspondent writes: "Judge Fiske was a justice of the peace and town
clerk in Williamstown from my earliest recollection until a brief period before
his death, and as such made public all the marriages, and did most of the marrying. He represented that town in the state legislature, I think, over twenty years
in succession, and afterward at various times. He was also judge of probate
at an early date, and continued in that office until his sight failed and until too old
and otherwise infirm to discharge its duties. He was also a deacon in the Congregational church at Williamstown further back than I can remember, and when he
died his mantle fell on two of his worthy sons now living." From a file of the
Wenham records it appears that Judge Jonathan Fiske was married to Mrs. Mary
Bragg by Rev. Joseph Swain in Dec., 1772. They were the parents of twelve children, eight sons and five daughters, all of whom except one matured, married, and
had families, and all excepting three lived to be over seventy years of age. Their
grandchildren number upward of seventy, fifty-three of whom are still living
(1867), including the fourth generation. Their living descendants will probably
reach one hundred souls. Judge Fiske, after living to see his children all married
and comfortably settled in life, died in 1825—his wife the following year—both at
the age of seventy-four. Their closing days were spent with their son, Samuel,
who then resided in Berlin, Vt., and after their deaths their remains were taken
to Northfield for burial. The sons, Nathaniel, William, John, Samuel, and daughters Elizabeth and Anna were married by their father in Williamstown, where most
of the family appear to have originally settled. Some of them afterward removed
to Northfield, where a number of their descendants yet remain. Amherst, N. H.,
is situated in Hillsborough County, forty-seven miles from Boston and twenty-
eight from Concord, the state capital. The town had its origin in a grant of the
general court of Massachusetts to the surviving officers and soldiers of the Nar-
ragansett war and to the posterity of those now living. The claimants had seven
towns awarded them. Amherst was principally settled by people from Wenham
and adjoining towns and incorporated in 1760. In 1771 Amherst became the shire
town of Hillsborough County, and after many years was one of the most flourishing villages in the state. Its residents contained many people who later attained
prominence in the state and nation, among the number being President Franklin
Pierce, Horace Greeley and Daniel Webster.

He d. 1825; res. Amherst, N. H., and Williamstown, Vt.

913. i.   JONATHAN. b. Sept. 6, 1773; m. ——— Livingston.

914. ii.   NATHANIEL, b. July 6, 1775; m. Mehitable Bates and ———

915. iii.   WILLIAM R., b. May 30, 1779; m. Hannah Martin.

916. iv.   MARY, b. May 13, 1781; m. Feb. 27, 1800, Daniel Worthington.
            They removed about 1830 to Wisconsin. They had eleven

children, and subsequently scattered through the states. They are now dead. Daniel Worthington died in Oconomowoc, Wis., Mar., 1866. His wife died there in the spring of 1851. One of their sons was a presiding elder in the M. E. Church for several years. Two daughters have resided at Northfield, and one of them is the wife of a clergyman in the same denomination. Ch.: Huldah, b. July 31, 1801; Elijah, b. July 31, 1803; Sophia, b. Apr. 9, 1805; Lyman, b. Feb. 16, 1807; Mary, b. Sept. 26, 1808; Rhoda, b. June 18, 1811; Daniel, b. Feb. 3, 1813; David, b. Feb. 13, 1815; Theodore, b. May 17, 1817; Elias, b. July 16, 1819; d. Jan. 12, 1824; Francis, b. Feb. 3, 1822; d. Sept. 2, 1823. Huldah Worthington, eldest daughter of Mary Fiske, was married to John Richardson, a farmer, at Northfield, Dec. 19, 1821. They had seven children, named Sarah Sophia, George Martin, John H., Marshal S., George Sullivan, Mary Jane, Daniel W. John Richardson d. Mar. 6, 1834. Widow Huldah was married to Rev. Hosea Clark in June, 1838. They had Lucia Ann and Stephen A. Clark. The latter was an officer in Sherman's army. John H. and Daniel W. Richardson married. The former had four and the latter two children. Elijah Worthington married in Stafford, Vt., Emily Rand, a school teacher. They had but one child, Francis, born at Northfield. Elijah emigrated west and died at Hart Prairie, Wis., June 4, 1858. He was a minister and farmer. Sophia Worthington married at Northfield Nathan S. Green, a manufacturer, May 7, 1833. They had three children, Mary Sophia, George and Charles, born at Northfield. Also two grandchildren. Lyman Worthington married, at Norwich, Vt., Caroline Blood, a school teacher. He was a millwright by trade. They had three children, Susan A., George and Charles, who are now in the West. Their father died in Michigan. Mary Worthington married at Northfield Moses Lane, a farmer, May 2, 1833. She resided in Northfield. Rhoda Worthington married, in Northfield, Gilman Cummings, a farmer, at Metuchen, N. J. They had three children, Elvira, George T. (was a Union soldier) and Daniel. Daniel Worthington, Jr., married, at Northfield, Miss Ann Paine, a teacher, in May, 1835. They had one child, Frances, born in 1837. He resided in Chicago, Ill. His daughter Frances, married a Mr. Hall. They had three or four children. Rev. David Worthington in early life identified himself with the M. E. Church, and at the early age of twenty-two entered upon the work of the ministry. His labors in this calling were mostly confined to the limits of the Iowa conference, where his zeal and talents soon placed him in the front rank of the clergy of that state. Several years since Mr. Worthington received the appointment of presiding elder for Mt. Pleasant district, and was continued in that position until his death, by consumption, which took place in Mar., 1866. A sound preacher, and a devoted evangelist, he went to his grave according to his wish with the harness on. Mr. Worthington was twice married, and left four children by his first wife, Arinda Lee, the eldest of whom, Jason, died while in the service of his country during the late war. Theodore Worthington was a farmer and lived in Oconomowoc, Wis., and had a family.

917. v. JOHN, b. Feb. 24, 1783; m. Elizabeth Martin.
918. vi. BENJAMIN, b. Nov. 17, 1784; m. Hannah Herrick.
919. vii. ELIZABETH, b. Oct. 15, 1786; m. Apr. 18, 1811, Miles Stebbins at Williamstown. They had two children: 1, Miles J., b. Apr. 29, 1813; 2, Pamela, b. Oct. 24, 1816. Miles J. Stebbins was married to Mehitable Olds at Williamstown, Sept. 21, 1844. One child, George, b. Jan. 29, 1845. Pamela Stebbins was married to Lyman Capron at Williamstown, Jan. 7, 1837. Ch : 1,

Lucy E., b. Dec. 19, 1843; 2, Dorcas A., b. Sept. 8, 1845; 3, May L., b. Nov. 29, 1851; 4, Martha L., b. Feb. 28, 1854. Miles Stebbins, the husband of Betsy Fiske, died in Williamstown about the time his youngest brother was born, and Betsy resided there a widow. She was the only daughter of Judge Fiske, who attained a venerable age.

920. viii. SARAH, b. Sept. 17, 1788; m. May 9, 1826, John White, of New Hampshire. They had born to them two daughters, Martha M. and Mary A. White. The first married John D., a son of Benjamin Fiske, elsewhere spoken of. Mary A. White was married to O. J. Walden, June 28, 1852. Ch.: 1, John H., b. May 15, 1853; d. October 12, 1862. 2, Frederick W., b. Sept. 16, 1855; d. Sept. 28, 1862. 3, Charles E., b. November 15, 1857; d. Oct. 1, 1862. 4, Frances, b. Aug. 14, 1863. 5, Elizabeth, b. Dec. 5, 1864. Mr. White removed to Black Rock, N. Y., in 1833, where he d. Oct. 8, 1839. His widow, Sarah, died there Nov. 9, 1843.

921. ix. ANNE, b. Oct. 12, 1790; m. Apr. 18, 1811, Allen White, a farmer in Williamstown. Mr. White d. Jan. 31, 1836, in his forty-seventh year, when Anne married a Mr. Staples, and d. in Mar., 1863, aged seventy-three years. By the first husband were the following children: 1, Caroline Ann, b. Oct. 11, 1812; d. young. 2, Cornelius Allen, b. Dec. 18, 1814; d. young. 3, Cornelius Allen, b. Mar. 21, 1816; 4, Horace Elliot, b. July 25, 1819; 5, Samuel Davis, b. Mar. 21, 1821; 6, George Hamman, b. Jan. 31, 1823; 7, Jonathan Perkins, b. Feb. 10, 1825; 8, Caroline Ann, b. September 17, 1827; 9, Mary Emeline, b. Aug. 4, 1829; 10, Abijah Prentis, b. July 24, 1831; 11, Cynthis Delphinia, b. Sept. 21, 1833. Cornelius Allen White m. Josephine Seapled, Aug. 8, 1841, at Williamstown, where he resided. Ch.: 1, Cornelius Allen, b. Sept. 21, 1842; 2, Henry Kirk, b. Jan. 13, 1852; 3, George Perkins, b. Aug. 17, 1855. Horace Elliot White m. a Miss Peck of Williamstown. Caroline Ann m. Lorenzo Downing of St. Albans. Mary Emeline m. Arthur Whitney of Montpelier. Cynthia m. P. F. Blanchard. Others have married.

922. x. DAVID, b. Feb. 2, 1793; m. Sarah Reed.
923. xi. SAMUEL L., b. Oct. 24, 1794; m. Lucy White.

565. HON. WILLIAM FISKE (William, Ebenezer, William, William, John, William, Robert, Simon, Simon, William, Symond), b. Wenham, Mass., Apr. 20, 1755; m. Oct. 28, 1773, Eunice Nourse, b. May 2, 1752, d. Mar. 13, 1819; m. 2d, Nov. 28, 1819, Hannah Walker of Concord, N. H.; d. Dec. 10, 1841. Deacon Francis Nourse of Danvers, Mass., whose eldest daughter, Eunice, and granddaughters Abigail and Harriet Nourse, married Amherst Fiskes, was a lineal descendant of Francis and Rebecca Nourse, original settlers in Salem, Mass. Francis Nourse died in 1695, aged 77 years; his wife, Rebecca, July 19, 1692—one of the sad victims of the Salem witchcraft. The jury—Capt. Thomas Fiske, foreman——— "were compelled to convict, against their better judgment and belief, through the singular infatuation and perversity of the judges." In Apr., 1779, Mr. Fiske located himself and wife on a farm situated on the turnpike leading from Amherst village to Bedford, and for some years occupied a small tolling house. His farm was limited in extent and his land rough and rocky. Mr. Fiske and wife became members of the Congregational Church in Amherst, Nov. 6, 1776, and lived exemplary Christian lives to the day of their death. Besides having for some years command of the military company, Mr. Fiske was in Mar., 1792, elected town clerk of Amherst and re-elected every year in succession for twenty years. In Mar., 1794, he was chosen chairman of the board of selectmen of Amherst and held that office till 1815, twenty-one consecutive years. He was chosen representative of the town at the general court in 1798-99, 1804-5-6-7-8-9. He was elected state senator for the Seventh senatorial district in 1810-11-12-13. He was then appointed one of the justices of the court of common pleas of the county of Hillsborough, but a remodeling of the courts by the state soon after by legislature (a political change occurring in that body), by which all the judges

were displaced to make room for new favorites, prevented his accepting the appointment. In 1815 he was appointed United States Assessor of direct taxes for the county of Hillsborough. In 1824 he was chosen one of the electors of president and vice-president, and cast his vote for John Quincy Adams. Having attained the good old age of three score and ten, he then retired from public life, and spent the remainder of his days in the quiet of home where he died. He was twice married. His first wife was Eunice Nourse and the mother of his children. A few years after he married Miss Hannah, daughter of James Walker, Esq., of Concord, N. H., but had no children by her. In personal appearance Mr. Fiske was rather commanding, being six feet in height and well proportioned. His features were strongly molded and intellectual. Of Puritan descent, he was in principles, habits and manners a Puritan of the straitest sect, rendered straiter perhaps by his severe and excessive labors. In his family and on his farm his right to rule no subordinate ever presumed to question. By his strict yet judicious exercise of authority his children were trained to admirable obedience. The homestead in which Hon. William Fiske resided was erected in 1795, and was ranked among the finest and most desirable in that section. It is located two and a half miles northeasterly from Amherst on the old stage road between that place and Manchester and Concord. To the south lies Walnut Hill, 200 feet high, to the north Chestnut Hills flanking them on the right and left and at a distance of from three to five miles tower the granite peaks of "Joe English" and "Uncanoonucks" and southeast Babboosack Pond. He d. June 4, 1831; res. Amherst, N. H.

924. i. EUNICE, b. Jan. 7, 1774; m. Dec. 30, 1795, Levi Dodge. She d. Aug. 3, 1861. He was son of Bartholomew and Martha (Kimball) Dodge, who was b. Feb. 26, 1771, and d. Nov. 21, 1842. She d. Aug. 3, 1861. Ch.: Martha, d. in infancy. Hiram, b. Jan. 2, 1803, and d. in 1876; m. Sarah Abbott. Calvin, b. Mar. 22, 1815, and d. June 6, 1853; m. Lucy Hubbard.

925. ii. EZRA, b. Apr. 2, 1776; m. Melinda Blake.
926. iii. WILLIAM, b. July 11, 1778; m. Margaret Cleave Dodge.
927. iv. FRANCIS NOURSE, b. June 12, 1780; m. Mary (Walker) Emery.
928. v. ABIGAIL, b. Oct. 9, 1782; d., unm., July 24, 1852. She res. at home, and later with her brother David for more than twenty years.
929. vi. MARY, b. Apr. 1, 1785; m. July 10, 1806, Bartholomew Dodge, Jr. She d. Oct. 15, 1857. Mary resided constantly with her father's family until twenty-two years of age, when in July she was united in marriage to Bartholomew Dodge, Jr., son of a neighboring farmer and two years her senior. Their children were: 1, Mary Ann, b. Feb. 8, 1807; d. May 1, 1813. 2, Francis P., b. Sept. 20, 1808; d. May 6, 1815. 3, David Nourse, b. Jan. 29, 1810; d. Apr. 16, 1829. 4, Allen F., b. May 22, 1812; d. Mar., 1814. 5, Mary Ann, b. May 2, 1814; m. July 24, 1848, to Jonathan Knight of Amherst, N. H., and d. Dec. 17, 1851, leaving a pair of twins two days old (Mary and George), who died respectively in Aug. and Oct. following. 6, Francis Fiske, b. May 28, 1816; m. Jan. 18, 1849, James Smith of Lowell, Mass., and d. in Mar., 1857. 7, Francis A., b. Sept. 8, 1818; d. Jan., 1820. 8, Harriet M., b. Oct. 4, 1820; d. Jan., 1821. 9, Horace N., b. Oct. 4, 1820; m. Dec. 14, 1845, Hannah H. Miller of Lamoille, Ill. One child, Cheever Kendall, b. Nov. 15, 1850. 10, Abby M., b. Dec. 14, 1821; m. Nov. 18, 1852, Stephen Ballard, now of Stearns & Ballard, New York City. 11, Martha A., b. Nov. 8, 1823; m. Aug. 12, 1852, Rev. Allen H. Brown, late of May's Landing, N. J. Their children were: Silas Belding, b. May 17, 1854. Allen Henry, b. Nov. 17, 1855; d. Dec. 12, 1859. Mary Dodge, b. Jan. 1, 1858. Louisa Matilda, b. Jan. 18, 1860. 12, Charles W., b. May 8, 1826; m. Aug. 15, 1853, Anna Eliza, dau. of George Fiske, Esq., of Lowell. Ch.: Florence M., b. Aug. 31, 1854; d. Jan. 4, 1860. Fanny A., b. May 12, 1857. Herbert C., b. July 28, 1859; d. Sept. 15, 1850.

Bartholomew Dodge was b. Dec. 26, 1784, and d. Oct. 7,
1838. Mrs. Mary Fiske Dodge d. in Hooksett, N. H., Oct. 15,
1857, aged 72 years.

930. vii. FANNY, b. June 6, 1787; d., unm., June 17, 1817.
931. viii. ALLEN, b. Apr. 10, 1789; m. Eliza Chapman and Mrs. Maria
           Stokes.
932. ix.   DAVID, b. May 4, 1791; m. Mrs. Lydia M. Holbrook.
933. x.   NANCY, b. June 17, 1794; m. Sept., 1815, Stephen Damon, son
           of Deacon Benjamin Damon. She d. Dec. 7, 1854. They
           were the parents of the following children: 1, Francis S., b.
           Apr. 16, 1816; d. Mar. 16, 1841. 2, Lucy Ann, b. June 1, 1818;
           d. June 14, 1853. 3, William F., b. Apr. 17, 1821; d. Aug. 5,
           1844. 4, Charles A., b. Aug. 28, 1823; d. July 4, 1863. 5, Ste-
           phen C., b. Mar. 21, 1826. 6, Sarah Jane, b. June 9, 1830; d.
           Jan. 10, 1853. The two eldest sons emigrated to Illinois, but
           died soon after their arrival there. Lucy Ann, the eldest
           daughter, married David P. Low of Amherst. Of this union
           two children were born: Wm. Damon, 1845, and Alphonso,
           1849, d. in 1851. Nancy Fiske Damon d. Dec. 7, 1854. Charles
           A. Damon m. Mary E. Low of Amherst, N. H., in June, 1845.
           Children born as follows: George W., b. Feb., 1847; Clara G.,
           b. July, 1849; Frank C., b. May, 1851; Charles Edgar, b. Sept.,
           1854; Nellie, b. Aug., 1856; Stephen C. Damon, b. Jan., 1854;
           m. Mrs. Mary J. McClelland. Dea. Benjamin Damon was a
           descendant of Dea. John Damon of Reading, Mass., freeman,
           1645, was born in that place June 4, 1760. The family prob-
           ably originated in Reading. Although but sixteen years of
           age at the commencement of the American Revolution, he
           enlisted, and continued fighting the battles of his country
           until the close of the war. In Jan. (16th), 1783, he married
           Polly Hosea, who was born in Plymouth, Mass., April 30, 1764.

566. DAVID FISKE (William, Ebenezer, William, William, John, William,
Robert, Simon, Simon, William, Symond), b. Wenham, Mass., June 25, 1757; m.
1786, Edith Tay, b. 1763, d. June 13, 1815. David Fiske, Sr., third son of William
Fiske, Sr., of Amherst, did good service to his country as a soldier in the war of
the Revolution. He enlisted at the age of eighteen for one year, and was stationed
first at Newcastle, N. H. In the fall of 1786 he was m. to Edith Tay of Chelsea,
Mass., and settled in Merrimack, N. H. They both united with the Congregational
Church. They had five children. In April, 1801, Mr. Fiske removed to Amherst
and settled on a farm in the eastern part of that town, where he lived a Christian
life. He lived in comfortable circumstances to quite a venerable age, respected
generally for his sterling merits, and died in peace among his children, at the age
of 86 years. He d. June 23, 1843; res. Amherst and Merrimack, N. H.

934. i.   BETSEY, b. Sept. 12, 1788; d., unm., Aug. 25, 1876.
935. ii.   EDITH, b. Mar. 1, 1790; m. Oct. 18, 1820. John Sprague of
           Bedford and rev. to Ohio and d. there.
936. iii. DAVID, b. Sept. 20, 1792; m. Abigail Nourse and Harriett
           Nourse.
937. iv.   GEORGE, b. Aug. 22, 1794; m. Arinda Lane.
938. v.   ARDELLA, b. Dec. 18, 1803; d. unm. Sept. 20, 1828.

568. DEA. EBENEZER FISKE (William, Ebenezer, William, William,
John, William, Robert, Simon, Simon, William, Symond), b. Nov. 11, 1762, in
Wenham, Mass.; m. at Mt. Vernon, N. H., 1782. Abigail Woodbury, b. March 7,
1766; d. Dec. 9, 1839. Deacon Ebenezer Fiske, fourth son of William and
Susanna Fiske, removed from Wenham to Amherst with his father when but
eleven years of age, and resided in that place until his majority. Owing to the
reduced circumstances of the family, caused by the bankruptcies of his father's
brother-in-law (White), for whom his father had largely endorsed, Eben lost the
opportunity for enjoying educational privileges. He, however, inherited a remarkable physical frame and strong intellect, and possessed good sterling
qualities and an indomitable will. Many and remarkable are the feats of strength
recorded of him when in the prime of his powers, while his excellent common
sense and well-known integrity made him a counselor among his fellow towns-

men in Mt. Vernon, where he subsequently resided and for many years filled
various local offices. In 1782 he married Abigail Woodbury, born in Beverly,
Mass., March 7, 1766, and second daughter of James Woodbury of Mt. Vernon.
N. H., near Amherst, to which place he at once removed. Miss Woodbury was of
an excellent family, and a relative of Judge Levi Woodbury of Portsmouth, N. H.,
a farmer of the state and secretary of the United States Treasury under President
Jackson. Mr. Fiske, like the most of his ancestors, was blessed with a large
family, six sons and six daughters, all of whom, except a son who died in infancy,
lived to mature age.

All of these except the two last were born in Mt. Vernon. After residing for
some years in this place, Mr. Fiske removed to Warner, N. H., where he purchased a farm, and later located on a farm on the "Wilmot Flat" in Wilmot, N. H.
Later in life he moved to the hills in the northwestern part of the town, called
North Wilmot, and near where a meeting house afterward stood. Here he and
the wife of his youth grew old together, sustained and cheered by the consola-
tions of the gospel, and by the tender love and care of their son, Calvin, who, with
most filial affection, watched over and cared for them to the day of their death.
Ebenezer Fiske was a man of decided and conscientious and fixed and exemplary
principles, and the resolute energy and courage that always rises superior to the
difficulties of the occasion. During the most of his life he was a member and
deacon of the Congregational Church. He d. May 8, 1838; res. Wilmot, N. H.

939.   i.   ABIGAIL, b. Dec. 22, 1783; m. Josiah Carrier of Warner, N. H.,
              March, 1808, and after his decease, Samuel Clark of Hopkin-
              ton, N. H., where she died.
940.   ii.   JOHN, b. Sept. 28, 1784; d. in infancy.
941.   iii. EBENEZER, b. Aug. 22, 1786; m. Hannah Proctor.
942.   iv.   JAMES, b. Aug. 4, 1788; m. Eleanor Ransom.
943.   v.   HANNAH, b. June 17, 1790; m. 1810 Dr. Charles Thompson of
              Andover, N. H.; res. Wilmont Centre and Concord, N. H.
              He d. Sept. 14, 1856. Ch.: Elvira, b. Nov. 16, 1810, d. March
              16, 1826. Sophronia, b. April 10, 1812; m. J. R. Palmer; res.
              Sandusky, Ohio. Franklin W., b. Nov. 20, 1813; res. Con-
              cord, N. H. Hannah, b. April 4, 1817; m. Isaac Youngman
              of Wilmot. Caroline, b. July 20, 1819; m ――― Stearns; res.
              Concord. Charles Harrison, b. Feb. 8, 1824; res. Minneapolis.
              Luther Fisk, b. July 7, 1828; res. Janesville, Wis.
944.   vi.   DESDEMONA, b. March 15, 1792; m. Abner Watkins and
              William Abbott of Concord, N. H. Ch.: Livonia, m. Abijah
              Watson of Warner. James. George, m. Abby Bean.
945.   vii. LUTHER, b. May 16, 1794, d. 1816.
946.   viii. CALVIN, b. June 15, 1796; m. Asenath Cross and Mary J.
              Thompson.
947.   ix.   JOHN, b. April 16, 1798; m. Mahala Rand and Sarah Goodhue.
948.   x.   MEHITABLE, b. April 18, 1800; m. March 14, 1819, James B.
              Straw of Salisbury, N. H. He removed to Lowell, Mass.,
              and entered the employ of the Appleton Mfg. Co., where he
              died Aug. 14, 1830. She removed to Manchester, where she
              afterwards resided. Ch.: Ezekiel Albert, b. Dec. 30, 1819.
              After availing himself of the best educational advantages in
              the city of Lowell, he entered Phillip's Academy at Andover,
              where he mastered practical mathematics. In 1838 he was
              assistant civil engineer in the Nashua and Lowell Railroad.
              Later he was civil engineer for the Amoskeag Mfg. Co. In
              1851 he was appointed agent for the company, and in 1858 he
              was given entire charge. In Nov., 1844, he visited England
              and Scotland on a tour of inspection. In 1859 he was elected
              Representative for Manchester to the Legislature and re-
              elected in 1860-61-62-63, and for some time chairman of the
              committee on finance. In 1864 he was elected to the State
              Senate and re-elected in 1865, and was president of that body.
              Later he was elected Governor of N. H. Governor Straw had
              the honorary degree of Master of Arts by Dartmouth College.
              He m. April 6, 1842, Charlotte Smith Webster of Amesbury,

Mass. He d. Oct. 25, 1882. She d. Mar. 15, 1852. Ch.: Albert, b. June 24, 1846; d. April 9, 1847. Charlotte Webster, b. Mar. 24, 1848; m. William W. Howard; res. Lowell, Mass.; 4 ch. Herman Foster, b. Dec. 30, 1849; m. Sept. 18, 1873, Mary O. Parker; res. Manchester, N. H.; ch : 1, Parker, b. June 18, 1878; 2, Harry Ellis, b. April 25, 1883; 3, Herman F., Jr., b. Mar. 12, 1894; he is agent of the Amoskeag Mfg. Co., at Manchester, N. H. Ellen, b. Feb. 15, 1852; m. Sept. 12, 1872, Henry M. Thompson; ch.: 1, Albert W., b. Feb. 16, 1874; 2, Herman E., b. Apr. 25, 1881; res. Lowell, Mass. He was at one time manager of the Manchester, N. H., print works, now proprietor of the Lowell felting mills. Luther Fiske, b. July 31, 1821, d. Aug. 2, 1825. Guy Eldridge, b. Feb. 12, 1823, d. Aug. 1, 1825. Miranda, b. Oct. 6, 1824; m.

Benj. F. Manning of Manchester, s. p. Abigail, b. Apr. 22, 1827; d. unm. July 13, 1895. James Brown, Jr., b. Dec. 23, 1828; d. Mar. 23, 1830. James Brown, 3d, b. Apr. 9, 1831; m. Oct. 12, 1858, Clara A. Hancock; 2 ch.: Minnie Fiske, b. Mar. 26, 1862; d. young; and Gertrude, b. July 24, 1864.

949. xi. MARY, b. Mar. 16, 1802; m. Abner Harvey of Warner, N. H.; res. Concord. Ch.: Caroline M., b. May 19, 1825; m. John Emerson of Wilmont; d. Jan. 25, 1852. Elvira T., b. Aug. 3, 1827; m. Henry Saltmarsh of Concord. Susan E., b. Nov. 23, 1830; m. D. Emerson of Warner. Lavona W., b. Nov. 5, 1835; m. Albert Davis of Warner.

950. xii. PLOMA, b. March 7, 1807; m. John Langley of Andover, N. H.; d. Sept. 11, 1834.

574¼. JOHN FISKE (John, John, Samuel, William, John, William, Robert, Simon, Simon, William, Symond), b. July 15, 1751; m. Hepzibeth ———. She m. 2d in 1776, Moses Pearson. He d. and she m. 3d ——— Burnet or Burnap. He d. Apr. 5, 1773; res. Andover, Mass.

    950¼.i. JOHN, b. Apr. 5, 1771; d. young.
    950½.ii. HEPZIBAH, b. Apr. 28, 1773; m. July 5, 1798. Isaac Abbott, Jr., of A., had son Isaac, Jr.

576. SAMUEL FISKE (Samuel, Daniel, Samuel, William, John, William, Robert, Simon, Simon, William, Symond), b. Upton, Mass., 1759; m. Rebecca Fiske, his cousin, dau. of Benjamin, b. 1765; d. Apr. 30, 1849. He d. May 14, 1828; res. Shelburne, Mass.

    951. iv. DAVID, b. July 17, 1791; m. Laura Seaverance.
    952. vii. SAMUEL, b. March 25, 1800; m. Mercy B. Smead.
    953. i. AUSTIN, b. Nov. 21, 1784; d. May 23, 1789.
    954. ii. HERVY, b. March 8, 1787; d. Dec. 25, 1789.
    955. iii. MELINDA, b. Jan. 16, 1789; m. November, 1831, James Lord Merrill. She d. s. p. July 23, 1833.
    956. v. REBECCA, b. Aug. 2, 1793; d. Oct. 8, 1794.

957. vi. REBECCA, b. Feb. 15, 1794; m. Solomon Bardwell. She d. leaving a dau., Fidelia, and her dau. is Mrs. Alfred Skinner; res. S.

958. viii. AUSTIN, b. Feb. 9, 1803; d. Sept. 25, 1815.

959. ix. PHILO, b. Sept. 23, 1806; d. Sept. 23, 1806.

578. DANIEL FISKE (Samuel, Daniel, Samuel, William, John, William, Robert, Simon, Simon, William, Symond), b. May 16, 1765, in Sherborne. Mass.; m. Polly Crosby, b. Jan. 17, 1773, d. Dec. 7, 1795; m. 2d in Upton, Sept. 15, 1796, Huldah Fiske, his cousin, b. Nov. 6, 1772; d. Jan. 14, 1866. He d. Oct. 25, 1842; res. Shelburne, Mass.

960. i. POLLY, b. June 23, 1793; m. ―――― Barnard.

961. ii. ELECTA, b. March 4, 1798; d. Sept. 1, 1811.

962. iii. PARTRIDGE, b. Dec. 18, 1799; m. Lydia B. Dickinson.

963. iv. CHLOE, b. Oct. 1, 1801; d. Oct. 21, 1802.

964. v. CHLOE, b. July 27, 1803; d. Oct. 22, 1841.

965. vi. DANIEL, b. Feb. 9, 1805; m. Anna Fiske.

966. vii. WILLIAM, b. May 13, 1807; d. May 8, 1808.

967. viii. MARIA, b. June 25, 1809; d. Aug. 25, 1811.

968. ix. ELECTA MARIA, b. July 10, 1813; d. April 5, 1815.

909. x. AUSTIN, b. Sept. 15, 1815; m. Lucy W. Barnard.

970. xi. BETSEY ALLEN, b. July 23, 1822; m. Edwin W. Stevens. She d. June 12, 1853. He res. Guilford, Vt., s. p.

971. xii. DAUGHTER, b. June 10, 1795; d. June 10, 1795.

972. xiii. A SON, b. Oct. 10, 1811; d. Oct. 10, 1811.

581. ROBERT FISKE (Daniel, Daniel, Samuel, William, John, William, Robert, Simon, Simon, William, Symond), b. Holliston, Mass., Feb. 24, 1746; m in Upton, Mass., Sept. 17, 1768, Mary Hall of Hopkinton, b. 1744. She d. in Upton, Feb. 7, 1822. He d. Sept. 25, 1820; res. Holliston and Upton, Mass.

973. i. ELISHA, b. Sept. 3, 1769; m. Lydia Robinson and Mrs. Margaret (Shepherd) Brown.

974. ii. DANIEL, b. Oct. 29, 1770; m. Ruth Chapin.

975. iii. WILLIAM, b. Nov. 8, 1776; m. Lucy Bradish.

976. iv. AMASA, b. Sept. 17, 1780; m ――――.

584. DANIEL FISKE (Daniel, Daniel, Samuel, William, John, William, Robert, Simon, Simon, William, Symond), b. Upton, Mass., in 1759; m. Jan. 16, 1783, Hannah Rockwood, d. May 6, 1785; m. 2d, Sept. 27, 1792, Hannah or Beulah Palmer; d. July 14, 1815. He d. Jan. 22, 1841; res. Upton, Mass.

977. i. HANNAH, b. Apr. 23, 1785; prob. d. young.

978. ii. ELIAS, b. May 24, 1789; d. Aug. 4, 1823.

979. iii. ANNA, b. Jan. 9, 1791; d. Aug. 10, 1802.

980. iv. EMELINE, b. Feb. 1, 1793; m. in Upton, May 14, 1819, Holland Forbush, of Upton; b. Aug. 18, 1800 (Elijah, Peter, Samuel, Thomas, Thomas, Daniel). He d. Nov. 4, 1856; res. Upton. She d. May 30, 1876. Ch.: Emeline M., b. July 19, 1820; d. Dec. 25, 1826; Holland E., b. Nov. 9, 1824, m. Martha Fiske, dau. of Levi; Daniel C., b. Aug. 26, 1826, m. Apr. 8, 1852, Nancy E. Perham, dau. of Reuben, of Milford; Aaron A., b. Feb. 10, 1832, m. Emily S. Holmes; she res. Gorham, Me.; William W., b. Jan. 12, 1834, d. Dec. 7, 1843.

981. v. LUCINDA, b. Dec. 1, 1794; m. in Upton May 8, 1822, Rufus Fletcher, of U., moved to Columbus, O., in 1852, but children all born in Upton: Alonso, last heard from in Texas during war; Charles, dead; Elias, last heard from 1895 in Galveston, Texas; Rodolphus, last heard from in Texas during war; Maria.

982. vi. EMMONS H., b. May 10, 1802; m. Anna M. Ward.

983. vii. AMELIA ANN, b. May 10, 1807; m. Louis Kallisch. She died in Sacramento, Cal., a few years since. Ch.: Levi. Louis, m. ――――, San Jose, Cal. Frank.

984. viii. CLARISA, b. July 16, 1796; m. in Upton, Feb. 5, 1820, Jonathan B. Bradish of U.; both dead; their children born in Upton: Frederick P., m. and with children at La Crosse, Wis.

Philander, d. young in 1850. Clarissa Ann, m., with two
daus. living in Upton, Mass. Harrison, m. twice, and died
in the west in 1895.

985.　ix.　JOANNA, b. Dec. 18, 1804; m. in U. Nov. 28, 1839, Newel Gore,
of U., both dead. She died in Winfield, Kan., in 1894. Child,
died young. Ellen, m. ———— Bills, now living in Winfield,
Kan.

586.　BENJAMIN FISKE (Benjamin, Daniel, Samuel, William, John, William, Robert, Simon, Simon, William, Symond), b. Upton, Mass., May 1, 1749; m.
there June 14, 1770, Jemima Holbrook; m. 2d, Mar. 7, 1782, Margery Wood; b.
1761. She d. in Upton Feb. 24, 1843. His will was probated Nov. 11, 1820; was a
miller by occupation. His son Clark was executor. He d. Nov., 1820; res. Upton,
Mass.

986.　i.　JOEL, b. Dec. 17, 1770; m. Hannah Turner.
987.　ii.　CLARK, b. Apr. 4, 1778; m. Chloe Bradish.
988.　iii.　JEMIMAH, b. Feb. 16, 1780; m. in Upton, June 3, 1800, Abner
Smith, of Bellingham.
989.　iv.　AZARIAH, b. Sept. 13, 1782; d. bef. 1820, unm. No heirs mentioned in father's will.
990.　v.　HANNAH, b. Apr. 10, 1784; m. ———— Durham.
991.　vi.　ZIBA, b. Nov. 24, 1785; m. in Auburn Nov. 30, 1806, Polly Phillips, of Ward.
992.　vii.　GALACIUS, b. Apr. 17, 1788; m. Mary Brown.
993.　viii.　EMORY, b. June 30, 1790; m. Sally Gross.
994.　ix.　ELVIA, b. June 30, 1790; m. Jan. 1, 1811, Rufus Sibley, of Grafton. She d. Oct. 5, 1811.
995.　x.　BENJAMIN, b. Nov. 24, 1792.
996.　xi.　DAVID, b. Aug. 30, 1794; d. Feb. 19, 1795.
997.　xii.　JONATHAN, b. Aug. 30, 1794; m. Gratia Wilson.
998.　xiii.　AUSTIN, b. Jan. 21, 1797.
999.　xiv.　HARVEY, b. Jan. 21, 1797; m. Sophia Warren.
1000.　xv.　MIRANDA, b. Apr. 1, 1799; m. in Upton, Mar. 10, 1818, David
Chapin, of Upton.
1001.　xvi.　REBEKAH, b. Mar. 10, 1801; m. June 12, 1817, Jesse Whitney, b.
Oct. 12, 1790, d. Feb. 1, 1850; res. Milford, Mass. She d. Aug.
10, 1871. Ch.: Rowanna Semira, b. Aug. 28, 1820; m. Sept. 18,
1872, Israel Patch, s. p.; res. East Main street, Milford.
1002.　xvii.　SALLEY, b. Mar. 12, 1804; m. Jan. 26, 1826, Milton Ruggles,
of Upton. He d. and she m. 2d, a Sutherland. She d. s. p.

600.　HON. ELISHA FISKE (William, Daniel, Samuel, William, John, William, Robert, Simon, Simon, William, Symond), b. Upton, Mass., Nov. 4, 1774;
m. June 20, 1799, Betsey Forbush, town record says Betsey "Sherman;" b. May 14,
1775; d. Aug. 19, 1863. He was a son of Lieut. William Fiske, who served in the
Revolutionary Army in an Upton company. He held several town offices there,
such as town clerk and selectman, and for some time was a representative in the
legislature. A meat tub brought over from England by William, the emigrant, fell
into possession of his father and is still preserved in the family. He died Jan. 24,
1851; res. Upton, Mass.

1003.　i.　ERAN, b. May 12, 1800; m. Sally Wood and Sally Whitney.
1004.　ii.　ELISHA, b. Apr. 16, 1802; m. Hannah Forbush.
1005.　iii.　LEVI, b. May 1, 1804; m. Amy Taft.
1006.　iv.　ESTHER F., b. June 7, 1806; m. June 8, 1826, Adams Rockwood of U.; d. s. p.
1007.　v.　ELIZABETH, b. June 20, 1808; d. Dec. 26, 1826.
1008.　vi.　LYDIA, b. May 22, 1810; m. Sept., 1834, Daniel Hunt, b. Dec.
12, 1806. She d. Oct. 29, 1879. He d. Oct. 3, 1854; res. Sterling,
Mass. Ch.: Geogianna, b. Dec. 13, 1836; m. Aug. 9, 1859, Dr.
John Q. A. McCollester, b. May 3, 1830; res. Waltham, Mass.
Ch.: Lucretia Isabelle, b. 1860-8-26th. Edward Q., b. 1863-1-
28th. Harry Grey, b. 1864-8-5th. Edith E. May, b. 1867-9-1st.
John Fred, b. 1871-7-27th. Helen Hortense, b. 1878-7-2d.
Lucretia Isabelle, d. 1863-2d-1st. Harry Grey, d. 1867-2d-27th.

Edith L. May, d. 1869-1st-27th. Edward Q. McCollester, m. 1887, Nov. 27th. P. O. Ad. Ayer, Mass. John F., 1894, Dec. 25th married. P. O. Ad. Waltham, Mass.

1009. vii. WILLIAM, b. July 2, 1812; d. June, 1830.
1010. viii. ADAMS, b. Apr. 19, 1814; m. Betsey Forbush.
1011. ix. JEMIMAH J., b. May 11, 1816; m. Oct. 10, 1839, Levi W. Taft. He is a farmer and was b. Dec. 8, 1809, res. Upton, Mass. Ch.: Frances L. Taft, Born 1841 Apr. died 1841 Sept. Sarah J. Taft, Born 1842 Sept 28 Calvin A Taft Born 1847, Aug. 1 (address Upton). Sarah J. married to Fiske Batchelor Nov. 21, 1866; present address Upton Mass.
1012. x. WESLEY L., b. June 3, 1823; d. s. p.

602. DAVID FISKE (William, Daniel, Samuel, William, John, William, Robert, Simon, Simon, William, Symond), b. Upton, Mass., Sept. 6, 1780; m. in Grafton Dec. 3, 1807, Sarah Stowe, of Grafton: d. Mar. 18, 1814; m. 2d, Lydia Allen, of Hardwick, dau. of David and Elizabeth (Fisk) Allen; b. 1784; d. 1864. He was a farmer and cooper. He d. in 1860; res. Shelburne, Mass.

1013. i. JONATHAN STOWE, b. June 8, 1808; m. Georgianna M. Keith.
1014. ii. WILLIAM ADAMS, b. Sept. 30, 1810; m. Mary Jane Heald.
1015. iii. SARAH STOWE, b. Feb. 11, 1816; m. 1845, Daniel Whitney. This was his second marriage. By his first wife, Nancy, he had three ch. (see Whitney Genealogy, by Fred C. Pierce). Ch. by second wife: Edward E., res. Grafton, Mass.; Esther Marletta, m. —— Howell, res. Westboro; Julia M., m. —— Pratt; res. Natick. She is dead.
1016. iv. DORINDA STOWE, b. July 31, 1817; m. Joseph Upton; d. s. p.
1017. v. DAVID ALLEN, b. Feb. 15, 1819; m. Caroline F. Smith.
1018. vi. LYDIA ALLEN, b. Feb. 11, 1821; m. Dwight Hardy. They had one ch., who d. young. She d. s. p.
1019. vii. MOSES ALLEN, b. July 16, 1825; m. ——; res. Conway, Mass.
1020. viii. ESTER ALLEN, b. Nov. 22, 1822; unm.

605. JOSIAH FISKE (Josiah, Daniel, Samuel, William, John, William, Robert, Simon, Simon, William, Symond), b. Upton, Mass., Oct. 20, 1764; m. there Mar. 24, 1785, Kezia Wood; res. Upton, Mass.

1021. i. JASPER, b. July 28, 1785.
1022. ii. COMFORT, b. Sept. 26, 1787.
1023. iii. ALEXANDER, b. Nov. 29, 1789; m. Mary Fisk.
1024. iv. There were also three other girls; two married two brothers, Obadiah and Josiah Tainter, and resided in the north part of Greenfield, Mass. The other sister married Aaron Partridge, of Upton, Mass., and one of their sons is Joseph Partridge, of Upton, Mass.

606. ABIJAH FISKE (Josiah, Daniel, Samuel, William, John, William, Robert, Simon, Simon, William, Symond), b. Upton, Mass., Dec. 8, 1766; m. Betsey ——. She d. Apr., 1816. Daniel Fisk was executor of the will of Abijah. The inventory of her estate was filed Apr. 3, 1816. Elisha and Asa Fisk were guardians of the children. He d. May 26, 1807; res. Upton, Mass.

1025. ii. ELIZABETH, b. Nov. 18, 1805; m. Nov. 19, 1827. Calvin Whitney Forbush. He was b. Sept. 8, 1805 (Silas, David, Thomas, Thomas, Daniel); d. Feb., 1881. He resided on his father's farm on George Hill in Grafton, Mass., until 18 years of age, when he went to Charlestown, S. C., remaining two years. In 1825 he returned and engaged in manufacturing boots and shoes on George Hill. Later he moved to Boston, where he resided for seven years. Returning to Grafton in 1832, he purchased the Hon. Samuel Wood place at the head of the common, where he resided for twenty-five years. During this time he was engaged in the manufacture of boots and shoes. He died at his home on Bowdoin street, Boston. It was to his persistent efforts more than any other person that the town of Grafton is indebted for its beautiful common. He was associated in procuring the first banking interests in the town and was among its enterprising business men. He was greatly interested in the cultivation of fruits (see Pierce's History of Grafton; Pierce's Forbush Genealogy and Pierce's Whitney Genealogy). Ch.: Elizabeth, b. Aug. 20, 1828, m. Jonathan C. Warren; he d. and she res. So. Evanston, Ill. Sarah W., b. July 24, 1831; m. Major Willard D. Wheeler; was paymaster in the army; res. Grafton. Calvin, b. Apr. 8, 1833, m. Eliza J. Gates; res. So. Evanston. William, b. Mar. 30, 1836, res. Chicago, Ill. Harrison, b. Nov. 6, 1839; d. Nov. 8, 1869. Horace, b. June 13, 1843, m. Adelaide Lines, res. 633 E. 15th street, New York City.

1026. i. HORACE, b. June 8, 1800.

611. AMOS FISKE (Daniel, Samuel, Joseph, William, John, William, Robert, Simon, Simon, William, Symond), b. ———; m. Apr. 25, 1762, Mary Wilbour, both of Swanzey. Amos Fisk was the grandson of Dr. Samuel Fisk and was born and reared in Rhode Island. In early life he owned and commanded a coasting vessel, until the breaking out of the Revolutionary war, which rendered his occupation too precarious. He then sold his vessel and bought lands in Guilford, Vermont; res. Swanzey, Mass.

1027. i. ISAIAH, b. Sept. 6, 1763; m. ——— ———.
1028. iii. CALEB, b. Dec. 24, 1768; m. and had sons Amos, Jesse and Caleb Stone.
1029. ii. MARY, b. Mar. 25, 1767.

622. DEA. EPHRAIM FISKE (Joseph, Samuel, Joseph, William, John, William, Robert, Simon, Simon, William, Symond), b. ———; m. in Johnston, R. I., Nov. 29, 1761, Lydia Mathewson, b. ———; d. 1765; m. 2d, ———.

Ephraim Fisk was born in Scituate, R. I. He early removed to Killingly, Conn., where he afterward resided. He was a prominent citizen, deacon for a number of terms, and held a number of important offices, and was respected and esteemed in the community where he lived. He was married twice. By his first wife he had six children, four being born at one time. The children all lived, but the mother died. By his second wife, ten children. He died above 80 years old, greatly respected; he was a man of superior physical and mental abilities, and like his brother Isaac, was known as a peacemaker in society.

Upon the alarm following the capture of Fort William Henry by Montcalm, four volunteer companies marched from Windham County commanded by Abner Baker, Ashford; John Carpenter, Woodstock; Isaac Coit, Plainfield; John Grosvener, Pomfret. These volunteers were mostly men advanced in life, the fathers of the towns, showing that most of the men were already in service. Among the number was Ephraim Fiske.

He d. ———; res. Johnston, R. I., and Killingly, Conn.

1030. i.   SAMUEL, b. ———.
1031. ii.   DAVID, b. ———.
1032. iii. DEBORAH, b. ———.
1033. iv.   MIRIAM, b. ———.
1034. v.   JOSEPH, b. July 14, 1765; m. and res. in De Kalb, N. Y., was there in 1807.
1035. vi.   EPHRAIM, b. July 14, 1765; m. and res. in De Kalb, N. Y., was there in 1807.
1036. vii. JEROD, b. ———.
1037. viii. ABRAM, b. ———; m. Mary Brown.
1038. ix.   JASON, b. 1764. The family tradition is that he was born in England. A son of his was Joel, b. 1794, m. 1827, Mary Locum, b. 1799, d. in Warsaw, Ind., Oct. 13, 1891. He d. in Greencastle, Ind., in 1854. Joel's only child was 1, John Wilbur, b. 1829, m. in Ashland, O., in 1858, Arminda A. Kaufman, b. Oct. 31, 1833. He was a teacher and d. in Jefferson Barracks Jan. 11, 1865. His ch. were 1, Wilbur A., b. Aug. 19, 1860; m. in Greencastle Nov. 7, 1889, Edna E. Bayne, b. July 17, 1864, s. p. He is Professor of Chemistry and Physics; res. 136 S. 13th St., Richmond, Ind. 2, Luella

F. Galentine, Warsaw, Ind., b. Oct. 31, 1863; m. Apr. 8, 1889.
3, Canning B. Fisk, b. May 25, 1862; d. Oct. 12, 1869.

1039. x. THOMAS, b. ———.
1040. xi. BENJAMIN B., b. Nov. 2, 1794; m. Lydia Aldrich.
1041. xii. MARY, b. July 14, 1765; m. ——— Greenwell.
1042. xiii. KEZIAH, b. July 14, 1765; m. Edward Beaty; res. at Ogdensburg, N. Y., and had one ch., Edward, now deceased.

624. JUDGE ISAAC FISKE (Joseph, Samuel, Joseph, William, John, William, Robert, Simon, Simon, William, Symond), b. Johnston, R. I., June 15, 1757; m. there in 1775, Marcy Fenner, dau. of Richard, b. Feb. 24, 1758, d. July 7, 1820.

He was born on the old homestead in Johnston, R. I., and received an excellent education for those early days. Before he had obtained his majority he enlisted in the Continental Army under Gen. Greene, of Rhode Island. He was stationed at Prospect Hill in Cambridge, not far from Bunker Hill in Charlestown. His grandson, Geo. R. Fiske, Esq., of Roxbury, has two letters of his written the time he was in the army. One is dated Sept. 3, 1775, and the other Oct. 26, 1775, which he sent to his father, Joseph Fiske.

This is the inventory of his estate: 1824, Aug 14 Inventory of Isaac Fiske $1303.40 viz. carding machine, turning lath, linen wheel, wooden wheel, quilt wheel, cash $38.50, silver watch, cooper's tools, blacksmith's tools, pepper mill, coffee mill, white horse, 2 cows, 1 heifer, chaise, writing desk, 27 stacks rye, 4 stacks clover, clover in barn, $100. It is evident that he left home against the will of his parents, or certainly not with their approval, for he says he will not enlist again when his time is up. He was then 18 yrs. old, and the letters are very pathetic, showing the lack of almost everything among the troops, especially ammunition. I have also another letter of his written five years later, when he was very active in religious matters, probably had become a member of the Society of Friends, which he certainly was later on. In later life he was always called Judge Fiske; twenty years Judge of Probate and later Judge of the Court of Common Pleas, and the high estimation in which he was held by his neighbors. "My father once took me to the graves of his father and mother, when I was a lad of about ten years, and I well remember with what great respect he spoke of his father and mother."

He d. June 17, 1824; res. Johnston, R. I.

1043. i SAMUEL, b. Apr. 4, 1797; m. Sally S. Kent.
1044. ii. ISAAC, b. Mar. 15, 1791; m. Anna Robinson.
1045. iii. JOSEPH, b. Oct. 29, 1785; m. Roby Baker, Mary Robbins, Maria Goddard and Maria Hall.
1046. iv. BENJAMIN, b. Dec. 3, 1794; m. Polly Van Der Marke.
1047. v. ARNOLD, b. Feb. 28, 1777; m. Mary A. Bunker.
1048. vi. ISRAEL, b. Apr. 4, 1782; m. Harriett Sheldon. She d. in Prov., R. I., he d. s. p. in New Orleans, La., in 1820.
1049. vii. EDMOND, b. Apr. 16, 1787; m. Abby Brown.
1050. viii. MARIETTA, b. Mar. 12, 1789; m. Apr. 23, 1809, Dr. Peleg Clark; res. Coventry, R. I. He was b. Aug. 5, 1784; d. Jan. 1, 1875, at East Providence; was a physician. She d. Apr. 14, 1867. Ch.: Lydia Fenner, b. July 16, 1810; m. Nov. 2, 1835; d. Feb. 27, 1883. John Lewis, b. Nov. 30, 1812; m. June 11, 1840; d. Oct 25, 1880. Erasmus Darwin, b. Sept. 8, 1815; m. Jan. 5, 1837; res. No. Scituate, R. I. Eunice Browning, b. Jan. 24, 1817; m. ———; d. May 9, 1861. Isaac Weeden, b. Feb. 3, 1819; m. Nov. 10, 1840; d. May 14, 1884. Alfred Sheldon, b. Mar. 1, 1821; m. June 5, 1842; d. Apr. 9, 1894. Horace, b. June 11, 1823; m. Sept. 29, 1852, Elizabeth Jane Wilbur, b. May 30, 1832; he is a real estate agent, res. Olneyville, R. I.; ch.: Walter Luther Clarke, b. Jan. 31, 1856; m. Mattie B. Alden, Nov., 1880; P. O., Providence, R. I.; Horace Eugene Clarke, b. Sept. 30, 1868; m. Lila E. Spencer, Sept. 30, 1891; P. O. Providence, R. I.; Jennie Lawton Clarke, b. Sept. 30, 1868; unm.; P. O., Olneyville, R. I. Peleg, Jr., b. Feb. 11, 1826; m. July 16, 1868; d. May 6, 1889. Henry Bradford, b. Oct. 18, 1827; m. Sept. 10, 1857; d. Mar. 6, 1888. George Augustus, b. July 22, 1830; unm.; d. Nov. 25, 1866.

10

1051. ix. FREELOVE, b. Apr. 2, 1784; m. Jacob Knight; res. Johnston, R. I. She had 11 ch., among them were: Israel; Arnold; Phebe, m. —— Reynolds; res. Olneyville, R. I.

1052. x. DANIEL, b. June 24, 1779; m. Polly Horton.

1053. xi. BETSEY, b. Dec. 28, 1800; m. Darius P. Lawton. They had three ch., and all d. in infancy; res. Seekonk, Mass.

1054. xii. BARBARA, b. Nov. 19, 1780; d. unm.

1055. xiii. MARCY, b. Oct. 31, 1792, died.

636. JOHN FISK (John, John, John, Nathaniel, Nathaniel, William, Robert, Simon, Simon, William, Symond), b. Waltham, Mass., June 10, 1716; m. at Worcester, Mass., June 1, 1748, Azubah Moore.
He d. about 1797; res. Worcester, Mass

1056. i. JOHN, b. Aug. 16, 1749; m. Irene Buck.

1057. ii. MARY, b. Dec. 22, 1751-2; m. —— Fisk; had son William (see) and second, —— Shattuck; res. Worcester; had five ch. by second wife.

1058. iii. SAMUEL, b. Sept. 2, 1753, d. young.

1059. iv. JAMES, b. Aug. 10, 1755; d. young.

1060. v. JAMES, b. Aug. 17, 1757; m. Azubah Moore.

1061. vi. SAMUEL, b. June 29, 1759; m. Olive —— and Priscilla ——.

1062. vii. ELIZABETH, b. Aug. 20, 1761; m. Sept. 26, 1779, Daniel Chaddick, of Worcester.

1063. viii. SARAH, b. Apr. 10, 1764.

1064. ix. AZUBA, b. June 13, 1768; m. Aug. 12, 1787, James Goulding, of Worcester. (According to the Worcester Probate Records on Apr. 14, 1786, her brother James was appointed her guardian. She was the minor dau. of John Fisk, of Worcester.)

638. JONATHAN FISKE (John, John, John, Nathaniel, Nathaniel, William, Robert, Simon, Simon, William, Symond), b. Waltham, Mass., June 27, 1729; m. Abigail ——. She d. in Wendall Oct. 8, 1792.
June 23, 1723, a precinct was erected, extending three miles into Worcester, three into Oxford, three into Leicester, and one mile and a half into Sutton, measured from the place designated for the new meeting house, along the roads then traveled. This district, which was denominated the South Parish of Worcester, was incorporated April 10, 1778, as the town of Ward, receiving its name from Artemus Ward, Esq., a brave general of the Revolution, member of the council of the Provincial Congress, judge of the County Courts, and representative in Congress. About thirty families were thus separated from Worcester. The boundaries of the parish and new town were nearly, though not precisely, coincident. The act provided that certain individuals included by the latter, but not within the limits of the former, might retain their relations to the towns of their original settlement, until it was their pleasure to express in writing, intention to unite with the new corporation. Ten persons by this exception were permitted to continue their former connections, and among this number was Jonathan Fiske.
He d. in Worcester and was buried there Jan. 8, 1781; res. Worcester and Ward, Mass.

1065. i. JONATHAN, b. Nov. 7, 1762.

1066. ii. EBENEZER, b. Mar. 17, 1765.

1067. iii. JONAS, b. Sept. 27, 1767; m. Matilda Leach.

1068. iv. SALLY, b. July 15, 1770.

1069. v. DANIEL, b. June 26, 1772, m. Dorcas Saunders.

1070. vi. MARY, b. July 30, 1775.

1070½. vii. BETSEY, b. Aug. 17, 1777.

639½. DANIEL FISK (John, John, John, Nathaniel, William, Robert, Simon, Simon, William, Symond), b. Waltham, Mass., about 1730; m. Sarah Kendall of Lexington, b. 1743; d. in Wendall Jan. 16, 1788. Daniel was born in Waltham, married his wife there, and at least four of his children were born there. He probably moved to Wendall not far from 1772-75. There is no record of his joining the church there, but he probably did. The pastor of the Congregational Church there, Rev. J. C. Wightman, under date of July 3, 1896, sends the following: "I find no record of Mr. Fisk or his wife joining the church, but I find the following: October 2nd, 1785, baptized four children of Daniel Fisk and wife, their names Abijah, Amos, Moses & Lydia.

"January 16th, 1788, Buried Sarah wife of Daniel Fisk in the 45th year of her age.

"November 30th, 1799. Daniel Fisk aged 69 he died Thanksgiving Day the 28th; going to public worship he was seized with a pain in his stomach, he had strength to return, and leave his body in his own house.

"I think, however, this which has been recorded leaves no doubt but that he was a member of the church, as it has not been customary to baptize children of those outside the church. Neither would there be any likelihood of the records of his wife's death, nor of his own."

In 1790, Daniel Fisk of Wendell conveyed land in Wendell. In 1792, Daniel Fisk of New Salem had land in Wendell conveyed to him. In 1793, Daniel Fisk of Deerfield conveyed land in Deerfield. In 1794, Daniel Fisk 3d of Wendell had land in Wendell conveyed to him. In 1798, Daniel of Wendell conveyed land in Wendell.

These are the earliest records on the Franklin County Registry of Deeds. Still earlier records of that county are in Springfield, where, perhaps, might find something more of Daniel Fisk. He d. Nov. 30, 1799, in Wendall; res. Wendall, Mass.

1071. i.   ZEDEKIAH, b. July 23, 1763; m. Lucy Sweetser.
1072. ii.   ABIJAH, b. 1766. He m. and had several ch. One son was Sullivan, who has a son S. L.; res. at 800 Crescent St., Brockton, Mass.
1073. iii. DANIEL, b. Oct. 1, 1768; m. Sally Partridge and Mrs. Lucy F. Robinson.
1074. iv.   AMOS, b. May 26, 1780; m. Mary Hubbard.
1075. v.   LYDIA, b. Dec., 1779; m. in Wendall, Mass., Abijah Wheeler; res. Templeton, Mass. She d. Mar. 9, 1853. He d. Feb., 1863; was a farmer. They had several children and all are dead except one son in Templeton and one in Portland, Me., and Abigail R., b. July 19, 1819; m Sept. 18, 1838, Josiah B. Goodnow, b. 1819; res. Templeton, Mass. Ch. b. in Templeton: June P. Goodnow, b. Aug. 1, 1839, d. Aug. 17, 1889. Ellen M. Goodnow, b. May 20, 1841, Templeton. David W. Goodnow, b. Apr. 23, 1843; d. Jan. 20, 1850. Henry O. Goodnow, b. Mar. 9, 1890; d. Oct. 16, 1891. Charles A. Goodnow, b. Templeton, Dec. 22, 1853. Ellen M. Goodnow, m. John McGuile, of Norwich; her postoffice address West Gardner, Mass. Charles A. Goodnow, railroad man, Chicago, Ill.
1076. vi.   LUCY, b. ———; m. Benjamin Southwick, and 2d, ——— Kellogg; res. Sangerfield, N. Y., in 1816. Abijah Southwick, d. in 1864, in Ashtabula, O.; Benjamin Southwick, resided in Waterville, N. Y.; Warren Kellogg; Daniel Kellogg, m. and had ch. A descendant of this family is Mrs. Senator Plumb of Atchison, Kan.
1077. vii. BEULAH, b. Mar. 4, 1770; m. Nathan Sweetser, b. Mar. 2, 1768. She d. s. p. and he m. 2d, Sept. 1, 1800, Lydia Johnson, of Acton, by whom he had ten children. He was a farmer and resided in Wendall, where he d. Mar. 8, 1842.
1077¼.viii. SALLY, b. Mar. 30, 1766.
1077½.ix.   LOIS, b. Jan. 16, 1772; m. and had 12 ch.; res. in Vermont.
1077¾.x.   MOSES, bap. Oct. 2, 1785; prob. d. young, prob. 1800, in New Salem.

643. DAVID FISKE (David, John, John, Nathaniel, Nathaniel, William, Robert, Simon, Simon, William, Symond), b. Windham, Conn., Dec. 17, 1726; m. there Mar. 26, 1747, Sarah Farnam. With his son, David, Jr., he served in the company from Windham, Conn., in the Rev. War (see Conn. Rev. reports). Res. Hampton, Windham Co., Conn.

1078. i.   AMAZIAH, b. Oct. 6, 1747; m. ——— ——— and Priscilla ———.
1079. ii.   SARAH, b. Apr. 13, 1749; d. unm. Feb. 4, 1796.
1080. iii. DAVID, b. Aug. 12, 1754; d. July 24, 1775, in the Revolutionary

army. He was in the company from Windham (see Conn. Rev. reports).

1081.   iv.   LUCY, b. Apr. 27, 1760.
1082.   v.   HANNAH, b. July 29, 1765.

645. JONATHAN FISKE (David, John, John, Nathaniel, Nathaniel, William, Robert, Simon, Simon, William, Symond), b. Windham, Conn., July 4, 1731; m. there Aug. 5, 1750, Elizabeth Scott; d. there Feb. 15, 1761; m. 2d there Mar. 18, 1762, Sarah Leach. Res. Windham, Conn.

1083.   i.   JONATHAN, b. Dec. 13, 1750; d. Oct., 1754.
1084.   ii.   DAVID, b. May 29, 1752; d. Nov., 1754.
1085.   iii.   JONATHAN, b. Aug. 15, 1755; m. Mehitable Smith.
1086.   iv.   MARY, b. Feb. 17, 1758; d. July 29, 1760.
1087.   v.   ELIZABETH, b. Jan. 22, 1761.
1088.   vi.   JOHN, b. Jan. 22, 1761. He was a celebrated singer, and died about 1810, leaving a son Nathan, who went to Vermont in 1824.
1089.   vii.   MARGERY, b. Oct. 9, 1763.
1090.   viii.   DAVID, b. June 9, 1770.
1091.   ix.   NATHAN, b. Oct. 7, 1772.

646. CAPT. ASA FISK (David, John, John, Nathaniel, Nathaniel, William, Robert, Simon, Simon, William, Symond), b. Windham, Conn., May 26, 1733; m. there Mar. 19, 1755, Elisabeth Knight of Norwich, Conn., dau. of Joseph and Elizabeth (Tracy) Knight. She d. Mar. 6, 1818. Capt. Asa Fisk emigrated to Wales from Hampton, Conn., thereafter abode and died there; when first he came or soon after he acquired the ownership of the premises constituting and connecting with the "Oliver Wales Tavern Stand." There he dwelt, and for some time kept an inn or house of public entertainment. Subsequently he disposed of that estate and purchased a large tract of land in the southern part of the town, upon which he established and through after life maintained his family home. That tract was upon the elevated ground or high land situated a little distance off the direct road to Stafford in our approachment of Stafford line. That elevation received from him the significant name of Fisk Hill. His old premises, or rather the central and main part thereof, are now owned by Moses Davis, and dwelt upon by him, and derive from him their modern name of Davis Place. He possessed much strength and penetration of mind, solidity of judgment and inflexibleness of purpose mixed up with some of the spirit of domination and arbitrariness. As an agriculturist he was judicious, skillful, thoroughgoing. As a townsman, he was prominent, conspicuous, influential. As a military officer, he was manly and commanding in his mien, well informed in tactics, resolute and efficient in discipline. One occurrence in his life opened a doorway through which to question his patriotism: In the time of "Shay's war" he took sides with the party opposed to the government and was appointed a captaincy in the opposing and rebelling forces, but as he had enough of that "better part of valor," discretion, to restrain him from the commission of any overt act of rebellion, he finally got out of the scrape without being overwhelmed or greatly damaged thereby. All things considered, Capt. Fisk must be set down as a very good man for this town. Let us not be found undervaluing his virtue, says the Wales historian: "Elizabeth, Fidelity is compelling us to say her virtues were many and must be unforgot." Another correspondent says: He kept a country store on the hill where he lived, and that he owned in his farm 400 acres, and that Shay's war cost him considerable property. Also that he sent two sons, aged 14 and 16, to the Revolutionary war. My grandfather Elisha was one. Both were drummers. The company that they were in arrived at Cornwallis surrender one hour after the surrender. He was lieutenant in the company of minute men which marched to the Lexington alarm, and was afterward and for some time captain in the Continental army. His gravestone is as follows:

Capt
Asa Fisk
died
9 Feby 1812 AE
78

Close by is a stone which reads thus:

Mrs. Elizabeth
Relict of
Capt Asa Fisk
died
3 Nov 1818 AE 86

He d. Feb. 9, 1812; res. Windham, Conn., Wales, Mass.

1092. i. STEPHEN, b. Apr. 28, 1763; m. Sarah Parker.
1093. ii. ELISABETH, b. Jan. 20, 1765; m. Nov. 20, 1784, Elisha Davis. Ch.: Philip, b. Nov. 8, 1784; Elisha, b. Aug. 8, 1786; Alfred, b. Jan. 13, 1789; Sally, b. Aug. 8, 1791; Porter, b. Aug. 2, 1794. Elisha Davis came from Mansfield, Conn., in 1783, and returned to Connecticut in 1796.
1094. iii. EUNICE, b. Oct. 24, 1768; m. May 30, 1787, Jonathan Needham; res. Wales, Mass. He died about the year 1813, aged 49 She died about the year 1797, aged 29. Ch.: Raysal. b. Aug. 8, 1787; Sally, b. Mar. 29, 1789; Asa, b. ———, 1791: d. 1871; Jonathan, b. June, 1793; Chester, b. ———, 1795.
1095. iv. OLIVE, b. June 5, 1770; m. Apr. 11, 1791, Samuel Fisk, and res. in Holland, Mass.
1096. v. ASA, b. Feb. 26, 1772; m. Amanda Cooley, Sally Colburn and Mary Jane Davidson.
1097. vi. SALLY, b. July 26, 1774; m. and res. N. Y. state.
1098. vii. LUCY, b. Mar. 24, 1776.
1099. viii. PERSY, b. Mar. 6, 1778. Res. Wales, Mass. Ch.: William, b. June 24, 1804; Austin, b. Feb. 14, 1806; m. there Sylvanus Bolton, from Taunton, Mass. Rhodolphus, b. Dec. 28, 1808; Washington, b. Mar. 9, 1810; Sylvanus, b. Apr. 28, 1811. They rev. to Vermont
1100. ix. HEZEKIAH, b. June 2, 1756; m. Eleanor Cooley.
1101. x. ELISHA, b. 1762; m. Zurvish Parker and Hannah Wheeler.
1102. xi. ASA, b. Windham, Conn., Dec. 21, 1757; d. before 1772.
1103. xii. HANNAH, b. Windham, Apr. 17, 1759; m. Sept. 3, 1777, Joseph Munger; res. Wales, Mass. Had ch.: Asa, Loving, Roysal, and rev. to Vermont.

651. JOHN FISKE (Thomas, William, John, Nathaniel, William, Robert, Simon, Simon, William, Symond), b. Wat. Apr. 24, 1728; m. Jan. 18, 1753, Elizabeth Harrington, b. Jan. 10, 1731, dau. of Jonas. He was a blacksmith in Waltham. He was in the expedition, against Lake George, in 1758, in Capt. Jonathan Brown's company. Res. Watertown, Mass.

1104. i. THOMAS, b. Apr. 11, 1758.
1105. ii. ELIZABETH, b. July 18, 1760.
1106. iii. ABIGAIL, b. May 12, 1763; m. Jan. 8, 1784, Joel Harrington, b. Oct. 31, 1754; d. Mar. 28, 1805; res. Wat. Ch.: Abigail, b. Dec. 19, 1784; d. Dec. 27, 1784. Joel, b. Dec. 19, 1784; d. Dec. 29, 1784. Joel, b. May 2, 1786; m. Jerusha Perry; res Weston.
1107. iv. ANNA, b. May 25, 1765.

652. ABIJAH FISKE (Thomas, William, John, Nathaniel, William, Robert, Simon, Simon, William, Symond), b. Wat. Mar. 12, 1729; m. May 24, 1753, Elizabeth Upham; b. Jan. 15. 1724. She m. 2d, Feb. 23, 1775, Col. John Trowbridge, of Fram. He left a will dated May 16, 1774, and it was proved July 12, following. At the time of his death he was an innholder in Waltham.

(Midd. Prob. records, v. 55, 380.) May 16, 1774, for Abijah Fiske, Waltham. In holder. Will. To wife Elizabeth, incpr of whole estate till Son Abijah 21—to sons Amos & Abijah, all remainder of estate—to 3 drs. Mary, Elizabeth, Aseneth. Wife Elizabeth, Ex'x.

He d. 1774; res. Watertown and Waltham, Mass.

1108. i. AMOS, b. Apr. 25, 1754; m. May 29, 1777, Mary Whitney, of Weston, b. Dec. 11, 1744, dau. of William. He was in the Rev. war and rev. to Ohio.
1109. ii. ABIJAH, b. Nov. 1, 1755; m. Alice Adams.
1110. iii. ELIAS, b. Feb. 3, 1757; d. July, 1757.

1111.   iv.   MARY, b. Sept. 9, 1759; d. 1760.

1112.   v.   MARY, b. Oct. 10, 1761; m. Zaccheus Weston, and d. 1809, leaving issue.

1113.   vi.   ELIZABETH, b. Apr. 3, 1763; m. 1783, Major Josiah Stone, Jr., of Fram., and had 11 ch. (See Barry's Hist. of Fram. [400].); b. Feb. 22, 1762; res. Fram.; ch.: Wm. Fiske, b. Apr. 10, 1784; m. Harriet Brigham, an M. D., was Reg. of Deeds of Mid. Co.; res. Camb. Luther, b. May 6, 1786; m. Mary Eaton. Nancy, b. ———. Abijah, b. ———; m. Martha Buckminster; res. Westboro. Aseneth, b. 1790; d. May 30, 1842. Mary, b. ———; m. Jabez G. Fisher, of West. Micah, b. ———; res. Fram.; at his death was Pres. of Fram. bank. Eliza F., m. Jos. Lothrop; d. 1844. Josiah, m. Sophia Brigham, of Wayland. He m. 2d, Nancy Stone. He was selectman in 1801 for 3 years.

1114.   vii.   ASANATH, b. Sept. 2, 1766; m. Nov. 18, 1794, Nathan Eaton, of Fram.; bap. Aug. 23, 1767; d. Apr. 26, 1812.

653.   DAVID FISKE (Thomas, William, John, Nathaniel, William, Robert, Simon, Simon, William, Symond), b. Lex. Oct. 8, 1731; m. Apr. 16, 1761, Elizabeth Mansfield, b. June 20, 1743; d. ———; m. 2d, at Lincoln, Oct. 31, 1765, Rebecca Garfield, of Lincoln; b. Sept. 23, 1745. He d. in 1800; res. Woburn and Lincoln, Mass.

1115.   i.   REBECCA, b. Oct. 26, 1766; m. Mar. 18, 1798, Caleb Cutler.

1116.   ii.   DAVID, b. Apr. 2, 1768; d. Oct. 22, 1780.

1117.   iii.   ELIJAH, b. Mar. 24, 1770; m. Anna Harrington and Bathsheba Brooks.

1118.   iv.   ABRAHAM, b. Apr. 4, 1773; m. Grace Hagar.

1119.   v.   THOMAS, b. Feb. 1, 1776; d. Aug. 6, 1778.

1120.   vi.   HANNAH, b. Nov. 7, 1777; m. Nov. 21, 1797, town records say Sept. 13, 1799, Daniel Wheeler, of Concord.

1121.   vii.   LUCY, b. Dec. 3, 1779; m. Oct. 14, 1802, Jesse Wheeler, of Concord.

1122.   viii.   SUKEY, b. Jan. 27, 1782; d. Nov. 7, 1803.

1123.   ix.   DAVID, b. May 4, 1784; d. July 26, 1806.

655.   JONATHAN FISKE (Thomas, William, John, Nathaniel, William, Robert, Simon, Simon, William, Symond), b. Lex. May 14, 1735; m. June 7, 1763, Abigail Lawrence, b. Dec. 6, 1744, d. Oct. 21, 1803. He was a Middlesex County farmer. He d. in Waltham. The inventory of his estate was taken May 28, 1787, and Apr. 5, 1794, his estate was divided, widow Abigail received her dower: To Phinehas, eldest son, double share; the other children mentioned are Jacob, Thomas, Susanna, Abigail and Avis. He d. Mar. 30, 1787; res. Watertown, Mass.

1124.   i.   PHINEHAS, b Dec. 27, 1765; m. Abigail Stearns.

1125.   ii.   JONATHAN, b. Dec. 14, 1767; m. Mary E. Baker.

1126.   iii.   JACOB, b. Jan. 13, 1770; m. Sarah Flagg.

1127.   iv.   SUSANNA, b. Jan. 30, 1774; m. Feb. 2, 1792, Amos Bemis, b. Oct. 6, 1760; res. Lincoln. She d. Nov. 12, 1827. Ch.: Maria, b. July 11, 1792; m. William Hoar; his name was changed to William H. Pierce; res. Phil. Jonathan, b. June 30, 1794; d. unm. Susanna, b. July 11, 1796; m. Major E. Flint. Eliza, b. ———; m. Oliver Hastings. Amos, b. Nov. 1, 1801; m. Lucy Wheeler. Caroline, b. June 6, d. July, 1804. Charlotte, b. June 6, 1804; m. Abel Wheeler; res. Lincoln. George, b. ———; m. Martha Field. Ellen, b. ———; m. John Prentiss, of Phil.

1128.   v.   ABIGAIL, b. Feb. 11, 1776; d. Oct., 1842.

1129.   vi.   AVIS, b. Apr. 6, 1778; m. May 3, 1798, William Wellington, son of William and Mary (Whitney), b. Dec. 11, 1769; res. Waltham and Lex. Ch.: Mary, b. Feb. 11, 1799; m. Aaron Holbrook. Jonathan Fiske, b. Jan. 5, 1801; m. Abigail Cope. Adaline, b. Mar. 8, 1803; m. Nathaniel W. Stearns. He was b. Dec. 3, 1795; m. Dec. 13, 1827, and d. in Waltham July 9, 1849; a dealer in West India goods. His wife d. Jan. 2, 1890; ch.:

Watson, b. Sept. 13, 1828; m. May 20, 1851. Charles Shepard, b. April, 1832: d. Jan. 9. 1849. Adeline Wellington, b. June 11, 1834; m. Jan. 4, 1860, Frank E. Stanley, b. Dec. 7, 1832; res. Waltham; is a provision dealer; ch.: 1, Nora Franklin, b. July 17, 1861; m. Mar. 8, 1884. 2, Bernard Watson, b. May 3, 1865; m. Sept., 1889. 3, Nora Franklin Smiley, Waltham, Mass. 4, Bernard Watson Stanley, Waltham, Mass. 5, Henry, b. Apr., 1837; d. Nov. 16, 1851. 6, Mary Crehove, b. May 17, 1840; unm.; P. O. address Waltham, Mass. Abigail, b. July 15, 1805; d. Oct. 15, 1806; Abigail, b. Feb. 11, 1806; m. Nov. 25, 1827, Nathaniel Pierce. William, b. Mar. 29, 1808; m. Rebecca Ames.

- 1130. vii. MARY, b. May 18, 1780.
- 1131. viii. THOMAS, b. Apr. 13, 1785: m. ——— ———.

669. SAMUEL FISKE (Samuel, William, John, Nathaniel, William, Robert, Simon, Simon, William, Symond), b. Wat. Nov. 2, 1741; m. Oct. 29, 1761, Abigail White, bap. Aug. 20, 1738. He was a farmer; res. Waltham, Mass.

- 1132. i. ABIGAIL, b. Feb. 9, 1762; m. Jan. 8, 1784, Joel Harrington.
- 1133. ii. ANNA, b. Apr. 11, 1764; m. June 7, 1783, Peter Edes, of Waltham.
- 1134. iii. ELIJAH, b. Sept. 26, 1765; m. Lydia Livermore.
- 1135. iv. JONATHAN, b. Dec. 14, 1767; d. in infancy.
- 1136. v. JONAS, b. Apr. 12, 1768; m. Ruth Pierce and Abigail Pierce.
- 1137. vi. SAMUEL, b. Sept. 24, 1769; m. Hannah Babcock.
- 1138. vii. WILLIAM, b. Dec. 20, 1770; m. Eunice White.
- 1139. viii. FRANCIS, b. Aug. 24, 1772; m. Sarah Livermore.
- 1140. ix. ROBERT, b. Mar. 15, 1774; d. June 30, 1774.
- 1141. x. ROBERT, b. June 9, 1775; m. Nancy Stratton.
- 1142. xi. POLLY, b. June 20. 1777; m. Sept. 13, 1798, Edward Child, b. Jan. 12, 1772: res. Weston.
- 1143. xii. NATHAN, b. Dec. 6, 1779; m. Anna L. Mason.

672. HON. WILLIAM FISKE (Samuel, William, John, Nathaniel, William, Robert, Simon, Simon, William, Symond), b. Wat. Dec. 28, 1753; m. Nov., 1776, Hannah Cook, b. Apr. 30, 1751, dau. of Samuel; m. 2d, Ruth Smith. He was b. in Watertown, was graduated at Harvard College in 1772; was for years Justice of the Peace at Waltham.

Wm. Fiske of Waltham was a mem Mass His Society "Was the son of Samuel Fiske, a worthy farmer of Waltham"—Supposed b. at Waltham in Dec 1753 studied with Rev Mr Woodward of Weston, "Who was at the time much esteemed, not only for his professional, but for his classical learning." Mr. F. gr at H. C. in 1772. Was Lawyer in Waltham, &c. (See Biographical notice vol 9, p 206 1st series Mass His Society's Coll.).

He d. Aug. 13, 1803; res. Waltham, Mass.

- 1144. i. WILLIAM, b. Mar. 13, 1777.
- 1145. ii. RUTH, b. Apr. 15, 1783; m. May 3, 1801, Abner Wellington, bap. Sept. 7, 1777, son of Samuel, of Waltham and Wat. He d. Apr. 24, 1804, and his wid. m. 2d, Oct. 13, 1805, Elisha Whitney Dana, of Wat. Ch.: Abigail, b. Apr. 10, 1802; m. Isaac Robbins, Esq. Ruth, b. Nov. 14, 1803.
- 1146. iii. CHARLES, b. July 15, 1785; gr. H. C. 1805; d. 1847.
- 1147. iv. CYRUS, b. Apr. 5, 1787.
- 1148. v. JAMES, b. June 14, 1789.
- 1149. vi. JOHN, b. Sept. 7, 1791.
- 1150. vii. EDWIN, b. Feb. 5, 1794.
- 1151. viii. BENJ. FRANKLIN, b. Aug. 17, 1796.
- 1152. ix. CAROLINE, b. Aug. 11, 1799.

675. NATHAN FISK (Nathan, Nathan, Nathan, Nathaniel, William, Robert, Simon, Simon, William, Symond), b. Wat. Feb. 25, 1701; m. Dec. 9, 1730, Anne Warren, b. Feb., 1711, dau. of Dea. John of Weston, d. Oct. 1. 1736; m. 2d, Feb. 21, 1738, Mary Fiske, bap. June 30, 1712, dau. of Dea. Jonathan Fiske of Lex. and Sudbury (see). After the death of her husband she was killed by a fall from a horse on a visit to Sudbury on horseback. His will is dated Oct. 13, 1765. In the Name of God Amen, the Thirtieth Day of October, anno Domini one thousand Seven

Hundred & Sixty five in the Sixth (&c year of the Reign of George the third king of Great Britain I Nathan Fisk of Weston in the County of Middlesex in the province of the Massachusetts Bay in New England yeoman.

Being advanced in age, but of perfect mind, and having my memory, thanks be to God, therefore, calling to mind the mortality of my Body, & knowing that 'tis appointed for all men once to Dy, do ordain and make this my last Will & Testament, that is to say, principally and first of all, I give and recommend my soul into the Hands of God that gave it, and my body, to the Earth, to be buried in a Christian decent manner, nothing doubting but at the general resurrection I shall receive, the same again by the mighty power of God: And as touching the world-things-or Estate wherewith it hath pleased God to bless me in this life; I give demise & dispose of the same in the following manner and form.

Imprimis I give & Bequeath to Mary my Beloved Wife, & to Her Heirs forever, all my indoor or House-hold Stuff (excepting Cash, Bonds & notes for money, my wearing apparrel Library one bed & bedding & my clock) and also I give to my s'd wife the improvement of one half of my Real Estate during the time she shall remain my widow, and if she shall see cause to marry, she shall Quit, all her right in my Real Estate, and also I Give to my s'd wife the use of my clock during her natural life, she keeping it in good repair.

Item. I give and bequeath unto Nathan Fisk my Eldest and Beloved son twenty pounds, L. money to be paid to him in one year after my decease by my Executors hereafter named.

Item. I give & bequeath to Jonathan Fisk my beloved son and to his heirs and assigns forever, the one half of my Real Estate, land, and buildings wherever it is to be found, and when it is divided he shall have the first choice, he making no charge for labour or building, he paying out what is hereafter mentioned.

Item. I give and bequeath to Ezra Fisk my Beloved son and to his Heirs one Hundred & Sixty pounds L. money, to be paid to him in two years after my decease by my Executors hereafter named. I also give my s'd son Ezra one bed & bedding, & liberty to dwell in my house so longe as he lives Single.

Item. I give & bequeath unto my beloved son Samuel Fisk, the other half of my Real Estate where ever it is to be found, he making no charge for buildings or labour done on my Real Estate he paying out what is hereafter mentioned.

Item. I give & bequeath unto Anna Bigelow my beloved daughter, ten pounds L. money, & to her heirs, to be paid to her, within Three years after my decease, by my Executors hereafter named.

Item. I give and bequeath to Mary Fisk, my beloved daughter, and to her heirs fifty pounds L. money if she arives to the age of twenty one years, or on her marriage day, to be paid to her, by my Executors hereafter named.

Item. I also give and bequeath to my afore's'd wife, and to all my children, my library. I do also give & bequeath to my four sons before named, my wearing apparil.

Item. I also give and bequeath to my two sons Jonathan & Samuel before named all my cash, bonds and notes for money, and all my personal estate or Stock, all my husbandry tools & utencils, and whatsoever is not heretofore given, and bequeathed, they namely, my two sons Jonathan and Samuel, paying out all the before mentioned legacies, and all my lawful debts & funeral charges.

Item. I also give and bequeath to my son Jonathan Fisk my clock, to be his after my wife deceases. I also constitute make & ordain my two sons Jonathan & Samuel Fisk to be the Sole Executors of this my last will and Testament, and I do hereby ratify and confirm this and no other to be my last will & Testament.

In witness whereof I have hereunto set my hand and seal the day and year above written.   Nathan Fisk & Seal.

Signed Sealed pronounced and Declared by the said Nathan Fisk to be his last will and Testament in the presence of——————
        Braddyll Smith
        Tho's Russell
        Joseph Russell
        Simeon Smith.
This will was proved June 27, 1769.
He d. Jan. 4, 1769; res. Weston, Mass.

1153. i. ANNE, b. Dec. 8, 1731; m. Oct. 24, 1751, Abraham Bigelow, b. 1713, son of Lieut. Thomas of Walth. and Marlboro. He res. Weston. Ch.: By 1st wife: 1. Isaac, b. Nov. 30, 1736; d. Jan. 1, 1748. 2. Joseph, b. Sept. 30, 1738; d. Dec. 20, 1748. 3. Abigail, b. Oct. 1, 1740; d. Jan. 7, 1748. 4. Abraham, b. Feb. 26, 1742; d. July, 1753. 5. Jesse, b. Mar., 1746; d. July, 1746. 6. Jesse, b. June 20, 1747; d. Jan. 12, 1748. 7. Isaac, b. May 2, 1750; gr. Harvard College, 1769, a clergyman; d. May 2, 1777. By Anne: 8, Abigil, b. Aug. 10, 1752; m. Rev. Thomas Prentice of Medfield. 9. Anna, b. Nov. 4, 1754; m. Rev. Thomas Haven of Reading. 10, Abraham, b. June 13, 1758; d. young. 11. Amos, b. Sept. 30, 1760; m. Lucy Savage. 12. Abraham, b. Sept. 18, 1762; gr. Harvard College, 1782; m. Hepzibah Jones; res. Camb. 13. John, b. Apr. 14. 1765; m. Lydia Spreig. 14. Samuel, b. Sept. 4, 1773.

1154. ii. NATHAN, b. Sept. 9, 1733; m. Sarah Hill, Mrs. Elizabeth (Breck) Treat and Mrs. Hannah (Wells) Reynolds.

1155. iii. SARAH, b. July 26, 1736; d. Nov. 7, 1743 of dysentery, "a lovely child."

1156. iv. JONATHAN, b. Dec. 15, 1739; m. Abigail Fiske.

1157. v. EZRA, b. Dec. 25, 1740; d. unm. non. comp. mentis.

1158. vi. SAMUEL, b. July 9, 1742; m. Mary Parkhurst and Abigail Murdock.

1159. vii. THADDEUS, b. Feb. 19, 1743; d. Jan. 20, 1748, scarlet fever.

1160. viii. MARY, b. Apr. 22, 1747; d. Jan. 4, 1748.

1161. ix. OLIVER, b. Sept. 14, 1748; d. young.

1162. x. MARY, b. Jan. 21, 1750; m. May 15, 1770, Samuel Learned of Camb.

1163. xi. HEPZIBAH, b. Aug. 10, 1754; m. Apr. 15. 1787. Abraham Jones, Jr., b. Feb. 12, 1762; res. Weston.

676. DEA. JOSIAH FISKE (Nathan, Nathan, Nathan, Nathaniel, William, Robert, Simon, Simon, William, Symond), b. Wat. Oct. 10, 1704; m. Sarah Lawrence, b. June 20, 1708, dau. of John and Anne (Tarball), of Lex.; d. 1798. He was selectman 1749-50, assessor 1743-44-48. He was dismissed to the Groton church May 13, 1753, and settled in Pepperell, where the births of his children (b. in Waltham) are recorded. He was deacon of the Congregational church, leading man in the town, and resided in that part of Groton incorporated later as Pepperell. For some years he was town clerk at Groton, and later the first town clerk of Pepperell for twenty years. His will is dated Sept. 1, 1778, and proved Jan. 23, 1779. He d. Oct. 27, 1778; res. Waltham, Groton and Pepperell, Mass.

1164. i. DAVID, b. Jan. 28, 1727; d. Oct. 28, 1729

1165. ii. SARAH, b. Aug. 7, 1729; d. May 19, 1731.

1166. iii. DAVID, b. Dec. 16, 1731; d. Feb. 1, 1766. He was accidentally killed by an apple thrown from a church window at an ordination in Lunenburg, Mass.

1167. iv. JOSIAH, b. Feb. 12, 1733; m. Sarah Colburn.

1168. v. SARAH, b. Oct. 7, 1736; m. Apr. 14, 1756, Simon Gilson, and had 10 ch.

1169. vi. AMOS, b. May 10, 1739; m. Mary Whitney.

1170. vii. DANIEL, b. May 18, 1742; m. Elizabeth Varnum.

1171. viii. ANNA, b. Feb. 16, 1744; d. Feb. 12, 1745.

1172. ix. ANNA, b. Dec. 16, 1747; m. Mar. 3, 1768, Dr. Ephraim Lawrence, of Pepperell. She d. June 12, 1774, ae. 27. He was b. Mar. 31, 1735; d. 1812. Was a physician; res. Pepperell. Ch.: Ebenezer, b. Jan. 9, 1770; gr. Harvard College in 1795; a physician; res. Hampton, N. H. Anna, b. July 26, 1772; m. Isaac B. Farrar; res. New Ipswich, N. H. Ruth, b. Apr. 8, 1777. Sarah, b. Apr. 18. 1779; d. Dec. 16, 1779. Dr. Lawrence m. 2d, and had 6 ch.

1173. x. ABEL, b. May 28, 1752; m. Anna Spalding and Sarah Putnam.

677. LIEUT. HENRY FISKE (Nathan, Nathan, Nathan, Nathaniel, William, Robert, Simon, Simon, William, Symond), b. Wat. Jan. 24, 1706; m. there Jan. 10, 1737, Mary Stone, b. Feb. 22, 1705, dau. of John. She d. June 2, 1805.

He was born in Watertown, where he resided for some time, finally moving to Medfield. With his brother Daniel he was one of the first proprietors of New Medfield, incorporated as Sturbridge and settled in that new town at an early date. He was elected selectman at the first meeting, Sept. 18, 1738, after the incorporation of the town; was often selectman, town clerk and treasurer. He was Lieut. in the colonial forces, member of the church, and a highly respected and esteemed citizen. His will is dated Dec. 13, 1789, and mentions grandchildren Mary Fay Durand and Sarah.

He d. Mar. 1, 1790; res. New Medfield, now Sturbridge, Mass.

1174.	i.	MARY, b. Jan. 29, 1738; m. John Fay, who was killed in battle at Bennington Aug. 16, 1777. She d. Aug. 31, 1777.
1175.	ii.	DANIEL, b. Jan. 12, 1740; d. Jan. 12, 1740.
1176.	iii.	HENRY, b. Nov. 13, 1740; d. Nov. 15, 1740.
1177.	iv.	SUSAN, b. Sept. 19, 1741; m. July 1, 1762, Stephen Fay, of Hardwick. She d. Dec. 26, 1812. He was b. 1739; d. May 26, 1804.
1178.	v.	ARMILLA, b. Aug. 24, 1743; d. Sept. 13, 1754.
1179.	vi.	HENRY, b. Aug. 16, 1745, m. Sarah Fiske.
1180.	vii.	ANNA, b. June 11, 1747; m. Dec. 30, 1766, Silas Corbin, of Woodstock. She d. Nov. 15, 1844.
1181.	viii.	SAMUEL, b. Mar. 30, 1749; d. Sept. 10, 1754.
1182.	ix.	THOMAS, b. Mar. 2, 1751, d. Sept. 16, 1754.
1183.	x.	RUTH, b. Feb. 17, 1754; d. Sept. 20, 1754.
1184.	xi.	SIMEON, b. Mar. 26, 1755; m. Mary Gould and Lydia Bugbee.
1185.	xii.	BULAH, b. Apr. 26, 1757; m. Jan. 27, 1780, Solomon Jones, of Brimfield. She d. Feb. 28, 1848. He d. Apr. 10, 1812.
1186.	xiii.	DAVID, b. Dec. 19, 1759; m. Eleanor Jones.
1187.	xiv.	EUNICE, b. Nov. 21, 1761, m. Feb. 18, 1784, Joshua Woodbury, of Sutton, b. Feb. 10, 1760; d. Aug. 8, 1825.

678. DEA. DANIEL FISKE (Nathan, Nathan, Nathan, Nathaniel, William, Robert, Simon, Simon, William, Symond), b. Wat. Aug. 19, 1709; m. in Weston, Mar. 31, 1743, Deliverence Brown, b. Nov. 11, 1720, dau. of Dea. Benj.; d. July 26, 1758; m. 2d, Feb. 19, 1760, Jemima Shaw, of Sturbridge.

He was born in Watertown, and with his brother, Lieut. Henry, became an early resident and one of the first proprietors of Sturbridge; was elected deacon of the church and held many town offices, selectman, assessor, etc. His will is dated Mar. 14, 1778, and is on record in the Worcester Probate office (see Barbour Hist. Collections of Massachusetts).

Henry and Daniel Fisk went from Watertown, Mass., to New Medfield, later called Sturbridge, Mass., and commenced a settlement on what is now called Fiskhill, in the year 1731. While clearing in the timber one day they heard some one chopping on the other side of the Quinnebog river. They did not know of any white man being near them, so they went to the bank of the river and shouted until a man replied and came to the opposite bank and said his name was Hyde. Daniel Fisk proposed to make a bridge so they could cross over and become acquainted, so Fisk and Hyde felled a tree from each bank of the river and the tops locked together so that persons could cross, for a number of years, and was therefore of great convenience to the people. When high water came this bridge would stir, or move down the river, therefore when they named the town they named it Sturbridge, after the above described bridge. Two joining towns are called Northbridge and Southbridge. The Fisks also named Fiskhill, Fiskdale and Fiskfactories, all of which they once owned and occupied.

Daniel Fisk kept a record of Remarkable Events, and in that book, among others, is found: Remarcable Dark Day May 19th 1780—Baptist Meeting House raised on Fiskhill, Sturbridge, Mass., June 3d, 1784—Terrible Huricane Aug. 23d 1786—Shase's Insurection in Mass. 1787—Very Hard Frost May 17, 1774. Remarcable Total Eclips of the Sun June 16, 1806—A Terrible Tornado Sep'r 23, 1815—Cold Summer but little corn 1816.

He d. Mar. 15, 1778, of smallpox, which he contracted in Boston while serving as representative of his town. His wid. m. 2d, Dec. 17, 1799, Dea. Samuel Green, of Leicester, where she d. July 2, 1810. She was buried in S. near the grave of Dea. Daniel. Res. Sturbridge, Mass.

1188.	i.	ANNE, b. May 9, 1744; d. Aug. 11, 1746.

1189. ii. SARAH, b. Aug. 12, 1746; m. May 5, 1774, her cousin. Dea. Henry Fiske, Jr. She d. Dec. 11, 1815. He d. Dec. 10, 1815. Both buried the same day.

1190. iii. DANIEL, b. May 12, 1748; m. Elizabeth Morse.

1191. iv. JOSHUA, b. Aug. 26, 1750; d. in the Rev. army in 1778.

1192. v. NATHAN, b. June 20, 1755; d. Aug. 25, 1756.

1193. vi. DELIVERENCE, b. July 31, 1757; m. 1778, Silas Marsh, of Sturbridge. She d. Dec. 19, 1842.

1194. vii. JEMIMA, b. Nov. 22, 1760; m. Feb. 6, 1783, Joshua Harding, Jr., of Sturbridge. She d. Dec. 7, 1841. A son, Daniel Fiske, gr. Brown University in 1809, a lawyer; res. Union, Me.

1195. viii. NATHAN, b. Apr. 4, 1762; m. Abigail Lyon.

1196. ix. LYDIA, b. Apr. 4, 1762; m. Feb. 6, 1783, Oliver Plimpton, b. Sept. 7, 1758; d. Apr. 26, 1832, a corporal in Rev. war. She d. Dec. 20, 1851, the oldest person in S. Both received pensions.

1197. x. SUSANNAH, b. Feb. 6, 1764; m. 1784 Capt. Samuel Newell, a soldier in the Rev. war. 8 ch., one Dolly, b. Dec. 25, 1788; m. Hon. William Larned Marcy. He was born Dec. 12, 1786, in Southbridge, Mass., and died in Ballston Spa., N. Y., July 4, 1857. He was graduated at Brown in 1808, and studied law in Troy, N. Y. Was later admitted to the bar there and at once began the practice of his profession. In the war of 1812 he served as First Lieutenant and achieved distinction by capturing the Canadian forces, being the first prisoners taken on land, and their flag was the first captured in the war. At the close of the war he had attained the rank of Captain, and returned to the practice of the law. He held minor political city offices, was at one time editor of the "Troy Budget." In 1821 he was appointed Adj. Gen. of the State Militia by Gov. Van Buren. In 1823 he was comptroller of the State, and in 1829 he was appointed one of the associate justices of the Supreme Court of New York. One of the most important cases before him was the trial of the alleged murderers of William Morgan, of anti-masonic fame. He continued on the bench until 1831, when he was elected to the United States Senate. He resigned in 1833 to become Governor of the State of New York, which office he held for three terms, until 1839. In 1840 he was appointed by President Van Buren one of the commisssioners to decide upon the claims against the government of Mexico. Upon the election of James K. Polk as President, he was appointed Secretary of War, which position he filled with great credit President Pierce selected him as Secretary of State. At the close of Pierce's administration he returned to private life, and four months afterward he was found dead one evening in his library with an open volume before him. Mr. Marcy had the reputation of being a shrewd politician and tactician, and probably has never been surpassed in this respect by any one in New York except Martin Van Buren. He was regarded among his countrymen of all parties as a statesman of the highest order of administrative and diplomatic ability.

1198. xi. HANNAH, b. Sept. 24, 1765; m. Mar. 27, 1789, Samuel Groves, of Monson, Mass. She d. Dec., 1836.

1199. xii. REBECCA, b. Mar. 20, 1768; m. May 10, 1795, John Streeter, and d. in Cambridge, N. Y.

1200. xiii. MIRIAM, b. Jan. 30, 1770; m. Salmon Hebard.

1201. xiv. KEZIA, b. Oct. 25, 1771; m. Sept. 29, 1792, Gershom Plimpton, Esq., b. Feb. 18, 1768; d. Apr. 20, 1823. She d. Oct. 8, 1808, leaving 5 sons and 2 daus. Their eldest son was Moses, b. Oct. 17, 1795; res. Boston. He d. Sept. 19, 1854, from injuries received by being run over by horses attached to an omnibus. He had several children. From 1816 to 1844 he was one of the leading men in Southbridge and largely interested in the welfare of the town.

1202. xv. SAMUEL, b. Dec. 30, 1773; m. Sally Lyon.
1203. xvi. LOIS, b. Feb. 8, 1776; m. July 29, 1795, Col. Asa Bacon, of Charleston. She d. Oct. 21, 1797, s. p.

679. HON. SAMUEL FISKE (Nathan, Nathan, Nathan, Nathaniel, William, Robert, Simon, Simon, William, Symond), b. Wat. Feb. 16, 1711; m. Mar. 21, 1744, Lydia Bond, b. May 21, 1718, dau. of Thomas. He was representative 1774-76 and justice of the peace for years; selectman 1751-3-4-5-6-7-8-71-2. Thomas Farrington and Samuel Jones, of Boston, were admr. of his estate. He d. Apr. 30, 1792; res. Watertown, Mass.

1204. i. LYDIA, b. June 21, 1747; d. 1769.
1205. ii. SARAH, b. Oct. 20, 1750.
1206. iii. ELIZABETH, b. July 15, 1753.
1207. iv. MARY, b. Mar. 15, 1755.
1208. v. LUCY, b. June 30, 1758; d. Aug., 1758.
1209. vi. SAMUEL, b. Oct. 19, 1762; d. 1764.
1210. vii. LUCRETIA, b. Sept. 15, 1764.

682. WILLIAM FISK (William, Nathan, Nathan, Nathaniel, William, Robert, Simon, Simon, William, Symond), b. in Watertown, Mass., Apr. 20, 1709; m. Willington, Conn., Jan. 23, 1729, Mary Blancher, d. abt. Jan., 1744; m. 2d, Mar. 6, 1744, Eunice Whitney. He d. in Conn.; res. Willington, Conn.

1211. i. WILLIAM, b. Apr. 26, 1732; m. ——— ———.
1212. ii. MARY, b. July 28, 1734.
1213. iii. EUNICE, b. Mar. 29, 1737.
1214. iv. SARAH, b. May 13, 1739.
1215. v. HANNAH, b. Mar. 26, 1740.
1216. vi. NATHAN, b. Dec. 13, 1743.
1217. vii. PETER, b. Dec. 24, 1745; d. Dec. 25, 1746.
1218. viii. BENJAMIN, b. Aug. 19, 1748.

683. STEPHEN FISK (William, Nathan, Nathan, Nathaniel, William, Robert, Simon, Simon, William, Symond), b. Sept. 14, 1714; bap. Weston, Mass., Apr. 17, 1715; m. at Willington, Conn., Aug. 5, 1742, Prudence Farley; m. 2d, (published) June 26, 1758, Anna (Bradish) Green, of Hardwick. He was baptized in Weston, Mass., with his brother. His father and his mother, whose maiden name was Eunice Jennings, moved to Willington, Conn., where her brother, Stephen Jennings, had previously located on a large tract of land. Stephen married his first wife in Connecticut, and resided in Willington, where he was town clerk for nine years, from 1744 to 1753 inclusive. After her death he married a second wife in Hardwick, Mass., and located in Greenwich, Mass., where he died. He resided in that part now Enfield, and was town clerk from 1758 to 1763.

Rev. Lucius R. Paige, of Cambridgeport, Mass., who wrote the History of Hardwick, Mass., writes, "on page 386 of that work it is suggested that Annie Green may have been the widow of John Green, and the mother of two children by him." John Green was the son of Thomas, and was born in Shrewsbury, Mass., Mar. 2, 1726. He m. Anna Bradish Dec. 7, 1751. She was b. June 6, 1729, the dau. of Dea. James and Damaris (Rice) Bradish (see Conant Genealogy, Hist. of Hardwick and Hist. of Shrewsbury). Stephen and his second wife were married in Hardwick, he of Greenwich and she of that town in Worcester County. There is a tradition in the family that Stephen's widow was married to a Mr. Chase, for her second husband. This, I think, is incorrect, for at Warwick, Mass., Jan. 16, 1770, the intention of marriage of Ezra Conant and Anna Fisk (Stephen's widow) was published. She died in Vermont, and lived to be nearly 100 years old

A descendant in writing of her says this: "My grandfather Fisks Mother, died in Claremont N. H. over one hundred years old. Dont know the date, but have heard my Father say so. When she was well along in life, and a widow, she married Mr Chase then a widower, and an old man Father of Bishop Philemon Chase. Dudley Chase, U. S. Senator from Vt. and Ithamar Chase, who was father of Salmon B Chase, the famous member of Lincolns Cabinet." Ezra Conant married for his first wife in Dudley, Mass., Jan. 1, 1745, Melicent Newell, b. Dec. 19, 1725, d. July, 1769. He married Mrs. Anna Fisk at Warwick. In

1772 Anna Conant, formerly Fisk, guardian of Stephen and James Fisk, sons of Stephen Fisk, late of Greenwich, Mass., in Hampshire County, petitions to sell land of her late husband. (Cheshire Co. Court Records, Ezra Conant, Dec. 7, 1804).

The children of Ezra and Anna were: 1, Anna, b. May 26, 1771; m. Sept. 13, 1791, Charles Conant, at Warwick, Mass. 2, Clark, b. June 23, 1773, at Warwick, Mass. Anna (Green) (Fisk) Conant, when very old, used to ride from Claremont, N. H., horseback, some 50 or 60 miles, to East Randolph, to visit her son Stephen, and always before going home again used to ride on horseback also three or four miles up to Randolph Centre Village, to see Dudley Chase, who lived there. Dudley was uncle to Judge Salmon P. Chase. Another brother of Dudley's was 70 years ago, or more, an Episcopal clergyman, Philemon, having a little wooden church, quite secluded, on the edge of the town of Bethel, some three miles up stream toward West Randolph, from Bethel Village. This Philemon Chase became first Episcopal bishop of Ohio. With him in Ohio lived for awhile his afterward famous nephew, when a boy, Salmon P.

The Hampshire, Mass., probate records show that April 7, 1767, Capt Jeremiah Powers was appointed guardian of Rufus Fisk a minor under 14 years. on July 7, 1767, said Powers resigned his trust for the reason that said Rufus was living in the Colony of Connecticut, on the 7th of April 1767 said Powers was appointed guardian of Olive Fisk and Mary Fisk minors over 14 years old, and on the 6 of November 1764 Anna Fisk was appointed guardian of Stephen Fisk and James Fisk minors under the age of 14 years all said minors are children of Stephen Fisk.

Stephen's Will.—In the name of God Amen. August ye 17th Anno. Dom 1764, I Stephen Fisk of Greenwich in the County of Hampshire, Yeoman of sound mind memory thanks be given to God tho very sick and weak, and calling to minde the mortality of my Body Knowing it is appinted for all men once to Dy. Do make and ordain this my Laste will and testament that is to Say principly and first of all. I, Give and Reccomend my Soul into the hands of God that Gave it, my Body I reccomend to the earth to Be Buried in Decent Christian Burial at the Discrsn of my executrix not Doubting But that I shall Receive the same again By the almighty power of God at the General Ressurrection, and as touching Such Worldly Eestate wherewith it hath pleased God to Bless me in this World. I give Devise and Dispse of the Same in manner and forme folliong:

Imprimis——— I give and Bequeeth to my Belovid wife Anna the one third part of all my Estate Both Real and Personal, whome I Do also hereby appoint Sole Heir and Executrix of this my last will and testament.

Item———
I Give and Bequeathe to my three Belovid Sons, Rufus Stephen and James two thirds of the Remaining Part of my estate, to Be Equilly Divided Between Them, when they arrive to ful age.

Item———
I Give and Bequeath to my three Belovid Daughters Prudence, Olive, and Mary the Remaining third part of my Estate when they arrive to full age. After Debts and Funeral Charges are Subducted out of my estate which I Do Give and Bequeath to all my belovid Children aforesaid; and I Do hereby utterly Revoke Disannul and make void all and every other will and testament of what name or nature soever; Ratyfying and Confirming this and no other.

In witness whereof I, have hereunto Set my hand and Seal the Day and Date above written

Stephen Fisk.   [Seal.]

Signed Sealed Published and pronounced and Declaried as the Last will and testament of the said Stephen Fisk in presence of

Nathan Fisk.
Nathan Fisk Jr.
Josiah Fisk.

Here followeth an Inventory of all the Estate both Real & Personal of Stephen Fisk of Greenwich Lately Deceased as shown by Anna Fisk Administratrix and Prized by us as the Subscribers (Viz) The Home Lot about 10 acres with No. 27, 2d Division

	£	s	d
50 acres adjoining in the west end of the said Home Lot.............	166	13	4
To about 20 acres of land adjoining on the south-east corner of the home lot being Part of the Lot No 57, 2d Division....	..	..	..
To about 30 acres of land Lying to the North East corner of the sd home lot origanely laid out to Nathan Fisk.............	6	10	0
To ten calves.............	1	4	0
"Two Oxen.............	9	10	0
One Brass Ketel..........	1	0	0
* " Fire sh'el & Tongs....	0	6	0
* " " "	0	8	0
a frying Pan..............	0	1	0
One fire lock.............	0	13	9
" Sadle & Bridle........	0	14	0
The wearing clothing of the Deceased...........	3	4	10
Sunday shoes.............	0	6	0
* Axes....................	0	9	0
an Iron bar..............	0	10	0
one cart and wheels........	2	0	0
Plows & *.............	1	11	0
one Pick Fork...........	0	0	8
one Muck fork...........	0	4	0
one Galon Botel..........	0	1	0
one Sith.................	0	2	0
6 Bushels of Rye.........	0	18	0
3 Bushels of Wheat.......	0	12	0
harrow teath.............	0	8	0
* a damaged lot of hay....	7	6	0
* three beds & the furneture	10	7	4
one table Cloth...........	0	2	8
Indigo *..................	0	1	6
*..................	0	2	8
10 Pound of hops..........	0	5	0
a Great Wheel.............	0	2	0
a dry Hogsed.............	0	2	0
Meal	0	8	0
2 Meal bags..............	0	2	0
one chest.................	1	6	0
Wedges & Rings.........	0	5	4
one chest.................	0	7	0
one table.................	0	2	6
one cheese Press.........	0	4	0
one clevis & Pin........	0	1	4
two Sithes..............	0	6	0
one chain................	0	2	8
* a sith tallon..........	0	1	0
Knives & forks..........	0	1	0
one hammer..............	0	0	4
7 Chairs.................	3	4	0
3 Cows.................	9	6	8
one hefer *..............	2	13	4
fifteen Sheep............	4	10	0
one Mare.................	6	10	0
one Swine.................	0	12	0
William Fisk Note........	16	14	9
John Bradish Note........	4	15	9
John Bradish Note........	3	4	6
Nathan Fisk bond.......	17	9	113
Nathan Fisk Note........	9	6	3
Indian Corn 16 bushels....	2	2	8
3 Picks of Beans & Pees...	0	3	0
a churn..................	0	1	6
one Lanthorne...........	0	3	0
* Enk horse.............	0	0	8
* for Bolts.............	0	8	4
Potatoes	0	12	0
* to a Pare of Fetorch.....	0	3	0
Meal Troves.............	0	2	0
Sole Leather.............	0	3	0
a looking Glass..........	0	3	6
Glass botels..............	0	6	0
an Iron Goose...........	0	2	8
Puter	1	4	0
Cofee Pot & Funel........	0	1	0
Pepper box & Grater......	0	0	4
Wooden Plators..........	0	0	2
Wooden Plates...........	0	1	6
" Dish	0	0	6
6 Traps................	0	5	0
Earthan Jars..............	0	1	6
2 Trowels................	0	6	8
one Iron Pot...........	0	3	0
one Iron Ketle..........	0	5	0
Monny in hand...........	0	16	0
To 14 books.............	0	9	8
Batemonds drops.........	0	9	0
1 Loam & Sucklen........	1	14	8
14 Pounds of Tallow......	0	7	0
To Pork................	1	12	0
To Beef................	1	13	0
Sope	0	4	9
Sadel Bages.............	0	6	8
Warmming Pan & Skilet..	0	5	0
horse chanes.............	0	8	0
a Tub of Butter..........	1	7	6
Oats	1	0	0
Sives	0	3	8
3 Tabels.................	0	2	6
one cow Hide............	0	7	8
one Note against William Rogers	0	2	0
one Box iron.............	0	1	6
2 tubs..................	0	2	0
6 yards all wool cloth 4s 5d per yd.................	1	7	0
one Pue in the meeting house	3	4	0
Joseph Hinds accompt....	0	8	0

Greenwich Dated November 19th 1764

Benjamin Cooley

Abr'm Gibbs

Wm Rogers

He d. Oct. 20, 1764; res. Willington, Conn., and Greenwich, Mass.

1219. i. PRUDENCE, b. Sept. 4, 1745.
1220. ii. OLIVE, b. Aug. 4, 1747.
1221. iii. MARY, b. Oct. 22, 1749.
1222. iv. RUFUS, b. Mar. 28, 1752; m. Dorcas Gleason.
1223. v. STEPHEN, b. Apr. 7, 1759; m. Esther Clark.
1224. vi. JAMES, b. Oct. 4, 1763; m. Priscilla West.
1224½.vii. HANNAH, b. 1764.

685. NATHAN FISK (William, Nathan, Nathan, Nathaniel. William, Robert, Simon, Simon, William, Symond), b. Willington, Conn., Feb. 13, 1722; m. there Feb. 14, 1743, Eleanor Whitney. He was a farmer. He was born in Willington, Conn., to which his parents had removed at an early day. He married his wife there, and in 1748 moved to Greenwich, Mass. He was a farmer all his life. He resided in that part afterward incorporated as Enfield, and was town clerk from 1743 to 1758. Res. Willington, Conn., and Greenwich, Mass.

1225. i. JOSIAH, b. Feb. 8, 1745; m. Elizabeth Morse.
1226. ii. NATHAN, b. Apr. 17, 1744; m. Ruth Burt.
1227. iii. OLIVER, b. June 13, 1750; d. Nov. 3, 1750.
1228. iv. EXPERIANS, b. Nov. 19, 1751; m. Mary Earl. They res. in Westminster, Vt. They subsequently resided in Brookfield, Vt. One of their children was Artemas, who married Catherine Colt. He died in Brookfield, Feb. 28, 1872. They had 1, Almira, who d. June 8, 1894; 2, Edward E., who d. Oct. 2, 1870; 3, Sophia, m. Jan., 1867, Joseph George Colt; 4, Roxanna, m. Nov. 29, 1866, John Lamson.
1229. v. MIRIAM, b. Apr. 8, 1758.
1230. vi. LURANA, b. May 13, 1759.
1231. vii. EUNICE, b. June 26, 1762.
1232. viii. STEPHEN, b. Jan. 26, 1747; m. ———— ————.
1233. ix. DINAH. b. Jan. 26, 1747.
1233½.x. SYLVANUS, b. ————. He d., unm., of wounds received in Battle at Guilford, Vt., at the time of the trouble with New York State.

689. ASA FISKE (Nathaniel, Nathaniel, Nathan, Nathaniel, William, Robert, Simon, Simon, William, Symond), b. Sherburne, Mass., Feb. 22, 1708; m. Jan. 30, 1734, Lois Leland, b. 1714, dau. of Timothy. She made her will Mar. 3, 1775; proved Feb. 25, 1801. His will is dated Nov. 6, 1770, and proved Jan. 8, 1781. In it he is styled gentleman, "Being very weak in body" etc. He gave his wife Lois, one-third of his estate. He d. 1781; res. Holliston, Mass.

1234. i. ABEL. b. 1743; m. Mehitable Rix; res. Medway.
1235. ii. AARON, b. Mar. 13, 1748; m. Tabatha Metcalf.
1236. iii. ASA, b. Sept. 3, 1746; m. Mercy Jones.
1237. iv. ABNER, b. 1754; m. Molly Grant; res. Lee, Oneida Co., N. Y.
1238. v. LYDIA, b. 1738; m. ———— Burbank; res. Holl.
1239. vi. HULDAH, b. 1740; m. Caleb Claflin; res. Hop.
1240. vii. LOIS, b. 1751; m. Amariah Marsh of Pawtucket, R. I. They were the ancestors of Mrs. Edward F. Jones of Binghampton, N. Y., wife of Ex-Lieut. Gov. Jones.

691. HON. MOSES FISKE (Nathaniel, Nathaniel, Nathan, Nathaniel, William, Robert, Simon, Simon, William, Symond), b. Sherburne, Mass., Jan. 29, 1713; m. in Needham, Apr. 11, 1745, Mehitable Broad, d. Feb. 13, 1773. He was born in Sherburne, but soon before marriage, probably about 1740, he moved to Needham, and was married there. Later he moved to Natick, where he afterward resided and was a prominent citizen. He held the office of selectman and was a deputy to the General Court. Late in life he resided in Needham and died there. He d. Feb. 18, 1770; res. Natick and Needham, Mass.

1241. i. MOSES, b. Natick, 1746; m. Rebecca Clark and Mrs. Sarah Stone.
1242. ii. JOSHUA, b. ————; m. Martha Smith.
1243. iii. ENOCH, b. ————; m. Sarah Bacon.
1244. iv. ELIJAH, b. Sept. 14, 1753; m. Elizabeth Binney.
1245. v. HEZEKIAH, b. Dec. 6, 1756; d. Apr. 24, 1757.
1246. vi. SARAH, b. ————; m. ————.

695. JOHN FISKE (John, Nathaniel, Nathan, Nathaniel, William, Robert, Simon, Simon, William, Symond), b. Sherburne, May 8, 1709; m. Sept. 21, 1731, Abigail (Leland) Babcock, d. Mar. 7, 1761. She was the widow of Ebenezer Babcock, and seems to have lived on or near the farm of her late husband at West Sherburn, where the heirs of the late William Leland (a gunsmith) now reside. Abigail Leland was a great-granddaughter of her grandaunt (by marriage), the wife of Henry Leland, Sr., of Sherborn (Margaret Babcock), and great-granddaughter of Robert Babcock of Dorchester, who was born 158— in Essex County, England, and removed with the Pilgrims to Holland, and came in the ship "Anne" in 1623 to Plymouth, Mass. John Fiske died of what was known in those days as the "great Holliston fever." He had to go to Boston on business for the town and was taken ill and died quite suddenly on his return home.

John Fisk of Sherburne Inv of his estate Mar. 12, 1754 £820 David his eldest son the adm'r rendered an acct of his adm'n Mar 17 1755 when the est owed an Isaac Fisk Guardian of the following children app'd June 10 1754 viz: Jonas who was then under 14 years of age and Amos, John & Joel who were all over 14 32:247 and 35:356.

He d. Jan. 3. 1754; res. Sherburne, Mass.

1247.   i.   DAVID, b. Apr. 16, 1732; m. Sarah Bullard.
1248.   ii.   AMOS, b. Mar. 5, 1735; m. Anne Bryant.
1249.   iii.   JOHN, b. Mar. 16, 1738; m. Sarah Hill and Abigail ———.
1250.   iv.   JOEL, b. Apr. 22, 1740; m. Ruth Reed and res. in Cambridge, Mass.
1251.   v.   JONAS, b. Feb. 4, 1742; m. Mary Hill.
1252.   vi.   MARTHA, b. Jan. 5, 1749; d. Nov. 19, 1750.
1253.   vii.   HANNAH, b. Jan. 24, 1734; m. ——— Fairbanks and Caleb Hill.
1254.   viii.   SALLY, b. ———; d., unm., July 8, 1780.

697. ISAAC FISKE (John, Nathaniel, Nathan, Nathaniel, William, Robert, Simon, Simon, William, Symond), b. Sherburne, Apr. 24, 1714; m. Nov. 11, 1736, Hannah Haven, b. June 10, 1716, dau. of Richard and Lydia (Whitney) Haven, of Fram., d. Feb. 21, 1800. He was born in Sherburne and was a weaver by trade. He resided first at Worcester and later at Framingham, first near Addison Dadmun's, after at Guinea end, and later on the Richard Fiske place. After his marriage for many years his wife taught school. His will is dated Aug. 24, 1789, and proved Mar. 17, 1800. He d. Dec. 22, 1799; res. Worcester and Framingham, Mass.

1255.   i.   ISAAC, b. 1736; m. Esther Mann.
1256.   ii.   HANNAH, b. Mar. 27, 1739; m. Dea. Everett of Attleboro. Ch.: 1, Samuel; 2, Hannah; 3 and 4, twins, Paul and Silas; 5, Gilbert, and other daus.
1257.   iii.   JOHN, b. Aug. 9, 1741; m. Abigail How.
1258.   iv.   RICHARD, b. (town records, Nov. 28, 1743,) Feb. 25, 1750; m. Zebiah Pond.
1259.   v.   DANIEL, b. 1751; m. Sukey Thurston and Alice Davis.
1260.   vi.   MOSES, b. ———; d. young.
1261.   vii.   LYDIA, b. Oct. 25, 1753; m. in Hop., 1779, Major Lawson Nurse of Fram. She d. before 1799, for he then m. 2d, Lydia Eaton. Ch.: 1, Nathan, b. Mar. 13, 1780; m. Esther ———; res. Thomaston. 2, Lawson, b. Dec. 15, 1781, a physician; res. Templeton, Mass., and Sparta. Tenn., where he d. unm. 3, Nancy, b. Mar. 21, 1784. 4, Fortunatus, d. Feb. 25, 1816. 5, Betsey, d. young. 6. Martha, d. ae. 18. 7, Sophia, m. Peter Brewer of Southbridge.
1262.   viii.   MOSES, b. July 12, 1755; m. Betsey Bullard.

700. PETER FISKE (John, Nathaniel, Nathan, Nathaniel, William, Robert, Simon, Simon, William, Symond), b. Sherburne, Mar. 12, 1723; m. in Grafton Nov. 15, 1758, Sarah Perry of Grafton, Mass. Res. Grafton and Warwick, Mass.

1263.   i.   PETER, b. July 1, 1758; d. July 2, 1758.
1264.   ii.   MOSES, b. June 11, 1760; m. ——— ———.
1265.   iii.   NATHANIEL, b. July 16, 1762; rev. to Tennessee.

1266. iv. PETER, b. Dec. 5, 1764; rev. to Tennessee.
1267. v. SARAH, b. Feb. 1, 1768; m. Jeduthan Willcox; res. Orford, N. H. Leonard, one of his sons, was one of the judges of the Supreme court of N. H. He d. in 1850.
1268. vi. JOHN, b. Oct. 26, 1770; m. Elizabeth Mellen.

708. ASA FISKE (Bezaleel, Jonathan, David, David, David, Jeffrey, Robert, Simon, Simon, William, Symond), b. Holden, Mass., Oct. 7, 1764; m. there Oct. 4, 1787, Dolly Warren, b. 1764, d. Dublin, N. H., Aug. 6, 1818. He was a farmer, was born in Holden, married there, and about 1789 moved to Rutland, Mass., and later in 1801 to Dublin, N. H., where he continued to reside until his death. He d. July 2, 1829; res. Holden and Rutland, Mass., and Dublin, N. H.
1269. i. LUCY, b. Aug. 9, 1788.
1270. ii. PARKER, b. ———; d. young.
1271. iii. BOY, b. ———; d. young.
1272. iv. BOY, b. ———; d. young.
1273. v. PARKER, b. in 1793; m. Mary B. Priest.
1274. vi. MARY.
1275. vii. DANIEL, b. June 18, 1798; m. Esther Eaton.
1276. viii. DORYTHA, b. ———.

709. NAHUM FISKE (Bezaleel, Jonathan, David, David, David, Jeffrey, Robert, Simon, Simon, William, Symond), b. Holden, Mass., May 11, 1762; m. there July 7, 1785, Sally Gay, d. 1801. He d. Oct. 26, 1803; res. Holden, Mass.
1277. i. SALLY, b. Oct. 17, 1786; m. James Pierce. They res. in Boylston, Mass. She d. 1871. Ch.: James Reed, b. 1815; d. Nov., 1876; m. Maria Stowell, b. 1825, d. Oct., 1871; three ch. Jarvis, unm. Lyman, b. ———; d. Feb., 1884; m. Louisa Vinton, b. ———, d. 1884. Abbie, b. 1825; d. June, 1893; m. Otis Knight, d. during the war. Nancy, unm. Charles F., m. Hannah F. Carpenter.
1278. ii. BETSEY. b. Sept. 11, 1787; m. William Woods. She d. 1865. They res. in Rutland, Mass. Ch.: Loring m. Mary Webb. Rev.; res. New Braintree, Mass. James.
1279. iii. ISAAC, b. May 27, 1789; m. ——— Davis.
1280. iv. BAZELEEL, b. July 9, 1791; m. Mary Rice.
1281. v. ABNER, b. Dec. 27, 1793; m. Mary Rice.
1282. vi. LEONARD, b. Dec. 19, 1795; m. and d. 1866.
1283. vii. NANCY, b. May 4, 1798; m. Oct. 13, 1819, Jonathan Wentworth of Newmarket, N. Y., b. Jan., 1793; drowned in Penobscot river, Maine, July 9, 1834; m. 2d, Apr. 5, 1835, George Dennison. She d. Dec. 1, 1879. 1, Charles A., b. Mar. 15, 1821; d. Mar. 29, 1854, unm. 2, John F., b. Oct. 31, 1822; d. at sea, Jan., 1848. 3, Nancy Maria, b. Sept. 27, 1825; m. Isaiah Dunster Russell, of Mason, N. H., b. Aug., 1820; d. Jan., 1887. They res. Worcester, where he was a merchant. Ch.: Addison C., b. Feb. 7, 1847; d. Aug. 10, 1851. Charles Addison, b. Mar. 2, 1852; m. Ella Frances Sayles, of Conn. Ch.: 1, Sabin S., b. Oct. 23, 1883; 2, Deborah, b. Feb. 28, 1889. He was born in Worcester, fitted for college at the public schools in that city, and was graduated at Yale College. For some time he was editor of one of the papers in his native city. Shortly after his marriage he was elected to congress as republican representative from the Killingly, Conn., district, embracing the counties of Windham and New London, and has been repeatedly re-elected ever since, which shows the confidence and esteem in which he is held by his constituents. Annie Maria, b. Aug. 10, 1864; m. Charles Marble; res. Worcester. 4, George F., b. Aug. 11, 1830; d. 1834. 5, Frances E., b. Jan. 9, 1833; d. July 1, 1875; m. Chas. Campbell. 6, George, b. 1836; m. Carrie Blanchard of N. H.; res. Worcester. 7, Mary Jane, b. 1838; m. Curtis Robinson. 8, Saphira, b. 1840; m. Harry Richardson. 9, Martha S.
1284. viii. CHARLES, b. June 19, 1800; d. 1801.

11

710. SAMUEL FISK (Samuel, Jonathan, David, David, David, Jeffrey, Robert, Simon, Simon, William, Symond), b. Sherborn, Mass., Feb. 8, 1762; m. Dolly Gleason, of Hubbardston, dau. of Bezaleel Gleason, formerly of Worcester; d. 1799; buried in ———; m. 2d, Mrs. Lydia (Brooks) Stone. Samuel Fisk came to Barre, Mass., with his parents and a brother and sister, Jason and Hepzibath. The parents died, also the sister, who was single. The farm was divided between Jason and Samuel. They both married, and brought up their respective families on the place. He d. Jan. 26, 1832; res. Barre, Mass.

    1285. i.   SEWALL, b. Dec. 17, 1788; m. Sally Norcross Smith.
    1286. vi.   SAMUEL, b. in 1797; m. Maria Williams, Lucy B. Allen and
          ———.
    1287. iv.   HARVEY, b. Dec. 18, 1792; m. Lydia Hastings.
    1288. viii.   LEVI, b. Sept. 4, 1806; m. Susan G. Felker.
    1289. v.   LYMAN, b. May 2, 1794; d. in Barre, Mar. 22, 1814.
    1290. ii.   DOLLIE, b. 1798; d. infancy.
    1291. iii.   GARDNER, b. Dec. 17, 1790; d. ae. 10.
    1292. vii.   ROXANNA, b. 1804; d. unm. 1846.
    1293. ix.   SARAH, b. 1808; d. unm.

711. JASON FISK (Samuel, Jonathan, David, David, David, Jeffrey, Robert, Simon, Simon, William, Symond), b. Sherborn, Mass., Sept. 1, 1754; m. Elizabeth ———. Jason was born in Barre, and always resided there. Worcester Register of Deeds, Vol 105 page 182 Nov. 8 1783. Jason Fisk of Barre for 23 £ sells to Samuel Fisk Jr of Barre, Yoeman part of the Great Farm No 2 in Barre, 12½ acres. Vol 217 p. 455 April 28 1818 Jason Fisk of Barre, Yoeman, for $15 sells to Samuel Fisk of Barre 23 rods. Res. Barre, Mass.

    1294. i.   HANNAH, b. Mar. 30, 1783; m. ——— King; res. Homer, N. Y.
          They had ch., but all died young.
    1295. ii.   JOHN, b. ———; m. ——— Fiske, his cousin. He was a farmer;
          res. Barre, Mass., and d. s. p. about 1825, ae. 40.
    1296. iii.   JOEL, b. ———; m., and had children, and res. in Ohio.

718. DAVID FISKE (David, Jonathan, David, David, David, Jeffrey, Robert, Simon, Simon, William, Symond), b. Holden, Mass., July 19, 1761; m. there July 11, 1782, Naomi Winch. She m. 2d, May 4, 1797, Asa Greenwood of H. The inventory of his estate was probated Aug. 20, 1794. His widow Naomi was admr. He d. 1794; res. Holden, Mass.

    1297. i.   BETSEY, b. Dec. 12, 1782; d. Apr. 16, 1783.
    1298. ii.   SAMUEL, b. Sept. 4, 1784; m. ——— ———.
    1299. iii.   JOHN, b. Oct. 24, 1786.
    1300. iv.   RUTH, b. Feb. 1, 1790.

730. SERGT. ROBERT FISK (Robert, Robert, David, David, David, Jeffrey, Robert, Simon, Simon, William, Symond), b. in Lexington, Mass., in 1758; m. near Poughkeepsie, in Dutchess County, N. Y. Elizabeth ———, b. 1750, d. 1849. He was a soldier in the Revolutionary Army. After the war he resided in Dutchess County, New York, and there married a wife who was born in Holland. She died in 1849 ae. 99. She drew a pension from the United States as the widow of Robert Fisk, a Revolutionary soldier. The pension was obtained in 1843-4 and continued until her death. Their oldest child was Abraham. From the Bureau of Pensions at Washington, D. C., it is ascertained that Robert Fisk was a soldier of the Revolutionary War, and he made an application for pension on June 8, 1819, at which time he was residing in Pope County, Ill., and sixty-one years of age, and his pension was allowed for eight years and one month's actual service as a sergeant in the Massachusetts troops, Revolutionary War; a part of the time he served under Capt. North and Col. Greaton. Place of enlistment not stated. His widow, Elizabeth, made application and received a pension for the service of her husband as above set forth. He d. in Illinois or Kentucky; res. Dutchess County, New York.

    1301. i.   ABRAHAM, b. about 1780; m. ——— ——— and Artimitia
          ———.
    1302. ii.   HENRY A., b. about 1778; m. Susanna Wiley.
    1303. iii.   PROBABLY OTHERS.

731. DR. DAVID FISKE (Robert, Robert, David, David, David, Jeffrey, Robert Simon, Simon, William, Symond), b. Lexington, Nov. 23, 1760; m. Abigail Harrington, dau. of Robert and Abigail (Mason), b. Aug. 9, 1754. He was a physician and resided at the corner of Elm avenue and Bedford street which place consisting of a house and an acre of land he bought of Mrs. Ruth Harrington in 1777. At his death he was buried by the Masonic order. "I will say in regard to my great-grandfather, the last Dr. David Fisk, that he was the only doctor the Americans had at the battle of Lexington, and that his brother-in-law, young Harrington, was the first one killed in that battle." M. M. Fisk, 39 Bowdoin street, Boston, Mass. He d. Nov. 20, 1803; res. Lexington, Mass.

    1304. i.   ROBERT, b. in 1780; m. Sally Robbins.
    1305. ii.   ABIGAIL, b. ———; d. young.
    1306. iii. BETSEY, b. Oct. 17, 1782; m. Nov. 29, 1810, Joseph Newell, of
                New Ipswich, N. H.
    1307. iv. JOHN, b. Jan. 22, 1789; m. Lydia Pierce.
    1308. v.   MARY, b. ———; d. young.
    1309. vi. CHLOE, b. ———; scalded to death Feb. 16, 1794.
    1310. vii. PETER, b. ———.

735. DR. JOSEPH FISKE (Joseph, Robert, David, David, Jeffrey, Robert, Simon, Simon, Simon, William, Symond), b. Lexington, Dec. 25, 1752; m. July 31, 1794, Elizabeth Stone, b. Nov. 13, 1770, d. Mar. 6, 1842. He was a young man at the battle of Lexington, not quite twenty-three years of age. He assisted his father who was also a doctor and whose name was the same, to dress the wounded soldiers on that day. He studied medicine and surgery with his father, and in later years with Dr. John Warren and his son, Surgeon J. C. Warren. He was led by his patriotic spirit to accept the commission of surgeon's mate in Col. Vose in the First Massachusetts of Foot in 1777. He was made full surgeon Apr. 17, 1779, and served in the Continental army seven years. He was present at the surrender of Burgoyne in 1777 and of Cornwallis in 1781, and of other intermediate battles. Rev. A. B. Muzzey in his "Reminiscences of Men of the Revolution," speaks of him: "He was frequently at my father's house and was very agreeable. I drank in greedily his accounts given to my grandfather, who was with him in the company of Capt. John Parker Apr. 19, 1775, and of his experience as a surgeon in the army. It was a time when all shared in the common privations. Gen. Washington would sit down with his highest officers to a small piece of beef with a few potatoes and some hard bread—a single dish of wood or pewter sufficed for a mess, with a horn spoon and tumbler passed around, and the knife was carried in the pocket. Sugar, tea and coffee were unknown luxuries, and if a ration of rum was given out—this was in the dead of winter—the question would be raised "Shall we drink it or put it in our shoes to keep our feet from freezing?" During the pursuit of Cornwallis the soldiers had not decent clothing, and an old cloak, they not having a blanket left, was shared with two other officers. Dr. Fiske would corroborate in my hearing accounts of the need of medicine and comforts for the wounded—wine, spirits and even the ordinary medicine could not be procured. Even after searching miles nothing of the kind could be found except small portions of snake-root, and as for bandages the case was still worse. Nothing of the kind could be found for their supply but to cut up a tent found on the field. He used to relate mirthful stories about the French officers and soldiers around Yorktown. Surgeon Fiske was one of the original founders of the Middlesex Medical Association, afterward and now the Massachusetts Medical Society, one of the original members of the Cincinnati. His son took his place in the society at his death, and after the son's death it reverted to his grandson, who is the eldest. Dr. Fiske was also a member of the Bunker Hill Monument Association. Dr. Fiske practiced his profession nearly forty years in Lexington after the close of the war, and was very skillful in his treatment of the small-pox, and he was among the foremost doctors to make use of vaccination, his old friend, Dr. Benj. Waterhouse, bringing it from Europe, from the discoverer, Jenner. Dr. Fiske held many town offices, having been town clerk and justice of the peace many years.

From the Revolutionary War records it is learned that Joseph Fisk was a second lieutenant in the Continental army from June 1 to Dec. 31, 1776; surgeon's mate June 1, 1777; surgeon Apr. 17, 1779, and served as such to the close of the war. He d. Sept. 25, 1837; res. Lexington, Mass.

1311. i.   ELIZABETH, b. June 15, 1795; m. Dec. 5, 1819, Richard Fisher, of Cambridge, who was a glass manufacturer; res. New York City. A dau., 1, Elizabeth, m. Charles S. Willet, b. May 31, 1811, d. Mar. 14, 1888. They have a dau., 1½, Lida, b. Apr. 3, 1858, who m. Prof. Frank Justus Miller, Professor of Languages of the Chicago University; res. 5410 Madison avenue. Ch.: Donald Philbrook Miller, b. May, 1887, d. July, 1887; Philip Davenport Miller, b. Dec. 28, 1889; Winifred Fiske Miller, b. Oct. 7, 1891. 2, Charles E., res. 406 Water street, Baltimore, Md. 3, Mary W., res. 79 Willet street, Bloomfield, N. J. 4, Jennie W., res. Bloomfield, N. J. 2, Angeline A.
1312. ii. JOSEPH, b. Feb. 9, 1797; m. Mary Gardner Kennard.
1313. iii. JONAS STONE, b. May 9, 1799; m. Pamela Brown.
1314. iv. SARAH, b. May 18, 1802; d. unm. Dec. 27, 1825.
1315. v.   FRANKLIN, b. Oct. 16, 1804; m. Hannah Peters.
1316. vi. ALMIRA, b. June 24, 1808; m. Mar. 5, 1828, Zadoc Harrington. She d. Jan. 22, 1834, leaving one son, George Frederic, b. June 14, 1829. Res. in Lincoln, Mass., and is a wealthy farmer.

743. DAVID FISKE (David, Robert, David, David, Jeffrey, Robert, Simon, Simon, William, Symond), b. Lexington, Nov. 23, 1760; m. Apr. 26, 1784, Sarah Hadley, b. Nov. 26, 1764, d. May 21, 1804; m. 2d, May 6, 1806, Mrs. Ruth Trask. He had ten children by his first wife and four by his second. He entered the Revolutionary Army as fifer in Capt. Edmund Monroe's company, and served to the close of the war. For the sake of distinction he was known as "Fifer David." He d. Aug. 17, 1820; res. Lexington, Mass.
1317. i.   RUTH, b. ———; m. 1804, Philip Thomas of Rindge, N. H.
1318. ii.   JONATHAN, b. Apr. 15, 1786; m. Rowena Leonard.
1319. iii. SARAH, b. ———; m. Henry Spear; rev. to New York.
1320. iv.   DAVID, b. ———; m. Aug. 25, 1820, Chloe Trask, dau. of Jonathan.
1321. v.   SAMUEL, b. ———; d. unm., ae. 30.
1322. vi.   BENJAMIN, b. Apr. 27, 1798; m. Sarah Deland.
1323. vii. ANNA, b. ———; m. Sept. 10, 1820, Oliver Winship; res. East Lexington, Mass.
1324. viii. CHARLES, b. ———; went to sea and never ret.
1325. ix.   PATTY, b. ———; m. Daniel Gray and moved to Keene, N. H.
1326. x.   BETSEY, b. ———; m. Samuel Clarke; rev. to Glover, Vt.
1327. xi.   ICHABOD, b. ———; went to Surry, N. H., on a visit, and d. there.
1328. xii. WILLIAM, b. ———; m.; res. in Boston; kept a lot there on Hanover street.
1329. xiii. JOHN, b. ———. He res. in Boston, was married, but died s. p. He was a shoe dealer.
1330. xiv. FREDERIC, b. ———; m.; had a family; was a carpenter, and res. in Charlestown.

746. EBENEZER FISK (Ebenezer, Ebenezer, David, David, David, Jaffrey, Robert, Simon, Simon, William, Symond), b. in New Hampshire, ———; m. ——— ———. She d., and he m. 2d, at Chester, Vt., Jan. 8, 1795, Azuba Hoyt. He was probably a farmer, and may have been a physician. He was very well educated for those early days, and by the death of his father, at an early age, was left largely upon his own resources. He visited his brother Cotton on one occasion while the latter was residing in Bolton, Canada. The tradition in the family is that after his visit he started for the west with considerable money in his possession, and that was the last his Canadian relatives ever heard from him. He married his first wife probably in New Hampshire and his children were brought up by her. While living in Chester, Vt., he married his second wife, and after his death, on Oct. 7, 1816, she was married in Chester, Vt., to Dr. Artemas Robbins by Judge Aaron Leland. He d. before 1816; res. Chester, Vt.
1331. i.   DAVID, b. Oct. 10, 1772; m. ——— Lewis and Abigail Sargent.
1332. ii. JONATHAN, b. ———; N. f. k.; went to northwestern part of New York state.
1333. iii. EBENEZER, b. ———; N. f. k.

747.   ISABELLA FISK, b. Aug. 2, 1757; m. Apr. 11, 1776, Gen.
Henry Butler, b. Apr. 27, 1754; d. July 20, 1813. She d. Jan. 17,
1808. He served in war of the Revolution. Was Captain of a
volunteer company and went to West Point. He was afterwards Major General of the first division of the N. H. militia,
which office he held for many years. General Butler was the
first postmaster of Nottingham; he was a prominent Mason.
He filled many offices of trust and honor in the State and
was highly esteemed for his usefulness as a citizen and his
integrity as a man. His wife was the dau. of Dr. Ebenezer Fisk
of Epping and grand dau. of Rev. Ward Cotton of Boston,
the first settled ordained minister in Hampton, N. H. Mrs.
Cotton's maiden name was Joanna Rand. After Rev. Cotton's
decease she married Capt. Jonathan Gilman of Exeter, and after
his death she m. Dea. Ezekiel Morrill of Canterbury, and
after his death Dea. Joseph Baker of Canterbury, where they
res. until his death, when she moved to Nottingham and
resided with her grand dau. Isabella Fisk Butler, and after her
death she continued to reside with Gen. Butler until her own
death Feb. 25, 1811, aged 93. Rev. Peter Holt of Epping
officiated at the funeral. Mrs. Baker, or "Grandmother
Baker" as she was called was a lady of remarkable attraction,
much personal beauty and ready wit. She never weighed over
100 pounds during her life and it is said never suffered from
sickness until at the time of her death. Her talent at enter-
taining friends and her readiness at repartee are proverbial. At
one time during the last year of her life a remark of surprise
was made that she had never used spectacles of any kind, her
reply was that she "might need them if she lived to be old
enough." Ch.: 1, Elizabeth, b. July 29, 1777; d. July 12, 1808; 2,
Benjamin, b Apr. 11, 1779; m. Hannah Hilton, and d.
Oct. 1, 1851; res. Cornville, Me. 3, Ebenezer, b.
Mar. 13, 1781; m. Sarah Hersey. Res. Sanbornton, N. H.
Was sheriff for many years; d. Dec. 25, 1850. 4, Henry, b.
June 30, 1783; m. Abigail Lord and Nancy Hersey. Res. Nottingham. A remarkable fact of his domestic experience is
that by his two wives he had seven daughters in succession and
then seven sons in succession. 5, Sarah Cotton, b. Aug. 12,
1785; m. John Haley of Lee. They had numerous and highly
respected descendants. 6, Dorcas, b. Apr. 15, 1787; m. Wm.
Furber of Nottingham. She d. Nov. 8, 1855. 7, Samuel A.,b.
July 19, 1789; d. Jan. 16, 1814, he enlisted as a soldier in
the war of 1812 in the company under command of Capt. John
Butler, a cousin of his father's. Samuel was soon made
First Sergeant and clerk of his company and stationed at Burlington, Vt. While there on duty he was ordered with eighteen
men under his command, to detect smugglers who were feed-
ing the army in Canada, and while in the town of Highgate,
near the Canada line they met a company of the enemy's infantry from the Dominion escorting owners with a large lot
of cattle. A fight ensued in which Sergt. Butler and men were
victorious. The British were routed, many cattle taken and
driven several miles to a bivouac where the British infantry,
re-enforced by cavalry came upon them. The result was the
killing of four of Sergt. Butler's men, while he received three
mortal wounds and a broken leg: yet he disdained the summons
to surrender and with his pistols and sword killed two of the
enemy before they could take him. He never surrendered.
Though weak and bleeding, the strength of his intellect and the
power of his courage so controlled his enemies that, as was
afterwards said by one of them. "We were afraid of him after
we had him," and another in speaking of him said, "We all
acted like cowards before him." He refused to receive any

services from the British surgeons and as was said died a few hours after the fight, his intellect all the while being perfectly clear. His body was taken to Burlington and buried. His death was much lamented by officers and men. 8 and 9, Twins, b. June 16, 1793; d. infancy. 10, Ward Cotton, b. Jan. 22, 1895; m. Margaret Anderson of Philadelphia, Pa. Res. there. 3 ch.

748. CAPT. COTTON FISK (Ebenezer, Ebenezer, David, David, David, Jeffrey, Robert, Simon, Simon, William, Symond), b. Epping, N. H., Aug. 8, 1779; m. at Weare, N. H., Feb., 1804, Sarah Fifield, of Weare, N. H., b. Aug. 7, 1780, d. Feb. 8, 1852. He was born in Epping, N. H., and on reaching his majority went to Magog Lake, Bolton, Eastern Canada. Four years later he went to Weare, N. H., and there married his wife. Returning to Bolton he resided there for a number of years, and later moved to Abbotsford. P. Q., where he was killed by a tree falling upon him. He was a United Empire Loyalist. He d. Apr. 14, 1826; res. East Bolton, P. Q., and Abbotsford.

1334. i. NATHANIEL, b. Nov. 17, 1802; m. Miriam Whitney.

1335. ii. SEWELL C., b. May 5, 1816; m. Mary Ann Gorton.

1336. iii. ABRAHAM, b. Feb. 8, 1811; m. Lauretta Buzzell.

1337. iv. SALLY, b. June 10, 1808; m. July 7, 1829, Richard Bradford; res. Granby, P. Q. He was b. Nov. 17, 1805; d. Dec. 15, 1878; res. Granby, P. Q. Ch.: 1, Rachel Sarah, b. Apr. 21, 1830; m. Mar. 8, 1859; d. Jan. 17, 1876. 2, Richard Cotton, b. Dec. 13, 1831; m. Mar. 10, 1863; d. ———. 3, John, b. Sept. 25, 1834; m. Sept. 14, 1858; d. ———; 4, Isabella Jane, b. Aug. 8, 1840; m. Feb. 15, 1877; d. ———. 5, Mary Ann, b. Apr. 22, 1843; m. Nov. 15, 1865; d. Apr. 14, 1888. 6, Elizabeth, b. Mar. 11, 1847; m. June 4, 1874; d. Sept. 27, 1878. 7, Jessie Abbott, b. Nov. 26, 1849; m. ———; d. Aug. 3, 1880.

1338. v. EBENEZER, b. Mar. 8, 1806; m. Eliza Bradford.

1339. vi. BETSEY, b. Aug. 23, 1813; m. ——— ———, dau. Sarah Bradford; res. Abbotsford, P. Q.

1340. vii. JANE, b. Nov. 21, 1818; m. ——— Stimson. Ch.: 1, Theodore.

1341. viii. ISABELLA, b. Mar. 29, 1822.

749. HON. BENJAMIN FISKE (Benjamin, Ebenezer, David, David, David, Jeffrey, Robert, Simon, Simon, William, Symond), b. Lexington, Aug. 20, 1774; m. in Chelmsford, May 16, 1797, Elizabeth Bridge, dau. of William and granddaughter of Rev. Ebenezer Bridge of Chelmsford. She d. Oct. 20, 1814; m. 2d, Nancy Adams of Westford, b. 1785, d. Sept. 6, 1865. Hon. Benjamin Fiske was born in Lexington, Mass., on a farm on the road to Concord, at a point known as "Fiske Hill," where there is now erected a tablet stating that a skirmish was there had between the British and American forces, and the former repulsed. Wm. B. Fiske has often heard his great-grandmother give an account of her flight to the woods on that day, and upon her return to her dwelling she found an Acton man dead at the doorstep and a red coat dead at the well, each having killed the other. Wm. B. at his house in Plainfield, N. J., has an elegant portrait by Frothingham of his great-grandmother, with a panel at the corner picturing her home and showing the two bodies as stated. He was married to Elizabeth Bridge, daughter of Rev. Wm. Bridge of Chelmsford, Mass. She died, and he again married Nancy Adams. He moved to Boston in 1808 and was actively engaged in shipping, his sails whitening every sea, until 1848. In the year 1843 he returned to Lexington where he purchased a large farm on Lowell street, where he died. He was elected an alderman in Boston in 1843, and served as representative from 1833 to 1838. He held a commission as justice and was always considered an upright and exemplary citizen. He d. Feb. 2, 1858; res. Lex., Boston, and Lexington, Mass.

1342. i. JOHN MINOT, b. July 15, 1798; m. Eliza Winn.

1343. ii. LOUISA, b. May 30, 1801; m. in Boston in 1826 Dr. Cyrus Briggs of Augusta, Me. He was b. Mar. 4, 1800; d. in Salem, Mass., June, 1871. She d. Dec. 4, 1890. Ch.: 1, Sarah Louisa, b. Feb. 25, 1828; m. Rev. Wheelock Craig; ch., Annie Briggs, b. Feb. 6, 1853; m. George P. Dutton; Louise, b. May 30, 1885.

2, Nancy Adams, b. Jan. 25, 1831; d. Aug. 4, 1882; m. George
Parkman Denny Nov. 9, 1852, d. Jan. 23, 1885; ch., Arthur
Briggs Denny, b. Apr. 24, 1855; res. Chestnut Hill, Brookline,
Mass.; m. Frances Anna Gilbert, Nov. 1, 1882; George Parkman Denny, b. June 2, 1887; Elizabeth Denny, b. Sept. 4, 1888.
3. Elizabeth Church, b. Nov. 18, 1832; m. Aug., 1859, Wm. A.
Dana. He was a banker; res. New Bedford, Mass., b. 1818;
d. 1871; 3, ch.: Elizabeth, Willie A., Alice Louise, b. Aug. 24,
1870. 4. Anne, b. July, 1843; d. May 1, 1851.

1344. iii. CHARLES, b. Nov. 17, 1807; m. Abigail M. Hayden and Mrs.
Elizabeth P. Davis.
1345. iv. BENJAMIN, b. Oct. 15, 1811; d. June 18, 1812.
1346. v. BENJAMIN, b. Nov. 20, 1820; m. Oct. 21, 1842, Maria Spear;
res. New York City and Medford, Mass.

751. SAMUEL FISKE (Aaron, Samuel, James, James, Phinehas, Thomas,
Robert, Simon, Simon, William, Symond), b. Newton, Mass., Nov. 19, 1766; m.
there Frances Swan, b. Nov. 13, 1768, d. Apr. 12, 1865. He was a farmer. He d.
Nov. 15, 1845; res. Claremont, N. H.

1347. i. AARON, b. Mar. 23, 1801; m. Hannah Laughton and Hannah
Fay.
1348. ii. MINERVA, b. Apr. 19, 1804; m., and d. s. p.
1349. iii. ORREN E., b. May 3, 1805. His son, A. O. Fiske; res. Lunenburg, Mass. (see).
1350. iv. WARREN DEXTER, b. May 3, 1805. He has a son Charles
in New York City.
1351. v. SARAH, b. Dec. 23, 1806; m., and d. s. p.
1352. vi. ATTERSON, b. Apr. 7, 1808; m. Catherine Lehman.
1353. vii. ERASTUS, b. June 1, 1808; m. Anna Perry.
1354. viii. FANNIE S., b. Nov. 23, 1810; m. Jan. 1, 1835, Daniel Perry; res.
Newport, N. H. He was b. May 5, 1809; d. July 14, 1882; was
a farmer. Ch.: George B. Perry, b. Sept. 6, 1833; m. Apr. 25,
1858, Sarah Cowles; d. at Faribou, Miss., June 5, 1866. Mary
J. Perry, b. Aug. 19, 1837; m. at Newport May 3, 1858; d. at
Henniker, N. H., Apr. 23, 1881. Wm. H. Perry, b. Oct. 12,
1840; m. Fannie S. Kidder Dec. 27, 1864, now residing at Newport, N. H. Frances M. Perry, b. Mar. 10, 1845; m. to Granvill
Rowell, living at Auburn, Me. Edwin A. Perry, b. Sept. 1,
1844; d. in Wyoming Territory Sept. 28, 1869. Horace F.
Perry, b. Feb. 12, 1849; m. Sarah Adams, living at Hillsboro,
N. H.
1355. ix. LUCY, b. July 15, 1814; m. —— Shoals; res. C. A son Warren res. in C.
1356. x. ROXANNA, b. Feb. 14, 1819. Her dau. is Mrs. Melvin Fletcher
of Croydon, N. H.
1357. xi. OLIVE, b. Sept. 9, 1812. A son Albert Fiske res. in Boston.
1358. xii. SAMUEL FRANKLIN, b. Feb. 9, 1814; m. Harriett Lehman.

761. SAMUEL FISK (Thomas, Thomas, Samuel, James, Phinehas,
Thomas, Robert, Simon, Simon, William, Symond), b. Nov. 28, 1768, Pepperell,
Mass.; m. Dublin, N. H., Jan. 17, 1793, Mary Twitchell, dau. of Samuel T., Esq.,
b. Jan. 23, 1771; d. Dec. 19, 1834. He was a farmer, settled in Dublin in 1791.
He d. Oct. 18, 1844; res. Dublin, N. H.

1359. i. ASA, b. May 8, 1794; d. Aug. 24, 1796.
1360. ii. MARY, b. Oct. 19, 1795; m. May 7, 1828, William D. Cogswell,
of Peterborough, N. H., where he died. His widow resided
later in Holly, N. Y. Ch.: 1, William F., b. Jan. 27, 1829; d.
June 27, 1847. 2, Francis D., b. June 10, 1830; m., and resides
in Holly; names of his children unknown. 3, Lucas, b. Dec.
10, 1834. 4, James B., b. Jan. 13, 1838; d. May 1, 1854.
1361. iii. SAMUEL, b. Apr. 1, 1797; m. Betsey Gleason.
1362. iv. ASA, b. Feb. 16, 1799; m. Priscilla Ranstead.
1363. v. ALICE WILSON, b. Sept. 16, 1800; m. Feb. 28, 1826, Elias
Hardy; rev. to Walpole, N. H., Apr. 6, 1842, thence to Marl-

borough, N. H. Ch.: 1, Samuel Albert, b. Nov. 18, 1827; m.
Jan. 3, 1854, Sarah Ann Hall, and d. June 29, 1858, leaving a
son named Alfred; res. in Boston. 2, Thomas Alfred, b. Nov.
27, 1829; d. Oct. 1, 1853. 3, Julia Sophia, b. Feb. 23, 1832; m.
William M. Tenney of Marlborough, N. H. 4, Mary Louisa,
b. May 20, 1834; m. Amariah Sawtell. 5, Lucy Maria, b. June
4, 1839. 6, Anna Elizabeth, b. June 8, 1844; m. Alvin Streeter.

1364 vi.   BETSEY, b. Sept. 21, 1802; m. June 9, 1829, Ephraim Foster;
            rev. to Walpole, N. H., in 1832, and returned to Dublin in
            1842, where he d. in 1855. Ch.: 1, Henry, b. Apr. 28, 1830; m.
            Caroline P. Fisk, and resided in Penn. 2, John, b. Nov. 9,
            1832; a graduate of Dartmouth College, and a teacher by pro-
            fession at Faribault, Minn. 3, Frederick, b. Nov. 2, 1834; d.
            Sept. 14, 1836. 4, Andrew B., b. Feb. 26, 1837; d. June 22, 1859.
            5, Frederick, b. Jan. 6, 1839; d. Feb. 26, 1858.
1365. vii. LOUISA, b. Oct. 17, 1804.
1366. viii. JULIA T., b. July 22, 1808; m. Apr. 16, 1835, Edward Foster;
            rev. to Lexington, Mass.; d. in Dublin July 25, 1842. Ch.:1,
            Mary T., m. Geo. H. Bennett; res. Burlington, Mass. 2,
            George, d. unm. 3, Deroy, m. and left 2 ch. 4, Julia A., d.
            unm.
1367. ix.   AMOS T., b. Jan. 23, 1811; d. May 29, 1814.

762. ASA FISKE (Thomas, Thomas, Samuel, James, Phinehas, Thomas,
Robert, Simon, Simon, William, Symond), b. Pepperell, Mass., July 1, 1771; m.
Aug. 4, 1800, Cynthia Mann, b. Marlboro, Mass., Oct. 5, 1778; d. Aug. 30, 1858.
Asa Fisk, Esq., settled in Dublin, N. H., in 1801, where he resided till he died. He
was by trade a mason, and for neatness and thoroughness in his work it is believed
he was excelled by few. He was for many years in commission as justice of the
peace, but never officiated in that capacity. He married Cynthia Mann, daughter
of Nathan M. and granddaughter of Rev. Elijah Mann, a former minister of
Wrentham, Mass. He d. Aug. 8, 1848; res. Dublin, N. H.

1368. i.   THOMAS, b. Dec. 29, 1802; m. Sophia Appleton.
1369. ii.   CYNTHIA M., b. Sept. 2, 1804; m. Oct. 11, 1838, Calvin Lear-
            ned, son of John W. Learned. They res. in Dublin. Ch.: 1,
            Sarah E., b. Oct. 8, 1839; d. Mar. 4-5, 1846. 2, Sarah E., b.
            Feb. 15, 1841; d. Aug. 3, 1843. 3, Emeline S., b. Dec. 31, 1842;
            m. Nov. 28, 1867, Allison T. Mason, a merchant of Boston, but
            a native of Dublin; son of Cyrus and Abigail (Allison) Mason,
            b. Aug. 13, 1839. She d. in Boston, Mass., Jan. 16, 1883. Ch.:
            1, Lucelia Learned, b. in Dublin, N. H., July 9, 1870; m. Mar.
            20, 1895, Morton Ellery Getchell; res. Dorchester, Mass. Mr.
            Learned d. in Dublin, Apr. 1, 1880. Mrs. Learned d. in Bos-
            ton Jan. 30, 1882, while spending the winter with her daughter.
1370. iii. ASA H., b. Mar. 23, 1812; m. Caroline Ranstead.
1371. iv.   SARAH, b. Sept. 30, 1815; d. unm. May 18, 1840.
1372. v.   AMOS, b. July 17, 1817; d. Aug. 15, 1819.

763. HON. LEVI FISK (Thomas, Thomas, Samuel, James, Phinehas,
Thomas, Robert, Simon, Simon, William, Symond), b. Feb. 16, 1775, Pepperell,
Mass.; m. in 1799, Hannah Mellen, May 27, 1775; d. July 22, 1861, in East Jaffrey.
Hon. Levi Fisk was of Jaffrey, N. H. He was by trade a cooper, but was also
engaged in farming. In his younger days, for many years in the winter season,
he taught public schools and was thought to excel as a teacher. Subsequently he
was much employed in public business, such as settling estates, surveying land,
as a justice of the peace and quorum, as a selectman and representative of the
town, and in 1835 and 1836 was state senator. He d. Aug. 16, 1857; res. Jaffrey,
N. H.

1373. i.   ADAMS, b. May 3, 1800; m. Mary Loring.
1374. ii.   MARY, b. Feb. 11, 1802; m. Jan. 1, 1838, Elbridge Baldwin, and
            resided in Jaffrey. Ch.: John E. F., b. July 21, 1842; m. Har-
            riette E. Pierce; res. Dublin, N. H.

1375. iii.   POLLY, b. Apr. 21, 1804; m. June 2, 1827, Eli Smith. She d.
Apr. 1, 1860. He was b. Feb. 21, 1805; d. Jan. 2, 1852; was a
farmer; res. East Jaffrey, N. H. Ch.: 1, Eli A. Smith, b. Apr.
22, 1828; d. May 15, 1877. 2, Mary A. Smith, b. Dec. 11, 1829;
d. May 13, 1880; m. Isaac R. Chase in 1859; res. in East Cambridge, Mass. 3, Sarah A. Smith, b. Feb. 10, 1834; d. Dec. 9,
1893; m. Charles W. Farnham in 1858; res. Newton, Mass. 4,
Levi A. Smith, b. May 15, 1837; m. Annie R. Blood in 1866. 5,
Nellie H., b. June 8, 1840; m. Daniel W. Parker, Aug. 31, 1863;
res. Cambridgeport, Mass., 23 Western avenue. Ch.: Samuel
Eli Parker, b. June 2, 1868; d. Sept. 26, 1868. 6, Julia A.
Smith, b. May 11, 1842.
1376. iv.   PARKER, b. Apr. 15, 1806; d. May 13, 1806.
1377. v.   AIR, b. Sept. 23, 1808; d. Oct. 1, 1825.
1378. vi.   EMILY, b. May 12, 1812; m. James Harvey of Marlboro, N. H.;
3 ch. She d. Aug. 28, 1844, and he rev. to Rochester, Minn.
Ch.: 1, Emma R., b. Apr. 28, 1839; d. Sept. 27, 1864. 2, Alphonso H., b. Mar. 29, 1841. 3, James F., b. July 25, 1844.
1379. vii. JOHN S., b. July 18, 1814; m. Anna Clark; d. Jan. 12, 1876.
1380. viii. LUKE, b. Oct. 29, 1817; d. Dec. 10, 1819.

767.   JOHN FISK (John, Thomas, Samuel, James, Phinehas, Thomas, Robert, Simon, Simon, William, Symond), b. Groton, Mass., Mar. 9, 1779; m. ———
———. He learned the mason's trade, worked in Boston and other places. He
d. in Boston; res. Boston, Mass. Had 3 ch., 1 son and 2 girls.

768.   BENJAMIN FISK (Benjamin, Benjamin, John, John, Phinehas,
Thomas, Robert, Simon, Simon, William, Symond), b. ———; m. in Scituate, R.
I., Dec. 3, 1758, Hannah Hammond. He d. Dec. 9, 1785; res. Scituate, R. I.
1381. i.   BENONI, b. in 1768; m. Barbara Colvin.
1382. ii.   BENJAMIN, b. July, 1770; m. Freelove Colvin and Polly Taylor.
1383. iii. REUBEN, b. May 10, 1765; m. Patty Wait.
1384. iv.   NANCY, b. ———; m. Israel Phillips and d. s. p.

772.   REV. NATHANIEL FISK (Benjamin, Benjamin, John, John, Phinehas, Thomas, Robert, Simon, Simon, William, Symond), b. prob. in Rhode Island
in 1735; m. prob. in Rhode Island Anna ———, d. in Danby, Vt., about 1770;
m. 2d, in Danby, Lois Rowley, d. Danby, Vt., about 1783; m. 3d, Sylvia ———,
d. about 1785; m. 4th, Sarah Arnold, b. 1753, d. at Brandon 1803. Rev. Nathaniel
Fiske was born probably in Rhode Island. Soon after his first marriage, and
shortly before the Revolutionary war, he moved to Vermont and located in 1768
in Danby. He was a Quaker preacher, and like all others of this particular
belief, did not believe in war, and was for peace first, last and all the time. When
the colonies had determined to be free and independent and throw off the yoke
of British oppression, the Quaker exhorter did not lend his aid or even influence,
and stoutly maintained that he would not participate in the war for independence.
As a result the town of Danby confiscated his entire property, of which he was
possessed of quite a little for those days. He made the statement to the authorities
then and there that he would live to be a wealthy man once more; they could
kill him if they saw fit, but the day would come when they would be penniless.
He moved to Brandon, followed farming, and died in 1816, having amassed a
large amount of property. He was grandfather of Hon. Stephen Arnold Douglass. Rev. Nathaniel Fisk was buried on his farm in the family burying ground.
The writer had an examination made of the little God's acre, but no monument
or headstone marks his last resting place. It was his wish, it is said, not to have
any stone or slab at his grave. He d. in 1807; res. Danby and Brandon, Vt.
1385. i.   SEMANTHA, b. ———; m. Stephen Smith; res. Sharon, Vt.
Ch.: Lois, Silva, Jeremiah and Alma. The ch. moved to Mich.
1386. ii.   RUFUS, b. July 30, 1777; m. Polly Tower.
1387. iii. BATEMAN, b. Sept. 19, 1780; m. Sarah Winchester.
1388. iv.   SYLVIA, b. Jan. 15, 1784; d. of a fever, unm.
1389. v.   EBER, b. Aug. 10, 1771; m. Betsey Gratten and Martha Bigelow.

1390. vi. NATHANIEL, b. Nov. 1, 1766; m. Hannah Smith.
1391. vii. EDWARD, b. Dec. 3, 1787; m. Emily Granger.
1392. viii. SARAH, b. Mar. 24, 1789; m. Jan. 10, 1811, Dr. Stephen A.
Douglas. He was b. in Stephentown, N. Y., in 1781; d. at Brandon, Vt., July 1, 1813. She d. May 30, 1869. Ch.: 1, Sarah, b. Oct. 29, 1811; m. Feb. 14, 1830, Julius N. Granger, b. June 22, 1810, d. Mar. 28, 1884. He was a farmer, and for 32 years a government official; res. Clifton Spa, N. Y.; ch., Adelaide B. Granger, b. Nov. 24, 1836; m. May 25, 1858; d. Apr. 12, 1860. Emma C. Granger, b. Aug. 20, 1839; m. Sept. 13, 1860; P. O. Clifton Spa, N. Y. 2, Stephen Arnold, b. Apr. 23, 1813; m. Apr. 7, 1847, ———; m. 2d, Nov. 20, 1856, ——— ———. He d. June 3, 1861; ch., Robert M.; res. Greensboro, N. C. Stephen A., Jr., attorney at law, unm.; res. Chicago, Ill.

HON. STEPHEN A. DOUGLAS.

That branch of the Douglas family from which the subject of this sketch is a descendant emigrated from Scotland, and settled at New London, in the province of Connecticut, during the earlier period of our colonial settlements. One of the two brothers who first came to America subsequently removed from New London, and settled in Maryland, on the banks of the Potomac, not very distant from the site of the present city of Washington. His descendants, now very numerous, are to be found in Virginia, the Carolinas, Tennessee, and other southern states. The other brother remained at New London, and his descendants are scattered over New England, New York, Pennsylvania and the northwestern states. Dr. Stephen A. Douglas was born at Stephentown, in Rensselaer County, New York, and when quite a youth removed with his parents to Brandon, Rutland County, Vt., where, after his regular course at Middlebury College, he studied medicine, and became distinguished in his profession. His wife was the daughter of an extensive farmer in Brandon, by whom he had two children—the first a daughter, and the second a son, Stephen A., Jr. On the first of July, 1813, without any previous illness or physical warning, he died suddenly of a disease of the heart. At the very moment of his attack and of his death, he was playing with the daughter at his knees, and holding his son Stephen A. in his arms.

In 1813 the country was at war with Great Britain—had undertaken a war with the most powerful nation in the world; at that time the United States, with an unprotected coast, with an overbearing, and insulting, and powerful enemy menacing both seaboard and frontier; with hostile navies swarming upon the lakes, and commanding every sea where the enterprise of American commerce had unfurled a sail, and veteran armies, fresh from Continental fields of renown, landing on our shores —at that time when the infant republic, trusting in the justice of her cause, had risked everything to preserve the sacred principle that an American citizen, no matter where he might be, who stood upon an American deck, was to be secured, at all hazards, in all the great rights guaranteed to him by the Constitution of his country—while this war was waging, and while the contest between absolute power and popular right was maintained with fire and sword from Detroit to Key West, in the midst of this struggle, on the 23d day of April, 1813, was born Stephen A. Douglas, who forty-one years thereafter became the great champion of that same sacred principle not, indeed, in behalf of the gallant men who tread the decks of the American fleets, but in behalf of those other and no less gallant heroes—the pioneers of American progress, the founders of American states, the builders of American sovereignties—the people of the American territories.

The grandmothers, maternal and paternal, of Mr. Douglas, were of the name of Arnold, and were both descended from William Arnold, who was one of the associates of Roger Williams in founding the colony of Rhode Island, and whose son was appointed governor of that colony by Charles the second, when he granted the famous charter under which the state continued to be governed until even after the establishment of the American Union, and until the adoption a few years later of the present constitution of Rhode Island. The descendants of Governor Arnold are at this day very numerous in Rhode Island, and, indeed, throughout the whole country.

AN EARLY PICTURE OF HON. STEPHEN A. DOUGLAS.

Immediately after the death of Dr. Douglas, his widow, with her two children, removed from their native village to a farm about three miles in the country, where she resided with her bachelor brother, Mr. Fisk, on their patrimonial estate.

From his earliest childhood, Stephen was raised to a regular course of life, attending the district school during the winter seasons, and working steadily on the farm the residue of each year. When fifteen years of age, finding that a number of his schoolmates of his own years were about to enter the academy to prepare for college, he applied to his uncle, whom he had always been taught to respect as a father for permission and means to enable him to take the same course. This request was made in pursuance of an understanding which he sup-

posed had existed in the family from his earliest recollection,
that he was to be educated and sent to college; so strongly
was this plan for the future impressed upon his mind, that it
had never occurred to him that his uncle's marriage a year previous, and the very recent birth of an heir to his estate, had in
the least changed their respective relations; nor had he seen
in these events that cloud which was to darken the hitherto
bright visions which had stimulated his youthful ambition.
An affectionate remonstrance against the folly of abandoning
the farm for the uncertainties of a professional life, accompanied by a gentle intimation that he had a family of his own to
support, and therefore did not feel able to bear the expense of
educating other persons' children, was the response made to
the boy's request. Instantly the eyes of young Douglas were
opened to his real condition in life. He saw at once that he
could not command the means requisite for acquiring a collegiate education without exhausting the only resources upon
which his mother and sister must rely; he also saw that if he
remained on the farm with his uncle until he became of age,
he would then be thrown upon the world without a profession
or a trade by which he could sustain them and himself. Realizing the full force of these considerations, and perceiving for
the first time that he must rely upon himself for the future,
he determined to leave the farm and at once learn a mechanical
trade, that being the most promising and certain reliance for
the future. Bidding farewell to his mother and sister, he set
off on foot to engage personally in the great combat of life;
on that same day he walked fourteen miles, and before night
was regularly indentured as an apprentice to a cabinet-maker
in Middlebury. He worked at his trade with energy and
enthusiasm for about two years, the latter part of the time at a
shop in Brandon, and gained great proficiency in the art, dis-
playing remarkable mechanical skill; but, in consequence of
feeble health, and a frame unable to bear the continued labor
of the shop, he was reluctantly compelled to abandon a business in which all his hopes and pride had been centered, and to
which he had become sincerely attached. He had often been
heard to say, since he had been distinguished in the councils
of the nation, that the happiest days of his life had been spent
in the workshop, and, had his health and strength been equal
to the task, no consideration on earth could have induced
him to have abandoned it, either for professional or political
pursuits.

He entered the academy of his native town, and commenced a course of classical studies, to which he devoted
himself for about twelve months with all that energy and
enthusiasm which were a part of his nature.

In the meantime his sister had married Julius N. Granger,
Esq., of Ontario County, New York, and shortly afterward
his mother was married to Gehazi Granger, Esq., father of
Julius, and at the close of his first year at Brandon Academy,
young Douglas, at the earnest solicitation of his mother and
stepfather, removed with them to their home near Canandaigua, New York. He at once became a student at that
place—an institution which for more than half a century has
been celebrated for its thorough academical course of studies,
and for the large number of eminent professional men and
statesmen whose names once appeared on her catalogue.

In December, 1832, he began the study of law; but, finding that his mother would be unable to support him through
the long course of legal studies prescribed by the state, he
determined upon going to the west, and on the 24th of
June, 1833, set out for Cleveland, O., where he was danger-

ously ill with fever for four months. He then visited Cincinnati, Louisville, St. Louis and Jacksonville, Ill., but failed to obtain employment. Finding his money exhausted, he walked to Winchester, where he arrived at night with only thirty-seven and a half cents. Here he secured three days' employment as a clerk to an auctioneer at an administrator's sale, and was paid six dollars. During the sale he made so favorable an impression that he at once obtained a school of about forty pupils, whom he taught for three months. During this time he studied law at night, and on Saturdays practiced before justices of the peace.

In March, 1834, he removed to Jacksonville, obtained his license, and began the regular practice of law. Two weeks thereafter he addressed a large Democratic meeting in defense of Gen. Jackson's administration. In a short sketch of his early life written in 1838, from which the foregoing facts have been taken, Mr. Douglas thus spoke of this event: "The excitement was intense, and I was rather severe in my remarks upon the opposition. . . . The next week the 'Patriot,' the organ of the opposition, devoted two entire columns to me and my speech, and continued the same course for two or three successive weeks. The necessary consequence was that I immediately became known to every man in the county, and was placed in such a situation as to be supported by one party and opposed by the other. . . . Within one week thereafter I received for collection demands to the amounts of thousands of dollars from persons I had never seen or heard of. . . . How foolish, how impolitic, the indiscriminate abuse of political opponents whose humble condition or insignificance prevents the possibility of injury, and who may be greatly benefited by the notoriety thus acquired! . . . Indeed, I sincerely doubt whether I owe most to the kind and efficient support of my friends (and no man similarly situated ever had better and truer friends), or to the violent, reckless, and imprudent opposition of my enemies." During the remainder of the canvass Mr. Douglas bore a prominent part, and on the assembling of the legislature, although not yet twenty-two years of age, he was elected attorney-general, an officer who then, in addition to his other duties, rode the metropolitan circuit. His opponent was Gen. John J. Hardin. This office he resigned in December, 1835, having been elected to the lower house of the Legislature, of which he was the youngest member. The mental vigor and capacity he there displayed, in striking contrast with his physical frame, which was then very slight, won for him the title of the "Little Giant," which followed him through life. In 1837 he was appointed register of the land office at Springfield. In 1838 he was the Democratic candidate for Congress; but his opponent was declared elected by a majority of five votes. Over fifty votes cast for Mr. Douglas were rejected by the canvassers because his name was misspelled. In December, 1840, he was appointed secretary of state of Illinois, and in the following February elected a judge of the supreme court. Here his decision of character was shown in the trial of Joseph Smith, the Mormon prophet. A mob had taken possession of the court room, intending to lynch the prisoner, and the officers of the court appeared powerless. In this emergency Judge Douglas saw a bystander idly looking on, whose great strength and desperate courage were well known. Above the shouts of the rioters rose the voice of the judge appointing this man a special officer and directing him to select his deputies and clear the court room. In ten minutes order was restored.

In 1843 Judge Douglas was elected to Congress by a majority of 400, and he was re-elected in 1844 by 1,900 and again in 1846 by over 3,000; but before the term began he was chosen United States senator, and took his seat in the Senate, March 4, 1847. He was re-elected in 1852 and 1858, and had served fourteen years in that body at the time of his death. His last senatorial canvass was remarkable from his joint discussions with Abraham Lincoln. Each was conceded to be the leader of his party and the fittest exponent of its principles, and the election of one or the other to the Senate was the real issue of the contest, which was for members of the Legislature. Mr. Buchanan's administration was understood to be hostile to Mr. Douglas. The result of the election showed a Republican popular majority of 4,000; but the Democrats returned a majority of eight members to the Legislature, which secured Senator Douglas' re-election. In 1852, at the Democratic national convention in Baltimore, he was strongly supported for the presidential nomination, receiving a plurality on the thirtieth ballot. In 1856 he was again a candidate at the Democratic national convention in Cincinnati, his friends throughout the convention controlling more than enough votes to prevent any nomination under the two-thirds rule. On the sixteenth ballot he received 121 votes; but, as he was opposed to the principle of the two-thirds rule, he at once withdrew in favor of Buchanan, who had received a majority, thus securing his nomination. At the Democratic national convention in Charleston in 1860, on the first ballot he received 145½ votes out of 252½ cast. On the twenty-third ballot he received 152½ votes, which was not only a large majority of the votes cast, but also a majority of all those entitled to representation. The convention having adjourned to Baltimore, he received on the first ballot 173½ out of 190½ votes cast. On the second ballot he received 181½ votes of 194½, and his nomination was then made unanimous. The seceding delegates nominated John C. Breckinridge. Abraham Lincoln was the nominee of the Republican party, and John Bell of the Constitutional Union party. Of the electoral votes only twelve were cast for Douglas, although he received 1,375,157 of the popular votes distributed through every state in the Union. Mr. Lincoln received 180 electoral votes and 1,866,352 popular votes. From the age of twenty-one till his death, with the exception of about two years, Mr. Douglas' entire life was devoted to the public service. During his congressional career his name was prominently associated with numerous important measures, many of which were the offspring of his own mind or received its controlling impress. In the House of Representatives he maintained that the title of the United States to the whole of Oregon up to latitude 54 deg. 40 min. N. was "clear and unquestionable." He declared that he "never would, now or hereafter, yield up one inch of Oregon, either to Great Britain or any government." He advocated the policy of giving notice to terminate the joint occupation, of establishing a territorial government over Oregon protected by a sufficient military force, and of putting the country at once in a state of preparation, so that if war should result from the assertion of our just rights we might drive "Great Britain and the last vestiges of royal authority from the continent of North America, and make the United States an ocean-bound republic." In advocating the bill refunding the fine imposed on Gen. Jackson by Judge Hall, he said: "I maintain that, in the exercise of the power of proclaiming martial law, Gen. Jackson did not violate the constitution nor assume to himself any authority not fully authorized and legalized by his position, his duty, and the unavoidable necessity of the case. . . . His power was commensurate with his duty, and he was authorized to use the means essential to its performance. . . . There are exigencies in the history of nations when necessity becomes the paramount law, to which all other considerations must yield." Gen. Jackson personally thanked Mr. Douglas for this speech, and a copy of it was found among Jackson's papers endorsed by him: "This speech constitutes my defense." Mr. Douglas was among the earliest advocates of the annexation of Texas, and, after the treaty for that object had failed in the Senate, he introduced joint resolutions having practically the same effect. As chairman of the committee on territories in 1846, he reported the joint resolution by which Texas was declared to be one of the United States, and he vigorously supported the administration of President Polk in the ensuing war with Mexico. He was for two years chairman of the committee on territories in the House (then its most important committee in view of the slavery question), and became chairman of the same committee in the Senate immediately upon entering that body. This position he held for eleven years, until removed in December, 1858, on account of his opposition to some of the measures of President Buchanan's administration. During this time he reported and carried through the bills organizing the territories of Minnesota, Oregon, New Mexico, Utah, Washington, Kansas and Nebraska, and also those for the admission of the states of Iowa, Wisconsin, California, Minnesota and Oregon.

On the question of slavery in the territories he early took the position, which he consistently maintained, that Congress should not interfere, but that the people of each state and territory should be allowed to regulate their domestic institutions to suit themselves. In accordance with this principle he opposed the Wilmot proviso when it passed the House of Representatives in 1847, and afterward in the Senate when it was offered as an amendment to the bill for the organization of the territory of Oregon. Although opposed to the principles involved in the Missouri compromise, he preferred, as it had been so long acquiesced in, to carry it out in good faith rather than expose the country to renewed sectional agitation; and hence, in August, 1848, he offered an amendment to the Oregon bill, extending the Missouri compromise line to the Pacific coast, thus prohibiting slavery in all the territory north of the parallel of 36 deg. 30 min., and by implication tolerating it south of that line. This amendment was adopted by the Senate by a large majority, receiving the support of every southern and several northern senators, but was defeated in the House by nearly a sectional vote. This action of the House of Representatives, which Mr. Douglas regarded as a practical repudiation of the principle of the Missouri compromise, together with the refusal of the Senate to prohibit slavery in all the territories, gave rise to the sectional agitation of 1849-50, which was temporarily quieted by the legislation known as the "compromise measures of 1850," the most famous of which was the fugitive-slave law (see Clay, Henry, vol. 1, page 644). Mr. Douglas strongly supported these measures, the first four having been originally reported by him from the committee on territories. The two others, including the fugitive-slave law, were added by the committee of thirteen, and the measures were reported back to its chairman, Henry Clay. On his return to Chicago, the city council passed resolutions denouncing him as a traitor, and the measures as violations of the law of God and the Constitution; enjoining the city police to disregard the laws, and urging the citizens not to obey them. The next evening a large meeting of citizens was held, at which it was resolved to "defy death, the dungeon and the grave," in resistance to the execution of the law. Mr. Douglas immediately appeared upon the stand, and announced that on the following evening he would speak at the same place in defence of his course. Accordingly, on Oct. 23, he defended the entire series of measures in a speech in which he defined their principles as follows: "These measures are predicted upon the great fundamental principle that every people ought to possess the right of framing and regulating their own internal concerns and domestic institutions in their own way. . . . These things are all confided by the Constitution to each state to decide for itself, and I know of no reason why the same principle should not be extended to the territories." This constituted the celebrated doctrine of "Popular Sovereignty," sometimes called by its opponents "squatter sovereignty" (see Butts, Isaac). At the close of the speech the meeting unanimously resolved to sustain all the compromise measures, including the fugitive-slave law, and on the following evening the common council repealed their nullifying resolutions by a vote of twelve to one. In December, 1853, Mr. Douglas reported his celebrated bill to organize the territories of Kansas and Nebraska, which formed the issues upon which the Democratic and Republican parties became arrayed against each other. The passage of this bill caused intense excitement in the non-slaveholders' states, and Mr. Douglas, as its author was bitterly denounced. He said that he travelled from Washington to Chicago by the light of his own burning effigies. The controversy turned upon the following provision repealing the Missouri compromise: "Which, being inconsistent with the principle of non-intervention by Congress with slavery in the states and territories, as recognized by the legislation of 1850 (commonly called the compromise measures) is hereby declared inoperative and void; it being the true intent and meaning of this act not to legislate slavery into any territory or state, nor to exclude it therefrom, but to leave the people thereof perfectly free to form and regulate their domestic institutions in their own way, subject only to the Constitution of the United States." In the Congressional session of 1857-58 he denounced and opposed the Lecompton constitution on the ground that "it was not the act of the people of Kansas and did not embody their will."

Mr. Douglas was remarkably successful in promoting the interests of his own state during his Congressional career. In 1848 he introduced the passage of the bill granting to the state of Illinois the alternate sections of land along the line of the Illinois Central railroad, which so largely contributed to developing the resources and restoring the credit of the state. He was one of the earliest and warmest advocates of a railroad to the Pacific. In foreign policy he opposed the treaty with England limiting the territory of Oregon to the forty-ninth parallel. He also opposed the Trist peace treaty with Mexico. He opposed the ratification of the Clayton-Bulwer treaty, chiefly because it pledged the faith of the United States never to annex, colonize, or exercise dominion over any part of Central America. He maintained that the isthmus routes must be kept open as highways to the American possessions on the Pacific; that the time would come when the United States would be compelled to occupy Central America;

and declared that he would never pledge the faith of the republic not do in the future what its interests and safety might require. He also declared himself in favor of the acquisition of Cuba whenever it could be obtained consistently with the laws of nations and the honor of the United States.

In 1855 he introduced a bill for the relief of the United States Supreme Court, giving circuit court powers to the district courts, requiring all the district judges in each circuit court to meet once a year as an intermediate court of appeals under the presidence of a justice of the supreme court, and providing for appeals from the district courts to these intermediate courts, and thence to the supreme court, in cases involving large amounts. In 1857 he declared that the only solution of the Mormon question in Utah was to "repeal the organic act absolutely and unconditionally, blotting out of existence the territorial government, and bringing Utah under the sole and exclusive jurisdiction of the United States."

In 1858 and again in 1860, he visited the Southern states, and made many speeches. Everywhere he boldly denied the right of secession, and maintained that, while this was a union of sovereign states independent of all local matters, they were bound together in an indissoluble compact by the Constitution, which established a national government inherently possessing all powers essential to its own preservation. During the exciting session of 1860-61, Mr. Douglas, as a member of the committee of thirteen, and on the floor of the Senate, labored incessantly to avert civil war by any reasonable measures of adjustment, but at the beginning of hostilities he threw the whole weight of his influence in behalf of the Union, and gave Mr. Lincoln's administration an unfaltering support. In public speeches he denounced secession as crime and madness, and declared that, in the new system of resistance by the sword and bayonet the result of the ballot-box shall prevail in this country, "the history of the United States is already written in the history of Mexico." He said that "no one could be a true Democrat without being a patriot." In an address to the Legislature of Illinois, delivered at its unanimous request, he urged the oblivion of all party differences, and appealed to his political friends and opponents to unite in support of the government. In a letter dictated for publication during his last illness, he said that but one course was left for patriotic men, and that was to sustain the government against all assailants. On his deathbed his last coherent words expressed an ardent wish for the preservation of the Union, and his dying message to his sons was to "obey the laws and uphold the Constitution."

Mr. Douglas was somewhat below the middle height, but strongly built, and capable of great mental and physical exertion. He was a ready and powerful speaker, discarding ornament in favor of simplicity and strength. Few equaled him in personal influence over the masses of the people, and none inspired more devoted friendship. While considering it the duty of Congress to protect the rights of the slave-holding states, he was opposed to slavery itself. His first wife was the only child of a large slave-holder, who, in his last will provided that, if Mrs. Douglas should die without issue, all her slaves should be freed and removed to Liberia at the expense of her estate, saying further that this provision was in accordance with the wishes of Judge Douglas, who would not consent to own a slave. He married April 7, 1847, Martha, daughter of Col. Robert Martin, of Rockingham county, N. C., by whom he had three children, two of whom, Robert

12

M., and Stephen A., both lawyers, are living (1887). She died Jan. 19, 1853. He married Nov. 20, 1856, Adele, daughter of James Madison Cutts, of Washington, D. C., who is now the wife of Gen. Robert Williams, U. S. A. The spot on the bank of Lake Michigan in Chicago that Mr. Douglas had reserved for his future home was bought from his widow by the state, and there his remains lie under a magnificent monument begun by private subscriptions and completed by the state of Illinois. It is surmounted by a statue executed by Leonard Volk. His life was written by James W. Sheehan (New York, 1860,) and by Henry M. Flint (Philadelphia, 1860).

MRS. HON. STEPHEN A. DOUGLAS.

Mrs. Robert Williams, wife of the general of that name, has had a romantic and interesting life and has been blessed with numerous homes which are all historic and famous. Mrs. Williams was, previously, the wife of Stephen A. Douglas.

When she was a girl she was known in Washington as "beautiful Addie Cutts." Her grandmother was a sister of President Madison's lovely wife, and her father, James Madison Cutts, was second comptroller of the treasury, while her mother was a Maryland belle and beauty. Adele Cutts, now Mrs. Williams, was born in the Cutts home, a stuccoed house on H street and Lafayette square, built early in the present century. When she was a baby her parents moved to another house. The homestead was taken by President Madison on a mortgage and after his death his widow lived in it. It is always spoken of as the Dolly Madison house, its first owner, who lived in it longest, rarely being mentioned. It is now the home of the Cosmos club.

When Adele Cutts entered society she became a belle on account of her beauty and brilliancy. Stephen A. Douglas, the young senator from Illinois, wooed and won her. They went to live in a gray, grouted brick house in a walled and terraced garden, a quaint old house, once a country place. Twenty-one years ago two houses were made of this and the grounds covered with new buildings. Soon after his marriage Senator Douglas built a new home—a large, plain brick house with a ball room at the back. During the war it was used as a hospital and is now the home of Cardinal Satolli. When Stephen A. Douglas died his wife and family went back to the old house, the gray one in the terraced garden, to live.

After the war closed Mrs. Douglas married Gen. Robert Williams. It was a love match and they were a handsome couple. Soon after the wedding he was sent west and they divided their time between Fort Leavenworth, Omaha and Chicago until about five years ago, when they went to Washington, Gen. Williams having retired. They took a new and handsome house on Hillyer place, unpacked treasured pictures and books stored because they were too heavy to carry around the country and stayed there a couple of years. At present they are in another house.

There are six children in the family—three boys and three girls. The eldest son is in the navy and the youngest went west the other day to try his luck at making a fortune. Two daughters are in society and are very popular. One is a striking brunette, the other a pure blonde with a fine complexion and masses of golden hair. The baby of the family is 14 and promises to be a second edition of her mother. Mrs. Williams has not changed much these years. Her heavy dark hair is lightly touched with gray and she wears it combed plainly back as when she .was a girl. Her large, dark eyes are kindly and show her gentle disposition. Her head is finely poised and, although she is a quiet dresser, she has a stately air about her which makes strangers pause to look at her again and ask who she is.

She has many treasures in her home. There are a number of family portraits and some rare old china, one set being of white sprayed in green which was used by her grandmother. Quaint chairs and inlaid tables, one of them having the portraits of Italian poets on it, marbles and bric-a-brac make her home a beautiful one.

777. HON. DANIEL FISKE (Daniel, Benjamin, John, John, Phinehas, Thomas, Robert, Simon, Simon, William, Symond), b. Rehoboth, Mass., Apr. 28, 1753; m. in Cranston Apr. 13, 1785, Freelove Knight, dau. of Stephen and Mary (Manchester) Knight, b. Jan. 21, 1766. She m. for 2d husband a man by the name of Thomas; d. May 20, 1819. He was a member of the Rhode Island Legislature; d. May 5, 1810; res. Scituate, R. I.

    1393. ix.   DAVID, b. about 1763; m. Faith Doty.
           x.   ANNA, b. Aug. 6, 1773.
    1394. i.   RHODA, b. Nov. 20, 1786; d. unm. July 13, 1872.
    1395. ii.   CELIA, b. Feb. 17, 1788; m. Nov. 16, 1815, Stephen Burlingame, of Scituate. She d. May 7, 1859. Ch.: all (probably) born in Coventry, R. I.: 1, Dilly, b. Jan. 6, 1817; d. Jan. 27, 1820. 2, Stephen, b. Dec. 3, 1819; d. Nov. 15, 1890; m. Oct. 30, 1841, Elsie Maria Tillinghast, b. Jan. 3, 1820; d. May 20, 1884, (3 ch.), dau. of Pardon and Sarah (Waite) Tillinghast of Killingly, Conn. Colonel Stephen (7) Burlingame (Stephen (6), Ebenezer (5), Stephen (4), Ballingston (3), John (2), Roger (1),), son of Stephen and (Celia Fiske) Burlingame, was born in Killingly,

Conn., Dec. 3, 1819. When he was three years of age his parents moved to the old Burlingame homestead in Coventry, R. I., where he passed his boyhood and early manhood. He enjoyed the advantages which the common schools had to give, and as he showed a peculiar aptitude for military affairs he was proffered a cadetship at West Point, but the death of his father made it necessary for him to abandon his cherished desires, and at the age of eighteen he took his father's place at the head of the family and managed a large estate successfully. At the age of seventeen he joined the militia as private. He was promoted in 1837 to sergeant, 1838 to lieutenant, 1841 to captain, 1841 to lieutenant-colonel, and subsequently colonel, when he was twenty-one years old. He was in command during the state embroglio entitled the Dorr war, being active in the field for the suppression of the rebellion. He was a firm disciplinarian, and conspicuous for his athletic build. About 1857 he, with his family, moved to East Greenwich, R. I., and became associated with the Providence Conference Seminary, and was one of its staunchest friends and supporters. He held various town offices, and in 1868-9 represented his district in the Rhode Island Senate. Having a mechanical turn of mind he made several valuable inventions, among which may be mentioned a packing for steam pipes, which has been in universal use for thirty years, a method by which illuminating gas is manufactured in one-fifth of the time formerly required; a system of sewerage, and other minor inventions, all of which are in common use at the present time in their respective spheres of practicability. Colonel Burlingame was a quiet man, thoughtful and reflective in disposition, conscientious and upright in character. He was deacon of the Baptist Church many years. On Oct. 30, 1841, he married Miss Elsie Maria Tillinghast, who died May 20, 1884, by whom he had three daughters, Anne Eliza, Adeline King and Sarah Maria. In 1888 he was married to Miss Ruth M. Spencer. He died Nov. 15, 1890, at East Greenwich, and is interred in the family burying ground at that place. 3 ch., all born in Coventry, R. I.: a, Anne Eliza Burlingame, b. Sept. 20, 1842; m. Aug. 21, 1865, Charles Edwin Guild, son of Harmon and (——) Guild of Attleboro, Mass.; no children; d. Feb. 1, 1885, at East Greenwich, R. I. b, Adeline King Burlingame, b. Aug. 11, 1845; m. Aug., 1866, Wilfred Parkins Taylor, b. Lowell, Mass., 1839, d. Lowell, Mass., Sept. 1, 1887, son of Peter and Catharine (Burbank) Taylor, of Lowell, Mass.; ch.: Harry Burlingame Taylor, b. Sept. 19, 1867, in Lowell, Mass.; Alice Burnette Taylor, b. in Lowell, Mass., May 8, 1871; d. Bethlehem, N. H., Sept., 1875; res. Lowell, Mass. c, Sarah Maria Burlingame, b. Feb. 10, 1854; m. Dec. 12, 1877, Prentiss Webster, b. in Lowell, Mass., May 24, 1851, son of Maj. Wm. Prentiss and Susan (Hildreth) Webster.

Prentiss (7) Webster (Wm. (6) Prentiss, Humphrey (5), Israel (4), John (3), John (2), Thomas (11) was born in Lowell, Mass., May 24, 1851. He was graduated from the Lowell public schools, and fitted for Harvard College. In 1869 he went to Germany with his father, who had received the appointment of Consul General of the United States at Frankfort-on-the-Main. He there attended the University of Heidelberg, and subsequently the University of Strassburg, from which institution he was graduated. In 1873 he was appointed United States Consul at Mayence in Germany, which position he held until 1877, when he resigned to return to Massachusetts in order to pursue the study of the law. While in Europe he traveled extensively, and familiarized himself with the German and French languages. In 1880 he was admitted to the bar, and since that time has been in active practice with offices in Lowell and in Boston. He has written extensively for the press and law magazines, and in 1890 published a work known as the "Law of Citizenship," and in 1895 published the "Law of Naturalization;" also a genealogy of "One Branch of the Webster Family." He was for several years a member of the City Hall Commission of the city of Lowell, and published its reports. In 1895 he received the degree of A. M. from Dartmouth College. Ch., all born in Lowell, Mass.: Susan Hildreth Webster, b. Jan. 2, 1879. Adiline Burlingame Webster, b. Mar. 18, 1883; d. Feb. 28, 1887, in Lowell. Prentiss Burlingame Webster, b. Jan. 6, 1885; d. Sept. 15, 1885, in Lowell. Helen Burlingame Webster, b. June 13, 1886. Dorothy Webster, b. Nov. 23, 1888; res. Lowell, Mass. 3, Celia, b. July 23, 1821; d. about 1851: m. Jason Vaughn; 4 ch. 4, George, b. Oct. 2, 1823; d. Nov. 19, 1870; m. Susan Rebecca Fiske, dau. of Arnold and Susan (Miller) Fiske; 2 ch. 5, Cynthia, b. Oct. 24, 1825; m. Job Burgess: 1 ch.; res. Moosup Valley, R. I. 6, Susan, b. Mar. 21, 1828; d. about 1849; m. Smith Gallup; no issue.

1396.	iii.	STEPHEN K., b. Apr. 26, 1789; m. Mercy Burlingame.
1397.	iv.	ISAAC, b. Mar. 4, 1792; m. Nabby Henry.
1398.	v.	HARDIN, b. Mar. 4, 1795; m. Rhoda Orswell.
1399.	vi.	BETSEY, b. July 7, 1798; d. Feb. 27, 1819.
1400.	vii.	ARNOLD, b. July 26, 1802; m. Susan R. Miller.

778. JONATHAN FISK (John, Benjamin, John, John, Phinehas, Thomas, Robert, Simon, Simon, William, Symond), b. Rhode Island in 1738; m. there Barbara Brown. Res. Providence, R. I.

1401.	i.	ABRAHAM, b. 1762; m. Elizabeth Arnold.
1402.	ii.	JACOB, b. 1774; m. Sarah Van Dreser.
1403.	iii.	JAMES, b. Dec. 9, 1777; m. Sally Chapman.
1404.	iv.	ISAAC, b. ———; m. ——— ——— and had Cynthia, Lavinia, Polly, William and John.
1405.	v.	JONATHAN K., b. ———; m. ——— ——— and Mrs. Anna Atwood.
1406.	vi.	JABISH, b. Jan. 25, 1781; m. Polly Wilkinson.
1407.	vii.	ROBY, b. ———; m. Tappin R. Johnson. She d. in Niles, Mich.
1408.	viii.	MARIBA, b. ———; m. M. H. Fairservice. She d. in Summit, Wis. Ch.: Harriet Fairservice Parks, Frances Fairservice Leavitt, Agnes Fairservice Alden, Mary Fairservice Lush, Marshal Fairservice Reed, and of the descendants of these accurate information can be obtained from Judge Warham Parks, Oconomowoc, Wis., and Miss Delia Leavitt, Summit, Wis.

779. PELEG FISKE (John, Benjamin, John, John, Phinehas, Thomas, Robert, Simon, Simon, William, Symond), b. Scituate, R. I., Jan. 24, 1740; m. in Cranston, R. I., May 1, 1763, Lydia Sheldon, dau. of Capt. Philip of Cranston. He was a justice of the peace for years, and member of the Legislature. He d. May 30, 1808; res. Scituate, R. I.

| 1409. | i. | PELEG, b. Apr. 25, 1769; m. Orpha Knight. |

780. DR. CALEB FISKE (John, Benjamin, John, John, Phinehas, Thomas, Robert, Simon, Simon, William, Symond), b. Scituate, R. I., Jan. 24, 1753; m. in Providence, June 24, 1776, Mary Manchester, b. 1753, d. Nov. 1, 1817. Caleb, a physician, was president of State Medical Society, and appointed a justice in Court of Common Pleas, 1780. He is said to have been surgeon in the Continental army (see Brown University Graduates). Dr. Caleb was fortunate in money matters, and liked a good mortgage. Some farmers were debating the all-important question whether the old lady's apron in the moon was or was not a bit of good land, and when the debate waxed warm they decided to leave it in this way—to search the land record, and if any there was, then Doctor Fiske must

182   FISKE GENEALOGY.

needs have a mortgage of it. He was versed in law as well as physic. I think,
too, I have heard of his wearing the ermine with as much grace as he was wont
to handle the scalpel. He d. Oct. 4, 1834; res. Scituate and Fiskville, R. I.

    1410. ii.   PHILIP M., b. Mar. 2. 1782; m. Eliza Andrews Taylor.
    1411. iii.   MARY, b. 1788; m. Aug. 5, 1811, James Le Baron. He was
             b. in Plymouth, Mass., 1780; d. in Brooklyn, N. Y., in 1856.
             She d. in Fiskville, R. I., in Dec., 1825. Ch.: 1, Harriett E.,
             b. Aug. 21, 1815; m. May 7, 1833, Geo. Lawton Willard, b.
             Sept. 11, 1808, d. Apr. 16, 1888. She d. July 29, 1881. Ch.:
             1, James Le B. Willard, b. Mar. 1, 1834; m. at Huntington, L.
             I., May 9, 1860, Mary Bryar, b. Dec. 28, 1839; s. p. He is a
             merchant in New York City at 43 Leonard street. 2, Chas.
             Frederick, b. Feb. 23, 1836; m. Mary C. Moore May 20, 1863.
             3. Wm. Henry, b. Aug. 14, 1841; d. June 10, 1842; unm. 4,
             Mary LeBaron, b. Dec. 2, 1844; d. Apr. 29, 1851; unm. 5, Edward
             Augustus, b. May 28, 1846; m. Caroline H. Sands Feb. 2, 1869.
             6, Harriett, b. Oct. 11, 1847; d. Apr. 30, 1851; unm. 7, George
             L., b. July 31, 1849; d. Apr. 29, 1851; unm. 8, Francis Arthur,
             b. Aug. 6, 1851; d. Jan. 12, 1895; unm. 9, Annie Louise, b.
             Jan. 28, 1853; unm. 10, Henry Bradford, b. June 28, 1855; m.
             Mary S. Hatch June 6, 1883. 11, Gordon Lewis, b. Aug. 6,
             1857; d. Mar. 14, 1861; unm.
    1412. i.   ABBY, b. ——; m. Cyrus Harris, b. ——; d. ——; m. 2d,
             Caleb Williams.
    1413. iv.   ELIZABETH, b. 1780; d. May 17, 1799. "She was engaging,
             affable and dignified in her manners." [Alden's Epitaphs.]
    1414. v.   HARRIETT, b. ——; m. Caleb Ray.

    782. JOB FISK (Job, Benjamin, John, John, Phinehas, Thomas, Robert,
Simon, Simon, William, Symond), b. Scituate, R. I., July 29, 1747; m. ——
——. He d. in B.; res. in R. I. and Booneville, N. Y.

    1415. i.   JAMES, b. 1771; m. Phoebe Leach, Frances Leach and Eleanor
             Pitcher.
    1416. ii.   THOMAS, b. ——; m. Waite Manchester.
    1417. iii.   JOB, b. ——; m. —— Dewey.
    1418. iv.   JEREMIAH, b. in 1788; m. Mary Manchester.
    1419. v.   ALTHEA, b. July 25, 1778; m. June 28, 1803, Hezekiah Jones,
             Jr., b. in Pittsfield, Mass., July 13, 1776; d. in Lee, N. Y. She
             d. Aug. 8, 1874. Ch.: 1, Betsy Maria, b. Jan. 1, 1804; m. Sept.
             1, 1824; d. Feb. 23, 1892. 2, Harry, b. Aug. 24, 1805; m. Mar.
             6, 1837; d. Sept. 27, 1870. 3, Hannah, b. Jan. 12, 1807; d. Dec.
             1, 1809. 4, Seymour, b. Dec. 12, 1808; d. May 19, 1809. 5,
             Ann, b. May 30, 1810; m. Mar. 16, 1833; d. Feb. 23, 1892. 6,
             Lucy, b. Mar. 16, 1812; m. May 10, 1835, Charles Wheelock,
             b. Dec. 14, 1812; d. Jan. 21, 1865; res. Booneville, N. Y. Ch.:
             1, Althea, b. June 29, 1837; m. June 27, 1860; d. May 23, 1863.
             2. Wrexiville, b. Sept. 23, 1839; d. June 27, 1841. 3, Morton
             D. Wheelock, b. May 8, 1841; m. 1861; res. North Adams,
             Mass. 4, Helen M. Clark, b. Feb. 12, 1843; m. Oct. 8, 1872;
             res. 600 Macon street, Brooklyn, N. Y. 5, Herbert M.
             Wheelock, b. Nov. 3, 1845; m. 1883; res. Cayuga, Cayuga Co.,
             N. Y. 6, Forrest J. Wheelock, b. Aug. 28, 1856; m. May 12,
             1886; res. Booneville, Oneida Co., N. Y.

    785. JEREMIAH FISK (Job, Benjamin, John, John, Phinehas, Thomas,
Robert, Simon, Simon, William, Symond), b. Scituate in Rhode Island in 1731; m.
in Swansey, Mass., Sept. 7, 1758, Rebekah Pierce, dau. of —— Pierce, b. Nov.
26, 1741, d. April 27, 1817. He was born in Rhode Island, married there and
soon afterwards moved to another town in that state. He had five children and
all his life followed farming. He lived to be over ninety years of age, as did his
brothers and sisters. He d. Mar. 13, 1823; res. Scituate, R. I.

    "Seeing your name 'Pierce' makes me think of hearing my father, Jeremiah,
say that in some way he was connected to Clothier Pierce who had some local
fame as a revolutionary soldier."

1420.   i.   JEREMIAH, b. Sept. 29, 1766; m. Elizabeth Green.
1421.   ii.   PRUDENCE, b. in 1761; m. Daniel Coomer; res. Cheshire,
               Mass. She d. Mar. 6, 1845. Prudence was married to a man
               in Cheshire, Mass., by the name of Franklin, when twenty
               years old; she lived with him forty years. She then lived single
               ten years, then married a man in the same vicinity by the
               name of Dea Coomer, and lived with him twenty years. He
               died leaving her, ninety years old, in the hands of his grand-
               children, who treated her shamefully. Her nephew, Richmond,
               was informed of it by the selectmen of the town where she
               lived, and he went and brought her away, and took care of her
               to her death, when she was in her ninety-sixth year.
1421¼.iii.   MIAL, b. ——, 1763; m. —— ——.
1421½.iv.   AARON, b. ——. Said to have moved to Vermont.
1421¾.v.   MOSES, b. in Rhode Island, 1759; m. —— ——.

790. NOAH FISKE (Noah, Benjamin, John, John, Phinehas, Thomas,
Robert, Simon, Simon, William, Symond), b. in Scituate about 1743; m. there
——. He d. in S.; res. Scituate, R. I.
1422.   i.   NOAH, b. ——; m. —— ——.

791. MOSES FISKE (Noah, Benjamin, John, John, Phinehas, Thomas, Robert, Simon, Simon, William, Symond), b. ——; m. Huldah ——. He d. Nov.
22, 1816; res. Scituate, R. I.
1423.   i.   RICHARD, b. ——.
1424.   ii.   STEPHEN, b. Jan. 14, 1784; m. Joanna Colegrove.
1425.   iii. ROBERT, b. ——. He was a farmer and in 1845 resided near
               Cleveland, O., forty miles from there.

792. AARON FISKE (Noah, Benjamin, John, John, Phinehas, Thomas,
Robert, Simon, Simon, William, Symond), b. in Rhode Island; m. —— ——;
res. Scituate, R. I.
1426.   i.   AARON, b. ——.
1427.   ii.   MOSES, b. ——.
1428.   iii. JEREMIAH, b. ——. Rev. E. Fiske, Auburn, N. Y., gt. gr.
               son of his.

794. REV. ICHABOD EBENEZER FISKE (Ebenezer, Ebenezer, John,
John, Phinehas, Thomas, Robert, Simon, Simon, William, Symond), b. New
Milford, Conn., Oct. 19, 1747; m. at Middletown, Conn., Aug. 16, 1773. Eleanor
Roberts, b. Middletown, Conn., Sept. 24, 1750; d. Isle La Mott, Vt., July 16, 1839.
Ichabod E. was born in New Milford, Conn., and moved with his parents to what
is now Southington, Conn., graduated at Yale College in 1770. At the breaking
out of the Revolutionary War he resided in Poultney, Vt. He went to Isle La
Mott, Vt., in Lake Champlain, in 1788. He was a surveyor at this time and sur-
veyed the Isle and taught the first school there before 1802. He was ordained
a minister in the P. E. Church, was the author of an English grammar in verse,
and died the rector of a parish in Macon, Ga., where he was buried. He went
south for his health.
    He graduated at Yale College with first honors, and soon after his marriage
was settled at Poultney, Vt., as pastor of a Presbyterian church. While residing
there he lost his property and a very valuable library by fire. He soon after gave
up preaching and followed teaching and surveying.
    From later information it is learned that he died at the Indian Agency, now
Crawford County, Ga., and lies buried on the east side of Flint River near the
site of the old agency. When he first went to Georgia he settled at St. Marys
and was the rector there, taught school and published an English grammar in
verse. He was a classmate in college with Col. Hawkins, the Indian agent, who,
hearing of him at St. Marys invited him to the agency, which was at that time at
Fort Hawkins, on the east side of the Ockamulgee River, opposite the city of
Macon. The Indian Agency was moved to Flint River in 1812.
    The following is a copy of a letter written Sept. 20, 1810, which gives an ac-
count of the death of Mr. Fisk:
    On the 16th Sept. Died at the residence of Col. Hawkins, the Agent for Indian
Affairs in the Creek department, Ichabod E. Fisk, A. M. and late tutor of St.

Maries Academy, Ga. This gentleman left his residence near the old British works on Lake Champlain in Vermont some years past, with an inflammation of the lungs and stomaik, as he expressed it, to try the effects of a southern climate. He came to the Creek agency in July in pretty good health apparently, on his way to the Mississippi Territory and stated his complaint and object for visiting a warm climate. His disorder seamed at times to be leaving him and again returned in the increased violence. He was invited to return to a seaside residence on the sea islands of Georgia till the spring and go thence by water. For a month or more he amused himself in visits to the Indians at their festivals or correcting for a new edition his practical Grammar, also commenced the study of the French language and flattered himself daily with a speedy recovery. On the 9th of Sept. he was confined to his bed; during the night he had frequent bad spells. Slept mostly in the day and was able to retain food or drink for a short time only on his stomaik. When he could eat he indulged himself in the heartiest high seasoned food and strongest drink. Every morning he reported himself better till the day of his ssialution, that morning he asked for some soup, complained of being hungry, took a spoonfull or two and drank sum sylabub. About twelve oclock he ceased to speak and half after nine he was dead. When asked whether he did not want to see his wife, he answered yes. He called her name several times and the last was "O death come." One of Col. Haskin's Family remained at his bedside during the day and two of them during the night at the period of his confinement to his bed and he was buried by the Colonel's Family at sunset on the 17th. As he gave no directions relative to his family affairs the adjutant agent, Major Linbough, by order took an inventory of his property.   BENJAMIN HASKINS.

    Creek Agency, Sept. 20th, 1810.

    He d. in Georgia, Sept. 16, 1810, but is buried in Isle La Mott, Vt.; res. Isle La Mott, Vt., Macon, Ga.

    1429. ii.   SOLOMON, b. Feb. 20, 1787; m. Sabina Worthington and Catherine Worthington.

    1430. i.   SARAH, b. Sept. 25, 1774, in Middleton, Conn.; m. Erastus Miles. They resided in a beautiful place in Amsterdam, N. Y., on the Mohawk river. The father of Erastus purchased the estate of Sir William Johnson, an officer in the British army, and who took a prominent part in the affairs of that state. The place was known as Guy Park. After Erastus' death the widow married again. Her ch. were: 1. Dr. Archibald, b. Amsterdam, N. Y., in 1800; d. in New York city in 1868; m. Mary Treese. They had several children and all are deceased except Mary. She m., in 1864, Christian Herter. He was born in Stuttgardt in 1841, and died in New York city in 1884. He was educated at the Polytechnic School in Stuttgardt, Germany, and afterwards studied at the Beaux-Arts in Paris for four years. He was graduated there as draftsman and went to New York where he founded the house of Herter Bros. He had two sons: a, Dr. Christian Archibald, b. 1865, who was educated in New York city, was graduated from the New York College of Medicine, studied afterwards at the Johns Hopkins University in Baltimore and then in Zurich, Switzerland. He now practices medicine in New York city. He has written several medical works, and is a distinguished physician. He m. Susan Dows and has three dau., Christine, Mary Dows and Susan. b, The second son, Albert, was born in 1871. He studied art in Paris, and first exhibited at the age of nineteen in the Salon in Paris, a picture for which he received honorable mention. He is at present still studying in Paris; m. Adele McGinnis, and has two sons, Everit and Christian Archibald. These are the only living des. of Sally Fiske. Her other ch. were: 2, Erasmus Mills; 3, Laura Mills, m. Dr. I. B. Badger, res. and d. in Atlanta, Ga., ch. a, Elvira, m. Col. Jno. Wood, Cass Co., Ga.; ch.: 1, Laura, m. Joseph Pitman. He was a lieutenant in the Confederate army. 2, Mary, m. ——— Alexander, res. Ft. Gaines, Ga.; 3, Preston. He was a captain in the Confederate army; 4, Ella Alvira, n. f. k. b, Alonzo, m.

and in 1866 res. Albany, Ga. 4, Sally Fisk Mills, d. in Cincinnati, O., in 1846.

1431. iii. SAMUEL, b. Aug. 16, 1776; m. Polly Scott.
1432. iv. IRA, b. Oct. 4, 1778; m. Chloe Holcomb.
1433. v. EBENEZER, b. Mar. 31, 1781; m. Ida Landing.
1434. vi. POLLY, b. Apr. 5, 1790; d. unm. at Isle La Mott June 17, 1842.
1435. vii. HANNA, b. May 16, 1794; d. unm. at Chazy, N. Y., Oct. 22, 1847.
1436. viii. LAURA, b. Feb. 11, 1784; m. Dr. Elijah Butts; res. Macon, Ga. She d. in Sumter, Ga. Sept. 15, 1862. He was b. in Canterbury, Conn., Dec. 26, 1794. Ch.: 1, James R., b. Aug. 22, 1802; m. Louisa Poehill; he d. Macon, Ga., July 26, 1859; ch.: 1, Catherine Grantland, m. 1867, Wm. H. Atwood; she d. in 1869, leaving Louise McIntosh. 2, Tallulah Ellen, m., in 1871, her deceased sister's husband, Wm. H. Atwood; they res. Crescent, Ga.; ch.: Henry Grantland, b. 1872; Maud Allen, b. 1875; James Roger, b. 1877; Jane C., b. 1878; Elliott McIntosh, b. 1884; Sibyl Jessie, b. 1890, and Catherine, b. 1885, deceased. 3, Elijah Poehill. 4, James Albert. 5, Jessie C. 6, John G. P. A granddaughter of Laura Fiske is Mrs. Lavinia Lewis, of Montezuma, Ga. b, Elijah, b. June 10, 1808; m. Ann J. Tomlinson. He d. Nov. 2, 1871, in Sumter, Ga., a dau. is Mrs. John F. Lewis, Montezuma, Ga. c. Laura, b. 1805; d. Nov. 14, 1806. d. Albert Gallatin, b. Aug. 10, 1813; m. Sarah C. Stovall; ch.: Laura E., b. Feb. 21, 1841; m. Dr. J. B. Hinkle, May 29, 1860, in Macon, Ga., address, Americus, Ga. Mary L., b. Jan. 18, 1842; m. T. J. Hunt, in 1869, Macon, Ga.; P. O. address Columbus, Ga. Arannah W., b. Jan. 14, 1844; d. Oct. 25, 1887. Albert G., Jr., and Armand L. (twins), b. in Macon, June 25, 1847. Albert G. d. in Confederate army, Jackson Artillery, Nov. 11, 1864, and Armand L. res. Macon, Ga. Carrie E., b. Mar. 1, 1850; m. in 1892; d. May 30, 1895, in Macon.

1437. ix. LAVINIA, b. Oct. 25, 1795; m. Noah Pomeroy, of Colchester, Conn. She d. in 1824, in Savannah, Ga. Ch.: a, Noah, nothing known. b, Woodbridge, nothing known. c, Ellen, b. Aug. 9, 1816, m. May 3, 1837, Fredk. E. Mather; ch. (b. in N. Y. city): 1, Elira, b. Feb. 25, 1838; m. Wm. C. Ludlow, Oct. 7, 1857; ch.: Belle Mather, b. Sept. 12, 1858; Henry A., b. Aug. 10, 1862. 2, Ellsworth, b. Feb. 3, 1839; drowned Apr. 7, 1845. 3, Ellen Lavinia, b. Oct. 30, 1840; m. Alfred H. Timpson, Sept. 22, 1863; ch.: Ellen, b. June 14, 1864; Annie H., b. Oct. 31, 1865. 4, Laura W., b. July 31, 1843; m. Alex. P. Miller, June 28, 1865, in New York city. 5, Ada E., b. Nov. 18, 1851. 6, Isabella P., b. Dec. 25, 1853. 7, Grace E., b. Apr. 22, 1859. 8, Fredk. E., b. Jan. 9, city. d. Jan. 26, 1863. Family lived (in 1867) in New York city. d, Abner, b. ———; m. and in 1866 was living on Cenhe is called only son. In 1792—93 he move to Grand Isle on tral railroad, 30 miles from Savannah, Ga.

797. JOHN FISK (Ebenezer, Ebenezer, John, John, Phinehas, Thomas, Robert, Simon, Simon, William, Symond), b. New Milford, Conn., Sept. 24, 1752; m. Lavinia Dean; res. Vermont and Little Fork, Canada.

1438. i. JOHN DEAN, b. ———. In his grandfather's will, in 1790, he is called only son. In 1792-93 he moved to Grand Isle on land given him by his grandfather.
1439. ii. CLAUDIUS LUCIUS, b. ———; m. Jemima W. Knapp.
1440. iii. CYNTHIA, b. ———.
1441. iv. CATHERINE, b. ———.
1442. v. CLARISSA, b. ———.

799. LIEUT. ISAAC FISK (Ebenezer, Ebenezer, John, John, Phinehas, Thomas, Robert, Simon, Simon, William, Symond), b. Southington, Conn., Feb. 26, 1756; m. Lucy ———, b. 1747; d. Aug., 1804. He was in the Revolutionary army and served as lieutenant in a Connecticut company and d. in Southington,

where he is buried. He had one son. According to the Conn. Rev. rolls he was Sergt. Major from Southington, Conn., in Col. Lamb's Artillery Company in service from 1777 to 1780. In 1781 he was appointed 2d Lieut. in Trabe's Artillery Company by the Governor and council of New York. The regiment in which he served was in service on the Hudson, was represented in nearly all the battles at the north, was at the siege of Yorktown and noted for its efficiency. It remained in the service until the close of the war (see Rev. records). He d. Feb. 1, 1801; res. Southington, Conn.

800. CAPT. SOLOMON FISK (Ebenezer, Ebenezer, John, John, Phinehas, Thomas, Robert, Simon, Simon, William, Symond), b. Southington, Conn., Dec. 26, 1757; m. Mar. 20, 1791, Mary Harris. "Solomon Fisk also held the military rank of Captain. He entered the army of the Revolution in 1780 as one of the short term men and served 5 months and 23 days, whether in the regular army or militia I do not know." Res. Southington, Conn.

    1443. i.   SOLOMON, b. July 20, 1798; m. Levincy Newton.
    1444. ii.   EBENEZER, b. Nov. 3, 1793; m. and had a son John. He d. at Bath, N. Y., in 1865.
    1445. iii. SAMUEL, b. Aug 14, 1796; died in the south.
    1446. iv. MARY, b. July 20, 1798; m. ——— Lake and d. in 1863 at Mt. Morris, N. Y.
    1447. v.   SARAH, b. June 22, 1800; m. but d. s. p.
    1448. vi. HARRIETT, b. Apr. 5, 1802; in 1866 res. unm. in Le Roy, Geneseo Co., N. Y.
    1449. vii. JOHN WHITING, b. ———; res. Grand Rapids, Mich. Had a son John.
    1450. viii. JEANNETTE, b. ———; m. ——— Barrows, and in 1866 was a widow res. in Geneseo, N. Y.
    1451. ix. GEORGE, b. ———; in 1866 res. Penn.
    1452. x.   CHESTER, b. ———, ———.

804. JOHN FISK (John, John, John, John, Phinehas, Thomas, Robert, Simon, Simon, William, Symond), b. in Chatham, Conn., about 1740; m. ———. He was born in Conn. and moved to Trenton, N. Y., about 12 miles north of Whitestone about 1796. He had only one child. He d. in Eaton, N. Y.; res. Conn. and Trenton and Eaton, N. Y.

    1453. i.   JOHN, b. about 1764; m. Elizabeth Wright

804. BAZALEEL FISK (John, John, John, John, Phinehas, Thomas, Robert, Simon, Simon, William, Symond), b. Middleton, Ct., ——— 1743; m. there Nov. 13, 1768, Margaret Rockwell, b. 1744, d. Jan. 6, 1810; m. 2d, Aug. 12, 1810, Abigail Dobson, b. 1762, d. Sept. 17, 1824. He was town clerk at Middletown and in public office for years. In 1798 he moved to New York State and resided at Holland Patent. He d. Aug. 6, 1830; res. Middletown, Conn.

    1454. i.   JOHN, b. Aug. 5, 1771; m. Polly Merrill.

810. JOHN FISK (Benjamin, John, John, John, Phinehas, Thomas, Robert, Simon, Simon, William, Symond), b. in Connecticut about 1755; m. in that State, Martha Goodrich, b. Mar. 3, 1759, d. Randolph, Vt., June 28, 1841. He was born in Connecticut and was a tailor by trade. About 1795 one day he left his shop and his family never saw or heard of him afterwards. It was supposed by the family at that time that he was impressed into the British marine service, for in those days citizens were caught and smuggled on board ship unceremoniously. There are no entries on the Ellington records as the following letter will explain: Ellington, Ct., July 27, '96.—F. C. Pierce.—Dear Sir: Have made search of records second time—there certainly are no name of Fisks or Fiskes on Ellington records nor any conveyance of property to or from a Fisk before 1850. This town was incorporated in 1786; from 1768 to 1786 it was East Windsor, before 1768 Windsor. As you will see by dates you might be able to find something at East Windsor. Very truly yours, M. H. Aborn, Asst. Town Clerk." Res. Ellington, Conn., and Randolph, Vt.

    1454—1. i.   SARAH, b. July 8, 1779; m. Capt. William Carley of East Randolph, Vt. She d. ———. Ch.: 1, Adeline, b. Sept. 3, in 1810 he moved to Lancaster, N. H. She d. Dec., 1865,

26, 1851. 3, Fanny, b. May 29, 1814; m. Silas Kendrick; res. Milwaukee, Wis. 4, Horace Fisk, b. 1816; d. Aug. 26, 1839. 5, Shubal C., b. 1819; d. Aug. 9, 1827.

1454—2. ii. MARY, b. Dec. 9, 1782; m. Joseph Holton of Ellington, Conn. In 1810 he moved to Lancaster, N. H. She d. Dec. ,1865. Ch.: 1, Albert, b. Oct. 19, 1807; d. Bangor, Me., Feb. 16, 1888. 2, Martha M., b. June 23, 1809; d. ———. 3, Dwight, d. infancy. 4, James, b. Nov. 20, 1812; res. 3214 St. Paul Av., Milwaukee, Wis. 5, Edward D., b. Apr. 28, 1815; d. Apr. 21, 1892. 6, Horace Fisk, b. Sept. 5, 1817; d. Dec. 9, 1893, at the old homestead in Lancaster, N. H. 7, Mary S., b. July 16, 1819; d. ———. 8, Eliza Sophia, b. Feb. 6, 1823; d. ———.

1454—3. iii. FANNY, b. Jan. 31, 1785; m. Asa Story of Randolph Centre, Vt. She d. Jan. 6, 1860. Ch.: 1, John Fisk, b. July 29, 1814; d. Jan. 9, 1837. 2, Horace Goodrich, b. Oct. 1, .1816. 3, Hiram Fitch, b. Nov. 10, 1818; d. Sept. 20, 1887. 4, Martha N., b. Sept. 4, 1820. 5, Albert L., b. Aug. 30, 1822; d. young. 6, Fanny Jennette, b. Oct. 10, 1824; m. ——— Davis; res. Milwaukee, Wis. 7, Lucy, b. Sept. 9, 1826; d. July 12, 1827.

1454—4. iv. LEONARD, b. Sept. 6, 1787; m. Lucy Billings.
1454—5. v. HORACE, b. Apr. 17, 1790; m. Mary A. Adams.
1454-6. vi. JOHN, b. Sept. 8, 1793. He m. and d. s. p.; a merchant in Ellington, Aug. 31, 1819.

812. WILLIAM FISKE, (Ebenezer, William, William, William, John, William, Robert, Simon, Simon, William, Symond), b. Tewksbury, Mass., Mar. 24, 1754; m. Rachel ———. He was a farmer; res. Tewksbury, Mass.
1455. i. JONATHAN, b. Sept 24, 1778.
1456. ii. RACHEL, b. Apr. 12, 1780.

816. BENJAMIN FISK (Ebenezer, Ebenezer, William, William, William, John, William, Robert, Simon, Simon, William, Symond), b. Jan. 2, 1762; m. Aug. 13, 1783, Lydia Kitteridge at Woburn. He was in the Revolutionary army, was taken prisoner and poisoned by the enemy; res. in Woburn when married.
1457. i. JOHN, b. ———.
1458. ii. EPHRAIM, b. ———.
1459. iii. BENJAMIN, b. ———.
1460. iv. DAVID, b. ———.

818. SAMUEL FISK (Ebenezer, Ebenezer, William, William, William, John, William, Robert, Simon, Simon, William, Symond), b. June 4, 1767; m. ———, ———. He was a sailor and rope maker; res. Newburyport, Mass.; two sons res. there 1835.

819. ISAAC FISK (Ebenezer, Ebenezer, William, William, William, John, William, Robert, Simon, Simon, William, Symond), b. Aug. 27, 1769; m. Molly Seaverance. He was a soldier in the Revolutionary army and was in many battles including Bunker Hill; res. in N. H.
1461. i. DAVID, b. ———.
1462. ii. MOLLY, b. ———.
1463. iii. ELIZABETH, b. ———.
1464. iv. RHODA, b. ———.
1465. v. ENOCH, b. ———.
1466. vi. ROSWELL, b. ———.
1467. vii. ISAAC, b. ———.
1468. viii. BENJAMIN, b. ———.
1469. ix. SALLY, b. ———.
1470. x. SILAS, b. ———.
1471. xi WALTER W., b. ———.

820. REV. DAVID FISK (Ebenezer, Ebenezer, William, William, William, John, William, Robert, Simon, Simon, William, Symond), b. Mar. 3, 1772; m. Feb. 20, 1794, Lydia Morse, b. Aug. 22, 1770; d. at New Hampton, N. H., Aug. 11, 1857.

He was a farmer, a clergyman (Free Baptist), a planter of churches and a pioneer in New Hampshire. He is buried in New Hampton, N. H. Ordained July 1, 1810. A brief biography of him will be found on p. 195 of the "Free Baptist Cyclopedia." The old Fisk family seat is in New Hampton, N. H., where Rev. David Fisk and wife died, where David Marks Fisk was born, as was also Rev. Daniel Moses Fisk. The buildings have gone into much decay. He d. Feb. 9, 1834; res. Boscowen and New Hampton, N. H.

    1472. i.   EBENEZER, b. Oct. 1, 1802; m. Miriam A. Gordon.
    1473. ii.   LYDIA MORSE, b. Oct. 27, 1794, m. Daniel Kennison. She
              d. May 12, 1823. Possibly of two children of Mrs. Daniel
              Kennison (Lydia) survive in Cambridge, Mass. (1) David,
              (2) Nancy, (3) and a Mrs. —— Snell, Cambridge, Mass.
    1474. iii. ELIZABETH, b. Mar. 21, 1796, m. John L. Gordon. She d.
              May 7, 1833.
    1475. iv. JOHN MORSE, b. Mar. 6, 1798; d. Mar. 5, 1823.
    1476. v.   HANNAH, b. ——; d. infancy.
    1477. vi. DAVID, b. ——; d. infancy.
    1478. vii. WILLIAM, b. ——; d. childhood.
    1479. viii. TIMOTHY, b. ——; d. childhood.
    1480. ix. MOSES, b. Jan. 6, 1808; d. May 15, 1823.
    1481. x.   POLLY GORDON, b. Apr. 6, 1810; m. Sanders Herbert. She
              d. Nov. 3, 1873. Of Polly Gordon (Mrs. Sanders Herbert)
              only Mrs. Sarah Fisk Herbert Ingalls survives, Bristol, N.
              H., with two daughters—Clara and Eudora (?), school teach-
              ers, Concord, N. H.
    1482. xi. SALLY MORSE, b. Feb. 20, 1812; d. May 6, 1840.
    1483. xii. NANCY KELLEY, b. Sept. 18, 1814; m. William Hale. She
              d. Jan. 28, 1859.

    821. EPHRAIM FISK (Ebenezer, Ebenezer, William, William, William, John, William, Robert, Simon, Simon, William, Symond), b. Boscowen, N. H., Apr. 19, 1774; m. in Newbury, Sally Morse, cousin to Prof. Samuel F. B. Morse, b. May 23, 1777. She d. in Vermont in June, 1848. He was a farmer. He d. in Geneva, Kan., in July, 1859; res. Stratford, Vt.

    1484. i.   DAVID, b. Oct. 24, 1814; m. Lucinda Platts.
    1485. ii.   JOSEPH M., b. Sept. 10, 1811; m. Phebe M. Densmore.
    1486. iii. EPHRAIM, b. Sept. 10, 1811; m. Elizabeth B. Trescott.
    1487. iv. MARY, b. Jan. 31, 1806; m. Sept. 7, 1824, William Preston, b.
              June 28, 1803; d. Nov. 10, 1881. She d. Feb. 10, 1888. Of her
              forefathers on her father's side, 28 were ministers, besides 18
              deacons, and that more than one hundred of them were
              graduates of various colleges, it will be readily understood
              why Mrs. Preston was so much of a Bible student and so de-
              voted a Christian. She was married in the state of Vermont,
              where they lived a few years, and then moved to western
              New York, then a new country. In Feb., 1864, they moved to
              Mt. Pleasant, Mich., where they lived for nearly a quarter of a
              century, both passing from life to death in the house in which
              they moved so long ago, Mr. Preston having died in 1881.
              They had nine children, of whom three—Mrs. S. Woodworth,
              Mr. W. W. Preston, and Mrs. I. A. Fancher—are yet living
              and residents of Mt. Pleasant. Mrs. Preston was uncommonly
              well preserved for one of her age. Ch.: Wallace W., b. Oct.
              9, 1837; res. Mt. Pleasant, Mich.; m. Sept. 24, 1861, Arsenath
              Woodworth, b. June 21, 1841; is a farmer; ch.: 1, Worth W.
              Preston, b. Sept. 19, 1864; m. May 15, 1889; P. O. Duluth,
              Minn. 2, Anna Belle Preston, b. Sept. 15, 1870; single; P. O.
              Mt. Pleasant, Mich. 3, Ralph E. Preston, b. June 10, 1874;
              single; P. O. Duluth, Minn. Sarah Almira, b. Jan. 16, 1826,
              m. Mar. 14, 1843, I. H. Fuller, and d. Feb. 16, 1854; had 4 ch.
              Albert Alonzo, b. Aug. 16, 1827; m. Apr. 13, 1851. Mary An-
              geline, b. Dec. 15, 1829; m. June 13, 1854, I. H. Fuller; she
              d. Mar. 13, 1862, and had 1 ch. Ellen Levinda, b. July 7, 1833;
              m. Apr. 13, 1851, Samuel Woodworth. Althea May, b. Dec.

HOME OF REV. DAVID FISK 1802-1834, OF HIS SON REV. EBENEZER FISK, 1802-1853; THE BIRTHPLACE OF ERV.

15, 1840; m. June 6, 1860, F. A. Fancher. Walter Scott, b. July 4, 1844; d. in infancy. Celia Eliza, b. June 26, 1846; m. Oct. 10, 1865, E. H. Bradley; she d. Mar. 25, 1867, s. p. Emma Amelia, b. July 18, 1848; m. June 6, 1866, Albert Fox; she d. June 8, 1878; had one girl, b. 1870, Edith J.; he d. Feb 28, 1873.

1488. v. LAVINDA HIDE, b. 1809; m. in Bethany, N. Y., Josiah R. Beckwith. He was b. in Lyme, Conn., Aug. 15, 1804; d. in Buchanan, Mich., in 1867. Ch.: Edgar H. Beckwith (not living); Edward A. Beckwith, Buchanan, Mich.; Fidelia Mary Moon, Buchanan, Mich.; Francelia Graham, Liberty, Ind.; John T. Beckwith, Benton Harbor, Mich.; Olive E. Weaves, Kirwin, Kan.; Almira Moon, Kirwin, Kan.

1489. vi. HANNAH, b. ———; m. ——— Thompson.
1490. vii. DOLLIE, b. ———; m. ——— Jenkins.
1491. viii. PHILENA, b. ———; m. ——— Wells.
1492. ix. SARAH, b. ———; m. ——— Eddy.

824. EPHRAIM FISKE (Ephraim, Ebenezer, William, William, William, John, William, Robert, Simon, Simon, William, Symond), b. Tewksbury, Mass., Aug. 27, 1758; m. Martha Sawyer, d. Concord, N. H. Ephraim, the son, when he enlisted was only sixteen years old, and rather small of his age; but he succeeded in passing muster by tying his hat-band tight around his hat, and putting his hat as high on his head as he could without having it fall off, and standing erect as he could. When he came to the inspector, the latter said "march on," while some of the others were rejected. In the battle of Bennington, he, with three others were ordered by a lieutenant to carry Captain Taylor from the field, who was wounded (his thigh being broken). This was a very dangerous and critical position. It was rising ground, and Captain Taylor fainting every few minutes. The cannon balls would plow furrows as large as those made by a breaking-up plow, yet a kind Providence protected them. He was a private in the N. H. Cont. line, and was granted a pension Mar. 16, 1823, ae. 70. He d. in Contoocook in 1849; res. Concord, N. H.

1493. i. RICHARD, b. Apr. 6, 1789; m. Rhapsyme Sargent and ——— Sargent.
1494. ii. JOHN, b. Jan. 2, 1787; m. Elizabeth Kittredge.
1495. iii. CHARLOTTE, b. Redding, Mass.; m. in Concord, N. H., Calvin Boutelle, of Contoocook, N. H. He d. July 15, 1890. She d. Dec. 30, 1866. Ch.: 1, John. 2, Horace. 3, Wm.; res. Manchester, N. H. 4, Charlotte Ann, b. July 16, 1828; m. Feb. 18, 1851, Henry Dow; res. C. He was b. May 5, 1829; d. July 7, 1892; ch.: William Henry Dow, b. June 28, 1854; m. Aug. 16, 1874, A. Pricilla Elliotte; d. July 17, 1876. Jeannette D. Dow, b. Oct. 17, 1856; m. Sept. 9, 1874, Frank D. Webster; d. May 30, 1879. Lizzie D. Dow, b. Oct. 16, 1859; m. Nov. 12, 1877, Walter Colby; d. Apr. 13, 1881. Sarah J. Dow, b. Feb. 16, 1865; m. July 9, 1880, William A. Currier; d. Nov. 8, 1882. 5, Nancy Ann.
1496. iv. MARTHA, b. 1795; m. John Elliott; res. Concord, N. H. She d. Oct. 10, 1889, ae. 94. Ch.: 1, Martha F., m. Alanson Gray and Mr. Chandler; ch.: Laura, Emma and George, all dead. Widow and dau. Emma, res. Contoocook, N. H. S. p. by 2d husband. 2, Augusta, m. Henry Barrett, of Manchester, N. H. One ch., Ella. Mother and ch. dead. Husband res. Manchester, N. H. 3, Mary, m. Charles Holmes, of Contoocook; both deceased.
     v. POLLY, b. ———; d. young.
1497. v. POLLY, b. ———; d. young.
1498. vi. EPHRAIM, b. Apr. 17, 1798; m. Margaret Dow.

827. EBENEZER FISKE (Ephraim, Ebenezer, William, William, William, John, William, Robert, Simon, Simon, William, Symond), b. Tewksbury, Mass., Jan. 26, 1766; m. Sarah Blanchard, b. Sept. 28, 1769; d. Nov. 11, 1848. Ebenezer Fiske, son of Ephraim, was born at Tewksbury, Mass., Jan. 26, 1766, and lived to

an advanced age. He was one of the first settlers at Little Pond, about 1787. He purchased one of the eighty-three acre lots, that belonged to the Rolfe Estate, and commenced at the west end of the lot; made an opening near the road, and put up a shanty, in which he lived about three years. He then built a house. Mr. Fiske possessed a large, muscular frame, which during his long life was subjected to severe labors, toils and hardships. When a young man about twenty-one he worked for a while for Joseph Colby, of New London, father of Ex-Gov. Anthony Colby. Going out together in a boat on a pond they were upset and Fiske saved Colby's life by catching him by the hair of his head, when sinking. Soon after this in raising the New London meeting house, both Colby and Fiske were on the frame, when, a board being suddenly moved, Fiske fell and Colby caught him by the hair of his head and saved his life. At another time young Fiske was threshing grain with Thomas Morse of Hopkinton, when Morse in sport struck the end or swingel of Mr. Fisk's flail and drove it into his left eye. He fell, and was thought to be dead, but recovering Dr. Philip Carrigain was sent for, who told him that his eye was spoiled, and said he, "if the eye should run out you would give all Hopkinton to get rid of the pain." Happily the eye did not run out, but the sight of it was completely destroyed for life. Dr. Carrigain charged but two shilings for his service. At the raising of a barn, at what is now Millville, when about 28 years old, Mr. Fiske says, "I fell from the top or plate to the bottom of the cellar; and a stick of timber I was lifting, fell across my breast. My shoulder was broken, and breast so much bruised that it was thought I could not recover; but by skillful means of a doctor, and a good constitution, I recovered, but felt the effects for three or four years after." About three years after Mr. Fiske was upset in a wagon on the road at the top of the hill west of Richard Bradley's and received a severe cut in the head, which for a considerable time benumbed his faculties. With no education in early life, he was ever a good calculator and manager of his affairs, and a reliable, substantial citizen. Res. Concord, N. H.

1499. i   BETSEY, b. Aug. 3, 1798; m. Andrew Seavy.

1500. ii. ABIRA, b. Mar. 8. 1800; m. Eunice B. Abbot, and settled on a part of the old homestead.

1501. iii. ELEANOR S., b. July 12, 1801; unm.

1502. iv. HENRY, b. Oct. 20, 1803; d. May 26, 1831; a school teacher; member of the First Congregational Church, and highly esteemed.

1503. v. SARAH B., b. June 8, 1805; m. Dea. Hazen Runnels, and d. Oct. 30, 1840.

1504. vi. METHITABLE F., b. May 4, 1809; d. Aug., 1832; school teacher.

836. ENSIGN SQUIRE FISKE (John, Josiah, Samuel, William, William, John, William, Robert, Simon, Simon, William Symond), b. Jan. 10, 1756; m. Nov. 23, 1777, Amey Lapham, dau. of Abner; b. Aug. 29, 1762; d. in the summer of 1843. There is a tradition in the family that Squire Fiske served as Colonel of a Rhode Island regiment during the Revolutionary War. The records of soldiers from that state during the struggle for Independence show that he was an Ensign in Richmond's Rhode Island State Regiment from Nov. 1, 1775 to April, 1776. He was later in life granted a pension for revolutionary service. When his daughter, Abby, died, Squire's wife, Amy, took her four children home and brought them up. She also brought up, for a while at least, Francis' two children, Ann Elizabeth and William. Squire Fisk's home at Cumberland, Rhode Island, was a brick cottage. This had never been transferred until some ten or fifteen yeads ago (perhaps twenty). Then there were many heirs to sign the deed although the property was not valuable enough to give much to each individual. I am not sure that every living heir did sign the deed, all did that could be found, but enough signed so that Mr. Burlingame, the purchaser, was willing to take the property. This deed is registered in the office of the town clerk of Cumberland. He d. Nov. 30, 1804; res. Cumberland, R. I.

1505. i. SAMUEL BARTLETT, b. Feb. 12, 1780; m. Vianna Estes.

1506. ii. ABBY, b. Oct. 23, 1782; m. Benjamin Hendrick and d. May 15, 1808. He was son of Dr. Stephen, and d. at Thompson, Conn., in 1832. Ch.: 1, Stephen, b. ——— ; m. Hannah Esty. He d. Feb. 14, 1880; ch.: a, Benjamin Otis; b, Stephen Potter; c,

George Russell; d, Joseph Warren, e, Amey Ann, d. Mar. 11, 1879; f, Samuel Truesdale! g, Asenath Caroline. All of these died young except Amey Ann, who married Samuel Sims associate publisher of the Woonsocket Patriot, who died August 6, 1879. They had at least two children, Herbert Sims, who died in childhood and Bertha Sims who married a man named Elliot. Bertha is now a widow with children and res. on Union St., Worcester, Mass. 2, Benjamin Wing, b. July 21, 1802; m. Sarah Wilcox Browning, b. Aug. 11, 1802; d. July 22, 1889. She d. July 13, 1889; ch.: 1, Celia Ann, b. Dec. 27, 1823; m. Dec. 25, 1845, Dr. Absolem Pride King, b. May 1, 1820; d. Oct. 10, 1868. She res. 51 Vernon, St., Prov., R. I., ch.: a, Asenath Caroline, b. September 19, 1846; d. Nov. 20, 1850. b. William Henry Herbert, b. Nov. 8, 1850; d. May 31, 1853. c, Eugene Pride, b. Nov. 5, 1854; he is connected with Prov. R. I. Health Department. d, Virginia May, b. April 28, 1859; d. Oct. 11, 1861. 2, Sarah Browning, b. July 17, 1825; m. Felix Augustus Peckham; res. Newport, R. I., P. O. box 285. 3, Henry, b. Jan. 1, 1830; m. Frances Campbell of Willimantic, Conn., a dau. is Harriett L. Hendrick of Middletown, N. Y.; he d. Dec. 23, 1891. 4, Benjamin Wing, b. July 8, 1840; d. July 16, 1842. 5, Abby Fisk, b. Jan. 17, 1842; d. unm., June 14, 1881. Benjamin Wing Hendrick was left motherless very young and his grandmother, Mrs. Amey Fisk, took him to live with her. He began life as operator in a cotton mill when a small boy and rose through various grades of the work to the position of overseer and superintendent and afterwards, in company with his brother, Stephen, and alone, he operated mills himself. They had ventures in the South as well as in the New England states. Benjamin's schooling was very little but he trained himself in higher mathematics when he was older and was something of a mechanic. He patented at least one "loom-motion." His experience at the South before the war made him acquainted with the Southern people, and although his politics was republican (and I think he always after Whig times voted the republican ticket) yet he had and would express such regard and admiration for the Southerners during the war time that his political orthodoxy was gravely doubted by many of his relatives. I think he was a rather admirable sort of a man who hadn't much chance in youth and who led a rather commonplace and uneventful life. During the last years of his life he took personal care of his wife. His death was quite sudden. His wife survived only nine days. 3, Olney, b. ———; m. 1st, Sarah Ann Remington; ch.: a, Harriet; b, Abby; c, Phoebe; d, Sarah; 2d wife a widow Steere. Address, Hendrick Olney, postal clerk, Boston to N. Y.) in care Olney Brothers, 16 South Water St., Providence, R. I. 4, Horace, b. ———; m. Maria Fuller; ch.: a, Abby; b, Wm. Henry, res. Newbury St., Worcester, Mass.; c, Fanny, m. ——— Cady, res. 182 Austin St., Worcester, Mass.; d, Horace Simmons.

1507. iii. MAJOR, b. Nov. 24, 1787; m. ———'———.
1508. iv. SQUIRE, b. Aug. 14, 1785; d. unm.
1509. v. CHARLES, b. Oct. 5, 1789; m. Alice Carpenter.
1510. vi. HALEY, b. Feb. 29, 1793; m. Judith Qureaux.
1511. vii. POLLY, b. ———; m. July 15, 1811, George F. Thorpe. He was in the war of 1812. Children were William, Angeline, Louisa, and Frederick. She died at Cumberland, R. I., and the town clerk of Cumberland might give information or address of some one of her descendants.
1512. viii. NANCY, b. July 18, 1799; d. unm.
1513. ix. FRANCIS M., b. Mar. 24, 1804; m. Ursula French.

838. JOHN FISKE (John, Josiah, Samuel, William, William, John, William, Robert, Simon, Simon, William, Symond), b. Cumberland, R. I., Aug. 20, 1761; m. Apr. 14, 1784, Abigail Ballou, dau. of Rev. Abner of Cumberland; d. Jan. 3, 1819. He d. in Northboro, Mar. 26, 1837; res., Westboro, Mass. Mr. Ballou was a worthy descendant of a French Huguenot family who were among the early settlers in this country. John Fiske occupied the old homestead farm in Cumberland until April, 1794, where his three eldest children were born. In April, 1794, it became necessary to sell the old homestead farm in Cumberland in order to effect a settlement of the estate, and John took his share of the proceeds, in Spanish milled dollars, and put them into his saddlebags and started on horseback into the interior of the country to look for a new home. Providence directed his steps to Westboro, Mass., where he purchased a farm, and immediately removed his family thither. Westboro was 28 miles from Cumberland, and the family connections of his wife felt that she was going to remove almost to the end of the world; in fact, the journey was thought more of at that time than a journey to Oregon or California is now. The family remained on the farm in Westboro seven years, until the year 1801, and here two more children were born. In April, 1801, the farm in Westboro was sold, and another farm in Northborough purchased, where the family removed and there remained until the death of John Fiske, in 1837, at the age of 76 years.

1514. i.   JAMES BALLOU, b. Dec. 14, 1784; m. Rebecca McGraw.
1515. ii.   NATHAN, b. Feb. 1, 1787; m. Sarah A. Arnold.
1516. iii. JOHN, b. Dec. 7, 1795.
1517. iv.   HORACE SUMNER, b. June 24, 1799.
1518. v.   BETSEY, b. Oct. 24, 1790.

841. DARIUS FISK (John, Josiah, Samuel, William, William, John, William, Robert, Simon, Simon, William, Symond), b. Cumberland, R. I., May 7, 1768; m. there Feb. 12, 1789, Patty Darling, dau. of Joshua of Bellingham; res., Cumberland, R. I.

JONATHAN FISK (Jonathan, Josiah, Samuel, William, William, John, William, Robert, Simon, Simon, William, Symond), b. Feb. 12, 1760, Rhode Island; m. Apr. 20, 1779, Mercy Robinson, b. Mar. 23, 1762; d. Dec. 12, 1833. He d. Nov. 2, 1853; res., Mayfield, N. Y.

1519. i.   NATHANIEL, b. Jan. 13, 1780; m. Lois Hall and Lydia Wells.
1520. ii.   JONATHAN, b. Jan. 5, 1798; d. Apr. 14, 1800.
1521. iii. STEPHEN, b. Feb. 24, 1796; d. Aug. 19, 1811.
1522. iv.   LUCY, b. Apr. 26, 1781; m. Apr. 27, 1797, Timothy Foot, Jr.
1523. v.   HANNAH, b. Feb. 9, 1784; m. July 5, 1801, James Woodworth. He d. Oct. 11, 1858. She d. Mar. 28, 1856.
1524. vi.   RUTH, b. Dec. 28, 1786; m. Mar. 19, 1807, William Green. He d. July 25, 1807. She m. 2d, Sept. 8, 1812, Edward H. Gaylord. She d. Apr. 7, 1866.
1525. vii. ESTHER, b. Sept. 28, 1788; m. Sept. 12, 1810, Nicholas Keysar.
1526. viii. THEODOSIA, b. Apr, 8, 1790 m. June 6, 1811, Truman Christie.
1527. ix.   LOIS, b. Dec. 18, 1791; m. Sept. 27, 1818, Sylvenus Keysar.
1528. x.   SAMUEL, b. Nov. 7, 1793; m. Esther Wood and res. Danville, N. Y.
1529. xi.   MERCY, b. Dec. 23, 1799; m. Dec. 8, 1819, Herman Pettit.
1530. xii. PATTY, b. Dec. 10, 1801; d. unm., July 11, 1841.
1531. xiii. CYNTHIA, b. Feb. 26, 1804; m. Dec. 11, 1822, John Wood.

847. DAVID FISK (Jonathan, Josiah, Samuel, William, John, William, Robert, Simon, Simon. William, Symond), b. June 17, 1769, Rhode Island; m. Dec. 26, 1790, Mary Green, b. May 4, 1775; d. June 27, 1828, in Arcadia, N. Y. He moved to Mayville, Saratoga Co., was married there and for many years kept hotel there, later he moved to Arcadia and was an extensive farmer. He d. Nov., 1849; res. Saratoga Co., N. Y., and Waterford, Mich.

1532. i.   JONATHAN D., b. Feb. 21, 1794; m. Lucy Codman and Mrs. Betsey Granger.
1533. ii.   JAMES G., b. Oct. 10, 1791; m. Mary S. Alexander.
1534. iii. WEAVER G., b. July 22, 1796; m. Eleanor Childs.
1535. iv.   DAVID, b. Mar. 26, 1801; m. Cynthia J. Chittenden.
1536. v.   LEWIS MOSES, b. Sept. 14, 1804; m. Mary Titus; d. N. Y. state.

13

1537. vi.   HYRAM, b. Aug. 14, 1813; m. —— Worden; d. N. Y. state.
1538. vii. POLLY, b. Oct. 26, 1798; m. Aug. 17, 1817, Silas Moon. She
             d. in Oakland, Co., Mich. Ch.: Luman, res. Waterford, Mich.;
             Lanson, Elizabeth, Stephen, Lerancy, Silas Ashley.
1539. viii. BETSEY, b. Jan. 22, 1807; m. July 22, 1824, Benjamin Green.
             She d. s. p., Newark, N. Y.
1540. ix.   MARY MARCELLA, b. Apr. 20, 1809; m. July 1, 1827, Adrian
             Conner Ch.: 1, Stephen, b. Aug. 4, 1828. 2, Lester, b. July
             4, 1832. 3, Mary M., b. Aug. 6, 1834. 4, Martha M., b. Aug.
             18, 1836. Mr. Conner died and she m. 2d, May 12, 1844 ——
             Miller res. Matanna Station, Ohio. She d. in Michigan.
1541. x.   ALMIRA, b. Apr. 14, 1811; m. in Rushford, N. Y. in 1849, Asa
             Putney She m. 2d in Freedom, N. Y., in 1856, Amos Tuttle.
             She d. in Knowlesville, N. Y.
1542. xi.   STEPHEN, b. Apr. 21, 1817; m. and s. p.
1543. xii. BOY, b. Sept. 1, 1803; died young.
1544. xiii. GIRL, b. Feb. 6, 1820; d. young.

851.   EZRA FISK (Jonathan, Josiah, Samuel, William, William, John, William, Robert, Simon, Simon, William, Symond), b. Schuylerville, N. Y., Apr. 26,
1778; m. in New Bedford, Lydia Hannibal, b. 1782; d. in 1871, in Pontiac, Mich.
He d. 1832; res. Saratoga and Port Gibson, N. Y.
1545. i.   JOHN HANNIBAL, b. Jan. 12, 1804; m. Jane Wells.
1546. ii.   STEPHEN, b. 1812; d. 1882, in White Lake, Mich.
1547. iii. JAMES, b. 1814; d. 1894.
1548. iv.   HANNAH, b. 1823; m. John Seeley; res. Newark, N. Y.
1549. v.   WILLIAM, b. 1806; m.; d. 1844. Ch.: dau. Lydia; res. Marion,
             N. Y.
1550. vi.   HARVEY, b. 1818; d. Waterford Centre, Mich.
1551. vii. HIRAM, b. 1800; m. Maria Fraser.
1552. viii. DANIEL B., b. Aug. 20, 1816; m. Elizabeth A. Sherman.
1553. ix.   EZRA, b. 1820; m. ——; d. 1875.

853.   STEPHEN FISK (Jonathan, Josiah, Samuel, William, William, John,
William, Robert, Simon, Simon, William, Symond), b. Saratoga Co., N. Y., 1782; m.
at Schuylerville, N. Y., Hannah Carry, b. in 1790; d. at Newark, N. Y., Jan. 14, 1849.
Stephen, with his wife, Hannah, and three children, Lonson, aged about 9, Samuel,
about 6 or 7, and William, an infant, emigrated from Schuylerville, Saratoga
Co., N. Y., in the winter of 1821, arriving in Newark, February 5, 1821, having come by wagon and eight days on the road. Some of Stephen's brothers
and sisters went to that locality (either before or after)—one or more settled in Michigan, and other remained in the locality of their early home. It
is said that one of the girls in the early days owned fifty acres of land upon
which a part of the city of Saratoga Springs is now located. He d. July 21, 1855;
res. Schuylerville and Newark, N. Y.
1554. i.   LONSON, b. Feb. 8, 1811; m. Adelia Wells.
1555. ii.   WILLIAM, b. ——; m.: res. Newark.
1556   iii. SAMUEL, b. 1814; d. ae. 18 years, in 1832.

856.   JOSEPH FISKE (Joseph, Mark, Joseph, William, William, John,
William, Robert, Simon, Simon, William, Symond), b. New Ipswich, N. H., Sept.
5, 1767; m. Dec. 27, 1790, Margaret Clark, b. Londonderry, N. H., Oct. 25, 1765;
d. Jan 17, 1852, at Eden Vt. During the war of 1812 he kept a huckster's store,
being honest and upright himself, trusted to others and therefore lost nearly
all his property; sold his home in Goffstown, N. H., and was again unfortunate
through dishonest people, lost nearly all of that. Came to Eden, Vt., about 1808
or 1809, the town then almost a forest, and settled on what is now known
as Cooper Hill. A few years later fell from his house (while fixing the chim-
ney) and broke his leg, never walking again without crutch or cane. That fall
finished his work, and after suffering for years, went out for the last time to
his son Washington's wedding, Jan. 14, 1834. He d. Jan. 31, 1834; res. Londonderry and Goffstown, N. H., and Eden, Vt.
1557. i.   JOSEPH, b. May 1, 1792; m. Fannie Brown.

1558. ii. JOHN, b. Apr. 16, 1794. He left home unknown to his parents,
           went to Albany, N. Y., and was in the war of 1812.
1559. iii. CLARK, b. May 29, 1797; m. Olive Atwell.
1560   iv. MARK, b. Sept. 15, 1799; d. Goffstown, June 13, 1802.
1561. v.   MARGARET, b. Dec. 14, 1801; m. Mar. 2, 1842, Jefferson Cob-
           leigh. He d. Hyde Park, Vt., Mar. 10, 1860. She d. Jan.
           17, 1868. Ch.: Lucilla; d. 3 years old.
1562. vi. WASHINGTON, b. Feb. 15, 1804; m. Hannah Whitney Alden.
1563. vii. MARY, b. Mar.. 15, 1807; m. Asaph Spalding of Morristown,
           Vt.; res. Hyde Park, Vt. She was his second wife. She
           d. s. p. in Sept., 1887.

   857. BENJAMIN FISKE (Joseph, Mark, Joseph, William, William, John,
William, Robert, Simon Simon, William, Symond), b. Ipswich, Mass., Nov. 15,
1768; m. ——— ———. He was a hotel keeper. He d. s. p.; res. Pembroke,
N. H.

   861. COL. MARK FISKE (Joseph, Mark, Joseph, William, John, William, Robert, Simon, Simon, William, Symond), b. Ipswich, Mass., June 21, 1778;
m. at Londonderry, N. H., Apr. 2, 1801, Eleanor Wilson, of Watertown; m. 2d.,
Mrs. Elizabeth (Stark) Kidder, granddaughter of Gen. John Stark. His parents
moved to Londonderry, N. H., were farmers, also kept tavern. Stages stopped there
on the route from Lowell to Deerfield. He was captain of the artillery at the time
of the war of 1812. The company was drafted and went to Portsmouth, N. H.;
remained there three months; never was in any.action. The British were at the Isle
of Shoals. He died at the age of 64. He d. Pembroke, N. H., Aug., 1840; res.
Londonderry, N. H.   .
1564. i.   BENJAMIN, b. Dec. 27, 1810; m. Mary B. Sawyer.
1565. ii. MARK, b. July 21, 1814; m. Elizabeth S. Gove and Mrs. Sarah
           E. (Reed) Cutter.
1566. iii. JOSEPH, b. Aug. 5, 1809; m. Sarah A. Stevens.
1567. iv. JAMES W., b. Oct. 6, 1818; m. Mary Webber.
1568. v.   ELIZABETH, b. Dec.. 1802; m. Henry Willey and Isaac Clem-
           ent. Res. ———. She d. s. p.
1569. vi. ELEANOR W., b. ———; m. Albury Mason. Res. ———.
           she d. ———. A daughter is Mrs. Dudley; res. E. Boston,
           Mass.
1570. vii. SARAH HOBBS, b. Apr., 1804; m. Dec. 26, 1825, John M.
           Stevens; res. Raymond, N. H. She d. Apr. 28, 1835. Ch.:/
           John Fisk Stevens, b. Dec. 5, 1827; res. Raymond, N. H.,
           dead. Hiram Wilson Stevens, b. Nov. 23, 1829. Sarah Helen
           Stevens, b. July 5, 1834; m. Dec. 15, 1861, Sewell Brown Pevear,
           b. July 18, 1839; res. 539 Western Av., Lynn, Mass.; ch.:
           Everett Sewell, b. Feb. 7. 1863; m. Dec. 2, 1885, address 69
           Park St., Lynn; Evelena Florence, b. Apr. 28, 1866; m. Mar.
           18, 1891, address, Pelham, N. H., Mrs. Charles de Chatnal;
           Helen May, b. Oct. 8, 1868; m. Oct. 16, 1895, address, Read-
           ing, Mass., Mrs. J. O. Newhall; Norman Melrose. b. Jan. 9,
           1871.   Mary Ellen Stevens, b. July 5, 1834, twins; m. Nov. 23,
           1853, Samuel Belcher, b. Jan. 1, 1821; Willey A. Belcher, b.
           Feb. 26, 1857; Alvah, H. Belcher, b. Dec. 27, 1859; Carrie E.
           Belcher, b. Oct. 28, 1862; Mamie F. Belcher, b. Jan 12, 1868;
           m. Jan. 12, 1890, now Mrs. Mamie F. Wyman, Winthrop, Mass.
           Mrs. Carrie E. Kent, East Derry. N. H.
1571. viii. MARY JANE, b. ———; m. Luther Mitchell and Fitch Cutter.
           She d. s. p.
1572. ix. STARK, b. ———; d. ———.
1573. x.   HIRAM. b. Oct. 15, 1807; m. Louisa Whitney.
1574. xi. PRISCILLA A., b. July 16. 1816; m. Sept. 3, 1837, James Shute,;
           res. Somerville, Mass. He was b. May 17, 1815; d. Jan. 1,
           1891; was a brick manufacturer. Ch.: Ellen Priscilla Angier,
           b. June 27. 1838; m. Aug. 29. 1872; now living; present name
           same; P. O. address, Derby St., Somerville, Mass. Boy, not
           named, b. Oct., 1840; d. in a few days. Mary Adelaide Shute,

b. May 22, 1842; d. Nov., 1842. Adelaide, b. Sept. 13, 1844; m. June 11, 1867; present name Adelaide Shute Bolton, res. No. 18 Temple St., Somerville, Mass. James Henry Shute, b. Feb. 9, 1847; unm.; res. No. 18 Temple St., Somerville, Mass. Benjamin Franklin Shute, b. May 16, 1851; m.; P. O. address, Forest St., Arlington, Mass.

862. JOHN FISK (John, Mark, Joseph, William, William, John, William, Robert, Simon, Simon, William, Symond), b. Kennebunk, Me., Apr. 28, 1786; m. at Waterboro, Me., May 3. 1811, Sarah Coffin of Waterboro, b. Apr. 14, 1794; d. Nov. 16, 1824; m. 2d. July 3, 1825. Nancy Davis of Alfred, Me., b. there Apr. 14, 1804; d. Dec. 18, 1863. He was a farmer. H d. Oct. 2, 1846; res. Waterboro, Me. Me.

　1575.　i.　BENJAMIN, b. Feb. 11, 1813; m. Mary Jane Marshall.
　1576.　ii.　JOHN, b. May 25, 1815; m. Mary Andrews.
　1577.　iii.　MARK, b. Mar, 22, 1817; d., unm., at W., Mar. 12, 1842.
　1578.　iv.　SAMUEL C., b. Mar. 12, 1820; m. Fanny Wilson.
　1579.　v.　GEORGE, b. June 10, 1822; m. Abigail Hill.
　1580.　vi.　CHARLES, b. Mar. 6, 1824; res. Col.
　1581.　vii.　NEHEMIAH, b. Sept. 4, 1827; d. Aug. 25, 1850.
　1582.　viii.　IVERY, b. Dec. 6, 1829; d. Feb. 2, 1832.
　1583.　ix.　IVERY, b. Jan. 20, 1836; d. June 17, 1853.
　1584.　x.　SARAH J., b. Apr. 18, 1833; m. Nov. 2, 1854, Daniel Warren; res. Waterboro. Ch.: John E., b. Dec. 5. 1858; d. unm. June 8, 1882. She m. 2d. Frank L. Libby of Limerick, Me.; ch.: 1, Elsworth S., b. June 12, 1865: 2, Edward E., b. July 27, 1867; 3, Warren S., b. June 11, 1871; res. New York city.
　1585.　xi.　USHER, b. Nov. 29, 1839; d. unm. Mar. 8, 1864.
　1586.　xii.　ELIZA, b. June 8, 1843; m. July 2, 1878, Joseph Chadbourne; res., Waterboro, s. p.

872. NATHANIEL FISKE (Nathaniel, Theophilus, Theophilus, William, William, John, William, Robert, Simon, Simon, William, Symond), b. Topsfield, Mass., Dec. 2, 1764; bap. June 9, 1765; m. Nov. 20, 1794, Mehitable Balch of Topsfield, b. June 26, 1771; d. Sept. 16, 1864. Nathaniel, Jr., son of Nathaniel and Lydia Gould Fiske, who m. Mehitable, dau. of John and Sarah (Baker) Balch, was a shoemaker by trade. He settled at first on the homestead in Topsfield; and died in that town, aged eighty-five; and his widow, who was born June 26, 1771, died, with her daughter Elsey, in Salem, aged 93 years. He d. Nov. 13, 1849; res. Topsfield, Mass.
He d. Nov. 13, 1849. Res., Topsfield, Mass.

　1587.　iv.　JONAS, b. Sept. 24, 1805; m. Apr. 14, 1841, Abigail Pettingill. Rev. Jonas Fiske, who was born in Topsfield, received his classical education in Bangor, Me., at Bowdoin College, graduated at the Theological Seminary in 1838, was ordained pastor over the Salem (N. H.) Church in 1840, and in 1843 removed to the state of Maine, to labor as an evangelist. For twenty years he preached to the feeble churches in that sparsely settled State and did good missionary work among them, being principally sustained therein by the Missionary Board of that State. He has recently retired from active service, and resided in Danvers, Mass. His wife was a daughter of Joseph and Lucy (Smith) Pettingill and was b. in Salem, Mass. They did not have any children.
　1588.　i.　MEHITABLE, b. Aug. 22, 1793; m. a John of Beverly, who soon died at sea, and she died a widow years after without issue.
　1589.　ii.　ELSEY, b. May 3, 1798; m. and res. on Mall St., Salem, in 1867.
　1590.　iii.　AMOS, b. May 26, 1801; m. Mercy Peabody.
　1591.　v.　REBECCA, b. June 1, 1812; d. Dec. 12, 1848.

873. JOHN FISKE (Nathaniel, Theophilus, Theophilus, William, William, John, William, Robert, Simon, Simon, William, Symond), bap. Aug. 20, 1769, in Topsfield; m. there, Huldah Woodbury, of Beverly, b. 1771; d. May 6, 1804. John Fiske of Beverly Shoreman Adm'n granted to Mrs. Huldah Fisk [his widow] June

8, 1803 and after his decease Adm'n De Bonis Non was granted to Ebenr Fiske of
Beverly trader June 5 1804 Inv of the Estate was taken July 15, 1803 Nov 5, 1805.
Acc't of Adm'n was given June 27, 1804, and Dec 4, 1805. Huldah the widow de-
ceased & adm'n of her Est was granted to Peter Woodbury, June 5 1804. Inv of
the Est was taken June 26 1804. Acc't of Adm'n of her Est was given Nov 6 1805.
Elbridge the only child of John & Huldah Fiske was five years old when Nath
Fiske was app'd his guardain June 27, 1804 and he received from the adm'rs of the
Estates of the father & mother Jan 13, 1806 the personal Estate amounting to
1817 when the minor was 14 years old. Same time Eben'r Fisk of Beverly a trader
$6442.29.   (Vol. 73, page 78.)   And rendered his acc't of Guardianship Oct 4,
1817, when the minor was 14 years old. Same time Eben'r Fisk of Beverly a
trader received the appointment of Guardian & received the Estate which then
amounted to $8254.90. Vol. 84, p. 154. After serving as guardian 6 ys 10 ms &
the minor having become of age he renders the acct. of his guardianship to the
Court Aug 1820, charging for his services $800. the whole amount of said Elbridge
Fisk's personal Est. was then $7536.84. Vol. 96, pages 242 & 259. He d. May 4,
1803; res., Beverly, Mass.

    1592. i.   LYDIA, b. Jan. 29, 1792; d. Jan. 4, 1798.
    1593. ii. JOHN, b. Dec. 27, 1794; d. Aug. 17, 1803.
    1594. iii. AYOR, b. Jan. 17, 1797; d. April 24, 1803.
    1595. iv. ELBRIDGE, b. June 27, 1799; d. Dec. 9, 1846, married July 12,
           1821, Hannah Kilham, daughter of Jonathan and Rebecca
           (Kilham) Dodge, who was born Nov. 19, 1798, and died
           May 15, 1850. No children. Elbridge Fisk of Beverly, trader
           made his will Nov 25 1846, which was proved Feb 2, 1847, in
           which he gives all his Estate to his wife Hannah Kilham Fisk
           & made her Ex'x and Edward Kilham & Charles A. Kilham
           of Beverly were bondsmen—among Items he gave her was his
           house, Store &c with the land on the southwesterly corner of
           Cabot & Winter Streets & Pew No 74, in the First Parish in
           Beverly. Inv. of Estate taken Nov. 29, 1847, amt. $5564.75.

    874. BENJAMIN FISKE (Nathaniel, Theophilus, Theophilus, William,
William, John, William, Robert, Simon, Simon, William, Symond), b. Topsfield,
Mass, Aug. 17, 1774; bap. Aug. 21, that year; m. Mar. 17, 1796, Lydia Hobbs, dau.
of Abraham, b. Aug. 25, 1774; d. June, 1847, in Danvers. Benjamin, son of Nathaniel and Lydia (Gould) Fiske, married Lydia, dau. of Abraham and Elizabeth
(Cummings) Hobbs; resided awhile in Topsfield, in Salem, Newburyport, and
removed to Peeling, now called Woodstock, N. H., where he deceased, aged
forty-seven years. He was a soldier in the war of 1812, and with his company
paroled the shore of Beverly. He d. Mar. 8, 1822; res. Woodstock, N. H.

    1596. i   BENJAMIN, b. ———; d. young.
    1597. ii. ABRAHAM H., b. Nov. 2, 1792; m. Joanna Ober Edwards and
           Mrs. Abigail Wingate.
    1598. iii. LYDIA, b. in 1800; m. Luther Thonnpson, from Keene, N. H.,
           for many years superintendent of the town farm and alms-
           house of Dedham, Mass., died in Concord, N. H., about 1858;
           she resided in Lynn, Mass. Ch.: 1, Laura Jane, who m.
           Fred. Nichols, of Lynn. 2, Alethea, who married her cousin,
           liam L., who was formerly a school-teacher, was in the U.
           3, Lydia, who married Otis Bauldwin, of Lynn; and 4, Wil-
           Samuel A. Southwick; res. 112 New Park St., Lynn, Mass.
           S. Army time of the rebellion, now a lawyer in Lawrence,
           Mass., and m. Aug., 1867, a wife from Woburn.
    1599. iv. BENJAMIN, b. ———; d. young.
    1600. v. JOHN, b. Mar. 2, 1804; m. Salley Haynes.
    1601. vi. MARY DODGE, b. Feb. 28, 1806; m. June 8, 1831, Samuel South-
           wick, b. in Danvers, May 15, 1806. Resided in South Danvers
           when their children were born, but she deceased about 1850, and
           he, who has resided in Ballardvale, Andover, and now in Law-
           rence, is married to his second wife. Ch.: 1, Samuel Au-
           gustus, b. March 20, 1832; married his cousin, Alethea Thomp-
           son; have children; 2, Mary, b. Jan. 25, 1834. who married a

Coulder, no children; and 3, Amos, b. Aug. 26, 1836, res., Lawrence.

1602.	vii.	ALETHEA, bap. in Limebrook Church (west parish in Ipswick, Aug. 7, 1808, who married first, Cyrus Fish, from Barnard, Vt., by whom had a dau., Martha Ann. He deceased in Strongville, Ohio, where she married a second husband named Elisha Taylor, and they now reside in North Camden, Ohio. A daughter of hers is Mrs. Martha Ann Robinson, 1116 19th St., West Superior, Wis.

1603.	viii.	EBENEZER, b. Aug. 18, 1809; m. Elizabeth Mudge and Mrs. Elizabeth (Stevens) Wilson.

1604.	ix.	SHADRACH, b. May 2, 1812; m. Lucy (Boden) Standley and Susan Raymond.

1605.	x.	MARTHA BYRON, b. May 23, 1816; m. James Johnson Mansfield, July 9, 1834, b. in Lynnfield, Mass., March 23, 1811. He is a son of William and Eunice (Johnson) Mansfield. They have, for most of the time since married, resided in South Reading, Mass. He has been connected with shoemaking, teaming, and now is in the wood and coal business, having his two sons in company with him. Their children are: 1, James Fiske, b. Oct. 20, 1835; m. June 6, 1858, Francis Olive Walton, in Wakefield, Mass., where they reside and have had a dau., Cora F., b. Feb. 13, 1860, who died Aug. 1, 1862. He served through the entire war, enlisting at first in company E., Mass. 16th regiment and afterwards belonged to the 11th regiment; was chosen sergeant, and came out a lieutenant colonel, and chosen Representative to the Mass. Legislature from South Reading, in 1866. 2, Mary Elizabeth, b. Aug. 27, 1837; d. Feb. 20, 1840. 3, Laura Matilda, b. Aug. 23, 1839; m. Dec. 31, 1863, Hoyt B. Parker, b. in Newport, N. H., Dec. 29, 1838, is a carpenter and cabinet maker; res., 9 Yale Av., Wakefield; place of business, Charlestown. 4, Joseph Henry, b. Nov. 8, 1841; enlisted into the same company with his brother, July 12, 1861, but died in Bellevue Hospital, N. Y., Sept. 14, 1862, with typhoid fever. 5, Albert Alonzo, b. in South Reading, Aug. 19, 1843; m. July 22, 1868, Carrie E. Newhall, b. July 8, 1844; res., Wakefield. 6, Mary Elizabeth, b. July 10, 1845; m. Cyrus E. Marshall, of Newbury, N. H., Jan. 31, 1867; b. Sept. 5, 1842, and is a provision dealer in Brighton, Mass. 7, Austin Le Roy, b. Mar. 31, 1856; m. May 16, 1880, Clara A. Noble, d. Apr. 12, 1882; m. 2d, Oct. 17, 1887, Harriet M. Peirson, b. Jan. 22, 1866; res. Wakefield.

875. DEA. MOSES FISKE (Nathaniel, Theophilus, Theophilus, William, William, John, William, Robert, Simon, Simon, William, Symond), b. Topsfield, Mass., Aug. 20, 1777; m. Dec. 12, 1802, Sukey Platts, b. Londonderry; d. Jan. 9, 1822; m. 2d, Oct. 1839, Abigail Platts. Dea. Moses, was son of Nathaniel and Lydia (Gould) Fiske, m. to Sukey, a dau. of James and Mary Platts; b. in Londonderry, d. at an advanced age, about 1833-6, her father having been a Revolutionary pensioner. They resided in Topsfield until the year 1805, in New Boston, N. H., until Mar. 1820, when they emigrated to Parishville, St. Lawrence county, N. Y., and remained about two months; and removed to Stockholm, same county, where Mrs. Fiske died and Deacon Fiske, the spring of that year, removed to Fort Covington, Franklin county, same state, and resided until his death, after marrying Abigail Platts, a sister to his first wife. He was an industrious farmer, and a shoemaker by trade; and from an obituary notice of him in the Franklin Gazette, published at Fort Covington, June 9, 1841, we learn that "In early life he made a profession of religion, and was set apart to the office of Ruling Elder in the Presbyterian church before his removal to this town, which office he continued to hold until his death. His deportment was uniformly that of a Christian." He d. June 2, 1841; res., Fort Covington, N. Y.

1606.	i.	SUSAN PLATT, b. at Topsfield, Mass., Mar. 22, 1804; m. Feb. 17, 1830, at Fort Covington, where they resided, to Humphrey

Russell, jr., b. at White Creek, Washington county, N. Y., May 12, 1802. Their children, who are all alive, and some married, with children, are: 1, Edwin Humphrey, b. Jan. 2, 1832. 2, Lovica Susan, Mar. 16, 1834. 3, Rodney Fiske, Dec. 28, 1836. 4, Hulda Eliza, Dec. 13, 1838. 5, Moses Fiske, June 12, 1841, 6, Mary Maria, Mar. 17, 1847.

1607. ii. MARY CLEVES, b. in New Boston, Oct. 17, 1807; m. Robert Young, who died at Massena, St. Lawrence county, N. Y., Feb. 17, 1862. She had no issue, but her husband had a large family by his first wife.

1608. iii. NATHANIEL, b. 1810; d. aged seventeen years, a worthy member of the Methodist Episcopal church, and of the same church where other members of this family are of like standing.

1609. iv. MOSES, JR., b. Apr. 27, 1813, in Boston; m. at Lisbon, St. Lawrence county, N. Y., Aug. 2, 1824. He is a farmer at Lisbon, but had no children.

1610. v. HARRIET NEWELL, b. Aug. 30, 1815; m. Hiram Russell, a brother of her sister, Susan P——'s husband, and born at same place, June 21, 1814; reside at Fort Covington, and their children are all living, and several of them have children. 1, Briggs, b. Dec. 8, 1836. 2, Fanny, b. Apr. 28, 1839. 3, Mary, b. May 4, 1843. 4, James, b. Feb. 4, 1848. 5, Daniel, b. Feb. 20, 1850. 6, George, b. Aug. 12, 1853. 7, Caroline, b. July 24, 1855.

1611. vi. HULDAH WOODBURY, b. Sept. 29, 1817; d. unm., Dec. 31. 1844; she left a diary of her Christian experience, which she kept, now held by the family as a sacred memento of her.

1612. vii. PUTNAM BRADFORD, b. Sept. 9, 1820 m. ——, ——.

877. DAVID FISKE (Nathaniel, Theophilus, Theophilus, William, William, John, William, Robert, Simon, Simon, William, Symond), b. Topsfield, Nov. 24, 1783; m. Apr. 8, 1813, Nancy Baker, dau. of Moses and Hepzibah (Card) Baker; b. Hamilton, Aug. 19, 1786; d. Nov. 30, 1856. David, son of Nathaniel and Lydia (Gould) Fiske, m. Nancy Baker, resided with his father in Topsfield until two children were born, when they removed to New Ipswich, N. H., where three more children were born; in Ashburnham, Mass., and in Nov., 1843, removed to Byron, Ogle county, Ill., where some of his children had removed. He d. and his wife d. at the same place. He d. Sept. 5, 1851; res. Byron, Ill.

1613. i. LYDIA GOULD, b. Feb. 21, 1814; m. in Ashburnham, Oct. 4, 1837, Phineas Brown Spaulding, b. in Ashburnham, Oct. 14, 1815. His parents were Isaac Spaulding and Lydia Brown, who were of New Ipswich, N. H., resided in Worcester one year after they were married, five years in Fitchburg, where he carried on his business of cabinet making. Ill health compelled him to give up that business, and several months subsequently removed to Byron, Ill., where he commenced in 1844 the nursery business; and, eleven years after, removed to Beloit, Rock Co., Wis., where he deceased, Nov. 1, 1864. Ch.: 1, Alfred Foster, b. at Byron, Ill., Sept. 28, 1849; 2, Charles Washburn, b. at Byron, Ill., Aug. 12, 1851, and, 3, Ann Elizabeth, b. at Beloit, Wis., Dec. 26, 1856.

1614. ii. NATHANIEL GOLDSMITH, b. Mar. 12, 1817; m. Hannah Z. Springer, from Hallowell, Maine, in 1846; has resided in Natick, in Hopkinton, etc., and is (1867) in East Holliston, Mass. A carpenter by occupation. No children.

1615. iii. HEZIBETH CARD, b. at New Ipswich, Apr. 3, 1820, died June, 1863; m. Isreal Stone Knowlton, son of Benjamin and Olive, and b. in Newfane, Vt., Jan. 29, 1815. Settled in Byron, Ogle Co., Ill., where their children were born, namely: 1. Tryphena M., b. June 2, and d. in Oct., 1843; 2, Alvah Benjamin, b. Feb. 28, 1847; 3, Elsie Cornelia, b. Feb. 4, 1849; 4, Willie Henry, b. Dec. 3, 1845.

1616. iv. ELIZABETH HUBBARD, b. Feb. 2, 1822, in New Ipswich; m. July 10, 1845, Milo H. Smith, son of Friend and Salley (Rowe)

Smith, b. in Amherst, Hampshire Co., Mass., May 20, 1812; settled in Byron, Ogle Co., Ill., where all their children were born. And she died March 3, 1857. Her children were: 1, Owen, b. May 5, 1846; 2, Mary Esther, b. March 12, 1848; 3, Eldbridge F., b. Sept 2, 1850; 4, Maria Elizabeth, b. Dec. 1, 1852; 5, Henry A., b. Dec. 7, 1854; d. January, 1855; 7, Abby Nancy, b. Oct. 13, 1856.

1617.   v.   MARY ANNA PERKINS, b. at N. Ipswich, Feb. 25, 1824; d. unm. at Byron, Oct. 20, 1844.

1618.   vi.   MOSES BAKER, b. at Ashburnham, Mass., Mar. 14, 1828; m. May 14, 1854, Abby J. Whitaker, of West Boylston, Mass., but have no issue.

881.   SAMUEL FISKE (Samuel, Theophilus, Theophilus, William, William, John, William, Robert, Simon, Simon, William, Symond), b. Ipswich, Mass., May 7, 1773; m. Oct. 19, 1795, Sarah Patch, dau. of Samuel of Hamilton, b. 1778, d. March 1, 1833. He was baptised the 29th of the August following, which was the day his father owned the church covenant. He settled in western part of Wenham, where he died on the day he was 73 years old; but she deceased, aged 55. He d. May 7, 1846; res. Wenham, Mass.

1619.   i.   PATTY, b. Jan. 3, 1799; d. unm. ae. 33.

1620.   ii.   WILLIAM, b. Sept. 6, 1804, deceased, aged 16 years.

1621.   iii.   PAULINE, b. April 21, 1810; m. May 16, 18—, Eldbridge G., son of Warren Peabody, was b. in Wenham, Sept. 9, 1810, where they resided until their first child was born, and removed to Beverly, where they afterwards resided. Ch: 1. Sarah L., who died, aged 7 years, and, 2, Adeline Mullet, b. in Salem, Feb. 5, 1852.

1622.   iv.   SAMUEL BLANCHARD, 14, b. July 8, 1812; d. Nov. 5, 1845. aged 32 years; settled on his father's homestead which his widow sold to James Cook, and afterwards owned by Geo. Kimball. His widow resided near the church in Wenham. Her name is Harriet Frances, a daughter of Rev. William and Frances (Costigan) Dodge, and a granddaughter of John Dodge, of that part of the town called Wenham Neck. She was b. Dec. 29, 1810, and d. Nov. 18, 1883. Their daughter and only child was Martha Madalena, who died May 1, 1855, aged 20 years and 2 months, after marrying Ezra, son of Amos and Bethiah (Goodell) Hobbs, of Wenham, who died Oct. 5, 1853. aged about 23 years, and they had an only child who resided with her grandmother Fiske, whose name is Eliza Jane, born in Wenham, July 4, 1851.

882.   CAPT. EZRA FISKE (Samuel, Theophilus. Theophilus, William, William, John, William. Robert, Simon, Simon, William, Symond), b. Ipswich, Mass., Jan. 7, 1776; m. Dec. 31, 1800, Polly Lakeman of Hamilton, dau. of James and Mary (Brown) Lakeman, b. Dec. 13, 1778, d. Dec. 20, 1857. Ezra, son of Samuel and Sarah (Perkins) Fiske, who married Polly Lakeman, of Hamilton, resided in Beverly at the time his first and his last child was born, and Salem the rest of his life, where he deceased. He was a master mariner, and commanded the barque "Speed," in time of war 1812, when in the employ of Joseph Peabody; was taken by the British and put in prison at Bermuda, where he was kept during most of the time until the war ended. He d. April 6, 1827; res. Salem, Mass.

1623.   i.   JOHN BROWN, b. Oct. 1, 1804; m. Sarah Smith.

1624.   ii.   MARY, born Oct. 2, 1806, married July 12, 1831, James, son of James and Abigail (Cheever) Perkins, of Salem, have since resided in Bangor, Me., where two or three of their children were born; in Salem, Boston. and now Melrose, near the Wyoming station, on the Boston and Maine Railroad. He learnt the trade of blacksmith of his father; for some time followed the same business, and has since been in the machinery business. Their children have been: 1, Wm. Francis, b. June, 1835. who d. unm., July, 1867; 2. Mary Louisa, who is a widow without children, m. Edward Thayer, of Boston, a master mariner, who d. at New York; 3, James Fisk, who was in the U. S. army at the time of the rebellion, and now a seaman; 4, Edward B., d. young; 5, Chas. F., who went to sea and supposed deceased; and 6, Stephen Jarvis, b. about 1847, who is at home.

1625. iii. SOPHRONIA, b. May 24, 1808, in 1837 m. Richard, son of Richard and Lois (Devereux) Lindsey, b. in Marblehead, Feb. 22, 1809; res. on Broad Street, and had a trading store of West India goods and groceries on Layfayette Street, Salem. Their children were all born in Salem, namely: 1, Elizabeth, b. Dec. 22, 1838, who was a deaf mute from a child (the misfortune caused by scarlet fever), married James Denison, from Royalton, Vt., and he is so deaf that his way of conversation is, for the most part, by signs. They are teachers in the asylum at Washington,, D. C., where they reside. Have had no children.

1626. iv. MERCY, b. July 10, 1811; d. young.

1627. v. LOUISA, b. Sept. 5, 1812; m. Sept. 15, 1835, Mark Webster, of Bangor, Me., a lumber surveyor, and resided in that place until about 1862, when they removed to Chicago, Ill. His father, who was born in Fryeburg, Me., d. Mar., 1836, aged 64 years; and his mother, Mary, the dau. of Rev. Dr. Porter, d. about 1855, aged 75 years. Dr. Porter was about 96 years of age. Ch.: 1, an infant, d. young; 2, Ezra Fiske, b. Apr. 25, 1848. 3, Emery Abbott, b. Feb. 28, 1851, and Percy L., b. Oct. 10, 1852.

1628 vi. SARAH ANN, b. Dec. 2, 1814; m. William Page, of Salem, a cooper, and went to Newton, Mass., about 1841, where she d. Jan. 9, 1846, and he m. a Lydia Smith for his second wife. Her children were: 1. Sarah Ann, who resides with her father, m. Charles Chamberlain, of Watertown, who d. in Charlestown, by whom she had a son, George William, b. in Charlestown. 2, William Henry, whose wife is Harriet, who belonged in Richmond, Ind., resides in a western state, and has a son Thomas. 3, Mary Jane. 4, Harriet, d. young; and 5 ,Edwin Chapen.

1629. vii. ABIGAIL, b. Sept. 23, 1816; m. June 6, 1839, John Emery Abbott Todd, son of Jeremiah and Rebecca (Fabens) Todd. b. in Salem, Nov. 18, 1817. He is a shipmaster, residence corner of Porter and Cherry streets, Salem. That city has been his residence most of the time, but they were a while in South America, at Rio Grande, in Boston and Brazil. Ch.: 1, Nathaniel Mayhew, b. in Salem, Mar. 29, 1840, who is a shoemaker in Boston, m. Helen Augusta, dau. of Bradstreet Parker Woodman, of Haverhill, whose father was Col. John Woodman, of Haverhill (see Hist. and Genealogical Researches of Merrimack Valley) and they have a dau., Mary Abby, b. in Haverhill, Aug. 22, 1864; and 2, Mary A., the other child of Mrs. Todd, died, aged eight years.

1630. viii. CHARLES, b. Oct. 8, 1818, who d. at Accra, on the coast of Africa, Aug. 30, 1847, m. Judith Rhue, by whom he had a dau., Sarah Ann, who d. young, and his widow m. Ephraim Allen, of Salem.

1631. ix. CHARLOTTE, b. in Beverly Sept. 11, 1822; m. William Williams Whitmore, b. in Salem Sept. 1, 1821, son of Stephen and Betsey (Noyes) Whitmore. He is a bookkeeper in Boston, but now resides on Essex street, Salem. Their children have been 1, Charlotte E., who d. young. 2, William Fiske, b. in Salem May 30, 1851. 3. Edith, b. in Charlestown Apr. 11, 1853. 4. Jennie Emerson, b. in Charlestown Feb. 11, 1856. 5, Catie Meservey, b. in Salem May 12, 1860; and 6, Earnest Drayton, b. in Salem Mar. 3, 1865.

888. CAPT. JONATHAN FISK (Simeon, Ebenezer, Ebenezer, William, William, John, William, Robert, Simon, Simon, William, Symond), b. Shelburne, Mass., Oct. 18, 1790; m. in Leverett, Mass., in May, 1813, Susanna Williams, b. May 25, 1790; d. July 17, 1841; m. 2d, 1843, Mrs. Maria Roberts, d. 1845; m. 3d, 1850, Releafy Blood, d. Sept., 1852. Jonathan Fisk, son of Simeon and Diana (Whitcome) Fisk, was born at Shelburne Falls, Mass. He grew to manhood on his father's farm. He was married to Susanna Williams, daughter of Rev. Henry Williams, of Leverett, Mass. In 1816 or 1817 he moved with his family, wife and one daughter, to the state of Georgia, settling in Wilks County. In 1819 he returned to the north, settling in Windham County, Vermont. About 1824 he removed to Goshen, Orange County, N. Y., and in 1834 to Coshocton, Ohio, where his wife died. In 1843 he was married to Mrs. Maria Roberts, who lived but two years after. In the fall of 1849 he went to Terre Haute, Ind., where in 1850 he was married to Miss Releafy Blood. He was a farmer and mechanic, a cooper by trade. He was a ruling elder in the Presbyterian Church. At the time of the War of 1812 he was a captain in the Massachusetts militia, and was called out in the service of the state, but was never engaged in battle in the national service. He d. Aug. 21, 1853. res. Goshen, N. Y., and Terre Haute, Ind.

　1632.　i.　ESTHER SUSANNA, b. Feb. 13, 1814; m. in Coshocton, O., July 14, 1836, Jacob Welsh. She d. 1873.

　1633.　ii.　GEORGIANNA F., b. Nov. 14, 1818; m. Sept. 26, 1839, Washington Burt; res. Flint, Ohio. He was b. Aug. 3, 1813; d. Mar. 13, 1888. Ch.: Ellen, b. July 25, 1840; m. Hiram A. Taylor Sept. 26; res. Penty, Pa. Georgianna, b. June 27, 1843; m. I. M. Voorhees Nov. 27, 1862; res. Coshocton, Ohio. Chas. H., b. Feb. 22, 1845; m. Ada Richmond; res. Arkansas City, Kan. Maria, b. Nov. 16, 1843; m. H. K. Johnson Sept. 26, 1867; res. Flint, Ohio. Emma, b. Nov. 21, 1848; m. Henry C. Johnson Dec. 25, 1866; res. Flint, Ohio. Sarah A., b. Nov. 24, 1850; m. J. N. Thompson Dec. 18, 1872; res. Westerville, Ohio. Susanna, b. Apr. 10, 1853; m. Oliver Moore Sept. 20, 1879. George K., b. Apr. 12, 1855; m. Ida M. Case; res. Eureka, Kan. Allan D., b. Apr. 9, 1857; m. Nora Case; res. Eureka. Clara, b. July 30, 1869; m. John Hambleton; res. Hanford, Cal.

　1634.　iii.　EZRA W., b. May 29, 1820; m. Mary Van Dyke.

　1635.　iv.　JONATHAN, b. Aug. 15, 1825; d. unm. in Reno County, Kansas, Mar. 28, 1879. He was born in Goshen, N. Y. The family removed to Coshocton, Ohio, when he was nine years old. His mother died at that place when he was sixteen. In May, 1846, he enlisted for twelve months' service in the Mexican war; was in the Third Ohio Regiment, Company B. This regiment was not in any of the great battles of that war, being much of the time in garrison. At the expiration of his term he returned to Ohio. Soon afterward he went to the southern part of Indiana, where he entered land (with his land warrant), but did not settle on it. In 1850 he was called to Princeton, N. J., by the serious illness of his eldest brother, who had just graduated from the college at that place. He remained in the east two years, then returned to Indiana, and soon after engaged in the marble business at Hutsonville, Ill. In the fall of 1854 he closed his business at that place, sold his land in Indiana, and went to Minnesota, then a new territory. He took up a claim on government land, as yet unsurveyed, and yet only sixteen miles from the site of the present city of Minneapolis. He obtained this land under the pre-emption law, and it was his home for twenty-one years. In the fall of 1861 he visited his brother at Greencastle, Ind., and there enlisted in Company H, Forty-third Indiana Volunteers. With this regiment he was in numerous battles, among which were New Madrid, Ruddles Point, Helena and Marks' Mill. Near the close of his three years' term he was examined by a military board and recommended for a captain's commission, to command colored troops. The commission was issued, but before it reached the regiment his brigade was sent in charge of a wagon train from Camden to Pine Bluff, Ark. On the way, at Marks' Mill, they were attacked by a strong force of rebels, and after one of the most fiercely contested battles of the war, though not on a large scale, the lines were broken up and they were captured man by man. Fisk, who was a sergeant, was in command of the company through this action, there being no commissioned officer with it. He with the rest was taken to Tyler, Tex., and imprisoned in a stockade. The treatment was not so severe as at Libby or Andersonville, but it was bad enough. The whole long summer was spent in this wretched place, from April till late in September. Near the end of the latter month he with three others escaped, and after a journey of forty-eight days, traveling at night and hiding during the day much of the time, suffering from exposure to the weather with only a single suit of clothing, and that worn to rags before they started, and from hunger almost to the point of starvation, they finally reached the Union lines at Little Rock, Ark. As it was then considerably beyond the expiration of his term of enlistment, he received his discharge, and did not accept the commission tendered him, but returned to his home in Minnesota. During his absence in the army the Indian war occurred in Minnesota, and when he got to his place he found nothing left but his land, not a trace of a building (except ashes) and not a rail of a fence. He went to work to restore his improvements. In this he succeeded, though it was evident that his constitution was permanently injured by his severe army service and his prison experience. He lived at his Minnesota home until the summer of 1875, at which time he sold out, and after nearly two years spent in travel and prospecting, he settled in Reno County, Kansas, where he again established a home, but his health soon after became impaired and he died on the 28th of March, 1879. He was never married.

1636. v. HARRIETT MARIA, b. Aug. 25, 1823; m. at Coshocton, Ohio, Dec. 24, 1840, Lewis D. Roderic. She d. at Claremont, Ill., in Sept., 1872.

1637. vi. HENRY WILLIAMS, b. Nov. 6, 1833; m. Mary J. Stevenson.

893. RUFUS FISKE (Ebenezer, Ebenezer, Ebenezer, William, William, John, William, Robert, Simon, Simon, William, Symond), b. Shelburne, Mass., Mar. 22, 1781; m. 1807, Hannah Woodward. He d. Sept. 24, 1840; res. Shelburne, Mass.

1638. i. ANNA, b. Apr. 22, 1808; m. Daniel Fiske, son of Daniel.
1639. ii. FIDELIA, b. Oct. 24, 1810; d. July 11, 1814.
1640. iii. LAURA, b. Oct. 30, 1813; d. Mar. 6, 1815. .
1641. iv. FIDELIA, b. May 1, 1816, united with the church at Shelburne, under the pastoral care of Rev. Dr. Packard, in Jan., 1831. She was a pupil and then a teacher at Mount Holyoke Female Seminary, and partaking largely of the spirit of Mary Lyon, thoroughly accepting her views of Christian education, she would probably have been connected permanently with that institution but for the conviction in her own mind that she was called to the missionary field. She embarked at Boston, for the Nestorian mission, Mar. 1, 1843, in company with Mr. and Mrs. Perkins and Mar Yohannan, returning to Persia, and Messrs. D. T. Stoddard and E. E. Bliss and their wives, and Miss C. E. Myers, reached Oroomiah, June 14, of the same year, and after laboring there for fourteen years, was constrained by impaired health to return to the United States in 1858, and died at the house of her brother in Shelburne, July 26, 1864.

One who had known Miss Fiske long and well, says of her character and influence: "That she was generally regarded by those who knew her as a remarkable woman, was not owing to the predominance of any one quality in her character, but to a combination of qualities, intellectual and emotional, surpassing anything, as it seems to me, that I have ever seen in any other man or woman. I remember enough of her uncle, Pliny Fiske, the companion of Parsons in commencing the Palestine mission, to believe that he owed the stronghold he had upon popular interest to the same cause. Her emotional nature was wonderfully sanctified; and each of her powers being well developed, and all nicely adjusted one to another, the whole worked with regularity and ease. Hence that singular accuracy of judgment, that never failing sense of propriety, for which she was distinguished. Hence the apparent absence of fatigue in her protracted conversations and conversational addresses. Hence the habitual control of her sanctified affections, over her intellectual powers, so that she seemed ever ready at the moment, for the call of duty, and especially to meet the claims of perishing souls around her. In the structure and the working of her nature, she was the nearest approach I ever saw to my ideal of the Saviour, as he appeared when on earth. "The amount of her usefulness is as extraordinary as her character. The book entitled 'Woman and her Saviour in Persia,' strikingly sets forth her influence on Nestorian character, and I doubt not it would be the judgment of the mission, that few of their number exerted so great a formative influence on the Nestorian mind, as did this departed sister. Certainly the tidings of no death could awaken so many voices of lamentation, as will the tidings of hers, over the plain of Oroomiah, and in the glens and fastnesses of Koordistan." At the time of her death was engaged in writing "Recollections of Mary Lyon" (Boston, 1866). See the memoir of Miss Fisk, by the Rev. Daniel T. Fiske, D. D., entitled "Faith Working by Love" (1868).

1642. v. LAURA, b. May 20, 1819.
1643. vi. HANNAH, b. 1822; d. Oct. 17, 1840.

895. DEA. EBENEZER FISKE (Ebenezer, Ebenezer, Ebenezer, William, William, John, William, Robert, Simon, Simon, William, Symond), b. Shelburne, Mass., Apr. 18, 1785; m. in Abington, Mass., 1809, Hannah Terrill, of Abington, b. 1785; d. May 11, 1866. Ebenezer, second son of Ebenezer and Sarah Fiske, married Hannah Terrill. He always lived in Shelburne, Mass. Brought up on a farm, he received a common education. His farm and saw mill together with the country tavern he ran occupied his time. He was an upright, honest man in all his business life, and was chosen deacon of the church in Shelburne in 1821, which office he held until his death in 1846. He d. Dec. 25, 1846; res. Shelburne, Mass.

1644. i. CLARISSA TERRILL, b. Feb. 18, 1811; m. May 7, 1835, Frank Mather. She d. Feb. 24, 1892, in Painesville, Ohio.
1645. ii. FRANCIS ALVAREZ, b. July 8, 1813; m. Melinda O. Bardwell.
1646. iii. EBENEZER, b. Aug. 28, 1815; m. Elizabeth Smead.
1647. iv. PLINEY, b. July 30, 1817; m. Orrilla Peck.
1648. v. DANIEL TAGGART, b. Mar. 29, 1819; m. Eliza P. Dutton and Mrs. Caroline Walworth Drummond.
1649. vi. CHARLOTTE TAGGART, b. Apr. 6, 1822; m. Apr. 1, 1847, Francis L. Slate; res. Bernardston, Mass. He was b. Feb. 23, 1818; d. June 2, 1874; was a farmer. Ch.: 1, Ann Eliza, b. Aug. 11, 1848; m. Sept. 17, 1873, —— Hall; res. Worcester, Mass. 2, Ellen E.; res. Bernardston, Mass.
1650. vii. ISAAC TERRILL, b. July 27, 1824; m. Hannah Parsons and Rosanna Crosby.
1651. viii. HENRY MARTYN, b. Aug. 21, 1827; m. Jan. 4, 1855, Ellen Gale; res. Heath, Mass.
1651¼. ix. LEVI PARSONS, b. Mar. 23, 1829; d. unm.

897. HON. LEVI FISKE (Ebenezer, Ebenezer, Ebenezer, William, William, John, William, Robert, Simon, Simon, William, Symond), b. Shelburne, Mass., Feb. 21, 1790; m. in Buckland, Apr. 27, 1819, Cynthia Coleman, b. May 18, 1779; d. July 12, 1851. He settled in Byron, Gen. County, N. Y., where he established himself as a successful woolen manufacturer. In 1851 and 1852 he represented his district in the State Legislature, and for above twenty years has been a deacon and elder in the Presbyterian Church. Of his six children, two were sons, John S. and Pliny B. A son-in-law, Loren Green, was also a member of the Legislature, in 1863 and 1864. He d. Sept. 16, 1878; res. Byron, N. Y.

 1652. i. JOHN SHELDON, b. Feb. 27, 1820; m. Sarah Green. He d. s. p. Jan. 2, 1894. She d. Mar. 12, 1866.
 1653. ii. CLARISSA, b. Sept. 8, 1822; d. Aug. 20, 1889.
 1654. iii. CYNTHIA C., b. Jan. 28, 1823; d. Jan. 22, 1894.
 1655. iv. EUSEBIA N., b. Apr. 19, 1829; d. Mar. 18, 1861.
 1656. v. PLINY BEYROOT, b. Dec. 8, 1830; m. Jane A. Walker.
 1657. vi. ABIGAIL, b. Oct. 25, 1825; m. Oct. 13, 1852, Loren Green; Station "D," Los Angeles, Cal. He was b. July 23, 1822; d. Feb. 12, 1879; was a farmer and miller. Ch.: 1, Andrew Fisk Green, b. Apr. 25, 1855; d. Mar. 25, 1873. 2, Arthur Hunter Green, b. July 3, 1856; now living at Los Angeles, Cal. 3, Levi Worthington Green, b. Mar. 1, 1858, Los Angeles, Cal., Station D.
   4, Herber Loren Green, b. Sept. 20, 1864, Los Angeles, Cal.

902. REV. PERRIN BACHELDER FISKE (Moses, Ebenezer, Ebenezer, William, William, John, William, Robert, Simon, Simon, William, Symond), b. Waitesfield, Vt., July 6, 1792; m. in Wardsboro, May 1, 1815, Azubah Blaisdell, dau. of Perrit and Ruth, b. Dec. 14, 1794, d. in Wardsboro, Vt., Mar. 19, 1846. Perrin B., eldest son of Deacon Moses and Hannah Fiske, commenced life as a mechanic, but the love of religion took him from a profitable employment and placed him in the ranks of missionary laborers. He was ordained a minister in the Baptist church; possesses good natural abilities, but never enjoyed the facilities for a liberal education. "Had he lived in these more favored days or enjoyed modern advantages, he would have richly adorned the ministerial calling." He was an acceptable preacher in his denomination, and lived to see the good results of his ministry. He d. Mar. 19, 1846; res. West Wardsboro, Vt., and Fort Covington, N. Y.

 1658. i. THOMAS BRIGGS, b. June 27, 1823; m. Amaritt Bartlett.
 1659. ii. MOSES, b. Oct. 20, 1817; m. Dec. 24, 1837, at Moretown, Vt., Orvilla Foster and had one dau. who died in childhood.
 1660. iii. ELLEN HANNAH, b. Sept. 4, 1832; m. 1850 Lewis Hart of Jamaica, Vt. Ch.: Louisa A., b. 1851; m., 1869, W. Irving Howard, res. E. Jamaica. Ellen, d. 1854; 2 ch., Dana I. and Lewis A., b. 1877.
 1661. iv. WILLIAM WALLACE, b. Mar. 5, 1816; d. July 16, 1826.

903. HON. MOSES FISKE (Moses, Ebenezer, Ebenezer, William, John, William, Robert, Simon, Simon, William, Symond), b. Waitesfield, Vt., July 25, 1794; m. ———————; m. 2d Rebecca Ferrin. Moses, son of Deacon Moses and Hannah Fiske, was a prominent citizen of Waterville, Vt., where he successfully held the office of Town Clerk for twenty-five years, Justice of the Peace, Representative eight years, State Senator and Judge. He was also a deacon of the Congregational Church in Waterville. He d. Feb. 18, 1853; res. Waterville, Vt.

 1662. ix. HENRY CLAY, b. July 22, 1852; m. Isabel M. Page.
 1663. i. INFANT, b. 1826; d. 1826.
 1664. ii. CORNELIA ANN PARMELEE, b. Aug. 19, 1828; m. 1850 Hon. Thomas Gleed; res. Morrisville, Vt. Hon. Thomas Gleed was son of the Rev. John Gleed of Lyme Regis and London, Eng., and was b. there in 1825. He had only a primary school education, became a lawyer, settled in Morrisville, Vt., became States Attorney, served several terms in the State Senate and died as he was preparing to enter the army. She d. Jan. 10, 1889. Ch.: 1, Thomas Fred, b. 1852; d. 1854. 2, Charles Sumner, b. Mar. 23, 1856. Charles S. Gleed m. June 28, 1888, at Lawrence, Kan., Mabel Edith Gore, b. Apr. 19, 1867. Ch.:

Cornelia Gleed, b. Oct. 7, 1891. He was educated in the common schools of Vermont and Kansas and the University of Kansas. Went from Vermont to Kansas in his tenth year, residing in Lawrence. Finishing school he became an editor, then entered the railway business, then became chief clerk of law department of Atchison, Topeka & Santa Fe R. R. company, then became (1884) editor in chief of the Denver Daily Tribune, then began private practice of the law in Topeka (1885) with his brother Prof. James Willis Gleed, formerly of the University of Kansas. Is regent of Kansas State University and director of Atchison, Topeka & Santa Fe Ry, and sundry other corporations. Is author of various magazine articles, pamphlets and addresses. 3, James Willis, b. Mar. 8, 1859; m. Aug. 25, 1886, Grace Greer, b. June 27, 1866; is a lawyer; ch.: Mary E. and Dorothy C.; res. Topeka. 4, Thomas Fisk, b. 1861, d. 1864.

1665. iii. JAMES HARVEY, b. 1830; d. 1855.
1666. iv. ANNA MARY, b. 1832; m., 1852, J. Coleman Burnett; res. Montpelier, Vt. Ch.: 1, Mary Cornelia, b. 1853; m. ——— Whitney; 2, Edward Fisk, b. 1855; 3, Walter Calvin; 4, Charles Harris; 5, Wm. C.; 6, John C.; 7, Frederick.
1667. v. JOSIAH MOSES, b. 1834; m. and had dau. Cornelia.
1668. vi. JOEL BATCHELDER, b. 1837; m. and had 2 ch. d. infancy.
1669. vii. HARRIS WM., b. 1840; d. 1841.
1670. viii. HARRIS MYRON, b. 1842.

904. REV. JOEL FISKE (Moses, Ebenezer, Ebenezer, William, William, John, William, Robert, Simon, Simon, William, Symond), b. Waitesfield, Vt., Oct. 16, 1796; m. Oct. 15, 1826, Clarinda Chapman, b. June 21, 1803; d. Jan. 15, 1878. Joel, third son of Deacon Moses and Hannah Fiske, fitted for college at Montpelier Academy. He read theology with Rev. Charles Walker, D. D., of Rutland, Vt., 1825-26, graduated at Middlebury College, Vermont, in 1825, in which State he principally labored in the ministry. He was distinguished for originality of thought rather than depth of research, but also for great zeal and devotion to his Master's service. In this, his efforts were greatly blessed, for many souls, through his instrumentality, were brought to the knowledge of redeeming grace. His discourses usually produced a marked impression. Sometimes a Scriptural truth would be presented in such relations that the congregation would be thrilled and set to thinking as for their lives. He began his ministry at about thirty years of age and was successively settled in Monkton 1826-30 and New Haven, Vt., 1830-32 Essex, N. Y., 1832-44 a missionary at Phillipsburgh, Canada East, 1844-45 and Plainfield, Vt., where his labors closed. He published one or more sermons. He d. Dec. 16, 1856; res. Plainfield, Vt.

1671. i. PLINY, b. May 10, 1828; m. Helen Burlay and Elizabeth C. Hall.
1672. ii. CLARINDA CHAPMAN, b. Nov. 27, 1829; m., 1852, L. W. Adgate. She d. May 13, 1854. Had one child who died young.
1673. iii. HARVEY, b. Apr. 26, 1831; m. Louisa Green.
1674. iv. SARAH J., b. Dec. 12, 1835; m. Henry Kinney; res. Plainfield, Vt. Ch.: Wm. C., b. 18—; m. 1890; add. 28 Nassau St., N. Y. City; and Sarah J., d. 1864.
1675. v. MARY I., b. Apr. 9, 1838; m., 1877,, L. W. Adgate; res. E. Hardwick, Vt. She d. 1878.
1676. vi. DANIEL C., b. Nov., 1840; m. ———, ———.
1677. vii. RICHARD HENRY, b. Nov. 17, 1842; m. and d. 1868.

905. REV. HARVEY FISKE (Moses, Ebenezer, Ebenezer, William, William, John, William, Robert, Simon, Simon, William, Symond), b. Waitesfield, Vt., Apr. 12, 1799; m. Feb. 17, 1829, Anna Mary Plumb. Harvey, fourth son of Deacon Moses and Hannah Fiske, graduated at Hamilton College, in 1826, and studied theology at Princeton—but had previously spent some years in that most practical and efficient of all training schools—the printing office, where he learned, not only the art of conducting a newspaper, but the secret of guiding and controlling the popular mind. He was never settled as a pastor, but labored as State missionary in New Jersey, principally in the cause of Sabbath-schools, and with the most

marked success, until his health, previously shattered by his great efforts to complete his education, gave way altogether, after three years of a most useful ministry. He was noted for vivacity yet soundness of mind, for quickness of apprehension and perseverance in application. His death suddenly closed a career of much promise at the age of thirty-one years. He d. Mar. 5, 1831; res. in New Jersey.

    1678. i.   HARVEY JONATHAN, b. July 2, 1830; res. Buffalo.

    906. DEA. LYMAN FISKE (Moses, Ebenezer, Ebenezer, William, William, John, William, Robert, Simon, Simon, William, Symond), b. Waitesfield, Vt., Oct. 15, 1801; m. at Moretown, Vt., Oct. 14, 1828, Mary Spofford, b. Nov. 14, 1801; d. Mar., 1879. Lyman Fiske, fifth son of Deacon Moses and Hannah Fiske, was a substantial citizen in Waitesfield, Vt., and a deacon of the Congregational Church in that place. He was a cooper by trade and followed farming most of his life. No one acquainted with the religious history of the town of Waitesfield can forget the constant part in it of Deacon Fisk. Almost from the beginning of the Congregational organization he has been identified with it. Deacon Fisk's very name is both an honored inheritance and an honored legacy. On the 8th of Nov., 1801, his father became a member of the church, and soon after was made deacon, a position which he held honorably for more than forty years. Lyman professed his Christian faith in his sixteenth year, and a few years before his father's death, which occurred in 1847, was also elected deacon, serving forty years. The family connection with this sacred office is perpetuated in his nephew, Deacon E. A. Fisk. He d. Dec. 14, 1884; res. Waitesfield, Vt.

    1679. iv.   PERRIN BATCHELOR, b. July 3, 1837; m. Harriett L. Bigelow.
    1680. i.   NORONA AUGUSTA, b. July 5, 1830; m. Hiram B. Cross; res. 21 Hubbard St., Montpelier, Vt. Ch.: Wm. Henry, b. 1858; d. 1858.
    1681. ii.   JONATHAN ALBIN, b. Jan. 12, 1832; d. Mar., 1842.
    1682. iii.   THERON EZRA, b. May, 1834; d. Mar., 1839.
    1683. v.   MARY ELINOR, b. Apr. 19, 1840; res. 21 Hubbard St., Montpelier, Vt.
    1684. vi.   BETSEY AMANDA, b. Feb. 5, 1842; res. 21 Hubbard St., St., Montpelier.
    1685. vii.   HARRIETT CLARINDA, b. Mar. 21, 1845; res. 21 Hubbard street, Montpelier.

    908. ANSON FISK (Moses, Ebenezer, Ebenezer, William, William, John, William, Robert, Simon, Simon, William, Symond), b. Waitesfield, Vt., Oct. 31, 1806; m. there Nov. 24, 1835, Joanna Barnard, b. Oct. 12, 1810; d. Dec. 21, 1891. She was dau. of Ebenezer. After becoming of age he worked at the cooper's trade three years, first at Williston, Vt., and then at Monkton, Vt. He then returned to Waitesfield and purchased a small farm, and for a time followed his trade in connection with it. In after years by various additions to the original purchase he became the owner of an excellent farm which fully occupied his time. He was a man of good business ability, and unblemished Christian character. His early opportunities for education were limited, but he kept himself well abreast with the times by thorough and systematic reading. For over fifty years he was a faithful member of Waitesfield Congregational Church, and was ever ready to give of his time, money or influence for its support, and, what is far better, his daily life was such that none could speak a word to his reproach. He d. Oct. 2, 1880; res. Waitesfield, Vt.

    1686. i.   CAROLINE SEMANTHA, b. Nov. 22, 1837; m. Sept. 8, 1868, Orrin H. Joslin. She d. Feb. 4, 1888. Ch.: 1, Ervin Stephen, b. June 5, 1870; m. Dec. 5, 1894, Elizabeth Ward; res. W. 2, Mabel Ruth, b. Aug. 22, 1871; res. W. 3, Fidelia L., b. June 25, 1873; res. W.
    1687. ii.   EDWARD ANSON, b. Feb. 1, 1842; m. Lilian A. Ramsay.
    1688. iii.   FIDELIA JOANNA, b. Jan. 14, 1845; d. Oct. 5, 1867.
    1689. iv.   PLINY BARNARD, b. May 6, 1850; m. Caroline Clarke.

    909. JONATHAN FISK (Moses, Ebenezer, Ebenezer, William, William, John, William, Robert, Simon, Simon, William, Symond), b. Waitesfield, Vt., May 6, 1809; m. at Allentown, N. J., Jan. 14, 1834, Mary A. Imlay, b. Mar. 23, 1814.

Jonathan Fiske was for many years cashier of the Mechanics' (National) Bank, Trenton, N. J., and also an elder in the Presbyterian Church. He d. Dec. 5, 1872; res. Trenton and Allentown, N. J.

    1690. i.   HARVEY, b. ———; d. young.

    913. HON. JONATHAN FISKE (Jonathan, William, Ebenezer, William, William, John, William, Robert, Simon, Simon, William, Symond), b. Amherst, N. H., Sept. 6, 1773; m. ——— Livingston. Jonathan, eldest son of Judge Jonathan Fiske, started from Williamstown, Vt., for New York City, where he supported himself for some years by teaching school, meantime devoting himself to a thorough study of the mystery of law. A good classical scholar, he had among his more distinguished pupils Theodosia, only daughter and child of Aaron Burr. After being admitted to the bar, Mr. Fiske established himself in a very successful practice of law at Newburgh, N. Y., until he was chosen a representative of Congress during the first term of President Madison's administration, by whom he was subsequently appointed to the office of the United States attorney for the southern district of New York. From the pecuniary emolument of his extensive practice, while in this position, he speedily acquired a handsome property.

Jonathan Fiske was a man of fine figure, tall, well proportioned, of courtly manners and elegant address. He was married to a descendant of the Livingston family of New York and had four children, Mary, the latter, a very lovely child. Theodore was a man of bright talents, educated at Columbia College, New York City, and settled in the practice of law with his father at Newburgh. Jonathan Fiske died in 1823, and his children, none of whom ever married, followed him some years later. The family has now become extinct. He d. 1823; res. Newburgh, N. Y.

    1691. i.   THEODORE DWIGHT, b. ———; d. unm.
    1692. ii.   JAMES LIVINGSTON, b. ———; d. unm.
    1693. iii. JOSEPHINE ADELIA, b. ———; d. unm.
    1694. iv. MARY, b. ———; d. unm.

    914. NATHANIEL FISKE (Jonathan, William, Ebenezer, William, William, John, William, Robert, Simon, Simon, William, Symond), b. Amherst, N. H., July 6, 1775; m. Dec. 1, 1796, Mehitable Bates; b. 1770; d. Aug. 13, 1826; m. 2d, ——— ———. She d. s. p. He was a farmer. He d. May 3, 1861; res. Williamstown and Northfield. Vt.

    1695. i.   JOSEPH WILLOUGHBY, b. Nov. 29, 1797; m. Louisa Carpenter and Clarissa Buck.
    1696. ii.   MARTHA, b. Feb. 6, 1800; m., 1823, Chester Buck. She d. Sept., 1865. Ch.: Chancey, Mashall, Martha and William, whose s. res. Clinton, Mass.
    1697. iii. JONATHAN, b. May 12, 1804; m. Dolly Carrier.
    1698. iv. DANIEL, b. Dec. 4, 1805; d. in 1831.
    1699. v.   SAMUEL BATES, b. Sept. 25, 1807; d. Nov. 10, 1810.
    1700. vi. DAVID ALLEN, b. June 8, 1810; m. Rhoda B. Putnam and Sarah Morrison.
    1701. vii. NATHANIEL CURTIS, b. July 3, 1813; m. Elizabeth Putnam.
    1702. viii. SAMUEL NEWELL, b. June 25, 1817; m. Lucy M. Gooch.

    915. DEA. WILLIAM ROBY FISKE (Jonathan, William, Ebenezer, William, William, John, William, Robert, Simon, Simon, William, Symond), b. Williamstown, Vt., May 30, 1779; m. there Dec. 4, 1800, Hannah Martin, b. 1781; d. Sept., 1824. William Fiske, third son of Judge Jonathan Fiske, resided as a merchant in Williamstown, where he was married by his father to Hannah Martin. In 1816-17 he removed thence to Newburgh, N. Y., where his eldest brother had been engaged in the practice of law, and there remained about three years, when he removed to the town of Liberty, Sullivan County, N. Y., and drove the stakes of his future home in what was then the depth of a primeval forest, but which is now the site of a flourishing village called Parksville. He cut down the first tree and erected the first building in the place. An original settler, he was for many years one of the leading men of the town; a deacon of the Baptist Church. During the latter years of his life he was surrounded by many of his descendants, venerable in years and greatly esteemed in the community. Nine of his grandsons

did good and loyal service in the Union armies. He d. July, 1867, in Parksville, N. Y.; res. Williamstown, Vt., Newburgh,and Parksville, N. Y.

1703. i. EUNICE, b. Oct. 7, 1802; m. Dec. 25, 1822, Henry David. They had eight children, named as follows: Hannah, Mary, Harriet, Daniel H., William E., Horace, Wallace, Plymouth and Eunice. Four grandchildren are also reported.

1704. ii. JONATHAN, b. May 12, 1804; d., unm., July 8, 1895.

1705. iii. MARY, b. Aug. 15, 1806; d. in 1808.

1706. iv. AARON MARTIN, b. Aug. 15, 1808; m. Elizabeth Carrier.

1707. v. WILLIAM R., b. Nov. 18, 1810; m. Sophia Stowell.

1708. vi. MARY, b. Nov. 22, 1812; m., 1830, G. M. L. Hardenburgh. Names of their children: Nancy M., Sarah Ann, William Martin, Arietta Caroline, Jaspar Newton, Hannah Elizabeth, Catherine Jaspar, Jonathan, Benjamin Franklin, Milton Lewis, Sophia Louisa, Elma Jane, Florence; res. Liberty, N. Y. Mary Hardenburgh d. Feb. 26, 1863. The names of twelve of her grandchildren have been reported.

1709. vii. SARAH F., b. Oct. 1, 1816; m. Ebenezer Bush. Their children were Abiel and Luther.

1710. viii. HARRIET F., b. Mar. 16, 1822; m. Apr. 6, 1836, William Bradley.Names of their children as follows: Walter, Napoleon B., Wolcott, William A., Frank M., Josephine,.Alma I., Carrie E.

1711. ix. LUKE, b. Jan. 16, 1825.

917. JOHN FISKE (Jonathan, William, Ebenezer, William, William, John, William, Robert, Simon, Simon, William, Symond), b. Williamstown, Vt., Feb. 24, 1738; m. there Nov. 16, 1805, Elizabeth Martin. He was the fifth son of Judge Fiske and resided in Williamstown until after his marriage, when he located in Northfield, where he was accidentally killed by the cars in 1860. His children were all born in Williamstown. He d. 1860; res. Williamstown and Northfield, Vt.

1712. i. OLIVE, b. Dec. 11, 1806; m. Mar. 24, 1829, Marvin Simons; res. Northfield, Vt. Ch.: Marcellus Lycergus, Darwin, Cordelia A., Olive M., Elmer A., William.

1713. ii. BETSEY, b. Dec. 28, 1808; d. Dec. 3, 1847.

1714. iii. SALOMA, b. May 28, 1810; m. Dec. 8, 1828, Isaac Hardin. Ch.. Dennison, Lucius, Elizabeth, Mark and Maria.

1715. iv. JOHN, b. Oct. 8, 1811; d. May 2, 1812.

1716. v. LYDIA, b. May 14, 1813; m. Charles Morton. Ch.: 1, Anna; 2, Lucinda.

1717. vi. LINDIA, b. Feb. 8, 1815; d. Apr. 16, 1823.

1718. vii. EUNICE, b. Dec. 27, 1816; m. Dec., 1837, Amaziah Williams. Ch.: 1, George; 2, Ellen; 3, Charles; 4, Warren.

1719. viii. AZRO J., b. Aug. 3, 1818; m. Almira Capron.

1720. ix. SARAH, b. May 18, 1820; m. 1853 Elijah Pride. Ch.: 1, Alvin, 2, Alanson; 3, George; 4, Willie O.

1721. x. LUCINDA, b. May 7, 1822; d. Mar. 22, 1825.

1722. xi. MARIA, b. Dec. 14, 1823.

1723. xii. MARY, b. Feb. 18, 1826.

1724. xiii. HANNAH, b. Nov. 27, 1828.

918. BENJAMIN FISKE*(Jonathan, William, Ebenezer, William, William, John, William, Robert, Simon, Simon, William, Symond), b. Williamstown, Vt., Nov. 17, 1784; m. at Barre, Hannah Herrick. Benjamin Fiske, sixth son of Judge Jonathan Fiske, married at Barre, Vt.; had seven children, five died young. Benjamin was for many years a merchant in Northfield and subsequently an inn keeper at Burlington, where for some time he held the position under the government as collector of public revenue. He died at Burlington in 1860, where his family afterwards resided. He d. 1860; res. Northfield and Burlington, Vt.

1725. i. DELPHINE, b. September 24, 1808; d. August 7, 1839.

1726. ii. BENJAMIN P., b. May 27, 1811; d. May 7, 1834.

1727. iii. JOHN DENNISON, b. May 3, 1813; d. September 6, 1828.

1728. iv. CAROLINE, b. September 10, 1815; d. December 23, 1831.

1729. v. SOPHIA, b. April 8, 1819; m. T. W. Lovell at Burlington, and

14

had five children. 1, Lucy S., born in 1843, married Capt. John T. Drew, served in the 2d Reg. Vt. Vols. in the civil war; they had one child. 2, Carrie E., born in 1845. 3. Helen, born in 1848. 4. George T., born in 1852; and 5, Eugene W., born in 1854.   (

1730. vi.   ROSINA, b. December 2, 1822; d. September 10, 1826.
1731. vii. JOHN DENNISON, b. Sept. 10, 1826; m. Martha M. White.

922. DAVID FISKE (Jonathan, William, Ebenezer, William, William, John, William, Robert, Simon, Simon, William, Symond), b. Williamstown, Vt., Feb. 21, 1793; m. Sarah Reed, of Weston, Vt. David Fiske, the seventh son of Judge Jonathan Fiske, pursued for many years the occupation of blacksmith, at Williamstown and at Northfield, in which trade he was instructed by his own father. His wife was a Sarah Reed, of Weston, Vt., by whom he had seven ch. David Fiske d. in Jan., 1864, aged 71 years. His widow lived with her children in Northfield, and had in her possession the old family Bible, brought from New Hampshire. Mr. Fiske was a man of powerful physical frame and good natural abilities, a class leader in the M. E. church, and generally respected by his townsmen. He d. Jan., 1864; res. Northfield, Vt.

1732. i.   SARAH ANN, b. Feb. 28, 1818; m. Robert Bolgar, b. Oct. 28, 1812, who d. some years since in Lowell. His widow m. 2d Abel S. Williams. He is a retired farmer; res. Northfield, Vt. Ch.: 1, Ellen E. Badger, b. Apr. 24, 1846; 2, Kneeland A., b. Feb. 28, 1839; d. Oct. 19, 1864, in the civil war; 3, Elizabeth, b. May 26, 1841; d. Aug. 29, 1868; 4, Carlton, b. Mar. 27, 1843; d. Aug., 1870.
1733. ii.   DAVID R., b. ———; m. Martha Moercroft, Northfield, Vt. Ch.: 1, Martha.
1734. iii. HARRY, b. ———; d. Boston.
1735. iv.   ANN ELIZA, b. ———; m. at Northfield, Sept. 8, 1845, William Moercroft, Jr., a woolen manufacturer of Montpelier. They have two boys and two girls; res. Barre, Vt.
1736. v.   GEORGE M., b. ———; b. Jane E. Nichols.
1737. vi.   FANNIE C., b. ———; m. Apr. 28, 1850, H. A. Brown of Northfield. They had two children.
1738. vii. VAN LOREN, b. ———; d. unm. Dec., 1863; was in the war.

923. DEACON SAMUEL LOLLEY FISKE (Jonathan, William, Ebenezer, William, William, John, William, Robert, Simon, Simon, William, Symond), b. Oct. 24, 1794; m. Mar. 11, 1823, Lucy White, b. Oct. 28, 1799, dau. of Deacon Paul. Samuel Lolly Fiske, youngest son of Judge Jonathan Fiske, was appointed register of probate by his father at the age of 16 years, which position he retained until his father retired from public life. In the spring of 1820 he removed with his aged parents to Berlin, Vt., and settled on a farm, ministering to their necessities until their death. In 1827 Mr. Fiske returned to Williamstown and resided there several years, filling in a measure his father's place in that community. In 1840, sensible of the importance of giving his children better educational facilities than were within reach at that point, he removed to Malone, N. Y., and placed them in the Franklin Academy, where his oldest son, Pliny, a promising student, was fitted to enter Burlington College the very year he died, and his two daughters were also qualified to become successful teachers, which they afterwards did for some years. Mr. Fiske was elected deacon of the Congregational Church in Williamstown in 1832, and upon his removal to Malone, he was re-elected to that position in 1844. Deacon Fiske was never a seeker for political emolument or distinction, but nevertheless has on various occasions been honored by the free preference of his townsmen for local or county offices. A man of the strictest integrity and sound judgment of benevolent Christian aims, he sought rather to do the work of a faithful servant of Christ than to win applause of men. The worthy scion of the Puritan stock, he lived a busy, useful life, and left to his surviving children a spotless name and example. Res. Berlin and Williamstown, Vt.

1739. i.   SAMUEL GEORGE PLINY, b. Dec. 11, 1823; d. June, 9, 1842.
1740. ii.   JOHN DENNISON, b. Feb. 9, 1825; m. Harriett Elizabeth Blaisdell.

1741. iii. MARY JANE, b. July 24, 1829; m. June 12, 1860, George D. Bell. Mr. Bell was born in Waybridge, Vt., June 11, 1817. He was formerly a teacher, and is now a farmer.

1742. iv. LUCY ANN, b. Dec. 22, 1832; m. Jan. 25, 1855, Adin Williams. Ch.: Winifred John, b. Jan. 1, 1856; Lucy Pamela, b. Jan. 20, 1860.

925. HON. EZRA FISKE (William, William, Ebenezer, William, William, John, William, Robert, Simon, Simon, William, Symond) b. Amherst, N. H., Apr. 2, 1776; m. May, 1799, Melinda Blake, b. 1784; d. 1868. Ezra Fiske, first son and second child of Hon. Wm. and Eunice Nourse Fiske, was born at Amherst, N. H. His father was a farmer and shoemaker. The sterility of the land, the poverty following the Revolution, and his father's having a large family of children, compelled him to assist in the support of the family. He worked on the farm in summer, on the shoe bench in winter, and received but a very limited education, being but a few months in the public schools of that day. He, however, gained much knowledge from reading by the light of pine knots during winter evenings. After he arrived at the age of twenty-one, he attended the Amherst Academy for over a year, taught school, and in May, 1799, moved to Maine and bought land in Fayette. He soon after married Melenda Blake, daughter of Robert and Martha Dudley Blake, who were natives of New Ipswich, N. H. He settled on his land, where he and his wife enjoyed a married life of over sixty-seven years, she dying at the age of eighty-four. He survived her two years and died at the age of ninety-four years and six months. There were born unto them sixteen children, twelve of whom grew to manhood and womanhood. Robert Blake was a Revolutionary soldier, and Martha Dudley, a descendant of the Dudley family of England, both being descendants of early New England colonists. Melenda Blake inherited the resolute and sterling qualities of her parents, and much of Ezra Fiske's success in life must be accredited to her assistance. Ezra Fiske in early life evinced mechanical ingenuity, and at sixteen, with but few tools to work with, made a violin without assistance. In after life he invented a number of useful machines, among which was the machine which first successfully molded brick. He made the models and many of the drafts of his inventions for the patent office. He entered the militia in the town of Fayette as drummer, and became successively Clerk and Lieutenant of the company, and served as Adjutant during two colonelcies. He taught in the public schools for twenty-one years and served on the board of school examiners for twenty-three years. He revised Fiske-Murray's "Grammar for Advanced Students," producing a work for the primary grades. He served for twenty-two years on the Board of Selectmen of his town. He served as Justice of the Peace successively for thirty-five years. He represented his town in the Massachusetts Legislature in 1812-13, and the Maine Legislature in 1829-31, and was also a member of the Constitutional Convention which formed the constitution of the State of Maine. He was a member of the Massachusetts Legislature when Elbridge Gerry introduced the first "Gerrymander Bill," and although of the same politics as Mr. Gerry, bitterly opposed the bill as not only outraging the rights of the people, but as being impolitic. He held political office over forty-five years. In politics, his admiration for the views held by Washington and Hamilton, and his fears of the French red republican influence over Jefferson, made him a stanch follower of the former and their successors. He afterwards became a Whig, and died a Republican. In his religious views he was reared a Congregationalist, the views of which church he early embraced; but afterwards became a Baptist, and lived an honored member of that denomination for sixty-seven years. In both his politics and religion he differed from the other members of his father's family. He was a member of the Masonic order for sixty-seven years, and at his death was the oldest Mason in the State of Maine. His funeral was conducted by the Masonic order. Although commencing with but limited education, by self-instruction, he succeeded in acquiring a great fund of general information.

The children of Ezra and Melinda Fiske inherited excellent constitutions and fine natural abilities, improved in some instances by a knowledge of books and familiar intercourse with the world. The sons were active, stirring and enterprising men, and the daughters comely and well favored personally. Francis Nourse, the eldest, was a substantial and respectable farmer in his native town.

Allen was for many years a member of the Kennebec bar and also served as Justice of the Peace. Franklin, perhaps the best educated of the family, was a successful teacher in several of the States, traveled extensively and possessed good literary abilities.

When the Rebellion broke out, the family of Ezra Fiske partook of the military spirit which swept through the North. Franklin early enlisted and became a Captain in one of the famous Illinois cavalry regiments. His brother Allen served as a Lieutenant in the Maine Twelfth Volunteers. Their nephews, Allen, William and Philip, sons of Francis Nourse, enlisted respectively in the Maine Seventh, and Twelfth, and Fifth Connecticut regiments, and did good service under the old flag. He d. Oct. 4, 1870; res. Fayette, Me.

The following is taken from the diary of Ezra Fiske, of Fayette, Me.:

"April 2nd, 1861. Tuesday. Morning cloudy and cold. P. F. Pike called and took my inventory this morning. I am permitted to enter upon the 86th year of my age. Yes, 85 years ago this morning I received existence from the same kind hand of Providence which has upheld me in life through this long series of years, and has dealt bountifully with me and towards me in every stage of my life, and now this morning I am numbered among the living, in the enjoyment of comfortable health. O, that I could render to the Lord all due returns of gratitude, thanksgiving and praise for his bountiful goodness unto me, in the kingdom of his providence and Grace. Amen."

1743. i.   WILLIAM, b. Nov. 22, 1801; d. Jan. 17, 1820.
1744. ii.   FRANCIS NOURSE, b. Mar. 30, 1803; m. Fanny Hilton.
1745. iii. EZRA, b. Apr. 19, 1805; d. Dec. 11, 1806.
1746. iv.   EZRA, b. Feb. 2, 1807; d. Mar. 13, 1815.
1747. v.   THOMAS GAGE UNDERWOOD, b. Sept. 26, 1809; m. Mary J. Johnson.
1748. vi.   FANNIE NOURSE, b. Feb. 9, 1811; d. June 10, 1840.
1749. vii. ROBERT BLAKE, b. Jan. 21, 1813; d. August 26, 1819.
1750. viii. ALLEN, b. Mar. 16, 1815; m. Miranda Farber.
1751. ix.   MELINDA, b. Jan. 26, 1817; m. 1837, William Campbell; religion, Baptist. They had one child, Viola Campbell-Pierce; Melinda dying at Lowell, Mass., in 1839. Viola married Charles E. Pierce, in 1862, at Fayette, Me. She had one child that died in infancy. Viola d. in Dec., 1880, in New York City. Charles E. Pierce is now a retired policeman in New York City.
1752. x.   DUDLEY BLAKE, b. July 19, 1819; m. Mary A. Ashton.
1753. xi.   LUCINDA, b. July 13, 1821; d. Nov. 22, 1843
1754. xii. DAVID, b. Mar. 15, 1823; d. Aug. 24, 1824.
1755. xiii. MARY WALKER, b. Nov. 4, 1824, at Fayette, Me.; was married to Stephen Taft, 1841; her religion was Baptist. She d. June 12, 1889. Ch.: Stephen Taft, Jr., b. in 1843, and is now a merchant in New York State; 2, Mary Elizabeth, who m. Charles Waters, a son of the inventor, of Boston, Mass.; Mr. Waters d., leaving one child, who d. in infancy, and one child, Edward Waters, who res. in Chicago. Mary Elizabeth Taft-Waters afterwards m. Henry M. Willey, a Chicago hotel man.
1756. xiv. JOSEPH ANDERSON, b. Aug. 31, 1826; m. Sarah Fifield.
1757. xv.   FRANKLIN, b. Feb. 10, 1829; m. Ellen M. Wakefield.
1758. xvi. SARAH WALKER, b. Jan. 9, 1831; m. Nov. 23, 1853, Gilman W. Johnson; res. Newburyport. She was a Baptist; add., 310 Fairview Av., North Denver, Colo.; politics, Republican. Gilman W. Johnson was b. Dec. 9, 1825, at Newburyport, Mass.; profession, civil engineer; religion, Baptist; he d. Dec. 9, 1893, at Denver, Colo. Ch.: 1, Gilman W., Jr., b. Dec. 4, 1855; d. Aug. 29, 1859. 2, Hannah Clark, b. June 24, 1861; d. Oct. 4, 1864. 3, Henry Fessenden, b. Aug. 11, 1874; d. Sept. 25, 1882.

926. WILLIAM FISKE (William, William, Ebenezer, William, William, John, William, Robert, Simon, Simon, William, Symond), b. Amherst, N. H., July 11, 1778; m. Sept. 4, 1802, Margaret Cleave Dodge, of Amherst, b. Oct. 12, 1780, d. Apr. 6, 1867. The eight children of Bartholomew Dodge, Sr., born in Wenham,

were among the earliest emigrants to Amherst, N. H. As three of them inter-married with the family of Hon. William Fiske, doubtless a number of the latter's descendants are equally interested in what relates to the Dodge ancestry. Of Mr. Dodge's parentage and family, the date of his birth and marriage, no account has been furnished us. He was descended from Richard Dodge, of Salem, Mass., who emigrated from England in 1638. According to Savage, he is the progenitor of all the name in New England. He had, by wife Edith, John, Mary, Richard, Samuel, Edward and Joseph. They, and their descendants, appear to have partici-pated largely in public affairs in Wenham and adjacent towns. Eighteen of this name have graduated at New England colleges since A. D. 1700. In Wenham, according to the records, several of this family married Fiskes.

William Fiske, of Concord, was the third child and second son of Hon. Wil-liam and Eunice Fiske. In features and in stature he resembled his father, but his disposition and character was more like his mother's. Like his brothers, he grew up amid the labors of his father's family, until he was 21 years of age. Then, after visiting Maine and looking about him, for two or three years, at the age of 24 he married Margaret C. Dodge, of Amherst, and settled at Concord, N. H. They became members of the Congregational Church in Concord at an early date. of 24 he married Margaret C. Dodge, of Amherst, and settled at Concord, N. H. They became members of the Congregational church in Concord at an early date. They first located themselves at Concord, "West Parish," where he erected several buildings, a public dwelling and store, and resided there several years. But, in 1832, he bought a lot and built him a house in the village of Concord. He died there, aged 76 years. His wife was the daughter of Bartholomew Dodge, of Amherst. He d. Oct. 9, 1854; res. Concord, N. H.

1759. i. MARY CLEAVES, b. Sept. 8, 1803; m. Edward M. Walker, Apr. 20, 1824, by the Rev. Dr. Butler, of St. Paul's Church, Troy. Edward M. Walker d. Feb. 19, 1831. Their children were: 1, Mary A., b. Sept. 16, 1825. 2, Edward M., b. Sept. 21, 1828; d. Aug., 1829. 3, Edwarda M., b. Mar. 22, 1831. In November, 1850, she was married to Charles T. Bradley, Esq., of Milwaukee, Wis. Mary A. Walker, the eldest daughter, lived with her parents. Mrs. M. C. Walker was married Oct. 21, 1836, to William Jennison. Charles T. Bradley was the sev-enth of a family of nine children, born in Haverhill, Mass. His father, Enoch B., was the son of Joseph Bradley, of Haverhill. His mother was a daughter of Dr. Samuel Hildreth, of Methuen, in that State. The Bradleys were among the first settlers in New England, but it is not known that the original families were all closely related. Mr. Joseph Bradley, above referred to, was quite probably a descendant of Daniel Brad-ley, who was a passenger by the ship "Elizabeth," 1635, who was killed by the Indians at Haverhill, 1689, and whose family for several generations experienced great sufferings at the hands of the savages. He had several children, and among them Daniel, Abraham, Joseph and Isaac—the latter was car-ried into captivity, 1695. Daniel, with his wife and younger children, and Joseph, with their sisters, Martha and Sarah, were massacred in 1697. In 1704 the garrison house of a grand-son, Joseph, son of Joseph, was surprised, burned down, and his wife (in delicate circumstances) taken a second time pris-oner, and carried to Canada, where she was sold into bond-age until redeemed the following year. In 1746, Jonathan and Samuel Bradley, sons of Abraham above, were massacred with others in New Hampshire, by the same relentless foe. Such were the perils and such the sufferings encountered by our fathers, in early days. Joseph Bradley, of Haverly, was the ancestor of Hon. John Bradley, of Concord, N. H.; also of Deacon Amos Bradley, of Dracut, Mass., and of Enoch Bradley, Esq., of Haverhill.

1760. ii. WILLIAM PORTER, b. Dec. 29, 1805; m. Sophia W. Parker, and Sarah A. Clifford.

1761. iii. DAVID DODGE, b. Aug. 28, 1808; m. Elizabeth B. Stevens.

1762. iv.   SARAH WHEELER, b. Dec. 20, 1810; m. Apr., 1831, Moses W.
            Grout; res. Worcester, Mass. He d. Mar. 27, 1836, and Nov.
            25, 1841, Mrs. Grout was married to Calvin Thayer, of Kings-
            ton, N. H. He was b. June, 1805, in Kingston, and d. in Con-
            cord, Feb., 1881. Their children are: 1, Eliha F., b. Feb. 25,
            1844; d. in Aug., 1863; 2, William Fisk, b. Mar. 13, 1846; m.
            Oct. 20, 1874, Sarah C. Wentworth. He is engaged in banking,
            in Concord, N. H. Ch.: Edith Jennison, b. Sept. 4, 1877; d.
            Mar. 28, 1881; Margaret, b. Aug. 9, 1892; William W., b. Apr.
            15, 1894. 3, Clara Eda, b. Oct. 1, 1848.

1763. v.   CLARA NOURSE, b. Oct. 23, 1812; m. to Asaph Evans, of
            Concord, May 3, 1836. Mr. Evans d. June 6, 1839, and in 1850,
            May 29, his widow was married to Calvin Howe, of Gilmanton,
            N. H. Res. Concord, N. H.

1764. vi.   FRANCIS ALLEN, b. Aug. 22, 1815; d. Dec. 18, 1815.

927. HON. FRANCIS NOURSE FISKE (William, William, Ebenezer, William, William, John, William, Robert, Simon, Simon, William, Symond), b. Amherst, N. H., June 12, 1780; m. May 1, 1813, Mary (Walker) Emery, d. Mar., 1847.
Hon. Francis N. Fiske was the third son and fourth child of Hon. William and
Eunice Fiske. Remained with his father until 1802, when he went to Maine;
taught school there most of time until 1809, when he returned to New Hampshire. In 1810 he located himself in trade at Concord, and continued in that business up to 1853. In March, 1819, he was elected town clerk of Concord, and was
elected to the same office fourteen consecutive years. In 1825, and also in 1826, he was
elected representative to the general court. In 1827-29-30 he was elected Counselor for the district of Rockingham. He was chosen president of the Merrimack
county bank in January, 1847, and continued the same for thirteen consecutive
years. He was also president of the New Hampshire savings bank in Concord, for
several years. He was married by the Rev. Dr. Asa McFarland, of Concord, to
Mrs. Mary Emery, daughter of Judge Timothy Walker, of Concord. They
both united with the First Congregational Church, Concord, in 1831. As a son and
brother, as a husband, father and citizen and in all the relations of life, if Francis
Nourse Fiske were not absolutely blameless, none were more nearly so. Besides
a good common school education he obtained at the academy of Amherst, a fair
introduction to the higher English branches. Mrs. Mary Emery was the daughter
of Judge Timothy Walker, of Concord, N. H. Judge Walker of Concord, was
descended from Deacon Samuel Walker, of Woburn, Mass., whose eldest son,
Timothy, born 1705, was a graduate of Harvard College, 1725, and ordained the
first pastor of the Congregational Church in Concord, in 1730, and died there in
1782, in the 52d year of his ministry. He married Sarah Burbeen, of Woburn,
and had five children. His only son, Judge Timothy Walker, born in 1737, was
for many years among the most prominent of the early public men in New
Hampshire. He was a colonel and paymaster in the army of the Revolution, a
member of both houses of Common Pleas, and, in 1798, the Republican candidate
for Governor, against John Taylor Gilman, a distinguished federalist. He married Esther, daughter of Rev. Joseph Burbeen, of Woburn, and of their fourteen
children, the thirteenth was Mary, born in 1786, who was married to Hon. Francis
N. Fiske, as above. The family and descendants of Rev. Timothy Walker have
been largely identified with the growth and prosperity of Concord, and in the
voluminous historical work of Rev. Dr. Nathaniel Bouton, of that city, they are
noticed at length. He d Oct. 7, 1870; res. Concord, N. H.

1765. i.   SARAH WALKER, b. Sept. 20, 1814; m. Aug. 20, 1834, Hon.
            James M. Tarlton. For many years she spent the winters in
            southern Alabama with her husband, where he was in business.
            In 1854 he was appointed United States Consul at Melbourne,
            Australia, and resided there for six years. She d. s. p. in New
            York, Feb. 28, 1882. He d. Dec. 23, 1880.

1766. ii.   MARY WALKER, b. Dec., 1815; d. in infancy.

1767. iii. JOSEPH WALKER, b. June 12, 1817; d. young.

1768. iv.   FRANCIS ALLEN, b. Apr. 26, 1819; m. Abby Gilman Perry
            and Abby Blake Parker.

1769. v.   TIMOTHY WALKER, b. Apr. 7, 1820; d. Feb. 18, 1845, while midshipman of the United States Navy at Philadelphia. He was a prominent and very promising young man.

1770. vi. JOSEPH WALKER, b. June 10, 1822; d. Aug. 2⅗, 1825.

1771. vii. SUSAN EUNICE, b. Nov. 17, 1825; d. July, 1828.

1772. viii. LUCRETIA MORSE, b. Nov. 26. 1826; m. Aug. 20, 1849, Dr. William G. Perry; res. Exeter, N. H. Ch.: 1, Frances Perry, b. Dec. 30, 1861; m. July 2, 1890, Albertus True Dudley, son of Rev. Horace F. Dudley; their ch.: 1, William Perry, b. July 11, 1891. Exeter; 2, Gardner Blanchard, b. in Exeter, Oct. 5, 1894: d. June 1, 1894.

Dr. William Gilman Perry was the eldest son of Dr. William and Abigail (Gilman) Perry. of Exeter, N. H. The Perry family is of English stock, and their ancestors were among the earliest emigrants who settled in the Old Colony. Nathan Perry, the father of Dr. William, of Exeter, was born in Attleboro, Mass. In early life he removed and settled in Norton, of that State, where he married Phebe Braman, and lived and died a respectable farmer.

931 ALLEN FISKE (William, William, Ebenezer, William, William, John, William, Robert, Simon, Simon, William, Symond), b. Amherst. N. H., Apr. 10, 1789. m. at Morristown, N. J., July, 1819, Eliza Chapman, b. Aug. 24. 1797, d. May 7, 1834, eldest daughter of Nathaniel Chapman, Esq., who was descended from an ancient and honorable family of that name in Connecticut. She was a lady of rare beauty and accomplishments, well fitted to adorn any station in life, was for some years eminently successful as a teacher of young women in the higher educational branches of study, and though called to an early grave, she left behind her a sweet memory that was cherished by a wide circle of admirers and friends. Nathaniel Chapman was one of a family of four sons and one daughter, children of Phineas Chapman. Esq., who was the son of Deacon Caleb, who was the son of Deacon Nathaniel, who was the youngest son of Hon. Robert Chapman, one of the original settlers of Saybrook, and who, besides filling other im-

ALLEN FISKE.

portant offices in the gift of his townsmen, represented that town for thirty consecutive years in the Connecticut Legislature, viz., from 1654 to 1684, numbering during that period over fifty separate sessions. His son, Deacon Nathaniel, of the Saybrook (Cong.) Church. represented the same town in twenty-four sessions of that body, from 1697 to 1723. His son, Caleb, succeeded him in the inheritance of the ancient Chapman homestead, and also as deacon of the Saybrook Church. Allen Fiske m. 2d, Sept., 1835, Mrs. Maria Stokes, b. 1796, in Montrose, Scotland, d. Oct., 1863. Allen, fourth son of Hon. William and Eunice (Nourse) Fiske, was born in Amherst, N. H. Delicate in his youth the plans of his life were left undecided until he was nineteen years of age, when he began his preparation for college, and soon after entering Dartmouth, at Hanover, N. H., he graduated in the summer of 1814. At college he held a very respectable standing, ranking as third in his class, and was honored by election to the Phi Beta Kappa Society, in recognition of his scholarship. Going to New York the following winter. he entered the law office of Hon. Jonathan Fiske in the spring of 1816, where he continued until he was admitted to the bar in 1819. Mr. Fiske was peculiarly well fitted for the office of instructor of youth, and tiring of the law after a brief practice. he betook himself to his favorite role as the principal of grammar schools, designed to prepare young men for college. Called to take charge of such departments in the academies located in Troy, Auburn and Skaneateles. N. Y., he made a brilliant success in this field, was largely instrumental in shaping the course of many young men who afterwards attained distinction, and probably more than any others of his day helped to raise the standard of education in the state. He was the author of several text books widely in use in the schools of New York and New England, notably Murray's English Grammar simplified and adapted to popular use, and Fiske's Elements of Latin Grammar for High Schools. Mr. Fiske, in addition to his rare gifts as teacher, also possessed the pen of a ready writer, and was a frequent and valued contributor to the columns of the eastern press. He was at different times on the editorial staff of several prominent journals of his day, was a leading writer for a number of popular magazines and quarterlies, and for several years conducted a very popular home journal. To the very last years of his life Mr. Fiske retained to a remarkable degree the vigor of his intellectual powers, and when past the age of three-score and ten years, was accustomed to keep up his familiar acquaintance with the classic authors, and even when the physical infirmities of an octogenarian prevented him from engaging longer in the activities of outdoor life, he occupied himself in writing full commentaries on the entire New Testament.

At the ripe age of 86 years, in the full possession of his faculties, with an unclouded trust and holy peace and saintly resignation, Allen Fiske, after a brief illness, on Sept. 18th, 1875, fell asleep in Jesus, and was gathered unto his fathers, "having the testimony of a good conscience, in the communion of the Holy Catholic Church, in the confidence of a certain faith, in the comfort of a reasonable, religious and holy hope, and in perfect charity with the world!" His remains were taken to Auburn, N. Y., for interment.

Allen Fiske was a well read man, not only in English literature, but the classics also, and Homer's Iliad was as familiar to him as Shakespeare. But the Holy Scriptures were his especial delight. From private papers it appears that before his seventieth year he had read the Bible through by regular course over forty times, and portions of the New Testament many more times. During his long career as a teacher he had received from his pupils many valued souvenirs of their regard, but the most touching testimony came at his decease, when about his remains were gathered at the cemetery in Auburn, N. Y., where the committal took place, nearly a score of prominent gentlemen, in middle life, who after more than thirty years had elapsed, came from their homes to testify by their presence their profound appreciation of the service he had rendered to them as their early instructor, and to pay this heartfelt homage to his memory. He d. Sept. 18, 1875; res. Troy, N. Y.

1773 i.   MARIA ANTOINETTE, b. in New York City, Feb. 26, 1821; m. Nov. 1, 1854, Dr. J. Asa Kennicott. Early manifesting a remarkable precocity and strength of character, she greatly resembled her mother also in personal charms and indomitable energy. At the age of thirteen, during her mother's illness and afterwards, she took charge of the female department of Auburn Academy, of which her father was then principal, and discharged her duties in this position with such dignity and ability as to attract the notice of other educators. At the age of sixteen she was engaged as preceptress of the Aurora (N. Y.) Female Academy, notwithstanding the rule in force of the board of trustees, which prescribed eighteen as the minimum age, and was eminently successful in that capacity. In 1841, when her father took charge of the academy in Skaneateles, N. Y., she again became his assistant, as head of the female department and filed the position with entire satisfaction. Subsequently, on the removal of the family to Troy, N. Y., she entered (1844-5) Mrs. Willard's Seminary, to perfect herself in music, painting, French, and higher mathematics, and graduating with credit eighteen months later, she became a teacher in that famous institution. In 1849, after a brief visit with friends in New York City, she went to Chicago, and established the Chicago Female Seminary, the pioneer of all such institutions in the great West, and for several years she conducted that school with signal popularity, having in the various departments instructors of the highest ability, and at one time a scholar-roll of over one hundred pupils. In 1854 she was united in marriage to Dr. J. Asa Kennicott, a leading dentist of the city, and well known in scientific circles, and for fifteen years retired to domestic life. In 1869, with the view of giving her three daughters the best educational advantages, she established in her own beautiful home at Kenwood, Chicago, a girl's school which soon became widely known as the Kenwood Female Seminary, with the patronage of the best Chicago families, and a large roll of pupils drawn from all quarters of the west and south. While in the full tide of prosperity, she was compelled, on account of ill health, to transfer the management of the school to other hands, and in 1878 she engaged to chaperon a good-sized class abroad, and with this charge spent a year in Europe, visiting the various places of interest, but more especially the art galleries and salons, where her class received instruction in art, music and modern languages. On her return from Europe she decided not to resume charge of the seminary, but opened a studio, in connection with her eldest daughter, Miss Maud Kennicott, who was a member of the class that went abroad, and gave instruction in the higher grades of art, with special favor and success. Mrs. Kennicott's work in crayon, pastel and oil has been catalogued and exhibited in the art galleries of the leading expositions of the country, especially those of Chicago, New York and New Orleans, and has been honored with distinguished commendation and patronage. Her productions in fruit work have not been excelled by any artist in this country or Europe, and are simply exquisite. And the same might be said of much of her other work, especially her canvas representations of the various specimens of the American flora, which have been much admired. Indeed, faultless gems from her easel may be found in the homes of the wealthy all through the land, associated with the best work of modern masters. In 1886 her husband, Dr. Kennicott, was stricken with paralysis, and as he became a hopeless and for years almost a helpless invalid, her studies in art from this date were practically ended in her devotion to him. Since his demise in 1893, Mrs. Kennicott has lived a very retired life, passing the evening of her days pleasantly, with her children all near her, solaced by the reflection that her busy life had been at least a very useful one, and representative of the highest grade of American womanhood. To her were born three daughters, as follows: Isabella Maud, born Dec. 21, 1856; married Dr. T. J. Reid. 2d, Mabel Blanche, born August 16, 1858; married Frederick Grant Gleason. 3d, Ada Mary Walker, born August 1, 1860; presides with grace as mistress of the homestead. Inheriting in a large degree the talents of their mother, they have by her judicious training acquired accomplishments which fit them for any station in life.

Dr. Kennicott is a younger son of Jonathan Kennicott, who was born in Warren, R. I., April 27, 1775, and a grandson of Robert, of that State, who was descended from Dr. Robert Kennicott, of London, a distinguished English scholar and savant, and presumed to be related to Benjamin Kennicott, D. D., regius professor in Oxford University during the last century, and a bishop in the Church of England. In 1832 the family removed to Illinois, before Chicago could boast of a hundred buildings, and when the great Northwest was a comparative wilderness. Establishing themselves upon a large tract of land, in one of the most desirable locations in the State (about twenty miles northwest of Chicago), they early became wealthy and very successful farmers, and gained a wide reputation as pioneers in western horticulture. There they built mills, erected a trading post, and founded the village of Mettawa—called (by its English translation) Half Day. There several of them married and settled, and have large families. Three brothers in this family graduated at medical universities, two of them were practicing physicians for several years, and two of them have been prominent as dental surgeons in Chicago. Drs. John and William Kennicott recently deceased, stood deservedly high as professional men, and they and others of their relatives are favorably known in scientific circles.

1774 ii   MARY FRANCES, b. Troy, N. Y., Jan. 20, 1823, d. Oct. 1, 1864.
1775. iii   WILLIAM ALLEN, b. Nov. 4, 1824, m. Susan M. Bradley.
1776. iv   DAVID EDWARD, b. Sept. 3, 1826, unm. res. Chicago, Ill. David

DAVID EDWARD FISKE.

Edward Fiske, second son of Allen and Eliza Fiske, was born in Troy, N. Y. At an early age he went to live with his uncle, David Fiske, in Amherst, N. H., on whose rugged farm and precipitous hillsides he readily acquired that robust health and constitution which served him so well in after years. There also he acquired, in the excellent schools of that town and vicinity, a good English education, and so much knowledge of Latin and Greek as is required to enter college. After teaching a couple of winters, he abandoned farm life and, returning to Troy, N. Y., became connected with the Family Journal in the spring of 1849. His excellent business talents soon placed the enterprise on a solid basis, and brought the Journal in the front rank of weekly newspapers. Subsequently he undertook the publication of the Troy Traveler. But not finding the publication of newspapers sufficiently remunerative to suit his views, he dissolved his connection with these enterprises, and, in 1856, removed to Chicago, where he engaged several years in the dairy business, at first on a small, but afterwards on quite a large scale, and in which, by energy, prudence and perseverance, he accumulated in a few years a handsome competence. In 1864 he parted with his dairy interests and for about thirty years has been engaged in the real estate and loaning business, in which with ample means and careful management, he has attained the goal of his early ambition— a recognized position among mean of wealth and influence.

Mr. Fiske, while not a man of letters, is nevertheless well versed in current literature, has decided and intelligent convictions on most subjects, and is not lacking in ability to express his views, by voice or pen, with clearness and force, and when occasion calls can maintain his ground with the best of disputants.

As the favorite legatee of his uncle, for whom he was named, and with whom he passed the greater part of his youth, Mr. Fiske has taken great and commendable delight in restoring to a highly productive and attractive condition the old farm and homestead, which has been now in possession of the family for over one hundred and fifty years.

William Fiske, Sr., youngest son of Deacon Ebenezer Fiske of Wenham, with Susanna Batchelder, his wife, and their nine children, emigrated from Wenham at an early day, and established themselves on the eastern slopes of Walnut Hill, in

the town of Amherst, N. H., when that portion of the country
was still a wilderness. There was founded the Amherst branch
of the Wenham Fiskes, whose descendants, wherever located,

OLD FISKE HOME, AMHERST, N. H.

have fully sustained the high character of their ancestry, have
been noted for their ability, probity and piety, and have filled
many official positions of honor and public trust. The hardships
of frontier life in a country heavily timbered and rocky, shortened the days of that sturdy pioneer, William Fisk, Sr., and he
died in 1777 in his fifty-second year, leaving a large family.
Stanch and stalwart, the elder sons soon cleared up a large tract
of land, and established homes for themselves and families. A
few years later Jonathan removed to Williamstown, Vt., where
he achieved a most honorable record; Ebenezer settled in Mt.
Vernon, where he became prominently identified with town
affairs; while William (Jr.) located himself on the old mail
route from Amherst to Manchester, on a plateau lying between Walnut and Chestnut Hills. Living for awhile in a plain
log house, at the close of the Revolutionary War, he built on
this spot a fine mansion, which has ever since been in possession of the family. Here was raised a large family of sons and
daughters, whose subsequent career reflected great credit on
their early training. And here Hon. William Fiske resided
until his death (June, 1831), very greatly respected by his
townsmen, being called for twenty-five years to represent them
in public life, both in town affairs and state government, legislative and judicial. The old homestead, which was willed first
to his son David, and subsequently to a grandson of that name,
is still in a most excellent state of preservation, and remains
a fine specimen of the commodious and hospitable New
England homes of the early days. Mr. David E. Fiske, of
Chicago, who is the present owner, takes great pleasure in re-
visiting his boyhood's home, where he usually spends his summers, superintending improvements, and exercising the tastes
of a gentleman farmer. It is his firm purpose to keep the old
homestead in the family as long as he can, as the best monument to the sterling worth of those who founded the Amherst
branch of the Wenham Fiskes.

1777. v.   ALBERT AUGUSTUS, b. Nov. 1, 1828; m. Amelia Goodyear.
1778. vi. ANN ELIZA, b. March 11, 1831; m. March 29, 1848.
1779. vii. CHARLES ASA CHAPMAN, b. Nov. 26, 1832; d. Dec. 9, 1833.

932. DAVID FISKE (William, William, Ebenezer, William, William, John, William, Robert, Simon, Simon, William, Symond), b. May 4, 1791; m. Mar., 1859, Mrs. Lydia M. Holbrook; d. Feb. 28, 1870. He was b. in Amherst, where he always resided. During a western trip he contracted fever and ague from which he never fully recovered. He was not married until 64 years of age. Often solicited to hold public office, he always declined. He d. June 29, 1882; res. Amherst, N. H.

1780. i.   ELLEN, his wife's dau. by former marriage. •

936. DEA. DAVID FISKE (William, William, Ebenezer, William, William, John, William, Robert, Simon, Simon, William, Symond), b. Amherst, N. H., Sept. 20, 1792; m. Jan. 19, 1823, Abigail Nourse, b. 1800; d. June, 1825; m. 2d, Jan. 17, 1828, Harriett Nourse, b. Aug. 21, 1799; d. Aug. 22, 1872. David, Jr., eldest son of David, Sr., of Amherst, inherited his father's homestead and was married to Abigail, dau. of Deacon Benjamin Nourse, of Merrimack, N. H., and a few years afterward, Nov. 18, 1836, he was chosen deacon of the Congregational Church, of Amherst, which office he held until his removal from that town. Deacon David Fiske, for many years an enterprising, industrious farmer by occupation, and an earnest, conscientious Christian in life, may justly be regarded as a fine specimen of the active New Englander. A man of sound and active mind and spotless integrity, zealous in the discharge of all good works. After the death of his first wife, Deacon Fiske married Harriett, another daughter of Deacon B. Nourse. His sons having attained maturity, bought for him a pleasant residence in Nashua, N. H., where he enjoyed a green old age. He d. June 22, 1873; res. Nashua, N. H.

1781. i.   THOMAS SCOTT, b. Nov. 22, 1823; m. Clara Isabel Pitman.
1782. ii.   JAMES PORTER, b. June 5, 1825; m. Sarah C. Hill.
1783. iii. GEORGE, b. Oct. 22, 1835; m. Elmira F. Morrill.
1784. iv.   ABBIE ARINDA, b. Nov. 24, 1838; m. July 26, 1860, George W. Ordway, of Bradford, Mass. He was b. May 8, 1835; d. Sept. 26, 1886. Her ch. d. in infancy; res. 4827 Vincennes Ave., Chicago, Ill., care E. W. Keyes.
1785. v.   MARY PORTER, b. Dec. 9, 1841; m. Dec. 10, 1867, Hon. George A. Marden of Lowell Mass., res. 84 Fairmount Ave. George Augustus Marden was born in Mount Vernon, N. H., Aug. 9, 1839; son of Benj. F. and Betsey (Buss) Marden. Graduated at Dartmouth College, class 1861; enlisted as private in Co. G., 2d Regiment, Berdan's U. S. Sharpshooters in Nov., 1861. Promoted to first lieutenant and regimental quarter master First U. S. Sharpshooters, July, 1862. Mustered out with regiment in Sept., 1864. Studied law at Concord, N. H., in 1865; edited Kanawha Republican at Charleston, W. Va., in 1865 and 1866; returned to Concord and edited histories of New Hampshire regiments for adjutant-general's report, and wrote for Concord Daily Monitor and corresponded with Boston Daily Advertiser; joined editorial staff of Boston Advertiser Jan. 1, 1867; Sept. 1, 1867, purchased one-half Lowell Daily Courier and Lowell Weekly Journal, which papers he has since edited; was elected member of Mass. house of representatives for 1873; elected clerk of same body annually, 1874-1882, inclusive; speaker of same body in 1883 and 1884, and member of Mass. senate for 1885; was elected treasurer and receiver general of Mass. for 1889-1893, inclusive; the constitution forbidding more than five successive elections; elected vice-president Hancock National Bank, Boston, in 1895, and still serving as an active manager of said bank; was elected a delegate to the national republican convention in Chicago in 1880, and was one of the 306 supporters of Grant; was trustee of Mass. Agricultural College two years, resigning when elected state treas-

urer. Ch.: Phillip Sanford, b. June 12, 1874; Robert Fiske, b. June 14, 1876.

937. GEORGE FISKE (William, William, Ebenezer, William, William, John, William, Robert, Simon, Simon, William, Symond), b. Amherst, N. H., Aug. 22, 1794; m. May 6, 1824, Arinda Lane of Bedford, Mass., b. May 29, 1793; d. Jan. 24, 1885. George, the younger son of David Fiske, Sr., of Amherst, m. Miss Arinda Lane, and settled in Lowell, Mass., where for a long period he filled a responsible position connected with the manufacturing interests in that city. He d. Feb. 20, 1869; res. Bradford and Lowell, Mass.

    1786. i.   GEORGE NOURSE, b. May 17, 1825; d. Apr. 28, 1861.
    1787. ii.   NATHAN LORD, b. Oct. 9, 1826; d. Aug. 21, 1847.
    1788. iii. DAVID ABBOTT, b. July 30, 1828; d. Sept. 8, 1847.
    1789. iv. ANN ELIZA, b. Aug. 27, 1830; m. Aug. 15, 1853, Charles W. Dodge of Lowell.
    1790. v.   SARAH MARIAH, b. Nov. 28, 1832; res. 61 Chapel St., Lowell, Mass.
    1791. vi. JONATHAN LANE, b. Oct. 8, 1834. He enlisted in one of the Massachusetts Volunteer Regiments at the breaking out of the Rebellion, and after doing good, loyal service for the country, d. Dec. 19, 1862, of a disease contracted while in the discharge of his military duties.

941. EBENEZER FISKE (Ebenezer, William, Ebenezer, William, William, John, William, Robert, Simon, Simon, William, Symond), b. Aug. 22, 1786; m. Sept. 23, 1807, Hannah Proctor, b. Mar. 5, 1784; d. Apr. 14, 1857. He was m. in Henniker, N. H., his wife having been born in Manchester, Mass., the dau. of Dea. John Proctor. She possessed an excellent mind and fine person. After his marriage, Mr. Fiske resided for a few years in Henniker, thence he removed to Salisbury, N. H., thence to Wilmot and afterward to Hopkinton. Mr. Fiske possessed great energy and decision of character. He d. July, 1842; res. Hopkinton, N. H.

    1792. i.   HANNAH COGSWELL, b. Aug. 8, 1809, at Henniker, N. H.; m. Jan. 13, 1838, Dea. Elias Lyman, a native of Easthampton, Mass., and resided in that place until his death, Apr. 4, 1866, at the age of 56 years. Ch.: 1, Carlos Parsons, b. Dec., 1838. 2, Ednah Maria, b. Apr., 1840. 3, Howard Fisk, b. Nov., 1841. 4, Zuinglius Paley, b. Aug., 1843. 5, Albert Taylor, b. Mar., 1845. 6, Lucy Ann, b. Sept., 1846. 7, Celia Augustus, b. June 13, 1848; d. Mar. 7, 1866. 8, Hannah Proctor, b. Mar., 1852. Ednah M., m. May 9, 1866, Dwight Lock Wilbur, and res. in Boonesboro, Iowa. Carlos P. enlisted for the war for the Union as private in the Sixth Regiment, Ohio Volunteer Cavalry, and rose to a captancy in the One Hundreth United States Colored Infantry, July 11, 1864. After honorably filling his term of service, he retired at the close of the war, Dec., 1865, to his home in Mesopotamia, where he engaged in farming. Howard F. entered the United States service in the Eighteenth Ohio Volunteer Infantry, Mar. 2, 1865, and was honorably discharged July 24, 1865.
    1793. ii.   EDNAH PROCTOR, b. Apr. 20, 1811, at Salisbury, N. H.; m. Apr. 15, 1834, Cyrus Dustin, of Hopkinton, N. H. Ch.: 1, Gilbert F., b. Feb. 11, 1835. 2, Clara Ann, b. Sept. 18, 1838. 3, Hannah Proctor, b. July 19, 1842. 4, Ebenezer F., b. Nov. 26, 1843. 5, Cyrus Herbert, b. January 28, 1855. Of these, Gilbert F., their only son of military age at the breaking out of the war for the Union, early enlisted in the Seventh N. H. Volunteer Regiment to assist in the putting down of the Rebellion. He died July 19, 1863; killed in the attack on Fort Wagner and died in the fort while uttering the words: "Come on, boys, let us be brave!"
    1794. iii. ABIGAIL WOODBURY, b. in Wilmot, N. H., Feb. 28, 1814; m. Nov. 13, 1837, Daniel Proctor, of Lowell, Mass. Immediately

after their marriage they removed to Chicopee and afterward to Springfield, Mass., where Mr. Proctor was employed in the service of the government in the United States armory. They had one child: Hannah Cogswell, b. July 10, 1840; m. June 6, 1866, Charles Conant, Gardner, Mass., where she resided.

1795. iv. ANNIE JUMPER, b. in Wilmot, N. H., Feb. 26, 1816; m. Erastus Woodruff; removed to Ohio. They subsequently went to reside in Wisconsin, at British Hollow, Grant Co. Ch.: Abby Ann, b. Apr., 1844. Harlan, b. Oct. 1849; d. in 1865. Clara Amelia, b. Mar., 1852.

1796. v. JOHN PROCTOR, b. in Wilmot, May 31, 1818; m. Abby R. Clark.

1797. vi. FRANKLIN WOODBURY, b. in Hopkinton, N. H., Feb. 16, 1820; m. Mrs. Amelia Allen (Bowen) Austin and Mrs. Jennette (Gardner) Hitchcock.

1798. vii. CLARA APPLETON, b. in Hopkinton, Aug. 26, 1825; d. Aug. 25, 1830.

942. JAMES FISKE (Ebenezer, William, Ebenezer, William, William, John, William, Robert, Simon, Simon, William, Symond), b. Wilmont, N. H., Aug. 4, 1788; m. in New York state, June 8, 1815, Eleanor Ransom, d. Mar. 18, 1856. When a young man he moved to New Platz, N. Y., and later to Coldwater, Mich., where he established himself on a fine farm a mile from the center of the town. He was a member of the M. E. Church; class leader and replete with good works. A Coldwater paper says: "James Fiske was born in Amherst, N. H., Aug. 4, 1788, of industrious and pious parents. Inheriting an excellent physical constitution, he developed into a man of rare physical and moral vigor. In June, 1815, he married Miss Eleanor Ransom, the death of which faithful wife preceded his by about 15 years. The name of "Father Fiske," by which he was familiarly and widely known, has long since become a synonym for religion.
He d. Aug. 10, 1870; res. New Platz, Ulster Co., N. Y., and Coldwater, Mich.

1799. i. BETSEY, b. Mar. 3, 1816; m. Apr. 16, 1836, William Aldrich, a substantial farmer. She d. Sept. 4, 1837.

1800. ii. LUTHER, b. July 9, 1817; m. Mahala Halsted.

1801. iii. PHEBE M., b. June 7, 1819; m. May 24, 1842, Rev. Dr. E. H. Pilcher. He was a clergyman of the M. E. Church, of considerable ability and scholarship and has held a number of important positions in that denomination. He was regent of the University of Michigan from 1845 to 1851; was born in Athens Co., Ohio, June 2, 1810. He was a student at the Athens University and was ordained a Methodist minister in 1829; from 1831 to his death he was a resident of Michigan, preaching at various places. He was ten years secretary of the conference and for nearly 25 years was a presiding elder. He was one of the founders of Albion College. He received several degrees, including D. D., and was admitted to the bar in 1846. He was the author of "Protestantism in Michigan." She d. Aug. 23, 1866. Ch.: 1, Ellen M., b. Aug. 21, 1843; gr. Ann Arbor, Mich., high school, 1863. 2, Lewis S., b. July 28, 1845; gr. 1863, Michigan University; A. M., 1864. 3, Leander Wm., b. Aug. 2, 1848; gr. Ohio Wesleyan University. 4, James E., b. Mar. 18, 1857.

1802. iv. SUSAN, b. Aug. 3, 1821; m. May 20, 1840, Dr. W. Matthew Gill. He is a physician in good standing in Marshall, Mich. She d. Sept., 1878. Ch.: 1, James F., b. Feb. 13, 1841; d. May 24, 1843. 2, Geo. M., b. June 17, 1843. 3, Ellen E., b. Sept. 3, 1845; d. Mar. 9, 1848. 4, Charles E., b. Aug. 5, 1848. 5, Wm. R., b. Aug. 30, 1853. 6, Ella Ann, b. Nov. 11, 1858.

1803. v. ELEANOR J., b. Sept. 7, 1823; m. May 29, 1883, Abram C. Fiske; res. Coldwater, Mich.

1804. vi. LEWIS R., b. Dec. 24, 1825; m. Elizabeth R. Spence and Mrs. Helen M. Davis.

1805. vii. JAMES A., b. Aug. 10, 1828; d. Nov. 4, 1828.

1806. viii. JOSEPH D. W., b. Sept. 24, 1829; m. Delia Babbitt.

1807. ix. HARRIETT A., b. Nov. 6, 1833; m. Dec. 28, 1852, Ives G. Miles. She d. Nov. 22, 1889. He was a successful merchant. Ch.: 1, Allah, b. Aug. 24, 1854; d. Sept. 8, 1856. 2, Lellah E., b. Sept. 8, 1857. 3, Jennie E., b. Oct. 21, 1862.

1808. x. ELMIRA E., b. May 7, 1838; m. Dec. 26, 1860, Capt. Isaac M. Cravath. He was b. in 1827; d. May 4, 1872. He was a native of New York state and went to Lansing, Jan. 1, 1855, as clerk in the auditor general's office. He retained the position until May, 1861, when he became editor of the Lansing State Republican, at which time he received authority to raise a company of the Twelfth Mich. Infantry. He succeeded in filling his company and went out with the regiment, which saw its first service at the battle of Shiloh. He was one of a reconnoitering party sent out by General Ben. Prentiss, and narrowly escaped both death and capture. Soon after the battle he was attacked with typhoid fever and chronic diarrhoea, and was reduced to borders of the grave. Finally he reached the family of his wife at Coldwater, where for many months he fought the battle between life and death, and for most of the time during two years was dangerously ill, and was honorably discharged from service. In 1870 he was elected senator, which duty he faithfully discharged until the time of his death. He was possessed of strong mental qualities, integrity of character, was a genial companion. He was a man of fine literary and poetic taste, had written several poems and lectures with great credit to himself and with general acceptance. He was also an elder in the Presbyterian Church, where he had a large Bible class.

946. DEA. CALVIN FISKE (Ebenezer, William, Ebenezer, William, William, John, William, Robert, Simon, Simon, William, Symond), b. June 15, 1796; m. May, 1840, Asenath Cross; d. May 11, 1857; m. 2d July 1, 1858, Mary J. Thompson. He lived with his parents and cared for them to the day of their deaths. He was deacon in the Congregational Church; res. Wilmont Centre, N. H.

947. JOHN FISKE (Ebenezer, William, Ebenezer, William, William, John, William, Robert, Simon, Simon, William, Symond), b. Apr. 16, 1798; m. Mahala Rand of Warner, N. H.; m. 2nd. Sarah Goodhue, of Enfield. He was killed by falling from a mill he was framing. He d. 1840; res. Warner, N. H.

1809. i. WOODBURY, b. ———; a dau. is Mrs. Fred Smith; res. 5th St., S. E. Minn.

1810. ii. ELIZABETH, b. ———; m. Wm. Andrews; res. St. Anthony Park, Minn.; a son is Geo. C. Andrews; res. 527 5th St., Minn.

1811. iii. JOHN, b. ———; d. ———.

1812. iv. MAHALA, b. Springfield, N. H., May 7, 1832; m. Nov. 3, 1856, Hon. John S. Pillsbury; res. Minneapolis. He was b. July 29, 1827; res. Minneapolis, Minn. Ch.: 1, Susan May, June 23, 1863; m. F. B. Snyder, Sept. 23, 1885; d. Sept. 3, 1891. 2, Sarah Belle, b. June 30, 1866; m. Edward Gale, June 28, 1892; res. Minneapolis, Minn. 3, Alfred Fisk Pillsbury, b. Oct. 20, 1869; unm.; res. Minneapolis, Minn.

John S. Pillsbury, Governor of Minnesota for two terms ending Jan., 1878, was born in Sutton, N. H., July, 1827. At the age of 16 he entered the store of his brother at Warner, N. H., as a clerk, and subsequently went into business with the ex-Governor, Walter Harriman. At a later period he was in business in Concord, N. H., but came west in 1854, and finally settled at St. Anthony Falls, Minn., where he engaged in the hardware business. He has been active and energetic and successful, and has taken a lively interest in public affairs in that State. He served in the Senate two terms, and was most of the time chairman of the committee on finance. He has held the position of president of the Board of Regents of the State University for several years. He was chosen Governor in 1875, and entered upon the duties of the office the following January.

1813. v.   JOSEPH, b. ——; drowned while bathing.
1814. vi.   SARAH, b. ——; Mrs. L. W. Campbell; res. 1100 5th St., Minn.
1815. vii. MARY, b. ——; Mrs. Mary F. Andrews; res. 527 5th St., Minn.

951. DEA. DAVID FISKE (Samuel, Samuel, Daniel, Samuel, William, John, William, Robert, Simon, Simon, William, Symond), b. Shelburne, Mass., July 17, 1791; m. Oct. 31, 1814, Laura Severance, b. 1795; d. July 6, 1870. David Fiske was born on the top of one of the beautiful hills of Shelburne, Franklin Co., Mass. He had a good common school education, and married Laura Severance, who was born in the same town. Previous to his marriage he had formed a partnership with two other young men for building and running a saw mill, a grist mill and a cloth factory at the falls of the Deerfield river, then called Salmon Falls, from the abundance of that fish caught there. These falls made a fine water power and the banks on either side were owned by Captain Martin Severance, Laura's father. For nearly twenty years he was the head of these establishments, and then chief owner. He built a pretty little house on the river side for his bride. In it were born his eight children, and there three of them died. There also their golden wedding was celebrated and there his beloved wife died, after 56 years of married life. In 1832 he sold out his manufacturing interests, having caught the western fever, and removed with his family to Ohio, making the long journey from Albany over the Erie canal by packet boat, then considered a rapid and luxurious mode of travel, and by lake to Cleveland, which was then but a pretty group of fourteen houses under the bluff by the river. There he first bought 180 acres on the bluff on which now stands the whole business part of Cleveland. But, he wanted a farm, and found better soil out at Strongsville, 18 miles southwest, and exchanged his purchase of the Cleveland site for twice as many acres, where into whose black soil he could thrust a "sabre's tail clear up to the head;" where into the hollow trunk of a fallen sycamore a man could walk upright with a tall hat on and where the black walnut trees made grand rails for fences. Six rails and posts, and rider high to keep the deer from the crops. He sold his farm on which he had built a fine house, the first between Cleveland and southern Ohio. The raising of that house was an event. He and his wife had seen too much of the baleful effects of rum in New England, it was wholly banished from their house and they determined to raise the heavy black walnut frame without its aid. They notified everybody for twenty miles around of this "raising" "without rum." Everybody said that nobody would come and the frame would have to go up on such terms. But everybody came to see and jest at the failure of these temperance cranks. When they came, however, they found a magnificent spread of mother's best cookery and long tables under fine trees and a half a dozen pretty girls to serve them and so knew that no stinginess was at the bottom of it and the boss and carpenters gave them a good report of the way they were treated by the new-comers, and all turned in to the work right merrily and the raising went off fine and after the jolly feast that crowned it the ringleader of the crowd which came to show them that they could not raise a house without rum, mounted a table and made a speech, saying that it was the best raisin' he had ever heard of, and that Mrs. Fiske was the handsomest woman and the best hostess in Ohio. At that the whole crowd thanked her and her husband for having raised their house without rum, so that they were all going home sober and yet jolly, and then the crowd gave a rousing cheer and swung their hats, and the impossible was achieved. Some kinsmen who had settled over in Michigan in Sarnia now, Jackson then, had written that there they had no fever and that there was a fine farm there for him, so they packed up their goods into covered wagons drawn by horses and cattle, and went across the black swamp, a trip of six weeks. Took the new farm and found their old enemy had followed them from Ohio so they were after a couple of years shaken out of Michigan and out of the western fever as well, and returned to Shelburne, where he bought a part of the large farm on which he was born. He ultimately exchanged it for a part of the farm on which his wife was born at the Falls, and finally, it still standing, he bought the identical house he had built for his bride, moved into it and there in 1867 his beloved wife died in the very

room where eight of her children had been born. After her death he lived for eight years (part of the time only, the summers) with his eldest son, Orlando, in Shelburne, or with his brother Samuel, yet spending about two thirds of his time with his son Asa in Rochester and with Mrs. Hart in Philadelphia or New Haven. He fell asleep at 85 in his brother's house in Shelburne, in the fall of 1875, after an hour or two of suffering, with his eldest son at his bedside. He was of a most gentle, genial, kindly nature, a lover of music, of fun, of man and of God, was for many years a deacon in the Congregational Church and respected and honored by all who knew him. In his old age he straightened up after his life of hard work, grew stouter, let his luxuriant silver beard grow full, and was a marvelously fine picture of hearty, alert and serene age. His two eldest daughters married clergymen, and the eldest son, for his first wife, a sister of Fidelia Fiske. Two others of the family attained merited distinction as clergymen and authors. He d. July 22, 1875; res. Shelburne, Mass., and Strongsville, Ohio.

1816. i. LAURA ARABELLA, b. Aug. 31, 1817; m. May 9, 1844, Rev. Henry Seymour. She d. Mar. 28, 1850. He was b. in Hadley, Mass., Oct. 20, 1816; d. Jan. 30, 1893. His mother was Mary Standish, a direct descendant of Myles Standish. He graduated from Amherst College in 1838, and from Union Theological Seminary in New York a few years later. Was settled as the pastor of the Cong. Church in Deerfield, Mass., Mar. 1, 1843. He preached here 6 years and Oct. 3, 1849, was installed pastor of the Cong. Church in East Hawley. He continued to serve this church with the exception of about 3 years till Mar. 2, 1890, when on his way to the Sabbath service he fell on the ice, breaking his hip and closing his active ministry. He was a frequent contributor to religious papers, keeping a scrap book containing several hundred of his printed articles. He was a man of most devoted piety. His first wife was Laura Arabella Fisk, by whom he had one son, Henry Martyn, b. Jan. 16, 1850; d. in Nov., 1876, s. p. His wife was Mary E. Smith. His second wife was Sophia Williams, by whom he had three sons: 1, James Standish, now living in Hawley, Mass.; 2, Charles Williams, of Brooklyn, N. Y., office, 527 Broadway, cor. Spring St., New York City; 3, Horace Dwight, d. at the age of 24.

1817. ii. DAVID ORLANDO, b. Mar. 14, 1821; m. Laura Fiske and Isabella Hawkes.

1818. iii. REBECCA WHEELOCK, b. Feb. 22, 1823; m. Aug. 21, 1849, Rev. Burdett Hart. He was b. Nov. 16, 1821; d. Nov. 25, 1892. He was a Congregational clergyman. Ch.: Frederick Burdett Hart, b. Aug. 2, 1850; d. Aug. 6, 1851. Arthur Burdett Hart, b. Sept. 5, 1852; m. Jan. 10, 1878, at New Haven, Conn., Estelle Lee White, b. July 29, 1855. Is a merchant in New York city; res. s. p., 58 W. 72d st. Mary Arabelle Hart, b. May 30, 1855; m. Oct. 25, 1893, Abraham Robinson Perkins; res. West Upsal St., Germantown, Pa. Minerva Lee Hart, b. Nov. 9, 1859; m. Oct. 18, 1882, Samuel Hemingway; res. 37 East Pearl st., New Haven Conn. Rev. Burdett Hart, D. D., was born in New Britain, Conn. He was graduated at Yale College in 1842 and from Yale Divinity School in 1846; was ordained as pastor of the Grand Avenue Church in New Haven, in 1846, and is now pastor emeritus of that church. He was appointed a corporate member of the A. B. Ct. M. in 1876. He has been a fellow of Yale University since 1885. He is the author of the works, "Aspects of Christ," "Always Upward," "Aspects of Heaven." Mrs. Rebecca Wheelock Fisk, wife of Dr. Burdett Hart, was b. in Shelburne, Mass., was graduated at Mt. Holyoke Seminary (College), and was a teacher then with Mary Lyon for two years. She organized the Philadelphia branch of W. B. M. and was its president as well as the president of the New Haven branch of W. B. Missions. She is the author of a number of Missionary pamphlets. She d. Nov. 25, 1892.

1819. iv. SAMUEL WHEELOCK, b. July 23, 1828; m. Lizzie Foster.
1820. v. JANE ISABELLA, b. Aug. 20, 1830; m. June 20, 1849, Dr. David B. Hawkes. She res. in Decatur, Ill. He d. in 1885. She res. with her dau., Mrs. Clay Dempsey.
1821. vi. ASA SEAVERENCE, b. July 8, 1819; d. May 6, 1823.
1822. vii. PHILO, b. June 3, 1837; m. Josephine Tyler.
1823. viii. PHILO, b. Dec. 6, 1815; d. Apr. 6, 1816.
1824. ix. PHILO SEAVERENCE, b. July 28, 1826; d. Sept. 12, 1827.
1825. x. ASA S., b. Mar. 2, 1833; m. Elizabeth W. Hand.
1826. xi. PLINEY, b. Dec. 24, 1835; d. Aug. 20, 1836.

952. SAMUEL FISK (Samuel, Samuel, Daniel, Samuel, William, John, William, Robert, Simon, Simon, William, Symond), b. Shelburne, Mass., Mar. 25, 1800; m. there Sept. 30, 1824, Mercy Bardwell Smead, b. Dec. 3, 1798; d. Feb. 20, 1890. He res. in Shelburne all his life and was a farmer. He d. May 16, 1882; res. Shelburne, Mass.
1827. i. SAMUEL AUSTIN, b. July 23, 1825; m. Henrietta Parmenter.
1828. ii. CHARLES EDWARD, b. Sept. 9, 1826; m. Luthera S. Sprout and Charlotte A. Rounds.
1829. iii. SOLOMON B., b. Nov. 22, 1827; m. Helen M. Anderson.
1830. iv. LOUISA SOPHIA, b. June 15, 1829; d. Apr. 10, 1831.
1831. v. SOPHIA ELLEN, b. Feb. 1, 1832; d. Jan. 1, 1857.
1832. vi. GEORGE WASHINGTON, b. Nov. 2, 1834; m. Margaret H. Whitehill.
1833. vii. LOUISA MELINDA, b. Apr. 8, 1842; m. Oct. 23, 1872, A. R. Perkins. She d. Apr. 25, 1884. Ch.: 1, Thomas J., b. Aug. 6, 1873; res. 27 W. 60th St., N. Y. City. 2, Penuse R., b. Apr. 11, 1880; res. W. Upsal street, Germantown, Pa. 3, Louis Fiske, b. July 26, 1875; d. Mar. 30, 1884.

962. PARTRIDGE FISKE (Daniel, Samuel, Daniel, Samuel, William, John, William, Robert, Simon, Simon, William, Symond), b. Dec. 18, 1799, in Shelburne; m. there Apr. 19, 1824, Lydia D. Dickinson, b. June 8, 1803; d. Oct. 12, 1877. He was a farmer. He d. Feb. 12, 1832; res. Shelburne, Mass.
1834. i. SARAH ELECTA, b. Apr. 9, 1826; d., unm., in June, 1841.
1835. ii. RHODA MARIAH, b. June 7, 1828; m. Nov., 1848, Levi Page, b. Jan. 21, 1821; d. Jan. 15, 1891. He was a farmer; res. Conway, Mass. Ch.: Sarah Elizabeth Page, b. May 25, 1850; m. John W. Tilton, Conway, Mass. Feb. 14, 1877; ch.: Leroy P., b. Aug. 16, 1891. Levi Page, Jr., b. Nov. 8, 1857; d Jan. 29, 1877. Harlan Page, b. Feb. 12, 1863; m. May 24, 1888, Mary Ferris, of Millville, Orleans County, N. Y.; they res. in Millville. James Fiske Page, b. ———; m. Dec. 31, 1892, Dora French; res. Amherst, Mass.
1836. iii. JAMES DICKINSON, b. Jan. 1, 1831; m. Harriet Loomis and Mary E. Sheldon.

965. DANIEL FISKE (Daniel, Samuel, Daniel, Samuel, William, John, William, Robert, Simon, Simon, William, Symond), b. Shelburne, Mass., Feb. 9, 1805; m. Anna Fiske, dau. of Rufus, b. Apr. 22, 1808; d. May 21, 1875. He was a farmer. He d. Nov. 28, 1882; res. Shelburne, Mass.
1837. i. A SON, b. May 4, 1833; d. May 4, 1833.
1838. ii. CLARA TIRRELL, b. Feb. 18, 1836; unm.; res. Shelburne, Mass.
1839. iii. LAURA ANN, b. Apr. 30, 1838; d. Nov. 24, 1889.
1840. iv. HANNAH WOODWARD, b. Sept. 3, 1841; m. Apr. 3, 1891, Eugene Trask; res. Shelburne, Mass.

969. AUSTIN FISKE (Daniel, Samuel, Daniel, Samuel, William, John, William, Robert, Simon, Simon, William, Symond), b. Shelburne, Mass., Sept. 15, 1815; m. Sept. 29, 1842, Lucy W. Barnard, of Charlemont, b. Aug., 1820; d. Feb. 19, 1891. He was a farmer. He d. Oct. 10, 1851; res. Shelburne, Mass.
1841. i. CHLOE AUGUSTA, b. May, 1844; d. Feb. 22, 1859.

1842. ii.   LUCY SEVERANCE, b. Nov. 1, 1845; unm.; res. Easthampton, Mass.
1843. iii. MARY ELLEN, b. June 11, 1848; unm.; res. Conway, Mass.
1844. iv.   SARAH DORINDA, b. June 3, 1850; m. at Conway, Mass., Dec. 31, 1885, Wm. C. Wilder, b. June 15, 1828. He is a farmer; res. Conway. Ch.: Austin Fiske Wilder, b. Dec. 23, 1887; d. Dec. 23, 1887. Lucie Ellen Wilder, b. Nov. 8, 1889. Lillian Grace Wilder, b. Nov. 8, 1889; d. Nov. 12, 1889.

973.   REV. ELISHA FISKE (Robert, Daniel, Daniel, Samuel, William, John, William, Robert, Simon, Simon, William, Symond), b. Holliston Sept. 3, 1769; m. Lydia Robinson, d. July 11, 1805; she was dau. of John and Susanna of Milford; m. 2d, Mrs. Margaret (Shepherd) Brown, dau. of Capt. Benjamin and Hepzibah (Blake) Shepherd, of Wrentham; she was b. 1779; d. Apr. 30, 1850. Rev. Elisha Fisk was the son of Robert and Mary (Hall) Fisk, and was born in that part of Holliston now included in West Medway. At a year and a half of age his parents removed to Upton, where he spent his youth, and where he became converted under the ministry of Rev. Elisha Fish, whose name differed from his own but by a single letter. At five years of age he had read the Bible through. He set himself to gain a liberal education with reference to the ministry and by dint of perseverance, entered Brown University, and graduated in 1795, an A. M. He was tutor the three years following. While here he was approbated to preach the Gospel. He preached the first time in Wrentham on the first Sabbath in May, 1798. It was the first sermon he wrote and the text was Gen. 1; 1. It proved to be the first of a long series of discourses to that people. Nov. 6 he received a call to settle among them. The prospect was dark, indeed, but circumstances appeared to make duty very plain. He was the forty-ninth candidate and but the second who had received a call. Imagining the interminable catalogue which might follow if he declined, he determined to break the non-apostolic succession, and accepted the invitation Apr. 25. He was ordained over the first church in Wrentham June 12, 1799. Rev. Dr. Hitchcock of Providence preached the sermon. After occupying the field alone nearly 45 years, he proposed that a colleague should be settled, and Rev. Horace James was inducted into this office Nov. 1, 1843. Mr. Fisk still continued to preach almost every Sabbath at home, in surrounding vacant places, or in the pulpits of his brethren. The last Sabbath he spent on earth was employed in preaching the Gospel and breaking the sacramental bread in the church of Attleboro. It was an intensely cold day in December and the fatigue and exposure of riding in an open sleigh some ten miles was more than a human frame of over four score years' standing could endure. A cold and fever was the result, running into a lethargic state, in which the ever busy spirit, having put its weary partner of dust to sleep, softly withdrew. He died in the 82d year of his age, and 52d year of his ministry, and was buried on the day of the regular meeting of the association at his house. It was appointed to be there at his request, and he had anticipated its coming with great satisfaction, not imagining that they should be convened for his funeral. At the time of Mr. Fisk's ordination, the church was reduced to ten members; and "they were divided in their religious opinions, and in many instances strongly excited against each other, on account of the different positions, which they had taken in the controversy with his predecessor, Rev. McAvery. Of an observing mind, careful and conciliating in his conversation and manners, interesting and popular in his pulpit performances, he succeeded, as few other men would, in uniting and holding together very discordant materials, not only at the commencement of his ministry, but through the vicissitudes of more than fifty years. He gained and kept the enviable reputation of peacemaker." (Funeral Sermon by Rev. Dr. Stoors, Braintree.) As a fact illustrative of Mr. Fisk's reputation the celebrated Hannah Adams once said that another question should be added to the well known interrogatories in New England, "Who is the first man," etc., viz.: "Who is the most prudent man? Parson Fisk, of Wrentham." He was blessed with additions to his church. In 1805, 51 were added to the church. In 1815-16, 64 made profession of religion. In 1821, 43 were gathered in. Again, 58 joined in 1832. The whole number of admissions during his sole ministry was 432.

Mr. Fisk possessed an iron constitution and great perseverance and was able to labor, even in his advanced age, beyond the ability of many young men. He frequently took long walks of five and even ten miles on his exchanges. He traveled much on foot over his extensive parish. He was seldom unable to preach—but two Sabbaths in forty years. He was seldom absent, or even tardy, at associate meetings. He attended over 150 ecclesiastical councils; and did a large part of the editing of the "Christian Magazine," during its four years' continuance, and was in all ministerial labors abundant.

Rev. Nathaniel Emmons, D. D., pastor of the church in Franklin, preached the sermon at the funeral of his first wife, Lydia, July 13, 1805. The sermon was printed by H. Mann of Dedham, in Aug., 1805. The compiler of this work has a copy of the sermon.

He d. Jan. 11, 1857; res. Wrentham, Mass.

1845.   i.   MARY HALL. b. ——; m. Rev. George Fisher of Harvard; she d. Apr. 29, 1852. He was a native of Wrentham, Mass., where he was born Nov. 7, 1796. He was graduated at Brown University in the class of 1819, sharing the highest honors of graduation with Horace Mann. His studies for the ministry were conducted under the direction of Rev. Elisha Fisk; was installed pastor of the Evangelical Congregational Society in Harvard, Mass., Sept. 12, 1821. He preached the sermon on the one hundredth anniversary of the incorporation of that town. This sermon is deposited with the Congregational Library Association in Boston. He was a most efficient pastor, and for thirty years was a member of the school board. He died Sept. 6, 1853.

1846. ii.   CHARLES ROBINSON, b. Oct. 27, 1804. He gr. Brown University 1824; was a clergyman in Ill. He d. in Delavan, Ill., Dec. 28, 1869 (see Coll. Grad.).

1847. iii.   CHARLOTTE BROWN, b. ——; m. Rev. Amos A. Phelps of Boston; she d. Aug., 1838

1848. iv.   EMILY FRANCES, b. Nov. 7, 1812; m. at Wrentham, Mass., Capt. Wm. Sturtevant of New Bedford. He was a master mariner, b. Sept. 20, 1802, in Rochester, Mass.; d. in May, 1879. Ch.: Charles, b. July 28, 1839; m. June 15, 1871. Bethia Hadley Delano, b. Feb. 18, 1848, M. D., physician and surgeon formerly U. S. Navy; res. Hyde Park, Mass. Ch.: Emil Frances Sturtevant, b. Oct. 17, 1872; res. Hyde Park, Mass Verona Hadley Sturtevant, b. Nov. 9, 1878; res. Hyde Park, Mass.

1849.   v.   WM. JONES, b. 1814; d. 1830.

1850. vi.   FRED'K A., b. Apr. 15, 1816; m. Anna A. Nelson and Mrs. Rebecca J. (Robbins) Haskell and Abbie Wheeler Woods.

1851. vii.   HARRIETT JOSEPHINE, b. ——; m. Rev. Erasmus D. Moore of Boston. A son, Geo. A. Moore, res. 70 Kilby street, Boston.

974. DEA. DANIEL FISKE (Robert, Daniel, Daniel, Samuel, William, John, William, Robert, Simon, Simon, William, Symond), b. Holliston, Mass., Oct. 29, 1770; m. at Mendon, Apr. 4, 1816, Ruth Chapin, of Mendon, Mass., b. Jan. 14, 1786; d. July 30, 1883. He held many town offices, as well as others; was deacon of the First Congregational Church for forty years. He had but little schooling, and that in the last century. He was brought up on a farm and when 17 years of age conducted a farm for a widow lady "on halves." He did not have a pair of boots until 18 years of age; drove turkeys to market, and put up over night when the turkeys went to roost by the wayside. Eventually he went into the village store; was a merchant some thirty years, and gave it up to his son, David B. Was Captain of the militia through the war of 1812 and 1815, but not called into active service. Was town clerk for many years; selectman, assessor, coroner, justice of the peace, treasurer, agent for procuring pensions for soldiers of the Revolution; first postmaster in Upton in 1818. In after years D. B. and D. E., his sons, were postmasters in the same town; the only case of the kind in the United States. Interested in anything that was of benefit to the town or citizens. He retired from all business in 1836, and died in 1840 in the 70th year of his age. He was born in Holliston, Mass., but resided nearly all his life in Upton, Mass., where he was an honored and respected citizen. At the time of his death Rev. Benjamin Wood, pastor of the Upton Church, officiated at his funeral. The sermon was printed in

Boston by Dutton & Wentworth, and from that discourse it is learned that the deceased was a constant attendant at public worship; as a husband and father, he was tender and affectionate; as a friend, open, candid, honest and sincere; as a neighbor, kind and obliging. Dea. Fiske had an extended acquaintance; being engaged for many years in the mercantile business. He d. Apr. 23, 1840; res. Upton, Mass.

and was highly respected and esteemed. He d. Apr. 23, 1840; res. Upton, Mass.

 1852. i. DAVID B., b. June 23, 1817; m. Lydia C. Wood.
 1853. ii. HANNAH P., b. Oct. 29, 1818; m. Oct. 26, 1840, George W. Wood.
 1854. iii. ALMIRA C., b. Apr. 22, 1820; m. in U., Aug. 22, 1839, Abner G. Wright.
 1855. iv. DANIEL E., b. Mar. 4, 1822; m. Harriot Billings.
 1856. v. JOHN MILTON, b. Jan. 17, 1824; d. 1825.

 975. DEA. WILLIAM FISKE (Robert, Daniel, Daniel, Samuel, William, John, William, Robert, Simon, Simon, William, Symond), b. Holliston, Mass., Nov. 8, 1776; m. Lucy Bradish, b. 1780; d. Dec. 29, 1860. He was a farmer, deacon in the church, a man of very high character and highly esteemed. He d. Dec. 15, 1862; res. Upton, Mass.

 1857. i. ALBERT WM., b. Jan. 16, 1802. Albert W. Fiske was born in Upton, Mass.; fitted for college at Wrentham Academy; graduated at Brown University, Providence, R. I., 1829; graduated at Andover Theological Seminary, in class 1832; began to preach in Alfred, Me., Sept. 30, 1832; after a service of twelve years resigned May 12, 1844; began to preach in Scarborough, Me., Sept. 8, 1844; labored three years and three months, closing labors Feb. 13, 1848; began to preach in Kittery, Me., May 12, 1850; was dismissed Apr. 1, 1857; began to preach in Pennacook, N. H., Dec. 21, 1856; service six years ten months, eleven days; resigned Oct. 16 1863. From his journal is copied the following: "By a kind Heavenly Father's overruling providence my lot has been cast in pleasant places and I have had a goodly heritage—been favored with general good health, taken great pleasure in the various kinds of pastoral labor, and especially enjoyed preaching Christ. To Him I owe an immense debt of gratitude for calling me by His grace and spirit and permitting me to labor so long in the delightful work of the Christian ministry. As an humble instrument in His service I will not pretend to say what I may have accomplished by my labors; but if any good to the welfare of His kingdom, to Him be all the glory." He published a book called "A New Year Offering." It consisted of miscellaneous articles, poetry and prose, and one or two sermons; m. Jan. 1, 1833, Mary Davis; d. June 2, 1850; m. 2d, June 18, 1851, Mary Ann Whipple, b. Oct. 24, 1813; d. May 26, 1896; res. Pennacook, N. H. Ch.: George William Fiske, b. Nov. 24, 1833; d. Sept. 28, 1834. Ellen Maria, b. July 20, 1835; m. Apr. 12, 1860, —— Shepperd; res. Lebanon, N. H. Charles Albert, b. Jan. 12, 1838; res. Greenwich, Conn.; he was born in Alfred, Me.; was a graduate of Dartmouth College, and is an artist by profession; he married in June 24, 1872, Miss Sarah B. Smith, dau. of Mr. William Smith, of Greenwich, Conn., and has two children, a daughter, Alice Belcher Fiske, and a son, William Smith Maynard Fiske. Henry Bardwell, b. Apr. 19, 1842; d. Nov. 12, 1842. Mary Caroline, b. Mar. 26, 1845; d. Mar. 31, 1846. George Whipple, b. May 9, 1852; d. Feb. 4, 1876. John William, b. May 24, 1853; res. Boston, Mass. Mary Anna, b. July 4, 1855; res. Pennsylvania. After finishing school she studied music for several years, spending one year at the Conservatory in Boston. For six years she occupied a nice position as organist and has also taught music several years. For the last few years she has given her time to the care of her aged father, who died of old age, Dec. 6, 1892. His widow passed away May 26, 1896.

1858. ii.   ELISHA B., b. Feb. 16, 1804; m. Mariam C. Starkweather.
1859. iii.   JUDSON HOPKINS, b. Aug. 30, 1807; d. in 1815.
1860. iv.   CHARLES A., b. Apr. 4, 1811; m. Salina Melita Ward.
1861. v.   GEORGE R., b. Jan. 5, 1821; m. Louisa M. Tyler.

976. AMASA FISKE (Robert, Daniel, Daniel, Samuel, William, John, William, Robert, Simon, Simon, William, Symond), b. Holliston, Mass., Sept. 17, 1780; m. —— ——. He graduated at Brown University; was a lawyer (see list College graduates). He d. Mar. 23, 1847; res. Dover, Vt.

982. EMMONS HOWARD FISKE (Daniel, Daniel, Daniel, Samuel, William, John, William, Robert, Simon, Simon, William, Symond), b. Upton, Mass., May 10, 1802; m. there, Nov. 12, 1825, Anna Marilla Ward, b. Aug. 1, 1805; d. Sept. 14, 1879. He was a farmer. He d. Apr. 7, 1885; res. Upton, Mass.

1862. i.   HARRISON LYSANDER, b. Nov. 28, 1828; m. Mary S. Hill.
1863. ii.   HYPOLLITUS CLAUSEN, b. Feb. 3, 1827; m. Philena A. Perry.
1864. iii.   CELIA ANN, b. Aug. 7, 1849; m. June 2, 1870, Wm. H. Wellington; res. Upton, Mass.; one ch. m. Joseph B. Chapin of Hopedale.
1865. iv.   ADALISA P., d in 7th year, in Upton.
1866. v.   CORNELIA A., d. in 5th year.
1867. vi.   CALVIN W., d. in 3d year.
1868. vii.   MELITA A., d. in 11th year, 1849, in E. Cambridge.
1869. viii. JONATHAN O., b. June 17, 1844; killed at Newberne, ae. 16.
1870. ix.   FRANCOIS T., d. in 6th year.

986. JOEL FISK (Benjamin, Benajmin, Daniel, Samuel, William, John, William, Robert, Simon, Simon, William, Symond), b. Upton, Mass., Dec. 17, 1770; m. Hannah Turner; res. Medway, Mass. Among his children was:

1870½. i.   JAMES JONES, b. Jan. 14, 1806; m. Rebekah Prouty and Miranda Prouty.

987. CLARK FISKE (Benjamin, Benjamin, Daniel, Samuel, William, John, William, Robert, Simon, Simon, William, Symond), b. Upton, Mass., Apr. 4, 1778; m. there Jan. 27, 1813, Chloe Bradish of Upton, b. Sept. 15, 1783. He d. in U., Nov. 10, 1835; res. Shelburne and Upton, Mass.

1871. i.   LUTHER B., b. Mar. 17, 1814; m. S. N. F. Leonard.
1872. ii.   HARVEY W., b. Jan. 13, 1816; m. Jerusha Adams.
1873. iii.   CHANDLER JUDSON, b. July 17, 1822; d. in U., May 2, 1828.

992. GALACIUS FISKE (Benjamin, Benjamin, Daniel, Samuel, William, John, William, Robert, Simon, Simon, William, Symond), b. Upton, Mass., Apr. 17, 1788; m. in Rutland, Mass., May 2, 1816, Mary Brown, b. Mar. 5, 1794; d. in Worcester, on Mar. 22, 1890. He was a farmer and miller. He d. in Ludlow, Mass., May 30, 1853; res. Shelburne, Mass.

1874. i.   GALACIUS F., b. Jan. 23, 1821; m. Margaret J. Brady.
1875. ii.   SARAH ELIZA, b. Apr. 19, 1824; m. —— Spunt. She d. Sept. 12, 1880.
1876. iii.   OTIS ALPHONZO, b. Nov. 25, 1826; m. Abby S. Gove.
1877. iv.   JULIA ANN MARIA, b. Nov. 24, 1828; m. Apr. 6, 1849, Jeremiah Dutton. She d. Oct. 23, 1866. He was b. in Ludlow, Mass., Aug. 21, 1822. He d. in Belchertown, Mass., Oct. 23, 1867; was a farmer. Ch.: Wilbur Fisk Dutton, res. Cleveland, Ohio; b. May 5, 1853; m. Nov. 27, 1884. Ora C. Dutton, res. Thorndike, Mass.; b. Nov. 11, 1855; m. Sept. 24, 1873, George A. Murdock, b. Jan. 19, 1850, is a merchant; ch.: Maude Julia Murdock, b. May 2, 1874. Eva Murdock, b. Oct. 25, 1876; d. Mar. 9, 1877. Victor Dutton Murdock, b. Jan. 29, 1878. Ada Josephine Murdock, b. July 14, 1880. Blanche Nancy Murdock, b. May 8, 1883. Florence Adelaide Murdock, b. June 20, 1886. Their P. O. add. is Thorndike, Mass., excepting Victor, who is in Cleveland, Ohio.
1878. v.   SEWALL AUGUSTUS, b. Aug. 3, 1831; m. Mary J. ——; res. 1 Dudley Place, Worcester, Mass. He d. Nov. 4, 1887; left two sons, Fred and Eugene.

1879. vi. HARRIETT ADELIA, b. Jan. 24, 1817; m. Aug. 4, 18—; Edward
Lucius Ward; res. Worcester, Mass., P. O. box 595. He was
b. Jan. 13, 1815; d. Apr. 20, 1890. She res. 9 Gardner St.,
Worcester. Ch.: 1, Julia Maria Ward Tompkins, b. Mar. 19,
1846; m. Sept. 19, 1865, in Worcester City and Co., Mass.; ch.:
Lucius Warren Tompkins, b. June 9, 1866; m. June 14, 1893;
one child b. Oct. 4, 1895; name of child Louisa Ward Tompkins; address of Lucius, 51 May St., Worcester, Mass. Mabelle
Ward Tompkins, b. May 8, 1870; d. Aug. 12, 1871. 2, Harriet
Louisa Ward King, b. Dec. 31, ——; m. Dec. 2, 1869, Worcester City and Co., Mass.
1880. vii. MARY BURNS, b. Nov. 2, 1818; m. —— Marshall. She d.
Sept. 15, 1861; a son, Julius Marshall, res. 36 Newbury St.,
Worcester, Mass.
1881. viii. FRANCIS WAYLAND, b. May 30, 1838; d. Dec. 27, 1868, from
effects of wounds in the civil war.

993. EMORY FISK (Benjamin, Benjamin, Daniel, Samuel, William, John,
William, Robert, Simon, Simon, William, Symond); b. Upton, Mass., June 30,
1790; m. Feb. 26, 1816, Sally Gross; b. Oct. 1, 1792; d. June 30, 1866, in Chicopee.
He was a farmer and millwright. He d. Feb. 11, 1852; res. Enfield, Mass.
1882. i. ERASTUS CLARK, b. Feb. 2, 1817; d. May 31, 1817.
1883. ii. GEORGE ARMORY, b. Sept. 29, 1818; m. Caroline H. Merrick.
1884. iii. SARAH CAROLINE, b. Jan. 21, 1821; m., in 1845, James S.
Blair. Ch.: Lizzie and Jennie. She d. 1894. Jennie m. ——
Buxton, res. Dartmouth St., Springfield, Mass.
1885. iv. ERASTUS HIRAM, b. July 12, 1823; m. Dency A. Sprout.
1886. v. CHARLES HORACE, b. Nov. 1, 1825; m. Sylvia J. Ward.
1887. vi. ELIZA ANN, b. Dec. 23, 1829; m. in 1848 John Q. Bailey. She
d. in 1893.
1888. vii. MELISSA JANE, b. Feb. 23, 1830; d. Oct. 6, 1839.

997. JONATHAN FISK (Benjamin, Benjamin, Daniel, Samuel, William,
John, William, Robert, Simon, Simon, William, Symond), b. Upton, Mass., Aug.
30, 1794; m. in Upton, 1816, Gratia Wilson, dau. of Samuel; b. Feb. 19, 1797; d.
July, 1876. He res. in Milford and his death was quite sudden. He d. Nov., 1857;
res. Milford, Mass.
1889. i. DAVID ANSON, b. Oct. 16, 1816; m. —— Handy.
1890. ii. PAULINE ANN, b. July 23, 1817; m. June 5, 1839, George S.
Lackey.
1891. iii. BENJAMIN W., b. Jan. 17, 1820; m. Frances Blake of Boston.
1892. iv. LUCIUS C., b. Aug. 3, 1821; m. Harriett E. Sheperd.
1893. v. ELIZABETH MELITA, b. Sept., 1823; m. David Saunders.
1894. vi. SARAH JANE, b. Sept., 1825; m. Oct. 5, 1849, Orlando J. Davis.
1895. vii. JONATHAN EDWIN, b. Oct., 1828; m. Martha Cummings.
1896. viii. CHARLES AUSTIN, b. Jan., 1831; res. Upton; unm.
1897. ix. WILLIAM PRENTICE, b. June, 1833; m. Mary Hilton.
1898. x. JAMES WOOD, b. Dec., 1835; m. Maria Smith.
1899. xi. HENRY P., b. Nov., 1840; m. Jan. 1, 1867, Elmira A. Ballard.

999. HARVEY FISKE (Benjamin, Benjamin, Daniel, Samuel, William,
John, William, Robert, Simon, Simon, William, Symond), b. Upton, Mass., Jan.
21, 1797; m. there Mar. 2, 1818, Sophia Warren; b. 1798. Res. Upton, Mass.
1900. i. MARGERY W., b. June 15, 1818; m. Sept. 1, 1844, George L.
Wood; res. Upton.
1901. ii. JULIA W., b. Nov. 23, 1819; m. Barnabas Snow; res. Ware.
1902. iii. ANN MARIA, b. June 24, 1821; m. Oct. 12, 1843, Sylvester
Whitney; b. June 2, 1819; res. U. Ch.: 1, Charlotte Marion, b.
Nov. 5, 1844; m. Nov. 14, 1866, Walter Bryant Clapp; res. Upton, Mass.; ch.: Edwin Blake, b. July 27, 1872. 2, Alfred Langdon, b. Jan. 22, 1848; res. Upton, Mass.; unm. 3, Edward Rice,
b. Apr. 24, 1851; d. May 7, 1851. 4, Jennie Eveline, b. Apr. 9,
1858; m. Sept. 26, 1878, Estus Warren Harback; res. Upton; ch.:
Frank Leonard, b. Jan. 13, 1879; Maud Ella, b. July 9, 1880;

Nellie May, b. Aug. 24, 1886; Fred Warren, b. Sept. 7, 1889; Charles, b. Nov. 3, 1891; d. July 31, 1892: a son, b. Sept. 7, 1893.

1903. iv. CHLOE S., b. May 15, 1823.
1904. v. JOSIAH A., b. 1828; d. Aug. 11, 1848.
1905. vi. HARRIETT F., b. 1835; d. 1835.

1003. ERAN FISK (Elisha, William, Daniel, Samuel, William, John, William, Robert, Simon, Simon, William, Symond), b. Upton, Mass., May 12, 1800; m. June 14, 1825, Sally Wood, b. 1802; d. Jan. 15, 1828; m. 2nd Apr. 1, 1829, Sally Whitney, b. Aug. 11, 1801, in Upton, dau. of Amos; d. Jan. 27, 1880. He was a carpenter and farmer. He d. Apr. 26, 1885; res. Upton, Mass.

1906. i. ERAN A., b. June 12, 1826; m. Jane E. Holbrook and Harriett S. Pearse.
1907. ii. PHILO WHITNEY, b. Apr. 5, 1832; m. Nov. 1856 and d. in Upton in June, 1879.
1908. iii. DENNIS TAFT, b. Apr. 7, 1837; m. Calista A. Fiske.
1909. iv. ELLEN L., b. May 18, 1839; m. Feb., 1864, Z. B. Grandy, res. Upton.
1910. v. LEONA WOOD, b. Jan. 31, 1842; m. Apr., 1865, J. Augustus Goddard; res. Grafton. He was b. Sept. 20, 1836; is a farmer and carpenter. Ch.: Maria A. Goddard, b. Feb. 10, 1866; m. Lucius R. Dodge of Sutton, Mass., June 18, 1889; P. O. Milford, Mass.; Silas B. Goddard, b. Feb. 2, 1868; Arthur F. Goddard, b. Aug. 26, 1869; Herbert A. Goddard, b. Mar. 24, 1871; Albert H. Goddard, b. Mar. 21, 1875; Bertha Fisk Goddard, b. July 12, 1879.

1004. ELISHA FISKE (Elisha, William, Daniel, Samuel, William, John, William, Robert, Simon, Simon, William, Symond), b. Upton, Mass., Apr. 16, 1802; m. there, Sept. 12, 1826, Hannah F. Forbush, b. May 12, 1808 (Elijah, Peter, Samuel, Thomas, Thomas, Daniel). He was a farmer. He d. in Upton; res. Upton, Mass.

1911. i. GEORGE WM., b. July 9, 1837; m. Sarah E. Lackey.
1912. ii. BETSEY MARIA, b. Mar. 9, 1827; m. Sept. 10, 1843, Alanson P. Rockwood; res. Upton, Mass.
1913. iii. GILBERT NEWELL, b. Nov. 7, 1839; d. young.

1005. LEVI FISK (Elisha, William, Daniel, Samuel, William, John, William, Robert, Simon, Simon, William, Symond), b. Upton, Mass., May 1, 1804; m. there Mar. 16, 1828, Amy Taft, b. Mar. 5, 1802; d. Aug. 16, 1863. He d. in Hopkinton, May 30, 1881; res. Upton, Mass.

1914. i. MARTHA, b. July 15, 1828; m. Holland E. Forbush, b. Upton, Nov. 9, 1824 (Holland, Elijah, Peter, Samuel, Thomas, Thomas, Daniel). He d. Feb. 6, 1865; res. Upton, Milford and Hopkinton, Mass. Ch.: 1, Arthur H., b. Jan. 17, 1863; m. Esther Worcester; res. Boston, Mass., 181 Devonshire St.
1915. ii SARAH ELIZABETH, b. Oct. 29, 1830; m. Feb. 17, 1858, Amos R. Adams. He is a farmer, was b. Feb. 22, 1830; res. Hopkinton, Mass. Ch.: Nellie E. Adams, b. Mar. 7, 1859; Emmie J. Adams, b. Aug. 18, 1862; d. May 20, 1872; Wilbur F. Adams, b. Mar. 6, 1865; m. Oct. 31, 1888, Hattie Phipps; add. 15 Vinsen St., Dorchester, Mass.; Grace Louise Adams, b. Mar. 31, 1871; m. June 10, 1891, to Geo. O. Wood; add. 333 Park St., Dorchester, Mass.
1916. iii. JANE ALMIRA, b. Sept. 21, 1832.
1917. iv. MARIETTA ADELAIDE, b. Sept. 23, 1835.

1010. ADAMS FISKE (Elisha, William, Daniel, Samuel, William, John, William, Robert, Simon, Simon, William, Symond), b. Upton, Mass., Apr. 19, 1814; m. Mar. 23, 1836, Betsey Forbush, b. May 30, 1818. (Herman, David, David, Thomas, Thomas, Daniel). Res. Upon, Mass.

1918. i. WALDO, b. May 30, 1839; d. June 5, 1855.

1013. JONATHAN STOWE FISKE (David, William, Daniel, Samuel, William, John, William, Robert, Simon, Simon, William, Symond), b. Grafton, Mass.,

June 8, 1808; m. there Mar. 5, 1838, Georgiana Maria Keith, b. Aug, 19, 1803; d. Aug. 21, 1851. Was a farmer and prominent citizen. He d. Apr. 9, 1872; res. Grafton, Mass.

    1919. i.   SARAH JANE, b. Dec. 22, 1838: m. Mar. 1, 1864, Henry Keith Southwick; d. s. p., 1864, and is buried in Providence, R. I.

    1920. ii.   DAVID L., b. July 19, 1840; m. Ella Williams.

    1921. iii. REBECCA ANN K., b. Jan. 15, 1843; m. Apr. 7, 1869, Orlando J. Davis; res. Upton. She d. Mar. 1, 1877, a son, Irving H., res. Hopedale, Mass.

    1922. iv. DORINDA LOUISA, b. Aug. 27, 1845; m. Jan. 21, 1874, Charles Henry Ballard; res. East Charlemont, Mass.

    1014. WILLIAM ADAMS FISKE (David, William, Daniel, Samuel, William, John, William, Robert, Simon, Simon, William, Symond), b. Upton, Mass., Sept 30, 1810; m. at Chester, Vt., May 16, 1854, Mary Jane Heald, b. Sept. 16, 1834. He was a farmer. He d. Feb. 17, 1875; res. Grafton, Mass.

    1923. i.   HARRY EDWARDS, b. Apr. 17, 1865; m. in Somerville, Mass., Apr. 4, 1888, Ella M. Beckwith, b. May 30, 1868. He is a seedsman; s. p.: add. 34 So. Market St., Boston, Mass.

    1924. ii.   WILLIE EUGENE, b. Nov. 25, 1856; m. Frances Hedstrom.

    1017. DAVID ALLEN FISK (David, William, Daniel, Samuel, William, John, William, Robert, Simon, Simon, William, Symond). b. Shelburne, Mass., Feb. 15, 1819; m. at Buckland, Sept. 5, 1850, Caroline Forbes Smith, b. Nov. 10, 1823; d. Jan. 23, 1891. He is a farmer, cooper and stock dealer; res. Shelburne, Mass.

    1925. i.   PRESTON ERVING, b. June 15, 1857; d. ae. 4.

    1926. ii.   ELISHA SMITH, b. Apr. 11, 1853: P. O. Waitsfield, Vt.

    1927. iii. LYDIA LOUISE, b. 1855; d. ae. 4 years.

    1928. iv. WILLIAM ALLEN, b. Sept. 21, 1857: P. O. Stamford, Conn.

    1929. v.   LYDIA LOUISE, b. Dec. 13, 1859.

    1930. vi. TWIN BOYS, one still born, 1861; one d. ae. 4.

    1931. vii. CARRIE ESTHER, b. Jan. 12, 1863; P. O. Shelburne, Mass.

    1023. ALEXANDER FISK (Josiah, Josiah, Daniel, Samuel, William, John, William, Robert, Simon, Simon, William, Symond), b. Upton, Mass., Nov. 29, 1789; m. in Chesterfield, Mary Fisk, his cousin, b. 1795; d. Shelburne Falls, Mass., in Aug. 1840. He was a farmer, carpenter and carriage builder and d. at Island Pond, Vt. He d. Aug. 20, 1877; res. Shelburne and Colerain, Mass.

    1932. i.   MARY ANN, b. in New York State. Feb. 21, 1812; d. in Shelburne, Apr. 19, 1813.

    1933. ii.   HORACE L., b. Oct. 3, 1813; m. Emily E. Cumming.

    1934. iii. MARIANNA, b. Dec. 21, 1815; m. Brigham M. Savage. They were m. in 1840 in Shelburne Falls, Mass. She d. in Independence, Ia., in 1890, s. p. He is living.

    1935. iv. EMELY AURELIA, b. Apr. 6, 1817: m. ——— Pettis. They had five children. She d. in Stanstead Plains, near Derby Line, Vt., in 1870.

    1936. v.   BETSY F., b. May 10, 1819: d. June 4, 1819.

    1937. vi. HANNAH E., b. June 24, 1820; d. May 10, 1826.

    1938. vii. SAMUEL W., b. Nov. 29, 1823: m. Lucina Pierce.

    1939. viii. HANNAH ELIZABETH, b. Mar. 31, 1827; d. Feb. 11, 1829.

    1940. ix. JOHN GOODALE, b. July 12, 1825; d. May 13, 1826.

    1941. x.   JOHN GOODALE, b. Sept. 1, 1831: m. Sarah Jane Horn.

    1942. xi. ELZORA DARLISKA, b. ———; m. William Havens at Spencer, Mass. She d. about 1872 and left a daughter, Mary, who m. John Cunningham, and resided near Worcester, Mass.

    1943. xii. DIANTHA ELIZABETH, b. ———; m. Simon Graves of Worcester, Mass. They had two children, Charles and Willie.

    1027. HON. ISAIAH FISKE (Amos, Daniel, Samuel, Joseph, William, John, William, Robert, Simon, Simon, William, Symond). b. Swanzey, Mass., Sept. 6, 1763; m. Mar. 2, 1786, Hannah Bacon. Her grandfather Bacon, with his brother, came from England. The brother, Rev. Jacob Bacon, was the pastor of the church at Plymouth, Mass. Her mother's name was Willbur. She was a lineal descendant of Rev. Samuel Mann, the first minister of the town of Wrentham, mentioned in Barber's Historical Collections of Mass. (Judge Fisk was born in Swansea, Mass., and was descended in both lines from that noble class of men who sought on "the wild New England shore" "freedom to worship God." There has been a tradition in the family that Benjamin Fisk, a brother of the great-grandfather of the subject of this sketch, was governor of the colony of Connecticut, but this has not been substantiated. A strong family likeness has always existed among the Rhode Island Fisks. In early life he resided in Rhode Island, but subsequently moved to Guilford, Vermont, a town which adjoined Brattleboro, where his father had some time before purchased land. By an unfortunate business venture he lost his patrimony, but by industry and frugality he accumulated sufficient for the purchase of new land in the interior of the State. He accordingly settled in Lyndon, Caledonia county, within 40 miles of the Canada line. In that county he ever after resided, respected and beloved by all who knew him. He received repeated proofs of the confidence of his fellow citizens, filling various important civil offices. Isaiah Fisk was one of the assistant judges of Caledonia county court, 1807, 1809, 1810, 1811, 1812. Chief judge of Caledonia county court, 1816, 1817, 1818, 1819, 1820, 1821, 1822; then the office was more important than it is now, under the revised constitution. He was a presidential elector from Vermont in 1817 and a delegate in the convention that nominated James Monroe for President. Isaiah Fisk was a member of the general assembly of Vermont for the following years from Lyndon, Vermont, Caledonia county: 1803, 1804, 1813, 1814, 1815, 1816, 1817, 1818, 1821, 1823. Besides these he filled various local offices involving more care and responsibility than emolument. Twice he was elected to the council of censors, which was then composed of thirteen members, chosen once in seven years, by a general vote. Its province was to revise all the official acts of the Legislature, executive and judiciary departments, during the past seven years, with power to send for persons, papers and records. It could pass censure, order impeachments and recommend the Legislature to repeal unconstitutional laws. Such a tribunal was a very important one. Judge Fisk remained comparatively poor where many would have amassed a fortune. It was his maxim that no man ought to enrich himself on the spoils of the public, a maxim which through life he carried to a romantic extreme. With his wife he early became a member of the church and took an active interest in it. Mrs. Fisk was very assiduous in impressing upon the minds of her children the principles of Christianity. He d. June 7, 1859; res. Brattleboro, Lyndon and Charlestown, Vt.

> 1943½.i.   DAUGHTER, b. ———; m. and had children.
> 1944. ii.   WILBUR, b. Aug. 31, 1/92; m. Miss R. Peek.
> 1944½.iii. ISAIAH, b. ———; d. æ 4.

1037. ABRAHAM FISK (Ephraim, Joseph, Samuel, Joseph, William, John, William, Robert, Simon, Simon, William, Symond), b. Providence R. I.; m. 1790, Mary Brown. He d. Mar. 14, 1855; res. Cherry Valley, N. Y.

> 1945. i.   ORIN M., b. Apr. 25, 1807; m. Sarah A. Cooper and Roxanna Priest.
> 1946. ii.   OBADIAH, b. ———; d. unm.
> 1947. iii. JESSE, b. ———; d. unm.
> 1948. iv.   CHARLES, b. ———; d. unm.
> 1949. v.   DARIUS b. ———.
> 1950. vi.   LYDIA, b. ———; m. Harris Lascelles.

1040. CAPT. BENJAMIN BIGFORD FISKE (Ephraim, Joseph, Samuel, Joseph, William, John, William, Robert, Simon, Simon, William Symond), b. Killingly, Conn., Nov. 2, 1794; m. there Apr. 12, 1816, Lydia Aldrich; b. Killingly, Conn., Apr 1, 1796; d. Mar. 2, 1879. She m. 2d William Smith. Benjamin B. Fisk was born in Killingly, Conn., where he learned the trade of a blacksmith. Having mastered his trade, he was soon afterward united in marriage to Lydia Aldrich. She came of Welsh descent, and in her veins flowed somewhat a sturdy feeling and marked courage and the unfailing will that her ancestors knew. In the fall of 1822, with his wife and two babies, he left Killingly for Livingston Co., New York. There he was a blacksmith, wagon builder and general mechanic for the country round about. Muscular and willing, equipped with fine physique, he did not shrink from hard toil. His shops became a source of mechanical supplies for farmers all up and down the valley. As a citizen he acquired local repute as a man of intelligence, enterprise and character. He was the captain of the militia, and was deferred to as a leading spirit in town affairs. He finally moved to Clinton, Mich., where he died after a short illness. He d. Sept. 28. 1832; res. Killingly, Conn., Greigsville, N. Y., and Clinton, Mich.

1951. i. CYRUS B., b. Nov. 29, 1871; m. Miss Powell.

1952. ii. LEANDER, b. Killingly, Conn., Jan. 22, 1820; m. in Clinton, Dec. 10, 1857, Fannie Wilson Ellis, b. Mar. 4, 1821; res. s. p., 671 3d St. Oakland, Cal. His life has not been a very eventful one. Born in 1820 in Connecticut, in 1821 or 1822, his parents moved to the State of New York, Livingston Co., town of York; in 1830 they moved to Michigan (Clinton, Lenawee Co), where in winter times he went to school three months, in summer worked out, sometimes driving from six to ten yoke of cattle before what was called a breaking-up plow. His father died in 1832, leaving his mother with six boys, the eldest only 14 years old. He went to a trade when he was 15 years old (fanning mill making). He worked at that until he was about 22, at which time he was elected constable and served one year. In 1843 he went into a store, where he worked until 1847, at which time he enlisted in the 1st regiment of Michigan Volunteers, and went to Mexico, where he remained until the close of the war. He returned to Detroit, got an honorable discharge, made his way back to Clinton and went into business. Gold was discovered in California and he got the fever and in 1853 he crossed the plains to California, where he has wandered up and down for nearly forty-three years. He has been in the mines where he did mining and kept a trading post. He has been well off and has been poor. He has had the sciatica and a stroke of paralysis, also had a stroke of footpads two years ago, which came very near killing him. He is drawing a pension for service in the Mexican war.

1953. iii. HORACE A., b. Feb. 16, 1825; m. Jane N. Brown.

1954. iv. CLINTON B., b. Dec. 8, 1828; m. Janette A. Crippen.

1955. v. BENJAMIN W., b. Apr. 20, 1831; d. June 21, 1840.

1956. vi. WELCOME V., b. June 29, 1822; m. Amanda Vaughn and Mary Felton.

1043. SAMUEL FISK (Isaac, Joseph, Samuel, Joseph, William, John, William, Robert, Simon, Simon, William, Symond), b. Johnston, R. I., Apr. 4, 1797; m. June 16, 1822, Sally Stone Kent, b. June 1. 1799; d. May 23, 1889. Samuel Fiske was b. Apr. 4, 1797, in Johnston, R. I.; lived there with the exception of one year, 1828, until 1840; lived in Cranston, R. I., until 1860, from there to Warwick, where he died in 1863. He was a farmer always. He d. in Cranston, Aug. 2, 1863; res. Providence, R. I.

1957. ii. MARY ANN, b. Jan. 1, 1825; m. July 5. 1853. H. W. Patt; m. 2d, June 16, 1862, Hardin Smith. He d. ———. She res. 68 Vernon St., Providence, R. I. Ch.: 1. Marietta C., b. Feb. 24. 1855; m. ——— Gardiner; res. Cor. Vinton and Vernon Sts., Providence, R. I.

1958. i. E. ARNOLD, b. May 16, 1823; m. Mary E. Battey.

1959. iii. JOSEPH B., b. Mar. 20, 1827; m. Eliza A. Pike.

1960. iv. ISAAC. b. Feb. 4, 1830; m. Abby Burke.

1961. v. JOHN C., b. Nov. 10, 1831; m. Rachel Thompson and Jemima Kane.

1962. vi. PHEBE ELIZA, b. Apr. 17, 1839; m. Sept. 6, 1870, Charles W. Whitfield of New York. She d. Dayton, O., Nov., 1891. Ch.: 1. Libbie, b. Aug. 28, 1872; m. Nov. 29, 1893. Bert Paxtun; 2. George; 3. Forrest.

1963. vii. MARIA KNIGHT, b. July 7, 1840; m. May, 1866, Joseph F. Esten; res. Rockland, R. I. Ch.: 1, Grace, b. Oct. 31, 1872; 2, Carrie F., b. Sept, 16, 1876..

1964. viii. ALBERT W., b. Nov. 26, 1842; m. Olive Kenyon.

1965. ix. ALBERT C., b. June 11, 1837; d. Mar. 5, 1838.

1044. DR. ISAAC FISKE (Isaac, Joseph, Samuel, Joseph, William, John, William, Robert, Simon, Simon, William, Symond), b. Johnston, R. I., Mar. 15, 1791; m. at Swansey, July 10, 1835, Anna Robinson, dau. of Gideon, now deceased, and Patience, now wife of Oliver Chase, of Fall River; at the time of his marriage he was of Scituate, R. I., and was married in Swansey according to the Friends' record. She was b. July 5, 1808, and d. Dec. 27, 1889. He was b. in Johnston, R. I., and died in Fall River in his 82d year. He received a liberal education for those days and early studied medicine, but did not practice until late in life. He was a fine penman and very fond of travel and taught penmanship in many places in the United States, largely to see the country. At the time of his marriage in 1835 he purchased a farm in Scituate, R. I., where he kept a private school, with a few day scholars, but mostly boarders. This school was patronized mostly by Friends and Quakers, who sent their sons there to be fitted for college or for a better education than could be obtained in the public schools in those days. In 1845 he decided to discontinue his school and practice medicine in Fall River. He was a practicing physician in that city for 25 years, highly esteemed by every one and very successful in his profession. He and his wife continued members of the Society of Friends till death and were noted for a large exercise of the old-fashioned style of genuine hospitality. No relative or friend of the family was ever allowed to go to a hotel when visiting Fall River, and Dr. Fiske's house was a rendezvous for the Abolitionist or escaping slave, and the Boston "Liberator," Garrison's paper, came to him as long as it was published. He left a homestead and quite a little property. He d. June 2, 1873; res. Fall River, Mass.

1966. i. GEORGE R., b. Jan. 18, 1837; m. Mary A. Anthony.
1967. ii. ANNA ROBINSON, b. Apr. 8, 1844; m. June 20, 1876, Harry Theodore Harding; res. Truro, Nova Scotia.
1968. iii. ISAAC GIDEON, b. Oct. 18, 1838; d. Apr. 2, 1840.
1969. iv. ISAAC, Jr., b. Nov. 28, 1841; d. Mar. 25, 1843.

1045. JOSEPH FISKE (Isaac, Joseph, Samuel, Joseph, William, John, William, Robert, Simon, Simon, William, Symond), b. Johnston, R. I., Oct. 29, 1785; m. there 1804, Roby Baker, b. 1780; d. Aug. 28, 1823, in Centreville, O.; m. 2d, in Centreville, Mary Robbins; d. Sept. 6, 1833; m. 3d, in Miamisburg, O., Maria Goddard, d. s. p.; m. 4th, Maria Hall, d. s. p. He was a blacksmith by trade. He d. Apr. 30, 1864; res. Providence, R. I., Bordentown, N. J., Centreville and Miamisburg, O.

1970. i. NATHAN PURSER, b. Dec. 6, 1806; m. Mrs. Rebecca (Whitehill) Cowan and Margaret K. Tate.
1971. ii. ISAAC, b. Oct. 13, 1815; d. unm.; was chief engineer on a man-of-war, in U. S. N.
1872. iii. AUGUSTUS, b. ———; he m. and d. s. p. in Miamisburg, O.
1973. iv. SHELDON FENNER, b. Jan. 26, 1825; m. Sarah Hurd.
1974. v. DE WITT CLINTON, b. Jan. 12, 1828; d. ae. 25, unm.
1975. vi. SAMUEL R., b. July 4, 1830; m. Sarah J. Miller.
1976. vii. ELVIRA F., b. May 3, 1833; m. Sept. 19, 1867, George Truman; res. Spring Valley, O. He was b. Mar. 1, 1833. Is a hardware merchant. Ch.: 1, Minnie Truman, b. June 14, 1868; d. Oct. 13, 1875; 2, Joseph Llewellyn Truman, b. Feb. 19, 1870; P. O. Columbus, O., 931 Atchison St.; 3, Abigail Cora Truman, b. Mar. 5, 1874; d. Dec. 5, 1876.
1977. viii. WILLIAM, d. young.
1978. ix. ABBY ANN, d. young.
1979. x. JOHN, d. young.
1980. xi. ELIZA, d. young.
1981. xii. JULIA ANN, d. young.
1982. xiii. ANN SMITH, d. young.
1983. xiv. MARIETTA, d. young.

1046. BENJAMIN FISKE (Isaac, Joseph, Samuel, Joseph, William, John, William, Robert, Simon, Simon, William, Symond), b. Johnston, R. I., 1794; m. Polly Van Der Marke; res. Oswego, N. Y.

1984. i. JOHN, b. ———.
1985. ii. BENJAMIN, b. ———.
1986. iii. CALEB I., b. ———.

St. John's Church of England, Parra matta, N.S.W. ... and first children here born in Hobart Town, Van Drieman's Land, Tasmania. From a letter sent to librarian dated Dec. 4, 1929 from Sophia Cartwright whose mother was the daughter of Arnold Fiske.

FISKE GENEALOGY 237

Her address: Imbarrang, 15 Hasstone, Arncliff, N.S.W. — Australia

(A.C.D. Jan 9, 193)

1047. ARNOLD FISKE (Isaac, Joseph, Samuel, Joseph, William, John, William, Robert, Simon, Simon, William, Symond), b. Johnston, R. I., Feb. 28, 1777; m. in New Zealand, Mary A. Bunker, dau. of Capt. Bunker. He raised quite a family, but there has been no correspondence or other intercourse with his family and connection there for many years. I have seen a letter from him dated Hobart Town, Van Deiman's Land, June 29, 1816, in which he speaks of having a wife (a dau. of a Capt. Bunker) and three children; res. New Castle, New South Wales.

1049. EDMOND FISKE (Isaac, Joseph, Samuel, Joseph, William, John, William, Robert, Simon, Simon, William, Symond), b. R. I. Apr. 16, 1787; m. in Johnston, R. I., May 11, 1808-9, Abby Brown. He went to sea in 1830. A grandson, James B., res. 989 Westminster St., Providence, R. I. Res. Johnston and Providence, R. I.

    1987. i.   HENRY, b. ———; m. and res. Providence; had a son James.
    1988. ii.   WILLIAM, b. July 18, 1809.
    1989. iii. AMY, b. ———.
    1990. iv. MARIETTA, b. ———.

1052. DANIEL FISKE (Isaac, Joseph, Samuel, Joseph, William, John, William, Robert, Simon, Simon, William, Symond), b. R. I., June 24, 1779; m. Polly Horton, dau. of Lyman Horton; res. South Scituate, R. I., and ———, Conn.

    1991. i.   FENNER, b. ———.
    1992. ii.   DANIEL ARNOLD, b. ———; res. in the west.
    1993. iii. BARBARA, b. ———.
    1994. iv. PHEBE, b. ———.
    1995. v.   ARVILLA, b. ———.
    1996. vi. MARCY, b. ———.
    1997. vii. MARY, b. ———.
    1998. viii. JULIETTE, b.

1056. JOHN FISK (John, John, John, John, Nathaniel, William, Robert, Simon, Simon, William, Symond), b. Worcester, Mass., Aug. 16, 1749; m. Aug. 30, 1777, Irena Buck, b. Aug. 26, 1754; d. in 1850, in Ellington, N. Y. He was born in Worcester, Mass., and d. in Brookfield, N. Y. His death was caused by a tree falling upon him on his premises, situate on lot 17, in the 19th township, town of Brookfield, N. Y. He was the eldest son in his father's family and in accordance with the family custom, was named after his father, whose name was John. He m. Irena Buck. They lived in York State during the Revolutionary war with England, at Crown Point, on Lake Champlain. The date of their leaving Worcester, Mass., and moving into York State I do not know. John was a commissary in the U. S. army. Just before the close of the war his dwelling house and outbuildings were burned by the enemy. After the war closed he sold or traded his place and moved back east. Some traditional accounts of him say he did not go back to Massachusetts, but settled in Connecticut and lived there until 1797, when he, with his family, removed back into the State of New York and settled in the town of Brookfield, N. Y. After the death of her husband, Mrs. Fisk lived with her son, David Fisk, in the town of Brookfield until 1840, when she went to Ellington, N. Y., and lived the remainder of her life with her grandson, James Fisk. She died there. He d. July 4, 1802; res. Worcester, Mass., Brookfield, N. Y.

    1999. i.   DAVID, b. Nov. 12, 1782; m. Lidia Bugbee.
    2000. ii.   JOHN, b. Aug. 4, 1778; m. Eunice Bugbee.
    2001. iii. JAMES, b. Aug. 21, 1780; m. Hannah Green.
    2002. iv. AZUBAH, b. Oct. 29, 1785; m. ——— Faulkner. She d. Mar. 23, 1869, in Brookfield, N. Y., leaving a large family.
    2003. v.   JONATHAN, b. Apr., 1790, d. in infancy.
    2004. vi. SALLY, b. Feb. 12, 1792; d. in 1825.
    2005. vii. OLIVE, b. Oct., 1788; m. ——— Fairbanks; res. Ellington, N. Y. Had a large family.

1057. WILLIAM FISKE (William, John, John, John, John, Nathaniel, William, Robert, Simon, Simon, William, Symond), b. Worcester, Mass., Mar. 13, 1777; m. in Worcester, Aug. 4, 1799, Dolly Wellington, b. 1780. She d. in Heath,

Mass., Oct. 28, 1840, and after her death he m. again, but the 2d wife d. s. p. He was born in Worcester, and by the death of his father at an early age was left with his mother's relatives. The widow soon married again and resided in Worcester, where he spent his boyhood days. Soon after his marriage he took up his present residence in Heath. He was twice married and had 12 children. He d. Dec. 25, 1862; res. Heath, Mass.

2006.   i.   JAMES, b. Apr. 5, 1805; m. Maria Nichols.
2007.   ii.   BETSEY, b. Mar. 7, 1803; m. Dec. 19, 1830, Joseph Hilton Dow, b. Epping, N. H., May 27, 1803, d. in Charlton, Mass., Aug. 29, 1880. He was a farmer. Ch.: 1, Amanda Fisk Dow, b. Aug. 14, 1832; d. June 19, 1850; 2, Daniel Webster Dow, b. Nov. 18, 1835; 3, Eleanor Emerson Dow, b. May 13, 1837; m. July, 1856; res. Oceanus. Fla.; 4, Ellen Mandana Dow, b. Oct. 26, 1838; m. June, 1858; res. Fitchburg, Mass.; 5, William Hilton Dow, b. Nov. 18, 1840; m. July, 1863; d. Feb. 12, 1875; 6, Louisa Allen Dow. b. July 8, 1834; m. Nov. 17, 1856, Reuben Wallin, b. Aug. 4, 1831; res. Harriman, Tenn. Ch.: Mortimer Fisk Dow Wallin, b. May 20, 1866; m. May 27, 1891; P. O. Harriman, Tenn.
2008.   iii.   DOROTHY CHARLOTTE, b. Apr. 14, 1818; m. in 1842, Aard Hale; res. Waterloo, Ia. He was b. Sept. 8, 1818; d. Jan. 2, 1884; was a farmer. Ch.: Ellen Maria Hall. b. Sept. 20, 1843; m. Sept. 20, 1865; d. 1893. Augusta Jane, b. Oct. 21, 1845; m. Oct. 21, 1869, Waterloo. Arthur William, b. July 7, 1847; m. Dec. 31, 1864; res. North Amherst, Mass. Boardman Judson, b. 1849; m. June 2, 1879, Waterloo, Ia. Charlene Fisk, b. May 26, 1851; m. May 1879, Waterloo, Ia. Charlene Fisk, b. May 26, 1851; m. May 20, 1879; d. May 1. 1883. Frank Fayette, b. Apr. 20, 1853; m. Jan. 29, 1873; res. Waterloo. Cyrus Emerson, b. Jan. 24, 1856; m. Oct. 23, 1889; res. Waterloo. Frederick, b. May 9, 1858; m. Dec. 31. 1891; d. Oct. 22. 1894; a teacher in the college Los Angeles, Cal.
2009.   iv.   JOSEPH E., b. Feb. 12, 1811; m. Rebecca A. Shattuck.
2010.   v.   WILLIAM BOYDEN, b. Dec. 25, 1799; d. unm. 1840.
2011.   vi.   DOLLY, b. Sept. 29, 1801; d. May 2, 1810.
2012.   vii.   MARY, b. Mar. 14, 1809; m. 1832, Samuel Hall. She d. Waterloo, Ia., in 1879.
2013.   viii.   LEVI, b. Feb. 17, 1813; d. Sept. 3, 1823.
2014.   ix.   SAMUEL CLARK, b. Dec. 1, 1815; m. Abigail Wait.
2015.   x.   CYRUS KINGSBURY, b. Jan. 22, 1820; m. Isabel Boyd.
2016.   xi.   JOHN SAWYER, b. Nov. 2, 1822. In 1865 he was unm., and res. at 26 Fourth Ave., New York City. N. Y.

1060.   JAMES FISK (John, John, John, John, Nathaniel, William, Robert, Simon, Simon, William, Symond), b. Worcester. Mass., Aug. 17, 1757; m. Apr. 12, 1789, Azubah Moore; res. Worcester, Mass. and Shutesbury, Mass.

2017.   i.   JAMES, b. ———. He res. in Shutesbury, Mass.

1061.   SAMUEL FISK (John, John, John, John, Nathaniel, William, Robert, Simon, Simon, William, Symond), b. Worcester, Mass., Jan. 29, 1759; m. Olive ———; m. 2d, Priscilla ———; res. Worcester and Shutesbury, Mass.

2018.   i.   LUCY, b. Oct. 22, 1792; m. in Shutesbury Peter Stowell, b. Dec. 23, 1790; d. Sept. 24, 1868; was a farmer. She d. Jan. 28, 1871. Ch.: 1, Samuel H., b. Feb. 16, 1821; m. Sept. 9, 1846, Mary A. Chandler, b. Aug. 22, 1824; res. New Salem, Mass.; is a farmer; ch.: Estella M., b. Nov. 1, 1853; m. ——— Billings; P. O. address, Gilbertville, Mass. Edwin F., b. July 19, 1857; P. O. address, New Salem. Ellen F., b. July 19, 1857; d. Feb. 20, 1891. Dwight A., b. Aug. 2, 1859; P. O. address, New Salem. 2, Franklin, b. Apr. 15, 1818; d. Aug., 1895. A son, Willard D., res. Leverett, Mass.
2019.   ii.   BETSEY, b. Apr. 27, 1794; m. Apr. 15, 1823, Joseph Nourse of Shrewsbury. He was b. Jan. 9, 1791, and d. in Princeton, Mass.

She d. Aug. 27, 1834. Ch.: Lucy A. Nourse, b. Feb. 12, 1824; m. May 11, 1848, Albert Bennett, b. Oct. 11, 1811; d. Feb. 12, 1888; she res. in Hubbardston, Mass.; ch.: Abbie Bennett, b Apr. 27, 1849; m. Seth P. Hale Dec. 3, 1867; d. Mar. 8, 1888. Emeline E. Nourse, b. Sept. 26, 1826; m. June, 1853, Edward Knight, and 2d, —— Edwards; she d. Apr. 6, 1883; a dau. is Emma L. Jenkins of Milford, Mass. Caroline M. Nourse, b. Oct. 29, 1828; m. John D. Ames; res. Binghamton, N. Y. Mary C. Nourse, b. July 7, 1830; d. Apr. 16, 1867; William H. Nourse, b. Oct. 23, 1832.

2020. iii. SARAH, b. Mar. 18, 1797.
2021. iv. JOHN, b. Apr. 22, 1801; m. Sally Nourse.
2022. v. OLIVE, b. May 26, 1803.

1067. JONAS FISK (Jonathan, John, John, John, Nathaniel, William, Robert, Simon, Simon, William, Symond), b. Worcester, Mass., Sept. 27, 1767; m. at Wendell, 1790, Matilda Leach, b. Mar. 2, 1770, at Hardwick, Mass.; d. Apr. 5, 1847, at Wendell; dau. of Ensign Lemuel Leach, by his wife Rebecca Washburn. Mr. Fisk was a farmer. He d. Dec. 1, 1850; res. Wendell, Mass.

2023. i. JOSEPH, b. Apr. 25, 1791; m. Martha Willis.
2024. ii. MARTIN, b. Apr. 8, 1795; m. Priscilla Leach.
2025. iii. REBECCA, b. Apr. 2, 1797; d. July 13, 1856.
2026. iv. STEPHEN, b. July 15, 1799; m. Elmira Johnson and Elcey Larry.
2027. v. LYMAN, b. Mar. 26, 1800; d. Wendell, Jan. 10, 1892. He was prominent in town affairs, and represented Wendell in the Legislature in 1846, and was a member of the Constitutional Convention in 1853.
2028. vi. ARTEMAS, b. Apr. 3, 1802; m. Susan Williams.

1069. DANIEL FISK (Jonathan, John, John, John, Nathaniel, William, Robert, Simon, Simon, William, Symond), b. June 26, 1772, in Worcester, Mass.; m. Dorcas Sanders, b. Aug. 28, 1772; d. Feb. 8, 1822, in Veteran, N. Y. He d. in Albany, N. Y., July 25, 1810; res. Wendell, Mass.

2029. i. JABEZ, b. June 3, 1794; m. Catherine Ten Brook.
2030. ii. ABIJAH, b. Nov. 11, 1795; m. Henrietta Hughes.
2031. iii. JOSEPH, b. ——; descendants res. Citronella, Ala.

1071. CAPT. ZEDEKIAH FISK (Daniel, John, John, John, Nathaniel, William, Robert, Simon, Simon, William, Symond), b. Waltham, Mass., July 23, 1763; m. in Wendell, Dec. 29, 1785, Lucy Sweetser, b. in Wendell Sept. 14, 1764; d. in Wendell Apr. 3, 1835. He was b. in Waltham, moved to Wendell, m. there, followed farming, enlisted in the Revolutionary army when 16 years of age. It is stated by his descendants that he was one of the guard who watched Andre and saw him executed, and how sorry he was to see such a fine young fellow suffer such a fate. ("I have tried to find confirmation of this in historical documents but have never yet discovered any list of the persons concerned in guarding Andre from the time of his capture to his execution." R. A. Smith, Washington, D. C.) Was later Captain in the State militia. He had a pension granted him which, however, was suspended Aug. 1, 1820, and regranted Sept. 4, 1832. His wife was the daughter of Capt. Henry Sweetser and Lucy Johnson. They resided in Wendell and took an active part in organizing the first church there; he was a farmer and his ancestor Seth came from England and settled in Charlestown, Mass. He d. Aug. 5, 1844; res. Wendell, Mass.

2032. i. LUCY, b. Oct. 16, 1794; m. July 20, 1818, Otis Gunn, b. July 12, 1793; d. Nov. 28, 1878; she d. Aug. 31, 1837. They lived and died in Montague, Mass.; she lived to be nearly 93 years of age, and was a representative woman and an honor to her Creator. Although she was slight and petite, she was possessed of wonderful vitality and her whole life was spent in a desire to do good. No call for sympathy or aid was ever passed by unheeded, whatever sacrifice to herself.
Otis Gunn was born in Montague upon a farm; kept hotel several years at Granite Corner, now Miller's Falls, in Mon-

tague; went upon the old homestead farm more than 60 years ago and lived there most of the time until his death Nov. 28, 1878. He was noted for great kindness and benevolence and as one who truly loved his neighbor as himself.

They res. Montague, Mass. Ch.: 1, Erastus Fisk Gunn, b. Aug. 21, 1819; m. Nov. 12, 1846, Nancy Bardwell, b. Aug. 27, 1818; d. May 7, 1859; res. Montague, Mass. He is a farmer and trial justice; ch.: Charles Bardwell Gunn, b. Sept. 20, 1847; m. Addie Cutter Freeman, Feb. 15, 1876; P. O. address Colorado Springs, Colo. George Ransom Gunn, b. Oct. 18, 1849; d. Oct. 26, 1889; unm. Mary Cayton Gunn, b. Nov. 28, 1851; m. Aug. 27, 1873, to Charles Orville Sawyer; P. O. address Orange Mass. Frank F. Gunn, b. Nov. 19, 1853; d. Dec. 30, 1853. Alice Parsons Gunn, b. Jan. 5, 1855; m. Jan. 1, 1880, to Frank O. Johnson; P. O. add. 7 Bulfinch St., Boston, Mass. Frank B. Gunn, b. Nov. 29, 1857; d. Mar. 18, 1859. 2, Ira Arms Gunn, b. Nov. 21, 1821; d. Nov. 6, 1839. 3, George Rodney Gunn, b. Mar. 5, 1824; d. May 30, 1825. 4, Lucy Ann Gunn, b. May 16, 1826; d. Aug. 27, 1841. 5, Otis Berthonde Gunn, b. Oct. 29, 1828; m. in Spencerport, N. Y., Dec. 15, 1853, Mary Helen Crosby, b. Aug. 26, 1831. Otis Berthonde Gunn was born in Montague, Franklin County, Mass., Oct. 29, 1828; attended district school and high school in Montague and in Prescott, Mass.; later at Williston Seminary, Easthampton, Mass.; taught school one year in Penn., near Harrisburgh, and one winter in Montague; began railway service in 1848 upon the Vermont and Mass. R. R. at Miller's Falls, Mass.; was rodman at Brattleboro; then was leveler at Greenfield; was assistant engineer on the Rochester and Niagara branch of the N. Y. Cent. R. R. In the spring of 1853, when 24 years old, was appointed division engineer of the 7th division of the Wabash R. R. from Lafayette, Ind., to the Ill. State Line. In 1857 moved to Kansas; was State Senator from Wyandotte County in 1861 and 1862; was appointed in 1861 on Governor Robinson's staff as chief engineer of the Kansas State Militia; later was appointed major of the 4th Kansas Volunteers; served six months and resigned to become engineer of the Kansas Pacific Railroad Company. In 1863 was appointed chief engineer of what is now the Central branch of the Union Pacific Railroad. In 1868 he was appointed superintendent of the road. In 1869 was appointed chief engineer of the Missouri, Kansas & Texas Railroad Company, and built about 900 miles of that road. In 1875 built the railway bridge across the Missouri River at Atchison. In 1878 was chief engineer of the Kansas Central Railroad Company. In 1879-80 was chief engineer of the Southern Kansas Railroad Company. In 1881 was contractor on the Kansas Central Railroad, and in 1882 contractor on the Atlantic & Pacific Railroad, and in 1885-86 contractor on the Union Pacific Railroad. In 1889 was city engineer of Kansas City, Mo.; since then retired from business. Of five children two are deceased. The elder daughter is the wife of the auditor of the Southern California Railroad Com- married and lives in San Francisco, Cal. The son is a prominent architect and is superintendent of the new custom house and postoffice building now being erected in Kansas City to cost $1,200,000; res. Kansas City, Mo.; was major in the late war; ch.: Charles Henry Gunn, b. Apr. 24, 1855; d. Mar. 19, 1880. Vara Helen Gunn, b. Oct. 6, 1857. Lucy Isabella Gunn, b. July 10, 1863; d. Mar. 12, 1865. Frederick Crosby Gunn, b. Nov. 6, 1865. Ellen Louise Gunn, b. Dec. 15, 1867. 6, Charles Henry Gunn, b. Mar. 10, 1831; d. Oct. 28, 1839. 7, Isabella Gunn b. Oct. 23, 1833; d. Nov. 23, 1839.

2033. ii. ZEDEKIAH, b. July 23, 1812; m. Sarah McDonald.

2034. iii. SARAH. b. May 23, 1790; m. Oct. 18, 1818, Levi Moore; she d. Aug. 24, 1840. He was b. in Sudbury Mar. 18, 1785, and d. in Leverett, Mass., June 7, 1838. She was his second wife. She d. in Greenfield, Mass. Ch.: 1. Edwin L., b. July 25, 1819; m. Sarah C. Reed. He was proprietor and principal of the Mt. Joy Seminary at Lancaster, Pa.; was M. A. from a Pennsylvania college; was paymaster in the United States service from 1862 to 1869 with rank of Colonel; was taken prisoner by the Mosby guerrillas and confined in Libby Prison. He d. in St. Peter, Minn., Apr. 22, 1874. 2, Stillman, b. Mar. 19, 1821; m. Oct. 28, 1843, Mary A. Preble, b. Mar. 15, 1821, a grandneice of Commodore Preble, U. S. N. Res. New Haven, Conn.; retired. One ch., Anna Fiske Preble, b. Dec. 5, 1851; m. Aug. 29, 1883, Robert Atwater Smith, b. July 2, 1849; he is a government clerk in war department in Washington, D. C., and res. 936 French street, N. W. 3, Leander, b. May 16, 1822; m. Roxanna Collins and d. s. p. in Brooklyn, Nov. 23, 1850. 4, Sarah F., b. July 9, 1824; m. Lewis H. Ganse; res. 122 Calder street, Harrisburg, Pa.; eight ch. 5, Fidelia, b. May, 1826; d. 1833. 6, Joseph K., b. Feb. 17, 1828; m. Clara Louise Hosley; res. Los Angeles, Cal.; was connected with the Greenfield, Mass., Gazette and Courier, Morristown, Pa., Republican, and later editor and proprietor of the St. Peter, Minn., Tribune; was appointed postmaster of St. Peter by President Lincoln in 1861, and held the office except for three years until 1886, when he resigned. In 1887 he was private secretary of Gov. McGill and later secretary and treasurer of the St. Paul & Minneapolis Loan & Trust Company. In 1890 Secretary Windom appointed him chief of the division of appointments in the treasury department at Washington, D. C. He is a man of sterling character and great decision and energy.

2035. iv. HENRY b. Aug. 17, 1792; m. Mary Perry.

2036. v. BEULAH. b. July 17, 1797; m. June, 1818, Martin Moore. He was b. Feb. 16, 1795; d. Nov. 13, 1871; was a miller and farmer; res. Leverett, Mass. Ch.: Alpheus, b. Mar. 26, 1819; m. Jan. 1, 1845, Maretta A. Whitney, b. Sept. 13, 1818; d. Feb. 13, 1885 (see Whitney Genealogy by F. C. Pierce). He is a builder; res. Montague, Mass.; ch.: 1, Gilman Alpheus Moore, b. Dec. 19, 1845, Montague, Mass.; 2, Wesley Fisk Moore, b. Sept. 28, 1854, Montague, Mass.; m. Elsie E. Greenwood, Oct. 24, 1886, b. June 2, 1858, Hubbardston, Mass.; P. O. address Montague, Mass. Clesson F., b. Feb. 5, 1821; m. Apr. 28, 1846, Mary A. Fuller; 4 ch. res. Montague. Beulah, b. Apr. 15, 1828; d. Mar. 25, 1831. Asa, b. Mar. 26, 1823; d. Aug. 13, 1841. Lucy F., b. Oct. 7, 1825; m. Feb. 2, 1846, Nathan A. Fitts; res. Northington, Mass.; 1 ch.

2037. vi. JOSEPH, b. Apr. 17, 1800; m. Martha Marsh, Eunice G. Sweetser and Mrs. Lucy Howe.

2038. vii. STILLMAN, b. May 7, 1805; d. Aug. 17, 1821.

2039. viii. DANIEL K., b. May 7, 1808; d. unm. in Saybrook, Ohio, May 24, 1842.

1073. DANIEL FISK (Daniel, John, John, John, Nathaniel, William, Robert, Simon, Simon, William, Symond), b. in Wendell, Mass., 1773; m. Sally Partridge; m. 2d, Mrs. Lucy F. Robinson, b. 1790; d. May 14, 1851. He d. Sept. 8, 1850; res. Erving, Mass.

2040. i. JAMES WILLARD, b. Aug. 15, 1814; m. Almina Kendrick.

2041. ii. DEXTER, b. Feb. 3, 1807; m. Lavina F. Robinson.

2042. iii. SALLY, b. Oct. 21, 1799; m. May 16, 1827, Felch Austin; res. Orange. He d. Dec. 18, 1837. She d. July 24, 1871. Ch.: 1, Perley, d. s. p. 2, Gilbert, b. ———. 3, Sophia. 4, Lorinda. 5, Dwight P., b. July 5, 1828; m. Nov. 6, 1851, Marie W. Stone, b. Oct. 5, 1828; res. Wendell, Mass.; ch.: Ella J. Austin, b. Aug.

16

4, 1854; m. to Frank F. Stoughton, Apr. 4, 1883; P. O. Gill, Mass. Geo. L. Austin, b. July 28, 1856; d. Dec. 15, 1868. William Henry Austin, b. Nov. 23, 1863; m. to Evelyn M. Beals July 5, 1893; P. O. Orange, Mass.

2043.   iv.   DANIEL P., b. May 23, 1803; m. Eliza Cheney.
2044.   v.   JOHN, b. Oct. 28, 1804. He went to California and nothing has been heard of him since.
2045.   vi.   CLARK, b. July 6, 1809; m. Rhoda Ward and Hulda Crossman.
2046.   vii. MILTON E., b. Sept. 27, 1832.

1074. HON. AMOS FISK (Daniel, John, John, John, Nathaniel, William, Robert, Simon, Simon, William, Symond), b. Wendell, Mass., May 26, 1780; m. Trenton, N. Y., 1807, Mary Hubbard, of Trenton, N. Y., dau. of Isaac and Ruth (Coleman) of Middletown, b. Aug. 26, 1789; d. Nov. 29, 1872. He came west from Wendell, Mass., in 1807; located at Erie, Pa.; married at Trenton, N. Y., in 1808; followed farming and salt business, i. e., brought salt from Syracuse up Lake Ontario around the falls of Niagara and up Lake Erie. In 1810 moved to Ashtabula, Ohio, the land upon which the present city of Ashtabula is located and his life was spent in farming, mercantile and stock raising. (His son, Edward W., is living on a part of the farm about one minute —— from Main street.) About 1833 he was elected to the Legislature. He d. Jan. 31, 1836; res. Ashtabula, Ohio.

2047.   i.   MARY ANN, b. Oct. 3, 1808; m. Jan. 31, 1837, J. D. Hulburt. She d. in A. Dec. 25, 1842, s. p.
2048.   ii.   ISAAC HUBBARD, b. Oct. 9, 1811; m. Mary Safford.
2049.   iii. ORIN, b. Sept. 30, 1814; d. Sept. 16, 1819.
2050.   iv.   RUTH K., b. Mar. 1, 1817; m. Nov. 1, 1836, Rev. Ashel Chapin, of Greenville, Ohio. She d. Oct. 5, 1838. A dau. m. Henry Stearns; res. Freeport, Ill. (see Forbush Genealogy by Fred C. Pierce).
2051.   v.   AMOS, b. Apr. 27, 1819; d. Sept. 4, 1819.
2052.   vi.   AMOS, b. Dec. 11, 1820; d. Sept. 2, 1821.
2053.   vii. AMOS C., b. Feb. 21, 1823; m. Sarah L. Paine.
2054.   viii. SARAH A., b. Apr. 18, 1825; m. Nov. 7, 1844, Dr. Stephen F. Selby; res. Williamson, N. Y. He was b. Aug. 16, 1815. Ch.: 1, Mary S. Selby, b. Oct. 12, 1845. 2, Emma H. Selby, b. Dec. 1, 1847; m. Mar. 4, 1873, James K. Stebbins; address Ashtabula, Ohio. 3, Amos Fisk Selby, b. Apr. 10, 1849; m. Apr. 10, 1884, Evalyn F. Warren; address Pultneyville, N. Y. 4, Ellen Selby, b. Apr., 1851; d. Oct. 1853. 5, Jared C., b. Feb. 11, 1859; m. Feb. 22, 1885, Lillian C. Whitborn; address Eaton Rapids, Mich. 6, Stephen F., b. Feb. 11, 1862; m. Sept. 4, 1889, Alice C. Sanborn; address Ashtabula, Ohio.
2055.   ix.   ELLEN M., b. Nov. 13, 1828; m. Aug. 27, 1851, Anson Groton. She d. in A., May 14, 1854. Ch.: Edward Fiske, b. May 6, 1854; m. June 9, 1879, Fanny Whitney, b. Feb. 1, 1855; res. Lake Forest, Ill.; address 51 Portland Block, Chicago, Ill.; s. p. He was b.

MAJOR EDWARD FISKE GORTON.

in Ashtabula, Ohio, but early moved to Rochester, N. Y., where he attended the public schools and was graduated at Wilson's private school. In 1871 he went to Columbus, Ohio, where he remained until 1883, when he came to Chicago. He studied law at the Union College of Law and was graduated with honors in June, 1886, and was at once admitted to the bar and began practice. He is an able and successful advocate and counselor. He is mayor of Lake Forest, where he resides. The Chicago Evening Post in commenting on his recent renomination said:

Since Mayor Gorton took charge of the affairs of Lake Forest's city government a number of improvements have been made in all parts of the town, and his administration has been so popular with all the residents that he was the first and unanimous choice for renomination at the late caucus. He has been unwilling to take the position, which is purely an honorary one, there being no salary provided for the mayor. Recently he handed his resignation to the city council, but it was torn up by his associates before it reached City Clerk Frazer.

2056. x. EDWARD WILLIAM, b. May 17, 1832; m. Mary H. Mygatt.
2056½.xi. ORIN, b. Jan. 16, 1831; d. May, 1831.

1078. AMARIAH* FISK (David, David, John, John, Nathaniel, William, Robert, Simon, Simon, William, Symond), b. Hampton, Conn., Oct. 6, 1747; m. ———— ————; m. 2d, Priscilla ————; d. Sept. 16, 1799, in Hampton; res. Hampton, Conn.

2057. i. EZRA, b. Apr. 13, 1778; m. Polly Downing.
2058. ii. DAU., b. ————; m. ———— Nichols; m. 2d, Dr. Ezra Hammond; res. Northfield, Minn., and Danielsonville, Conn.
2059. iii. LUCY, b. Aug. 2, 1780.
2060. iv. PATTY, b. Apr. 28, 1783; d. July 10, 1784.
2061. v. ELBA, b. Mar. 5, 1787; d. Feb. 16, 1788.
2062. vi. ELBA, b. Jan. 30, 1789.
2063. vii. PATTY, b. Mar. 11, 1791; d. Aug. 8, 1792.
2064. viii. BRIGHAM, b. July 12, 1792; m. Lydia M. ————.
2065. ix. SARAH, b. Jan. 11, 1796.
2066. x. AMANDA, b. May 22, 1798.

1085. JONATHAN FISK (Jonathan, David, John, John, Nathaniel, William, Robert, Simon, Simon, William, Symond), b. Hampton, Conn., Aug. 15, 1755; m. there Feb. 8, 1781, Mehitable Smith, b. Nov. 3, 1755; d., ae. 82. He was a soldier in the Revolutionary war. He d., ae. 81; res. Hampton, Windham County, Conn., and Otsego, Cooperstown, N. Y.

2067. i. RUFUS, b. Dec. 17, 1781.
2068. ii. ELBA, b. Apr. 26, 1799; m. Nancy Eddy and Phebe C. Ruby.
2069. iii. STEPHEN, b. Apr. 8, 1788.
2070. iv. ANNIE, b. May 24, 1792.
2071. v. DAVID, b. ————.
2072. vi. PHILENA, b. June 9, 1786.
2073. vii. PATTY, b. ————.
2074. viii. ASA, b. Nov. 11, 1783; m. Lucinda Shelly.
2075. ix. MEHITABLE, b. Mar. 20, 1790.

1092. STEPHEN FISK (Asa, David, John, John, Nathaniel, William, Robert, Simon, Simon, William, Symond), b. Wales, Mass., Apr. 28, 1763; m. there Apr., 1784, Sarah Parker, sister of Zurviah who m. Elisha Fisk. He fell into a well while assisting in excavating it near his father's house and was killed. He d. Aug. 23, 1785; res. Wales, Mass.

2076. i. PHILA, b. May 29, 1785.

*Town Clerk in his copy calls him Amariah—Amasa.

1096. CAPT. ASA FISK (Asa, David, John, John, Nathaniel, William, Robert, Simon, Simon, William, Symond), b. Wales, Mass., Feb. 26, 1772; m. Nov. 27, 1792, Amanda Cooley; she d. s. p.; m. 2d, Sally Colburn of Stafford, b. 1774; d. Oct. 2, 1807; m. 3d, May 25, 1808, Mary Jane Davidson, b. Mar. 12, 1779; d. Dec. 15, 1824. The epitaph on his tombstone is as follows: "Asa Fisk died May 8, 1817, aged 45.

> "In faith he died, in dust he lies,
> But faith forsees that dust shall rise
> When Jesus calls while hope assumes
> And boasts his joys among the tombs."

He d. May 8, 1817; res. Wales, Mass.

2077. i. ELETHEA, b. Nov. 2, 1796; m. Oct., 1822, Linus Davidson. She d. Oct. 27, 1838. Ch.: 1, Sarah C., b. Mar. 15, 1824; m. Orren West of Stafford, Conn.; went west and d. They had four children, viz.: Eugene D. West, Adelbert Fisk West, Frances West, Sarah C. West. Two of the above are now living. Mrs. Sarah Black, who resides in South Des Moines, Ia.; and Adelbert at Hillside Ave., who has 4 ch. 2, William Fisk, b. Nov. 13, 1825; d. Aug. 13, 1846. 3, Roswell D., b. Feb. 13, 1830; m. May 21, 1879, Jane Ives. He was a lawyer in Stafford, and d. s. p. in Stafford, Aug. 16, 1885. She res. in Colchester, Conn. 4, Mary Jane, b. Oct. 20, 1834, never married, was adopted by a Mr. Goodell, but wants her name called Mary Jane Davidson, and now lives in Agawam, Mass.

2078. ii. STEPHEN, b. July 27, 1799. He was m. in Wales, Mass., but later resided in Bangor, Me.

2079. iii. EBENEZER, b. Aug. 13, 1801; m. Emily Moore, and removed to New York State and d. in St. Louis, Mo., leaving 2 ch.

2080. iv. EUNICE, b. Apr. 4, 1804; m. in Wales, Jonathan Durfee of Brimfield, Mass.: she d. June 15, 1853. Ch.: 1, Henry Dwight, b. ———. 2, Jane Maria, b. Jan. 11, 1831; in Southbridge; m. Lyman Fisk of Ludlow (See). 3, Anna Louise, b. ———.

2081. v. ROSWELL, b. Jan. 13, 1806; m. Sally Vinar of No. Adams, Mass. He was a cotton manufacturer in No. Adams, Mass., and later moved to St. Louis.

2082. vi. ERVINE, b. May 21, 1809. After the death of his parents he resided with Sewell Shaw in Wales, later went away to Troy, N. Y.

2083. vii. SALLY, b. Mar. 31, 1811: m. and her husband d.; she then m. in 1831, Christopher Conrad, and had six children; res. Mahwah, N. J. Ch.: 1, Sarah E. Conrad, b. Sept. 6, 1836; unm. res. Mahwah, N. J. 2, Christopher Fisk Conrad, b. Dec. 19, 1838; m. in Colorado a widow named Anna Galbraith, in 1886; no ch. 3, Anna Maria Conrad, b. Apr. 25, 1841, widow of Charles L. Atwood, of Pittsfield, Mass.; no ch. 4, Henry Clay Conrad, b. Aug. 3, 1845; d. July 7, 1846. 5, Charles Sandford Conrad, b. Jan. 29, 1846; unm. 6, Jennie Louisa Conrad, b. July 6, 1848; d. June 26, 1850.

2084. viii. SANFORD, b. Oct. 22, 1813; m. Lucy Ann Tourtellotte and adopted a little girl by law, named her Abbie Francese Fisk. She m. Orville W. Judd in 1872 and inherited her father's property after her mother's death. She is now living in Westboro, Mass.; no children. Lucy Ann (Tourtellotte) Fisk, d. in Mar., 1889, in Webster, Mass. Sanford Fisk, d. in June, 1881, in Webster, Mass. Both buried in Webster, Mass.

2085. ix. ASA, b. Mar. 10, 1816; m. Sarah Bridgeford of Fisherville, R. I. They had two children, George W. and Albert Fisk, both d. Asa is buried with his wife and two sons (both of whom were m.) in Springfield Cemetery, Mass. George W. Fisk, one of the sons, left a widow and one child named Hattie Viola Fisk, at one time teaching near Springfield, Mass. His widow died not long ago. Hattie m. E. D. Olds; res. Meriden,

Conn., Albert Fisk m. his 2d wife, Kate Elwell, of Danbury, Conn., no ch., and she still lives in Springfield, Mass.

2086. x. DANIEL SHAW, b. Nov. 13, 1820.

1100. HEZEKIAH FISK (Asa, David, John, John, Nathaniel, William, Robert, Simon, Simon, William, Symond), b. Windham, Conn., June 2, 1756; m. Eleanor Cooley, b. Sept. 4, 1757; d. Mar. 5, 1825. She was dau. of Azaria and Eleanor (Warrenner) Cooley, of Brimfield, Mass. He was a Revolutionary soldier in Capt. John Samson's company of Connecticut men; fought under Arnold and Gates at Saratoga, and was serving at New London when the garrison was massacred, but his company escaped. He moved from Stafford, Conn., to Wales, Mass., in 1784, and settled where the Wales Manufacturing Company's mills now stand, where he erected a saw mill that was standing and used in 1834. He was a Free Mason. After his death the following was copied from papers found among his effects:

This may certify that Hezekiah Fisk served in the army the following terms:

1775. At Roxbury 5 months under Capt. Cotton. Col. Brewers regiment, Gen. Washington, Commander.

1776. At Ticonderoga 4 months under Capt. Munger, Col. Woodbridge regiment; Gen. Gates, Commander.

1777. At Ticonderoga 3 months, Capt. Charles Company; Col. Robinson regiment. Gen Wane, Commander.

1777. At Stillwater and Saratoga under Capt. Lawson; Col. Cooks regiment; Gen. Gates, Commander.

He d. June 14, 1819, in South Brimfield, Mass.; res. Stafford, Conn.; Wales, Mass.

2087. i. DAVID, b. Apr. 18, 1776; m. Dolly Rood and Polly Sykes.
2088. ii. ELEANOR, b. June 25, 1777; m. —— Parker. She d. Dec. 9, 1841, in Mansfield, Conn.
2089. iii. ELI, b. Apr. 9, 1781; m. Margaret Moore.
2090. iv. LENA, b. June 25, 1783; m. —— Pratt and —— Perry; she d. Mar. 16, 1848.
2091. v. CLINA, b. June 6, 1785; she d. June 13, 1867, deaf and dumb.
2092. vi. STEPHEN, b. Apr. 8, 1787; m. Lucina Thompson.
2093. vii. WILLIAM HEZEKIAH, b. Mar. 4, 1789; m. Lois Wales.
2094. viii. ASA, b. Mar. 18, 1794; m. Catherine Shaw.
2095. ix. JAMES L., b. Apr. 2, 1797; m. Laura Hamlin.
2096. x. CHAUNCEY, b. June 22, 1799; m. Eliza Aldrich.
2097. xi. BETSEY, b. Feb. 11, 1791; d. young of smallpox.

1101. ELISHA FISK (Asa, David, John, John, Nathaniel, William, Robert, Simon, Simon, William, Symond), b. Wales, Mass., 1762; m. Mar. 25, 1782, Zurviah Parker, b. 1760; d. Aug. 30, 1805; m. 2d, 1806, Hannah Wheeler, b. 1772; d. May 7, 1865. Soon after the death of his first wife, Mrs. Zurviah Parker, he married Miss Hannah Wheeler of Warren, Mass., and he owned a large farm close by the cemetery. He farmed it considerably, kept an inn or tavern and attended a toll gate by his house. There were the house, three barns and cider mill, all of which are now gone or replaced by new buildings. He served in the Revolutionary war as a drummer boy; with his company he arrived where Cornwallis surrendered, one hour after that surrender. In a cemetery near the northeast part of Stafford on a knoll overlooking a reservoir of water, on the old turnpike from Hartford to Boston, close by where Elisha Fisk lived, one stone reads, "In memory of Mrs. Zurviah, the wife of Mr. Elisha Fisk, who died Aug. 30, 1805, in the 45th year of her age." On another stone is this: "Mr. Elisha Fisk, died Jan. 25, 1816, in the 54th year of his age." On another stone it reads, "Hannah Wheeler, widow of Elisha Fisk, died May 7, 1865, age 93 years." Also on same stone, "Their son Calvin, buried in Sonora, Cal.; died Jan. 8, 1853, age 45 years. Their daughter, Mrs. Orrel Thomson, buried in Middleburg, Va., died Aug. 8, 1873, Age 63 years." He d. Jan 25, 1816; res. Stafford, Conn.

2098. i. MARY, b. 1783; m. Jonathan Stowell and Sullivan Barnes. He was b. Stafford, Conn., in 1781, and d. Wilbraham, Mass., in Oct., 1877. She d. in 1841, in Union, Conn. Ch.: 1. Leonard Barnes, a son James; res. in Webster, Mass. 2. Charles

Barnes. b. June 6, 1818; m. Loretta Stowell; ch.: Arceus M.,
b. '1844; res. Barnes Block, Springfield, Mass. Sullivan B.,
b. Oct. 1, 1854; m. Cora L. Clarke and Mary A. Squier; res.
Three Rivers, Mass. 3, Arseno Stowell. 4, Lucius. 5, Zurviah.
6, Pliny. 7, Moriah. 8, Lewis. 9, Luretta; m. Charles Barnes
(see above). 10, Mary. 11, Martin.

2099. ii. RHODA, b. ———; m. J. Shaw.
2100. iii. CALVIN, b. Dec. 16, 1807; m. Nancy Ann Young.
2101. iv. ORREL, b. 1810; m. Mr. Thomson. She d. s. p. in Middleburg,
Va., Aug. 8, 1873. Orrel Fisk went first to Baltimore. Md.,
thence to Middleburg, Va., where she married a Mr. Thomson, and d. childless, and was buried in the Thomson family
lot on their plantation. The colored people were warm in
their gratitude to her for her sympathetic help in their times
of need.

1109. ABIJAH FISKE (Abijah, Thomas, William, John, Nathaniel. William,
Robert, Simon, Simon, William, Symond), b. Wat. Nov. 1. 1755; m. Sept. 11, 1783,
Alice Adams, b. Dec. 9, 1763. He was in the Revolutionary war; res. Waltham,
Mass.

2102. i. ALVAREZ, b. Jan. 19, 1784. He d. unm. in Natchez, Miss.,
where he was a prominent merchant.
2103. ii. ABIJAH, b. Dec. 2, 1785. He went south to Natchez; was in
business with his brother, and d. unm.
2104. iii. ALICE, bap. Nov. 18, 1787; d. in Weston, unm., Jan. 1, 1842.
2105. iv. ISAAC, bap. Feb. 28, 1790.
2106. v. SERENO, bap. Nov. 11, 1792; d. young.
2107. vi. BETSEY, b. Mar. 31,' 1795.
2108. vii. STEBBINS, b. Dec. 4, 1798.
2109. viii. SERENO, b. Feb. 21, 1802; m. July 22, 1833, Elizabeth S. Pierce
of Needham; was a clergyman.

1117. ELIJAH FISKE, ESQ. (David, Thomas, William, John, Nathaniel,
William, Robert, Simon, Simon, William, Symond), b. Mar. 24, 1770; m. in Weston Nov. 28, 1799, Anna Harrington, b. 1779; d. Oct. 11, 1812; m. 2d, Dec. 15, 1814,
Bathsheba Brooks, b. Feb. 18, 1789, dau. of Dea. David of Lincoln; d. 1871. He
d. in 1854; res. Lincoln, Mass.

2110. i. THOMAS, b. Oct. 26, 1800.
2111. ii. ELIZA, b. July 3, 1802.
2112. iii. GEORGE, b. Aug. 22, 1804.
2113. iv. CHARLES, b. Feb. 23, 1807.
2114. v. SUSANNA, b. Sept. 28, 1812; d. Mar., 1813.
2115. vi. MARTHA EMELINE, b. Feb. 8, 1816; m. ——— Tarbell; res.
Lincoln, Mass.
2116. vii. LUCY B., b. Aug. 10, 1819; m. ——— Hartwell; res. Lincoln,
Mass.
2117. viii. AUGUSTA, b. Jan. 20, 1822; d. Oct. 28, 1826.
2118. ix. CAROLINE, b. Aug. 15, 1824; d. Jan., 1828.
2119. x. CORNELIUS, b. Mar. 24. 1830; m. Mary A. Greenwood.

1118. ABRAHAM FISKE (David, Thomas, William, John, Nathaniel, William, Robert, Simon, Simon, William, Symond), b. Apr. 4, 1773; m. Nov. 26, 1794,
Grace Hagar, b. May 10, 1774; res. Waltham, Mass.

2120. i. LORENZO, b. Oct. 15, 1796.
2121. ii. ABRAHAM, b. Mar. 23, 1798.
2122. iii. HORATIO N., b. Aug. 28, 1799; m. Ann Smith.
2123. iv. POLLY, b. Apr. 16, 1801.
2124. v. SAMUEL, b. 1803; d. 1804.
2125. vi. LOIS, b. May 28, 1804.
2126. vii. THEODORE, b. Feb. 21, 1807.
2127. viii. WASHINGTON, b. Oct 5, 1808.
2128. ix. NAPOLEON, b. Jan. 22, 1810.
2129. x. JACOB GALE, b. May 6, 1811.

1124. PHINEHAS FISKE (Jonathan, Thomas, William, John, Nathaniel, William, Robert, Simon, Simon, William, Symond), b. Dec. 27, 1765; m. Feb. 1, 1783, Abigail Stearns, b. July 13, 1760; d. 1843; she was dau. of Daniel of Waltham. He d. Oct. 24, 1846; res. Waltham and Lincoln, Mass.

2130. i. PHINEHAS, b. Apr. 29, 1785; m. Mary Hart and Isabella B. Redington.

2131. ii. PRISCILLA, b. Sept. 17, 1787; m. Sept. 16, 1807, Elisha Hagar of Lincoln, b. Dec. 20, 1782, son of Nathan. Ch. b. in Lincoln: 1, Elisha, b. June, 1808; m. Elizabeth Johnson of Boston. 2, Phinehas Fiske, b. Feb., 1810; res. Philadelphia, Pa. 3, Priscilla, b. 1812; m. 1837 Edmund Wheeler of Lincoln, and d. same year. 4, Albert, b. Apr., 1817. 5, George, b. Feb., 1820; res. Colusa, Cal. 6, Lucia, b. Apr., 1823. 7, Sarah, b. 1827; d. young. 8, Edward, b. May, 1830.

2132. iii. ABIGAIL, b. Oct. 10. 1789; m. Mar., 1817, Jonas Smith of Weston, b. Feb. 6, 1788; d. Nov. 21, 1874. She d. Apr. 13, 1862. Ch.: 1, Sarah Hart, b. Jan. 13, 1820; d. Oct. 9, 1822. 2, Francis, b. Apr. 8, 1822; m. Nov. 19, 1850, Abigail Prescott Baker, b. Sept. 13, 1823; res. Lincoln, Mass.; ch.: Frank Webster Smith, Westfield, Mass., b. June 27, 1854; m. ———. Charles Sumner Smith, Lincoln, Mass., b. Dec. 19, 1857; m. Mar. 6, 1888, Mary Isabel Smyth of Lincoln. Sumner Smith, son of Chas. S. S., b. Sept. 26, 1889. Jonas Waldo Smith, Montclair, N. J. 3, Webster, b. May 24, 1825; res. Lexington. 4, Sarah Caroline, b. June 7, 1828; m. Samuel H. Pierce; res. Lincoln.

1125. JONATHAN FISKE (Jonathan, Thomas, William, John, Nathaniel, William, Robert, Simon, Simon, William, Symond), b. Watertown, Mass., Dec. 14, 1767; m. Feb. 18, 1808, Mary E. Baker, of Lincoln, Mass., b. Mar., 1782; d. Jan. 5, 1851. He was a farmer during his entire life, which was quiet and uneventful. He d. Jan. 20, 1843; res. Waltham, Mass.

2133. i. MARY ELIZABETH, b. Feb. 11, 1810; m. Aug. 5, 1832. Elijah Brown: she d. June 22, 1892. Ch.: 1, Lizzie Mary, b. May 12, 1856; m. Feb. 24. 1887, Arthur W. Bryant, b. Mar. 14, 1859; res. Harvard, Mass.; ch.: Winifred Louise Bryant, b. Oct. 23, 1890. Amy Elizabeth Bryant, b. Apr. 25, 1893.

2134. ii. MARIA, b. Apr. 30, 1812; m. Nov. 12, 1835, Edwin Hobbs; res. Weston. He was b. Apr. 11, 1811; d. Mar. 24, 1893; was a farmer. Ch.: 1, Elmira Maria Hobbs, b. July 24, 1838. 2, George Edwin Hobbs, b. Jan. 5, 1841; m. May 24, 1868. 3, Grace Elizabeth Hobbs, b. Dec. 1, 1843. These three addresses Weston, Mass. 4, John Louis Hobbs, b. Apr. 21, 1847; m. Nov. 6, 1878, Cambridge, Mass.; address, No. 56 Bay St., Springfield, Mass.

2135. iii. GRACE, b. Dec. 10, 1813; res. Waltham, Mass.
2136. iv. J. DEXTER, b. Oct. 14, 1815; m. Mary Clark.
2137. v. CALVIN, b. Feb. 21, 1817; m. Caroline M. Wellington.
2138. vi. ABIGAIL, b. Oct. 29, 1819; she d. Aug. 28, 1891.

1126. JACOB FISKE (Jonathan. Thomas, William, John, Nathaniel. William, Robert, Simon, Simon, William, Symond), b. Jan. 13, 1770; m. (pub.) Oct. 24, 1790, Sarah Flagg, b. about 1770, dau. of William. She m. 2d, 1813, Stephen Mead of Waltham, by whom she had four ch. She d. 1851. He was a yeoman, and d. intestate, Sept. 7, 1802, the administrator requested allowance for the support of the ch. He d. 1801; res. Weston, Mass.

2139. i. MARY, b. Mar. 21, 1790; d. young.
2140. ii. HENRY, b. July 24, 1792; d. in New Orleans in 1818.
2141. iii. ABIGAIL, b. Nov. 3, 1794; m. Aug. 14, 1817; Henry Bright, b. Aug. 31, 1793. She d. in Mobile, Ala., Nov. 26, 1833. He began a course of study preparatory to a collegiate education, but ill health compelled him to relinquish it. In 1815 he went to New Orleans, La., in business. The following year he

moved to St. Stephens, Ala. In 1824 he went to Mobile, where his wife died. In 1837 he moved to Cambridge, Mass., and in 1842, settled in Northampton. Ch.: 1, Abby Anne, b. July 4, 1818; d. July 6, 1818. 2, Henry, b. and d. Mar. 27, 1820. 3, John Henry, b. May 6; d. May 10, 1821. 4, Elizabeth Anne, b. Nov. 9, 1822; d. July 26, 1825. 5, Sarah Emily, b. Jan. 8, 1826; m. Dec. 18, 1852, Rev. Henry N. Hudson of New York, the lecturer on Shakespeare and editor of the Churchman. 6, Henry, b. Feb. 19, d. July 22, 1828. 7, Henry John, b. Aug. 9, 1829. His name was changed by the Legislature to Henry. Entered Yale College in 1846, but by an accident which affected his sight he was obliged to relinquish his studies; was a merchant in Boston. 8, William Ellery, b. Apr. 26, 1831. The father m. for a second wife, Feb. 10, 1835, Emeline M. Pinney, b. Apr. 21, 1808, in Simbury, Conn., by whom he had one dau. 9, Julia S., b. Mar. 12, 1839.

2142.   iv.   ISAAC, b. Aug. 9, 179-; m. Maria Pearce.

1131.   THOMAS FISK (Jonathan, Thomas, William, John, Nathaniel, William, Robert, Simon, Simon, William, Symond), b. Waltham, Mass, Apr. 13, 1785; m. ——— ———; res. Sudbury, Mass., and Rutland, Vt.

2143.   i.   MOSES, b. in 1807; m. Susan Hurd and Sarah Huntress.
2144.   ii.   JACOB, b. Dec. 2, 1808; m. Maria Louise Cushman.
2145.   iii.   WALTER H., b. ———; m. ———; and d. in 1886 in Boston, Mass.
2146.   iv.   SUSAN, b. ———; d. unm.
2147.   v.   THOMAS L., b. ———.
2148.   vi.   SARAH H., b. ———.
2149.   vii.   ABIGAIL P., b. ———.
2150.   viii.   ADALINE, b. ———.

1134.   ELIJAH FISKE (Samuel, Samuel, William, John, Nathaniel, William, Robert, Simon, Simon, William, Symond), b. Waltham, Sept. 26, 1765; m. Sept. 8, 1793, Lydia Livermore, b. Nov. 5, 1774, dau. of Lieut, Elisha; d. in Waltham, July 11, 1862. He was a plain, honest, industrious farmer. He d. July 15, 1843; res. Waltham, Mass.

2151.   i.   LUKE, b. Feb. 6; bap. Feb. 9, 1794; m. Susanna S. Piper.

1136.   JONAS FISKE (Samuel, Samuel, William, John, Nathaniel, William, Robert, Simon, Simon, William, Symond), b. Apr. 12, 1768; m. May 26, 1793, Ruth Pierce, b. May 30, 1773; d. Jan. 19, 1799; m. 2d her sister, May 27, 1800, Abigail Pierce, b. Dec. 30, 1830, daus. of Samuel and Ruth (Lee) Pierce; res. Weston, Mass.

2152.   i.   HENRY, b. Jan. 10, 1795.
2153.   ii.   NANCY, b. July 7, 1797.
2154.   iii.   ABIGAIL, b. Feb. 4, 1802.
2155.   iv.   RUTH SOPHIA, b. Sept. 27, 1803; m. Isaiah Dunster. He was b. Dec. 10, 1798; res. Weston, Mass. After his death she m. ———Haywood. She d. Oct. 6, 1875. Ch.: 1, Eliza Sophia, b. Apr. 5, 1824; m. Aug. 29, 1844, Moses Mason. He d. Aug. 7, 1866. Had 8 ch. 2, Henry, b. Apr. 13, 1831; m. Oct. 6, 1851, Jane Mellen; 2 ch.; res. Providence, R. I.
2156.   v.   EMILY, b. Aug. 13, 1806.
2157.   vi.   REBECCA ADAMSON, b. Apr. 16, 1808.
2158.   vii.   SUSAN, b. Feb. 20, 1812.
2159.   viii.   JONAS, b. Mar. 14, 1817; m. Charlotte Harrington, in Weston, Mass. He died and his widow resides in Brighton. They had one child, Charlotte Althea, who died young.

1138.   WILLIAM FISKE (Samuel, Samuel, William, John, Nathaniel, William, Robert, Simon, Simon, William, Symond), b. Dec. 20, 1770; m. May 8, 1794, Eunice White, b. June 24, 1769; d. 1860. He was a cabinet maker. He d. 1844; res. Boston, Mass.

2160.   i.   WILLIAM, b. Feb. 3, 1795; d. unm., Oct. 28, 1827.
2161.   ii.   LUCY WHITE, b. Mar. 25, 1797; m. Sept. 10, 1818, Aaron Chapin, b. Ludlow, Mar. 21, 1791; d. Jan. 31, 1833. Ch.: 1, Lucy

White, b. Dec. 4, 1819. 2, Harriette Maria, b. Sept. 22, 1821; m. Thomas Emmons, who d. June 14, 1844. 3, George Amon, b. Jan. 18, 1824; m. 1846, Sarah H. Davis. 4, Caroline Louisa, b. Jan. 9, 1826; m. 1845, Charles A. Hewins.

2162. iii. HARRIETT, b. Jan. 3, 1799; m. June 13, 1822, Chester Guile, leather manufacturer of Rox., b. Walpole. Apr. 19, 1791. Ch.: 1, Chester, b. Dec. 13, 1823. 2, Charles Henry, b. June 11, 1825; m. 1848, Margaret J. Fox. 3, George Alfred, b. Dec. 14, 1826. 4, Harriette Maria, b. Jan. 28, 1829. 5, Josiah Fiske, b. May 20, 1831.

2163. iv. MARY ANN, b. Sept. 10, 1800; d. May 8, 1802.

2164. v. CAROLINE, b. Jan. 12, 1803; d. Sept. 22, 1803.

2165. vi. SAMUEL, b. Aug. 11, 1804; m. Abigail S. H. Clapp.

2166. vii. MARIA, b. Aug. 4, 1806; m. Dec. 4, 1832, William Fowle, a merchant in Boston, b. Aug. 17, 1794. Ch.: 1, William Fiske, b. Sept. 17, 1833. 2, Josiah Fiske, b. Oct. 20, 1835.

2167. viii. CAROLINE, b. July 21, 1808; d. May 18, 1809.

2168. ix. JOSIAH, b. Aug. 17, 1810; m. Helen M. Bridge.

2169. x. GEORGE ALFRED, b. Oct. 11, 1812; m. Sarah W. Clapp.

1139. FRANCIS FISKE (Samuel, Samuel, William, John, Nathaniel, William, Robert, Simon, Simon, William, Symond), b. Waltham, Aug. 24, 1772; m. there Oct. 21, 1798, Sarah Livermore; b. Jan. 1, 1781; dau. of Lieut. Elisha; d. at Malden, Mar. 29, 1865. He d. Feb., 1859; res. Saugus, Mass.

2170. i. LYDIA, b. Apr. 12, 1799; m. ——— Paull. She d. in Boston; a son is H. H. Paull; res. 7 Cedar Park, Roxbury, Mass.

2172. ii. SAMUEL, b. Apr. 17, 1801; a son is Dudley B. Fiske, Cliftondale.

2173. iii. ABIJAH LIVERMORE, b. Dec. 11, 1803; a son is W. L. Fiske; res. C.

2174. iv. ANNA MARIA, b. Mar. 17, 1807; m. ——— Anthony; had several ch., all dead.

2175. v. SARAH JANE, b. Apr. 27, 1814.

2176. vi. FRANCIS, b. June 30, 1824; m. Sarah E. Houghton.

2177. vii. HARRIETT, b. ———; m. ——— Newhall. She is deceased; a son is Geo. Francis Newhall; res. Lynn, Mass.

2178. viii. LUCY W., b. ———; m. ——— Baker; d. in Nebraska; left a child.

1141. ROBERT FISKE (Samuel, Samuel, William, John, Nathaniel, William, Robert, Simon, Simon, William, Symond), b. June 9, 1775; m. May 21, 1801, Nancy Stratton, of Weston, b. July 31, 1780; dau. of Daniel. He d. Feb. 18, 1843; res. Waltham, Mass.

2179. i. GEORGE, b. Apr. 25, 1802.

2180. ii. MARY, b. Nov. 14, 1803.

2181. iii. PATTY, b. Apr. 9, 1805.

1143. NATHAN FISKE (Samuel, Samuel, William, John, Nathaniel, William, Robert, Simon, Simon, William, Symond), b. Dec. 6, 1779; m. July 13, 1804, Anna Livermore Mason, of East Cambridge; dau. of Josiah, b. 1784; d. Sept. 12, 1861. Nathan was a grain dealer near West Boston bridge, and afterwards deputy sheriff, and otherwise engaged in public business. Late in life he res. on Holyoke place and on North avenue, Cambridge. He d. Apr. 27, 1868; res. East Cambridge, Mass.

2182. i. CLEMENTINA, b. Aug. 12, 1805; d. young.

2183. ii. FREDERICK WM., b. Nov., 1806; d. young.

2184. iii. SARAH RUSSELL MASON, b. Dec. 16, 1808; m. Oct. 8, 1834, James Munroe, Jr.

2185. iv. ELIJAH, b. Feb. 1, 1811; m. Charlotte D. Endicott.

2186. v. MARY LOIS, b. May 1, 1813; m. Apr. 8, 1835, Alexander H. Ramsey.

2187. vi. MARGARET, b. Apr. 1, 1815; m. Nov. 15, 1837, David Humphrey.

2188. vii. BENJAMIN, b. May 9, 1817; d. young.

2189. viii. ELBRIDGE GERRY, b. July 26, 1819; m. Nov. 24, 1842, Sarah
               P. Teele.
2190. ix.   JOSEPH BRADLEY VARNUM, b. Aug., 1821; d. young.
2191. x.   JOSIAH MASON, b. Oct. 23, 1823; m. Martha T. Smith.
2192. xi.   ANNA ABIGAIL, b. July 10, 1826; m. May 4, 1844, Nathaniel
               Prentiss.
2193. xii. CHARLES CARROLL, b. June 11, 1828. He was gr. at Har-
               vard in 1849; m. ———— ————.

1154. REV. NATHAN FISKE, D. D. (Nathan, Nathan, Nathan, Nathaniel,
William, Robert, Simon, Simon, William, Symond), b. Weston, Sept. 9, 1733; m.
Oct. 19, 1758, Sarah Hill of Camb.; d. 1774; m. 2d, Mrs. Elizabeth (Breck) Treat; d.
1786; m. 3d, Mrs. Hannah (Wells) Reynolds. The place of his nativity was Weston, Mass.; born Sept. 9, 1733. In early life he was fond of reading; graduated at
Harvard College, Cambridge, 1754; ordained to the work of the gospel ministry
in Brookfield, May 28, 1758. The title of D. D. was conferred on him from Harvard College in 1792. He preached his last sermon from the text, Prov. 4: 18, "But
the path of the just is as a shining light," etc. In the evening of the same day,
Nov. 24, 1799, he spent in company with friends in apparent health, retired to
rest and sleep, which proved the sleep of death, at the age of 66. He published a discourse on the settlement and growth of Brookfield, 1775; a feast sermon,
1776; a sermon on the death of Mr. Joshua Spooner, 1778; an oration on the capture of Lord Cornwallis, 1781; a funeral sermon of Mr. Josiah Hobbs, who was
killed by lightning, 1784; a volume of sermons on various subjects, 1794; Dudleian
Lecture at Harvard College, 1796; two volumes of essays, entitled the "Moral Monitor," 1801, after his decease. He was married first, to Sally Hill, who died 1774;
next to Mrs. Elizabeth Treat (originally Breck), who died 1786; after this to Mrs.
Hannah Reynolds (originally Wells), who survived him. He had six children,
five sons and one daughter. The eldest son died while a member of Harvard
College. Of the two other sons who graduated there, Oliver became a physician,
and Samuel first studied law and afterwards engaged in mercantile persuits. As
a preacher, it is said, he was not distinguished so much for the powers of oratory,
as for purity of sentiment and perspicuity and elegance of style. He was modest
and unassuming; and few men with his advantages have acquired a greater store
of rich and varied knowledge. He was highly esteemed by the people of his
charge and by his clerical brethren; as a learned divine, a reputable author, acceptable preacher and devoted to the various duties of his profession. He d. Nov. 24,
1799; res. Brookfield, Mass.

2194. i.   OLIVER, b. Sept. 2, 1762; m. Sarah Duncan.
2195. ii.   SALLY, b. ————; m. Dec. 25, 1781, Lieut. Samuel Jennison, who
               was b. 1759. He was graduated at Harvard College in the class
               of 1774. When the Revolutionary war broke out he enlisted in
               the Sixth Mass. Regiment; was Lieut. and later Quarter-
               master. After the war he studied law; was admitted to the
               bar at Worcester Mass.; practiced in Oxford, Mass., and died
               in Thomaston, Me., Sept. 1, 1826. Ch.: 1, Nathan Fiske, b. 1783;
               d. unm. 2, Sally, b. Aug. 25, 1785; d. unm. 3, Samuel, b. Feb.
               24, 1788; m. 1815, Mary Gould Ellery. He res. Worcester,
               Mass., and d. Mar. 11, 1860. At the age of 12 he res. in Wor-
               cester with his uncle, Hon. Oliver Fiske, a physician there, who
               was also engaged in trade and employed his nephew in his
               store till Apr., 1810, when he became teller in the Worcester
               Bank. In 1812 he was chosen cashier and held the office until
               he resigned, in 1846. Was also treasurer of the Worcester
               County Institution of Savings from 1828 to 1853, besides this
               he held various city and state offices. He was a member of the
               American Antiquarian Society and the N. E. Hist. and Gen.
               Society. He had five children; was a man of fine education,
               and greatly interested in history and biography. 4, William, b.
               June, 1790. He m. for his second wife, Mrs. (Fiske) Walker,
               of Concord, N. H.; two ch. (see elsewhere).
2196. iii. WILLIAM, b. 1764; m. Frances Rice.
2196¼. iv.   SAMUEL, b. ————; went to Claremont, N. H. He was gradu-

ated at Harvard College in the class of 1793; studied law and practiced it for a short time at Claremont, but relinquished it and engaged in mercantile business. He was soon elected Representative and soon afterwards Senator, he filled both offices alternately for many years. Catharine Fiske, daughter of Hon. Samuel Fiske, of Claremont, N. H., now Mrs. Bradley, wife of Amos Bradley, lived at Detroit, Mich. Mr. B. was in the nursery business and is out of the city about one mile. Phillips Fiske, Esq., son of Sam. Fiske, lived at Claremont, N. H., could give information of his father's family, and perhaps also of his uncle, George Fiske, who had but one child, a son, very promising, who died immediately after graduation as a physician and surgeon. Another son of Hon. Samuel was Samuel P., who res. at Claremont.

2196½. v. NATHAN, b. ——: fitted for college; entered Harvard and died there in his senior year.

2196¾. vi. GEORGE, b. ——; m. and had a son, who died just as he was entering on the practice of medicine.

1156. CAPT. JONATHAN FISKE (Nathan, Nathan, Nathan, Nathaniel, William, Robert, Simon, Simon, William, Symond), b. Weston, Dec. 15, 1739; m. Apr. 30. 1760, Abigail Fiske, dau. of Thomas and Mary (Pierce) Fiske of Waltham. Capt. Jonathan Fiske, who was Captain of the Weston Company in Feb., 1776, was in the Revolutionary war. His company, with others, was in the regiment commanded by Col. Eleazer Brooks of Lincoln, Samuel Lamson of Weston, Major. This regiment, with other troops, was ordered to take possession of Dorchester Heights. Res. Weston and Medfield, Mass.

2197. i. NATHAN, b. Sept. 7, 1760; m. Mary Stearns.
2198. ii. THADDEUS, b. June 22, 1762: m. Lucy Clark.
2199. iii. MICAH, b. Aug. 12, 1764; m. Lydia Upham.
2200. iv. EBENEZER, b. Dec. 3, 1766; m. Dolly Gould.
2201. v. ABIGAIL, b. Apr. 4, 1769; m. Dec. 23, 1788, Isaac Lamson, b. July 7, 1765. Ch.: 1, Nabby, d. unm. 2, Horatio, d. Mar., 1874, unm. 3, Mary, b. Feb. 27, 1803: m. Feb., 1822. Rev. Joseph Bennett of Woburn. He gr. at Harvard College in 1818 and d. Feb. 11, 1846. His son, Joseph L., gr. at Amherst College in 1844; his dau. Mary m. Rev. Thomas Morong, of Pepperell, Mass. Mr. Lamson d. and his wid. m. 2d, July 1, 1810, Dea. Isaac Warren of Charlestown, by whom she had two children. 3. George Washington, who was graduated at Harvard College in 1830, was a lawyer in Charlestown and Mayor of that city. 4, Henry. who d. young.
2202. vi. JONATHAN, b. Dec. 28, 1771; d. Jan. 12, 1772.
2203. vii. JONATHAN, b. Jan. 19, 1774; m. Sally Flagg.
2204. viii. ABIJAH, b. July 28, 1776: d. unm.
2205. ix. ISAAC, b. Dec, 1, 1778; m. Sukey Hobbs.

1158. SAMUEL FISKE (Nathan, Nathan, Nathan, Nathaniel, William, Robert, Simon, Simon, William, Symond), b. Weston, July 9, 1742; m. Mar. 21. 1764, Mary Parkhurst, b. Mar. 3, 1743, dau. of Josiah. She d. in childbed, June 18, 1773; m. 2d. (pub. Apr. 3), 1774. Abigail Murdock of Newton; res. Weston, Mass.

2206. i. HEPZIBAH, b. June 7, 1765; m. Apr. 15, 1787, Abraham Jones, Jr., b. Feb. 12, 1762.
2207. ii. LOUISA, b. Apr. 20, 1767; m. Nov. 2, 1787, Nahum Traine, b. Apr. 10, 1759, son of Samuel. Ch.: 1, Polly, b. Sept. 10, 1788. 2, Marshall, b. Sept. 15, 1790. 3, Oliver, b. July 28, 1792. 4, Louisa, b. Jan. 7, 1794.
2208. iii. POLLY, b. Mar. 6, 1771; m. Nov. 19, 1791, Joseph Parker of Weston.
2209. iv. ANNA, b. June 13, 1773; m. Apr. 8, 1794. Jonathan Rand of Hopkinton.
2210. v. ABIGAIL, b. Jan. 16, 1775: m. Micah Clark of Sherborn.
2211. vi. EZRA. b. July 21, 1776: d. Feb., 1777.

2212. vii.   EZRA, b. Jan. 16, 1778; m. Lydia Sanderson.
2213. viii. SAMUEL, b. Mar. 6, 1781; m. Lydia Travis.
2214. ix.   LYDIA, b. Nov. 21, 1782; m. Feb. 23, 1728, Abel Cummings of
              Wat.
2215. x.   SALLY, b. July 31, 1784; m. May 8, 1806, Jonathan D. Dix of
              Newton.
2216. xi.   OLIVER, b. Aug. 3, 1786; m. Abigail ———. She d. Feb. 18,
              1820; m. 2d, Nov. 9, 1820, Eliza Park; res. Sherborn, Mass. Ch.:
              Mary, b. Feb. 24, 1815; Samuel, b. Nov. 10, 1816.
2217. xii.   REBEKAH, b. Aug. 23, 1788.

1167. JOSIAH FISKE (Josiah, Nathan, Nathan, Nathaniel, William, Robert,
Simon, Simon, William, Symond), b. Walth., Feb. 12, 1733; m. Sarah Colburn of
Dracutt, Mass., b. 1737; d. 1825. His estate was admr. on by his wid., Sarah, Apr.
11, 1767. He received a good education and taught school for several winters. He
died when only 33 years of age, "beloved by all." After his death his widow married Levi Blood of Groton. He died Apr. 14, 1766; res. Groton, Mass.
       2218. iv.   PHINEHAS, b. Jan. 29, 1765; d. young; not mentioned in
                     father's will.
       2219. v.   SUBMIT (posthumous), b. 1767.
       2220. i.   JOSIAH, b. Sept. 3, 1755; m. Mary Caldwell.
       2221. ii.   DAVID, b. 1756; m. ——— ———.
       2222. iii.   SARAH, b. about 1760.

1169. AMOS FISKE (Josiah, Nathan, Nathan, Nathaniel, William, Robert,
Simon, Simon, William, Symond), b. Walth., May 10, 1739; m. May 29, 1777, Mary
Whitney, b. Dec. 11, 1744; dau. of William of Weston. Lieut. Joseph Craft (son of
Lieut. Moses) (38) (Ancestry Samuel, Samuel, Lieut. Griffin); b. in Newton, Mass.,
June 12, 1736; m. in Brookline, Mass., Oct. 19, 1762, Elizabeth Davis, dau. of Dea.
Ebenezer and Sarah (White) Davis of Brookline. She was b. in Brookline, Aug.
30, 1742, and d. in Newton Mar. 13, 1776, aged 33. He m. 2d in Newton, Jan. 23,
1777, Sarah Fuller, dau. of Jonathan and Eleanor (Hammond) Fuller of Newton.
She was b. there Mar. 26, 1752, and d. there in Mar., 1808, aged 56. He m. 3d the
widow Mary Fiske of Newton, in 1808. She d. in Newton, Sept., 1829. He d. in
Newton, Apr. 21, 1821, aged 85. Lieut. Joseph Craft, like his brothers, was a
smart, active, business man, and was held in high esteem by his townsmen. He
was an ardent patriot, and was in active service during a long period of the war
of the Revolution. He was present at the battle of Lexington, and was Lieutenant
in command of the company of Newton minute men at that time. They remained on duty for four days following that battle. Again, in 1776, we learn from
the records that by order of the council, he marched as Lieutenant in command of
his company, Dec. 9, 1776, to join Col. Thomas Craft's regiment at Boston, and
among the privates in his company was Samuel Craft. Again, in 1778, he was
Lieutenant of the company of Capt. Edward Fuller, Col. Thrasher's regiment, detailed to guard the British troops, Sept. 2, 1778. Finally, in 1780, he once more
went into the field, and marched with his company to reinforce the Continental
army. He took an active part in town affairs. On Dec. 18, 1776, he was chosen on
a committee to adjust matters relative to "an allowance for soldiers for services
done in the war since Apr. 19, 1775, and also to consider in what manner the war
shall be supported by the inhabitants in the future." He gave substantial aid in
the cause of liberty by loaning £200 to the town, Jan. 6. 1777, for the purpose of
paying the soldiers. He was also a selectman in Newton during that year, 1777,
and doubtless held many other positions of trust and responsibility, of which we
are not informed. With his brother, Samuel, he was a residuary legatee of his
father's estate, which was very large. From the town records we learn that
he was taxed in Newton, Oct. 1, 1798, for seventy-eight acres of land, valued at
$2,612. By his first wife he had five children, besides an infant which cost the life
of its mother, and did not survive. By his second marriage he had ten children,
and none by his third wife. He was a soldier in the Revolutionary war. He d. in
1785, in Pennsylvania, where he had gone on business. Res. Waltham, Mass.
       2223. i.   POLLY, b. Aug. 23, 1778; m. Mar. 29, 1801, Samuel Harrington
                     of Wat., b. July 17, 1775; m. 2d, 1809, Jeremiah Wiswell of
                     Newton; had five ch. A granddaughter is Mrs. C. K. Thomas,
                     118 Princeton St., East Boston, Mass. Sarah Craft (dau. of

Joseph) (87) (Ancestry, Moses, Samuel, Samuel, Lieut. Griffin), b. in Newton, Mass., June 14, 1764; m. June 10, 1784, Dea. Jeremiah Wiswall, son of Capt. Jeremiah and Elizabeth (Murdock) Wiswall of Newton. He was b. Aug. 23, 1760. They lived in Newton, where she d. Jan. 26, 1809, aged 44. He m. 2d, in 1809, Mary, widow of Samuel Harrington, and dau. of Amos Fiske. She d. Sept. 26, 1856. He d. in Newton, June 22, 1836, aged 76.

2224. ii. AMOS, b. ———; he was twice married, but never had children. For twenty years he was an invalid. He d. in 1828.

2225. iii. HANNAH, b. ———; m. ——— Stearns.

2226. iv. BETSEY, b. ———; m. ——— Fletcher.

2226½.v. JOSIAH, b. ———; he married and resided in Keeseville, N. Y., was a member of the Legislature and prominent citizen; a dau. was Mrs. W. S. Hascoll, 63 E. Twenty-seventh St., New York City, and another Mrs. Rev. Conant Sawyer, Gloversville, N. Y.

1170. DEA. DANIEL FISKE (Josiah, Nathan, Nathan, Nathaniel, William, Robert, Simon, Simon, William, Symond), b. May 18, 1742; m. in Pepperell, Apr. 22, 1766, Elizabeth Varnum, b. Mar., 1742; dau. of Jonas of Groton. He was a delegate to the convention to adopt the Federal Constitution. Res. Pepperell, Mass.

2227. i. MARY, b. Mar. 13, 1767.

2228. ii. NATHAN, b. Jan. 3, 1769; m. Dorothy J. Holt.

2229. iii. MICAH, b. June 11, 1771; d. Aug. 10, 1772.

2230. iv. WALTER, b. June 17, 1773; m. Phebe Abbott.

2231. v. MICAH, b. Jan. 9, 1775.

2232. vi. DANIEL, b. Mar. 9, 1777.

2233. vii. BETTY, b. Feb. 17, 1779.

2234. viii. SARAH, b. July 1, 1781.

2235. ix. JOSIAH, b. Jan. 3, 1783; m. Betsey Harvey.

2236. x. VARNUM, b. Sept. 13, 1786; m. Sally Eames.

1173. REV. ABEL FISKE (Josiah, Nathan, Nathan, Nathaniel, William, Robert, Simon, Simon, William, Symond), b. Pepperell, Mass., Mar. 28, 1752; m. Aug. 19, 1783, Anna Spalding, dau. of Rev. Sampson Spalding, of Tewksbury, b. Jan. 19, 1755; d. July 8, 1796; m. 2d, Sarah Putnam, b. 1773. She d. Nov. 26, 1838, in Wilton, N. H. He was graduated at Harvard College in the class of 1774, and four years later, Nov. 18, 1778, ordained as the successor of Rev. Jonathan Livermore at Wilton, N. H., where he remained until his death. At the time of his ordination 27 male members of the church in a solemn manner renewed their covenant engagements. Mr. Fiske continued in the ministry a little more than twenty-three years, and died Apr. 21, 1802, aged 50. Rev. Abel Fiske was born at Pepperell, Mass., May 28, 1752. During his ministry, including short vacancy between the time of his death and the settlement of his successor, 224 persons were added to the church, and 745 children and others were baptized. Greatly beloved by his flock, who manifested their love by every family in the parish following him to his grave. His wife was appointed administrator Apr. 30, 1802. He d. Apr. 26, 1802; res. Wilton, N. H.

2237. i. ABEL, b. July 24, 1784; m. Abigail Dale.

2238. vi. THEOPHILUS, b. Dec. 4, 1801; m. ——— Dwinelle.

2239. ii. ANN SPALDING, b. Apr. 17, 1786; m. Apr. 26, 1808, David R. Clark. A dau., Mary Ann, b. May 19, 1810, m. John Perkins Nichols, b. Aug. 19, 1798; d. Oct. 27, 1891. She d. Dec. 27, 1885; res. Boston, Mass. Ch.: Arthur Howard, b. Sept. 9, 1840; m. Nov. 11, 1869, Elizabeth Fisher Homer, b. Dec. 22, 1844; is a physician; res. 55 Mt. Vernon St., Boston; ch.: Rose Standish, b. Jan. 11, 1872. Marian Clarke, b. Dec. 21, 1873. Sidney Homer, b. Nov. 14, 1875; d. July 6, 1881. Margaret Homer, b. Oct. 30, 1879. Add. 55 Mt. Vernon St., Boston.

2240. iii. ACHSAH, b. Jan. 28, 1788; m. Dec. 20, 1810, Jacob Farrar. A descendant is Hamilton Farrar, of Jamaica Plains, Mass.

2241. iv. ALLETHINA, b. June 30, 1792; m. Asa Holt; d. Sept. 4, 1838.

A grandson is Q. A. Hartshorn, 23 Maple Ave., Somerville, Mass.

2242. v. ALLETHEA, b. ———. See will.

1179. DEA. HENRY FISKE (Henry, Nathan, Nathan, Nathan, Nathaniel, William, Robert, Simon, Simon, William, Symond), b. Aug. 16, 1745; m. May 5, 1774, Sarah Fiske, his cousin, b. Aug. 1, 1746, dau. of Dea. Daniel and Deliverence (Brown) Fiske, d. Dec. 11, 1815. He was born in Sturbridge, on Fiske Hill, where his father settled before the town was incorporated. He was an active citizen in the affairs of the town and church and much trusted with the business of both. He married his cousin who died one day after he passed away. Their bodies were buried in one grave. He carried on a large farm and owned other real estate to a large extent. He was a very liberal man and deacon in the Baptist Church, and conducted what was called in those days a "Baptist Hotel." He entertained a great many people free of charge. A short distance from his house and on the top of Fisk Hill was the old fashioned Baptist meeting house with the high back square pews and the sounding board over the pulpit. He d. Dec. 10, 1815; res. Sturbridge. Mass.

2243. i. ARMILLE, b. Feb. 12, 1775; d. Feb. 22, 1779.
2244. ii. MOSES, b. June 27, 1776; d. Mar. 15, 1777.
2245. iii. JOSHUA, b. June 16, 1778; m. Betsey Cheever.
2246. iv. ICHABOD, b. July 19, 1779; d. Aug. 14, 1779.
2247. v. MARY, b. July 19, 1780; m. Aug. 19, 1804, David Taylor, b. Apr., 1779. She d. Oct. 5, 1827, leaving three ch.
2248. vi. SALLY, b. Apr. 4, 1782; m. Sept. 1, 1799, Rev. Zenas Lockwood Leonard. His ancestry is as follows: 1, Solomon (Duxbury, 1637), m. Mary ———; d. 1686. 2, John (s. of Solomon) Bridgewater, m. Sarah ———; d. 1699. 3, Joseph, s. of John, Bridgewater, m. Hannah Jennings, d. of Richard Jennings, 1712. 4, Joseph, s. of Joseph, b. 1713, m. Mary, d. of Nath'l Packard. 5, David (twin), s. of Joseph, b. ———; m. Mary Hall of Taunton, 1769; was with Gen. Winslow at taking of French in N. Scotia, 1755. Ch. of David above: David, Zenas L., Mary, Bernard, Caleb F., Linus, George W., Sarah, Fanny, James, Charles Frederick, Olive, Hannah. He was b. June 16, 1773; d. June 24, 1841; a Baptist minister, who preached in the meeting house on Fisk Hill for a good many years and until his health failed, and he gave up preaching. He was college educated and a very talented man, none superior or equal to him in the very large association. He owned and worked on his farm. It is remembered how in the winter season Rev. Leonard and many of the congregation would go to Dea. Fisk's hotel to spend the noon hour in the large old house. Three rooms would be well warmed, one for men, where apples and cider would be freely passed round and the minister and perhaps one or two or more of the old people invited to the pantry for a lunch. Then tobacco and pipes passed round. The minister was quite a smoker, and two of the old deacons took snuff. One of them lived to be 104 years old, and he was summoned as a witness after he was 100 years old to the court in Worcester in the case of a pauper between two towns when he was one of the selectmen of Sturbridge. Another of the rooms was for the women, where the deacon's wife would furnish some warm drink and apples. The other room was for the children and they had apples. There was no Sunday school in those days, not in that church. The children of Sally and Rev. Zenas L. Leonard were: 1, Henry F., b. Aug. 14, 1800; m. Ann F. Burrough; d. June 23, 1831. 2, Mary Ann Hall, b. Jan. 4, 1803; m. Aug. 31, 1829, Rev. Francis W. Emmons; five ch. She d. Nov. 19, 1889. 3, Vernera, b. June 20, 1805; m. Apr. 25, 1831, Francis E. Corey. He was b. Sept. 25, 1804; d. Mar. 19, 1892. She d. July 10, 1892; res. Chicago, Ill.; ch.: a, Helen M. Corey, b. Sept. 28, 1832; m. James Mix, Chicago, Apr. 27, 1854.

b, Sarah M. Corey, b. Dec. 3, 1834; m. B. F. Carver (now deceased), Chicago, Apr. 30, 1857. c, Josephine Corey, b. Apr. 16, 1843; m. John B. Drake (now deceased), Chicago, Feb. 24, 1863; ch.: Tracy Corey Drake, b. Sept. 12, 1864; m. Annie Colton Daughaday Jan. 12, 1893; Helen Vernera Drake, b. Feb. 23, 1867; John B. Drake, Jr., b. May 19, 1872; Lillian Carver Drake, b. Sept. 30, 1874; Francis Edwin Drake, b. May 9, 1876, all of Chicago. d, George Henry Corey, b. May 24, 1839; d. Aug. 13, 1847. 4, Sarah, b. June 19, 1810; m. Sept. 5, 1842, Thomas Spooner. She d. July 31, 1850; three ch. 5, Manning, b. June 1, 1814; m. Sept. 15, 1840, Mary Fiske Ammidown, b. Aug. 23, 1817; d. May 31, 1892.; ch.: Charles Henry, b. Dec. 29, 1841; m. Mary Grace Beecher. Bernard Ammidown, b. July 25, 1844; m. Nellie T. Burr; m. 2d, Ermina E. Newton; res. De Pere, Wis. George Manning, b. Sept. 4, 1846; d. Sept. 8, 1863. Anna Rebekah, b. Apr. 8, 1849. Mary Frances, b. Aug. 2, 1851. Sarah Catherine, b. Dec. 16, 1854; m. Wm. H. Green. David Fiske, b. July 26, 1857; d. May 31, 1864. Manning Leonard was at the time of his death preparing a history of the Leonard family, which he was unable to finish. His son, Bernard A. Leonard, and daughter, Miss Anna R. Leonard, have greatly added to his work and it is now ready for publication. 6, Linus, b. Dec. 29, 1819; m. Sarah P. Harridon, and d. Aug. 12, 1862. 7, Frances Maria, b. Apr. 17, 1826; m. Oct. 9, 1851, Thomas Spooner; she d. Nov. 30, 1855; two ch. Sally Leonard d. at the residence of her son Manning Leonard, Esq., in the adjoining town of Southbridge, July 18, 1868, aged 86 years 3 months and 12 days. "Mrs. Leonard's extreme age made her an interesting link with the past. She was granddaughter of the two first settlers of Sturbridge—Lieutenant Henry Fiske, and his brother, Deacon Daniel Fiske, who pitched their tent in 1731 on what has been known ever since as 'Fiske Hill'."

"Her father was Deacon Henry Fiske, son of the first named, who was the sixth of a family of 14 children, and her mother, Sarah, daughter of the last named, and the second of a family of 16 children, and they were married May 5, 1774. Her father died Dec. 10, 1815, aged 70, and her mother next day, aged 69, and they were both buried in one grave in the old cemetery in Sturbridge. They had nine children, Mrs. L. being the sixth, and was born in 1782, a year celebrated for the birth of a great number of prominent men in this country, the last of whom—Gov. Levi Lincoln—died May 29, 1868. She was married Sept. 1, 1799, to Rev. Zenas L. Leonard, a native of Bridgewater, who had then been pastor of the Baptist Church on Fiske Hill more than four years, with which church she united. Although she was very young when she assumed the responsible duties of a minister's wife, which position, like that of the minister, was no sinecure at that period, yet she developed at once a remarkable capacity for the position. Though not rapid in her movement yet her wonderful tact, perfect system, untiring industry, enabled her to accomplish a vast amount of work. She was free from eccentricity, selfishness and hypocrisy, just what she professed and appeared to be, and every day alike. Their new home was established in sight of her birthplace during the first year of this century, and was the center of attraction to her for nearly sixty-eight years. In addition to his pastoral duties, her husband was for many years much engaged in instructing the youth of the neighborhood, having students in his family who were fitted for college and the prominent positions of business life. She sympathized with him, and aided him in all his labors, and was indeed a helpmate. A very interesting sketch of his life was published by Dr. Wm. Sprague, of Albany, in his 'Annals of the American Pulpit,' 6th vol., pages

347-354, to which the writer referred for many of the prominent events of her life. Suffice it to say, in this delightful home, where was always dispensed a courteous and bounteous hospitality, friend and stranger alike welcomed and needs supplied, they reared a family of seven children, three of whom only survived their mother. The father died June 24, 1841, so that she has had a widowhood of more than twenty-seven years. She remained at the homestead where her son Linus Leonard deceased Aug. 12, 1862, until her 86th birthday—the 4th of Apr., 1868, when she made a brief visit to her daughter, Mrs. Emmons, and then came to her son's in Southbridge, where an accident befel her on the 12th of June, which caused her five weeks of intense suffering, and with her other maladies and weaknesses of age, resulted in her death. She bore her pains with wonderful patience and resignation, and as characteristic of her whole life seemed more interested for others' comfort than her own. Her obsequies were attended at her son's house, Sunday afternoon, July 19, 1868, at three o'clock, and it was pleasant to look upon her calm and placid features which seemed to have renewed comparative youth, and to feel that she had attained eternal rest. She was buried beside her husband and eldest son in the new cemetery in Sturbridge.

"Two sisters survive her, and she left quite a number of descendants to the third generation, in whose hearts, and those of numerous relatives and friends who knew her excellencies, her memory is sacredly enshrined. She will be sadly missed, with her cheerful, cordial greeting, tender inquiry and constant interest, but we could not wish her back to the sufferings and wearinesses of age. She has lived a long and active, useful and somewhat eventful life, and her rest must be sweet and glorious." Southbridge Journal.

Fisk Hill is the most beautiful swell of land in the town, possessing fertility, and commanding an extensive and delightful view, in every direction. Here you have to the west, a full view of the village of Sturbridge Centre, one mile, and beyond in the same direction the view of Fiskdale appears to very good advantage; at the north as far as the vision can extend, you catch a view of the azure Monadnock, hardly distinguishable from the surrounding atmosphere; very much nearer, about twenty-seven miles away, the Wachuset appears head and shoulders above her neighbors; nearer still, the town of Leicester presents a beautiful appearance twelve miles distant. At the east you have a view of the village of Charlton, on a graceful swell of land, presenting a stately, and no less beautiful appearance. Thence southerly, the eye sweeps over an expansion of varied and lofty scenery, exhibiting spires, churches, villages, and scattered residences, intermixed with the beauties of nature. Take it all in all, the eye may dwell with a high degree of pleasure on a rare assemblage of natural and artificial attractions.

Transporting ourselves back to that period, when our Fisk ancestors first commenced a settlement here, we may, in imagination, catch a view of the almost unbroken forest, which was spread out around them. Contrasting that scene with the present, the change has lessened the sublimity of the prospect, but not its beauties. This selection by the original settlers, viz. —Henry and Daniel Fisk—is a manifestation of good taste and sound judgment. The breezes here are somewhat searching, but not too much so for health and a vigorous constitution. First settled by them, the land comprising this very fertile hill, continued in their possession and that of their descendants more than a century before any of it passed into the hands of others except such persons as had married into the Fisk families. This section of the town has probably exceeded every other in point of strength and productiveness of soil. The farms still exhibit a neat appearance, and evidence of skillful

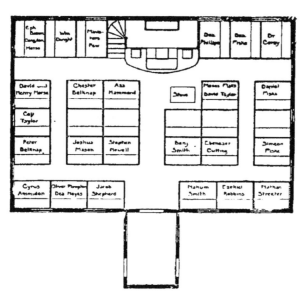

OLD MEETING HOUSE ON FISKE HILL, STURBRIDGE, MASS.

cultivation. If the soil at the commencement of the spring is so wet as to delay tillage, the autumn almost invariably presents heavy crops. The original highway was laid out directly over the highest point of Fiske Hill, and it is still the favorite drive. A new highway shunning and passing around it to the southeast was built in 1839, and the rapid traveler, for a little more ease, foregoes the pleasure of an admirable landscape, spread out before him, in passing over Fiske Hill.

2249. vii. MATILDA, b. Jan. 16, 1784; d. July 15, 1880.
2250. viii. AMY, b. Nov. 9, 1785; m. Oct. 11, 1812, her cousin, Daniel Fiske, son of Daniel and Elizabeth (Morse), b. May 10, 1786; d. Dec. 7, 1859. She d. Dec. 14, 1859 (see).
2251. ix. MELISCENT, b. Sept. 6, 1789; m. June 3, 1830, John Plimpton, b. Sept. 9, 1789; d. June 24, 1864. She d. June 24, 1871. Had one ch.; res. Sturbridge.

On page 17, Historical Sketch of Sturbridge and Southbridge, Hon. George Davis says: "On the southern declivity of this elevation was situated the neat and comfortable Baptist Church. Here those families [of the Fisks], with others of that denomination in various parts of the town, worshiped more than half a century. The Rev. Zenas L. Leonard was the watchman on this watch tower. Mr. Leonard was 'in season and out of season' in his devotion to the spiritual interests of his charge."

The church building was raised June 3, 1784, on the land of Henry Fisk, and in it several ministers preached previous to August, 1795, in which month Rev. Z. L. Leonard first preached. During a period of thirty-six years he had immediate charge of the congregation. Rev. Addison Parker followed him, preaching in this building, and he then preached in a new building that was raised in Sturbridge Centre in 1832.

The late Henry Morse Fisk (deceased Apr. 13, 1896) said: "The old building was on the farm of Mr. John McKinstry, and when he sold his farm in the winter of 1832 or spring of 1833 to Leonard Upham, he bounded on the land of Daniel Fiske without naming the meeting-house lot, and Mr. Upham said he should hold the house and lot. The society did not want the house and Mr. McKinstry paid for the building and land to the church or society. Mr. Upham soon after took the building down, but what use was made of the material is not known."

1184. CAPT. SIMEON FISK (Henry, Nathan, Nathan, Nathan, Nathaniel, William, Robert, Simon, Simon, William, Symond), b. Sturbridge, Mass., Mar. 26, 1755; m. there Oct. 21, 1779, Mary Gould, b. Aug. 24, 1753; d. Sept. 10, 1813; m. 2d, Nov. 23, 1815, Lydia Bugbee of Woodstock, b. Feb. 20, 1760; d. Apr. 18, 1830, s. p. He was a thrifty farmer, and an amiable and upright man. As a neighbor, a townsman, a citizen, and a Christian, he was kind, liberal and exemplary. He resided northerly on the elevation of Fisk Hill. He possessed a strong intellect, and a memory, in which were treasured very many important facts and events of the stirring times in which he lived. The causes of the Revolution, and subsequent transactions, were fresh in his memory. He was a prominent and efficient man in civil and religious concerns. He left an extensive diary, which is a valuable reference work. His conversation was always edifying and calculated to make a salutary impression. Not only in his conversation but in the transactions of life was clearly manifested his implicit dependence on Divine guidance in regard to the path of duty. To this may be traced no doubt in no small degree, that cheerfulness and serenity which uniformly marked his deportment. Capt. Fisk's personal appearance was manly and commanding. He died at an advanced age. He was in active service during the Revolution about six months, and received a wound in a battle which affected him through life. He d. Feb. 28, 1840; res. Sturbridge, Mass.

2252. i.   ELIAS, b. Oct. 29, 1782; m. Melissa C. Wilder.
2253. ii. SUBMIT, b. Feb. 14, 1781; d. Feb. 14, 1781.
2254. iii. ANNA, b. Feb. 14, 1781; m. Moses Marsh; she d. Apr. 29, 1845; had ch.: 1, Simeon Fisk; 2, John Elliot; 3, Lewis Wheelock; 4, Mary Ann; 5, Louisa.

1186. LIEUT. DAVID FISKE (Henry, Nathan, Nathan, Nathan, Nathaniel, William, Robert, Simon, Simon, William, Symond), b. Fiske Hill, Sturbridge, Mass., Dec. 17, 1759; m. in Sturbridge Nov. 13, 1783, Eleanor Jones, b. Dec. 26, 1764; m. 2d, Mr. Elliott, of Thompson, Conn. She d. in Thompson July 14, 1846. He was a farmer; was born in Sturbridge, and always resided there; was a man of the strictest integrity; was prominent in the affairs of both church and town. He settled on the highest point of Fisk Hill. His numerous family were trained up in habits of industry, and were favored with common school instruction requisite for the transaction of business. Three of his sons received a collegiate education, and became professional men. He d. Aug. 19, 1817; res. Sturbridge, Mass.

2255. i. HENRY, b. Apr. 8, 1795; m. Susan H. Fales.

2256. ii. JOSIAH JONES, b. Nov. 28, 1785; m. Jerusha Norton.

2257. iii. BETSEY, b. July 26, 1784; d. Dec. 14, 1819; she slipped and fell, breaking her neck.

2258. iv. AMASA, b. June 6, 1783; d. July 8, 1788.

2259. v. AMASA, b. Apr. 27, 1789; d. at sea Oct. 18, 1811.

2260. vi. RILLA, b. Jan. 20, 1791; d. June 28, 1793.

2261. vii. CYNTHIA, b. Mar. 19, 1793; m. Nov. 6, 1813, Darius Dwight; d. in Jackson, Mich., Aug. 28, 1842. Her children are dead. Two of her grandchildren are Cynthia Sager of Ann Arbor, Mich., and Percy Dwight of Detroit, Mich., the Jefferson Flats, Jefferson Ave.; the latter son of David Dwight, deceased.

2262. viii. AMARYLLIS, b. Aug. 6, 1797; m. July 22, 1818, William Dwight of Sturbridge. She d. May 27, 1854. Her children: Amasa F. Dwight, of Chicago, Ill., deceased; his son, Walter T. Dwight, Chicago, Ill. Mrs. Lucia D. Dwight, of Springfield, Mass; her son, Theo. F. Dwight, 186 Buckingham St., Springfield, Mass. Miss Elizabeth C. Dwight, of Detroit, Mich. Mrs. Dr. Hendrickson, Oakland, Cal., and Alfred, 781 Jefferson Ave., Detroit, Mich.

2263. ix. LYMAN, b. Oct. 9, 1799; d. Aug. 17, 1832.

2264. x. DAVID W., b. Nov. 2, 1801; m. Eliza S. Coggeshall.

2265. xi. ELEANOR JONES, b. July 10, 1804; m. Apr. 18, 1831, Simeon Bailey, of New Bedford. He is deceased. Her address, 365 County St., New Bedford. Ch.: Josiah F. Bailey, Peoria, Ill., and Mrs. Ada B. Cornwell, 365 County St., New Bedford.

2266. xii. CALVIN PARK, b. July 27, 1806; m. Laura Wallace and Mrs. Mary A. Hetfield.

2267. xiii. LEWIS WHEELOCK, b. July 15, 1809; d. Mar. 29, 1809.

1190. DANIEL FISKE (Daniel, Nathan, Nathan, Nathan, Nathaniel, William, Robert, Simon, Simon, William, Symond), b. Sturbridge May 12, 1748; m. Woodstock, Conn., Dec. 26, 1781, Elizabeth Morse (cousin of S. F. B. Morse, the inventor of the telegraph), b. Apr. 29, 1757; d. Cazenovia, N. Y., ae. 87, July 1, 1839. He was a soldier in the Revolutionary war, serving in a Sturbridge company; was a farmer; resided many years on Fisk Hill. He was an honest and exemplary man, more retiring in his habits than some of his relatives. He removed in advanced life into the State of New York. He had a numerous and respectable family. He d. Dec. 23, 1836; res. Sturbridge, Mass., and Cazenovia, N. Y.

2268. i. DANIEL, b. May 10, 1786; m. Amy Fiske, his cousin, dau. of Henry.

2269. ii. SILAS, b. Mar. 1, 1788; m. Susanna Wight.

2270. iii. DELIVERENCE, b. June 1, 1784; m. June 8, 1806, Penuel Belknap. He was b. June 1, 1774; d. Mar. 5, 1847; was a farmer. She d. Dec. 31, 1877. Ch.: 1, Daniel Fiske, b. Apr. 13, 1807; d. Sept. 3, 1850. 2, James Madison, b. Apr. 19, 1809; d. Dec. 23, 1891. 3, Sarah, b. Feb. 7, 1811; m. Henry Fiske. 4, Lydia, b. Nov. 12, 1815. 5, Lois, b. June 2 1819; d. Oct. 26, 1838. 6, Bulah Marsh, b. Jan. 10, 1821; n. May 30, 1851, Rev. Salem Marsh Plimpton, b. Apr. 27, 1820; d. Sept. 14, 1866. He fitted for college at Monson Academy and was graduated at Amherst in 1846 and at Andover in 1849. His first service in the ministry was at Fayetteville, Vt., where he was acting pastor during the year 1850. He was ordained at Wells River, Vt., in 1851, and labored in that field for ten years with marked fidelity and success when he was dismissed at his own request. Soon after he received the appointment of chaplain of the 4th Vermont Regiment Volunteers, in which capacity he served from

1861 to 1802, when failing health compelled him to resign. He then supplied the pulpit in St. Johnsbury during the absence of the pastor. Afterward he supplied a church in East Douglass for a considerable time. In the fall of 1865 he became acting pastor in Chelsea, Vt., where he endeared himself to all classes. The widow m. 2d, Oct. 11, 1881, Dea. Samuel M. Lane, of Southbridge, a banker, b. Nov. 19, 1800; d. s. p. Nov. 6, 1886. She res. Globe Village, Mass. Ch.: Herbert F. Plimpton, b. Apr. 9, 1853; unm.; Globe Village, Mass. Mary C. Plimpton, b. Apr. 17, 1856; unm.; Jackson Sanitarium, Dansville, Livingston County, N. Y. Arthur S. Plimpton, b. Dec. 13, 1857, Hollis, Long Island, N. Y. 7, Penuel, b. Oct. 23, 1824; d. Dec., 1853. 8, Lyndon Freeman, b. Mar. 19, 1828; d. Dec. 9, 1834. 9, Albert Morse, b. Aug. 31, 1813; d. Mar. 10, 1892.

2271. iv-v. LYDIA, b. Nov. 7, 1789; m. Nov. 18, 1824, Abram Hart, b. Mar. 30, 1784. She d. Dec. 16, 1836; res. Cazenovia, N. Y. Ch.: 1, Adeline Morse, b. Sept. 23, 1826. 2, Frances Granger, b. Oct. 13, 1830.

2272. vi. JOSHUA M., b. Sept. 25, 1795; m. Maria Benedict.
2273. vii. LOIS, b. Oct. 7, 1797; m. Feb. 23, 1830, Elias Mason. He was b. Nov. 21, 1784; d. Nov. 21, 1859. She d. Dec. 13, 1865. Res. Cazenovia, N. Y. Ch.: 1, Frances Amelia, b. July 2, 1834. 2, Elias Fiske, b. Dec. 16, 1835. 3, Jeremiah, b. Mar. 13, 1838; m. and res. Fort Atkinson, Wis.

2274. viii. LUCY, b. Aug. 4, 1799; m. Sept. 7, 1824, Joseph Beach. He was b. Jan. 26, 1795; d. Oct. 1, 1873. She d. Aug. 21, 1879. Ch.: 1, Elizabeth, b. Oct. 4, 1826; m. Jan. 26, 1848, —— Hutchins; she d. June, 1892. 2, Albert Fiske, b. Mar. 28, 1830; m. Sept. 1869; d. Oct. 3, 1880. 3, George Emerson, b. May 14, 1832; m. Jan., 1854; d. Dallas, Texas, Oct. 25, 1893. 4, Frances Henrietta, b. Mar. 17, 1834. 5, Joseph Stiles, b. Sept. 31, 1836. m. and res. Rochester, N. Y. 6, Julia Mariah, b. Dec. 22, 1838; m. Jeremiah Mason, res. Antigo, Wis. 7, Charlotte, b. Feb. 13, 1843; m. —— Callen; res. Charlton, N. Y.

2275. ix. JOHN, b. June 17, 1791; m. Mary P. Peck.
2276. x. MOSES, b. Oct. 19, 1782; m. Esther Cheever.

1195. NATHAN FISKE (Daniel, Nathan, Nathan, Nathan, Nathaniel, William, Robert, Simon, Simon, William, Symond), b. Apr. 4, 1762; m. Feb. 2, 1792, Abigail Lyon, dau. of Abner. He was in the war of the Revolution and during the latter part of his life was granted a pension. He d. Nov. 2, 1829. Res. Sturbridge, Mass.

2277. i. BATHSHEBA, b. Nov. 20, 1792; m. —— Fay.
2278. ii. JULIA, b. May 8, 1794; m. Dec. 19, 1819, Samuel L. Newell (her cousin). He d. Jan. 30, 1823, from injuries sustained in an accident. She m. 2d, Dea. George Sumner of Southbridge.
2279. iii. NATHAN, b. Feb. 25, 1796; d. Oct., 1815.
2280. iv. LEVIUS M., b. Feb. 2, 1799.
2281. v. ABIGAIL, b. 1801; d. unm. 1847.
2282. vi. CALISTA, b. 1895; d. 1810.

1202. MAJOR SAMUEL FISKE (Daniel, Nathan, Nathan, Nathan, Nathaniel, William, Robert, Simon, Simon, William, Symond), b. Sturbridge, Dec. 30, 1773; m. June 18, 1801, Sally Lyon, dau. of Abner. He resided in Sturbridge near the north end of the large brick factory now in Globe Village. He d. Dec. 27, 1833. Res. Strubridge, Mass.

2283. i. MARY ANN, b. Dec. 23, 1802; m. —— Pierce.
2284. ii. A CHILD, b. and d. Apr. 19, 1804.
2285. iii. VERNEY, b. Oct. 12, 1805; m. Manillee McKinstry.
2286. iv. ALBERT, b. Aug. 30, 1807; d. ——.
2287. v. SALINE, b. Sept. 16, 1808; m. Simeon Folsom; res. Detroit, Mich.
2288. vi. ELIZA, b. June 4, 1811; d. s. p.

2289. vii. A CHILD, b. and d. June 28, 1813.
2290. viii. SAMUEL LYON, b. 1814; m. Maria Louise Hodges.

1211. WILLIAM FISK (William, William, Nathan, Nathan, Nathaniel, William, Robert, Simon. Simon, William, Symond), b. Willington, Conn., Apr. 26, 1732; m. ———. She died and he married a second wife. He was in the Revolutionary war with his two brothers; res. Stanwich, Fairfield Co., Conn., and Genoa, N. Y.

2291. i. WILLIAM, b. Sept. 5, 1779; m. Christena Piper.
2292. ii. DAVID, b. ———. He was a chairmaker and res. in Michigan; died and left two daus.
2293. iii. SYLVANUS, b. Feb. 17, 1775. He was a farmer, res. Buffalo, N. Y., and d. there June 18, 1864.
2294. iv. HENRY, b. Apr. 2, 1782. He was a house builder; res. Greenwich, O.; m. and d. there Apr. 2, 1844, leaving four daus. A grandson is Henry F. Kellogg, Esq., of Hillsdale, Mich., a lawyer.
2295. v. NATHANIEL, b. ———. He m., res. in New York State and d. there leaving a son John.
2296. vi. ABBY, b. ———; m., in 1799, Silas Howe; res. Patriot, Ind., and she d. there in 1836, leaving four sons: Sylvanus, David, William and Jonathan
2297. vii. JERUSHA, b. ———; m. Ezra Webb; res. and d. in Cincinnati, O., leaving two sons, Ezra and Nathaniel, the latter res. Louisville, Ky.
2297¼.viii. JONATHAN, b. ———; was a farmer; res. in Cincinnati, O.; d. in 1792, the year he settled there.
2297⅜.ix. LEMUEL, b. ———; m. Julia Applegate.
2297½.x. JOSEPH, b. Conn. He always res. there at Stanwich, unm.
2297¾.xi. SALLY, b. Conn.; res. unm. Stanwich, Conn.

1222. LIEUT. RUFUS FISKE (Stephen; William, Nathan, Nathan, Nathaniel, William, Robert, Simon, Simon, William, Symond), b. Willington, Conn., Mar. 28, 1752; m. there Dorcas Gleason. He was born in Willington Conn., where he resided nearly all his life, and where he was a leading and prominent citizen. He served in the Revolutionary war as Corporal and later was a representative in the General Court for some years. He was called Lieut. Fiske. He was a Revolutionary pensioner, was at the campaign of Long Island and White Plains with Col. Parsons' regiment, and with Col. Latimer's regiment at the two battles of Stillwater and capture of Burgoyne, and nine years a member of the Conn. Legislature. He d. Dec. 2, 1813; res Willington a d Stafford Conn.

2298. i. STEPHEN, b. Jan. 8, 1786; m. Lucy Chandler.
2299. ii. RUFUS, b. Feb. 10, 1774; m. Irene Scripture.
2300. iii. DORCAS, b. ———.
2301. iv. HANNAH, b. ———.
2302. v. ELI, b. May 27, 1795; removed to N. Y. State.
2303. vi. POLLY, b. ———.

1223. ESQUIRE STEPHEN FISK (Stephen, William, Nathan, Nathan, Nathaniel, William, Robert, Simon, Simon, William, Symond), b. Greenwich, Mass., Apr. 7, 1759; m. in Claremont, N. H., May 1, 1788. Esther Clark, b. Lebanon, Conn., May 1, 1770; d. in Bethel, Nov. 13, 1847. He was born in Hampshire Co., Mass., and while yet in his teens enlisted in the Revolutionary army. His father died when he was but five years of age and ever after took care of himself. While in the army he rose to the rank of Ensign in a Massachusetts company. Shortly after the close of the war with his brother he migrated to Vermont and settled at Randolph, on land he made a farm of, about a mile up the "Branch" (of White river, as the little stream was called, above where is now the village of East Randolph. I have been told he cut the first tree cut down in clearing up the town of Randolph. Here several of his older children were born. After a few years he moved down into the village of East Randolph and kept "tavern" (hotel was a name not in use in those days) there. Was appointed and reappointed for many years "Justice of the Peace;" was always after that universally called "Esquire" Fisk by everybody who knew him, till his death. After some years he moved again ten miles up the "Branch" to East Brookfield, where his younger children were born. In 1820 he moved to Bethel, Vt., where he died. He enlisted at Greenwich in the Revolutionary army in which he served three years and six months. He served in the Indian campaign, participated in the battle of Stillwater and was in Monmouth when the British surrendered. He d. in Bethel, Vt., Dec. 13, 1848; res. Randolph, Vt.

2304. i. LEONARD, b. Sept. 10, 1799; m. Julia Colt.
2305. ii. FANNY, b. Mar. 17, 1790; m. Martin Tullar of Royalton. He res. in 1820 to Bethel. Ch.: 1, Daniel, d. in Texas; 2, Alden, m. Eliza Packard; 3, Eliza, m. Sanford Pinney; 4, Jane; 5, Isabelle, m. Hon. A. H. Cragin, for 18 years he was United States Senator from N. H. He now res. in Washington, D. C.; 6, One other child.
2306. iii. THOMAS JEFFERSON, b. Apr. 19, 1803; m. Caroline Clapp.
2307. iv. HARRISON, b. Mar. 1, 1812; m. Lucinda Bean.
2308. v. DAU, b. ———; m. Orville Bowen; a son is Albert Bowen, of Bethel, Vt.
2309. vi. SARAH ANN, b. Aug. 25, 1810. res. Highgate, Vt.
2310. xii. ESTHER CAROLINE, b. Feb. 25, 1805; m. Loren Carpenter.
2311. vii. CYNTHIA, b. Sept. 10, 1791.
2312. viii. MELINDA, b. July 13, 1793.
2313. ix. JAMES, b. Apr. 30, 1795; m. Eliza Colt.
2314. x. STEPHEN C., b. July 10, 1796; m. Angelina Gardner.
2315. xi. NANCY, b. June 22, 1801.

1224. HON. JAMES FISK (Stephen, William, Nathan, Nathan, Nathaniel, William, Robert, Simon, Simon, William, Symond), b. Oct. 4, 1763, Greenwich, Mass.; m. there Apr. 27, 1786, Priscilla West, b. Tolland, Conn., Nov. 20, 1763; d. Swanton, Vt., Aug. 19, 1840. She was dau. of Caleb West who res. in Greenwich, Mass. He was born at Greenwich, Mass., Oct. 4, 1763. His father died before the subject of this sketch was old enough to realize the loss. A short time before he was sixteen he joined the Continental army under Gen. Washington as a private soldier, and during the remainder of the war cheerfully bore his share of the sufferings and hardships of those who fought for freedom.

At his discharge from the army he returned to his native town, and, after attending a district school the first winter, was employed in teaching school during several subsequent winters and labored by the month the rest of the time until he was married, when he moved onto a piece of forest land which he cleared and reduced to a state of cultivation by his own labor. He was elected a member of the Assembly of Massachusetts, from Greenwich, when in his 22d year, and continued a member of that body for six or seven years, serving during 1791-92-93-95 and 1896. Soon afterward he began to preach the doctrines of Universalism. When 35 years of age, in 1797, he removed to Barre in Vermont, and continued in the clerical profession for some time. Later he was elected to the General Assembly in the fall of 1801 which sat at Newbury.

Soon after taking his seat in that body, by his talent, energy and integrity, he gained the confidence of his political party and the respect and esteem of his political opponents.

He continued to be annually elected to the Assembly until he was chosen a Representative to Congress in 1805, and continued a member of that body until Mar. 4, 1815. During his career in Congress he was ever found the firm supporter of his country's honor. He was in favor of a resort to arms rather than resort to the haughty dictation of the self styled "Mistress of the Seas." He voted for the declaration of war in 1812 and supported that measure in the hall of Congress, and among his fellow citizens at home. Many now living well remember with what interest, in 1812 and 1813 in assemblies of the people, they listened to his voice, the voice of a Revolutionary soldier, as he vindicated the measures of the general government, described the insults and indignities which had been heaped upon our government and people by a foreign power, and called upon them to vindicate their rights and fame. He enjoyed the confidence and esteem of Jefferson, Madison and Monroe and their prominent supporters. In June, 1812, he was offered by President Madison the position of Postmaster General, but declined.

In July, 1812, he was appointed Judge of the territory of Indiana by James Madison with the advice and consent of the Senate, but declined the office. The strenuous opposition of his friends to his leaving the State induced him not to accept the appointment. He was possessed of a good mind, sound judgment, and was an excellent reasoner. He was of great integrity, and one of the few who held and was offered positions of trust without seeking them; he was a man of unusual ability. He was both a personal and political friend of President Monroe, and at Montpelier on the morning of July 24, 1817, at eleven o'clock, he had the pleasure of delivering the address of welcome in behalf of the citizens of Montpelier and vicinity to the President on reaching Montpelier on his tour through the New England States. In 1802 he was Assistant Judge and in 1809 Chief Judge, of Orange County, Vermont, and in 1815 and 1816 he was appointed one of the Judges of the Supreme Court of Vermont. In 1817 he was elected a Senator in Congress, which office he held but one year and resigned. He was afterward Collector of Customs for this district for eight years. He was marked for his decision of character, his strict integrity, his powers of persuasion and his kind, affable deportment. He was a selfmade, a selftaught man. He has filled many offices with honor to himself and to his constituents. His last days were tranquil and serene. In describing the speakers at the great war meeting in 1812, Mr. Thompson in his history of Vermont says: "On one side sat the small-sized, keen-eyed, ready-witted and really talented James Fisk of Barre, who was then a member of Congress and who had now come on to act as the champion of the Democrats at this meeting." In 1809 the degree of A. M. was conferred upon him by Middlebury College. He enlisted for service in the Revolutionary war in Nov., 1781, in Capt. Wm. Willis' Company in Col. John Brooks' Regiment of the Mass. line. He resided in Hardwick and Greenwich, Mass. He applied for a pension July 23, 1832, from Swanton, Vt., where he was then residing. He was then 68 years of age. His pension was granted and he drew $70.66 per annum (see Coolidge and Mansfield's History of New England, p. 916). He d. Nov. 17, 1844; res. Swanton, Vt.

2316. i.   STEPHEN, b. Sept. 20, 1787; d. Mar. 9, 1795.

2317. ii.   JAMES, b. Feb. 9, 1790. He d. at Swanton, Vt., s. p., Sept. 30, 1827.

2318. iii. SUSANNA, b. July 25, 1791; m. 1810, Capt. Thomas M. Tyrrell. He was b. Feb. 4, 1786. She d. in Texarkana, Ark., Oct., 1878. Ch.: Priscilla, b. ——; m. —— Church. A son is A. E. Church; res. in Atlanta, Ill. Mary, b. Dec. 15, 1812; m. Oct. 24, 1830, Heman K. Hopkins, b. Dec. 31, 1803; d. Apr. 9, 1861. Both d. at Glens Falls, N. Y. Susanna was born in Greenwich, Mass. After her marriage she resided in New York for some forty years. Her husband died there and she returned to Vermont. In 1855 with her daughter, Mrs. Ira A. Church, she moved to Atlanta, Ill., where she resided for twenty-two years, then moving to Texarkana, where she died.

2319. iv.   ROSWELL, b. Jan. 19, 1793. He d. at Swanton, Vt., June 22, 1837.

2320. iv½. PRISCILLA, b. Jan. 29, 1795; d. Apr. 4, 1795.

2321. v.   PARIZADE, b. Mar. 27, 1796; m. Mar. 24, 1820, Peter P. Payne. She d. in Brooklyn, Ia., Jan. 17, 1884. He was b. in Lebanon, N. H., Nov. 4, 1795; d. Chelsea, Ia., Nov. 19, 1875. Ch.; 1, Paraizade, b. Dec. 28, 1820, in Highgate, Vt.; m. Samuel L. Squires; res. Brooklyn, Ia.; he d. in 1892. 2, Cornelia, b. Dec. 10, 1823; m. Thomas Seller; res. Aurora, Ill.; six ch. 3, Maria L., b. Sept. 15, 1825; m. —— Walton; res. California. 4, Cecellia Ann, b. Nov. 15, 1830; m. Apr. 22, 1845, Dudley Redfield, at Aurora, Ill.; res. Rockford, Ill.; he d. Mar. 4, 1884. They had four ch.; a dau. is Nellie E., m. July 28, 1868, Cyrus W. Wheeler; res. Rockford. 5, Versa, b. Aug. 31, 1835; m. Walter Gardner; res. Aurora, Ill.; she d. 1860.

2322. vi.   VERSA, b. Dec. 6, 1798; m. Mar. 9, 1823, Dr. Franklin Bradley; she d. Swanton Mar. 27, 1835; res. Swanton, Vt., and Patriot, Ind. He was b. in Vermont, and d. in Indiana Dec. 18, 1882, ae. 83 years and 2 months. Ch. by first wife: Stephen R., d. June 22, 1885, ae. 60 years and 6 months. Dr. Bradley m. a second time in Vermont and had nine ch. His second wife d. Sept., 1892.

2323. vii. ALICE, b. June 15, 1802; m. Oregon, Ill., 1829, Matthias R. Conroy. He was b. 1799; d. Nov. 19, 1831. She m. 2d, July, 1834, Horace Leffingwell, of Alburgh, Vt.; he was b. Jan. 26, 1802; d. Oregon, Ill., Oct. 27, 1847. She d. there Jan. 6, 1877. Only one child by first marriage, Alice Ross, b. June 4, 1831; m. July 1, 1845, Dr. E. S. Potter, b. June 4, 1831; res. 1026 Washington St., Waterloo, Ia. Ch. by 2d marriage: Albert Rosil, b. Oct. 27, 1835; d. June 19, 1840. Ellen Priscilla, b. Mar. 2, 1837; m. Dec. 7, 1850, N. B Choate; res. Waterloo, Black Hawk County, Ia. Julia Allen, b. Feb. 28, 1841; m. Jan. 1, 1862, Theodore McKenny; res. Chicago, Ill. Smith Potter, b. Oregon, Ill., May 28, 1846; d. there Jan. 28, 1848

2324. viii. ZAROASTER, b. Jan. 22, 1804; m. Sarah E. —— and Ann Miretta Vail.

2325. ix. PARMA, b. Oct. 11, 1805; m. Swanton Falls, Vt., Apr. 11, 1822, Judge Orlando Stevens, b. Rutland, Vt., Oct. 11, 1797; res. St. Albans, Vt., and d. there Mar. 25, 1879. She d. at Winona, Minn., Dec. 3, 1854. He studied law and was admitted to the bar at Franklin County Court (Vt.) in Nov., 1819. He commenced practice in Swanton, where he held the office of Deputy Collector of Customs. He then removed to East Highgate and engaged in the lumber business for a short time, but about the year 1829 resumed active practice at St. Albans, where he continued to reside until about 1850, when he removed to Winona. After having dwelt there a few years, he was stricken with paralysis, and then returned to St. Albans, where he lived until his death. He was State Attorney from 1839 to 1842, and again in 1845. He represented St. Albans in the House in 1845, and was Senator from Franklin County one term. He was also a member of the Minnesota Legislature while a resident of that State. As a lawyer and legislator he took high rank. His ability was comprehensive, ready and strong. He conducted cases with original tact and uncommon shrewdness. He was a prominent member of the Masonic fraternity. They had four children, all born in Vermont, two of them sons and two daughters; one son died when quite a young man, and the other, Orlando Stevens, Jr., died in Minnesota, where he was a lawyer of recognized ability. His daughters were both married. Ch.: 1, Zaroaster Fisk, b. Jan. 9, 1823; d. suddenly Feb. 24, 1854. 2, Orlando Fassett, b. Aug. 18, 1825; m. 1852; he was an attorney at law and was prosecuting attorney for two terms in Iowa; d. Winona, Minn., Aug. 21, 1856; left two sons, Orlando and David. 3, Parma Elmira, b. May, 1829; d. Jan. 1831. 4, Parma West, b. Jan. 18, 1833; m. Sept. 30, 1851, David Olmstead, of St. Albans; she d. Nov. 19, 1879; he d. Mar. 25, 1870; ch : David; Alice, res. 2920 Stevens Ave., Minneapolis, Minn. Hon. David Olmstead was the first Mayor of St Paul, Minn., and one of the most influential men among the early pioneers of the west. His portrait hangs in the City Hall, St. Paul. He assisted largely in framing the constitutions of the States of Iowa and Minnesota. He was an excellent looking man and a fine specimen of the gentleman of the old school. 5, Polly Craits, b. Aug. 19, 1838; m. Martin J. King June 12, 1850; res. McKeesport, Pa.; has several ch.: Parma d. at Clayton City, Ia., and was buried at Garnovillo, Ia., Dec. 4, 1854. Her husband d. in St. Albans, Vt., Mar 25, 1870

1225 JOSIAH FISK (Nathan, William, Nathan, Nathan, Nathaniel, William, Robert, Simon, Simon, William, Symond), b. in Willington, Conn., Feb. 8, 1745; m. in Worthington, Mass., Elizabeth Morse.; she d in Chesterfield, Mass., in her 54th year. Josiah Fisk was son of Nathan, who was born in Willington, Conn. He was married in that State and soon after moved to Greenwich, Mass., where his father and uncle Stephen had settled. While residing in Greenwich, with his father and brother Nathan he witnessed the will of his uncle Stephen. He was a farmer all his life. He d. in Chesterfield in 1826; res. Greenwich, Partridgefield and Chesterfield, Mass.

2326. i.   MOSES, b. Nov. 12, 1786; m. Emily Lucretia Todd, Martha Pratt and Olive Porter.
2327. ii. JOSIAH, b. ———; m. Penelope Pierce and Rebekah Cole.
2328. iii. REBECCA, b. ———; m. in Chesterfield, Mass., Mar. 3, 1803, Job Taylor; res. New York State, Genesee County.
2329. iv. NATHAN, b. Nov. 30, 1774; m. Rebecca Canfield.
2330. v.   SALLY, b. ———; m. Thomas Moore; he was a soldier in the Revolutionary army and d. s. p.
2331. vi. JOSIAH, b. ———; d. young.
2332. vii. ELIZABETH, b. ———; m. ——— Perrin; res. New York and Michigan.

1226. NATHAN FISK (Nathan, William, Nathan, Nathan, Nathaniel, William, Robert, Simon, Simon, William, Symond), b. in Willington, Conn., Apr. 17, 1744; m. ———, Ruth Burt. Nathan Fisk was a soldier in the Revolutionary army. He resided in Northfield, Mass., and in 1782 moved to Westminster, Vt., and later to Newfane. At one time he resided in Newfane, Vt., and was keeper of the county jail. He contracted consumption while serving in Revolution and for many years suffered with this disease. After his death his widow resided with his brother Experians. She died ae. 96. He d. s. p. in E. Brookfield, Vt., res.: Northfield, Mass. and Newfane, Vt.

1228. EXPERIANS FISK (Nathan, William, Nathan, Nathan, Nathaniel, William, Robert, Simon, Simon, William, Symond), b. Greenwich, Mass., Nov. 19, 1751; m. Oct. 12, 1785, at Westminster, Vt., Mary Earll. Was in the Revolutionary war (see pension roll). He d. June 2, 1825; res. Brookfield, Vt.

2333. i.   SOPHIA, b. in Westminster, July 5, 1786.
2334. ii. ROXANA, b. in Westminster, Dec. 12, 1787.
2335. iii. SYLVANUS, b. in Westminster, Jan. 9, 1790; d. May 2, 1792.
2336. iv. NATHAN, b. in Brookfield, Sept. 2, 1791. Nathan moved to Irasburg, Vt. He filled several prominent offices and was considered a very capable man. He finally died at Hartford, Vt., Mar. 3, 1857.
2337. v.   POLLY, b. in Brookfield, June 8, 1794.
2338. vi. EXPERIANS, b. in Brookfield, Aug. 25, 1796. Experians was a graduate of college and went to South Carolina as a teacher, and on his voyage home was shipwrecked off Roanoke Island, in 1825. I think the name of the vessel was "The Herald."
2339. vii. ARTEMAS, b. in Brookfield, June 9, 1798. Artemas Fisk lived in Brookfield, Vt. He had a family of eleven children; two died quite young, leaving five girls and four boys arriving at maturity. Of the sons, Elisha C. resided in Woodbury, Vt., on his farm. Artemas Jr. died in the State of Iowa in 1857. George M. commenced the study of medicine in 1857 with one James M. Woodworth, an eminent practitioner, in West Bethel, Vt.; he attended three full courses of medical lectures at the Dartmouth Medical College, Hanover, N. H., graduating in 1859. He then settled in the practice of medicine at Barton Landing, Vt., where he practiced nearly three years, and in 1863 moved to East Randolph, Vt., where he afterwards resided. He was married in Jan., 1862, to Georgianna Updike, of the State of New York, and as to the younger brother, he was (1865) some 17 years old, Earl F., he is stopping on the old farm.
2340. viii. ALMYRA, b. in Brookfield, Dec. 17, 1800.
2341. ix. EARL, b. in Brookfield, June 13, 1804; d. 1808.

1232. STEPHEN FISK (Nathan, William, Nathan, Nathan, Nathaniel, William, Robert, Simon, Simon, William, Symond), b. Willington, Conn., Jan. 26, 1747; m. there ——— ———. He was a farmer; res. Willington, Conn., Northfield, Mass., and Windsor, Vt.

2341¼. i.   STEPHEN, b. Jan. 8, 1786; m. ——— Chandler and Sarah Ingersoll.
2341½. ii.   DAU., b. ———; m. ——— Brooks.
2341¾. iii. DAU., b. ———, m. ——— Brooks; two brothers married two sisters.

1235. AARON FISKE (Asa, Nathaniel, Nathaniel, Nathan, Nathaniel, William, Robert, Simon, Simon, William, Symond), b. Holliston, Mass., Mar. 13, 1749; m. at Worcester, Mass., Feb. 18, 1773, Tabatha Metcalf. He d. in 1839; res. Templeton, Mass., Chesterfield and Franconia, N. H.

2342.   i.   ASA, b. Apr. 19, 1775; m. Betsey Henry.
2343.   ii.   AARON, b. June 23, 1777; m. Abigail Chandler.
2344.   iii. LAVINA, b. Oct. 27, 1773.
2345.   iv.   ANSON, b. ———.
2346.   v.   JOSEPH, b. Sept. 2, 1782; m. ——— ———.
2347.   vi.   ABEL, b. Feb. 17, 1785; m. Sally Phillips and Jerusha Johnson.
2348.   vii. ELIJAH, b. Apr. 29, 1789.
2349.   viii. EZRA, b. May 23, 1791; m. ——— ———.
2350.   ix.   LEVI, b. July 23, 1793; m. Marian Bacon.
2351.   x.   LOIS, b. Dec. 11, 1795; d. in Chesterfield, N. H., 1813.
2352.   xi.   BETSEY, b. Oct. 26, 1797; m. in 1824, James A. Sheridan, b. 1800; d. Jan. 12, 1870. He was a carpenter by trade and served in the late war. Ch.: Harriet Lobine Sheridan, b. 1831; m Apr. 24, 1861, Geo. L. Ismon, res. Sandwich, Ill.; ch.: Willie, b. b. 1864; d. Apr. 20, 1883. Aaron A. Sheridan, b. 1834; d. 1877; four children living; Charlie Sheridan, Yorkville, Kane Co.

1236. ASA FISKE (Asa, Nathaniel, Nathaniel, Nathan, Nathaniel, Jeffrey, Robert, Simon, Simon, William, Symond), b. Holliston, Mass., Sept. 3, 1746; m. Mercy Jones; d. ae. 75. He d. 1830; res. Holliston, Mass.

2353.   i.   LYDIA, b. 1769; m. Elias Knowlton. She d. in 1800, leaving: 1, Simeon, b. 1789; res. Warwick, Mass. 2, James, b. 1791; m. ——— Cheney. 3, Lyman, b. 1793; m. ——— Jackson; res. Warwick, Mass. 4, Linda, b. 1798; unm.
              After her death, her husband m. her sister, Hannah. Ch.: 5, Mercy, m. ——— Bideford; res. Charlestown, Mass. 6, Mary, m. ——— Bird; res., Lunenburg, Mass. 7, Sally, m. ——— Swift; res. Holliston, Mass. 8, Hannah, m. ——— Howard; res. Holl. 9, Lydia, d. young. 10, Asa; res. Chelsea. 11, Emerline; res. Holl.
2354.   ii.   HANNAH, b. 1771; m. Elias Knowlton.
2355.   iii. ELIJAH, b. 1773; m. Perley Forster and Experience Wheelock; res. Warwick, Mass., where he d. in 1843.
2356.   iv.   AARON, b. 1777; m. Lucy Woods.
2357.   v.   ASA, b. Feb. 18, 1779; m. Susanna Partridge and Ruth P Leland.
2358.   vi.   POLLY, b. ———; m. Abner Johnson; res. Holliston; farmer.

1241. HON. MOSES FISKE (Moses, Nathaniel, Nathaniel, Nathan, Nathaniel, William, Robert, Simon, Simon, William, Symond), b. Natick, Mass., in 1746; m in Natick, Rebecca Clark, b. Framingham, Mass.; d. in Natick in 1800; ae. 55; m. 2d, the Widow Sarah Stone, b. May, 1749; d. Oct. 17, 1841. He was a farmer and removed from Needham to Framingham and there sold his farm to his son Moses. He was born in Natick and always resided there. Before the stirring events of the Revolution a military company had been formed in Natick, and officers chosen for any emergency. A muster-roll of this company has fallen into my hands, and I give it to readers now for the first time. It was under the command of Captain James Mann, in Colonel Samuel Bullard's regiment, and marched on the alarm of the Battle of Bunker Hill. They were all residents of the town of Natick, and were allowed 1d. per mile traveled for their services, which amounted, for the whole company for two days' services, to £11 8s. 9d. The original roll is in the hands of Eben Mann, Myrtle, corner of Belknap St., Boston, who is great-grandson of Captain James Mann. Captain Mann's place was that now owned by Mr. Calvin Leland. Among the names enrolled is found that of Moses Fiske, private. He was Selectman, Member of the Legislature, and held other town offices. He d. Oct. 2, 1810; res. Framingham, Mass.

2359. i. SAMUEL, b. July 21, 1781; m. Nancy Stone.
2360. ii. MOSES, b. Jan. 4, 1776; m. Sybil Jennison.
2361. iii. SARAH, b. 1787; m. 1814, Rev. Martin Moore of Natick. She d. in Boston, Feb. 4, 1858; a son, Edward Payson Moore, res. New York City, and Sarah, res. Cambridgeport, Mass.
2362. iv. RUFUS, b. June 15, 1779; m. Feb. 13, 1811, Hitty Fiske. Res. Cambridge, Mass.
2363. v. WILLIAM, b. Nov. 6, 1783; m. Jane Farriss.

1242. CAPT. JOSHUA FISKE (Moses, Nathaniel, Nathaniel, Nathan, Nathaniel, William, Robert, Simon, Simon, William, Symond), b. Natick, Mass., ———; m. Mar. 24, 1774, Martha Smith, of Sherborne, Mass.; d. Apr. 17, 1796. He was born in Natick, where he always resided. When the Revolutionary war broke out he enlisted in the company commanded by Capt. Mann in Col. Bullard's regiment. About the time of the Revolution he was a Selectman and as such signed the following: "We, the subscribers, do truly and sincerely acknowledge, profess, testify, and declare, that the Commonwealth of Massachusetts, is and of right ought to be, a free, sovereign, and independent State; and we do swear that we will bear true faith and allegiance to the said Commonwealth, and that we will defend the same against traitorous conspiracies and all hostile attempts whatsoever. And that we do renounce, and abjure all allegiance, subjection, and obedience to the King, Queen, or Governor of Great Britain (as the case may be), and every other foreign power whatsoever. And that no foreign prince, person, prelate, state or potentate, hath or ought to have any jurisdiction, superiority, pre-eminence, authority, dispensing or other power, in any matter, civil, ecclesiastical, or spiritual, within this Commonwealth, except the authority or power which is or may be vested by their constituents in the Congress of the United States. And we do further testify and declare, that no man, or body of men, hath or can have any right to absolve or discharge us from the obligations of this oath, declaration, or affirmation. And that we do make this acknowledgment, profession, testimony, declaration, denial, renunciation and abjuration, heartily and truly, according to the common meaning and acceptation of the foregoing words, without any equivocation, mental evasion, or secret reservation whatsoever. So help us God." He held other town offices and at one time was a member of the Legislature. He died intestate and his estate was divided Apr. 28, 1797; Calvin F. received all the real estate and he paid the other ch., viz.: David, Joseph, John, Mehitable and Betsey. He d. Mar. 27, 1796; res. Natick, Mass.

2364. i. JOHN, b. Nov. 20, 1793; m. Joanna Damon, b. Jan., 1791; d. Jan., 1834. He d. in Newton, in Jan., 1867. A son is John, b. July, 1832. Res. Newton.
2365. ii. HANNAH, b. Nov. 16, 1791. In 1796, an accident of a most distressing character occurred at the house of Joshua Fisk, now that of the heirs of Moses Fisk. Hannah Fisk, 4 years old, was shot by her brother, a few years in advance of her in age. John (the name of the brother who committed the act) had been out with a still older brother in hunting excursions, and at this time leveled the gun, which happened to be loaded, at his infant sister, remarking that "he would kill a wild goose." The contents of the gun were lodged in the side of the girl, who fell instantly over the warping bars, in the northeast chamber of the house. The stains of the blood on the floor were not many years since plainly to be seen.
2366. iii. MEHITABLE, b. May 5, 1775.
2367. iv. ELIZABETH, b. Oct. 15, 1776.
2368. v. CALVIN, b. Feb. 25, 1779; m. Patty Pratt.
2369. vi. PATTY, b. Jan. 28, 1781.
2370. vii. HITTY, b. Jan. 4, 1783; d. young.

2371.   viii. DAVID, b. Mar. 8, 1785.
2372.   ix.   JOSEPH, b. Dec. 19, 1787; d. Apr. 14, 1816, in Bellingham, Mass.

1243. ENOCH FISKE (Moses, Nathaniel, Nathaniel, Nathan, Nathaniel, Jeffrey, Robert, Simon, Simon, William, Symond), b. Natick, Mass., Apr. 10, 1750; m. May 18, 1780, Sarah Bacon, b. 1758; d. Sept. 17, 1800. May 21, 1776, he signed the following paper with a number of others from Newton, Natick, and vicinity: "We whose names are underwritten do hereby severally Inlist ourselves into the service of the United American Colonies, and severally promise and engage to continue in such service until the first day of December, 1776, unless sooner discharged, and to furnish ourselves each with a good, effective fire arm, and if possible a Bayonet fitted thereto, a cartridge-box and blanket, or in lieu of a bayonet, a hatchet or tomahawk;—We also, in like manner, promise and engage to obey all the lawful commands of the officers appointed, or to be appointed over us, pursuant to the resolves of the General Court of the Colony of Massachusetts Bay; and under the direction of such officers, to march when ordered, with the utmost despatch to the Northern Department or Canada, and to be subject to all such rules and regulations, in every respect as are provided for the Continental Army." He d. Oct. 2, 1827; res. Needham and Natick, Mass.

2373.   i.   ENOCH, b. Jan. 28, 1781; m. Grace Seaverns.
2374.   ii.   SARAH, b. Nov. 11, 1782; m. Feb. 28, 1808, Jesse Kingsbury.
            She d. in 1848; res. Boston, Mass. Ch.: 1, Sarah M., b. 1812;
            m. Luther Crane; res. Somerville. 2, Jesse F., b. 1813; m.
            Mary O. Stevens; res. Sherburne. 3, Caroline H., b. 1817; m.
            E. H. Wakefield; res. Chelsea.   4, Charles A., b. 1819; m.
            Sarah Hoyt; res. Nottingham, N. H.
2375.   iii. MEHITABLE, b. July 5, 1784; m. July 8, 1804, Ebenezer Fuller.
            She d. in 1820; res. Needham. Ch.: 1, Mehitable, b. 1805; d.
            1805. 2, William, b. 1806; d. 1831. 3, Sarah F., b. 1809; d. 1810.
            4, Mehitable J., b. 1812; m. Daniel Morse, Jr.
2376.   iv.   MARY, b. Mar. 12, 1786; d. Oct. 28, 1818.
2377.   v.   ANNA, b. Dec. 5, 1787; m. Nov. 12, 1809, Alvin Fuller. She d.
            in 1819; res. Needham, Mass. Ch.: 1, Angelina, b. 1810; m.
            Isaac Flagg; res. N. 2, Rebecca B., b. 1811; m. Granville
            Fuller; res. Brighton. 3, Caroline F., b. 1812; m. Marshall
            Smith; res. Boston. 4, Alvin, b. 1814; m. Judith Wellington;
            Natick. 5, Nancy, b. 1816; m. Sabin Felch; res. Ann Arbor,
            Mich. 6, Persis W., b. 1817; d. 1835. 7, Mary F., b. 1819; m.
            Thos. E. Wakefield; res. Fairhaven, Vt.
2378.   vi.   CAROLINE, b. Dec. 12, 1789; d. Oct. 1, 1812.
2379.   vii. ISAIAH, b. Dec. 17, 1791; m. Elizabeth B. Fiske. They res. in
            Levant, Me. He d. s. p. in 1855.
2380.   viii. JEREMIAH, b. Mar. 29, 1794; d. at Nat., July 5, 1828.
2381.   ix.   HULDAH, b. June 25, 1796; d. at Nat., May 30, 1818.
2382.   x.   JOSHUA, b. Sept. 25, 1798; d. at Nat., Mar. 9, 1826.

1244. ELIJAH FISKE (Moses, Nathaniel, Nathaniel, Nathan, Nathaniel, William, Robert, Simon, Simon, William, Symond), b. Natick, Mass., Sept. 14, 1753; m. in Weston, Mass., Sept. 27, 1781, Elizabeth Binney, b. Lincoln, Mass., June 22, 1756; d. Jan. 2, 1798. He was born in Natick, Mass., where he was living when the Revolutionary war broke out. He went at once to Cambridge, enlisting Apr. 20, 1775, and served through the entire struggle. Soon after his marriage he moved to Hillsboro, N. H., where he afterwards resided and where he was an early settler. He d. Sept. 6, 1818; res. Hillsboro, N. H.

2383.   i.   JOHN, b. Aug. 19, 1789; m. Lucy Howe and Susan Craige
2384.   ii.   ELIJAH, b. ———; res. Me.
2385.   iii. MOSES, b. ———; m. and removed to Wis. Had a son Nathan.
2386.   iv.   NATHAN, b. ———; removed to Wis.
2387.   v.   ELIZABETH, b. ———; m. Isaiah Fiske of Natick, Mass.
2388.   vi.   MARY, b. ———; m. James Mann of Hillsboro, N. H.; 4 ch.
2389.   vii. CHARLES, b. ———; m. and res. St. Croix Falls, Wis.

1247. ENSIGN DAVID FISKE (John, John, Nathaniel, Nathan, Nathaniel, William, Robert, Simon, Simon, William, Symond), b. Holliston, Mass., Apr. 16,

1732; m. Sarah Bullard, of East Medway; dau. of John; d. in 1830. David Fiske, son of John and Abigail Leland Babcock, b. Apr. 16, 1732, was a noted descendant from many noted English families, viz.: Fiskes, Lelands and Babcocks; the latter name being among those old. noted and true Pilgrims who sailed from Holland in ship Anne, and came to this country to worship God according to the dictates of their own consciences. Mr. Fiske was a man of great energy of character; faithful to the trusts confided to him; an active business man; a large and successful farmer; owner of large tracts of land in this vicinity. He was a man of military attainments and ambitious to serve his country and State in the early wars with the Indians, and it is recorded in his private daily diary of his marching from his native town, May 22. 1758, through many of the western towns of the State to New York, there meeting other regiments and troops from other states. They captured many forts and dispersed enemies, and their raid was a success. Returning home he settled on his farm again, where he prospered in his chosen vocation, rearing and educating a large family; and it is said of him that when the sons became of age he gave each one of them a farm, except the youngest, Timothy (to him he gave a college education), who graduated at Harvard as M. D. In his diary are found receipts for goodly sums of money given to all his children at their majority. He d. Dec. 23, 1817; res. Holliston, Mass.

2390. i.   DAVID, b. Apr. 19, 1763; m. Hannah Eames.
2391. ii.   JOHN, b. Mar. 15, 1760; m. Abigail Albee.
2392. iii. NATHAN, b. May 3, 1761; m. Jemima Leland and Julia Daniels.
2393. iv. LEVI, b. Feb. 23, 1765; m. Jemima Underwood.
2394. v.   NATHANIEL, b. Mar. 9, 1767; m. ——— Allen.
2395. vi. AMOS, b. Nov. 23, 1769; d. Nov. 6, 1776.
2396. vii. SALLY, b. Dec. 17, 1771; m. Simeon Newton; res. Templeton, Mass.
2397. viii. GAD, b. Jan. 31, 1774; d. Oct. 26, 1776.
2398. ix. KEREN, b. July 24, 1776; d. Sept. 17, 1778.
2399. x.   TIMOTHY, A. M., M. D., b. Nov. 3, 1778; m. Rhoda Daniels of Medway.
2400. xi. ANER, b. Sept. 20, 1780; m. Martha Fairbanks.

1248. AMOS FISKE (John, John, Nathaniel, Nathan, Nathaniel, William, Robert, Simon, Simon, William, Symond), b. Sherburne, Mass., Mar. 5, 1735; m. there Jan. 2, 1765, Anne Bryant. Res. Sherburne, Mass.

2401. i.   DAVID, b. June 1, 1769.
2402. ii.   PEGGE, b. July, 16, 1771.
2403. iii. HANNAH, b. Nov. 4, 1773.
2404. iv. POLLY, b. Nov. 17, 1775.
2405. v.   JOHN HANCOCK, b. Oct. 23, 1777.

1249. JOHN FISKE (John, John, Nathaniel, Nathan, Nathaniel, William, Robert, Simon, Simon, William, Symond), b. Sherburne, Mass., Mar. 16, 1738; m. there Oct. 25, 1764, Sarah Hill, b. 1742; d. Sept. 27, 1813, in Sherburne; m. 2d, Abigail ———. He d. Nov. 20, 1817. Res. Sherborn. Mass.

2406. i.   ABIGAIL, b. June 29, 1766; m. Mar. 31, 1785, Capt. Samuel Learned of S.
2407. ii.   SARAH, b. July 8, 1772; m. Tapley Wyeth, A. M., M. D., of Sherborn.
2408. iii. EDE, b. Apr. 24. 1774; m. Apr. 30. 1794, Aaron Whitney by Daniel Whitney. Esq. Aaron Whitney, b. 1772; d. 1818. Res. Sherborn. and Providence, R. I. Ch.: 1, John F., b. in 1795; d. in 1814. 2, Mary, b. in 1801; m. Moses Stratton, of Natick, and d. 1822; ch.: Mary W., b. 1822. 3, Elizabeth, b. in 1803; d. in 1824. 4. Daniel, b. in 1805; m. Hannah Smith. 5. Aaron, b. in 1809; m. Marie E. Delavie. 6, Miriam L., b. in 1811. 7, Sarah H., b. in 1813. 8, John F., b. in 1816; d. in 1816.
2409. iv. ELIABETH, b. Feb. 3, 1776; m. Jan. 3, 1806, Lewis Bullard.
2410. v.   JOHN, b. Dec. 2, 1778.
2411. vi. LUKE, b. Feb. 26, 1781.
2412. vii. SALLEY, b. Jan. 19, 1783.

1251. JONAS FISKE (John, John, Nathaniel, Nathan, Nathaniel, William, Robert, Simon, Simon, William, Symond), b. Sherborn, Mass., Feb. 4, 1742; m. there, Feb. 6, 1766, Mary Hill. Res. Sherborn, Mass.

    2413. i.   JONAS, b. Feb. 4, 1779.
    2414. ii.   MARY, b. Nov. 11, 1781.

1255. ISAAC FISKE (Isaac, John, Nathaniel, Nathan, Nathaniel, William, Robert, Simon, Simon, William, Symond), b. in 1736; m. Esther Mann of Wrentham; she m. 2d, Ebenezer Marshall. He was a weaver by trade. The inventory of his estate was taken May 3, 1780. His wife Esther was admn. In 1780, Oct. 5, her name was Esther Hide He d. Sept. 19, 1778; res. Framingham and Wrentham, Mass.

    2415. i.   OLIVE, b. ———; d. ae. 20, unm.
    2416. ii.   JAMES, b. Sept. 19, 1773; d. in Savannah, Ga., about 1799, unm.
    2417. iii. POLLY, b. Aug. 6, 1777; d. young, living in 1789.
    2418. iv. ISAAC, b ———. In 1780, when he was about 14 years of age, he chose John Fisk of Sherborn, tanner, his guardian. He was also appointed guardian to James and Polly, under 14 years of age.

1257. HON. JOHN FISKE (Isaac, John, Nathaniel, Nathan, Nathaniel, William, Robert, Simon, Simon, William, Symond), b. Farmingham, 1741; m. Abigail Howe, b. 1752; d. Apr. 1829. He was b. in Framingham, where he always resided; lived near the Isaac Warren place on the Silk Farm, and built the house of Rufus Brewer Esq. For years he was Justice of the Peace, for six years was Representative in the Legislature and for twelve years Selectman He d. Dec. 17, 1819; res. Framingham, Mass.

    2419. i.   NAT, b. Aug. 12, 1772; m. Catherine Slack.
    2420. ii.   THOMAS, b. Mar. 22, 1774; m. Lucinda Trowbridge.
    2421. iii. SALLY, b. July 17, 1776; d. young.
    2422. iv. JOHN BOYLE, b. Dec. 2, 1778. He res. in New York City. He gr. at Dartmouth College in 1798, studied law, was admitted to the bar and practiced in N. Y. He d. there Dec. 11, 1805.
    2423. v.   SUSANNA, b. Feb. 26, 1781; m. Ebenezer M. Ballard. Ch.: 1, Susan, d. young. 2, Caroline, m. Obed Winter of Fram. 3, Marshall S., m. Priscilla Hubbard of Worcester and res. there. 4, George, m. Lucy Hunt of Sud.; res. Fram. 5, Charles, m. 1842 Maria Goddard of Worcester. 6, Mary Ann, m. Charles M. Briggs of Boston. The widow Susanna m. 2d, Phinehas Rice.
    2425. vi. SALLY, b. July 19, 1783; m. Sept. 16, 1806, William Larrabee, of Framingham. Ch.: 1, William F., a merchant in New York, unm. 2, Edward W., d. ae. 24. 3, Charles M., m. Eliza Colton, and d. 1842, leaving one child. 4, Abigail Howe, b. Sept. 7, 1814; m. June 23, 1833, Cornelius Cadle of N. Y. He was b. Mar. 11, 1809; d. Nov. 11, 1886. She d. Sept. 11, 1847; both buried in Muscatine, Ia. Ch.: a, Col. Cornelius Cadle, b. May 22, 1836, in New York City, m. Sept., 1867, Lucy Anna Barnes, Providence, R. I., b. Oct., 1841. They res. in Cincinnati, O. He is chm. of the Shiloh Commission and rec. sec. of the Society of the Army of the Tennessee. b, Edward Fiske Cadle, b. Aug. 5, 1838, in New York City; m. Dec. 31, 1863, Delia Emeline Elsemore of East Machias, Me., b. July 27, 1837; ch.: Lucy Abigail, b. Dec. 14, 1864, in Stockton, Cal; m. June 19, 1894, Arthur Henry Ashley. Frank Fiske, b. Feb. 17, 1868, in Stockton, Cal.; m. Oct. 8, 1890, Anna Fairbank. Cornelius William b. Feb. 1, 1890. All reside in Stockton. c, William Larrabee Cadle, b. Oct. 19, 1841, in New York City; m. Nov., 1880, Jessie Bowers, of Peru, Ill., b. 1859; ch.: Jessie Bowers, b. Nov. 28, 1881, in Chicago, Ill. William Larrabee, b. Apr. 3, 1884, in Chicago, Ill. Charles Edward, b. May 13, 1892, in Chicago, Ill. Reside at La Grange, Ill.; Chicago office, 524 Home Ins.

Bldg., Chicago, Ill. d, Charles Frances Cadle, b. Feb. 1, 1846, in Muscatine, Ia.; m. May 31, 1876, Harriet Maria Swan, b. July 31, 1846, in Lockport, N. Y.; 1 child Cornelius Cadle, b. Nov. 14, 1878, at Victor, Ia. Res. at Muscatine, Ia. 5, George, 6, John Fiske. He was the youngest son of William, and for years suffered with consumption. Born in Framingham, he was closely connected, says a San Francisco, Cal., paper (where he d.), with the well known and prominent Fisk family, that ancient English family so well known in the State and elsewhere. His father owned the house at Framingham Center, where now the Home for the Aged is located, and his grandmother, Abigail Howe Fisk, was one of the five original members of the First Baptist Church, Framingham. Deceased was born in 1820. After leaving Framingham he settled in Worcester, then at Woonsocket, R. I., finally going west as one of the first of the forty-niners in search of gold.

2426. vii. EDWARD, b. May 25, 1786; m. Eliza Porter of Boston; res. New York City. S. p.

2427. viii. NANCY, b. Jan. 26, 1789; m. Col. James Brown of Framingham. Ch.: 1, Maria m. Rev. James A. Kendall, gr. Harvard College in 1823. 2, Lucy Ann, m. Agustin Leland, gr. Brown University in 1834. He d. leaving one dau. The wid. m. 2d, Benjamin Brown. 3, Ellen, m. Anson L. Hobart, gr. Williams College, 1836. 4, James W., m. Mary J. Brewer, gr. Williams College, in 1840. He was a banker and supt. of schools in Framingham, and a prominent citizen. 5, Nancy, unm.

2428. ix. WILLIAM, b. 1791; d. Nov. 19, 1805.

2429. x. GEORGE B., b. Sept. 23, 1793; m. Mrs. Honora Bolton.

1258. CAPT. RICHARD FISKE (Isaac, John, Nathaniel, Nathan, Nathaniel, William, Robert, Simon, Simon, William, Symond), b. Fram., Feb. 25, 1750; m. Zebiah Pond of Franklin, b. 1749; d. Jan. 25, 1837. He was Captain of the militia company and served in the Revolutionary war; for five years was Selectman. He d. Mar. 9, 1824; res. Framingham, Mass.

2430. i. LUTHER, b. Nov. 12, 1772; m. Sally Wait and ——— Webster. He d. s. p., June 26, 1797. He was a trader. Inventory of his estate filed Oct. 10, 1797.

2431. ii. MARTIN, b. Apr. 8, 1774; m. ——— Gilbert.

2432. iii. PATTY, b. June 3, 1776; m. Dec. 26, 1803, Ebenezer Freeman, of Barre. She d. June 4, 1823. He m. Nabby Morse and res. in Fram. Ch.: 1, Charles, b. Nov. 24, 1804; m. May, 1832, Louisa Caroline Pharo; res. Camden, N. J. She d. Dec. 15, 1840; m. 2d, Ann E. Sloan. 2, Mary F., b. Mar. 24, 1807; m. Nov. 1834, Ira M. Collom of Phil. 3, Nancy F., b. June 14, 1809. 4, Martha, b. Jan. 8, 1815.

2433. iv. DANIEL, b. Mar. 20, 1778; d. Norfolk, Va., Mar. 23, 1800.

2434. v. NANCY, b. July 6, 1780; d. 1789.

2435. vi. RICHARD, b. Jan., 29, 1783; m. Mrs. Elizabeth (Lampry) Lowell,

2436. vii. MARY, b. Jan. 29, 1783; m. 1809, Samuel Valentine, Jr., of Hopkinton. Ch.: 1, John T. 2, Samuel W. 3, Dan., m. Philip W. Bixby. 4, Eliza, m. Benjamin Stow Farnsworth, of Detroit, Mich., and had: a, Harriett Eliza Prescott; b, Henrietta Lynde, unm., res. 567 East Congress St., Detroit, Mich.; and c, Mary Susan, m. Wm. Wirt Smith, of Chicago, Ill., a child is Edna Valentine Smith. Stephen Valentine, Jr., m. for his first wife, Frances Clark. Samuel, Jr., was son of Samuel and Elizabeth Jones, and grandson of Thomas Valentine and Elizabeth Gooch of Hopkinton.

2437. viii. JOSIAH, b. Feb. 22, 1785; m. Martha Coolidge.

2438. ix. DAVID, b. Feb. 16, 1791; d. Nov. 24, 1817. By his will he left to the Baptist Church at Framingham, $570, which he had saved of his earnings as a teacher in that town.

1259. DR. DANIEL FISKE (Isaac, John, Nathaniel, Nathan, Nathaniel, William, Robert, Simon, Simon, William, Symond), b. Framingham, Mass., in 1751; m. Nov. 10, 1772, Sukey Thurston, b. 1753; dau. of Rev. David Thurston, of Medway; d. Nov., 1798; m. 2d, 1800, Alice Davis, of Oxford, dau. of Elisha, b. 1761; d. July 28, 1844. David was born in Framingham, Mass. His father, Isaac, purchased land in Oxford, opposite Town's Pond, upon which he went to reside. There he was married to his wife, the daughter of the local clergyman. He had studied medicine elsewhere, and was well versed in physics in all its intricate branches. He soon became the leading physician of the town and was also well known in all the country round about. He had many students, for in those early days the prospective physician was obliged to study with a regular practitioner. Among his students who later became celebrated were Drs. Holbrook, of Thompson, Conn., and Dr. Bullard of Sutton. Besides being a successful practitioner he was very active and public spirited in town affairs. He was an active free mason and one of the leading men in the formation of the Oxford society, a stockholder in the Central Cotton Mfg. Co., an adherent of Shay's in the famous incipient rebellion. He went to Cambridge at the time of the siege of Boston, had, it is related, an interview with Gen. Washington, and was offered a surgeon's appointment, which he declined. He was Selectman in 1782-3-4. Erected the residence he resided in in 1791, which is still standing. At his death, by his request, no Masonic services were held at his grave. The funeral was very largely attended and was a remarkable occasion. He d. Aug. 6, 1815; res. Oxford, Mass.

2439. i. WILLIAM T., b. July 6, 1778; m. Alice Hudson and Betsey Hudson.

2440. ii. SOPHIA, b. Sept. 18, 1773; m. Apr. 8, 1792, John Russell, son of Ephraim. Ch.: 1, Sally, b. ———; m. Amos Woodbury of Charlton, where they res. and where she died. 2. Daniel F., b. Feb. 23, 1797; m. Nov. 10, 1817, Louisa Rider; ch.: 1, Salem T., b. Oct. 18, 1818; m. Oct. 10, 1840, Adaline Davis; was a banker in New York City; 2, Maria L., b. Oct. 12, 1822; in 1840 m. Abraham Firth, of Leicester; 3, William P., b. Aug. 24, 1825; unm.; 4, George E., b. Aug. 28, 1831; m. Mary A. Wallis and Hellen E. Ross. Daniel d. Feb. 11, 1883. She d. 1886.

2441. iii. SALLY, b. Sept. 2, 1776; m. Feb. 6, 1796, John Butler of Rutland, Vt. In 1804 he was in trade at Spencer, Mass. In 1806 he went to St. Louis, Mo. In a letter to a friend he says, after mentioning the States he had passed through, "I think of all the places in my travels, no one equals this. It is without exception the finest country I ever heard or saw for goodness, but the inhabitants are indolent, living from hand to mouth. Millions of acres of land in this, the Northwest Territory, are as level as a floor, without a tree upon it, but grass as high as your head on horseback, and very thick; 100 bushels of corn to the acre; wheat good, but no good mills at present; through idleness. Can keep 200 hogs, 100 cows, 50 horses here as easy as you can five hogs. I have been to the lead mines and find there is made in this territory 3,000 tons of lead per year." He remained west until the war of 1812 and enlisted. Was acting Adjutant at Newport, Ky. In Aug., 1814, was in command of a company at the attack on Fort Mackinaw, later returned to Oxford and resided near his father, where he died, Sept. 25, 1824. His wife d. May 23, 1823. Ch.: 1, Celia, b. Nov. 22, 1796; m. Lament Bacon, of Southbridge; removed to Chelsea, Vt., and both d. there. 2, Susanna F., b. Oct. 21, 1798; m. May 20, 1816, Capt. Wm. Sears, of Rochester, Mass.; res. there. 3, Mary, b. May 28, 1803; m. Capt. Blodget, of Southbridge; res. there; one son, Fred, who removed to New Orleans, La.

2442. iv. ABIJAH, b. May 8, 1780. He d. unm.; was a soldier in Capt. Jones' company of Miller's regiment in the war of 1812, and died of camp fever in Greenbush, N. Y., in 1813.

2443. v. SUKEY, b. June 28, 1782; m. Apr. 10, 1806, Alpheus Eddy, son of Jonas. She d. Mar. 2, 1829. Ch.: 1, Clementine, b. 1807; d.

1809. 2, Susan F., b. Oct. 23, 1809; unm. 3, Celia B., b. June 21, 1811; m. Amasa Alton, of Thompson, Conn.; rev. to Cape Jorado, Mo.; ch.: Laura Fiske and Wilbur Fiske. 4, Sophia, b. 1813; d. 1813. 5, John F., b. 1814; d. 1816. 6, James F., b. May 3, 1817; d. June 23, 1863; unm. 7, Daniel F., b. June 6, 1821; unm.; was a railroad contractor and quite wealthy, was drugged and robbed in Philadelphia, Pa., and died from effects of poison, July 23, 1858. 8, Sarah, m. Wm. J. Hancock; d. in Rome, N. Y.

2444. vi. MARY, b. Feb. 1, 1785; m. Nov. 12, 1809, Amos Hudson, son of William; b. June 22, 1781; was a scythe manufacturer; in 1811 he purchased of Jonathan Davis the scythe shop and six acres of land in Oxford, formerly owned by Thaddeus Hall and with his brother-in-law began the scythe business. The same time he began keeping store with Dr. Wm. T. Fiske. He resided near her father in Oxford, finally moving to Ellisburgh, N. Y.; there he built a scythe factory and continued the business until his death, Feb. 12, 1830. She d. Oct. 10, 1856, at her son's home, in Janesville, Wis. Ch.: 1, Lucian F., b. Dec. 14, 1810; m. Adeline Stearns. 2, Amos B., b. 1812; d. 1813. 3, Mary L., b. July 26, 1814; d. Feb. 14, 1845. 4, Sanford A., b. May 16, 1817; m. Sarah D. Canfield; res. Oxford, Mass.; Ellisburgh, N. Y.; Janesville, Wis.; and Fargo, N. Dak.; studied law and while res. in Janesville was city attorney, and mayor for two years; in 1881 was appointed by President Garfield, Justice of the Supreme Court of Dakota: 5 ch.: one, Rev. Theodore C.; res. Fairmount, Minn. 5, Abijah T., b. May 1, 1819; m. J. M. Luff; is a physician; res. Stockton, Cal.; was surgeon of the Twenty-sixth Iowa Regiment in late war; since res. in Cal. has been elected State Senator. 6, Abisha S., b. May 1, 1819; m. Rose Elliott; was Sergeant during the war of the Thirty-fourth Regiment Illinois Infantry; res. Stockton, Cal. 7, Celia M., b. Nov. 16, 1821; m. Rev. Oscar Park. She d. Waukesha, Wis., July 6, 1862, leaving: 1, Mary, b. May 21, 1849; res. Stockton, Cal.; 2, Goddard, b. Oct. 12, 1850; m. Blanche E. Newell; was a lawyer; d. Feb. 5, 1885; 3, Sarah C., b. Aug. 5, 1852; d. same day; 4, Hudson, b. Oct. 14, 1853; m. Charlotte B. Kentfield; res. Bakersfield, Cal.; 5, Anna L., b. Oct. 8, 1855; m. Hugh A. Blodget; 6, Frank C., b. Dec. 6, 1857; m. Belle McDonald; res. Bakersfield, Cal; 7, Henry C., b. Oct. 21, 1859; d. Apr. 22, 1860; 8, Martha L., b. Feb. 20, 1861; m. Wm. F. Dougherty; res. Glenwood, Minn.

1262. MOSES FISKE (Isaac, John, Nathaniel, Nathan, Nathaniel, William, Robert, Simon, Simon, William Symond), b. Fram., July 12, 1755; m. in Hopk., Apr. 13, 1780, Betsey Bullard (his cousin), b. 1759. She was living in Framingham in 1843. He d. Mar. 1, 1828; res. Hopkinton, Mass.

2445. i. MOSES MADISON, b. Nov. 25, 1780. He was graduated at Dartmouth College in 1802; m. Mary Temple, of Fram. They both d. at Knoxville, Tenn., in 1805, s. p.

2446. ii. ISAAC, b. May 26, 1782; m. Betsey Johnson.

2447. iii. HANNAH, b. Aug. 2, 1784; m. Joseph Ballard, Esq., of Brighton, bro. of Ebenezer M. Ch.: 1, Albert, m. Caroline Fiske, dau. of Josiah. 2, Olivia Ann. 3, Richard.

2448. iv. ASENETH, b. July 29, 1786; d. May 9, 1809.

2449. v. BETSEY, b. June 13, 1788; d. unm., in 1806.

2450. vi. OLIVIA, b. July 20, 1790; m. Elias Temple, Esq., of Fram. Their only child, Ellen, m. Charles E. Horne, of Fram.

2451. vii. EBENEZER, b. June 5, 1792; m. Emily Willard.

2452. viii. SOPHIA, b. ———; d. in infancy.

1264. PROF. MOSES FISKE (Peter, John, Nathaniel, Nathan, Nathaniel, William, Robert, Simon, Simon, William, Symond), b. Grafton, Mass., June 11,

18

1760; m. ——— ———. He was graduated at Dartmouth College in 1786; was licensed and preached for some time, but never ordained to a pastorate. He was tutor in Dartmouth College from 1788 to 1795, when he removed to Pelham, Tenn., and died there, aged 83. He remained single until he was 50 years of age, when he married and reared a family of nine children. He ever manifested a strong disapprobation of involuntary servitude; was never the owner of a slave, although surrounded by slaves all his life. He was the author of several published works on negro slavery. He d. 1842; res. Pelham, Tenn.; had 9 children

1268. REV. JOHN FISKE (Peter, John, Nathaniel, Nathan, Nathaniel, William, Robert, Simon, Simon, William, Symond), b. Warwick, Mass., Oct. 26, 1770; m. 1796, Elizabeth Mellen, of Milford, Mass. He was graduated at Dartmouth College, in 1791; studied theology with Rev. Dr. Lyman, at Hatfield, and was ordained to the ministry at Hadley in May, 1794. For some time he preached as an evangelist in Geneva, N. Y.; Milford, Conn., and North Brookfield, Mass. He declined these calls, but accepted one to New Braintree, Mass., where he was installed pastor in Aug., 1796. In 1809 he had a revival which was prolonged two years, and this was repeated in 1818-19-26-31-42, by which large numbers were gathered in the church. He preached his half-century discourse in the New Braintree church, Oct. 26, 1846, which was published. He was interested in education, was one of the efficient helpers in the building up of Amherst College, and received the degree of D. D. from that institution in 1844. He continued to preach and perform pastoral duties, with the assistance of a colleague, until Oct., 1854. He spent sixty-one years in the actual ministry, and above sixty-eight with the same people. In person he was tall, well-proportioned, of dignified manners, of serene and intelligent countenance. He possessed a clear, well balanced mind, and a general completeness of character seldom found. His pulpit efforts were marked by eminent good sense and great appropriateness, especially in prayer. A number of his discourses were published. He d. Mar., 1855; res. New Braintree, Mass.

    2453. i.   JOHN MELLEN, b. 1798. In 1852 he res. in West Brookfield, Mass., and d. in 1854.

    2454. ii.   MARY WARREN, b. 1800; m. 1826, William R. Dwight, of New York, and had six children, viz.: Elizabeth Russell; d. 1831; Julia Porter; Elizabeth Fiske; d. 1865; George Spring; Mary Edwards; Sarah Mellen.

    2455. iii. ELIZABETH RUSSELL, b. 1802; d. 1833.

    2456. iv. EDWARD WHIPPLE, b. 1805.

    2457. v.   WILLIAM, b. 1807; m. and res. in the South; was a clergyman there. William Fiske married in 1838, Pamell Coan, of Mobile (who died 1841), and had one child, Laura Hitchcock, who died 1841; married again in 1855, Nancy Parsons, of Amherst, and had two children: John Fiske died 1862, and Pamell Coan. William Fiske, the father, was ordained at Mr. Beecher's church. He returned south two years ago, and has been in the employ of the government as superintendent of schools in a district about New Orleans. He has always felt a deep interest in the blacks, and since he has been among them he has preached constantly, as well as taught them. But he felt that he could be of more use and have more influence, if he were an ordained minister, and as he was obliged to come North, on account of ill health, he improved the opportunity of having the rite performed.

    2458. vi. SARAH, b. 1809; m. John M Fisk.

    2459. vii. ABBY, b. 1812; m. 1831, George Spring, of Brooklyn, N. Y., who. d. in 1835: leaving two ch.: Helen and Henrietta: m. 2d, 1841, George Merriam, of Springfield, Mass. Ch.: Geo. S., James Fiske. Edward Fiske, Susan Raymond, Abby Little, and Celia Campbell.

    2460. viii. JAMES, b. 1814; m. Mary Godfrey.

1273. PARKER FISK (Asa, Bezaleel, Jonathan, David, David, David, Jaffrey, Robert, Simon, Simon, William, Symond), b. Rutland, Mass., in 1793; m. Feb. 29, 1820, Mary B. Priest, b. 1789; d. Apr. 27, 1863. He was a farmer. He d. Oct. 8, 1866; res. Dublin, N. H.

 2461. i. LEVI W., b. Apr. 29, 1825; m. Sarah J. White.
 2462. ii. EUNICE P., b. Feb. 18, 1822; m. Oct. 6, 1860, and d. May 27,
     18 ?.
 2463. iii. MARY EVELINE, b. Apr. 15, 1830; d. Oct. 13, 1874.

1275. DANIEL FISKE (Asa, Bezaleel, Jonathan, David, David, David, Jaffrey, Robert, Simon, Simon, William, Symond), b. Rutland, Mass., June 18, 1798; m. Dublin, N. H., Mar. 16, 1820, Esther Eaton, b. Aug. 6, 1798; d. Dec. 2, 1858. Daniel Fiske, son of Asa Fiske, went to Dublin, N. H., with his father in 1801, at the age of about four years, and lived there until his death. He always took a great interest in the welfare and prosperity of the town, and was a prominent member of the Unitarian Church and society, and labored faithfully for its success both financially and otherwise. He d. Aug. 9, 18,8.

 2464. i. LAURA A., b. Sept. 4, 1821; m. Apr. 26, 1847, Mark True; she d.
     May 8, 1852.
 2465. ii. DIANTHA L., b. Aug. 25, 1823; unm.
 2466. iii. WARREN·L., b. Mar. 12, 1826; m. Emily M. Mathews.
 2467. iv. SARAH M., b. Apr. 13, 1828; m. Charles C. Martin.
 2468. v. GEORGE D., b. Sept. 27, 1850; d. unm. Jan. 12, 1892.
 2469. vi. CHARLES W., b. June 14, 1833; m. Mary L. Frasier.

1279. DEA. ISAAC FISKE (Nahum, Bezaleel, Jonathan, David, David, David, Jaffrey, Robert, Simon, Simon, William, Symond), b. Holden, Mass., May 27, 1789; m. ——— Davis. Deacon Isaac Fiske was the son of Mr. Nahum Fisk, and was born at Holden; a blacksmith by trade; married to the daughter of Ethan Davis, Esq., and soon after her death he engaged as a lay missionary among the Choctaw Indians. He arrived at Elliot, Aug., 1819, and died in 1820. In his will he bequeathed about $800 to the American Board. He was chosen deacon Apr. 3, 1818. He d. 1820, s. p.; res. ———.

1280. BEZALEEL FISK (Nahum, Bezaleel, Jonathan, David, David, David, Jaffrey, Robert, Simon, Simon, William, Symond), b. Holden, Mass., July 9, 1791; m. May 25, 1819, Mary Rice, of Holden, dau. of Peter and Mary (Hart) Rice, b. Apr. 14, 1796; d. Dec. 6, 1872, in Worcester, Mass. His will was probated Jan. 28, 1850, and allowed. The inventory was filed in the Probate Court June 8 following. He d. Feb., 1850; res. Worcester, Mass.

 2470. i. EDWARD R., b. Aug. 31, 1822; m. Rebecca H. Sumner.
 2471. ii. ISAAC, b. Oct. 23, 1820; m. Clara M. Wood.
 2472. iii. CHARLES, b. July 5, 1825; he d. unm. Sept. 16, 1848.
 2473. iv. MARTHA LEE, b. Aug. 22, 1827; m. Thomas Baird, of Auburn;
     she d. s. p. Jan. 26, 1852.
 2474. v. MARY JANE, b. Mar. 19, 1831; m. Philetus Cook; she d. s. p.
     July 29, 1857.
 2475. vi. ELIZABETH WOODS, b. Feb. 6, 1834; d. unm. Apr. 23, 1854.
 2476. vii. WALTER LEE, b. July 19, 1836; d. Nov. 13, 1855.

1281. ABNER FISK (Nahum, Bezaleel, Jonathan, David, David, David, Jeffrey, Robert, Simon, Simon, William, Symond), b. Holden, Mass., Dec. 27, 1793; m. Mary Rice, of Holden, b. May 11, 1800; d. Feb. 25, 1875; she was dau. of Ezra and Rebecca (Gardner) Rice. His will was probated July 3, 1866. He d. in 1865; res. Hubbardston and Princeton, Mass.

 2477. i. MARY ELIZABETH, b. 1839; m. Isaac Newton Rice. He d. in
     1864 in the Civil war.
 2478. ii. ELLEN AUGUSTA, b. 1841; m. Ephraim Matthews, of Hubbardston, Mass.

1285. SEWALL FISK (Samuel, Samuel, Jonathan, David, David, David, Jeffery, Robert, Simon, Simon, Wil.iam, Symond), b. Barre, Mass., Dec. 17, 1,88; m. in Boston, in 1813, Sarah Norcross Smith, dau. of Benjamin, b. Apr. 16, 1750, and Sarah (Norcross), b. July 6, 1753; d. May 13, 1800, in Boston. Sarah, b. Sept. 23, 1,90, d. Jan., 1883. He was born in Barre, Mass., where he resided until 21 years of age when he went to Boston, where he lived about ten years (married there in 1813). Then moved to New York, lived there until his death on August 12, 1868. He was formerly in the produce commission business, but retired many years before his death. He was a very domestic man, devoted to his family—a most genial and kindly nature. Those who knew him speak of his kindly nature and say they don't believe he had an enemy in the world, and he had many, many friends. He was not active in politics, nor did he accumulate a large fortune, but that is not all of life. He was an active Mason, and had a Masonic funeral. One of the obituary notices published at the time of his death says that "he was held as authority on disputed matters relative to Masonic usage, and his opinion was held in high respect by the craft." He d. Aug. 12, 1868; res. New York City.

SEWALL FISK.

2479. i. HANNAH AUGUSTA, b. Mar. 12, 1821; m. Nov. 7, 1842, Davis Collamore, son of Col. John, of Scituate, Mass. He was b. Oct. 7, 1820; d. Nov. 13, 1882, at "Belhurst," Orange Mt., Orange, N. J. He was a merchant and dealer in china and glassware in New York City. Ch.: Lucinda Fuller, d. ———. 2, Davis, d. ———. 3, Emma Augusta, m. ——— Partridge. 4, Marion Davis, b. May 23, 1856; unm.; res. 2 W. 36th St., New York City. Col. John was a descendant of Peter Collamore, who received a grant of land (twenty-five acres) at Scituate, Plymouth Co., Mass., in 1640. His home, Brook Hall, was on the road to Scituate Harbor.

2480. ii. SARAH ELIZABETH, b. Jan. 11, 1814; m. May 17, 1845, Charles Gardner; res. New York City. They had a dau. Eleanor, m. Wm. P. Miller; ch.: Charles and Arthur; res. Nally, L. I.

2481. iii. SEWALL, b. Apr. 15, 1816; d. young.

2482. iv. SEWALL THOMAS, b. Jan. 5, 1818; unm. 1884.

2483. v. EMELINE AMANDA, b. Mar. 13, 1823; m., May 23, 1845, William Macdonough, Jr.; res. 59 Norman St., East Orange, N. J. They had three ch.: William, Henry, and Emeline, who m. ——— Conklin and res. 34 Jackson St., Plainfield, N. J., all of whom married.

2484. vi. HELEN MARIA, b. May 15, 1825; m. May 9, 1846, Wm. Desendorf, b. Nov. 25, 1827. She died June 8, 1863, and he married twice afterwards. Helen had Helen Maria, b. Nov. 12, 1846; m. Apr., 18 o. William, b. Dec. 17, 1848; m. 18,0; res. Waverly Place, New York City. Sewell Fiske, b. 1852; d. 1855. Pauline Augusta, b. Aug. 11, 1855; m. ——— Brown; res. Maplewood, N. J. Ida Fisk, b. July 26, 1857; m. Sept. 8, 1880, Harry Duhring Miller, b. Sept. 10, 1857; is a merchant; res. 134 Walnut St., East Orange, N. J.; ch.: Ida Pauline Miller, b. May 4, 1881; George Channing Miller, b. July 13, 1884; Roland Van Gieson Miller, b. June 26, 1893. Mary Louisa, b. May 24, 1859; m. Feb. 9, 1880, ——— Macdonough; res. 54 Carlton St., East Orange, N. J. Florence, b. July 4, 1861; m. Oct. 5, 1880, ——— Hewtell; res. Waverly Place, New York City.

1286. SAMUEL FISK (Samuel, Jonathan, David, David, David, Jeffery, Robert, Simon, Simon, William, Symond), b. Barre, Mass., in 1797; m. there Feb. 17, 1810, Maria Williams, b. in 1799; d. in Barre July 23, 1847; m. 2d, June 19, 1850, Lucy B. Allen, b. 1803; m. 3d, —— ——. He was a speculator. He d. Apr. 30, 1882; res. Hubbardston, Mass., and Northport, L. I.

    2485. i. DOLLY, b. Jan. 19, 1818; m. —— Beekman; a son is Edward L.; res. Hackensack, N. J.

    2486. ii. TRYPHENA, b. Jan. 2, 1820; m. —— Vandewater; a son is Joseph E., connected with Equitable Insurance Company in New York City.

    2487. iii. SARAH, b. Aug. 9, 1821; m. Sept. 2, 1846, Rev. Israel Bryant Smith; res. N. He was b. Sept. 12, 1822, in Woodbury, L. I., and d. July 6, 1878, in Green Lawn, L. I.; was a Presbyterian clergyman. Ch.: 1, Lyman Augustus, b. Mar. 12, 1849; d. ——. 2, Julia Josephine, b. Oct. 16, 1850; d. ——. 3, Edwin Wilberforce, b. Oct. 18, 1853, Northport, L. I.

    2488. iv. LYMAN, b. July 20, 1823. He was a physician in New York City; a son is Lyman who res. in Hackensack, N. J.

    2489. v. SUSAN, b. May 2, 1825; d. May 3, 1825.

    2490. vi. CHARLES, b. ——; d. in infancy.

    2491. vii. JOHN, b. ——; d. in infancy.

    2492. viii. SAMUEL NELSON, b. ——. He was a physician in Brooklyn, N. Y.; a son is Dr. Eugene, connected with the Equitable Life Insurance Company in St. Louis, Mo.

    2493. ix. MARY JANE, b. ——; m. Gen. Wm. Gurney; res. 209 W. 21st St., N. Y. City.

    2494. x. ANNIE MARIA, b. ——; m. Myron Fox; res. 93 High St., Brooklyn, N. Y.

    2495. xi. ALONZO W., b. Mar. 31, 1832; m. Martha E. Crispin.

1287. HARVEY FISK (Samuel, Samuel, Jonathan, David, David, David, Jeffrey, Robert, Simon, Simon, William, Symond), b. Barre, Mass., Dec. 18, 1792; m. Apr. 25, 1822, Lydia Hastings, b. 1794; d. Feb. 19, 1863. He d. Apr. 29, 1861; res. Barre, Mass.

    2496. i. HARRIOT ANGELINE, b. Sept. 3, 1825; d. Sept. 20, 1857.

    2497. ii. SARAH ADALINE, b. June 5, 1831. She d. unm. of consumption, as did her sisters.

    2498. iii. ALICE RICE, b. Aug. 15, 1836; d. Apr. 14, 1859.

1288. LEVI FISK (Samuel, Samuel, Jonathan, David, David, David, Jaffery, Robert, Simon, Simon, William, Symond), b. Barre, Mass., Sept. 4, 1806; m. in Boston Mar. 22, 1838, Susan Gilpatrick Felker, of Biddeford, Me., b. 1818; d. in Everett, Mass., June 2, 1890. She was b. in 1818. He lived at home until his father died, Jan. 26, 1832; then he left home at the age of 26 to go to Boston to seek his fortune. He learned the carpenter's trade and was a contractor and builder until he retired at the age of 72. He moved from Boston six years ago to Everett, where he at present resides; res. Everett, Mass.

    2499. i. LYDIA MARIA, b. Feb. 20, 1839; m. June 15, 1864, William Wallace; res. 98 Garden St., Pawtucket, R. I. They had six children, four deceased. Those living are: 1, Fred Lincoln, b. 1865; m. Mary McKenna, of Pawtucket, R. I., s. p. 2, Jennie F., b. 1874; res. P.; unm.

    2500. ii. SUSAN AUGUSTA, b. June 5, 1847; m. Feb. 4, 1869, George M. Wilson; res. 7 Pleasant St., Everett, Mass. Ch.: 1, Helen Hardy, b. Dec. 30, 1868; d. Mar. 5, 1881. 2, Edith Hallie, b. Jan. 21, 1882; d. Jan. 22, 1885. 3, Marion, b. Apr. 23, 1887.

    2501. iii. FRED'K LINCOLN, b. May 28, 1843; m. Sarah E. Balch.

1301. MAJOR ABRAHAM FISK (Robert, Robert, Robert, David, David, Jeffery, Robert, Simon, Simon, William, Symond), b. in Dutchess County, New York State, about 1780; m. —— ——; she d., and he m. 2d, in Orleans, Ind., in 1808, Artimitia ——. She m. 2d, in Bedford, Ind., Mr. McLane. She d. in 1850. Abraham Fisk served in the war of 1812 as a Major of infantry in a Kentucky or Illinois regiment. He had married prior to that time and had four children:

Robert Wilson, James, Eliza and Miranda. Upon his return from the army to his home (I think in northern Kentucky, opposite Golconda, Ill. Golconda is in Pope County, Ill., and Livingston County, Ky., is opposite, the Ohio river running between) he and his wife separated, he keeping the children. His wife married a man named McLane in Orleans, Orange County, Ind. Abram Fisk married a second wife and lived with her in Kentucky in Livingston County and died there. By the second wife he had two sons. McLane moved to Bedford, Ind., where he prospered and raised a large family of boys and girls. His eldest son, Hiram H. McLane, now lives in San Antonio, Tex. He d. in Kentucky in 1830; res. Dutchess County, New York, Indiana and Kentucky.

    2502.   i.   ROBERT WILSON, b. July 14, 1807; m. Mary O. Ransom and Rachel ———.
    2503.   ii.   JAMES, b. ———; d. ae. 21.
    2504.   iii.   ELIZA, b. ———; m. Geo. W. Heap; res. Olney, Ill. Ch.: John P., b. ———; res. Nashville, Tenn.; is an attorney. H. S., b. ———; res. 7124 Wentworth Ave., Chicago, Ill.
    2505.   iv.   MIRANDA, b. ———; m. ——— Courtney. Ch.: Robert, b. ———; res. St. Joe, Mo.
    2506.   v.   ST. JOHN, b. ———.

    1302. HENRY A. FISK (Robert, Robert, Robert, David, David, Jaffery, Robert, Simon, Simon, William, Symond), b. in New York State about 1778; m. Susanna Wiley; she d. in Montgomery County, Ky. He was a farmer and d. in Putnam County, Ind. He d. in 1844; res. Virginia.

    2507.   i.   JAMES, b. Jan. 5, 1807; m. Casander Frakes and Camilla C. Clover.
    2508.   ii.   WILEY B., b. Oct. 24, 1819; m. Julia N. Spratt and Malinda Lasswell.
    2509.   iii.   JOHN, b. ———.
    2510.   iv.   HENRY, b. ———.
    2511.   v.   ROBERT, b. ———.

    1304. ROBERT FISKE (David, Robert, Robert, David, David, Jeffrey, Robert, Simon, Simon, William, Symond), b. Lexington, Mass., in 1780; m. Sally Robbins, of West Camb., b. 1781; d. of consumption in Woburn, Dec. 14, 1848. He d. in Boston, in 1820; res. Woburn, Mass.

    2512.   i.   CAROLINE, b. Nov. 15, 1801; m. William Snow, of Lunenburg, Mass.; d. Nov., 1842. She d. Feb. 8, 1890. Ch.: a, Mary Caroline, b. Nov., 1824; m. Thomas S. Scales. M. D., Sept., 1858; d. Jan., 1859. b, Anne Maria, b. Apr., 1831; m. William M. Miller, Edinboro, Scotland, July, 1890. c, Sarah Fisk, b. Mar., 1839; m. Stephen, Thompson, Sept., 1867; ch.: i., Benjamin Franklin, b. Dec. 4, 1868; ii., William Snow, b. May 10, 1873; res. 12 Pine St., Winchester, Mass. d, William Francis, b. Mar., 1842; m. May Diggs, of England; ch.: i., Caroline Fisk, b. July, 1879; ii., Marion King, b. Apr., 1881; iii., Stephen Thompson, b. May, 1884.
    2512¼.   ii.   CATHERINE, b. Apr. 22, 1803; m. Whitney Vinal, b. Jan., 1799; d. Apr., 1855. She d. June 4, 1886. Ch.: 1, Sarah Elizabeth, b. May, 1825; d. Sept., 1891. 2, Ann Louisa, b. Aug., 1829; d. Nov., 1833. 3, Anne Louisa, b. June, 1837. 4, Charles Arthur, b. June, 1841; d. May, 1852. Sarah Elizabeth, m. George Ezra Willis, 1845; d. Oct., 1890. 5, Mary Ella, b. Sept., 1846; m. July, 1871, Oliver Alonzo Leaver. 6, Ada Hayward, b. June, 1850; d. 1873. 7, Charles Arthur, b. Feb., 1853; d. 1857.
    2512½.   iii.   PETER, b. Nov. 28, 1804; d. Oct. 10, 1805.
    2512¾.   iv.   PETER, b. Aug. 21, 1806; d. July 20, 1854.
    2513.   v.   JONAS CLARK, b. July 21, 1809; d. May 10, 1812.
    2513⅛.   vi.   SALLY, b. Sept. 28, 1810; d. Sept. 30, 1810.
    2513¼.   vii.   SARAH ANN, b. Aug. 9, 1813; d. Nov. 9, 1833.
    2513½.   viii.   ELIZABETH NEWELL, b. Oct. 4, 1819; m. Elijah Pierce Fisk, her cousin; res. 39 Bowdoin St., Boston, Mass. (See.)
    2513¾.   ix.   SUSAN PAGE, b. Oct. 17, 1820; d. Jan. 17, 1821.

1307. JOHN FISK (David, Robert, Robert, David, David, Jeffrey, Robert, Simon, Simon, William, Symond), b. Lex., Jan. 22, 1,89; m. in Woburn, July 20, 1809, Lydia Pierce, of Woburn, b. 1789; d. Aug. 26, 1880. John Fisk was born in Lexington and resided in that vicinity all his life. He was a farmer, and followed agricultural pursuits all his life. He died in Boston, at the home of his son, Elijah P. He d. in Boston, 1858; res. Winchester, Mass.

    2514. i.   ABIGAIL, b. Jan. 4, 1810; m. Oct. 9, 1828, Baxter B. Otis, of Woburn. Ch.: 1, Bradford, b. ———; d. ———. 2, Timothy, b. ———; d. ———.

    2515. ii.   ELIJAH PIERCE, b. Aug. 25, 1814; m. Elizabeth Newell Fisk.

    2516. iii. LYDIA ANN, b. Mar. 8, 1817; m. June 30, 1840, Dr. Walter Bailey, of Woburn. She left one dau,. Abby Ann, who died young.

    2517. iv. CLARA WYMAN, b. Jan. 16, 1822; m. July 30, 1840, Thomas Waterman Kimball, b. ———; d. ———; m. 2d, Nathan Chandler. Ch.: 1, Curtis Kimball, b. ———; res. Boston. 2, Oscar Chandler, b. ———; res. Boston.

    2518. v.   MARY, b. Feb. 16, 1826; m. William Henry Colburn. He d. s. p., 1885. She res. Boston.

    2519. vi. JOHN, b. 1811; d. Sept. 22, 1816. "In Memory of John Fisk, Jr., son of John Fisk, Who died Sept. 22, 1816, Aged 5 Years. "No prayers, nor tears, nor sighs, could save This lovely Infant from the grave."—Woburn Town Records.

    2520. vii. MARY, b. 1819; d. Dec. 1, 1822.

    2521. viii. JOHN W., b. Oct. 29, 1827; m. Ann E. Seates.

    2522. ix. DAVID BRAINERD, b. Feb. 19, 1830; m. ———.

1312. JOSEPH FISKE (Joseph, Joseph, Robert, David, David, Jeffrey, Robert, Simon, Simon, William, Symond), b. Lex., Feb. 9, 1797; m. Nov. 12, 1829, Mary Gardner Kennard, of Eliot, Me., b. in Kittery, Me., Oct. 17, 1795; d. Jan. 12, 1874. He was a farmer. He d. May 4, 1860; res. Lexington, Mass.

    2523. i.   JOSEPH ALEXANDER, b. Mar. 8, 1830; m. Love Langdon Dodge.

    2524. ii.   TIMOTHY KENNARD, b. Aug. 5, 1833; m. Barbara Peters.

1313. JONAS STONE FISKE (Joseph, Joseph, Robert, David, David, Jeffrey, Robert, Simon, Simon, William, Symond), b. Lex., May 9, 1799; m. May 8, 1823, Pamela Brown, dau. of James Brown, b. July 29, 1800. He d. Mar. 23, 1828; res. Lexington, Mass., and West Cambridge.

    2525. i.   MARY ELIZABETH, b. June 2, 1824; m. Apr. 3, 1845, Nehemiah Munroe Fessenden, of Arlington, Mass.; b. Jan. 20, 1821; d. Apr. 7, 1867; he was a merchant in the spice business. She d. May 15, 1890, leaving quite a family. Ch.: Phillip Winslow, b. Feb. 14, 1846; d. Dec., 1848. Edward Stanley, b. Mar. 21, 1848; Selectman in Arlington. Lelia Crafts, b. Feb. 10, 1851. Horace Chapman, b, Mar. 15, 1853. Mary Pamelia, b. Mar. 26, 1855. Evelyn Rebecca, b. Apr. 27, 1857. Nellie Munroe, b. Apr. 25, 1859. Marion Brown, Mar. 15, 1861. E. S. Fessenden, Arlington, Mass.; Mrs. E. C. Prescott, Arlington, Mass.; H. C. Fessenden, Arlington, Mass.; Mrs. B. A. Norton, Arlington, Mass.; Mrs. F. C. Howe, 10 Ellsworth, Ave., Cambridge, Mass.; Mrs. N. C. Nash, 19 Craigie St., Cambridge, Mass.; Miss Marion B. Fessenden, 19 Craigie St., Cambridge, Mass.

    2526. ii.   JAMES FRANCIS, b. Dec. 31, 1825; m. Mar. 9, 1848, Lydia Hastings Ingraham, b. Apr. 18, 1829; d. Sept. 21, 1877. He d. 1880. Ch.: 1, Emma I., b. Sept. 18, 1848; unm. 2, Carrie Francis, b. Feb. 28, 1851; unm.; res. East Lexington, Mass. 3, Louie Theodore, b. Mar. 22, 1853; d. July 31, 1872.

1315. FRANKLIN FISKE (Joseph, Joseph, Robert, David, David, Jeffrey, Robert, Simon, Simon, William Symond), b. Lex., Oct. 16, 1804; m. Oct. 3, 1839, Hannah Peters, of Newport, N. H. He left two sons, who served in the

Eleventh Massachusetts Infantry during the war of the Rebellion, and gave their young lives to their country. Their names were Chas. Albert., who was wounded at Gettysburg, and died at Hampton, Va.; Joseph Henry, joined the regular army and died in Ark. He d. Mar. 23, 1868; res. Lexington, Mass.

2527. i. CHARLES A., b. Dec. 25, 1842; d. unm.

2528. ii. JOSEPH H. R., b. Sept. 8, 1843; d. unm.

1318. JONATHAN FISKE (David, David, Robert, David, David, Jeffrey, Robert, Simon, Simon, William, Symond), b. Lex., Apr. 15, 1786; m. in Walpole, N. H., Rowena Leonard, of Keene, N. H., b. 1786; d. May 17, 1871. He was born in the historic old town of Lexington, Mass., where he always resided and where his children were all born. He was a shoemaker by trade, which he followed with farming. During the latter part of his life he resided with his son, John, in Billerica, where he died. He d. in Billerica, Dec. 19, 1871; res. Lexington, Mass.

2529. i. ELIZA, b. Dec. 13, 1810; m. Mar. 6, 1833, Nathaniel Bridgman Pierce; res. Cavendish, Vt. He was b. Mar. 18, 1808, in Weathersfield, Vt.; d. in Cavendish in May. 1882. She d. Feb. 11, 1886. Ch.: 1, Charles J., b. Nov. 21, 1833; d. Mar. 14, 1841. 2, Sarah A., b. June 21, 1836; m. Oct. 28, 1857, Dr. Charles F. Kingsbury; res. Boston and Harvard Aves., West Medford, Mass.; ch.: Ella Sarah, b. Oct. 29, 1858; m. June 7, 1884, J. W. Bean; res. W. Medford. 3, Silas, b. Mar. 20, 1840; d. Mar. 22, 1840. 4, George, b. Jan. 21, 1843; d. Jan. 23, 1843. 5, Edwin, b. Aug. 17, 1844; d. Nov. 4, 1845. 6, Henry Dutton, b. May 26, 1846, in Cavendish, Vt.; m. in Toledo, O., July 2, 1874, Mary Elizabeth Hill, b. Nov. 14, 1848; ch.: Helena Elizabeth. b. May 28, 1875; now traveling abroad; Edith Van Nostrand, b. Aug. 17, 1876; d. Ian. 5, 1878; Henry Kingsbury, b. Dec. 29, 1881; res. 133 South Grove Ave., Oak Park, Ill.

HENRY D. PIERCE
President of the Town of Cicero.

2530. ii. GEORGE, b. 1814; d. unm. in 1830.

2531. iii. MARIA, b. Nov. 30, 1819; m. in 1845, Dr. M. F. Haley, who was b. in York, Me.; rev. to New Orleans and Jackson Co., Texas, where he d. Nov. 17, 1849. Ch.: Jael M., res. Edna, Texas. She m. 2d. J. McIver. She res. in Edna, Texas. McIver was b. in Kentucky; he was killed while sheriff of Jackson Co., May 1, 1871; d. s. p. He held the office for four years and was a farmer by occupation.

2532. iv. SARAH, b. 1817. She d. in Boston, in 1862; unm.

2533. v. CAROLINE M., b. in Billerica 1821; m. Asa C. Chase. He Was a merchant in Boston and d. in 1881. One dau., Frances S., res. 55 Walnut St., Waltham, Mass.

2534. vi. ROWENA, b. 1825; m. David J. Mackie; res. Boston and 618 Larkin St., San Francisco, Cal.; two ch.

2535. vii. JOHN, b. Nov. 6, 1827; m. Judith Decrow.

1322. BENJAMIN FISKE (David, David, Robert, David, David, Jeffrey, Robert, Simon, Simon, William, Symond), b. Lex., Apr. 27, 1798; m. at Woburn,

Mar. 20, 1827, Sarah Deland, of Woburn or Westford, b. Jan. 18, 1806; res. Lexington, Mass.

2536. i. BENJAMIN ICHABOD, b. Oct. 6, 1828; m. Caroline Wood, of Leominster; res. W. Cambridge, Mass.
2537. ii. LOUISA D., b. Feb. 21, 1830; m. George Reed, of Auburn N. H.
2538. iii. FREDERIC C. D., b, Oct. 3, 1831; killed in the second battle of Bull Run.
2539. iv. HANNAH E. D., b. June 5, 1834; m. Nathan Brown; res. Walth.
2540. v. DAN GRAY, b. Dec. 6, 1836.
2541. vi. CHARLES HENRY, b. Apr. 23, 1838; killed in the army.
2542. vii. SARAH LOVINA, b. Apr. 2, 1841.
2543. viii. MARY MARIA, b. Mar. 16, 1843; m. Mar. 24, 1861, George G. Wheeler.
2544. ix. OLIVER O., b. Apr. 3, 1845; d. Apr. 5, 1845.

1331. DR. DAVID FISK (Ebenezer, Ebenezer, Ebenezer, David, David, David, Jeffery, Robert, Simon, Simon, William, Symond), b. Oct. 10, 1772; m. at Hanover, N. H., —— Lewis, dau. of Dr. Lewis of that place (nothing on Hanover town records of this marriage): m. 2d, July 19, 1804, in Chester, Vt., Abigail Sargent, dau. of Jabez, of Chester, Vt., b. Jan. 2, 1779, d. Oct. 27, 1848. Sargent Geneology says Miss Abigail Sargent. Chester, Vt., town records say: "State of Vermont Windsor ss Be it Remembered that at Chester in the County aforsd on the nineteenth day of July 1804 Dr. David Fisk of Cavendish and Mrs. Abigail Sargeant of Chester were duly joined in marriage By me Jabez Sargeant J't Peace A true record of the return Aaron Leland Clerk." The Town Clerk of Cavendish. Vt., writes that there is nothing on the records of Fisks. Chester was never any part of any other town. It first received its charter in 1763 as New Flamstead. Afterwards the name was changed to Chester. He was born in New England and was a successful physician. He settled in Genesee Co., N. Y. His eldest son, Dr. David Lewis Fisk, located in Kentucky and the father paid him a visit. Being much pleased with the country he decided to locate there himself. He resided for some time in Kentucky before sending for his family. He boarded with John Carlisle, the grandfather of John G. Carlisle (not then born), the present Secretary of the Treasury. Dr. Fisk on his way back to New York stopped at Mount Vernon, O., to visit some friends he had known in the east, and there he died. He had resided in what was then Pomfrey Hollow, now Oran, and in Manlius Square, both in Onondaga County, N. Y. He resided but a very short time in Genesee County, N. Y., and then returned to Onondaga County, N. Y. He was a handsome man, six feet, well proportioned, healthy, and quite an athlete. He was a natural doctor and became eminent in his profession. In making a diognosis he exhibited rare ability. He was of a rather roving disposition and acquired property slowly. He d. Feb. 28, 1829; res. Genesee Co., N. Y., and Ky.

2545. i. JOHN FLAVEL, b. Dec. 14, 1815; m. Elizabeth Sarah Johnson.
2546. ii. HARRISON DEARBORN, b. Mar. 25, 1813; m. Maria E. Goss.
2547. iii. DAVID LEWIS, b. ——; m. —— Abercombie and Mary Griffing.
2548. iv. NAOMI, b. Sept. 6, 1805; d. unm. Apr. 18, 1859.
2549. v. ZELINDA, b. May 12, 1809; d. Apr. 11, 1830, in her wedding garments on her appointed wedding day.
2550. vi. EBENEZER, b. June 29, 1819; m. Eliza A. Stephens.
2551. vii. LUCY, b. ——; m. —— Cutter. of Bellows Falls, Vt.
2552. viii. EMELINE, b. Jan. 2, 1806; d. Feb. 19, 1808.

1334. NATHANIEL FISK (Cotton, Ebenezer, Ebenezer, David, David, David, Jeffrey, Robert, Simon, Simon, William, Symond), b. East Bolton, P. Q., Nov. 17, 1802: m. at Abbotsford, Canada, Jan. 28, 1827, Miriam Whitney, dau. of Capt. Benjamin Whitney, of Three Rivers, Canada, b. Sept. 19, 1799, d. Sept. 20, 1881. Nathaniel Fisk was the eldest son of of Capt. Cotton Fisk, and settled on a farm at Abbotsford where he died at the age of 37, in 1840, leaving a widow and four children, who experienced many privations in those early days before railroads and steamships were known to the farmers of the present date. Capt. Whitney was born in Petersham, Mass., and served in the Revolutionary army. At its close he moved to Three Rivers, Canada, and engaged extensively in the lumber business. He d. Dec. 5, 1840; res. Abbotsford, P. Q.

2553. i. JOHN M., b. Dec. 13, 1836; m. Ellen M. Knowlton.
2554. ii. NATHANIEL C., b. Nov. 17, 1828; m. Helen Bangs.
2555. iii. NEWELL, b. Mar. 11, 1839; m. Clara Lucelia Fisk.
2556. iv. ELIZABETH, b. Nov. 18, 1827; d. Nov. 20, 1827.
2557. v. INFANT DAU., b. and d. Oct. 29, 1829.
2558. vi. LOVINA E., b. Oct. 10, 1832; d. June 15, 1848.
2559. vii. BENJAMIN SEWELL, b. May 14, 1834; d. May. 31, 1834.
2560. viii. MARY ANN, b. Mar. 3, 1835; d. Mar. 29, 1835.
2561. ix. SARAH MARIA, b. Dec. 13, 1836; d. Oct. 27, 1840.

1335. CAPT. SEWELL COTTON FISK (Cotton, Ebenezer, Ebenezer, David, David, David, Jeffery, Robert, Simon, Simon, William, Symond), b. Abbotsford, P. Q., May 5, 1816; m. there, in 1846, Mary Ann Gorton, b. Aug. 10, 1818; d. Aug. 26, 1854. He was a carpenter and farmer. A Captain in the Canadian militia and an honest, respectable citizen. He d. Aug. 27, 1889; res. Abbotsford, P. Q., and Seymour, Wis.

2562. i. ERASTUS SEWELL, b. May 18, 1843; unm.; res. Chicopee Falls, Mass.
2563. ii. NATHANIEL B., b. Mar. 6, 1848; m. Katherine S. Gillespie.
2564. iii. BELLONCE M., b. Oct. 6, 1851; m. Rev. Emanuel E. Charlton; res. Gloucester, Mass. Ch.: Charles Magnus, b. Maynard, Mass.; res. G. He is a theological student.
2565. iv. MARY ANN, b. Feb. 19, 1853; m. Alfred G. Fuller; res. Seymour, Wis. A son is Clinton; res. Seymour.
2566. v. JOHN, b. Aug. 6, 1854; d. Aug. 30, 1854.

1336. ABRAHAM FISK (Cotton, Ebenezer, Ebenezer, David, David, David, Jeffery, Robert, Simon, Simon, William, Symond), b. Bolton, P. Q., Feb. 8, 1811; m. Jan. 7, 1834, Lauretta Buzzell, b. Dec. 8, 1811; d. Feb. 18, 1888. He was a farmer. He d. Feb. 26, 1888; res. Abbotsford, P. Q.

2567. i. ANDREW MURRAY, b. Nov. 7, 1834; m. Mary A. Edmunds.
2568. ii. COTTON ORREN, b. Sept. 7, 1836.
2569. iii. HARLOW WINDSOR, b. Jan. 14, 1840.
2570. iv. CLARA LUCELIA, b. Jan. 6, 1845; m. Dr. Newell Fisk.
2571. v. SARAH LOVINIA, b. Sept. 20, 1846.
2572. vi. WILLARD ABRAHAM, b. July 3, 1849.
2573. vii. WILLIAM ALBERT, d. in infancy.

1338. EBENEZER FISK (Cotton, Ebenezer, Ebenezer, David, David, David, Jeffery, Robert, Simon, Simon, William, Symond), b. Bolton, P. Q., Mar. 8, 1800; m. at Abbotsford, P. Q., Feb. 14, 1839, Eliza Bradford, dau. of Rev. Robert Bradford, b. May 20, 1804. He was an enterprising, active farmer and trader; dealt largely in lumber; had much mechanical skill and ingenuity, and filled the government office of ostmaster acceptably for some twenty years. He d. 1861; res. Abbotsford, P. Q.

2574. i. JOHN J., b. Feb. 23, 1844; m. Aleyda Eliza David.
2575. ii. WM. CALDWELL, b. Jan. 29, 1830; d. unm. in 1851.
2576. iii. JESSIE H. ELIZA, b. Dec. 9, 1831; res. Gouverneur, N. Y.
2577. iv. EMMA SARAH, b. May 12, 1834; res. A.
2578. v. HENRY CHAS., b. Oct. 20, 1836; m. Isabella Graham.
2579. vi. LAURA AMELIA, b. Feb. 25, 1838; d. s. p. in 1891.
2580. vii. EDWARD FRANCIS, b. Sept. 5, 1841; m. Emma Elliott.

1342. COL. JOHN MINOT FISKE (Benjamin, Ebenezer, Ebenezer, David, David, David, Jeffery, Robert, Simon, Simon, William, Symond), b. Lex. July 15, 1798; m. at Salem, Eliza Maria Wine, of Salem, dau. of Joseph, b. June 30, 1800; d. Dec. 17, 1784. He was educated in Lexington, Mass., entered Harvard College and was graduated in the class of 1815; studied law and was subsequently admitted to the bar, having offices in Boston and Charlestown; was interested in the State militia and rose to the rank of Colonel; was quite active in politics; was a Democrat and warm admirer and supporter of President Jackson; died in Chelmsford Aug. 16, 1841. He d. Aug. 16, 1841; res. Chelmsford, Mass.

2581. i. JOSEPH, b. ———; d. in infancy.
2582. ii. BENJ. MINOT, b. ———; m. Elizabeth A. Parkhurst.
2583. iii. JOSEPH W., b. May 22, 1832; m. Caroline Gould.
2584. iv. JOHN M., b. Aug. 17, 1834; m. Isabella L. Goodrich.

1344. CHARLES FISKE (Benjamin, Ebenezer, Ebenezer, David, David, David, Jeffery, Robert, Simon, Simon, William, Symond), b. Chelmsford, Mass., Nov. 17, 1807; m. Nov. 8, 1831, Abigail Malvina Hayden, of Boston, dau. of Daniel and Sarah, b. June 9, 1812; d. Mar. 28, 1859; m. 2d, May 20, 1861, Mrs. Elizabeth Priscilla Davis, of Nashua, N. H.; she d. there Oct. 8, 18/3. He was born in Chelmsford, Mass. His father was quite well to do, and having plenty of means was never engaged in any business and has always lived a quiet, uneventful life; res. Milford, Me., and Lexington, Mass., and 70 Chandler St., Boston, Mass.
    2585. i. FRANCES ALBERTINE, b. Nov. 1, 1832; m. June 8, 1852, Thomas B. Davenport, of Hopk.
    2586. ii. CHARLES, b. May 27, 1834; m. Adeline W. Shaw and Annie I. Crafts.
    2587. iii. WILLIAM B., b. June 23, 1836; m. Henrietta S. Lyford.
    2588. iv. HENRY A., b. Apr. 23, 1840; d. ———.
    2589. v. MARION A., b. Jan. 28, 1846; d. Jan. 12, 1864.
    2590. vi. ABBIE JOSEPHINE, b. Nov. 18, 1848; m. Nov. 18, 1869, Alonzo Austin Goddard, b. Apr. 1, 1847. Ch.: Henry Austin, b. Mar. 25, 1875; res. 70 Chandler St., Boston, Mass.

1347. AARON FISK (Samuel, Aaron, Samuel, James, James, Phinehas, Thomas, Robert, Simon, Simon, William, Symond), b. Claremont, N. H., Mar. 23, 1801; m. there Nov. 30, 1828, Hannah L. Laughton, b. Unity, N. H., Aug. 21, 1804; d. Sept. 3, 1847, in Lowell, Mass.; m. 2d, Hannah Fay. He was a farmer. He d. Feb., 1861; res. Dalton and Jaffrey, N. H.
    2591. i. JAMES W., b. Oct. 19, 1835; m. Mary Jane Sharp.
    2592. ii. ROSATTHA A., b. ———; m. Harvey Clark. Ch.: Janette Clough; res. Windsor, Vt. Hellen Bacon; res. Bellows Falls, Vt.
    2593. iii. FRANCES M., b. ———; m. Samuel G. Baldwin; res. Charlestown, N. H.
    2594. iv. ORRISIA A., b. ———; m. George Fuller. Ch.: Millie Toothacre; res. Minot, Me.
    2595. v. ARTEMISSIA, b. Dec., 1832; m. Albert O. Fisk; res. Lunenburg, Mass. He was b. Grafton, Mass., Sept., 1831. She was b. in Jaffrey, N. H., and m. there. Ch.: 1, Albert Lawton, b. 1860; m. May, 1889; res. L. 2, Harry Jackson, b. 1865; res. L. Albert O. was son of Oren E. (see elsewhere) who was b. in 1805 in Claremont, N. H.; m. there Sept., 1830, Mariah H. Jackson, b. Apr., 1808; d. Jan. 27, 1892. Oren d. in Grafton, Mass., Aug. 25, 1836, where he was a shoemaker.
    2596. vi. JOHN W., b. Feb. 25, 1834; m. Arvilla L. Dodge.
    2597. vii. ORIN E., b. Sept. 4, 1837; m. Blindia D. Eaton.

1352. ATTERSON FISK (Samuel, Aaron, Samuel, James, James, Phinehas, Thomas, Robert, Simon, Simon, William, Symond), b. Claremont, N. H., Apr. 7, 1808; m. in Dayton, Ohio, Apr. 23, 1844, Catherine Lehman, b. Jan. 17, 1820. He d. Sept. 17, 1871; res. St. Marys, Ohio.
    2598. i. LEHMAN, b. ———; res. St. Marys, Ohio.
    2599. ii. PERRY, b. Apr. 13, 1846; m. Eliza J. Baker.

1353. ERASTUS FISK (Samuel, Aaron, Samuel, James, James, Phinehas, Thomas, Robert, Simon, Simon, William, Symond), b. Claremont, N. H., June 1, 1808; m. Anna Perry; d. 1891. He d. 1891; res. Claremont, N. H.
    2600. i. SAMUEL E., b. Sept. 20, 1842; m. Carrie A. Dodge, Hattie A. Haselton and Jennie Renfrew.
    THREE OTHER BOYS.

1358. SAMUEL FRANKLIN FISK (Samuel, Aaron, Samuel, James, James, Phinehas, Thomas, Robert, Simon, Simon, William, Symond), b. Claremont, N. H., Feb. 9, 1814; m. in Dayton, Ohio, Harriett Lehman, b. Apr. 5, 1822. He was a farmer, and when the war broke out enlisted in an Ohio regiment. He died in the service at Barbersville, Ky. He d. Feb. 22, 1864; res. St. Marys, Ohio.

2601. i.   FRANCES E., b. Apr. 25, 1843; m. Oct. 13, 1864, Joseph W. Wise; res. 735 W. North St., Lima, Ohio. He was b. June 20, 1841. Ch.: Dellia Wise, b. Sept. 22, 1865; d. Oct. 15, 1865. Harry Wilber Wise, b. Mar. 20, 1867; add. Lima, Ohio. Clyde Wise, b. May 28, 1871; d. Jan. 14, 18,8. Birdie Wise, b. July 1, 1874; d. June 22, 1875. Daisy Bell Wise, b. Feb. 17, 1874, Lima, Ohio. Elsie May Wise, b. Apr. 7, 1881; add. Lima, Ohio. Roy Wise, b. May 28, 1883; add. Lima, Ohio.

2602. ii.   WILBUR, b. Nov. 14, 1844; m. Laura B. Wise.

2603. iii. JANE, b. Sept. 29, 1846; m. June 20, 1869, George Myers; res. 131 N. Metcalf St., Lima; he was b. May 24, 1837; s. p.

2604. iv. ALMA, b. Dec. 14, 1850; m. Dec. 7, 1876, Geo. W. Whitley, b. Sept. 10, 1849; d. Oct. 5, 1881. Ch.: Floyd, b. June 7, 1878; m. 2d, J. D. Nagers, Rockford, Ohio.

2605. v.   MARY, b. Sept. 6, 1853; m. Nov. 14, 1876, Emanuel Crist; res. 130 N. McDonald St., Lima. Ch.: Pearl Crist, b. 1877; d. July 21, 18;8. Ethel Crist, b. May 13, 1880; d. July 7, 1880. Clifford Crist, b. Aug. 27, 1882; d. Jan. 8, 1883. Hoyt Crist, b. Apr. 8, 1885; d. Mar. 5, 1887. Walter A. Crist, b. Sept. 29, 1889; res. 130 N. McDonald St., Lima, Allen County, Ohio.

2606. vi. GEORGE I., b. Oct. 1, 1860; m. Della Hinkle.

1361. SAMUEL FISK (Samuel, Thomas, Thomas, Samuel, James, Phinehas, Thomas, Robert, Simon, Simon, William, Symond), b. Dublin, N. H., Apr. 1, 1797; m. Mar. 29, 1825, Betsey Gleason, dau. of Phinehas; res. Dublin, and Peterboro, N. H.

2607. i.   ELIZABETH S., b. May 18, 1826; d. unm.

2608. ii.   MARIA L., b. July 11, 1828; m. Frank Eaton, of Gardner, Mass., and lived in Gardner, Mass., for a time. Then they removed to California, where she died, leaving several children. He came back to Gardner afterwards and is now dead.

2609. iii. AMOS T., b. Aug. 27, 1831; d. unm.

1362. ASA FISK (Samuel, Thomas, Thomas, Samuel, James, Phinehas, Thomas, Robert, Simon, Simon, William, Symond), b. Dublin, N. H., Feb. 16, 1799; m. there Apr. 12, 1835, Priscilla Ranstead, b. June, 1813, d. Sept., 1891. Asa Fisk, with the exception of a short time spent in teaching school in New York, lived his whole life on the farm where he was born, devoting his time and attention to farming. He was a respected citizen of the town, was always interested in the affairs of the town and neighborhood, but never held office. He d. Aug., 1868; res. Dublin, N. H.

2610. i.   CHARLES R., b. Apr. 25, 1843; m. Abbie M. Jones.

2611. ii.   FRANK H., b. Mar. 28, 1855; res. Forrest City, Ia.

1368. HON. THOMAS FISKE (Asa, Thomas, Thomas, Samuel, James, Phinehas, Thomas, Robert, Simon, Simon, William, Symond), b. Dublin, N. H., Dec. 29, 1802; m. there Apr. 19, 1832, Sophia Appleton, dau. of Dea. Francis and Mary (Ripley) Appleton, b. Nov. 15, 1806, d. Oct. 2, 1890. Hon. Thomas Fisk was bred a farmer, having few advantages for an education besides those furnished by the common school. In the winter seasons from 1822 to 1840 he was mostly employed in teaching public and private schools. For nearly twenty years, commencing Mar., 1824, he was a member of the Superintending School Committee of his native town; and during that time he had the satisfaction of seeing the common schools of Dublin rise from the lowest to the highest rank among similar institutions in the State. While farming was his principal business, he has been employed more or less in surveying lands, and routes for roads, in settling estates and in taking care of funds belonging to individuals. He was one of the compilers of the "History of Dublin," published in 1855, which is regarded as a work of some merit. He has held several positions of honor and trust, among them are that of Town Clerk; agent to defend the town in several long and perplexing law suits; agent having charge of the town funds ($18,768.80) from Mar., 1842, till he was 70 years of age; moderator, having presided over more annual and other meetings of the town than any other individual that has ever resided there; representative in 1847, 1857, 1858; State Senator 1859, 1860; State commissioner to prevent the spread of contagious diseases among cattle, 1864-1865; Justice of the Peace from 1842 to 1857, and from 1857 has been Justice of the Peace and Quorum throughout the State. He has devoted much time and attention to promote the causes of education, temperance and universal freedom. He d. Apr. 30, 1889; res. Dublin, N. H.

2612. i. JESSE APPLETON, b. June 7, 1836. He volunteered in Aug., 1862, and entered the service as a Sergeant in Company A, Fourteenth Regiment, New Hampshire Volunteers. Nov. 2, 1863, he was commissioned Second Lieutenant of Company E, Fourteenth Regiment, and May 27, 1864, he was promoted to First Lieutenant of Company K, in the same regiment. On being mustered in as First Lieutenant he took command of the company which he held to his death. He was killed in the battle of Winchester, Va., Sept. 19, 1864. An officer of the regiment said of him: "Lieutenant Fisk will be remembered as a dutiful son, an affectionate brother, a dear friend, an agreeable companion, a kind neighbor, a true soldier, and a brave officer. His townsmen bear ample testimony to his worth as a citizen and a man. In the army too, officers and men keep his memory green, and sadly call to mind that he will no more join them on the march, at bivouac, in camp or where death shots fall thick and fast He was ever ready to do a kind deed, both at home and abroad, and many a soldier remembers him kindly for attentions received at his hands while on a sick bed. He was prompt to do his duty and 'died at his post' in the van of the fight. A patriot's honors rest upon his brow."

2613. ii. ARABELLA SOPHIA, b. May 29, 1844; m. May 25, 1880, Dr. Henry Hillard Smith, son of Rev. Henry S. and Mary (Hillard Smith, born in Liverpool, Medina County, O., June 16, 1837. Afterwards moved with his parents to Claremont, N. H. Studied medicine with Prof. Dixi Crosby, M. D., and A. B. Crosby, M. D., of Hanover, N. H. Graduated at Dartmouth Medical College in 1859. Commenced the practice of medicine in the State of Vermont. Served in the late Civil war as Acting Assistant Surgeon in United States navy. Settled in Dublin, N. H., in 1865, where he continued in his profession and now resides; res. s. p., Dublin, N. H.

1370. CAPT. ASA HARVEY FISK (Asa, Thomas, Thomas, Samuel, James, Phinehas, Thomas, Robert, Simon, Simon, William, Symond), b. Dublin, N. H., Mar. 23, 1812; m. May 24, 1838, Caroline Ranstead. They settled on the homestead. He taught school several winters, practiced surveying; settled estates and was a Justice of the Peace and Quorum, also a Captain in the N. H. Militia. In 1850 he removed with his family to Pennsylvania, and died at Fallen Timber. Cambria Co., Pa. He d. Sept. 28, 1885; res. Dublin, N. H., and Frugality (Fiske P. O.), Pa.

2614. i. CAROLINE P., b. Dec. 7, 1841; m. 1862, Henry Foster, son of Betsey (Fiske) Foster; res. Frugality, Cambria Co., Pa.
2615. ii. JOHN H., b. Jan. 15, 1844; m. Mary A. Mullen.

1373. ADAMS FISK (Levi, Thomas, Thomas, Samuel, James, Phinehas, Thomas, Robert, Simon, Simon, William, Symond), b. May 3, 1800, in Jaffrey, N. H.; m. in Groton, Mass., Jan. 7, 1835, Mary Loring, of Rindge, b. Mar. 23, 1805; d. Mar. 26, 1892. He was a farmer and resided on the property inherited from his father. For a short time he resided in Groton, Mass. He d. Aug. 23, 1890; res. Jaffrey, N. H.

2616. i. MARY EMELINE, b. May 20, 1837; m. Apr. 11, 1858, Benjamin F. Prescott. He was b. in Westford, Mass., Apr. 19, 1837; d. Mar. 2, 1895; res. East Jaffrey, N. H. Ch.: 1, Herman Frank-

lin, b. Jan. 7, 1859. 2, Mary Ada, b. Nov. 30, 1860. 3, Fred
Adams, b. May 3, 1863. 4, Henri Mansfield, b. Dec. 7, 1865.
5, Carrie Howard, b. Nov. 22, 1868. 6, Helen, b. Nov. 6, 1872.
7, Belle, b. July 6, 1876; d. July 6, 1876.

2617.   ii.   JOHN ADAMS, b. Sept. 5, 1839; d. Dec. 20, 1844.
2618.   iii. HENRY HARRISON, b. Apr. 5, 1842; d. June 20, 1843.
2619.   iv.   EMILY HARVEY, b. June 20, 1845; d. June 20, 1845.

1379. JOHN S. FISKE (Levi, Thomas, Thomas, Samuel, James, Phinehas,
Thomas, Robert, Simon, Simon, William, Symond), b. Jaffrey, N. H., July 18, 1814;
m. May 18, 1836, Anna Clark, of Nelson, N. H. He was a machinist; has been
an agent for several manufacturing companies, and res. in Peterborough, Claremont and Suncook, N. H., Knoxville, Tenn., Cleveland, O., Meadville, Pa., and
several other places. He d. Jan. 12, 1876; res. Cleveland, O.

2620.   i.   MARY E., b. Jan. 8, 1841.
2621.   ii.   HENRY M., b. July 23, 1842.

1381. BENONI FISK (Benjamin, Benjamin, Benjamin, John, John, Phinehas, Thomas, Robert, Simon, Simon, William, Symond), b. Scituate, R. I., 1768;
m. there Jan. 21, 1790, Barbara Colvin, b. Dec. 14, 1769; d. Nov. 17, 18——. He emigrated from Scituate, R. I., with his two brothers, in 1789, and settled on a farm
in Danby, Vt., where he ever after resided. He d. Mar. 13, 1840; res. Danby ,Vt.

2622.   i.   ROYAL, b. Oct. 20, 1808; m. Harriett A. Mead.
2623.   ii.   NANCY, b. Nov. 30, 1790.
2624.   iii.   JOAB, b. Feb. 5, 1793.
2625.   iv.   BENONI, b. Sept. 6, 1795; m. Betsey Lake.
2626.   v.   REUBEN, b. June 6, 1798; m. Sabra Phillips and res. Peru, N. Y
2627.   vi.   CALEB, b. Feb. 18, 1801.
2628.   vii.   COLONEL, b. Mar. 6, 1802.
2629.   viii. BENJAMIN, b. June 26, 1803.
2630.   ix.   LINUS, b. June 16, 1805.
2631.   x.   MARSENA, b. Aug. 26, 1811.

1382. BENJAMIN FISK (Benjamin, Benjamin, Benjamin, John, John,
Phinehas, Thomas, Robert, Simon, Simon, William, Symond), b. Scituate, R. I.,
July, 1770; m. in E. Scituate, R. I., July 13, 1793, Freelove Colvin, b. June 16, 1771;
d. May 24, 1844; m. 2d, Polly Taylor. He went to Danby, Vt., in 1789, and settled
on a farm, where he lived for seventy-nine years, or until his death. He went to
the Green Mountain State with his two brothers. In 1790 he returned to Rhode
Island, was married, and soon returned, bringing the household effects and wife
in an ox team. He lived in a log house twenty years, when he erected the frame
house now standing. He possessed a rugged constitution and was remarkably
fitted to encounter the obstacles and endure the privations necessarily experienced
during the establishment of a home in the wilderness. Mr. Fisk was a great hunter
and trapper in the early days, and many good stories are related of his adventures
with wild game. He led a laborious and industrious life, always peaceable and
unassuming, and died at the ripe age of 96. He d. ae. 96, in 1867; res. Danby, Vt.

2632.   i.   HIRAM PHILLIPS, b. Jan 15, 1806; m. Olive Smith.
2633.   ii.   BENJAMIN J., b. Jan. 21, 1796; m. Catherine Colvin.
2634.   iii. LIZZIE M., b. Mar. 16, 1794; m. in Danby, Vt., Benjamin Col-
              vin; res. Clarendon Springs, Vt. She d. Sept. 15, 1822. He
              was b. in Clarendon, Vt., Mar. 16, 1793; d. June 22, 1874. Was
              a farmer. Ch.: 1, Linus F. Colvin, b. ——; m. ——; ch.:
              John C. Colvin, res. Chippenhook, Vt. Erastus J. Colvin, b.
              ——; m. ——; ch.: Linus E. Colvin, res. Keeseville, N. Y.
              3, Rosetta B. Colvin, b. ——; m. —— Francis; ch.: Eliza-
              beth R., res. Chippenhook, Vt. 4, Elizabeth Fisk, b. Jan. 29,
              1822; m. Sept. 3, 1846, Geo. W. Cougdon, b. Feb. 6, 1820; res.
              Chippenhook, Vt.; ch.: 1, Joseph E., b. Aug. 12, 1858; d. July
              18, 1860.
2635.   iv.   LUCY R., b. Mar. 10, 1800; m. Apr. 8, 1824. Joseph Warren Pot-
              ter, of Clarendon, b. Aug. 7, 1801; d. Dec. 31, 1849; was a
              farmer. She d. Jan. 30, 1879. Ch.: Alonzo H., b. Apr. 17, 1825;

m. ———; d. Mar. 8, 1870. Melissa P., b. June 5, 1827; m. Henry Brewster; add., Wesley, Iowa. Sally J., b. Feb. 14, 1829; d. Feb. 27, 1893. Polly E., b. Apr. 19, 1831; m. H. Tower; add. Fort Atkinson, Iowa. Darius E., b. July 21, 1834; add. 2254 Sixth Ave., Troy, N. Y. Noel, b. Jan. 19, 1841; add. Chippenhook, Vt.; m. Nov. 14, 1865, Lydia Potter, b. July 5, 1842. He is a farmer; ch.: H. Blanche Potter, b. Nov. 7, 1872; Warren E. Potter, b. Feb. 23, 1875; William R. Potter, b. Feb. 23, 1875; Noel Ralph Potter, b. Mar. 28, 1877; H. Percy Potter, b. Nov. 22, 1881; none married; P. O. add., Chippenhook, Vt.

2636. v. LYMAN R., b. Nov. 28, 1803; m. Mrs. Lucy Colvin.

2637. vi. JOEL, b. June 16, 1810; m. Laura Fitz and ——— ———.

2638. vii. CHLOE, b. Dec. 3, 1801; m. in Danby, Vt., Jeremiah Ormsby; res. Ellenburgh, N. Y. Lucy P., b. Apr. 11, 1832; m. Nov. 14, 1802, and d. in Ellenburgh, Apr. 25, 1878. She d. Dec. 4, 1888. Ch.: Addison C., b. Apr. 22, 1826; m. Mar. 30. Emily M., b. Sept. 22, 1827; m. Oct. ———. Oliver F., b. Mar. 30, 1829; m. May 5, 1857; d. May 6, 1878. Harriet A., b. Aug. 22, 1830; m. Dec. 25, 1856; d. Feb. 11, 1871; a dau. is Mrs. Laura J. Garlick; res. Ellenburgh, N. Y. Lucy P., b. Apr. 11, 1832; m. Nov. 14, 1855. Eliza, b. Sept. 20, 1834; d. Jan. 2, 1835. Warren P., b. Feb. 18, 1836; d. June 6, 1857. Laura A., b. May 20, 1838; m. Aug. 15, 1858. Edwin L. Warner, b. May 27, 1835; d. Apr. 2, 1874; res. St. Albans, Vt., P. O. box 270; ch.: 1, Edwina, b. Apr. 7, 1861; d. Apr. 7, 1861. Wm. H. Harrison, b. July 4, 1840; m. July ———. Emeline, b. Apr. 20, 1843; d. July 9, 1845.

2639. viii. LUCRETIA, b. Jan. 11, 1798; m. Perry Knight. Ch.: 1, Mary J., b. Mar. 11, 1831; m. John C. Wade; she d. Mar. 6, 1852; ch.: Geo. H., b. Oct. 12, 1849; m. Perry Knight. Ch.: 1, Mary b. July 1, 1852; res. s. p., Danby, Vt.; is a farmer.

2640. ix. DANIEL, b. Mar. 10, 1808; m. Eunice Spaulding.

2641. x. FREELOVE, b. Jan. 3, 1816; m. in 1836, Perry W. Johnson. She d. Sept. 15, 1893. He was b. July 3, 1815; d. June 6, 1888; res. Danby, Vt.; was a farmer and mason. Ch.: Emily K., b. May 28, 1837; m. Nov. 20, 1855; d. Apr. 3, 1890. Agnes Faxon, b. Jan. 6, 1839; res. Paulet, Vt. Harriett W., b. Jan. 6, 1839; m. Mar. 4, 1865; P. O. Clarendon Springs, Vt. Laura A., b. Jan. 3, 1844; m. Dec. 23, 1868, Wm. H. Lyon; is a farmer; res. Danby Four Corners, Vt.; ch.: Marriette J. Lyon, b. Aug. 22, 1874; m. Dec. 20, 1893, ——— Herrick; res. Danby Four Corners, Vt. m. Dec. 23, 1868, Wm. H. Lyon; is a farmer; res. Danby Four Corners, Vt. Marrietta T., b. Dec. 3, 1854; m. Dec. 9, 1878; P. O. South Wallingford, Vt.

2642. xi. OLIVER, b. Mar. 14, 1813; m. Sarah Parris.

1383. DR. REUBEN FISK (Benjamin, Benjamin, Benjamin, John, John, Phinehas, Thomas, Robert, Simon, Simon, William, Symond), b. Scituate, R. I., May 10, 1765; m. in Danby, Vt., June 2, 1786, Patty Wait of Rhode Island, b. Apr. 2, 1768; d. in Brandt, N. Y., Mar. 1, 1855. He went from Scituate, R. I., with his two brothers, he was a farmer, a hard working man and a worthy member of society. He possesed a peculiar characteristic of healing the sick by laying on of hands. From this he received the appellation of the "stroking doctor." This virtue he possesesd in an eminent degree and was successful in healing and curing many sick people. Dr. Fisk practiced it for many years; was widely and extensively known. He removed to Holland Purchase, N. Y., and died quite advanced in years. He d. in Brandt, N. Y., Apr. 18, 1849; res. Danby, Vt., and Holland Purchase, N. Y.

2643. i. ISRAEL, b. May 2, 1787; m. Lucy Colvin. He was a farmer and settled on the old homestead in Danby, Vt.; was Captain of the local militia; d. 1869.

2644. ii. ABIGAIL, b. Mar. 30, 1789; m. Febin Colvin.

2645. iii. PATTY, b. Apr. 6, 1794; m. in Danby, Vt., George Matteson, b. Oct. 21, 1790. He d. Sept. 16, 1861, in Brandt, N. Y. She d. Apr. 14, 1874. Ch.: 1, Thomas E. P.; res. Wonewoc, Wis. 2, Cleymer G. P.; res. Bolivia, N. Y. 3, Francis, d. s. p. 4, Judah H., d. ——. 5, D. 6, Martha Caul; res. Buffalo, N. Y. 7. Fidelia; a dau. is Irena Bromley; res. Angola, N. Y. 8, Philena, 9, Wm. F., b. Oct. 31, 1813; m. July 18, 1837, Jane Baxter, b. Nov. 13, 1818; res. Angola, N. Y.; he d. June 5, 1864; ch.: 1, Wm. H., b. Nov. 9, 1841; d. unm, Jan. 24, 1890; 2, Thomas B., b. Oct. 15, 1845; m. ——; add. Angola, N. Y.; 3, George W., b. June 18, 1848; m. ——; d. Dec. 1, 1882; s. p.; 4, John Q. A., b. Oct. 5, 1850; m. ——; add. Elgin, Ill.; 5, Albert F., b. Nov. 2, 1861, d. unm. May 22, 1887; 6, Peter W., b. July 17, 1855; d. Jan. 10, 1863; 7, Mary I., b. Nov. 21, 1852; m. Bert Burtis; a ld. Merna, Cus er Co., Neb.; 8, Henry C., b. Nov. 15, 1839; m. Aug. 9, 1863, Olevia V. Anderson, b. July 23, 1842; res. Pierport, Mich.; ch.: Wm. H., b. July 21, 1864; m. May 29, 1890; add. Lake Ann, Mich.; Mary I., b. Aug. 17, 1866; m. Walter Harmer, Oct. 17, 1893; add. Arcadia, Mich.; Thomas G., b. Aug. 29, 1870; unm.; Charles P., b. Sept. 27, 1875; unm.; res. Pierport, Mich.

2646. iv. CHRISTIANA, b. June 15, 1797; m. Orin Taylor.

2647. v. NANCY, b. Sept. 20, 1799; m. Henry Matteson.

2648. vi. LOVICA, b. June 12, 1802; m. Jan. 17, 1823, Albert Matteson; res. Angola, N. Y. He was b. Feb. 6, 1803; d. Oct. 14, 1864. Ch.: Martha M. Matteson Eddy, b. July 11, 1824; m. Apr. 9, 1848; add. Angola, Erie Co., N. Y. Louisa J. Matteson White, b. Sept. 23, 1827; m.; res. Wonewoc, Juneau Co., Wis. Reuben F. Matteson, b. Jan. 7, 1831; d. Apr. 24, 1855. Jay H. Matteson, b. July 2, 1834; m. 1857; add. Bradford, Pa. Lucy Ann Matteson, b. Mar. 6, 1839; d. Mar. 17, 1840.

2649. vii. SALLY, b. June 12, 1802; m. Unite Keith; and 2d, Levi Clark.

2650. viii. LUCY, b. Apr. 11, 1805; m. Ezekiel Eddy.

2651. ix. CELINDA, b. July 19, 1810; m. Albert White; res. Wonewoc, Mich.

2652. x. RHODA, b. Jan. 27, 1808; m. —— Edmunds; res. Rutland, Vt.

2653. xi. REUBEN, b. Jan. 27, 1808; m. Phebe Spaulding.

2654. xii. MARSENA, b. ——; m. Benjamin Colvin. He settled on his father's homestead in Danby, and m. 2d, Elsie Northrup and rev. to Dorset. Ch.: Barbary; m. Russell Streeter; Reuben, Stephen and William.

2655. xiii. VALLERIAH, b. Oct. 8, 1792.

1386. RUFUS FISK (Nathaniel, Benjamin, Benjamin, John, John, Phinehas, Thomas, Robert, Simon, Simon, William, Symond), b. Brandon, Vt., July 30, 1777; m. there Polly Tower. A descendant says Rufus m. Mary Wright, and that she d. aged 44. May have been his first wife. He was a farmer. He d. in Malone, ae. 87; res. Brandon, Vt., and Malone, N. Y.

2656. i. FITZ WILLIAM, b. Oct., 1808; m. Lucy Howe Perry.

2657. ii. ALMON ARNOLD, b. Brandon, Vt.; m. Fannie A. Clough.

2658. iii. POLLY, b. ——; m. Simon Smith. He was b. in Grafton, N. H., and d. in Moira, N. Y.; was a farmer. Ch.: 1, Mary A. Morril, b. Dec. 3, 1828, add. Ashland. N. H. 2, Charity M. Gile, b. Mar. 22, 1830; m. Nov. 1, 1849, James Gile. b. June 5, 1823; d. farmer; res. Santa Clara, N. Y.; ch.: Richard Gile, b. Oct. 1, 1850; Tupper Lake, N. Y.; Lewis W. Gile, b. July 15, 1853; d. Feb. 25, 1872; Loren D. Gile. b. Feb. 20, 1858; East Hartford, Conn.; Louisa Gile, b. Dec. 12, 1868; m. John Fleming, June 15, 1880; P. O. add., Santa Clara, Franklin Co., N. Y. 3, Jessie Buckland, Santa Clara, Franklin Co., N. Y.

2659. iv. CHARITY, b. ——; m. —— Mears; res. Bangor, N. Y.; a son is Horatio Mears; res. St. Regis Falls, N. Y.

1387. BATEMAN FISK (Nathaniel, Benjamin, Benjamin, John, John, Phinehas, Thomas, Robert, Simon, Simon, William, Symond), b. Danby, Vt., Sept.

19, 1780; m. Sarah Winchester. About 1815 his wife died and for a few years he lived with his children. One day he started to a neighboring town with considerable money to make a payment on his farm. Two other men accompanied him, and they returned, but nothing was ever heard of Mr. Fisk afterwards. It is supposed by his relatives that he was murdered for his money. The persons who accompanied him would give no satisfactory answers. Res. Danby and Brandon, Vt., and Batavia, N. Y.

  2660. i. ALANSON, b. ———; m. Lydia Knight.
  2661. ii. IVERS, b. ———; res. Madrid, N. Y.
  2662. iii. NATHANIEL, b. ———; m. Sarah A. Blatchly.
  2663. iv. ELMINA, b. ———; res. Stockholm, N. Y.

  1389. EBER FISK (Nathaniel, Benjamin, Benjamin, John, John, Phinehas, Thomas, Robert, Simon, Simon, William, Symond), b. Danby, Vt., Aug. 10, 1771; m. 1790, Betsey Grattan. She d. in 1795; m. 2d, Oct. 30, 1796, Martha Bigelow, b. May 3, 1781, in Salisbury, Vt.; d. June 25, 1861. He was a blacksmith by trade, but later in life followed farming. He was a prominent member of the Masonic fraternity. Moved to Schroon, N. Y., in 1819. He d. Mar. 7, 1843; res. Brandon, Vt., and Schroon, N. Y.

  2664. i. LEVI, b. Mar. 15, 1809; m. Lois Ann T. Wolcott.
  2665. ii. LYMAN JACKSON, b. July 11, 1805; m. Betsey Stowell.
  2666. iii. LURA, b. May 21, 1811; m. Sept. 5, 1831, William Mills. They had nine children; five died; the living are: Dr. N. J., Helen, Will and Sarah.
  2667. iv. JULIA ANN, b. June 24, 1813; m. Sept. 5, 1830, Orson Richards. He was b. Dec. 13, 1811; d. at Schroon Lake, N. Y., Sept. 4, 1879; was a lumberman. She d. May 14, 1881, at Sandy Hill, N. Y. Ch.: 1, Lydia, b. Sept. 11, 1831; m. Dec. 31, 1849, to John F. Howe. 2, Nelson, b. Aug. 2, 1833; m. Erie White, Sept. 28, 1853; d. May 12, 1854. 3, Eber Richards, b. May 6, 1836; m. Mary E. Culver, Sept. 24, 1857; he is a pulp and paper maker; res. Sandy Hill, N. Y.; ch.: a, Caroline Berry Richards, b. July 23, 1858; b, Nelson James, b. Dec. 14, 1861; c, Frederick Barnard, b. Aug. 1, 1865; d, Orson Culver, b. June 7, 1873; Nelson James d. May 5, 1862; Caroline Berry d. Oct. 2, 1890; Frederick Barnard m. June 12, 1895; lives now Ticonderoga, N. Y.; Orson Culver Richards, Sandy Hill, N. Y. 4, Ralph P. Richards, b. Jan. 2, 1843; m. Francelia J. Harding, Dec. 24, 1862. 5, Martha, b. Dec. 17, 1844; m. Silas B. Ambler, Jan. 9, 1867; d. May 29, 1870; Sandy Hill, N. Y., is the P. O. add.; those who died left no children.
  2668. v. RUFUS, b. Apr. 3, 1820; m. Eliza Wickham.
  2669. vi. EBER, b. Nov. 17, 1815; m. Eleanor Dexter.
  2670. vii. MARTHA, b. Apr. 21, 1818; m. Mar. 17, 1836, David Able; res. Granville, Vt. He was b. June 11, 1811. He enlisted in the civil war, and was killed at Harper's Ferry, Oct. 30, 1862; m. 2d, Cellucious Garfield, b. Oct. 11, 1798; d. Sept. 1, 1877. Both were farmers. She res. Granville, Vt. Ch.: 1, Orlando W. Able, b. Sept. 4, 1837. 2, Elizabeth Adelia, b. Apr. 5, 1840. 3, Lura Ellen, b. Nov. 17, 1848. 4, David Jr., b. Jan. 3, 1852. 5, Orsen Abel, b. May 22, 1854. 6, Levi Fisk Abel, b. Jan. 30, 1859; he res. Schroon Lake, N. Y., and is proprietor of the Hotel Emmet. The daughters live in Joliet; the oldest married Henry P. Van Benthuysen; the other m. John Gosselin; res. 902 Second Ave. 7, Eber, d. young. 8, Rufus, d. young.
  2671. viii. STEPHEN BIGELOW, b. Nov. 25, 1824; m. Nov. 2, 1845, Mary Auree. He d. s. p., in Canada.
  2672. ix. LOIS, b. Sept. 22, 1797; m. Apr. 6, 1814, John Moore. She d. at Waterford, Pa., 1883. Two girls d. young. The boys were Chauncy, who res. in Waterford, and John L., who d. in Plover, Wis.
  2673. x. SOLOMON, b. Feb. 19, 1798; m. Almira Huntley.

2674. xi.   FANNY, b. Oct. 19, 1800; m. Jan., 1821, Cellucious Garfield. She
            d. Feb. 17, 1866. Ch.: Lyman, Silas, Delia, Ann, Martha and
            Elijah.
2675. xii. SAMANTHA, b. May 12, 1803; m. Nov. 11, 1819, William Stow-
            ell. She d. Apr. 1, 1859. They had twelve ch., and all died in
            infancy.
2676. xiii. ANSEL, b. Apr. 25, 1807; d. Feb. 25, 1813.
2677. xiv. MARTHA, b. bef. 1796; d. young.
2678. xv.   BETSEY, b. bef. 1796; d. young.
2679. xvi. ANSON, b. bef. 1796; d. young.

1390. NATHANIEL FISK (Nathaniel, Benjamin, Benjamin, John, John,
Phinehas, Thomas, Robert, Simon, Simon, William, Symond), b. Danby, Vt., Nov.
1, 1766; m. in Leicester, Vt., Hannah Smith, b. 1775; d. in Brandon, June 8, 1864.
He d. Mar. 22, 1827; res. Brandon, Vt.
2680. i.   JOHN, b. June 1, 1803; m. Almira H. Soper.
2681. ii.   HIRAM, b. ———; one of his dau. m. Gilbert Judkins; res. Iron-
            ton, Mich.
2682. iii. NATHANIEL, b. ———.
2683. iv.   HORATIO S., b. ———.
2684. v.   ANNA, b. ———.
2635. vi.   BETSEY, b. Sept. 29, 1798; m. Dec. 2, 1824, Salathiel Patch; res.
            Brandon, Vt. He was b. Mt. Holly, Vt., Mar. 31, 1800; d.
            Dec. 10, 1886. She d. Dec. 31, 1856. Ch.: 1, Henry W., b.
            Mar. 16, 1833; m. Mar. 7, 1860, Nancy Mariah Haff, b. Oct. 13,
            1840; he is a farmer; ch.: Cora May Patch, now Cora May Fay,
            Brandon, Vt.; b. Apr. 22, 1871; m. to Dan C. Fay of Brandon,
            Vt., Apr. 12, 1893; 2, a son, b. 1828; d. about 1830.
2686. vii. ABIGAIL, b. ———.

1391. EDWARD FISK (Nathaniel, Benjamin, Benjamin, John, John, Phinehas, Thomas, Robert, Simon, Simon, William, Symond), b. Danby, Vt., Dec. 3,
1787; m. Emily Granger, of Geneva, N. Y. He was a well-to-do farmer, and at
his death left an estate valued at about $70,000. Res. in Vermont.
2687. i.   JULIUS, b. ———. He went to California at an early day and
            resided there for several years; returned to Cleveland, O., and
            was murdered.
2688. ii.   EDWARD, b. ———. He m. and resided in Chicago, where he
            kept hotel for years. His health failed, and going to Battle
            Creek, Mich., to visit his sister, died there s. p. For some time
            he was private secretary for Hon. Stephen A. Douglas.
2689. iii. MARIAH, b. ———; m. a Methodist clergyman; moved to Battle
            Creek, Mich, and died there.

1393. DAVID FISKE (Nathaniel, Benjamin, Benjamin, John, John, Phinehas, Thomas, Robert, Simon, Simon, William, Symond), b. in R. I. prob., in 1763;
m. ———, Faith Doty. He was b. probably in Rhode Island, went to Danby, Vt.,
where he resided for some time; later was at Danby, Vt., and finally settled on
Bemis Heights, at Stillwater, N. Y. It is said he served in the Revolutionary
war and was given land in Vermont for services performed in that heroic struggle.
He d. Orwell, Vt.; res. Stillwater, N. Y.
2690. i.   GIDEON MEAD, b. Nov. 25, 1786; m. Sophia Wallace and
            Emily Austin.
2691. ii.   WILLIAM, b. Mar. 16, 1788; m. Abigail Razey.
2692. iii. ELIJAH DOTY, b. June 1, 1791; m. Anna Sutphin.
2693. iv.   CHARLOTTE, b. ———.
2694. v.   DAVID, b. ———.
2695. vi.   ASENITH, b. ———.

1396. HON. STEPHEN KNIGHT FISKE (Daniel, Daniel, Benjamin, John,
John, Phinehas, Thomas, Robert, Simon, Simon, William, Symond), b. Scituate,
R. I., Apr. 26, 1789; m. in Scituate, Mar. 2, 1817, Mercy Burlingame, of Clemence,
b. Apr. 8, 1800; d. July 19, 1857. He was left fatherless at the age of 21, and being
the eldest son of a large family, carried on the home farm with the help of some

of the other sons to support the family; at the age of 28 he and a brother bought the farm of the other heirs and he married and staid there until moving to said Hope village; the mother died in 1857. Stephen afterward gave a part of the farm to his youngest son, Almond, and made his home with him for a number of years (never marrying again), then went to live with another son in the same village, remaining there until his death, in his 83d year, being a very well preserved man for one of those years. He died, after a brief illness, of cholera morbus. He was a man held in high esteem by his townspeople, being Representative to State Legislature two years, also town councilman for a long time, besides settling a great many estates and holding many positions of responsibility. He d. Aug. 18, 1871; res. Scituate, R. I.

2696. i.   ALMOND W., b. Aug. 23, 1830; m. Amy Cahoon.
2697. ii. DANIEL, b. May 27, 1817; m. Ruth Burlingame.
2698. iii. CLARINDA ANN, b. Mar. 23, 1818; m. Feb., 1838, Zephaniah Ramsdell; d. Jan. 26, 1885. He was b. in Scituate, R. I., Sept. 24, 1810; res. Olneyville, R. I. She d. Jan. 26, 1885. Ch.: Stephen F., b. Oct. 13, 1840; m. Ruby A. Munsell, of Vermont, July, 1866; res. St. Louis, Mo. Alfred B., b. Dec. 4, 1842; m. May 5, 1866, Hattie M. Simmons, b. Dec. 4, 1847; res. Olneyville, R. I. He is a broker and real estate dealer; ch.: Lucy E., b. Mar 17, 1867; m. Aug. 29, 1888; d. Dec. 3, 1894; John, b. June 14, 1869; m. Sept. 3, 1893; Ada B., b. Mar. 8, 1871. Clara E., b. Aug. 1, 1852; m. Sept. 18, 1877; d. Mar. 6, 1881; her issue: Zephaniah M. Richardson; P. O. add., Brookfield, Mass.
2699. iv. STEPHEN, b. June 21, 1819; m. Cynthia Colvin.
2700. v.   ·EBENEZER, b. Aug. 31, 1821; m. Amy Colvin.
2701. vi. CYNTHIA, b. Aug. 30, 1824; d. July 22, 1828.
2702. vii. ELIZABETH, b. Sept. 3, 1828; d. July 14, 1844.

1397. ISAAC FISKE (Daniel, Daniel, Benjamin, John, John, Phinehas, Thomas, Robert, Simon, Simon, William, Symond), b. Scituate, R. I., Mar. 4, 1792; m. Dec. 31, 1815, Nabby Henry, b. July 4, 1797; d. Jan. 30, 1887. He was a farmer. He d. Nov. 27, 1867; res. South Scituate, R. I..

2703. i.   ASAHEL, b. Mar. 17, 1823; m. Rachel S. Parkhurst.
2704. ii.   JOHN, b. Aug. 12, 1837; m. Nov. 3, 1864, Phebe A. Hopkins; res. s. p. Anthony, R. I.
2705. iii. WILLIAM N., b. Oct. 29, 1819; m. Phebe H. Luther.
2706. iv.   ALFRED, b. Aug. 2, 1821; d. Nov. 20, 1823.
2707. v.   ALFRED, b. July 22, 1825; d. Sept. 17, 1826.
2708. vi.   HARRIET, b. Mar. 6, 1827; d. Jan. 18, 1831.
2709. vii. GEORGE, b. Sept. 16, 1828; d. Oct. 19, 1830.
2710. viii. DELINDA, b. Oct. 25, 1830; d. Mar. 15, 1836.
2711. ix.   ALBERT D., b. Mar. 15, 1833; m. Roxanna S. Johnson.
2712. x.   STEPHEN, b. Dec. 4, 1835; d. Dec. 16, 1857.
2713. xi.   REUBEN HENRY, b. Mar. 1, 1817; m. Sarah Wilbor.
2714. xii. MARIA, b. May 7, 1818; d. Dec. 22, 1861.

1398. DR. HARDIN FISKE (Daniel, Daniel, Benjamin, John, John, Phinehas, Thomas, Robert, Simon, Simon, William, Symond), b. in Scituate, R. I., in 1795; m. Rhoda Orswell. In 1842 he began the practice of homoeopathy, and was very successful. He was a Justice of the Peace, Selectman and held many town offices. He d. May 25, 1871; res. Hope, R. I.

2714¼.i. F. AMEY, b. ——; m. Rev. Wm. T. Anderson. They d. s. p. He was a preacher in the Christian denomination, and edited a temperance paper in New Bedford.
2714½.ii. SARAH RHODES, b. ——; m. Horatio N. Angell, of Providence. Ch.: Arthur Everett and Hardin Fiske, both d. young. He was a real estate dealer.

1400. ARNOLD FISKE (Daniel, Daniel, Benjamin, John, John, Phinehas, Thomas, Robert, Simon, Simon, William, Symond), b. Scituate, R. I., July 26, 1802; m. East Greenwich, Susan R. Miller, b. Oct. 29, 1807; d. Jan. 11, 1880. He was a cordwainer. He d. Aug. 14, 1867; res. East Greenwich, R. I.

2715. i. EGBERT H., b. Mar. 23, 1840; m. Frances Jane Harris.
2716. ii. SUSAN R., b. Sept. 19, 1823; m. Oct. 27, 1844, —— Burlingame; res. Newport, R. I., P. O. box 393. He was b. Oct. 3, 1823; d. Nov. 19, 1870. He was a farmer. Ch.: 1, Lorenzo A., b. Apr. 13, 1847; m. Dec. 25, 1867; P. O. add., Newport, R. I., box 393. 2, Frank Sumner, b. May 5. 1854; d. Mar. 3, 1883, leaving two ch., Mabel Fiske Burlingame and Mary Eliza Burlingame.
2717. iii. SARAH JANE, b. Aug. 18, 1836; m. June 6, 1883, Henry G. Reynolds, b. Sept. 16, 1832; res. s. p., Newport, R. I., box 393.

1401. ABRAHAM FISKE (Jonathan, John, Benjamin, John, John, Phinehas, Thomas, Robert, Simon, Simon, William, Symond), b. Rhode Island, 1762; m. in Providence, R. I., in 1787, Betsey Arnold, b. 1763; d. Watertown, N. Y., 1853. He was born in Rhode Island and when quite young served in the Revolutionary army. He migrated to New York State with his brothers James and Jabez and took up 500 acres of land. For a long time he was engaged in the manufacture of salt. He was much respected for his strict integrity and untiring energies. He d. 1828; res. Sacket's Harbor and Watertown, N. Y.

2718. i. ABRAM, b. Mar. 18, 1797; m. Sarah King.
2719. ii. JOHN, b. in 1789; m. Betsey Morgan.
2720. iii. EPHRAIM J., b. 1794; m. Catherine Chapman.
2721. iv. DANIEL, b. June 10, 1792; m. Sallie D. Brown.
2722. v. WM. RILEY, b. ——; m. Susanna King.
2723. vi. IRA, b. in 1799; m. Joanna Holbrook.
2724. vii. CHARLES, b. ——; m. Lucy Strong; d. in Wisconsin leaving Chester, Anson and Martha.
2725. viii. ANSON, b. ——; m. Sally Holbrook; he was drowned in the Indian river.
2726. ix. BETSEY, b. ——; d. unm.
2727. x. SYBIL, b. ——.
2728. xi. VIANNA, b. ——.

1402. JACOB FISK (Jonathan, John, Benjamin, John, John, Phinehas, Thomas, Robert, Simon, Simon, William, Symond), b. Providence, R. I., in 1774; m. in Lee, N. Y., Sarah Van Dreser, b. 1791; d. Apr. 10, 1832. He was a farmer. He d. Apr. 7, 1841; res. Lee, N. Y.

2729. i. SQUIRE GILBERT, b. Aug. 5, 1816; m. Christiana M. Borst.
2730. ii. LEANDER, b. ——.
2731. iii. ARBA, b. ——.
2732. iv. HANNAH, b. ——.
2733. v. ANDREW J., b. ——. Son Chas. A. res. Oswego Centre, N. Y.

1403. JAMES FISK (Jonathan, John, Benjamin, John, John, Phinehas, Thomas, Robert, Simon, Simon, William, Symond), b. Providence, R. I., Dec. 9, 1777; m. in Junius, N. Y., in 1805, Sally Chapman, b. Nov. 11, 1786; d. 1872. He was a farmer. He d. Sept. 5, 1846; res. Junius, N. Y.

2734. i. HIRAM, b. Oct. 13, 1804; m. at St. Catherines, Canada, in 1842, Sarah Ann Fiske, b. Feb. 25, 1818; d. Feb. 21, 1888, s. p. He is a shoemaker; res. Francisco, Mich.
2735. ii. FRANKLIN, b. 1806.
2736. iii. BARBARA, b. 1808.
2737. iv. JAMES, b. 1811.
2738. v. ELIZA, b. 1814.
2739. vi. SOMER, b. 1817.
2740. vii. JABEZ, b. 1820.
2741. viii. DANIEL, b. 1824.
2742. ix. JOHN, b. Nov. 22, 1818; m. Phebe Sloan and —— ——.

1405. JONATHAN KNIGHT FISK (Jonathan, John, Benjamin, John, John, Phinehas, Thomas, Robert, Simon, Simon, William, Symond), b. near Scituate, R. I., Sept. 7, 1787; m. —— ——; m. 2d, June 11, 1850, Mrs. Anna Atwood; res. Scituate, R. I.

2742-1.i.   REBECCA, b. ———.
2742-2.ii.   JOHN, b. ———.
2742-3.iii.   SAMUEL K., b. June 30, 1826; m. Ann Eliza Bishop.
2742-4.iv.   STERRY, b. ———.
2742-5.v.   ROBY, b. ———.
2742-6.vi,   MARY, b. ———,
2742-7.vii.   SARAH, b. ———.
2742-8.viii. NATHAN, b. ———.
2742-9.ix.   JEREMIAH, b. July 25, 1824; m. Sarah Ann Davis.
2742-10.x.   RACHEL, b. ———.
2742-11.xi.   LOUISA, b. ———.

1406. JABISH FISK (Jonathan, John, Benjamin, John, John, Phinehas, Thomas, Robert, Simon, Simon, William, Symond), b. Lee, N. Y., Jan. 25, 1781; m. there Mar. 7, 1810, Polly Wilkinson, b. Oct. 14, 1794; d. Nov. 13, 1874. He was a farmer. He d. Nov. 25, 1817; res. Lee, N. Y.

2743. i.   MARSHALL HUTCHINSON, b. Nov. 3, 1811; m. in Westernville, N. Y., Mar. 7, 1849, Phebe C. Badgley, b. Aug. 15, 1816; d. Aug. 16, 1884. He was a shoemaker and later a farmer, and d. s. p. Dec. 21, 1893; res. Rome, N. Y.
2744. ii.   MARIA, b. July 19, 1813; m. Feb. 22, 1838, John L. Martin, of Clinton. She d. June 16, 1883. Ch.: Edward L. Martin, res. Clinton, N. Y.; George Martin, res. Clinton, N. Y.; Delia Martin Willard, res. Clinton, N. Y.; John Martin, res. Clinton, N. Y.; Julia Martin Wilkinson, res. Clinton, N. Y.; Newton Martin, res. Clinton, N. Y.
2745. iii. MARIBA, b. Apr. 11, 1817; m. Apr. 12, 1838, Thomas J. Brown. She d. June 15, 1883. Ch.: Edwin F. Brown, res. Somerville, N. J.; Helen Brown Colman; Marshal H. Brown.
2746. iv.   ETHAN BROWN, b. Mar. 15, 1815; m. Adaline Sanborn.

1409. PELEG FISKE (Peleg, John, Benjamin, John, John, Phinehas, Thomas, Robert, Simon, Simon, William, Symond), b. Scituate. R. I., Apr. 25, 1769; m. 1789 Orpha Knight, b. 1770; d. Mar. 22, 1826. He d. July 30, 1821; res. Providence, R. I.

2747. i.   PELEG, b. Jan. 10, 1808; m. Caroline A. Green and Mary B. Graves.
2748. ii.   SOPHIA, b. Apr. 4, 1790.
2749. iii. SAMUEL HENRY, b. May 30, 1792.
2750. iv.   MARIA DYE, b. Oct. 30, 1794.
2751. v.   CLARISSA HARLOW, b. July 12, 1797.
2752. vi.   JOHN, b. Nov. 21, 1799.
2753. vii. PHILLIP, b. Aug. 6, 1802; m. Caroline Briggs.
2754. viii. BETSEY COLLINS, b. May 11, 1805.
2755. ix.   LYDIA SHELDON, b. May 28, 1811.

1410. PHILIP MANCHESTER FISKE (Caleb, John, Benjamin, John, John, Phinehas, Thomas, Robert, Simon, Simon, William, Symond), b. Fiskville, R. I., Mar. 2, 1782; m., Oct. 8, 1817, Eliza Andrews Taylor of Providence, b. Sept. 3, 1797, d. Apr. 17, 1876. He was graduated at Brown; he was a cotton manufacturer. He d. Jan. 31, 1828; res. Fiskville, R. I.

2756. i.   JOHN THOMAS, b. Jan. 30, 1819; m. Abby A. Eddy.
2757. ii.   PHILIP M., b. Sept. 5, 1820; m. Almira F. Balles.
2758. iii. ELIZABETH TAYLOR, b. Dec., 27, 1822; m,. Mar. 6, 1844, Walter C. Simmons. He was b. Sept. 12, 1821; d. Apr. 16, 1887. He was a cotton manufacturer and merchant; res. Providence, R. I. She d. Oct. 23, 1895. Ch.: 1, Walter Cook, Jr., b. Mar. 9, 1845; he res. in Providence; is Commissioner of Dams and Reservoirs. 2, Eliza, b. Mar. 5, 1848; m. Alex. Duncan Chapin; res. Providence, care Webster & Brownell, 20 Market Sq. 3, Kate Fowler, b. Mar. 11, 1856; res. Providence. 4, Henry Bradford, b. May 3, 1861; res. 428 E. 144th St., New York City.

2759. iv. MARY MANCHESTER, b. July 28, 1825; m., Apr. 30, 1846, Robert Manton. He was a merchant; was b. Apr. 12, 1824; d. Sept. 24, 1871; they res. in Providence, R. I. She d. Oct. 20, 1895. Ch.: 1, Annie, b. Nov. 1, 1847; m., Feb. 3, 1872, Henry T. Grant; res. Providence, R. I. 2, Francis, b. Nov. 3, 1851; Providence. 3, Robert Gallup, b. Dec. 5, 1854; m. Emily S. Ballou, and d. Dec. 16, 1894. 4, Jeannie, b. Dec. 28, 1864; m. Feb. 18, 1890, Francis Fisher Flagg; res. 65 Broadway, N. Y. City. 5, Mary, b. Apr. 12, 1864; d. Apr. 28, 1882. 6, Louise Miller, b. June, 1864; d. June 25, 1893.

2760. v. ABBIE WILLIAMS, b. Aug. 21, 1827; m. Robert W. Watson. She d. Aug. 2, 1893; res. Providence. Ch.: 1, ——, b. ——. 2, Matthew, b. ——; res. Providence, R. I.; P. O. box 1553.

1415. JAMES FISK (Job, Job, Benjamin, John, John, Phinehas, Thomas, Robert, Simon, Simon, William, Symond), b. in Rhode Island in 1771; m. there, Dec. 25, 1800, Phoebe Leach, b. Dec. 25, 1781, d. Apr. 14, 1802; m. 2d, 1803, Frances Leach, b. 1786, d. 1812; m. 3d, 1813, Eleanor Pitcher, b. Feb. 2, 1795. He was a farmer. He d. Apr. 9, 1849; res. Booneville, N. Y.

2761. i. JEREMIAH, b. Sept. 17, 1825; m. Margaret Comstock.

2762. ii. JOB W., b. Oct. 4, 1819; m. Emily Pitcher and Sarah A. Pitcher; res. Booneville, N. Y.

2763. iii. MILTON E., b. Dec. 3, 1831; m., Sept. 17, 1860, Anna S. Traffarn; res. Booneville, N. Y.,; one dau., Emma, res. there. He is dead.; was a clergyman. He d. June 9, 1876.

2764. iv. ELIJAH P., b. Sept. 20, 1823; m., Feb. 28, 1865, Harriet P. Jackson. He d. in Booneville, N. Y., Jan. 15, 1890; only child Emma res. there.

2765. v. ACHSAH O., b. Oct. 15, 1821; m., Jan. 6, 1841, Horace Pitcher; m. 2d, Dec. 3, 1851, Stephen Murphy. Pitcher was a farmer, b. Sept. 21, 1819; d. May 27, 1844. Murphy was b. Oct. 17, 1802; was a farmer; d. Apr. 9, 1885. The widow res. Port Leyden, N. Y. Ch.: 1, Mary E., b. Jan. 17, 1842; m. Nov. 13, 1871, James Moore; res. P. L.; she d. July 17, 1876. 2, James F., b. Dec. 17, 1843; m., June 19, 1873, Jennet Tallcott; res. Booneville, N. Y. 3, Stephen H., b. Feb. 27, 1853; m., Aug. 26, 1875, Mary A. Dorn; res. B. 4, Smith D., b. July 13, 1863; m., June 17, 1885, Abbie A. Hovey; res. P. L.

2766. vi. JOHN L., b. Jan. 9, 1804; m. Feb. 6, 1825; d. Mar., 1867; res. ——.

2767. vii. ALVIRA, b. Nov. 6, 1805; m. Jan. 23, 1825, Noah Nelson; res. Booneville, N. Y. She d. Aug. 12, 1870.

2768. viii. CHARLES B., b. Sept. 1, 1806; d. unm. Mar. 1, 1847.

2769. ix. LOUISA, b. Sept. 19, 1808; d. unm. ——.

2770. x. PHOEBE, b. Mar. 11, 1802; d. unm. ——.

2771. xi. CHLOE, b. Feb. 6, 1814; m., Feb. 17, 1835, Fordice M. Rogers. She d. May 22, 1859.

2772. xii. JAMES, b. Jan. 13, 1816; m. Barbary Bellinger, and July 15, 1845, Betsey E. Pool; res. ——. He d. Apr. 9, 1849.

2773. xiii. REBECCA, b. July 5, 1818; m. Jan., 1838, Benjamin H. Nelson, She d. Apr. 29, 1849.

2774. xiv. MELISSA A., b. Nov. 23, 1828; m., May 28, 1851, Sylvester H. Dewey; res. Leyden.

1418. JEREMIAH FISKE (Job, Job, Benjamin, John, John, Phinehas, Thomas, Robert, Simon, Simon, William, Symond), b. in Scituate, R. I., in 1788; m., Jan. 2, 1805, Mary Manchester, b. 1791, d. Booneville, Jan. 1, 1868. He was born in Scituate, R. I. After his marriage he moved to Booneville, N. Y., early in 1800. He was a carpenter by trade and lost his life from the falling of a tree upon him when he was about 42 years of age. He d. Feb. 20, 1830; res. Booneville, N. Y.

2775. i. JOHN MANCHESTER, b. Oct. 1, 1809; m. Eliza A. Burgess and Delia Felt.

2776. ii. ISAAC, b. ———, 1808; m. Elizabeth Morris.
2777. iii. PHILANDER, b. 1805; m. Mary A. Boyd.
2778. iv. MARY, b. ———; m. ———; has one child; res. in Dix., Ill
2779. v. JULIA, b. ———; m. ———; had three ch.: Mary, m. P. B. Ward; Ann, m. J. P. Babcock, res. Booneville, N. Y.; William, res. Dolgeville, N. Y.

1420. JEREMIAH FISKE (Jeremiah, Job, Benjamin, John, John, Phinehas, Thomas, Robert, Simon, Simon, William, Symond), b. Scituate, R. I., Sept. 29, 1766; m. Feb. 18, 1790, Elizabeth Green, b. Mar. 26, 1771; d. in Shaftsbury, Vt., July 4, 1821. He settled in Shaftsbury, Bennington County, Vt., where he died in the 57th year of his age. His wife was Elizabeth Greene. She was the daughter of a Baptist clergyman who lived in Cheshire, Mass., near a place once called Muddy Brook. She died July 4, 1821, about 50 years of age. He d. Oct. 26, 1823; res. Shaftsbury, Vt.
2780. i. RICHMOND, b. Aug. 7, 1804; m. Lurana Matteson.
2781. ii. RUSSEL, b. May 11, 1791. He m., and d. s. p. Oct. 28, 1860.
2782. iii. MIAL, b. Feb. 9, 1798; m. Annie Cumstock Hicks.
2783. iv. ELIZA, b. Sept. 29, 1806; m. Apr. 9, 1829, Jonas Galusha. He was b. Aug. 3, 1805; d. Aug. 12, 1871. She d. Feb. 27, 1877. He was a farmer. Ch.: 1, Richmond F., b. Feb. 5, 1830; res. Shaftsbury Centre, Vt. 2, Ruth Eleanor, b. Aug. 14, 1832; m. Oct. 27, 1853, Columbus Buell, b. Aug. 10, 1829; he was a farmer when married, and for twenty years; miller for ten years; farmer for a few years again; since then various occupations, dealing in real estate, etc., etc.; a republican; res. Batavia, N. Y.; ch.: Edward G. Buell, b. July 2, 1857; Lizzie F. C. Buell, b. Aug. 21, 1860. The address of each is 533 E. Main St., Batavia, N. Y. 3, Francesca C., b. Feb. 12, 1835; d. Mar. 8, 1851. 4, J. Edward, b. Nov. 7, 1838; m. ———; d. Dec. 19, 1864; he was a soldier in the late war and died at Annapolis. 5, Seymour F., b. June 1, 1843; m. Dec. 16, 1869; d. Sept. 3, 1880. 6, Charles E., b. Aug. 7, 1846; m. ———; res. Bennington, Vt. The three deceased had no children.
2784. v. PHEBE, b. ———.
2785. vi. SILENCE, b. Aug. 21, 1793; m. ——— Cole; she d. Nov. 16, 1865.
2786. vii. JEREMIAH, b. July 29, 1802; m. Sarah Matteson.
2787. viii. PELEG, b. Dec. 27, 1808; m. ——— ———.
2788. ix. WARREN G., b. Feb. 15, 1815; m. ——— ———.
2789. x. HANNAH, b. Nov. 9, 1795; m. Dec. 7, 1815, William Johnson, b. Mar. 26, 1796. He d. Oct. 2, 1875. She d. Sept. 17, 1858. Ch.: Betsey, b. Nov. 13, 1821; m. Sept. 20, 1855, Francis L. Childs, b. Sept. 22, 1824; res. Greeley, Colo.; he is a carpenter; ch.: William J., b. Dec. 16, 1857; m. Dec. 17, 1879; res. Greeley.
2790. xi. TRUMAN, b. July 23, 1800; m. Freelove Andrus and Phebe A. Stratton.

1421¼. MIAL FISKE (Jeremiah, Job, Benjamin, John, John, Phinehas, Thomas, Robert, Simon, Simon, William, Symond), b. Scituate, R. I., about 1763; m. there ——— ———. He d. in Rhode Island; res. Scituate, R. I.
2790-1.i. JOHN, b. ———; m. ——— ———.
2790-2.ii. CHARLES, b. ———; m. Mary Leach.

1421¾. MOSES FISK (Jeremiah, Job, Benjamin, John, John, Phinehas, Thomas, Robert, Simon, Simon, William, Symond), b. Rhode Island, 1759; m. ——— ———; res. Cranston, R. I.
2790-3.i. JOB WILBUR, b. 1780; m. Cyrena Atwood.

1422. NOAH FISKE (Noah, Noah, Benjamin, John, John, Phinehas, Thomas, Robert, Simon, Simon, William, Symond), b. Rhode Island; m. ——— ———; res. Scituate, R. I.
2791. i. CALEB, b. ———; m. Isabella Yeaw.

1424. STEPHEN FISK (Moses, Noah, Benjamin, John, John, Phinehas, Thomas, Robert, Simon, Simon, William, Symond), b. Scituate, R. I., Jan. 14, 1784; m. there Jan. 22, 1809, Joanna Colegrove, dau. of William, b. May 1, 1792; d. Mar. 20, 1838. He d. Nov. 30, 1852; res. Scituate and Pawtucket, R. I.

    2792. i.   STEPHEN PERRY, b. Oct. 16, 1813; m. Sarah Marchant.
    2793. ii.   ALFRED W., b. Nov. 24, 1809; d. Nov. 10, 1881.
    2794. iii. CLARISSA, b. ———.
    2795. iv. JOHN P. A., b. ———.
    2796. v.   JOANNA, b. ———.

1429. SOLOMON FISKE (Ichabod E., Ebenezer, Ebenezer, John, John, Phinehas, Thomas, Robert, Simon, Simon, William, Symond)), b. Chazy, N. Y., Feb. 20, 1787; m. Feb. 1, 1808, Sabina Worthington; she d. ———; m. 2d there, Apr. 23, 1809, Catherine Worthington, b. Mar. 12, 1793; d. Sept. 24, 1861. Solomon Fiske was a son of Rev. Ichabod E. Fiske and settled in northern Vermont. Two of his sons graduated at Burlington, in that State, and another, Joel S. Fiske, Esq., was for some years a Judge of Probate, and Register in the United States land office, at Green Bay, Wis. He d. Mar. 23, 1859; res. Chazy, N. Y.

    2797. i.   JOEL S., b. Oct. 24, 1810; m. Charlotte A. Green.
    2798. ii.   SOLOMON N., b. Apr. 11, 1811; m. Mariah North and Mrs. Phebe Ann (Raymond) Fiske.
    2799. iii. ALMOND D., b. Apr. 26, 1818; m. Phebe Ann Raymond.
    2800. iv. MARTHA ELLEN, b. Mar. 15, 1821; m. May 9, 1843, Rev. Newton B. Wood; res. 101 Division Ave., Brooklyn, N. Y. He was b. Nov. 8, 1814; d. Dec. 7, 1876; was a clergyman of the M. E. Church. Ch.: 1, Ellen Amelia, b. Aug. 24, 1844; d. May 19, 1846. 2, Martha Amelia, b. Apr. 6, 1847; m. May 7, 1873, William H. McLenathen, M. D.; d. Mar. 17, 1893. 3, Charles Newton, b. June 26, 1849; m. Oct. 21, 1874, Olive Clark; d. June 14, 1877. 4, Frances Fisk, b. May 18, 1852; m. Apr. 9, 1883, Charles Hagar; P. O. Plattsburg, Clinton County, N. Y. 5, Ellen Juliet, b. Oct. 10, 1854; m. Jan. 19, 1882, Henry Gibbud; P. O. 309 Hickory St., Syracuse, N. Y. 6, Wilbur Fisk, b. July 4, 1858; m. Jan. 13, 1889, Katherine Witler; P. O. 519 W. Walnut St., Springfield, Mo. 7, Lucian Worthington, b. Aug. 7, 1861; P. O. 519 W. Walnut St., Springfield, Mo.
    2801. v.   WILLIAM C., b. 1814; d. s. p. Apr. 12, 1844; was a physician at Oxford, Miss.
    2802. vi. WILBUR WORTHINGTON, b. Sept., 1833; d. s. p. June 5, 1855.
    2803. vii. SABINA A., b. Dec. 24, 1812; m. Dec. 24, 1833, John Scott. Ch.: John O., b. Apr. 24, 1835. Julia E., b. Apr. 30, 1837; d. Apr. 30, 1841. Caroline S., b. Aug. 25, 1839; m. Henry Raymond Jan. 9, 1861. Chas. M., b. Jan. 24, 1842; d. Jan. 11, 1843. Martha E., b. May 5, 1844; m. Geo. T. Corbin June 13, 1865. Winfield S., b. Mar. 30, 1847; d. July 24, 1848. Cornelia, b. Sept. 13, 1849. Chas. A., b. Apr. 18, 1852. Catherine F., b. Apr. 25, 1855. Martha d. at Chazy, N. Y., in 1866. The rest of the family all came to Waupaca, Wis., in 1866, and still live there (1896).

1431. HON. SAMUEL FISK (Ichabod E., Ebenezer, Ebenezer, John, John, Phinehas, Thomas, Robert, Simon, Simon, William, Symond), b. Aug. 16, 1776; m. at Isle La Motte, Vt., Polly Scott, dau. of Henry, b. 1787; d. Jan. 23, 1864. Samuel Fisk, Esq., was born Aug. 9, A. D. 1776; came to Isle La Motte, in the State of Vermont, with his father Ichabod Ebenezer Fisk, a collegiate in the year A. D. 1788, said family being one of the first families who settled said Isle La Motte and located upon the real estate which afterward developed into the Fisk Marble Quarry in said Isle La Motte. Through the opportunities afforded by his father, Samuel became well educated. He had a very peculiar manner of expressing his ideas in language that indicated a large degree of magnanimity which he actually possessed. His sayings and aphorisms were remembered by his contemporaries and handed down to posterity. Those who knew him in his lifetime say that he was never known to distress or to attempt to distress or injure a person no matter how much he might be aspersed, maligned or traduced; retaliation and vindictiveness being foreign to his nature. He was always affable and generous in his impulses. The writer hereof lived a near neighbor to Samuel Fisk fifty years ago and knows that the statements above narrated are true. Samuel Fisk was one of the first organizers of the Methodist Episcopal Church, in said Isle La Motte, and always gave liberally from his large resources for the maintenance of said church during his lifetime. He represented his town in the General Assembly of the State of Vermont in the year A. D. 1802, and gave his town a name at said Legislature, calling it "Vineyard." It bore that name until 1830, when it was changed and named "Isle La Motte." The said Samuel was the first of the Fisk family who originated and developed the noted Fisk Marble Quarry in Isle La Motte. By this industry and his large farming operations he became wealthy and was the richest man in town for a number of years and up to his death, which occurred at Isle La Motte Jan. 25, 1858. In his lifetime he married Polly Scott, and their children's names were Sylvia, Laura, Julia, Ira E., Nelson, Henry S., Hiram C., Sarah and Julius S., who are all deceased. Samuel Fisk was 81 years 5 months and 16 days old at his decease. He d. Jan. 25, 1858; res. Isle La Motte, Vt.

2804. i. HIRAM C., b. Aug. 16, 1818; m. Cynthia Clark.

2805. ii. IRA E., b. May 29, 1810; m. Louisa Brownson.

2806. iii. SYLVIA, b. Oct. 30, 1804; m. Jan. 5, 1824, Jared Pike; he d. Dec. 23, 1858; res. Ellenburgh, N. Y. Ch.: 1, Wm. S., b. Oct. 27, 1825; m. Amanda Reynolds 1851; ch.: Thomas H., b. Mar., 1852; Louisa E., b. Oct., 1856; Cynthia F., b. 1858; Hiram F., b. ———. 2, Amasa H., b. Jan. 28, 1828; m. Mary Ashline, 1854; six boys. 3, Benj. Franklin, b. Nov. 9, 1830; m. Cornelia Hartford Jan. 5, 1865. 4, Mary P., b. Sept. 24, ———; m. Wm. Reynolds 1853; two ch. 5, Calvin H., b. Oct. 31, 1834; m. Jennie Angell 1859; one dau.; was Captain in 153d Regiment, New York Volunteers. 6, Laura F., b. May 22, 1840; m. Michael Dewell 1859; three ch. 7, Elliott, b. Jan. 7, 1848.

2807. iv. LAURA, b. July 18, 1806; m. Thomas Hodgson; she d. s. p. Dec. 13, 1861, at Lacale, C. E., his second wife.

2808. v. NELSON W., b. Apr. 23, 1814; m. Anette W. Fisk.

2809. vi. HENRY S., b. June 25, 1816; m. Mary Ann Sewell.

2810. vii. JULIA DIANA, b. Feb. 26, 1805; m., Feb. 8, 1830, John Miller Johnson, b. Aug. 4, 1840. He d. Apr., 1852. She d. July 7, 1861; res. Brasher, N. Y. Ch.: 1, Samuel Johnson, b. Apr. 10, 1831; m. Wealthia Hall Aug. 2, 1856; d. Nov. 15, 1893. 2, Theron, b. Jan. 10, 1833; m. 1866. 3, Henry F., b. Apr. 27, 1835; m. Mary Clark Feb. 16, 1864; P. O. add. Northfield, Minn.; ch.: a, Annie Cynthia Johnson Burlon, b. Mar. 8, ———; m. Mar. 8, 1887; P. O. add. Brasher, N. Y.; b, Wyman Henry, b. Apr. 24, 1868; d. ———; c, Leonie Ellen, b. Dec. 2, 1869; m. Sept. 27, 1888; P. O. add. Great Falls, Mont.; d, William Agustus, b. Aug. 20, 1872; d. ———; e, Lydia Mabel, b. June 8, 1880; f, Myra Alta, b. Sept. 13, 1882. 4, Nelson, b. Apr. 1, 1837; m. Dec. 31, 1866; d. ———. 5, Ellen P., b. Feb. 16, 1839; m., Oct. 10, 1857, Alonzo Eldredge; P. O. add. Brasher, N. Y. 6, Sarah, b. Oct. 10, 1844; d. Mar. 31, 1854; Fred M. Johnson, son of Nelson, P. O. add. Plattsburgh, N. Y.; Asa Johnson, son of Samuel, P. O. add. St. Paul, Minn.

2811. viii. JULIUS S., b. June 15, 1826; m. Fannie C. Fisk.

2812. ix. SARAH, b. Apr. 30, 1824; m., Aug. 24, 1849, Rev. A. F. Fenton. Ch.: Maggie F., b. Oct., 1851. George W., b. Sept. 11, 1853; m. and res. Broadalbin, N. Y. Sarah d. in Broadalbin, N. Y., Apr. 5, 1864.

1432. IRA FISKE (Ichabod E., Ebenezer, Ebenezer, John, John, Phinehas, Thomas, Robert, Simon, Simon, William, Symond), b. Isle La Motte, Vt., Oct. 4, 1778; m. there Feb. 4, 1810, Chloe Holcomb, b. Aug. 30, 1781, at Granby, Conn.;

d. Mar. 28, 1850, at Chazy. Ira Fisk was a son of Ichabod E. Fisk, who moved with his family to Isle La Motte, Grand Isle Co., Vt., when his father was a boy. He was born in Conn. Was married to Chloe Holcomb. Had five children, one girl and four boys. Moved to Chazy, Clinton Co., N. Y., 1813. He was industrious, temperate, a good calculator, of sound judgment, fleshy, good looking, and acquired a good property. He was a farmer. He and his wife became religious, and drew around the children such associates, he being a class leader in the M. E. Church from earliest recollection. He, his wife and seven others left the M. E. Church and joined in forming the First Wesleyan Methodist Church in that town in 1843, which was organized by their son. He remained a worthy member until death, in 1852. His wife died the year previous. He d. Apr. 4, 1851; res. Chazy, N. Y.

2813.   i.   OLIVE MARIA, b. Mar. 24, 1814; m. Jan. 27, 1837, Charles Bishop Minkler; res. Ft. Covington, N. Y. He was b. July 16, 1811; is a retail grocer. Ch.: Miles Fiske, b. Apr. 6, 1839, Ft. Covington, N. Y. Phebe Ann, b. Aug. 9, 1842, Ft. Covington, N. Y. Wilber Solomon, b. Jan. 10, 1846, Ft. Covington, N. Y. Miles, m. Apr. 31, 1865, Flora Carpenter, present add. Ft. Covington, N. Y. Phebe, m. Jan. 12, 1863, Elam C. Burch; present add. Ft. Covington, N. Y. Wilbur's present add. 1021 Market St., San Francisco, Cal.

2814.   ii.   MILES, b. Oct. 26, 1815; m. Laura Newell and Mrs. Betsey (Tuttle) Newell.

2815.   iii.   NEWELL WILBUR, b. Oct. 5, 1817; m. Maranda Hansing and Elvira Ransom.

2816.   iv.   SOLOMON WOODBRIDGE, b. Jan. 7, 1824; m., May 25, 1852, Martha Doane at Chazy. She d. Nov. 10, 1857; m. 2d, Nov. 10, 1858, Frances Darling; one son, Almond D., b. Aug. 27, 1865.

2816½.v.   IRA WOODARD, b. Jan. 7, 1824; m. Martha Potter.

1433. EBENEZER FISK (Ichabod E., Ebenezer, Ebenezer, John, John, Phinehas, Thomas, Robert Simon, Simon, William, Symond), b. Mar. 31, 1781; m. Feb. 25, 1806, Ida Landing; d. in 1839. He d. Aug. 31, 1824; res. Dickinson, N. Y.

2817.   i.   DAVID L., b. Nov. 4, 1806; m. and was probably drowned.

2818.   ii.   LUCINIA, b. Mar. 18, 1810; m. Mar. 3, 1825, Peter Whitney. She d. 1839. Ch.: Hellen, b. Jan. 25, 1829; m. Dexter Hutchins; she was living in 1866 in National, Clayton Co., Ia.; ch.: Clayton, b. Jan. 6, 1848; also two others. Barney, b. June 9, 1832; m. Jane Wilbur. Allen C., b. Dec. 20, 1837; d. Sept. 30, 1860.

2819.   iii.   HIRAM, b. Oct. 15, 1808; m. Diantha Russell.

2820.   iv.   LAVINIA, b. Oct. 11, 1812; m. Dr. Dudley Waller, 1832. Had two children. She d. 1842. Dr. Waller lived in 1866 at No. 77 Christopher St., N. Y.

2821.   v.   ORRELLIA, b. Oct. 25, 1813; m. Wm. R. Davenport, July 13, 1830; m. Eliza Deyso, July 17, 1852. Ch.: Warren, b. Sept. 18, 1832; d. May 19, 1862. Chloe L., b. Jan. 12, 1834. I. Sabina, b. Oct. 12, 1835; d. Nov. 21, 1852. Cynthia L., b. May 9, 1837; m. Cyrus P. Whitney Sept. 3, 1865. Aurilla F. Davenport lived (1866) in West Bangor, Franklin Co., N. Y.

2822.   vi.   IDA MARIAH, b. Nov. 21, 1815; m. Robt. Hay. Oct. 30, 1840, at Moira, N. Y., but res. at Moores, Clinton, Co., N. Y.; she d. Sept. 13, 1855. Ch.: Rodney, b. Dec. 4, 1844; d. Mar. 12, 1850. Ida, b. Oct. 23, 1847. Hellen, b. Jan. 22, 1849; d. June 27, 1858.

2823.   vii.   HARRIET, b. July 24, 1817; m. Rev. Jno. Wallace July 14, 1839. Ch.: Benj. Nevin, b. June 8, 1840. Sarah Eugenia, b. Oct. 4, 1841. Jno. L., b. Dec. 6, 1843; d. June 10, 1862. Spencer Alex, b. Feb. 22, 1845, Wm. Hawkins, b. Dec. 2, 1846. Mary Orr, b. Feb. 11, 1848. Ebenezar, b. Mar. 28, 1851. Martha b, Oct. 21, 1854. Marriett Jos., b. Mar. 11, 1856.

1439. CLAUDIUS LUCIUS FISK (John, Ebenezer, Ebenezer, John, John, Phinehas, Thomas, Robert, Simon, Simon, William, Symond), b. Vermont; m. Jemima W. Knapp; d. Nelsonville, Ohio, ae. 96. He d. in Ashley, Ohio, ae. 65; res. Nelsonville, Ohio.

2824. i. PEARLEY B., b. Aug. 6, 1836; m. Lois F. Thornburg.
2825. ii. LUCIUS K., b. ———; res. Nelsonville, Ohio.

1443. SOLOMON FISK (Solomon, Ebenezer, Ebenezer, John, John, Phinehas, Thomas, Robert, Simon, Simon, William, Symond), b. in Southington, Conn., July 20, 1798; m. in Cheshire, Conn., Mar. 5, 1821, Lavincy Newton, b. 1801; d. Cheshire, Conn., in spring of 1885. He d. in 1884; res. Cheshire, Conn.

2826. i. JAMES H., b. Nov. 10, 1833; m. Queen V. Whitcomb.
2827. ii. ELMER, b. ———; res. Grass Valley, Cal.
2828. iii. SARAH J., b. Oct. 13, 1835; m. June 4, 1861, Capt. Roswell M. Waterman; res. 18 Meridian St., New London, Conn.
2829. iv. CAROLINE, b. Mar. 8, 1824; m. Jan. 12, 1845, Joseph Lewis; res. New London, Conn.; had one child which died.
2830. v. AUGUSTUS N., b. Mar. 31, 1822; drowned Feb. 26, 1848.
2831. vi. SILAS W., b. July 2, 1826; m. Julia A. Edgcomb.
2832. vii. JOHN WHITING, b. Apr. 7, 1828; m. Oct. 15, 1849, M. B. Latham; he d. Mar. 9, 1853, in Georgetown, Cal.
2833. viii. MARY E., b. Feb. 24, 1830; m. Sept. 27, 1849, Reuben R. Bristol; res. Cheshire, Conn. Ch.: 1, Walter R., b. Oct. 18, 1851; res. Meriden, Conn. 2, John N., b. July 26, 1853. 3, James F., b. Oct. 23, 1855. 4, Joseph L., b. Oct. 23, 1855. 5, Cornelia B., b. Sept. 15, 1860.
2834. ix. SAMUEL, b. Jan. 28, 1838; d. May, 1838.
2835. x. SOLOMON, b. Feb. 28, 1832; d. May, 1832.

1453. JOHN FISKE (John, John, John, John, John, Phinehas, Thomas, Robert, Simon, Simon, William, Symond), b. in Connecticut about 1764; m. Elizabeth Wright (see History of Madison County, New York); res. Eaton, N. Y.

2836. i. WRIGHT, b. ———; left descendants in Allegany County, New York.
2837. ii. ELIZABETH, b. ———.
2838. iii. MAHALEY, b. ———; a descendant is Edward Gale; res. Wellsville, N. Y.
2839. iv. HARVEY, b. ———.
2840. v. JOHN, b. Aug. 16, 1796; m. Mildred A. Stevens.
2841. vi. POLLY, b. ———; a descendant is Edward Hewitt, of Waterville, N. Y.
2842. vii. SARAH, b. Nov., 1800; m. Jobe Omans. She d. 1828. Ch.: 1, Betsey, d. ———. 2, Riley, d. Apr. 9, 1848. 3, Morris, b. Jan. 4, 1822; m. July 9, 1844, Nancy Foster, b. Apr. 25, 1825; res. West Eaton, N. Y.; ch.: a, Merril D. Omans, b. Apr. 9, 1845; m. June, 1868; d. Oct. 26, 1886, Cortland, N. Y. b, Sarah S. Omans, b. Nov. 19, 1848. c, Elsie L. Omans, b. Nov. 29, 1850; m. Mar. 17, 1869; present name Mrs. L. Hamilton.
2843. viii. ALTA, b. ———; a descendant is Porter Omans, of West Eaton, N. Y.

1454. JOHN FISKE (Bazaleel, John, John, John, John, Phinehas, Thomas, Robert, Simon, Simon, William, Symond), b. Middletown, Conn., Aug. 5, 1771; m. Aug. 10, 1793, Polly Merrill, of Killingworth, Conn.; d. Oct. 21, 1837; m. 2d, Dec. 25, 1838, Olive Cone, of Middletown; she d. s. p. in Mar., 1868. He was Town Clerk fifty years, Treasurer twenty-four, and Clerk of the County and Supreme Court about the same time. He d. Feb. 15, 1847; res. Middletown, Conn.

2844. i. JOHN JAY, b. Jan. 22, 1794; m. ——— Stetson and Mrs. ——— Eaton.
2845. ii. POLLY, b. Mar. 11, 1795; m. 1817 John Bound. He d. in Montgomery Ala., about 1835. She d. in Windsor, Vt., in Aug., 1874. Ch.: 1, John Fiske, b. Mar., 1819; founder of Bound &

Co., bankers, 36 Wall St., New York, cit. 1860—cit. 1890; m. Hannah Johnson, of Middletown; res. Hackensack, N. J.; ch.: Walter Bound, b. 1846, of Hackensack, N. J.; and Charles Fiske Bound, b. 1848, of New York City. 2, Mary Fiske, b. June 21, 1821; m. Sept. 4, 1840, Edmund Brewster Green, b. Jan. 3, 1815, at Smyrna, Del. He was the son of Humphreys Green, by his second wife, Hannah Heaton. "My father was born Jan 3, 1815; studied at Wilbraham Academy, Mass.; was in the class of 1837 at Wesleyan University, Middletown; studied law for a while; was associated for a short time with J. G. Whittier in the editing of a paper at Hartford. I think it was called New England Review. Afterward edited a short lived paper in New York, called Saturday Review; was private secretary to Henry Clay; died in Panama July 11, 1852." She m. 2d. Hon. Edwin Wallace Stoughton, of New York, Minister to Russia 1877-79. He was born at Windsor, Vt., in 1817; practiced law in New York until his death Jan. 7, 1882. He was appointed Minister to Russia by President Hayes in 1877; resigned and came home in 1879 on account of ill health; ch.: Edmund Fiske, b. Mar. 30, 1842 (in 1855, by act of Connecticut Legislature, took the name of great-grandfather, but restored the final e.—JOHN FISKE); m. at Appleton Chapel, Harvard University, Sept. 6, 1864, Abby Morgan Brooks, b. Aug. 4, 1839; ch.: Maud Fiske, b. Jamaica Plains, Mass., July 21, 1865. Harold Brooks Fiske, b. Cambridge, May 13, 1867. Clarence Stoughton Fiske, b. Cambridge, May 10, 1869; m. to Margaret Gracie Higginson, in New York City, June 1, 1895; add. 112 Brattle St., Cambridge, Mass. Ralph Browning Fiske, b. Cambridge, Nov. 16, 1870. Ethel Fiske, b. Cambridge, July 22, 1872. Herbert Huxley Fiske, b. Cambridge, Aug. 20, 1877. All except C. S. have same address. John Fiske, author, was born in Hartford, Conn., Mar. 30, 1842. He is the only child of Edmund Brewster Green, of Smyrna, Del., and Mary (Fiske) Bound, of Middletown, Conn. The father was editor of newspapers in Hartford, New York and Panama, where he died in 1852, and his widow married Hon. Edwin W. Stoughton, of New York, in 1855. The son's name was originally Edmund Fiske Green. In 1855 he took the name of his maternal great-grandfather, John Fiske. He lived at Middletown during childhood and until he entered Harvard, where he was graduated in 1863. He was graduated at the Harvard Law School in 1865, having been already admitted to the Suffolk bar in 1864, but has never practiced law. His career as author began in 1861, with an article on "Mr. Buckle's Fallacies," published in the "National Quarterly Review." Since that time he has been a frequent contributor to American and British periodicals. In 1869-71 he was university lecturer on philosophy at Harvard; in 1870 instructor in history there, and in 1872-79 assistant librarian. On resigning the latter place, in 1879, he was elected a member of the board of overseers, and at the expiration of the six years' term was re-elected in 1885. Since 1881 he has lectured annually on American history at Washington University, St. Louis, Mo., and since 1884 has held a professorship of American history at that institution, but continues to make his home at Cambridge. He lectured on American history at University College, London, in 1879, and at the Royal Institution of Great Britain in 1880. Since 1871 he has given many hundred lectures, chiefly upon American history, in the principal cities of the United States and Great Britain. The largest part of his life has been devoted to the study of history; but at an early age inquiries into the nature of human progress led him to a careful study of the doctrine of evolution, and it was as an expounder of this doc-

John Distler

trine that he first became known to the public. In 1871 he arrived at the discovery of the causes of the prolonged infancy of mankind, and the part played by it in determining human development; and the importance of this contribution to the Darwinian theory, now generally admitted, was immediately recognized by Darwin and Spencer. His published books are: "Tobacco and Alcohol" (New York, 1868); "Myths and Myth-Makers" (Boston, 1872); "Outlines of Cosmic Philosophy, based on the Doctrine of Evolution" (2 vols., London, 1874, republished in Boston); "The Unseen World" (Boston, 1876); "Darwinism, and Other Essays" (London, 1879; new and enlarged edition, Boston, 1885); "Excursions of an Evolutionist" (Boston, 1883); "The Destiny of Man Viewed in the Light of His Origin" (Boston, 1884); "The Idea of God as affected by Modern Knowledge" (Boston, 1885); and "American Political Ideas Viewed from the Standpoint of Universal History" (New York, 1885); "Critical Period of American History" (1888); "Beginnings of New England" (1889); "The War of Independence, for Young People" (1889); "Civil Government in the United States" (1890); "American Revolution," 2 vols. (1891); "Discovery of America," 2 vols. (1892); "History of the United States, for Schools" (1894). All the above published by Houghton, Mifflin & Co. Also "Edward Livingston Youman's Interpreter of Science for the People" (New York, D. Appleton & Co., 1894); "A Japanese Translation of The Destiny of Man" was published at Tokio in 1893.

He received degree of doctor of letters from the University of Pennsylvania, 1894; doctor of laws, Harvard University, 1894; has been a fellow of the American Academy of Sciences, member of the American Oriental Society, American Folk-Lore Society, British Folk-Lore Society, Massachusetts Historical Society, Military Historical Society of Massachusetts, Essex Institute, American Geographical Society, American Antiquarian Society, Historical Societies of Virginia, Missouri, California, Oneida County, N. Y.; was president of the Boylston Club, a club of singers in Boston, from 1877 to 1882.

2846. iii. FRED'K REDFIELD, b. July 14, 1798; d. at sea Oct. 6, 1836.
2847. iv. WM. HENRY, b. June 8, 1800; d. Sept. 6, 1836.
2848. v. CHARLES, b. May 20, 1803; d. Feb. 26, 1804.
2849. vi. DAUGHTER, b. and d. Mar. 29, 1805.
2850. vii. MARGARET, b. Dec. 15, 1810; d. Jan. 1, 1827.
2851. viii. HENRY WM., b. Apr. 28, 1813.
2852. ix. CHARLES BEZALEEL, b. June 14, 1806.
2853. x. DAUGHTER, b. and d. Oct. 9, 1809.

1454-4. LEONARD FISKE (John, Benjamin, John, John, John, Phinehas, Thomas, Robert, Simon, Simon, William, Symond), b. Sept. 6, 1787; m. Lucy Billings of Royalton, Vt.; res. East Bethel, Vt.

2853-1.i. BENJAMIN GOODRICH, b. ———; m. Nov. 22, 1837, Delia Electa Chandler, b. Nov. 13, 1817; d. Sept. 11, 1839, in East Bethel. Ch.: Wm. Leonard, b. Mar. 19, 1839; m. Eliza Barlow. She d. Mar., 1870. He d. also in Mar., 1870, leaving son Leonard, b. in 1867.
2853-2.ii. LUCY, b. ———.
2853-3.iii. JOHN, b. ———.
2853-4.iv. OLIVE, b. ———.
2853-5.v. MARY, b. ———.

1454-5. ELDER HORACE FISK (John, Benjamin, John, John, John, Phinehas, Thomas, Robert, Simon, Simon, William, Symond), b. Apr. 17, 1790, Ellington, Conn.; m. in Albany, N. Y., Oct. 4, 1827, Mary A. Adams, of Albany, N. Y., b. May 24, 1806; d. Jan. 6, 1889. Horace Fisk(e) was born April 17, 1790. In 1827 he married Mary Adams, who was born in Mass., May 24, 1806. Of his early life there is no record. He told his children that when traveling on business through Canada, he was imprisoned in a guard-house for some time on suspicion of being a spy, probably during the war of 1812. He also told of carrying on business in Albany, N. Y. He was a hotel keeper many years in Waterford, and later had charge of the express business between Waterford and Troy, until he died. His integrity was such that for years he carried an immense amount of money between the Waterford and Troy banks without the requirement of written receipts. He was an elder in the Presbyterian Church, which office he held for thirty years. He d. Dec. 24, 1864; res. Waterford, N. Y.

2853-6.   i. JOHN B., b. Oct. 10, 1828; m. Mary Gregory and ——— ———.
2853-7. ii. MARY BRITTON, b. Dec. 21, 1831; m. Apr. 4, 1859, Albert C. Bridges; res. 3018 Wells St., Milwaukee. He was b. Mar. 18, 1831; is a merchant of Milwaukee, Wis. They have had four ch., viz.: a, Mary Stewart Bridges, b. Apr. 1, 1860; m. Jan. 27, 1886, George Lord Graves (his second wife); they have one son, Harold Bridges Graves, b. June 27, 1888. b, Mabel Fidelia Bridges, b. Sept. 11, 1863; m. Sept. 22, 1887, George A. Messer of Milwaukee, Wis. c, Henry Flint Bridges, b. Dec. 24, 1864; d. Sept. 12, 1869. d, Hattie Fiske Bridges, b. Apr. 7, 1874.
2853-8. iii. MARTHA AUGUSTA, b. Mar. 16, 1834; d. Aug. 24, 1865.
2853-9. iv. HARRIET CAROLINE, b. Jan. 26, 1837; d. June 24, 1837.
2853-10. v. HARRIET ANNA, b. Sept. 26, 1844; m. Mar. 16, 1870, Wm. Wirt Watkins; res. 175 Fifteenth St., Milwaukee. He was b. Oct. 16, 1833. Is retired.
2853-11. vi. HORACE, b. June 10, 1850; d. Feb. 21, 1852.
2853-12. vii. SARAH CRAMER, b. July 21, 1839.

1472.   REV. EBENEZER FISK (David, Ebenezer, Ebenezer, William, William, William, John, William, Robert, Richard, William, Symond), b. Boscawen, N. H., Oct. 1, 1802; m. at New Hampton, N. H., June 12, 1828, Miriam Atwood Gordon, b. June 12, 1807; d. June 17, 1880. Ebenezer Fisk, b. Oct. 1, 1802; d. Oct. 5, 1890, was born in Boscawen, taken at six months to New Hampton N. H.; was for a short time a student in the (old) New Hampton Institution. He was a farmer; licensed to preach, 1828, and ordained to the Free Baptist ministry on Nov. 4, 1830. He preached in N. H. with power for fifty years. He was a successful evangelist as well as pastor. He was State Representative (in Legislature) for five terms. President of corporation of New Hampton Institution. He observed his golden wedding with 400 guests. He was greatly esteemed by all who knew him. Rev. E. Fisk closed his life in the home (for ten years) of his son Daniel; died at Jackson, Mich., and is buried in Hillsdale, Mich. He d. Oct. 5, 1890; res. New Hampton, N. H., and Jackson, Mich.

2854.   i. OLIVER BLAKE, b. July 14, 1832; d. Oct. 25, 1861. Oliver Blake Fisk was the genealogist and biographer of the family in so far as anything has ever been done. His MSS. survive and are in the hands of his brother. The substance of the genealogical side has been given in the preceding pages. The biography of Rev. David Fisk is quite full, so also the early and middle life of Rev. Ebenezer Fisk. Oliver died of consumption.
2855. ii. DAVID MARKS, b. July 29, 1834; d. Oct. 12, 1854.
2856. iii. DANIEL MOSES, b. Apr. 10, 1846; m. Alma H. Moore.

1484.   DAVID FISK (Ephraim, Ebenezer, Ebenezer, William, William, William, John, William, Robert, Simon, Simon, William, Symond), b. Stratford, Vt., Oct. 24, 1814; m. at Buchanan, Mich., Jan. 7, 1838, Lucinda Platts, b. May 19, 1819; d. Aug. 3, 1855. He was a farmer, but learned the carpenter's trade, which he followed occasionally. He d. Jan. 29, 1878; res. Buchanan, Mich.

2857.   i. BENJAMIN F., b. May 21, 1840; m. Amanda H. Batchelor.
2858. ii. SARAH ELLEN, b. May 7, 1842; m. Mar. 27, 1866, B. F. Galeener, b. Apr. 7, 1838; d. Feb. 23, 1873; m. 2d, Mar. 27, 1875, A. B. Downing; res. Galien, Mich. He was b. Mar. 16, 1834. Ch.: 1, Nellie Elizabeth Galeener, b. Aug. 26, 1867; m. Sept. 5, 1886;

present name, Nellie Keefer, P. O. Galien, Mich. 2, Bertha
Lucinda Downing, b. Aug. 11, 1880; Galien, Berrien Co., Mich.
3, Alice Mary Downing, b. May 23, 1888; Galien, Berrien Co.,
Mich.

2859. iii. MARY ALICE, b. Jan. 7, 1844; m. Apr. 2, 1864, Miles Crippen;
res. Alton, Kas. He was b. Apr. 1, 1843. Ch.: 1, Arthur W.,
b. Jan. 14, 1865; m. June 24, 1888; Fairfield, Ill. 2, Clarence
E., b. May 24, 1867; m. May 5, 1891; Indianapolis, Ind. 3,
Roland F., b. Aug. 23, 1871; d. Feb. 14, 1872. 4, Adelbert M.,
b. Apr. 22, 1873; Fairfield, Ill. 5, Alice I., b. Dec. 1, 1879; d.
Mar. 27, 1880. 6, Crestus L., b. Sept. 23, 1881; Alton, Kas.

2860. iv. MARTHA M., b. Mar. 19, 1846; m. June 28, 1868, James M.
Swank; res. Galien. He was b. July 4, 1845. Ch.: 1, Richard
E. Swank, b. Aug. 20, 1869; P. O. add., Galien, Berrien Co.,
Mich. 2, Orrilla Swank. b. June 13, 1875; d. Dec. 16, 1881. 3,
Olive Swank. b. May 26, 1886; Galien, Berrien Co., Mich.

2861. v. ORRILLA A., b. Dec. 13, 1849; m. Sept. 16, 1866, Sutliff Bates;
res. Taylor, Ore. He was b. Sept. 23, 1841. Is a farmer. Ch.:
1, Anna L. Bates, b. July 12, 1867; m. Nov. 12, 1885; present
add., Anna L. Thomas, Alton, Osborne Co., Kas. 2, Etta M.
Bates, b. Mar. 31, 1869; m. Dec. 25, 1884; present add., Etta M.
Bell, Taylor, Ore. 3, Frank E. Bates, b. Dec. 27,
1871; Taylor, Ore. 4, Alta L. Bates, b. Apr. 8, 1874; Taylor,
Ore. 5, Harley A. Bates, b. Mar. 6, 1889; Taylor, Ore.

2862. vi. ALEXIS A., b. June 7, 1853; d. Feb. 13, 1872.

2863. vii. CRESTUS L., b. Jan. 1, 1855. He is a farmer, unm.; res. Seneca,
So. Dak.

2864. viii. ALZINA, b. Oct. 30, 1847; d. Sept. 24, 1851.

1485. JOSEPH MORSE FISK (Ephraim, Ebenezer, Ebenezer, William,
William, William, John, William, Robert, Simon, Simon, William, Symond), b.
Strafford, Vt., Sept. 10, 1811; m. in Sharon, Mar. 17, 1835, Phebe Miller Dens-
more, b. Apr. 18, 1814; d. Aug. 9, 1892. He was an invalid the most of his life
from a spinal complaint. He worked for several years in the factories in Lowell,
Mass.; removed to a farm in Tunbridge, Vt., about 1853, and in 1864 he removed
to Kansas, where he followed farming till his health compelled him to abandon it. He died while on a visit to his son in Freeborn, Minn. He d. Feb. 25,
1879; res. Kansas.

2865. i. WILBUR, b. June 7, 1839; m. Angelina S. Drew.

2866. ii. MARY JANE, b. Aug. 30, 1836; d. Oct. 8, 1853.

2867. iii. SARAH ANN, b. Oct. 6, 1837; d. Oct. 29, 1863.

2868. iv. JOSEPH FRANKLIN, b. June 22, 1841; d. May 27. 1864.

2869. v. EPHRAIM, b. Sept. 27, 1847; killed by lightning, Sept. 6, 1867.

2870. vi. PHILENA, b. Feb. 14, 1851; m. Mar., 1870, E. W. Pomeroy;
res. Northcott, Kas.

2871. vii. PLINEY H., b. Dec. 14, 1854; m. Emma Lampman, Alice Calahan and Charlotte Scoville.

1486. DEA. EPHRAIM FISK (Ephraim, Ebenezer. Ebenezer, William,
William, William, John, William, Robert, Simon, Simon, William, Symond), b.
Strafford, Vt., Sept. 10, 1811; m. in Thetford, Vt., June 20, 1840, Elizabeth B. Tres-
cott, b. Dec. 6, 1812; d. June 20, 1875. He is a farmer. Res. s. p. Geneva, Kas.

1493. RICHARD FISK (Ephraim, Ephraim, Ebenezer, William, William,
William, John, William, Robert, Simon, Simon, William, Symond), b. Concord,
N. H., Apr. 6, 1789; m. at New London, Rhapsyme Sargent, b. Nov. 20, 1797; d.
Dec. 20, 1838; m. 2d, —— Sargent. They were from New London, N. H. He
was a blacksmith. He d. Nov. 5, 1847; res. Contoocook, N. H.

2872. i. MARY ANN, b. Mar. 22, 1821; m. Nov. 2, 1842, Lorenzo Merrill; res. Burnett, Wis. He was b. June 21, 1818; d. Aug. 15,
1895. He was a farmer. Ch.: George Fisk Merrill, b. Feb.
17, 1847; m. Oct. 13, 1875; Ashland, Wis. Sarah Jane Merrill,
b. Jan. 12, 1849; m. Nov. 26, 1868, —— Cole; add.,
Burnett, Dodge Co., Wis. Frank H. Merrill, b. June 17, 1850;

m. Nov. 18, 1874; Pasadena, Cal. Edgar P. Merrill, b. Oct. 14, 1854; m. Oct. 13, 1886; Burnett, Dodge Co., Wis. Charles L. Merrill, b. Apr. 25, 1858; m. Apr. 20, 1882; Miles City, Custer Co., Mont.

2873. ii. SARAH, b. Apr. 21, 1824; m. Nov. 27, 1846, Amos Parker, res. Madison, Wis. She d. Jan 1, 1891; son Fred res. M.

2874. iii. JOHN SARGENT, b. Apr. 11, 1830; m. and d. Sept. 7, 1891, in Penacook, N. H.

2875. iv. MARTHA JANE, b. Nov. 29, 1833; m. 1851, David Noyes, son Frank res. Cambridgeport, Mass.

1494. JOHN FISK (Ephraim, Ephraim, Ebenezer, William, William, William, John, William, Robert, Simon, Simon, William, Symond), b. Concord, N. H., Jan. 2, 1787; m. in Dracut, Mass., June 15, 1829, Elizabeth Kittredge, b. May 23, 1801; d. Apr. 28, 1858. He was a farmer. He d. Sept. 1, 1870; res. Concord, N. H.

2876. i. HARRIET W., b. Oct. 4, 1833; d. Jan. 8, 1838, in Concord, N. H.

2877. ii. JOANNA G., b. Aug. 24, 1843; m. Apr. 5, 1864, George Abbott, Jr.; res. C.; one son, Herbert G., res. C.

2878. iii. MARY ANN, b. Feb. 10, 1840; m. June 21, 1866, James H. Rowell, res. s. p. School St., Concord. He was b. May 10, 1838. Is a contractor.

2879. iv. CHARLES H., b. Mar. 5, 1836; m. Sept. 6, 1864, Emma Clough; res. Lowell, Mass. Is a dry goods dealer.

2880. v. ANGELINE K., b. July 29, 1831; m. Nov. 24, 1853, John James Wallace. She d. Nov. 1, 1854.

2881. vi. HARRIETT W., b. Apr. 19, 1838; unm.; res. C.

1498. EPHRAIM FISK (Ephraim, Ephraim, Ebenezer, William, William, William, John, William, Robert, Simon, Simon, William, Symond), b. Concord, N. H., Apr. 17, 1798; m. there, Margaret Dow, b. 1804; d. Mar. 27, 1870. He was a clothier, and later railway station agent. He d. in Lowell, Mass., Oct. 31, 1891; res. Chichester, N. H.

2882. i. CYRUS MENTOR, b. Jan. 9, 1825; m. Amanda M. Putnam.

2883. ii. GEORGE LEWIS, b. Apr. 27, 1831; m. in Lindsay, Ont., Jan. 17, 1859, Maria Jewett. She was b. May 3, 1837. He is a railway station agent; res. Loresville, Ontario. Ch.: Lillian Eva, b. Oct. 24, 1859; m. Dec. 17, 1879; d. Aug. 31, 1889. Charles Holmes Fisk, b. Nov. 16, 1861; unm.; P. O., 955 Court Circle, Los Angeles, Cal. Emma Leith, b. Nov. 30, 1864; m. Apr. 15, 1891; P. O. Midland, Ontario. William Kervin Fisk, b. Nov. 24, 1866; m. 1895; 137 Abbott St., Detroit, Mich. Frank Mentor, b. July 2, 1869; m. June 13, 1894, Lorneville, Ont. Edward Major, b. Aug. 19, 1887; m. Dec. 30, 1892; Midland, Ont. George Dow, b. Apr. 13, 1876; Lorneville, Ont.

2884. iii. MARY JANE, b. ———; d. Aug. 30, 1849.

2885. iv. TWO INFANTS, b. ———; d. young.

1505. SAMUEL BARTLETT FISKE (Squire, John, Josiah, Samuel, William, William, John, William, Robert, Simon, Simon, William, Symond), b. R. I., Feb. 12, 1780; m. June 3, 1802, Vianna Estes, dau. of Zacheus. She d. in Adams, Mass. He was born in Rhode Island, married there and soon afterwards moved to So. Adams, Mass., where he was a millwright. He died in Rochester, N. Y., and his widow married an Alger, by whom she had one son, Franklin Alger. He d. in Rochester, N. Y.; res. Providence, R. I.

2886. i. VIANA, b. ———; m. John Randall and had two daus., one m. Dr. James Priest and res. N. Y., and the other m. Dr. Thurston; res. 1803 Michigan Ave., Chicago, Ill.

2887. ii. JOHN POND, b. Jan. 8, 1806; m. Charlotte Gray, Laurina Orton and ——— Bunker.

2888. iii. JAMES, b. 1812; m. Love B. Ryan.

2889. iv. SAMUEL B., b. 1813; m. Louisa Smith.

2890. v. STEPHEN, b. ———; m. ———.

2891. vi. ABIGAIL, b. ———; m. ——— Tallmadge; res. Blissfield, Mich.; four ch.

2892. vii. LUCINDA, b. ———; m. Gilbert Frazer and ——— Hurlbert.
She d. s. p.

2893. viii. LAURA, b. ———; m. Bateman Randall.

1507. MAJOR FISKE (Squire, John, Josiah, Samuel, William, William, John, William, Robert, Simon, Simon, William, Symond), b. R. I., Nov. 24, 1787; m. ——— ———. He d. Oct. 25, 1829; res. in R. I.

2894. i. WILLIAM, b. ———; d. young.
2895. ii. RUSSELL, b. ———.
2896. iii. PRUCIA, b. ———.
2897. iv. DIANA, b. ———.

1509. CHARLES FISKE (Squire, John, Josiah, Samuel, William, William, John, William, Robert, Simon, Simon, William, Symond), b. R. I., Oct. 5, 1789; m. in Cumberland, R. I., Dec. 31, 1811, Alice Carpenter, town records say Elsey Carpenter. Res. Cumberland, R. I.

2898. i. ASQUIRE, b. June 24, 1812.
2899. ii. NABBY ANN, b. July 3, 1818.
2900. iii. JOSEPH CARPENTER, b. Jan. 22, 1821; res. Valley Falls, R. I.

1510. JUDGE HALEY FISK (Squire, John, Josiah, Samuel, William, William, John, William, Robert, Simon, Simon, William, Symond), b. Cumberland Hill, R. I., Feb. 29, 1793; m. in Paterson, N. J., in 1815, Judith Qureaux, b. 1801; d. 1865. Haley Fisk was born in Cumberland, R. I., in 1793. He was a machinist and engineer by trade, and while in Paterson, N. J. during the war of 1812, raised a company, of which he was Lieutenant, and went to Cape May for duty as a member of the State Militia; was not called on to go further. He was an expert swordsman and a good musician. During his life he had charge of a powder mill at Spotswood, N. J., which blew up after he left there. He was also in charge of the work of building the lower lock of the Delaware and Raritan canal at that city, when the canal was built, and afterward started the first iron foundry in that city and built the boiler and engine with which it was run. Before this was finished he ran the foundry by horse power. He was a friend of Henry Clay and other prominent Whig politicians and was a power in politics in the 40's, and up to the war, in that city and county, was Justice of the Peace for over thirty-five years. For a number of years he was a county judge, and was prominent in social affairs. His honesty was a proverb and as Justice he preferred to have litigants settle their differences rather than throw money into his hands by litigation. He was a Mason and when the two lodges of F. & A. M's. in that city were broken up during the anti-Masonic craze he was the means of gathering the members together and forming what was called the Union Lodge, which is still in existence. He was ever after called the "Father of the Lodge." He was buried in that city with Masonic honors. He d. in Greenpoint, N. Y., 1877; res. New Brunswick, N. J.

2901. iv. STEPHEN M., b. 1822; m. Mary Flynn of Cavan, Ireland; res. Washington, D. C. They had a son, Henry Clay.
2902. i. SQUIRE WHITTAKER, b. Sept., 1816; m. Mary Jordan, of Philadelphia. He d. s. p.
2903. ii. CORNELIA, b. 1819; m. Capt. Haggerty, 24 Peck Slip, New York. Ch.: 1, William, b. ———. 2, Henry, b. ———.
2904. iii. CAROLINE, b. Feb. 17, 1825; unm.; res. 90 Redmond St., New Brunswick, N. J.
2905. v. WILLIAM HENRY, b. Apr. 6, 1818; m. Sarah Ann Blakeney.
2906. vi. MARY, b. ———; d. infancy.
2907. vii. CATHERINE, b. ———; d. infancy.
2908. viii. ELIZA JANE, b. 1820; m. Laurence Van Buskirk. She d. 1893.

1513. FRANCIS MELBOURNE FISKE (Squire, John, Josiah, Samuel, William, William, John, William, Robert, Simon, Simon, William, Symond), b. Mar. 24, 1804, Rhode Island; m. Ursula French. Res. New Orleans, La.

2909. ii. WILLIAM HENRY, b. 1828; m. ———; d. about 1875. Ch.: 1, William. 2, Georgie Helen: res. S. F.; m. ——— Mayhew; res. 1517 Post St.; ch.: Henry Clay, aged 17; Joseph Reno,

20

aged 13; William Worth, aged 11, and Georgie Elizabeth, aged 7.

2910. iii. ANNE ELIZABETH, b. Cumberland, R. I., June 10, 1830; m. at Mobile, Ala., May 13, 1849, William Greene; res. 1357 Post St., San Francisco, Cal. He was b. May 30, 1812; d. Aug. 1, 1871. Ch.: 1, Clay Meredith, b. Mar. 12, 1850; m. Alice Randolph Wheeler; res. Bayside, L. I., N. Y., s. p.; 2 ch. d. 2, Harry Ashland, b. Jan. 12, 1852, m. Arabella Little; res. Monterey, Cal.; ch.: Wm. and Ursula. 3, Clement Herbert, b. Oct. 31. 1853; d. 1861. 4, Lizzie E., b. 1860; d. 1864. 5, Francis M., b. Dec. 23, 1866; res. London, Eng., 88 Abingdon Road.

2911. i. FRANCIS M., b. 1825; d. ———.

1514. JAMES BALLOU FISKE (John, John, Josiah, Samuel, William, William, John, William, Robert, Simon, Simon, William, Symond), b. Cumberland, R. I., Dec., 1784; m. in Merrimack, N. H., Jan. 18, 1814, Rebecca McGraw, of Merrimack, N. H., b. 1783; d. Mar. 27, 1851. In the year 1806, James Ballou Fiske, eldest son of John Fiske, went to Bangor, Me., and commenced business, and there remained until his death in 1854. In January, 1814, he was married to Rebecca McGraw, of Merrimack, N. H., by whom he had five children; three of whom are still living; namely, James B. Fisk, merchant of Bangor; John O. Fiske, of Bath, and Prentice D. Fiske, of New York. He d. 1854; res. Bangor, Me.

2912. i. JOHN ORR, b. July 13, 1819; m. Mary A. Tappan.
2913. ii. PRENTICE D., b. ———; res. Bangor, Me., and New York, N. Y.
2914. iii. REBECCA, b. ———; m. ——— Sandford. Son, Wm. F., res. St. Louis.
2915. iv. JAMES B., b. ———; m. ———. He d. in Bangor, Me., s. p.
2916. v. ROBERT, b. ———; d. unm.

1515. NATHAN FISKE (John, John, Josiah, Samuel, William, William, John, William, Robert, Simon, Simon, William, Symond), b. Feb. 1, 1787, Cumberland R. I.; m. Mar. 25, 1816, Sarah Ann Arnold, b. 1788; d. in Northboro, Sept. 8, 1864. He d. Sept. 18—; res. Northboro, Mass.

2917. i. JOHN ARNOLD, b. July 10, 1822; m. Georgiana E. Perry.

1519. NATHANIEL FISK (Jonathan, Jonathan, Josiah, Samuel, William, William, John, William, Robert, Simon, Simon, William, Symond), b. Broadalbin, N. Y., Jan. 13, 1780; m., Nov. 22, 1801, Mrs. Lois Van Buren Hall, d. Apr. 1, 1822; m. 2d, in Mayfield, Jan. 6, 1823, Lydia Wells, b. 1793; d. 1869. He was a farmer. Nathaniel Fisk possessed a remarkable mind and was no ordinary orator at Masonic festivals. But like all the rest of the Fisk family of whom one has any knowledge, was exceedingly modest and unpretending, being content to lead a quiet life on his farm. Nathaniel Fisk was an active, zealous Mason, as also were all his sons by his first wife, Lois Van Buren Hall. During the days of anti-Masonry, by the appointment of the Grand Lodge he had much to do in tracing out the life of Morgan, who was said to have been murdered by the Masons for being untrue to his Masonic obligations. Mr. Fisk found positive proof that Morgan was not murdered, but left the United States, went to Germany, where he lived many years and died there. One of our foreign Ministers saw Morgan in Germany, recognizing him and conversed with him concerning the reports of his murder. He d. in West Bush, N. Y.; res. Mayfield, N. Y.

2918. i. STEPHEN, b. Apr. 13, 1816; m. Sophrona Lowe and Mrs. Laura C. Birdier.
2919. ii. CHARLES P., b. July 17, 1834; m. Catherine Morrison.
2920. iii. WM. W., b. Mar. 13, 1830; m. Annie T. Empie.

1532. JONATHAN D. FISK (David, Jonathan, Josiah, Samuel, William, William, John, William, Robert, Simon, Simon, William, Symond), b. Saratoga Co., N. Y., Feb. 21, 1794; m. at Manchester, N. Y., in 1817, Lucy Codman, d. Aug., 1832; m. 2d, Mrs. Betsey Granger. He was a tanner and shoemaker by trade, but during the last years of his life followed farming. He d. July 29, 1874; res. Arcadia, N. Y., and Ovid, Mich.

2921. i.   LEONARD, b. Jan., 1820; res. Saginaw, Mich.
2922. ii. EDWARD, b. Apr. 17, 1821; m. Elmina Dolph and Sarah C.
             Parker.
2922½.iii. HARRIETT, b. 1823; m. —— Prescott: res. Newark, N. Y.
2923. iv. JONATHAN WYMAN, b. ——: d. Nov., 1856.
2924. v.   WM. HENRY, b. ——; d. Feb., 1848.
2925. vi. MARY JANE, b. ——.

    1533. JAMES GREENE FISK (David, Jonathan, Josiah, Samuel, William,
William, John, William, Robert, Simon, Simon, William, Symond), b. Stillwater, N.
Y., Oct. 10, 1791; m. in Arcadia, Mar. 3, 1814, Mary Smith Alexander, b. July 29,
1795, d. Oct. 9, 1887. He was a farmer. He d. Oct. 10, 1863; res. Somerset, N. Y.
2926. i.   EMILY, b. Jan. 20, 1815; m. Nov. 26, 1831, Joseph Raze. He
             was b. in Stamford, Vt.,; d. in Buffalo, N. Y., Aug. 27, 1879.
             She d. July 5, 1871. Ch.: Hamilton Delos Raze, Elma Jane
             Raze, Leonard Raze, Mary Raze, James Lorenzo Raze, all
             dead. B. Franklin Raze, b. Dec. 5, 1847; m. Mar. 30, 1881,
             Estella Julia Hayes, b. Apr., 1856; d. May 21, 1882; res. 219
             State St., Albany, N. Y.; is an accountant; ch.: Franklin James,
             b. May 14, 1882; d. Oct. 16, 1882, Marinda Francelia, b. ——;
             m. J. C. Ellis; res. 71 Chestnut St., Lockport, N. Y.
2927. ii. CATHERINE, b. June 2, 1817; m. May 23, 1838, John Van
             Wagoner: d. Apr. 6, 1874; a son is Neal J.; res. Somerset, N. Y.
2928. iii. MARCUS R.. b. July 7, 1819; m. Emily Polly Huntington and
             Mary S. Peryne.
2929. iv. CLARINDA, b. July 30, 1821; m. Mar. 2, 1844, Orange Hogle;
             m. 2d, Apr. 28, 1858, Sidney Smith, d. Mar. 2, 1870. A child
             is Wilford R. Hogle; res. Somerset, N. Y.; Clarinda res. S.
2930. v.   CAROLINE, b. Aug. 15, 1823.
2931. vi. ALFRED D., b. Feb. 11, 1826; m. Eliza J. Robinson.
2932. vii. MARY NANCY, b. Aug. 4, 1828; m. Jan. 5, 1854, William
             Millis, b. Feb. 25, 1828; d. Sept. 7, 1881; was a farmer and
             school teacher; res. Lyndonville, N. Y. Ch.: Samuel Buck-
             master Millis, b. Mar. 13, 1860; m. 1st, Jan. 1, 1884, ——; m.
             2d, Jan., 1896, ——; add., Lyndonville, Orleans Co., N. Y.
             Forrest Hugh Millis, b. Nov. 25, 1864; res. Lyndonville, Or-
             leans Co., N. Y.
2933. viii. JAMES A., b. Oct. 9, 1830; m. Elenor Powell.
2934. ix. ALLEN, b. Dec. 20, 1832; d. Aug. 12, 1834.
2935. x.   MYRON H., b. June 7, 1836; m. Apr. 3, 1855, Margarett Fitts,
             b. Mar. 27, 1835. He d. Nov. 27, 1863: was killed in battle at
             Mine Run, Va. Ch.: Jenette Loveland, b. Nov. 15, 1855; m.
             Apr. 17, 1872; d. Mar. 11, 1893. Ida M. Wiles, b. Mar. 10, 1858;
             m. Aug. 30, 1872; add. Elk P. O., Genesee Co., Mich. Ella
             Hamilton, b. May 2, 1859; m July 12, 1875; add. 820 Lyon St.,
             Flint, Mich. Estelle, b. June 4, 1861; m. Albert Levi McDon-
             ald Jan. 18, 1880; add. Johnson Creek, Niagara Co., N. Y.,; he
             is a farmer; was b. Aug. 27, 1859; ch.: Josephine McDonald, b.
             Jan. 4, 1881; Edgar Powell McDonald, b. Mar. 27, 1886;
             Hattie May McDonald, b. Aug. 3, 1890; Florence Irene Mc-
             Donald, b. Dec. 7, 1892. Jenette Loveland's oldest child's
             name is Adelbert Loveland, Flint, Mich.

    1534. WEAVER E. FISK (David, Jonathan, Josiah, Samuel, William, John,
William, William, Robert, Simon, Simon, William, Symond), b. Vermont, July 22,
1796; m. there, Mar. 22, 1820, Elenor Childs, b. Nov. 1, 1795, d. in East Arcade,
N. Y., Nov. 4, 1877. He d. in Elton, N. Y., Mar. 28, 1873; res. Yorkshire and Me-
chanicsville, N. Y.
2936. i.   SAMUEL A., b. ——; m. Hannah Holmes.
2937. ii. CHESTER C., b. ——; res. Yorkshire Corners, N. Y.
2938. iii. MARY H., b. ——; m. —— Dibble; res. Mt. Pleasant, Mich.
2939. iv. GEORGE C., b. Oct. 8, 1833; m. Martha Winslow.
2940. v.   JAMES G., b. ——; res. Charles City, Ia.

2941. vi.   LUCY, b. ———; m. ——— Dennis; res. Elsa, Mich.
2942. vii. ROXEY P., b. ———; m. ——— Deahing. She d. ———.
2943. viii. BENJAMIN, b. ———.

1535. DAVID FISKE (David, Jonathan, Josiah, Samuel, William, John, William, William, Robert, Simon, Simon, William, Symond), b. Mar. 26, 1801, in New York State; m. Dec. 24, 1820, Cynthia Jane Chittenden, b. Mar. 29, 1800; d. Jan. 7, 1877. He was a farmer. He d. Feb. 3, 1889; res. Cattaraugus, N. Y., and Mantua, O.

2944. i.   NATHAN INGRAHAM, b. Jan. 30, 1825; m. Loiza J. Hill.
2945. ii.   NORMAN G., b. Jan. 19, 1822; m. Philura C. Marinon.
2946. iii. JEFFERSON, b. Feb. 9, 1828; m. Delesta M. Moseley.
2947. iv.   ORSON, b. Aug. 24, 1832; m. E. M. Dewey.
2948. v.   ALDOMERON, b. June 14, 1834; m. Frances Imfield.
2949. vi.   JASON PIERCE, b. Feb. 14, 1839; d. May 28, 1858.
2950. vii. OLIVER CROMWELL, b. Nov. 20, 1830; m. June 20, 1851, Sophia P. Dewey.
2951. viii. MARY MASENA, b. Oct. 19, 1823; m. Mar. 25, 1856, John Hector Ross. He was b. May 14, 1806; d. July 15, 1889. He was a cabinetmaker and undertaker. Ch.: 1, Ida Mary Ross Ritter, b. Dec. 26, 1856; m. Dec. 13, 1874; d. Dec. 15, 1893. 2, Royal Hector Ross, b. Apr. 17, 1860. All res. Julia, O
2952. ix.   PHOEBE MARIA, b. Apr. 1, 1836; m. in Portage Co., O. James Mott Folger; res. Mantua Station, Portage Co., O. He was b. 1823. Is station agent. Ch.: 1, Walter A. Folger, b. July 13, 1858; m. Oct., 1883, Lola Russell; res. Akron, O.; he is treasurer of B. F. Goodrich Co.; ch.: Florence P. Folger, b. Nov. 18, 1886; Elizabeth Folger, b. Aug. 25, 1891; Mary Joy Folger, b. May 25, 1894; all b. at Akron, O. 2, Mary Folger Wilson, b. Dec. 30, 1860; m. Jan, 1882, Charlestown, O. 3, Julia Folger Corson, b. ———; m. Oct. 1, 1884, Akron, O. 4, Carrie Ladd Folger, b. ———; living in Brooklyn, N. Y. 5, Harriette Emily Folger, b. ———; living in Akron, O. 6, Geo. Mayhew Folger, b. 1875; living at Mantua, O.
2953. x.   CYNTHIA JANE, b. May 15, 1841; m. ——— Cadwell.
2954. xi.   LUCY, b. Jan. 8, 1827; d. June 8, 1828.

1536. LEWIS MOSES FISK (David, Jonathan, Josiah, Samuel, William, John, William, Robert, Simon, Simon, William, Symond), b. Arcadia, N. Y., Sept. 14, 1804; m. in Ontario, May 27, 1827, Mary Titus, b. Sept. 28, 1806; d. Mar. 16, 1885. He was a clothier in early life and afterwards a farmer. He d. Dec. 15, 1890; res. Ontario, N. Y., and Dodgeville, Wis.

2955. i.   SAMUEL W., b. Apr. 28, 1829; m. Mary W. Webb.
2956. ii.   CELIA J., b. 1828; m. ——— Campbell. She d. 1893. Son L. D. Campbell res. Duluth, Minn.
2957. iii. ALBERT, b. ———.
2958. iv.   OSCAR C., b. ———; d. ———.
2959. v.   EMMA ROSELL, b. Feb. 25, 1832; m. May 19, 1859, George Wilson, b. Feb. 22, 1836. He is a farmer and owns hotel; res. Osceola, Wis. Ch.: Harriet A. Wilson, b. Feb. 19, 1860; d. Mar. 25, 1862. Bert Grant Fisk Wilson, b. Dec. 12, 1862. Claribelle May, b. May 31, 1864; m. Geo. Knapp, Dubuque, Ia. Grace E. Wilson, b. Mar. 10, 1867; m. C. M. Truesdell, Los Angeles, Cal. George Wilson, b. June 13, 1870, Chicago.

1537. HIRAM FISK (David, Jonathan, Josiah, Samuel, William, John, William, Robert, Simon, Simon, William, Symond), b. Aug. 14, 1813, in Arcadia, N. Y.; m. in Springfield, Mich., July 4, 1837, Mary Ann Worden, b. July 4, 1819. He was a farmer. He d. July 30, 1895; res. Springfield, Mich., and Portville, N. Y.

2960. i.   WM. ELLIOTT, b. Sept. 4, 1838; m. Mahala A. Rolph.
2961. ii.   ELIZA ANN, b. May 14, 1840; m. Feb. 20, 1864, James Marvin. She d. Feb. 25, 1865, in Franklinville, N. Y. Infant dau. d.

2962. iii. CLARINDA HARRIET, b. May 10, 1842; d. Oct. 20, 1842.

2963. iv. RHODA SABRINA, b. Aug. 4, 1843; m. Dec. 23, 1867, William Austin; res. Franklinville, N. Y., b. Dec. 27, 1810; d. Nov. 17, 1894. He was a farmer. Ch.: Mary Odell, b. May 30, 1871; m. Apr. 3, 1890. Jenet Ethel, b. Jan. 28, 1874; d. Jan. 19, 1875. Geo., b. Nov. 3, 1875. Nathan R., b. July 25, 1877. E. Mae, b. Jan. 9, 1880. Julia Ett, b. May 15, 1882. Frances Margaret, b. May 2, 1886.

2964. v. JONATHAN SILAS, b. June 8, 1846; d. Feb. 14, 1872.

2965. vi. MERTON DELANCY, b. May 26, 1850; d. May 13, 1864.

2966. vii. JULIA HELEN, b. May 26, 1852; m. Sept. 2, 1872, Alfred W. Howard; one son, Jonathan G., b. Aug. 27, 1875, d. Oct. 10, 1884; res. Franklinville, N. Y. She d. Oct. 10, 1884.

2967. viii. GEO. WEAVER, b. Sept. 17, 1857.

1545. JOHN HANNIBAL FISK (Ezra, Jonathan, Josiah, Samuel, William, William, John, William, Robert, Simon, Simon, William, Symond), b. Saratoga, N. Y., Jan. 12, 1804; m. in Manchester, N. Y., Jane Wells, b. Sept. 29, 1808; d. Sept. 13, 1850. He was a farmer and cabinetmaker by trade. He d. Feb. 17, 1880; res. Manchester and Chapinville, N. Y.

2968. i. JOHN S. C., b. Nov. 24, 1831; m. Adelphia Huntoon.

2969. ii. CLARISSA A. J., b. Feb. 5, 1828; m. Apr. 3, 1857, Lewis P. Henry, b. Nov. 23, 1824; d. Jan. 9, 1867. He was a farmer. She m. 2d, W. L. D. Barde, b. Nov. 1, 18—; d. Jan. 24, 18—. He was a lawyer. Res. Chapinville, N. Y. Ch.: 1, Spencer L. Henry. b. May 10, ——; d. ——. 2, Jennie J., b. Nov. 22, ——; d. ——. 3, J. James, b. Mar. 5, 1862. 4, May M., b. Nov. 27, 1864; d. ——. 5, Georgia E., b. Nov. 26, 1866. Add. J. J. Henry, Chapinville, Ontario Co., N. Y.; Georgia E. Hubbard, Caton Centre, Steuben Co., N. Y.

1551. HIRAM FISK (Ezra, Jonathan, Josiah, Samuel, William, William, John, William, Robert, Simon, Simon, William, Symond), b. in Saratoga, N. Y., in 1800; m. in Palmyra, N. Y., about 1824, Maria Fraser, b. 1803; d. Jan. 5, 1892, in Ypsilanti, Mich. She was a dau. of Oris Fraser and Mary Lee, of Green River, Columbia Co., N. Y. She was a member of a family of nine, five girls and four boys. The oldest of the brothers became a Methodist minister, and his twin brother, Oris, who died at Florida, this county, in 1877, was a minister in the Presbyterian Church. She was a descendant of Alexander Fraser, his great-grandfather, who settled in Guilford, Conn., in 1745. This Alexander was the second son of Simon Fraser, twelfth Lord Lorat. A Pierce Fraser went with William the Conqueror into England. His grandson settled in the south of Scotland, whence the family branched off into Aberdeenshire and Invernesshire, the latter branch furnishing most of the Frasers of this country, who now number about 7,000. He was a farmer. He d. in Romulus, Mich., June, 1845. In an early day he lived in Palmyra, Wayne Co., N. Y. He had four brothers, Hiram, Harvey, Ezra and James. Harvey moved to Oxford, Oakland Co., Mich. Res. Cattaraugus Co., N. Y., and Romulus, Mich.

2970. i. HORACE F., b. Mar. 15, 1832; m. Anna L. Montgomery.

2971. ii. HIRAM, b. Dec. 18, 1829; m. Martha A. Harmon.

2972. iii. DARWIN B., b. Oct. 19, 1837; m. Lovina Thayer.

2973. iv. CHARLES H., b. Aug. 24, 1843; m. Mira Thayer.

2974. v. JULIA ANN, b. ——; d. Romulus, Mich., in 1838.

2975. vi. MARY A., b. in 1838; d. Toledo, O., in 1854.

2976. vii. HELEN MARIA, b. June 22, 1830; m. at Toledo, O., Apr. 23, 1857, Frank Braisted, b. Apr. 5, 1827; d. Jan. 6, 1892. He was assistant auditor of Mich. Cent. R. R.; res. Port Chester, N. Y. Ch.: Edward Thayer Braisted, b. Jan. 28, 1858; d. Mar. 10, 1860. Annie Earl Braisted, b. June 5, 1859; d. Mar. 25, 1860; Charlotte Augusta Braisted, b. Feb. 7, 1861; d. Mar. 4, 1865. William Clarence Braisted, b. Oct. 9, 1864; m. Lillian Mulford Phipps, Apr. 2, 1888, Philadelphia, Pa.; add. Port Chester, N. Y. Frank Alfred Braisted, b. Feb. 12, 1889. Helen Louise Braisted, b. Sept. 6, 1892. Evelyn Virginia Braisted, b. Feb. ~ 1891

1552. DANIEL B. FISK (Ezra, Jonathan, Josiah, Samuel, William, William, John, William, Robert, Simon, Simon, William, Symond), b. Saratoga Co., N. Y., Aug. 20, 1816; m. in Canandaigua, Mar. 2, 1847, Elizabeth A. Sherman, b. Jan. 22, 1827. He is retired from active work and business; res. Newark, N. Y.

    2977. i.   JULIA A., b. Aug. 12, 1850; d. Oct. 13, 1857.
    2978. ii.   EBEN D., b. Feb. 8, 1852; m. Nettie E. Hughson.
    2979. iii. WATSON A., b. Sept. 20, 1853; m. 1877, Nettie Wheeler.
    2980. iv. PEARLIE L., b. Aug. 8, 1855.
    2981. v.   SHERMAN G., b. June 5, 1862; m. Ella M. Ratliffe.
    2982. vi. MAY F., b. May 18, 1865; m. Mar. 11, 1883, Henry Proscus; res. N.

1554. DEA. LONSON FISK (Stephen, Jonathan, Josiah, Samuel, William, William, John, William, Robert, Simon, Simon, William, Symond), b. Schuylerville, N. Y., Feb. 8, 1811; m. at Manchester, N. Y., June 14, 1832, Adelia Wells, b. Mar. 7, 1812; d. July 27, 1888. Lonson and his brothers went to Newark at such an early age that important links in the history back of Jonathan were either not known to them or were lost or forgotten. The old family homestead is located about three miles southwest of Newark, N. Y., and on this farm nine children were born, all now (1895) alive, although the father and mother are dead. The father was deacon of the Newark Baptist Church forty years; held town and village offices, and, although one of the early settlers there, accumulated a very respectable property. He and his wife lived to celebrate the fiftieth anniverssary of marriage, enjoying the occasion in the presence of their unbroken family, together for the first time in twenty years. Lonson Fisk was a farmer's son, and chose farming as a life occupation for himself. At the age of 21 he located on a farm adjoining his father's, near Newark, in the southwest part of Wayne Co., New York. He had a good common school education, and by reading kept pace with the times in knowledge of the world's doings. He was a Christian man in the full sense of the word, and gave liberally of his time and means to the church. He, though interested in political affairs, never held office. In 1873 he left the farm in the care of one of his sons and resided in the village of Newark until his death. He d. Dec. 19, 1885; res. Newark, N. Y.

    2983. i.   GEO. W., b. Apr. 29, 1833; m. at Manchester, N. Y., Alice A. Southworth, b. Sept. 8, 1834. He is a farmer; res. Coldwater, Mich. He held town and county offices.
    2984. ii.   SAMUEL, b. Oct. 13, 1834; m. Clara S. Conover.
    2985. iii. WILLIS P., b. Apr. 1, 1836; m. Mary E. Field and Julia L. Sherman.
    2986. iv. WM. H., b. Sept. 27, 1838; m. and res. 371 State St., Brooklyn, N. Y. William H. has been engaged in the mercantile business, and is now occupying a government position in New York in the United States Barge office, living in Brooklyn.
    2987. v.   HANNAH JENNIE, b. May 1, 1844; unm.; res. Mayville, N. Y.
    2988. vi. A. JUDSON, b. July 19, 1849; m. Julia A. Hunt.
    2989. vii. H. HUDSON, b. July 19, 1849; unm; res. Newark, N. Y. H. Hudson taught school, was corresponding clerk in the old Traders National Bank, Chicago; was vice principal six years of the Newark Union School, and during the past ten years (until three months ago, Aug., 1895,) was publisher and owner of the "Union," published at Newark, N. Y.
    2990. viii. FRANCES A., b. May 1, 1853; unm.; res. Omaha, Neb., 539 Park Av. Is connected with the public schools there.
    2991. ix.   ARABELLE, b. Dec. 20, 1854; m. V. E. Welcher; res. Newark, N. Y. He is a prosperous farmer.

1557. JOSEPH FISKE (Joseph, Joseph, Mark, Joseph, William, William, John, William, Robert, Simon, Simon, William, Symond), b. Londonderry, N. H., May 1, 1792; m. May 29, 1813, Fannie Brown, b. 1787; d. at Round Grove, Ill., in 1872. He was a farmer. He d. Aug. 25, 1834; res. Springville, Pa.

    2992. i.   JOSEPH W., b. Feb. 12, 1824; m. Rhoda E. Strickland.
    2993. ii.   CLARK S., b. Dec. 4, 1832; m. Adelia E. Reynolds.
    2994. iii. MARY, b. ———; m. R. A. Champlin. Ch.: 1, Oren, b. ———; res. Sterling, Ill. 2, Almon, b. ———; res. Clinton, Ia.

2994¼.iv. NANCY, b. ———; m. Phillip Reynolds; had two children, a boy and a girl. 1, Elizabeth, m. Herman Reynolds; res. Morrison, Ill. 2, James.

2994½.v. SARAH, b. ———; m. Anan Place and d. s. p.

2994¾.vi. RENA, b. ———; m. Earl Smith and d. s. p.

1559. CLARK FISKE (Joseph, Joseph, Mark, Joseph, William, William, John, William, Robert, Simon, Simon, William, Symond), b. Londonderry, N. H., May 29, 1797; m. July 15, 1832, Olive Atwell, b. Mar. 25, 1808. He was a farmer. He d. in Montpelier; res. Montepelier, Vt.

2995. i. MARGARET C., b. in Eden, Vt., 1840; m. 1868. Alfred L. Carlton, d. 1874; m. 2d, 1888, George S. Turner; res. La Cygne, Kan. He is a banker; s. p

2996. ii. JOEL, b. ———. His dau., Mamie Fisk, res. Independence, Mo.

2997. iii. LYDIA, b. ———.

2998. iv. JOSEPH, b. ———.

2999. v. HOMER, b. ———.

3000. vi. CAROLINE, b. ———. Her son, Amos Hale, res. Trading Pass, Kan.

3001. vii. JOHN, b. ———.

3002. viii. LOVINIA, b. Mar. 30, 1846; m. Mar. 31, 1871, Russell Amos Corey, b. 1847; d. Nov. 9, 1895, Elwood, Neb. He was a lumber dealer Ch.: 1, Clark Fiske, b. Mar. 17, 1872; asst. cashier Citizens Bank, La Cygne, Kan. 2, Amos J., b. ———; res. Elwood, Neb. 3, Homer Russell, b. ———; res. La Cygne, Kan. 4, Hobert Chester, b. ———; res. La Cygne, Kan.

1562. WASHINGTON FISKE (Joseph, Joseph, Mark, Joseph, William, William, John, William, Robert, Simon, Simon, William, Symond), b. Goffstown, N. H., Feb. 15, 1804; m. in Eden, Vt., Jan. 14, 1834. Hannah Whitney Alden, dau. of William and Susannah (Whitney) Alden, b. Needham, Mass., Sept. 13, 1806; d. Nov. 16, 1885, in Ashland. He remembers back to the age of two and a half years when a company of militia were passing the house, and the family had assembled at the windows leaving no place for him. So he thrust his head out of the cat-hole near the floor. The captain saw his head and wishing a little sport rode up and drawing his sword said, "Take your head in or I shall cut it off." At his advanced age of nearly 92 he laughs about it now and says it is needless to say his head went in. When 4 years of age his father moved to Eden, Vt., on a two-horse sled. He rode on one side of the sled while his sister Margaret sat upon the other side so no points of interest should be passed unnoticed on the way, At the age of 14 he and his sister Margaret were bound out to their brother Clark, until they became of age, to work out the old debt Clark had paid for his father when he lost so much as a huckster. He came to Boston at 21, and drove stage from Boston to Worcester for a few years. During that time became acquainted with Hannah Whitney Alden, bought a farm, and returned to Eden, bought a farm, erected buildings (near his father's home), and married, Jan. 14, 1834. There his six children were born, and in 1855 moved to Hyde Park, on account of better schools for his children. He returned to his own home in Eden in 1861. Sold and bought a farm in Ashland, Mass., in Apr., 1865, where he now (1895) lives at the age of 91 years and 7 months. He was always and even now is fun-loving, believing that it is better to not watch for the solemn shadows that will surely find us, but make the most of life as we go along. Honest and upright in his dealings, often telling his children that no Fiske was ever behind the bars. Is a Congregationalist in creed, Republican in politics. An Ashland paper in referring to its aged citizen says: "Four Score and Twelve Years.—Our honored townsman, Washington Fiske, reached the age of 92 years last Saturday, and was able to be up and receive his friends who called upon him with congratulations for a life so well rounded out in years, strength and usefulness. Your correspondent was shown the photographic group of four generations which are now represented in this household—Mr. Fiske, senior, the central figure; at his right his son, G. C. Fiske; his granddaughter, Mrs. Nina (Fiske) Prouty; and at his left his great-grandson, Claude Granville Prouty. Among the guests was his niece, Mrs. Lizzie Bassett, of Worcester. Mr. Fiske bids fair to round out the century, although he has for many years suffered from infirmity to which ordinary men would have succumbed." Res. Eden, Vt., and Ashland, Mass.

    3003. i.   INFANT SON, b. Dec. 13, 1834; d. Dec. 14, 1834.
    3004. ii.   INFANT DAUGHTER, b. Dec. 2, 1835; d. Dec. 2, 1835.
    3005. iii. GEORGE WASHINGTON, b. Jan. 21, 1839; d. Ashland, Mar. 10, 1860. He moved to Hyde Park, Vt., in 1855; was educated in the public school and Lamoille Central Academy; gifted with a remarkable musical ability; also possessed a tenor voice so clear and powerful, that, had he been so disposed, would have been his support through life, if that life had been given to him for years. He went to Ashland, Mass., Apr. 1, 1859, to work for his cousin, Chas. Alden, in the emery business. Died of typhoid fever in Ashland, where, during his short stay, he had made many friends.
    3006. iv.   EDWIN AUGUSTUS, b. May 9, 1843; d. Mar. 1, 1844.
    3007. v.   GRANVILLE CLARK, b. Aug. 21, 1845; m. Susan S. Aldrich.
    3008. vi.   JOSEPHINE LUCILLA, b. Feb. 5, 1848; unm.; res. Ashland.

    1564. BENJAMIN FISK (Mark, Joseph, Mark, Joseph, William, John, William, Robert, Simon, Simon, William, Symond), b. Derry, N. H., Dec. 27, 1810; m. at Haverhill, Mass., Aug. 1, 1832, Mary B. Sawyer, b. at Haverhill, Dec 23, 1808; d. Mar. 17, 1890. He was a farmer; res. Shirley, Mass.
    3009. i.   HARRIET FRANCES, b. Apr. 11, 1833; d. June 10, 1835.
    3010. ii.   MARY FRANCES, b. Feb. 13, 1835; d. Feb. 12, 1889.
    3011. iii. JAMES WILSON, b. Feb. 26, 1838; m. Christy Morrison. He d. Oct. 6, 1874, in Boston, Mass.
    3012. iv.   THOMAS KING, b. Oct. 25, 1839; res. S.
    3013. v.   ANNIE MARIA, b. Sept. 11, 1844.

    1565. MARK FISK (Mark, Joseph, Mark, Joseph, William, John, William, Robert, Simon, Simon, William, Symond), b. Derry, N. H., July 21, 1814; m. in Boston, Nov. 14, 1838, Elizabeth S. Gove, b. Aug. 24, 1811; d. May 27, 1848; m. 2d, at Burlington, Mass., Sept. 30, 1840, Mrs. Sarah E. (Reed) Cutler, b. Sept. 30, 1828. He resided at home in Londonderry until he was 20 years of age, when he went to Boston, where he was first engaged in the construction of wharves, and shortly afterwards turned his attention to cooperage. Later brick manufacturing and operations in real estate occupied most of his time and attention. However, he found time to successfully operate a quarry and till a large acreage for farm purposes. Before Somerville became a city he was for a number of years one of its selectmen and prominent in its affairs. He was one of the heaviest tax payers, as his interests in real estate were large. Being too old he was not drafted, but paid a man $500 to serve in the army at the time of the late war. One fact occurs as being important: He owned the patent and built the first kiln for the manufacture of bricks with one side glazed or marbleized. Bricks so treated are in quite general use today. Gen. James Dana and he owned and developed a large part of the northeasterly side of Somerville. He was abstemious, honest, frugal, of intense activity, and a very successful man of business in those days. Fruit culture was his hobby. He d. Apr. 12, 1869; res. Somerville, Mass.
    3014. i.   SUSAN E., b. Aug. 17, 1840; m Jan. 1, 1866, Eber Henry Lawrence. She d. July 19, 1876. He d. Sept. 23, 1874. Ch.: Geo. Fisk, b. Jan. 28, 1867; d. Aug. 3, 1867. Elizabeth Gertrude, b. Oct. 31, 1870; d. Nov. 7, 1872.
    3015. ii.   CHARLES HENRY, b. May 31, 1843; d. Aug. 10, 1843.
    3016. iii. ANDREW P., b. July 22, 1845; d. unm. in San Francisco Jan. 2, 1872.
    3017. iv.   MARY E., b. Mar. 17, 1848; m. Feb. 18, 1869, Forest Greenleaf Hawes. She d. Aug. 20, 1880. He was born in Hanover, Mass., Dec. 27, 1845; is a mercantile broker. Ch.: Laura Willard, b. Nov. 8, 1872; m. Oct. 28, 1895, Winslow Armitage Parsons, b. Dec. 19, 1870; is a designer; res., s. p., Waban and Newton, Mass.
    3018. v.   SARAH J., b. Mar. 17, 1851; d. July 3, 1851.
    3019. vi.   MARK, b. Oct. 9, 1853; unm.; res. at home.

3020. vii. EMMA A., b. Nov. 13, 1856; m. Apr. 29, 1880, Edward Stevens Lincoln. He d. Apr. 15, 1890. Ch.: Mildred Fisk, b. Aug. 27, 1883; Madeline Ellsworth, b. Oct. 20, 1889.

3021. viii. ELLSWORTH, b. Aug. 4, 1861; unm.; res. Somerville, Mass. He attended the public schools and graduated in June, 1879, from the high school. The following day after graduation he went to work in an office and since then has been occupied in office labors; was compelled to resign his position as book-keeper in a large manufactory, owing to poor health. Since that time has been in real estate business. He has traveled a moderate amount—California, the Southwest, Canada, Nova Scotia, New Brunswick, etc.

3022. ix. FREDERICK A., b. Apr. 14, 1867; res. at home.

1566. JOSEPH FISK (Mark, Joseph, Mark, Joseph, William, John, William, Robert, Simon, Simon, William, Symond), b. Derry, N. H., Aug. 5, 1809; m. Mar. 28, 1832, at Raymond, Sarah A. Stevens, b. Nov. 16, 1804. Joseph Fisk was born in Derry, N. H., lived there until 18 years of age; then moved to Pembroke, N. H.; was married and lived in Pembroke twelve years; then moved to Raymond Mar. 14, 1844, where he lived the life of a successful farmer until his death. He d. Nov. 15, 1885; res. Raymond, N. H.

3024. i. JOSEPH W., b. Dec. 27, 1838; m. Abbie M. Hardy.

1567. JAMES W. FISK (Mark, Joseph, Mark, Joseph, William, John, William, Robert, Simon, Simon, William, Symond), b. Derry, N. H., Oct. 6, 1818; m. in Somerville, Mass., Oct., 1841, Mary Webber, b. Jan. 5, 1822. He was a brick maker. He d. Mar. 26, 1876; res. Somerville, Mass.

3025. i. ALBERT, b. Aug. 21, 1847; m. Mary Lizzie Emery.

3026. ii. MARY ADENA, b. Oct. 14, 1852; m. Apr. 27, 1871, ―― Wakefield; res. 35 Temple St., Somerville, Mass.

3027. iii. FRANK HAYES, b. Jan. 27, 1860; m. Oct. 15, 1884, Annie F. Page, b. 1860; d. July 8, 1885; m. 2d, Sept. 29, 1887, Margaret A. Smith, b. Jan. 18, 1863. He is in the dairy business; res. 97 Jaques St., Somerville, Mass.; s. p.

1573. HIRAM FISK (Mark, Joseph, Mark, Joseph, William, John, William, Robert, Simon, Simon, William, Symond), b. Derry, N. H., Oct. 15, 1807; m. in Lowell Mar. 15, 1835, Louisa Whitney, b. June 8, 1812; d. Nov. 1, 1892. He was a carpenter. He was born in New Hampshire. When a young man he went to Massachusetts and married in Lowell. He was a carpenter by trade. He is now, 1896, 88 years old, and is a smart old man; can see to read without glasses, and reads the papers and is very much interested in politics; res. Woburn, Mass., and Long Beach, Cal.

3028. i. HIRAM WILSON, b. Feb. 1, 1837; m. Sarah Perry and Diana Cameron.

3029. ii. LOUISA F., b. July 24, 1838; m. Dec. 24, 1857, Jonathan P. Downing; he d. Oct. 16, 1894. She res. L. B.

3030. iii. CAROLINE A., b. May 7, 1840; m. July 20, 1866, John Perley Green, and Charles M. Gowing; res. Wilmington, Mass.

3031. iv. MARY JANE, b. Sept. 6, 1841; m. Oct. 4, 1860, at Woburn, Daniel W. Skelton; res. Stoneham, Mass.

3032. v. ADALINE D., b. Aug. 18, 1843; d. June 8, 1854.

3033. vi. GEORGIANNA, b. July 20, 1846; m. July 18, 1866, Stephen R. Bennett, of Woburn; res. L. B.

3034. vii. SARAH E., b. Aug. 9, 1852; d. June 30, 1853.

1575. BENJAMIN FISK (John, John, Mark, Joseph, William, William, John, William, Robert, Simon, Simon, William, Symond), b. Waterboro, Me., Feb. 11, 1813; m. Mary Jane Marshall; res. Alfred, Me.

3035. i. MARSHA, b. ――――; d. ae. 3 months.

3036. ii. GEORGE, b. May 17, 1846; unm.; res. Alfred.

3037. iii. MARY, b. Mar. 17, 1851; m. George Tripp; res. Alfred. Ch.: Louisa R., b. Oct., 1879; Frederick, b. Mar., 1882.

3038. iv. FRANK, b. ――――; d. ae. 1½ years.

1576. JOHN FISK (John, John, Mark, Joseph, William, William, John, William, Robert, Simon, Simon, William, Symond), b. Waterboro, Me., May 25, 1815; m. Mary Andrews, of Waterboro. He d. Oct. 27, 1875; res. Waterboro, Me.

    3039. i.   CHARLES, b. ———; res. Waterboro.
    3040. ii.   FRANK, b. ———; res. Saco, Me.; has 2 ch.

1578. SAMUEL COFFIN FISK (John, John, Mark, Joseph, William, William, John, William, Robert, Simon, Simon, William, Symond), b. Mar. 12, 1820, So. Waterboro, Me.; m. in Princeton, May 16, 1843, Fanny Ripley Wilson, of Princeton, Mass., b. May 3, 1820; d. Jan. 1, 1891. He was in the express business. He d. Sept. 10, 1880; res. Boston, Mass.

    3041. i.   ADELAIDE, b. Aug. 21, 1844; d. unm. Apr. 17, 1895.
    3042. ii.   GEORGIANNA, b. Sept. 1, 1846; m. Sept. 1, 1867, Frank Robinson. She d. Feb. 22, 1894. He was of Montreal, Canada; b. Apr. 23, 1844; d. Mar. 8, 1894; was a silk importer. She is buried in Englewood, N. J. Ch.: 1, Blanch Alice, b. at Boston, Mass., June 14, 1869; m. June 12, 1894, William Esterbrook; res. 162 W. 96th St., New York City; ch.: William, b. Apr. 26, 1895. 2, Florence Adelaide, b. at Boston, Mass., Nov. 7, 1873; m. Richard Kimball; res. Concord, N. H. 3, Mabel Fiske, b. at Boston, Mass., Sept. 14, 1875; d. at St. Albans, Vt. 4, Ethel White, b. at Boston, Mass., Dec. 30, 1876; d. at St. Albans, Vt.; buried at St. Albans, Vt. 5, Mildred, b. at Boston, Mass., Sept. 8, 1878; res. Concord, N. H. 6, Marion, b. at Boston, Mass., Sept. 8, 1878; res. Concord, N. H.
    3043. iii. SARAH, b. Mar. 30, 1848; d. Sept. 10, 1848.
    3044. iv. FRANKLIN PIERCE, b. Dec. 23, 1851; d. Dec. 30, 1853.
    3045. v.   ALBERT, b. Oct. 20, 1850; d. Dec. 1, 1850.
    3046. vi. FLORENCE WILDER, b. Feb. 20, 1855; d. Feb. 24, 1856.
    3047. vii. ALICE MAY, b. Apr. 30, 1861; m. Sept. 17, 1888, Arthur H. Chase; res. Concord, N. H. He was b. Feb. 10, 1864; is an attorney at law and librarian of the State Library of New Hampshire, at Concord. Ch.: Marjorie Fisk, b. June 12, 1892.

1579. GEORGE FISKE (John, John, Mark, Joseph, William, William, John, William, Robert, Simon, Simon, William, Symond), b. June 10, 1822, Waterboro, Me.; m. June 22, 1847, Abigail Hill, of Waterboro. He is a teamster; res. 374 W. Fourth St., So. Boston, Mass.

    3048. i.   OSCAR, b. Jan. 1, 1852; d. Sept. 8, 1852.
    3049. ii.   EMMA L., b. Sept. 26, 1855; m. Benjamin T. Leuzarder, of Lincoln, Me.; res. Milwaukee, Wis. Ch.: Annie B., b. Nov. 18, 1876.
    3050. iii. FRANK C., b. Feb. 3, 1857; res. at home.
    3051. iv. WILBUR S., b. Jan. 3, 1859; d. in Chicago Nov. 30, 1893.
    3052. v.   GEORGE E., b. Mar. 13, 1862; d. Sept. 6, 1862.

1590. AMOS FISKE (Nathaniel, Nathaniel, Theophilus, Theophilus, William, William, John, William, Robert, Simon, Simon, William, Symond), b. Topsfield, Mass., May 26, 1801; m. Dec. 16, 1834, Mercy Peabody, dau. of Capt. Ebenezer and (Perkins) Peabody, near relations of the Perkinses, who married into the family. He settled at first in Topsfield where all their children were born, and died in Boxford near the border of Topsfield. He d. Sept. 9, 1850; res. Boxford, Mass.

    3053. i.   JOSEPH BATCHELDER, b. Jan. 5, 1837.
    3054. ii.   JOHN, b. June 7, 1839.
    3055. iii. MARY HERBERT, b. June 23, 1841.
    3056. iv. SARAH ABIGAIL, b. Mar. 8, 1843; m. Leonard Killam; res. Boxford.
    3057. v.   JAMES, b. June 24, 1845.

1597. ABRAHAM HOBBS FISKE (Benjamin, Nathaniel, Theophilus, Theophilus, William, William, John, William, Robert, Simon, Simon, William, Symond), b. Salem, Mass., Nov. 2, 1792; m. Joanna (Ober) Edwards, b. Oct. 17, 1802; d. Nov. 5, 1865; m. 2d, Mrs. Abigail Wingate. Abraham, son of Benjamin and Lydia (Hobbs) Fiske, married Joanna Ober, dau. of Benjamin and Joanna

(Ober) Edwards, of Beverly. She died and he married second, widow Abigail Wingate; resided in Beverly, at a place on the north side of the town called Dodge's Row; a farmer. He d. Feb. 6, 1881; res. Beverly, Mass.

3058. i. ELBRIDGE L., b. Oct. 9, 1824; d. Aug. 25, 1825.
3059. ii. ALBERT RICHARD O., b. Apr. 30, 1826; m. Elizabeth (White) Safford and Mrs. Jennie L. (Clay) Seavey.
3060. iii. BENJAMIN, b. Jan. 6, 1832; d. young.
3061. iv. ABRAHAM ALVIN, b. Dec. 28, 1832; m. Lucy Ann Philbrook.
3062. v. GEO. FRANKLIN, b. Feb. 29, 1828.
3063. vi. CAROLINE ELSA, b. Apr. 17, 1830; d. young.
3063¼.vii. JOANNA O., b. July 15, 1835; m. Luther Foster, b. Jan. 30, 1830.
3063½.vii. ELBRIDGE, b. May 16, 1837.
3063¾.ix. WILLIAM, b. Oct. 16, 1839.

1600. JOHN FISKE (Benjamin, Nathaniel, Theophilus, Theophilus, William, William, John, William, Robert, Simon, Simon, William, Symond), b. Mar. 2, 1804; m. Sally Haynes, dau. of James Haynes, of Compton, N. H.; res. Woodstock, N. H.

3064. i. ELBRIDGE GERRY, b. ———.
3065. ii. BENJAMIN, b. ———; res. Haverhill, Mass.
3066. iii. SULLIVAN, b. ———; res. Maine.

1603. EBENEZER FISKE (Benjamin, Nathaniel, Theophilus, Theophilus, William, William, John, William, Robert, Simon, Simon, William, Symond), b. Salem, Mass., Aug. 18, 1809; m. June 8, 1835, Elizabeth Mudge, dau. of Simon and Fanny, b. Aug. 22, 1813; d. July 6, 1860; m. 2d, Mrs. Elizabeth (Stevens) Wilson. Ebenezer, son of Benjamin and Lydia (Hobbs) Fiske, married Elizabeth, dau. of Simon and Fanny Mudge, of Danvers. His occupation was that of a farmer. He was born in Salem. About the time of his marriage he removed to Lyndeboro, N. H., where he afterward resided. He d. Mar. 30, 1883, in Milford, N. H.; res. Lyndeboro, N. H.

3067. i. FRANCES MUDGE, b. Mar. 30, 1836; m. Levi P., son of Page and Mary Spalding, of Lyndeboro, July 1, 1863; a farmer in that town. Ch.: Fred Willis, b. Apr. 25, 1864; Lizzie, b. July 23, 1865, now Mrs. L. P. Spalding; res. Lyndeboro.
3068. ii. LYDIA JANE, b. Dec. 3, 1837; d. Sept. 10, 1840.
3069. iii. HERBERT AUGUSTUS, b. Oct. 18, 1839; m. Sarah E. Cutler.
3070. iv. JAMES OSCAR, b. Nov. 21, 1841; m. Sarah O. Jones.
3071. v. BENJAMIN MUDGE, b. Mar. 5, 1844; m. Sarah Fletcher.
3072. vi. JANE CATHERINE, b. Apr. 8, 1846; m. Jan. 31, 1871, William D. Deadman; res. Wakefield, Mass.
3073. vii. JULIA AUGUSTA, b. May 8, 1848; m. Mar., 1880, Edwin Stark; res. Wakefield, Mass.
3074. viii. WILLIAM EBEN, b. Aug. 22, 1850; m. Phebe C. Cutler.
3075. ix. ALMIRA ELIZABETH, b. Aug. 23, 1852; unm.; res. 16 Church St., Wakefield, Mass.

1604. SHADRACH FISKE (Benjamin, Nathaniel, Theophilus, Theophilus, William, William, John, William, Robert, Simon, Simon, William, Symond), b. Woodstock, N. H., May 2, 1812; m. Jan. 15, 1832, Mrs. Lucy (Boden) Standley, widow of Thomas, b. Oct. 3, 1805; d. Nov. 11, 1867; m. 2d, Dec. 10, 1868, Susan Raymond, b. July 23, 1808; d. Apr. 4, 1887. Shadrach, son of Benjamin and Lydia (Hobbs) Fiske, was the tallest in stature of all the family, who in that respect follow their grandfather, who was a shoe manufacturer on Central St., Beverly, close by his residence. Lucy, his wife, was a dau. of Thomas Boden, and widow of Thomas Standley, born in Beverly. He d. Jan. 20, 1886; res. Beverly, Mass.

3076. i. CHARLES EDWIN, b. Apr. 3, 1834; d. May 31, 1839.
3077. ii. BENJAMIN PORTER, b. Apr. 7, 1836; d. at Amherst, Mass., Jan. 1, 1858, in the 22d year of his age, unmarried. The sad death was caused by breaking his back in a fall of about thirty feet from a shellbark hickory tree, the limb that he was upon breaking; but he endured intense suffering from the time of the accident, in October, until the following January. He was a student in Amherst College in his third year.
3078. iii. LUCY JANE, b. Dec. 10, 1837; d. Feb. 28, 1839.

3079. iv. JOHN MILTON, b. June 25, 1839; d. June 22, 1850. He met his
           death in a singular manner. He went out on the seashore one
           evening after supper with his comrades, and as they had fre-
           quently done before, gathered mussels, baked and ate them, and
           it is supposed he happened to eat one that was diseased, or had
           undergone a partial decomposition. As soon as he felt sick he
           started for the house, and just as he reached home lost the en-
           tire use of his limbs, was unable to speak, and at nine o'clock
           that same evening died.

3080. v.   ELIZABETH BODEN, b. Apr. 20, 1841; m. July 31, 1864, Isaac
           Henry, son of Handyside P. and Ruth Edgett, from Eastport,
           Me., b. in Hillsboro, N. B., Mar. 13, 1838, a cabinet maker.
           She res. with her father. Ch.: 1, Horace Peirce, b. Mar. 3,
           1866; 2, Carrie Cousins, b. July 22, 1870; 3, Grace Lawrence, b.
           May 12, 1874; 4, Ruth Eleanor, b. October 31, 1876. All un-
           married, living at 329 Cabot St., Beverly, Mass.

1612. JUDGE PUTNAM BRADFORD FISKE (Moses, Nathaniel, Theophilus, Theophilus, William, William, John, William, Robert, Simon, Simon, William, Symond), b. Sept. 9, 1820; m. Feb. 25, 18—, ————— —————. Putnam Bradford
was born in Stockholm, St. Lawrence County, N. Y.; was brought up in a little log
house, in a new settlement adjoining the forests on the land reserved to the St.
Regis Indians. He early formed a determination to acquire an education, though
having scarcely any means as regards schools, or the funds, in consequence of his
father not being able to provide them on account of his feeble health. Like the
"Bobbin Boy," and others, he succeeded in acquiring an excellent education and
won the confidence and esteem of his fellow citizens generally, for they gave him
places of honor and trust. He commenced school-teaching, when seventeen years
of age; practiced law in the courts of the State; has been Inspector of Schools,
Deputy Sheriff, and for two years one of the Associate Justices of the Court of
General Sessions of Franklin County. He resided and had his law office in Fort
Covington until 1850, when he removed to Chateaugay, same county. He was
married at Le Roy, Jefferson County, N. Y.; res. Chateaugay, N. Y.

3081. 1.   KATE AMELIA, b. Sept. 1, 1854.
3082. ii. GEORGE ARTHUR, b. Feb. 12, 1857.

1623. JOHN BROWN FISKE (Ezra, Samuel, Theophilus, Theophilus, William, William, John, William, Robert, Simon, Simon, William, Symond), b. Beverly, Oct. 1, 1804; m. Jan. 10, 1832, Sarah Smith, dau. of Andrew and Lucretia
Derby (Mansfield) Smith, b. May 28, 1812. John B., son of Capt. Ezra and Polly
(Lakeman) Fiske, who married Sarah Smith, was a seaman from a child 15 years
old to 1856, when his health failed. He was a ship commander from the age of 23,
consequently has seen rough times, having sailed around the stormy Cape Horn
over a half dozen times, more often around Good Hope, and into cold and hot
climes, requiring courage and fortitude. His place of residence has been (excepting a while in Brooklyn, N. Y.) in Salem, and some time in the house on Boston
Street, with his grandfather, George Smith, and since 1852 in a house he then
built on Mason, northwest corner of Buffum Street, in North Fields, Salem; res.
Salem Mass.

3083. i.   GEORGE ALEXANDER, b. Aug. 2, 1833; m. Elizabeth Mor-
            ton.
3084. ii.   CHARLES BROWN, b. May 6, 1836, in Brooklyn, is a farmer
            in "Bealaratt," Australia, where he has been since 1852; prob-
            ably unm.
3085. iii. AUGUSTUS, b. Sept. 17, 1838, in Salem, is a seaman.
3086. iv.   JOHN BROWN, b. in Salem Sept. 10, 1843, commenced a sea-
            man's life, but was drowned in the Black Sea Apr. 10, 1863.

1634. REV. EZRA WILLIAMS FISK, D. D. (Jonathan, Simeon, Ebenezer,
Ebenezer, William, William, John, William, Robert, Simon, Simon, William, Symond), b. May 29, 1820, Wilmington, Vt.; m. at Princeton, N. J., May 22, 1855,
Mary Van Dyke, b. June 18, 1825. He was born in the Green Mountain State and
when 14 years of age moved with his parents to Coshocton, Ohio, where he grew
to manhood. He worked part of the time with his father at the cooper trade and
was prepared for college in a private school in that place taught by Prof. B. C.

Woodward. He entered college at Princeton, N. J., in the winter of 1846-47 and was graduated in the summer of 1849. His graduation was followed by a singular and very severe and protracted illness, unfitting him for any labor for three years. In the autumn of 1852 he had so far recovered that he gradually resumed his studies, having removed in the meantime to Terre Haute, Ind. He was licensed to preach in the spring of 1854 and immediately took charge of the Presbyterian Church at Greencastle, Ind.; was ordained and installed a year later and continued in this pastorate for more than twenty years. He received the degree of D. D. from the State University of Indiana. He was for some years president of the Indiana Female College. Since leaving that he has been engaged in ministerial work at different points, at present at Rockport, Ind., though he still retains his home at Greencastle, Ind.; res. Greencastle, Ind.

1637. REV. HENRY WILLIAMS FISK (Jonathan, Simeon, Ebenezer, Ebenezer, William, William, John, William, Robert, Simon, Simon, William, Symond), b. Goshen, N. Y., Nov. 6, 1833; m. at Paris, Ill., Aug. 12, 1862, Mary J. Stevenson, b. Sept. 6, 1834. Henry W. Fisk was the youngest son of Jonathan and Susanna (Williams) Fisk, and was born at Goshen, Orange County, N. Y. The family moved to Coshocton, Ohio, in the autumn of 1834. His mother died in July, 1841. Henry's home for the succeeding eight years was with one or the other of his sisters, Mrs. Esther S. Welsh or Mrs. Georgiana Burt. In Oct., 1849, he went with his father to Terre Haute, Ind., where he spent about four months as a clerk in a grocery store, and four months in school, after which he entered the shop of Barton & Co., as an apprentice, to learn the marble cutting trade. After two years at this work he entered Waveland Academy as a student. Near the close of his second year at this institution his health became so much impaired as to necessitate his leaving school and it was four years before he returned to it. A part of this time was spent in work at his former trade, one year of which was in Iowa, at Sigourney and Marion—this was the year 1855. In the spring of 1856 he went to St. Paul, Minn., where he spent six months at the same work. In Oct., 1856, he returned to Indiana, where he engaged in teaching until the summer of 1858. At the opening of the fall term 1858 he re-entered the school, then Waveland Collegiate Institute, where he graduated July 8, 1859, receiving the degree of B. S. In Sept. following he taught in the public schools of Paris, Ill., and afterward in Edgar Academy at the same place. From there he went to the Waveland (Ind.) Institute as professor of mathematics. In the fall of 1861 he took charge of Maple Grove Academy, near Vincennes, Ind., where he continued for about four years. In the fall of 1864, having read the course in theology under the guidance of his pastor, Rev. F. R. Morton, and passed the customary examination, he was licensed to preach by the Presbytery of Vincennes, Sept. 10. In the spring of 1865 he took charge of a home mission field with headquarters at Petersburg, Ind., continuing in this work for five and one-half years, when failing health necessitated a change. In the fall of 1870 he took charge of Beulah Church, Rock Island County, Ill. After nearly two years in this charge he removed to Hamlet, Mercer County, Ill., becoming pastor of Hamlet and Perryton Churches. He continued in this field thirteen years, resigned, and in Sept., 1885, was called to the pastorate of Peniel and Millersburg Churches; he remained with them seven years, when, having been partially disabled by the grippe and compelled to seek lighter work, he obtained charge of the Viola (Ill.) Church and moved there in Oct., 1892. And is there yet, Nov., 1896; res. Viola, Ill.

    3087. i.   CHARLES EZRA, b. Nov. 9, 1863; m. Lulu A. Johnson.

    3088. ii.   SUSAN, b. Apr. 24, 1866, Petersburg, Ind.; m. May 24, 1887, Rev. Wm. W. Carlton; res. Independence, Ia. She graduated at the Lenox College in the same class with her brother and her future husband. He is a Methodist clergyman. Ch.: Florence, b. Nov. 11, 1888; d. Oct., 1892. Mabel E., b. Sept., 1890. Henry F., b. Sept., 1892.

    3089. iii. EMMA, b. July 12, 1873; now, 1895, a student at Lenox College, Hopkinton, Ia.

1645. FRANCIS ALVAREZ FISKE (Ebenezer, Ebenezer, Ebenezer, Ebenezer, William, William, John, William, Robert, Simon, Simon, William, Symond), b. Shelburne, Mass., July 8, 1813; m. there Apr. 2, 1840, Melinda Ophelia Bardwell. When a boy he assisted his father in his business. As he attained his majority he taught school for a number of years, some of the time at home and the remainder in the west. Later he returned from the west to Shelburne; was married, bought the farm where he afterward lived and died. He was honest and upright in all his dealings with his fellowmen, a church member and an officer in the church. He d. June 26, 1881; res. Shelburne, Mass.

3090. i.   FRANCIS ALVAREZ, b. June 3, 1841; m. Hattie Allen.
3091. ii.   WILLIAM BARDWELL, b. Nov. 20, 1842; m. Luella Emma Herrick and Mrs. Hannah R. (Naylor) Jones.
3092. iii. FIDELIA, b. Oct. 31, 1844; m. Nov. 12, 1867, Charles Elliston Slate, of S. He was b. Oct. 22, 1841. They now reside in Greenfield, Mass. Ch.: Francis Clark Slate, b. in Shelburne July 26, 1870. Ella Fidelia Slate, b. in Shelburne Feb. 9, 1874.
3093. iv.   MELINDA WAIT, b. Nov. 18, 1847; d. Jan. 1, 1849.

1646. EBENEZER FISKE (Ebenezer, Ebenezer, Ebenezer, Ebenezer, William, William, John, William, Robert, Simon, Simon, William, Symond), b. Shelburne, Mass., Aug. 28, 1815; m. Adrian, Mich., Nov. 18, 1841, Elizabeth Smead, b. Jan. 11, 1817. He went to Michigan in 1838 where he remained for a year. He then returned to Shelburne and lived two years, finally returning to Michigan in Nov., 1841. Purchasing a farm of 160 acres he has resided upon it ever since; res. Adrian, Mich.

3094. i.   RUFUS HENRY, b. Aug. 17, 1844; m. Eliza C. Horder.
3095. ii.   EBENEZER, b. Oct. 31, 1846; d. Mar. 30, 1849.
3096. iii. EDWARD PAYSON, b. Nov. 15, 1848; m. Frankie J. Poucher.
3097. iv.   HERMAN SMEAD, b. Aug. 3, 1853; m. Dora E. Gambee.
3098. v.   ANNA ELIZABETH, b. Sept. 17, 1856; m. Nov. 10, 1881, Clarence Frost, b. Feb. 6, 1856. She d. July 23, 1891. Ch.: Mildred, b. Aug. 21, 1890; res. A.

1647. PLINEY FISKE (Ebenezer, Ebenezer, Ebenezer, Ebenezer, William, William, John, William, Robert, Simon, Simon, William, Symond), b. Shelburne, Mass., July 30, 1817; m. Aug. 29, 1844, Orilla Peck, b. Feb. 21, 1822. He was a teacher. He d. Dec. 12, 1872; res. Shelburne, Mass.

3099. i.   PLINEY, b. Oct. 26, 1862; res., unm., Arlington, Mass.
3100. ii.   HARRIET AMELIA, b. May 17, 1847; res. A.
3101. iii. MARY PACKARD, b. July 23, 1865; res. A.; unm.
3102. iv.   JOHN PECK, b. June 6, 1870.

1648. REV. DANIEL TAGGART FISKE (Ebenezer, Ebenezer, Ebenezer, Ebenezer, William, William, John, William, Robert, Simon, Simon, William, Symond), b. Shelburne, Mass., Mar. 29, 1819; m. in 1849, Eliza P. Dutton, of Boston, b. May 3, 1827; d. Oct. 21, 1862; m. 2d, Feb. 14, 1867, Mrs. Caroline Walworth Drummond, b. Aug. 31, 1828. Daniel Taggart, fourth son of Deacon Ebenezer Fiske, of Shelburne, graduated at Amherst College in 1842, and at Andover Theological Seminary, in 1846, was licensed, and supplied the same year, at Andover, Exeter, N. H., and St. Johnsbury, Vt., and Aug. 18, 1847, was ordained as pastor over Belleville Church, Newburyport, the late professor preaching the sermon, which position he has retained almost fifty years. In 1862 Mr. Fiske received the degree of D. D., from Amherst College, as a theologian. He is much esteemed in Newburyport as a preacher, pastor and citizen; was married to Eliza Dutton, of Boston, and after her death to Mrs. Drummond. He still continues in the same pastorate to which he was ordained Aug 18, 1847, but since 1887 he has had a colleague and is senior pastor. Res. Newburyport, Mass.

REV. DANIEL TAGGART FISKE.

3103. i.   MARY FIDELIA, b. Aug. 11, 1850; m. May 8, 1882, Rev. Charles A. Savage; res. Orange, N. J. b. Stowe, Vt., July 10, 1849; son of Reuben A. and Elizabeth D. Savage. His early years were spent on his father's farm. He graduated from Dartmouth College in 1871. Taught in St. Johnsbury, Vt.

Academy for three years, and in Robert College, Constantinople, for four years more; traveling extensively meanwhile through Europe and the Orient. Returning to this country in 1878, he took his theological course in Yale Divinity School, and then went to Berkeley, Cal., as pastor of the First Congregational Church in that place. That pastorate lasted for some six years; his second, in Enfield, Mass., for three years, and his present one, in Orange, N. J., has now lasted five years. Two children; Theodore Fiske Savage, b. in Berkeley, Cal., June 8, 1885, and Marion Dutton Savage, b. in Enfield, Mass., June 18, 1888.

3104. ii. GEORGE DUTTON, b. Mar. 9, 1859; d. Oct. 13, 1871.

1650. ISAAC TERRILL FISKE (Ebenezer, Ebenezer, Ebenezer, Ebenezer, William, William, John, William, Robert Simon, Simon, William, Symond), b. Shelburne, Mass., July 27, 1824; m. in 1847, Hannah Parsons, of Vernon, Vt.; m. 2d, Sept. 15, 1858, Rosanna Crosby, b. June 6, 1839. He was born and brought up in Shelburne and there spent most of his life. Taught school several winters, working on the home farm summers.* Soon after his marriage he moved to Guilford, Vt., where he engaged in the lumber business. On the death of his younger brother, Levi, he returned to the old home in Shelburne, Mass., where he lived until his death, Aug. 29, 1895. He took great pleasure in improving the place, erecting modern buildings and bringing the land under a high state of cultivation; making the old homestead one of the finest places in the town. He was known throughout the country as a successful farmer and breeder of choice Jersey stock. He was always active in church and Sunday school work and influential in town affairs. An obituary notice says: "Of quiet demeanor, yet force of character, his influence was a potent factor in the history of the town. He was self reliant and could not by fear or flattery be swerved from principle. He was sincere, conscientious, reliable. His word was as good as his bond. In home life he was genial, pleasant, kindly; as a citizen, large minded, public spirited." He d. Aug. 29, 1895; res. Vernon, Vt.

3105. i. FREDERICK F., b. Jan. 8, 1867; m. at Hoosick Falls, N. Y., Sept. 27, 1895, Alice L. Bell, b. July 20, 1879. He is a farmer; res. E. Shelburne, Mass. He was born on the old place, has always resided there and expects to as long as he lives.
3106. ii. ELLA, b. ———; m. Albert Wright; res. Hardy, Neb.
3107. iii. CHARLES S., b. Oct. 27, 1859; m. Addie Gilbert.
3108. iv. LEVI L., b. Mar. 10, 1861; m. Jessie E. Miner.
3109. v. ALICE B., b. Aug. 22, 1864; res. E. Shelburne.
3110. vi. ROSA B., b. July 5, 1869; m. Oct. 2, 1891, Edward T. Cutting; res. E. Shelburne, Mass. Ch.: Raymond F., b. Apr. 1, 1893.

1656. PLINY BEYROOT FISK (Levi, Ebenezer, Ebenezer, Ebenezer, William, William, John, William, Robert, Simon, Simon, William, Symond), b. Byron, N. Y., Dec. 8, 1830; m. there Oct. 14, 1857, Jane A. Walker, b. Jan. 24, 1836. He is a farmer; res. Byron, N. Y.

3111. i. LEVI W., b. June 21, 1859; m. Nellie E. House.
3112. ii. HENRY C., b. Oct. 3, 1870; d. Sept. 27, 1875.

1658. CAPT. THOMAS BRIGGS FISK (Perrin B., Moses, Ebenezer, Ebenezer, William, William, John, William, Robert, Simon, Simon, William, Symond), b. Fort Covington, N. Y., June 27, 1823; m. Shushan, N. Y., July 26, 1842, Amarett Bartlett, b. Aug. 8, 1824; d. July 31, 1879. He settled in Shushan, town of Salem, Washington Co., N. Y., in early life, where his father preached as a Baptist minister; married Amarett Bartlett, in that town; enlisted in Civil war, 1861; being the first volunteer in the county; served five years, and was honorably discharged. Was Second Lieutenant, First Lieutenant, and finally Captain before the war closed. His trade in early life was harness and saddle making. He d. Feb. 20, 1868; res. Jackson, N. Y.

3113. i. WM. WALLACE, b. Sept. 4, 1843; d. Sept. 26, 1846.
3114. ii. PERRIN BARTLETT, b. Oct. 27, 1845; m. Hannah M. Wing, Mary E. Gleason and E. J. Sugden.
3115. iii. CORNELIA ANN, b. Feb. 29, 1847; m. Nov. 30, 1861.

Elbert H. Wing; res. No. Hoosick, N. Y. Ch.: I, Lillian M.,
b. Aug. 10, 1863; d. Dec. 10, 1873. 2, E. Otto, b. July 26, 1873.
3, Martha F., b. May 31, 1883.

3116.   iv.   CHAS. HENRY, b. Dec. 29, 1850; m. Mary A. Soterege.
3117.   v.   JULIA AMARETT, b. May 6, 1853; d. Dec. 17, 1864.
3118.   vi.   THOMAS OTTO, b. Jan. 27, 1857; m. Ida M. Andrus.

1662. HON. HENRY CLAY FISK (Moses, Moses, Ebenezer, Ebenezer, William, William, John, William, Robert, Simon, Simon, William, Symond), b. Morristown, Vt., July 22, 1852; m. at Hyde Park, Vt., Mar. 15, 1876, Isabel Martha Page,

HON. HENRY CLAY FISK.

b. Mar. 25, 1857. Hon. Henry C. Fisk,
of Morristown, Republican, trustee, was
born in Morristown. He is a lawyer,
and the editor of the "News and Citizen;"
was educated at People's Academy and
Peacham Academy. He was page in the
Senate in 1867 and 1868 and executive
clerk in 1869, and has been register of
probate for the district of Lamoille from
1880 to 1884, and a member of the First
Congressional District Committee since
1882. He represented Morristown in the
House of Representatives in 1886, when
he served on the committee on the judi-
ciary and the joint special committee on
State and Court expenses; in December
of that year he was appointed a trustee of
the Vermont Reform School, which position he now holds. Religious preference, Congregationalist. Add. Morrisville. Was State Senator in 1888-9. Res.
Morrisville, Vt.

3119.   i.   MARY MALVINA, b.
               Oct. 16, 1877.
3120.   ii.   GERTRUDE REBEC-
               CA, b. Dec. 14, 1879;
               d. Dec. 16, 1887.
3121.   iii.   LILLIAN ELLEN, b.
               May 29, 1884.
3122.   iv.   CARROLL PAGE, b.
               May 31, 1887.

3123.   v.   HENRY CLAY, b. Sept. 19, 1888.
3124.   vi.   MARJORIE CORNELIA, b. June 30, 1891; d. Nov. 16, 1893.
3125.   vii.   HAZEL ISABEL, b. Apr. 6, 1895.
3126.   viii. GEORGE HENDEE, b. Apr. 6, 1895.

1671. PLINY FISK (Joel, Moses, Ebenezer, Ebenezer, William, William,
John, William, Robert, Simon, Simon, William, Symond), b. Monkton, Vt., May
10, 1828; m. in Allenton, N. J., May 12, 1852, Helen Burlay, b. Apr., 1828; d. Dec.
15, 1871; m. 2d. at Trenton, N. J., Oct. 22, 1874, Elizabeth C. Hall, b. July 9, 1840.
The limited salary his father received, forced him at an early age to seek employment. He was a clerk in a hardware store in Montreal and New York; bookkeeper for an insurance company, and secretary and treasurer of a trust company. Later a coal operator in Schuylkill Co., Pennsylvania, and then president of
a national bank in New York; director of a railroad in Virginia; president of a pot-
tery manufactory, Trenton. Res. Trenton, N. J.

3127.   i.   HORACE E., b. Aug. 25, 1856; m. Julia S. Atterbury.
3128.   ii.   MARY HELEN, b. July 6, 1859; res. New Haven, Conn.
3129.   iii.   WM. I., b. Nov. 16, 1861; m. Fannie B. Norris.
3130.   iv.   JOHN H., b. Oct. 22, 1876; d. July 24, 1882.
3131.   v.   ANNIE HALL, b. Aug. 6, 1878.
3132.   vi.   ELIZABETH C., b. Dec. 6, 1880.

1673. HARVEY FISK (Joel, Moses, Ebenezer, Ebenezer, William, William, John, William, Robert, Simon, Simon, William, Symond), b. Apr. 26, 1831, at New Haven, Vt.; m. at Trenton, N. J., Dec. 13, 1853, Louisa Green, b. Aug. 8, 1834. He was a banker. His sons have failed to send biographical sketch, though requested repeatedly to do so. He d. Nov. 8, 1890; res. Greensburgh, N. J.

3133. i. HARVEY EDWARD, b. Mar. 28, 1856; m. Mary Lee Scudder.
3134. ii. CHARLES J., b. June 16, 1858; m. Lillie Richie.
3135. iii. PLINY, b. Aug. 26, 1860; m. Mary Chapman.
3136. iv. ALEXANDER GREEN, b. Sept. 26, 1862; unm.; add. 24 Nassau St., New York City.
3137. v. WILBUR C., b. Feb. 22, 1868; m. Julia H. Allen.
3138. vi. LOUISA, b. Sept. 10, 1864; d. Sept. 26, 1865.
3139. vii. FREDERICK H., b. May 18, 1866; d. Aug. 22, 1867.
3140. viii. MARY LOUISA, b. Feb. 23, 1870; unm.
3141. ix. EDITH, b. Mar. 11, 1872; d. Sept. 27, 1880.
3142. x. BERTHA, b. Aug. 30, 1874; unm.
3143. xi. EVELYN LOUISE, b. Oct. 29, 1878; res. at home.

1676. DANIEL C. FISK (Joel, Moses, Ebenezer, Ebenezer, William, William, John, William, Robert, Simon, Simon, William, Symond), b. in Nov., 1840; m. in 1860; res. Brooklyn, N. Y., 1198 Bushwick, Ave.

3144. i. CLARINDA C., b. 1861; m. 1881, W. P. Gesner. Ch.: 1, Frank Whitney, b. 1882; d. 1882.
3145. ii. SAMUEL M., b. 1864.
3146. iii. DANIEL C., b. 1866.
3147. iv. MARION R., b. 1867; d. 1868.
3148. v. LOUISA, b. 1869.
3149. vi. GEO. W., b. 1871; d. 1873.

1679. REV. PERRIN BATCHELDER FISK (Lyman, Moses, Ebenezer, Ebenezer, William, William, John, William, Robert, Simon, Simon, William, Symond), b. Waitsfield, Vt., July 3, 1837; m. there Aug. 25, 1863, Harriett Laura Bigelow, b. Nov. 8, 1840. He graduated from Bangor Theological Seminary in 1863; was ordained pastor in Dracut (now Lowell), Mass., Oct. 1, 1863; served the first church, Rockport, Mass., from Nov., 1865, to June, 1866; was fourth pastor of Congregational Church, Peacham, Vt., from 1866 to 1870; was appointed to take up the new work in Lyndonville in the same county in 1870-75. In 1869-72 was chaplain of Vermont Senate; 1875-78 pastor Springfield, Vt.; 1878-82 pastor Lake City, Minn.; 1882-83 field agent Carleton College, Northfield, Minn.; 1883-84 Home Mission pastor, Plano, Ill.; 1884-86 H. M. pastor Mount Dora and Tangerine, Florida, Orange County (later Lake County); 1886-89 H. M. pastor Altemonte, Orange County, Fla. (during this time he was also trustee of Rollins College, Winter Park, Fla.); 1889-92 acting pastor Morrisville, Vt.; 1882 to the present time pastor of First Church of Lyndon and St. Johnsbury Center, Vt. It was by him while in Lake City, Minn., that the discovery was made of the true Congregationalism of the Swedish Mission Churches, and the clue given to Secretary Montgomery, which led to his beautiful life work. His native church in June, 1896, chose him to give its Centennial discourse, and one item in that discourse mentioned the fact that there had now been for ninety-five years a Deacon Fisk in that church; res. Lyndon, Vt.

3150. i. FLORA IMLAY, b. Jan. 4, 1865; m. Jan. 4, 1885, George Leslie Zimmerman. He d. June 26, 1892. They were m. in Florida, and have two ch.: Vernon and Nina.
3151. ii. GEO. SHEPARD, b. Aug. 10, 1868; m. Dec. 25, 1894, Alice Morgan, b. Oct. 18, 1868. He d. s. p. of quick consumption Sept. 25, 1895. George S. Fisk died at Burlington after a long illness. He had an attack of typhoid fever in Mar., and came near to death's door then. Early in the summer he recovered sufficiently to be removed to his father's home in Lyndon, where he seemed to improve for a time, but when he returned to Burlington he began to fail in health again. He was married to Miss Alice Morgan, of Burlington. He had been in newspaper work for about half a dozen years, during which time he had

21

worked on the Morrisville Citizen, both the St. Johnsbury papers, the Bennington Banner, Burlington Clipper and Burlington News. He was a bright and easy writer and a splendid newsgatherer.

3152. iii. FIDELIA, b. June 1, 1870; clerk; res. Room 40, No. 1 Beacon St., Boston, Mass.
3153. iv. GRACE HARRIETT, b. Jan. 29, 1876; kindergarten.

1687. DEA. EDWARD ANSON FISK (Anson, Moses, Ebenezer, Ebenezer, William, William, John, William, Robert, Simon, Simon, William, Symond), b. Waitsfield, Vt., Feb. 1, 1842; m. there Nov. 28, 1876, Lilian A. Ramsay, b. St. Johnsbury, Vt., July 28, 1852. He received his education at the common schools and at Barre (Vt.) Academy. His student life was cut short by the war, however. He enlisted as private in Company B, Thirteenth Vermont Regiment. At the battle of Gettysburg, under Gen. Stannard, he took part with the Second Vermont Brigade in movements that good judges pronounce the "turning points" of this battle, which is called the "turning point" of the war. On the second day of the fight when the confederates had well nigh pierced our center, the Thirteenth Vermont was called into action and made a charge against a brigade of the enemy, driving it back and following it up for some distance and capturing many prisoners although the regiment was unsupported on either flank. Mr. Fisk was slightly wounded in this charge but did not leave the field, and the next day took part in the famous movement of Gen. Stannard's troops when they fell upon the flank of Gen. Pickett's advancing column and completed its discomfiture. Soon after this battle Mr. Fisk had an attack of typhoid fever which nearly cost him his life and left him unfitted for further army service. He settled upon the old homestead in Waitsfield and cared for his parents in their declining years. He has held several important offices in his native town, with acceptance. He was chosen deacon of the Congregational Church at the age of 24, which office he still holds. He has frequently written acceptable articles for the press, especially upon agricultural and Grand Army topics; res. Waitsfield, Vt.

3154. i. ANNIE LOWISA, b. Sept. 2, 1878.
3155. ii. CHARLES EDWARD, b. Mar. 25, 1880.
3156. iii. ANSON HUBERT, b. Nov. 5, 1882.
3157. iv. HAROLD HAYES, b. Nov. 24, 1890.

1689. REV. PLINY BARNARD FISK (Anson, Moses, Ebenezer, Ebenezer, William, William, John, William, Robert, Simon, Simon, William, Symond), b. Waitsfield, Vt., May 6, 1850; m. in Gettysburg, So. Dak., Jan. 3, 1888. Caroline Clarke, b. near Piqua, Ohio, Apr. 9, 1841. He was born in Waitsfield, Vt.; graduated from Barre Academy in 1873; entered Vermont University, Burlington, Vt., the same year; graduated from college in 1877; spent one year teaching in the graded schools in Essex, N. Y.; entered Yale Divinity School in 1878; spent his summer vacations in the employ of the Vermont Domestic Missionary Society; also a portion of the summer of 1881, after the close of his seminary course. In the fall of 1881 he went to Dakota as a member of the Yale Dakota Band, with a company of nine students who pledged themselves to go into the Home Missionary work in the then new territory of Dakota. He worked one year in Egan (Moody County); two years in Letcher (Sanborn County); four years in Gettysburg (Potter County); seven years in Myron (Faulk County); and is now situated at Ree Heights (Hand County), having charge of four churches in that county and two in Buffalo County; res. Sweetland and Ree Heights, So. Dak., Hand County, s. p.

1695. JOSEPH WILLOUGHBY FISKE (Nathaniel, Jonathan, William, Ebenezer, William, William, John, William, Robert, Simon, Simon, William, Symond), b. Williamstown, Vt., Nov. 29, 1797; m. at Northfield, Mar. 25, 1823, Louisa Carpenter; m. 2d, 1833. Clarissa Buck. He d. May, 1864; res. Williamstown, Vt.

3158. i. JOSEPH B., b. Apr., 1825.
3159. ii. MARY U., b. May 14, 1828.
3160. iii. SAMUEL B., b. Dec. 30, 1829.
3161. iv. ROSWELL C., b. Apr. 9, 1831; d. in 1860.
3162. v. GEORGE, b. Nov. 18, 1832.
3163. vi. RUTH M., b. Apr. 3, 1835; d. young.
3164. vii. ANGELINA B., b. Aug. 27, 1838; d. young.

3165. viii. HARRIET ADELINE, b. Feb. 23, 1843; m. Edward Misener; he d. ———.

1697. JONATHAN FISKE (Nathaniel, Jonathan, William, Ebenezer, William, William, William, John, William, Robert, Simon, Simon, William, Symond), b. Williamstown, Vt., May 12, 1804; m. 1838 Dolly Carrier. He d. Dec. 25, 1883; res. Parksville, N. Y.

3166. i. JOEL CARRIER, b. ———; is a lawyer; res. Liberty, N. Y.
3167. ii. MARTHA MEHITABLE, b. ———; unm.; res. Liberty, N. Y.
3168. iii. CURTIS LEE, b. ———; killed accidentally.

1700. DAVID ALLEN FISK (Nathaniel, Jonathan, William, Ebenezer, William, William, John, William, Robert, Simon, Simon, William, Symond), b. June 8, 1810, in Williamstown, Vt.; m. Mar. 25, 1834, Rhoda Bates Putnam, b. Feb. 13, 1806; d. in Northfield, Vt., Sept. 25, 1865; m. 2d, at East Boston, Apr. 4, 1867, Sarah Morrison. David Allen Fisk was employed by the Vermont Central Railroad, having charge of a gang of men on the construction of the road. The company having decided on Northfield, Vt., as their headquarters, he went there to work in the shops and yard. His wife having died in 1865, in 1866 he left Vermont and went to Boston to work in the same capacity for the Eastern Railroad, now a part of the Boston & Maine. In 1868 the company transferred him to Salem, Mass., where he lived until he died. He d. Dec. 25, 1884; res. Williamstown and Northfield, Vt., Salem, Mass.

3169. i. RUSSELL PORTER, b. Dec. 21, 1836; res. Dover and Village Sts., Boston.
3170. ii. DANIEL D., b. June 11, 1839; d. May 3, 1840.
3171. iii. CHARLES DENNISON, b. Sept. 11, 1841, Cliftondale, Mass.
3172. iv. WILLIAM PORTER, b. Nov. 20, 1843. He d. Aug. 24, 1864, a prisoner of war in Andersonville prison.
3173. v. GEORGE W., b. Mar. 20, 1850; m. Eloise M. Farnsworth and Isabel A. Ashley.
3174. vi. MARY LOUISE, b. Mar. 30, 1869; m. William Taylor; res. Bridge St., Salem, Mass.
3175. vii. WILLIAM PORTER, b. Dec. 10, 1871; res. Bridge St., Salem.

1701. NATHANIEL CURTIS FISKE (Nathaniel, Jonathan, William, Ebenezer, William, William, John, William, Robert, Simon, Simon, William, Symond), b. Williamstown, Vt., July 3, 1813; m. Mar. 3, 1833, Elizabeth Putnam. He d. Feb. 25, 1893; res. Williamstown, Vt.

3176. i. M. VAN BUREN, b. Nov. 8, 1835.
3177. ii. HARRIET, b. Aug. 22, 1837.

1702. SAMUEL NEWELL FISKE (Nathaniel, Jonathan, William, Ebenezer, William, William, John, William, Robert, Simon, Simon, William, Symond), b. Williamstown, Vt., June 25, 1817; m. Dec. 28, 1840, Lucy Maria Gooch, b. Braintree, Vt., Nov. 20, 1814. He is a painter by trade; res. Williamstown and Randolph, Vt.

3178. i. ALMIRA MELORA, b. Oct. 30, 1841; res., unm., R.
3179. ii. GILBERT EBENEZER, b. Aug. 6, 1843; enlisted in the First Vermont Cavalry at the commencement of the Civil war; was taken prisoner at Gettysburg, taken to Belle Isle, and being transferred to Andersonville was left at Augusta, Ga., and died the next March in a rebel prison.

1706. AARON MARTIN FISK (William, Jonathan, William, Ebenezer,
3180. iii. JOHN BATES, b. Mar. 4, 1848; m. Almy Rumrell.
William, William, John, William, Robert, Simon, Simon, William, Symond), b. Williamstown, Vt., Aug. 15, 1808; m. at Liberty, N. Y., May 10, 1838, Elizabeth Carrier, b. June 1, 1821; d. July 3, 1852. He is a farmer; res. Williamstown, Vt., and Liberty, N. Y.

3181. i. DENNISON, b. Mar. 31, 1839; m. Sarah E. Crary.
3182. ii. CATHARINE, b. July 4, 1841; m. June 1, 1865, Daniel K. Le Roy; res. Hancock, N. Y. He was b. July 15, 1835. Ch.: Ina Eliza, b. Mar. 6, 1866; m. Leon E. Vatet, July 18, 1889. Ressa

Jane, b. Aug. 18, 1867. Edmond Herman, b. Feb. 19, 1869; m. Evalyn Thomas. Cyrus D., b. Jan. 18, 1870. Emma Rosalie, b. Dec. 22, 1872. Anna Augusta, b. Feb. 12, 1877; d. Mar. 26, 1877.

3183. iii. DELIA SOPHRONA, b. Sept. 27, 1844; m. Nov. 7, 1872, R. C. Young; res. Liberty.

3184. iv. HARRIET AUGUSTA, b. Oct. 9, 1847; m. June 4, 1872; she d. June 11, 1892.

3185. v. EMMA LOUISA, b. Sept. 28, 1850; m. June 10, 1874, Geo. H. Carpenter; res. Liberty.

1707. WILLIAM ROBY FISKE (William, Jonathan, William, Ebenezer, William, William, John, William, Robert, Simon, Simon, William, Symond), b. Williamstown, Vt., Nov. 18, 1810; m. Nov. 17, 1836, Sophia Stowell; res. Williamstown, Vt.

3186. i. CLARK N., b. Feb. 6, 1838.
3187. ii. RACHAEL I., b. Apr. 20, 1839.
3188. iii. MARY A., b. Jan. 6, 1840.
3189. iv. WILLIAM S., b. Mar. 23, 1841; d. Mar. 23, 1843.
3190. v. CHAUNCEY S., b. Mar. 27, 1843.
3191. vi. HANNAH E., b. Mar. 23, 1845.
3192. vii. MARTIN D., b. Aug. 11, 1846; d. Aug. 18, 1856.
3193. viii. GEORGE H., b. July 25, 1848.
3194. ix. HARRIET A., b. July 5, 1850; d. 1852.
3195. x. WILLARD F., b. Mar. 25, 1852.

1719. AZRO J. FISKE (John, Jonathan, William, Ebenezer, William, William, John, William, Robert, Simon, Simon, William, Symond), b. Williamstown, Vt., Aug. 3, 1818; m. Nov. 1, 1840, Almira Capron; res. Montpelier, Braintree, Frendon, Chittenden and Pittsfield, Vt.

3196. i. JAMES HENRY, b. July 24, 1843.
3197. ii. FOREST CAPRON, b. June 21, 1845.
3198. iii. SEREPTA ALMINA, b. July 25, 1847.
3199. iv. CHARLES ELLIOT, b. June 1, 1849.
3200. v. EMMA EDWYNA, b. Feb. 14, 1852.
3201. vi. JOHN EDWIN, b. May 10, 1853.
3202. vii. ELLEN MARIA, b. July 16, 1855.
3203. viii. ANNA ELIZABETH, b. June 25, 1858.
3204. ix. ALMA SUSAN, b. Apr. 14, 1860.
3205. x. ERNEST FRANKLIN, b. July 22, 1863.

1731. JOHN DENNISON FISKE (Benjamin, Jonathan, William, Ebenezer, William, William, John, William, Robert, Simon, Simon, William, Symond), b. Northfield, Sept. 10, 1826; m. his cousin Mar. 31, 1853, Martha M. White, dau. of Sarah Fiske.

3206. i. MARY, b. Jan. 24, 1858.
3207. ii. KATIE, b. Jan. 9, 1860.
3208. iii. JOHN O., b. Jan. 15, 1863.

1736. HON. GEORGE M. FISKE (David, Jonathan, William, Ebenezer, William, William, John, William, Robert, Simon, Simon, William, Symond), b. Northfield, Vt., ———; m. 1856 Jane E. Nichols, of Northfield. He is a lawyer in Northfield and was admitted to the bar in 1863. He represented his town that year in the State Legislature; res. Northfield, Vt.

1740. JOHN DENNISON FISKE (Samuel L., Jonathan, William, Ebenezer, William, William, John, William, Robert, Simon, Simon, William, Symond), b. Berlin, Vt., Feb. 9, 1825; m. Sept. 17, 1851, Harriett Elizabeth Blaisdell, b. Fort Covington Jan. 15, 1829. Mr. Fiske was for some time the publisher of a weekly newspaper in Franklin County, N. Y., but subsequently turned his attention to commercial pursuits and later was connected with the mercantile house of Baldwin, Fisher & Co., 25 Park Row, New York City; res. New York, N. Y.

3209. i. ELIZABETH VRILENA, b. in Malone July 1, 1852.
3210. ii. ELMIRA CORDELIA, b. July 7, 1856.
3211. iii. CHESTER DENNISON, b. Jan. 15, 1859.

1744. FRANCIS NOURSE FISKE (Ezra, William, William, Ebenezer, William, William, John, William, Robert, Simon, Simon, William, Symond), b. Fayette, Me., Mar. 30, 1803; m. there in 1828 Fanny Hilton, b. Aug. 11, 1808; d. Mar., 1892. His occupation was that of a farmer; religion, Baptist; politics, Republican. Her religion was Baptist. He d. Apr., 1876; res. Fayette, Me.

    3212. i.   JOSEPH DAVIS, b. Apr., 1830; d. May, 1832.

    3213. ii.   PHILIP DAVIS, b. Apr. 20, 1832; m. Mary M. Hitchcock.

    3214. iii.   WM. HILTON, b. Bath, Me., May 10, 1835; m. there Mary E. Chase, b. Feb. 1, 1837; d. June 23, 1895, s. p. He was formerly a farmer; is now a merchant; res. Bath, Me.

    3215. iv.   MARY MARSTON, b. Apr. 14, 1836; m. June 30, 1868, William H. Hitchcock, at Fayette, Me.; religion, Congregationalist; husband b. June 20, 1836; is a machinist, and superintendent of bolt factory; religion, Congregationalist; in politics, a Republican; res. 417 Pearl St., Cleveland, Ohio. Ch.: 1, Fanny Louise, b. Mar. 2, 1869; d. Aug. 18, 1869. 2, Mary Louise, b. July 11, 1872; m. Aug. 18, 1894, Henry A. Anthony, at Cleveland, O. His occupation, printer; religion, Protestant; politics, Republican; add. 417 Pearl St., Cleveland, O. 3, Paul Dombey, b. Feb. 2, 1876; add. 417 Pearl St., Cleveland, O.

    3216. v.   HANNAH, b. May 16, 1838, at North Wayne, Me.; m. Orrin Foss in Fayette, Me., Nov. 26, 1863; b. Sept. 14, 1838. He was a brick mason and contractor. In politics a Republican; a member of Baptist Church. He d. Nov. 9, 1895, at Fitchburg, Mass.; res. Fitchburg. Ch.: 1, Frank Herbert Foss, b. Sept. 20, 1865; m. Dec. 2, 1891, at Livermore Falls, Me.; add. Fitchburg, Mass. 2, Charles Waters, b. Dec. 9, 1876; add. Fitchburg, Mass.

    3217. vi.   ALLEN C., b. Wayne, Me., Aug., 1840; left home after he became of age; m.; had several children, all but one dying in childhood; this one is named Arthur, and with his mother is supposed to be living in Lowell, Mass. Allen Fiske went to the Bermuda Islands, several years ago and has not been heard from since. Letters to him and his family have been returned undelivered.

    3218. vii.   FANNY N., b. Nov. 23, 1844; m. June 6, 1866, George E. Chase at Fayette, Me.; d. Mar. 16, 1872. Religion, Baptist; husband's add. Jacksonville, Fla.; business, ship-chandler; religion, Baptist; politics, Republican. Ch.: 1, Addie Frances Chase, b. at Bath, Me., Dec. 31, 1868; m. at West Bath, Me., Dec. 14, 1892, to Miles Stanley Purington; religion, Protestant; husband's occupation, farmer; politics, Republican; b. at West Bath, Me., Dec. 21, 1868; add. Bath, Me. 2, Willie Chase, b. in 1869, at Fayette, Me.; d. 1870 at Fayette, Me.

1747. THOMAS GAGE UNDERWOOD FISKE (Ezra, William, William, Ebenezer, William, William, John, William, Robert, Simon, Simon, William, Symond), b. Fayette, Me., Sept. 26, 1809; m. at Lowell, Mass., Mary Jane Thurston, b. July 11, 1821, in N. H., and d. at St. Louis, Mo., Sept. 26, 1867. His occupation was music instructor and inventor; religion, Baptist; politics, Republican; d. at Elkhorn, Mont. He d. Jan. 1, 1893; res. Elkhorn, Mont.

    3219. i.   CELIA AUGUSTA, b. Sept. 7, 1843, at Manchester, N. H.; m. Dec. 25, 1862, to Rensellar Worthing, at Great Falls, N. H. Names of family changed by Probate Court, Middlesex County, to Worthing. Ranford Worthing, b. Sept. 14, 1839; add. Mr. and Mrs. Worthing, Otay, Cal. Ch.: 1, Edwin Ellsworth Worthing, b. Jan. 3, 1865; m. to Ella A. Parker, Oct. 26, 1888; add. Winchester, Mass. 2, Eula Velma, b. Sept. 22, 1867; m. to Chas. S. Palmetter June 10, 1886; add. San Diego, Cal. 3, Louisa May, b. Oct. 20, 1869; d. May 23, 1888. 4, Frederic Howard, b. Oct. 15, 1873; add. Otay, Cal. 5, Grace Marina, b. Sept. 1, 1877; d. Feb. 26, 1879. 6, Daisy Maud, b. Aug. 8, 1880;

add. Otay, Cal. 7, Eva Augusta, b. Oct. 26, 1882; add. Otay, Cal.

3220. ii. AVIS MARINA, b. June 9, 1853; m. to John M. Hussey Nov. 15, 1875. He d. 1880; m. 2d to John H. Barnicoate Nov. 16, 1890. He was b. Mar. 17, 1852; religion, Protestant; politics, Republican; add. Missoula, Mont. He is a miner.

1750. LIEUT. ALLEN FISKE (Ezra, William, William, William, Ebenezer, William, William, John, William, Robert, Simon, Simon, William, Symond), b. Fayette, Me., Mar. 16, 1815; m. at Great Falls, N. H., May 23, 1843, Miranda E. Furber, b. Nov. 11, 1816; d. Apr. 12, 1871. His profession was that of a manufacturer, trial justice and compounder of medicines; add. 78 Middle St., Portland, Me. Religion, Baptist; politics, Whig, Republican; he voted for both Harrisons; res. Portland, Me.

3221. i. HOMER W., b. Mar. 18, 1844; m. Jennette L. Abbot and Ida J. Richards.

3222. ii. MILTON, b. Aug. 26, 1850; machinist.

3223. iii. BYRON, b. June 12, 1852; machinist.

3224. iv. HENRY PAYNE, b. Aug. 20, 1857, at Fayette, Me.; m. at Waterbury, Conn., June 29, 1886, Henrietta Ford, b. Granby, Conn., July 4, 1852. He is an inventor and machinist; res. Waterbury, Conn.

1752. DUDLEY BLAKE FISKE (Ezra, William, William, Ebenezer, William, William, John, William, Robert, Simon, Simon, William, Symond), b. Fayette, Me., July 19, 1819; m. at Lowell, Mass., Sept. 7, 1846, Mary Ann Ashton, b. Liversage, Eng., Nov. 12, 1826; d. at Providence, R. I., Aug. 9, 1880. He was a mechanic; his religion was Baptist; his politics, Whig. He died in Dec., 1851, of yellow fever, on his way to California, leaving two sons, William Francis, who was killed by the explosion of an engine, and Charles Dudley Blake, now a merchant of No. 23 and 25 Boylston St., Boston. He d. Dec., 1851; res. Littleton, Mass., and Hookset, N. H.

3225. i. WILLIAM FRANCIS, b. Nov. 11, 1847; d. s. p., killed in a railroad accident at Prov., R. I., Nov. 30, 1876.

3226. ii. CHARLES D. B., b. Feb. 17, 1850; m. Susan E. Sparhawk.

1756. JOSEPH ANDERSON FISKE (Ezra, William, William, Ebenezer, William, William, John, William, Robert, Simon, Simon, William, Symond), b. Fayette, Me., Aug. 31, 1826; m. in 1857, Sarah Elizabeth Fifield, b. Feb. 29, 1828; d. Mar. 11, 1875. He was a farmer and manufacturer; he was married to Sarah Elizabeth Fifield, of Fayette, Me., and died at Auburn, Me.; his religion, Baptist; politics, Republican. He d. Mar. 1, 1892; res. Auburn, Me.

COL. FRANKLIN FISK.

3227. i. WILLIS CLIFTON, b. Sept. 18, 1858; res. 212 Thirty-first St., Chicago, Ill.

3228. ii. CHARLES EZRA, b. Oct. 16, 1860; d. Nov. 22, 1881.

3229. iii. FRANKLIN DUDLEY, b. July 21, 1862; d. Mar. 14, 1880.

3230. iv. HATTIE MORRELL, b. May 7, 1866; m. at Lynn, Aug. 5, 1888, Wm. Fry Burbank, b. Feb. 23, 1867. He is a jeweler. Ch.: 1, Frank Charles, b. Apr. 2, 1889; d. Sept. 17, 1889. 2, Flossie Elizabeth, b. Aug., 1889; res. 75 East Ave., Lewiston, Me.

1757. COL. FRANKLIN FISK (Ezra, William, William, Ebenezer, William, William, John, William, Robert, Simon, Simon, William, Symond), b. Fayette, Me., Feb. 10, 1829; m. at Kingsville, Ohio, May 1, 1870, Ellen Margaret Wakefield, dau. of Nathan B. and Ruth W. (Leffenwell) Wakefield, b. Apr. 18, 1841. Franklin Fisk was born on his father's farm, in Fayette, Me., Feb. 10, 1829. His family failing, his boyhood life was one of hard work, with little education. At 21 he was employed in a mill yard at Manchester, N. H., at 75 cents a day, working twelve hours at very hard work, out of which he paid board and expenses. After working in the mill yard, in a hotel and family, he returned to Maine; attended a private school eight weeks, the Maine Wesleyan Seminary twenty-three weeks, and the Waterville Academy fifteen weeks, working on a farm and teaching during vacations. He was compelled to use rigid economy, and for thirteen weeks carried his week's provision in a basket on his arm, while at the Wesleyan Seminary, and lived during two terms at the Waterville Academy on crackers, West India molasses and cold water, six days out of seven, and for a rarity had baked meat and beans, coffee and brown bread for Sundays. Hard work, hard study, the sudden change from school to hard work and from hard work to school, began to undermine his health, and in 1852 he came to Mt. Pulaski, Ill., and after peddling books awhile, he taught school until Apr., 1857, when he came to Lincoln, Ill., to complete his law studies (which he had commenced while teaching), at the same time writing in the office of the clerk of the courts. In Nov., 1857, he was elected Justice of the Peace, which office had yielded his predecessor $350 per year. He was appointed notary public in 1857, which office he has held for thirty-eight years, and was admitted to the bar of the State of Illinois, in 1858. In four years his office of Justice of the Peace and his other business yielded him over $7,000, which laid the foundation for a competence. His next move in life was a great sacrifice in health and financial success. In Aug., 1861, he entered the service as First Lieut., in Company H., Fourth Regiment of Cavalry, Illinois Volunteers.; was promoted to Captain, July 1, 1862; appointed Lieutenant-Colonel of the Third United States Colored Cavalry, by the President, in 1864, but declined and was mustered out of service in Nov., 1864, after serving three years and three months, his health having been completely broken down by the hardships of the service. He returned to Lincoln, where he has since resided. During his service, he took part in the capture of Fort Henry, Fort Donelson, the battle of Shiloh, siege of Corinth, advance into Mississippi under Grant, and many other sharp engagements. At Fort Henry, Lieutenant-Colonel McCollough, his commander, with 150 men, marched to the rear of the fort; the garrison, except those at the water-battery, fled up the river. McCollough entered the fort; about twenty men under the Captain of Company H went to the water-battery, while McCollough (Fisk in command of Company H.) charged the retreating rebels, over 2,000 strong; stampeded them; chased them ten miles, capturing all their cannon, baggage and rear guard. This taught Captain Fisk to fight his cavalry with a dash and desperation. Three incidents we will relate. Nov. 30, 1862, he was ordered, with his command of 125 dismounted men to develop the enemy, who were in a thicket. Moving in line to within close range, he ordered the men to hold their fire and charged the thicket. The enemy gave a volley, but with a yell Fisk's men dashed on, stampeded the rebels, who fled. The rebels proved to be a Texan regiment of 450 infantry. The Texan Colonel said he had believed one Southerner could whip three "Yankees," but he found one Yankee could whip three Texans. In May, 1863, with twenty men, half raw recruits, he suddenly met eighteen picked rebels. Fisk instantly ordered the charge, stampeded them, and captured five. Aug. 8, 1864, in Concordia Parish, La., 300 Texas rebels were about to surround forty of his regiment. With sixty men he galloped in column to close range, deployed in line at a gallop, ordered his men to hold their fire for close quarters, and charged without halting. The onslaught was so sudden, the rebels fled. His instructions to his men were: "If you are ever in close quarters, with nine chances of death, and one to escape, take the tenth chance and you will escape." Following these instructions, although many times in close quarters, he never had a man captured. His discipline over and kindness to his men were noted. But one man under his command deserted, although twenty-eight of his men deserted while under the command of his successor. He received an honorable mention in Davidson and Stuvee's "History of Illinois" for a reconnoissance on the flank of the enemy at the battle of Shiloh. In 1865 he was elected a member of the first city council of Lincoln, and served as chairman of the finance committee, and the other most important committees. In 1867 he was elected Justice of the Peace for four years. Finding his health would not permit a general practice of the law, he, in 1866, opened a real estate and counsellor-at-law office, which vocation he has followed to the present time. He married Miss Ellen M. Wakefield, daughter of Nathan B. and Ruth (Leffingwell) Wakefield, of Kingsville, Ohio, by whom he has two children, Ruth Melenda, and Franklin, Jr. He is giving his children a liberal education, of which he was denied, his daughter having taken graduate and postgraduate courses and a course in music, and his son entering college as freshman at 16. In politics, he was a conservative Whig, up to 1856, when being an eyewitness to the United States Marshal's border ruffian posse's acts at Lawrence, Kan., he became, and remained, a stanch Republican. His religious motto is: "Do right in all things, and trust God for the result." Res. Lincoln, Ill.

3231.   i.   RUTH MELENDA, b. June 1, 1871.
3232.   ii. FRANKLIN, b. Feb. 23, 1879.

1760.   WILLIAM PORTER FISKE (William, William, William, Ebenezer, William, William, John, William, Robert, Simon, Simon, William, Symond), b. Concord, N. H., Dec. 29, 1805; m. June 3, 1833, Sophia W. Parker, b. 1811; d. July, 1855; m. 2d, Oct., 1856, Sarah A. Clifford. He was born in Concord; learned the printer's trade and became an expert. He worked in various places and finally established himself at Nashville, Tenn., where he became part owner in the Union and American. He continued there until the Civil war broke out, when his property was confiscated and after many dangers he finally returned to the North and settled in Worcester, Mass.; res. Worcester, Mass.

3233.   i.   WILLIAM W., b. Sept. 16, 1837; d. Aug. 20, 1839.
3234.   ii. EDWARD L., b. Feb. 17, 1841.
3235.   iii. MARY W., b. July 31, 1845.
3236.   iv. NELLIE C., b. Aug. 7, 1859.

1761.   HON. DAVID DODGE FISKE (William, William, William, Ebenezer, William, William, John, William, Robert, Simon, Simon, William, Symond), b. Concord, N. H., Aug. 28, 1808; m. July 11, 1833, Elizabeth B. Stevens, b. 1815; d. Brooklyn, N. Y., Jan. 5, 1882. He was born in Concord, learned the printing trade and established himself in business in Portsmouth, Va., where he acquired wealth and distinction and became publisher and editor of The Transcript. In 1855, during the epidemic of yellow fever, he was Mayor of the city and by his courageous efforts much suffering was prevented. At the breaking out of the rebellion he found himself most unhappily situated. He d. July 22, 1870; res. Portsmouth, Va.

3237.   i.   EMMA, b. Apr. 13, 1834; m. W. H. Morrill, of Concord, N. H., Oct. 22, 1851; d. Sept. 5, 1855.
3238.   ii. CHARLES E., b. Nov. 19, 1837; m. Rosalby Porter.
3239.   iii. WILLIAM A., b. May 9, 1840; res. unm. Portsmouth, Va.
3240.   iv. MELZAR A., b. Dec. 17, 1845; d. July 3, 1862. He was killed in battle near Richmond, Va., during Gen. McClellan's campaign.

1768.   FRANCIS ALLEN FISKE (Francis N., William, William, Ebenezer, William, William, John, William, Robert, Simon, Simon, William, Symond), b. Concord, N. H., Apr. 26, 1819; m. Feb. 22, 1849, Abby Gilman Perry, dau. of Dr. William Perry of Exeter, N. H., b. Nov. 14, 1824; d. Oct. 18, 1858; m. 2d, Nov. 7, 1872, Abby Blake Parker, dau. of Rev. Leonard S. Abby (Blake) Parker. Francis Allen Fiske was a successful merchant in Concord for many years, retiring in 1875 from active business. He was a trustee in the New Hampshire Savings Bank, and served as one of the committee of investment. He did not hold any public offices, but was of a quiet, retiring nature, fond of books, spending much of his last years in their companionship. He d. Oct 7, 1887; res. Concord, N. H.

3241.   i.   MARY WALKER, b. Jan. 30, 1850; d. Nov. 20, 1877.
3242.   ii. FRANK WALKER, b. Sept. 19, 1851; m. Hattie E. Hubbard.
3243.   iii. WILLIAM PERRY, b. Dec. 6, 1853; unm.; res. Concord, N. H. William Perry Fiske attended school in his native city, spending a year at Phillips Andover Academy. Entered the New Hampshire Savings Bank as clerk, in 1872, and in 1875 was chosen treasurer, and still continues as such at present time. Has held positions as president of board of water commissioners of the city, also a member of the board of park commissioners from the inception of same. He has also held positions as

treasurer of various local and state organizations, also director in First National Bank of Concord. Is unmarried and lives in the old homestead with his sister, Abbie Gilman Fiske, who keeps house for him. Is fond of books and has a good library. Does not seek office; lives in a quiet way, devoted to home and finds much pleasure in doing for others.

3244. iv.   SARAH TARLTON, b. Apr. 4, 1856; d. Apr. 10, 1857.
3245. v.   NATHANIEL GILMAN, b. Dec. 1, 1857; d. Oct. 17, 1860.
3246. vi.   ABBIE GILMAN, b. Apr. 19, 1862; res. Concord, N. H.
3247. vii. JOHN TAYLOR, b. Oct. 29, 1864; m. Mary Amelia Lillie.
3248. viii. HARRY TARLTON, b. Oct. 9, 1863; d. May 6, 1873.
3249. ix.   HELEN, b. Oct. 9, 1868; d. Oct. 10, 1868.
3250. x.   ELEANORE P., b. Mar. 29, 1874; res. 13 Humboldt St., No. Cambridge, Mass.
3251. xi.   GEORGE LIVERMORE, b. Nov. 15, 1875; res. 13 Humbolt St., No. Cambridge, Mass.

1775. REV. WILLIAM ALLEN FISKE, LL.D. (Allen, William, William, Ebenezer, William, William, John, William, Robert, Simon, Simon, William, Symond), b. Troy, N. Y., Nov. 4, 1824; m. in Brownville, N. Y., Sept. 22, 1852, Susan Mathews Bradley, b. May 18, 1831. John Brad-

REV. WILLIAM ALLEN FISKE.

ley was a native of Cheshire, Conn. The ancestors of the Connecticut Bradleys appear to have been William and Isaac, both of whom settled in New Haven, the former in 1645, the latter (spelled Bradlee) in 1683, having stopped some time in Bradford, Mass. Both families have numerous descendants. Savage says twenty-three of this name had graduated at N. E. colleges before 1835. Col. John Bradley was born in Cheshire, Conn., in 1793. His parents were —— Bradley and Susan Mathews. Their children were John, Susan, Esther, and Roxana. Col. Bradley entered the military service of the United States during the war of 1812, and for meritorious conduct was promoted to the rank of Captain in the regular army. He was for some time in command of the military force stationed at Fort Dearborn, Chicago. In 1837 he retired from the service, having previously married Miss Sarah Brown, of Brownville, N. Y., in which place he settled, engaged in business, and acquired property. Upon the election of Hon. Wm. H. Seward as Governor of New York, he was offered and accepted a position on his staff, with the rank of Colonel.

Rev. Dr. William Allen Fiske was graduated at the Episcopal Theological Seminary in the City of New York, in 1849. On Sept. 22, 1852, he was married to Susan Mathews Bradley, daughter of Col. John and Sarah Bradley, of Brownsville, N. Y. In Nov., 1849, he was appointed missionary to Theresa and Redwood, Jefferson county, New York, where he remained two years and three months, built churches and gathered in congregations. In Jan., 1852, he was called to the rectorship of St. Stephen's Church, New Hartford, N. Y. There he remained two years and later obtained a parsonage for the church. In 1854 he was called to Lyons, N. Y., where he remained five years. In 1859 he was called to Grace Church, Cleveland, O. He was called to St. Paul's Church, Cincinnati, O., in the winter of 1865-6. He built up this parish, until it was the largest in the diocese of Ohio; but his health failed in 1874, and he then gave up the parish, and retired for about a year to his farm in Indiana, near Rei. His health improved considerably here, so that he was able, in 1875, to accept a call to the rectorship of St. John's Church in Quincy, Ill. In 1876 he became rector of St. John's parish, Naperville, Ill., where he remained for four years, increasing largely the parish membership and doubling the size of the church edifice. While residing here the Northwestern College conferred the degree of LL.D. on him. In 1881 he was called to the rectorship of St. John's Church, Bangor, Me., where he remained until 1886. He was now 61 years old, and he gave up the parish and went to Boston, where he lived for about a year, doing light work in filling occasional pulpits. In 1887 he and his wife went to Brooklyn, to be near their children; and for three years he assisted the bishop and archdeacon in missionary work among the struggling parishes in the growing parts of the city. In 1890 he was called as rector of St. Andrew's parish, Brooklyn; and though he was 65 years old, he undertook the work, and pushed it ahead with extraordinary vigor. Not content with merely enlarging the parish as it was, he determined, after he had made the congregation too large for the edifice, to purchase land, and build a church and chapel on a scale commensurate with the future which he foresaw to be certain for that part of Brooklyn. He succeeded in his self-allotted task, aided in every way by the devotion of his wife and his youngest son, John, and actually bought the ground and superintended the designs for the church and chapel. But he overtaxed his strength, and did not live to see the completion of the work that crowned his latter days. He died on the 12th of March, 1894; died in the harness, as he always wished to do, died in the very midst of his work, died in the fullness of years; and the new St. Andrews Church is a lasting monument. He lived a noble and useful life; his aims were always pure and lofty; his ideals were exalted; he lived for others more than for himself, and he died for his Master, whom he had so long and so devotedly served. In a publication, "The Bishop's Address," in a lengthy obituary of Dr. Fiske, it is said: "Though in declining health for some months, his death at last was a surprise to his family and his people. It might be enough to say of him, in his somewhat secluded ministry and in his young and struggling parish, that he was a good pastor and a faithful preacher, and as such gave himself largely to the task of thoroughly grounding his flock upon the principles of the church's faith and order. He worked with a cheerful faith and undaunted courage which, under God, are always the sure pledges of ultimate triumph. Others will enter into his labors and build on his foundations; but let us hope, it will be with an unfailing memory of the debt of gratitude which St. Andrew's parish owes to its first rector." He d. Mar. 12, 1894; res. Cleveland, O. and 216 Fifty-third St., Brooklyn, N. Y.

3252. i.   BRADLEY ALLEN, b. June 13, 1854; m. Josephine Harper.
3253. ii.   FRANCES ELIZA, b. Dec. 5, 1855; m. June 3, 1885, at Bangor, Me., Noah Hallowell Holt, b. Taunton, Mass., Feb. 14, 1841. Ch.: 1, Kathryn Fiske, b. Apr. 12, 1886; res. Providence, R. I., P. O. add. box 1330. He is connected with the Jewelers' Mercantile Agency.
3254. iii. SOPHIA HURLBURT, b. July 19, 1859; d. May 13, 1863.
3255. iv.   WILLIAM CLARENCE, b. January 17, 1861; unm.; res. at home.
3256. v.   JOHN BROWN BRADLEY, b. Feb. 7, 1863; unm.; res at home. His New York address is 52 Wall St. John Brown Bradley Fiske was born at Cleveland, Feb. 7, 1863, and is a son of the Rev. William Allen Fiske, LL.D., and Susan Bradley Fiske. His father was at the time rector of Grace Church, Cleveland, and left there in 1865 to become rector of St. Paul's Church, Cincinnati, where John's common school education was chiefly procured. A year and a half on the farm at Delaware, Ind.; a year at Quincy, Ill., and four years at Naperville, Ill., where he attended Northwestern College, gave him the experience of country and Western life which, together

JOHN BROWN BRADLEY FISKE.

with seven years in New England, prevent him from being at all narrow. He nevertheless remembers that he is an Ohio man and will doubtless use this for all he is worth when occasion arises. While in Bangor, Me., where he moved with his father, in 1880, he studied law with Peregrine White an Hon. Frederick M. Laughton, and was admitted to the bar in 1884, and for two years practiced law there and argued a case in appeal before the full bench in 1885, in Trainor vs. Morrison, 78 Maine, 160, where the opposing counsel was an ex-Governor of the State. Strange to say, he was beaten, but his contention as to the powers of traveling salesmen has since become recognized as the law. Becoming convinced that a law school course was a proper one to fit a lawyer for his profession, he took the three years' course at the Boston University Law School in one year, and graduated among the first ten in his class, receiving his degree magna cum laude, in 1887. He then came to New York City, and was admitted to the New York bar, and acted as managing clerk for Hon. Peter B. Olney, Messrs. Kelly & Mackae, Cravath & Houston and Hays & Greenbaum. Since 1893 he has been connected with the firm of Messrs. Evarts, Choate & Beaman, 52 Wall St., New York City, and is the assistant of Hon. Charles C. Beaman, who headed the reform ticket in 1895 as candidate for Justice of the Supreme Court of the State of New York. Mr. Fiske is also attending to the legal wants of South Brooklyn, where he resides. He always, since a lad, evinced a strong love for music, and as a boy soprano won considerable attention. When in Bangor he sang tenor in the quartette choir at his father's church, and was quite prominent in the councils of the Cecilia Club, a local musical society. He studied the voice for three years under J. C. Bartlett and Clarence A. Marshall, of Boston, and while at Law School sang at St. Paul's Church. Coming to New York he sang for over a year in Trinity Church, and afterwards held solo positions in Calvary Church, New York, and Trinity, Hoboken. His father's health commencing to fail in the fall of 1893, he deemed it his duty to take charge of the choir of St. Andrew's Church, Brooklyn, of which his father was rector, and otherwise sustain him in his work. This move proved a very wise one, as the revival of the choir invigorated the energies of the parish, and kept the work going on during his father's illness, so that at his death the people of the church united with his son in the work of building a new church edifice. Mr. Fiske is a trustee of St. Andrew's parish, and a delegate to the diocesan convention, where he is a member of the standing committee on the incorporation of new parishes. He is treasurer of the local Y. M. C. A., and represents the Eighth Ward of Brooklyn in the councils of the Citizen's Union, of Brooklyn, a non-partisan organization. He is not married, but resides with his mother at 216 Fifty-third St., Brooklyn.

REV. ALBERT AUGUSTUS FISKE.

1777. REV. ALBERT AUGUSTUS FISKE (Allen, William, William, Ebenezer, William, William, John, William, Robert, Simon, Simon, William, Symond), b. Troy, N. Y., Nov. 1, 1828; m. Nov. 23, 1859, Amelia Goodyear. Rev. Albert Augustus Fiske, third son of Allen and Eliza Fiske, was born in Troy, N. Y. The youngest of the brothers, the first fifteen years of his life was spent with his father, a student most of that time in his school, and fitted under his excellent training to enter upon an advanced collegiate course at the age of 16. Such had been his early purpose, but overruled by what was then deemed to be wiser counsels, he was persuaded to betake himself to the more practical training of the printing office, which he did, in the winter of 1844-5, at Auburn, N. Y., in the office of the Northern Christian Advocate, an organ of the M. E. Church, of extensive circulation. After serving his apprenticeship in this establishment, in the fall of 1847 he returned to his native city, and soon afterward commenced, in connection with his father, the publication of a weekly newspaper, called the Family Journal. In the fall of 1848 his brother, David E., from Amherst, joined them, and proved a most efficient ally. From this time onward, for more than twelve years, the Family Journal prospered, both in means and influence, recognized by its many thousands of readers, and by its contemporaries, as an able, popular, and influential newspaper, which result was largely due to the gifted pen of its principal editor, Allen Fiske, Esq. In 1854, David, and shortly afterward his father, severally retired from the concern, and soon the publication of "Fiske's Family Journal" was brought to a close. Albert A. Fiske married Miss Amelia, the accomplished daughter of Rev. George Goodyear, of Temple, N. H., and in the summer of 1862 they removed to Chicago, Ill., where shortly afterwards Mr. Fiske began the preparation and compilation of materials for a genealogical work, which was finally completed and published in 1867, entitled: "A History of the Family (ancestral and descendant), of William Fiske, Sr., of Amherst, N. H." with brief notices of other branches springing from the same stock. This was the first attempt to publish a work on the Fiske genealogy in this country, and though the details mostly concerned certain branches descended from the Wenham Fiskes, yet so comprehensive was its view, that it has probably served as the nucleus of this larger and more elaborate work*

In 1864-5 Mr. Fiske began his preparation for holy orders in the Protestant Episcopal Church, and in 1869 he graduated from the Nashotan Theological Seminary, Wisconsin. On Trinity Sunday of that year he was ordained to the diaconate by Bishop Whitehouse, and in November following was called to the rectorship of Zion Church, Oconomowoc, where he was advanced to the priesthood by Bishop Kemper, of saintly memory, in the spring of 1870. He remained for several years there, and was greatly prospered in his work. In 1875 he resigned his charge to give his invalid wife the benefit of a change of climate. In 1876 he returned to Chicago, and took missionary service for awhile under Bishop McLaren. In Jan., 1877, he was called to Christ Church, Harvard, Ill., where in 1881, he built a new and beautiful house of worship, and presented it to the diocese all paid for. He continued in charge, serving the people most acceptably, until Easter, 1886, when he was called to St. Paul's Church, Austin, Ill., a suburb of Chicago, where he remained about six years. In this field also he was signally successful, the membership of the church increasing threefold, but his health failing, he resigned in the fall of 1892, in order to secure much needed rest. In Nov., 1895, he was recalled to the church in Harvard, where he now resides, respected and beloved by the people. Several of Mr. Fiske's sermons have been published by request, and received flattering commendation from the Church Press. Although serving continuously in the ministry for over twenty-five years, Mr. Fiske has had but three parishes during that time, and is pleasantly remembered in them all. A very valuable heirloom came into the possession of Rev. A.A. Fiske, on the death of his uncle, David Fiske, Esq., of Amherst. It is an old

---

*The compiler, as stated in the introduction, expresses his appreciation of the valuable assistance rendered by the work of Rev. A. A. Fiske. When his book was compiled it was indeed a most difficult task. But few town histories and genealogies had then been printed and nearly everyone was diffident and indifferent as to their origin. A friend writing of Mr. Fiske says: "It would be entirely just and proper to recognize in some fitting way the fact of obligation to one who, as pioneer, had 'blazed the way' thro' the trackless jungle where reposed the ashes of buried generations. The fathers took little pains to keep track of their kindred in their migrations and ever widening groups of descent. It is only with a truer appreciation of its value that an interest in genealogical matters has revived. Hence the difficulty in this country of compiling a general family history. It is a big job, as he happened to know, for he spent the best part of two years at it and considerable money without pecuniary reward. Doubtless what he did has been some help to you."

English clock, of large dimensions and superior workmanship, which undoubtedly belonged originally to the Wenham Fiskes, as far back as the beginning of the last century (1700), as it is distinctly mentioned in testamentary documents signed by Dea. Ebenezer Fiske, of date 1764, and described as his "old clock," which came to him along with the homestead, from his father, Dea. William, whose will was probated 1725. As Dea. William, of Wenham, was the sole legatee of William the emigrant, it probably was bequeathed to him as part of his marriage portion (1662). There can be no question as to the venerable age of this clock, for its works are of chilled brass, harder than the hardest steel, and the process of such rare alchemy became a lost art a long while ago. It is perfectly safe to say that this clock is at least 150 years old, for in 1764 it was spoken of as an old English timepiece; was willed at that date by Ebenezer Fiske to his son William; was brought to Amherst from Wenham in 1771, and for ninety years stood in the mansion of Hon. William Fiske, firmly bolted against the oaken crossbeams. It is an excellent timepiece even now, and is greatly prized.

Rev. George Goodyear, of Temple, N. H., was a lineal descendant of Hon. Stephen Goodyear, who came to this country in 1630, and was descended from an ancient English family of that name, entitled to coat armor as appears by a royal grant dated 1569. In the records of the Herald Office, it is thus described: "Gules, a fesse bet. 2 chev. vair—Crest, a partridge, holding in its beak three ears of wheat." Res. s. p. Austin, Ill., and Harvard, Ill.

1781. THOMAS SCOTT FISKE (David, William, William, Ebenezer, William, William, John, William, Robert, Simon, Simon, William, Symond), b. Nov. 22, 1823; m. Clara Isabel Pittman, of New York, b. Brooklyn, 1840; is a descendant of the old R. I. family of Pittmans. He went to St. Louis in 1846, and soon afterward to New Orleans. He engaged in the banking business the greater part of his life. In 1852 he went to California and entered the firm of Page, Bacon & Co., and two years later organized the banking house of Thomas S. Fiske & Co., of San Francisco and Sacramento. At the beginning of the war he transferred his business interests to New York. He d. Feb. 18, 1885; res. 328 W. 57th St., New York, N. Y.

    3257. i.   THOMAS SCOTT, b. May 12, 1865; unm. He was educated at the Pingry school, of Elizabeth, N. J., and at Columbia College, New York, entering the latter institution in 1881. He was graduated from Columbia College in 1885, taking the degree of A. B. with the highest honors, and was appointed to a fellowship which he held for three years, studying part of the time at Cambridge, England, and obtaining the degree of Ph. D. from Columbia in 1888. He was then appointed tutor in mathematics, being promoted in 1891 to an instructorship, and in 1894 to a professorship. He was one of the founders of the New York Mathematical Society, which has since become the American Mathematical Society, being the secretary of the society from its begining in 1888 to the end of the year 1895. He is now editor of the Bulletin of the American Mathematical Society, a fellow of the American Association for the Advancement of Science, a member of the London Mathematical Society, and a member of the New York Academy of Sciences.

    3258. ii.   JAMES PORTER, b. Nov. 22, 1866; unm.; occupation, physician and surgeon; educated by private tutors, and at Columbia College. After graduating from the College of Physicians and Surgeons, in 1891, was appointed "chief of staff" at the famous Charity Hospital, New York City. He has devoted himself for several years to a special study of the deformities of children, and has established clinics in several parts of New York City, where these deformities in the children of the poor are treated gratuitously.

    3259. iii.   CLARA DULCE, b. 1868.

1782. JAMES PORTER FISKE (David, William, William, Ebenezer, William, William, John, William, Robert, Simon, Simon, William, Symond), b. June 5, 1825, Amherst, N. H.; m. Jan. 4, 1866, Sarah Coffin Hill, of Groton, Mass., b.

there Aug. 31, 1838; d. Sept. 26, 1886, in Fitchburg, Mass. He established himself in St. Louis in the boot and shoe trade and prospered. He was before his death a member of the firm of Fiske, Knight & Co., of St. Louis, and Fiske, Kirtland & Co., of Chicago. His wife was the daughter of Deacon Henry Hill, of Groton, Mass. He d. May 10, 1873; res. St. Louis, Mo.

    3260. i.   JAMES HILL, b. Sept. 19, 1870; d. Jan. 24, 1871.

    1783. GEORGE FISKE (David, William, William, Ebenezer, William, William, John, William, Robert, Simon, Simon, William, Symond), b. Oct. 22, 1835, Amherst, N. H.; m. Apr. 16, 1873, Elmira F. Morrill, of San Jose, b. Chichester, N. H., Mar. 4, 1845. George, the youngest son of Deacon David Fiske, has pursued for some years the occupation of a photographic artist, principally in California, with good success; res. San Jose, Cal., and Yosemite Valley, Mariposa County, Cal.

    3261. i.   CARLETON W., b. Aug. 8, 1874; d. Sept. 6, 1877.
    3262. ii.   WALTER HOWARD, b. Feb. 24, 1878; d. July 6, 1878.

    1796. DEA. JOHN PROCTOR FISKE (Ebenezer, Ebenezer, William, Ebenezer, William, William, John, William, Robert, Simon, Simon, William, Symond), b. May 31, 1818, in Wilmont; m. Apr. 9, 1850, Abby Richardson Clark, b. Jan. 3, 1825, in Tewksbury, Mass. John Proctor, the fifth and eldest son of Ebenezer and Hannah Fiske, desiring to fit himself for the profession of teaching, entered a teacher's department of Phillips Academy. After teaching two or three winters he took charge of a select school in Cedarville, N. J., from 1840 to 1842. He then entered the classical department of the Phillips Academy and completed the preparatory course in the languages. For two years he taught in St. Johnsbury, Vt., and for the following nine years was principal of the Hancock school, in Lowell, Mass. For many years subsequently he was principal of the preparatory department of the Beloit, Wis., College, which institution conferred the degree of M. A. upon him in 1857. In 1865 he was elected deacon of the First Congregational Church in Beloit. He left off teaching in the preparatory department of Beloit College in June, 1871, and went to Chicago to engage in business. After four years he began to sell books and continued in that business until Mar., 1893, when he went to Chicago to live with his son, and since then he has not been able to do anything; res. Beloit, Wis., and Chicago, Ill.

DEA. JOHN PROCTOR FISKE.

    3263. i.   ABBY CLARK, b. June 17, 1851; m. ——— Eaton; res. Madison, Wis.
    3264. ii.   HARRIETT PROCTOR, b. June 23, 1853; unm.; res. 2803 N. Paulina St., Ravenswood, Ill.
    3265. iii. FRANKLIN LUTHER, b. June 24, 1855; m. Vera Ida Brown.
    3266. iv. JOHN PROCTOR, b. Sept. 11, 1857; m. Mrs. Elizabeth H. Eddy.
    3267. v.   EDWARD OLIVER, b. Dec. 30, 1859; m. Mary F. Miller.
    3268. vi. EDNAH ANNA, b. May 14, 1862; d. May 28, 1862.
    3269. vii. GEO. FRED'K, b. Aug. 21, 1863; m. Mary E. Zimmerman.

    1797. PROF. FRANKLIN WOODBURY FISK (Ebenezer, Ebenezer, William, Ebenezer, William, William, John, William, Robert, Simon, Simon, William, Symond), b. Feb. 16, 1820; m. Mar. 9, 1854, Mrs. Amelia Allen (Bowen) Austin, dau. of George Bowen, of Woodstock, Conn., b. May 1, 1822; d. May 10, 1881; m. 2d, Dec. 23, 1885, Mrs. S. Jennette (Gardner) Hitchcock, b. Aug. 13, 1832, dau. of Dea. Elijah Gardner. Prof. Fisk was born in Hopkinton, N. H.; he left home at an early age and for some time worked in the factories of the Merrimack corporation in Lowell, Mass. Later he entered the Phillips Academy in Andover in the fall of 1835, being then 16 years of age. Until he completed his

PROF. FRANKLIN WOODBURY FISK.

course he attenuated between teaching and study. He taught schools in Methuen and East Abington, Mass.; Fairton, Bridgeton and Burlington, N. J. In Sept., 1845, he entered Yale College; he was graduated in 1849, and at once entered the theological department of the school. He was licensed to preach in 1852; was a tutor at Yale from 1851-53; student in Andover Theological Seminary during part of 1853, and also traveled in Europe. Compelled by disease of the eyes to abandon the idea of entering the ministry, he refused several calls to take a pastorate. He however, accepted the professorship of rhetoric and English literature in Beloit, Wis., College, to which he had been appointed while abroad and entered upon his duties Apr., 1854, where he continued until 1859, having previously been appointed to the chair of sacred rhetoric in the Chicago Theological Seminary, in which institution he has since continued. In 1865 he received the degree of Doctor of Divinity from Olivet College, Mich., and from Yale University in 1888; also the degree of Doctor of Laws from Beloit College in 1888. In the autumn and winter of 1871-72 he attended lectures in the University of Berlin, Germany, and in 1872 traveled in Arabia, Egypt, Greece and Palestine. In 1887 he became president of the Chicago Theological Seminary, with which he has been connected as professor and president for thirty-seven years. His work entitled "Manual of Preaching," published in 1884, has reached a third edition, and is used as a text-book in several institutions. In 1891 he went as delegate to the "International Congregational Council," which met in London in July of that year, and also traveled extensively in Europe. As a student in college he took the highest honors, being valedictorian of his class. As a scholar, writer and preacher he enjoys an enviable reputation; res. 532 W. Adams St., Chicago, Ill.

    3270. i.   FRANKLIN PROCTOR, b. Oct. 27, 1857; m. Katherine Tanner.

    3271. ii.   AMELIA MARIA, b. Feb. 3, 1860; m. Dec. 29, 1892, Dr. Walter May Fitch; res. 640 W. Monroe St., Chicago, Ill. Ch.: Edith May, b. Oct. 17, 1893.

    3272. iii.   HENRY EDWARD, b. Sept. 11, 1862; m. Hannah S. Mac Neish.

    1800. LUTHER FISKE (James, Ebenezer, William, Ebenezer, William, William, John, William, Robert, Simon, Simon, William, Symond), b. July 9, 1817; m. Aug. 29, 1841, Mahala Halstead. He d. in Homestead, Mich.; res. Coldwater, Mich.

    3273. i.   JAMES C., b. ——.
    3274. ii.   CATHERINE M., b. ——.
    3275. iii.   FRANKLIN B., b. ——.
    3276. iv.   LORENZO D., b. Apr. 2, 1854; m. Ella T. Gates.
    3277. v.   C. B., b. ——; res. Coldwater.

    1804. REV. LEWIS RANSOM FISKE (James, Ebenezer, William, Ebenezer, William, William, John, William, Robert, Simon, Simon, William, Symond), b. Penfield, N. Y., Dec. 24, 1825; m. at Howell, Mich., Aug. 19, 1852, Elizabeth Ross Spence, formerly teacher in Albion, Mich., Female College, b. Howell, Mich., July 19, 1827; d. Feb. 26, 1879; m. 2d, June 29, 1880, Mrs. Helen M. Davis; d. 1896. The remains were taken to Detriot for

REV. LEWIS RANSOM FISKE.

burial. Mrs. Fiske was a most admirable woman and deeply beloved by her friends and very influential in society; a cultured, Christian woman. When nine years of age he studied as opportunity presented, and before he was 17 years of age was given the management of the public school. In 1846 he entered the Michigan State University and was graduated in 1850 with the intention of studying law. He accepted a professorship in the Wesleyan Seminary and Female College, and remained there three years, then accepting the professorship of natural sciences in the Michigan State Normal School. In 1857 he resigned and took the chair of chemistry in Michigan State Agricultural College, where he remained until 1863. During the last four years he acted as president. In 1852 he was licensed to preach, and subsequently was ordained deacon and elder. In 1863 he was appointed pastor of the Methodist Episcopal Church in Jackson, Mich. At the end of his pastorate he was appointed pastor of the Central Methodist Episcopal Church of Detroit, Mich. As a public speaker and writer he holds a commanding position; res. Detroit and Albion, Mich.

3278. i. LEWIS ROSS, b. July 23, 1853; m. Luella J. Tillotson.
3279. ii. JOS. HENRY, b. Feb. 20, 1857; unm.; res. Aspen, Colo.
3280. iii. FRED'K IRVING, b. May 18, 1860; d. July 19, 1862.
3281. iv. HERBERT ELWOOD, b. June 23, 1863; m. Marie Mater.
3282. v. CLARENCE ADELBERT, b. July 30, 1868; res. Chicago, Ill.; is connected with Callahan & Co., law book publishers, Monroe St.
3283. vi. ELIZABETH ISABELLA, b. Aug. 14, 1870; m. Oct. 26, 1893, Otis A. Leonard; res. Albion.

1806. DEA. JOSEPH D. W. FISK (James, Ebenezer, William, Ebenezer, William, William, John, William, Robert, Simon, Simon, William, Symond), b. Sept. 24, 1829, Penfield, N. Y.; m. June 9, 1859, Delia Bobbitt, at one time preceptress in Iowa Female Seminary, b. Feb. 17, 1831. When a lad less than 6 years of age he came to Michigan with his parents, the late Mr. and Mrs. James Fisk, reaching Coldwater June 17, 1835. There he obtained such an education as the home schools afforded, but his thirst for knowledge did not permit him to be content with this; his inquiring mind continued to improve as long as he lived. What he read he remembered, and, being a man of studious habits, he soon became well informed in all matters of general importance. In religious views Mr. Fisk was a Presbyterian, and had been a life long and consistent member of that church. He was at one time ruling elder and superintendent of its Sunday school. To be constantly on the alert, seeking improvements, and then imparting to others the valuable results of his investigation and experience, was a ruling habit of his life. He d. Nov. 30, 1893; res. Coldwater, Mich.

3284. i. BESSIE FRANCES, b. Apr. 24, 1860; d. Oct. 12, 1860.
3285. ii. WALTER JAMES, b. July 20, 1862; m. July 12, 1884, Adelle Bassett; res. Coldwater.
3286. iii. CARRIE LOUISE, b. Oct. 15, 1866; m. Mar. 27, 1895, Terwilliger Clark; res. Coldwater.

1817. DAVID ORLANDO FISKE (Samuel, Samuel, Daniel, Samuel, William, John, William, Robert, Simon, Simon, William, Symond), b. Shelburne, Mass., Mar. 14, 1821; m. Mar. 19, 1845, Laura Fiske; m. 2d, Feb. 8, 1853, Isabella Hawkes, b. Sept. 7, 1828. He was a farmer. He d. Dec. 27, 1878; res. Shelburne, Mass.

3287. i. LAURA ISABEL, b. Nov. 7, 1859; unm.; res. Shelburne.
3288. ii. EDWARD H., b. Jan. 8, 1854; m. Lucy E. Hale.
3289. iii. HARVEY O., b. Dec. 23, 1855; m. Mary Emily Thompson.

3290. iv. WALTER E., b. Aug. 23, 1861; m. Julia Pascoe.
3291. v. CLARA A., b. Oct. 29, 1865; res. S.
3292. vi. ZERAH H., b. Jan. 31, 1869; res. Chicago.
3293. vii. DAVID, b. Apr. 7, 1872; res. Chicago.
3294. viii. SAMUEL A., b. Aug. 5, 1875; res. Amherst, Mass.

1819. REV. SAMUEL WHEELOCK FISKE (David, Samuel, Samuel, Daniel, Samuel, William, John, William, Robert, Simon, Simon, William, Symond), b. Shelburne, Mass., July 23, 1828; m. at East Charlemont, Feb. 15, 1859, Elizabeth Leavitt Foster, b. Mar. 5, 1840. She m. 2d, H. S. Kelsey; res. 416 La Salle Av., Chicago, Ill. He is a technical optician at 44 Madison St. Samuel Fiske graduated from Amherst College in 1848, and from Andover Theological Seminary in 1851, after which he returned to Amherst College as tutor for three years. He then passed more than a year in extensive travels in Europe, Egypt, Syria and Turkey. In 1857 he was installed pastor of the Congregational Church in Madison, Conn., and this relationship continued until his death. In 1862 he enlisted as private in the Fourteenth Connecticut Volunteers, but received the commission of Second Lieutenant in Company G before leaving Hartford in August. (The Fourteenth Regiment Connecticut Volunteers served in the Second army corps to the close of war. Mr. Fiske took with him a large number of young men from his parish.) In December he was promoted to First Lieutenant, and in the following month to Captain. During the spring and summer of 1863 he was Acting Assistant Inspector General on the staffs of Gen. Carroll and Gen. Alexander Hayes, of the Third Divison, Second Corps. During the battle of Chancellorsville, May 3, he was captured and taken to Libby Prison. In June he was exchanged and returned to camp. (In September, at his own request, he again took command of Company G.) He distinguished himself in several battles. He received a fatal wound in the battle of the Wilderness, May 6, 1864, while at the head of his company, and died in Fredericksburg on May 22. During the time he was abroad, and also while in the army, he was a correspondent of the Springfield Republican under the nom de plume of Dunn Browne, and the letters were afterward republished in the volumes "Dunn Browne Abroad" and "Dunn Browne in the Army." He d. May 22, 1864; res. Madison, Conn.

3295. i. GEORGE F., b. Jan. 26, 1860; m. Gertrude Bass.
3296. ii. ARTHUR SEVERANCE, b. Sept. 19, 1862, in East Charlemont; d. Meran, Austria, Oct. 11, 1891. Arthur S. Fiske graduated from Amherst College in 1884, and from Hartford Theological Seminary in 1887. Took a high position as a scholar in college, and won the fellowship in the seminary. By advice of the faculty spent three years in the University of Berlin, studying oriental languages, specially Arabic. Was ready to return and enter upon a professorship at Hartford when his health, which by constant study had been seriously impaired, suddenly failed, and he died at the age of 29. As a lad he was deeply interested in ornithology. While in college he had charge of the ornithological collection, arranging and classifying it, and adding sixty-seven varieties to the number. Many of his drawings of birds and eggs were published by the Smithsonian Institute, and were helpful in settling some disputed points in New England ornithology. While in the seminary he made a Hebrew vocabulary of the Psalms. His proficiency in Arabic was very marked, and he left extensive translations from the literature of that people. He was interesting and instructive as a preacher, but important offered pulpits failed to lure him from his chosen course. Through native gifts and high attainments a promising career was open before him. "Flebilis multis occidit," and by a wide circle his death was regarded as a serious loss to American scholarship. "He was an enthusiast in Christian work as in study. He was an artist in soul, as well as with pencil, pen, and brush; a student of architecture, a keen naturalist, proficient especially in ornithology. In the vacations of his theological course, he had won an enviable reputation as writer, speaker and preacher, and important pulpits had been open for his pastoral charge. He turned,

Yours

Dumm Browne.

REV. SAMUEL W. FISKE.

however, from all such offers, in his zeal for the highest Christian scholarship. The Hebrew Bible, with all the Orientalism in customs, language, literature, and monuments, which should interpret and illustrate it, was his chosen field. By special advanced studies in the seminary and by his subsequent years of work abroad he had become signally equipped for these lines of instruction."

1822. PHILO FISKE (David, Samuel, Samuel, Daniel, Samuel, William, John, William, Robert, Simon, Simon, William, Symond), b. Shelburne, Mass., Jan. 3, 1837; m. at Haddam, Conn., Apr. 1, 1861, Josephine Hortense Tyler, b. Dec. 4, 1834; she d. Sept., 1895. He died at Cleveland, Ohio. He removed with his wife to Beloit, Wis., where he remained in mercantile pursuits for some years. Thence he was clerk for some time in Milwaukee, Wis. From there he went to Cleveland, Ohio, where he was chief clerk in the great house of Baldwin & Hatch, until his death in 1864. His daughter Fannie lived in Madison, Conn., and his son Philo in St. Louis, Mo. Neither of them is married. His widow died at Madison, Conn. He d. Jan. 26, 1864; res. Madison, Conn.

3297.　i.　FANNIE A., b. Sept. 30, 1862; res., unm., Madison, Conn.
3298.　ii.　EDWARD PHILO, b. Sept. 14, 1863; res., unm., St. Louis, Mo.

1825. REV. ASA SEAVERENCE FISK (David, Samuel, Samuel, Daniel, Samuel, William, John, William, Robert, Simon, Simon, William, Symond), b. Mar. 2, 1833, in Strongsville, Ohio; m. at Madison, Conn., Sept. 6, 1859, Elizabeth, Worthington Hand. He was born at Strongsville, Ohio, in a big storm of snow and wind, in a pioneer log house; was brought back to Massachusetts when about six years old; went to common schools; worked on the farm; taught school in New Jersey a year when he was 15 and when 17 got into college at Amherst in 1851. He taught school winters, got through with a house appointment at graduation; taught afterward at Canandaigua boys' boarding and day school. Went to Andover Theological Seminary; was called back to Amherst as tutor; was licensed to preach by the Franklin County Congregational Association in 1857; was tutor at Amherst and preached all through western Massachusetts for two years; leaving there went to St. Paul, Minn., for rest; preached there for a new First Congregational Church—the Plymouth; was ordained and installed first pastor in 1859; married in 1859; enlisted in the army in 1861; was elected chaplain of the Fourth Minnesota Volunteer Infantry same year; went into the field first after the battle of Shiloh; served through the war with his regiment or on detailed service, by special order of Gen. Grant. He returned to civil life in the summer of 1865; entered at once on the pastorate of the Second Congregational Church of Rockville, Conn., which was nearly doubled in strength in the course of a five years' ministry there; was called thence to St. Peters Presbyterian Church of Rochester, N. Y., in 1870; the church grew and he paid off an old debt of $30,000. Then he was unexpectedly called to the Harvard Church, San Francisco, Cal. In that city he remained in the pastorate of the Harvard Street Church for nine years. Thence he was called to the pastorate of the First Church, Ithaca, N. Y., where he still is. In the war times with Gen. John Eaton, Jr., he had a large hand in organizing freedmen's affairs on the Mississippi River; armed and equipped the first colored company of soldiers; built two log house towns of more than 1,000 houses each, and married 119 couples in half an hour. He was sent by Gen. Grant to Washington to endeavor to prevent the transfer of freedmen's affairs to a civil department, and to keep it in the department of war. Sumner's bill for such transfer was defeated and the Freedmen's Bureau was organized in the war office as was desired. He was employed afterward by the Bureau of Education to visit and report on the various penal and reformatory institutions of New England and the Middle States. Papers published in Reports of Bureau of Education, Washington, D. C. He was afterward invited to go as Government Commissioner to an International Conference in London, of the departments of education of the various governments of Europe and the United States, and to examine and report on the European National Educational systems, and their working. But, as he had only lately accepted a call to the church at Rochester and as it was anxious for his immediate service, he was constrained to decline so inviting an appointment. He has been too busy to try to write any books. A good many sermons and addresses on various occasions have been published and he has tried to do his duty by the newspapers—

religious and others—as well as he could, and in all the reforms, temperance, civil service and civic federation lines as well as he has been able; res. Ithaca, N. Y.

3299. i. EDWARD SEAVERENCE, b. Nov. 8, 1860.
3300. ii. ZOE WORTHINGTON, b. Apr. 4, 1864; she is an artist.
3301. iii. CHRISTABLE FORSYTHE, b. Dec. 24, 1869.

1827. SAMUEL AUSTIN FISKE (Samuel, Samuel, Samuel. Daniel, Samuel, William, John, William, Robert, Simon, Simon, William, Symond), b. Shelburne, Mass., July 23. 1825; m. in Greenfield Apr. 26, 1854, Henrietta B. Parmenter, b. Jan. 13, 1837; she d. Jan. 27, 1866. He is a solicitor. He res. at 30 Fourth St., St. Paul, Minn.

3302. i. CORA S., b. Sept. 2, 1855; res. Shelburne, Mass.
3303. ii. ABBIE ISADORE. b. Oct. 10, 1856; res. Newtonville, Mass.
3304. iii. HENRIETTA PARMENTER b. Jan. 9, 1866; res. Mont Clair, N. J.
3305. iv. HERBERT EUGENE b. Mar. 21, 1861; d. Sept. 17, 1861.

1828. CHARLES EDWARD FISKE (Samuel, Samuel, Samuel. Daniel, Samuel, William, John, William, Robert, Simon, Simon, William, Symond), b. Shelburne, Mass., Sept. 9, 1826; m. Springfield, Mass., Sept. 9, 1852, Luthera Saloma Sprout, b. Apr. 25, 1833; d. Nov. 6, 1859; m. 2d. at Truxton, N. Y., May 30, 1861, Charlotte Augusta Rounds, b. Oct 15, 1836; d. Mar. 25, 1882. He resided in Shelburne until 21 years of age and worked on his father's farm. Then went to Enfield, Mass., and worked as a millwright during the summer of 1849; went to Holyoke, Mass., in the fall of 1849 and worked at same trade until Sept., 1850; from there went to Middletown, Conn., and stayed about two months. Then went to Beach Island. Edgefield District. South Carolina, and worked until the following July as millwright. Then returned to Massachusetts and worked in Cohasset until Mar., 1852. Then to Greenfield; worked until 1854 making wood planes; commenced at carriage-making in Mar., 1854; went to Chicago, Ill., in May, 1865, and worked in J. Estey & Co.'s organ factory until Apr., 1866; then returned east and worked for same company in Brattleboro, Vt., until the following spring; then went to Greenfield in Apr., 1867, and worked in Gunn & Amidon's bit-brace factory until the spring of 1868. At that time resumed the carriage-making business; purchased farm of ten acres in Deerfield, Mass., in the spring of 1872 and carried on same in connection with carriage business in Greenfield; kept Jersey cows and secured first premiums ($100) on butter at State Board of Agriculture Butter Show in Greenfield in 1878; sold farm in 1884 and moved to Greenfield; res. No. 45 Pleasant St., Holyoke, Mass.

3306. i. ELLEN LOUISE, b. Sept. 1, 1854; m. May 2, 1873, James Joseph Gault; res. 45 Pleasant St. Ch.: Harry Samuel, b. May 21, 1874; Arthur Charles, b. Feb. 20, 1876; Edith Luthera, b. Nov. 4, 1878, Edna Alfreda, b. Oct. 6, 1880. All living.
3307. ii CHARLES HIRAM, b. Nov. 1, 1856; d. May 12, 1875.
3308. iii. ROSE DELL. b. Mar. 18, 1864; m. Sept. 27, 1885, Adolphus Joseph Landry, s. p.; res. 373 Elm St., W. Somerville, Mass.
3309. iv. EDWIN BURTON. b May 10, 1869; res. H.
3310. v. HAL CARPENTER, b. Oct. 7, 1871; d. Sept. 9, 1894.
3311. vi. WM. GRANT, b. Feb. 13, 1874; res. H.

1829. SOLOMON BARDWELL FISKE (Samuel, Samuel, Samuel, Daniel, Samuel, William, John, William, Robert, Simon, Simon, William, Symond), b. Shelburne, Mass., Nov. 22, 1827; m. there June 11, 1857, Helen M. Anderson, b. at Lysander, N. Y., Oct. 17, 1835. He died suddenly of heart failure as the result of the shock he sustained by being thrown from his carriage in a runaway accident. Mr. Fiske accompanied by his daughter started to drive from their home to Greenfield. The horses were a pair of lively colts which had given some trouble before. Mr. Fiske was driving. When near the Col. Wells' place the colts became frightened and dashed down the hill at a lively pace. Mr. Fiske was thrown out but picked himself up apparently uninjured and followed the team. His daughter pluckily took the reins and after going some distance succeeded in reining the frightened animals into an open lot. She was thrown out and the horses stopped. Mr. Fiske came up and saw his daughter and then fell to the ground, dying almost instantly. The young woman was not seriously injured. Dr. F. J. Canedy, of Shelburne Falls, the family physician, and Dr. Deane, of Greenfield, were summoned. Dr. Canedy said that Mr. Fiske had shown symptoms of heart trouble for three years. He was a highly respected citizen and had always lived in Shelburne. Besides his daughter Mr. Fiske is survived by a widow, two brothers living in the West and a brother Charles Fiske of Holyoke. He d. Oct. 25, 1895; res. Shelburne, Mass.

3312. i. ALPHEUS ANDERSON, b. June 28, 1858; d. Mar. 14, 1859.
3313. ii. HARRIET LOUISE, b. Aug. 31, 1860; unm.; res. S.

1832. GEORGE WASHINGTON FISKE (Samuel, Samuel, Samuel, Daniel, Samuel, William, John, William, Robert, Simon, Simon, William, Symond), b. Shelburne, Mass., town records say Nov. 2, 1834; he says Oct. 28, 1837; m. at Manteno, Ill., Aug. 10, 1868, Margaret H. Whitehill, b. July 25, 1849. He is a farmer; res. Robbinsdale, Minn.

3314. i. GEORGE W., b. June 18, 1873.
3315. ii. LOUISE M., b. Nov. 18, 1881.

1836. JAMES DICKINSON FISK (Partridge, Daniel, Samuel, Daniel, Samuel, William, John, William, Robert, Simon, Simon, William, Symond), b. Shelburne, Mass., Jan. 1, 1831; m. 1857 Harriet Loomis, b. 1836; d. 1858; m. 2d, 1867, Mary E. Sheldon, b. Nov. 1, 1832. He is a farmer; res. Lyndon, Ill.

3316. i. HARRIET R., b. Apr. 8, 1858; m. Sept. 22, 1879, Mark A. Root; res. Morrison, Ill.
3317. ii. GEO. PLINEY, b. Oct. 6, 1868; m. Eva E. Brewer.
3318. iii. JAMES ADELBERT, b. Apr. 2, 1870; res. L.
3319. iv. EDITH MAY, b. Mar. 4, 1874; res. L.

1850. REV. FREDERIC A. FISKE (Elisha, Robert, Daniel, Daniel, Samuel, William, John, William, Robert, Simon, Simon, William, Symond), b. Wrentham, Mass., Apr. 15, 1816; m. in Amherst Sept. 24, 1839, Anna A. Nelson, dau. of Rev. Stephen Smith Nelson; d. May 7, 1848; m. 2d, 1852, Mrs. Rebecca J. (Robbins) Haskell, dau. of Dea. Josiah Robbins of Plymouth; she d. in North Carolina July 23, 1865; m. 3d, Jan. 5, 1869, Abbie Wheeler Woods, dau. of Samuel Woods, of Malden, Mass., b. Nov. 7, 1834; res. 2 Chestnut St., Boston. Rev. Frederic Augustus Fiske, son of Rev. Elisha and Margaret Shepard Fiske, was born in Wrentham, Mass., Apr. 15, 1816; fitted at Day's Academy in his native town at so early an age that it was not deemed advisable for him to enter college then, so he taught school for a year or so and then entered Amherst College from which he graduated in 1836 and received his A. M. in 1837, after which, as his health did not then permit of his taking a theological course, he at once engaged in teaching, first as assistant in Washington Institute, New York City, then in Norwalk, Conn., next as principal of Monson (Mass.) Academy, 1833-34, and later in Fall River, Mass. While in Fall River his wife died and he then decided to enter the ministry in accordance with his original plan, and much to the regret of his patrons in Fall River he entered Yale Theological Seminary, taking the full course from 1847 to 1850, when he entered upon the work of the ministry, being ordained pastor of the Congregational Church of Ashburnham, Mass., Dec. 30, 1851, where he remained until Apr. 17, 1854, when he resigned. For about three years, from November 16, 1854, he was pastor of the Congregational Church in East Marshfield, after which at the solicitation of friends he resumed his former occupation of teaching, first as principal of the high school at Clinton, Mass., and for the next eight years as principal of a boys' boarding school in Newton, Mass., which grew in numbers and popularity under his care. In 1865 on account of a severe illness his physician insisted upon his leaving his school and strongly recommended his moving at once to a warmer climate, so that from 1865 to 1868 he was Superintendent of Education for the State of North Carolina under the Freedmen's Bureau, receiving his appointment from Gen. O. P. Howard. Having now regained his health he returned to Massachusetts, where he was for a short time pastor of the church in Raynham, Mass. The remainder of his life was spent in the service of the Protestant Episcopal Church, being ordained as deacon on June 25, 1870, and as priest on Nov. 5 of the same year. From July, 1870, to May, 1873, he was rector of Trinity Church, Van Deusenville, Mass.; from May, 1873, to Sept., 1876, rector of St. Paul's Church, Brookfield, Conn.; from Sept., 1876, until his death rector of Grace Church, North Attleboro, Mass., which joins his native town. He died of nervous prostration induced by overwork in his efforts to relieve his parish from a load of pecuniary indebtedness, but not until he had raised the last dollar. His bishop (Paddock), who officiated at his funeral, said of him in his annual address to the convention of 1879, as follows: "In the rectory that with the church at its side crowns the little knoll of an ample lot in a pretty village of Bristol County, one of our best rural pastors lay down to die soon after he had given God thanks for the good example of dear Dr. Wells. This man coming to his parish two years before, had found the wise and far-sighted work of his predecessor burdened with such honest, but partially unexpected indebtedness as changed times had brought upon many of the parishes all over the land. The time came last autumn when about $2,000 of this indebtedness must be raised to avert disaster. He did not create the obligation; but it was Christ's cross that lay athwart his path, to remove it. First letting it cost himself more, perhaps, than he would expect of any one else, he then roused the hearts of all, even to the children, of his flock and they responded nobly. Then strengthened as he supposed in his gentleness and modesty, by a statement and commendation from his bishop, he went from door to door in Boston, to let others bear the burden with him, and so fulfill the law of Christ. From a few he received refusals which pained him; from a few, good advice against parishes getting into debt; from others modest offerings toward his longed-for getting out of debt and saving a valuable church property. Twice he broke in his weary rounds; but at last he succeeded and went home with a church property saved and his life given for it." After a few weeks of exhaustion and suffering the Rev. Frederic Augustus Fiske, rector of Grace Church, North Attleboro, died Dec. 15, 1878, and was buried by one and other brethren amidst a town full of mourners. He was a man of manly and strong piety, clear and happy in his convictions and of willing and unwearying labor. His wife and son Frederic Elisha Fiske survive him. He d. Dec. 15, 1878; res. New Haven, Conn.; Ashburnham, Mass., and Boston, Mass.

    3320. i.   FRED. E., b. July 25, 1840; m. Marion A. Cutter.
    3321. ii.   MARGARET SHEPPARD, b. ———; d. ae. 12.
    3322. iii. WILLIAM, b. ———; d. in infancy.

1852. DAVID BRAINERD FISK (Daniel, Robert, Daniel, Daniel, Samuel, William, John, William, Robert, Simon, Simon, William, Symond), b. Upton, Mass., Jan. 23, 1817; m. there June 12, 1838, Lydia C. Wood. Mr. Fisk was born at Upton, Mass., and received a common school education. At the age of sixteen he entered upon his business career by accepting a clerkship. He married Lydia C. Wood, and soon after embarked in business for himself. In 1853 Mr. Fisk came to Chicago, and with B. M. Fisk and J. E. L. Fraser opened the first millinery house in Chicago on Wells St., between Lake and South Water, under the now familiar firm name of D. B. Fisk & Co. The business continued to grow through Mr. Fisk's energy, until it became the largest millinery establishment in the world. Mr. Fisk had never known a sick day until about three weeks before his death when he caught a bad cold, which developed into bronchitis. He was not, however, confined to his home. Nothing serious was anticipated until a short time before he died when a decided change for the worse occurred. He became unconscious and so remained until death came. Mr. Fisk was a lover of outdoor sports, and a member of the Chicago, Calumet and Washington Park Clubs, yet he was in no sense a club man, nor was he what is known as a society man. He was devoted to his home, and there were very few pleasures that could draw him away from his fireside. The remains were taken from the family residence, 2100 Calumet Ave., to Rosehill, for burial. None but the family and a few intimate friends were present. The funeral services were held at the residence, Rev. Thomas C. Hall, pastor of the 41st Street Presbyterian Church, officiating. The members of the old Tippecanoe Club were present. He d. July 29, 1891; res. Upton, Mass., and 2100 Calumet Ave., Chicago, Ill.

    3323. i.   DANIEL MILTON, b. Dec. 6, 1839; m. Martha E. Sharp.
    3324. ii.   HENRY EZRA, b. Oct 18, 1841; unm.; res. 2100 Calumet Ave.
    3325. iii. ALMIRA C., b. Mar. 18, 1851; m. Sept. 2, 1869, Bennett B. Botsford, b. Aug. 3, 1840; res. 2100 Calumet Ave., Chicago. Ch.: Bertha Fisk Botsford, b. Oct. 2, 1875, 2100 Calumet Ave., Chicago, Ill.; Marion Kent Botsford, b. Feb. 20, 1884; d. Dec. 30, 1887.

1855. DANIEL E. FISKE (Daniel, Robert, Daniel, Daniel, Samuel, William, John, William, Robert, Simon, Simon, William, Symond), b. Upton, Mass., Mar. 4, 1822; m. at Leominster Oct. 26, 1872, Harriot Billings, b. Jan. 23, 1834; d. May 11, 1887. He was born in Upton and has always resided there; has held various town offices and is highly esteemed and respected by the entire community; has been engaged in business all his life; res. Upton, Mass., s. p.

1858. ELISHA B. FISKE (William, Robert, Daniel, Daniel, Samuel, William, John, William, Robert, Simon, Simon, William, Symond), b. Upton, Mass., Feb. 16, 1804; m. there Sept. 17, 1829, Mariam Clay Starkweather, b. Sept. 22, 1809. He was a boot manufacturer. He d. Dec. 25, 1869; res. Upton, Mass.

  3326. i. LUCY MERIAM, b. Aug. 29, 1830; d. July 10, 1876.
  3327. ii. GEORGIANNAH BLISS, b. Dec. 14, 1832; m. Jan. 21, 1858, Joshua M. Marshall; res. 784 Merrimack St., Lowell, Mass.
  3328. iii. SARAH ELLEN, b. Jan. 13, 1836; unm.; res. 165 Salem St., Lowell, Mass.

1860. CHARLES A. FISKE (William, Robert, Daniel, Daniel, Samuel, William, John, William, Robert, Simon, Simon, William, Symond), b. Upton Apr. 4, 1811; m. there Sept. 18, 1832, Salina Melita Ward; res. Upton, Mass.

  3329. i. CALVIN JUDSON, b. Nov. 5, 1835.
  3330. ii. EDWIN WINSLOW, b. June 30, 1839.

1862. HARRISON LYSANDER FISK (Emmons H., Daniel, Daniel, Daniel, Samuel, William, John, William, Robert, Simon, Simon, William, Symond), b. Nov. 28, 1828, Upton. Mass.; m. June 23, 1855, Mary Submit Hill, b. June 23, 1829; d. Sept. 13, 1888. His early life was spent in Maine, near Union; then he served an apprenticeship to a druggist in Greenfield, Mass.; then in the early fifties he went south as traveling agent for J. C. Ayer Pill Manufactory of Lowell, and after several years settled in Nacogdoches, Tex., with his wife, where Harry was born. She came north in 1859 with her baby son, and the second child was born in Upton. His store was seized by the Confederate army and he was forced into the ranks as a surgeon; was captured by the Federal army in Red River, and was in prison some time; finally exchanged, and came north in 1865; lived in Upton about one year; then he moved to Springfield, where he went into the publishing business (subscription books), D. B. Fisk & Co. In a few years went into the grocery business on North Main St., for several years, then took in a partner who took him in and did him up. In 1874 went to Worcester and took charge of a drug store, oldest in the city; remained there until 1891, when, owing to ill health and change in firm, he resigned, and did nothing until 1895, now running drug store in Worcester; res. 351 Park Ave., Worcester, Mass.

  3333. i. HARRISON RANSON, b. Apr. 19, 1858; m. Emma S. Cady.
  3334. ii. WINTHROP WARD, b. Oct. 26, 1859; m. Caroline C. Swasey.

1863. HYPOLLITUS CLAUSEN FISK (Emmons H., Daniel, Daniel, Daniel, Samuel, William, John, William, Robert, Simon, Simon, William, Symond), b. Upton, Mass., Feb. 3, 1827; m. Philena A. Perry; res. Hyde Park, Mass., 12 Pond St.

  3335. i. HELEN, b. ———; m. Marshall T. Burnett; res. H. P.

1870½. JAMES JONES FISK (Joel, Benjamin, Benjamin, Daniel, Samuel, William, John, William, Robert, Simon, Simon, William, Symond), b. Medway, Mass., Jan. 14, 1806; m. in Charlestown, N. H., Nov. 20, 1832, Rebekah Prouty, dau. of Artemas and Rebekah (Perrin) Prouty, b. Langdon, N. H., Feb. 20, 1813; d. June 12, 1853; m. 2d, Aug. 10, 1854, Miranda Prouty, b. July 11, 1815. He was a shoemaker by trade; resided in Mendon, Bellingham, and So. Milford. His second wife was probably sister of his first. He married the second time in Bellows Falls, Vt.; res. Bellingham, Mass., and Milford, Mass.

  3335¼.i. MARION ELIZA, b. Nov. 15, 1835; m. Nov. 15, 1856, Alvan A. Sweet; res. Hopkinton, Mass. Ch.: 1, Annie Rebekah, b. Aug. 26, 1857. 2, Gertrude Marion, b. Dec., 1863; d. June 2, 1873.
  3335½.ii. HAMBLET BARBER, b. Mar. 27, 1838; m. Eliza Hawes.

1871. LUTHER B. FISKE (Clark, Benjamin, Benjamin, Daniel, Samuel, William, John, William, Robert, Simon, Simon, William, Symond), b. Mar. 17, 1814; m. Aug. 1, 1837, S. N. F. Leonard; res. Upton, Mass.

3336.   i.   CALISTA A., b. July 3, 1838.
3337.   ii.   ELIZA A., b. June 7, 1840.
3338.   iii. CHLOE A., b. Feb. 25, 1842.
3339.   iv. CHANDLER C., b. Mar. 3, 1844.
3340.   v.   FRED'K A., b. May 25, 1846.
3341.   vi. CALVIN BRADISH, b. June 3, 1849; d. July 16, 1849.

1872. HARVEY W. FISKE (Clark, Benjamin, Benjamin, Daniel, Samuel, William, John, William, Robert, Simon, Simon, William, Symond), b. Jan. 13, 1816; m. Jan 9, 1842, Jerusha Adams; res. Upton, Mass.

3342.   i.   ADIN WARREN, b. Apr. 10, 1850; d. Apr. 11, 1852.

1874. FRANKLIN GALATIOUS FISK (Galacious, Benjamin, Benjamin, Daniel, Samuel, William, John, William, Robert, Simon, Simon, William, Symond), b. Shelburne Falls, Mass., Jan. 23, 1821; m. New York City, Oct. 2, 1850, Margaret J. Brady, b. June, 1830. He was a map engraver, and succeeded to the business of Sidney E. Morse, inventor of relief plate map engraving, in New York, in 1850. He d. Nov. 13, 1889; res. New York, N. Y.

3343.   i.   EDWARD F., b. June 27, 1857; m. Sadie B. Roberts.
3344.   ii.   IDA MABEL, b. Apr. 14, 1866; m. at Mont Clair, N. J., Sept. 22, 1892, William H. Johnson, b. Oct. 30, 1864. He is a druggist; res. 38 Yankee Road, Middletown, O. Ch.: Edna Margaret, b. Feb. 26, 1894.
3345.   iii. FRANCELIA J., b. Sept. 16, 1851; m. May, 1875, Chauncey W. Ames, b. Aug., 1841. He d. Oct. 19, 1894; was a printer, designer and engraver; res. Salt Lake City, Utah. Ch.: Mabel, b. Brooklyn, Apr. 2, 1876; d. Sept., 1889, Denver, Colo. Bessie, b. Mont Clair, N. J., Feb. 14, 1882. Chester Fisk, b. Mont Clair, N. J., Sept. 24, 1885.

1876. OTIS ALPHONSO FISK (Galacious, Benjamin, Benjamin, Daniel, Samuel, William, John, William, Robert, Simon, Simon, William, Symond), b. Nov. 25, 1826, in Ludlow, Mass; m. there Sept. 9, 1846, Abby Sophia Gove, b. Aug. 5, 1826; d. Jan. 28, 1863. He was a farmer. He d. Apr. 1, 1870; res. Palmer, Mass.

3346.   i.   ABBY LOUISA, b. Dec. 30, 1847; d. Aug. 30, 1848.
3347.   ii.   MARIA LOUISA, b. Sept. 12, 1849; d. Mar. 24, 1850.
3348.   iii. CLARA FIDELIA, b. Apr. 26, 1851; m. Nov. 25, 1868, Everett D. Stebbins; res. 11 Mosher St., Holyoke, Mass.
3349.   iv. OTIS GALACIOUS, b. Jan. 1, 1855; m. Carrie L. Davis.
3350.   v.   GEORGE HENRY, b. Nov. 4, 1858; d. June 29, 1859.

1883. GEORGE ARMORY FISK (Emory, Benjamin, Benjamin, Daniel, Samuel, William, John, William, Robert, Simon, Simon, William, Symond), b. Upton, Mass., Sept. 29, 1818; m. Caroline H. Merrick.

3351.   i.   GEORGE MERRICK, b. Mar., 1847; res. Springfield, Mass.
3352.   ii.   HENRY GROSVENOR, b. ———.
3353.   iii. ———, b. ———; d. ———.

1885. ERASTUS HIRAM FISK (Emory, Benjamin, Benjamin, Daniel, Samuel, William, John, William, Robert, Simon, Simon, William, Symond), b. Enfield, Mass., July 12, 1823; m. Jan. 1, 1846, in Greenwich, Mass., Dency Aurelia Sprout, b. June 6, 1825. He was a millwright and later a carpenter. He d. Feb. 20, 1889; res. Sterling, Ill.

3354.   i.   CHARLES CHAPIN, b. Aug. 4, 1848; m. Mary Fannie Wilson.
3355.   ii.   ERLON HIRAM, b. Aug. 9, 1851; d. Sept., 1852.
3356.   iii. EMMA AMELIA, b. May 2, 1855; m. Oct. 7, 1875, Stewart Wilson. He was b. Jan. 14, 1849. Is a farmer; res. Prairieville, Lee Co., Ill. Ch.: Lorena Amelia, b. Aug. 13, 1877.

3357. iv. NELLIE LUTHERIA, b. May 12, 1858; m. May 10, 1886, William
Sprout; d. July 18, 1892. She had three ch., two d. young, and
Ethelwyn, b. 1889 (blind).

3358. v. CORA AURELIA, b. Jan. 28, 1863; m. Oct. 18, 1888, Nathan J.
Bush; res. Sterling, Ill. Ch.: Gladys Grace, b. Feb. 1, 1891.
Ethelyn Reid, b. May 15, 1893; d. Sept. 2, 1894.

3359. vi. LOGAN EMORY, b. Sept. 4, 1866; d. Dec. 15, 1871.

1886. CHARLES HORACE FISKE (Emory, Benjamin, Benjamin, Daniel,
Samuel, William, John, William, Robert, Simon, Simon, William, Symond), b.
Enfield, Mass., Nov. 1, 1825; m. there Nov. 13, 1849, Sylvia J. Ward, b. Sept. 23,
1828. He is a carpenter; res. Germantown, Pa., 234 West Chelton Ave.

3360. i. EDWARD R., b. Dec. 30, 1850; m. Caroline P. Holland.

3361. ii. CHARLES H., b. Dec. 18, 1856; m. Nellie L. Osborn.

1892. LUCIUS CAREY FISK (Jonathan, Benjamin, Benjamin, Daniel,
Samuel, William, John, William, Robert, Simon, Simon, William, Symond), b.
Milford, Mass., Aug. 3, 1821; m. Jan. 8, 1851, Harriett E. Shepherd, dau. of Abraham and Hannah (Webb) Shepherd, b. Plainfield, Conn., May 29, 1829. He was
born in Milford, Mass.; resided in Brooklyn, Conn., Keene, N. H., and finally
settled in Hopedale, a village in Milford, Mass., and was employed in Walker's
boot factory. Res. Hopedale, Mass.

3362. i. HARRIETT LUELLA, b. Brooklyn, Conn., Oct. 14, 1851; m.
Charles A. Miller.

3363. ii. ESTHER ESENOR, b. July 24, 1853.

3364. iii. GEORGE IRVING, b. Nov. 10, 1863.

1897. WILLIAM PRENTISS FISKE (Jonathan, Benjamin, Benjamin, Daniel, Samuel, William, John, William, Robert, Simon, Simon, William, Symond),
b. Milford, Mass., June 7, 1833; m. July 13, 1863, Mary Adaline Hilton, b. in Holliston, July 2, 1845. He is a shoemaker; res. Boston, Mass., 367 Tremont St.

3365. i. LIZZIE ADELIA, b. 1869

3366. ii. GEO. WM., b. 1865.

3367. iii. ULYSSES GRANT, b. 1871.

1898. JAMES WOOD FISKE (Jonathan, Benjamin, Benjamin, Daniel,
Samuel, William, John, William, Robert, Simon, Simon, William, Symond), b.
Milford, Mass., Dec. 1, 1835; m. in Woonsocket, R. I., July 5, 1856, Maria Smith,
of Acton, b. June 19, 1837. He is a dealer in small fruits; res. Acton Centre, Mass.

3368. i. HERBERT BYRON, b. Oct. 25, 1857; m. Sept. 25, 1880, Hattie
F. Whittemore, b. Sept. 25, 1860. Res. Acton Centre, Mass.
He is a tool dresser. Ch.: Inez Gertrude, b. Apr. 11, 1889.

3369. ii. JAMES WILBUR, b. Dec. 14, 1860; m. Dec. 7, 1884, Mary
Hattie Dockendorff, b. Jan. 5, 1858. Res. 282 Dudley St.,
Roxbury, Mass. Is a musician; s. p.

3370. iii. FLORIAN WALTRON, b. Jan. 21, 1868; m. May 20, 1886,
Iva Louise Larrabee. She was b. June 29, 1869. Res. 44
Chestnut St., Haverhill, Mass. He is an engineer. Ch.: Liz-
zie May Fisk, b. Aug. 10, 1887. Retar Verner Fisk, b. May 20,
1889. Cora Methel Fisk, b. Mar. 14, 1892; d. Mar. 22, 1894.
Ethel Florian Fisk, b. Feb. 18, 1895.

3371. iv. BERTHA I., b. May 15, 1866.

3372. v. FRANK E., b. Oct. 31, 1869; m. Sept. 6, 1892, Bertha May
Roberts. She was b. May 1, 1874. He is a farmer; res. s. p.
Acton, Mass.

1906. EVAN AUGUSTUS FISK (Evan, Elisha, William, Daniel, Samuel,
William, John, William, Robert, Simon, Simon, William, Symond), b. Upton,
Mass., June 12, 1826; m. there Sept., 1850, Jane Elizabeth Holbrook, b. Apr., 1828;
d. May, 1856; m. 2d Nov. 19, 1859, Harriet S. Pearse, b. Sept. 20, 1832. He was
formerly a boot and shoe manufacturer; res. Milford, Mass.

3373. i. WALTER A., b. Nov. 13, 1864; d. June 25, 1868.

3374. ii. CORA L., b. May 29, 1869; d. Apr. 21, 1872.

1908. DENNIS TAFT FISKE (Evan, Elisha, William, Daniel, Samuel,
William, John, William, Robert, Simon, Simon, William, Symond), b. Upton,
Mass., Apr. 7, 1837; m. Aug. 8, 1860, Calista A. Fiske, b. July, 1838. He is a
carpenter; res. Upton, Mass.

    335 i.   NELLIE ISABELL, b. May 27, 1861; m. Jan. 1, 1889, Wm.
              C. Whitney; res. Mont Clair, N. J.
    336 ii. WILBUR GEORGE, b. Sept. 14, 1862; m. at Worcester, July,
              1884, Sadie M. Goddard; res. Upton.

1911. GEORGE WILLIAM FISKE (Elisha, Elisha, William, Daniel, Samuel, William, John, William, Robert, Simon, Simon, William, Symond), b. Upton,
Mass., July 9, 1837; m. Aug. 25, 1858, Sarah E. Lackey, b. July 11, 1839. He is in
the wholesale produce commission business in Boston; res. Danvers, Mass.

    3376¼.i. MAUD E., b. Sept. 27, 1882.
    3376½.ii. ETHEL C., b. Feb. 22, 1887.

1920. DAVID LUTHER FISKE (Jonathan S., David, William, Daniel,
Samuel, William, John, William, Robert, Simon, Simon, William, Symond), b.
Grafton, Mass., July 19, 1840; m. in Shrewsbury, Mass., June 9, 1879, Ella Maria
Williams, b. July 24, 1849. He was born on Keith Hill, in Grafton, on the old
Fiske place. His father was an extensive farmer and the son pursued the same
vocation. At one time he was in the provision business. He has held numerous
town offices and is much esteemed and respected by his fellow citizens; res.
Grafton, Mass.

    3377. i.   MAVIDA, b. May 24, 1880.
    3378. ii. REBECCA CUTLER, b. Jan. 12, 1882.
    3379. iii. GEORGIANNA KEITH, b. Oct. 25, 1885.

1924. WILLIE EUGENE FISKE (William A., David, William, Daniel,
Samuel, William, John, William, Robert, Simon, Simon, William, Symond), b.
Grafton, Mass., Nov. 25, 1856; m. there Aug. 7, 1885, Frances Hedstrom of Kan-
sas City, Mo.; res. Kansas City, Mo.

    3380. i.   FRANCIS EUGENE, b. Feb. 17 1890.
    3381. ii. LUCILE GEORGIE, b. Feb. 24, 1887.
    3382. iii. RICHARD IRWIN, b. Feb. 3, 1891.
    3383. iv. FORREST WILBUR, b. Sept. 20, 1894.

1933. HORACE LEONARD FISK (Alexander, Josiah, Josiah, Daniel,
Samuel, William, John, William, Robert, Simon, Simon, William, Symond), b.
Shelburne, Oct. 3, 1813; m. July 24, 1843, in Bellingham, Mass., Emily Eveline
Cumming, b. Apr. 2, 1822. He was a farmer. He d. Dec. 25, 1891; res. Spencer,
Mass.

    3384 i.   HATTIE IDELLA, b. Oct. 1, 1857; m. Apr. 17, 1881, Fred J.
              Underhill; res. 19 Wendell St., Providence, R. I., s. p.
    3385. ii. MARY JANE, b. May 5, 1844; m. John Wheeler; res. 195 Sum-
              mer St., Worcester, Mass.
    3386. iii. MARTHA ANN, b. July 29, 1845; m. George Ullrich. She d.
              in 1872.
    3387. iv. HORACE LEWIS, b. ay 11, 1849; m. ———; d. in 1892. Had
              six ch.; one, Gertie, res. in Paxton, Mass.
    3388. v.   GEORGE EDWARD, b. Sept. 31, 1850; res. Colorado.
    3389. vi. HELEN MARIA, b. July 18, 1854; d. ———.
    3390. vii. CHARLES H., b. Aug. 13, 1855; m. Delia E. Gotha.
    3391. viii. HATTIE IDELLA, b. Sept. 29, 1857.
    3392. ix. CHARLES LEONARD, b. Oct. 20, 1852; d. ———.

1938. DR. SAMUEL WARFIELD FISKE (Alexander, Josiah, Josiah,
Daniel, Samuel, William, John, William, Robert, Simon, Simon, William, Symond), b. Nov. 29, 1823, Shelburne Falls, Mass.; m. in Thompson, Conn., Apr. 29,
1848, Lucina Pierce, b. Aug. 17, 1828. He was born in Shelburne Falls, Mass.,
where he received an excellent education. He studied medicine, was graduated,

and since 1856 has very successfully practiced his profession; res. Norwich, Conn., 53 Oak St.

3393. i. PERSIS M., b. Dec. 29, 1849; m. July 1, 1876, Washington M. Vars; res. N.

3394. ii. CHARLES S., b. July 1, 1858; m. Jan. 21, 1885, Ellen E. Mason; res. N.

3395. iii. WILLIE E., b. May 22, 1860; d. unm. May 19, 1882.

1941. JOHN GOODALE FISK (Alexander, Josiah, Josiah, Daniel, Samuel, William, John, William, Robert, Simon, Simon, William, Symond), b. Colerain, Mass., Sept. 1, 1831; m. at Stanstead, P. Q., Aug. 31, 1848, Sarah Jane Horn, b. Jan. 3, 1832. He is a farmer; res. Rock Island, P. Q.

3396. i. MARY E., b. May 25, 1849; d. Feb. 5, 1878.

3397. ii. ELLEN M., b. June 6, 1851; m. James B. Cox; res. Morgan Corner, Vt.

3398. iii. WM. THOS., b. Mar. 9, 1855; m. Martha Pelow.

1944. REV. WILBUR FISK, D. D. (Isaiah, Amos, Daniel, Samuel, Joseph, William, John, William, Robert, Simon, Simon, William, Symond), b. Brattleboro, Vt., Aug. 31, 1792; m. June 9, 1823, Miss R. Peck; d. Middletown, Conn., 1886. He studied law, but after a long and serious illness abandoned the profession and entered the itinerant ministry in 1818, when he was licensed as a local preacher in the Methodist Episcopal Church. He took high rank as a pulpit orator, was pastor for two years in Craftsbury, Vt., and in 1819, removed to Charlestown, Mass. At the conference of 1820 he was admitted into full membership, ordained as a deacon in 1822, and from 1823 till 1827 was presiding elder of the Vermont district, which then comprised the whole of Vermont east of the Green Mountains. He was placed upon the superannuated list, but was requested, in so far as health would allow, to act as agent for Newmarket Academy, at that time the only Methodist institution in New England. dress of welcome to Lafayette in 1824. He was also a delegate to the general conference in that year, and was chosen to write the address to the British conference. He was chaplain of the Vermont Legislature in 1826, and was one of the founders and principal of the Wesleyan Academy in Wil- While here he was chosen to make the ad- braham, Mass., 1826-31, and a delegate to the general conference of 1828, when he

REV. WILBUR FISK, D. D., LL.D.

was elected bishop of the Canada conference but declined. In 1829 he also refused the presidency of La Grange College, Alabama, and a professorship in the University of Alabama. In 1830 he was chosen first president of the Wesleyan University, in whose organization he had materially aided. The duties of that office were entered upon in 1831; the institution under his direction became the most influential of any in the Methodist denomination in America. At the general conference in 1832 his appeals in behalf of Indian missions resulted in the organization of the Oregon mission, and he was at this time instrumental in founding Williamstown Academy. For years he was useful to educational interests at large by recommending or furnishing professors and presidents to the rapidly multiplying colleges of the far west. In search of health, he passed the winter of 1835-6 in Italy, and the summer of 1836 in England, when he also represented the M. E. Church of the Wesleyan conference as a delegate. He was elected bishop of that church in 1836, but declined. In 1839 he became a member

of the board of education of Connecticut. He was said to be unsurpassed in elo-
quence and fervor as a preacher, and was often compared to Fenelon, being endowed with like moral and mental traits. The degree of D. D. was conferred
on him by Augusta College, Kentucky, in 1829, and LL. D. by Brown in 1835. His
published works are: "Inaugural Address" (New York, 1831); "Calvinistic Controversy" (1837); "Travels in Europe" (1838); "Sermons and Lectures on Universalism: Reply to Pierpont on the Atonement, and other Theological and Educational Works and Sermons." His account of his European travels had a wide circulation and was greatly admired. His "Life and Writings" were published by
the Rev. Joseph Holdich, D. D. (New York, 1842). He d. s. p., Feb. 22, 1839; res.
Middletown, Conn.

    1945. ORIN MORRIS FISK (Abraham, Ephraim, Joseph, Samuel, Joseph,
William, John, William, Robert, Simon, Simon, William, Symond), b. Cherry Valley, N. Y., Apr. 25, 1807; m. at De Kalb, Dec. 11, 1826, Lydia Ann Cooper, b.
Nov. 13, 1804; d. Aug. 22, 1837; m. 2d, Oct. 24, 1839, Roxanna Priest, b. Dec. 11,
1815, in Rutland, Vt. Among the truly representative men of St. Lawrence county,
whose life and character entitle them to record on the pages of history, was the late
Orin M. Fisk, Esq., who during his life deservedly held a prominent position in
the community in which he lived. He was born in De Kalb, N. Y., Apr. 25, 1807,
and after a brief life of usefulness died at his home in De Kalb, Jan. 20, 1857, much
lamented by kindred and friends, he was a man of more than ordinary ability in
all the vocations of life, and could never say no to the needy and destitute. His
adhesions to the principles of honor were so strong that nothing could break them,
and money would not tempt him to do a wrong act. In early life he devoted considerable time to teaching and bore the enviable reputation of being one of the
finest penman in St. Lawrence county, consequently under the earnest solicitations
of the various school districts of De Kalb he gave instructions which were long
cherished by those who were so fortunate as to come under his tuition. In later
years he was successful in doing business as a merchant in De Kalb, as one of the
firm of Fisk & Slosson; still later he opened a store at Cooper's Falls. At the organization of the De Kalb works at this place he was chosen as its head manager, investing $10,000 of his capital towards a grist mill, which was said to be
one of the finest in the county, but was subsequently burned down some years
after his death. He was for a long period agent for several of the original proprietors of land in St. Lawrence county, among which were Frederic De Peyster
and W. C. H. Wadell, of New York City. In politics he was formerly a member
of the Whig party, but joined the Republican organization on its formation. He
held the office of Justice of the Peace for many years, and in 1847 was elected
supervisor of the town of De Kalb, which office he held till his death, in 1857.
It is needless to add any encomium to Orin M. Fisk's reputation as a man
and worthy citizen, as the foregoing record amply testifies to his worth, and the
estimation in which he was held by his fellow citizens. Although not a member
of any church, he exhibited a Christian principle in all his dealings, and many
can testify to the timely aid received from his hands in their direst extremity.
He d. Jan., 1857; res. De Kalb, N. Y.
      3399. i.   CHARLES H., b. Oct. 6, 1827; m. Mary F. Smith.
      3400. ii.   THEODORE, b. Mar. 8, 1829; m. Jane Morris.
      3401. iii. MATILDA ADALINE, b. Jan. 30, 1831; m. Feb. 22, 1855.
                   Henry C. Newcome; res. Osage, Iowa.
      3402. iv.   ELIZABETH, b. May 14, 1833; m. May, 1858, Charles H. Lamp-
                   son; res. Green Bay, Wis.
      3403. v.   ELVIRA, b. Apr. 1, 1835; m. Nov., 1857, Dr. Joseph Hastings.
                   She d. ———. Ch.: Clara; res. Palermo, Kan.
      3404. vi.   ORIN LEE, b. July 1, 1842; d. Aug. 20, 1865. Orin L. Fisk was
                   the eldest son (by a second marriage) of the late O. M. Fisk,
                   Esq. When war was declared, in 1860, Orin L. was a prom-
                   inent druggist, doing business at Watertown, Jefferson county,
                   N. Y., and subsequently was on a visit to his half brothers and
                   sisters west, when he enlisted in the Fourth Iowa Cavalry.
                   In obedience to the promptings of true patriotism and
                   loyalty the son went forth to serve his imperiled country in the

gloomiest hour of its struggle for an existence. Gallantly he shared its fortunes under Sherman and other Generals at Vicksburg, Memphis and Cairo. Possessing a delicate constitution, he soon fell a victim to that relentless scourge, chronic diarrhoea. He lingered for many months, subject to sanitary treatment, till at length an honorable discharge relieved him from the stern duties of military life. Buoyed up by his indomitable will, though physically incapacitated to endure the fatigue of travel, he soon reached the home of his childhood. Here, the mere shadow of his former presence, he greeted his doting mother, a loving sister, and a younger brother.

3405.   vii.   WM. C. H. WADELL, b. Nov. 29, 1855; d. Jan. 21, 1860.
3406.   viii. FRED'K DE PEYSTER, b. Dec. 5, 1848; unm. He is a resident of De Kalb. He was born in De Kalb and has always resided there. Educated at the public schools on attaining his majority he engaged in business on his own account. At present he is general agent for books, various publications and novelties.
3407.   ix.   ELLA WINSLOW, b. June 7, 1850.

1951. CYRUS B. FISK (Benjamin B., Ephraim, Joseph, Samuel, Joseph, William, John, William, Robert, Simon, Simon, William, Symond), b. Nov. 29, 1817, in Killingly, Conn., m. 1842, Miss Powell, dau. of Rev. Robert Powell. She d. 1844. He always lived at home; learned the fanning mill trade in Clinton and worked at that for a few years. Later he bought a farm and continued farming until his health failed. He sold his farm to his brother, Horace. He d. s. p. Oct. 9, 1846; res. Bridgewater, Mich.

1953. HORACE A. FISK (Benjamin B., Ephraim, Joseph, Samuel, Joseph, William, John, William, Robert, Simon, Simon, William, Symond), b. York, Livingston Co., N. Y., Feb. 16, 1825; m. in Bridgewater, Mich., Mar. 13, 1851, Jane U. Brown, b. Oct. 7, 1830, in Monroe Co., N. Y., dau. of Kinner Brown, who was b. in Dec., 1802, and d. Apr. 1, 1875, and Margaret Smith, b. 1803; d. 1883. He was born in Livingston Co., N. Y., and went to Michigan from New York State, with his parents and brothers, when he was but 5 years of age. His father, Benjamin B. Fisk, died two years after they went to Clinton, and left the mother with six boys. She put them out to live with farmers in the neighborhood. Horace was sent to live with a man by the name of James Nichols, in Pittsfield. There he remained until he was 19 years of age, when he went to Spring Arbor to reside with his mother, who had married William Smith. After four years he purchased the farm recently owned by his brother, Cyrus B. He has resided there ever since; res. Clinton, Mich.

3408.   i.   FLORA L., b. May 26, 1852; m. Oct. 8, 1890, Porter I. Maddox; res. Neb. Ch.: 1, Candace Anna, b. Aug. 18, 1891. 2, Jane Emma, b. Nov. 26, 1892.
3409.   ii.   JEFFERSON C., b. Feb. 20, 1854; m. Mary A. English.
3410.   iii. THERON B., b. Jan. 31, 1856. He has always lived at home with the exception of a few months spent in Dakota and Kansas. He is living at home now.
3411.   iv.   JENNIE C., b. June 27, 1857; d. Aug. 31, 1883.
3412.   v.   EMILY T., b. June 23, 1862; m. Mar. 2, 1887, Hubert Beach, b. Sept. 1, 1886. Ch.: 1, Hazel Belle, b. May 19, 1888. 2, Jennie Marguerite, b. Nov. 13, 1889. 3, Irving Judson, b. Mar. 15, 1892. 4, Leander Horace, b. Feb. 8, 1894.
3413.   vi.   MAMIE V., b. Oct. 10, 1866; m. Benjamin Feldkamp. Ch.: 1, Otto B., b. Mar. 18, 1888. 2, Robert E., b. Dec. 16, 1890. 3, John G., b. Nov. 8, 1892. 4, Roy Fisk, b. Sept. 5, 1894.
3414.   vii. CLINTON B., b. July 30, 1868; m. Mary Wilcox.
3415.   viii. MARGUERITE N., b. Mar. 27, 1874; unm.; res. Clinton, Mich.

1954. GEN. CLINTON BOWEN FISK (Benjamin B., Ephraim, Joseph, Samuel, Joseph, William, John, William, Robert, Simon, Simon, William, Symond), b. Clapp's Corners, N. Y., Dec. 8, 1828; m. at Coldwater, Mich., Feb. 20,

1850, Janette A. Crippen, b. Nov. 24, 1832. Clinton Bowen Fisk.—A Life-Sketch of the Prohibition Party's Probable Standard-Bearer. — A Typical American Life—From a Log Cabin to Positions of National Honor — His Early Struggles for an Education — Walking Twenty Miles to Learn How to Pronounce a Latin Diphthong—His Creditable Record in the Civil War and After—Endearing Himself to Whites and Blacks in the South—His Intimate Friendships with Lincoln, Grant and Greeley — A Splendid Business Career Side by Side With Noble Christian Activities. The Voice, New York City, May 15, 1888, said: In a conspicuous box at the Metropolitan Opera House, on Monday night, May 14, as the great Prohibition rally there drew near its close, a man sat down and looked out with swift interest upon that vast assemblage. It was near eleven o'clock, and he had just come from a down-town appointment so binding he could not sooner get release. At the wide street entrance only some stragglers appeared, and he had sought the special box assigned him, half believing that because of storm and small attendance the meeting had early broken up, and he should find but vacancy and darkness. When he entered and took his seat, his beaming blue eyes ranged over the stage below him, packed with well-known Prohibitionists, and thence over the spacious auditorium facing them, crowded in all its five great galleries with men and women whose enthusiasm was electric. Scores of people near by observed this man, with whose form they had grown familiar. The attention of hundreds more was speedily drawn to him. And all whose gaze turned that way beheld a gentleman of portly build, with rather short gray beard, partly veiling a face roundish in outline, rising to a forehead high and intellectual. The rather rotund figure and the genial countenance were suggestive of comfortable living, little care and happy temperament. From the gray whiskers, and the bald crown above them, one might have guessed this gentleman past middle life, though surely not yet old.

Who was he? The crowd soon told his name. When Professor Dickie's clear, masterful voice rang out its final word, with one mighty volume of sound the shout went up for "Fisk!" "Fisk!" The man in the box was wanted upon the platform. These many years, indeed, he has been wanted there, at any gathering of which he might form part, whatever its occasion or character. His wonderful aptness of extempore address, his choice command of language, his unfailing good humor, and his magnetic charm, have made him a general favorite in ecclesiastical bodies, in party gatherings, and in commercial assemblies, whenever speech-making came in order.

There is no man in all our country more popular as an off-hand talker than Gen. Fisk; no man, it may be added, whose talking gifts have been tested in more various ways, or on wider fields. He could speak to his newly recruited regiment of soldiers in St. Louis with such persuasiveness that they agreed he should do all their swearing, well aware he would not swear a word. In camp, at the front, he could lead a prayer meeting with tender exhortation and fervent appeal. When reconstruction days came on he could gather thousands, white and black, upon some Southern plantation, and win them to ready acceptance of the great change from slavery to freedom. And in these later years, South and North, at the general conference of his church, as a fraternal delegate with Southern brethren, in the great convention at Pittsburg which nominated St. John, at some great business banquet where capital massed itself, or where old army comrades met in annual reunion—oftener than almost any other American he has been called to say the word most fitting, to lend the final grace of flowing rhetoric and felicitous quotation. Upon this night of particular reference, in the great opera house of this great metropolis, it was not so much that another speech was wanted—for four speeches had been heard already—as that the vast audience desired to recognize and salute, in this genial man of gracious manner and warm heart, the next probable standard bearer of Prohibition—the almost inevitable nominee for President by the Prohibition party. And their greeting was such as to honor and exalt the most princely. Under its inspiration thousands of pulses leaped aflame and glowed with sudden fire. It was magnificent. It was thrilling. Could she have lived to see it, how glad and proud one woman must have been! Her name was Lydia Aldrich when a girl in Rhode Island; she was the wife of Capt. Benjamin Fisk when on the 8th of December, 1828, she gave to the world a boy they christened Clinton Bowen. That was in the little hamlet known as Griggsville, town of York, Livingston County, N. Y. Clinton Bowen was the fifth male child born to this pair of young Puritans since they had settled in the Genesee Valley. Half his patronymic came from New York's "Canal Governor," De Witt Clinton; the other half was from the mother's family tree. It was a humble home wherein the boy saw daylight first, but in a region beautiful and fertile, though sparsely peopled then. His father was a man of local reputation, and getting on fairly well for one in so new a country. He was a blacksmith, wagon-maker, and miscellaneous manufacturer, for quite an area round about. He trained with the military, as was natural, for his grandfather had been under Washington. And sometimes, on general training days, as was also natural, he took a little stronger drink than his son ever takes, for even a deacon could do it then and not lose religious caste. When his fifth and youngest boy was less than two years old, Capt. Fisk removed to Michigan. Better opportunities were there to be found, in his opinion, for building the fortune his growing family must need. He turned some modest savings into timber land in the wilderness county of Lenawee, bought out a mechanic who had located five mile north of Tecumseh, on the river Raisin, and there, surrounded by not unfriendly Pottawattomie Indians, set about fortune-making. The new place thus established he called Clinton, in honor of the Governor left behind and the baby brought along. Two years later, poisoned with the malaria then so pervading that whole region, he sickened and died, leaving his wife Lydia with yet another babe to care for, and at the mercy of conditions most unkind. Mistress Lydia did the best she could for her six fatherless boys and with her untilled lands. Losses came, lands went, times grew hard. One by one the lads were put out to earn their own support, and Clinton's turn to go came at last. He was then but 9 years old, yet eager to help his mother and to make a chance for himself. When Farmer Wright offered a horse, a saddle, a bridle, two suits of clothes, one hundred dollars, and three months of "schooling" every year, if he would serve him till 21, Clinton saw his chance. To him the "schooling" was powerful inducement. He hungered for knowledge, young as he then was. He left mother and home even cheerfully, and wondered why his mother so often put her apron to her eyes after he bade her good-bye, as he rode away. He lived with Deacon Wright between two and three years, busied in the many ways a chore-boy can be occupied on the farm. But he grew ambitious for wider things. He craved better chances still. By hook and crook (though he hooked none of them) he had obtained a few books, and read them stretched out upon the broad hearthstone before a huge fireplace. There he had learned to write—that handsome back-hand script his correspondents know so well—using the hearthstone for a copy-book: and on this novel slate he had wrought out the problems Daboll gave. Verily, "a little knowledge is a dangerous thing." It made this young lad restless, dissatisfied and eager. Then his younger brother died, and the widowed mother grew so lonesome that she secured his release from the contract binding him out, and Clinton returned to her, sure the broader chances which he hungered for were waiting not far ahead.

We have not the space here to detail his varied struggles to secure an education during the next ten years. They form a long and interesting chapter in the full biography which has been written. He had pluck, push and perseverance. Chiefly he was self-taught. He earned his own text-books and studied them in his own way much of the time. As he had secured his first coveted volume —a mutilated Shakespeare—by hoeing corn for a neighbor, so he bought a Latin grammar by special effort and sacrifice. He caught a coon, like many another lad of twelve, but hoping, as few lads would, to realize upon him for educational ends. By patient applications he made the coon expert at many things, and came to love him as a boy might. Then he walked with his pet to Jackson, a half-day's journey, and sold him as a trick animal to the circus which exhibited there, that "Anthon's Latin Lessons" might be his. So he lost the pet he loved, but gained the book he coveted. It was not easy to study Latin alone, unaided. But at night, in front of the fireplace, and by day while a-field, with the help of written slips prepared for such field service the night before, he plodded on through nouns and verbs, declensions and conjugations. The Latin dipthong troubled him as to pronunciation, but his pluck conquered it. Nobody near him knew a Latin word, but by chance he learned of another boy studying the language who was to be at a camp-meeting ten miles distant. To meet that boy he walked the twenty miles of that round trip, and he fairly hugged himself the whole way home because of his success in pumping the boy dry of Latin information without telling how little he really knew himself. When he was 13 years old his mother married William Smith, a well-to-do farmer living at Spring Arbor, in Jackson county, and for awhile he had better advantages, which faithfully he improved. His stepfather liked him, and wished him to have the most liberal college education. All the plans were laid for him to enter Wesleyan Seminary at Albion, in preparation for Michigan Central College, now at Hinsdale, when Mr. Smith died. Again his dream of fine opportunities was broken, but again he set manfully about making the best of things. His twice-widowed mother removed to Albion, where and near where Clinton studied and labored and taught. He achieved first place in Latin and Greek, and, spite of many obstacles, was going forward well toward graduation there, when utter disaster befell him on this line. Hard study by night, and the intense heat of firelight, by which, as a boy, so much study had been done, bore fruit in disease of the eyes, so acute and continued that study became impossible, and with keen, lasting regret, he abandoned his fondest hope.

At Albion he met Miss Jeanette A. Crippen and her brother, fellow-students, and after college dreams were over he took up mercantile business with Miss Crippen's father and brother at Coldwater. In 1850 he married Miss Crippen, whose bright black eyes had fascinated him in recitation hours, and so perfected a partnership which brought him compensation for loss of college honors. Mr. Crippen was the leading merchant and banker of that region, and the firm of Crippen & Fisk kept and increased the commercial standing and enterprise of L. D. Crippen & Co. Clinton B. Fisk's adaptability, goodfellowship and swift business sagacity came into full play. He grew prosperous rapidly, and was known through all that country round. Success attended every step he took. He mingled in or led every social and religious movement. He bought a farm near Coldwater and made it the premium farm of that county. He was versatile, far-sighted, fortunate. Then came the financial crash of 1857. Banks went down on every hand. Business firms failed everywhere. Creditors could not pay. Loans were not collected. Friends advised him to suspend and so protect himself; but Mr. Fisk would not. His bank paid dollar for dollar to the end. But when the end came, though he had some money left, he was without health. That year of constant overwork and terrible strain had broken his hardy constitution and bankrupted his nervous resources. He lay by some months ensuing, and in 1858 took up residence in St. Louis, as western financial agent of the Etna Insurance Company. For a year more he traveled widely the whole length and breadth of the Mississippi Valley and contiguous States. He made broad acquaintance with men, from Abraham Lincoln at his home in Illinois to the humblest planter on a Mississippi bottom. Health came back. New opportunities for usefulness opened before him. He was growing ripe for the richest work a patriot could do. The business men of St. Louis knew and admired him. In the church life there he was a vital force. With 1860 came mutterings of war. Mr. Fisk knew the South and the North. He foresaw conflict and helped make ready for it. He enlisted as a private for three months, and helped capture a camp secretly formed outside the city. The Merchants' Exchange, of vast commercial influence, grew doubtful for the Union and was likely to cast all its weight upon the disunion side. He called a meeting of seceders from the Exchange and organized a Union rival to it which swallowed the old organization completely. He spoke, he wrote, he worked for the cause of right. By birth a Puritan and an Abolitionist, he could do no less. Even as a boy he had been with the Abolition army in politics, small as it was. In 1840 the boys all round him were Whigs, and carried their banner "for Tippecanoe and Tyler, too;" but he raised a solitary flag for Birney and Morris, and bore it to victory. To victory, because he had to fight for the privilege to carry it at all, and won his first conflict in life on that very issue. It wasn't much of a flag—three-fourths of a yard of white cotton cloth, bought with the sale of molasses candy, painted with axle grease, and affixed to a broomstick—not much of a flag, but dear to the boy whose ingenuity devised and whose patriotism bore it. A little dearer than ever, may be, after his mother had spanked him for spoiling her broom. In July of 1862, at President Lincoln's request, he set about recruiting a regiment. Back of him loyally stood the Union Merchants' Exchange, with money to assist. September saw it mustered in and at the front. Then he recruited a brigade, and was commisisoned Brigadier-General, Nov. 24, 1862. One month later he proceeded with his full command to Helena, Ark., and until June, 1863, he was on duty in the Department of the Tennessee, where Grant was seeking to capture Vicksburg. After that his service was continuously in Missouri till the war closed. He was some months in command of all southeast Missouri, with headquarters at Pilot Knob, and for a time had charge of certain very lawless northwestern counties, which he made orderly and inhabitable. Later he commanded the District of St. Louis, comprising all the territory before in separate districts. When Sterling Price attacked the State capital, General Fisk was ordered to protect it, and met the emergency with cool tact and judgment. The forces of Price were led by Marmaduke and Shelby, and commanded in person by Price. General Fisk had only a handful of troops, but, by strategy, he multiplied them to the ears of Price, and raised such defenses as gave color to these fictitious reports. The first assault was met gallantly, and Price retreated with his large force. Fisk ordered a pursuit and Shelby and Marmaduke were captured; the capital was saved. In February, 1865, he was made Major-General of the Missouri militia, and one month later Andrew Johnson commissioned him Major-General by brevet "for faithful and meritorious services during the war." In May that year he was assigned to special duty as Assistant Commissioner of the Freedmen's Bureau, in which important and delicate capacity he served till September, 1866. The entire States of Kentucky and Tennessee, and parts of Alabama, Mississippi and Arkansas were under his jurisdiction. Through all that once rich territory devastation reigned. The negroes, freed, were largely unwilling to work, and their notions of what they should have and should do, were extravagant, often absurd. To restore confidence between white and black, to readjust the relations of society, and to bring about that industrial status which was imperative, was the task General Fisk took up. He gave it the best work in his power. Mild in his methods, calm always in judgment, decisive as to conclusions, judicial in mental habit, he was at once in his own person a court of just appeal, and a commission to execute. He won common respect. Going up and down the region under his command, he invited before him the former master and slave, set forth to their mutual understanding the law governing both, and the whole facts relating to their mutual interest. He made each his friend. More than any other one man, it is safe to say, he made possible the rehabilitation of Southern fields, and the sure beginning of a better future. Out of this work grew, naturally, the institution of learning for colored youth, known now as Fisk University, at Nashville. General Fisk early saw the need of such liberal helps for the Freedmen, and his influence has been constant in their behalf. Throughout the South today his name is held in reverence among the blacks, and is mentioned in terms of candid respect and confidence by the whites. General Fisk resigned from the army in the fall of 1866, after over four years' unremitting service, and since then has been busily occupied with railroad,

2

banking and ecclesiastical affairs. For eight years he was treasurer of the Missouri and Pacific Railroad; since 1879 he has resided in New Jersey, with headquarters in New York. In Missouri he declined all political honors when urged upon him. In 1884 he came out from the Republican party, whose great leaders—Lincoln, Grant, Greeley, and others—had been his intimate friends, and supported St. John. Two years ago he consented, as a matter of duty and sacrifice, to lead the Prohibition campaign in New Jersey, and as candidate for Governor polled about 20,000 votes—a three-fold increase of the vote previously cast. In that campaign he made one hundred and twenty-five engagements to speak, filled them all, and was never five minutes late. To meet these he traveled five thousand miles. Scrupulous of his every duty, considerate of all men, the soul of personal honor, sensitive as a woman, Clinton B. Fisk shrinks from political warfare, and protests against his preferment as a political leader. The most conspicuous layman in the Methodist Church, to which, as a boy of 10, he gave himself, he gives to religious and denominational progress his chief concern; but he sees how closely the church of God is related to this question of the ages, and his whole heart is alive, his entire nature consecrated, to the fight now up for settlement along political lines. He will refuse no clear call of duty, whatever to him the cost

Gen. Fisk actively aided, as stated above, in establishing Fisk University, Nashville, Tenn., in 1865, and it was named for him. He had been identified with its financial and educational interests, and was president of its board of trustees. He was also a trustee of Dickinson College, of Drew Theological Seminary, and also of Albion College, Michigan. He was trustee of the American Missionary Association, and also a member of the book committee of the M. E. Church. He rendered conspicuous service in Methodism in his efforts toward a reunion of the Northern and Southern branches of the church. He was also identified with the temperance movement. From 1874 to his death he was president of the board of Indian commissioners. He was the Prohibition nominee for President of the United States at one time. He d. July 9, 1890; res. New York. N. Y.

    3416. i.   MARY, b. Oct. 13, 1852; m. May 29, 1873, Dr. Edgar Park; res. 175 West Fifty-eighth St., New York, N. Y. He was b. Apr. 21, 1840; d. Aug. 12, 1892. He was a dental surgeon. Ch.: Jeannie Fisk, b. Mar. 15, 1874; m. Mar. 28, 1894, G. F. Hodgman. Edgar, b. July 15, 1875. Mary Edith, b. Jan. 10, 1877. Fisk (one of twins), b. Jan. 23, 1879. Elizabeth Frances, b. Sept. 15, 1880. Mabel, b. May 8, 1883.

    3417. ii.   CHARLES ATWOOD, b. Aug. 29, 1851.

    3418. iii. HARRY GIBSON, b. Oct. 4, 1855; d. June 11, 1862.

    3419. iv. JEANNIE LEWIS, b. Feb. 16, 1867; d. Feb., 1869.

    3420. v.   CLINTON BOWEN, b. Mar. 3, 1871; m. May Isabel Taylor.

    1956. WELCOME V. FISK (Benjamin B., Ephraim, Joseph, Samuel, Joseph, William, John, William, Robert, Simon, Simon, William, Symond), b. June 29, 1822, York, N. Y.; m. Mar. 13, 1850. Amanda M. Vaughn, b. Feb. 28, 1831; d. Mar. 15, 1866; m. 2d, Mary Felton, b. Jan., 1830; d. s. p. 1887. Welcome V. Fisk came to Michigan at the same time his parents and brothers came from New York. He was eight years of age. He lived with his mother until after his father died, then he went to live with a man by the name of Dennis Lancaster for a couple of years. He lived in Clinton after that and learned the mason's trade. He worked at that for several years, then clerked in a dry goods store for Snow & Kies for some time. Afterward he went into the speculating business and was quite successful. He retired from business about fifteen years ago. His second wife died eight years ago, and since then he lived in Iowa with his step-children, until the past few years he has lived with his daughter Grace in Clinton. He is now 73 years of age and will no doubt live to be an old man; res. Clinton, Mich.

    3421. i.   LEANDER D., b. Mar. 22, 1851; d. Aug. 7, 1852.

    3422. ii.   LEANDER D., b. Aug. 21, 1853; d. Apr. 7, 1884.

    3423. iii. FRANK, b. Oct. 24, 1855; res. Newton, Ia.

    3424. iv. GRACE, b. Feb. 14, 1858; m. Nov. 20, 1878, Porter C. Smith, b. Dec. 25, 1857; res. Clinton. Ch.: 1, Eva Belle, b. Jan. 16, 1882; 2, Leander Vaughan, b. Apr. 12, 1884; d. June 29, 1889; 3, Willie Jacob, b. June 11, 1887.

1958. EDMUND ARNOLD FISKE (Samuel, Isaac, Joseph, Samuel, Joseph, William, John, William, Robert, Simon, Simon, William, Symond), b. May 16, 1823, Johnston, R. I.; m. in Providence May 14, 1846, Mary Elizabeth Battey, b. Sept. 8, 1825, dau. of Henry, of Providence. He was a carriage builder. He d. Oct. 3, 1873; res. Fiskville, R. I.

 3425. i. LAURA ANNA, b. May 2, 1848; m. Jan. 23, 1879, Frank Herbert Newton; res. s. p. 37 Hoyle St., Providence, R. I.

 3426. ii. MARY FRANCES, b. Jan. 29, 1850; m. Nov. 28, 1876. Edward H. Potter, of Providence, R. I.; he d. ———. Ch.: 1, Louella Frances, b. Nov. 25, 1877; 2, Bessie Harris, b. Jan. 8, 1881; 3, Mollie Arnold, b. Mar. 3, 1888.

 3427. iii. ESTHER ELIZABETH, b. Jan. 18, 1852; m. Oct. 16, 1880, Wm. Henry Winslow; res. Belleville, N. J. Ch.: 1, Leon Arnold, b. Feb. 17, 1883; 2, Blanche Annette, b. May 24, 1884; 3, Marjorie Pearl, b. Mar. 27, 1886; 4, Lorimer Alton, b. July 27, 1894.

 3428. iv. JOSEPH S., b. Nov. 4, 1861; m. Sept. 29, 1884, Carrie Mabel Muller; res. s. p. 208 Pavillion Ave., Providence, R. I.

 3429. v. GEO. ARNOLD, b. June 10, 1854; d. Dec. 10, 1866.

 3430. vi. SUSAN BATTEY, b. Apr. 4, 1856; d. Aug. 23, 1857.

 3431. vii. HENRY BATTEY, b. Feb. 8, 1858; d. Feb. 27, 1858.

 3432. viii. EDMUND ARNOLD, b. Apr. 26, 1859; d. Oct. 26, 1859.

1959. JOSEPH FISKE (Samuel, Isaac, Joseph, Samuel, Joseph, William, John, William, Robert, Simon, Simon, William, Symond), b. Mar. 20, 1827, in Johnston, R. I.; m. in Providence Feb. 14, 1848, Eliza Ann Pike, dau. of Abisha, of Thompson, Conn., b. June 8, 1821; d. Jan. 8, 1894. He d. while in the Civil war; res. Providence, R. I.

 3433. i. WALTER CLINTON, b. Aug. 27, 1855; m. Emily Dunning.

 3434. ii. CHARLES FREDERICK, b. Nov. 16, 1851.

1960. ISAAC FISKE (Samuel, Isaac, Joseph, Samuel, Joseph, William, John, William, Robert, Simon, Simon, William, Symond), b. Feb. 4, 1830; m. 1861 Abby Burke; d. 1865. He d. Dec. 20, 1868. He had two daughters, but both died in infancy.

1961. JOHN CADY FISKE (Samuel, Isaac, Joseph, Samuel, Joseph, William, John, William, Robert, Simon, Simon, William, Symond), b. Nov. 10, 1831, Johnston, R. I.; m. July 2, 1859, Rachel Thompson, b. Dec. 25, 1837; d. Nov. 8, 1865; m. 2d, Dec. 28, 1867, Jemima Liddle, b. Jan. 22, 1837; res. 27 Capitol St., Pawtucket, R. I.

 3435. i. SAMUEL, b. Feb. 22, 1866; m. Nov. 25, 1886, ——— ———.

 3436. ii. CORA BELLE, b. Sept. 16, 1872.

 3437. iii. EDNA GERTRUDE, b. Mar. 27, 1879.

 3438. iv. CHARLES L., b. Apr. 10, 1863; d. young.

 3439. v. GEO. A., b. Dec. 9, 1869; d. 1874.

1964. ALBERT WILSON FISKE (Samuel, Isaac, Joseph, Samuel, Joseph, William, John, William, Robert, Simon, Simon, William, Symond), b. Nov. 26, 1842, Cranston, R. I.; m. in Providence Apr. 17, 1867, Olive Kenyon, b. Oct. 4, 1849. He is overseer in a wool carding factory; res. Belleville, R. I.; Allentown P. O.

 3440. i. EDWIN A., b. Apr. 20, 1868.

 3441. ii. WALTER H., b. Aug. 8, 1869.

 3442. iii. OLIVER F., b. Mar. 15, 1871.

 3443. iv. HANNAH LOUISE, b. Jan. 5, 1876.

 3444. v. MAY VIOLA, b. May 27, 1887.

1966. DEA. GEORGE ROBINSON FISKE (Isaac, Isaac, Joseph, Samuel, Joseph, William, John, William, Robert, Simon, Simon, William, Symond), b. South Scituate, R. I., Jan. 18, 1837; m. at Providence June 23, 1868, Mary Amanda Anthony, dau. of David of Fall River, b. Jan. 17, 1843. His father-in-law, David Anthony, was one of the earliest cotton maufacturers in the country, and a pioneer of the now immense cotton manufacturing interests of Fall River. He was highly esteemed in the church and State, and very successful in business. The

subject of this sketch was educated in the Fall River schools, which are most
excellent, finishing with a six years' course in the high school. At 18 years of age
he entered the Massasoit bank in Fall River as clerk; was in the banking business for
eighteen years, the last ten of which he was cashier of the Fall River National bank.
Having acquired quite a little property and being tired of the routine of bank life,
he improved the opportunity which was opened by the great fire of 1872 in Boston,
to go into the firm with which he is now connected, North, Fiske & Co., Mrs.
North having lost largely by the fire and needing capital. Roxbury (suburb and
part of Boston) has been his home ever since coming to Boston in Feb., 1873.
He has tried to exert a good influence in a quiet way, and lead an upright, honest
life. He has held many offices in the Congregational Church, deacon, superintendent of Sunday school, etc. He has had ups and downs in business for the last
twenty years, but has enough to live on comfortably if spared to old age; res. 50
Elmore St., Roxbury, Mass.; Boston office, 51-53 Chauncy St.

    3445. i.   HENRY ANTHONY, b. May 16, 1870; m. Frances E. Thomas.
    3446. ii.   GEORGE ISAAC, b. Nov. 28, 1875; unm.; res. at home. He
                    was born in Boston. He is a graduate of the Roxbury Latin
                    school and is now taking a five-year course in electrical en-
                    gineering at the Massachusetts Institute of Technology, having
                    completed about one-half the course. He is of a very religious
                    turn of mind, being president of a branch of the Y. M. C. A.
                    at "Tech," which is doing a grand, good work.
    3447. iii. MARY BURDEN, d. in infancy.

    1970. NATHAN PURSER FISK (Joseph, Isaac, Joseph, Samuel, Joseph,
William, John, William, Robert, Simon, Simon, William, Symond), b. Bordentown, N. J., Dec. 6, 1806; m. at Centreville, Ohio, June 17, 1828, Mrs. Rebecca
(Whitehill) Cowan, b. 1796; d. Apr. 13, 1838; m. 2d, Feb. 10, 1840, Margaret K.
Tate, b. Feb. 16, 1818, who d. in Toledo, Ohio, Aug. 20, 1882. He was a farmer.
His parents were Quakers and while he was quite young emigrated west, settling
in Centreville, Montgomery County, Ohio, where he lived the remainder of his
life. His father was the village blacksmith as well as farmer. Nathan received a
liberal education for the times, learned his father's trade but took to farming after
his marriage in 1828 to Rebecca Whitehill Cowan. He was frequently elected or
appointed to local office by his neighbors and friends, who held him in high
esteem. He was one who had a happy faculty of looking on the bright side of
passing events and was charitable to a fault. The following incident was characteristic: Hearing a noise at the corn crib one night, he went out and found a
ne'er-do-well neighbor helping himself from the crib. Watching him until at least
two bushels were in the sack, he stepped up and said, "I guess that is as much
as you can carry," and regardless of the plea of the pilferer, who wished to empty
the sack, made him tie it up and take it home. He d. Nov. 15, 1863; res. Centerville, Ohio.

    3448. i.   MARIETTA, b. Mar. 1, 1829; m. 1854 Henry J. Vaughn; res.
                    Minneapolis.
    3449. ii.   WM. COWAN, b. Oct. 13, 1830; m. Apr. 1, 1865, Louisa C. Stahl;
                    res. Toledo, Ohio; had a son who d. in infancy; dau. Florence
                    Elizabeth, b. Jan. 14, 1872.
    3450. iii. SUSAN JANE, b. Oct. 13, 1832; d. Oct. 13, 1833.
    3451. iv. LAFAYETTE, b. June 22, 1833; m. Harriett J. Hancock.
    3452. v.   JOSEPH BAKER, b. Mar. 13, 1838; m. Mary Shaw.
    3453. vi. THOMAS WHITEHILL, b. Feb. 13, 1836; d. Mar. 23, 1850, in
                    Lebanon, Ohio.
    3454. vii. FRANKLIN AUGUSTUS, b. Aug. 11, 1844; m. Cornelia E. B.
                    Sebring.
    3455. viii. SAMUEL TATE, b. Nov. 23, 1848; m. Lillian M. Higbie.
    3456. ix. LAURA BELL, b. Mar. 23, 1846; m. —— Williams; she d.
                    s. p. 1880.
    3457. x.   JOHN ALBERT, b. Nov. 10, 1851; m. Clara Hawthorn.
    3458. xi. ANNIE ELVIRA, b. Oct. 10, 1853; d. Nov. 20, 1866.
    3459. xii. MARY VIRGINIA, b. May 27, 1850; res. Toledo, Ohio; is em-
                    ployed in the county clerk's office.

1973. SHELDON FENNER FISKE (Joseph, Isaac, Joseph, Samuel, Joseph, William, John, William, Robert, Simon, Simon, William, Symond), b. Centreville, Ohio, Jan. 26, 1825; m. at Miamisburg, Ohio, Aug. 12, 1846, Sarah Hurd, b. Chenango County, New York, Dec. 5, 1826; d. July 7, 1871. He was a shoemaker by trade, a strong Abolitionist and a Methodist. He d. Aug. 23. 1855; res. Springsboro and Dayton, Ohio.

3460.   i.   EMILY FRANCES, b. Feb. 9, 1848; m. at Vienna Cross Roads, Ohio, Edward Everist Buvinger. He was b. May 12. 1844, at Dayton, Ohio; is a manufacturer; res. Dayton. Ch.: Hurd Edward Buvinger, b. Mar. 6, 1873; d. Sept. 27, 1879.

3461.   ii.   DE WITT CLINTON, b. ——; m. and rev. to Mineral Wells, Tex.; had eight ch.; one son was Edward Fenner.

3462.   iii.   LEAVENWORTH HURD, b. Oct. 29, 1851; d. Springsboro Aug. 26, 1852.

3463.   iv.   WM. FENNER, b. Jan. 25, 1856 (posthumous); m. Dec. 25, 1882, Julia Lee Jones. He d. in Colorado City, Tex., July 2, 1884. Ch.: Alfred Lee, b. May 30, 1884; res. Dayton, Ohio.

1975. SAMUEL R. FISK (Joseph, Isaac, Joseph, Samuel. Joseph, William, John, William, Robert, Simon. Simon, William, Symond), b. Miamisburg, Ohio, July 4, 1830; m. in Springboro, Ohio, July 14, 1855. Sarah J. Miller, b. Aug. 14, 1826; d. Dec. 13, 1891. He was a cordwainer by trade and later a farmer; res. Springboro and Jacksonville, Ohio, and Virginia, Ill.

3464.   i.   ROLLA C., b. ——; d. in infancy.

3465.   ii.   SUSANNA M., b. ——; d. in infancy.

3466.   iii.   MARY E., b. June 1, 1859; unm.; res. at home.

3467.   iv.   JOSEPH L., b. June 17, 1867; m. Sept. 20, 1894, Elizabeth Miles; res. Virginia. Ill.

1999. DAVID FISK (John, John, John, John, John, Nathaniel, Nathaniel, William, Robert, Simon, Simon, William, Symond), b. Nov. 12, 1782, in Worcester, Mass.; m. in Brookfield, N. Y., Dec. 18, 1803, Lidia Bugbee, b. Mar., 1784; d. July 10, 1838. He was a farmer. He d. in Ellington, 1862; res. Brookfield and Ellington, N. Y.

3468.   i.   DENNISON, b. Apr. 1, 1807; m. Polly P. Bush.

3469.   ii.   JOHN, b. Apr. 5, 1821; m. Clarinda Main.

3470.   iii.   FRIEND LYMAN, b. Sept. 24, 1804; m. Perley Farman; d. 1868.

3471.   iv.   DAVID, b. Jan. 5, 1812; m. Mary Maria L. Wentworth.

3472.   v.   SALLY, b. Apr. 1, 1809; m. —— Golding; d. 1861; res. Ellington, N. Y.

3473.   vi.   JAMES, b. Aug. 3, 1815. Four ch.; one is Irving; res. Ellington, N. Y.

3474.   vii.   CHARLES, b. Oct. 17, 1823. Four ch.; a son is George; res. Ellington.

3475.   viii.   IRENA, b. July 4, 1818; m. 1836 Geo. Pierce. Ch.: 1, John Pierce, b. 1837; had two ch.; one son was drowned in the Connecticut River soon after graduating at Wesleyan University; res. Corry, Pa. 2, Charles Le Roy, b. Aug. 28, 1841, served in the war in the Ninth New York Cavalry; wounded at Five Forks in Apr., 1865, losing his right leg before he was discharged. He was commissioned Captain just a few days before Lee surrendered. Of course he was never well after that, although he lived until Jan. 11, 1880. He left five children: Gertrude Ruth Pierce, b. Nov. 29, 1868; Bertha Garetta Pierce, b. Mar. 7, 1870; Lucy Irene Pierce, b. Aug. 26, 1874; Samuel Hatch Pierce, b. Aug. 10, 1876; Charles Roy Pierce, b. Feb. 17, 1879. Of these Gertrude and Bertha have graduated and received a college A. B. Lucy starts for college this fall. The boys are in high school. His widow is Garetta H. Pierce, res. 461 W. Seventh St., Erie, Pa. 3, Martha A., b. Feb. 14, 1845; unm. 4, Mary A., b. Feb. 14, 1845; m. Randall Lyman; res. Lockport, Ill.; has three ch.: George, Harry and Grace. 5, George Miner, b. Sept., 1853; m. and res. near Wesleyville, Pa.; ch.: Callie, Frank, Edith and Ethel.

2000. JOHN FISK (John, John, John, John, John, Nathaniel, Nathaniel, William, Robert, Simon, Simon, William, Symond), b. Aug. 4, 1778, Worcester, Mass.; m. at Brookfield, N. Y., Eunice Bugbee, b. Apr. 10, 1779; d. at Racine, Wis., ae. 72. He was born in the beautiful city of Worcester, Mass., but migrated west with his parents. He was a pioneer in western New York; landed proprietor; followed farming; died early in life. He d. Feb. 22, 1811; res. Brookfield, N. Y.

    3476.   i.   JAMES B., b. Sept. 17, 1809; m. Jerusha T. Loveland.
    3477.   ii.   JOHN, b. Nov. 30, 1802; m. ―― ――.
    3478.   iii. ORIN, b. May 15, 1806.
    3479.   iv. LEVI, b. June 28, 1804; m. Susannah Bixby.
    3480.   v.   ORIL, b. May 15, 1806.
    3481.   vi. CHARLES L., b. Feb. 13, 1808; d. Nov. 13, 1827.
    3482.   vii. JONATHAN, b. ――; d. in infancy.

2001. JAMES FISK (John, John, John, John, John, Nathaniel, Nathaniel, William, Robert, Simon, Simon, William, Symond), b. Worcester, Mass., Aug. 21, 1780; m. in Brookfield, N. Y., 1803, Hannah Green, b. 1781; d. at Alfred, N. Y., ae. 67, Aug. 28, 1848. He was born in Worcester, Mass., emigrated to New York with his parents and followed farming. James Fisk was called into United States service to guard prisoners of war at Albany, N. Y. He took the camp fever, and lived only a few days after reaching home. He d. Nov. 11, 1814; res. Brookfield, N. Y.

    3483.   i.   JONATHAN, b. Oct. 27, 1804; m. Achsah Rowley.
    3484.   ii.   IRENA, b. May 25, 1811; m. July 3, 1827, Luke Green, b. Aug. 3, 1802. He d. Feb. 13, 1876; was a merchant. She d. Apr. 7, 1890; res. Alfred, N. Y. Ch.: David C. Green, b. Apr. 8, 1828; d. Apr. 18, 1877. Maxson J. Green, b. Nov. 22, 1829; d. Nov. 3, 1895. Hannah A., b. July 1, 1831; m. Rev. Darwin E. Manson. Susan J., b. July 19, 1833; d. June 16, 1895. Miranda S., b. Feb. 19, 1835; m. Jas. R. Livingston. Orson C., b. June, 29, 1836; unm.; res. Alfred, N. Y. Selenda I., b. Sept. 20, 1841; unm.; Henry S., b. Aug. 29, 1848; d. Oct. 4, 1849. Byron L., b. Oct. 20, 1850; d. Nov. 19, 1885.
    3485.   iii. EDWARD, b. ――.

2006. JAMES FISK (William, William, John, John, John, John, Nathaniel, William, Robert, Simon, Simon, William, Symond), b. Worcester, Mass., Apr. 5, 1805; m. in West Boylston, Apr. 1, 1828, Maria Nichols, of Holden, Mass., b. Jan. 28, 1810; d. Apr. 6, 1893. He was a farmer. He d. July 24, 1868; res. West Boylston, Mass.

    3486.   i.   SARAH E., b. May 5, 1829; m. May 7, 1851, Cyrus Hubbard; res. W. B. He was b. Dec. 21, 1824; d. Nov. 26, 1892. Is a farmer. Ch.: Louesa Maria Hubbard, b. Mar. 30, 1854; m. June 21, 1872, ―― Sawyer; P. O. add. West Boylston, Mass.
    3487.   ii.   HENRY A., b. Dec. 5, 1831; m. Jennie Richardson.
    3488.   iii. GEO. A., b. Dec. 29, 1834; m. Rebecca D. Renton.
    3489.   iv. LOUISE FRANCES, b. Mar. 28, 1836; d. Dec. 17, 1844.
    3490.   v.   MARY A., b. Apr. 15, 1841; d. Oct. 31, 1863.
    3491.   vi. JAMES FRANK, b. Jan. 7, 1845; d. Apr. 27, 1881.
    3492.   vii. EDWIN E., b. Aug. 24, 1847; m. M. Louise Reed.
    3493.   viii. CLARA L., b. Dec. 4, 1850; m. June 18, 1872, ―― Murdock; res. 11 Whitman St., Dorchester, Mass.

2009. DR. JOSEPH EMERSON FISKE (William, William, John, John, John, John, Nathaniel, William, Robert, Simon, Simon, William, Symond), b. Heath, Mass., Feb. 12, 1811; m. in Bradford, Mar. 9, 1837, Rebecca Ann Shattuck, of Bradford, b. Mar. 10, 1837; d. July 17, 1884, in Salem. He was born in Heath, but left there when quite young to seek his fortune. He applied himself first to the study of medicine at the College in Philadelphia, but somehow drifted into dentistry (after having taken his diploma as an M. D.) and commenced to practice in Troy, N. Y. He did not remain there very long, but came to Salem; here he settled and had a successful practice for many years. He was of an inventive turn of mind and took out several patents, but never made much use of any of them. He d. Aug. 31, 1882; res. Salem, Mass.

3494. i. JOSEPHINE ELIZABETH, b. Jan. 1, 1838; m. Apr. 24, 1860, John Hill Belcher. He was b. in Boston, Apr. 20, 1828; is quartermaster in the U. S. Army; res. 148 Washington St., Salem, Mass. Ch.: Gertrude Belcher, b. Sept. 23, 1862, in California; m. Sept. 4, 1883, Dr. Thomas H. Pleasants; add. Helena, Mont. Allen Belcher, d. in infancy. Mabel Belcher, b. May 22, 1867; Fort Leavenworth, Kan.

3495. ii. ELLA WHEELOCK, b. May 22, 1840; unm.; res. Salem.

3496. iii. CHORLINE SHATTUCK, b. Jan. 27, 1842; unm.; res. S.

3497. iv. MARIA EUSTACE BACON, b. July 31, 1847; d. unm. May 23, 1884.

3498. v. CAMILLA LELAND, b. Jan. 4, 1849; d. May, 1876.

3499. vi. LOUISA PARKER, b. Sept. 20, 1851; d. unm. May, 1883.

2014. SAMUEL CLARK FISKE (William, William, John, John, John, John, Nathaniel, William, Robert, Simon, Simon, William, Symond), b. Worcester, Mass., Dec. 1, 1815; m. 1837, Abagail Wait, of West Boylston, Mass. He d. May 17, 1861; res. Waterbury, Conn., and Waterloo, Iowa.

3499-1. i. JANE A., b. Jan. 5, 1840.

3499-2. ii. CHARLOTTE A., b. Dec. 2, 1842.

3499-3. iii. A. FAYETTE, b. Dec. 9, 1846.

3499-4. iv. SARAH C., b. June 27, 1853.

3499-5. v. GEORGE S., b. Mar. 5, 1858.

2015. CYRUS KINGSBURY FISKE (William, William, John, John, John, John, Nathaniel, William, Robert, Simon, Simon, William, Symond), b. Worcester, Mass., Jan. 22, 1820; m. in 1845, at St. Andrews, N. B., Isabel Boyd of that place. Res. St. John, N. B.

3499a. i. JOHN McKENZIE CAMPBELL, b. in 1847; entered Harvard College, Sept. 1, 1864.

3499b. ii. MARY D., b. 1849.

3499c. iii. CYRUS V., b. 1857.

2021. JOHN FISK (Samuel, John, John, John, John, Nathaniel, Nathaniel, William, Robert, Simon, Simon, William, Symond), b. Apr. 21, 1801; m. Apr. 11, 1827, Sally Nourse, b. 1808; d. Ayer, Mass., Oct., 1868. He d. Sept. 10, 1836; res. Princeton and Worcester, Mass.

3500. i. JOSEPH ALONZO, b. Dec. 15, 1828; m. Serena N. Metcalf.

2023. JOSEPH FISK (Jonas, Jonathan, John, John, John, Nathaniel, Nathaniel, William, Robert, Simon, Simon, William, Symond), b. Wendell, Mass., Apr. 25, 1791; m. June 3, 1823, Martha Willis, of Leverett; d. May 15, 1857. He d. June 24, 1882; res. Wendell, Mass.

3501. i. ASA S., b. Apr. 2, 1827.

3502. ii. AUGUSTA, b. Nov. 2, 1828.

2024. MARTIN FISK (Jonas, Jonathan, John, John, John, Nathaniel, Nathaniel, William, Robert, Simon, Simon, William, Symond), b. Wendell, Mass., Apr. 8, 1795; m. Apr. 16, 1821, his cousin, Priscilla Leach, dau. of Gardner Leach, Esq., and Susanna (Macomber). He d. June 29, 1868; res. Wendell and Salem, Mass.

3503. i. WELLINGTON MARTIN, b. June 7, 1823.

3504. ii. DIANA PRISCILLA, b. Feb. 5, 1827; m. Sept. 17, 1847, Austin W. King, at New Salem, Mass. He was son of Austin W. King and Polly Basset. Ch.: 1, Melvin Diana King, b. Shutesbury, Mass., Aug. 3, 1847. 2, Emma Agnes King, b. New Salem, Mass., May 7, 1848. 3, Willis Austin King, b. Athol, Mass., Dec. 2, 1861.

3505. iii. GARDNER LEACH, b. May 14, 1832; d. Jan., 1849.

2026. STEPHEN FISKE (Jonas, Jonathan, John, John, John, Nathaniel, Nathaniel, William, Robert, Simon, Simon, William, Symond), b. Wendell, Mass., July 15, 1799; m. there May 25, 1836, Almira Johnson, of Wendell, d. Jan. 10, 1845; m. 2d, Elcey Larry, of Erving. He was a farmer. He d. Aug. 10, 1882; res. Wendell, Mass.

3506. i. WILLIAM WALLACE, b. Dec. 24, 1837.
3507. ii. EMMA JANE, b. Jan. 7, 1844.
3508. iii. ALBURN, b. Feb. 23, 1848; m. Emily Stevens.
3509. iv. JULIETTE, b. 1846; m. Alonzo Granger; res. Lock Village, Mass.

2028. ARTEMAS FISK (Jonas, Jonathan, John, John, John, Nathaniel, Nathaniel, William, Robert, Simon, Simon, William, Symond). b. Wendell, Mass., Apr. 3, 1802; m. Apr. 3, 1830, Susan Williams, of Montague. Mass., who d. June 9, 1859; res. Wendell, Mass.
3510. i. GEO. COOLEY, b. Apr. 27, 1831.

2029. JABEZ FISK (Daniel, Jonathan, John, John, John, Nathaniel, Nathaniel, William, Robert, Simon, Simon, William, Symond), b. Mass., June 3, 1794; m. Sept 23, 1819, Catherine Ten Brook, b. Oct. 12, 1798; d. Jan., 1870. He was a farmer. He d. May 11, 1867; res. Horseheads, N. Y., and Dover, Mich.
3511. i. AUGUSTUS GEORGE, b. May 30, 1820; m. Cassandra Howard.
3512. ii. JOHN T., b. July 8, 1821.
3513. iii. REBECCA, b. Aug. 12, 1822.
3514. iv. DORCAS, b. Dec. 18, 1823; m. Mar. 22, 1854, Hon. Richard H. Whitney, son of Cyrus Whitney, of Harvard, Mass., was born at Harvard, Mass., 1808, and died at Adrian, Mich., July 11, 1867. He was a self made man and successful in life as to accumulating property and making and holding funds. He left an estate of $125,000 which was divided 1-3 to his second wife Dorcas Fisk Whitney and the remaining 2-3 divided among each of his six children. He was mayor of Adrian in 1857 and held the office of Justice of the Peace many years, and died at the age of 57, honored and respected by all who knew him. He d. July 11, 1867; res. Albany, N. Y., and Adrian, Mich. Ch.: 1, Richard Harris, b. Sept. 22, 1856, unm.; res. Adrian Mich. He has since 10 years of age been afflicted with epilepsy and unfitted for active business life although at times bright and smart and active. 2, Henry Hart, b. Jan. 18, 1858; d. Sept. 22, 1860.
3515. v. DANIEL, b. Feb. 1, 1825; m. Elizabeth Quick.
3516. vi. GARRETT T., b. Oct. 6, 1826; res. Addison, Mich.
3517. vii. JOSEPH, b. Mar. 17, 1828; d. unm.
3518. viii. ANDREW J., b. Dec. 12, 1829.
3519. ix. AMOS, b. Nov. 17, 1831; d. ———.
3520. x. WILLIAM, b. Jan. 5, 1834; d. ———.
3521. xi. MARGARET, b. Oct. 14, 1836; d. ———.
3522. xii. LYMAN C., b. Nov. 22, 1839; d. ———.
3523. xiii. JAMES J., b. Jan. 20, 1844; res. Woodland, Cal.

2030. ABIJAH FISK (Daniel, Jonathan, John, John, John, Nathaniel, Nathaniel, William, Robert, Simon, Simon, William, Symond), b. Wendell, Mass., Nov. 11, 1795; m. in Veteran, N. Y., Apr. 24, 1821. Henrietta Hughes, b. June 5, 1802; d. Dec. 4, 1876. He was a farmer. He d. Mar. 27, 1872; res. Veteran, N. Y.
3524. i. WILLIAM F., b. Oct. 8, 1822; m. Mrs. Martha (Putnam) Fisk.
3525. ii. MALISSA C., b. Feb. 28, 1835; m. Dec. 24, 1863, Samuel S. Sayre; res. Horseheads, N. Y. He was b. Dec. 31, 1831. Is a farmer. Ch.: William Fisk Sayre, b. Sept 8, 1865; m. Nov. 18, 1891. Blanche Hall; one child, Seely H. Sayre, b. Dec. 5, 1895; add. Horseheads, N. Y. Charles Sayre, b. Nov. 20, 1870; d. Oct. 16, 1881; nearly 11 years old.
3526. iii. SANFORD N., b. Oct. 9, 1837; m. Clementine Hooley.
3527. iv. SARAH M., b. Oct. 7, 1824; m. Mar. 25, 1846, Myron Humphrey. He d. July 1, 1862. Sarah M. Fisk Humphrey d. Apr. 20, 1880. Ch.: Alice Humphrey, b. Mar. 16, 1847; m. Rev. D. P. Leas; P. O. add. Philadelphia, 400 South Fortieth St., West Philadelphia, Pa. Edwin B. Humphrey, b. July 7, 1857; m. Apr. 8, 1880; lives at Philadelphia.

3528. v.   LUCY C., b. May 5, 1827; m. I. C. Roberts. She d. ———.
3529. vi.   FRANCES A., b. Mar. 7, 1840; d. ———.

2033.   ZEDEKIAH FISK (Zedekiah, Daniel, John, John, John, Nathaniel, Nathaniel, William, Robert, Simon, Simon, William, Symond), b. Wendell, Mass., July 23, 1802; m. at Ashtabula, O., Sarah McDonald, b. Mar. 26, 1810; d. Feb. 2, 1862. He was a farmer. He d. Sept. 7, 1867; res. Ashtabula, Ohio.
3530. i.   •CORNELIA B., b. Aug. 12, 1828; m. Mar. 9, 1847, Asa Gillett. She d. June 7, 1866. Ch.: Frank E., b. Jan. 7, 1848; m. Anna F. Brown; 5 ch.; res. El Reno, Ok. Preston B., b. July 9, 1860; res. Kingman, Kan. Charles E., b. Jan. 20, 1850; d. Feb. 20, 1873. Russell R., b. Feb. 20, 1853; d. Aug. 20, 1854. Cornelia, b. Mar. 15, 1855; d. Mar. 25, 1855. Alice Helen, b. July 10, 1858; m. Whitley C. Fullen; 3 ch.; res. Burlington, Kan. Guy Russell, b. Sept. 15, 1862; m. Myrtle Finley; res. Hennessey, Okla.; 1 ch. Donald A., b. Dec. 20, 1870.
3531. ii.   JAMES S., b. June 9, 1831; m. Ella J. Cook.
3532. iii.   LUCY SWEETSER, b. Apr. 6, 1834; m. Nov. 10, 1852, in Saybrook, O., Lewis B. Brackett, b. May 7, 1828; res. Saybrook, Ohio, where he is postmaster. Ch.: 1, Cornelia A., b. Nov. 27, 1853; d. May 13, 1857. 2, Haddie C., b. Feb. 10, 1858; m. Oct. 2, 1878, Chas. C. Parker; res. Trenton, Mo.; he was b. Mar. 28, 1852, is claim agent for the C. R. I. & P. railroad; ch.: 1, Elbridge Tracy Parker, b. Mar. 5, 1880; 2, Lucy Fisk Parker, b. Jan. 16, 1882; d. Mar. 2, 1882; 3, Haddie Parker, b. Oct. 2, 1883; 4, Lois Parker, b. Jan. 1, 1886; 5, Vara Parker b. June 11, 1887; 6, Marcia Parker, b. Dec. 31, 1893. 3, James D., b. Nov. 14, 1859; res. Lincoln, Kan. 4, Sarah H., b. Jan. 11, 1862; d. 1862. 5, Benton L., b. Sept. 5, 1864; res. Atchison, Kan. 6, Fletcher, b. Sept. 29, 1867; res. S. 7. Amy, b. May 15, 1870; res. S. 8, Ellen Fiske, b. Oct. 25, 1873; res. S.
3533. iv.   HADASSAH, b. Feb. 28, 1836; m. Sept. 20, 1855, James Camp; d. Apr. 18, 1858; s. p.
3534. v.   HELEN OPHELIA, b. May 29, 1839; m. Apr. 10, 1856, Dr. P. G. Barrett; d. Sept. 5, 1860; s. p.

2035.   HENRY FISK (Zedekiah, Daniel, John, John, John, Nathaniel, Nathaniel, William, Robert, Simon, Simon, William, Symond), b. Wendell, Mass., Aug. 17, 1892; m. Oct. 6, 1822, Mary Perry. He d. Aug. 8, 1861, and was buried Wendell; res. Leverett, Mass.
3535. i.   HARRIET MARIA, b. June 24, 1825; m. Aug. 22, 1843, Samuel W. Glover; res. L. He was b. Sept. 5, 1821. Ch.: Harriet W., b. Mar. 17, 1845. Samuel W., b. Dec. 1, 1848; d. Jan. 21, 1852. Henry J., b. July 28, 1851; d. Feb. 2, 1852. Irene G., b. Aug. 7, 1854; d. Oct. 11, 1861.

2037.   JOSEPH FISK (Zedekiah, Daniel, John, John, John, Nathaniel, Nathaniel, William, Robert, Simon, Simon, William, Symond), b. Wendell, Mass., Apr. 17, 1800; m. at Montague, Mass., May 16, 1826, Martha Marsh, b. July 25, 1801; d. Dec. 12, 1842; m. 2d. at Wendell, Nov. 22, 1843, Eunice G. Sweetser, b. Apr. 29, 1808; d. Nov. 22, 1867; m. 3d, Dec. 24, 1868, Mrs. Lucy Howe, d. Mar., 1880. He d. Dec. 28, 1887; res. No. Leverett, Mass.
3536. i.   ASA L., b. Apr. 2, 1827; d. Jan. 19, 1830.
3537. ii.   MARTHA AUGUSTA, b. Nov. 2, 1828; m. May 31, 1848, Willard H. Fleming. He was b. Nov. 19, 1823; res. Northfield Farms, Mass. She d. Oct. 9, 1893. Ch.: Inez Electa, b. Nov. 16, 1852; m. Sept. 19, 1876, Frank Henry Holton, b. Mar. 1, 1852; res. Northfield Farms, Mass.; ch.: Henry Willard, b. Jan. 29, 1883.
3538. iii.   ELECTA THOMPSON, b. Feb. 9, 1834; m. in Greenfield, Feb. 26, 1861, George Hall. She res. The Montague, Kansas City, Mo. He was b. in Ashfield, Mass., Aug. 23, 1833; d. Jan. 7, 1885. Was agent for the Red Line Transit Co., New York City. Ch.: George Fisk Hall, b. June 9, 1867 (only child);

profession, actor; add. 447 West Twenty-second St., New York City.

3539. iv. JOSEPH SWEETSER, b. Feb. 3, 1845; d. Dec. 21, 1862.
3540. v. LUCY EUNICE, b. Nov. 21, 1846; m. Dec. 15, 1867, Edwin C. Rice, b. June 22, 1843. He was in the Union army for three years in Company B., Twenty-first Massachusetts Regiment, and Company H, United States Cavalry; res. Westboro, Mass. She d. Nov. 1, 1890. Ch.: Gertrude E., b. June 2, 1870; res. Westboro, Mass. Edith L., b. Feb. 17, 1873; res. W. Leon E., b. Apr. 3, 1884; res. W.
3541. vi. HENRY Z., b. Jan. 15, 1849; m. Ella Marvell.

2040. JAMES WILLARD FISKE (Daniel, Daniel, John, John, John, Nathaniel, Nathaniel, William, Robert, Simon, Simon, William, Symond), b. Aug. 15, 1814, Wendell, Mass.; m. in Rowe, Almina H. Kendrick, b. Mar. 18, 1822; d. Feb. 14, 1893; res. Rowe, Mass.
3542. i. HENRY JAMES, b. June 30, 1848; m. Ida A. Clark.
3543. ii. HILAND P., b. ———; d. ———.
3544. iii. WM. WILLARD, b. Sept. 1, 1855; m. Lizzie G. Liebecker.
3545. iv. ELLA ALMINA, b. June 6, 1857; res. R.
3546. v. FRANK ARTHUR, b. ———; res. R.
3547. vi. ROSCOE ROYAL, b. ———; res. R.

2041. DEXTER FISKE (Daniel, Daniel, John, John, John, Nathaniel, Nathaniel, William, Robert, Simon, Simon, William, Symond), b. Feb. 3, 1803, in Wendell, Mass.; m. there Luvina Flint Robinson, b. Orange Nov. 28, 1815; d. Sept. 23, 1877. He was a mechanic. He d. Sept., 1879; res. Erving, Mass.
3548. i. EMELINE LUVINA, b. Apr. 15, 1832; m. Nov. 27, 1850, Phinehas Baldwin, of Erving. He was born in Heath; was a farmer. She d. Sept. 6, 1867. Ch.: Loriston Baldwin, b. Aug. 19, 1851, Heath, Franklin County, Mass.; d. Nov. 22, 1867. Alice Luella Baldwin, b. at Heath, Mass., Nov. 9, 1855; m. at Charlemont June 1, 1879, Lucino Freemont Hillman, b. at East Charlemont, Franklin County, Mass., Jan. 3, 1856; ch.: Madeline Baldwin Hillman, b. at East Charlemont, Mass., Oct. 4, 1880; Allen Baker Hillman, b. at East Charlemont, Mass., June 13, 1884; their present res., Grand Junction, Greene County, Ia. Nellie Luvina Baldwin, b. at Colerain, Franklin County, Mass., May 5, 1862; m. at Charlemont, Mass., May 5, 1884. William Ballard Avery, b. at East Charlemont, Franklin County, Mass., July 11, 1856; ch.: Francis William Avery, b. at East Charlemont, Mass., Aug. 22, 1885; Grace Prudence Avery, b. at East Charlemont, Apr. 5, 1888; present res. East Charlemont, Mass.
3549. ii. ARNOLD, b. June 27, 1835; d. Oct. 22, 1836.
3550. iii. FANNY JOSEPHINE, b. May 19, 1837; d. Sept. 27, 1864.
3551. iv. DAUGHTER, b. and d. June 17, 1839.
3552. v. MARCUS MORTON, b. Aug. 31, 1840; m. Sarah A. White and Laura M. Eaton.
3553. vi. MARSHALL, b. May 17, 1843; d. Aug. 2, 1843.
3554. vii. PHILA JANE, b. Sept. 15, 1844; unm.; is a dressmaker; res. 43 Crescent St., Northampton.
3555. viii. SON, b. and d. Aug. 14, 1849.
3556. ix. DAUGHTER, b. and d. Feb. 7, 1851.

2043. DANIEL PARTRIDGE FISK (Daniel, Daniel, John, John, John, Nathaniel, Nathaniel, William, Robert, Simon, Simon, William, Symond), b. Erving, Mass., May 28, 1803; m. in Heath in 1831 Eliza Cheney, b. May 28, 1803; d. May 14, 1879. He was a painter by trade and resided in many places. Just prior to the war he went west and his family lost all trace of him. Some time in 1856 his family heard a rumor of his death, but after looking up the evidence they were not satisfied. He d. in Cairo, Ill., in 1856; res. Heath, Mass.
3556½. i. MILTON EMERSON, b. Sept. 14, 1837; res., unm., in Lunenburg, Mass.

3557. ii. SARAH ELIZA, b. July 14, 1839; m. Nov. 17, 1859, Malon S. Heath; res. Lunenburg.

3558. iii. NOBLE, b. June 4, 1842; m. Lucy A. Pelton.

3559. iv. HEZEKIAH, b. ———; d. in infancy.

3560. v. JOSEPHINE, b. ———; d. in infancy.

2045. CLARK FISK (Daniel, Daniel, John, John, John, Nathaniel, Nathaniel, William, Robert, Simon, Simon, William, Symond), b. July 6, 1890, Wendell, Mass.; m. Rhoda Ward, d. Aug., 1838; m. 2d, Mar. 19, 1839, Hulda Crossman, b. Mar. 28, 1814; d. Sept. 18, 1891. He was a farmer. He d. June 16, 1858; res. Orange, Mass.

3561. i. EMORY DANIEL, b. July 5, 1841; unm.

3562. ii. GEORGE WARNER, b. Apr. 20, 1851; unm.

3563. iii. EDWARD, b. Mar. 5, 1844; unm.

3564. iv. FRANK, b. ———; unm.

3565. v. EMERSON CLARK, b. Jan. 27, 1846; m. Lydia Waldron; res., s. p., 554 Main St., Worcester, Mass.

3566. vi. MARTHA ANN, b. Dec. 14, 1833; m. July 1, 1860, Marshall Collins. She d. Sept. 16, 1863. Ch.: Albert, b. June 18, 1861; m. Dec., 1885, Alice Shepard, of Phillipston; res. Athol Centre, Mass.; two ch. He (Marshall) d. July 13, 1863, and she d. Sept. 16, 1863.

3567. vii. ALBERT, b. Dec. 15, 1836; d. Mar. 25, 1858.

3568. viii. SARAH REBECCA, b. Mar. 5, 1840; unm.; res. Orange.

3569. ix. MARY ELIZA, b. Nov. 5, 1842; m. Dec. 31, 1870, Joseph Warriner; res., s. p., Leicester, Mass.

2048. ISAAC HUBBARD FISK (Amos, Daniel, John, John, John, Nathaniel, Nathaniel, William, Robert, Simon, Simon, William, Symond), b. Oct. 9, 1811, Ashtabula, Ohio; m. in Watertown, N. Y., Oct. 3, 1836, Mary Safford, d. Dec. 21, 1876. He d. Feb. 1, 1877; res. Watertown, N. Y.

3570. ii. SUSAN, b. Nov. 30, 1839; m. Dec. 3, 1863, John C. Knowlton; res. W.; s. p.

3571. i. JOHN SAFFORD, b. Jan. 18, 1838; res. Alassio, Italy. He was graduated at Yale.

3572. iii. ISAAC ROCKWELL, b. Jan. 17, 1841; res. 19 W. 46th St., New York, N. Y.

3573. iv. MARY HUBBARD, b. July 14, 1844; res. Wat.

2053. AMOS C. FISK (Amos, Daniel, John, John, John, Nathaniel, Nathaniel, William, Robert, Simon, Simon, William, Symond), b. Feb. 21, 1823, Ashtabula, Ohio; m. in Royalston, Mass., Aug. 21, 1861, Sarah Leonard Paine, b. Aug. 21, 1835. He was a flour merchant. He d. Dec. 23, 1891; res. Ashtabula, Ohio.

3574. i. AMOS PAINE, b. July 28, 1874; unm.; res. A.; is studying (1896) for an electrician.

2056. EDWARD W. FISK (Amos, Daniel, John, John, John, Nathaniel, Nathaniel, William, Robert, Simon, Simon, William, Symond), b. Ashtabula, Ohio, May 17, 1832; m. in Canfield, Ohio, Mary H. Mygatt, b. Sept. 23, 1841. He was born May 17, 1832, followed mining, mercantile and manufacturing until ill health compelled him to retire about 1892. He resides on land his father settled on in 1810; res. Ashtabula, Ohio.

3575. i. ELLA M., b. Aug. 19, 1861; m. Sept. 23, 1886, F. J. Morris, b. Nov. 10, 1860.

3576. ii. MARY A., b. Sept. 14, 1862; m. July 9, 1884, S. H. Dawson. She d. Apr. 15, 1885. He was b. Sept. 17, 1861.

3577. iii. GEO. M., b. July 16, 1864.

3578. iv. GERTRUDE H., b. Feb. 24, 1867; m. Sept. 5, 1888, Edward G. Ducro and d. Feb. 27, 1893. He was b. Aug. 9, 1867.

3579. v. FANNIE C., b. May 4, 1868; m. Mar. 26, 1890, Herman R. Baptiste, b. June 7, 1866.

3580. vi. EDWARD A., b. July 8, 1873.

2057. EZRA FISK (Amariah, David. David. John. John, Nathaniel, Nathaniel, William, Robert, Simon, Simon, William, Symond), b. Hampton, Conn., Apr. 13, 1778; m. there Apr. 3, 1798, Polly Downing, b. Jan. 4, 1776; d. Nov. 3, 1841, in Brookfield, Vt. He was a merchant. He d. Oct. 31, 1831; res. Chaplin, Conn.

    3580½.i.   DANIEL, b. Nov. 3, 1798; d. 1808.

    3581. ii.   BETSEY, b. Sept. 30, 1800; m. Sept. 20, 1818, Rufus Bill, son of Roswell and Rebecca (Burgess) Bill, b. Feb. 26, 1794; d. Aug. 24, 1841, in Woodstock Vt. She d. Sept. 20, 1879. Ch.: 1, O. W., b. Apr. 13. 1823; add. Garden Grove, Orange Co., Cal. 2, Charles B., b. June 15, 1825; add. Franklin Grove, Ill.; m. Dec. 18, 1844, Elizabeth W. Wright, b. Apr. 12, 1824; d. Aug. 6, 1852; m. 2d, July 24, 1853, Catherine Woodruff, b. Aug. 3, 1831; d. Aug. 12, 1882; ch.: 1, Idella, b. Sept. 8, 1850; m. at Franklin Grove, Ill., ——— Trilly; add. Chickasha, Ind. T.; 2, Mary A., b. Apr. 11, 1856; add. Franklin Grove, Lee Co., Ill.; 3, Ella E., b. Apr. 10, 1858; m. Elmer E. Miller; add. Franklin Grove, Ill.; 4, Martha J., b. Oct. 24, 1860; m. James H. Lincoln; add Franklin Grove; 5. Chas. D., b. Mar. 17, 1864; add. Franklin Grove, Ill. 3. Joseph N., b. Aug. 16, 1831; add. Garden Grove. Orange Co.. Cal. 4. Wm. Henry, b. Sept. 13, 1829; d. Aug. 6, 1831. 5. Screpta, b. Oct. 7, 1827; d. Feb. 14, 1832. 6, Edward S., b. Dec. 2, 1833; add. Northfield, Minn. 7, David K., b. Feb. 24, 1839; add. Hillsboro, Ore. 8, Martha Boardman, b. Aug. 10, 1836; d. Oct. 8, 1895.

    3582. iii.   WM. A., b. Jan. 8, 1803; m. Selyma S. Whittemore.

    3583. iv.   CHAS. LEE, b. Dec. 26, 1804; m. Emeline Moulton.

    3584. v.   LUCY M., b. Jan. 14, 1806; m. Sept., 1829, Hiram Wolbridge.

    3585. vi.   LOWENA, b. Apr. 14, 1807.

    3586. vii.   DANIEL D., b. July 25, 1813; m. Martha Hutton and Mary Jane Johnson.

    3587. viii.   NELSON, b. Feb., 1815.

    3588. ix.   JOHN, b. 1817.

    3589. x.   AMANDA, b. Apr. 21, 1821; m. May 1, 1838, Samuel Nichols.

2064. BINGHAM FISK (Amaziah. David. David, John, John, Nathaniel, Nathaniel, William, Robert, Simon, Simon, William, Symond), b. Hampton, Conn., July 12, 1792; m. Lydia M. ———; res. Hampton, Conn.

    3590. i.   MAY SMITH, b. Aug. 31, 1832.

    3591. ii.   LAURA WEBB, b. June 22, 1835.

2068. ELBA FISK (Jonathan, Jonathan, David, John, John, Nathaniel, Nathaniel, William, Robert, Simon, Simon, William, Symond), b. Hardwick, Otsego Co., N. Y., Apr. 26, 1799; m. in 1817 at Hardwick, Nancy Eddy, d. July 24, 1820; m. there 2d, Phebe C. Ruby, b. Aug. 11. 1804; d. Jan. 2, 1894, in Saginaw, Mich. He was a farmer. He d. Aug. 21, 1874; res. Arcade, N. Y.

    3592. i.   JOSEPH D., b. Jan. 20, 1822; m. Jane M. Eaton.

    3593. ii.   ASA H., b. Jan. 17, 1824; d. in Freedom, N. Y., July 8, 1844.

    3594. iii.   BETSEY L., b. Mar. 8, 1828; m. Royal Alden, and 2d, Jan. 27, 1857, Joseph Barber, b. Dec. 30, 1829. He was a boatman. Ch.: 1, Victoria Alden, b. May 22, 1845; m. 1864, Norman Wood, present name Anson Jones; add. Clio, Mich. 2, Marie Alden. b. May 25, 1849; m. Joachim Valiquet, Sept. 20, 1867; add. Clio, Mich.

    3595. iv.   JANE L., b. May 28, 1830; m. Nov. 6, 1850, Edward Tate. He was b. Jan. 28, 1826; d. Mar. 26, 1877. She res. Saginaw, West Side., Mich. Ch.: 1, Louisa A. Tate, b. Aug. 10, 1851; m. Aug. 3, 1883; present name Louisa A. Ketcheson. 2, Henrietta J. Tate. b. Sept. 14, 1853; d. Sept. 5, 1858. 3. Alice R. Tate, b. June 4, 1860; m. Aug. 1, 1886, ——— Reynolds. 4, Elvie F. Tate, b. Aug. 5, 1868.

    3596. v.   HENRIETTA, b. 1835; d. Oct. 14, 1836.

    3597. vi.   ORLANDO B., b. Apr. 15, 1841; d. Nov. 28, 1843.

    3598. vii.   MARCELLUS A., b. Aug. 13, 1845; m. Feb. 20, 1871, Rhoda A.

Cappell, b. Feb. 10, 1851. He is a farmer; res. Arcade, N. Y.; s. p.

3599. viii. ORVIN V., b. June 11, 1820; m. Emily H. Moore.
3600. ix. ELBA, b. 1818.
3601. x. JAMES BIRD, b. ———.

2074. ASA FISK (Jonathan, Jonathan, David, John, John, Nathaniel, Na. thaniel, William, Robert, Simon, Simon, William, Symond), b. Windham, Conn., Nov. 11, 1783; m. in Springville, Pa., Lucinda Shelly, b. 1786; d. Nov. 8, 1842. He was a farmer and miller. He d. Sept. 10, 1849; res. Springville, Pa.

3602. i. ASA, b. Dec. 16, 1813; m. Sally Blowers and Caroline Cottrell.
3603. ii. JONATHAN, b. Dec., 1814; m. Sally Clapp.
3604. iii. ABIGAIL b. Dec., 1816; m. ———. Post; res. Skinners Eddy, Pa.
3605. iv. EBENEZER, b. Nov., 1818; a dau. is Mrs. John Smith, Golden Hill, Pa.
3606. v. GEORGE, b. Mar., 1826; d. ———; a son is Willis Fisk, Wilbur St., Binghamton, N. Y.
3607. vi. JAMES, b. ———; res. Franklin Forks, Pa.
3608. vii. HARRIETT, b. 1817; m. ——— Farr. She d. July 28, 1877; a dau. is Lemira Inman, Nimble, Pa.
3609. viii. ALIZA, b. ———; m. ——— Snow; a son is John Snow, Fairdale, Pa.
3610. ix. LUCINDA, b. 1823.
3611. x. SAMUEL S., b. Apr. 11, 1810; m. Martha Wylie and Hannah Brown.

2087. DAVID FISK (Hezekiah, Asa, David, John, John, Nathaniel, Nathaniel, William, Robert, Simon, Simon, William, Symond), b. Wales, Mass., Apr. 18, 1776; m. Dolly Rood; m. 2d, Polly Sykes. He d. Mar. 19, 1848; res. Ludlow, Mass.

3615. i. QUARTUS, b. ———.

2089. ELI FISK Hezekiah, Asa, David, John, John, Nathaniel, Nathaniel, William, Robert, Simon, Simon, William, Symond), b. Stafford, Conn., Apr. 9, 1781; m. at Union, Conn., Feb. 12, 1813, Margaret Moore, b. May 13, 1787; d. Feb. 12, 1857. He was born at Stafford, Conn., on the old homestead. His father moved to Wales, Mass., three years after his birth. He married the eldest daughter of John Moore, of Union, Conn., an old comrade of his father's while in the Continental army, on May 13, 1813. Her mother, Maria, was a daughter of their father's Captain, John Lawson. They lived on the Moore farm, in Union, Conn., until 1817. Their only daughter was born there. In 1817 Eli and family moved to Indiana county, Pennsylvania. When he settled there he improved a farm and set up a shoemaker's shop. He made the first pairs of pegged shoes and boots that were made in that county. He also erected several mills and dwelling houses. In 1824 he moved to Cincinnati, O. When he went there he engaged in the grocery business, but as he was not busy all the time, he put in his spare time at his old trade, shoemaking, but he was interrupted so much that he soon quit it. Soon after he went to work at the joiner's trade; from that to pattern making in David Powell's machine shops; soon afterwards he was transferred to the construction of steam engines department. For several years he was foreman of the shop. His son, Eli Cooley, was born there. In 1834 he was burned out, while Mrs. Fisk and Eli C. went back East. He had not even a pair of pants left after the fire. In 1835 he moved to Havana, Ill. He lived there two years, then he moved, in Aug., 1837, to the farm, where his son now lives. He entered it May, 1837, and it came to Eli by will. He died and is buried in the old graveyard in Havana. He d. Feb. 21, 1861; res. Wales, Mass., and Havana, Ill.

3616. i. ESTHER LAWSON, b. Feb. 5, 1814; m. in Cincinnati, Apr. 26, 1832, Frederick Buck. He was born in Copenhagen, Denmark, July 26, 1800. The marriage was crowned with six sons and four daughters. Four sons died in infancy or early life. Henry Hoffmire, the second son, b. Aug. 21, 1835, was killed in battle at Kenesaw, June 27, 1864. He taught school several years, was preparing himself for college, enlisted in the Eighty-fifth Illinois Infantry, and was killed as above stated. The other son, George Rotvil, served three years with the Seventeenth Illinois Infantry, and came back First Lieutenant of Company K. He lives at Normal, Ill. The eldest daughter married Hiram Lindley, and lives in Havana, Ill. Their only son, Fred, lives in Chicago, Martha Margaret, the second daughter, married Louis Aubere. She died Nov. 3, 1881, leaving one son and two daughters. Jewel is in Peoria, on the editorial staff of the Peoria Journal. The elder daughter, Pearl, is teaching in Havana. Ruby, the other, teaches in Chandlerville, Ill. Mr. Aubere keeps a furniture store in Havana. Ann Maria Buck, the third daughter, married Bernard Rodgers, and lives in Nebraska. Esther Elizabeth, the fourth daughter, b. Mar. 11, 1849, was married to Lewis W. Ross. He is a druggist and lives in Chicago. They have no children.

3617. ii. JOHN MOORE, b. Sept. 17, 1822; m. Sarah Ann McReynolds; d. Pa.
3618. iii. ELI COOLEY, b. Aug. 22, 1825; m. Rosanna Wagoner.

2092. STEPHEN FISKE (Hezekiah, Asa, David, John, John, Nathaniel, Nathaniel, William, Robert, Simon, Simon, William, Symond), b. Wales, Mass., Apr. 8, 1787; m. there Aug. 11, 1810, Lucina Thomson, b. May 28, 1794; d. Aug. 22, 1880. Stephen Fiske was born in Hampton, Conn., removed to Wales at 4 years of age, attended school and worked on his father's farm till he was married, then he bought a farm of his own, with saw mill and grist mill attached, continued to occupy it till 1841; then he sold and built a new house on another farm that he owned, and occupied till his death. He was a member of the Congregational Church for over fifty years, and a respected citizen. He d. Oct. 25, 1863; res. Wales, Mass.

3619. i.   MARY W., b. Jan. 22, 1812; m. June 21, 1831, ——— Gale. She d. Feb. 9, 1889; dau., Carrie Dodge; res. Charlton, Mass.
3620. ii.   WILLIAM T., b. Feb. 27, 1814; m. Sept. 11, 1840 and d. Dec. 27, 1883. His ch. d. before he did.
3621. iii. WARREN COOLEY, b. Sept. 21, 1816; m. Harriett M. Parsons.
3622. iv.   ASA, b. Dec. 20, 1818; m. Mary L. Graves.
3623. v.   DEXTER, b. Feb. 20, 1821; d. Feb. 16, 1822.
3624. vi.   ALFRED E., b. Mar. 18, 1824; m. ——— ———.
3625. vii. LYMAN A., b. Feb. 27, 1827; m. Cordelia Smith.
3626. viii. DEXTER, b. May 14, 1829; d. Wales, Mass., June 13, 1829.
3627. ix.   ELI BUEL, b. Nov. 27, 1831; m. Martha Flint.
3628. x.   DEXTER P., b. Feb. 13, 1834; d. Wales, Nov. 20, 1850.
3629. xi.   EMELINE B., b. Mar. 2, 1836; d. Apr. 15, 1841.

2093. WILLIAM H. FISK (Hezekiah, Asa, David, John, John, Nathaniel, Nathaniel, William, Robert, Simon, Simon, William, Symond), b. Wales, Mass., Mar. 4, 1789; m. there Nov. 5, 1810, Lois Wales, b. July, 1793; d. in Agawam, May 4, 1865. He was a clothier by trade. He d. Sept. 27, 1869, in Agawam; res. Wales, Mass.

3630. i.   EMELINE, b. Nov. 4, 1811; d. Oct. 5, 1834.
3631. ii.   ORRIN WALES, b. Mar. 25, 1814; m. Hannah M. Tucker.
3632. iii. DORCAS WALES, b. Nov. 25, 1815; m. Apr. 11, 1837, Elijah Dudley; res. Millbury, Mass.
3633. iv.   LOREN W., b. Oct. 25, 1817; m. Eunice Barnes.
3634. v.   WM. WARNER, b. Sept. 1, 1819; d. unm.
3635. vi.   DAVID H., b. Dec. 23, 1821; m. Eunice M. Robberts.
3636. vii. GORDAN M., b. May 9, 1825; m. Sarah A. Putnam.
3637. viii. DANFORTH W., b. Sept. 25, 1827; m. July 9, 1850, Elizabeth Hindman. He d. Sept., 1867.
3638. ix.   LYMAN E., b. Jan. 1, 1830; m. Jane M. Durfee.
3639. x.   ELIZA, b. Dec. 25, 1831; d. Feb. 16, 1832.
3640. xi.   MARIA, b. Jan. 21, 1833; d. Sept. 11, 1833.

2094. CAPT. ASA FISKE (Hezekiah, Asa, David, John, John, Nathaniel, Nathaniel, William, Robert, Simon, Simon, William, Symond), b. Wales, Mass., Mar. 18, 1794; m. in Brimfield, Apr. 25, 1819, Catherine Shaw, of Brimfield, b. Feb.

15, 1801; d. Apr. 11, 1892, in No. Brookfield, Mass. Asa Fiske was an Ensign and Captain in the Massachusetts State Militia; enrolled as Ensign, May 18, 1819, Fifth Regiment, First Brigade, Fourth Division. The papers are signed by Gov. John Brooks, Sec. Alden Bradford. He served in the war of 1812, and the company was never discharged, as peace was declared while it was home on furlough. He was a strong Abolitionist, and a perfectly honest, upright man. His widow was a pensioner of the War of 1812. With his wife he celebrated his golden wedding Apr. 25, 1869. He d. Feb. 7, 1874; res. Sturbridge, Mass.

3641. i. DANIEL SHAW, b. Nov. 13, 1820; m. Louisa E. Glazier.

3642. ii. EUNICE BROWN, b. Sept. 14, 1822; m. Nov. 24, 1847, Lucius Hebard. She d. Sept. 26, 1855. Ch.: 1, Lucius Fisk. 2, Ida Frances; m. Geo. C. Ward, one child, Mary Frances. 3, Anna Violet. 4, Willie Brown.

3643. iii. LUCY ELEANOR, b. Oct. 18, 1824; m. Sept. 15, 1846, Elias Larkin. He was b. Aug. 14, 1826. Is a tailor; res. Atlantic, Mass. Ch.: 1, Rinaldo Gildroy, b. May 11, 1848; d. Sept. 22, 1859. 2, Rosalia Jane, b. July 10, 1849; d. Aug. 26, 1849.

3644. iv. MILTON ASA, b. Dec. 4, 1827; m. Nov. 24, 1855, Mary A, McFarland, and d. in Springfield, Mass., Mar. 8, 1882, s. p. He was an inventor and a very skilled machinist.

3645. v. OLIVET CATHERINE, b. Sept. 29, 1829; m. Sept. 1, 1850, Joel Bartlett, b. July 4, 1830. Is a shoe cutter; res. North Brookfield, Mass., s. p.

3646. vi. MARY JANE, b. Apr. 28, 1832; d. unm. June 17, 1865.

3647. vii. ANN LLOYD, b. Feb. 8, 1836; d. unm. Feb. 17, 1863.

3648. viii. SARAH CAROLINE, b. Nov. 27, 1838; m. Sept. 7, 1864, Worthington Jennings. She d. Sept. 28, 1876. Ch.: 1, Lloyd W.; res. Nevada City, Cal. 2, May Fisk, m. —— Deble; one ch., Daniel. The mother is dead.

3649. ix. FRANCES ABBOTT, b. Apr. 30, 1845; m. May 2, 1867, Edmund Lyman Lackey; res. Natick, Mass. He was b. Mar. 27, 1846; s. p.

2095. JAMES LAWRENCE FISK (Hezekiah, Asa, David, John, John, Nathaniel, Nathaniel, William, Robert, Simon, Simon, William, Symond), b. Brimfield, Mass., Apr. 2, 1797; m. in Columbia, Conn., Oct. 14, 1819. Laura Hamlin, b. Dec. 14, 1800; d. Mar. 18, 1888. He was a mechanic. He d. Jan. 3, 1875; res. Wales, Mass., and Omro, Wis.

3650. i. JAMES DARIUS, b. Oct. 7, 1820; m. Sept. 24, 1842, and d. Mar. 27, 1891.

3651. ii. JOHN L., b. Jan. 3, 1832; m. Adaline D. Houston.

3652. iii. AUSTIN C., b. Sept. 3, 1822; m. Lucy Hollester.

3653. iv. LAURA M., b. July 20, 1824; m. Aug. 13, 1840.

3654. v. ELIZA C., b. Oct. 14, 1826; m. Nov. 18, 1844, —— Cole; res. Watertown, Wis.

3655. vi. ELEANOR L., b. Oct. 16, 1829; d. N. Y., Oct. 6, 1836.

3656. vii. FIDELIA A., b. Mar. 16, 1834; m. Feb. 21, 1850, —— ——. She d N. Y., July 25, 1870.

3657. viii. GEO. F., b. Jan. 4, 1837; d. in Ohio, Sept. 5, 1855.

3658. ix. ALBERT L., b. Dec. 22, 1839; d. Arlington, Va., Feb. 6, 1862.

3659. x. ELLEN V., b. Aug. 16, 1843; d. in Wis., Sept. 1, 1844.

2096. CHAUNCY FISK (Hezekiah, Asa, David, John, John, Nathaniel, Nathaniel, William, Robert, Simon, Simon, William, Symond), b. Wales, Mass., June 22, 1799; m. Eliza Aldrich. He d. Aug. 16, 1859; res. Wales, Mass., and Watertown, N. Y.

3660. i. EMILY COOLEY, b. Aug. 27, 1821.

3661. ii. JANE E., b. Feb. 19, 1823.

3662. iii. DAVID COOLEY, b. Sept. 12, 1824.

3663. iv. LESLIE TURNER, b. May 28, 1829.

3664. v. ANN LESLIE, b. Dec. 8, 1833.

3665. vi. MARY HELEN, b. Dec. 27, 1835.

3666. vii. HOWARD CHAUNCY, b. Oct. 23, 1842.

2100. CALVIN FISK (Elisha, Asa, David, John, John, Nathaniel, Nathaniel, William, Robert, Simon, Simon, William, Symond), b. Stafford, Conn., Dec. 16, 1807; m. there Nov. 27, 1829, Nancy Ann Young, b. Aug. 27, 1805; d. Feb. 21, 1895. Calvin Fisk, born at Stafford, Conn., Hall district, educated at Monson Academy, Mass.; married Thanksgiving, 1829, to Nancy Ann Young. He was a surveyor and civil engineer, also deputy sheriff for several terms. He lived on a farm on the street in his native town. At the time of the California gold fever he went West via Charges, Panama, and was in Nevada City and California for about three years, until the time of his death, Jan. 8, 1853. He left a widow and five sons. He d. in Sonora, Cal., Jan. 8, 1853; res. Stafford, Conn.

    3667. i.   NANCY ANN, b. Aug. 30, 1830; d. Dec. 11, 1836.
    3668. ii.   MARSHALL C., b. Feb. 19, 1832; d. July 30, 1838.
    3669. iii. EVERETT Y., b. Jan. 16, 1834; m. Louisa Bartlett.
    3670. iv. JAMES H., b. Apr. 3, 1836; m. Sophronia R. Hiscox.
    3671. v.   ALBERT E., b. Dec. 2, 1841; d. Mar. 1, 1846.
    3672. vi. JOHN L., b. Sept. 22, 1843; unm.; res. Stafford.
    3673. vii. FRANCIS E., b. Feb. 14, 1846; m. Charlotte C. Cutler.
    3674. viii. GEO. L., b. Sept. 10, 1849; m. Abbie S. Tyler.

2119. CORNELIUS FISKE (Elijah, David, Thomas, William, John, Nathaniel, Nathaniel, William, Robert, Simon, Simon, William, Symond), b. in Lincoln, Mass., Mar. 24, 1830; m. N. Y. City, Aug. 24, 1858, Mary Amanda Greenwood, b. Dec. 12, 1832. Of excellent ancestry, Mr. Cornelius Fiske was born at Lincoln, Mass., completed his preparatory studies at the Lawrence Academy, Groton, Mass., and at the Phillips Exeter Academy, entered Harvard College, and was graduated in the class of 1853. Among his classmates were President Charles W. Eliot, John Quincy Adams, John Davis Washburn, Justin Winsor, and others well known to the public. He studied law in Boston, and later in New York City, in the office of Hon. Erastus C. Benedict (the then leading admiralty lawyer in the United States), of the firm of Benedict, Burr & Benedict, who, together with Beebe, Dean & Donohue, were the leading admiralty lawyers in New York. After leaving the office of Benedict, Burr & Benedict, Mr. Fiske took an office on his own account, and commenced practice in the United States District and Circuit Court, and acquired a large practice in all the courts of New York. Among his clients were many of the leading merchants. For eighteen years he was attorney and counsel to Ball, Black & Co., as long as they were in business, the leading merchants in watches, jewelry and gas fixtures, occupying the place in the mercantile world which Tiffany & Co. now occupies; also to the leading dry goods houses for many years, such as A. T. Stewart & Co., Strang, Adriance & Co., Arnold, Constable & Co., and several silk firms and sugar houses. With this mercantile practice, Mr. Fiske also represents several corporations and is entrusted with the investments of large sums of money upon real estate, and in other first-class ways. It is said that he has never lost a case of which he had the management, except one: in which latter case his client reports that Mr. Fiske strongly advised, not only that the case was extremely doubtful, but that he would lose the case and costs, and expenses. Mr. Fiske stands high in the profession, and is universally respected. Res. New York City; add. 120 Broadway.

    3675. i.   GREENWOOD, b. Feb. 6, 1860.
    3676. ii.   CORNELIA, b. July 17, 1861.
    3677. iii. MARTHA T., b. Dec. 12, 1863.
    3678. iv. MARY LOUISE, b. ———.
    3679. v.   KITTIE L., b. ———.
    3680. vi. GEORGE G., b. ———.

2122. HORATIO NELSON FISKE (Abraham, David, Thomas, William, John, Nathaniel, Nathaniel, William, Robert, Simon, Simon, William, Symond), b. Waltham, Aug. 28, 1799; m. Sept. 29, 1822, Anna Smith, of Weston, b. Aug. 16, 1800; d. May 17, 1887. He was a farmer and cordwainer. He d. Aug. 26, 1864; res. Weston, Mass.

    3681. i.   GRANVILLE M., b. Dec. 7, 1833; m. and res. Richmond St., Dorchester District, Boston, Mass.
    3682. ii.   MARCUS MORTON, b. Feb. 2, 1840; m. Abbie A. Cooper.
    3683. iii. GRACE A., b. Jan. 23, 1825; d. Aug. 25, 1828.
    3684. iv. ADALINE A., b. Sept. 19, 1827; d. Sept. 5, 1828.

3685. v.   HORATIO NELSON, b. Aug. 3, 1829; m. Feb. 22, 1849, Eunice
Arvilla Livermore, b. Oct. 3, 1829. He is in the wholesale
provision business; res. Waltham, Mass. Ch.: 1, Ellen Augusta, b. Dec. 7, 1855; m. W. E. Shedd; res. 238 Bacon St.,
Waltham. 2, Horatio Francis, b. Nov. 14, 1867; unm.; travels for wholesale drug house; res. Providence, R. I.

3686. vi.   SAMUEL N., b. Oct. 11, 1831; d. Dec. 19, 1831.

2126. THEODORE FISKE (Abraham, David, Thomas, William, John,
Nathaniel, Nathaniel, William, Robert, Simon, Simon, William, Symond), b. Waltham, Feb. 21, 1807; m. ———; res. Waltham, Mass.

3687. i.   LOIS, b. ———; m. ——— Sargent; res. Waltham, Mass.

2130. PHINEHAS FISKE (Phinehas, Jonathan, Thomas, William, John,
Nathaniel, Nathaniel, William, Robert, Simon, Simon, William, Symond), b. Waltham, Apr. 29, 1786; m. in 1812 Mary Hart, d. June, 1821; m. 2d, Nov. 18, 1824, Isabella Brigham Redington, b. Feb. 22, 1798, dau. of Isaac, d. Apr., 1841. He was a
merchant in Boston and retired in 1826, passing the remainder of his life in Keene,
N. H. He d. Oct. 27, 1842; res. Keene, N. H.

3688. i.   MARY HART, b. Oct. 29, 1812; m. May 26, 1840, Thomas Mc-
Key Edwards, Esq., of Keene, N. H. He was b. Dec. 16,
1795; graduated Dartmouth College in 1813; was a lawyer in
Keene, N. H. He rose to the head of the bar of Cheshire
County; was postmaster and pension agent for many years;
president of the Cheshire Railroad Company, and was active
in its construction; president of the Ashuelot Bank; representative to the State Legislature and to Congress in 1859-60-
61-62. Ch.: 1, Julia, b. June 28, 1841. 2, Thomas Chandler,
b. Oct. 6, 1843; res. Chicago, Ill. 3, Isabella Fiske, b. Dec. 25,
1845; m. Gen. Thomas Sherwin; res. Dedham, Mass. 4, Henry
Fiske, b. Nov. 1, 1847; d. Feb. 10, 1848. 5, Mary Fiske, b. June
15, 1849. 6, Sarah Louisa, b. Nov. 10, 1851. 7, Helen Fiske,
b. Sept. 5, 1853.

3689. ii.   JULIA ANN, b. 1815; m. William Dinsmore. She d. Jan. 4,
1854.

3690. iii. SAMUEL WARREN, b. 1816; d. 1834.

3691. iv. PHINEHAS STEARNS, b. Dec., 1819; m. 1843 Helen Clapp,
of Boston. He d. Sept. 11, 1869. They had one ch., d.

3692. v.   FRANCIS SKINNER, b. Nov. 9, 1825; m. Annie Farnsworth
Wilson.

2136. JONATHAN DEXTER FISKE (Jonathan, Jonathan, Thomas, William, John, Nathaniel, Nathaniel, William, Robert, Simon, Simon, William, Symond), b. Waltham, Mass., Oct. 14, 1815; m. there Oct. 20, 1842, Mary Clark, dau.
of Daniel, b. Mar. 29, 1817; d. Oct. 12, 1891. He is a farmer; res. Waltham, Mass.

3693. i.   MARY CLARK, b. Aug. 3, 1843; m. Aug. 31, 1871, Geo. Foster
Barnes; res. 25 Harvard St., Waltham.

3694. ii.   CHAS. DEXTER, b. Nov. 12, 1844; m. Ella F. Haynes.

3695. iii. ADELAIDE SUSANNA, b. Mar. 29, 1847; d. May 29, 1880.

3696. iv. ABBIE BAKER, b. July 8, 1849; m. Sept. 15, 1870, Alfred Warren; res. 33 Adams St., W.

3697. v.   LELIA MARIA, b. May 5, 1853; res. at home.

3698. vi.   EMMA GERTRUDE, b. Feb. 27, 1856; res. at home.

2137. CALVIN FISKE (Jonathan, Jonathan, Thomas, William, John, Nathaniel, Nathaniel, William, Robert, Simon, Simon, William, Symond), b. Feb. 21,
1817, Waltham, Mass.; m. Nov. 20, 1850, Caroline M. Wellington. He remained on
the old homestead and carried on farming until about the year 1859. At that time he
sold his farm to his brother-in-law, Mr. Elijah Brown, and removed to the center
of the town, where for a time he was engaged in the stock business. Later he was
engaged in the grain and produce business for several years. The last seven or
eight years of his life he was connected in various ways with the Waltham Water
Works. He served five years as water commissioner, being chairman of the
board at the time of his death. "The Waltham Water Commissioners in making

21

their seventh annual report are reminded that they have sustained a great loss in the death of Mr. Calvin Fiske, the Chairman of the Board. His late associates bear willing testimony to his industry, his fidelity to the best interests of the water works, as well as his earnest desire to act impartially and justly to all the water takers. His death is a great loss to the town, and a sad bereavement to his family." He d. Oct. 24, 1879; res. Waltham, Mass.

3699. i. MARY ETTA, b. Mar. 4, 1852; res. 56 Pond St., Waltham.
3700. ii. ELLIOT W., b. Nov. 17, 1862; m. Oct. 8, 1890, S. Grace Randall; res., s. p., W.

2142. ISAAC FISKE (Jacob, Jonathan, Thomas, William, John, Nathaniel, Nathaniel, William, Robert, Simon, Simon, William, Symond), b. Aug. 9, 179(6), in Weston, Mass.; m. in St. Stephens, Ala., Maria Pearce, an English lady. He d. at St. Stephens, Ala.

3701. i. THOMAS STRONG, b. ———; res. at St. Stephens.

2143. MOSES FISKE (Thomas, Jonathan, Thomas, William, John, Nathaniel, Nathaniel, William, Robert, Simon, Simon, William, Symond), b. Waltham, Mass., 1807; m. in Dover, N. H., 1827, Susan Hurd, b. 1811; d. in Dover in 1848; m. 2d, Sarah Huntress. He was born in Waltham, Mass., but lived with his grandfather. He learned the trade of pattern making and followed that calling through life. He was mostly self-taught, remarkably intelligent, and well read and a thorough musician, a fine tenor singer and at one time the soloist of the Boston Handel and Haydn Society. He was what one would call an old-fashioned man, conscientious and very religious. He never used tobacco or intoxicating liquors and all his habits were of the simplest. He had seven children by his first wife (Susan Hurd), all boys; two children (both girls) by second marriage to Sarah Huntress. He died in 1863 of softening of the brain. He was for a long time second lieutenant of the Second Regiment New Hampshire Militia, and his honorable discharge is dated Feb. 26, 1846. He d. in Hartford, Conn., 1863; res. Dover, N. H.

3702. i. JEROME H., b. Apr. 7, 1841; m. Sarah D. Bemis and Nellie G. Long.
3703. ii. MOSES W., b. ———. He was a well known actor.
3704. iii. HOWARD, b. ———.
3705. iv. MARIA HUNTRESS, b. ———.
3706. v. WALTER BALFOUR, b. 1834; m. Matilda H. Bruen.

2144. JACOB FISKE (Thomas, Jonathan, Thomas, William, John, Nathaniel, Nathaniel, William, Robert, Simon, Simon, William, Symond), b. Sudbury, Mass., Dec. 2, 1808; m. Belvidere, Ill., Dec. 25, 1838, Maria Louise Cushman, b. July 29, 1821; d. Waverly, Ia., Feb. 16, 1893. He was born in Massachusetts, was married in Illinois, and resided for a time in Iowa; he died in Minnesota. He d. Mar. 9, 1893; res. Belvidere, Ill., and Granite Falls, Minn.

3707. i. WALTER LESLIE, b. Jan. 8, 1855; m. Mary A. Briggs.
3708. ii. HENRY CUSHMAN, b. July 16, 1844; m. Elizabeth Ray.
3709. iii. HARRIETT ADELAIDE, b. Aug. 6, 1840; d. Oct. 11, 1841.
3710. iv. ALICE ELIZABETH, b. Apr. 5, 1845; d. Sept. 10, 1845.
3711. v. ADA EMALINE, b. Apr. 5, 1845; d. Sept. 12, 1845.

2151. HON. LUKE FISKE (Elijah, Samuel, Samuel, William, John, Nathaniel, Nathaniel, William, Robert, Simon, Simon, William, Symond), b. Waltham, Mass., Feb. 6, 1794; m. there Nov. 23, 1817, Susanna Sweetzer Piper, of Boston, b. Sept. 25, 1796; d. Apr. 30, 1876. Luke Fiske was a remarkable man and one respected and talked about by the people of Waltham while living and his loss was much felt when he died. He was spoken of as one of the intelligent and distinguished men of Middlesex County. He was popular. Broad paths to distinction and eminence lay open before him, were thrown open to him, and smoothed for his footsteps, onward and upward, and few knew why he never took full advantage of them. Luke Fiske might have been one of the great men of the country—a Senator of the United States—had he but stepped forward and used the means and advantages that absolutely stood begging at his side, and wide open for him. Much reliance was placed on his judgment and opinions. During his life he was commissioned to carry out many public measures, but before he acted, every measure was fully canvassed in all its bearings. He always seemed to give with cheerful alacrity his time to the public whether the duty to be performed was an agreeable one or not. He had pride, but placed himself on a footing of equality with all. There was a time in his life when it would have been difficult to provide a man with a more advantageous passport into the political world than a favorable word spoken by Luke Fiske. He entered Harvard College when quite young, and graduated with a good deal of honor. In 1819 he was the orator of the day for the Fourth of July in the town of Waltham. He was an open-hearted, honest man, generous and free in his sympathies, a genial companion, a lover of the social circle, and when roused was a debater of power. He would probably have studied a profession, but being an only child, his father and mother were not willing to have him leave them and he would not disappoint them, and as his father owned two farms adjoining each other he went on to one of them, but did very little but oversee it, as his time was taken up in other ways. He cared very little for money excepting for what it would buy.

In referring to the organization of the Waltham Bank a local paper says: "The Hon. Luke Fiske was chosen from the board of directors as the president of the bank. Mr. Fiske retained his office until a short time before his death, when declining health induced him to resign. He will long be remembered as one of our leading citizens in his day and generation. Possessed of great energy, of will and independence of character he was one of that class of men who are sure to exercise a controlling influence over the community in which they reside. In all matters relating to the well being of the town he took a lively interest. From occupying the most important of town offices he had risen to the position of a Senator for the county of Middlesex and to the honor of a seat in the council of Governor Lincoln. He died in the midst of his usefulness." He d. Feb. 26, 1845; res. Waltham, Mass.

 3712. i. JOHN T. K., b. May 1, 1819; m. Lydia A. Stone.
 3713. ii. LYDIA E., b. Mar. 27, 1821; d. Apr. 22, 1843.
 3714. iii. GEORGIANNA ELOISA, b. Aug. 20, 1823; m. Mar. 12, 1848, Amasa Coye, of Boston, b. Apr. 25, 1822; d. June 10, 1868; was a merchant. She res. 527 Main St., Waltham. Ch.: 1, Helen Maria Coye, b. Apr. 17, 1849, in Boston; m. Feb. 2, 1876, in Waltham, Merrick L. Richardson, of Sudbury, Mass.; res. 527 Main St., Waltham, Mass. They have no children.
 3715. iv. AGNES EDES, b. Dec. 6, 1825; m. May 8, 1847, Lucius D. Ashley. She d. Feb. 11, 1892.. He was a broker's clerk, and was killed by the cars at the Fitchburg railroad station in Boston in 1854. Ch.: 1, Clara Ashley, d. in infancy. 2, Lizzie Ashley, b. June 27, 1851; m. Melvin M. Flint, of Newton, carpenter; ch.: Mary Ashley Flint, b. Dec. 31, 1874; unm. 3, Luke Fiske Ashley, b. Nov. 30, 1853 (is now provision dealer in Newton, Mass.); m. Nov. 8, 1882, Emma F. Clough, of Annisquam, near Gloucester, Mass.: no children. 4, Edith Adelaide Ashley, b. Mar. 29, 1855; m. Clarence L. Wentworth, of Waltham; d. Jan. 30 or 31, 1892; she has three young children. Mrs. Flint's and Mrs. Wentworth's addresses are both Waltham, Mass.
 3715¼.v. ELIJAH, b. Sept. 6, 1830; d. unm.; was a farmer.
 3715½.vi. SUSAN S., b. Nov. 22, 1828; d. Dec. 11, 1828.

 2165. SAMUEL FISKE (William, Samuel, Samuel, William, John, Nathaniel, Nathaniel, William, Robert, Simon, Simon, William, Symond), b. Aug. 11, 1804; m. June 20, 1833, Abigail Sever Hewes Clapp, b. Sept. 23, 1808, dau. of Wm. T., of Boston. He was a merchant of Boston; res. Boston, Mass.
 3716. i. SAMUEL WHITE, b. Mar. 17, 1834.
 3717. ii. WM. HENRY, b. Sept. 14, 1837.
 3718. iii. ALBERT MINOT, b. Feb. 22, 1842; d. Nov. 17, 1842.
 3719. iv. ABIGAIL HEWES, b. Oct. 17, 1848.
 3720. v. JOSEPH HEWES, b. Oct. 17, 1848.

 2168. JOSIAH FISKE (William, Samuel, Samuel, William, John, Nathaniel, Nathaniel, William, Robert, Simon, Simon, William, Symond), b. Aug. 17, 1810; m. Aug. 16, 1832, Helen Maria Bridge, b. Nov. 23, 1810, dau. of Joseph of Boston. He was a prominent merchant; res. Boston, Mass.

3721. i.   SARAH BRIDGE, b. Nov. 4, 1834.
3722. ii.   ELIZA ANN BRIDGE, b. Feb. 22, 1838.
3723. iii. JOSEPH BRIDGE, b. Dec. 8, 1841; d. Jan. 3, 1844.

2169. GEORGE ALFRED FISKE (William, Samuel, Samuel, William, John, Nathaniel, Nathaniel, William, Robert, Simon, Simon, William, Symond), b. Boston, Oct. 11, 1812; m. there Mar. 23, 1837, Sarah Warland Clapp, b. Boston, Dec. 20, 1818, dau. of William Clapp of Boston, where she d. Apr. 23, 1883. Geo. A. Fiske was a Boston boy, educated at the English high school, and early entered the hardware business with Fairbanks, Loring & Co., and for many years was one of the firm of Loring, Fiske & Co., successors to Fairbanks, Loring & Co., with whom was also Oakes Ames, of Union Pacific fame, as special partner. After visiting California in the interest of the firm, he withdrew from the hardware business and engaged in the manufacture of fish oil and guano at Bristol Ferry, R. I., where he and others erected a large factory for that purpose. In this business he was not successful, and finally withdrew and engaged in a general commission business until his death. He d. Jan. 15, 1883; res. Boston, Mass.

3724. i.   HELEN MARIA, b. Oct. 15, 1838; d. unm. Jan. 21, 1873.
3725. ii.   GEORGE ALFRED, b. Aug. 14, 1841; m. Kate Washburn.
3726. iii. WILLIAM, b. June 10, 1848; d. unm. in Liverpool, England, Mar. 28, 1873.

2176. FRANCIS FISKE (Francis, Samuel, Samuel, William, John, Nathaniel, Nathaniel, William, Robert, Simon, Simon, William, Symond), b. Bedford, Mass., June 30, 1824; m. at Saugus, Nov. 16, 1850, Sarah E. Houghton, b. Aug. 7, 1832. He was a provision dealer. He d. Dec. 16, 1889; res. Cliftondale and Saugus, Mass.

3727. i.   WILBUR, b. Oct. 26, 1851; res. C.
3728. ii.   HENRIETTA, b. Dec. 28, 1852; d. ———.
3729. iii. E. FRANK, b. Sept. 14, 1854; res. C.
3730. iv.   GEO. W., b. Sept. 6, 1857; res. Charlestown, Mass.
3731. v.   E. P., b. Mar. 13, 1859; res. Everett.
3732. vi.   HENRY F., b. Jan. 10, 1861; res. C.; proprietor of a livery stable.
3733. vii. FRED M., b. Jan. 9, 1863; d. ———.

2185. ELIJAH FISKE (Nathan, Samuel, Samuel, William, John, Nathaniel, Nathaniel, William, Robert, Simon, Simon, William, Symond), b. Feb. 1, 1811; m. Oct. 5, 1837, Charlotte D. Endicott, b. June 16, 1816; d. New York in Apr., 1878. He was a merchant. He d. Dec. 4, 1859; res. New York, N. Y.

3734. i.   KATHERINE, b. May 6, 1839; d. Aug. 22, 1840.
3735. ii.   WM. ENDICOTT, b. Jan. 8, 1841; m. Caroline E. Hartwell.
3736. iii. ARTHUR D., b. Aug. 21, 1843; m. Caroline W. Whitney.
3737. iv.   ELIZABETH, b. Apr. 6, 1847; d. Dec. 27, 1847.
3738. v.   GEO. HENRY, b. Sept. 6, 1849; m. Jennie Douglass.

2194. DR. OLIVER FISKE (Nathan, Nathan, Nathan, Nathan, Nathan, Nathaniel, Nathaniel, William, Robert, Simon, Simon, William, Symond), b. Sept. 2, 1762; m. at Worcester, June 9, 1796, Sarah Duncan, b. 1775; d. Apr. 22, 1855, in Roxbury at her daughter's home. She was the daughter of Mr. Andrew Duncan, a native of Glasgow, Scotland, who in company with his countryman, Wm. Campbell, established himself in trade in Worcester before the Revolution and married Sarah, daughter of Joseph Lynde, Esq., of Charlestown. The loyalty of Mr. Campbell compelled him to leave the country and settle in Nova Scotia, where for more than twenty years he was Mayor of St. John. He died in 1823, aged 82. Mr. Duncan shared the same political feeling, but continued to reside in Worcester under unfavorable influences. He was drowned in a fishing excursion on Quinsigamond Lake, soon after the termination of the war. Mrs. Fiske was his only daughter.

Dr. Oliver Fiske, son of Rev. Nathan Fiske, was born in Brookfield, Mass. His early education was superintended by his father, whose productive farm, during most of the Revolutionary war was from necessity, principally confided to his management. In the summer of 1780 a requisition for recruits for the Revolutionary war was made. The quotas of men had thus far been furnished without compulsory process; but levies had been so frequent that none would enlist freely, at a season so busy. The company then commanded by the late Major General John Culter, was ordered to met for a draft. Exempted by the courtesy extended to clergymen from military duty, and never having been enrolled, Dr. Fiske offered himself as volunteer, with the approbation of his father, who applauded the patriotic spirit, while the personal sacrifice it involved was severely felt Animated by the example, the requisite number came from the ranks on the parade. The regiment in which they were embodied was ordered to West Point, and was stationed in the vicinity of that post at the defection of Arnold and the capture and execution of Andre. On being discharged he returned to the farm, and was employed in its cultivation until the close of the war in 1783, when he entered Harvard College.

At the breaking out of Shays' insurrection he was instrumental in reorganizing the Marti-Mercurian Band of the university, in obtaining an order from Gov. Bowdoin for sixty stands of arms at Castle William, and was second officer of the company. When the court commenced at Concord he was the organ of a petition from this corps, to march in support of government, which was properly declined by the authorities of the institution.

In the winter vacation (1786-7) he took a school at Lincoln, but hearing of the threatened movements of the malcontents to stop the judicial tribunals at Worcester, he procured a substitute to assume his engagements, exchanged the ferrule for an appropriate weapon and hastened to Worcester. Finding the enemy dispersed and the troops on their way to Springfield he set out to visit his father. On the heights of Leicester the report of Gen. Shepherd's artillery diverted him from his course. Uniting himself to a body of light horsemen, then en route, he joined Gen. Lincoln's army. When the rebellion was suppressed he resumed his studies, without censure for the long absence, and graduated in 1787. After the usual preparation, under the tuition of Dr. Atherton of Lancaster, he commenced business in Worcester in October, 1790.

He was active in forming a county medical association, and in obtaining the establishment of the present district organization of the Massachusetts Medical Society. Soon after the formation of the last named body in the second medical district, he was elected president and held the offices of councillor and censor until he retired from the profession. In February, 1803, he was appointed special justice of the court of common pleas. During five years succeeding 1809 he was member of the executive council. The commissions of Justice of the Peace, of the Quorum, and throughout the commonwealth, were successively received, and the latter has been renewed to the present time.

Dr. Fiske was corresponding secretary of the Linnaean Society of New England in 1815, of the Worcester Agricultural Society from 1824, and councillor of the American Antiquarian Society. He was Register of Deeds during the triennial term from 1816 to 1821. From this period an increasing defect in the sense of hearing induced him to retire from busy life and devote himself to the pursuits of horticulture and agriculture, those employments, in his own graceful language, the best substitute to our progenitors for their loss of Paradise, and the best solace to their posterity for the evils they entailed. The results of that taste and skill in his favorite occupations, early imbibed, ardently cherished and successfully cultivated, have been freely and frequently communicated to the public in many essays, useful and practical in matter and singularly elegant in manner. He published an oration delivered at Worcester in 1797, an essay on "Spotted Fever," forming part of the "Transactions of the Massachusetts Medical Society," and other writings.

By the exertions of Dr. Oliver Fiske the most respectable and influential physicians of the country assembled and formed the Worcester Medical Society Dec. 18, 1794. Dr. John Frink, of Rutland, was elected president and Dr. Fiske, of Worcester, secretary. At an early meeting a petition presented to the Legislature for incorporation was referred to a joint committee of physicians and resulted in an arrangement to enlarge the numbers of the general society and a proposal to create district associations. This system, removing the evils which had been felt was mutually satisfactory, was carried into effect, and on the 26th of Sept. 1804, the Worcester District Society was organized. The succession of presidents has been as follows: 1794, John Frink; 1803, Israel Atherton; 1806, Oliver Fiske. He d. in Boston, Jan. 25, 1837: res. Worcester and Boston, Mass.

3739. i. ANDREW WM. DUNCAN, b. Apr. 8, 1797.

3740. ii.   ROBT. TRENT PAINE. b. Jan. 1, 1799; m. Mary Otis Gay and
            Anna L. Baker.
3741. iii. SARAH DUNCAN. b. Sept. 16, 1801; m. Apr. 5, 1826, Otis
            Pierce of Dorchester; res. Roxbury, Mass.

2196. MAJOR WILLIAM FISKE (Nathan, Nathan, Nathan, Nathan, Na-
than, Nathaniel, Nathaniel, William, Robert, Simon, Simon, William, Symond), b.
Brookfield, Mass., 1764; m. Mar. 12, 1792, Frances Rice, b. Oct. 29, 1770; d. Oct. 26,
1840. He was born in Brookfield, Mass., and for several years resided in Worcester,
where he followed his trade, that of silversmith. Later he moved to Brookfield
and died when only 35. He was a prominent citizen and Major in the State Militia.
He d. Jan. 16, 1800, ae. 35; res. Worcester and Brookfield, Mass.
      3742. i.   WILLIAM E., b. June 15, 1796; m. Eliza M. Olcott.
      3743. ii.   MARY BUCKMINSTER, b. Mar. 19, 1799; m. at Brookfield,
                  Mass., Nov. 10, 1818, Francis T. Merrick, of Worcester, b.
                  in Brookfield, Mass., June 29, 1792, and died in Worcester
                  July 28, 1863. She d Jan. 31, 1863, in Worcester. Ch.: 1, Hen-
                  ry, b. ———— ; d. on the Rock of Gibraltar. 2, Mary B., b. ————.
                  3, Sarah Reed, b. ————. 4, Frances Fiske, b. Oct. 5, 1819; m.
                  Nov. 30, 1841, Hon. D. Waldo Lincoln, b. Jan. 16, 1813; d.
                  July 1, 1880. Daniel Waldo Lincoln was born in Worcester,
                  Mass., Oct. 16, 1813. He was the third son of the Hon. Levi
                  Lincoln, Governor of Massachusetts from 1825 to 1832. He
                  was graduated at Harvard University in the class of 1831; was
                  admitted to the bar in 1834, and practiced for a few years,
                  after which he gave his attention to horticulture and farming.
                  He was called into public service in 1856 as a member of the
                  Legislature, and was a member of the Board of Aldermen in
                  1858-59, and was elected Mayor of the city in 1863-64. He be-
                  came a director in the Boston & Albany Railroad corporation
                  in 1858, and was its vice-president and president in 1878, which
                  office he held at his death which took place accidentally at
                  New London, Conn., in 1880. During his term of Mayor the
                  duties of the office were quite arduous owing to the Civil war.
                  Gov. Andrew regarded Mayor Lincoln as a model Mayor and
                  of great assistance to him in many ways during those trying
                  times; ch.: Frances Merrick, b. July 1, 1843; res. 39 Cedar St.,
                  Worcester. Waldo, m. 1873 Fanny Chandler; res. 49 Elm St.,
                  Worcester. Mary Waldo, b. Sept. 15, 1845; m. Oct. 18, 1870,
                  Joseph E. Davis; res. 154 Beacon St., Boston, Mass. He was
                  born at Worcester, Mass., Sept. 27, 1838, son of Hon. Isaac
                  Davis, of said city; graduate of Worcester Academy; entered
                  foreign import and export trade in Montevideo and Buenos
                  Ayres, and returned to the United States after an absence of
                  six years, and entered a manufacturing corporation for the
                  manufacture of railroad iron and wheels; ch.: Lincoln Davis,
                  b. Mar. 31, 1872; graduated at Harvard College in 1894; add.
                  154 Beacon St., Boston, Mass. Mabel Davis, b. Mar. 24, 1875.
                  5, Wm. Pliny, b. ————.
      3744. iii. NATHAN, b. Jan. 15, 1798; d. Jan. 16, 1798.

2197. CAPT. NATHAN FISKE (Jonathan, Nathan, Nathan, Nathan, Nathan, Nathaniel, Nathaniel, William, Robert, Simon, Simon, William, Symond),
b. Weston, Sept. 7, 1760; m. 1787, Mary Stearns, b. Oct. 25, 1761, dau. of Hon.
Isaac of Billerica; d. Sept. 13, 1834. Nathan Fiske when a boy of the age of 18 years
seized his gun at the first alarm of the British troops going out of Boston, and did
yeoman's service in the war of the Revolution. His wife's father, Stearns, raised and
equipped at his own expense an entire company of volunteers. I think this was
done in the town of Billerica, Mass. He d. Jan. 24, 1852; res. Weston, Mass.
      3745. i.   POLLY, b. May 9, 1788; d. unm. Jan. 4, 1813.
      3746. ii.   HARRY, b. Apr. 29, 1790; a merchant; d. unm. Sept. 11, 1826.
      3747. iii. SEWALL, b. Sept. 8, 1792; m. Martha Stearns.
      3748. iv.   NATHAN WELBY, b. Apr. 17, 1798; m. Deborah W. Vinal.
      3749. v.   MARIA, b. May, 1800; unm.

2198. REV. THADDEUS FISKE (Jonathan, Nathan, Nathan, Nathan, Nathan, Nathaniel, Nathaniel, William, Robert, Simon, Simon, William, Symond), b. June 22, 1762, in Weston; m. June 17, 1787, Lucy Clarke, b. May 2, 1767, dau. of Rev. Jonas Clarke, of Lex.; d. Mar. 9, 1855. Her great-grandmother was Lucy Hancock, sister of Rev. John Hancock, father of the signer of the Declaration of Independence. The Rev. Thaddeus Fiske, in an account of himself and ancestry appended to a "Sermon delivered at West Cambridge, Apr. 13, 1828," at the close of his ministry, and published at Boston by Charles C. Little and James Brown, 1843, states: "I was born on the 22d of June, 1762. At the age of 17 I began to prepare for college under the tuition of Rev. Mr. Samuel Woodward, who was an able instructor and linguist, the minister of Weston, my native town. I was offered by him for examination, and was admitted a student of Harvard University in July, 1781, and graduated in 1785."

After he had taken his degree, he taught a grammar school in Lexington, and boarded in the family of the Rev. Jonas Clark. He returned to the university in Cambridge, and studied divinity under Rev. Prof. Wigglesworth, and was licensed to preach Aug. 8, 1786, by the "Association of Ministers in and about Cambridge." He preached his first sermon in his native town, and after supplying several vacant parishes, was invited in March, 1787, to preach to the Second Congregational Church and Society in Cambridge, then called Menotomy, now "West Cambridge." On July 16, 1787, he received a call to settle as their minister. "I hesitated," he said, "for some time, whether to decline or to accept their invitation. The parish was very small and poor and considerably involved in debt, having been destitute of a settled minister about six years, and was in a broken state, very much reduced in numbers and property. It was generally thought doubtful whether they would be able to support a minister, or pay the small salary they offered me. But it was feared by many, and so stated to me, that if I gave a negative answer, the church and society would not make any further effort to obtain a minister, and would be broken up and dissolved."

He accepted their invitation, and was ordained Apr. 23, 1788. Having cast his lot with the "Second Church and Congregation in Cambridge," he immediately endeavored to allay the difficulties that obstructed their prosperity. He began by relinquishing a part of his salary. To supply the deficiency of his support, he boarded and instructed children and youth, and some he prepared for admission to college; he instructed many daughters of his parishioners, and other young ladies of the neighboring towns.

Though this employment occupied much of his time, yet he was enabled to perform the usual duties of a minister, and to study and write and preach upward of twelve hundred sermons during his ministry. He visited and taught his flock from house to house, gave religious instruction to youth, and continued the practice adopted by his predecessor, the Rev. Samuel Cooke, of meeting the children annually, and oftener, for the purpose of examining and assisting them in their knowledge of the assembly's catechism, which was universally taught then by their parents and heads of families. Sabbath schools were designed at first to aid this practice. He assisted in defraying the current expenses of the parish; he contributed fifty dollars toward furnishing a new house of worship, built in 1805; he remitted annually, during his ministry, the parish taxes of many individuals who were either unable or unwilling to pay their annual assessments; he gave fifty dollars in aid and support of a singing school for the service of the house of worship, and ten dollars toward purchasing an octavoviol for the use of the singers; had a set of curtains put in the foreseat of the front gallery for the singers' convenience, and the pulpit painted at his expense. He commenced, in 1806, the establishment of a social library, and took the entire care of it in his house, and delivered books to the proprietors for more than twenty years without compensation. This and other things he did; and hence, in a few years, "the appearance of the town, and the morals, and habits of the people," were changed for the better, and "its favorable aspect induced many individuals and families of other towns to come and settle in the place and aid and share in its growing prosperity." He received from his people at the same time "many tokens of their respect and benevolence," and enjoyed his full share of "their regards and affections."

In 1788 the Rev. Mr. Fiske became a member of the Board of Overseers of Harvard University. In 1821 he was honored with the degree of Doctor of Divinity by Columbia College, New York. He voluntarily resigned his pastoral office and charge Apr. 23, 1828, leaving a church of about one hundred members and a congregation of about five hundred souls for his successor.

Such is the substance of the narrative of this aged minister, appended to the discourse delivered at the close of his ministry. The text of this farewell discourse was Acts xx, 18-21. Subject: The Life and Character of St. Paul, a Model for Christian Ministers., During his ministry he baptized 749; number of funerals he attended, 666; admissions to the church (including those owning their covenant), 288; joined in marriage, 386 couples. He lived to see five ministers successively ordained over this society, three of whom died before him; was at the time of his death the oldest clergyman in Massachusetts. A marble monument marks the spot of his burial in Arlington's old burying ground, amid the members of his flock.

In 1788 he wrote as follows in accepting the call to the church: "To the people of the Church and Congregation of the North West Parish in Cambridge. In answer to the invitation you have given me to settle with you in the work of the ministry. I, in the first place return you my most hearty thanks, especially for the many instances of your friendship, esteem and affection. The sincerity and ardency of your desires are completely manifested in the disposition you have shown, and your willingness to do whatever the heart of a reasonable man can wish. And in considering your invitation in every point of view, I find my duty and happiness unite in the acceptance. And as you have agreed to be satisfied in the choice of me as your minister, and being induced by the encouragement you have offered, and in confirmation of the contract we have made, I now accept of your invitation. And being fully convinced that in the promotion of your prosperity, peace and happiness, I shall increase my own, I do cheerfully devote myself, my strength and future years to you, my fathers and brethren, in the service of my Maker, and our common Lord and Master. Under the protection and blessing of Almighty God, being assisted by Him who is the Great Shepherd and head of the Church, and being indulged with your prayers. I hope I may be a happy instrument as a minister of the Gospel, to advance the Redeemer's kingdom, and promote the glory of God in the world, that I may serve you faithfully all the appointed time of my days. And that in the morning of the Resurrection, I may be enabled to appear, and say, here, Lord, am I, and here are the souls which Thou hast given me.   Thaddeus Fiske."

Rev. Dr. Fiske's Resignation. May 8, 1828. The Rev. Dr. Fiske having previously signified his wish to the parish to resign the pastoral office, he was this day regularly dismissed by vote of the parish. The parish at the same time gave an affectionate and respectful testimonial of the good character and long and faithful services of their pastor. For a full account of all the proceedings relative to the resignation of Dr. Fiske, see the Parish Records.

May 14, 1828. At a meeting of the church—chose Jeduthun Wellington moderator and Miles Gardner clerk pro tem. On motion, voted unanimously that the following resolve be accepted and a copy of the same given to the Rev. Doctor Fiske, viz.:

To all whom these presents may come. Whereas it has become expedient for reasons stated in a communication made to the church and congregation of West Cambridge, by the Rev. Dr. Fiske. Pastor of said church, that his pastoral relation be dissolved by mutual consent, and that Mr. Miles Gardner, the parish clerk, be a committee from the church to express to him the due sense we have of his long and faithful services among us and the deep regret we feel that existing circumstances should dissolve a union which has been so endearing to us by time. And during forty years of his ministry he has maintained a fair character as a man and as a Christian in the performance of his various and arduous duties; and has been an example of the believer in the word, in conversation, in faith, in benevolence, in humility, in purity, and in piety. And it is our ardent and fervent wish that his life may be prolonged to do good; that the infirmities of age may rest upon him with joy and hope. And that many blessings and comforts may attend him in his retirement from his pastoral labors among us. He d. Nov. 14, 1855; res. West Cambridge, Mass.

        3750. i.   HORATIO HANCOCK. b. June 22, 1790; m. Letitia Whittemore.

        3751. ii.   ELMIRA. b. Apr. 23, 1792; m. Nov. 19, 1811, Joseph Adams, Esq. (H. U. 1803), son of Moses Adams (H. U. 1771), minister of

Acton. The father, a student, was adm. Camb. ch. (First Parish) 21 Apr. 1771. Joseph, b. Acton 25 Sept. 1783, m. Elmira, dau. of Rev. Thaddeus Fiske, at W. Camb. 19 Nov. 1811, and d. here 9 (10) June, 1814, a. 31 (g. s.). Elmira, his wife was adm. W. Camb. ch. 14 Aug. 1814, and dism. "to Episcopal ch., Boston, Rev. Mr. Potter's," 15 Dec. 1828. She d. 13 of June, 1854 (monument), s. p.

2199. MICAH FISKE (Jonathan, Nathan, Nathan, Nathan, Nathan, Nathaniel, Nathaniel, William, Robert, Simon, Simon, William, Symond), b. Aug. 12, 1764; m. Feb. 5, 1789, Lydia Upham, b. Feb. 7, 1765; d. Mar., 1816, dau. of Dea. Thomas and Susanna (Myrick) Upham. He was selectman for four years; was a tanner and currier. He d. Dec. 9, 1819; res. Framingham, Mass.

3752. i.   CHARLES, bap. 1792; m. Anne Buckminster, b. July 4, 1790; s. p. He d. May 6, 1874. She was dau. of Thomas and Hannah (Rice) Buckminster.
3753. ii.   CYNTHIA, b. 1794; d. 1796.
3754. iii. CYNTHIA, b. ———; m. 1821. Ralph Plympton, b. Mar. 5, 1800; d. Feb. 22, 1863. She d. 1826. He m. 2d, Alma Terrel; res. Richmond, Va., and Boston, Mass.

2200. EBENEZER FISKE (Jonathan, Nathan, Nathan, Nathan, Nathan, Nathaniel, Nathaniel, William, Robert, Simon, Simon, William, Symond), b. Dec. 3. 1766; m. Dolly Gould, b. Mar. 14, 1774; d. in Weston, May 24, 1858. He d. Nov. 29, 1839; res. Weston, Mass.
3755. i.   CELENDA, b. Feb., 1796; m. Harvey Fuller, of Weston. Ch.: Augustus, Sarah, Mary (m. Allen Jordan) and three others.
3756. ii.   CYNTHIA, b. ———; m. ———.
3757. iii. ISAAC, b. ———; m. Polly Fiske. He d. in Baltimore.
3758. iv.   ABIGAIL, b. ———; d. unm.
3759. v.   WILLIAM, b. ———; m., and d.; seven ch.; res. Charlestown.
3760. vi.   SARAH ANN, b. ———.

2203. MAJOR JONATHAN FISKE (Jonathan, Nathan, Nathan, Nathan, Nathan, Nathaniel, Nathaniel, William, Robert, Simon, Simon, William, Symond), b. Weston, Jan. 19, 1774; m. there Apr. 7, 1799, Sally Flagg, b. July 8, 1772, dau. of Isaac; d. Medfield, Mar. 18, 1865. Jonathan was a tanner and farmer, born at Weston, Mass.; married Sally Flagg, of Weston, and removed to Medfield. He was a man honored and respected, holding various town offices; was a deacon in the church. He was also at one time Major in the Massachusetts State Militia. While none of this branch of the family or immediate ancestors have reached very high positions of public honor, the family has been remarkably free from any who have in any way brought reproach or disgrace on the name. They have been upright and honorable and have been respected in the community in which they have resided; they have been intelligent and in several cases have received college educations. He d. June 19, 1864; res. Medfield, Mass.
3761. i.   SALLY, b. Jan. 13, 1800; m. Dec. 24, 1818, Francis D. Ellis. She d. Aug. 23, 1878. He was b. 1796; d. Medfield, Mass., Apr. 26, 1882. Ch.: 1. Ellen Amand, b. Dec. 30, 1824; m. May 25, 1848, Rev. Thomas Laurie, D. D., of Providence, R. I. He was b. May 19, 1821; ch.: Martha Ellen, b. Aug. 12, 1850; m. James O. Yatman; res. Dedham, Mass. Annie Laurie, b. Aug. 23, 1857; m. May 22, 1878, Dr. Lawton S. Brooks; res. 126 Chestnut St., Springfield, Mass. 2, Abbie Warren, b. ———; m. Richard B. Smith, of W. Roxbury, Mass.; ch.: Lucy M., unm.; res. W. Roxbury. 3, Caroline Louisa. 4, Sarah Jane. 5, Harriett Newell; her dau. is Mrs. H. C. Waters, Providence, R. I. 6, Sarah. 7, Mary Francis.
3762. ii.   CLARISSA, b. Nov. 4, 1801; m. Sept. 3, 1828, Phinehas Allen; res. Newton, Mass. He was b. Oct. 15, 1801; d. May 25, 1885; was a teacher. Ch.: 1, Francis Eugene, b. Feb. 27, 1830; d. May 2, 1830. 2, Horatio Fiske, b. Aug. 4, 1831. Cleveland, O. 3, Robert Alfred, b. July 29, 1833. Pomona, Cal. 4, Clarissa

Fiske, b. Oct. 6, 1835; d. Sept. 2, 1837. 5, George Edgar, b.
Mar. 2, 1838; M. D., Youngstown, O.; m. Mar. 27, 1868, Fannie
Marshall Phillips, b. Oct. 5, 1840; ch.: Frank Fiske Allen, b.
June 9, 1869; m. at Youngstown, Ohio, Oct. 11, 1891; add. 112
Market St., Youngstown, Ohio. 6, Chas. Eugene, b. July 20,
1841; d. Feb. 11, 1864. 7, Clara Everett. b. Aug. 25, 1846, Pas-
saic Bridge, N. J.; m. June 11, 1867, Chas. C. Chamberlain, b.
Jan. 21, 1837; ch.: Clara Lizzie, b. Apr. 4, 1868; m. Edw. S.
Hulbert, June 29, 1893; add. Passaic, N. J. Effie Eugenia, b.
June 29, 1872. Anna Louise, b. Oct. 22, 1880.

3763. iii.   GEORGE, b. Apr. 20, 1803; m. Anny P. Mann.
3764. iv.   AMOS FLAGG, b. Aug. 1, 1805; m. Eliza Stone.
3765. v.   ABIGAIL LAMSON, b. Feb. 3, 1803; d. unm.
3766. vi.   ISAAC, b. Nov. 6, 1813; m. Mary Manson; res. Medfield, Mass.
            He had a child who m. Sept. 5, 1871, George S. Stone, and she
            d. s. p.
3767. vii.   CHARLES A., b. Mar. 7, 1816; m. Abby Waldron and Ellen
            Boyd.

2205. ISAAC FISKE, ESQ. (Jonathan, Nathan, Nathan, Nathan, Nathan,
Nathaniel, Nathaniel, William, Robert, Simon, Simon, William, Symond), b.
Weston, Dec. 4, 1778; m. Nov. 2, 1802, Sukey Hobbs, b. Mar. 19, 1782, dau. of
Ebenezer and Eunice, of Weston; d. Jan. 8, 1831; m. 2d, 1832, Sophronia Hobbs,
sister of his first wife, b. Oct. 27, 1796. He was born in Weston; was graduated at
Harvard College in 1798; was a lawyer in Weston, and for more than thirty years,
from 1817 to 1851, was Register of Probate of Middlesex County; was Town Clerk
in Weston from 1805 to 1826. He d. Nov. 11, 1861; res. Weston and Cambridge,
Mass.

3768. i.   ISAAC, b. ———; d. young.
3769. ii.   AUGUSTUS HENRY, b. Sept. 19, 1805; m. Hannah R. Bradford.
3770. iii.   ISAAC LAMSON, b. Mar. 8, 1810; d. unm. Mar. 18, 1868.
3771. iv.   GEORGE, b. Nov. 19, 1813; d. unm. Mar. 23, 1843.
3772. v.   SUSAN ANN, b. Oct. 22, 1815; d. unm. July 10, 1832.
3773. vi.   ANDREW, b. May 8, 1817; d. unm. June 7, 1841.
3774. vii.   EDWARD, b. Dec. 17, 1819; d. unm. May 20, 1828.
3775. viii.   CHARLES FRED'K. b. June 3, 1808; d. June 1, 1835.
3776. ix.   DAUGHTER, b. 1812; d. 1812.

2212. EZRA FISKE (Samuel, Nathan, Nathan, Nathan, Nathaniel, William,
Robert, Simon, Simon, William, Symond), b. Jan. 16, 1778; m. 1820, Lydia
Sanderson, of Cambridge, dau. of Samuel, of Lancaster. He d. Oct. 17, 1831.

3777. i.   ABIGAIL, b. Oct. 12, 1823.
3778. ii.   EZRA, b. Aug. 21, 1825.

2213. SAMUEL FISKE (Samuel, Nathan, Nathan, Nathan, Nathaniel, Will-
iam, Robert, Simon, Simon, William, Symond), b. Weston, Mar. 6, 1781; m. there
June 3, 1804, Lydia Travis, b. Aug. 19, 1781, dau. of Elijah and Lydia (Pierce), of
Waltham; d. Feb., 1861. He d. July, 1870; res. Sturbridge, Mass.

3779. i.   HENRY, b. Aug. 17, 1808; m. Sarah Belknap.
3780. ii.   HORATIO, b. ———; res. Amherst, Mass.
3781. iii.   SOPHRONIA, b. May 27, 1810; m. in Southbridge, Daniel Fay
            Bacon, b. in Charlton. She d. Oct., 1892. He d. in South-
            bridge in 1866. He was an extensive manufacturer, having
            cotton and woolen mills at Westville, Mass.; was also post-
            master at Southbridge, Mass. Ch.: 1, Mary Caroline, b. May 5,
            1845; m. Wm. Chas. Archdale; res. 57 Union Av., South Fram-
            ingham, Mass. 2, Ellen Sophronia, b. May 20, 1833; m. Nov.,
            1859, Henry Dame; res. 16 Mellen St., Cambridge, Mass.; ch.:
            Marion Bacon Dame, b. Dec. 17, 1866; Grace Katharine Dame,
            b. Sept. 22, 1873.
3782. iv.   LYDIA, b. ———; d. ———.
3783. v.   SALLIE, b. ———; d. ———.

2220. JOSIAH FISKE (Josiah, Josiah, Nathan, Nathan, Nathaniel, William, Robert, Simon, Simon, William, Symond), b. Pepperell, Mass., Sept. 3, 1755; m. there Nov. 25, 1779, Mary Caldwell, of Cambridge, Mass., b. Apr. 20, 1755; d. Dec. 25, 1834. In the Revolutionary war he joined the company commanded by Capt. Dow, of Hollis; fought in Prescott's regiment at the battle of Bunker Hill and was afterwards a fifer at Saratoga. At Bunker Hill he took a register from the body of a British officer, which, with his fife, is still kept by his descendants. In 1782 he moved from Pepperell, Mass., to Temple, N. H., and settled on the Searles farm. About 1787 he purchased the Lieut. Jonathan Marshall farm, which was immediately north of the other. His son, Jeremiah, resided there afterwards. He was a man highly esteemed and was never known to omit family worship from his marriage to his death. He d. May 29, 1832; res. Groton and Pepperell, Mass., and Temple, N. H.

3784. i.   JOSIAH, b. Nov. 14, 1781; m. Betsey Kimball.
3785. ii.   SARAH, b. Apr. 19, 1784; d. Aug. 27, 1784.
3786. iii. POLLY, b. Oct. 12, 1785; m. William Patterson, who d. in Francistown, N. H., May 13, 1832, ae. 48. She d. in Nashua, N. H., Jan. 6, 1854.
3787. iv.   SALLY, b. Feb. 25, 1788; m. there about 1809 Earl Boynton; res. New Ipswich. He was b. Apr. 20, 1788; d. at New Ipswich, N. H., Aug. 26, 1881. Ch.: 1, Mary C. Boynton, b. Mar. 19, 1810; d. May 21, 1892. 2, Sally Boynton, b. Jan. 2, 1816. 3, William Boynton, b. Jan. 15, 1818; res. New Ipswich, N. H. 4, Isabel M. B. Boynton, b. Dec. 20, 1821; d. Jan. 10, 1892. 5, Francis Boynton, b. June 25, 1824; d. Sept. 3, 1888. 6, Emily M. B. Boynton, b. Aug. 16, 1828. 7, Charles F. Boynton, b. Nov. 10, 1830. 8, George F. Boynton, b. Nov. 21, 1832; two children died quite young.
3788. v.   JEREMIAH, b. Aug. 17, 1790; m. Sarah Heald and Mrs. Cemina Munro.
3789. vi.   ARTEMAS, b. Sept. 11, 1792; m. Lucy Jones.
3790. vii. DAVID, b. May 12, 1795; d. July 10, 1795.
3791. viii. DAVID, b. Jan. 12, 1797; m. Milly Sheldon.
3792. ix.   SETH H., b. Sept. 20, 1800; M. Lydia Putman and Hannah J. Miles.

2221. DAVID FISK (Josiah, Josiah, Nathan, Nathan, Nathaniel, William, Robert, Simon, Simon, William, Symond), b. in Groton or Waltham, Mass., about 1756; m. —— ——. His four sons, Benjamin, David, John and Jonas, moved from Massachusetts to Camden, Me., in 1800. He d. ——; res. Waltham or Cambridge, Mass.

3792-1. i.   JOHN, b. Oct. 23, 1777; m. Clynthia Howe.
3792-2. ii. BENJAMIN, b. Mar., 1780; m. Roxanna Harrington.
3792-3. iii. DAVID, b. ——; m. —— Brecket.
3792-4. iv. JONAS, b. ——.
3792-5. v.   AND SEVERAL GIRLS.

2228. NATHAN FISKE (Daniel, Josiah, Nathan, Nathan, Nathaniel, William, Robert, Simon, Simon, William, Symond), b. Pepperell, Mass., Jan. 3, 1769; m. at Weston, Vt., about 1800, Dorothy Johnson Holt, b. ——; d. at Landgrove, Vt., Nov. 26, 1882. He was a farmer. He d. in 1831; res. Landgrove, Vt.

3793. i.   DANIEL, b. Mar. 31, 1803; m. Floretta Wyman.
3794. ii.   BETSEY, b. Jan. 18, 1805; d. unm.
3795. iii. DOROTHY, b. Sept. 7, 1806; d. unm.
3796. iv.   NATHAN, b. Oct. 7, 1808; d. unm.
3797. v.   ABEL, b. Feb. 5, 1810; d. unm.
3798. vi.   JOHN D., b. Feb. 10, 1812; m. Emily Olin.
3799. vii. ANNE DALE, b. Feb. 12, 1814; res. Roxbury, Mass., 3 Burton Ave., in the Old Ladies' Home.

2230. WALTER FISKE (Daniel, Josiah, Nathan, Nathan, Nathaniel, William, Robert, Simon, Simon, William, Symond), b. Pepperell, Mass., June 17, 1773; m. there Phebe Abbott, d. in Weld, Me. He d. in Pepperell, in 1821; res. Pepperell, Mass., and Wilton, N. H.

3800. i.   WALTER, b. May 26, 1796; m. Abigail Dickson.
3801. ii. BENJ. NUTTING, b. Jan. 22, 1798; m. Susannah S. Shedd.
3802. iii. JEREMIAH, b. Jan. 3, 1800; m. Peggy Burton.

2235. JOSIAH FISK (Daniel, Josiah, Nathan, Nathan, Nathaniel, William, Robert, Simon, Simon, William, Symond), b. Pepperell, Mass., Jan. 3, 1783; m. at Marlboro, N. H., Betsey Harvey, b. Oct. 23, 1786; d. Mar. 1, 1865. He was a clothier. He d. Jan. 15, 1866; res. Londonderry, N. H.

3803. i.   GEO. W. H., b. May 10, 1809; m. Mary Cadwick.
3804. ii. HORATIO A., b. Nov. 26, 1814; d. unm. Jan. 17, 1872.
3805. iii. HIRAM F., b. Oct. 27, 1816; m. Dec. 8, 1844, Lucy Hurlbert. He d. s. p. May 17, 1881.
3806. iv. CHARLOTTE H., b. May 30, 1819; m. Jan. 21, 1838, George Walker. He was b. Feb. 4, 1813; d. Aug. 30, 1886; was a shoemaker and tanner. She res. Westminster, Vt. Ch.: 1, Mary E. Walker, b. Aug. 8, 1839; d. Mar. 4, 1841. 2, Charlotte E. Walker, b. Mar. 23, 1844; d. Feb. 24, 1845. 3, Geo. H. Walker, b. Aug. 20, 1854; P. O. Westminster, Vt.
3807. v.   MARY V., b. Aug. 30, 1810; m. Dec. 28, 1832, Dwight Tyler. She d. Nov. 20, 1884, only ch., H. D., res. So. Londonderry, Vt. He has two ch., Minnie and Frank.

2236. VARNUM FISK (Daniel, Josiah, Nathan, Nathan, Nathaniel, William, Robert, Simon, Simon, William, Symond), b. in Pepperell, Mass., Sept. 13, 1786; m. in Dublin, N. H., July, 1809, Sally Eames, b. 1789; d. Sept 12, 1838, in Potsdam, N. Y. He d. in Syracuse, N. Y., in 1849; res. Wilton, N. H.

3808. i.   ARNOLD H., b. June 4, 1814; m. Martha M. Van House.
3809. ii.   DANIEL V., b. ———.
3810. iii. LORENZO B., b. ———.
3811. iv.   CYNTHIA E., b. ———.
3812. v.   VARNUM M., b. ———.
3813. vi.   SARAH B., b. ———; m. ——— Hicks. She d. in Logan, Utah. Ch.: Esther R., b. ———; m. ——— Ellis; res. 244 Fern St., Salt Lake City, Utah.
3814. vii. ALEX E., b. ———.
3815. viii. ESTHER E., b. ———.

2237. DEA. ABEL FISKE (Abel, Josiah, Nathan, Nathan, Nathaniel, William, Robert, Simon, Simon, William, Symond), b. Wilton, N. H., July 24, 1784; m. there Apr. 12, 1804, Abigail Dale, of Wilton, N. H., b. 1781; d. Jan. 26, 1852. He entered Phillips Academy at Exeter at an early age, but was obliged to return home on account of severe illness. He returned to college when able, but was called home on account of the sudden death of his father and it was necessary for him to remain with the family. After his marriage he went to Weld, Me., and spent eleven years. He then returned to Wilton and spent the remainder of his life there. He was a teacher twenty-five years in succession, during the winter months and never missed a winter. His last school, the winter he was 52. He was deacon of the Second Congregational Church in Wilton, N. H., twenty-four years, retiring from the office because he thought it belonged to the younger members. He retained all his mental faculties in a remarkable degree; dying at the age of 93 years, one month, one day. It could be said of his as of Moses: "His eye was not dim," for he never wore spectacles. Was a great reader and read to the very last of his life. He had a large gathering of friends to celebrate his 90th birthday. There were ninety of the members of the family, including ten great-grandchildren, sat down to the dinner. He d. Sept. 25, 1877; res. Wilton, N. H.

3816. i.   ABEL, b. Oct. 10, 1804. He d. in Alstead, N. H., in Sept. 1873; a descendant is Nellie M. Fiske, of Alstead.
3817. ii. SARAH PUTNAM, b. May 12, 1806; m. Oct. 5, 1837, Ichabod Gibson. She d. in Brighton, Mass., in 1879. Ch. is Mrs. Geo. R. Spaulding, of Allston, Mass.
3818. iii. ANN SPALDING, b. Mar. 18, 1808; d. in Boston, Nov. 11, 1878.
3819. iv. JOHN DALE, b. Weld, Me., Dec. 17, 1809; m. in Pepperell,

Mass., Jan. 4, 1832, Almira Shattuck, b. there Nov. 20, 1813; d. in Brookfield, Mass., Nov. 30, 1892. He was a prominent citizen; deacon of the Congregational Church; d. there Aug. 1, 1892. Ch.: 1, Almira Elizabeth, b. Nov. 20, 1833. 2, John Cornelius. 3, Timothy Abbott. 4, Henriette Achsah. 5, Antoinette Sarah, b. Mar. 25, 1846, in Pepperell; m. at Brookfield, Oct. 30, 1867, Henry L. Butterworth, b. Apr. 17, 1845; d. Aug. 10, 1884; was a shoe manufacturer there; ch.: 1, Anthon Fiske Butterworth, b. in Brookfield, Sept. 20, 1869; P. O. add. Brookfield, Mass; 2, Louis Henry Butterworth, b. Nov. 14, 1876, in Brookfield; P. O. add. Yale College. 6, Abbie Ann. 7, Harriett Farrar.

3820. v. ACHSAH FARRAR, b. May 29, 1812; d. in Wilton, N. H., Mar. 7, 1847.

3821. vi. ABBA DALE, b. Jan. 3, 1815; m. Oct. 11, 1836, Nathan R. Marden, of Wilton; res. Peterboro. He was b. Mt. Vernon, N. H., Oct. 17, 1812. Is a shoe manufacturer. Ch.: R. Fiske, b. July 25, 1837; m. Sarah Evans; res. in Marblehead, Mass. Sarah C., b. July 7, 1839; m. Reed P. Ordway; res. in Hartland, Vt. Edwin S., b. July 25, 1841; unm.; res. in Lowell, Mass. Abbie E., b. June 17, 1849; m. Sewell S. Brown; d. June 26, 1889. Jane M., b. Feb. 9, 1845; m. W. P. Hopkins; res. in Goffstown, N. H. Hattie A., b. June 6, 1853; d. Oct. 2, 1862. Wm. R., b. Apr. 2, 1843; d. at Annapolis, Md., Sept. 12, 1863. Jessie F., b. Sept. 1, 1857; m. M. E. Osborne; res. in Petersboro, N. H. Charles N., b. Mar. 25, 1847; m. Rebecca Bartlett; res. in Revere, Mass. Nathan Marden, b. New Boston, N. H.

3822. vii. HARRIETT NEWELL, b. May 4, 1817; unm.; res. Wilton, N. H.

3823. viii. ALLILHIMA HOLT, b. May 20, 1819; m. Rev. John Jones; res. Ventura, Cal.

3824. ix. MARIAH ANTOINETTE, b. Sept. 2, 1821; m. Sept. 30, 1841, Lowell Whitcomb. He was b. in Swansea, N. H., July 25, 1816; was a shoemaker and d. in Dunstable, Aug. 27, 1879. Ch.: 1, Charles Loring Whitcomb, b. Nov. 4, 1842; d. Dec. 13, 1864. 2, Mary Frances Whitcomb, b. Aug. 30, 1844; unm.; res. Dunstable, Mass. 3, George Hamilton Whitcomb, b. Aug. 28, 1847; d. July 29, 1852. 4, Franklin Whitcomb, b. May 17, 1853; d. July 30, 1853. 5, a daughter, b. Mar. 3, 1857. 6, a daughter, b. June 8, 1862; d. July 30, 1863. 7, a daughter, b. Aug. 6, 1865; d. Sept. 2, 1865.

3825. x. HENRY A., b. May 22, 1833; m. Sophronia Kidder, Ella L. Prince and Theo. E. Tower.

2238. REV. THEOPHILUS FISKE (Abel, Josiah, Nathan, Nathan, Nathaniel, William, Robert, Simon, Simon, William, Symond), b. Wilton, N. H., Dec. 4, 1801; m. in 1851 —— Dwinelle, dau. of Judge Justin Dwinelle. He was a Universalist minister; res. Utica, N. Y.

3826. i. LOUISE, b. ——; m. —— Bryson; a dau. is Louisa Fiske Bryson; res. No. 70 W. 46th St., New York City.

3827. ii. JOHN DWINELLE, b. ——.

2245. JOSHUA FISKE (Henry, Henry, Nathan, Nathan, Nathan, Nathaniel, William, Robert, Simon, Simon, William, Symond), b. Sturbridge, Mass., June 16, 1778; m. Feb. 18, 1801, Betsey Cheever; d. Jan. 22, 1848, in Norwich, Conn. He was born in Sturbridge on Fiske Hill and always resided in that town. He d. Dec. 28, 1835; res. Sturbridge, Mass.

3828. i. SAMUEL CHEEVER, b. Apr. 12, 1804; m. Celestina W. Bottom.

3829. ii. FIDELIA, b. 1803; m. —— Parkhurst; d. s. p. 188—.

2252. ELIAS FISKE (Simeon, Henry, Nathan, Nathan, Nathan, Nathaniel, William, Robert, Simon, Simon, William, Symond), b. Sturbridge, Mass., Oct. 29, 1782; m. Melissa Cassandana Wilder, of Vermont, b. Nov., 1785; d. Apr. 29, 1818;

m. 2d, ——— ———. She d. s. p. He was a farmer. He d. Dec. 8, 1841; res. Sturbridge and Wilbraham, Mass.

3830. i. CARLISLE A., b. Feb. 7, 1808; m. Eliza Ann Davis and Caroline M. Ely.

3831. ii. EMILY, b. May 7, 1813; m. Sept. 18, 1836, Edward A. Royce, b. June 17, 1811; d. Mar. 16, 1881; res. Lee, Mass.; s. p.

3832. iii. REBECCA, b. Aug. 1, 1816; m. Oct. 1, 1842, Samuel Harris Butler, d. Dec. 18, 1847; m. 2d, Nov. 23, 1864, John Rice Hoar, d. May 13, 18—, s. p.

3833. iv. MARY ELIZA, b. Dec. 30, 1810; m. July 15, 1832, Solomon Cushman; he d. Apr. 29, 1848; m. 2d, July 29, 1860, Wm. Hasting Estes. He d. in 1879. She d. Feb. 29, 1892.

2255. JUDGE HENRY FISKE (David, Henry, Nathan, Nathan, Nathan, Nathaniel, William, Robert, Simon, Simon, William, Symond), b. Sturbridge, Mass., Apr. 8, 1795; m. Apr. 8, 1822, Susan Helen Fales, of Wrentham, b. Jan. 6, 1794; d. Feb. 27, 1882, at Keene, N. H. He d. Dec. 24, 1845; res. Sturbridge, Mass., and Leslie, Mich.

3834. i. HENRY M., b. Dec. 10, 1823; m. Rose Smith.

3835. ii. ELVIRA ELIZABETH, b. Mar. 28, 1835; d. in Leslie, Nov. 14, 1838.

3836. iii. FRANK LYMAN, b. Aug. 8, 1832; m. Eliza Ann Freeman.

3837. iv. WM. DWIGHT, b. Jan. 24, 1829; m. ———; d. Apr. 28, 1872, in Knoxville, Cal., leaving Edwin and Kittey.

3838. v. SUSAN FALES, b. Jan. 11, 1831; m. Nov. 4, 1850, S. Allen Gerould; res. Keene, N. H. He was a merchant, b. Feb. 1, 1821. Ch.: 1, Frances Elisabeth Gerould, b. Sept. 9, 1851; res. 46 High St., Worcester, Mass. 2, Henry Fiske Gerould, b. Jan. 30, 1853; res. 43 West St., Keene, N. H. 3, Joseph Bowditch Gerould, M. D., b. Feb. 20, 1856; m. Apr. 16, 1890; res. North Attleboro, Mass.

3839. vi. GEORGE D., b. July 31, 1827; m. Elizabeth C. Loring.

3840. vii. DAVID FALES, b. Feb. 22, 1825; d. in Leslie Sept. 17, 1841.

2256. HON. JOSIAH JONES FISKE (David, Henry, Nathan, Nathan, Nathan, Nathaniel, William, Robert, Simon, Simon, William, Symond), b. Sturbridge, Mass., Nov. 28, 1785; m. at Wrentham, May 6, 1813, Jerusha Norton, b. there Apr. 5, 1779; d. in Boston Apr. 1, 1867. Mr. Fiske graduated from Brown University, in the class with Gov. Wm. L. Marcy, whose friendship he enjoyed. After graduation he became preceptor in an academy in Maine, but shortly determined to study law, and entered the office of Nathaniel Searle, LL. D., of Providence, and later, that of Timothy Bigelow, Esq., of Boston. Mr. Fiske became an able and successful lawyer. His office at Wrentham, Mass., was noted, and a large number of students acquired their knowledge of law under his care and instruction. Mr. Fiske was a man of great energy, quick perception, and a fluent speaker. His ability to analyze a case and properly present its strong points, contributed largely to his success, and if he had devoted himself exclusively to the law, he would undoubtedly have ranked among the distinguished in that profession. Early in life he became interested in cotton manufacturing. He built a mill at Sturbridge in 1827 and later erected a mill containing 10,000 spindles and 200 looms. The village of Fiskedale, Mass., commemorates his name. Men of Mr. Fiske's stamp have molded the generation in which they lived. He was active and enterprising and earnest in promoting the general welfare. That he was deemed a public spirited man by his townsmen is evidenced by the fact that he was repeatedly elected to office. He was State Senator from 1823 to 1826 inclusive; was member of the Governor's Council in 1831 and was a member of the first board of railroad commissioners created by the State. From 1823 to 1827 he was aid de camp to Major-General Crane. He was a prominent Mason, being District Deputy Grand Master and member of the Grand Lodge, F. & A. M. of Massachusetts. He was far seeing in his thought and plans, and subsequent events in Sturbridge and Wrentham proved the wisdom of his judgment. He was courteous and kindly in his disposition, and these traits were marked in his family intercourse He married Jerusha, daughter of Dr. Jenckes Norton and Jerusha Ware of Wrentham. His death occurred at Sturbridge, his birthplace, Aug. 15, 1838. His brothers, David Woodward, a lawyer who settled in Detroit and died in 1871, and Calvin P., a physician who lived most of his life in Sturbridge and died in Chicago in 1874, were both graduates of Brown University. Of his ten children Josiah Jones and George Jenckes were members of the well known firm of James M. Beebe & Co., of Boston, and contributed largely to its success. Josiah was unmarried and died in 1850. George died in Nice, France, in 1868, leaving a widow Frances Lathrop, daughter of James M. Beebe, a son George Stanley, born in Paris in 1867, and a daughter Esther Lathrop, born in Nice in 1868. He d. Aug. 15, 1838; res. Sturbridge, Mass.

3841. vii. ELIZABETH STANLEY, b. Oct. 16, 1822; res. 121 Commonwealth Ave., Boston, Mass.

3842. i. JOSEPH NORTON, b. Mar. 4, 1814; m. in Detroit, Mich., May 24, 1849, Charlotte M. Morse, dau. of Dr. Elijah Morse, of Mt. Vernon, Me., for several years member of the Senate and House of Representatives of Maine. He d. in Boston, s. p., June 18, 1892. Joseph Norton received his early education at Day's Academy. In 1833 he entered the counting-room of Shaw, Patterson & Co., where he remained five years, and afterward became confidential clerk of the banking house of Geo. B. Blake & Co. In 1846 he became a member of the Boston Broker's Board, and opened a banking office on State Street. He met with great success during his active business life, his ventures proving very lucrative. He enjoyed the highest confidence of the business public in a wonderful degree. This was due not only to his unquestionable personal integrity, but also to his well known business methods and careful arrangement of his financial matters. While at times his operations were immense, his capital was invested in assets only of the highest character, so that he could in every emergency meet his obligations without inconvenience or sacrifice. He never speculated, and his connection with an enterprise was a guarantee that it was founded on sound business principles. He retired from active business in 1870, spending the next three years in Europe, during which time he studied the financial affairs of Europe, making himself familiar with the moneyed interests of the old world. He was among the first of the large property holders to inaugurate the erection of the modern, palatial office buildings. In 1888 he erected on State Street the well known Fiske building, one of the finest buildings in Boston, a model of beauty and convenience. In richness of interior finish and beauty of architecture it is unsurpassed in New England. Mr. Fiske devoted the remaining years of his life to the care of his extensive private business. Up to the very last of his life he enjoyed remarkable vigorous health, and his well preserved faculties of mind and body were a source of comment and congratulation. The illness which terminated in his death, June 18, 1892, was the result of a severe cold, which confined him to the house only ten days. Mr. Fiske was retiring in his disposition, finding his chief enjoyment in his family. His sunny and kindly disposition rendered his home life a very happy one. His charities were unostentatious and seldom extended where publicity would be given to his acts. Deserving young people struggling to improve their condition strongly appealed to his sympathies. He was a firm believer in the cardinal doctrines of Christianity and all his life was guided by their teachings and precepts. Though a Republican in politics, he was never an intense partisan, nor did he have the least desire for public office. His aim was to discharge conscientiously the duties of a private citizen

3843. ii. HARNDON I., b. ———— ; d. Feb. 24, 1816.

3844. iii. HENRY A., b. Jan. 18, 1816; d. Feb. 21, 1840, in Liverpool, England. He was in business in Boston and went to Europe for his health, but did not live to return, dying in Liverpool after a short illness.

3845. iv. MARIA J., b. Dec. 8, 1817; d. Feb. 8, 1876, in Boston.
3846. v. SARAH N., b. July 19, 1819; d. Oct. 28, 1821.
3847. vi. ELLEN J., b. Apr. 9, 1821; d. Dec. 31, 1844.
3848. viii. JOSIAH JONES, b. Nov. 15, 1824; d. Mar. 11, 1850. He was born in Wrentham and at an early age engaged in business on his own account with James M. Beebe & Co. He was very successful and a man of strict integrity, and by his early death a most successful future was cut short.
3849. ix. FRANCES S., b. Mar. 4, 1827; d. Nov. 7, 1836.
3850. x. GEORGE J., b. Aug. 4, 1829; m. Frances L. Beebe.

2264. DAVID WOODWARD FISKE (David, Henry, Nathan, Nathan, Nathan, Nathaniel, William, Robert, Simon, Simon, William, Symond), b. Sturbridge, Mass., Nov. 2, 1801; m. at New Bedford, Mass., Oct. 28, 1834, Eliza Slocum Coggeshall, of New Bedford. b. Dec. 20, 1813; res. 564 Brush St., Detroit. He was a graduate of Brown University, practiced law with his brother Isaiah Fiske, in Wrentham, Mass., until 1836, when he came to Detroit, and went into the hardware business with his relative Coggeshall, thinking a more active life better for his health. Afterward he engaged in the lumber business until a year or two before his death, failing health obliging him to give up all care. He d. July 12, 1871; res. 564 Brush St., Detroit, Mich.

3851. i. AVIS COGGESHALL, b. Sept. 6, 1835; m. June 25, 1856, Charles Henry Locke; d. Feb. 4, 1887; res. 564 Brush St., Detroit. He was a dry goods merchant. Ch.: 1, Charles Edward, b. Mar. 9, 1858; m. Sarah Whistler Hinchman, June 20, 1889; ch.: Edward Hinchman, b. July 17, 1890; add. care of W. A. McGraw & Co., Detroit. 2, Elizabeth Fiske, b. Jan. 11, 1866; add. 564 Brush St., Detroit.
3852. ii. LYMAN DAVID, b. Dec. 10, 1844; d. May 19, 1851.

2266. DR. CALVIN PARK FISKE (David, Henry, Nathan, Nathan, Nathan, Nathaniel, William, Robert, Simon, Simon, William, Symond), b. Sturbridge, Mass., July 27, 1806; m. Dec. 27, 1835, Laura Wallace, of Munson, Mass., who d. Sept. 10, 1866; m. 2d, 1870, Mrs. Mary A. Hetfield. Calvin Park Fiske was born in that section of the town of Sturbridge, Worcester County, Mass., known as Fiske Hill. He graduated from Brown University in 1826 at the age of 20, and from Harvard medical in 1829. He commenced the practice of medicine in his native town, continuing in active practice till about 1864. He was prominently connected with the educational and agricultural interests of the town as well as the medical societies of the county, in all of which he was elected to positions of honor and trust. After the death of his wife, in 1866 he came to Chicago, Ill., and in 1870 was married to Mrs. Mary A. Hetfield, who still survives him. He was a great sufferer, both physically and financially, by the Chicago fire. In 1872 he resumed practice in Hinsdale, Ill., and there passed away. He d. July 16, 1874; res. Hinsdale, Ill.

3853. i. CALVIN JONES, b. Nov. 24, 1838; unm.; res. 3640 Cottage Grove Ave., Chicago, Ill. He was born and educated in Sturbridge, Mass., attended the public schools there, Monson Academy, and later at Hitchcock high school at Brimfield. He went to Chicago, Ill., in Jan., 1867, and since has resided there. He is a pharmacist.
3854. ii. LAURA ANN, b. May 27, 1842; d. 1847.
3855. iii. CHARLES HENRY, b. Feb., 1841; d. July 4, 1843.

2268. DANIEL FISKE (Daniel, Daniel, Nathan, Nathan, Nathan, Nathaniel, William, Robert, Simon, Simon, William, Symond), b. May 10, 1786, in Sturbridge, Mass.; m. there Oct. 12, 1812, Anny Fiske, b. Nov. 9, 1785; d. Dec. 14, 1859. He was a carpenter by trade but always followed farming. The will of Anny Fiske, of Sturbridge, widow of Daniel, was probated Feb. 7, 1860. Mentions son, Lucius C., Henry M., and George D. and daughter Sarah. In the town of Sturbridge, Mass., is a rise of land (and a very sightly place, too,) which has gone by the name of "Fisk Hill" for more than 150 years. Henry M. was born there and lived on a farm fifty-six years. His father and mother were born, lived and died there. His father's father was born and lived there between fifty and sixty years, but died in Woodstock, N. Y. His mother's father and mother were born, lived and died there. They, together with his father and mother, died on the same farm that Henry lived on fifty-six years. At one time there were seven families by the name of Fisk living on the Hill, and there was no family by any other name. Henry can recollect when there were five families of Fisk's, and only two by any other name. His sister Sarah and himself were the last ones to leave the Hill, but they still live in plain sight of the old farm, about two miles away. They have outlived all their relatives that are nearer than cousins; no uncles or aunts, nephews or nieces. He d. Dec. 7, 1859; res. Sturbridge, Mass.

    3856. i.   LUCIUS COLWELL, b. Sept. 3, 1813; d. Placerville, Cal.,
                 Oct. 17, 1874, unm.
    3857. ii. SARAH, b. Apr. 13, 1817; unm.: res. Southbridge.
    3858. iii. HENRY MORSE, b. July 2, 1818; m. Apr. 3, 1847, Lydia Bel-
                 knap, b. Nov. 12, 1815; d. s. p. Apr. 24, 1887; res. in S.
                 He d. Apr. 13, 1896, in one of the houses on a farm on Fisk
                 Hill, Sturbridge. He was born and lived and worked at farm-
                 ing the first fifty-six years of his life. He presumes
                 if his mother was living she would say that he made
                 more work than he did in the first years of his
                 life; still he lived there. He sold the farm and moved
                 to Southbridge and spent the rest of his life there.
                 For a few years after he went there he worked in a machine
                 shop and kept a hotel. The rest of the time he has been in no
                 business. On that farm his mother, a daughter of Henry Fiske,
                 was born, and lived there till she was married. He was a man
                 of thoroughly upright, honorable, Christian character, a loyal
                 citizen and a true and faithful friend. His kindly, genial
                 nature endeared him to all who came into contact with him,
                 and his integrity commanded universal respect.
    3859. iv. GEO. DANIEL, b. June 22, 1823; was frozen to death in Yank-
                 ton, Dakota Territory, Feb. 10, 1861; unm.

    2269. SILAS FISK (Daniel, Daniel, Nathan, Nathan, Nathan, Nathaniel, William, Robert, Simon, Simon, William, Symond), b. Sturbridge, Mass., Mar. 1, 1788; m. Feb. 20, 1815, Susanna Wright, b. Oct. 24, 1790; d. July 8, 1847, in Council Bluffs, Ia. He was a farmer, and was a soldier in the war of 1812. He d. Dec. 16, 1865; res. Sturbridge, Mass., and Sullivan, N. Y.

    3860. i.   LIBERTY B., b. Mar. 14, 1818; m. Amey Ann Foster and
                 Nancy Foster.
    3861. ii. LUCIUS W., b. July 29, 1816; m. Mary Alling.
    3862. iii. HARRIETT NEWELL, b. May 21, 1824; m. Oct. 7, 1845,
                 Phinehas Caldwell. She d. in Logan, Ia., Sept. 1, 1892. Ch.:
                 Charles F. Cadwell, b. Feb. 29, 1848. William, b. June 28,
                 1853. Edgar Fiske, b. Aug. 4, 1855; res. Logan, Ia.
    3863. iv. ELIZABEH, b. Aug. 16, 1826; m. Oct. 7, 1845, Linus L. Bel-
                 knap; res. 1013 South Forty-eighth St., Philadelphia, Pa. He
                 was b. Aug. 13, 1822; d. Dec. 2, 1890; was a merchant. Ch.: 1.
                 Anna Marsh Belknap, b. Mar. 27, 1847; m. Jan. 17, 1867,
                 Frank A. Beale, attorney; add. 315 W. 104th St., New York;
                 ch.: Frank A. Beale, Jr., b. Apr. 29, 1868; res. Chicago, Ill.;
                 Fredrick Wight Beale, b. Mar. 3, 1872; res. New York City;
                 a student at Steven's Institute; mechanical and electrical en-
                 gineering. 2. Lothrop Fiske Belknap, b. Dec. 22, 1850; d. May
                 28, 1805. 3. Amy Elizabeth Belknap, b. Nov. 23, 1852; m. June
                 7, 1888, William A. Zur Lippe, of Philadelphia, Pa., only sur-
                 viving child of the late Adolph (senior) Count Zur Lippe,
                 Weistenfeld, Beistenfeld, of Lippe Detmold, Germany, who
                 came to America in the year 1838; was one of the pioneers
                 and leading physicians in homeopathy in the world, and known
                 in America as Dr. Adolph Lippe, of Philadelphia, Pa.; was
                 quoted in Hof-Calender-de-Gotha as the senior count of Lippe
                 family up to the time of his death, Jan. 23, 1888. His family

25

is one of the oldest sovereign families of Europe, dating back to 1129 A. D. (see encyclopedias); the present head of the family is, or was, Prince Waldemar, of Lippe, who died March 20, 1895, and the family is now under contention as to who shall next reign. 4, Frederick Wight Belknap, b. Aug. 25, 1854. 5, Clara F. Belknap, b. May 22, 1856; m. Jan. 14, 1889, Thomas R. Brown; add. 315 W. 104th St., New York City.

3864. v.   SARAH VENERA, b. June 20, 1830; m. Jan. 20, 1850, Henry Morey; res. in Burlington, Wis. Ch.: Louisa N., b. Oct. 24, 1852. She d. June, 1865.

2272. JOSHUA MORSE FISK (Daniel, Daniel, Nathan, Nathan, Nathan, Nathaniel, William, Robert, Simon, Simon, William, Symond), b. Sturbridge, Mass., Sept. 25, 1795; m. Feb. 17, 1829, Maria Benedict, b. Apr. 21, 1807. He d. Apr. 29, 1873; res. Utica, N. Y.

3865. i.   ROMEYNE, b. Apr. 19, 1830.
3866. ii.   ADALAIDE LOUISA, b. May 2, 1832.
3867. iii. MIRANDA, b. May 5, 1834.
3868. iv.   SULLIVAN, b. Sept. 23, 1839.
3869. v.   MARIA AMELIA, b. Sept. 17, 1840.
3870. vi.   MARY JANE, b. Sept. 24, 1842.

2275. JOHN FISKE (Daniel, Daniel, Nathan, Nathan, Nathan, Nathaniel, William, Robert, Simon, Simon, William, Symond), b. Sturbridge, Mass., June 17, 1791; m. at Cazenovia, N. Y., Sept. 20, 1821, Mary P. Peck, b. Jan. 25, 1804; d. Dec. 10, 1855. He was a farmer. He d. Aug. 27, 1866; res. Cazenovia, N. Y., and Detroit, Mich.

3871. i.   MARY A., b. Dec. 2, 1823; res. Upper Sandusky, Ohio.
3872. ii.   SARAH ELIZABETH, b. Apr. 24, 1826; m. Nov. 24, 1853, Solon Prentiss. He d. Aug. 8, 1882; was a hardware merchant. Ch.: Mary Elizabeth, b. July 30, 1856; unm.; is a music teacher; res. 83 Pitcher St., Detroit, Mich.
3873. iii. JULIA M., b. Apr. 22, 1828; d. Sept. 28, 1867.
3874. iv.   JOHN P., b. Sept. 2, 1830; m. Lucy A. Fuller.
3875. v.   EDWIN D., b. Nov. 8, 1835; m. ——— ———.

2276. MOSES FISK (Daniel, Daniel, Nathan, Nathan, Nathan, Nathaniel, William, Robert, Simon, Simon, William, Symond), b. Sturbridge, Mass., Oct. 17, 1782; m. May 2, 1811, Esther Cheever, b. Jan. 19, 1786. He d. July 5, 1857; res. Utica, N. Y.

3876. i.   ELIZABETH MORSE, b. Feb. 20, 1812.
3877. ii.   HARRIET CHEEVER, b. Nov. 5, 1817; d. Jan. 6, 1857.
3878. iii. JULIA ANN, b. Aug. 27, 1825; d. Sept. 28, 1826.
3879. iv.   WM. MOSES, b. Oct. 8, 1827; d. Aug. 17, 1846.

2285. VERNEY FISKE (Samuel, Daniel, Nathan, Nathan, Nathan, Nathaniel, William, Robert, Simon, Simon, William, Symond), b. Sturbridge, Mass., Oct. 12, 1805; m. Manilee McKinstry; res. Southbridge, Mass.

3880.   i.   JOHN D., b. ———; m. 1857; res. Chelsea, Mass.
3881.   ii.   WILLIAM, b. ———; res. Southbridge.
3881½. iii. THEY had nine children; one daughter and two sons d. young.

2290. SAMUEL LYON FISKE (Samuel, Daniel, Nathan, Nathan, Nathan, Nathaniel, William, Robert, Simon, Simon, William, Symond), b. Southbridge, Mass., in 1814; m. at Buffalo, N. Y., Maria Louise Hodges, of Warren, Mass., b. Apr. 4, 1814; d. Aug., 1889. Samuel Lyon Fiske, son of Samuel and Sally Lyon Fiske, was born at Southbridge, Mass. As a youth remarkably precocious and with maturity developed remarkable ability and strength of character. Associated with Sayles & Merriam, he became at 21 agent of the Hamilton Woolen Company, and planned and built that company's water power, mill building and houses. The crisis of 1846 when the change in tariff prostrated so many woolen industries compelled the company to make great changes in plant and make worsted delaines, then a new fabric, instead of broadcloth, which had been their product. At this period his genius was especially demonstrated, as the change was successfully inaugurated, and later the plant was greatly increased by the building of print works. Unfortunately the strain on his system was so great that his health broke down and the death, at this critical period in his career, of his firm friend, Willard Sayles, the head of and largest stockholder in the company created changes in the organization and put another man in control. His future career was varied, but he never failed in successfully conducting any undertaking. He died in Philadelphia at the early age of 54. He was always a stanch Republican, and an advocate of protection principles. A strong temperance advocate, never touched intoxicating liquors or tobacco. He was honored and respected by all who knew him. He d. in Sept., 1869; res. Southbridge, Mass.

    3882. i.   LOUIS SAMUEL, b. Feb. 14, 1844; m. Mary Dobson and Katherine Holmes Tucker.

    2291. WILLIAM FISK (William, William, William, Nathan, Nathan, Nathaniel, William, Robert, Simon, Simon, William, Symond), b. in Connecticut, Sept. 5, 1778; m. Christena Piper, b. Sept. 1, 1779; d. Nov. 22, 1873. He was a farmer and chair maker, a Free-Will Baptist, and an old time Democrat. He was born in Connecticut, moved to New York State, and died in Indiana. He d. in Ohio County, 1837; res. Lock, Cayuga County, N. Y.

    3883. i.   SAMUEL, b. Sept. 14, 1806; m. Elvira Campbell.
    3884. ii.   NELSON, b. Oct. 19, 1814; m. Francina Baker and Julia A. Hannah.
    3885. iii. HIRAM, b. Oct. 8, 1816; m. Cynthia Griswold.
    3886. iv. NATHANIEL, b. June 30, 1810; m. Icephena Morris.
    3887. v.   DAVID, b. Aug. 5, 1804; m. Prilla Humphrey.
    3888. vi. HULDAH, b. May 7, 1801; m. Hiram Hunter. Seven ch.
    3889. vii. MARY, b. Dec. 10, 1802; m. Hiram Scranton. Three ch.
    3890. viii. ELIZA, b. July 14, 1808; d. unm.
    3891. ix. PETER, b. July 5, 1812; d. unm.
    3892. x.   AMY, b. June 4, 1819; m. ——— McKlusky.
    3893. xi. ELIZA, b. Mar. 26, 1822; d. unm.
    3894. xii. SALLY (twin), b. Oct. 19, 1814; m. Orin Keith.

    2293. SYLVANUS FISKE (William, William, William, Nathan, Nathan, Nathaniel, William, Robert, Simon, Simon, William, Symond), b. Stanwich, Conn., Feb. 17, 1775; m. in Cayuga County, July, 1799, Salley Avery, d. Nov. 29, 1816; m. 2d, Oct., 1818, Elizabeth (Bud) Franklin, b. Sept., 1788. Sylvanus Fiske of Stanwich left his father's when 20 years of age and emigrated to Cayuga County, New York, where he married, but record of the date of his marriage is lost. From there he emigrated to Brownville, Jefferson County, then almost a wilderness. In 1813 he removed and tarried a short time in Ogden, Monroe County. He then made himself a home in Stafford, Genesee County, all in the State of New York. All his beginnings were on wild land. He was a decided farmer, a true Republican, and member of the Calvinistic Baptist Church. His wife died in Stafford. He then married Mrs. Sylvanus Franklin (Elizabeth Bud), who was born in Killingworth, Middlesex County, Conn., in Sept., 1788. There she married Sylvanus Franklin of the same town and with him emigrated to Genesee County, State of New York, 1806, and settled in the then almost wilderness. Her husband died from exposure in the war of 1814. He d. June 18, 1864; res. Watertown and Buffalo, N. Y.

    3894-1. i.   FREDERICK, b. May, 1800; was a farmer; res. Swan, Noble County, Ind.
    3894-2. ii.   ALFRED W., b. Apr. 25, 1802; m. Sally Gillett and Abigail Randall.
    3894-3. iii. HENRY ALVA, b. Sept. 5, 1803; m. Eliza Parker.
    3894-4. iv. JESSE H., b. Apr. 20, 1804; m. Amanda Parker.
    3894-5. v.   SYLVANUS MAXON, b. Mar., 1811; res. Texas, Mich.; was a farmer; d. Mar., 1864; left one son and four daughters.
    3894-6. vi. EARL, b. Mar., 1813.
    3894-7. vii. AMOS H., b. May, 1812; m. Nancy A. Gillett.
    3894-8. viii. WILLIAM, b. July 1, 1814; res. in Eureka, Cal., but later in Rosalie, Wash.

3894-9.   ix.   ASA PORTER, b. Dec. 8, 1821; was a farmer, and d. Feb. 17, 1858.

3894-10.   x.   DANIEL BUEL, b. Nov. 19, 1826; m. and res. Neenah, Wis.; served three years in the Federal army in the Seventh Minnesota Regiment; was honorably discharged.

3894-11.   xi.   SARAH, b. Aug., 1819; res. Rosalie, Wash.

3894-12.   xii. ALMEND LUCRETIA, b. Mar., 1823.

3894-13.   xiii. ANN JANE, b. July 3, 1825; m. Sept. 27, 1852, Franklin Lathrop. She d. in Jackson, Mich., Oct. 9, 1852.

3894-14.   xiv. LYMAN FRANKLIN, b. Aug. 3, 1828: was a farmer and res. Yuba, Cal.

2298. STEPHEN FISKE (Rufus, Stephen, William, Nathan, Nathan, Nathaniel, William, Robert, Simon, Simon, William, Symond), b. Stafford, Conn., Jan. 8, 1786; m. Lucy Chandler, b. Apr. 19, 1794, in Pomfret, Conn. (Silas, David, Joseph. John, William); d. Sept. 29, 1821; m. 2d, ——— ———; res. Stafford, Conn.

3895.   i.   STEPHEN CHANDLER, b. Sept. 16, 1810; m. and res. in So. Kingston, R. I.; is a manufacturer.

3896.   ii. LEMUEL, b. Jan. 26, 1813.

3897.   iii. MARY ANN, b. Mar. 4, 1815: m. Apr. 11, 1837, Uriah P. Marcy, b. Nov. 25, 1814; is a farmer; res. Holland, Mass. Ch.: 1, David Henry, b. June 7, 1838; d. 1843. 2, Hollowill P., b. Jan. 10, 1840; m. 1863 Ellen Baker. 3, Oscar C., b. Sept. 9, 1842. 4, Lucy Louisa, b. May 3, 1844. 5, Charles U., b. May 26, 1846. 6, David U., b. Dec. 10, 1847; d. 1848. 7, Sybil Zulette, b. July 10, 1851. 8, Frank F., b. Dec. 22, 1852.

3898.   iv. LATHROP, b. Feb. 10, 1820: d. in Willington, Conn., 1825.

2299. RUFUS FISKE (Rufus, Stephen, William, Nathan, Nathan, Nathaniel, William, Robert, Simon, Simon, William, Symond), b. Stafford, Conn., Feb. 10, 1774; m. Irene Scripture, b. Mar. 24, 1779, dau. of Elizier Scripture; d. Aug. 31, 1861, in Willington, Conn. He d. at Willington, Conn., Sept. 22, 1848; res. New Bethel, Conn.

3899.   i.   JOHN, b. Feb. 9, 1799; m. Anna O. Stillman.

3901.   i½.   RUFUS, b. 1801; d. June 19, 1819.

3901.   ii.   LOVING, b. 1802; d. 1862.

3902.   iii. ARK, b. June, 1804: m.; a son is Edward Fiske, of Springfield, Mass.

3903.   iv.   LEANDER, b. 1806.

3904.   v.   IRA, b. Sept., 1808; m. ——— ———, and d. in Feb., 1877; a son is Adoman Fiske, of Stafford Springs, Conn.

3905.   vi.   MARVIN, b. 1811; m. ——— ———, and d. in Nov., 1841; a dau. m. Edward Fiske, son of Ark.

3906.   vii. LUCIUS HANKS, b. June, 1813; m. Elizabeth Eldridge at Willington, Sept. 25, 1879. She was b. Apr. 4, 1822; d. Apr. 19, 1887. He was a farmer and mechanic, and d. in Hartford, Conn., Apr. 1, 1874. Ch.: 1, Theodore D., b. Sept. 29, 1840; m. Mar. 11, 1861, Edna Gardiner. 2, Jane Elizabeth, b. Oct. 30, 1841; m. Jan. 1, 1863, Jeremiah Haley. 3, Eugene D., b. Willington, Conn., Jan. 14, 1844; m. at Hartford, Mar. 31, 1868, Kate Daniels, b. Dec. 5, 1841; d. July 1, 1881; m. 2d, in New York, Nov. 24, 1893, Margaret Ellen Dwyer, b. Dec. 27, 1866. He is a lawyer; res. Sachem's Head, Guilford, Conn.; ch.: a, Leonard Daniels Fisk, b. Hartford, Conn., Sept. 4, 1869. b, Clifford E. Fisk, b. Hartford, Conn., Nov. 2, 1870; d. July 16, 1871. c, James V. Fisk, b. Hartford, Conn., Mar. 16, 1872; d. Aug. 16, 1872. d, Louis Agassiz, b. Hartford, Conn., Nov. 14, 1873. e, Blanche E. Fisk, b. Hartford, Conn., Mar. 14, 1875; d. July 15, 1875. f, Emanuel Kant Fisk, b. Guilford, Conn., Aug. 28, 1894. Leonard Daniels Fisk married Gertrude B. Judd, at Hartford, Conn., Aug. 4, 1891, and has son Leonard Daniels Fisk, Jr., b. May 17, 1895; West Hartford, Conn.

4, Emily Ann, b. Aug. 21, 1849; d. Aug. 14, 1863. 5, Ella La Von, b. Apr. 7, 1852; unm.

3907. viii. JAMES M., b. July 15, 1815; m. Mary Ann Hinman.
3908. ix.   MARCUS LYON, b. Dec. 16, 1817; m. Frances A. Tinker and Mrs. Emeline L. Frazier.
3909. x.   LODICA, b. Aug., 1819; d. May, 1820.
3910. xi.   RUFUS, b. June, 1824; d. 1851.
3911. xii. HORACE, b. July, 1826; d. Nov., 1841.
3912. xiii. IRENE, b. ——; m. —— Converse, of Somers, Conn.; a grandson is Arnold Converse, of Somers.
3913. xiv. LAVINIA b. ——; m. —— Tibbals; m. 2d, —— Moore. Ch.: 1, Marshall V. Tibbals; res. 31 Woodbridge St., Hartford, Conn.; his son is Wm. A.; res. 15 Bellevue St., H. 2, Mrs. Albert Phiney; res. Ellington, Conn. 3, Mrs. Henry Phiney; res. Ellington, Conn. 4, Mrs. Ella J. Doane; res. Rockville, Conn.

2297⅛. LEMUEL FISK (William, William, William, Nathan, Nathan, Nathaniel, William, Robert, Simon, Simon, William, Symond), b. Stafford, Conn., June 1, 1785; m. Julia Applegate, b. 1794; d. Feb. 12, 1880. He was a school teacher. He d. in Perrineville, N. J., in 1835; res. N. J.

3914. i.   SARAH ANN, b. Dec. 5, 1813; m. —— Thompson, and d. Dec., 1895.
3915. ii. MATILDA, b. Mar. 2, 1816; m. —— Cruser.
3916. iii. LEMUEL, b. Feb. 9, 1817; m. Elizabeth Wallace. Ch.: 1, Mrs. William Hollingshead; res. 95 Griffith St., Jersey City Heights, N. J. 2, Thomas Fisk; res. 224 Washington St., Trenton, N. J. 3, Mrs. Sarah Maple; res. Orange, N. J. 4, Mrs. J. F. Zimmerman; res. Catskill, N. Y. 5, Seth N. Fisk; res. Elsa, Ill. 6, William Fisk. 7, Mrs. J. J. Higgins, b. Nov. 9, 1844; m. Jan. 11, 1865, William P. Bastedo, b. Dec. 25, 1838; d. Nov. 3, 1884; m. 2d, Nov. 26, 1890, J. J. Higgins; he is a carpenter; res. Kingston, N. J.; ch.: Ella Florence Bastedo, b. May 1, 1868; m. Dec. 31, 1888; add. Mrs. W. S. Miller, Trenton, N. J., Box 277. Clarence Bastedo, b. Aug. 17, 1875; d. May 8, 1876. Annie Elizabeth Bastedo, b. Oct. 10, 1878. Mary Louise, b. May 20, 1881. Harriet, b. Oct. 30, 1883; add. Kingston, N. J.
3917. iv. WM. HENRY, b. Oct. 22, 1818; res. Indianapolis, Ind.; m. Apr. 1, 1863, at Milroy, Ind., Lucy Ellen Story, b. Aug. 6, 1836; d. Oct. 8, 1881; is a carriage manufacturer. Ch.: Usa Fisk, b. Aug. 7, 1865; d. Feb. 2, 1866. Mary C. Fisk, b. Apr. 10, 1868; m. Dec. 23, 1894; present name Hunter; add. 309 E. Ohio St., Indianapolis. Mariah Blanche Fisk, b. Nov. 24, 1869; d. Sept. 14, 1890.
3918. v.   CATHERINE, b. Feb. 18, 1820; res. South Amboy, N. J.; m. at Little Washington, N. J., John Meginis. He was a farmer, and d. Oct. 12, 1844. Ch.: John Meginis, b. Sept. 9, 1839; add. South Amboy. Maggie Eaton, b. Mar. 20, 1837; add. Rudger St., Newark, N. J.
3919. vi. ELMIRA, b. Nov. 12, 1823; res. Rocky Hill, N. J.; m. —— Higgins.
3920. vii. MARY ANN, b. Feb. 2, 1826; res. New Sharon, N. J.; m. Jan. 30, 1851, Samuel Killey, Jr., b. Feb. 2, 1823; is a carpenter; res. New Sharon, N. J. Ch.: Wm. Henry Killey, b. Mar. 14, 1852; m. Apr., 1882. Annie M. Killey, b. May 8, 1854; m. Mar., 1877. Mary Elizabeth Killey, b. June 29, 1856; m. Feb. 4, 1883. Alaphozo A. Killey, b. Mar. 24, 1858; m. Apr. 25, 1888. Florentine Tulane Killey, b. Apr. 4, 1860; unm. Amy K. Killey, b. Dec. 29, 1861; m. Sept., 1880. Julia Killey, b. Feb. 13, 1863; d. Aug. 10, 1863. Holmes J. Killey, b. Feb. 25, 1864; d. Sept. 4, 1877. Laura Smith Killey, b. Aug. 25, 1866; m. Oct. 31, 1886. Edward R. Killey, b. Apr. 26, 1870; d. Sept. 1, 1877.

3921. viii. CHARLOTTE A., b. Feb. 8, 1830; res. Hightstown, N. J.; m. —— Pullen.

3922. ix. DAVID V., b. Oct. 3, 1831; res. Hightstown, N. J.; m. Jan. 28, 1858, Mary Jane Dey, b. Dec. 26, 1834; d. May 5, 1864; m. 2d, Jan. 13, 1869, Achsah C. Gravatt, b. July 14, 1844. He was a mason and builder, and d. Dec. 24, 1890. Ch.: John B. Fisk, b. May 24, 1859; unm.; res. Hightstown, N. J. Mary Louise Fisk, b. Jan. 20, 1862; m. Dec. 25, 1889; now Mary Louise Scott; res. 728 N. Forty-ninth St., Philadelphia, Pa.

3923. x. SUSAN JANE, b. Jan. 3, 1834; d. ——.

2304. LEONARD FISK (Stephen, Stephen, William, Nathan, Nathan, Nathaniel, William, Robert, Simon, Simon, William, Symond), b. Sept. 10, 1799, Randolph, Vt.; m. Dec. 13, 1824, Julia Colt, b. Oct. 25, 1805; d. July 30, 1841. She was own cousin of Col. Sam Colt, inventor of the revolver; m. 2d, 1852. Her mother, whose maiden name was Hopkins, had a wide connection with clergymen, generally of the orthodox Congregational variety, from Jonathan Edwards, senior, down to Rev. Joseph Worcester, of Chicago, whose grandmother, wife of Rev. Leonard Worcester, D. D., of Peacham, Vt., was sister of the wife of Benjamin Colt, of Brookfield, Vt. Rev. Jeremiah Porter, who died a year or so ago in Chicago, over 80 years of age, who, it is said, preached the first sermon ever delivered in Chicago, was also a relative. The first twenty-five years of Leonard's life were spent in Randolph and in the adjoining town of Brookfield. After his marriage in 1824 he lived for about two years in Albany, Vt., then returned to Brookfield. Learned trade of cutting marble gravestones, and went into that business in Montpelier about 1830. In 1835 removed to Castleton, Rutland Co., Vt., where he remained till the death of his wife there in 1841. He married again in 1852 in Concord, N. H. Had one son of this marriage, Frank P. Fisk, born June 14, 1857, in Guernsey Co., Ohio (This Frank P. is now (1895) teacher of piano and organ in Kansas City, Mo.). He followed his son Solon to Bloomington, Ill., and died there very suddenly, dropping on the street while walking to his son's house and dying without speaking. He d. Dec. 6, 1878; res. Albany, Vt.

3924. i. SOLON, b. Jan. 12, 1826; m. Josephine K. Griffin and Ellen M. Frink.

3925. ii. AMELIA, b. Sept. 8, 1827; m. June, 1846, Otis E. Stevens. She d. Nov. 13, 1851, in Concord, N. H. He was master mechanic of the Northern railroad. Amelia left two children, a son, Frank E. Stevens, now of Bow Mills (near Concord), N. H., and a daughter, Ella H., now the wife of Rev. T. C. Moffatt, now preaching in Nebraska; he is a graduate of Wheaton College, near Chicago. They have no children.

3926. iii. LEONARD H., b. Nov. 27, 1829; d. Nov. 23, 1832.

3927. iv. GEORGE L., b. Mar. 1, 1835; d. June 13, 1836.

3928. v. CHAUNCEY, b. May 7, 1838; d. Apr. 5, 1839.

3929. vi. FRANK PIERCE, b. Jan. 14, 1857; m. May 11, 1891, Stella A. Connely, b. Sept. 5, 1857; res. Kansas City, Mo., s. p. He is a concert organist and pianist.

2306. THOMAS JEFFERSON FISKE (Stephen, Stephen, William, Nathan, Nathan, Nathaniel, William, Robert, Simon, Simon, William, Symond), b. Apr. 19, 1803, in Randolph, Vt.; m. at Royalton, Caroline Clapp. He was a farmer. He d. Oct., 1892; res. Hancock, N. H.

3930. i. EDGAR H., b. Aug. 30, 1838; m. Daniel L. Gage.

3931. ii. DAUGHTER, b. ——; m. J. B. Darling; res. Cambridge, Mass.

3932. iii. DAUGHTER, b. ——; m. J. E. Turner; res. Cambridge.

3933. iv. CHARLES J., b. ——; res. Hancock, N. H.

2307. HARRISON FISK (Stephen, Stephen, William, Nathan, Nathan, Nathaniel, William, Robert, Simon, Simon, William, Symond), b. Brookfield, Vt., Mar. 1, 1812; m. Jan. 7, 1836, Lucinda Bean, b. Aug. 18, 1816; d. Feb. 27, 1884. He died in the army; he was a member of Company E. Seventy-second Regiment Illinois Volunteers, and was sick in the hospital with erysipelas, which he contracted in the service. He d. at La Grange, Tenn., Jan. 31, 1863.

3934. i.   LOUISA ROSELLE, b. Jan. 22, 1843; m. Apr. 25, 1869, John S. Gibbs; res. Retreat, Wis. He was b. Aug. 2, 1843; is a farmer. Ch.: John H., b. Apr. 29, 1870. Herbert L., b. July 25, 1872. Alfred S., b. July 13, 1874. Edith L., b. Feb. 2, 1876. Charles R., b. Aug. 2, 1881.

2313. JAMES FISK (Stephen, Stephen, William, Nathan, Nathan, Nathaniel, William, Robert, Simon, Simon, William, Symond), b. Brookfield, Vt., Apr. 30, 1795; m. there Dec. 14, 1821, Eliza Colt, b. May 4, 1795, in Brookfield. Vt.; d. Dec. 18, 1858, at Hancock, Vt. He was a farmer all his life. He d. Aug. 5, 1877; res. Albany, Brookfield, Vt., and Chicago. Ill.

3935. i.   JAMES FREDERICK, b. Jan. 7, 1822; d. Jan., 1822.
3936. ii.   JULIA ELIZA, b. May 20, 1823; m. Dec. 12, 1847, Francis A. Stevens. She d. Feb. 2, 1883, in Chicago, leaving one son, Frank L., res. 2939 Michigan Av.
3937. iii. JOHN COLT, b. Sept. 13, 1825; m. Sarah M. Hubbard.
3938. iv. CYNTHIA, b. Apr. 17, 1828; d. Feb. 11, 1829.
3939. v.   ANDREW JEFFERSON, b. Mar. 8, 1832; m. Clara ———.
3940. vi. JAMES HARRIS, b. Apr. 12, 1834; m. Mary Jane Darling.
3941. vii. EMILY MELVINA, b. Sept. 5, 1839; d. Apr. 1, 1843.
3942. viii. STEPHEN EUGENE, b. Nov. 19, 1844; d. Jan. 6, 1855.
3943. ix. EMILY MELVINA, b. Dec. 2, 1830; d. Apr. 17, 1831.

2314. STEPHEN C. FISK (Stephen, Stephen, William, Nathan, Nathan, Nathaniel, William, Robert, Simon, Simon, William, Symond), b. Vermont, July 10, 1796; m. Angeline Gardner. She d. in Centralia. Ill. He was a farmer. He d. in Brookfield, Vt., Feb. 26, 1859; res. Sparta, Ill.

3944. i.   STEPHEN, b. Aug. 4, 1847; m. in Galena, Ill., Alice F. Edwards; res. Galena, Ill. Ch.: 1, James Otis, b. Mar. 19, 1871; res. Galena, Ill. 2, Nellie, b. June 15, 1876; m. Nov. 7, 1891. Geo. W. Green, b. Dec. 30, 1872; res. Galena, Ill.: ch.: Nellie Maria, b. Feb. 6, 1895; d. Sept. 23, 1895. 3, Caroline, b. Sept. 15, 1874; m. Apr. 25, 1894, Henry Rapp, b. Nov. 25, 1869; res. Galena, Ill.; ch.: Henry, b. Mar. 4, 1895.
3945. ii.   DALLAS M., b. Aug. 27, 1845; m. at Cheyenne, Wyo., Sarah Jennette Smith. He is conductor on C., M. & St. P. railway; res. s. p. 221 Seventeenth Av., Council Bluffs, Ia.
3946. iii. FRANCIS, b. ———; d. in Sparta, Ill.
3947. iv. EDWARD, b. ———; d. in Sparta, Ill.

2324. ZAROASTER FISK (James, Stephen, William, Nathan, Nathan, Nathaniel, William, Robert, Simon, Simon, William, Symond), b. Swanton, Vt., Jan. 22, 1804; m. Sarah E. ———, b. 1805; d. May 16, 1832; m. 2d, at Swanton, Oct. 20, 1834, Ann Miretta Vail, b. Montpelier, Vt., May 12, 1813; d. Dec. 10, 1858, in Montpelier, Vt.: dau. of Joshua E. Vail, of M. He d. at Pacific, Mo., Aug. 9, 1875; res. Swanton, Vt., and Ada Falls, Ia.

3948. i.   JAMES EDGAR, b. Swanton, Vt., Apr. 24, 1841. He entered the naval academy at Annapolis, Md., and was there when the war broke out. He resigned and joined the Confederate army. In 1864 he resided in St. Louis, Mo., and later moved to Fort Scott, Kan. He had three children, and after his death his widow res. in Washington, D. C. He was an unusually bright and interesting boy, and at the age of 17 was sent to the naval academy at Annapolis, Md. There he associated largely with southern gentlemen and lads of his own age, and became imbued with southern prejudices and principles. This feeling was fostered largely by frequent visits from ex-Governor Hunter, of North Carolina, who took special pains to gain the confidence and corrupt the principles of the students. He visited them often and of course presented his views in persuasive language and brilliant colors. He succeeded but too well. One hundred and fifty resigned at one time, James among them, which nearly killed his father.

3949. ii.   SARAH ELVIRA, b. June 26, 1852; she res. with her aunt, Mrs.
             Horace G. Storey, in 1886, in Milwaukee, Wis.

2326. MOSES FISK (Josiah, Nathan, William, Nathan, Nathan, Nathaniel,
William, Robert, Simon, Simon, William, Symond), b. Worthington, Mass., Nov.
12, 1780; m. in W. Chesterfield, Mass., in 1803, Emily Lucretia Todd, dau. of Rev.
Elder Todd, of Chesterfield, b. 1782; d. 1816 in W. Chesterfield, Mass.; m. 2d, in
1817, Martha Pratt, of Charlton, b. 1788; d. July, 1821; m. 3d, Dec. 11, 1821, Olive
Porter, of Worthington, b. Oct. 3, 1786; d. Feb. 24, 1876. He was a farmer. He d.
in No. Chester, Mass., Feb. 22, 1851; res. Chesterfield, Mass.

3950. i.   MOSES, b. Nov. 12, 1805; m. Lucretia Prentice, Lorinthia Pearl
             and Mrs. Stanton.
3951. ii.   EMILY, b. Nov. 29, 1807; m. Oct., 1829, Austin Pease. He was
             b. in Middlefield, Mass., and d. Apr. 30, 1850. She d. May 3,
             1854. Ch.: Russell, b. Aug. 23, 1835; m. Sept. 18, 1860, Corne-
             lia A. Hawkes, b. Sept. 11, 1838; res. Turner's Falls, Mass.; ch.:
             1. Stella A. Pease, now Mrs. W. B. Van Valkenburg, b. Aug.
             4, 1861; m. June 27, 1888; add. Mount Vernon, Ia. 2, Delia A.,
             b. Dec. 15, 1865. 3, Arthur C., b. Oct. 29, 1867; d. Jan. 11,
             1870.
3952. iii. ADDISON, b. May 26, 1826; d. unm. Oct. 30, 1846.
3953. iv.   MARTHA, b. June 8, 1824; m. Sept. 30, 1849, Benjamin Blair
             Eastman; res. 21 Leonard Ave., Westfield, Mass. He was a
             carpenter and wheelwright, b. June 23, 1816; d. Dec. 13, 1886.
             Ch.: Sarah Olive, b. July 3, 1850; m. Jan., 1886, ——— Hickox;
             res. 101 Oak St., Springfield, Mass. Oliver Addison, b. Sept. 11,
             1851; unm.; res. 21 Leonard Av., Westfield, Mass. Martha, b.
             Feb. 28, 1853; d. Mar. 17, 1853. Edwin Blair, b. Mar. 22, 1854; m.
             Apr., 1878, and May, 1886; res. Littleville, Mass. Austin, b.
             July 26, 1856; m. Dec. 25, 1882; res. Littleville, Mass. Benja-
             min, b. Apr. 26, 1859; d. Jan. 29, 1885. John Porter, b. June 2,
             1864; d. Mar. 6, 1883. Mary Emily, b. Oct. 29, 1867; unm.; res.
             21 Leonard Ave., Westfield, Mass.

2327. JOSIAH FISK (Josiah, Nathan, William, Nathan, Nathan, Nathaniel,
William, Robert, Simon, Simon, William, Symond), b. Chesterfield, Mass., ———;
m. Penelope Pierce, b. about 1780, in Scituate, Mass., dau. of Jonathan and Mary
(Litchfield) Pierce, of Scituate and Chesterfield, Mass.; m. 2d, Apr. 12, 1819, Re-
becca Cole, of Chesterfield. He d. Feb. 15, 1837; res. Potsdam, N. Y., and No.
Adams, Mass.

3954. i.   BUSHROD W., b. Apr. 7, 1807; m. Relief Holmes.
3955. ii.   MALINDA, b. ———; m. James Elder. She d., s. p., in No.
             Chester, Mass.
3956. iii. RODNEY, b. Mar. 11, 1809; m. Mary Cady.
3957. iv.   RALPH HALE, b. ———; m. ———.
3958. v.   ORIN, b. ———; d. ae. 10.

2329. NATHAN FISK (Josiah, Nathan, William, Nathan, Nathan, Nathaniel, William, Robert, Simon, Simon, William, Symond), b. Nov. 30, 1774, Chesterfield, Mass.; m. Oct. 4, 1798, Rebecca Canfield, b. Mar. 3, 1781; d. Oct. 13, 1853.
He was a carpenter and farmer. He d. July 27, 1829; res. Penfield, N. Y.

3959. i.   JOSIAH, b. Nov. 12, 1812; m. Narcissa L. White.
3960. ii.   JOSEPH, b. Oct. 13, 1818; m. Elizabeth H. Sibley.
3961. iii. GREENLEAF, b. May 19, 1807; m. Mary A. Manlove and Mrs.
             Mary (Piper) Hawkins.
3962. iv.   ABRAM CANFIELD, b. Feb. 19, 1816; m. Catherine Smith.
3963. v.   NATHAN, b. Jan. 6, 1804; res. Brockport, N. Y.
3964. vi.   LUCY, b. Oct. 31, 1799; m. Jan., 1819, John Wilbur. He was b.
             in Massachusetts in 1803; d. in Pulaski, Mich., in 1878. She d
             in 1881. He was a farmer. Ch.: 1, Mary Wilbur Dresser, de-
             ceased; ch.: Mary Cayword; add. Pulaski, Mich. 2. Almira
             Wilbur Wheeler, deceased; ch.: Jane Wheeler; add. Pulaski,
             Mich. 3, Ann Wilbur Brown, deceased; ch.: John Brown;
             add. Cambria, Mich. 4, Susan Wilbur Thorn, deceased. 5,

Lucy Wilbur, deceased. 6, John Wilbur; add. Jackson, Jackson County, Mich. 7, Goodal Wilbur; add. Grundy, Grundy County, Ia. 8, Nathan F. Wilbur; add. Chippewa Lake, Mecosta County, Mich. 9, Joseph J., b. Jan. 14, 1839; m. Jan. 18, 1862, Elizabeth A. Piper, b. Apr. 29, 1842; res. Concord, Mich.; is a farmer; ch.: Clyde L. Wilbur, b. Nov. 18, 1862; m. Oct., 1882; add. Pulaski, Jackson County, Mich. Gertrude M. Wilbur, b. Dec. 24, 1867; m. Dec. 23, 1886; present name Gertrude M. Bell; add. 88 Park St., Detroit, Mich.

3965. vii. AUGUSTUS, b. Apr. 3, 1801; d. Apr. 16, 1801.
3966. viii. SARAH, b. Mar. 26, 1802; m. Dec. 30, 1821, Bur Northrup. Ch.: Beach Northrup; res. Penfield, N. Y.
3967. ix. JOEL, b. Oct. 7, 1805; m. Sarah Crippen.
3968. x. PHILANDER, b. Jan. 15, 1809; m. Sarah Van Scouton.
3969. xi. SAMUEL, b. Dec. 6, 1810. His sons res. Monroe, Mich.

2341¼. HON. STEPHEN FISK (Nathan, Nathan, William, Nathan, Nathan, Nathaniel, William, Robert, Simon, Simon, William, Symond), b. Willington, Conn., Jan. 8, 1786; m. ——— Chandler, b. ———; d. ———; m. 2d, in Tolland, Conn., Sarah Ingersoll, b. Apr. 11, 1802, in Tolland; d. in Auburn, Mass., Mar. 6, 1885. He d. Oct. 4, 1847; res. Willington, Conn.

3970. i. HIRAM INGERSOLL, b. Oct. 14, 1823; m. Sarah A. Pott. He is a doctor; res. Guilford, Conn. Ch.: Catherine and Elverton.
3971. ii. ALVIRA BROOKS, b. Oct. 20, 1825; m. Darwin Whittaker. She d. in Gardner, Mass., Oct. 11, 1891. Ch.: Mrs. Albert Copeland; res. Palatine, Kas. Mrs. Joseph Drugan; res. Walpole, Mass.
3972. iii. AMANDA, b. July 29, 1827; m. Mar. 13, 1854, Dea. George Brancroft. She d. in Auburn, Mass., June 8, 1873. Ch.: Willis H. Brancroft; res. Auburndale, Mass. P. O. Box 356. Mrs. L. B. Gowen; res. 16 Harvard Place, Brookline, Mass.
3973. iv. DORCAS, b. Sept. 16, 1829; m. Sept. 19, 1855, D. B. Nichols. She d. May 15, 1884. Ch.: 1, Ella D., b. Oct. 11, 1856; m. Jan. 8, 18-8, Fred E. Ripley; res. Springfield, Mass. She d. Apr. 6, 1880. 2, Es'ella C., b. Aug. 25, 1858; m. May 16, 1881, Geo. S. Young; res. 72 Beacon Ave., Holyoke, Mass.; three ch. 3, Emma O., b. June 17, 1860; d. Nov., 1863.
3974. v. CORDELIA, b. May 22, 1832; d. unm. July 12, 1878.
3975. vi. MARY ELIZA, b. Dec. 18, 1838; m. in Auburn, Mass., May 31, 1873, Alpha M. Ward, b. Mar. 20, 1847; is a mechanic; res. Newhall, Cal.; ch.: Ida Eliza, b. Dec. 9, 1878; res. at home.
3976. vii. STEPHEN CHANDLER, b. ———; m. and res. in South Kingston, R. I. He was a woolen manufacturer and had one daughter by the name of Louisa. He died very suddenly and the daughter died the next day, leaving two small children.
3977. viii. LEMUEL, b. ———; m. ———; a son is Mahlon M. Fisk, of Poplar Bluff, Mo.
3978. ix. MARY ANN, b. ———; m. Uriah Marcey; res. Holland, Mass.; a son, Oscar, res. Palmer Depot, Mass.

2342. ASA FISKE (Aaron, Asa, Nathaniel, Nathaniel, Nathan, Nathaniel, William, Robert, Simon, Simon, William, Symond), b. Templeton, Mass., Apr. 19, 1775; m. Betsey Henry, b. Worcester, Mass., Oct. 29, 1774; d. Whitefield, N. H., Sept. 16, 1858. He was born in Massachusetts on a farm; learned the trade of mason which occupation he followed when not farming. He went from Templeton, Mass., at the beginning of the century, locating first at Chesterfield, N. H., with relatives across the river in Brattleboro, Vt., afterward at Lunenburg, or Guildhall, Vt.; then across the river again in Lancaster, N. H., and for a time in Whitefield. He had a family of twelve children. He d. Mar. 29, 1849; res. Chesterfield, N. H.; Lunenburg, Vt.; Lancaster, N. H., and Whitefield, N. H.

3979. i. HENRY, b. Feb. 27, 1802; m. Lucinda Keyes and Mrs. Dorothy B. (Keyes) Fiske.
3980. ii. LOIS, b. May 7, 1803; d. Guildhall, Vt., Nov. 29, 1822.

3981. iii. RALPH, b. May 7, 1804; m. Polly Abbott Walker and Mrs. Esther Ann (Turner) Hall.

3982. iv. MARIA, b. Sept. 7, 1805; m. Joseph Child, of Boston, Mass.; d. Apr. 2, 1879. They had one child who died young. She d. Apr. 2, 1879.

3983. v. ERASTUS, b. Apr. 4, 1807; m. Sarah Cleveland.

3984. vi. FREDERICK, b. Sept. 3, 1808; m. Sarah Clark.

3985. vii. NANCY, b. Feb. 24, 1810; m. 1830 Solomon Kenison. She d. in Dalton, N. H., Feb. 15, 1865. Ch.: 1. Hiram, b. May 21, 1831; res. in Kansas. 2, Charles, b. Feb. 14, 1833; res. Lancaster, N. H. 3, George S., b. Mar. 14, 1838; res. in Lancaster, N. H. 4, Jane, b. Mar. 8, 1840; res. in Vermont, and m. 5, Asa, b. Nov. 4, 1843; res. in San Francisco, with family. 6, Francis Edwin, b. Feb., 1849; d. Apr 5, 1867.

3986. viii. FRANCIS, b. Mar. 8, 1811; m. Dorothy B. Keyes.

3987. ix. CHARLES, b. Feb. 17, 1814; m. Mary Ann Eaton.

3988. x. ROYAL, b. July 26, 1815; d. unm. in San Francisco, Cal., Dec. 18, 1873. Royal, who had been in business in Boston, preceded Charles to California by some months, leaving no family, but they were interested together in a lumber venture. Royal established himself in business at Sacramento, where he was burned out twice and had his property swept away by flood once, and then engaged in commission and brokerage business in San Francisco. He made and lost two or three moderate fortunes, and finally left comparatively little property.

3989. xi. PASCHAL, b. Aug. 26, 1819; m. ———— ———— and ———— ————.

3990. xii. ADELINE, b. June 2, 1823; m. Jan. 6, 1847, Lorenzo C. Johnson; res. Rockford, Minn. He was b. Nov. 16, 1822; was a merchant. Ch.: Arianna F. Johnson, b. Feb. 10, 1848; res. Rockford, Minn. George W. Johnson, b. May 26, 1849; res. Hillyard, Wash. Royal F. Johnson, b. Nov. 29, 1850; res. Chicago, Ill. Edward L. Johnson, b. Oct. 5, 1853; d. May 26, 1884. Helen S. Johnson, b. Oct. 21, 1855; res. Monticello, Minn. Frank M. Johnson, b. Oct. 9, 1857; res. Rockford, Minn. Chester M. Johnson, b. Sept. 19, 1859; res. Rockford, Minn. Arianna F. Johnson m. Franklin W. Clifford; Helen S. Johnson m. William W. Bagley.

2343. AARON FISKE (Aaron, Asa, Nathaniel, Nathaniel, Nathan, Nathaniel, William, Robert, Simon, Simon, William, Symond), b. June 23, 1777, Chesterfield, N. H.; m. there Feb. 11, 1799, Abigail Chandler, of Putney, Vt., b. Brimfield, Mass., June 21, 1778 (John, Joseph, Joseph, William); d. May, 1866. He d. Sept. 10, 1822; res. Chesterfield, N. H.; Lunenburg, Vt., and Guildhall, Vt.

3991. i. MARY, b. Oct. 24, 1810; d. June 10, 1813.

3992. ii. ELIJAH, b. Aug. 13, 1811; d. Mar., 1826.

3993. iii. ANSON, b. Sept. 28, 1801; m. Prudence How.

3994. iv. ADELINE, b. May, 1804.

3995. v. WILLIAM, b. July 25, 1806; m. Catherine H. Hudson.

3996. vi. HENRY, b. Jan. 8, 1808; d. ————.

3997. vii. ELIJAH, b. Jan. 9, 1810; d. ————.

3998. viii. GEORGE W., b. Mar. 3, 1812; m. Eliza Brewer Cutler.

3999. ix. CLIMENA, b. Feb. 21, 1814; m. James Crane; res. Danville, Vt. Ch.: 1. George Hilland, b. Dec. 28, 1837. 2, Henry Alonzo, b. Mar. 27, 1839. 3. Solon Lycurgus, b. Sept. 22, 1842; d. May 14, 1844. 4, Eva Jane, b. Jan. 22, 1855.

4000. x. LOUISA, b. Feb. 11, 1816; m. Benjamin F. Boynton; res. Lowell.

4001. xi. MARILLA, b. Apr. 10, 1818; m. William Hoyt; res. Danville, Vt.

4002. xii. MARY, b. July 13, 1820; m. Charles Crane; res. Danville, Vt. Ch.: 1, John Henry, b. Feb. 27, 1843; 2, Celesta Jane, b. Dec. 2, 1845; 3, Danzill M., b. Feb. 19, 1848; 4, Edwin E., b. Sept. 20, 1850; 5, Emma Louisa, b. May 28, 1856.

2346. JOSEPH FISK (Aaron, Asa, Nathaniel, Nathaniel, Nathan, Nathaniel, William, Robert, Simon, Simon, William, Symond), b. Chesterfield, N. H., Sept. 2, 1782; m. ——— ———; res. Chesterfield, N. H.

    4003. i.   HANNAH S., b. 1811; d. Mar. 14, 1841.
    4004. ii.   ELVIRA, b. ———.

2347. ABEL FISKE (Aaron, Asa, Nathaniel, Nathaniel, Nathan, Nathaniel, William, Robert, Simon, Simon, William, Symond), b. Chesterfield, N. H., Feb. 17, 1785; m. there Nov. 26, 1807, Sally Phillips, b. Jan. 14, 1787; d. May 10, 1835; m. 2d, 1837, Jerusha Johnson, b. Aug. 15, 1798; d. Mar. 29, 1872. He was a carpenter, a Whig, and afterward a Republican. He d. Mar. 28, 1872; res. St. Albans, Vt., and Chicopee, Mass.

    4005. i.   LARNED P., b. Aug. 31, 1808; m. Maria White.
    4006. ii.   AARON A., b. May 19, 1810; d. Aug. 10, 1810.
    4007. iii. LEVINA, b. Aug. 1, 1811; d. Jan. 3, 1833.
    4008. iv.   ABNER, b. Apr. 17, 1813; m. Mary L. Smith.
    4009. v.   AARON WILSON, b. June 24, 1815; d. Dec. 14, 1816.
    4010. vi.   MARY M., b. Jan. 28, 1817; m. 1841 James O. Lord; res. Los Angeles, Cal.
    4011. vii. LAURA B., b. Apr. 6, 1819; d. Mar. 29, 1872.
    4012. viii. ELIZA H., b. Aug. 12, 1821; m. Samuel P. Bryant. She d. June 15, 1875. Ch.: Flora, b. ———; res. Granby, Conn.
    4013. ix.   EMILY S., b. Nov. 3, 1823; m. Charles H. Barrett; res. W. Brattleboro, Vt.
    4014. x.   LEWIS L., b. Oct. 19, 1825; m., and d. Dec. 24, 1868.
    4015. xi.   JOHN L., b. Feb. 7, 1828; m. Cornelia H. Woodruff.
    4016. xii. EDMUND D., b. June 17, 1838; m. and res. Chicopee, Mass.
    4017. xiii. JAMES O., b. Apr. 25, 1841; m. Annie M. Parsons.

2349. EZRA FISK (Aaron, Asa, Nathaniel, Nathaniel, Nathan, Nathaniel, William, Robert, Simon, Simon, William, Symond), b. Chesterfield, N. H., May 23, 1791; m. ——— ———. He d. Dec. 18, 1834; res. Chesterfield, N. H.

    4018. i.   EMELINE H., b. Apr. 25, 1818; d. Jan. 2, 1856.
    4019. ii.   CAROLINE W., b. Dec. 10, 1820.
    4020. iii. CHARLES B., b. Apr. 15, 1822; d. Jan. 11, 1835.
    4021. iv.   HARRIETT M., b. Jan. 10, 1824; d. July 23, 1858.
    4022. v.   MARIA A., b. Dec. 13, 1825.

2350. LEVI FISK (Aaron, Asa, Nathaniel, Nathaniel, Nathan, Nathaniel, William, Robert, Simon, Simon, William, Symond), b. Chesterfield, N. H., July 23, 1793; m. there Mariam Bacon, b. Jan. 25, 1794; d. Aug., 1853. He was a farmer. He d. in Victor, De Kalb County, Ill., Aug., 1853; res. Chesterfield, N. H., and Martinsburg, N. Y.

    4023. i.   FOSTER A., b. Oct. 4, 1821; m. Harriett E. Bliss.
    4024. ii.   MARCIA M., b. Dec., 1815; m. ——— ———; she d. Feb. 10, 1886; a dau. is Adaline Ingersoll; res. Oswego County, N. Y.
    4025. iii. EUNICE BACON, b. Mar. 12, 1817; m. Apr., 1844, Thomas Esterbrook. He was a blacksmith. and d. in 1860. Ch.: 1, Julia, b. 1846; d. 1846. 2, Frances S., b. May 14, 1848; m. Frank Wilcox Sept. 25, 1873; res. Sandwich, De Kalb County, Ill.
    4026. iv.   ADALINE L., b. Dec. 20, 1821; m. Woodrough Hough; res. 303 Blue Island Ave., Chicago.
    4027. v.   ELIZABETH CAROLINE, b. Nov. 21, 1826; m. Nathaniel Smith; res. Aurora, Ill. Ch.: Eva M., Clara L., Mabelle, and Addie L., b. Oct. 11, 1863.
    4028. vi.   LAURA LYDIA, b. Apr., 1828; m. Oct. 28, 1847, Eli Merrit Kinne. He was b. Apr. 12, 1816; d. May 16, 1888; res. Storm Lake, Ia. Ch.: Palmer Fisk Kinne, b. Sept. 12, 1851; m. Sept. 19, 1874, and again in Dec., 1882; add. Storm Lake, Ia.
    4029. vii. NORMAN C., b. Nov. 3, 1824; d. Aug., 1852.
    4030. viii. MARY ANN, b. Dec. 30, 1819; d. May 4, 1836.
    4031. ix.   BRADLEY E., b. Mar. 3, 1832; d. Jan. 27, 1837.
    4032. x.   LEVI J., b. Mar. 26, 1834; d. Jan. 21, 1837.

2356.　AARON FISKE (Asa. Asa, Nathaniel, Nathaniel, Nathan, Nathaniel, Jeffrey, Robert, Simon. Simon. William. Symond). b. Holliston, 1777; m. Lucy Woods; res. Holliston, Mass.

4033.　i.　　ELIZA, b. ———; m. Lawson Amsdale; res. Milford, Mass. Ch.: 1, Harriett; 2, Caroline; 3, Herbert W.

4034.　ii.　　JONES, b. ———; m. Aseneth Thompson.

2357.　ASA FISKE (Asa. Asa, Nathaniel, Nathaniel, Nathan, Nathaniel, Jeffrey. Robert. Simon, Simon, William, Symond), b. Holliston, Mass., Feb. 18, 1779; m. in Holliston Susanna Partridge, b. Nov. 30, 1784; d. Nov., 1844; m. 2d, Ruth P. Leland. He was a farmer. He d. Oct. 29, 1853; res. Holliston, Mass.

4035.　i.　　PAMELIA, b. Aug. 22, 1805; d. in Holliston in 1842.

4036.　ii.　　FRANCIS, b. Feb. 26, 1807; m. Caroline Cooper and Anna A. Aldrich.

4037.　iii.　　CHRISTOPHER COLUMBUS, b. Aug. 26, 1809; d. unm. in 1835.

4038.　iv.　　SUSAN PARTRIDGE, b. Apr. 15, 1811; m. Nov. 20, 1833, Gilbert Dean Cooper; res. Charlestown, Mass. He was b. in Sutton, Mass., Sept. 13, 1808; d. in Northboro. July 4, 1887. He was in the real estate business. Ch.: 1, Ellen Francis, b. Dec. 30, 1835; m. June 23, 1864, Ezra Wood Chapin, b. June 7, 1836; he is a woolen manufacturer; ch.: Janet Chapin, b. May 28, 1870; m. Geo. B. Cutting, Dec. 19, 1894; add. Chapinville, Worcester County. 2, Charles Gilbert Cooper, b. in Boston June 27, 1840; d. in Boston Nov. 17, 1842. 3, Susan Lee Cooper, b. in Boston Nov. 20, 1843; m. George R. Kelso, Jan. 1, 1866; d. May 27, 1893. leaving two daus.: eldest Mrs. Will F. Ingraham; add. 47 High St., Charlestown, Mass. 4, Abner Gilbert Cooper, b. Charlestown, June 16, 1846; d. in Charlestown, Dec. 31, 1850.

4039.　v.　　JULIA A., b. Aug. 19, 1814; m. in 1841 John L. Hunt; res. Holl. He was a farmer, b. May 6, 1815; d. Dec., 1869. Ch.: 1, Amelia Jane, b. Sept. 7, 1842; m. ——— Travis, Nov. 28, 1868; res. Holliston, Mass. 2, Althea Maria, b. Sept., 1844; m. J. H. Dewing, Oct. 25, 1867; res. Holliston, Mass. 3, Geo. Lincoln, b. Nov. 22, 1850; m. ———: res. 307 Hennepin Ave., Minneapolis. Minn.

4040.　vi.　　ASA, b. Dec. 25, 1817; m. Pamelia Hollis.

2359.　MAJOR SAMUEL FISKE (Moses, Moses, Nathaniel, Nathaniel, Nathan, Nathaniel, William, Robert, Simon, Simon, William, Symond), b. Framingham. Mass., July 21, 1781; m. July 13, 1806, Nancy Stone, of Needham. She d. Feb. 22, 1863. He was a leading citizen; was deacon of the church, and major in the militia. Mr. Fiske was a man of marked character and clear intellect. He was chosen deacon Aug. 20, 1828. For many years he had charge of the Indians remaining in the town; was public spirited, and chosen to many positions of trust. He was benevolent and a wise counselor. His integrity was unquestioned. He lived the uneventful life of a New England farmer who slowly acquired a competence. For many years he was Town Clerk and Selectman, and for twenty-eight years Justice of the Peace. He d. Oct. 16, 1869; res. Natick. Mass.

4041.　i.　　CHARLES ELLIS, b. Oct. 12, 1807; m. Harriet Haven.

4042.　ii.　　EMILY, b. Sept. 22, 1810; m. Nov. 3, 1834, Rev. Samuel Lee, of Shelburne, Mass. He was b. Mar. 18, 1803, in Berlin, Conn. In 1836 Mr. Lee became pastor of the Congregational Church in New Ipswich, N. H. She d. Mar. 5, 1843. He d. Aug. 27, 1881. Ch.: Sarah Fiske, b. Sept. 14, 1838; res. New Ipswich, N. H.

2360.　MOSES FISK (Moses, Moses, Nathaniel, Nathaniel, Nathan, Nathaniel, William, Robert, Simon, Simon, William, Symond), b. Natick, Mass., Jan. 4, 1776; m. there, June 14, 1801, Sybil Jennison, of Natick, b. Mar. 18, 1776; d. Sept. 1, 1867. Moses Fisk was born in Natick. Mass. Their eight children all lived to celebrate their parents' golden wedding. On that occasion were present all the children, and all the grandchildren (about thirty). He died ten weeks thereafter of erysipelas, in the 76th year of his age. His wife lived to her 93d year. He followed farming all his life. He d. Aug. 22, 1851; res. Framingham and Natick, Mass.

4043.　i.　　EMERY, b. Feb. 27, 1803; m. Eunice Morse.
4044.　ii.　 MOSES, b. Nov. 29, 1804; m. Abigail T. Bryant and Aurelia Wight.
4045.　iii.　AARON, b. Nov. 29, 1804; m. Sally M. Mallery.
4046.　iv.　SALLY, b. Aug. 9, 1806; res. now in Natick.
4047.　v.　　ISAAC JENNISON, b. June 30, 1809, He was m. Nov. 4, 1834, to Lucretia Green; d. May 28, 1873, s. p.. He adopted a son, David Fuller; name changed to Fiske, who m. Dec. 21, 1856, Elizabeth W. Hammond; ch.: 1, Homer, b. in Wayland; m. Dec. 31, 1880, Alice Bird, of Natick. Isaac was a farmer in Natick.
4048.　vi.　ELBRIDGE, b. Sept. 22, 1811; m. Mary Thornton.
4049.　vii.　FRANKLIN, b. June 21, 1814; m. Chloe C. Stone.
4050.　viii.　LUCY, b. June 5, 1817; res. Natick, Mass.

2363.　WILLIAM FISKE (Moses, Moses, Nathaniel, Nathaniel, Nathan, Nathaniel, William, Robert, Simon, Simon, William, Symond), b. Needham, Mass., Nov. 6, 1783; m. at Natick, June 6, 1811, Jane Fariss, of Natick, b. Jan. 11, 1788; d. Feb. 9, 1865. He d. Apr. 18, 1864; res. Cambridge, Mass.

4051.　i.　　JANE ELIZABETH, b. Oct. 12, 1812; m. July 19, 1837, Rev. Charles S. Porter. She d. Dec. 7, 1843, s. p.
4052.　ii.　WM. PATESHALL, b. Dec. 23, 1813; m. Lucy Folsom.
4053.　iii.　ROB'T PATESHALL FARRIS, b. Nov. 17, 1815; d. Aug. 6, 1818.
4054.　iv.　HARRIETT MARIA, b. Oct. 22, 1817; d. June 5, 1818.
4055.　v.　　ROBERT FARRIS, b. May 5, 1819; m. Narcissa P. Whittemore.
4056.　vi.　SAMUEL AUGUSTUS, b. Mar. 26, 1821; m. at New York, June 5, 1851, Harriett Burger Bininger. He d. at Northampton, Mass., Nov. 16, 1884, s. p.; physician.
4057.　vii.　HORACE MOORE, b. Apr. 9, 1823; m. June 28, 1847, Susan W. Nichols. He d. Feb. 10, 1886. Ch.: 1, Charlotte Maria, b. Mar. 2, 1852; d. Oct. 24, 1852.
4058.　viii.　JAMES CHAPLIN, b. Aug. 2, 1825; m. Mary Grant Daniell.
4059.　ix.　LYMAN BEECHER, b. Sept. 6, 1827; d. unm., Apr. 30, 1853.
4060.　x.　　HARRIETT ANN, b. Oct. 4, 1829; d. Oct. 31, 1832.
4061.　xi.　HARRIETT ANN, b. Aug. 4, 1834; m. Sept. 5, 1860, Charles Mellen. She d. July 26, 1870. Ch.: 1, Charles P., b. Aug. 20, 1862; add. 100 Chauncey St., Boston, Mass. 2, Elizabeth Rollins, b. Feb. 9, 1864. 3, Herbert Farris, b. Dec. 8, 1866. 4, Susan Nichols, b. June 16, 1868. 5, William Fisk, b. July 10, 1870.

2368.　CALVIN FISKE (Joshua, Moses, Nathaniel, Nathaniel, Nathan, Nathaniel, William, Robert, Simon, Simon, William, Symond), b. Natick, Mass., Feb. 25, 1779; m. Sept. 18, 1809, Patty Pratt. She d. in Newton, Apr. 28, 1875. He was a farmer. He d. June 23, 1863; res. Needham, Mass.

4062.　iii.　DAVID, b. Oct. 31, 1810; m. Lucinda Austin.
4063.　iv.　MARTHA, b. June 13, 1812; m. Robert Prentice.
4064.　v.　　HANNAH, b. Dec. 21, 1813; d. unm., Mar. 15, 1835.
4065.　vi.　OLIVIA, b. Feb. 13, 1816; m. Dec. 22, 1836, Horatio Nelson Hyde; res. Newton. Mass. He was b. Jan. 26, 1814; d. Dec. 15, 1890. He was a merchant. Ch.: 1, Horatio Nelson Hyde, b. June 26, 1840; m. Anna Mary (Wills) Davis, 1876; son, Henry Nelson Hyde, b. Dec. 15, 1877; res. Newton. Mass. 2, Hosea Hyde, b. Oct. 4, 1842; m. Henrietta M. Beals; a dau., Andelia Elizabeth Hyde, b. Aug. 2, 1870; Newton. Mass. 3, Andelia Elizabeth Hyde, b. Sept, 14, 1844; d. May, 1869. 4, Sarah Fiske (Hyde) Ivy, b. Sept. 7, 1854; m. Jesse C. Ivy, July 28, 1881; son, Malcolm Hyde Ivy, b. Aug. 14, 1883; Mildred and Florence Ivy, b. Apr. 1, 1885; Ruth Ivy, b. June 26, 1892; P. O. Newton, Mass.
4066.　vii.　JOSEPH, b. Dec. 3, 1817; m. Mary Allen and Nancy A. Darling.

4067.   viii.   MEHITABLE, b. Nov. 21, 1819; m. Henry S. Stimson. She d. Aug. 9, 1882.

4068.   ix.   ELIZABETH S., b. June 16, 1821; m. ―――― Windgate. She d. Feb. 12, 1843.

4069.   x.   CAROLINE, b. Feb. 28, 1823; d. Oct. 16, 1823.

4070.   xi.   CAROLINE S., b. Aug. 16, 1824; m. Lucius Pinkham. She d. Dec. 18, 1890.

4071.   i.   IRENE F., b. July 25, 1826; m. Albert A. Conner. She d. in Newton, Mass., May 6, 1882.

4072.   ii.   ANDELIA, b. Oct. 26, 1828; d. Nov. 20, 1840.

4073.   xii.   SARAH B., b. Mar. 26, 1832.

4074.   xiii.   JOSHUA WILLARD, b. Jan. 10, 1835; m. Katie Murphy; res. Holliston.

2373.   ENOCH FISKE (Enoch, Moses, Nathaniel, Nathaniel, Nathan, Nathaniel, William, Robert, Simon, Simon, William, Symond), b. Needham, Mass, Jan. 28, 1781; m. there Grace Seaverns, b. 1781; d. Oct. 31, 1822. He d Sept. 10, 1827; res. Needham, Mass.

4075.   i.   AMANDA MALVINA, b. Jan. 2, 1806; m. Samuel Ayer. Ch.: Amanda V., b. 1836; res. Charlestown, Mass.

4076.   ii.   ADELINE MARY ANN, b. May 3, 1808; m. Asa Kingsbury. Ch.: 1, Charles H., b. 1831; d. 1842. 2, Amanda, b. 1833; res. Detroit, Mich.

2383.   DEA. JOHN FISKE (Elijah, Moses, Nathaniel, Nathaniel, Nathan, Nathaniel, William, Robert, Simon, Simon, William, Symond), b. Hillsboro, Aug. 19, 1789; m. July 5, 1812, Lucy Howe, dau. of Otis, of Hillsboro, d. Dec. 29, 1815; m. 2d, Dec. 31, 1820, Susan Craige, of Bradford, d. Sept. 10, 1873. He was born in Hillsboro, N. H. The year of his marriage his father deeded to him thirty acres of land, upon which the lower part of East Washington Village, N. H., was built. In 1812 he erected a house. In 1832 he moved away and resided elsewhere, until 1856, when he returned to Washington and resided until 1864. That year he moved with his sons to Webster, N. H., where he afterwards resided. He was an active member of the church for years and was deacon. He died in Webster, May 24, 1878; res. Washington, Bradford, and Webster, N. H.

4077.   i.   CALVIN, b. Apr. 26, 1813; d. Apr. 28, 1813.

4078.   ii.   LUTHER, b. Apr. 26, 1813; d. Apr. 26, 1813.

4079.   iii.   ELIZABETH BINNEY, b. May 22, 1814; m. Sept. 14, 1848, Alden Walker; res. Hillsboro. She d. there, June 6, 1850. Ch.: Wm. Eddy and Charles Edwin, twins, b. July 14, 1849; Wm. E. m. Jan. 20, 1882, Jane M. Mansfield, b. May 6, 1848. He is a salesman; res. 63 Pine Grove Ave., Lynn, Mass.; ch.: Marion Gerrish, b. Dec. 3, 1883; d. July 31, 1887; Eleanor Elizabeth, b. June 28, 1889. Charles E., m. Apr. 13, 1881, Josephine M. Gage, of Washington, N. H., who d. s. p., Jan. 9, 1894. He res. with his brother.

4080.   iv.   JOHN NEWTON, b. Nov. 2, 1821; m. Margaret M. Morse.

4081.   v.   LUCY HOWE, b. Sept. 15, 1815; m. Dec. 26, 1837, E. N. Gage. She d. Feb. 19, 1868. Ch.: 1, George N., b. Nov. 27, 1851; physician; res. E. Washington, N. H. 2, E. Franklin, b. Mar. 19, 1839; d. ――――. 3, Lucy Ann, b. Feb. 14, 1844.

4082.   vi.   CHARLES CALVIN, b. Apr. 10, 1823; d. Jan. 6, 1825.

4083.   vii.   MERCY GAVETT, b. Dec. 18, 1825; m. Oct. 9, 1853, James B. Goodhue; res. Webster, N. H. He was b. May 19, 1831; is a farmer. Ch.: 1, Charles Fuller Goodhue, b. Dec. 24, ―――― ; m. Sept. 1, 1883, Mattie George; res. Webster. 2, Gavnetta Maria Goodhue, b. May 1, 1859; m. Aug. 15, 1894, Harvey C. Sawyer; res. Munsonville, N. H. 3, Will Gould Goodhue, b. Aug. 2, 1861; m. Nov. 16, 1890, Nettie M. Sargent; res. Boscawen, N. H. 4, Senter Macurdy Goodhue, b. Dec. 18, 1865; m. June 2, 1892, Nellie A. Wright; res. Webster. 5, Forrest Gould Goodhue, b. June 23, 1869; d. Sept. 25, 1877.

4084.   viii.   FRIEND FULLER, b. Apr. 6, 1828; m. Jane B. Smith.

4085. ix. WM. TAYLOR, b. Mar. 19, 1830; unm.; res. Webster, N. H
4086. x. ANN MARIA J., b. Apr. 8, 1832. d. Nov. 30, 1842.
4087. xi. SUSAN CAROLINE, b. Sept. 16, 1834; d. Feb. 14, 1865.

2390. DAVID FISKE (David, John, John, Nathaniel, Nathan, Nathaniel, William, Robert, Simon, Simon, William, Symond), b. Holliston, Mass., Apr. 15, 1763; m. there Apr. 17, 1800, Hannah Eames, b. there Jan. 24, 1774; d. there Feb. 12, 1856. She was dau. of Lieut. Reuben Eames, of Revolutionary fame and direct descendant of Thomas Eames, of Dedham, who came to America as early as 1634. David Fiske, Jr., descended from good Puritan stock from three lines, Fiskes, Babcocks, Lelands, and was a noble speciman of manhood of the times; honorable, quiet, unassuming in his manners and dealings, and acquired property sufficient to purchase a large farm, and occupied and improved well. In the year 1815, there occurred a very severe storm of wind, very much like the western cyclones, but at that time such storms were unknown here, and never have occurred since. At that time there was a very great damage to buildings, orchards and forest trees. He was the owner of a large forest of pine, hemlock and other woods, which was destroyed and laid low; and this storm has always been designated by the men of those days as the Great Blow. In trying to recuperate his fallen fortunes he set himself to converting the fallen trees into lumber as speedily as possible, and thus overworked his natural strength and he died of typhoid fever at the age of 53 years. He d. May 24, 1816; res. Holliston, Mass.
4088. i. REUBEN E., b. Feb. 28, 1809; m. Betsey Plympton.
4089. ii. WILLIAM, b. Nov. 6, 1813; m. Rhoda Pike.
4090. iii. TIMOTHY, b. June 20, 1804; m. Lucretia Batchelder.
4091. iv. BETSEY, b. Aug. 23, 1801; m. Joseph P. Leland, and settled in Sherborn. Ch.: 1, Jane Maria, b. ———; m. Nathan Stearns, soldier in the Rebellion. 2, Gilbert Howard, a brave soldier; d. prisoner of war at Andersonville, N. C.
4092. v. HANNAH, b. July 8, 1806; m. John Coombs and res. in Sherborn.

2391. JOHN FISKE (David, John, John, Nathaniel, Nathan, Nathaniel, William, Robert, Simon, Simon, William, Symond), b. Holliston, Mass., Mar. 15, 1760; m. in Medway, Feb. 26, 1799, Abigail Albee, b. Medway; d. in 1849. He d. Dec. 16, 1833; res. Holliston, Mass.
4093. i. LOVETT, b. June 13, 1814; m. Alma R. Greenhalge.
4094. ii. HORACE, b. Sept. 2, 1800; m. Melissa Newton.
4095. iii. ANER, b. Feb. 16, 1804; m. Betsey Dix.
4096. iv. JOHN, b. July 25, 1806; m. Mary Rockwood.
4097. v. ABNER, b. Aug. 5, 1808; m. Lorinda Bellows.
4098. vi. SEWALL, b. Dec. 20, 1810; m. Angeline Bartlett, of Woonsocket, R. I. He d. s. p. Sept. 18, 1862.
4099. vii. NABBY, b. June 6, 1802; d. Feb. 17, 1803.

2392. NATHAN FISKE (David, John, John, Nathaniel, Nathan, Nathaniel, William, Robert, Simon, Simon, William, Symond), b. Sherborn, Mass., May 3, 1761; m. in Sherburne, June 1, 1786, Jemima Leland, b. 1762; d. 1789; m. 2d, Julia Daniels; res. Holliston, Mass.
4100. i. JEMIMA, b. 1788; m. Luke Daniels of Franklin, Mass. Ch.: 1, Jemima L., b. 1812; d. unm. 2, Charles, b. 1816; m. Eliza Phipps. 3, Eliza, b. 1821; m. Horace S. Morse; res. Franklin, Mass.
4101. ii. ISIAH DANIELS, b. 1791; res. Medway; d. s. p.
4102. iii HORATIO, b. 1794; m. Ellen Learned, Sally Learned and Elizabeth Adams.

2393. LEVI FISKE (David, John, John, Nathaniel, Nathan, Nathaniel, William, Robert, Simon, Simon, William, Symond), b. Holliston, Mass., Feb. 23, 1765; m. there, Jemima Underwood, b. 1773; d. Mar. 6, 1819. He d. June 20, 1819; res. Holliston, Mass.
4103. i. LEWIS, b. Feb., 1793; res. Lowell, Mass. Lewis Fiske, b. Feb., 1793, and his brother, Levi, both settled in Lowell. Lewis was employed many years in the carpet mills as superintendent; was

a very excellent business man; and Levi was in the Middlesex mills for many years; both married and had children of note and education, and some of them are now living in L.; while the original ones are dead. His children were Oliver, Amos, Charles and David; all dead but Oliver, who res. in Lowell, Mass.

4104. ii.   SALLY, b. Sept. 2, 1794.
4105. iii.   MARTIN, b. Oct. 23, 1796; m. Sophia Howe.
4106. iv.   ANNA, b. Dec. 24, 1798.
4107. v.   LEVI, b. ———; m. Margaret ———; res. Lowell.
4108. vi.   AMOS, b. Jan. 19, 1801; m. Sarah Waterman.
4109. vii.   JEMIMA, b. ———.

2394. NATHANIEL FISKE (David, John, John, Nathaniel, Nathan, Nathaniel, William, Robert, Simon, Simon, William, Symond), b. Holliston, Mass., Mar. 9, 1767; m. ——— Allen; res. Dover, Mass.

4110. i.   AMOS, b. Nov. 23, 1796; res. Prov. R. I.
4111. ii.   NATHANIEL, b. ———.
4112. iii.   NOAH, b. ———.

2399. TIMOTHY FISKE, A. M., M. D. (David, John, John, Nathaniel, Nathan, Nathaniel, William, Robert, Simon, Simon, William, Symond), b. Holliston, Mass., Nov. 3, 1778; m. Rhoda Daniels, b. July 19, 1780; d. Aug. 14, 1874. Rev. Abner Morse, A. M., in his history of inhabitants of the towns of Sherborn and Holliston, on page 86, writes as follows: Timothy Fisk, A. M., M. D., M. M. S. S., graduated from Harvard University 1801, subsequently studied medicine, settled in his native town and was her first regularly educated physician. His course from the first was marked with that modesty and gentlemanly bearing which cultivation insures, and which are equally removed from the swaggering pretensions of empiricism and the low and vile arts of rude and jealous rivalry. His skill was soon appreciated and his conduct rewarded in a wide practice. This he retained to the great advantage of the public, for a series of years, seldom attained by a laborious physician. He has long held a high reputation abroad, shared largely in the confidence of the faculty; ever maintained the strictest regard for moral virtue; and he cannot fail of being long remembered as the beloved physician. He had sons: 1, Frederick. 2, Ferdinand. He d. Dec. 17, 1863; res. Holliston, Mass.

4113. i.   FRANCIS FREDERICK, b. Mar. 9, 1805; m. ——— Lovering, dau. of Col. Wm. Lovering, of Holliston. He d. Oct. 12, 1871.
4114. ii.   FERDINAND, b. Oct. 20, 1806; m. Sarah A. Clark.
4115. iii.   DAVID D., b. July 3, 1808; d. May 27, 1824.
4116. iv.   EVELINE, b. June 20, 1810; d. Jan. 24, 1832.
4117. v.   RHODA D., b. May 31, 1814; d. Dec. 14, 1832.

2400. ANER FISKE (David, John, John, Nathaniel, Nathan, Nathaniel, William, Robert, Simon, Simon, William, Symond), b. Holliston, Mass., Sept. 20, 1780; m. there, Martha Fairbanks. Aner was one of the enterprising men of his day; excellent business man; superintendent and manufacturer of woolen goods in H., and accumulated a fair fortune. He was selected by the business men of Holliston, about the year 1820, to go to South America to look after some very important business, as their financial agent, which proved successful in the end. But not being accustomed to the living and climate, he sickened and died with fever in 1822. A noble man, beloved by all who knew him, his friends erected a marble monument to his memory in the Central Cemetery in Holliston. He d. in Santa Martha, South America, in 1822; res. Holliston, Mass.

2419. COL. NAT. FISKE (John, Isaac, John, Nathaniel, Nathan, Nathaniel, William, Robert, Simon, Simon, William, Symond), b. Fram., Aug. 12, 1772; m. in Needham, June 4, 1795, Catherine Slack, of Needham. He was born in Framingham, Mass., but soon after marriage moved to Westmoreland, N. H. During the war of 1812 he commanded a regiment of militia ordered to Portsmouth, and later moved back to Framingham. He died while on a visit to New Hampshire, Aug. 20, 1841; res. Westmoreland, N. H., and Framingham, Mass.

4118. i.   MARY P., b. ———; m. July 1, 1824, Peter Coolidge, of Fram., b. July 2, 1787; son of David of Wat. He had four children by his first wife. Ch.: 1, Catherine D., b. July 27, 1825; d. July 11, 1826. 2, Catherine F., b. July 9, 1828. 3, John Mayward, b. Nov. 2, 1834.

4119. ii. CATHERINE, b. ———; m. Dr. George F. Dunbar, of Westmoreland, N. H.; had four ch.; 1, Fisk D.

4120. iii. JOHN, b. ———; d. ac. 14.

4121. iv. WILLIAM, b. ———; m. Susan F. Manson, of Framingham; res. Buffalo, N. Y.: had three sons.

4122. v. MARTHA, b. ———; m. Henry Parker, of Fram., and had ch.: 1, William F., and 2, Florence D.

2420. THOMAS FISK (John, Isaac, John, Nathaniel, Nathan, Nathaniel, William, Robert, Simon, Simon, William, Symond), b. Framingham, Mass., Mar. 22, 1774; m. in Westmoreland, N. H., Lucinda Trowbridge, of Pomfret, Conn., b. 1782; d. in Chesterfield, N. H., Apr. 14, 1869. In 1807 he went to Chesterfield and settled on the farm now owned and occupied by his son, John B. Fisk, Esq., building the large house in which the latter now lives. When about 2 years old he had an attack of scarlet fever, which caused him to be deaf, and, consequently, dumb. He learned, nevertheless, to read and cipher in the four fundamental rules of arithmetic. At the age of 50 years he was admitted to the school for deaf mutes at Hartford, Conn., for the term of one year. He made rapid progress and acquired knowledge that was of great use to him during the remaining years of his life. He d. July 25, 1861: res. Chesterfield, N. H.

4123. i. THOMAS T., b. Nov. 27, 1806; m. Emily H. Hildreth and Mrs. Adeline Goodnow.

4124. ii. LUCINDA D., b. Mar. 14, 1809; m. 1830, Nathaniel Hildreth, Jr. Ch.: ———, b. ———; m. Lucius Luddington; res. East Pearl St., New Haven, Conn.

4125. iii. MARY ANN B., b. June 28, 1814; m. Jan. 12, 1837, Hosea N. Newton; res. Keota, Ia., b. Feb. 18, 1814; d. Oct. 10, 1883. She d. Dec. 6, 1880. Ch.: 1, Hanno Prentice, b. Sept. 17, 1838: res. Keota, Ia.; he is secretary of the Farmers' Pioneer Mutual Insurance Association there. 2, a daughter, ———; d. in 1848.

4126. iv. JOHN B., b. Apr. 10, 1816: m. Arabell Robertson and Elizabeth A. (Chandler) Pierce.

2429. GEORGE B. FISKE (John, Isaac, John, Nathaniel, Nathan, Nathaniel, William, Robert, Simon, Simon, William, Symond), b. Sept. 23, 1793; m. Mrs. Honora Bolton, b. in the West Indies. George B. Fisk went to Georgia; m. Wid. Honora Bolton, in Brooklyn, N. Y.; was president of the Long Island Railroad at the time of his death. Res. Brooklyn, N. Y.

2431. MARTIN FISKE (Richard, Isaac, John, Nathaniel, Nathan, Nathaniel, William, Robert, Simon, Simon, William, Symond), b. Fram., Apr. 8, 1774; m. ——— Gilbert. He was a merchant; res. Norfolk, Va.

4127. i. DANIEL, b. ———.

4128. ii. MARY, b. ———.

4129. iii. GEORGE, b. ———.

2435. RICHARD FISKE (Richard, Isaac, John, Nathaniel, Nathan, Nathaniel, William, Robert, Simon, Simon, William, Symond), b. Fram. Jan. 29, 1783; m. Mrs. Elizabeth (Lampry) Lowell, of Kensington, N. H.; res. ———.

4130. i. HARRIET, b. ———; m. Elias Grout, of Fram.

4131. ii. SARAH, b. ———; m. David Fiske (her cousin).

4132. iii. RICHARD, b. ———.

2437. JOSIAH FISKE (Richard, Isaac, John, Nathaniel, Nathan, Nathaniel, William, Robert, Simon, Simon, William, Symond), b. Feb. 22, 1785; m. Martha Coolidge, b. July 23, 1789; dau. of Joel, of Fram. He d. May 3, 1832; res. Framingham, Mass.

4133. i. CAROLINE, b. ———; m. Albert Ballard.

4134. ii. DAVID, b. ———; m. Sarah Fiske.

4135. iii. MARTHA, b. ———; unm.

26

2439. DR. WILLIAM THURSTON FISKE (Daniel, Isaac, John, Nathaniel, Nathan, Nathaniel, William, Robert, Simon, Simon, William, Symond), b. Oxford, Mass., July 6, 1778; m. there, Nov. 1, 1801, Alice Hudson, dau. of Wm. and Ruth, b. Sept. 8, 1776; d. Nov. 10, 1827; m. 2d, Betsey Hudson, sister of first wife, b. Mar. 27, 1791; d. Mar. 27, 1863. He was born in Oxford, Mass.; was educated at the public schools; studied medicine with his father, and began the practice of his profession there. He was a prominent citizen, and for several years kept a general store in company with his brother-in-law, Amos Hudson; was a leading man in the Central Mfg. Co., and resided in Oxford, near his father. In 1820 he moved to Ellisburg, N. Y., where he continued to practice his profession. He died in Fulton, N. Y., Dec. 12, 1842; res. Oxford, Mass., and Fulton and Ellisburg, N. Y.

4136. i.   DANIEL H., b. Aug. 13, 1802; m. Caroline Willard.
4137. ii.   ABIJAH, b. 1804; d. infancy.
4138. iii. WILLIAM H., b. Nov. 4, 1805; m. May, 1830, Mary Stearns. He was a physician and d. s. p., Apr. 5, 1835.
4139. iv.   SOPHIA, b. Jan. 13, 1808; m. Nov. 9, 1835, John Shaw. He was a merchant at Ellisburg, Ia.; d. at Maquoketa, Aug., 1853, to which place they moved in 1849. She d. in 1886. Ch.: 1, Sophia F., b. 1836; m. 1870, Joseph Kelso, judge and banker; res. Bellevue, Ia.; three ch.: Carrie, Joseph and Jennie. 2, Laura, b. 1841; m. 1873, James C. Brocksmit; res. Cedar Rapids, Ia., 828 Second Ave.; three ch.: Eugenie, Helen and John. 3, Carrie E., b. 1844; m. 1873, Dr. W. H. C. Moore; res. Essex, Ia.; six ch.: Lilian, Austin, Roy, Charles, Lawrence and Bernard. 4, Mary C., b. 1848; res. Maquoketa, Ia.; unm. 5, Austin Fiske, b. ———; m. Isadore Roy; res. Vinton, Ia.; ch.: John Austin and Guy Roy.
4140. v.   CYNTHIA, b. Dec. 6, 1810; m. Jan. 26, 1843, Dr. Charles W. Eastman. He d. in 1880. During the war he was a hospital surgeon. She d. in 1885, in Sterling, Ill. Ch.: 1, William F., b. Nov. 11, 1844; m. June 18, 1872, Frances Adams, d. Feb. 22, 1876; m. 2d, June 8, 1880, at Byron, Ill., Myra F. Christopher; ch.: 1, Cynthia Louise, b. Oct. 28, 1886; res. Moline, Ill.; he was b. in Ellisburg, N. Y.; graduated at Union Academy, Belleville, N. Y., in 1863, at Union College, Schnectady, N. Y., 1866; taught school in Iowa and Illinois till 1872; owned and edited Red Oak (Iowa) Express, Apr., 1872, to Nov., 1872; half owner and one of the editors of Sterling (Ill.) Gazette, Jan., 1873, to Sept. 1882, went to Huron, Dak., in 1882; editor Farmers' Budget, Sterling, Ill., 1886 and 1887; Western Plowman, Moline, Ill., 1889 to 1890; half owner and editor Daily and Weekly Dispatch, Moline, since Nov., 1890.
4141. vi.   LAURA, b. July 22, 1813; m. Nov. 9, 1842, Nathaniel White, of Ellisburg. He was b. Sept. 24, 1797; d. Oct. 9, 1865; was a merchant. She res. 828 Second Ave., Cedar Rapids, Ia.; s. p.
4142. vii. AUSTIN THURSTON, b. Nov. 16, 1818; m. at Ellisburg, N. Y. Sept. 9, 1850, Mary R. Myres. He d. in Syracuse, N. Y., s. p., Oct. 11, 1863. She m. 2d, John Maner, of Manersville, N. Y., and d. Aug., 1895.
4143. viii. WILBUR HENRY, b. July 21, 1832; m. Myra Shaw.

2446. ISAAC FISKE (Moses, Isaac, John, Nathaniel, Nathan, Nathaniel, William, Robert, Simon, Simon, William, Symond), b. May 26, 1782; m. in 1806, at Nashville, Tenn., Betsey Johnson, of Nashville, b. 1784. She d. in Framingham, Mass., Apr. 12, 1853. Isaac Fisk was a civil engineer in early life, later on a soap manufacturer; was at one time one of the Selectmen of Framingham. He d. in Fram., Dec. 3, 1846; res. Nashville, Tenn., and Framingham, Mass.

4144. i.   MOSES M., b. Aug. 30, 1807; m. Harriett Herring.
4145. ii.   OLIVER J., b. Jan. 24, 1809; m. Louisa Brown.
4146. iii. CHARLES C., b. ———; m. Lucy Frost, of Framingham, Mass.
4147. iv.   THOMAS, b. ———; m. Harriet Adams.
4148. v.   EBENEZER W., b. Oct. 22, 1819; m. Caroline M. Smith.

2451. EBENEZER FISKE (Moses, Isaac, John, Nathaniel, Nathan, Nathaniel, William, Robert, Simon, Simon, William, Symond), b. June 5, 1793; m. Emily Willard, of Boston. He died on the passage from New Orleans; was a merchant. He d. 1831; res. New Orleans, La.

2460. DR. JAMES FISKE (John, Peter, John, Nathaniel, Nathan, Nathaniel, William, Robert, Simon, Simon, William, Symond), b. New Braintree, Mass, 1814; m. May 17, 1837, Mary Godfrey, b. Oct. 12, 1816; d. in Princeton, Kan., Nov. 22, 1878. James Fiske, M. D., youngest child of Rev. John, D. D., and Betsey, alias Elizabeth (Mellen) Fiske, b. in New Braintree (where his father was a venerated pastor for half a century), 1814; grad. from Dartmouth College, or certainly from the medical school therewith connected, Hanover, N. H., about the year 1835; came to Mil. soon afterwards, and commenced the practice of medicine with fair success; m. Mary Godfrey, dau. of William and Nancy (Stearns) Godfrey, by Rev. D. Long.

Dr. Fiske fell an early victim of consumption at the outset of a promising career. He d. here, July 1, 1843, ae. 29 years. His worthy consort was spared to see her two children well started in connubial and business life. She lived in exemplary widowhood over twenty-five years, and d. quite suddenly at last of typhoid fever, in Princeton, Kan., Nov. 22, 1878. Her son, Edward W., is engaged in the cattle raising business in Kansas. He m. a lady b. in the State of Delaware; and they have one daughter, named after his mother, Mary Godfrey. (History Milford, Mass.) He d. July 1, 1843; res. Milford, Mass.

4149. i. ELIZABETH R., b. Milford, Dec. 18, 1838; m. Major Samuel P. Lee.

4150. ii. EDWARD W., b. Milford, Aug. 29, 1841; m. Annie D. Lathrope; res. Kansas. One ch.: Mary Godfrey.

2461. LEVI W. FISK (Parker, Asa, Bezaleel, Jonathan, David, David, David, Jeffrey, Robert, Simon, Simon, William, Symond), b. Dublin, N. H., Apr. 29, 1825; m. there, Feb. 26, 1857, Sarah J. White, b. Aug. 16, 1824; d. Oct. 7, 1885. He was a farmer. He d. May 27, 1887; res. Dublin, and Harrisville, N. H.

4151. i. FRANK P., b. May 31, 1858; m. Hannah M. Spofford.
4152. ii. FANNIE W., b. May 27, 1862; d. Nov. 21, 1881.

2466. HON. WARREN L. FISKE (Daniel, Asa, Bezaleel, Jonathan, David, David, David, Jeffrey, Robert, Simon, Simon, William, Symond), b. Dublin, N. H., Mar. 12, 1826; m. Faribault, Minn., July 9, 1857, Emily M. Mathews, b. Aug. 8, 1835. Warren L. Fiske, son of Daniel Fiske, was born in Dublin, N. H., Mar. 12, 1826, and after receiving the advantages of the common schools and high school of Dublin, attended three terms of the Hancock Literary and Scientific Institution, prepared himself as a school teacher, which occupation he followed nine years. July 9, 1857, he married Emily M. Mathews, of Faribault, Minn., and since then has resided in Dublin. Has been a member of the New Hampshire Legislature, a Justice of the Peace, clerk of the Unitarian Society twenty-five years, and has held other important offices, and is now serving his thirty-fifth year as town clerk and town treasurer of his native town; res. Dublin, N. H.

HON. WARREN L. FISKE.

4153. i. CLARENCE L., b. Mar. 8, 1860; d. Apr. 9, 1864.

4154. ii. WILFRED M., b. Dec. 27, 1863; m. Mabel J. Carey, Oct. 20, 1887.

4155. iii. IDELLA M., b. May 6, 1868; m. Hiram A. Carey, May 9, 1888.

4156.   iv.   HENRY F., b. Apr. 28, 1870.
4157.   v.   HERBERT L., b. Dec. 12, 1871; m. Mar. 11, 1896, Hattie B.
                Lewis.
4158.   vi.   ALBERT P., b. Feb. 24, 1877.

2469. CHARLES W. FISKE (Daniel, Asa, Bezaleel, Jonathan, David,
David, David, Jeffrey, Robert, Simon, Simon, William, Symond), b. Dublin, N. H.,
June 14, 1833; m. at Lynn, Mass., Nov. 21, 1864, Mary L. Frasier, b. Nov. 18, 1846.
He is a gardener; res. Monadnock, N. H.
      4159.   i.   FLORA M., b. June 2, 1865; m. Nov. 7, 1889, L. H. Rabone; res.
                     209 Ash St., Waltham.
      4160.   ii.   FRANCIS D., b. Oct. 14, 1866; d. Feb. 12, 1867.
      4161.   iii. LESTER A., b. July 28, 1868; m. Jan. 17, 1895; Boston, Mass.
      4162.   iv.   ALICE M., b. Dec. 29, 1869; d. Aug. 13, 1871.
      4163.   v.   ERNEST L., b. Dec. 23, 1871; m. Jan. 18, 1893; Wall, Pa.
      4164.   vi.   CARROLL E., b. Sept. 16, 1873; d. Jan. 19, 1888.
      4165.   vii. EDNA C., b. Nov. 23, 1877.
      4166.   viii. MERTON C., b. Aug. 13, 1879.

2470. EDWARD RICE FISKE (Bezaleel, Nahum, Bezaleel, Jonathan,
David, David, David, Jeffrey, Robert, Simon, Simon, William, Symond), b. Holden,
Mass., Aug. 31, 1822; m. at Worcester, June 20, 1844, Rebecca Haskell Sumner, b.
Apr. 20, 1825; d. Aug. 18, 1883.   Edward R. Fiske was a printer and publisher of
assured position in Worcester, one of the oldest in the city, and once a prominent
newspaper man.   He was born in Holden, Worcester county, Mass., and spent
his boyhood there.   In Oct., 1837, he came to Worcester, and commenced working at the printer's trade with Mirick & Bartlett, on the Worcester Palladium and
Worcester Republican, the latter being afterward merged in the Palladium.   The
papers were published in the Central Exchange.   In May, 1841, Mr. Fiske formed
a partnership with Samuel D. Church, and in connection with job printing, published the Worcester Waterfall, a temperance paper, afterward burned in the
fire of the Central Exchange, 1843.   After the fire, Church & Fiske having sold
the Waterfall, printed the Palladium in the Central Exchange, which was rebuilt.
From this time until 1851 he spent a few months printing the State Sentinel, a year
as bookkeeper in Clinton, and the remainder of the time as bookkeeper in the
office of the Worcester Spy.   In 1851 he began business as a book and job printer
in Flagg's block, opposite the Bay State House, and was burned out there in
1853.   In Apr., 1855, he purchased the daily and weekly Transcript, with Werden
Reynolds, which they published for one year.   From this time until his death he
continued uninterruptedly the book and job printing business, publishing in
connection with it the Worcester Daily Press, from Apr., 1873, to Dec., 1874, when,
on account of ill health he relinquished his interest in the Press to his partner,
J. A. Spalding.   His printing office was widely known as "The Franklin Printing
Office."   Mr. Fiske was a member of All Saints' (Episcopal) Church, and was at
one time largely identified with its interests.   He was a member of the vestry for
nine years, from 1870 to 1879, being its clerk in 1870.   He was also
active in the Sunday school, serving as superintendent for awhile.   He
was a member of the City Council for two years, 1872 and 1873; of
Montacute Lodge A. F. & A. M.; and of the Worcester Typothetae, the organization of master printers of the city of Worcester.   He was in ill health for some
months before his death, which occurred at Mt. Holyoke, Northampton, Mass.,
June 29, 1891.   On June 20, 1844, he married Rebecca Haskell Sumner, of Beverly,
Mass., who died Aug. 18, 1883.   He d. June 29, 1891; res. Worcester, Mass.
      4167.   i.   EDWARD SUMNER, b. Sept. 23, 1845; m. Nettie Gray Smock.
      4168.   ii.   SARAH ELIZABETH WOODS, b. Jan. 28, 1848; d. Aug. 1,
                     1848.
      4169.   iii. ELLA MARIA, b. Feb. 24, 1849; m. Nov. 17, 1870, Benjamin M.
                     Pevey.   She d. Oct. 15, 1871.   Ch.: 1, Franklin Fiske, b. Aug.
                     22, 1871; d. Sept. 21, 1871; res. Worcester.
      4170.   iv.   ELIZABETH GERTRUDE, b. Oct. 20, 1855; unm; 67 Chatham
                     St.
      4171.   v.   CHARLES WALDO, b. Jan. 23, 1859; m. Martha L. Gunderson.

2471. ISAAC FISKE (Bezaleel, Nahum, Bezaleel, Jonathan, David, David, David, Jeffrey, Robert, Simon, Simon, William, Symond), b. Holden, Mass., Oct. 23, 1820; m. Dec. 11, 1844, Clara Maria Wood, of Westboro, b. Aug. 12, 1823. He was a manufacturer of band instruments. He d. Sept. 17, 1894; res. Holden, Mass.

    4172. i.   MABEL ESTELLA, b. Aug. 1, 1860; m. Jan. 12, 1892, Albert E. Hall; res. 324 Pleasant St., Worcester, Mass., s. p. He was b. June 11, 1855.

    4173. ii. ADELIZA MARIA, b. Oct. 25, 1850; d. Nov. 6, 1856.

    4174. iii. MARION LOUISE, b. Sept. 22, 1853; m. Oct. 21, 1873, Frank Waldo Bemis, of Spencer, b. May 8, 1848. Ch.: 1, Harry Fiske, b. Aug. 6, 1880; res. 97 Piedmont St., Worcester.

    4175. iv. ALICE MARIA, b. Feb. 13, 1864; d. May 8, 1864.

    4176. v.   NELLIE GERTRUDE, b. Aug. 27, 1867; m. Aug. 6, 1892, Edward D. Landry, of Plattsburg, N. Y., b. July 3, 1865. Ch.: 1, Kenneth Wood, b. Aug. 24, 1893. 2, Earl Fiske, b. Sept. 26, 1894; res. 97 Piedmont St., Worcester.

2495. CAPT. ALONZO WILLIAMS FISKE (Samuel, Samuel, Jonathan, David, David, David, Jeffrey, Robert, Simon, Simon, William, Symond), b. New York City, Mar. 31, 1842; m. in Brooklyn, July 24, 1861, Martha E. Crispin, b. Nov. 11, 1840. He was born in New York City; graduated from Henry St. public school, New York City; served four years in the late war, from June, 1861, to July, 1865, as private and Sergeant in Company C., Sixty-fifth New York Volunteers, and as Lieutenant and Captain of Company C., One Hundred and Twenty-seventh New York Volunteers; was severely wounded in forehead; lost sight of right eye at battle of Deveaux Neck, S. C., Dec. 6, 1864; was connected with the police department of New York City and Brooklyn, from 1865 to 1885, since that time has been in the employ of the Williamsburg Savings Bank, of Brooklyn, N. Y.; res. Brooklyn, N. Y., and Rockville Centre, L. I.

    4177. i.   ALONZO W., b. Apr. 30, 1866; m. Mamie I. Smith.

    4178. ii. ALFRED NELSON, b. Jan. 16, 1868; d. ———.

    4179. iii. CHARLES, b. Oct. 29, 1869; d. ———.

    4180. iv. FLORENCE A., b. Nov. 21, 1871; res. Rockville Centre.

    4181. v.   SAMUEL R., b. Oct. 28, 1873; res. Rockville Centre.

    4182. vi. ALBERT GIRDLER, b. Nov. 5, 1875; d. ———.

    4183. vii. MARTHA E., b. Dec. 27, 1877; d. ———.

    4184. viii. LEWIS ELMER, b. July 7, 1881; res. Rockville Centre, L. I.

2501. FREDERICK LINCOLN FISKE (Levi, Samuel, Samuel, Jonathan, David, David, David, Jeffrey, Robert, Simon, Simon, William, Symond), b. Boston, Mass., May 28, 1843; m. at Cambridge, Nov. 17, 1869, Sarah Elizabeth Balch, b. at Lynn, Jan. 1, 1844. He is a clerk; res. Everett, Mass., 7 Pleasant St.

    4185. i.   WM. LINCOLN, b. Jan. 29, 1873; m. Sept. 9, 1894, Clara E. Deihl; res. Everett, Mass., Ferry St., s. p.

    4186. ii. GEO. FRED, b. Sept. 18, 1877; unm., res. Everett, is a clerk in Boston.

2502. DR. ROBERT WILSON FISK (Abraham, Robert, Robert, Robert, David, David, Jeffrey, Robert, Simon, Simon, William, Symond), b. Dutchess Co., N. Y. July 14, 1807; m. in Cincinnati, O., Aug. 17, 1834, Mary Orpha Ransome, b. Oct. 29, 1817; d. Feb. 10, 1859; m. 2d, Rachel ———. She now res. in San Antonio, Tex. Poverty embarrassed the early aspirations of Dr. Robert Wilson Fisk, but industry and frugality kept pace with his ambition. He educated himself, studied medicine, and became a prominent and successful physician in Ripley Co., Indiana. In 1857 was elected to the State Senate on the Democratic ticket. In 1860 he moved with his family to Olney, Ill., where he died July 22, 1874; res. Old Milan, Ind., and Olney, Ill.

    4187. i.   FRANCIS HOSEA, b. Jan. 15, 1836; m. Mrs. Lizzie E. (Heasht) Witcher.

    4188. ii. RODMAN NORTH, b. May 15, 1848; m. and res. Grand Island, Neb.

    4189. iii. REDFORD WALKER, b. June 20, 1846. Redford W. Fisk was apprenticed to learn the carpenter's trade at the age of 14.

When the call for volunteers was made in 1863 he was one of the first to enlist in Company E., Fifth Illionis Volunteer Cavalry, and served until the close of the war. Returning home with honors, he worked at his trade and studied medicine, believing that he was better fitted for the latter vocation in life. In 1871 he began the practice of medicine at Springfield, Mo., under the able tutorship of his brother, Francis H. Fisk, M. D. In 1873 he returned to Olney, Ill., to assist his father, whose health was rapidly declining. After his father's death, which sad event occurred July 22, 1874, he took up the entire practice, continuing successfully until 1878, when, feeling that the invigorating gulf breeze of the southwest would rebuild his overtaxed constitution, he decided to move to Texas, since which time he has devoted his exclusive attention to the study and treatment of nervous diseases of men and women, building up an enviable reputation over his competitors, and today Dr. R. W. Fisk stands pre-eminently at the head of his well chosen profession in the special branches he has outlined. The Fort Worth (Texas) Gazette, says editorially: "Dr. R. W. Fisk.—This distinguished physician, located permanently in Fort Worth about three years ago, and has built up an enviable reputation in the treatment and cure of chronic nervous diseases of men and women and catarrh. His success has been marvelous in curing diseases that baffled the skill of the best physicians in our city or State. Hundreds in this and adjoining States who have been cured by this skillful physician will long sing his praises. Dr. Fisk is an affable gentleman, modest and unassuming for one of his ability and attainments. In his relations with all with whom he comes in contact he is uniformly courteous and kind. Dr. Fisk has cured many who were without hope, languishing on the bed with disease that baffled the most learned physicians. Under his treatment they improve, as if by the magical touch of one inspired. Dr. Fisk has carried sunshine and gladness into many households where once the dark gloom of disease enshrouded the hearthstone. Many friends and patients join in their approving voice to swell the grand chorus that goes up from all over the land in his praise and honor. May he live long to do much good for his skill is marvelous."

4190. iv.   MARY ELIZABETH, b. Feb. 29, 1844; m. Mar. 11, 1862, Wm. H. Gunn; res. Emporia, Kan. He was b. Oct. 7, 1839; is a farmer and stockman. Ch.: Robert West Gunn, b. Dec. 31, 1862; d. July 28, 1864. Perlie Wilbur Gunn; b. Jan. 1, 1866; think he was lost in the South Sea in 1889. George Rodman Gunn, b. Feb. 24, 1870; d. Feb. 3, 1891. Olive Snow Gunn, b. Feb. 26, 1870; d. May 19, 1874. Hattie Cy Belle Gunn, b. May 26, 1874; res. Sylvan St., Emporia Kan. All born in Olney.

4191. v.   ROBERT WEST, b. Jan. 8, 1838; d. Mar. 8, 1858.
4192. vi.   HIRAM RIPLEY, b. Sept. 4, 1841; d. Apr. 10, 1859.

2507.   COL. JAMES FISK (Henry A., Robert, Robert, Robert, David, David, Jeffrey, Robert, Simon, Simon, William, Symond), b. Virginia Jan. 5, 1807; m. in Montgomery Co., Ky., in 1825, Casander Frakes, d. 1837; m. 2d, in Putnam Co., Ind., Sept. 15, 1839, Camilla Catherine Clover, b. Oct. 11, 1817; d. Aug. 10, 1878. He is a farmer; res Greencastle, Ind.

4193. i.   JAMES WM., b. July 10, 1834; m. Sarah J. Dodd.
4194. ii.   ROBT. W., b. Jan. 13, 1838; res. Tascola, Ill.
4195. iii. RICHARD S., b. Sept. 12, 1841; m. Mary M. Wood.
4196. iv.   WILBUR W., b. Jan. 1, 1857; res. Kansas City, Mo.
4197. v.   JAMES L., b. Dec. 24, 1858; res. Greencastle, Ind.
4198. vi.   LOUISA HANNAH, b. July 29, 1828; m. —— Soper; res, Leon, Iowa.

4199. vii. SOPHRONIA E., b. Aug. 23, 1848; m. Wm. E. Starr; res. Greencastle. Ind.

4200. viii. CAMILLA C., b. Aug. 13, 1850; m. ——— Falls; res. Altoona,
Kan.

4201. ix. DEMARIUS R., b. Oct. 31, 1853; m. ——— Armstrong; res.
Ladoga, Ind.

4202. x. FIDELIA, b. June 2, 1867; m. ——— Barrier; res. New Market, O.

4203. xi. FRANCIS M., b. Mar. 30, 1843; m. Mary C. Matkin.

4204. xii. MARTHA ANN, b. Oct. 16, 1826; m. ——— Clover.

4205. xiii. PHEBE, b. Apr. 1, 1836; m. ——— Layton. She d. ———. Her
dau. is Mrs. Cassie Warrington, High Point, Ia.

4206. xiv. SARAH ELIZABETH, b. Sept. 2, 1836: d. s. p.

4207. xv. JOHN HENRY, b. Nov. 15, 1829; d. s. p.

4208. xvi. MARGARET, b. ———; s. p.

4209. xvii. MANDY ANN, b. Jan. 27, 1845; d. s. p.

4210. xviii. ALBERT W., b. Oct. 2, 1846; d. s. p.

4211. xix. JOSEPHINE, b. July 22, 1852; d. s. p.

2508. REV. WILEY BENNINGTON FISK (Henry A., Robert, Robert,
Robert, David, David, Jeffrey, Robert, Simon, Simon, William, Symond), b. in
Ky., Oct. 24, 1819; m. in Montgomery Co., Ky., Julia Ann Spratt, dau. of An-
drew, b. July 3, 1818; d. Oct. 8, 1854; m. 2d, June 22, 1855, Malinda Lasswell, b.
Aug. 25, 1834. He is a clergyman. Res. Bannoch, Kan.

4212. i. MARY E., b. Aug. 6, 1836; m. ——— St. John; res. Arroyo
Grande, Cal.; d. ———.

4213. ii. JOHN R., b. Sept. 15, 1839; m. Emily Walters and Julia A. Colliver.

4214. iii. WILEY R., b. ———; res. Bannoch, Edwards Co., Kan.

4215. iv. JAMES F., b. Dec. ———; d. ———.

4216. v. JULIA ANN, b. 1852; d. ———.

4217. vi. MARTHA KATHERINE, b. 1855; d. ———.

4218. vii. HENRY ANDREW, b. 1857; res. Oklahoma.

4219. viii. LEVINA JANE, b. in Ky. in 1859; m. in Dayton, Mo., Lafayette
Warner; res. Coffeyville. Kan. He was b. Syracuse, N. Y.,
in 1843: is a farmer. Ch.: Alice Warner, b. in Mo., 1880.
George Warner, b. in Mo., 1882. Frederick Warner, b. in Mo.,
1884. Andy Warner, b. in Kansas, 1887. Nora Warner, b.
in Kansas, 1890; d. ———. Walter Warner, b. in Kansas, 1894.

4220. ix. FRANCIS MARION, b. Dec. 3, 1856; res. Coffeyville, Kan.

4221. x. FRANK BELLIE, b. Oct. 24, 1862; m. Caroline Lasswell.

4222. xi. COLLINS M., b. ———; res. Arroyo Grande, Cal.

4223. xii. GEORGE WALKER, b. Sept. 25, 1858; res. Watsonville, Cal.;
m. July 8, 1886, Lizzie Castee, b. Apr. 1, 1866. Is a policeman.
Ch.: Leroy Fisk, b. May 3, 1887. Frank Leslie, b. Oct. 16,
1889. Grace Benella, b. Jan. 6, 1895.

4224. xiii. CHARLES LILLIE, b. ———; res. Arroyo Grande, Cal.

2515. ELIJAH PIERCE FISK (John, David, Robert, Robert, David, David,
Jeffrey, Robert, Simon, Simon, William, Symond), b. Woburn, Mass., Aug. 25,
1814; m. in Boston, Sept. 19, 1839, Elizabeth Newell Fisk, b. Oct. 4, 1818; res.
Boston (his cousin). He was a merchant; went to Boston when young, and was
a very successful business man. He d. Nov. 3, 1859; res. 39 Bowdoin St., Boston,
Mass.

4225. i. MARCUS M., b. Apr. 1, 1842; m. ——— ———.

2521. JOHN WARREN FISK (John, David, Robert, Robert, David, David,
Jeffrey, Robert, Simon, Simon, William, Symond). b. Woburn, Mass., Oct. 20,
1827; m. in Boston, Oct. 17, 1859, Anna Elizabeth Peates, b. Oct. 17, 1837. He was
a merchant tailor. He d. Feb. 3, 1887; res. 306 Shawmut Ave.. Boston, Mass.

4226. ii. ANNIE HOLDEN, b. Sept. 20, 1869; res. at home.

4227. i. EDITH CUSHING, b. Jan. 4, 1868; d. Aug. 4, 1868.

2522. DAVID BRAINERD FISK (John, David, Robert, Robert, David, David, Jeffrey, Robert, Simon, Simon, William, Symond), b. Woburn, Mass., Feb. 19, 1830; m. ———— ————; res. Boston, Mass.

    4228. i.   DELIA, b. ————.
    4229. ii.   KITTY, b. ————.

2523. JOSEPH ALEXANDER FISKE (Joseph, Joseph, Joseph, Robert, David, David, Jeffrey, Robert, Simon, Simon, William, Symond), b. Lex., Mar. 8, 1830; m. Love Langdon Dodge, of Methuen; res. Lawrence and Lynn, Mass.

    4230. i.   CLARENCE ELLSWORTH, b. 1860; res. Manchester, N. H.
    4231. ii.   MARY ETTA, b. Apr. 2, 1856.
    4232. iii. LEOLA ALFARRETT, b. 1866.

2524. TIMOTHY KENNARD FISKE (Joseph, Joseph, Joseph, Robert, David, David, Jeffrey, Robert, Simon, Simon, William, Symond), b. Lex., Aug. 5, 1833; m. there Dec. 25, 1857, Barbara Peters, b. Nov. 2, 1834. He is a house painter; res. Lexington, Mass.

    4233. i.   WILLIAM E., b. Nov. 11, 1858; unm.
    4234. ii.   ANNIE L., b. Dec. 11, 1859.
    4235. iii. GEORGIE L., b. July 29, 1862; m. Sept. 18, 1880, F. F. Jackson.
    4236. iv. ADALINE A., b. Dec. 1, 1865; m. Oct. 20, 1892, Richard S. Coffin, of Wiscasset, Me.; d. May 13, 1895.
    4237. v.   JOHN T., b. Nov. 23, 1867; unm.
    4238. vi. JOSEPH HOWARD, b. Mar. 28, 1870; unm.
    4239. vii. MARY ABBY, b. Jan. 21, 1872; unm.
    4240. viii. ARTHUR IRVING, b. Feb. 16, 1874; unm.
    4241. ix. HATTIE EVELYN, b. Apr. 19, 1876; unm.

2535. JOHN FISK (Jonathan, David, David, Robert, David, David, Jeffrey, Robert, Simon, Simon, William, Symond), b. Lex., Nov. 6, 1827; m. Mar. 13, 1856, Judith Decrow, of Lincolnville, Me., b. June 8, 1828. He was one of the California pioneers in 1849, going around Cape Horn—a six months' passage. He returned in 1850 and started again from Wilmington, sixty miles west of Chicago, Ill., with a train of three wagons, across the great plains—a six months' tramp. He returned in 1855 and settled in Billerica on his place which he has named "Elmore," from the fact that a group of four large American elms overshadow a beautiful lawn. The youngest tree was planted the same year as the erection of the house, in 1796. There he has for forty-one years tried to add to the agricultural products of our great and almost boundless country; res. Billerica, Mass.

JOHN FISK.

    4242. i.   JOHN L., b. Jan. 15, 1857.
    4243. ii.   HARRIET C., b. Dec. 1, 1858.
    4244. iii. ALICE M., b. Aug. 8, 1860; d. ————.
    4245. iv. AUGUSTA R., b. Apr. 18, 1863.
    4246. v.   MERTON L., b. Dec. 6, 1865.
    4247. vi. ALBERT E., b. Apr. 21, 1868; d. ————.

2545. EX-GOV. JOHN FLAVEL FISK (David, Ebenezer, Ebenezer, Ebenezer, David, David, David, Jeffrey, Robert, Simon, Simon, William, Symond), b. Dec. 14, 1815, Genesee County, N. Y.; m. in Cincinnati, Ohio, Oct. 25, 1842, Elizabeth Sarah Johnson, b. Jan. 1, 1822. He was born in Genesee County, N. Y., and when quite small moved with his parents to Kentucky. His father, Dr. Fisk, died in Mt. Vernon, Ohio, while on a journey from Kentucky to New York. The subject of this sketch received an excellent education, studied law and was in due course of time admitted to the bar. He has practiced since continuously, until his retirement, in the courts of the State of Kentucky. He has been one of the most prominent citizens in Covington, Ky. He has been president of two academies in Kentucky, president of the school board in Covington, Ky.; several times attorney of the city—called city attorney; several times county attorney; eight years State Senator; part of the time president of the Senate and thus ex-officio Lieutenant-Governor. He has been through all the grades of Odd Fellowship, including Grand Master of this State—that is of the I. O. O. F., and Grand Representative of the Sovereign Grand Lodge, I. O. O. F., of the United States; at present a director in the Covington and Cincinnati (Suspension) Bridge Company; director in the Covington Gas Company; director in the First National Bank of Covington, Ky.; president of Highland Cemetery; president of the board of trustees of the First Christian Church, and vice-president of the Covington Protestant Children's Home. One of the religious papers in Kentucky in referring to Gov. Fisk says: "Last Saturday, Gov. John F. Fisk celebrated his 80th birthday by a family reunion, at the old home on Eleventh Street. It was a very enjoyable affair. Brother Fisk has held many honorable positions in the gift of the people, and his family is one of which he can be justly proud. He has been one of the pillars of this church for many years, and we all hope he may be spared yet a long while to aid us by his counsel and timely advice. As was truly said at the reunion, he is the highest of God's creation—a Christian gentleman." In Jan., 1879, at the invitation of the Mexican minister, a company of merchants and others visited Mexico. There were nearly one hundred of them. The first night out of Chicago—the starting point—they organized under the name of "The American Industrial Deputation," elected officers, and appointed Governor Fisk president. Under this organization they visited Mexico as the guests of the Republic, remained there one month, being feasted by cabinet officers, by Hon. John W. Foster, the then American minister, and others. They returned via Vera Cruz and Galveston. Several years since, Diaz, the president of Mexico, visited several cities of the United States, Chicago among them. Governor Fisk was invited to meet President Diaz in Chicago, and did so. A banquet was given at the Palmer House, at which the Governor responded to one of the toasts: res. 13 W. 11th St., Covington, Ky.

4248. i. CHARLES HENRY, b. Aug. 31, 1843; m. Margaret A. Emmal.
4249. ii. VIRGINIA ALLENE, b. Nov. 15, 1846; m. Nov. 15, 1869, Andrew R. Scovill; res. 1135 Madison Ave., Covington, Ky.
4250. iii. SARAH CLARABELLE, b. Oct. 6, 1849; m. 2d, May 25, 1876, Sicilian C. Speers; res. Ashland Ave., Norwood, Ohio. He is a traveling salesman; b. Nov. 5, 1842. Ch.: Elizabeth Sarah Speers (by former marriage), b. June 20, 1869; res. Norwood, Ohio. James Gordon Speers, b. Sept. 8, 1878; res. Norwood, Ohio. Isabel Andrews Speers, b. June 5, 1891; res. Norwood, Ohio.
4251. iv. ROBERT BROWN, b. Mar. 2, 1852; m. Julia C. (Green) Ross.
4252. v. ISABELLA HILL, b. Mar. 17, 1854; m. Oct. 2, 1881, Byron Andrews; res. 152 W. 105th St., New York, N. Y.
4253. vi. JOHN FLAVEL, b. Nov. 27, 1858; m. Grace Gatch.
4254. vii. ELIZABETH SARAH, b. Apr. 8, 1863; d. unm. Oct. 10, 1880.

2546. DR. HARRISON DEABORN FISK (David, Ebenezer, Ebenezer, Ebenezer, David, David, David, Jeffrey, Robert, Simon, Simon, William, Symond), b. Eagle Village, Manlius, N. Y., Mar. 25, 1813; m. Sept. 15, 1845, Maria Edlam Goss, b. 1816; d. 1858. Dr. Fisk was born in Manlius, N. Y., moved to Ohio with his parents, obtained a good common school education, studied medicine and in due course of time was graduated at the Cincinnati Eclectic College. He taught school in Germantown, Ky., before and after graduation, but soon entered upon the practice of his profession at Covington, Ky., and later at Franklin, Ind. At the latter city his wife died, and becoming somewhat impaired in his hearing finally gave up his practice, and for several years past has made his home with his daughter, Mrs. Johnson, in Englewood; res. 6606 Yale Ave., Englewood, Ill.

4255. i. ADA ELLENE, b. Aug. 11, 1847; m. Jan. 17, 1866, John Mitchell Johnson, general freight agent of the Chicago, Rock Island & Pacific Railroad. He was b. Cincinnati, Ohio, May 13, 1845;

res. 6606 Yale Ave. Ch.: 1, Wm. S., b. June 19, 1867; d. unm. Apr. 22, 1896. He was in the grain business in Kansas City. 2, Clara Maud, b. Sept. 14, 1869; m. June 7, 1893, Wm. Edwin Nichols; res. Windemere Hotel, Chicago, Ill. 3, John M., b. Jan. 17, 1872; d. Feb. 3, 1873. 4, Margaret Emeline, b. Dec. 17, 1876; d. Oct., 1879. 5, Ada B., b. June 6, 1880; d. July 6, 1881. 6, Mary Winnifred, b. Feb. 20,. 1884.

4256. ii. GINEVRA, b. Feb. 2, 1849; unm.; res. 6606 Yale Ave.

4257. iii. CARRIE F., b. Sept. 18, 1851; m. Oct. 18, 1870, Samuel W. Cox; res. 238-67th St., Chicago, Ill. Ch.: 1, Ellene, b. Oct. 4, 1872. 2, Harrison Flavel, b. May 2, 1876. 3, Jennie, b. Apr. 20, 1884.

2547. DR. DAVID LEWIS FISK (David, Ebenezer, Ebenezer, Ebenezer, David, David. David, Jeffrey, Robert, Simon, Simon, William, Symond), b. ———; m. ——— Abercombie; m. 2d, Mary Griffing; res. Fiskburg, Kenton County, Ky.

4258. i. WILLIAM R., b. ———; captain; res. Fiskburg, Kenton County, Ky.

4259. ii. JOSEPH, b. ———; res. California; has a large family.

2550. EBENEZER FISK (David, Ebenezer, Ebenezer, Ebenezer, David, David, David, Jeffrey, Robert, Simon, Simon, William. Symond), b. June 26, 1819, Onondaga County, N. Y.; m. in Cincinnati, Ohio. June 11, 1843, Eliza A. Stephens, b. Oct. 10, 1819. He was a school teacher and quite noted. He died in Florence, Ky., though his school was in Nashville, Tenn. He d. Jan. 14, 1853; res. Fiskburg, Ky.

4260. i. ALBERT GALLATIN, b. May 4, 1844; m. Mary A. Conner.

4261. ii. SARAH S., b. Sept. 9, 1848; m. Dec. 6, 1871, Chas. M. Riggs. Two ch.: Eva and Albert; res. Erlanger, Ky.

4262. iii. JOHN S., b. Aug. 20, 1850; d. June 16, 1851.

4263. iv. HENRIETTA E., b. July 23, 1852; d. Aug. 13, 1853.

2553. JOHN MANSON FISK (Nathaniel, Cotton, Ebenezer, Ebenezer, David, David, David, Jeffery, Robert, Simon, William, Symond), b. Abbotsford, P. Q., Dec. 13, 1836; m. at Knowlton, Canada. June 5. 1860, Ellen Maria Knowlton, b. Feb. 8, 1836. John Manson Fisk, the subject of this sketch, was born at Abbotsford, P. Q., Dec., 13, 1836, and is the third son of Nathaniel Fisk and grandson of Capt. Cotton Fisk, a United Empire Loyalist, who came from Epping, N. H., to Canada in 1788. John, one of the four, as soon as he was old enough, worked on the farm during the summer months and attended school in winter, finishing his education at the age of 18 at the Granby Academy. Coming into possession of his father's farm in 1840, he married Ellen Maria Knowlton, by which marriage there were ten children born, five sons and five daughters, all attaining maturity, excepting the two youngest sons who died in infancy. As one of the leading agriculturists of his county, he has been called to fill various positions of trust, doing duty for thirteen years as a member of the local council, a member of the school board, and filling other minor positions in municipal office. He was appointed a Justice of the Peace by the Lieutenant-Governor of the Province in 1882. At an early period of his life he developed a taste for horticultural pursuits, and for many

JOHN MANSON FISK.

years has been engaged in the nursery business, and as a fruit grower becoming an authority of some note on the fruits of his Province. United with others of similar tastes, who, in 1874, succeeded in organizing a Fruit Grower's Association at Abbotsford, he was elected one of its chief officers, and for several years has filled the position as president. This society published the first fruit list for the Province of Quebec in 1875, and for many years entered largely into experimental work and the introduction of new fruits, which have become widely known through the dissemination of its trees and collections of fruits which have appeared on most of the exhibition tables of the Province from time to time, as well as on those of the Centennial at Philadelphia in 1876, the Intercolonial and Indian at London, England, in 1886, and the World's Fair in Chicago in 1893. Feeling the need of a Provincial organization and associating himself with other leading fruit growers of the Province, application was made to the Provincial Legislature for incorporation, which was granted by the government in January, 1894, under the name of "The Pomological and Fruit Growing Society of the Province of Quebec." A meeting was convened during the following month at Abbotsford for the purpose of organizing and electing a board of directors, when Mr. Fisk was honored by becoming the first president of the new society. In politics a liberal conservative, and in religion an Episcopalian, having from early childhood been closely associated with St. Paul's Church, Abbotsford, and for over thirty-five years served as secretary-treasurer to the vestry, and for many years representing that body as lay delegate to the synod for the Diocese of Montreal; res. Abbotsford, P. Q.

4264. i.   ALICE MARIA, b. Apr. 28, 1861; m. Nov. 18, 1884, E. A. Buzzell; res. Abbotsford.

4265. ii.   ARTHUR NEWELL, b. May 26, 1862; m. Sept. 30, 1895, Florence Overmeyer, b. Nov. 27, 1873; res. 118 Ashland Boul., Chicago, Ill. He was educated at the district school, Abbotsford and Granby Academy, Granby, Quebec; moved to Chicago, Sept., 1887, taking up the study of architecture, and at time of writing is in the employ of Henry Ives Cobb, architect; was married at Chicago to Florence, daughter of Col. Jno. B. Overmeyer, of Chicago. Ch.: 1, John Knowlton, b. Aug. 31, 1896.

ARTHUR NEWELL FISK.

4266. iii.   MIRIAM LAURA, b. May 5, 1863; m. Apr. 8, 1885, E. F. Carter; res. A.

4267. iv.   WM. HENRY, b. Dec. 10, 1864; res. Chicago, Ill.; educated at Abbotsford public school; remained on the old homestead until Oct., 1883; went direct to Chicago, entering the retail dry goods business in the employ of James Taylor, remaining with the firm until Dec., 1892; entered the wholesale firm of Jas. H. Walker & Co., Jan. 1, 1893, who failed and went into liquidation Jan., 1894; entered the firm of John M. Locke & Co., importers and jobbers of dry goods, Jan. 7, 1894, as their Pacific coast representative, still being in their employ.

4268. v.   KATHERINE ELLEN, b. May 21, 1867; m. Nov. 5, 1890, G. W. Buzzell; res. A.

4269. vi.   EDITH SARAH, b. Oct. 19, 1868.

4270. vii.   LAURA WHEELER, b. Aug. 29, 1870.

4271. viii.   WALTER MANSON, b. Sept. 6, 1872; res. 1823 Ontario St., Montreal, Canada. When old enough he was sent each winter to the district school until the fall of 1888, when he went to Knowlton, P. Q., to attend the academy, returning home in the spring to help his father on the farm at Abbotsford. He went to Knowlton again the following fall for another winter in the academy, and it was after returning to Abbotsford again that he decided to study medicine, and immediately commenced work on the subjects necessary for his matriculation in the College of Physicians and Surgeons of the Province of Quebec, studying evenings after the day's work on the farm was over. In Oct., 1890, he entered the high school at Granby, P. Q., and the following spring he took with honors the degree of associate in arts from McGill University. He continued his studies during the winter of 1891-92 at the Granby high school, and in May, 1892, successfully passed his matriculation for the study of medicine in the Province of Quebec. In Oct., 1892, he commenced the four years' course of medical study at McGill University, Montreal. During his final year there he was elected by his fellow students to the position of president of the Undergraduates Medical Society. Graduating with first class honors, he received from the university on the 31st of March, 1896, the degree of doctor of medicine and master of surgery. Dr. Fisk then applied for the position of resident medical officer in the Montreal General Hospital, and stood first in the entrance examination given to the twenty-eight applicants by the Hospital Medical Board, thereby receiving the appointment for one year.

4272. ix.   JOHN KNOWLTON, b. Oct. 16, 1876; d. Apr. 18, 1880.

4273. x.   ERNEST MORGAN, b. Oct. 22, 1878; d. Oct. 26, 1878.

2554. NATHANIEL COTTON FISK (Nathaniel, Cotton, Ebenezer, Ebenezer, David, David, David, Jeffrey, Robert, Simon, Simon, William, Symond), b. Abbotsford, P. Q., Nov. 17, 1828; m. there Dec. 16, 1856, Helen Bangs, b. Mar. 1, 1838. He is a farmer; in religion an Episcopalian; res. Abbotsford, P. Q.

4274. i.   MARIA, b. Nov. 10, 1857; m. Sept. 6, 1870; d. May 1, 1889.

4275. ii.   EDGAR NATHANIEL, b. Jan. 17, 1859; d. Dec. 13, 1864.

4276. iii.   MARY, b. May 30, 1862.

4277. iv.   FRED'K C., b. June 13, 1866

4278. v.   GEO., b. Jan. 10, 1869.

4279. vi.   CHARLES A., b. Oct. 9, 1873.

2555. DR. NEWELL FISK (Nathaniel, Cotton, Ebenezer, Ebenezer, David, David, David, Jeffrey, Robert, Simon, Simon, William, Symond), b. Abbotsford, P. Q., Mar. 11, 1839; m. Nov. 20, 1867, Clara Lucelia Fiske, b. Jan. 6, 1845. His education was obtained at the public schools at Abbotsford, Granby, Lennoxville and McGill College, Montreal, all in the Province of Quebec, Canada. While at Lennoxville, in the fall of 1857, he unfortunately met with an accident to his right knee which necessitated his using crutches for the two following years. In June, 1860, he went to England for a trip for his health, returning much benefited. In Dec., 1860, he went to Montreal and entered the office of Dr. Aldis Bernard, surgeon dentist, to study said profession, and became a pupil of Dr. Bernard. After remaining with the doctor until the 21st of February, 1861, he was accepted and indentured to him for two years, having to pay him $200 and board himself; also having to attend lectures at McGill College, with the understanding that he was to become a partner at the end of the two years. Unfortunately when his time was up his health was so broken from hard study and work that his doctor ordered him out of the city and to take a long holiday. In May, 1863, he left the city and went knocking about the townships, returning every few months to Dr.

Bernard to see how he could stand the city practice. After remaining for some time he found he was obliged to go to the country again. This went on until Oct., 1866, when he went to Waterloo, P. Q., and bought out A. A. Knowlton, dentist, and remained there until May, 1888, when he returned to Montreal, where he is at present located in the practice of his profession at No. 2 Cathcart St.; res. 2 Cathcart St., Montreal, Canada.

DR. NEWELL FISK.

4280. i. BENJAMIN NEW-ELL, b. Dec. 10, 1868; res. Chicago.

4281. ii. HENRIETTA, b. Sept. 19, 1871; is a trained nurse; graduated from the Western Hospital of Dorchester St., Montreal, where she is living at present.

4282. iii. CLARENCE AN-DREW, b. Jan. 4, 1878; d. Sept. 18, 1883.

4283. iv. PERCEY WALTER, b. July 13, 1885; res. Montreal.

4284. v. EDGAR HARLOW, b. Apr. 1, 1887; res. Montreal.

2563. REV. NATHANIEL BENJAMIN FISK (Sewell C., Cotton, Ebenezer, Ebenezer, David, David, David, Jeffrey, Robert, Simon, Simon, William, Symond), b. Abbotsford, P. Q., Mar. 6, 1848; m. there June 4, 1872, Katherine S. Gillespie, b. there Nov. 12, 1849. Rev. Nathaniel B. Fisk was born in Abbotsford, P. Q., Mar. 4, 1848, son of Sewell Cotton Fisk and Mary Ann Gorton. In 1866 he entered the New Hampshire Conference Seminary, where he graduated, taking immediately thereafter the theological course at the Boston University, from which he graduated in 1871. He was ordained a deacon in the Methodist Episcopal Church at Lynn, Apr. 6, 1873, and an elder at Springfield, Apr. 11, 1875. He has occupied stations in the New England Conference since 1871, all his pastorates being three years. He has had a grand record as pastor, winning all hearts to himself, and directly leading multitudes to the Savior of men. His preaching is strong, pathetic, convincing. He moves men. He is a man of intense energy and tireless industry. This is his fourth year at Chicopee Falls, and the church under his lead has reached its most prosperous history, with a Sunday school of more than 300 members and a church membership of 275 members in full and 43 probation. It has today the largest Sunday school and largest congregation of any church in the city. He built a fine church at Upton, Mass. The elegant Grace Church at Cambridge, a $6,000 parsonage at Ashburnham, besides raising $14,000 to pay off the debt on the Ashburnham Church. He secured the gift of a $7,000 parsonage from his personal friend, Hon. Luman Tufts at Hudson. While at Grace Church, Cambridge, Mr. Fisk was invited by the pastor, official board and the presiding elder to take the assistant pastorate of People's Church, Boston, but declined. He was also offered the business management of the New England Conservatory of Music, having 2,250 pupils. Since coming to Chicopee Falls he has declined an offer of $4,000 per year, with a guarantee for five years, and also an interest in the business, if he would take charge of a stock company in Boston, as business manager. His record of 2,200 pastoral calls last year shows him to be abundant in labors. In 1872 Mr. Fisk was married to Miss Katherine Gillespie, who has labored with him earnestly in the gospel. In 1878 he enjoyed a protracted vacation in Europe, visiting Scotland, England, Ireland, Belgium, Holland, Switzerland, Germany, Prussia, Italy and France; res. Chicopee Falls, Mass.

4285. i. HARRIET MAY, b. Graniteville, Mass., Apr. 4, 1874.
4286. ii. WINNIFRED ALICE, b. Upton, Mass., Sept. 16, 1875.
4287. iii. WILBUR WARREN, b. Marlboro, Mass., Nov. 25, 1877.
4288. iv. ERNEST R,, b. Woburn, Mass., May 22, 1884; d. June 30, 1885.
4289. v. RAYMOND JOHN, b. Cambridge, Mass., May 4, 1888.
4290. vi. ARTHUR GILLESPIE, b. Chicopee, Mass., Feb. 26, 1893.

2567. ANDREW MURRAY FISK (Abraham, Cotton, Ebenezer, Ebenezer, David, David, David, Jeffrey, Robert, Robert, Simon, Simon, William, Symond), b. Abbotsford, P. Q., Nov. 7, 1834; m. there Apr. 11, 1860, Mary Amelia Edmunds, b. Nov. 13, 1835, in East Weare, N. H. He is a farmer; res. Abbotsford, P. Q.

4291. i. ELWOOD ALFRED, b. May 1, 1861.
4292. ii. ALBERT HENRY, b. Jan. 19, 1863.
4293. iii. HORACE MURRAY, b. May 4, 1869.

2574. JOHN JEFFREY FISKE (Ebenezer, Cotton, Ebenezer, Ebenezer, David, David, David, Jeffrey, Robert, Simon, Simon, William, Symond), b. Abbotsford, P. Q., Feb. 23, 1844; m. at Montreal, Feb. 20, 1873, Aleyda Eliza David, dau. of Lieut.-Col. E. B. David, b. July 29, 1852. His life up to the death of his father in 1861 was a very easygoing, uneventful one, his time being mostly spent at the schools of the district and adjacent towns. Being the youngest son and at that period the only one at home, his father's death threw the care of the farm and postoffice upon him, and his life for a few years was an active and rather laborious one, but he found leisure to prosecute his studies and in 1865 he was indentured to Mr. Houghton, barrister of Montreal, and entered upon the study of law at McGill College. In 1866 his articles of indenture were transferred to his cousin, John J. C. Abbott, Q. C., then the leading lawyer in the city and afterward Sir John Abbott, premier of the Dominion of Canada. In May, 1868, he received the degree of B. C. L. from McGill College, and in the month of December following was admitted to the practice of the law. After spending two years in the practice of his profession in Montreal, he removed to Coaticook in 1871 where he has since resided. He married Aleyda E. David, daughter of the late Lieutenant-Colonel David, of Montreal. After an active and successful practice of his profession for ten years he became interested in manufacturing industries, and in 1881 assumed the management of an extensive knitting industry in his town and is at present at the head of the Lenman Manufacturing Company there, a wealthy corporation controlling a number of factories both in this Province and in Ontario. He has taken an active interest in politics, and usually directs the political contests in his section of that county in the interests of the liberal conservative party; res. Coaticook, P. Q.

4294. i. ERNEST JEFFERY, b. Nov. 26, 1873.
4295. ii. AMY GOLDA, b. Nov. 28, 1874.
4296. iii. LUCY FLORENCE, b. Feb. 21, 1876.
4297. iv. NINA BEATRICE, b. July 27, 1877.
4298. v. EDITH BRENDA, b. Jan. 8, 1879.
4299. vi. GRACE MURIEL, b. Jan. 23, 1880; d. in infancy.
4300. vii. MORRICE GORDON, b. Feb. 4, 1881; d. in infancy.
4301. viii. BROOKS ARCHIBALD, b. Feb. 4, 1881; d. in infancy.
4302. ix. KENNETH REGINALD, b. Jan. 12, 1882.
4303. x. LEILA MARGUERITE, b. Oct. 26, 1883; d. in infancy.

2578. HENRY CHARLES FISKE (Ebenezer, Cotton, Ebenezer, Ebenezer, David, David, David, Jeffrey, Robert, Simon, Simon, William, Symond), b. Oct. 20, 1836; m. Isabella Graham. Henry married in Boston. He was a successful speculator in the oil regions of Pennsylvania, and after spending some years in travel on this continent and in Europe is now located in Los Angeles, Cal.; res. Los Angeles, Cal.

2580. EDWARD FRANCIS McKENZIE FISKE (Ebenezer, Cotton, Ebenezer, Ebenezer, David, David, David, Jeffrey, Robert, Simon, Simon, William, Symond), b. Sept. 5, 1841, Abbotsford, P. Q.; m. at Montreal, Oct. 2, 1867, Emma

EDWARD FRANCIS McKENZIE FISKE.

E. S. Elliott, b. Montreal, May 28, 1848. After acquiring a thorough knowledge of business in a wholesale hardware house in Montreal, he married Emma, a daughter of John Elliott, of Montreal, wholesale merchant, and after spending some years in New York State and in Chicago, settled in Joliette, Province of Quebec, Canada, and is now engaged in the manufacture of lumber in which he has been very successful; res. Joliette, P. Q.

4304. i. EDWARD ELLIOTT JOHN, b. Aug. 8, 1870.

2582. BENJAMIN MINOT FISKE (John M., Benjamin, Ebenezer, David, David, David, Jeffrey, Robert, Simon, Simon, William, Symond), b. Charlestown, Mass., ———; m. at Chelmsford, Mass., Elizabeth Ann Parkhurst, b. June 11, 1823. He is in the custom house in Boston; res. Sumner cor. Cherry St., Somerville, Mass.

4305. i. JOHN MINOT, b. Dec. 31, 1853; m. Katie S. Westervelt.

4306. ii. JOSEPH WINN, b. Mar. 5, 1857; m. Mary S. Harrington.

4307. iii. FRED'K A. P., b. Oct. 4, 1859; m. Harriet L. Locke.

4308. iv. ELIZABETH MINOT, b. Oct. 14, 1860; m. ——— Warren; res. Chelmsford.

2583. JOSEPH WINN FISKE (John M., Benjamin, Ebenezer, David, David, David, Jeffrey, Robert, Simon, Simon, William, Symond), b. May 22, 1832; m. in Geneva, Switzerland, Aug. 15, 1872, Caroline Gould, b. Aug. 2, 1851, in Cincinnati, Ohio; res. 1672 Broadway, New York City.

4309. i. CAROLINE ELIZA, b. May 24, 1873.

4310. ii. MAUD BROOKS, b. Oct. 27, 1874.

4311. iii. JOSEPH WINN, b. Oct. 21, 1878.

2584. JOHN MINOT FISKE (John M., Benjamin, Ebenezer, David, David, David, Jeffrey, Robert, Simon, Simon, William, Symond), b. Boston, Mass., Aug. 17, 1834; m. at Stockbridge, June 1, 1864, Isabella Landon Goodrich, dau. of Hon. John Z., b. Apr. 13, 1845. He was born in Boston. Fitted for college at Phillips Academy, Andover, Mass., in class of 1852. Entered Yale College same autumn, and graduated in 1856. Subsequently at Harvard Law School; admitted to the Suffolk bar in 1858; opened office in Boston, and there practiced until May, 1863, when he was appointed deputy naval officer of the port of Boston. In November of that year was appointed deputy collector of customs, port of Boston, and has been connected with the customs at this port ever since. At present holding the position of special deputy collector. Was chairman of civil service examiners at Boston, during the administration of President Arthur, which office he resigned voluntarily, on the advent of President Cleveland, in 1885. Was a member of the Common Council of the city of Boston, in 1863 and 1864; res. Boston, Mass., add. care Custom House.

4312. i. SALLIE GOODRICH, b. Mar. 17, 1870; m. Nov. 16, 1892, J. L. Liecty, Jr.; res. 10 Webster St., Brookline, Mass.

4313. ii. JOHN LANDON, b. Nov. 6, 1873; res. 139 Oxford St., Cambridge, Mass. He fitted for college at the Boston Latin School and Phillips Academy, Andover; entered Harvard College in

1891, in the class of 1895. He left in one year to engage in business.

2586. CHARLES FISKE (Charles, Benjamin, Ebenezer, David, David, David, Jeffrey, Robert, Simon, Simon, William, Symond), b. Lex., May 27, 1834; m. Apr. 4, 1855, Adeline W. Shaw, of Augusta, Me.; m. 2d, Mar. 25, 1868, Annie I. Crafts, b. Sandwich, Mass., June 25, 1846. She was the daughter of Rev. Eliphalet Porter Crafts. Ancestry: (Thomas, John, Staples, Moses, Samuel, Samuel, Lieut. Griffin). Born in Sandwich, Mass., married in Eastport, Me., Charles Fiske. He is son of Charles and Abigail Melvina (Hayden) Fiske, of Lexington, Mass. He was born in Milford, Me. During the years 1861 and 1862 he served in the United States Navy, and was attached to the "San Jacinto." After leaving the Navy he was at Lexington for a short interval, and then went to Chicago, Ill., where he was engaged in the commission business. In 1865 he removed to New York City, and was a resident there for fourteen or fifteen years, being connected with the house of J. L. Cobb & Co. In 1879 he removed to Boston, since which time he has been connected with the Boston postoffice; res. Boston, Mass., 70 Chandler St.

    4314. i.   ELLEN MARION, b. Nov. 19, 1870.
    4315. ii.   FREDERICK PORTER, b. Feb. 27, 1874; d. Dec. 7, 1879.
    4316. iii. EDWARD CHARLES, b. Jan. 19, 1876; d. Sept. 6, 1876.

2587. WILLIAM B. FISKE (Charles, Benjamin, Ebenezer, David, David, David, Jeffrey, Robert, Simon, Simon, William, Symond), b. Milford, Me., June 23, 1836; m. in Boston, Oct. 15, 1855, Henriette S. Lyford, of Boston, b. Jan. 8, 1838. He has been in the mercantile business since he was 13 years of age, and has been fairly successful. His office is in the Mercantile Building, cor. Hudson and Harrison Sts., New York City; res. Boston, Mass., and New York, N. Y.; add. Mercantile Exchange Building, Hudson and Harrison Sts.

    4317. i.   WILLIAM B., b. Jan. 28, 1857; m. Claire E. Acorn.
    4318. ii.   FRANK HARRY, b. Mar. 24, 1859.
    4319. iii. FRANCES A., b. Apr. 10, 1861; m. in Brooklyn, Nov. 10, 1886, Archibald A. Smith, b. Jan. 6, 1860.
    4320. iv. MARION E., b. Sept. 29, 1864; m. in Brooklyn, Nov. 10, 1887, Sidney C. Ormsby, b. Dec. 26, 1860.

2591. JAMES W. FISK (Aaron, Samuel, Aaron, Samuel, James, James, Phinehas, Thomas, Robert, Simon, Simon, William, Symond), b. Dalton, N. H., Oct. 19, 1835; m. at Windsor, Vt., Apr. 28, 1860, Mary Jane Sharp, b. Mar. 15, 1837. He is a farmer; res. Charlestown, N. H.

    4321. i.   ELMER W., b. Feb. 26, 1863; d. Sept. 20, 1865.
    4322. ii.   EDGAR FREEMAN, b. Jan. 11, 1865; m. Nov. 13, 1889, Leema M. Sparrow. He is in the provision business; res. Charlestown, N. H. Ch.: 1, Charles S., b. Feb. 23, 1891.
    4323. iii. DICKIE G., b. Sept. 19, 1866; res. C.
    4324. iv. ALVIN W., b. Aug. 11, 1868.
    4325. v.   JOHN H., b. Nov. 16, 1870.
    4326. vi. GEO. S., b. Aug. 25, 1873.
    4327. vii. SABIN E., b. Aug. 6, 1876.

2596. JOHN WARREN FISK (Aaron, Samuel, Aaron, Samuel, James, James, Phinehas, Thomas, Robert, Simon, Simon, William, Symond), b. Dalton, N. H., Feb. 25, 1834; m. Bellows Falls, Vt., Dec. 31, 1861, Arvilla Lorina Dodge, b. Oct. 13, 1840. He is a carpenter and joiner; res. So. Acworth, N. H.

    4328. i.   ALGENE AARON, b. Mar. 19, 1863; m. Aug. 13, 1884; South Acworth, N. H.
    4329. ii.   LEON NAUM, b. Nov. 27, 1864; m. Dec. 25, 1885; Claremont, N. H.
    4330. iii. FLORA ROSINA, b. May 9, 1870; South Acworth, N. H.

2597. ORIN E. FISK (Aaron, Samuel, Aaron, Samuel, James, James, Phinehas, Thomas, Robert, Simon, Simon, William, Symond), b. Charlestown, N. H., Sept. 4, 1837; m. there, Mar. 2, 1865, Blindia D. Eaton, b. at Acworth, Sept. 29, 1840; d. May 20, 1894. He is a farmer; res. Charlestown, N. H.

    4331. i.   MARTENA H., b. Dec. 12, 1865.

4332. ii. NELLIE L., b. July 19, 1868.
4333. iii. FANNIE M., b. Nov. 1, 1870; m. Frank L. Adams, Nov. 1, 1895.
4334. iv. WESLIE H., b. Apr. 15, 1874.
4335. v. WINNIE E., b. Apr. 13, 1876.
4336. vi. JESSE M., b. Oct. 27, 1878.
4337. vii. J. ORTON, b. Mar., 1881.

2599. PERRY FISK (Atterson, Samuel, Aaron, Samuel, James, James, Phinehas, Thomas, Robert, Simon, Simon, William, Symond), b. St. Marys, O., Apr. 13, 1846; m. there, June 21, 1887, Eliza J. Baker, b. there Feb. 2, 1868. He is a dealer in buggies and carriages; res. St. Marys, O.
4338. i. OWEL, b. Mar. 30, 1888.
4339. ii. MAY, b. Oct. 21, 1889.

2600. COL. SAMUEL E. FISKE (Erastus, Samuel, Aaron, Samuel, James, James, Phinehas, Thomas, Robert, Simon, Simon, William, Symond), b. Claremont, N. H., Sept. 20, 1842; m. Carrie A. Dodge, d. 1867; m. 2d, Hattie A. Hazelton, d. 1876; m. 3d, Jennie Renfrew. He is a publisher; res. Fall River, Mass.
4340. i. CARRIE A., b. June 16, 1870.
4341. ii. MAMIE A., b. Oct. 6, 1871.
4342. iii. ANNIE G., b. Oct. 19, 1873.
4343. iv. MABEL R., b. Feb. 27, 1881.

2602. WILBUR FISK (Samuel F., Samuel, Aaron, Samuel, James, James, Phinehas, Thomas, Robert, Simon, Simon, William, Symond), b. Nov. 14, 1844, Dayton, O.; m. in Troy, O., Feb. 25, 1867, Laura B. Wise, b. in Troy. He is a merchant; res. 420 No. Main St., Lima, O.
4344. i. SAMUEL F., b. Mar. 10, 1872; d. Feb. 22, 1880.
4345. ii. MAGGIE D., b. 1870.
4346. iii. AMYIE, b. 1876.

2606. GEORGE IRVIN FISK (Samuel F., Samuel, Aaron, Samuel, James, James, Phinehas, Thomas, Robert, Simon, Simon, William, Symond), b. Oct. 1, 1860, St. Marys, O.; m. in Rockford, O., Apr. 4, 1886, Della Hinkle, b. Oct. 24, 1867. He is a clerk; res. 402 No. Main St., Lima, O.
4347. i. OPAL NINA, b. Oct. 11, 1887.

2610. CHARLES RANSTEAD FISK (Asa, Samuel, Thomas, Thomas, Samuel, James, Phinehas, Thomas, Robert, Simon, Simon, William, Symond), b. Dublin, N. H., Apr. 25, 1843; m. Oct. 18, 1868, Abbie Maria Jones, b. Aug. 11, 1850. Charles R. Fisk, born and lived on the old homestead until June, 1882, when he sold the farm and removed to Dublin village. He served three years in the army, enlisting Aug. 11, 1862, in Company A., Fourteenth Regiment, New Hampshire Volunteers; mustered out June 16, 1865. For the last half of this term he was on detached service at division headquarters of the Second Division, Nineteenth Army Corps; was on duty at Savannah, Ga., when Jeff Davis was sent a captive from Augusta Ga., and saw him transferred from a river to an ocean steamer on his way to Hilton Head and North. Charles R. Fisk was mustered into A. T. Stevens Post No. 6, G. A. R., Department of New Hampshire, June 6, 1871, of which he was still a member in 1896. Since Mr. Fisk has lived in the village he has been employed about some of the summer residences of which there are a number in town; res. Dublin, N. H.
4348. i. MABEL, b. Aug. 17, 1873; d. Dec. 7, 1874.
4349. ii. HARRY, b. Mar. 11, 1876; d. Aug. 11, 1879.
4350. iii. CHARLES, b. Jan. 2, 1880; d. Jan. 7, 1880.
4351. iv. MARY E., b. Oct. 14, 1877.
4352. v. ROBERT H., b. Mar. 17, 1881.
4353. vi. HOLLIS R., b. Dec. 25, 1882.

2615. JOHN HARVEY FISKE (Asa H., Asa, Thomas, Thomas, Samuel, James, Phinehas, Thomas, Robert, Simon, Simon, William, Symond), b. Dublin, N. H., Jan. 15, 1844; m. at St. Augustine, Pa., May 1, 1870, Mary Ann Mullen, b. Mar. 25, 1846. He is a merchant; res. Altoona, Pa.
4354. i. CHARLES HENRY, b. Feb. 12, 1871; d. June 19, 1884.
27

4355. ii.   CAROLINE MAUDE, b. Jan. 6, 1874; res. at home.
4356. iii. JOHN RANSTEAD, b. Feb. 2, 1883; d. Dec. 2, 1884.
4357. iv.   ADA MARY, b. June 23, 1885; res. at home.

2622. CAPT. ROYAL FISK (Benoin, Benjamin, Benjamin, Benjamin, John, John, Phinehas, Thomas, Robert, Simon, Simon, William, Symond), b. Danby, Vt., Oct. 20, 1808; m. there Harriet Ann Mead, b. Oct. 2, 1810; d. Dec. 31, 1880, at Freedom, Wis. Royal Fisk was a man of very steady habits, was converted to Christianity at the age of 18 years, and joined the Methodist Church, of which he remained a consistent member until his death, aged 69 years. He followed farming in the summer season and teaching in the winter; taught over forty terms. He also preached sometimes. He held the offices of Justice of the Peace and Town Clerk for several years. He was not a large man, but generally enjoyed good health until his last sickness, which lasted several months and gradually wore him out. He resided for some time in Danby, Vt., moved to Dorset, thence to Collins, N. Y., and finally to Wisconsin, where he died. He d. Mar. 29, 1878; res. Danby, Vt., and Freedom, Wis.

4358. i.   PRUSIA MARIA, b. May 17, 1830; m. Oct. 11, 1848, Comfort H. Knapp, res. No. Freedom. He was born in Collins, N. Y., Feb. 19, 1828. Ch.: 1, Merritt Adelbert, b. Brant, N. Y., May 22, 1849; m. and res. North Freedom. 2, Edwin Leander, b. Collins, N. Y., May 16, 1851; m. and res. Latah, Wash. 3, Harriett Deborah, b. Gowanda, N. Y., Sept. 14, 1854; m. Luther Deaborn; res. Copeland, Mo. 4, Frank Comfort, b. Reedsburg, Wis., Mar. 16, 1858; m. and res. Waitsburg, Wash. 5, Mary Elvira, b. Ada Co., Idaho, Aug. 2, 1866; m. James B. Randall; res. Reedsburg, Wis. 6, Laura Bell, b. Reedsburg, Wis., Nov. 3, 1869; m. Wilson W. Randall; res. North Freedom. 7, Walter Roscoe, b. Reedsburg, Wis., Dec. 8, 1871. 8, Alma Bertha, b. Reedsburg, Wis., Apr. 1, 1873; m. Frank Nelson; res. Baraboo, Wis. Present address is No. Freedom, Wis.

4359. ii. PHEBE ELVIRA, b. June 22, 1832; m. Aug. 17, 1854, Geo. Barnhart; res. North Freedom. He was born in Hoosic, N. Y., Nov. 30, 1827. Their present P. O. add. is North Freedom, Wis. Ch.: 1, Herbert Melvin, b. Excelsior, Wis., Mar. 28, 1856; d. Feb. 10, 1883. 2, Clara Estelle, b. Freedom, Wis., May 30, 1867; m. Wm. H. Hackett; res. North Freedom.

4360. iii. WARREN N., b. Feb. 11, 1834; m. Cordelia R. Harris.
4361. iv. SYLVANUS WHITE, b. Mar. 7, 1836; d. Oct. 12, 1837.
4362. v.   ALBERT MEAD, b. July 7, 1838; m. Myra E. Douglas.
4363. vi. MARY LUCINA, b. Mar. 28, 1840; m. Nov. 23, 1862, Newton M. Burt; res. Baraboo, Wis. He was born in Medina Co., Ohio, June 6, 1838. Their present P. O. add. is Baraboo, Wis. Ch.: 1, Lester Milton, b. Excelsior, Wis., Mar. 1, 1865. 2, Ralph Malcome, b. Excelsior, Wis., Oct. 8, 1869. 3, Royal Searles, b. Wis., Jan. 11, 1877.

4364. vii. BESEY ANN, b. Jan. 6, 1842; m. July 28, 1860, Milton Addison Burt. She d. June 29, 1861, s. p. He was born June 6, 1838.

4365. viii. MARTHA JANETTE, b. Mar. 12, 1850; m. Dec. 25, 1871, Samuel J. Carpenter. He was born in St. Lawrence Co., New York. Her present P. O add. is Baraboo, Wis. Ch.: 1, Harriett Nancy, b. Excelsior, Wis., Nov. 15, 1872; m. Clinton Apker; res. Baraboo. 2, Luverne De Ette, b. Freedom, Wis., May 29, 1879. 3, Grace Mildred, b. Freedom, Wis., Oct. 5, 1886; Samuel J. d. Oct. 19, 1893.

4366. ix. CHARLES WILBUR, b. Nov. 9, 1853; m. Lillian E. Dearborn.

2625. BENONI FISK (Benoni, Benjamin, Benjamin, Benjamin, John, John, Phinehas, Thomas, Robert, Simon, Simon, William, Symond), b. Sept. 6, 1795, Danby, Vt.; m. Betsey Lake. He was a farmer. Settled with his father and later moved to Dorset, where he died. Res. Danby and Dorset, Vt.

2632. HON. HIRAM PHILLIPS FISK (Benjamin, Benjamin, Benjamin, Benjamin, John, John, Phinehas, Thomas, Robert, Simon, Simon, William, Symond), b. Danby, Vt., Jan. 15, 1806; m. there Oct. 12, 1828, Olive Smith, b. Jan. 30, 1804; d. Nov., 1888. He was born in Danby and has always resided there. Was a successful farmer. He took great interest in politics, and was quite a party man. He held responsible offices in the town and positions of trust until his death. He represented his town in the state legislature in 1861. He d. Feb. 8, 1874; res. Danby, Vt.

    4367. i.   DANIEL, b. Sept. 9, 1833; d. unm. Nov. 21, 1855.
    4368. ii.   ROSINA, b. Aug. 16, 1836; m. Jan. 15, 1866, Hosea Benson. She d. June 25, 1869.
    4369. iii. ROZOLOO, b. Oct. 17, 1839; d. May 10, 1842.
    4370. iv. RUTH, b. June 6, 1843; m. Dec. 13, 1862, Cantlin G. Herrick; res. Danby Four Corners.
    4371. v.   HIRAM, b. Apr. 1, 1846; m. Helen Forbes.
    4372. vi. BENJAMIN A., b. Feb. 17, 1831; m. Mary J. Green.

2633. BENJAMIN J. FISK (Benjamin, Benjamin, Benjamin, Benjamin, John, John, Phinehas, Thomas, Robert, Simon, Simon, William, Symond), b. Jan. 21, 1796, Danby, Vt.; m. there Catherine Colvin, dau. of Daniel Colvin. He d. Nov. 8, 1884; res. Clarendon, Vt.

    4373. i.   MERRITT, b. Clarendon, Vt., Apr. 19, 1829; res. Clarendon Springs, Vt.
    4374. ii.   BENJAMIN J., b. June 2, 1825; m. Nov. 25, 1862, at Stockholm, N. Y., Mrs. Hannah Bresee Everest, b. Feb. 29, 1840; res. s. p. 253 South Main St., Rutland, Vt. Is a farmer.
    4375. iii. LEANDER, b. ———.
    4376. iv. LORETTA, b. ———.
    4377. v.   MARY C., b. ———.

2636. HON. LYMAN R. FISK (Benjamin, Benjamin, Benjamin, Benjamin, John, John, Phinehas, Thomas, Robert, Simon, Simon, William, Symond), b. Nov. 28, 1803, Danby, Vt.; m. there 1826, Mrs. Lucy Colvin, wid. of John, b Sept. 24, 1788; d. in 1864. He settled on the homestead in Danby. Was a man of steady habits and possessed the confidence and esteem of his fellow-citizens He was a carpenter and housebuilder as well as farmer. He was a grand juror three years from 1848, selectman in 1855, also represented the town in the Legislature in 1855, and served with credit in all the positions. He was well known as a man of standing and integrity and a worthy citizen. He was for many years a member of the Masonic fraternity, exemplifying the tenets of the order in his daily conduct and intercourse with mankind. He d. May 13, 1885; res. Danby, Vt.

    4378. i.   NOAH, b. May 26, 1827; m. Olive Ridlon.
    4379. ii.   LYMAN R., b. Feb. 8, 1832; d. unm. Sept. 24, 1886.
    4380. iii. JOSEPH, b. Nov. 26, 1829; res. unm. Tinmouth, Vt.

2637. JOEL FISK (Benjamin, Benjamin, Benjamin, Benjamin, John, John, Phinehas, Thomas, Robert, Simon, Simon, William, Symond), b. June 16, 1810; m. Laura Fitz; m. 2d, ———. He d. about 1875; res. Colchester and Winooski, Vt.

    4381. i.   MARION, b. Winooski, Vt. ———.

2640. CAPT. DANIEL FISK (Benjamin, Benjamin, Benjamin, Benjamin, John, John, Phinehas, Thomas, Robert, Simon, Simon, William, Symond), b. Danby, Vt., Mar. 10, 1808; m. Jan. 27, 1830, Eunice Spaulding, dau. of Nathan, of Danby, Vt., b. Sept. 15, 1813; d. Apr. 3, 1860. He was a farmer. Died from heart disease, being found dead in the road, but a few rods from his house. He d. Jan. 7, 1849: res. Danby, Vt., and Wonewoc, Wis.

    4382. i.   SALLY ANN, b. ———.
    4383. ii.   PERRY, b. ———.
    4384. iii. PHILLIP, b. ———.
    4385. iv. ISRAEL, b. ———.
    4386. v.   CHESTER, b. ———.
    4387. vi. CHARLES, b. ———.
    4388. vii. DANIEL, b. ———.

2642. CAPT. OLIVER FISK (Benjamin, Benjamin, Benjamin, Benjamin, John, John, Phinehas, Thomas, Robert, Simon, Simon, William, Symond), b. Danby, Vt., Mar. 14, 1813; m. Sarah Parris, dau. of Caleb 2d; d. 1869. He was a farmer and located near his father's farm, was an industrious farmer and good citizen; res. Danby, Vt.

    4389. i.   CALEB P., b. ——; m. Olive Ann Hulett.
    4390. ii.   BETSEY ANN, b. ——.
    4391. iii. VALARIAH, b. ——; m. Joel Colvin, of Danby.
    4392. iv.   GEORGE, b. ——; m. Helen Barrett; res. Castleton, Vt.

2653. REUBEN FISK (Reuben, Benjamin, Benjamin, Benjamin, John, John, Phinehas, Thomas, Robert, Simon, Simon, William, Symond), b. Danby, Vt., Jan. 27, 1808; m. Dec. 24, 1829, Phebe Spaulding, dau. of Nathan, of Plainfield, Conn., and Danby, Vt., b. Mar. 7, 1811; d. Oct. 4, 1889. He was a farmer and located on the old homestead. He was a noted musician; moved to New York and finally to Wisconsin. He d. July 13, 1870; res. Danby, Vt.; Evans, N. Y., and Wonewoc, Wis.

    4393. i.   NATHAN, b. Oct. 29, 1830; m. Rhoda Fuller.
    4394. ii   MARTHA M., b. Apr. 19, 1845; m. Feb. 7, 1864, —— Leonard; res. Washburn, Wis.
    4395. iii. REUBEN, b. Feb. 7, 1833; m. ——.
    4396. iv.   ALPHONSO, b. Mar. 5, 1840; d. Sept. 27, 1864.

2656. FITZ WILLIAM FISK (Rufus, Nathaniel, Benjamin, Benjamin, John, John, Phinehas, Thomas, Robert, Simon, Simon, William, Symond), b. Brandon, Vt., Oct., 1808; m. in Moira, N. Y., Lucy Howe Perry, b. May, 1811; d. Aug., 1893. He was a blacksmith. He was born in Brandon, Vt., near the old Fisk place at Otter Creek. He moved to Moira, N. Y., married there, and in 1840 went West to Michigan. As no tidings have ever been received of him the family always supposed he was murdered. He d. in Michigan; res. Moira, N. Y.

    4397. i.   ALMON PERRY, b. July 10, 1835. It is probable that Mr. Fisk has the distinction of being the oldest dry goods merchant in Rock Island county, Ill. He is a native of Northern New York and spent the first ten years of his adult life in railway service. He then went to Geneseo, Ill., and engaged in the dry goods business for ten years after, which he located in Moline, the date being 1873. As proprietor of the Boston Store he has had several of the best locations in the city and his removals have been due to the changing course of business. The new store in the Rosenstein bock, which he will occupy before Nov. 1, 1896, is to be the most elegantly fitted and furnished store in that city. Mr. Fisk is a shrewd buyer. As a merchant he is successful and as a citizen has hosts of friends who hold him in high esteem.

ALMON PERRY FISK.

    4398. ii.   AARON WM., b. July 24, 1831; m. Hannah Sweet Phillips.

2657. ALMON ARNOLD FISK (Rufus, Nathaniel, Benjamin, Benjamin, John, John, Phinehas, Thomas, Robert, Simon, Simon, William, Symond), b. Brandon, Vt., m. in Bangor, N. Y., Fannie M. Clough, b. June 19, 1809. He was a farmer. He d. in Nicholville, N. Y.; res. Franklin, N. Y.

    4399. i.   LUCY MOULTON, b. ———.
    4400. ii.   MARTHA AMADON, b. ———.
    4401. iii. HATTIE McWAINE, b. ———.
    4402. iv. ADALINE, b. ———; d. ———.
    4403. v.   JULIA STOWE, b. ———.
    4404. vi. CHARLES, b. ———.
    4405. vii. GREELEY, b. ———.
    4406. viii. FULTON, b. ———.
    4407. ix. FRED, b. ———.
    4408. x.   WILLIAM, b. ———; d. ———.
    4409. xi. ROBERT FULTON, b. May 22, 1841; m. in Stockholm, N. Y., Sarah Maria Freeman, b. Sept. 17, 1841. He is a wheelwright and farmer. Ch.: Charles J. Fisk, b. Nov. 10, 1870. Aggie C. Fisk, b. Feb. 5, 1869; m. ——— Benham. Fannie M., b. Oct. 29, ———; d. ———. Alice E., b. Aug. 2, 1880. Bessie B., b. Nov. 28, 1887.

2660. ALANSON FISKE (Bateman, Nathaniel, Benjamin, Benjamin, John, John, Phinehas, Thomas, Robert, Simon, Simon, William, Symond), b. in Danby, Vt., ———; m. Lydia Knight. She d. at West Exeter, N. Y., ae. 70. He d. ae. 73; res. Plainfield, N. Y.

    4410. i.   ALANSON, b. ———; m. Abigail Lewis.
    4411. ii.   WILLIAM, b. ———.
    4412. iii. CHARLOTTE, b. ———.

2662. NATHANIEL FISK (Bateman, Nathaniel, Benjamin, Benjamin, John, John, Phinehas, Thomas, Robert, Simon, Simon, William, Symond), b. in Danby, Vt., ———; m. in Vt., Sarah Amanda Blatchly, b. Vt.; d. 1893. He d. 1875; res. Malone, N. Y.

    4413. x.   EMMA E., b. ———; unm.; res. Hammonton, N. J.

2664. LEVI FISK (Eber, Nathaniel, Benjamin, Benjamin, John, John, Phinehas, Thomas, Robert, Simon, Simon, William, Symond), b. Schroon, N. Y., Mar. 15, 1809; m. in Shoreham, Vt., Mar., 1835, Lois Ann T. Wolcott; d. May 5, 1890. He was a lumberman. He d. July 18, 1876, in Angus, Canada; res. Schroon, N. Y.

    4414. i.   LEVI J., b. Apr. 25, 1836; m. Marie A. Wolcott.
    4415. ii.   WASHINGTON D., b. in 1838; m. in 1870; res. Lock Haven, Pa.
    4416. iii. PHEBE, b. Apr., 1840; m. Sept., 1865, Isaac Purvis; had 1 ch.: Annie.
    4417. iv. MARTHA, b. Mar. 2, 1849; m. Judge Love; res. Bellfonte, Pa. She d. Feb., 1877, s. p.
    4418. v.   RICHARD, b. in 1856; d. 1868.

2665. LYMAN JACKSON FISK (Eber, Nathaniel, Benjamin, Benjamin, John, John, Phinehas, Thomas, Robert, Simon, Simon, William, Symond), b. July 11, 1805, in Vermont; m. Apr. 3, 1825, Betsey Stowell. He was a farmer; was born in Vermont; moved to New York and settled near Tioga, Pa., in 1845, and died in Canada. He d. Mar. 17, 1857; res. Tioga, Pa.

    4419. i.   EZRA WILSON, b. ———; d. ———.
    4420. ii.   ANSEL JASON, b. June 16, 1829; m. Jane E. Spencer.
    4421. iii. WM. JACKSON, b. Jan. 2, 1833; m. Harriet H. Hamner.
    4422. iv. LYMAN WATSON, b. ———; d. ———.
    4423. v.   BETSEY MARIAH, b. ———; d. ae. 12.
    4424. vi. ANDREW W., b. ———; res. Tioga, Pa.
    4425. vii. TWO CH.; d. young.

2668. RUFUS FISK (Eber, Nathaniel, Benjamin, Benjamin, John, John, Phinehas, Thomas, Robert, Simon, Simon, William, Symond), b. Apr. 3, 1820, Schroon, N. Y.; m. Oct. 12, 1847, Eliza Wickham, b. Mar. 5, 1827; d. Apr. 22, 1894. He is a lumberman and farmer; res. North Hudson, N. Y.

4426. i. FRANK R., b. July 14, 1848.
4427. ii. SILVIA, b. —— 29, 1852; d. Sept. 12, 1854.
4428. iii. WM. R., b. Mar. 11, 1856.
4429. iv. FLORENCE I., b. Nov. 2, 1857.
4430. v. GEORGE, b. Oct. 17, 1866; d. Jan. 28, 1868.
4431. vi. BENJ. L., b. Aug. 30, 1870.

2669. EBER FISK (Eber, Nathaniel, Benjamin, Benjamin, John, John, Phinehas, Thomas, Robert, Simon, Simon, William, Symond), b. Nov. 17, 1815, in Brandon, Vt.; m. Nov., 1835, Eleanor Dexter. She d. in 1863; m. 2d, in 1864, —— ——. He d. 1881; res. ——. First wife, six children; all dead but one. Second wife, five more.

2673. SOLOMON FISK (Eber, Nathaniel, Benjamin, Benjamin, John, John, Phinehas, Thomas, Robert, Simon, Simon, William, Symond), b. Feb. 19, 1798, in Brandon, Vt.; m. Feb. 18, ——, Almira Huntley. He d. Apr. 2, 1857; res. Des Moines, Ia.
4432. i. EVELINE, b. ——.
4433. ii. RUTH, b. ——.
4435. iii. ALMIRA, b. ——.
4436. iv. JASON, b. ——.

2680. JOHN FISK (Nathaniel, Nathaniel, Benjamin, Benjamin, John, John, Phinehas, Thomas, Robert, Simon, Simon, William, Symond), b. Brandon, Vt., June 1, 1803; m. there, Feb. 13, 1834, Almira H. Soper, b. Apr. 19, 1810; d. Feb. 23, 1893. He was a farmer. He d. May 23, 1843; res. Brandon, Vt.
4437. i. JAMES F., b. June 2, 1835; m. Lois R. Clark.
4438. ii. ABIGAIL CHARITY, b. Feb. 23, 1838; m. Jan. 1, 1863, Benjamin F. Huff; res. Sudbury, Vt. He was b. Apr. 11, 1832. Is a farmer. Ch.: Wilbur James Huff, b. Nov. 6, 1864; Sudbury, Vt. Frank Leslie Huff, b. Aug. 6, 1870, Tilton, N. H. Arthur David Huff, b. Nov. 6, 1871, Tilton, N. H. Stella Maria Huff, b. June 8, 1879, Sudbry, Vt. None married.

2690. GIDEON MEAD FISKE (David, Nathaniel, Benjamin, Benjamin, John, John, Phinehas, Thomas, Robert, Simon, Simon, William, Symond), b. Stillwater, N. Y., Nov. 25, 1786; m. at Williston, Vt., May, 1816, Sophia Wallace, b. Holland, Mass., Dec. 22, 1789; d. Oct. 24, 1841; m. 2d, in So. Hero, Vt., Apr. 15, 1843, Emily Austin, b. Waterbury, Vt., Apr. 29, 1807. He was born in New York State, but shortly after marriage resided at South Hero, an island in Lake Champlain. He sold out there in 1852 and moved to Moira, N. Y., where he purchased a farm. The following winter he met with an accident that incapacitated him from any kind of manual labor. In splitting wood the axe glanced and went into the left foot. Gangrene set in before many weeks, and on Apr. 29, just three months after the accident, it was amputated; even then it did not get along well, for the arteries broke out and another operation was performed about four weeks after the first. He slowly regained his health, and for a few years could get around some on his crutches, when a more terrible affliction overtook him; for the last five or six years of his life he was totally blind. At one time he had a fulling mill, on Otter Creek, in Vermont, while residing in Weybridge, but it was swept away in a freshet. He d. Dec. 18, 1863; res. Moira, N. Y.
4439. i. LORENZO CHAPIN, b. Aug. 29, 1824; m. Sarah Louise Young.
4440. ii. GEORGE WALLACE, b. Dec. 29, 1827; m. Jane A. Reynolds and Cornelia Rowe.
4441. iii. ISAAC APLIN, b. Dec. 27, 1831; m. Marion Fruto.
4442. iv. JULIA ANN RUTH, b. Jan. 29, 1844; m. Apr. 10, 1866. George Mitchell; res. 1313 Fifth St., S. E. Minneapolis, Minn., s. p.
4443. v. JANE, b. Aug. 29, 1817; d. Feb. 29, 1818.

2691. WILLIAM FISK (David, Nathaniel, Benjamin, Benjamin, John, John, Phinehas, Thomas, Robert, Simon, Simon, William, Symond), b. Stillwater, N. Y., Mar. 16, 1788; m. at Jay, July 11, 1813, Abigail Razey, b. Aug. 13, 1795; d. Mar. 30, 1875. He was a cabinet maker and house joiner. He was apprenticed when 15 years of age to a Mr. Stephens, of Shoreham, Vt., at the cabinet maker's trade. He served an apprenticeship of five years, and then worked in Albany, N. Y., and Montreal, Canada. He was married in Jay, N. Y., and was at once drafted into the United States service, taken to Plattsburg, N. Y., and set to work constructing barracks for the soldiers. After the battle of Plattsburg, he was discharged from the service. He raised a family of nine children, seven boys and two girls, three of the boys are still living and one girl. He was a staunch Democrat. He was a consistent Christian from his youth. He died in the town of Jay, N. Y. He d. Apr. 29, 1861; res. Jay, N. Y.

4444.	i.	ADONIRAM JUDSON, b. July 18, 1829; d. in army, 1863.
4445.	ii.	RUFUS, b. Aug. 26, 1832; d. in army of wounds, 1863.
4446.	iii.	ELIJAH DOTY, b. Jan. 8, 1827; m. Phebe Briggs.
4447.	iv.	WM. RILEY, b. Feb. 12, 1817; m. June 1, 1842, ——. He had one son, Wilbur; res. Crary's Mills, N. Y. He d. in 1892.
4448.	v.	JOSHUA P., b. May 3, 1835; m. Pamelia C. Somers.
4449.	vi.	JAMES H., b. Sept. 18, 1841; m. Mary A. Smith and Margaret Simpson.
4450.	vii.	ALZINA MARY, b. Feb. 11, 1838; m. Nov. 29, 1876, Charles Blanchard; res. Salida, Col. He is a farmer; was b. Mar. 1, 1844. Ch.: 1, Eva L. Blanchard, b. July 21, 1878. 2, Ward L. Blanchard, b. June 26, 1880; going to school at Salida, Colo.
4451.	viii.	CHARLOTTE, b. Apr. 14, 1825; d. June 5, 1826.
4452.	ix.	AURILLA, b. Feb. 27, 1822; m. Feb. 4, 1839, —— ——. She d. June 6, 1842.
4453.	x.	ALONZO, b. June 23, 1820; d. Apr. 7, 1827.

2692. ELIJAH DOTY FISK (David, Nathaniel, Benjamin, Benjamin, John, John, Phinehas, Thomas, Robert, Simon, Simon, William, Symond), b. Bemis Heights, Stillwater, N. Y., June 1, 1791; m. at Northumberland, N. Y., Anna Sutphin, b. Oct. 16, 1792; d. Aug., 1869. He was born on the historic Bemis Heights, in Stillwater, Saratoga county, New York. Received an excellent education for those early days, and for some time was engaged in teaching school. Learned the clothier's trade, which he followed for some time, but during the latter part of his life was an extensive farmer. He d. Jan. 7, 1870; res. Orwell, Vt.

4454.	i.	CHARLES, b. Jan. 28, 1832; m. Frances J. Coburn.
4455.	ii.	JOHN, b. Jan. 6, 1826; d. unm., July 9, 1865.
4456.	iii.	ANN, b. June 28, 1834; d. unm., Dec. 18, 1878.

2696. ALMOND W. FISKE (Stephen K., Daniel, Daniel, Benjamin, John, John, Phinehas, Thomas, Robert, Simon, Simon, William, Symond), b. Scituate, R. I., Aug. 23, 1830; m. there, Jan. 1, 1853, Amy Cahoon, b. Apr. 8, 1831. He is a farmer; res. Hope, R. I.

4457.	i.	MERCY E., b. May 13, 1860; m. —— Brayton; res. Fiskville, R. I.

2697. DANIEL FISK (Stephen K., Daniel, Daniel, Benjamin, John, John, Phinehas, Thomas, Robert, Simon, Simon, William, Symond), b. Scituate, R. I., May 27, 1817; m. at East Killingly, Conn., July 3, 1842, Ruth Burlingame, b. June 20, 1820. He was born on a farm in Scituate, R. I., and his education was mostly through the country schools. By studying at home he fitted himself for the high school, mathematics being his favorite study. He then went to high school in South Scituate, returning home and teaching a school of eighty odd scholars without any assistant in the village of Hope, town of Scituate. At the age of 25 he moved with his father to said village of Hope, and was married the following summer. His father and he carried on the farm together. He was a Justice of the Peace and lived there until Feb., 1848. Then he bought a good farm of 150 acres in Brookfield, Mass., and went there with his wife and three children to live, remaining there until the year 1876, at which time he gave up business and removed to 56 Coral St., Worcester, Mass. Res. 56 Coral St., Worcester, Mass.

4458.	i.	JULIA ANN, b. Aug. 13, 1844; m. Nov. 15, 1865, Geo. R. Hamant; P. O. North Brookfield, Mass.
4459.	ii.	MARY ELIZABETH, b. Jan. 19, 1846; m. Nov. 16, 1865, Moses Hobbs; P. O. North Brookfield, Mass.

4460. iii. SUSAN MARIAH, b. ———; unm; P. O. Worcester, Mass.
4461. iv.   STEPHEN BURLINGAME, b. Oct. 30, 1849; m. Alice N. Stebbins.
4462. v.   CELIA JANE, b. Apr. 7, 1854; unm.; P. O. 56 Coral St., Worcester, Mass.
4463. vi.   CHAS. DANIEL, b. Mar. 13, 1856; m. Melinda Brooks.
4464. vii. SARAH FRANCES, b. Dec. 15, 1858; m. June 1, 1887, John Chas. Hawkins; P. O. Fiskeville, R. I. Ch.: 1, Clara Maud, b. May 17, 1888; d. Oct. 1, 1888. 2, Arthur Fiske, b. Jan. 17, 1891.

2699. STEPHEN FISKE (Stephen K., Daniel, Daniel, Benjamin, John, John, Phinehas, Thomas, Robert, Simon, Simon, William, Symond), b. June 21, 1819, in Scituate, R. I.; m. at Coventry, Apr. 15, 1841, Cynthia Colvin, b. June 26, 1817; d. Sept. 10, 1892. He was a farmer. He d. Nov. 24, 1882; res. Scituate, R. I.
4465. i.   STEPHEN K., b. Aug. 28, 1842; m. Hannah M. Carr.
4466. ii.   CHARLES FRED'K, b. Nov. 10, 1855; P. M. Fiskeville, R. I.
4467. iii. CLARINDA ANN, b. Feb. 18, 1844; m. Mar. 29, 1862, ——— Colvin; res. Hope, R. I.
4468. iv.   ELIZA ALMY, b. Nov. 7, 1847; m. June 4, 1865, ——— Young; res. Hope.

2700. EBENEZER FISKE (Stephen K., Daniel, Daniel, Benjamin, John, John, Phinehas, Thomas, Robert, Simon, Simon, William, Symond), b. Scituate. R. I., Aug. 31, 1821; m. in Coventry, R. I., in 1840, Amy Colvin, b. Apr. 16, 1820. He was a farmer. He d. Nov. 5, 1883; res. Hope, R. I.
4469. i.   NATHAN, b. Dec. 6, 1841; m. Melissa E. Matteson.
4470. ii.   EBENEZER B., b. May 23, 1850; m. Oct. 10, 1869; res. Fiskdale, R. I.

2703. ASABEL FISK (Isaac, Daniel, Daniel, Benjamin, John, John, Phinehas, Thomas, Robert, Simon, Simon, William, Symond), b. South Scituate, R. I., Mar. 17, 1823; m. in Warwick, R. I., Rachel S. Parkhurst, b. Apr. 16, 1830. He is a house carpenter. Res. 90 Sycamore St., Providence, R. I., s. p.

2705. WILLIAM NILES FISK (Isaac, Daniel, Daniel, Benjamin, John, John, Phinehas, Thomas, Robert, Simon, Simon, William, Symond), b. So. Scituate, R. I., Oct. 29, 1819; m. Apr. 14, 1849, Phebe H. Luther, of Scituate, b. Oct. 11, 1820. He is a farmer; res. Greene, R. I.
4471. i.   CHARLES EDWIN, b. Aug. 11, 1850.
4472. ii.   DULINDA, b. Dec. 27, 1851.
4473. iii. ABBIE FRANCES, b. July 3, 1853.
4474. iv.   WHEATON LUTHER, b. Feb. 4, 1855.
4475. v.   MARY ELLEN, b. Sept. 25, 1856.
4476. vi.   JOHN A., b. Mar. 2, 1863.
4477. vii. HATTIE MARIA, b. Sept. 20, 1861.
4478. viii. IDA M., b. Jan. 15, 1859.

2711. ALBERT DANY FISKE (Isaac, Daniel, Benjamin, John, John, Phinehas, Thomas, Robert, Simon, Simon, William, Symond), b. Mar. 15, 1833, in So. Scituate, R. I.; m. in Coventry, Apr. 4, 1858, Roxanna S. Johnson, b. Apr. 2, 1836; d. Dec. 3, 1888. He was a farmer. He d. Oct. 21, 1895; res. Coventry, R. I.
4479. i.   INFANT, b. July 22, 1864; d. July 22, 1864.
4480. ii.   GEO. R., b. Oct. 27, 1866; m. Harriett E. Knight and Mary A. E. Johnson.
4481. iii. CHARLES ALBERT, b. Aug. 3, 1871; res. Washington, R. I.

2713. REUBEN HENRY FISK (Isaac, Daniel, Daniel, Benjamin, John, John, Phinehas, Thomas, Robert, Simon, Simon, William, Symond), b. Coventry, R. I., Mar. 1, 1817; m. Scituate, Dec. 9, 1838, Sarah Maria Wilbor, b. Mar. 31, 1818; d. Apr. 4, 1888. He was a farmer. He d. July 21, 1858; res. Coventry, R. I.
4482. i.   JAMES HENRY, b. Feb. 2, 1849; d. Mar. 5, 1849.
4483. ii.   HENRY PERRY, b. July 13, 1851; d. Nov. 13, 1852.
4484. iii. GEO. W., b. Mar. 8, 1841; d. Dec. 27, 1862.

4485. iv. FRANK, b. Dec. 9, 1855; d. Sept. 9, 1865.
4486. v. ISAAC, b. Nov. 24, 1858; m. June 14, 1883, Lucy Elizabeth Andrews, b. June 14, 1863. He is a wheelwright and blacksmith; res. Greene, R. I., s. p.

2715. EGBERT HARDIN FISKE (Arnold, Daniel, Daniel, Benjamin, John, John, Phinehas, Thomas, Robert, Simon, Simon, William, Symond), b. Mar. 23, 1840, East Greenwich, R. I.; m. Apr. 25, 1859, Frances Jane Harris, b. Oct. 5, 1839; d. Dec. 13, 1892. He is a railway postal clerk; res. 30 Hudson St., Providence, R. I.

4487. i. FREDERICK HARRIS, b. Dec. 8, 1861; m. Dec., 1892, ——— ———; s. p.; res. 724 Cranston St., Providence.
4488. ii. EGBERT ARNOLD, b. Nov. 23, 1859; d. in infancy Oct. 11, 1860.
4489. iii. WM. SALISBURY, b. June 27, 1863; d. Aug. 11, 1865.
4490. iv. CHAS. WAYLAND, b. Apr. 23, 1865; m. Lizzie May Hawkes.
4491. v. ELISHA ARNOLD, b. Sept. 4, 1866; d. Mar. 27, 1875.
4492. vi. JAMES, b. Jan. 28, 1871; d. Apr. 2, 1875.

2718. ABRAM FISKE (Abram, Jonathan, John, Benjamin, John, John, Phinehas, Thomas, Robert, Simon, Simon, William, Symond), b. Whitestown, N. Y., Mar. 18, 1797; m. at Rochester, Nov. 29, 1818, Sarah King, b. Dec. 25, 1798; d. Mar. 3, 1851. He was a farmer and lumberman. He d. Aug. 11, 1874; res. Rochester, N. Y., and Girard, Pa.

4493. i. CHAS. ABRAM, b. July 8, 1826; m. Lucile J. Detchon.
4494. ii. BRYANT HENRY, b. Apr. 18, 1836; m. Alice S. Barrett.
4495. iii. LYMAN THOMAS, b. Sept. 14, 1830; m. Sallie A. Clark.
4496. iv. SARAH JANE, b. Nov. 22, 1824; m. Jan. 1, 1847, James McConnell; res. Painesville, Ohio, and 33 Marvin Ave., Cleveland, Ohio. He was b. Dec. 25, 1816; was a farmer. Ch.: 1, W. G. McConnell, b. Apr. 22, 1848; m. May 20, 1873. 2, W. E. McConnell, b. Oct. 24, 1849; m. ———, 1880. 3, Henry B. McConnell, b. Feb. 4, 1851; d. Mar. 29, 1870. 4, Lillian McConnell Cook, b. May 18, 1853; m. May 1, 1874; d. Jan. 15, 1888. 5, Jas. F. McConnell, b. May 1, 1855; m. 1880. 6, Dan J. McConnell, b. Mar. 10, 1860; d. Nov., 1881. 7, Jennie McConnell Cook, b. Feb. 28, 1866; m. June 8, 1889.
4497. v. DANIEL D., b. Aug. 24, 1833; m. Fannie J. Van Dorn.
4498. vi. LEONARD P., b. Feb. 7, 1828; m. Bulah Ann Wells.
4499. vii. ETHELINDA M., b. Oct. 17, 1820; unm.; res. 228 W. 20th, Erie, Pa.; is a fashionable dressmaker.
4500. viii. MATTHEW D., b. Aug. 20, 1823; m. Lucy A. Mitchell.
4501. ix. MARY ANN, b. Sept. 20, 1819; m. June 20, 1835, Jacob Madole. She d. in Ringwood. Ill., Mar. 26, 1852. He was b. Sept. 5, 1814; d. Nov. 13, 1885, in Ringwood. Ill. He was a farmer. Ch.: Marietta Madole, b. May 20, 1836, Chautauqua County, New York; m. Oct., 1854, Wm. Lumley. She d. leaving Dr. Wm. Alison; res. Renfield, Minn.; George, res. Ringwood. Ill. 2, Infant, b. ———, Clymer, N. Y.; lived 38 hours. 3, Sally Madole, b. July 6, 1838; is a teacher in Salt Lake City, Utah. 4, Anson Madole, b. ———; d. ae. 6 months. 5, Hugh Madole, b. ———; d. ae. 9 months. 6, Henry Madole, b. ———; d. ae. 18 months. 7, Eunice Madole Taylor, b. Mar. 30, 1845, Corry, Concord Township, Erie County, Pa.; d. ———. 8, Emily Madole, b. July 28, 1847; m. ——— Lyon; res. Des Moines, Ia. 9, Alvin Madole, b. May 13, 1849; res. Landrum, N. C. 10. Andrew Madole, b. Dec. 16, 1850; res. Des Moines, Ia.
4502. x. ADELINE ESTHER, b. Mar. 28, 1838; m. 1864 George J. Squier. She d. Jan. 19, 1866.
4503. xi. FRANKLIN NORMAN, b. Aug. 12, 1841; m. Ida S. Craig.
4504. xii. WILLIAM D., b. June 30, 1822; d. 1825.

2719. JOHN FISK (Abram, Jonathan, John, Benjamin, John, John, Phinehas, Thomas, Robert, Simon, Simon, William, Symond), b. in Massachusetts in

1789; m. in Vermont, Nov. 14, 1813, Betsey Morgan, b. in 1796; d. Oct. 1, 1873, in Francisco, Mich. He taught school in the early part of the present century. He was in the War of 1812, and received a land warrant for 160 acres. He was a member of the Baptist Church fifteen years, and studied the Scriptures until he became convinced that they were not of Divine origin; then he became an infidel. He became a spiritualist a few years before his death. He was up to the times in the age in which he lived. He was a Whig and Republican. He d. Sept., 1871; res. Cheshire, Mich.

    4505. i.   WM. WALLACE, b. ———; res. Cheshire.
    4506. ii.   ALFRED, b. Sept. 2, 1814; m. Sarah Miller.
    4507. iii. MARIE, b. ———; m. ——— Baker.
    4508. iv. SARAH ANN, b. ———; m. Hiram Fisk. She d., s. p., in Francisco, Mich.
    4509. v.   ELIZA, b. ———; m. ——— French; res. Three Rivers, Mich.
    4510. vi. DELIA, b. ———; m. ——— Thatcher.
    4511. vii. CAROLINE F., b. ———; m. ——— Jones.
               Clinton Fisk French, son of Eliza Fisk French, is living in Summit County, Ohio, near Cuyahoga Falls, and Ritchfield; Mrs. Adelia Bean, daughter of Caroline Fisk Jones, is living in Ravenna, Portage County, Ohio.

    2720. EPHRAIM J. FISK (Abram, Jonathan, John, Benjamin, John, John, Phinehas, Thomas, Robert, Simon, Simon, William, Symond), b. Sackets Harbor, N. Y., in 1794; m. there Catherine Chapman, b. July 17, 1801; d. Nov., 1869. He was a farmer. He d. June 15, 1875; res. Watertown, N. Y., and Altoona, Mich.

    4512. i.   ANSON A., b. Feb. 24, 1832; m. Rachel Jane Broaght.
    4513. ii.   ALBERT b. ———; d. unm.
    4514. iii. JOHN, b. ———; m., and d. s. p.
    4515. iv. ORVILLE, b. Aug. 2, 1819; m. Esther Ann Vandyke and Mrs. Anna E. Ovitt.
    4516. v.   ELIZABETH, b. ———.
    4517. vi. HEPSIBETH, b. ———.

    2721. DANIEL FISK (Abraham, Jonathan, John, Benjamin, John, John, Phinehas, Thomas, Robert, Simon, Simon, William, Symond), b. Whitesboro (Utica), N. Y., June 10, 1792; m. May 29, 1816, Sarah Doolittle Brown, b. St. Johnsbury, Vt., Dec. 24, 1798; d. in Sparta, Wis., in July, 1877. Daniel Fisk, second son of Abram and Elizabeth (Arnold) Fisk, was born at Whitesboro, N. Y. (now Utica), June 10, 1792, and reared there and at Watertown, N. Y., on his father's farm receiving only the rudiments of an education. He served an apprenticeship at the trade of a molder which he afterward followed at divers times. He served in the War of 1812 at Sacketts Harbor. In 1816 he married Sarah D. Bowen, of St. Johnsbury, Vt., a daughter of Pelig and Eusebia (Harvey) Bowen. After marriage he owned and operated a farm in Jefferson County, N. Y., until 1820, when he moved to Ohio and on to a farm purchased at Conneaut, Ashtabula County. In 1823 he sold the farm and returning to New York was connected with a foundry and furnace at Rossie until 1826, when he moved to Springfield, Ohio, where he purchased lands containing a bed of potter's clay and built a pottery which he operated very successfully until 1835, when he sold the Springfield property and purchased an interest in a pottery at Hamilton, Ontario, Canada, and a gypsum bed near that place. In 1836 he built a pottery at Cleveland, Ohio, and moved his family there into a fine home located on the city square, opposite the court house. He was now a wealthy man but in 1838 the business failure of a partner with whom he had become connected in Cleveland swept away a large portion of his property, and refusing to take advantage of the newly enacted bankrupt laws, he gave up everything, including his home in Cleveland, except his interests in Canada. He went to Canada, built a mill at his gypsum beds, and commenced what proved a profitable business; but the locality proved very unhealthful; his eldest son, Lorenzo, coming over to assist in the business, was taken sick and died there, and his own health failing he disposed of this and his Hamilton property in 1842-43 and purchasing wild lands near Middleburg, Ohio, returned to his old occupation —molding—at that place, improving his lands from time to time as the opportunity offered. In 1852 disposing of his property he removed with his own and the family of his son-in-law, W. W. Robinson, to Sparta, Monroe County, Wis., where he secured lands and continued to live, with the exception of a short sojourn in Minnesota, 1859-60, until his death in April, 1868, devoting his attention to farming, though not exclusively, as he claimed to have found a valuable bed of potter's clay in Monroe County and was gathering means to purchase the lands containing it when he died, the secret of its location dying with him. He was a man of wonderful energy and pluck, of a happy and rollicking disposition, never cast down or discouraged. He died without a moment's indisposition, seated in his easy chair, nearly 76 years of age, but in manner and carriage not more than 50. His widow survived him ten years, dying in 1878. He d. in Apr., 1868; res. Watertown, N. Y., and Sparta, Wis.

4518. i. DANIEL LORENZO, b. 1817; d. unm. 1841.

4519. ii. SARAH JANE, b. Sept. 18, 1819; m. Feb. 5, 1842, Col. William Wallace Robinson. He was b. Fair Haven, Vt., Dec. 14, 1819; res. Wildwood, Wis. William Wallace Robinson (husband of Sarah Jane Fisk), son of John Williams and Rebecca (Merritt) Robinson, is a descendant in the seventh generation from John Robinson of Leyden, Holland, Fame ("the Puritan Father"). Born at Fair Haven, Vt., Dec. 14, 1819, he received his education in the common schools of Vermont and Castleton Seminary and Rutland Academy, graduating from the last named when 19 years of age. He also took a course at the Norwich Military Academy. From 1838 to 1840 he taught school in his native State and New Jersey, when he went to Cleveland, Ohio, and in company with Wm. Murphy, a professor of languages from Philadelphia, opened and conducted for some years the "Cleveland High School and Academy." Feb 5, 1842, he married Sarah Jane, the eldest daughter of Daniel Fisk, and continued to teach until war was declared with Mexico in 1846. He promptly enlisted with Ohio volunteers and was elected First Lieutenant of his company which was assigned to the Third Regiment Ohio Volunteers, as Company G, his commission bearing date June 12, 1846. Oct. 26, 1846, he was promoted Captain of his company. He served at Fort Brown and Matamoras, Carnargo, Monterey and Buena Vista, though his command took no part in those battles being engaged on detached service. In July, 1847, the terms of enlistment of the regiment expiring, the entire command was mustered out of the service at New Orleans and he returned to Ohio and engaged in farming and teaching until the summer of 1851, when he made a trip to Wisconsin, locating lands for himself and father-in-law, Daniel Fisk, at Sparta, Monroe County. Returning to Ohio in the fall, intending to move his family to Wisconsin in the spring, he changed his plans, and went to California himself, leaving his family with Mr. Fisk who removed with them to Wisconsin in Sept., 1852. The trip to California, overland, consumed six months to a day, he arriving at Whiskey Diggings, Sierra County, in September. He engaged in mining for a few weeks but soon with several partners took a contract to construct a flume, some eleven miles in length, for the Minnesota Water Company, which was to conduct water from a mountain stream for use at "Smiths" and the "Minnesota Diggings." After completing this job he engaged in various enterprises of a more or less remunerative character until the fall of 1855, when he rejoined his family at Sparta, Wis., and removing during the winter of 1855-56 to Waseca County, Minnesota, founded the town of Wilton which for a time became the county seat. In 1858 he ran for the State Legislature on the Democratic ticket, but was defeated, and was appointed Colonel of the Ninth Regiment Minnesota Militia, by Governor Sibley. In 1859 selling his Minnesota property he returned to Sparta, Wis., and built a home

on his lands near that village. At the breaking out of the
Civil war he was engaged in drilling the first company raised in
the county, and Aug. 15, 1861, was commissioned Lieutenant-
Colonel of the Seventh Regiment Wisconsin Volunteer Infantry, and with this regiment, which with four others constituted
the famous Iron Brigade, he served, taking part in every battle
fought by the Army of the Potomac except the first Bull Run,
Antietam (fought while he was in hospital with a severe wound
received at battle of Gainesville) and Five Forks. He was promoted Colonel of the regiment in Feb., 1862, and was frequently in command of the brigade by reason of his seniority before
1863, but from the morning of the first day's fight at Gettysburg, when Brigadier-General Meredith was wounded, he commanded the Iron Brigade through the bloody campaigns of
1863-64 and until the army sat down in the trenches around
Petersburg, when suffering from sickness and the breaking
out of his wound received in 1862 he resigned in July, 1864.
He had taken part in over thirty battles and "affairs" and
though "hit" three times, received but one serious wound, that
at Gainesville. His regiment, the Seventh Wisconsin, lost
more men killed and wounded by four than any other taking
part in the war, as is shown by the records of the War Department and recently published. At the close of the war he was
tendered a Brevet Brigadier-General's commission, but declined it. After somewhat recovering from his wounds (1865),
he engaged in farming and lumbering, removing to Chippewa
Falls, Wis., in 1874. In 1875 he was appointed United States
Consul to Madagascar by President Grant, and undisturbed
by succeeding administrations held that office until the fall of
1886, when, heeding the remonstrances of his children, he resigned and came home to spend his old age surrounded by his
children and grandchildren. During his service in Madagascar
he made the treaty with that government which the French
at this writing are attempting to set aside, and at the urgent request of the Queen of Madagascar was directed by our State
Department to accompany the Malagassy Embassy on its visit
to the courts of Europe and to the United States in 1882-83
during its vain search for peace. He and his wife are now living with his youngest son in Wisconsin, hale and hearty,
though both are in their 77th year. He is a descendant of the
Rev. John Robinson, the Leyden pastor, b. in Lincolnshire,
England, 1575; emigrated to Leyden, Holland, in 1608, with his
congregation, and there formed the nucleus of the Plymouth
Colony of 1620. He is a direct descendant of his through his
son Isaac, b. 1610; Peter, b. 1660; Peter, Jr., b. 1697; Eliab, b.
1742; John William, b. 1782; William Wallace. Ch.: 1, Edward Lorenzo, b. Nov. 26, 1842; d. 1851 in Ohio. 2,
Leonora Colista, b. Aug. 10, 1844; m. 1862, at Washington, D.
C., to General Hollan Richardson; present add. Chippewa
Falls, Wis. 3, William Wallace, Jr., b. Apr. 21, 1846; graduated West Point, N. Y., June, 1869; now Captain and Quartermaster of United States Army; add. The Presidio, San Francisco, Cal.; m. Aug., 1869, Ella L. Winsor; m. 2d, Mar. 31, 1887,
Minnie Ten Eyck; ch.: Ella Nora, b. Nov. 28, 1873; add. Sparta, Wis. Edward Winsor, b. Feb. 18, 1875; add. West Point,
N. Y. May Josephine, b. May or June, 1880; add. Sparta, Wis.
4, Herbert Fisk, b. Aug. 2, 1858; m. at Chippewa Falls, Wis.,
Dec. 31, 1879; add. Wildwood, Wis. 5, Inez Euseba, b. Aug.
27, 1860; d. Aug. 5, 1864.

4520.   iii.   SOPHIA, b. Mar. 19, 1826; m. Sept. 5, 1842, Dr. Wm. Murphy.
               She d. Apr. 4, 1891. He was b. County Armagh, Ireland, Oct.
               7, 1815; d. at Wilton, Minn., May 16, 1859. He was a homeo-
               pathic physician. Ch.: John Fisk, b. Jan. 7, 1850; m. Nov. 15,

1871, Emma Jane Hiller, b. Sept. 12, 1853. He is editor and publisher of the Waseca, Minn., Herald; ch.: Mattie Inez, b. Nov. 7, 1872. Clementina S. Murphy, b. Oct. 31, 1843; m. Jan. 10, 1863; d. Dec. 14, 1888. Charles H. Murphy, b. Apr. 11, M. Murphy, b. Jan. 21, 1852; m. Oct. 20, 1878; add. 1332 Hewitt 1845; d. June 8, 1859. Sarah A. Murphy, b. June 15, 1847; m. May, 1868, —— Ascott; add. 627 Wilson St., Winona, Minn. William M. Murphy, b. Jan. 21, 1852; m. Oct. 20, 1878; add. 1332 Hewitt Ave., Hamline, St. Paul, Minn. Susan H. Murphy, b. Sept. 4, 1854; m. Apr. 2, 1874, —— Young; add. Holloway, Swift County, Minn. Frank S. Murphy, b. Apr. 12, 1857; m. July 31, 1885; add. Austin, Minn. Address of Clementina S. Murphy's (deceased) daughter, Mrs. Nellie Hale, Turney's Station, Clinton County, Mo.

4521. iv. MARY CORDELIA, b. 1828; m. Alpheus Lansdale. She d. 1886; a son Arthur res. Weston, Ore.

4522. v. WILBUR F., b. 1829; m., and d., s. p., 1859. He was the first Register of Deeds of Menominee County, Wis.

4523. vi. GEO. AUGUSTUS, b. Aug. 5, 1831; m. Catherine E. Walrath.

4524. vii. MARTHA E., b. 1834; d. 1838.

4525. viii. EDWIN FRANKLIN, b. 1835; d. in infancy.

2722. WM. RILEY FISKE (Abram, Jonathan, John, Benjamin, John, John, Phinehas, Thomas, Robert, Simon, Simon, William, Symond), b. ——; m. Susanna King. He d. in Minnesota; res. Watertown, N. Y.

4526. i. RUSSELL, b. ——.

4527. ii. WILLIAM, b. ——.

2723. IRA FISK (Abram, Jonathan, John, Benjamin, John, John, Phinehas, Thomas, Robert, Simon, Simon, William, Symond), b. Whitestown, N. Y., in 1799; m. Joanna Holbrook. She was b. near White River, Vt., 1798; d. in Watertown, N. Y., in 1869. He was a farmer. He d. in 1871; res. Watertown, N. Y.

4528. i. JOHN HOLBROOK, b. Oct. 26, 1824; m. Oct. 13, 1852, Calista M. Heath, b. June 4, 1822; d., s. p., Dec. 31, 1875. Is a farmer; res. Watertown, N. Y., s. p.

4529. ii. IRA, b. Aug. 26, 1826; m. Nov. 26, 1867, Mary C. Snell, b. Sept. 17, 1841. They res. Watertown, N. Y., s. p. Is a retired farmer.

4530. iii. ANN, b. Aug. 26, 1826; d. unm., Nov. 7, 1893.

4531. iv. ABRAM, b. June 12, 1828; unm.

4532. v. SUSAN, b. Nov. 27, 1829; unm.

4533. vi. LORINDA M., b. Dec. 12, 1831; d. May 2, 1859.

4534. vii. DUANE T., b. June 8, 1833; m. Adelaide F. Heath.

4535. viii. JEROME. b. Feb. 14. 1839; d. Aug. 20, 1840.

4536. ix. MELISSA ELIZABETH, b. Feb. 12, 1835; m. Oct. 15, 1854, Clark Edward Freeman, b. Dec. 30, 1831. He d. July 16, 1866, leaving three children: 1, Fannie Annette Freeman, b. July 24, 1856; d. Sept. 29, 1861. 2, Ira J. Freeman, b. July 7, 1861; m. Mary Elizabeth Wylie. Mar. 26, 1884; she was b. Nov. 23, 1861; they have three children, Wylie Fisk Freeman, b. Nov. 25, 1888; Emily Melissa Freeman, b. Sept. 7, 1890; Clark Edward Freeman, b. Dec. 8, 1894. 3, Dora May Freeman, b. Dec. 6, 1862; m. Smith Allen Persons, Feb. 9, 1881; he was b. in Ellisburg, Nov. 23, 1856; d. Dec. 28, 1891, in Sandy Creek, Oswego Co., N. Y.; he was a Republican in politics; in religion they were both Baptists; they have two children, Ethel Elizabeth Persons, b. Oct. 28, 1883; Smith Clark Persons, b. Nov. 10, 1890.

2729. SQUIRE GILBERT FISK (Jacob. Jonathan, John, Benjamin, John, John, Phinehas. Thomas, Robert, Simon, Simon, William, Symond), b. Lee, Oneida Co., N. Y., Aug. 5, 1816; m. Mar. 23, 1845, Christiana M. Borst, b. Sept. 3. 1827. Squire Gilbert Fisk inherited his father's farm in Oneida Co., N. Y., but while the parent enjoyed country life and succeeded in fancy farming and stock breeding, the son preferred another line of occupation. Gilbert, as he was called, had, in search of education, found city life more congenial than the lonely and drear days and nights on a farm. He soon disposed of the farm and removed to Oswego, N. Y. He here established a teaming business, which he conducted with fair success for many years. He had a thorough knowledge of horses, and in his string of teams, private and draft horses, he had the pride of the city, and was noted for his fine stock. He was a very conservative man, strong in his political preferences, yet would never consider political preferment. But his Republicanism was very pronounced. When nearing 50 years of age, his health became poor, and he gave up business cares, and sought many sources for the restoration of physical forces, with limited success. In this way he spent the last ten years of his life, and after about four years of serious throat trouble, partial paralysis developed, and he died at the age of 64 years. He d. Sept. 10, 1880; res. Oswego, N. Y.

4537. i.   GEORGE H., b. Jan. 28, 1846; d. Aug. 7, 1862.
4538. ii. MARY, b. Aug. 17, 1847; d. Feb. 21, 1848.
4539. iii. EDWIN JAY, b. Dec. 26, 1848; m. at Round Lake, N. Y., Sept.

17, 1894, Hattie A. Newton, b. Mar. 8, 1849. Dr. Edwin Jay Fiske, of Troy, N. Y., was born at Rome, N. Y., Dec. 26, 1848. While he was an infant his people removed to Oswego, N. Y. where he attended the schools of that city (rated the best in the state), finishing there his studies in Oswego, in 1867, after which he went to a preparatory school for one year, at Hannibal, N. Y. He spent the spring and summer of 1865 as a clerk in the Oswego postoffice, thus being a government clerk at the time President Lincoln was shot, and wore for thirty days the customary evidence

DR. EDWIN JAY FISKE.

of mourning, crape on the left arm. In the spring of 1868 he went to Albany, N. Y., to prepare for a medical course. Prior to entering upon the full course of medicine, he took the advanced course in the Boys' Academy, Albany, N. Y., and following this course he took a six months' private course in study with Professor Swan, principal of the above named school. Following this course he entered the office of Dr. Andrew Wilson, of Albany, then the president of the Albany County Medical Society. He soon became a favorite of Dr. Alden March, the founder of the Albany Medical College, and accompanied this great surgeon to most of his capital surgical operations up to the time of his death, which occurred in the fall of 1869, the doctor favoring young Fiske, owing to his steady nerve, placing him in the fore when there were several bleeding arteries to pick up and tie. While yet a student, in May, 1870, he was offered and accepted a posi-

tion, with large advantages for study, in the Marshall Infirmary, Troy, N. Y. He remained here until Sept., 1871,
when he went to the City Hospital, Albany, N. Y., and took
the final course at the college, graduating the same year,
Dec. 26, 1871, the anniversary of his birthday. As a medical
student young Fiske was very popular in classes, being chairman of the first quiz class, and one of the foremost and officers
of the football and baseball teams. He was elected poet of
his class, and on two occasions replied in witty verse to newspaper criticisms of exposure of canned and dried anatomical
specimens, for a short time exposed in the museum windows,
while cleaning the museum. After graduating, he returned to
the Marshall Infirmary as assistant physician, which position
he held until Apr., 1874, when he was appointed by the Mayor
of Troy (without his knowledge) city physician, May 10, 1874,
He accepted the office, left the Infirmary, and located in the city.

He held this office four years, when he resigned and accepted
the editorial head of the New York Medical Brief. He held
this position but one year, finding journalistic work too severe
and trying. He returned to Troy, and has since confined himself to the advancement of his knowledge of medicine, keeping in active practice. Dr. Fiske is a recognized authority
on diseases of throat and lungs, and has a large practice in
this line, being much called, near and far, in consultation.

4540. iv. CHARLES W., b. July 12, 1851; res. Rochester, N. Y.
4541. v. FRANK J., b. Mar. 8, 1853; res. Rochester, N. Y.
4542. vi. CHAUNCEY M., b. June 19, 1855. Is a merchant tailor in
Rochester, N. Y.
4543. vii. JULIA M., b. July 24, 1858; d. July 31, 1883.
4544. viii. CLARA L., b. Sept. 1, 1862; res. Rochester, N. Y.

2742. JOHN FISK (James, Jonathan, John, Benjamin, John, John, Phinehas, Thomas, Robert, Simon, Simon, William, Symond), b. Nov. 22, 1818, Janius,
N. Y.; m. there, Phebe Sloan, d. Sept., 1848; m. 2d, ——— ———. He d. in
Pinckney, Mich.
4545. i. MARSHAL, b. ———.
4546. ii. ELIZA, b. ———; m. ——— Weybred.
4547. iii. PHEBE, b. July 26, 1848; m. Dec. 10, 1874, ——— Shell, b. Jan.
3, 1844; res. Francisco, Mich. Ch.: W. Scott, b. Sept. 27, 1880.

2742-3. SAMUEL KNIGHT FISK (Jonathan K., Jonathan, John, Benjamin,
John, John, Phinehas, Thomas, Robert, Simon, Simon, William, Symond), b.
Scituate, R. I., June 30, 1826; m. Ann Eliza Bishop, b. Jan. 17, 1826; d. May
2, 1895; res. Providence, R. I., 38 Oak St.
4547-1.i. STILLMAN K., b. Nov. 19, 1849; m. Mrs. Belle H. White.
4547-2.ii. CLARA ADELAID, b. ———; m. ——— Huber; res. 38 Oak St.
4547-3.iii. JAMES STEPHEN, b. ——— m. and res. 77 Byers St., Denver,
Colo.

2742-9. JEREMIAH FISKE (Jonathan K., Jonathan, John, Benjamin, John,
John, Phinehas, Thomas, Robert, Simon, Simon, William, Symond), b. Scituate,
R. I., July 25, 1824; m. Oct. 31, 1847, Sarah Ann Davis, b. S., Jan. 21, 1825. He
is a farmer; res. No. Scituate, R. I.
4547-4.i. ELMER SCOTT, b. Apr. 19, 1861; m. Mary C. Smith and Mrs.
Lina Florence (Orr) Thompson.
4547-5.ii. CHARLES H., b. Nov. 1, 1851; m. Mary A. Goodhue.
4547-6.iii. GEO. W., b. Feb. 22, 1854; res. Swansea, Mass.
4547-7.iv. WILLIS WARREN, b. Feb. 23, 1857; m. Minnie L. Bowen.
4547-8.v. ANNAH ELIZABETH, b. Oct. 5, 1849; d. 1851.
4547-9.vi. CARRIE, b. Jan. 14, 1860; d. 1860.

2746. EDWIN BROWN FISK (Jabish, Jonathan, John, Benjamin, John,
John, Phinehas, Thomas, Robert, Simon, Simon, William, Symond), b. Mar. 15,

1815, in Lee, N. Y.; m. in Summit, Wis., Jan. 30, 1844, Adaline Sanborn, b. Dec. 11, 1825. He was a farmer. He d. Nov. 28, 1891; res. Utica and Oshkosh, Wis.

4548. i. ALMEDA, b. Jan. 14, 1851; m. Oct. 29, 1872, Ernest Henry Gallup; res. 96 Church St., Oshkosh, Wis. He was b. Dec. 18, 1846, and for twenty-five years was in railway postal service; he is now retired; s. p.

4549. ii. HELEN MARIA, b. Aug. 28, 1845; d. Jan. 5, 1846.

4550. iii. FRANCES H., b. Dec. 20, 1846; m. Aug. 13, 1865, ——— Cornish; res. 92 Park St., Oshkosh.

4551. iv. MARSHAL SANBORN, b. Mar. 22, 1849; d. Feb. 21, 1876.

4552. v. CHARLES JAY, b. Dec. 23, 1853; d. unm., Sept. 15, 1881.

4553. vi. EDWIN D., b. June 27, 1862; d. unm., Dec. 9, 1882.

2747. CAPT. PELEG FISKE (Peleg, Peleg, John, Benjamin, John, John, Phinehas, Thomas, Robert, Simon, Simon, William, Symond), b. Providence, R. I., Jan. 10, 1808; m. June 21, 1827, Caroline Augusta Green, b. July 8, 1806; d. Aug. 28, 1833; m. 2d, June 21, 1834, Mary Berkley Graves, b. May 19, 1817; d. Sept. 25, 1883. He was a machinist and at one time was government gauger and steamboat captain. He d. Aug. 29, 1895; res. New Albany, Ind.

4554. i. CHARLES A., b. Aug. 10, 1828; m. Rose Paul.

4555. ii. CAROLINE AUGUSTA, b. Aug. 27, 1835; m. Thomas Moore; res. New Albany, Ind. Son, Frank A., b. ———; res. New Albany, Ind.

4556. iii. MARY ORPHA, b. May 14, 1840; m. July 16, 1863, Benjamin F. Bounds; res. Magnolia, Colo. He was b. May 12, 1832; is a farmer and stock raiser. Ch.: One daughter, Minnie C. Bounds, b. in Louisville, Ky., May 24, 1870.

4557. iv. ELIZABETH RANDALL, b. Oct. 11, 1842; m. A. D. Croxall; res. New Albany, Ind.

4558. v. SAM'L HENRY, b. Sept. 10, 1844; res. Louisville, Ky.

4559. vi. ADA ALSWITHA, b. Sept. 19, 1850; m. Apr. 29, 1875, Wm. A. Fowler; res. Marion, Ind. He was b. May 14, 1848. Is a hardware clerk. Ch.: Herbert B., b. Sept. 30, 1876. Ada L., b. May 15, 1880. Earl G., b. May 24, 1878; d. June 19, 1879. Bertha A., b. June 21, 1886.

4560. vii. PELEG, b. Mar. 27, 1847; m. Kate Stephens.

4561. viii. JOSEPHINE EVA, b. Apr. 23, 185—; m. John Cannon; res. Deland, Fla.

4562. ix. ANNA LORENA, b. Oct. 1, 185—; m. Henry Kenney; res. New Albany, Ind.

4563. x. JULIA SLOAN, b. Jan. 29, 185—; m. Frank Parks; res. Sparksville, Ind.

2753. PHILLIP FISKE (Peleg, Peleg, John, Benjamin, John, John, Phinehas, Thomas, Robert, Simon, Simon, William, Symond), b. Rhode Island, Aug. 6, 1802; m. at Providence, May 20, 1827, Caroline Briggs, b. Nov. 8, 1808; d. Sept., 1852. He was a machinist by trade. When the gold craze broke out in California, in 1849, he was an early argonaut. He was drowned in the Sacramento River. He d. 1851; res. Providence, R. I.

4564. i. ALEXANDER SEABURY, b. Apr. 6, 1828.

4565. ii. FRANCIS HENRY, b. Nov. 25, 1831; d. Sept. 6, 1831.

4566. iii. FRANCES AMALIA, b. Apr. 2, 1833; d. May 30, 1834.

4567. iv. ALBERT HENRY, b. June 26, 1834; m. Mary J. Brawner.

4568. v. SAMUEL ANTHONY, b. May 6, 1840.

4569. vi. SARAH AMELIA, b. Jan. 1, 1842; d. 1852.

4570. vii. GEORGE ERASTUS, b. 1844; d. May 27, 1862.

2756. JOHN THOMAS FISKE (Philip M., Caleb, John, Benjamin, John, John, Phinehas, Thomas, Robert, Simon, Simon, William, Symond), b. Scituate, R. I. Jan. 30, 1819; m. in Gloucester, R. I., Apr. 4, 1843, Abby Ann Eddy, b. Nov. 16, 1821; d. Oct. 28, 1860; res. Pascoag, R. I.

4571. i. ELIZA TAYLOR, b. Jan. 14, 1844; m. May 5, 1868, Charles E. Paine; res. Prov., R. I.

4572. ii. CALEB, b. Apr. 13, 1846; d. Apr. 15, 1846.
4573. iii. MARY ELIZABETH, b. Dec. 24, 1848; d. Aug. 14, 1850.
4574. iv. JOHN THOMAS, b. May 21, 1847; m. Kate E. Arnold.
4575. v. FRANK, b. Sept. 30, 1850; m. Maranda Barnes.
4576. vi. FANNIE, b. Sept. 16, 1852; m. Nov. 20, 1879, Octavus I. Norris.
She d. Mar. 3, 1881.
4577. vii. MARY OWEN, b. July 16, 1854; m. Sept. 25, 1889, Dr. Sayer Hasbrook; res. Prov.

2757. PHILIP MANCHESTER FISKE, JR. (Philip M., Caleb, John, Benjamin, John, John, Phinehas, Thomas, Robert, Simon, Simon, William, Symond), b. Fiskville, R. I., Sept. 5, 1820; m. in Prov., Sept. 13, 1843, Almira Field Bolles, d. Dec. 18, 1846. He d. Dec. 18, 1893; res. Providence, R. I.
4578. i. ——, b. ——.
4579. ii. PHILIP MANCHESTER, b. June 12, 1844; unm.; res. Boston, Mass.; is an accountant at 89 State St.

2761. JEREMIAH FISK (James, Job, Job, Benjamin, John, John, Phinehas, Thomas, Robert, Simon, Simon, William, Symond), b. Sept. 17, 1825, at Booneville, N. Y.; m. at Booneville, N. Y., June 8, 1852, Margaret Cumstock, b. at Rome, N. Y., Sept. 3, 1834; d. Apr. 8, 1867. He was in the general merchandise business. He d. Dec. 26, 1878; res. Booneville, N. Y.
4580. i. FLORA MAY, b. May 1, 1853; m. Feb. 14, 1871, Dwight W. Miller; res. Leyden, N. Y.
4581. ii. GEO. EARL, b. June 3, 1856; m. June 5, 1883, Francis E. Saunders, b. Sept. 22, 1859. He res. 16 Clifton St., Worcester, Mass., s. p. Is in the grocery business.
4582. iii. OLIVER ROBBINS, b. Feb. 16, 1859; m. June 27, 1886, Fannie Elizabeth Farr, b. Nov. 11, 1860; res. 151 Lee Ave., Brooklyn, N. Y., s. p. Is baggage agent for D., L. & W. R. R.
4583. iv. ALICE MELISSA, b. Jan. 11, 1865; adopted by Hollis R. Murdock and his wife, Sarah A. Murdock, of the city of Stillwater, Minn., Oct. 29, 1867, and is named Alice Rice Murdock; unm.
4584. v. CLINTON W., b. Mar. 8, 1867; was adopted by Hollis R. Murdock, and his wife, Sarah A. Murdock, of the city of Stillwater, Minn., Oct. 13, 1868, and is called and named Robert Clinton Murdock. He has been married twice.

2775. JOHN MANCHESTER FISKE (Jeremiah, Job, Job, Benjamin, John, John, Phinehas, Thomas, Robert, Simon, Simon, William, Symond), b. Booneville, N. Y., Oct. 1, 1809; m. July 10, 1834, Eliza A. Burgess, b. Apr. 3, 1815; d. Mar. 9, 1855; m. 2d, Delia Felt. He was a farmer and manufacturer, and held many town offices. He d. Aug. 20, 1887; res. Booneville, N. Y.
4585. i. LEANDER W., b. Sept. 30, 1835; m. Margaret M. Ward.
4586. ii. JENETTE J., b. Sept. 26, 1837; m. J. H. Smith; res. San Diego, Cal.
4587. iii. JOHN C., b. ——; d.——.
4588. iv. EDGAR L., b. Sept. 3, 1848; m. Marie C. Knudsen.
4589. v. EUGENE W., b. Mar. 8, 1851; m. Kate I. Bailey.
4590. vi. EDITH, b. Sept. 3, 1853; m. Peter Peirce. She d. ——.
4591. vii. JERRY A., b. Aug. 13, 1864; res. B.
4592. viii. MARY A., b. Apr. 1, 1861; res. B.
4593. ix. MARTIN, b. Sept. 14, 1869; res. B.

2776. ISAAC FISKE (Jeremiah, Job, Job, Benjamin, John, John, Phinehas, Thomas, Robert, Simon, Simon, William, Symond), b. Booneville, N. Y., in 1808; m. there Elizabeth Morris, b. Jan. 13, 1814. He was a hotel proprietor. He d. June, 1855; res. Booneville, N. Y.
4594. i. WILSON, b. Feb. 11, 1836; m. Harriet Seckerson.

2777. PHILANDER FISKE (Jeremiah, Job, Job, Benjamin, John, John, Phinehas, Thomas, Robert, Simon, Simon, William, Symond), b. Booneville, N. Y., 1805; m. Mary Augusta Boyd, b. Nov. 15, 1809; d. Dec. 11, 1890. He was an honorable gentleman of good education, reared a large family of girls and boys.

His conduct in this life as a citizen and a father was exemplary. He stood over six feet tall, weighed over 200 pounds, but in morality, integrity and all the other attributes that go toward making the perfect man, he stood as tall as Washington monument. He sent four of his sons to the army, William, John, Jeremiah and James, to help put down the accursed Rebellion. They all served with honor, and each was honorably discharged at the close of the war. William Manchester Fiske as Captain of the Seventy-third New York Volunteers; John Boyd Fiske, private in the Ninth New York Volunteer Infantry; Jeremiah Fiske, private in the Seventy-third New York Volunteer Infantry; James B. Fiske, private in the Fifth and One Hundred and Forty-sixth New York Volunteer Infantry. He d. in New York City; res. 229 Rivington St., New York, N. Y.

4595. i. WILLIAM M., b. Jan. 8, 1830; unm.; res. 83 Lewis St., New York City; is scroll sawyer. When the war broke out he was engaged in a successful business on his own account. He served ten years as a member of the old New York Fire Department of Volunteers, as foreman of Bunker Hill Engine Company No. 32. In 1861 he raised a regiment for the war and the command went into service as the Second Fire Zouaves, Seventy-third New York Volunteers, and commanded a company. He remained in the service until the war closed.

4596. ii. JEREMIAH, b. Oct. 31, 1837.

4597. iii. JAMES BOYD, b. Oct. 30, 1845; m. June 14, 1875, Mrs. Jane Elizabeth (Magaw) Jeffcott, b. June 24, 1847; res. s. p. 317 W. 27th St., New York City. He was quite young when he enlisted in 1862 as private in Company K, Fifth New York Volunteers, Duryee Zouaves. On May 14, 1863, he was transferred to the One Hundred and Forty-sixth Regiment New York Volunteers, and served until the close of the war; became a manufacturer of school books in 1874; made lots of money and lost lots. Today is employed by the American Book Company, New York City, as secretary.

4598. iv. EDWIN FORREST, b. Sept. 29, 1852.

4599. v. MARGARET ANN, b. June 7, 1833; d. Nov. 4, 1883.

4600. vi. JOHN BOYD, b. June 7, 1835; d. July 4, 1869.

4601. vii. MARY, b. Oct. 26, 1831; d. Feb. 16, 1833.

4602. viii. MARTHA ADELAIDE, b. Sept. 8, 1848.

4603. ix. AUGUSTUS PHILANDER, b. Nov. 18, 1839; d. Feb. 25, 1840.

4604. x. EDWARD AUGUSTUS, b. Nov. 12, 1841; d. Dec. 11, 1841.

4605. xi. MARY AUGUSTA, b. July 29, 1843; d. Mar. 5, 1873.

2780. RICHMOND FISK (Jeremiah, Jeremiah, Job, Benjamin, John, John, Phinehas, Thomas, Robert, Simon, Simon, William, Symond), b. Shaftsbury, Vt., Aug. 7, 1804; m. Mar. 7, 1824, Lurana Matteson, b. Feb. 10, 1805; d. Oct. 23, 1886; dau. of George Matteson of Shaftsbury. Richmond Fisk, b. Aug. 7, 1804, in Shaftsbury, Vt., was for many years Deputy Sheriff and then Sheriff of Bennington County. Was a man of great energy and incisive mind and large benevolence and sympathy. On the expiration of his term as Sheriff he returned to farming, and also engaged for many years in the lumber business, owning a saw mill at foot of the Green Mountains in Shaftsbury. In about 1847 he moved to Mapletown, Renss. County, N. Y., and thence in 1849 to Hoosick Falls, N. Y., still continuing in the lumber business. He became interested with Horace Greeley in a Colorado colony, and was a member of the committee which located the site and founded Greeley, Colo., where he became a prominent resident. He d. Oct. 16, 1877; res. Bennington, Vt., and Greeley, Colo.

4606. i. RICHMOND, b. Feb. 23, 1836; m. Adelaide Bartle.

4607. ii. RUSSELL, b. Mar. 22, 1827; m. Martha C. Ranney.

4608. iii. LURANA, b. Sept. 27, 1829; m. Rufus Johnson of Hoosick Falls, N. Y.; m. 2d, Frank Childs. She d. s. p., 1854.

4609. iv. ANGELA SKINNER, b. Apr. 26, 1832; m. Geo. H. Robson. She d. s. p. 1853, in Hoosick Falls, N. Y.

4610. v. GEORGE W., b. May 30, 1838; m. Lucy E. Ames and Katherine L. Moody.

4611. vi. MARY VANDELLA, b. Apr. 25, 1840; m. Nov. 19, 1861,

Lemuel Burke Ball; res. Hoosick Falls, N. Y. They have three ch.: Fred C., of Boston; Richmond, of Minneapolis, Minn., and Dr. Russell, at head of Minnesota Hospital, near St. Paul, Minn.

4612.　vii.　JEREMIAH M., b. Mar. 6, 1845; m. Abby J. Wilson.

4613.　viii.　ARTHUR W., b. Dec. 19, 1848; m. Eloise Ingalls.

2782. MIAL FISK (Jeremiah, Jeremiah, Job, Benjamin, John, John, Phinehas, Thomas, Robert, Simon, Simon, William, Symond), b. Feb. 9, 1798, in Shaftsbury, Vt.; m. at Hartford, N. Y., Annie Cumstock Hicks, b. Oct. 14, 1802; d. Nov. 24, 1881. He was a farmer. He d. South Shaftsbury, Vt., in Mar., 1877; res. Bennington, Vt.

4614.　vi.　LESTER MIAL, b. Sept. 2, 1836; m. Sarah Jane Bradley and Alzina Surdam.

4615.　i.　PATIENCE D., b. Aug. 29, 1825; m. Truman Eddy; res. 315 County St., Bennington.

4616.　ii.　ELIZA ANN, b. May 12, 1827; m. Clark Elwell. She is d. He res. in B.

4617.　iii.　WARREN M., b. May 19, 1829; unm.

4618.　iv.　SARAH, b. Nov. 25, 1832; unm.

4619.　v.　HANNAH H., b. May 21, 1834; m. Charles Elwell. She d. He res. 315 County St., B.

4620.　vii.　EVERETTE E., b. June 17, 1841; m. Andrew Slocom; res. South Shaftsbury, Vt.

4621.　viii.　HIRAM HICKS, b. Aug. 29, 1845; m. Mary Rice.

4622.　ix.　JANE H., b. Jan. 4, 1824; m. July 5, 1847, Andrew M. Johnson. He was b. Feb. 1, 1824; d. Apr. 23, 1887; was a wheelwright; res. 221 North St., Bennington, Vt. Ch.: Herbert M., b. May 27, 1850; m. Mar. 24, 1880; res. as above.

2786. JEREMIAH FISK (Jeremiah, Jeremiah, Job, Benjamin, John, John, Phinehas, Thomas, Robert, Simon, Simon, William, Symond), b. Shaftsbury, Vt., July 29, 1802; m. there Sarah Matteson of Arlington, b. July 9, 1809; d. Sept. 5, 1873. He was a carpenter by trade. He d. Aug. 13, 1844; res. Arlington and Shaftsbury, Vt.

4623.　i.　HENRIETTA M., b. Dec. 25, 1826; m. Oct. 2, 1844, David C. Wheelock; res. Shaftsbury Centre, Vt. He was a farmer, b. May 15, 1818; d. Dec. 22, 1889.

2787. PELEG FISK (Jeremiah, Jeremiah, Job, Benjamin, John, John, Phinehas, Thomas, Robert, Simon, Simon, William, Symond), b. Dec. 27, 1808; m. ———— ————. He d. Jan. 2, 1891; res. Vermont.

4624.　i.　CHARLES, b. ————; res. North Bennington, Vt.

2788. DEA. WARREN G. FISK (Jeremiah, Jeremiah, Job, Benjamin, John, John, Phinehas, Thomas, Robert, Simon, Simon, William, Symond), b. Shaftsbury, Vt., Feb. 15, 1815; m. ———— ————. Warren G. Fisk, 81 years old, died at his residence, 3038 Bryant Avenue, S. Three years ago the deceased had a limb amputated and he seemed to rally from all the effects of the operation. He was taken very ill and Dr. Golden was summoned to the bedside. All was done that possibly could be for the aged sufferer, but he sank rapidly, and last his suffering ended. Mr. Fisk was born in Vermont and came to Minneapolis fourteen years ago. He was one of the founders of the Lyndale Avenue Congregational Church and has been a deacon in the church ever since. The deceased leaves two sons, William and George Fisk, and a wife. He was a contractor and builder. The eldest son, William, who is now in Atlanta, Ga., was telegraphed to.—Obituary in Minn. paper. He d. Dec. 19, 1895; res. 3038 Bryant Ave., So. Minneapolis, Minn.

4625.　i.　WM. BURNHAM, b. ————; res. Mankato, Minn.

4626.　ii.　GEORGE, b. ————.

2790. TRUMAN FISK (Jeremiah, Jeremiah, Job, Benjamin, John, John, Phinehas, Thomas, Robert, Simon, Simon, William, Symond), b. Shaftsbury, Vt.,

July 23, 1800; m. Oct. 14, 1828, Freelove P. Andrus, b. June 13, 1807; d. Jan. 3, 1841; m. 2d, Feb. 2, 1841, Phebe A. Stratton, b. Feb. 18, 1808; d. May 19, 1887. For years he was a tailor, but late in life followed farming. He d. Apr. 2, 1874; res. Castile. N. Y.

  4627. i. HELLEN E., b. Mar. 7, 1831; unm.; res. Perry, N. Y.
  4628. ii. ABI E., b. June, 1833; m., 1851, Myron Barton; res. Shaftsbury, Vt.
  4629. iii. HORATIO P., b. Mar. 11, 1835; m. Iris A. Chapin.
  4630. iv. WARREN J., b. Jan. 21, 1846; m. Jane S. Kelsey.

2790-1. JOHN FISKE (Mial, Jeremiah, Job, Benjamin, John, John, Phinehas, Thomas, Robert, Simon, Simon, William, Symond), b. Rhode Island, ——; m. —— ——. John settled in Gillespie County, Tex., after 1849, soon after the Mexican war, and became well off, having a large cattle ranch and a great many called. He died somewhere about 1868 or 1870. His family must be in that State or in California now. He d. about 1869; res. Gillespie County, Tex.

  4630-1.i. JOHN L., b. ——; m. —— ——.

2790-2. CHARLES FISKE (Mial, Jeremiah, Job, Benjamin, John, John, Phinehas, Thomas, Robert, Simon, Simon, William, Symond), b. Scituate, R. I.; m. Mary Leach. She d. ae. 92; res. Scituate, R. I.

  4630-2.i. ALFRED L., b. Dec. 4, 1807; m. Abby A. Locke.
  4630-3.ii. CHARLES, b. ——; m. —— ——.
  4630-4.iii. STERRY, b. Sept. 16, 1801; m. Mary P. Spencer.
  4630-5.iv. CORNELIA, b. ——; m. Oliver Matt.
  4630-6.v. PHEBE, b. ——; m. Albert G. Sprague.
  4630-7.vi. MARY, b. ——; m. Albert G. Sprague. Ch.: Albert G., b. ——; is a physician; res. River Point, R. I.

2790-3. CAPT. JOB WILBUR FISKE (Moses, Jeremiah, Job, Benjamin, John, John, Phinehas, Thomas, Robert, Simon, Simon, William, Symond), b. Cranston, R. I., 1780; m. Cyrena Atwood, b. 1785; d. June 15, 1866, in No. Scituate, R. I. He d. Sept. 6, 1856; res. Scituate and No. Scituate, R. I., and Gloucester.

  4630-8. i. EMORY, b. Feb. 26, 1807; m. Sophia A. Waterman.
  4630-9. ii. HARLEY, b. Dec. 12, 1809; m. Susan B. Greene.
  4630-10.iii. ALBERT, b. ——; m. Jennet Burlingame.
  4630-11.iv. WILLIAM H., b. ——.

2791. CALEB FISKE (Noah, Noah, Noah, Benjamin, John, John, Phinehas, Thomas, Robert, Simon, Simon, William, Symond), b. Scituate, R. I., ——; m. Isabella Yeaw, d. in Anthony, R. I., ae. 79. He d. ae. 63; res. So. Scituate, R. I.

  4631. i. NOAH, b. Oct. 5, 1820; m. Huldah Bennett.
  4632. ii. DANIEL BAKER, b. Dec. 14, 1822; m. Mercilea Salisbury.
  4633. iii. MATILDA, b. ——; m. —— Monroe; res. Norwood, R. I.
  4634. iv. FREELOVE, b. ——; m. W. H. H. Place; res. Anthony, R. I.
  4635. v. PHEBE, b. ——; m. —— Salisbury; a son, Horace, res. in Anthony.

2792. STEPHEN PERRY FISK (Stephen, Moses, Noah, Benjamin, John, John, Phinehas, Thomas, Robert, Simon, Simon, William, Symond), b. Scituate, R. I., Oct. 16, 1813; m. at Smithfield, R. I., Sarah Marchant, b. Sept. 5, 1814. Mr. Fisk was born in Scituate, R. I., Oct. 16, 1813. He learned the trade of carpenter in Providence, and went to Pawtucket in 1836. For a year or two he was foreman of the building operations at the Dunnell Print Works, and then went into business with Nathaniel Lewin, under the firm name of Lewin & Fisk, carpenters and builders. Subsequently Charles E. Kenyon was taken into the firm, when the name became Lewin, Fisk & Kenyon. This firm built some of the largest mills in the State of Rhode Island at that time, among them being the Atlantic Delaine Mill in Olneyville. Mr. Fisk retired from this firm in 1868, and entered the employ of the Providence, Washington, Equitable, Atlantic and Hope insurance companies as adjuster and examiner. With the two

STEPHEN PERRY FISK.

companies first named he remained until the day of his death, twenty-five years, but the Atlantic and Hope companies went out of business at the time of the Chicago fire, at which time Mr. Fisk settled claims amounting to over $1,000,-000. During his connection with these companies he settled thousands of claims, and was one of the oldest and best known insurance adjusters in New England. He was elected one of the directors of the Pawtucket Mutual Fire Insurance Company in 1859, and held that position as long as he lived, a period of thirty-four years, being the oldest director in the company. He was one of the trustees of Park Place Church from its organization, and one of the building committee of the church. He was a member of the Knights Templar and in his younger days took an active part in that order. He took no part in politics, but gave his whole attention to business and was active and energetic, showing little of the marks of advancing age up to the time he was taken ill. His wife was Miss Sarah Marchant, of Yarmouth, Mass. She and two sons, Stephen F. and Frank D., survive him. He d. May 18, 1893; res. Pawtucket, R. I.

4636. i.   JOANNA FRANCES, b. 1840; d. 1842.
4637. ii. FRANK DUANE, b. Dec. 13, 1843; d. Mar. 19, 1895. He was born in Pawtucket, and was a son of the late Stephen P. Fisk. For many years he was connected with the firm of J. E. Caldwell & Co., silversmiths, of Philadelphia, and later he was of the firm of Fisk & Co., druggists, of Pawtucket. Of late years he had not been engaged in active business pursuits. He was greatly attached to his family, being especially devoted to his aged mother, with whom he lived, making brighter her declining years. During the War of the Rebellion he was a member of the Ninth Rhode Island Regiment, and when Tower Post, No. 17, G. A. R., was formed, he was consequently qualified to become one of its charter members, and for two years he served as its commander. He was also a charter member of the Pawtucket Veteran Firemen's Association. He never held public office, although deeply interested in whatever concerned the Democratic party, and he was frequently selected as a delegate to city and State conventions. He was kind of heart, true to his friends, and many will join the bereaved family in mourning his loss.
4638. iii. STEPHEN FRANCIS, b. Dec. 13, 1843; m. Susan J. Sheldon.

2797. JUDGE JOEL S. FISK (Solomon, Ichabod E., Ebenezer, Ebenezer, John, John, Phinehas, Thomas, Robert, Simon, Simon, William, Symond), b. St. Albans, Vt., Oct. 24, 1810; m. at Plattsburgh, N. Y., Nov. 24, 1831, Charlotte Ann Green, dau. of Joseph I., b. Dec. 17, 1809; d. Apr. 5, 1877. He was born in St. Albans, Vt., and was a son of Solomon Fisk, who settled in northern Vermont. At an early age he became a merchant's clerk, and followed that occupation for several years in New York State, when, upon reaching man's estate, he married. Deciding to come west he journeyed to Ohio. Two years later he came further west, and in 1835 stopped in Green Bay, where he engaged in the lumber business and also opened a mercantile establishment. In 1836 he went after his wife and son, and brought them to his new home. He was the pioneer lumberman in certain sections of northern Wisconsin, and built the first mill at De Pere. He also erected the first grist mill at Fond du Lac. In inspecting the timber lands of Wisconsin in 1835, he walked over the territory between Green Bay and Chicago by Indian trail. He was admitted to the bar soon after his arrival at Green Bay, and during his younger years was an active politician. He was Judge of Probate at Green Bay in 1836; was appointed Postmaster at Green Bay in 1836 and again in 1846, and also appointed Register of the United States Land Office in 1848. He laid out and platted the original site of the city of Fort Howard, recently consolidated with Green Bay. He later abandoned the legal profession for more active mercantile pursuits, and in these, and real estate investments, amassed a fortune. He was an active worker in the Baptist Church. He d. May 27, 1877; res. Brunswick, Ohio, and Green Bay, Wis.

4639.   i.   WILLIAM JUSTAN, b. June 25, 1833; m. Mary J. Driggs.
4640.   ii. VALENTINE SATERLEE, b. Feb. 15, 1837; Lieutenant in Civil War for three years; d. unm. Dec. 28, 1872.
4641.   iii. MALANCTHON H., b. May 28, 1843; m. Mary J. Lawton.
4642.   iv. FRANCES C., b. Mar. 21, 1835; m. Feb. 2, 1856, Julius S. Fisk. She d. Sept., 1875.
4643.   v.   CATHERINE PARMELIA, b. Oct. 24, 1838; d. May 14, 1863.
4644.   vi. ELIZABETH SMITH, b. Oct. 9, 1841; m. Oct. 17, 1861, Albert Johnson; res. Murray, Idaho. He was b. Nov. 4, 1837; is a banker. Ch.: 1, Frank Fisk Johnson, Wallace, Idaho, b. Nov. 15, 1862; m. and has three ch.; is president of the First National Bank of Wallace, Idaho. 2, Annie Rosalie Johnson, b. Apr. 27, 1865; m. Dr. Jones; res. 2002 2d Avenue South, Minneapolis, Minn.
4645.   vii. JOEL H., b. Oct. 2, 1845; d. Aug. 11, 1846.

2798. DR. SOLOMON NEWELL FISKE (Solomon, Ichabod E., Ebenezer, Ebenezer, John, John, Phinehas, Thomas, Robert, Simon, Simon, William, Symond), b. Chazy, N. Y., Apr. 11, 1811; m. 1st, Maria North; she d. s. p. in 1850; m. 2d there July 18, 1852, Mrs. Phebe Ann (Raymond) Fisk, b. Sept. 5, 1821; d. May 29, 1880, at Brooklyn, N. Y. He was the first child of Solomon Fisk and Sabina Worthington, his wife. He was born in Chazy, N. Y., Apr. 16, 1809. His mother, Sabina, died Apr. 23, 1809. He was then taken care of by his mother's sister, Catharine Worthington, and she was married to Solomon Fisk Sept. 26, 1809. On July 18, 1852, he married Phebe Ann Fisk, the widow of his brother Almond D. He was a very successful physician and surgeon and had a large practice. He was an active member and official of the Methodist Episcopal Church. He was a fine French scholar, having spent some time in Canada acquiring a knowledge of the language. He d. June 11, 1856; res. Chazy, N. Y.

4646.   i.   HARVEY N., b. Aug. 2, 1854; m. Florence Dean.

2799. ALMOND DUNBAR FISKE (Solomon, Ichabod E., Ebenezer, Ebenezer, John, John, Phinehas, Thomas, Robert, Simon, Simon, William, Symond), b. Chazy, N. Y., Apr. 26, 1818; m. May 13, 1840, Phebe Ann Raymond, b. Sept. 5, 1821; she m. 2d, Dr. Solomon N. Fiske, her brother-in-law; she d. May 29, 1880. After leaving school at the age of 15 he was apprenticed to a jeweler in Troy; was given his time at 20; came to New York; started in the stove business at 109 Water St.; invented the first air tight coal stove, the first heating drum for second floor, the movable top to cooking stoves, and was at work on the base burner self-feeding stoves at the time of his death. He also was the inventor of the Fisk metallic burial case, and the first to introduce steam power in his foundry at Newtown. While on a trip to Cuba he saved the vessel by his ingenuity, when it was given up for lost by the captain. He brought on a hemorrhage of the lungs by jumping into the East River and saving a drowning boy, and from this he never recovered, and finally succumbed to lung and bowel troubles. This is a brief history of a man, who, if he had lived, would have been a man of mark among inventors. A peculiar fact in his inventions they were dreamed out, and upon awakening he immediately arose and put the facts or points in writing, then returned to sleep again. He was six feet four inches tall, of magnificent physique, and sacrificed his health and life for others. He d. at Newtown, L. I., Oct. 13, 1850; res. New York, N. Y.

4647.   i.   WILLIAM M. L., b. May 10, 1841; m. Julia P. Sage.
4648.   ii. HELEN M. C., b. May 28, 1843; m. Austin Adams.
4649.   iii. JOSEPHINE J., b. Jan. 18, 1845; m. ———— Wagner.
4650.   iv. ALMOND DUNBAR, b. Mar. 7, 1850; he is with the N. Y.
             World, N. Y. City.
4651.   v.   PHOEBE ANN, b. ————; d. young.

2804. HON. HIRAM CYRUS FISK (Samuel, Ichabod E., Ebenezer,
Ebenezer, John, John, Phinehas, Thomas, Robert, Simon, Simon, William, Symond), b. at Isle La Motte, Vt., Aug. 16, 1818; m. in South Hero, Feb. 25, 1850,

HON. HIRAM CYRUS FISK.

Cynthia Clark, dau. of Wm. A., b.
July 28, 1828; d. May 18, 1886. Hiram
Cyrus Fisk, son of Samuel Fisk, was
born in Isle La Motte, Vt., Aug. 19,
1818, and attended several academies and
seminaries of learning and obtained a
good education. Before the period of
adolescence in his life history had passed
he united with the Methodist E. Church
in Isle La Motte, and during his life
was one of the principal supporters of
that church. Held town office in Isle La
Motte the greater part of the time he
lived there. He represented the town of
Isle La Motte in the Legislature of Vermont in the years 1867 and 1868. Upon
the death of his father, the said Samuel,
Hiram C. Fisk became the main proprietor of the said Fisk marble quarry,
and worked the same more successfully
than his father did before him and accumulated more property than his
father had, being the wealthiest man in
Isle La Motte at the time he removed
therefrom. He bought the farm or
homestead once owned by his uncle,
Solomon Fisk, in Chazy, N. Y., and
moved there in 1876. He, like his father,
was the furthest estranged from male-
olence, unkindness and enmity to other
persons under any circumstances. He

was always social, generous and forbearing in his nature, and was a public benefactor. He d. Sept. 7, 1884; res. Isle La Motte, Vt., and Chazy, N. Y.

4652.   i.   ANNA CYNTHIA, b. Jan. 28, 1852; m. Feb. 7, 1880, Dr. Homer
             Crowell. She d. s. p. Sept. 2, 1888.
4653.   ii. NELSON WILBUR, b. Aug. 5, 1854; m. Feb. 25, 1880, Eliz-
             abeth Beckwith Hubbell, b. Aug. 31, 1859. Res. s. p. Fisk,
             Vt. The Hon. Nelson Wilbur Fisk, son of Hiram C. Fisk,
             Esq., was born Aug. 5, 1854, in Isle La Motte, Vt., and at-
             tended the Montpelier Seminary and Fort Edward Institute,
             and is a graduate of Eastman's Business College, Pough-
             keepsie, N. Y., and obtained a good education. His father,
             the said Hiram C., deceased when Nelson W. was quite young,
             when the large property and business operations of the father
             devolved upon the son, Nelson W. He administered in a re-
             markable manner upon his father's estate, being so young in
             years. He afterwards became sole proprietor of the Fisk
             marble quarry, and owns it at this time, and has been very suc-
             cessful in that enterprise; is a general merchant and owns a
             large amount of real estate. He is the ablest man, pecuniarily,
             in said Isle La Motte. His property in value far transcends that
             of his father's and grandfather's combined. The said Nelson W.
             has held the principal town offices in town and represented

his town in the Legislature of Vermont for two terms, from 1882 to 1886. He afterward in 1888 was elected a Senator from Grand Isle County in the Legislature of Vermont for two years. While in the Senate he introduced bills that became important laws of the State. He was appointed by the Governor of Vermont chairman of the Industrial School. an institution run by the State at Vergenus, Vt., He is also one of the trustees of the Montpelier Seminary, also a trustee of the State Normal School at Johnson, Vt. Was a member of the delegation in the National Convention, held in Chicago, 1888. Also a delegate from Vermont to the National Convention, held at Min-

LIEUT.-GOV. NELSON W. FISK.

neapolis, 1892. Mr. Fisk is eminently a public spirited man; pays liberally of his large resources for pious, charitable and beneficent purposes. He also inherited the virtue from his ancestors and progenitors of being possessed of no ill-will, prejudice or bias toward his fellowmen. The Hon. Nelson W. Fiske is one of the best business men in the State of Vermont. His advice and counsel are sought after by high State officials in matters of municipal concerns and the policy of State affairs. When said Fisk was Senator, as aforesaid, the Chaplain of the Senate said to the writer hereof that he (Fisk) was one of the best business men, one of the best Senators in that Senate. Mr. Fisk is a young man now, comparatively, and will accomplish a great deal of life's attainments if permitted to live to a tolerably good age.

When he was being urged by his friends as a candidate for Lieutenant-Governor of Vermont, the Burlington Free Press said editorially: "He has yielded to the wish of many of his warm friends throughout Vermont in that he will be a candidate for the second place on the ticket. The announcement will be gratifying to a large proportion of the Republicans of the State. Mr. Fisk is a staunch Republican. He is an honorable, genial and popular gentleman. As a Representative in the House in '82 and '84; Senator from Grand Isle County in '88; trustee of the Vermont Reform School, and leading member of the Fish and Game League, and in other public capacities, he has shown ability, sound judgment and large capacity for business. He has not asked for support, nor shown any eagerness to become a candidate for Lieutenant-Governor. In fact, it is the simple truth that he has up to this time resisted a very considerable amount of pressure from many quarters, urging him to permit the use of his name. His candidacy is thus an honorable one and every way creditable to him. His name, when placed upon the ticket, will add strength and popularity to it; and when he is elected the office will have sought the man, and it will be a source of gratification to many in other sections of the State that the good Island County has at last been recognized by the bestowal of an important elective State office." At the Republican State Convention, held in 1896, he was nominated by acclamation for Lieutenant-Governor and elected by a very handsome majority. At the joint session of the Vermont Legislature Lieutenant-Governor-elect Fisk was administered the oath of office. On assuming the president's chair the Lieutenant-Governor said: "The most agreeable duty assigned me by the people of the State of Vermont is that which brings me into official relations with the Senate. At this, the commencement of the session, I am forcibly reminded of the importance of the position we occupy. On us is centered criticism as well as the good wishes of our fellow Vermonters. I bring to the discharge of this chair but little experience, and shall, therefore, be compelled to rely largely upon that forbearance which has always characterized the courtesy shown by the Senate to its presiding officer. I indulge in the hope that the session upon which we are now entering will result in such beneficial legislation as the people have the right to expect and demand. My ambition is to so preside over and govern your deliberations as to merit at all times your commendation and assistance. I await the pleasure of the Senate." The speech was greeted with applause.

4654. iii. MYRA WILLARD, b. Nov. 15, 1856; m. Sept. 22, 1884, Sidney Howard Graves; res. Shelton, Neb. Ch.: 1, Fannie. 2, Frank. 3, Nelson Fisk.

4655. iv. HIRAM C., b. May 5, 1863; d. Nov. 6, 1865.

4656. v. NELLIE B., b. Jan. 14, 1869; m. Jan. 14, 1893, Charles H. Whitcomb; res. Manchester, N. H., P. O. box 215. He was b. May 16, 1868; is in the insurance business, being general agent for the Equitable Life Assurance Society, of New York, N. Y.

2805. IRA E. FISK (Samuel, Ichabod E., Ebenezer, Ebenezer, John, John, Phinehas, Thomas, Robert, Simon, Simon, William, Symond), b. May 29, 1810; m. Sept. 30, 1833, Louisa Brownson. He d. in Ellensburgh, N. Y., in June, 1888; res. Chazy, N. Y., and Isle La Motte, Vt.

4657. i. JONATHAN HASLON, b. ———. He was shot at Winchester, Va., Sept. 19, 1864. Was Sergeant of the Eleventh Regiment Vermont Volunteers. He was married, but d. s. p.

4658. ii. JULIUS ALMOND, b. ———. He was shot in battle at Savage Station, Va., June 29, 1862. Was serving in the Fifth Regiment Vermont Volunteers.

4659. iii. SAMUEL, b. ———. He died at Camp Griffin, Va., Dec. 3, 1861; was in the Fifth Regiment Vermont Volunteers.

4660. iv. LORET, b. June 29, 1848.

2808. NELSON W. FISK (Samuel, Ichabod E., Ebenezer, Ebenezer, John, John, Phinehas, Thomas, Robert, Simon, Simon, William, Symond), b. Isle La Motte, Vt., Apr. 24, 1814; m. Oct., 1846, Annette W. Fisk, dau. of Hon. Josiah Fisk, of Keesville, N. Y. She d. Oct., 1853. He resided in New York City, where he was in business and on the advice of his physician decided to go to a warmer climate. In 1849 he left for Chagres, Panama, where he engaged in business, doing a large trade with the California pilgrims or '49ers. His goods he had taken with him to South America. His health being greatly improved in the spring of 1850, he returned to New York City, where he remained until fall. He then returned to Chagres, taking his wife with him, and leaving his only child in New York City with relatives. Not long after their arrival in Chagres, Mrs. Fisk was taken dangerously ill with the "isthmus fever." The press of business and care and anxiety for his sick wife proved too much for his nervous system.

He was later attacked with the fever, Feb. 1, 1851, and died on the 25th. Soon after he had been taken on board the line steamer for New York City. His body was interred at Chagres temporarily and the following year were interred in Greenwood Cemetery, New York. In Oct., 1853, the widow passed away, and her remains were placed beside those of her husband. He d. Feb. 25, 1851; res. New York, N. Y.

    4661. i.   ELBRIDGE NELSON, b. July, 1849; res. New York City, 153 Fifth Ave., Scribner & Co.

2809. HENRY SCOTT FISK (Samuel, Ichabod E., Ebenezer, Ebenezer, John, John, Phinehas, Thomas, Robert, Simon, Simon, William, Symond), b. Isle La Motte, Vt., June 25, 1816; m. there, May, 1844, Mary Ann Sewell, of Alburgh, Vt., b. 1820; d. 1885, dau. of Hon. Joseph. He was in the quarry business at Isle La Motte, and died in New York, but interred at Isle La Motte. He d. Mar. 28, 1850; res. Isle La Motte, Vt.

    4662. i.   HENRY JULIUS, b. Dec. 11, 1848; m. at Toronto, Canada, Jan. 6, 1894, Adelaide Beardmore, b. 1860. He res. s. p. at Lemoine St., Montreal, Canada. He is a leather merchant.

    4663. ii.   ANNETTE W., b. Sept., 1847; d. 1853.

2811. JULIUS SCOTT FISK (Samuel, Ichabod E., Ebenezer, Ebenezer, John, John, Phinehas, Thomas, Robert, Simon, Simon, William, Symond), b. Isle La Motte, Vt., June 15, 1826; m. there, Feb. 2, 1856, Fanny C. Fisk, dau. of Joel S., of Green Bay, Wis., b. Mar. 21, 1835; d. Sept. 15, 1875. He was born on Isle La Motte, Vt., married there, and for some time was engaged in farming and stone quarrying. Later he was in the grocery trade, and died in Fort Howard, Wis. He d. Jan. 9, 1890; res. Isle La Motte, Vt.

    4664. i.   ANNETTE L., b. Nov. 20, 1858; m. June 26, 1883, John H. McLeon; res. Iron Mountain, Mich. He was b. June 6, 1860. Ch.: 1, Ethel Fanny, b. May 15, 1884. 2, J. Howard, b. Feb. 12, 1888. 3, Wilbur Fisk, b. Dec. 13, 1890. 4, Gertrude Annette, b. Oct. 28, 1892; all reside at Iron Mountain, Mich.

    4665. ii.   HENRY GREY, b. Jan. 16, 1857; m. Aug. 21, 1878; a son, Frank, res. Iron Mountain, Mich.

    4666. iii.   KATE, b. June 5, 1861; m. Apr. 17, 1894, W. H. Harvey; res. Iron Mountain, Mich.

    4667. iv.   JULIUS JOEL, b. Sept. 28, 1865; m.; res. unknown.

2814. REV. MILES FISK (Ira, Ichabod E., Ebenezer, Ebenezer, John, John, Phinehas, Thomas, Robert, Simon, Simon, William, Symond), b. Grand Isle, Vt., Oct. 26, 1815; m. Oct. 7, 1842, at Jordan, N. Y., Laura Newell, d. June 10, 1856; m. 2d, Aug. 20, 1856, Mrs. Betsey (Tuttle) Newell, d. May 24, 1873. He was the oldest son of Ira Fisk; was born on Isle La Motte, Grand Isle Co., Vt., Oct. 26, 1815, of pious parents, and brought up in Chazy, Clinton Co., N. Y., after he was 2 years old. Was a steady, obedient, truthful, reliable, persevering, diffident, courageous, religiously inclined boy, and never had a bad habit. He was called to preach at 18, and yielded, after passing through great mental agony. A few months after he entered the traveling ministry, and at the end of three years, with others, in consequence of slavery in that church, united in organizing the anti-slavery Wesleyan Methodist Connection, and was then, June 7, 1843, ordained elder at Utica, N. Y., which position he still occupies. Most of his life has been spent in preparation and labor to benefit the human family. It has been in pastorates, anti-slavery work, college agency, peace work against the horrid custom of war. Some years have been spent in recovery of wasted energies, in excessive work; also in efforts without financial success, though appearances were flattering, to recover from losses that in appearance incapacitated to carry out a written pledge, that in the end was to reach the establishment of a central point of mission work on heathen soil. Also in missionary work, pleading for the poor heathen, in going to Jerusalem as missionary, where he had the pleasure of seeing fifty Jews and one Arab seeking God, when there about two weeks. After a few months he returned to America, to secure a few of the right kind of workers, and means necessary. Persons have been secured, but there is delay in lack of means. In the meantime he is holding missionary meetings, mostly in behalf of Jews and Arabs. Rev. Fisk writes: "I should be pleased to have God honor our name by others taking a part in the accomplishment of this blessed work and share with Pliny and Fidelia Fiske in forming a bright galaxy around the throne of God." Res. Burlington, Vt.

4668. i.   WM. MILES, b. Aug. 20, 1845; res. 697 Fulton St.. Chicago, Ill.
4669. ii. LAURA NEWELL, b. May 10, 1855; m. Oct. 30, 1884, Rev. Dr. J. H. McCarty; res. 834 Eleventh St.. N. E. Washington. D. C. She received her preliminary education in the public schools of Adrian, and also attended the Methodist College in that city. Ch.: 1, Laura Clarim McCarty, b. of this union, June 17, 1886. 2, Joseph Vernon, b. Apr. 7, 1891. Mr. McCarty was born in Pennsylvania, educated at Allegheny College, Meadville, Pa., graduated in medicine at the Western Reserve University; subsequently entered the ministry of the Methodist Episcopal Church, and has filled many pulpits in several principal cities. He now holds a position under the government and resides with his family in Washington, D. C.

2815. NEWELL WILBUR FISK (Ira, Ichabod E., Ebenezer, Ebenezer, John, John, Phinehas, Thomas, Robert, Simon, Simon, William, Symond), b. Isle La Motte, Oct. 5, 1817; m. Jan. 21, 1847, Miranda Housinger, d. Aug. 3, 1854; m. 2d, Dec. 13, 1856, Elvira Ransom, b. June 12, 1826. He is a farmer; res. Alden, Ia.

4670. i.   ELLEN, b. Nov., 1847; d. Mar., 1849.
4671. ii. ELLSWORTH, b. July 21, 1850; m. Feb. 26, 1873. He d. May 3, 1877; leaving a son, Edgar; res. A.
4672. iii. CARRIE, b. July 8, 1858; m. July 16, 1886, ———— Clapp. Ch.: Wilbur and Ella; res. A.
4673. iv. RANSOM, b. Aug. 18, 1862; res. A.
4674. v.   WILBUR, b. Oct. 21, 1864; m. Feb. 6, 1895; res. A.

2816½. DR. IRA WOODARD FISKE (Ira Ichabod E., Ebenezer, Ebenezer, John, John, Phinehas, Thomas, Robert, Simon, Simon, William, Symond), b. Chazy, N. Y., Jan. 7, 1824; m. at Keesville, Apr. 29, 1851, Martha Potter, b. 1828. She res. 700 Cumberland Ave., Knoxville, Tenn. He died very suddenly in Daytona, Fla., of apoplexy. He was born in Clinton county, N. Y. His early life was spent on a farm. He commenced the study of medicine at 20 years of age and graduated from the Physicians' College of Medicine, Philadelphia, Pa., in 1851. He practiced medicine in Au Sable, northern New York, for thirteen years and then moved to Kalamazoo, Mich., where he was engaged in the active practice of his profession until a few days before his death. Dr. Fiske was one of the prominent physicians in that city, having been an active practitioner for twenty-eight years. He was in partnership for some years with the late Dr. H. O. Hitchcock. He had been a prominent member of the Kalamazoo Academy of Medicine since its inception. He always stood very high among his professional brethren. Dr. Fiske was a member of the First Presbyterian Church. He was an upright, straightforward citizen, and a good neighbor. His loss is one, says the Kalamazoo paper, which will be felt not only by his immediate relatives and friends, but also by the entire city and by his professional friends. Mrs. Fiske is the only immediate member of his family who survives him, a daughter having died some years ago, and his son, Arthur, about two years ago. He d. Dec., 1891; res. Au Sable, N. Y., and Kalamazoo, Mich.

4675. i.   ARTHUR POTTER, b. Apr. 23, 1865; m. Constance M. Parker.
4676. ii. GRACE POTTER, b. July 25, 1869; d. Feb. 9, 1878.

2819. HIRAM FISKE (Ebenezer, Ichabod E., Ebenezer, Ebenezer, John, John, Phinehas, Thomas, Robert, Simon, Simon, William, Symond), b. Dickinson, N. Y., Oct. 15, 1808; m. there, Diantha Russell. She d. in Dickinson. He d. in Dickinson, Nov. 20, 1844.

4677. i.   ABRAHAM, b. Dec. 24, 1832; res. Hayden. Colo. He m. July 4, 1855, at Canton, N. Y., Adelaide Leonard, b. Feb. 17, 1837. He is a blacksmith and farmer. Ch.: C. R. Fiske, b. May 20, 1858; m. Jan. 1, 1833; P. O. Hayden, Routt Co., Colo. De

Ette, b. Mar. 19, 1860; m. Aug. 12, 1886, —— Hooker; res. Hayden, Colo. Hiram, b. June 12, 1864; m. May 5, 1891; res. Hayden, Colo. Gertrude, b. May 18, 1866; drowned, May 9, 1884. Nellie, b. June 18, 1868; m. Dec. 20, 1887, —— Clark; res. Steamboat Spring, Colo., Le Neve, b. Mar. 4, 1873; m. Aug. 10, 1893, —— Ralston; P. O. Watson, Pitkin Co., Colo. Martin A., b. Apr. 5, 1862; d. Sept. 10, 1863.

4678. ii. KELLY, b. ——; res. Fort Scott, Kan.

4679. iii. SIMON, b. ——; res. Palmer, Kan.

4680. iv. HIRAM F., b. Sept. 5, 1840; res. Washington, Kan. He m. at Neponset, Ill., Apr. 10, 1868, Martha H. Parks, b. June 10, 1848. He is a farmer. Ch.: William F., b. Feb. 23, 1869. Chas. R., b. Sept. 28, 1871. Liew S., b. Dec. 23, 1873. Maggie J., b. Oct. 12, 1875. Andrew E., b. May 30, 1879. Alex. J., b. Mar. 19, 1881. Estella D., b. Jan. 28, 1883. Guy, b. Dec. 28, 1886. Inez, b. Sept. 26, 1889.

4681. v. FREEMAN K., b. Jan. 19, 1831; m. June 6, 1866, Mary R. Hawkins, b. Oct. 9, 1846. He d. Apr. 11, 1894; res. Haigler, Neb. He was a farmer. Ch.: Cora F., b. Aug. 15, 1867; d. Sept. 5, 1868. William K. Fisk, b. Feb. 5, 1869; res. Haigler, Neb. Dec. Kittie Fisk, b. Dec. 20, 1870; d. Apr. 5, 1892. Harry Fisk, b. June 2, 1872; P. O. Haigler. Frank Fisk, b. Apr. 28, 1874; P. O. Haigler. Freeman F., Jr., b. Apr. 29, 1876; P. O. Haigler. Myron F., b. Apr. 25, 1879; P. O. Haigler. Wilber F., b. Oct. 19, 1880; P. O. Haigler. Arthur F., b. June 4, 1883; P. O. Haigler. Walter F., b. June 16, 1887. Clinton F., b. July 28, 1890. Marry B. F., b. Aug. 28, 1892.

4682. vi. NEWEL, b. Oct. 15, 1829; m. Oct. 2, 1856, Elizabeth Rickel, b. Oct. 5, 1837. He was a farmer. He d. Aug. 18, 1891, at Trade River, Wis. Ch.: Warren Fisk, b. Aug. 29, 1857; m. Sept. 9, 1880; res. Hunter, N. Dak. Edward Fisk, b. May 24, 1860; res. Wolf Creek, Wis. Freeman Fisk, b. Dec. 3, 1863; m. Nov. 27, 1885; res. Wolf Creek, Wis. William Fisk, b. Apr. 3, 1869; m. May 5, 1889; res. Seebarsee, Colo. Hellen Fisk, b. Apr. 18, 1868; m. Oct. 8, 1885; res. Franconia, Minn. Fred W. Fisk, b. July 3, 1871; res. Wolf Creek, Wis. Ettie Fisk, b. May 8, 1875; m. Oct. 17, 1895; res. St. Croix Falls, Wis. Effie Fisk, b. July 18, 1877; d. Nov. 30, 1878.

4683. vii. LAVINIA, b. ——; m. —— Hepburn; res. New Haven, Conn.

4684. viii. SAMANTHA, b. ——; m. —— Short; res. St. Regis Falls, N. Y.

4685. ix. SIMON, b. ——.

2824. PEARLEY BROWN FISK (Claudius L., John, Ebenezer, Ebenezer, John, John, Phinehas, Thomas, Robert, Simon, Simon, William, Symond), b. Nelsonville, O., Aug. 6, 1836; m. in Westfield, O., May 29, 1864, Lois Farabe Thornburg, b. Oct. 4, 1846. He is a merchant; res. Ohio and Mich.

4686. i. P. LEE, b. Apr. 11, 1865; m. July 8, 1891, Rosalind Cotton, b. May 12 1890. He is manager for the Western Union Telegraph Co. there, also general agent for the Mutual Reserve Fund Life Association; res. Luddington, Mich., s. p.

4687. ii. L. LEONA, b. Aug. 2, 1866; d. June 26, 1877.

4688. iii. JOSEPH IMLACK, b. Nov. 21, 1868; m. Nov. 14, 1891, Nellie M. Solean, b. Feb. 19, 1867. He is a painter and decorator; res. Manistee, Mich., s. p.

4689. iv. JOHN C., b. July 10, 1870.

4690. v. EMELINE L., b. Dec. 15, 1872; d. Nov. 21, 1873.

4691. vi. EMERSON C., b. Jan. 8, 1875.

4692. vii. EFFIE GERTRUDE, b. Apr. 12, 1877.

4693. viii. DAISY PEARL, b. Jan. 21, 1880.

4694. ix. IDA MAY, b. June 23, 1883.

2826. JAMES HARVEY FISKE (Solomon, Solomon, Ebenezer, Ebenezer, John, John, Phinehas, Thomas, Robert, Simon, Simon, William, Symond), b. Cheshire, Conn., Nov. 10, 1833; m. at Portland, Ore., Oct., 1866, Queen V. Whitcomb, b. 1847. He is a chemist and assayer; res. Portland, Ore.

4695.   i.   BERTRAND E., b. May 24, 1869; m. Laura V. Beard.
4696.   ii.   ELIZABETH, b. July, 1868; d. Jan., 1869.

2831. SILAS W. FISK (Solomon, Solomon, Ebenezer, Ebenezer, John, John, Phinehas, Thomas, Robert. Simon. Simon, William, Symond), b. July 2, 1826; m. in Groton, Conn., May 15, 1850, Julia A. Edgcomb. He was drowned at sea, Feb. 27, 1864; res. Groton, Conn.

4697.   i.   SILAS E., b. Apr. 5, 1851.
4698.   ii.   JULIA A., b. May 18, 1857.
4699.   iii.   WM. W., b. Oct. 17, 1860; drowned at Groton, July 7, 1864.
4700.   iv.   HENRY T., b. Sept. 29, 1862.

2840. JOHN FISKE (John, John, John, John, John, Phinehas, Thomas, Robert, Simon, Simon, William, Symond), b. Aug. 16, 1796, in Conn.; m. in Conn., Oct. 20, 1816, Mildred A. Stevens, dau. of Capt. Gaylord Stevens, b. Jan. 5, 1795; d. Nov. 16, 1864. He was a most successful farmer, carried on a very large business. By his efforts he acquired farm after farm, and at one time he owned thirteen hundred acres, all of which were connected. He had a wonderful memory, kept all of his numerous accounts on tablets, and he never omitted an item. In his time he was considered a rich man. His real estate was divided among his sons and his personal property was left to the management of his eldest living son. He was a member of the Universalist Church. His last illness was of short duration. He contracted a cold, which developed into pneumonia. One of his last wishes was that Cora Etta, then a babe of a few months old, be brought to his bedside. The wish was granted, the dying old man patted the child lovingly, and said: "I meant to have had many a good time with you, but it has all gone by now." It was his request that he should be buried on his own ground. A pretty plat within sight of the house, overlooking the pond, was chosen. His wife, who died a short time before him, was buried there, also his son Ephraim's first wife, Nancy Campbell. He d. Mar. 21. 1866; res. Lebanon, N. Y.

4701.   i.   ALBERT, b. Aug. 28, 1817; d. unm., in 1850, in Wis.
4702.   ii.   PHEBE, b. Nov. 28, 1819; m. Sept. 15. 1837, Alonzo Sabin; res. Sabinsville, Pa.
4703.   iii.   JOHN, b. Dec. 6, 1840; m. Nettie A. Morrow.
4704.   iv.   OLIVE, b. June 26, 1821; m. Nelson Slocum. She d. Aug., 1891.
4705.   v.   HARRIETT, b. Feb. 12, 1823; m. Mar. 18, 1847, Elisha Steadman; res. St. John, Mich. He d. Aug. 20, 1890. Only ch.: David, b. Mar. 16, 1857; m. Nov. 20, 1883; res. St. John, Mich.
4706.   vi.   ANNE, b. June 25, 1825; m. 1847, Oscar Stewart. She d. May 26, 1890. Ch.: Adelbert, b. ———; res. ——— N. Y.
4707.   vii.   EPHRAIM, b. Feb. 10, 1827; m. Sept. 11, 1851, Nancy Campbell and ——— ———; res. Lebanon. N. Y.
4708.   viii.   LUMAN, b. July 16, 1829; m. Angeline R. Close.

2844. JOHN JAY FISKE (John, Bezaleel, John, John, John, John, Phinehas, Thomas, Robert, Simon, Simon, William, Symond), b. Jan. 22, 1794; m. ——— Stetson, of Charlestown, Mass; m. 2d, Mrs. ——— Eaton; res. ———.

4709.   i.   CHARLOTTE, b. 1822.
4710.   ii.   SARAH, b. ———.
4711.   iii.   MARGARET, b. ———; unm.; res. Framingham, Mass.

2853-6. REV. JOHN B. FISKE (Horace, John, Benjamin, John, John, John, Phinehas, Thomas, Robert. Simon, Simon, William, Symond), b. Waterford. N. Y., Oct. 18, 1828; m. at Northville, Mich., Mary Gregory, b. Nov. 23. 1829; d. Jan. 27, 1890; m. 2d, ——— ———. After an academic course in the Waterford Academy, he entered Union College, Schenectady, N. Y., and was graduated with the class of 1848, gaining as a reward of scholarship an honorary election by the faculty to membership in the Phi Beta Kappa Society. He was a classmate of President Chester A. Arthur's. After a brief clerkship at Detroit, Mich., in an iron foundry, he took a theological course at Kalamazoo, Mich., and Princeton, N. J., and was ordained minister of the gospel over the Congregational Church at Dexter, Mich., in 1855. Since then he has had pastoral care of churches at North Amherst, Mass., Grand Haven and Manistee, Mich., and at Anamosa, Ia , where his pastorate continued sixteen years. He is now pastor of the First Congregational Church at Bonne Terre, Mo., where he has remained for six years. He has been twice married; has had four children (by first wife), the only living one being Horace S. Fiske, now lecturer in English literature in the University of Chicago; res. Bonne Terre, Mo.

4711-1.i.   MATTIE S., b. 1856; d. 1858.
4711-2.ii.   HORACE SPENCER, b. Nov. 4, 1859; m. Ida M. Nettleton.
4711-3.iii.   DAVID, b. 1861; d. 1862.
4711-4.iv.   CARRIE, b. 1864; d. 1865.

2856. REV. DAVID MOSES FISK (Ebenezer, David, Ebenezer, Ebenezer, William, William, William, John, William, Robert, Simon, Simon, William, Symond), b. New Hampton, N. H., Apr. 10, 1846; m. at Wilton, Aug. 29, 1870, Alma Henrietta Moore, of Wilton, b. Apr. 10, 1850. Professor Fisk fitted for college in his native town, New Hampton, 1866. He graduated from Brown University (B. P.) in 1869, with an "honor-part" on commencement. He took a post-graduate course in Harvard University, 1869-1870; taught in Douglas, Mass., one year, married; taught in Fall River, Mass., one year, and was elected to the professorship of biology in Hillsdale College, Mich., in 1872. He held this chair of instruction fourteen years. Has been twice in Europe; is the author of three text books in his department; was during his life as a professor in much demand as a platform speaker; was twice elected president of colleges, but did not accept; was called to the First Congregational Church, Jackson, Mich., in 1886, and served that church for a little over five years. From there he was called to the First Congregational Church of Toledo, O., May, 1891, at a salary of $4,000. He is still serving that church. Professor Fisk has the academic degrees of A. M. (from Brown University) and Ph. D. (Findlay College). He has a library of nearly 2,000 volumes; holds important official positions denominationally, and is still called to speak on commencement and other occasions up to the limit of his strength. The First Congregational is perhaps the most important church in size, position, social standing in Toledo; res. Toledo, O., 2024 Robinwood Ave.

4712.   i.   ETHEL MIRIAM, b. Apr. 25, 1874.
4713.   ii.   EARL, b. July 29, 1881; d. Sept. 30, 1881.
4714.   iii.   AGNES, b. Feb. 18, 1883.
4715.   iv.   DANIEL MOORE, b. Apr. 2, 1885.

2857. BENJAMIN F. FISK (David, Ephraim, Ebenezer, Ebenezer, William, William, William, John, William, Robert, Simon, Simon, William, Symond), b May 21, 1840, Niles Mich.; m. July 1, 1874, Amanda H. Batchelor, b. June 12, 1846. He is a farmer and mechanic; res. Buchanan, Mich., s. p.

2865. REV. WILBUR FISK (Joseph M., Ephraim, Ebenezer, Ebenezer, William, William, William, John, William, Robert, Simon, Simon, William, Symond), b. Sharon, Vt., June 7, 1839; m. at Nashua, N. H., Feb. 27, 1863, Angelina S. Drew, b. Aug. 23, 1837. His father was an invalid from his earliest remembrance. His mother was the mainstay of the family. They owned thirty acres of hilly, unproductive land. The mother did the work, with the help of the children, outdoors and in. It was a struggle for the necessaries of life. She took wool just as it was clipped from the sheep, worked it up on shares and from her share carded by hand, spun, wove, cut and made up nearly all the clothing that was used in the family during the 40's. His brother, Franklin, next younger than he, was early accustomed to labor. He could not be spared to go to school in the summer time, after he was 9 years of age. In the spring of 1852 they moved to Lowell, Mass., where the mother and all the children old enough, found work in the factory. They remained in Lowell two years and had much sickness. His oldest sister died and was buried in Lowell. In the spring of 1854 his father bought another farm, and they moved back again to Vermont. The boys were now old enough to do the most of the work required, and what was too hard they exchanged work, and got their neighbors to do. Sept. 5, 1861, he enlisted in Company E., Second Regiment Vermont

REV. DAVID MOSES FISK.

Volunteers, and served till the end of the war. He was discharged July 24, 1865. He was married to Miss Angelina S. Drew, to whom he had been some time engaged, while home on a furlough, in the winter of 1863. At the close of the war he removed to a farm he had purchased in Kansas, where he contended with drouth and chinch bugs till the spring of 1875. As opportunity offered, he held meetings at different places near his home, and in the winter of 1875 was invited to go to Freeborn to do home missionary work in the Congregational denomination here. In connection with Freeborn he has had several other points. He has preached at Hartland, Berlin, Lemond, New Richland, Alden, Manchester, Minnesota Lake, Freedom, St. Clair and Janesville. He has been pastor of the church at Freeborn over twenty years, at Freedom over twelve, Hartland eighteen, and Manchester eight. He has received into the various churches by baptism and confession over one hundred persons. He now preaches at Freedom, St. Clair and Byron, besides regularly at Freeborn. Last March a stock company was organized for the Bank of New Richland, of which he was made president; res. Freeborn, Minn.

    4716. i.   NINA S., b. Sept. 10, 1867; m. May 1, 1890, Elmer E. Cram; res. New Richland, Minn. He is cashier of the bank there.

    4717. ii.   HARLAN W., b. Sept. 26, 1869; he graduates next spring (1896) from Carleton College, Northfield, Minn.; is County Surveyor of Freeborn County, Minn.

    4718. iii. J. FRANKLIN, b. July 4, 1872; d. Oct. 7, 1874.

    4719. iv. EDITH M., b. Dec. 25, 1874.

    4720. v.   LUCIEN D., b. Oct. 13, 1878.

2871. REV. PLINY HENDERSON FISK (Joseph M., Ephraim, Ebenezer, Ebenezer, William, William, William, John, William, Robert, Simon, Simon, William, Symond), b. Tunbridge, Vt., Dec. 14, 1854; m. at Independence, Kan., Apr. 2, 1879, Emma Lampman, b. June 6, 1857; d. Sept. 1, 1879; m. 2d. at Independence, Nov. 12, 1882, Alice Calahan, b. Feb. 17, 1856; d. Oct. 30, 1891; m. 3d. at Freeborn, Minn., June 9, 1893, Charlotte C. Scoville, b. Apr. 8, 1867. Removed with his father's family to Geneva, Kan., in 1864. Lived on a farm till 1881. Married Miss Emma Lampman, in Apr., 1879, she dying the following September. In 1881 he entered the South Kansas Conference of the Methodist Episcopal Church, as a minister of the gospel. Was married in Nov., 1882, to Miss Alice Calahan, of Lima, Ind., from whom his five children were born. He removed to Minn. in 1888, and in the following year entered the home missionary work of the Congregational Church, in which he is at present engaged. In Oct., 1891, while living at New Richland, Minn., his wife died when the youngest boy was five weeks old. His brother, Wilbur, took him to raise. His next oldest boy, Earl, was adopted by a family by the name of Lattin, living in Freeborn, Minn., the town in which his brother lives; res. North Branch, Minn.

    4721. i.   CLINTON BOWERS, b. Aug. 15, 1883.

    4722. ii.   SARAH ELLEN, b. Jan. 22, 1885.

    4723. iii. WILBUR MILLS, b. Feb. 6, 1887.

    4724. iv. EARL DENNIS, b. Aug. 13, 1888.

    4725. v.   PLINY FRANKLIN, b. Sept. 26, 1891.

2882. DR. CYRUS MENTOR FISK (Ephraim, Ephraim, Ephraim, Ebenezer, William, William, William, John, William, Robert, Simon, Simon, William, Symond), b. Chichester, N. H., Jan. 9, 1825; m. at Contoocook, N. H., Dec. 8, 1848, Amanda M. Putnam, b. July 8, 1831. Dr. Fisk was born in Chichester, N. H., the eldest son of Ephraim and Margaret Dow Fisk; studied medicine at Contoocook with the late Charles A. Savory, M. D., took his degree at Dartmouth College, and in 1847 returned to Contoocook to begin the practice of medicine. The following year he married Amanda M. Putnam, and with his young bride removed to Bradford, where they remained for twenty-four years, he having a large and constantly increasing business, making himself one of the leading men of the town, loved and respected by all. He was a man of generous heart and genial disposition, ever bringing sunshine and confidence into the sick room; and was universally considered a most reliable and skillful physician. In 1863 he enlisted in the Sixteenth Regiment, New Hampshire Volunteers; was appointed Assistant Surgeon and promoted to Surgeon. Served under Gen. Banks in the

DR. CYRUS MENTOR FISK.

expedition before Port Hudson. In August, the following year, was mustered out of service and returned home to resume his practice. In 1872, with his family, he removed to Lowell, there to engage in broader fields of usefulness. He then entered the office, as an associate of his old instructor, Dr. Savory; who had preceded him many years. After a time the partnership was dissolved and Dr. Fisk continued the practice of his profession alone, winning for himself the name and reputation of a skillful physician, second to none in that city. He was a member of Ladd and Whitney Post, No. 185, G. A. R.; Massachusetts Medical Society; Middlesex North District Medical Society, at different times being president, vice-president and counselor; was on the medical staff of St. John's Hospital; advisory board of Lowell Hospital; served on the school board for a time; was chairman of the board of pension examiners for twelve years; one of the board of trustees of the Lowell Institution for Savings; was also an active member of the Medical Journal Club, in which he took much interest. After a residence of twenty-two years in Lowell, he conceived the happy thought of returning again to Bradford, hoping to enjoy for a few years the rest and quiet which his active life and close attention to his arduous and trying profession so richly entitled him. "We have watched with interest and pleasure during the past summer, the progress made in building and decorating the new home. At last it was finished, and they were cozily settled. All were rejoiced at their coming, and ready to stretch a welcoming hand across this gulf of many years. Our fond anticipations were realized only a few days ago, the occasion being the 70th anniversary of his birth. Congratulations and good wishes were heartily extended by many and hopes expressed, that this happy couple might live to reach their fifty years of wedded life, which seemed so near at hand; but, alas, that was not so to be. It is easy to realize the sorrow and disappointment so keenly felt by all, at his untimely death."

Possibly no young M. D. was ever more uniquely started upon his career than was the doctor, when, in the winter of 1848, the western part of the town was smitten with the scourge of small-pox. Even Dr. Ames, another physician, fell a victim to the horrible disease. It was then that the boy, Dr. Fisk, came to the rescue. Rising to the occasion he showed the stuff that was in him. He went into quarantine with Bradford's afflicted townspeople, caring for and ministering to them as physician and nurse, and coming forth from the ordeal with flying colors, and the confidence and respect of the whole community. He was married just previously, and he often laughingly remarked that this was his honeymoon, spent among small-pox patients, as he was isolated for weeks from his then young bride. The doctor's sense of humor carried him successfully through many a dark scene and served to brighten many a dismal sick chamber. He had for many years been much interested in ornithology, not only as a scientific study, but pleasant pastime, and had, for a private one, a large collection of birds, which he enjoyed showing and explaining to his friends. He d. Jan. 21, 1895; res. Lowell, Mass., and Bradford, N. H.

4726. i.   MARY JANE, b. June 18, 1850; d. Apr. 18, 1854.
4727. ii. CLARA EVA, b. Dec. 28, 1857; m. June 21, 1876, Geo. Henry Blanchard; res. Bradford, N. H.

2887. JOHN POND FISK (Samuel B., Squire, John, Josiah, Samuel, William, William, John, William, Robert, Simon, Simon, William, Symond), b. Rhode Island, Jan. 8, 1806; m. in 1825, Charlotte Gray, b. 1806; d. Dec. 15, 1845; m. 2d, May, 1846, Laurina Orton, b. 1822; d. s. p., May, 1862; m. 3d, Aug., 1864, ——— Barker. She went to Mexico, Mo., but returned East and died in Kalamazoo, Mich., s. p. He was born in Rhode Island, where he learned the trade of a blacksmith. Later he moved to Cheshire, Mass., where he married his wife, and then moved to Williamstown, Mass. In May, 1843, he moved to Lawrence, Mich., where he ever after resided. He followed farming, and also kept a country store. He was a strong Democrat; attended the Methodist Church, and was highly esteemed and respected. He d. Oct. 8, 1865; res. Lawrence, Mich.

4728. i.   ANN ELIZA, b. 1828; m. Edmond M. Preston; res. Bangor, Mich.
4729. ii. JAMES MONROE, b. Aug., 1832; m. Anna Haynes.
4730. iii. CHARLES WESLEY, b. Mar. 17, 1834; m. Adaline A. Norton.
4731. iv. SARAH ELIZABETH, b. 1837; m. Thomas Van Brunt. She d. in Paw Paw, Mich., s. p., in Sept., 1856.
4732. v.   GEO. WHITFIELD, b. 1841; m. Kittie Smith.
4733. vi. JOS. MANNING, b. 1843; m. Nellie Torrey; res. Lawrence, Mich.
4734. vii. MARY, b. May, 1845; m. Enoch Southwell; res. Brooklyn, N. Y.

2888. JAMES FISK (Samuel B., Squire, John, Josiah, Samuel, William, William, John, William, Robert, Simon, Simon, William, Symond), b. Providence, R. I., 1812; m. at Brattleboro, Vt., in 1832, Love B. Ryan, b. 1809; d. July 2, 1892. He was a manufacturer in Adams, Mass.; was burned out, and as the business at that time was unsatisfactory, he went to Brattleboro, his wife's home, and started what he called a "traveling emporium." He had twenty teams and a salesman on each one. His own team was very handsome; on it he drove four horses, a coachman in livery. He also had another four horse team, which was the "wholesale wagon." In this way he traveled all over New England. Each Saturday every salesman reported to him, at a given place. His bookeeper was there, and, in fact, the business was carried on then as the large stores are now in the city; everything was systematized. He carried only silks and handsome shawls and wraps on his own team; he had his regular customers all over the country, who waited for him, and in many towns he would stay from two to three weeks. He was a very handsome man, six feet two inches, and the "pink" of neatness; very careful about his dress, and of a very elegant, courtly manner. His wife used often to say laughingly: "I first met Mr. Fisk in a stage coach, and was attracted by his fine clothes and noble bearing." He was a strong Prohibitionist, and built the Revere House in Brattleboro and opened it, the first temperance house ever opened and kept in the State of Vermont. After the death of his son he was ill for a year, in fact, out of his head, made so by the shock of his sudden death. He was walking up Broadway and heard the newsboys crying the murder on the street. He fell unconscious and remained so for twenty-four hours; he never saw his dearly loved boy again. He recovered his mind, but never his health. He d. June 4, 1881; res. Brattleboro, Vt.

4735. i.   JAMES, b. Apr. 1, 1835; m. Lucy D. Moore.
4736. ii. MARY GRACE, b. May 20, 1843; m. Jan. 28, 1868, George W. Hooker, b. Feb. 6, 1838. He is a manufacturer; res. B. Ch.: James Fisk, b. New York City, May 1, 1873; graduated at Yale University, June, 1895; now in Columbia College Law School, New York City; add. Plaza Hotel.

2889. SAMUEL BARTLETT FISK (Samuel B., Squire, John, Josiah, Samuel, William, William, John, William, Robert, Simon, Simon, William, Symond), b. Providence, R. I., 1813; m. in So. Orleans, Mass., Laura Smith; res. Monroe, Vt.

4737. i.   STEPHEN WINSLOW, b. Aug. 15, 1831; m. Emma Dyer.
4738. ii. JOHN P., b. ———.

2905. WILLIAM HENRY FISKE (Haley, Squire, John, Josiah, Samuel, William, William, John, William, Robert, Simon, Simon, William, Symond), b

Spotswood, N. J., Apr. 6, 1818; m. in New York City, 1840, Sarah Ann Blakeney, of New York City, b. Dec. 15, 1818; d. Feb. 14, 1884. Wm. H. Fiske, Sr., learned the moulders' trade in his father's foundry in New Brunswick, N. J., and afterward, with his brother, Squire, took the business, his father retiring, and ran it until after the war. He was a good draughtsman and musician, he, his father and brothers having belonged to a band when the sons were young men. After the war William was an inspector of streets in New York, and afterward held a position in the postoffice, but for a few years before he died was not in business, his health having failed him. When a young man his father obtained a place for him in a New York liquor store, but only remained one day, as he did not like the business. He never drank or used tobacco in any form, though the latter was not offensive to him. He early joined the Presbyterian Church (old school) and for nearly twenty years was librarian of the Sunday school, being assisted at times by his sons, Stephen and William. He d. May 28, 1892; res. New Brunswick, N. J., and New York, N. Y.

4739. i. STEPHEN RYDER, b. Nov. 22, 1840; unm.; add. 11 Frankfort St., New York, N. Y. On the third story of the Lotos clubhouse there is a square, high cardroom, fronting on Fifth avenue, and here, on his working mornings, Mr. Stephen Fiske may be found seated at a table-desk writing "copy" for the numerous papers to which he contributes. As he rises to welcome the interviewer, he displays a large, stout, portly figure, above the medium height—a strong, pleasant English face, with frank, mischievous blue eyes and dark brown hair and mustache tinged with gray. His manner is straightforward; his voice clear and honest. He pushes aside his papers, offers a box of choice cigars to his visitor, and, with a laugh and a jest at the idea of a hunter being hunted, glances over my notes and fills up the gaps in reply to my questions. "Yes," he says, in response to a remark about his surroundings, "having seen many writers, from Dickens down, annoyed by the absence of a particular chair, table, kind of pen or paper, I have always tried to be independent of such fads, and can write anywhere with equal facility. Give me a flat table and the light on my left hand, and I am comfortable in any room or company. I do not care to be alone; in fact, the talk of people about me, so long as they don't whisper, is a sort of inspiration. My writing is only a transcription and correcting of phrases already formed in my mind, and, therefore, is very rapid and seldom altered. But, if I have a choice, it is to write in a printing office, with the presses rumbling below me, and the printer's boy taking my pages as fast as I can scribble them. There is no music for a writer like the rumble of the press, and the jarring is like a series of beneficent electric shocks." Stephen Fiske was born November 22, 1840, at the little old Dutch city of New Brunswick, N. J., about thirty miles from New York. His parents had moved out from the metropolis and settled there. His grandfather, Haley Fiske, was a Judge, and a prominent leader of the Whig party. His father was a partner in a large iron foundry. He was educated at Rutgers College in his native city. As a schoolboy, his compositions were published in the local papers. He commenced his paid contributions before he was 12 years old, and at 14 he was the editor of a small daily paper, the Times, which, much enlarged, is still prosperous. He used to hear his father laugh over his editorials while he was afraid to avow their authorship; for his father was a Republican in politics, and the Times was the Democratic organ. The precocious journalist edited the Times during his collegiate studies. Before his year of graduation he contributed to the College Magazine the opening chapters of a satirical novel, called "Charles Herndon, a Modern American Student's

Progress," in which the professors and their antiquated methods of teaching were keenly caricatured. The professors demanded his resignation; but the reforms which he had suggested in his novel were carried out, and the caricatured professors were soon retired, and the college thoroughly reorganized. Alluding to this incident in a speech at the Delmonico banquet of the Rutgers Alumni, Mr. Fiske said: "I graduated, not exactly at the head of my class, but two years ahead of it." Then, for the first time in his life, the venerable President Campbell, D. D. and LL. D., was heard to laugh, and the speech thus became historical. Stephen Fiske first attracted attention outside of local circles by an article upon "Sunshine," which was extensively copied and which a New York paper accused him of plagiarizing from Dickens. The works of Dickens were searched in vain, and the paper was forced to apologize and explain that the writing was so like Dickens' that the editor could not detect the difference. This high compliment to a boy resulted in the departure of the young writer for New York to seek his fortune. Horace Greeley, his grandfather's friend, offered him a position upon the Tribune; but he preferred to become a reporter upon the Herald. In a few months he was promoted to be a special correspondent, and in that capacity he accompanied the Prince of Wales on his American tour, from Newfoundland to Portland. He used the telegraph exclusively, and his despatches were published in the English papers a fortnight in advance of the English correspondents' letters. At Niagara Falls, he telegraphed to the Herald chapters of Matthews and Revelations in order to hold the wires against all rivals, and Jules Verne has adapted this incident in a well-known novel and play. Afterwards he accompanied Abraham Lincoln, "The Martyr President," in his memorable trip from Illinois to Washington, and he relates with great glee the introduction of Mr. and Mrs. Lincoln to Washington society. "Here," said Mr. Lincoln to the brilliant company assembled to greet him at Willard's Hotel, "here is the long and the short of the Presidency," and Lincoln bent his tall figure as he held his little wife by the hand. In 1866 Mr. Fiske was an editorial writer on the Herald and the editor of the Leader, a local Democratic organ. He had produced a play at Wallack's, and wrote regularly for Bonner's Ledger and the leading magazines. Without hesitation he threw up all his engagements to go with Mr. James Gordon Bennett on the Henrietta in the first ocean yacht race which was sailed in December. The Henrietta arrived at Cowes on Christmas day after a stormy passage, and won the race. Hurrying up to London, Mr. Fiske wrote a report of the race for the Times, and then cabled a full account of it to the Herald. He refused to accept the seventy-five guineas offered him by the Times for his report; but the elder Bennett sent him a check for $1,000 by way of compensation. This is the largest sum ever received for a two-column article.

After a brief rest, Mr. Fiske was sent to Ireland to explode the Fenian conspiracy. He traveled over most of the country on a jaunting-car, interviewed all the leading Fenians, and cabled to the Herald not only the results of his investigations, but the editorials upon his reports, and the effect was that the Fenian movement was thoroughly discredited in America. From Ireland Mr. Fiske went to Paris to describe by cable the opening of the Paris Exposition; to Buda-Pesth to witness the coronation of the Emperor of Austria as King of Hungary; to Rome, to picture in words the canonization of the Japanese martyrs; to Naples to see an eruption of Mt. Vesuvius, and to Spain to report the war which threatened to break out with England on account of the "Vittoria" affair. Subsequently he went to Italy and took part in Garibaldi's campaign against Rome, which was settled by the French chassepots. His were the only despatches which came through from the seat of war at that time, the other correspondents being locked up in Rome, and they were recabled from New York to the London papers. Settling down in London as the Herald correspondent, Mr. Fiske became intimate with Charles Dickens, Wilkie Collins, Charles Reade, and other literary celebrities. One day, at Boucicault's the question was discussed whether the art of writing in character was not lost. Mr. Fiske proposed to write an article in the character of an American Fenian, if Mr. Yates would publish it in Tinsley's magazine, which he was then editing. The article, called "Ireland for the Irish," created an immense sensation, the London journals reviewing and denouncing it in elaborate leaders. Several similar articles followed in the magazine and in the Pall Mall Gazette, and the authorities searched Mr. Fiske's rooms, at the Queen's Hotel, for incendiary documents. For the same magazine Mr. Fiske wrote a series of papers called "English Photographs, by an American," dedicated by permission to Charles Dickens. These were republished in book form; obtained a wide popularity; were quoted in Parliament, and were so much esteemed by Dickens that he carried the book with him on his railway journeys, and "dipped in to it," as he said, constantly. Mr. Fiske contributed several papers to All the Year Round, and had arranged for the publication of his first novel in that periodical, when the death of Dickens ended the project.

"English Photographs" is still a readable book, full of suggestions of practical reforms, many of which have been adopted. The advance sheets of it were published in Harper's Magazine. With its profits Mr. Fiske purchased the Hornet, a satirical paper with a small city circulation, and attempted to open the way to what is now called society journalism. He also edited and published the Home Journal, to which Miss Braddon contributed a new novel, and a trade paper, called the News Vendor. As if his hands were not full enough of work, he undertook to manage the St. James' Theatre for Mrs. John Wood, and succeeded in running "She Stoops to Conquer" for 200 nights, and in delighting the town with the humors of that best of burlesques, "La Belle Sauvage." Afterward, he organized the Royal English Opera Company, with Rose Hersee and Belle Cole as his prima donnas, and sent out this troupe for a tour of Great Britain and Ireland. In 1874 Mr. Fiske returned to America and took charge of the Fifth Avenue Theatre, New York, which he saved from ruin and conducted for four years against the disadvantages of hard times and an unpopular house. There he first introduced to the public Mary Anderson, whom he advertised so boldly as to command attention and success. "I do not say that she is a great actress," he remarked to an interviewer, "but it is worth the money to see such a lovely girl." There, also, he brought out Madame Modjeska, who, a failure on the first night in "Adrienne," soon achieved an extraordinary success in "Camille." In 1878 Mr. Fiske withdrew from the theatre and returned to journalism, his first love. He accepted the position of dramatic critic of the Spirit of the Times, and Col. Buck, the editor and proprietor, made an engagement with him for life. His work upon that paper is almost as well known on the other side of the Atlantic as on this, so extensively is it read and quoted. Almost alone among writers in English, he has made criticism a fine art. For two years he was the editor-in-chief of the New York Star, and when he left that paper it waned and died. Editors and compositors always welcome his "copy," which is as clear as print, and, beneath the plainest statement of facts, has a sub-acid of satire and humor which precisely suits the tone of modern journalism. He has published three books, "English Photographs," "Holiday Stories," and "Off-Hand Portraits," in which he predicted Cleveland's election to the Presidency two years beforehand, and he has produced "Martin Chuzzlewit" (Olympic), "Corporal Cartouche" (Winter Garden), "My Noble Son-in-Law" (Wallack's) and "Robert Rabagas" (London) dramatizations or adapted plays, all very successful. In the prime of life, and with enormous capacities for work, Stephen Fiske's future is likely to be as varied and eventful as his past. "I used to think," he says, as he concluded the long chat from which these particulars have been gleaned, "that I had been everywhere and seen everybody and everything; but the world renews itself every year, and I often feel like beginning life all over again. I have lived every minute of my time, and I find that the only thing which really fatigues me is to stop and try to rest." Nov., 1896, he is writing a series of articles of intense interest on "The Personal Side of Dickens" for The Ladies' Home Journal.

4740. ii. WILLIAM HENRY, b. May 13, 1845; m. Mary E. Houghton.
4741. iii. HALEY, b. Mar. 18, 1852; m. Mary Garrettena Mulford and Marione C. Cushman.
4742. iv. FANNY ELIZABETH, b. Jan. 4, 1854; m. Dr. Clinton De Witt Van Dyck; res. 47 West Ninety-third St., New York, N. Y., s. p.
4743. v. WALTER, b. ———; d. ———.
4744. vi. MARY, b. ———; d. ———.
4745. vii. SARAH, b. ———; d. ———.

2912. REV. JOHN ORR FISKE (James B., John, John, Josiah, Samuel, William, William, John, William, Robert, Simon, Simon, William, Symond), b. Bangor, Me., July 13, 1819; m. Sept. 19, 1848, Mary Augusta Tappan, dau. of Rev. Dr. Tappan, of Augusta, b. Sept. 26, 1821. He was graduated at Bowdoin College in the class of 1837, and subsequently at the Bangor Theological Seminary, and was ordained pastor of the Congregational Church, in Bath, Me., in 1843; he was recognized as one of the leading clergymen of Maine. He was chairman of the committee of the National Congregational Council, held in 1865, to prepare a paper embodying a declaration of faith, according to the doctrinal standards, as anciently established by this denomination. He d. Dec. 18, 1893; res. Bath, Me.

4743. i. CATHARINE T., b. Sept. 10, 1849; d. unm., Jan. 31, 1877.
4744. ii. JOHN WINTHROP, b. Oct. 1, 1856; attorney at law; unm.; res. 33 Sidney Place, Brooklyn, N. Y.
4745. iii. MARY M., b. May 28, 1860; unm.; res. Bath.

2917. JOHN ARNOLD FISKE (Nathan, John, John, Josiah, Samuel, William, William, John, William, Robert, Simon, Simon, William, Symond), b. Westboro, Mass., July 10, 1822; m. in New York City, Georgianna Elizabeth Perry, b. July 5, 1829.

4746. i. THOMAS PERRY, b. July 2, 1848; res. New York City.
4747. ii. JOHN ARNOLD, b. Jan. 7, 1850; d. Nov. 26, 1884.
4748. iii. GEO. PERRY, b. Mar. 4, 1856; res. New York City.
4749. iv. FRED'C B., b. Dec. 13, 1857; m. Louise Palmer.

2918. DR. STEPHEN FISK (Nathaniel, Jonathan, Jonathan, Josiah, Samuel, William, William, John, William, Robert, Simon, Simon, William, Symond), b. Mayfield, N. Y., Apr. 13, 1816; m. Townsend, Vt., Sophrona Lowe, b. 1826; d. 1871; m. 2d, Mar. 12, 1878, Mrs. Laura C. Birdier, b. June 21, 1848. His early education was with primary reference to foreign missionary work; he therefore took a university course and before he left the medical department of the university it was found that he had extraordinary capacity as a surgeon. He is the author of "Fisk's-Smith's Operative Surgery," also author of a small work on "The Ear," and has written much on many subjects—in all fifty-two volumes. He is a graduate of two European colleges and has traveled extensively in Europe, Palestine and Egypt. Since he was 30 he has devoted the most of his time to the ministry and lecturing on various subjects. He has just completed the revision of his "Scriptural Analysis," published many years ago. He is not a sectarian. He has preached in all the Protestant churches of this city. He is not a pessimist but a wide-awake optimist; res. Jacksonville, Fla.

    4750. i.   FANNIE V., b. Jan. 3, 1842; m. Jan. 3, 1874; res. Aspen, Colo.
    4751. ii.   WILBUR L., b. July 17, 1844; m. Florence Van Peet.
    4752. iii. STEPHEN W., b. Jan. 3, 1847.
    4753. iv.   SEVERINUS CANOVA, b. Jan. 8, 1879.
    4754. v.   STAPHANES P., b. Oct. 19, 1880.
    4755. vi.   NORMAN J., b. Nov. 1, 1888.

    2919. CHARLES PLINY FISKE (Nathaniel, Jonathan, Jonathan, Josiah, Samuel, William, William, John, William, Robert, Simon, Simon, William, Symond), b. Mayfield, N. Y., July 17, 1834; m. there Catherine Morrison, b. Dec. 20, 184-. Chas. Pliny Fiske was born at Mayfield, Fulton County, N. Y., July 17, 1834; attended schools of said village. The first twenty-one years of his life was spent on a farm. His life since 1855 has been spent in the various departments of dressing glove leather and the manufacturing of leather gloves; res. Gloversville, N. Y.

    4756. i.   EDWARD W., b. Mar. 16, 1861; m. Aug. 18, 1880, Emma E.
                 Kelley; res. s. p. in G.
    4757. ii.   EUGENE, b. Sept. 7, 1863; d. Feb. 25, 1866.
    4758. iii. CHARLES P., JR., b. July 1, 1867; m. Minerva Steele.
    4759. iv.   ANNA B., b. June 18, 1871; res. G.
    4760. v.   CLARA E., b. Apr. 9, 1882; res. G.

    2920. WILLIAM W. FISK (Nathaniel, Jonathan, Jonathan, Josiah, Samuel, William, William, John, William, Robert, Simon, Simon, William, Symond), b. Mayfield, N. Y., Mar. 13, 1830; m. June 25, 1863, Annie T. Empie, b. Oct. 20, 1842; d. June 26, 1879. He is a salesman in furniture business; res. Fort Wayne, Ind.

    4761. i.   WILLIAM B., b. Jan. 25, 1871; is bookkeeper; res. unm. 4210
                 Berkely Ave., Chicago, Ill.
    4762. ii.   MARY LOUISE, b. June 19, 1874; res. Ft. W.

    2922. EDWARD FISK (Jonathan D., David, Jonathan, Josiah, Samuel, William, John, William, Robert, Simon, Simon, William, Symond), b. Arcadia, N. Y., Apr. 17, 1821; m. Oct. 6, 1844, Elmina Dolph, b. Jan., 1821; d. May 22, 1863; m. 2d, Oct. 15, 1863, Sarah C. Parker. He is a retired farmer; res. Newark, N. Y.

    4763. i.   CORNELIUS EDWARD, b. Aug. 15, 1853; m. and res. Man-
                 chester Centre, N. Y. Ch.: Edward C., b. June 12, 1872; m.
                 Mary F. Fisk.
    4764. ii.   LEONARD MONROE, b. Dec. 21, 1846; d. Mar. 27, 1864.
    4765. iii. WM. HENRY, b. Aug. 8, 1848; d. July 28, 1865.
    4766. iv.   FANNIE AMELIA, b. Aug. 22, 1850; m. ——— Fuller; res. 13
                 Beacon St., Rochester, N. Y.
    4768. v.   EMMA E., b. Oct. 11, 1854.
    4769. vi.   OLNEY H., b. Mar. 1, 1858.
    4770. vii. LUCY ELIZABETH, b. July 3, 1859; m. ——— Tibbits; res.
                 Rochester, N. Y.
    4771. viii. ADELBERT F., b. Apr. 11, 1863; d. Oct. 30, 1863.
    4772. ix.   FREDERICK L., b. June 15, 1865.
    4773. x.   ANNA C., b. Mar. 11, 1872; res. 210 Franklin St., Buffalo, N. Y.

    2928. MARCUS REYNOLDS FISK (James G., David, Jonathan, Josiah, Samuel, William, John, William, Robert, Simon, Simon, William, Symond), b. Arcadia, N. Y., July 7. 1819; m. at Somerset, N. Y., Mar. 27, 1844, Emily Polly

Huntington, d. Sept. 22, 1847; m. 2d, Nov. 9, 1847, Mary S. Peryne. He was a farmer. He d. Dec. 30, 1887; res. Somerset, N. Y., and Lyons, Mich.

 4774. i. ALLEN G., b. Feb. 5, 1845; m. Julia Etta Spencer.

 2931. ALFRED D. FISK (James G., David, Jonathan, Josiah, Samuel, William, John, William, Robert, Simon, Simon, William, Symond), b. Arcadia, N. Y., Feb. 11, 1826; m. Wayne, Nov. 26, 1851, Eliza J. Robinson, b. Dec. 10, 1827. He was a farmer. He d. Jan. 15, 1894; res. Somerset, N. Y.

 4775. i. EMMA C., b. Nov. 24, 1854; m. Dec. 20, 1871; m. 2d, Feb. 29, 1883, Andrew T. Pease. She d. Mar. 29, 1892; res. S.

 2936. SAMUEL A. FISK (Weaver G., David, Jonathan, Josiah, Samuel, William, John, William, Robert, Simon, Simon, William, Symond), b. —— New York State; m. Hannah Holmes. He was a carpenter; res. Freedom, N. Y.

 4776. i. SAMUEL EBER. b. Dec. 23, 1846; m. in Pike, N. Y., June 29, 1871, Asenath M. Campbell. He is a farmer; res. Pike, N. Y.; s. p.

 2939. GEORGE C. FISK (Weaver G., David, Jonathan, Josiah, Samuel, William, John, William, Robert, Simon, Simon, William, Symond), b. Yorkshire, N. Y., Oct. 8, 1833; m. at Wadham's Grove, Ill., June 16, 1853, Martha Winslow, b. Oct. 9, 1834. He is a carpenter; res. Wolf Creek, Wis.

 4777. i. MAY ELLA, b. Jan. 15, 1854.
 4778. ii. ORRILLA, b. Nov. 30, 1859.
 4779. iii. MASON B., b. Apr. 30, 1861.
 4780. iv. ROSE ELLA, b. Nov. 30, 1859.
 4781. v. CLINTON, b. May 18, 1863.
 4782. vi. BERT, b. June 26, 1868.
 4783. vii. DORA, b. Sept. 1, 1870.
 4784. viii. OSCAR, b. Aug. 6, 1874.
 4785. ix. TINNA, b. May 15, 1877.
 4786. x. BELL, b. Sept. 16, 1872.
 4787. xi. CHESTER, b. May 12, 1880.

 2944. NATHAN INGRAHAM FISKE (David, David, Jonathan, Josiah, Samuel, William, John, William, Robert, Simon, Simon, William, Symond), b. Arcadia, N. Y., Jan. 30, 1825; m. Oct. 18, 1849, at Ravenna, O., Loiza Jane Hill, b. May 15, 1828; d. May 17, 1886. He is a farmer; res. Rapids, Portage County, O.

 4788. i. EMMA M., b. Oct. 5, 1850; m. Apr. 14, 1880; res. Auburn, O.
 4789. ii. MARCIA A., b. Nov. 21, 1853; res. at home.
 4790. iii. NEWTON G., b. Mar. 31, 1858; res. at home.

 2945. NORMAN GREEN FISK (David, David, Jonathan, Josiah, Samuel, William, John, William, Robert, Simon, Simon, William, Symond), b. New York State Jan. 19, 1822; m. in Hartford, Ohio, Sept. 16, 1857, Philura C. Marimon, b. Granby, Conn., Jan. 11, 1827; d. Feb. 9, 1886. He was a farmer. He d. Oct. 25, 1894; res. Hartford, Ohio.

 4791. i. WILLARD E., b. Feb. 22, 1866; m. Apr. 29, 1885, Jennie T. Eich, b. Aug. 28, 1858. He is a farmer; res. s. p. Nutwood, Ohio.

 2946. JEFFERSON FISK (David, David, Jonathan, Josiah, Samuel, William, John, William, Robert, Simon, Simon, William, Symond), b. Feb. 9, 1828; m. at Unionville, Ohio, Feb. 25, 1857, Delesta Marinda Moseley, b. Feb. 22, 1837. After his death she married I. S. Sawdey; res. No. Madison, Ohio. He was a farmer. He d. Sept. 19, 1863; res. Galva, Ill.

 4792. i. IDA M., b. Mar. 18, 1858; m. Dec. 4, 1878, Dellie C. Winchester; res. No. Geneva, Ohio. They have four children.
 4793. ii. SARAH J., b. June 7, 1860; m. Nov. 22, 1876, Dwight H. Richmond; res. No. Madison, Ohio; s. p.

 2947. ORSON FISK (David, David, Jonathan, Josiah, Samuel, William, John, William, Robert, Simon, Simon, William, Symond), b. Yorkshire, N. Y., Aug. 24, 1832; m. Aug. 1, 1857, at Cambridge, Ill., E. M. Dewey, b. Jan. 3, 1835. He is a farmer; res. Latham, Kan.

4794. i. FRANK, b. Dec. 11, 1860; res. L.
4795. ii. LAURA E., b. May 13, 1858; m. Mar. 18, 1879, —— McClellan; res. L. Ch.: Hugh D., b. Apr. 25, 1880; Elsie M., b. Sept. 30, 1883.

2948. ALDOMERON FISK (David, David, Jonathan, Josiah, Samuel, William, John, William, Robert, Simon, Simon, William, Symond), b. Cattaragus, N. Y., June 14, 1834; m. Aug. 15, 1864, Frances Imfield, b. July 26, 1841. He is a billing clerk for the Lake Shore & Michigan Southern Railroad; res. 407 So. St. Clair St., Painesville, Ohio.
4796. i. ANNA BELLE, b. June 29, 1865; m. July 20, 1894, E. N. Dundass; res. Ludington, Mich.
4797. ii. LEA AURORA, b. June 21, 1880.

2950. OLIVER CROMWELL FISK (David, David, Jonathan, Josiah, Samuel, William, John, William, Robert, Simon, Simon, William, Symond), b. Cattaragus, N. Y., Nov. 20, 1830; m. June 20, 1851, in Montville, Ohio, Sophia Polly Dewey, b. Mar. 5, 1831. His business was railroading. He d. Feb., 1875; res. Auburn, Ohio.
4798. i. FRANCIS, b. ——; d. ——.
4799. ii. GEO. EMMIT, b. ——; d. ——.
4800. iii. JOSEPH HARRY, b. ——; d. ——.
4801. iv. JOSEPHINE CARRIE, b. ——; d. ——.
4802. v. CHARLES WILLIE, b. Aug. 4, 1861; m. Aug. 21, 1882, Nettie R. Morse, b. Oct. 7, 1859; res. Bellevue, Ohio; is conductor on New York Central & St. Louis Railroad. Ch.: 1, J. Carrie, b. Dec. 4, 1883; 2, Leo Oliver Wm., b. Jan. 10, 1888.
4803. vi. ELLA VIOLA, b. June 23, 1852; m. Feb. 12, 1871, William C. Dunn, b. Oct. 30, 1850; res. Anthony, Kan. Ch.: 1, Guy Franklin, b. Jan. 1, 1872. 2, Rose Viola, b. Aug. 13, 1875; d. July 6, 1880. 3, Charles Perry, b. Nov. 5, 1878. 4, Jay Cormo, b. Apr. 13, 1882; d. Feb. 6, 1891.

2955. SAMUEL W. FISK (Lewis M., David, Jonathan, Josiah, Samuel, William, John, William, Robert, Simon, Simon, William, Symond, b. Yorkshire Forks, N. Y., Apr. 28, 1829; m. Bradford, Pa., Sept. 16, 1849, Mary W. Webb, b. May 3, 1830. He is a farmer; res. Kalamazoo, Mich.
4804. i. DE WITT H., b. June 27, 1851; m. Adda C. Ashelman.
4805. ii. STANLY W., b. ——.
4806. iii. FRANK R., b. ——; res. Spokane, Wash.
4807. iv. ELLA M., b. ——; m. —— Martin; res. 515 Ontario St., S. E., Minneapolis, Minn.

2960. WILLIAM ELLIOTT FISK (Hiram, David, Jonathan, Josiah, Samuel, William, John, William, Robert, Simon, Simon, William, Symond), b. Springfield, Mich., Sept. 4, 1838; m. at Olean, N. Y., Apr. 1, 1868, Mahala Abigail Rolph, b. Dec. 6, 1840. He is a farmer; served three years in the late war; res. Olean, N. Y.
4808. i. EMMA GRACE, b. Sept. 15, 1869; m. Sept. 15, 1891, W. S. Clark; res. Kilbuck, N. Y.
4809. ii. CORA BELLE, b. Dec. 15, 1870; m. June 14, 1893, W. P. Hatten; res. Fullerton, Neb.
4810. iii. FRANCIS W., b. Mar. 24, 1872; m. Sept. 18, 1895, Emma Jane Ingalls, b. Oct. 3, 1874; res. s. p. Bolivar, N. Y.; is a farmer.
4811. iv. KITTIE CHARLOTTE, b. Apr. 1, 1874; d. Sept. 15, 1874.

2968. JOHN SPENCER CALHOUN FISK (John H., Ezra, Jonathan, Josiah, Samuel, William, William, John, William, Robert, Simon, Simon, William, Symond), b. Manchester, N. Y., Nov. 24, 1831; m. Nov. 5, 1850, Adelphia Huntoon, b. Jan. 20, 1834. He is a farmer; res. Newark, N. Y.
4812. i. CHARLES H., b. Nov. 24, 1863; m. Edna F. Beal.
4813. ii. EDWIN S., b. ——; res. Elmira, N. Y.
4814. iii. FRANK J., b. ——; res. Rochester, N. Y.
4815. iv. CLARA A., b. Jan. 7, 1858; m. June 13, 1880, Manley A. Chap-

man. He was b. Nov. 13, 1857; is a farmer; res. Sterling, N. Y.
Ch.: 1, Charlie Fisk Chapman, b. Dec. 3, 1882; res. Sterling,
N. Y. 2, Judson S. Chapman, b. Feb. 1, 1885; res. Sterling,
N. Y. 3, Bessie A. Chapman, b. Oct. 19, 1891; res. Sterling,
N. Y.

4816. v.   ETTA, b. ———; m. Judson Snyder; res. Port Gibson, N. Y.
4817. vi.   JENNIE M., b. Apr. 24, 1856; m. Jan. 13, 1877, Elias Burchard;
            res. 74 Groton Ave., Cortland, N. Y. He was b. Sept. 20,
            1846. Ch.: 1, Etta A. Burchard, b. June 16, 1878; 2, Josephine
            Burchard, b. Aug. 24, 1882; 3, William E. Burchard, b. Sept.
            26, 1885; 4, Claire A. Burchard, b. Jan. 22, 1894.
4818. vii. ASBRAH H., b. ———; res. Champion, Mich.

2970. HORACE FRASER FISK (Hiram, Ezra, Jonathan, Josiah, Samuel,
William, William, John, William, Robert, Simon, Simon, William, Symond), b.
Mar. 15, 1834, Cattaraugus Co., N. Y.; m. in Marshall, Mich., July 13, 1877, Anna
Louisa Montgomery, b. July 31, 1846. He is a broker; res. 53 W. Ninety-fifth St.,
New York City, and 123 No. Pryor St., Atlanta, Ga.
4819. i.   MONTGOMERY SCHUYLER, b. July 19, 1878. He is now
            attending St. John's Military Academy, at Manlius, N. Y.

2971. HIRAM FISK (Hiram, Ezra, Jonathan, Josiah, Samuel, William, William, John, William, Robert, Simon, Simon, William, Symond), b. Palmyra, N. Y.,
Dec. 18, 1829; m. in Tiffin, Ohio. Oct. 28, 1858, Martha A. Harmon, b. Nov. 22,
1842. He is a contractor; res. Upper Sandusky, Ohio.
4820. i.   FRANK, b. Nov. 2, 1859.
4821. ii.   EDA, b. May 28, 1861.
4822. iii. JOHN, b. July 22, 1865.
4823. iv.   ELLA, b. July 31, 1870.

2972. DARWIN B. FISK (Hiram, Ezra, Jonathan, Josiah, Samuel, William,
William, John, William, Robert, Simon, Simon, William, Symond), b. Oct. 19,
1837, Wayne County, Mich.; m. in July, 1861, at Dearborn, Lovina Thayer, b. Feb.,
1838; d. July 21, 1881. He was a stone and brick mason; res. Romulus, Mich., and
Findlay, Ohio.
4824. i.   MARY MARIA, b. July 31, 1874; is a school teacher.

2973. CHARLES H. FISK (Hiram, Ezra, Jonathan, Josiah, Samuel, William, William, John, William, Robert, Simon, Simon, William, Symond), b. Canton, Mich., Aug. 24, 1843; m. July 4, 1869, Elmira M. Thayer, b. July 16, 1853. He
is an employe of the Michigan Central Railroad; res. 717 Lowel St., Ypsilanti,
Mich.
4825. i.   LILLIAN M., b. 1871; m. Oct. 14, 1895, B. A. Robison; res. 256
            W. 39th St., New York, N. Y.
4826. ii.   WM. C., b. ———; res. at home.

2978. EBUN D. FISKE (Daniel B., Ezra, Jonathan, Josiah, Samuel, William, William, John, William, Robert, Simon, Simon, William, Symond). b. Newark, N. Y., Feb. 8, 1852; m. there Jan. 27, 1886, Nettie E. Hughson. He is captain
and owner of a steam barge; res. 17 South St., New York, N. Y.
4827. i.   D. W., b. Apr. 6, 1889.

2979. WATSON A. FISK (Daniel B., Ezra, Jonathan, Josiah, Samuel, William, William, John, William, Robert, Simon, Simon, William, Symond), b. Newark, N. Y., Sept. 20, 1853; m. there in 1877 Nettie Wheeler. He is captain and
owner of a steam barge; res. 17 South St., New York, N. Y.
4828. i.   GEORGIA MAY, b. 1881.
4829. ii.   PEARL, b. 1884.

2981. SHERMAN G. FISK (Daniel B., Ezra, Jonathan, Josiah, Samuel,
William, William, John, William, Robert, Simon, Simon, William, Symond), b.
Newark, N. Y., June 5, 1862; m. May 29, 1886, Ella M. Ratliffe. He is a captain
and owner of a steam barge; res. 17 South St., New York, N. Y.
4830. i.   HESTER E., b. Apr. 6, 1887.
4831. ii.   WATSON A., b. Dec., 1891.

2984. SAMUEL FISK (Lonson, Stephen, Jonathan, Josiah, Samuel, William, William, John, William, Robert, Simon, Simon, William, Symond), b. Oct. 13, 1834, Arcadia, N. Y.; m. at Coldwater, Mich., Oct. 15, 1874, Clara S. Conover, b. Apr. 6, 1849. Samuel lives near Coldwater, Mich., and has been continuously elected supervisor of the town for seventeen or eighteen years; res. Coldwater, Mich.

    4832. i.   ALBERT JEROME, b. Dec. 18, 1875.
    4833. ii. CHARLOTTE BELLE, b. Dec. 15, 1883.

2985. WILLIS PETER FISKE (Lonson, Stephen, Jonathan, Josiah, Samuel, William, William, John, William, Robert, Simon, Simon, William, Symond), b. Newark, N. Y., Apr. 1, 1836; m. at Canandaigua, Sept. 14, 1865, Mary E. Field, b. June 23, 1842; d. Feb. 27, 1871; m. 2d, at Newark, Oct. 9, 1873, Julia L. Sherman, b. Apr. 23, 1847. Willis P. Fiske spent his early years until the age of 17 on his father's farm, attending the district school, and doing such work on the farm as was required. In addition to the common school education, he was allowed a few terms at the Macedon Academy, to fit himself for teaching. He "taught his first school" while in his 18th year (1853-54), and continued in the profession until June, 1864, when he resigned his position in the Canandaigua Academy to accept a position as bookkeeper in the Bank of Ontario in Canandaigua. At the end of a year he was made assistant cashier, and for a considerable time had charge of the bank, whose business was large and the responsibility of his position great. He continued to fill responsible positions in the banking line until the spring of 1874, having been cashier of banking houses in Marathon, N. Y., Herkimer, N. Y., and Newark, N. Y., and for three years held positions in the Merchants Savings, Loan & Trust-Co. of Chicago, and the Traders National Bank of Chicago. In 1874 he went to Buffalo and engaged in insurance business in partnership with Stephen F. Sherman. In October, 1875, he entered the office of Richard Bullymore as bookkeeper, continuing in that capacity until December, 1878, when he resigned this position to become cashier of the Buffalo Grape Sugar Co. He remained with this company and its successor, the American Glucose Company, until the summer of 1894, nearly sixteen years. In April, 1894, the American Glucose Company's plant in Buffalo was destroyed by fire, which resulted in the severing of his connection with that company. He now (1896) holds the position of chief bookkeeper in the office of the Comptroller of the city of Buffalo. In politics he is a Republican, though never taking active part in politics, except as a voter. As a proof of the regard in which he is held, it may be said that in the several important financial positions held by him, involving the handling and care of large sums of money, he was never required to give bonds; res. 34 Fifteenth St., Buffalo, N. Y.

    4834. i.   LIZZIE FIELD, b. July 30, 1866; res. Lyons, N. Y.
    4835. ii. ADELIA LOUISE, b. June 5, 1868; d. Aug. 1, 1868.
    4836. iii. MARY FIELD, b. Dec. 2, 1870; m. Edward C. Fisk; res. Mayville, N. Y.
    4837. iv. DAISY SHERMAN, b Aug. 28, 1875.
    4838. v.   CHAS. POMERY, b. Mar. 18, 1882.
    4839. vi. ELIZABETH SHERMAN, b. Apr. 14, 1884.

2988. A. JUDSON FISK (Lonson, Stephen, Jonathan, Josiah, Samuel, William, William, John, William, Robert, Simon, Simon, William, Symond), b. Newark, N. Y., July 19, 1849; m. there Oct. 5, 1870, Julia Alice Hunt, b. Oct. 27, 1850. A. Judson lives near Newark, N. Y., and is quite largely engaged in farming and as a milk dealer; res. Newark, N. Y.

    4840. i.   JUDSON ELBERT, b. Mar. 16, 1875.
    4841. ii. LORA ADELIA, b. Apr. 30, 1877.
    4842. iii. LESLIE HUNT, b. Jan. 29, 1883.

2992. JOSEPH W. FISK (Joseph, Joseph, Joseph, Mark, Joseph, William, William, John, William, Robert, Simon, Simon, William, Symond), b. Springville, Pa., Feb. 12, 1824; m. Sept. 24, 1847, Rhoda E. Strickland, b. Dec. 18, 1820; d. Mar. 8, 1887. Joseph W. Fisk was born in Susquehannah County, Pa. He was the eldest son of Joseph and Fanny (Brown) Fisk who were among the pioneers that helped to develop the northeastern part of Pennsylvania. He had four sisters and one brother. His sisters with himself have all passed to the higher life. His brother, Clark S. Fisk, lives at Morrison, Ill. When Joseph was but ten years old his father died of consumption leaving a widow with six small children with **very** limited means of support, therefore his chance for education was small. We do not know that he ever attended school a day in his life, yet we take it for granted that he must have done so some time somewhere, as he possessed a knowledge of the three "R's." Soon after the death of his father Joseph went to live with his uncle Washington Fisk in Vermont, making a trip of three hundred miles on foot through the woods and over the mountains of Pennsylvania, New York and Vermont, with his wardrobe in a bandana. When about 20 years old his uncle advised him to return to Pennsylvania and take possession of the farm his father had settled on and this he did. Joseph W. Fisk and Rhoda E. Strickland were married. Miss Strickland had been devoted to teaching school for nearly eight years at the time of their marriage. With her superior education, active temperament and ambitious energy, she brought to her husband the qualities he so much needed. His judgment was sound and had he had the benefit of an education he would have been a strong man. He had an acute ear for music and could play almost any instrument. He was about six feet tall and well proportioned, in his palmy days weighing two hundred and forty pounds. His family consisted of twelve children, nine sons and three daughters, seven of whom are living, viz.: Wilmot, Melvin, Calvin, Everett, Mrs. Harriet E. Emery, Theron and Alfred. In 1860 he built the Union Hotel at Niven, Pa. In 1861 was made postmaster of that place, under Lincoln's administration, which office he held until he moved west in 1865. In the autumn of 1864 he went to Whiteside County, Ill., and bought a farm near where his brother and eldest sister (Mrs. Mary Champlin) lived. The following spring he moved his family there and continued the vocation of farming the balance of his life. In his early life he was religiously inclined, but as his family grew his son Calvin brought a class of free thought literature such as the "New York Truth Seeker," Prof. John Fiske's "Unseen World," Paine's "Age of Reason," Ingersoll's "Lectures," "Boston Investigator," etc., into his house, the reading of which somewhat changed his mind on dogmatic theology. His faithful wife died Mar. 8, 1887. This was a greater calamity than he could well bear, and three years one month and two days later he followed her to their long home. He d. May 10, 1890; res. Fisk Corners, Pa., and Morrison, Ill.

4843. i. WILMOT, b. Sept. 9, 1850; m. Sarah E. Humphrey.
4844. ii. THERON S., b. July 20, 1860; m. Ella Capron.
4845. iii. MELVIN, b. Dec. 12, 1851; m. Jennie E. Brumagin.
4846. iv. CALVIN R., b. Jan. 2, 1853; m. Stella A. Martindale.
4847. v. ALFRED L., b. Feb. 12, 1862; m. and res. 4014 Wright St., Chicago, Ill.
4848. vi. W. EVERETT, b. May 24, 1855; m. Eva Curtis and ———— ————; res. Lily, So. Dak.
4848½.vii. HARRIET ELIZA, b. Jan. 24, 1857; m. Frank O. Emery; res. Lovewell, Kans.

2993. CLARK S. FISK (Joseph, Joseph, Joseph, Mark, Joseph, William, William, John, William, Robert, Simon, Simon, William, Symond), b. Susquehanna County, Pa., Dec 4, 1832; m. Sept. 17, 1857, Adelia E. Reynolds, b. Dec. 12, 1839. Clark Fisk was born in eastern Pennsylvania about sixty years ago. He came west at about the age of 20 and located near Morrison in Whiteside County, Ill., where he has since resided, being engaged during the greater portion of said time in farming. At about the age of 30 he was married to Adelia E. Reynolds, whose parents removed from Vermont a short time prior thereto; res. Morrison, Ill.

4849. i. ADDIE N., b. June 2, 1857; m. May 14, 1891, G. L. Hollinshead; res. Ustick, Ill.
4850. ii. FRED WALLACE, b. Mar. 25, 1861; d. Oct. 24, 1870.
4851. iii. CHARLES J., b. Mar. 11, 1862; m. Ida M. Myers.
4852. iv. HENRY RAYMOND, b. Dec., 1864.
4853. v. EMMA JANE, b. Oct. 30, 1865; m. Jan. 16, 1890, William McFarlane; res. Wyzata, Minn.; b. Dec. 22, 1858; s. p. He is station agent for Great Northern Railway Company.
4854. vi. FRANK EDWARD, b. Nov. 30, 1877.
4855. vii. MYRTLE LOELLA, b. Dec. 7, 1872.
4856. viii. IDA MAY, b. Dec. 26, 1874.
4857. ix. LESTER CLARK, b. Apr., 1867.

3007. GRANVILLE CLARK FISKE (Washington, Joseph, Joseph, Mark, Joseph, William, William, John, William, Robert, Simon, Simon, William, Symond), b. Eden, Vt., Aug. 21, 1845; m. in Providence, R. I., June 27, 1871, Susan Seagraves Aldrich, b. Leicester, Mass., Apr. 26, 1848. Granville Clark Fiske was born in Eden, Vt.; moved to Hyde Park, Vt., at the age of 10 years; educated in the public schools of Hyde Park, Lamoille Central Academy of Hyde Park and Boston Business College, Boston, Mass.; enlisted June 14, 1862, in Company H, Ninth Vermont Volunteer Infantry; mustered into United States service July 9, 1862; discharged June 14, 1865, at Richmond, Va.; regiment mustered out; went to Ashland, Mass., June 25, 1865; worked on farm, in store, ran a bakery and ice business until 1893; is now New England agent for Boston Woven Hose & Rubber Co., 275 Devonshire St., Boston, Mass.; has been selectman of Ashland for seven years, and is at present one of them; represented the Twenty-seventh Representative District, composed of Hopkinton and Ashland, in Legislature in 1892; has been chief engineer of fire department three years; commander of Col. Prescott Post, No. 18, G. A. R., for nine years; worthy master North Star Lodge, A. F. & A. M., 1884-85; councilor of Mayflower Council, O. U. A. M., 1893; grand patron Order of Eastern Star of Massachusetts, 1887-88; res. Ashland, Mass.

4858. i. NINA BARNARD, b. Apr. 27, 1872; m. Dec. 2, 1891, in Ashland, Geo. N. Prouty. Ch.: Claude Granville, b. July 23, 1893; res. Jamaica Plain, Mass.

4859. ii. IVA ELATA, b. June 30, 1875.

4860. iii. ERROL WASHINGTON, b. June 4, 1882.

4861. iv. ALDEN CLARK, b. Sept. 2, 1884.

3024. HON. JOSEPH WILSON FISK (Joseph, Mark, Joseph, Mark, Joseph, William, John, William, Robert. Simon, Simon, William, Symond), b. Pembroke, N. H., Dec. 27, 1838; m. at Raymond, June 2, 1860, Abbie M. Hardy, b. Nov. 5, 1836. Joseph Wilson Fisk was born in Pembroke, N. H. At the age of 5 years moved to Raymond, N. H.; when 21 married Abbie M. Hardy. Five children were the fruits of the union, three daughters and two sons; has always been a farmer; represented the town of Raymond in the State Legislature of 1874 and 1875. At the present time he and his two sons are engaged in extensive farming operations, cultivating three farms; res. Raymond, N. H.

HON. JOSEPH WILSON FISK.

4862. i. LIZZIE C., b. June 6, 1861; m. Sept. 5, 18—, J. H. Harriman; res. R. Ch.: 1, Clarence W., b. June 6, 1881. 2, Ethel E., b. Sept., 1883. 3, Abbie L., b. May 22, 1890.

4863. ii. ELEANOR W., b. Nov. 9, 1863; m. Nov. 25, 1884, Williani A. Elliott; res. R. Ch.: 1, Albert F., b. June 6, 1885. 2, Harry E., b. Oct. 3, 1890.

4864. iii. JOSEPH H., b. July 23, 1870; m. Belle L. Patten.

4865. iv. LUCY B., b. July 5, 1873; m. Lewis G. Gilman; res. 452 Merrimac St., Manchester, N. H. Ch.: 1, Rosamond, b. Mar. 3, 1894.

4866. v. MARK, b. Apr. 6, 1867; m. Nellie F. Maloon.

3025. ALBERT FISKE (James W., Mark, Joseph, Mark, Joseph, William, John, William, Robert, Simon, Simon, William, Symond), b. Aug. 21, 1847, Somerville, Mass.; m. at Hyde Park, Dec. 25, 1872, Mary Lizzie Emery, b. Feb. 8, 1852. He is a cracker dealer; res. s. p. 47 Prescott St., Somerville, Mass.

3028. HIRAM WILSON FISK (Hiram, Mark, Joseph, Mark, Joseph, William, John, William, Robert, Simon, Simon, William, Symond), b. Feb. 1, 1837, in Derry, N. H.; m. there Sarah Perry; m. 2d, Diana Cameron. She m. 2d, ———. Thomas; res. Stroudsburg, Pa. He d. s. p. Apr. 19, 1881; res. Long Beach, Cal.

3059. ALBERT RICHARD FISKE (Abraham H., Benjamin, Nathaniel, Theophilus, Theophilus, William, William, John, William, Robert, Simon, Simon, William, Symond), b. Beverly, Mass., Apr. 30, 1826; m., 1846, Elizabeth (White) Safford, dau. of Henry and Elizabeth (Cook) Safford, b. Salem, Mass., Oct. 17, 1825; d. Aug., 1879; m. 2d, Sept. 11, 1880, Mrs. Jennie L. (Clay) Seavey, b. Lee, N. H., Jan. 20, 1835. Albert Richard Ober Fiske was born in Beverly, Mass., on what was then "Dodge's Row." His father, Abraham Fisk, was a farmer who moved afterward to Beverly Cove where the children were brought up, helping their father to pay for their home at the Cove, which was at the foot of Woodbury Street. The boys numbered five, all but the subject of this sketch following the sea. Albert was apprenticed to learn the shoemaker's trade at the early age of 11 years. He was courageous and active, and was early in life in business for himself. Failing in this, his first endeavor, he became foreman cutter in the factory of Francis Dane in So. Danvers, after which he was a partner in the business, having a separate factory on the corner of the "Square" and Chestnut Street. He was in business with varying fortunes at this stand for many years, removing to Wenham in 1870, eight miles away, where the workmen were mostly located, and where he continued to do business for himself until the great Boston fire, which swept away so many fortunes, so seriously impaired his business that he never fully recovered from the blow. He struggled on, however, for several years, when he was obliged to give up. He has lived since then in West Peabody, in Lynn and in Beverly, where he now resides. Albert R. Fisk is much respected wherever he is known, and is a man of sterling integrity, honest and incorruptible. In politics he was active in his younger days, serving two terms as Postmaster in So. Danvers, under Democratic administrations. He was loyal to the Union during the Civil War period, and though never joining the army, was a good friend of the soldier at the front, and their waiting families at home. He married, in 1846, Elizabeth White Safford, of Salem, who was born in 1825. In Aug., 1879, this truest of wives and fondest of mothers died. He subsequently married, at Lynn, Mrs. Jennie Seavey, a friend and acquaintance of many years. They resided for a time in Lynn, moving later to his native town of Beverly, where they live at 14 Home Street; res. South Danvers, Mass., and 14 Home Street, Beverly.

    4867. i.   ALBERT FRANKLIN, b. Aug. 27, 1847; m. Oct. 10, 1869, Emily Leighton Spiller; res. s. p. 71 Eastern Ave., Lynn, Mass.

    4868. ii.   HENRY SAFFORD, b. Mar. 27, 1849; m. Annie F. Longfellow.

    4869. iii.   GEORGE A., b. in 1850; d. in 1851.

    4870. iv.   EMMA CAROLINE, b. Oct. 11, 1853; m. A. L. Babbidge; res. No. Beverly, Mass.

    4871. v.   SARAH LIZZIE, b. Oct. 21, 1860; m. James B. Eaton, of West Peabody, and res. there now.

    4872. vi.   CLARENCE RUSSELL, b. July 2, 1863; res. Atlantic St., So. Boston.

    4873. vii.   WARREN BURTON, b. June 4, 1866; res. at home.

3061. ABRAHAM ALVIN FISKE (Abraham H., Benjamin, Nathaniel, Theophilus, Theophilus, William, William, John, William, Robert, Simon, Simon, William, Symond), b. Beverly, Mass., Dec. 28, 1832; m. Nov. 7, 1854, Lucy Ann Philbrook, dau. of Wm. H., b. Rockland, Me., Dec. 6, 1835. He was in his brother Albert R.'s manufactory, and was born at "The Point," in Beverly, and is now in the real estate and insurance business at Wenham Depot, Mass.; res. South Danvers, Mass., and Wenham Depot, Mass.

    4874. i.   CHARLES ALVIN, b. Jan. 24, 1856; m. Dec. 24, 1889; d. Apr. 10, 1891.

    4875. ii.   EVELEEN AUGUSTA, b. Mar. 28, 1858; res. Salem.

4876. iii. HARRIETT LOVETT, b. Aug. 22, 1860; res. Malden.
4877. iv. LUCY F., b. ———; d. young.
4878. v. MABEL P., b. ———; d. in infancy.
4879. vi. ELLA WILSON, b. May 12, 1872; m. May 29, 1890; res. Wenham Depot, Mass.

3083. GEORGE ALEXANDER FISKE (John B., Ezra, Samuel, Theophilus, Theophilus, William, William, John, William, Robert, Simon, Simon, William, Symond), b. Aug. 2, 1833, in Brooklyn, N. Y.; m. Elizabeth Morton, b. Liverpool, England. He was a machinist by trade; was called for his maternal grandfather; res. New York, N. Y.
4880. i. SARAH ELIZABETH MANSFIELD, b. Aug. 18, 1854; res. Salem.

3087. REV. CHARLES EZRA FISK (Henry W., Jonathan, Simeon, Ebenezer, Ebenezer, William, William, John, William, Robert, Simon, Simon, William, Symond), b. Vincennes, Ind., Nov. 9, 1862; m. Feb., 1889, Lulu A. Johnson at Greencastle, Ind. He was graduated at Lenox College, at Hopkinton, Ia., June, 1884, and from Princeton Theological Seminary in 1888; was licensed to preach in 1887 and ordained in the fall of 1888. He has charge of the Presbyterian Church at Alta; res. s. p. Alta, Ia.

3090. FRANCIS ALVAREZ FISKE (Francis A., Ebenezer, Ebenezer, Ebenezer, Ebenezer, William, William, John, William, Robert, Simon, Simon, William, Symond), b. Shelburne, Mass., June 3, 1841; m. there June 17, 1875, Hattie Allen, dau. of Loren and Hannah Allen, of Hadley; d. June 23, 1883.
4881. i. MAY WORTHINGTON, b. July 18, 1878.
4882. ii. HENRY HERBERT, b. Jan. 15, 1880.
4883. iii. HATTIE ALLEN, b. Aug. 13, 1881.

3091. WILLIAM BARDWELL FISKE (Francis A., Ebenezer, Ebenezer, Ebenezer, Ebenezer, William, William, John, William, Robert, Simon, Simon, William, Symond), b. Shelburne, Mass., Nov. 20, 1842; m. at Minneapolis, Sept. 15, 1870, Luella Emma Herrick, dau. of William W. and Garaophelia Herrick, d. Mar. 13, 1877; m. 2d, at Tiffin, Ohio, Sept. 26, 1894, Mrs. Hannah Rebecca (Naylor) Jones, dau. of James and Ann Naylor, and widow of Richard H. Jones, b. Alexandria, Ohio, Dec. 10, 1848. He is a broker on the Board of Trade; res. Chicago, Ill.; add. 323 Rialto.
4884. i. WILLIAM HERRICK, b. Oct. 27, 1874; d. Mar. 12, 1875.
4885. ii. LUELLA HERRICK, b. Dec. 1, 1876.

3094. RUFUS HENRY FISK (Ebenezer, Ebenezer, Ebenezer, Ebenezer, Ebenezer, William, William, John, William, Robert, Simon, Simon, William, Symond), b. Adrian, Mich., Aug. 17, 1844; m. June 11, 1873, Eliza Cordelia Harder; res. Adrian, Mich.
4886. i. BERTHA E., b. Apr. 27, 1874.
4887. ii. GEO. EBENEZER, b. Dec. 21, 1876.
4888. iii. OLIN HARDEN, b. Feb. 19, 1879.

3096. EDWARD PAYSON FISKE (Ebenezer, Ebenezer, Ebenezer, Ebenezer, Ebenezer, William, William, John, William, Robert, Simon, Simon, William, Symond), b. Adrian, Mich., Nov. 15, 1848; m. June 13, 1883, Frankie J. Poucher; res. Adrian, Mich.
4889. i. ANNA LAURA, b. Apr. 22, 1884.
4890. ii. NELLIE ELIZABETH, b. May 25, 1889.

3097. HERMAN SMEAD FISKE (Ebenezer, Ebenezer, Ebenezer, Ebenezer, Ebenezer, William, William, John, William, Robert, Simon, Simon, William, Symond), b. Adrian, Mich., Aug. 3, 1853; m. Oct. 30, 1888, Dora Estelle Gambee; res. De Witt, Mich.
4891. i. E. G., b. July 19, 1889.
4892. ii. ANNA LOUISE, b. Aug. 3, 1892 (adopted).

3107. CHARLES S. FISKE (Isaac T., Ebenezer, Ebenezer, Ebenezer, Ebenezer, William, William, John, William, Robert, Simon, Simon, William, Symond),

b. Oct. 27, 1859, Shelburne, Mass.; m. Sept. 27, 1881, Addie Gilbert, of Brattleboro; res. East Shelburne, Mass.

4893. i. BERTHA M., b. Dec. 15, 1882.
4894. ii. GRACE E., b. Feb. 11, 1884.
4895. iii. CHESTER E., b. July 17, 1888.
4896. iv. CHAS. CLAYTON, b. Aug. 2, 1893.

3108. LEVI LINCOLN FISKE (Isaac T., Ebenezer, Ebenezer, Ebenezer, Ebenezer, William, William, John, William, Robert, Simon, Simon, William, Symond), b. Mar. 10, 1861, Shelburne, Mass.; m. in Greenfield, Dec. 31, 1884, Jessie Eugenia Miner, b. Oct. 6, 1864. He is a farmer; res. Greenfield, Mass.

4897. i. LEON MINER, b. Aug. 4, 1886.
4898. ii. WALTER LEVI, b. Mar. 21, 1888.
4899. iii. HAROLD ELSWORTH, b. June 13, 1892.
4900. iv. MABEL ALICE, b. Aug. 21, 1894.

3111. LEVI W. FISK (Pliny B., Levi, Ebenezer, Ebenezer, Ebenezer, William, William, John, William, Robert, Simon, Simon, William, Symond), b. Byron, N. Y., June 21, 1859; m. Oct. 12, 1881, Nellie E. House; res. Byron, N. Y.

4901. i. CORA E., b. Aug. 6, 1882; d. Sept. 9, 1887.
4902. ii. PLINY B., b. Sept. 16, 1886.
4903. iii. JOHN S., b. Oct. 3, 1890.

3114. PERRIN BARTLETT FISK (Thomas B., Perrin B., Moses, Ebenezer, Ebenezer, William, William, John, William, Robert, Simon, Simon, William, Symond), b. Jackson, N. Y., Oct. 27, 1845; m. Nov. 30, 1865, Hannah M. Wing; m. 2d, May 25, 1870, Mary E. Gleason; m. 3d, Oct., 18—, E. J. Sugden. He is superintendent of a paper mill; res. No. Hoosick, N. Y.

4904. i. MINNIE MAY, b. Feb. 22, 1873.
4905. ii. IRA THOMAS, b. Dec. 24, 1874.
4906. iii. EDITH W., b. Dec. 14, 1876.
4907. iv. AMERETTE H., b. Feb. 7, 1879; d. Dec. 20, 1880.
4908. v. CLARENCE A., b. Feb. 12, 1881.
4909. vi. IDA G., b. Nov. 22, 1884.
4910. vii. FRANKIE S., b. Apr. 22, 1887.

3116. CHARLES HENRY FISK (Thomas B., Perrin B., Moses, Ebenezer, Ebenezer, William, William, John, William, Robert, Simon, Simon, William, Symond), b. Dec. 29, 1850; m. Nov. 27, 1873, Mary A. Soterege, at Whitehall. He d. in Shushan, Nov. 27, 1878; res. No. Hoosick Falls, N. Y.

4911. i. LURA AMARETT, b. July 15, 1875; unm.; res. No. H.

3118. THOMAS OTTO FISK (Thomas B., Perrin B., Moses, Ebenezer, Ebenezer, William, William, John, William, Robert, Simon, Simon, William, Symond), b. Salem, N. Y., Jan. 27, 1857; m. Dec. 10, 1885, Ida M. Andrus, b. Dec. 10, 1857. Thomas Otto Fisk, son of Thomas Briggs and Amarett Bartlett Fisk, born in Shushan, town of Salem, Washington Co., New York, on Jan. 27, 1856. Principal of Union graded school, No. Hoosick, Renss. Co., 1875 and 1876; graduated from State Normal School, at Albany, N. Y., 1879; principal of graded schools of Stillwater, N. Y., 1879 to 1881; engaged in mercantile business in Aurora, Ill., 1882; marble and granite merchant, 1885 to 1896; member of Baptist Church from 1867; married Ida M. Andrus, of Aurora, Ill. One child, girl, died in infancy. Add. 185 No. Lake St.; res. Aurora, Ill.,

3127. HORACE E. FISK (Pliny, Joel, Moses, Ebenezer, Ebenezer, William, William, John, William, Robert, Simon, Simon, William, Symond), b. Aug. 25, 1856, in Philadelphia, Pa.; m. in Trenton, N. J., Oct. 4, 1887, Julia Stimson Atterbury, b. Mar. 3, 1856. He is connected with John A. Roebling Son's Co., on Lake St.; res. Chicago, Ill., 474 No. State St.

4912. i. BEULAH LIVINGSTON ATTERBURY, b. July 15, 1888.
4913. ii. LIVINGSTON ATTERBURY, b. Mar. 28, 1892.
4914. iii. CALDWELL HALE, b. Oct. 14, 1894.

3129. WILLIAM IMLAY FISK (Pliny, Joel, Moses, Ebenezer, Ebenezer, William, William, John, William, Robert, Simon, Simon, William, Symond), b.

Nov. 16, 1861, Pottsville, Pa.; m. in Trenton, N. J., Fannie Bennett Norris, of Trenton, N. J., b. June 25, 1861; res. East Orange, N. J., 115 W. Fourteenth St.

4915. i.   HELEN IMLAY, b. Apr. 10, 1891.
4916. ii.   MARGARET, b. Apr. 22, 1892.

3133. HARVEY EDWARD FISK (Harvey, Joel, Moses, Ebenezer, Ebenezer, William, William, John, William, Robert, Simon, Simon, William, Symond), b. Jersey City, N. J., Mar. 26, 1856; m. at Scudder's Falls, N. J., Oct. 1, 1879, Mary Lee Scudder, b. Dec. 1, 1861. Is of the firm of Harvey Fisk & Sons, bankers; add. 24 Nassau St., New York, N. Y.

4917. i.   HARVEY EDWARD, b. Jan. 19, 1891.
4918. ii.   KENNETH, b. Nov. 17, 1895.

3134. CHARLES JOEL FISK (Harvey, Joel, Moses, Ebenezer, Ebenezer, William, William, John, William, Robert, Simon, Simon, William, Symond), b. June 16, 1858; m. Dec. 11, 1879, Lillie Richie. Is of the firm of Harvey Fisk & Sons, bankers; add. 24 Nassau St., New York, N. Y.

4919. i.   LOUISA GREEN, b. 1880.
4920. ii.   AUGUSTUS RICHIE, b. 1881.
4921. iii. CHAS. WILBUR, b. Jan., 1883.
4922. iv.   HARVEY, b. July 3, 1884.
4923. v.   ANNIE GRAY, b. Dec., 1888.

3135. PLINY FISK (Harvey, Joel, Moses, Ebenezer, Ebenezer, William, William, John, William, Robert, Simon, Simon, William, Symond), b. Aug. 26, 1860; m. Oct. 4, 1882, Mary Chapman. Is of the firm of Harvey Fisk & Sons, bankers; add. 24 Nassau St., New York, N. Y.

He has two children.

3137. WILBUR CHAPMAN FISK (Harvey, Joel, Moses, Ebenezer, Ebenezer, William, William, John, William, Robert, Simon, Simon, William, Symond), b. Feb. 22, 1868, New York, N. Y.; m. there, Feb. 9, 1893, Julia Herrick Allen, b. Sept. 9, 1867. Is of the firm of Harvey Fisk & Sons, bankers; add. 24, Nassau St.; res. New York, N. Y., s. p.

3173. GEORGE WASHINGTON FISK (David A., Nathaniel, Jonathan, William, Ebenezer, William, William, John, William, Robert, Simon, Simon, William, Symond), b. Northfield, Vt., Mar. 20, 1850; m. at Lincoln, Mass., Apr. 12, 1877, Eloise Moore Farnsworth, b. at Lincoln, June 20, 1849; d. Dec. 1, 1881, dau. of Joseph R. and Emeline (Moore) Farnsworth; m. 2d, Apr. 9, 1885, Isabel Agnes Ashley, at Hudson, Mass. He was born in Northfield, Vt. At the age of 12 he was put out to work on a farm for his board and clothes and three months' schooling per year. In the spring of 1867 he went to Boston, and lived with his brother, Charles D. Fisk, and worked whenever he could get a chance. In 1868 he went to Salem, Mass., to work, to learn the tinplate and sheet iron worker's trade. In 1872 he went to Hyde Park, Mass., where he went into business for himself, having a partner by the name of Fall; the firm name was Fall & Fisk. In 1879 he sold out his share of the business to Mr. Fall. Going to Boston to work at his trade. In 1883 he went to Hudson, Mass., and started in the stove and plumbing business, remaining there until 1891. Sold out to take a position as traveling salesman. In 1894 bought out a grocery and provision business in Lynn, where he at present resides; res. Lynn, Mass., 13 Arthur St.

4924. i.   GEO. FARNSWORTH, b. Sept. 27, 1878.

3180. JOHN BATES FISK (Samuel N., Nathaniel, Jonathan, William, Ebenezer, William, William, John, William, Robert, Simon, Simon, William, Symond), b. Williamstown, Vt., Mar. 4, 1848; m. Jan. 31, 1871, Alma Rumrell. He d. Nov. 26, 1876; res. Randolph, Vt.

4925. i.   NELLIE EMORY, b. June 20, 1873.
4926. ii.   WALTER NEWELL, b. Dec. 9, 1875.

3181. DENNISON FISK (Aaron M., William, Jonathan, William, Ebenezer, William, William, John, William, Robert, Simon, Simon, William, Symond), b. Liberty, N. Y., Mar. 31, 1839; m. there, Jan. 23, 1872, Sarah C. Crary, b. Apr. 24, 1845. He was a miller by trade and was killed by a horse running away. He was out sleighriding with his wife and son; the horse took fright and ran, throwing them all out, and he was hurt internally, so that he only lived two hours. He d. Mar. 13, 1884; res. Liberty, N. Y.

4927. i. RALPH M., b. Sept. 9, 1879.
4928. ii. DENCIA, b. Oct. 13, 1884 (posthumous).

3213. PHILIP DAVIS FISKE (Francis N., Ezra, William, William, Ebenezer, William, William, John, William, Robert, Simon, Simon, William, Symond), b. Apr. 20, 1832, in Fayette, Me.; m. at Winsted, Conn., June 10, 1863, Mary Melvina Hitchcock, b. Aug. 11, 1842. He is a mechanic and engineer; is a Republican. He was a policeman while residing in Winsted, Conn., and is now connected with the New Haven fire department; res. New Haven, Conn., 372 Grand Ave.

4929. i. ALFRED, b. Nov. 2, 1864; d. July 14, 1866.
4930. ii. CORA LUCIA, b. July 2, 1867; m. June 23, 1892, to Frank Leslie Arnold. They have one child. Leslie Philip Arnold, b. Aug. 28, 1893. Religion of family, Protestant; politics, Republican; P. O. add., No. 372 Grand Ave., New Haven, Conn.
4931. iii. FLORENCE EVA, b. Sept. 6, 1872; m. Frank Archer Southwerth, Nov. 24, 1892. Religion of family, Protestant; politics, Republican. Occupation of husband, editor; P. O. add., No. 169 Whalley Ave., New Haven, Conn.
4931½.iv. SARAH HITCHCOCK, b. May 19, 1880; P. O. add. No. 169 Whalley Ave., New Haven, Conn.

3221. HOMER WRIGHT FISKE (Allen, Ezra, William, William, Ebenezer, William, William, John, William, Robert, Simon, Simon, William, Symond), b. Fayette, Me., Mar. 18, 1844; m. at Lawrence, Mass., Nov. 22, 1866, Jennette L. Abbot, b. Feb., 1845; d. 1889; m. 2d, Aug. 29, 1894, Ida J. Richards, of Milan, O., b. Apr. 8, 1858. Mr. Fiske is a mechanical engineer and quite an expert in his line. Last year he came very near losing his life while at work in Washington, D. C., because of the carelessness of some individual unknown. In company with several other workmen, Mr. Fiske, who is an erecting engineer in the employ of the Providence Steam Engine Company, was engaged in fitting a portion of one of the Greene engines connected with the multipolar generator which supplies the motive power for the new electric system of propulsion being introduced by the Metropolitan company. While standing on the axle of the immense fly wheel, with his mind fixed on the work, Mr. Fiske was startled to feel that the axle was revolving. In the hope of saving himself he jumped to a wooden beam nearby, but it gave way with a crash, and the engineer was precipitated to the bottom of the wheel pit. Before he could move he was dragged beneath the revolving wheel, the space between the same and the cement flooring being less than one foot. In less time than it takes to tell it the unfortunate man had suffered a compound fracture of the right leg, a lacerated wound on the left hand, contusions of the back and shoulders and an abrasion of the left leg. A heavy iron casting which fell at the same time as did Mr. Fisk was smashed. The wheel, which had been set in motion by the shifting of a lever by some person among the many spectators watching the erection of the engine, was quickly stopped, and half a dozen of his fellow workmen lifted the injured man from his precarious position. The fact that the man had been badly injured quickly spread about the neighborhood, and in a few moments a surgeon with several members of the ambulance corps reached the scene from the hospital of the Washington Barracks, which is but half a block distant from the new power house. Several other physicians were also summoned, but it was decided to send Mr. Fiske to the Emergency Hospital. At the latter institution his injuries were attended to. Res. Providence, R. I., and Milan, O.

4932. i. FRANK HAMILTON, b. Sept. 29, 1870; res. Lawrence, Mass.
4933. ii. HOMER RICHARDS, b. June 1, 1895.

3226. CHARLES DUDLEY BLAKE FISK (Dudley B., Ezra, William, William, Ebenezer. William. William, John, William, Robert, Simon, Simon, William, Symond), b. Hookset, N. H., Feb. 17, 1850; m. Apr. 8, 1875, Susan Elizabeth Sparhawk, b. Oct. 20, 1854, dau. of Edward Carey and Susan Elizabeth (Greenwood) Sparhawk, of Brighton, Mass. Charles Dudley Blake Fiske, second son of Dudley Blake and Mary Ann Ashton Fiske, was born at Hookset, N. H., Feb. 17, 1850. His father died in 1851, leaving his mother destitute, with two small boys, his brother, William Francis, and himself. The first seven years of his life were passed at the home of his grandparents, in Lowell, Mass., his mother working hard to earn sufficient to care for her children. When Charles was nearly 7 years of age, his mother married an honest, hard working mechanic, who proved kind to the children, but of a roving nature, consequently Charles' early life was passed in various places, remaining in each hardly long enough to form any personal friends, and too short a time to acquire an education. At the age of 11 he worked in the early morning on a milk route, and in the evening sold papers on the streets of Providence, R. I. Two years later he had a cheap jewelry stand on Central St., Lowell, Mass., and later, at the age of 15, worked in a paper box factory. Again returning to Providence, Mr. Fiske, at the age of 16,

CHARLES DUDLEY BLAKE FISK.

drove a grocery order wagon. Realizing fully his ignorance, he attended a commercial evening school for about a year, learning bookkeeping, and laying the foundation for what knowledge he acquired later. Going to California at the age of 18, he soon spent what little he had saved, and went to work laying track for the Central Pacific Railroad at Sacramento, at $1.50 per day. After that he worked in the car shops, building cars, and yet later secured a position as clerk in the motive power department, at a salary of $1,500 a year, all the changes occurring within a year from his arrival in California, although when he landed he was an entire stranger to everybody. His last position carried him to the wilds of Nevada, where he mingled with the hardest set of men that could be gathered together from the four quarters of the globe. There might was law, and pistols and knives settled many a dispute. He dabbled in mines more or less, and became interested in a patent, which he thought would make his fortune. He returned East in 1871, soon became stranded, and was compelled to begin life anew as entry clerk in a large clothing house of J. B. Barnaby & Co., of Providence, R. I., at a salary of $6 per week. A year later he entered the employ of the Howe Sewing Machine Company, as bookkeeper; became their temporary general agent of Rhode Island and Connecticut, settled up their broken busines and returned as head bookkeeper of the said clothing firm. In 1874 he went to Portland, Me., and opened a clothing store under the name of C. D. B. Fiske & Co., being backed by J. B. Barnaby & Co., his former employers. In 1879 Mr. Fiske was elected to the common council of Portland, and in 1880, was elected president of that body. In 1881 he removed to Boston, and opened a much larger store, under the name of J. B. Barnaby & Co. In 1893, as Mr. Barnaby had died, the business was sold, and in April of the same year, taking a partner, he opened a very large store as Fiske & Goff, clothiers. Since then the firm added a store in Portland,

Me. In 1875 Mr. Fiske married Susie E. Sparhawk, of Brighton, Mass., daughter of Edward C. Sparhawk, a wealthy and honored citizen of that place; res. Boston, Mass.

4934.   i.   WM. FRANCIS, b. Mar. 2, 1878.
4935. ii.   CLARENCE AMES, b. Jan. 4, 1887.

3238.   CHARLES EDWARD FISKE (David D., William, William, William, Ebenezer, William, William, John, William, Robert, Simon, Simon, William, Symond), b. Sanbornton, N. H., Nov. 19, 1837; m. at Portsmouth, Va., Sept. 19, 1865, Rosalby Porter, b. Jan. 1, 1843. Charles E. Fiske was born at Sanbornton, N. H., Nov. 19, 1837. He was educated in Brooklyn, N. Y., and when quite a young man made a tour around the world, being absent about three years. On his return he was married to Miss Rose Porter, of Portsmouth, Va., and moved to New York, where he engaged in the wholesale wine business. He subsequently moved to Brooklyn, N. Y., where he died, Apr. 6, 1888, at the age of 50 years. He was a man beloved by all who knew him; was a loving husband and father, and a kind, faithful and generous friend. Of his five children, two daughters died when quite young, and one, Anita, resides in Brooklyn. He d. Apr. 6, 1888; res. 20 Ft. Green Place, Brooklyn, N. Y.

4936.   i.   ANITA L., b. ———.
4937. ii.   CHARLES EDMUND, b. Oct. 17, 1869; unm.; res. B. He was born in Portsmouth, Va., Oct. 17, 1869. He attended St. John's College, in Brooklyn, and the Columbia College Law School, in New York City. He was admitted to the bar of New York State, in 1892, and is now practicing law in Brooklyn.
4938. iii.   EDWARDA B., b. ———; d. ———.
4939. iv.   ROSE E., b. ———; d. ———.
4940.   v.   EDWIN HOWE, b. Jan. 23, 1877. He is a student in the class of 1897, at St. Francis Xavier College, New York City.

3242.   FRANK WALKER FISKE (Francis A., Francis N., William, William, Ebenezer, William, William, John, William, Robert, Simon, Simon, William, Symond), b. Concord, N. H., Sept. 19, 1851; m. Oct. 27, 1875, Hattie E. Hubbard, of Golden, Colo. Frank Walker Fiske attended school at Phillips Exeter Academy; studied law in Concord; went west in 1872 and located in Colorado; chose railroading for his work and served in various capacities with Colorado Central Railroad. The last years of his life he acted as agent for the Kanawha Fast Freight Line, with office at Kansas City, Mo. He d. June 11, 1886; res. Kansas City, Mo.

4941.   i.   HARRY HUBBARD, b. Nov. 29, 1877.

3247.   JOHN TAYLOR FISKE (Francis A., Francis N., William, William, Ebenezer, William, William, John, William, Robert, Simon, Simon, William, Symond), b. Concord, N. H., Oct. 29, 1864; m. in Savannah, Ga., Apr. 12, 1888, Mary Amelia Lillie (Lewis Converse, Lewis, Samuel, David,) [eldest daughter of Lewis Converse (7) and Julia (Frye) Lillie,] was born at Troy, N. Y., Apr. 2, 1862. She was married at 170 Hall St., Savannah, Ga.; res. Concord, N. H. John Taylor Fiske attended school in Concord; went south, spending a few years in Savannah, Ga.; also in business in New York City; now in Concord, living at the old homestead in the employ of the Concord Light and Power Company.

4942.   i.   DOROTHY LILLIE, b. Mar. 31, 1889, at Elizabeth, N. J.
4943. ii.   SARAH TARLETON, b. July 5, 1894, at Concord, N. H.

3252.   LIEUT. BRADLEY ALLAN FISKE (William A., Allen, William, William, Ebenezer, William, William, John, William, Robert, Simon, Simon, William, Symond), b. Lyons, N. Y., June 13, 1854; m. in New York City, Feb. 15, 1882, Josephine Harper. Born at Lyons, N. Y., June 13, 1854; appointed as cadet midshipman, United States Navy, and entered United States Naval Academy, Annapolis, Md., Sept. 22, 1870; graduated second in class and appointed midshipman, May 30, 1874; assigned to United States Flagship Pensacola, and made cruise of two years in North Pacific fleet; promoted to ensign in June, 1876; served on U. S. S. Plymouth and Powhatan in North Atlantic fleet, as ensign. During cruise in Plymouth, invented and perfected detaching apparatus, for lowering and hoisting boats in a seaway. This apparatus is now (1895) in use in may of the ships of the navy; promoted to master Jan. 10, 1881. The

LIEUT. BRADLEY ALLAN FISKE.

title of master changed to that of lieutenant, junior grade, Mar. 3, 1883; promoted to lieutenant Jan. 26, 1887. On Feb. 15, 1882, he married Josephine Harper, daughter of Mr. Joseph W. Harper, head of the publishing firm of Harper & Brothers. On Oct. 1, 1882, obtained leave of absence for one year, to study electricity. During this year he wrote "Electricity in Theory and Practice," which Van Nostrand published. This book in 1895 was still selling, in its tenth edition. On duty in Bureau of Ordnance, Navy Department, from Oct., 1883, to Oct., 1885. During this time, i. e. in Oct. and Nov., 1884, was member of International Conference of Electricians at Philadelphia, and also was detailed in charge of the Naval Exhibit at the International Electrical Exhibition; made cruise in U. S. S. Atlanta, the first modern cruiser of the United States Navy, from July, 1886, to Dec., 1888. During this cruise invented electrical range finder for measuring distances at sea and in forts. This instrument is now in use in the principal ships of the navy; carried on, also, while on this cruise a number of experiments in electrically signalling through the water and the air. Up to the present time these experiments have not borne fruit in the shape of practical apparatus. From Dec., 1888, to Nov., 1890, engaged in shore duty in New York and Philadelphia, and also perfecting in leisure moments the range finder. In Oct., 1890, received a year's leave, most of which spent in Europe with wife and daughter. In Oct., 1891, ordered to U. S. S. Yorktown and went in her to Chile; was in Valparaiso during the height of the crisis there, under the command of Captain R. D. Evans (Fighting Bob), whose conduct during the episode gained so much honor for himself, his ship, and the United States; went from Chile, after the crisis had passed, to Bering Sea, and spent the summer in the Yorktown, then flagship of the patrol fleet for suppressing seal poaching. In July, 1893, the Yorktown being then at New York, was transferred to the Flagship San Francisco. Shortly after this, the San Francisco was ordered to Rio de Janeiro, Brazil, to watch over American interests during the rebellion of the navy, under Admirals Mello and da Gama against the government; was on board the San Francisco, under Admiral Benham, when that gallant admiral cleared his fleet for action and forced the Brazilian navy to agree to the just demands of the United States. After the conclusion of hostilities, the San Francisco was ordered to Bluefields, Nicaragua, to protect American interests in the triangular dispute going on between England, Nicaragua and the Mosquito Indians; detached from the San Francisco in Oct., 1894. During this cruise perfected range finder, and invented new form of position finder; invented also stadimeter, range telegraph, helm indicator, steering telegraph, telescope sight, electric telescope-sighting-system, and electric engine-telegraph. At the present moment, the range finder has been adopted by the navy and is placed in all the new ships; the stadimeter has proved a complete success in service and is being supplied to all the ships. The range indicator, helm indicator, steering telegraph and electric engine telegraph have passed successful tests in service at sea, and are being installed in the new battleships. The telescope sight is being tested now in various ships. In the summer of 1895 invented electric lachometer for continuously indicating on the bridge of a ship the direction and speed of revolution of the ship's engines. This instrument is now undergoing a test in service on board the

United States armored cruiser New York; res. The Beresford, 1 W. 81st St., New York, N. Y.

  4944. i. CAROLINE HARPER, b. June 29, 1885.

  3265. REV. FRANKLIN LUTHER FISK (John P., Ebenezer, Ebenezer, William, Ebenezer, William, William, John, William, Robert, Simon, Simon, William, Symond), b. Lowell, Mass., Jan. 24, 1855; m. at West Minneapolis, June

REV. FRANKLIN LUTHER FISK.

18, 1890, Vera Ida Brown, a grandniece of John Brown, of Harper's Ferry. In 1856 he went to Beloit, Wis., with his parents, where he resided until the winter of 1876; graduated from Beloit College in June, 1876, and three years after took the degree of Master of Arts. He taught school in Ogle County, Ill., till 1880, when he entered Chicago Theological Seminary. During the three years' course at this institution, aside from the regular work, he taught a Chinese night school in Farwell Hall, preached many Sabbaths, and did other labor. In vacation preached at Blair and Kearney, Neb., graduated from above named seminary in May, 1883; was ordained and installed by council Nov. 20, 1883, at Downer's Grove, Ill., where he was pastor of the Congregational Church till July, 1885. After a successful year with the Congregational Church at Baraboo, Wis., he was called to the pastorate of the Congregational Church, Lake City, Minn., where he aided in a union with the Presbyterians (the latter disbanding their organization). After three years of hard and very fruitful work with the Congregational Church, Worthington, Minn., he undertook the new enterprise at Garner, Ia. In three years' time built up a strong, efficient church, having a new and well equipped building. Oct. 20, 1894, he began work with the new church at Elkader, Clayton County, Ia.; res. Elkader, Ia.

  4945. i. JOHN LEWIS, b. June 25, 1891.
  4946. ii. FRANKLIN DOUGLASS, b. May 26, 1893; d. Jan. 1, 1896.
  4947. iii. WILLIAM HALL, b. Oct. 17, 1895.

  3266. JOHN PROCTOR FISK (John P., Ebenezer, Ebenezer, William, Ebenezer, William, William, John, William, Robert, Simon, Simon, William, Symond), b. Beloit, Wis., Sept. 11, 1857; m. at Redlands, Cal., Dec. 5, 1890, Mrs. Elizabeth H. Eddy, widow of Rev. S. W. Eddy, b. Springville, N. Y., Sept. 25, 1860. Mr. Fisk went through the public and high schools of Beloit, Wis., and graduated from Beloit College in 1880. After two years of teaching at Richmond, McHenry County, Ill., he resumed study at the Chicago Theological Seminary, but a severe illness interrupted his studies and he then taught for four terms in the academy connected with Beloit College. His health then broke down, so that he was obliged to go south for the winter, and the following fall, in 1885, he went to California to regain his health; was for a time in Riverside, Cal., and then moved to Redlands, Cal., just as the place began to be built up. Here he engaged in the real estate and insurance business which he has since prosecuted successfully; res. Redlands, Cal.

  3267. EDWARD OLIVER FISKE (John P., Ebenezer, Ebenezer, William, Ebenezer, William, William, John, William, Robert, Simon, Simon, William, Symond), b. Beloit, Wis., Dec. 30, 1859; m. at Racine, Wis., Sept. 15, 1891. Mary Frances Miller, dau. of Moses and Frances Augusta Miller, b. Racine, Jan. 31,

MRS. KATHERINE TANNER FISK.

1865. He was graduated from Beloit high school in 1875, and for two years taught district school at Newark, Wis., and Shirland, Ill., laboring also during vacations on farms near Beloit. He entered Beloit College in Sept., 1877, and was graduated therefrom in June, 1881, and in 1884 received the degree of Master of Arts from the same institution. From Sept., 1881, until June, 1883, Mr. Fiske served as principal of the high school at Lake Geneva, Walworth County, Wis.; from Sept., 1883, until June, 1884, was head master of Markham Academy, Milwaukee, Wis., and from Sept., 1884, until June. 1887, was associate principal of Misses Grant's Seminary at Chicago, Ill. In Sept., 1887, he removed to Minnesota, to act as principal of Excelsior Academy at Excelsior, Hennepin County, Minn. In July, 1888, he established himself in the business of life insurance in which he is yet engaged in Minneapolis, Minn. Mr. Fiske is now the general agent for the Washington Life Insurance Company, of New York. His office is room 304, Bank of Commerce building, and his res. 1208 Southeast Seventh St. Mary Miller Fiske was graduated from McMynn's Academy at Racine in June, 1882, and from Misses Grant's Seminary at Chicago in June, 1885. Mr. and Mrs. Fiske are members of the First Congregational Church of Minneapolis, Minn; res. Minneapolis, Minn.

  4948. i. PROCTOR MILLER, b. Oct. 6, 1892.
  4949. ii. FRANCES, b. Aug. 5, 1894.

  3269. GEORGE FREDERIC FISKE (John P., Ebenezer, Ebenezer, William, Ebenezer, William, William, John, William, Robert, Simon, Simon, William, Symond), b. Beloit, Wis., Aug. 21, 1863; m. in Chicago, Oct. 22, 1891, Mary E. Zimmerman, dau. of John S. and Henrietta Ebell Cherry Zimmerman, b. Maryville, Tenn., July 23, 1866. He was graduated from the Beloit High School in 1880 and from Beloit College in 1885. In Oct., 1885, he came to Chicago and found employment in the office of George M. Clark Company, manufacturers of gas and gasoline stoves. In 1894 he was made secretary of the above company. Mr. and Mrs. Fiske are members of the First Congregational Church of Ravenswood, Chicago. Mr. Fiske is independent in politics; res. 2803 N. Paulina St., Chicago, Ill.

  4950. i. FREDERIC EBELL, b. Dec. 21, 1892.

  3271. PROF. FRANKLIN PROCTOR FISK (Franklin W., Ebenezer, Ebenezer, William, Ebenezer, William, William, John, William, Robert, Simon, Simon, William, Symond), b. Chicago, Ill., Oct. 27, 1857; m. Dec. 27, 1881, Katherine Tanner, of Rockford, Ill. She was born in Wisconsin, but when quite young moved with her parents to Rockford, Ill., where she always resided. When 12 years of age she entered the Rockford College, where she graduated in 1881, only six months before she was married to Frank Fisk. Very soon after removing to Chicago, she began her musical career as a pupil of Miss F. A. Roots, and she there enlisted the interest of Professor Tomlins, who was her next teacher. After much solo work, Mrs. Fisk sought the advice and guidance of Mrs. S. H. Eddy, who admired her wonderful voice, but said that she must give years to study before she could expect to do much with it. She accepted the verdict, and studied for four years intently under Mrs. Eddy. From that time she became the most popular singer in the West. She soon determined to go to London, and having been heard by Mr. Daniel Mayer, was induced to sign a three years' engagement with him. After her arrival there she studied French and German songs under Mr. Henschel and Mr. Blume and passed her oratorios with Signor Randegger, making her debut at St. James' Hall at the close of 1892. Her success was such that before the end of January, 1893, she had been heard in that hall fourteen times, as well as at the Crystal Palace, Albert Hall and the London Symphony Concerts. After a short visit to her native country she returned to London, which will be her headquarters, though she will sing throughout Europe. In private life Mrs. Fisk is as charming as she is in her professional, for she is singularly gifted both mentally and physically, has most excellent taste in dress, speaks French fluently, and has a good knowledge of German and Italian. The rise to her position as one of the leading American contraltos is really a record of labor, perseverance and patience. Prof. Fisk was born in Chicago and in referring to him the Post says: "Abreast of the times, keeping along with all requirements at the recognized Chicago pace, is the Northwest Division high school, at Potomac Avenue and Davis Street. Dominated by the idea that sound practical sense and reason may be drilled into the young as well as Greek, Latin, mathematics or history, and possessed of a curriculum which is far more elaborate and attractive than that of a large number of the small colleges in the West, this Chicago school is growing in popularity, and has come to be the ideal school for the thousands of children who live in the northwest section of the city. The pride which Principal Franklin B. Fisk takes in his school is indeed pardonable. He has stamped his individuality indelibly on the institution over which he presides and the credit of it all is his, to have and to hold. Northwest Division high school is now a little more than six years old and it is a prodigy. Seven hundred scholars attend it regularly and nineteen teachers assist Mr. Fisk in their instruction. Studying is a business under Mr. Fisk's regime. His pupils go to school to learn, and not simply to be where they cannot annoy their parents for a day. The hours in school are short, only one session being held from 9 o'clock a. m. to 2 o'clock p. m., with a half-hour for luncheon and a whispering recess of five minutes. The best of order is maintained in the class and recitation rooms, and nothing distracts the attention of any pupil. To describe Northwest Division high school, its rooms, its departments and its course of study would be simply going over old ground. It is a complete school from alpha to omega, and it is a great institution. It fills a place in Chicago's educational facilities which no man attempts to dispute and it affords children who would be compelled to stop with finishing at the graded schools an opportunity for a higher education, which they and their parents most assuredly appreciate. It is asserted that at least thirty per cent of the seven hundred pupils in the school would have been compelled to go to work for a living this fall had not Mr. Fisk's school been available, simply because their parents couldn't afford to send them to a college or a university. And an education means more than dollars and cents to the average child of school age. As an example of the plan upon which Mr. Fisk conducts this school one scene in the big gymnasium in the basement may be thus described: Thirty girls, of all sizes and forms, dressed in blue trousers, very full, blouses of the same material, stockings to match and light shoes, romping and racing, jumping, leaping, laughing, swinging on ropes hung from the ceiling, with rings attached, turning on the horizontal bar, climbing ladders, their feet higher than their heads half the time and every mother's daughter of them ruddy-faced and seemingly not exhausted. No unseemly behavior, no rough jesting, no false modesthood. Just healthy girlhood effervescent." Res. s. p. Chicago, Ill.

3272. HENRY EDWARD FISK (Franklin W., Ebenezer, Ebenezer, William, Ebenezer, William, William, John, William, Robert, Simon, Simon, William, Symond), b. Sept. 11, 1862, Chicago; m. there, Dec. 31, 1885, Hannah S. MacNeish. He is a commission broker in wholesale groceries. Was graduated at Yale College (Academic department), in the class of 1883 and at once engaged in business. Is at 42 River St.; res. 532 W. Adams St., Chicago, Ill.
    4951. i.   HENRY BOWEN, b. Nov. 1, 1886.

3276. LORENZO D. FISKE (Luther, James, Ebenezer, William, Ebenezer, William, William, John, William, Robert, Simon, Simon, William, Symond), b. Coldwater, Mich., Apr. 2, 1854; m. there, Ella T. Gates, b. May 9, 1857; res. Coldwater, Mich.
    4952. i.   MILDRED, b. Oct. 16, 1880.
    4953. ii. LLOYD, b. Jan. 1, 1885.
    4954. iii. ROBERT H., b. Dec. 16, 1890.
    4955. iv. DONALD D., b. Dec. 9, 1891.

3278. LEWIS ROSS FISK (Lewis R., James, Ebenezer, William, Ebenezer, William, William, John, William, Robert, Simon, Simon, William, Symond), b. Albion, Mich., July 23, 1853; m. May 28, 1882, Luella Josephine Tillotson, b. Harrisville, Mich., Feb. 12, 1866. He was a clerk and finally a merchant. He d. s. p. Sept. 8, 1895; res. Oneida, N. Y.

3281. HERBERT ELWOOD FISKE (Lewis R., James, Ebenezer, William, Ebenezer, William, William, John, William, Robert, Simon, Simon, William, Symond), b. June 23, 1863; m. June, 1893, Marie Mater; res. Leadville, Colo.
    He has two children.

3288. EDWARD H. FISKE (David O., Samuel, Samuel, Daniel, Samuel, William, John, William, Robert, Simon, Simon, William, Symond), b. Shelburne, Mass., Jan. 8, 1854; m. June 5, 1889, Lucy E. Hale; res. Shelburne, Mass.

3289. HARVEY ORLANDO FISKE (David O., Samuel, Samuel, Daniel, Samuel, William, John, William, Robert, Simon, Simon, William, Symond), b. Shelburne, Mass., Dec. 23, 1855; m. in Warehouse Point, Conn., Nov. 16, 1882, Mary Emily Thompson, b. May 1, 1859. He is a farmer; res. Shelburne, Mass.

    4956. i.   ESTELLE LEE, b. July 4, 1886.

3290. WALTER E. FISKE (David O., Samuel, Samuel, Daniel, Samuel, William, John, William, Robert, Simon, Simon, William, Symond), b. Shelburne, Mass., Aug. 23, 1861; m. there, Nov. 5, 1886, Julia Pascoe; res. Shelburne, Mass.

3295. DR. GEORGE FOSTER FISKE (Samuel W., David, Samuel, Samuel, David, Samuel, William, John, William, Robert, Simon, Simon, William, Symond), b. Madison, Conn., Jan. 26, 1860; m. at Peterboro, N. H., Aug. 9, 1888, Gertrude Bass, b. May 14, 1863.

Geo. F. Fiske obtained the degrees of B. A., at Amherst College, in 1881, of A. M., in 1886, and of M. D., at the Yale Medical School in 1883. Spent three years in Germany and France studying ophthalmology and otology. Was assistant surgeon to Prof. Graefe, in the University Ophthalmological Hospital, at Halle, Prussia. in 1884-85. Settled in Chicago in 1886 as an eye and ear specialist. In 1891 built a private hospital for treatment of his own patients. Visited European hospitals in 1890 and 1895. Res. Chicago, Ill., 438 La Salle Ave.

    4957. i.   SAMUEL PERKINS, b. May 27, 1889.

    4958. ii.   GEORGE FOSTER, b. Sept. 28, 1891.

    4959. iii.   CLARA BASS, b. Nov. 9, 1892; d. Mar. 25, 1893.

3317. GEORGE PLINY FISK (James D., Partridge, Daniel, Samuel, Daniel, Samuel, William, John, William, Robert, Simon, Simon, William, Symond), b. Oct. 6, 1868; m. Dec. 20, 1892, Eva E. Brewer; res. Lyndon, Ill.

DR. GEORGE FOSTER FISKE.

3320. FREDERIC ELISHA FISKE (Frederic A., Elisha, Robert, Daniel, Daniel, Samuel, William, John, William, Robert, Simon, Simon, William, Symond), b. Norwalk, Conn., July 25, 1840; m. in Boston, Mar. 31, 1870, Marion Austin Cutter, b. Nov. 22, 1848. Frederic Elisha Fiske, son of Rev. Frederic Augustus Fiske and Anna A. (Nelson) Fiske, was born in Norwalk. Conn.; was educated and received his preparatory course at his father's schools. In 1863 he entered the quartermaster's department of the army, spending most of the time at the post of Morehead City, N. C. In 1865 was transferred to the Freedmen's Bureau, in Raleigh, N. C., where he remained till 1868, when he resigned to return north, since which time he has resided in Taunton, Mass., except in the years 1885 and 1886, when he went to Garden City, N. Y., where he was business manager of the Cathedral School of St. Paul. Res. Taunton, Mass., s. p.

3323. DANIEL MILTON FISK (David B., Daniel, Robert, Daniel, Daniel, Samuel, William, John, William, Robert, Simon, Simon, William, Symond), b. Upton, Mass., Dec. 6, 1839; m. in Chicago, Nov. 16, 1865, Martha E. Sharp, b. Baldwinsville, N. Y., Feb. 22, 1844. He was born in Upton, where his father was in business. He attended the public schools and Wilbraham (Mass.) Seminary.

In 1850 he entered his father's employ as clerk, and on attaining his majority, was admitted a member of the firm of D. B. Fisk & Co., importers, manufacturers and wholesale dealers in millinery and straw goods. In the spring of 1871 he went to New York City, and had charge of the business of the company there. He remained there until 1893, when he returned to Chicago. His firm organized a stock company, and he was made a director in the same. He is still connected with the company; res. Chicago, Ill., 2100 Calumet Ave.

  4960. i. MATTIE BELL, b. Oct. 11, 1869; m. 1895, Edmund Crafts
       Green; res. 55 Astor St., Chicago, Ill.

  1861. GEORGE ROBERT FISK (William, Robert, Daniel, Daniel, Samuel, William, John, William, Robert, Simon, Simon, William, Symond), b. Upton, Mass., Jan. 5, 1821; m. Louise M. Tyler. He is a member of the firm of Geo. R. Fisk & Co., millinery goods, Boston and New York; res. New York, N. Y., add. 621 Broadway.

  3331. i. G. HERBERT, b. ———; m. Belle Delabough.
  3332. ii. LOUIS ISBEL, b. ———.

  3333. HARRISON RANSOM FISK (Harrison L., Emmons H., Daniel, Daniel, Daniel, Samuel, William, John, William, Robert, Simon, Simon, William, Symond), b. in Texas, Apr. 19, 1858; m. Oct. 21, 1884, Emma Azelia Cady, b. Mar. 6, 1860. He is a carpenter; res. Upton, Mass., P. O box. 275.

  4961. i. ETHEL F., b. July 23, 1885.
  4962. ii. THEODORE ORSON, b. Sept. 5, 1892.

  3334. WINTHROP WARD FISK (Harrison L., Emmons H., Daniel, Daniel, Daniel, Daniel, Samuel, William, John, William, Robert, Simon, Simon, William, Symond), b. Upton, Mass., Oct. 26, 1859; m. at Cincinnati, O., Dec. 22, 1885, Caroline Collier Swasey, b. Nov. 1, 1855. Winthrop Ward Fisk, born in Upton, Mass., Oct. 26, 1859. Named after Winthrop Ward, of Charlestown. 1860—At one year old, with the assistance of brother, one and a half years older, upset clothes frame into the open fire, and burned the house down; they saved us for further mischief; nothing else was saved. 1865—At six years of age was attending primary school, one mile from home. At seven we moved to Springfield, Mass., where I attended the Hooker grammar school, and later the high. 1875—Moved to Worcester, Mass., to attend the Worcester Polytechnic Institute. 1878—Graduated as Bachelor of Science, having given special attention to practice in chemistry. Height, 5 feet 11½ inches; weight, 130 pounds. 1879—Came to Boston to try my luck. 1880—The mining excitement struck Maine; I went to New York, bought an assay outfit, and went to Ellsworth, Me.; stayed about two years. Maine mines shut down; returned to Boston, and went to work with a corporation to manufacture lactic acid and lactate of lime. 1882—Moved to Littleton, Mass., and built a large factory. Present weight, 180 pounds. 1883—Went to Europe to perfect the lactic patents by producing the article in most of the European countries. While in Europe studied the mineral deposits of the countries; visited also the mineral specimens in the natural history museums. 1884—Spent some time writing up the Alabama iron and coal regions; visited the New Orleans Exposition, with an exhibit of lactic acid. 1885—Established an office in Boston to handle mining machinery; acted as chemist for Bay State Steel Works, built a gold mill at Milford, Mass.; married Dec. 22, 1885. 1886—Opened mine and repaired and operated eight-stamp mill, in Nova Scotia. 1888—Connected with mining company; opening mine and erecting eighty-stamp mill in Alaska; as assayer and consulting engineer for several years. 1891—Returned to Boston and opened permanent office as mining engineer; since which time have had charge of work in Alaska, New Mexico, Colorado, New Brunswick, and Cape Breton. Height, 5 feet 11 inches; weight, 180 pounds; health good; res. Boston, Mass., 12 Pearl St.

  4963. i. WINTHROP SWASEY, b. Nov. 10, 1889.
  4964. ii. MARY BARTOL, b. Feb. 16, 1893.

  3335½. HAMBLET BARBER FISK (James J., Joel, Benjamin, Benjamin, Daniel, Samuel, William, John, William, Robert, Simon, Simon, William, Symond), b. Bellingham, Mass., Mar. 27, 1838; m. at So. Milford, Oct. 21, 1874, Eliza Hawes, dau. of Samuel and Eliza Hawes, b. Pawtucket, R. I., Nov. 29, 1836. He is in the retail grocery business; res. So. Milford, Mass.

3343. EDWARD F. FISK (Franklin E., Galacious, Benjamin, Benjamin, Daniel, Samuel, William, John, William, Robert, Simon, Simon, William, Symond), b. Brooklyn, N. Y., June 27, 1857; m. there, Feb. 24, 1886, Sadie B. Roberts, b. Jan. 27, 1866, in Hummetstown, Pa. He is a map engraver; res. Ridgefield Park, N. J.

    4965. i. EDWARD T. F., b. Oct. 17, 1886.
    4966. ii. HELEN B., b. Jan. 18, 1890.
    4967. iii. ARTHUR E., b. Apr. 16, 1891.
    4968. iv. DOROTHY, b. Sept. 23, 1893.

3349. OTIS GALACIUS FISK (Otis A., Galacious, Benjamin, Benja-Daniel, Samuel, William, John, William, Robert, Simon, Simon, William, Symond), b. Ludlow, Mass., Jan. 7, 1855; m. in Belchertown, Mass., Jan. 12, 1876, Carrie Lilla Davis, b. Apr. 27, 1857. He is in the provision business; res. Holyoke, Mass., 123 Oak St.

    4969. i. FRANCES LILLIAN, b. Apr. 9, 1877.
    4970. ii. CARRIE LOU, b. Sept. 16, 1879.

3354. CHARLES CHAPIN FISKE (Erastus H., Armory, Benjamin, Benjamin, Daniel, Samuel, William, John, William, Robert, Simon, Simon, William, Symond), b. Aug. 4, 1848, Greenwich, Mass.; m. Oct. 15, 1874, Mary Fannie Wilson, b. Apr. 14, 1850. He was a dry goods merchant. He d. May 7, 1882; res. Sterling, Ill.

    4971. i. CLARENCE WILSON, b. July 19, 1879.

3360. EDWARD R. FISKE (Charles H., Emory, Benjamin, Benjamin, Daniel, Samuel, William, John, William, Robert, Simon, Simon, William, Symond), b. Dec. 30, 1850, Enfield, Mass.; m. in Belchertown, Mass., Dec. 20, 1876, Caroline P. Holland, b. Mar. 18, 1849. He is a merchant; res. s. p. 234 W. Chester Ave., Germantown, Pa.

3361. CHARLES H. FISKE (Charles H., Emory, Benjamin, Benjamin, Daniel, Samuel, William, John, William, Robert, Simon, Simon, William, Symond), b. Dec. 18, 1856, Richmond, Ind.; m. at Sedan, Kan., Oct. 1, 1893, Nellie Leonore Osborn, b. May 15, 1875. He is a contractor and builder; res. Virgil, Kan.

    4972. i. BERYL BRADY, b. July 9, 1894; d. Sept. 4, 1894.
    4973. ii. NELLIE OSBORN, b. June 26, 1895.

3390. CHARLES HENRY FISK (Horace L., Alexander, Josiah, Josiah, Daniel, Samuel, William, John, William, Robert, Simon, Simon, William, Symond), b. Bellingham, Mass., Aug. 13, 1855; m. at Paxton, Aug. 12, 1882, Delia E. Gotha, b. in Leicester, Oct. 26, 1866. He is a shoemaker; res. Spencer, Mass.

    4974. i. CHACES E., b. Aug. 18, 1883.
    4975. ii. ALICE I., b. May 12, 1886.
    4976. iii. THEODORE A., b. Sept. 18, 1893; d. Oct. 8, 1893.

3398. WILLIAM THOMAS FISK (John G., Alexander, Josiah, Josiah, Daniel, Samuel, William, John, William, Robert, Simon, Simon, William, Symond), b. Rock Island, P. Q., Mar. 9, 1855; m. at Holland, Vt., Mar. 19, 1884, Martha Pelow, b. Apr. 22, 1863. He is a carpenter; res. Derby Line, Vt.

    4977. i. ROY B., b. Feb. 10, 1885; d. May 3, 1889.
    4978. ii. EARNEST R., b. May 20, 1887; d. Dec. 28, 1892.
    4979. iii. SIDNEY H., b. Sept. 5, 1890.
    4980. iv. SARAH R., b. Mar. 22, 1892.
    4981. v. ELIZABETH E., b. Dec. 4, 1894.

3399. CHARLES HENRY FISK (Orin M., Abraham, Samuel, Ephraim, Joseph, Samuel, Joseph, William, John, William, Robert, Simon, Simon, William, Symond), b. Oct. 6, 1827, in De Kalb, N. Y.; m. Jan. 1, 1853, Mary F. Smith. She res. in Maywood, Ill. Charles H. Fisk, a brother of Theodore Fisk and Mrs. Henry Newcome, died suddenly at Maywood, near Chicago, on Saturday, July 12, 1884, from ulceration of the stomach, aged 57 years. His remains are buried in a beautiful spot in Forest Home Cemetery. He was an excellent man, well known as a one time honored resident and was greatly loved by all who knew him. A large attendance was present to render the last sad service mortals can bestow upon their fellows. He. d. July 17, 1884; res. Maywood, Ill.

4982. i. CHARLES H., b. ———; m., and res. 78 Osgood St., Chicago; is a florist at 167 Wabash Ave.

3400. THEODORE FISK (Orin M., Abraham, Samuel, Ephraim, Joseph, Samuel, Joseph, William, John, William, Robert, Simon, Simon, William, Symond), b. De Kalb, N. Y., Mar. 8, 1829; m. there June 22, 1854, Jane Norris, b. Feb. 25, 1831. He is a dealer in wood. Theodore Fisk enlisted in the cavalry arm of the service in the War of the Rebellion and remained till its close, enduring many hardships and hairbreadth escapes; res. Osage, Ia.

4983. i. CHARLES WM., b. Oct. 27, 1855.
4984. ii. FRED'K GEO., b. June 14, 1859; m. Adelaide S. Hill.
4985. iii. ALICE JANE, b. Oct. 31, 1866.
4986. iv. WESLEY EUGENE, b. May 7, 1870.

3409. JEFFERSON C. FISK (Horace A., Benjamin B., Ephraim, Joseph, Samuel, Joseph, William, John, William, Robert, Simon, Simon, William, Symond), b. Feb. 20, 1854, in Clinton, Mich.; m. Apr. 1, 1880, Mary A. English. Jefferson C. Fisk lived and worked on his father's farm until 20 years of age, when he went to the State of Oregon where he worked on a farm for four years. He then came back to Michigan and lived at home for a year and a half, when he married. He has always been a farmer and is now living on a farm three miles west of Clinton, Mich.; add. Clinton, Mich.

4987. i. FRED, b. Jan. 14, 1881.
4988. ii. HARRY, b. Apr. 12, 1882.
4989. iii. ARTHUR, b. Nov. 4, 1886.
4990. iv. HAZEL I., b. Feb. 13, 1891.

3414. CLINTON B. FISK (Horace A., Benjamin B., Ephraim, Joseph, Samuel, Joseph, William, John, William, Robert, Simon, Simon, William, Symond), b. July 30, 1868, in Clinton, Mich.; m. Nov. 5, 1893, Mary Wilcox. He lived and worked on the farm at home, going to school winters until he was 19 years of age, when he went to Nebraska with his sister, Mrs. Hubert Beach. After staying a year there, he came home and lived two or three years, then went to Jackson, Mich., where he has lived ever since; res. s. p. Jackson, Mich.

3420. CLINTON BOWEN FISK (Clinton B., Benjamin B., Ephraim, Joseph, Samuel, Joseph, William, John, William, Robert, Simon, Simon, William, Symond), b. St. Louis, Mo., Mar. 3, 1871; m. Jan. 28, 1894, in New York City, May Isabel Taylor, b. May 22, 1873. He removed from St. Louis at an early age; was educated at private school and by tutor in New York City; entered class of '92 at Columbia College, but left at the beginning of his junior year because of the death of his father; entered business in a desultory way, and formed the partnership now existing—Van Note & Fisk, No. 36 Union Square, New York, makers of stained glass and church goods—in 1849; res. s. p.; add. 36 Union Square, New York, N. Y.

3433. WALTER CLINTON FISK (Joseph, Samuel, Isaac, Joseph, Samuel, Joseph, William, John, William, Robert, Simon, Simon, William, Symond), b. Providence, R. I., Aug. 27, 1855; m. at East Prov., May 21, 1885, Emily Dunning, b. Sept. 30, 1864. He was a clerk; res. 10 Lavangher St., Providence, R. I.

4991. i. CHARLES DUNNING, b. Nov. 2, 1889.
4992. ii. MABEL ELIZA, b. June 18, 1892.

3445. HENRY ANTHONY FISKE (George R., Isaac, Isaac, Joseph, Samuel, Joseph, William, John, William, Robert, Simon, Simon, William, Symond), b. Fall River, Mass., May 16, 1870; m. in Boston, May 29, 1894, Frances Elizabeth Thomas. He was born in Fall River, but passed his boyhood years in Roxbury, where he had all the educational advantages that the place afforded. He passed through the celebrated Roxbury Latin school, which ranks high as an educational institution. Later he passed five years in the Massachusetts Institute of Technology and has two diplomas from that school—chemical engineering and electricity. He is special agent of the Imperial Fire Insurance Company of London, for New England, and has a brilliant career before him; res. s. p. 11 Sanborn Ave., Dorchester, Mass.

3451. LAFAYETTE FISKE (Nathan P., Joseph, Isaac, Joseph, Samuel, Joseph, William, John, William, Robert, Simon, Simon, William, Symond), b. Centerville, Ohio, June 21, 1833; m. Jan. 21, 1862, Harriett J. Hancock, b. West Jefferson, Ohio, July 27, 1838. He was born in Centerville; has resided in Ottawa and West Jefferson, Ohio; Bloomington, Stewarts and Chicago, Ill. For the past five years, since 1890, has resided in the latter city and now lives at 169 So. Hoyne St. He is employed by the Northwestern Railway Company as flagman; res. Chicago, Ill.

4993. i. MEEDHAM, b. Feb. 4, 1863; m. Amelia O. Kapelski.
4994. ii. JOHN ALBERT, b. Dec. 11, 1868; m. June 3, 1893, Dora Lake; is employed in railroad work; res. s. p. Decatur, Ill.
4995. iii. NELLIE A., b. June 1, 1873; res. Chicago.
4996. iv. HARRIETT J., b. July 27, 1878; res. 155 Dickey Ave., Chicago, Ill.

3452. JOSEPH BAKER FISKE (Nathan P., Joseph, Isaac, Joseph, Samuel, Joseph, William, John, William, Robert, Simon, Simon, William, Symond), b. Centreville, Ohio, Mar. 13, 1838; m. Oct. 8, 1867, Mary Shaw, b. June 6, 1839. He was born on a farm near Centreville, Montgomery County, Ohio. His mother's death occurring when he was but four weeks old, he was placed around at neighbors and relatives until his father remarried. He attended the district school and Centreville Academy; at age of 16 went to Philadelphia to attend school. His health failing after eighteen months he went to Ohio and spent a year in a flouring mill and in farming. In 1857-58 was with an engineering party surveying a new railroad in Illinois. Afterward went to New York City to take charge of a lumber interest; was married in New York in 1867; went to Toledo; engaged in hardwood lumber shipping and commission. In 1876 went into laundry business. In 1889 organized a stock company and since served it in capacity of secretary, treasurer and general manager; res. Toledo, Ohio.

4997. i. WILLIAM HARPER, b. July 31, 1869.
4998. ii. CAMILLA ISABEL, b. Jan. 18, 1872.
4999. iii. JOSEPH BAKER, b. Aug. 16, 1874.
5000. iv. HARRY JOHN, b. Feb. 25, 1877.
5001. v. ARTHUR SHAW, b. Oct. 19, 1879.

3454. FRANKLIN AUGUSTUS FISK (Nathan P., Joseph, Isaac, Joseph, Samuel, Joseph, William, John, William, Robert, Simon, Simon, William, Symond), b. Centreville, Ohio, Aug. 17, 1844; m. at Bloomington, Ill., Sept. 8, 1869, Cornelia Edwarda Barnetta Sebring, b. Feb. 20, 1849. He is a bookkeeper; res. 1421 G. St., Lincoln, Neb.

5002. i. SEBRING C., b. June 14, 1870, National Guard Armory, Toledo, Ohio.
5003. ii. EDITH CLARKSON, b. June 15, 1874, 1421 G St.
5004. iii. LAURA BELLE, b. Oct. 27, 1877, 1421 G St.

3455. SAMUEL TATE FISK (Nathan P., Joseph, Isaac, Joseph, Samuel, Joseph, William, John, William, Robert, Simon, Simon, William, Symond), b. Centreville, Ohio, Nov. 23, 1848; m. at Elizabeth, N. J., May 25, 1876, Lillian Marsh Higbie, b. Jan. 5, 1855. He is a railway ticket broker; res. 311 Madison St., Toledo, Ohio.

5005. i. VIRGINIA MAY, b. Mar. 22, 1877; res. Ann Arbor, Mich.
5006. ii. SAMUEL TATE, b. July 7, 1878; res. cor. 5th and Chestnut Sts., St. Louis, Mo.
5007. iii. ETHEL ZOE, b. Mar. 23, 1880; res. Ann Arbor, Mich.

3457. JOHN ALBERT FISKE (Nathan P., Joseph, Isaac, Joseph, Samuel, Joseph, William, John, William, Robert, Simon, Simon, William, Symond), b. Nov. 10, 1851, Centreville, Ohio; m. Nov. 8, 1877, Clara Hawthorne; res. Toledo, Ohio.

5008. i. ALBERT ELMER, b. Aug. 19, 1878.
5009. ii. ALFA HAWTHORNE, b. Feb. 24, 1880.
5010. iii. GEORGE MEREDITH, b. Apr. 4, 1884.

3468. DENNISON FISK (David, John, John, John, John, John, Nathaniel, William, Robert, Simon, Simon, William, Symond), b. Brookfield, N. Y., Apr. 4,

1807; m. at Sangerfield, Mar. 18, 1827, Polly P. Bush, b. Nov. 15, 1804; d. Jan. 6, 1892. He was a farmer. He d. Mar. 7, 1883; res. Brookfield, N. Y.

5011. i. MARY J., b. July 2, 1839; m. Nov. 26, 1884, Charles M. Cope; res. West Barre, N. Y. He is a farmer. Ch.: Wm. B., b. Nov. 30, 1887.
5012. ii. CHARLES C., b. Sept. 13, 1844; m. Laretta E. Collins.
5013. iii. MARY, b. Apr. 22, 1833; d. Sept. 22, 1838.
5014. iv. THERESIA A., b. June 29, 1847; d. Sept. 19, 1850.
5015. v. DAVID L., b. Jan. 1, 1829; m. Frances E. Green.

3469. JOHN FISK (David, John, John, John, John, John, Nathaniel, William, Robert, Simon, Simon, William, Symond), b. Apr. 5, 1821, in Brookfield, N. Y.; m. there Jan. 3, 1841, Clarinda Main. He is a farmer and wagonmaker. Res.. Brookfield, N. Y.

5016. i. FRANCES L., b. Dec. 8, 1841; m., 1870, —— Mane.
5017. ii. MARY LOUISA, b. Apr. 24, 1848; m., 1866, A. D. Poppleton; res. Hanover Court House, Va.
5018. iii. MILO L., b. Nov. 3, 1852; m. in 1873, Mrs. Frances Avery Main; res. B.

3470. FRIEND LYMAN FISK (David, John. John, John, John, John, Nathaniel, William, Robert, Simon, Simon, William, Symond), b. Brookfield, N. Y., Sept. 24, 1804; m. Jan. 1, 1824, Parley Farman, b. 1801; d. 1873. He was a farmer. He d. Mar. 3, 1868; res. Ellington, N. Y.

5019. i. EMILY, b. ——; m., 1845, L. Johnson.
5020. ii. BETSEY, b. ——; m., 1847, George Lane.
5021. iii. DAVID H., b. Apr. 25, 1831; m. Saloma Johnson.

3471. DAVID FISK (David, John, John, John. John, John, Nathaniel, William, Robert, Simon, Simon, William, Symond), b. Brookfield, N. Y., Jan. 29, 1812; m. there Apr. 12, 1832, Mary Maria Lord Wentworth b. Aug. 7, 1813; d. June 3, 1895. He was a farmer and speculator. He d. May 30, 1880; res. Forestville, N. Y.

5022. i. MARY M., b. Aug. 14, 1833; m. Nov. 17, 1854, Rev. D. E. Steadman; res. Beech Tree, Pa. He was b. May 1, 1831. Is a clergyman in the M. E. Church. Ch.: 1. Alice E., b. July 11, 1856; d. Dec. 20, 1856. 2, Miriam E., b. Apr. 22, 1859; m. Sept., 1877, B. V. Sherwood; P. O. Union City, Pa. 3, Helen M., b. Apr. 27, 1861; m. May, 1887, Dr. G. D. Thomas; P. O. Chicora, Butler Co., Pa.
5023. ii. W. HENRY, b. June 30, 1840; m. ——; d. Jan. 31, 1888, leaving a dau., Carrie C., who m. —— Glasford; res. Forestville, N. Y.
5024. iii. EDWIN, b. June 10, 1848; d. Feb. 22, 1851.
5025. iv. HELEN, b. May 16, 1852; m. Feb. 26, 1873. J. C. Hutchinson, b. Sept. 17, 1851; res. Forestville, N. Y. Ch.: 1, Harry Fisk, b. Oct. 26, 1873.

3476. JAMES BYRON FISK (John, John, John, John, John, John, Nathaniel, William, Robert, Simon, Simon, William, Symond), b. Brookfield, N. Y., 1809; m. at Mendon in 1830, Jerusha Theresa Loveland, b. May, 1814; d. Nov. 7, 1876. James Byron Fisk was married in the State of New York; removed to Ohio; studied law; admitted to the bar under Judges Joshua R. Giddings and Benj. F. Wade; practiced in the courts of Ohio, New York, Pennsylvania; later a resident of Indiana, and last of Minnesota. Died at St. Paul; burial place, Oak Hill Cemetery. He d. Jan. 30, 1864; res. Pierpont, O., and St. Paul, Minn.

5026. i. JOHN H., b. July 7, 1831; m. Mary E. Hamlin.
5027. ii. MARIA JANE, b. May, 1833; d. 1851.
5028. iii. JAMES LIBERTY, b. in 1835; m. Lydia Brerson.
5029. iv. ROBERT EMMET, b. Aug. 9, 1837; m. Elizabeth Chester.
5030. v. DANIEL WEBSTER, b. Apr. 5, 1839; m. Julia F. Walker.
5031. vi. VAN HAYDEN, b. in 1841; m. Ellie Reed.
5032. vii. ANDREW JACKSON, b. Jan. 8, 1849; m. Clara A. Wilcox.

3477. COL. JOHN FISK (John, John, John, John, John, John, Nathaniel, William, Robert, Simon, Simon, William, Symond), b. Brookfield, N. Y., Nov. 30, 1802; m. ——— ———. He was a noted Indian scout and at one time presented President Lincoln with a nugget of gold that resembled a human face. Res. in the west.

  5033. i. CORA F., b. ———; m ——— Anderson; res. Kansas City, Mo.

3479. LEVI FISK (John, John, John, John, John, John, Nathaniel, William, Robert, Simon, Simon, William, Symond), b. Brookfield, N. Y., June 28, 1804; m. at Royalton, N. Y., Oct. 22, 1828, Susannah Bixby, b. Feb. 28, 1807; d. Feb. 27, 1875. He is a farmer. Res. Lockport and Alabama, N. Y.

  5034. i. CHARLES L., b. July 22, 1829; m. June 19, 1866, Emily Benedict, b. Apr. 4, 1837. He d. s. p. June 20, 1891. Was a lumber dealer. Res. Royalton.
  5035. ii. HANNAH, b. Jan. 7, 1832; m. H. F. Douglass; res. Princeton, Ill.
  5036. iii. EUNICE, b. Sept. 10, 1833; d. unm.
  5037. iv. WILBUR, b. Mar. 10, 1835; m. in Princeton, Ill., May 24, 1871, Mary Frances Ripley, b. Jan. 26, 1844. Is a machinest. Res. Grand Island, Neb. Ch.: 1, Edwin Ripley, b. Mar. 6, 1880. 2, Bradford Truesdale, b. Feb. 16, 1883.
  5038. v. AMANDA L., b. Dec. 14, 1837; unm.; res. Alabama.
  5039. vi. MARTHA, b. Feb. 11, 1840; d. unm.
  5040. vii. NEWTON, b., Apr. 17, 1842. He died a soldier in the Civil war.
  5041. viii. ORRIL, b. Apr. 10, 1845; m. Geo. W. Duel; res. Alabama, N. Y. Two children.
  5042. ix. LUCY A., b. Oct. 7, 1847; m. H. J. Bateman; res. Webster, N. Y.
  5043. x. LEVI B., b. Nov. 14, 1849; m. Rachel Cope; res. Alabama.

3483. JONATHAN FISKE (James, John, John, John, John, John, Nathaniel, William, Robert, Simon, Simon, William, Symond), b. Brookfield, N. Y., Oct. 27, 1804; m. Achsah Rowley, b. July 6, 1807. He was a farmer. He d. in Somerset, Minn., Oct. 26, 1872; res. Milton, Wis., and Alfred, N. Y.

  5044. i. ESTHER EMMA, b. Aug. 10, 1849; m. Oct. 9, 1872, Calvin Dwight Reynolds, b. Feb. 24, 1846. He is a wholesale dealer in cheese. Ch.: 1, Sophie, b. Apr. 13, 1875. 2, Raymon F., b. May 27, 1887. 3, Fred C., b. Mar. 12, 1883. 4, Herbert, b. July 4, 1877; d. July 19, 1879.
  5045. ii. JAMES, b. Sept. 27, 1833; m. 1856; res. Owatonna, Minn.
  5046. iii. HANNAH, b. Mar. 6, 1836; m. Silas R. Bliven. and in 1854 L. H. Stratton: res. Langdon, N. Dak. Ch.: 1, Hiram Bliven, b. Osheria Co., Wis., June 3, 1861. 2, Esther Bliven, b. Jan. 8, 1862; d. 1884. 3, Rebecca Bliven, b. Osheria Co., Wis., Jan. 17, 1864; d. Nov., 1888. 4, Cornelia I. Bliven, b. Osheria Co., Wis., Jan. 14, 1869. 5, Mary J. Bliven, b. Osheria Co., Wis., July 4, 1871.
  5047. iv. MARY J., b. Apr. 26, 1838. She was b. in Hayfield, Pa.; m. in Westport, Wis., Daniel S. Bacon, b. Apr. 10, 1832; d. May 7, 1862; m. 2d, at Waseca, Minn., Delos Bardwell, b. Aug. 10, 1838; d. June 27, 1895. Res. Scriven, Minn. Ch.: 1, Alice R. Bacon, b. Mar. 23, 1855; m. Jan. 23, 1873, Jacob Cutsinger. 2, Albert Bacon, b. Mar. 22, 1857; m. Nov. 27, 1888, Mary Penner. 3, Willard Bacon, b. Feb. 24, 1860; m. Feb. 23, 1882, Amanda Gonser. 4, Walter Bardwell, b. Mar. 9, 1876. Their P. O. add. is Scriven, Minn.
  5048. v. IRENA, b. Dec. 28, 1840; m. 1860, ——— Lee. She d. ———. Ch.: Willard H., b. ———; res. Minneapolis.
  5049. vi. CHAS. M. G., b. Jan. 1, 1844; m.; d. in army in May, 1863.
  5050. vii. HIRAM, b. July 20, 1846; d. in the army in July, 1864.

3487. HENRY A. FISK (James, William, William, John, John, John, John, Nathaniel, William, Robert, Simon, Simon, William, Symond), b. West Boylston, Mass., Dec. 5, 1831; m. in Malden, June 20, 1868, Jennie Richardson; res. Charlestown, Mass., 72 High St.

5051. i. WILLIAM A., b. ———.
5052. ii. MARION B., b. ———.
5053. iii. J. H., b. ———.

3488. GEORGE ALBERT FISKE (James, William, William, John, John, John, John, Nathaniel, William, Robert, Simon, Simon, William, Symond), b. West Boylston, Mass., Dec. 29, 1834; m. in Groveland, Mass., Rebecca D. Renton (Palmer), b. Nov. 9, 1826. He is a blacksmith and farmer; res. Worcester, Mass., 154 Main St.
5054. i. WILLIAM VAUGHN, b. Mar. 10, 1863: m. Bertha M. Ball.
5055. ii. MARY AUSTRY, b. Sept. 18, 1864; res. at home.

3492. EDWIN E. FISKE (James, William, William, John, John, John, John, Nathaniel, William, Robert, Simon, Simon, William, Symond), b. Aug. 24, 1847, West Boylston, Mass.; m. Oct. 16, 1872, M. Louise Reede, b. Oct. 9, 1848. He is a grocer; res. Worcester, Mass., 407 Chandler St., s. p.
3500. JOSEPH ALONZO FISKE (John, Samuel, John, John, John, John, Nathaniel, William, Robert, Simon, Simon, William, Symond), b. Princeton, Mass., Dec. 15, 1828; m. in Worcester, Serena Nancy Metcalf, b. Jan. 26, 1835. Was a merchant. He d. June 15, 1869; res. No. Leominster, Mass.
5056. i. FRANK MORSE, b. Aug. 21, 1857; m. Nov. 8, 1881, Fannie Williams; res. No. L.
5057. ii. JOHN METCALF, b. Apr. 5, 1860; unm.; res. Boston., 502 Columbus Ave.

3508. ALBURN FISKE (Stephen, Jonas, Jonathan, John, John, John. John, Nathaniel, William, Robert, Simon, Simon, William, Symond). b. Wendell, Mass., Feb. 23, 1848; m. in Orange, Oct. 22, 1874, Emily Stevens, b. Apr., 1853. He is a prominent citizen; has been assessor and selectman; res. Wendell, Mass.
5058. i. NELLIE M., b. 1875.
5059. ii. ALLIE, b. 1877.
5060. iii. ALACE, b. 1882.
5061. iv. CHARLIE, b. 1888.

3511. AUGUSTUS GEORGE FISK (Jabez, Daniel, Jonathan, John, John, John, Nathaniel, William, Robert. Simon, Simon, William, Symond), b. N. Y., May 30, 1820; m. Dover, Mich., Nov. 21, 1844, Cassandra Howard, b. Mar. 30, 1823. Mar. 20, Mrs. Cassandra Fisk celebrated her seventy-third birthday, with the aid of twenty-five of her neighbors. In the morning she received a basket from Mrs. J. C. Holden, of Reed City, which contained fruit, a very handsomely decorated tea set, and a birthday cake. At the top of the cake was written "Mother," and in the center appeared "1823-1896." At the bottom was written. "Many blessings crown your head." The neighbors, who assembled in time for tea, presented the astonished woman with a very handsome swinging chair, the speech being made by Mrs. W. A. Stillwell. It was a very pleasant gathering, and was greatly appreciated by the good woman. He is a mechanic; res. Grand Rapids, Mich., 431 W. Bridge St.
5062. i. ANDREW TENBROOK, b. Dec. 3, 1845; d. Oct. 8, 1864.
5063. ii. MARTHA JANE, b. Mar. 25, 1848; m. Dec. 20, 1864, ——— Tuttle. She d. May 23, 1873.
5064. iii. EDGAR EUGENE, b. Jan. 4. 1850; m. at Hastings. Mich., July 4, 1877, Emma Hotchkiss. She d. Nov., 1892. He d. June 13, 1895. Was a carpenter. Ch.: Archie, b. May 29, 1878: res. Big Rapids, Mich. George Burnice, b. Mar. 20, 1890; res. B. R.
5065. iv. KATE, b. Feb. 16, 1857; m. Feb. 12, 1874, ——— Stickney: res. Gowen, Mich.
5066. v. CORA MAY, b. Aug. 15, 1867; m. Dec. 21, 1887, ——— Stillwell; res. Big Rapids, Mich.
5067. vi. JABEZ KENDALL, b. June 17, 1852; d. Oct. 18, 1870.
5068. vii. IDA BELL, b. Aug. 19, 1869; d. May 25, 1872.
5069. viii. MAE JOSEPHINE, b. Sept. 25, 1855; unm.; res. Big Rapids, Mich.

31

3515. DANIEL FISK (Jabez, Daniel, Jonathan, John, John, Nathaniel, William, Robert, Simon, Simon, William, Symond), b. Horseheads. Chenung Co., N. Y., Feb. 1, 1825; m. at Waverly, Oct. 23, 1852. Elizabeth Quick, b. May 6, 1829; d. Jan. 27, 1893. He is a farmer; res. Adrian, Mich.

   5070. i.   FRED M., b. Oct. 27, 1855; m. Lillie M. Blair.
   5071. ii.   CARRIE M., b. Oct. 7, 1858; res. A.
   5072. iii. HARRY JABEZ, b. Apr. 9, 1867; res. London, Eng. Is a manufacturing chemist; add. 21 No. Audley St.

3524. WILLIAM F. FISK (Abijah, Daniel, Jonathan, John, John, John, Nathaniel, William, Robert, Simon, Simon, William, Symond), b. Veteran, N. Y., Oct. 28, 1822; m. Feb. 1, 1860, Mrs. Martha (Putnam) Fisk, b. Apr. 22, 1826; d. Apr. 18, 1869. He is a farmer; res. Fairfield, Mich.

   5073. i.   LE ELLA C., b. Oct. 19, 1861; unm.; res. F.
   5074. ii.   JOSEPHINE, b. Feb. 3, 1865; m. Sept. 15, 1882, Llewellyn Be Dell; res. 665 Hanover St., Milwaukee, Wis.

3526. SANFORD NORRIS FISK (Abijah, Daniel, Jonathan, John, John, John, Nathaniel, William, Robert, Simon, Simon, William, Symond), b. Veteran, N. Y., Oct. 9, 1837; m. there, Clementina Hooley, b. Nov. 6, 1844. He is a farmer; res. Elmira, N. Y., 706 W. Water St.

   5075. i.   HARRY A., b. Jan. 2, 1870.
   5076. ii.   WM. L., b. June 26, 1875.
   5077. iii. FRED C., b. Oct. 26, 1880.

3531. JAMES STILLMAN FISK (Zedekiah, Zedekiah, Daniel, John, John, John, Nathaniel, William, Robert, Simon, Simon, William, Symond), b. Ashtabula, O., June 9, 1831; m. May 23, 1872. Ella Josephine Cook, b. Apr. 23, 1851. He d. in Osawatomie, Kan., Dec. 8, 1885; res. Atchison, Kan.

   5078. i.   LUCY STELLA, b. Nov. 27, 1873; res. Atchison.
   5079. ii.   CLAUDE B., b. Nov. 18, 1875; res. A.
   5080. iii. HADDIE BELL, b. Sept. 27, 1877; d. June 6, 1888.
   5081. iv. ROY STILLMAN, b. May 3, 1881.

3541. HENRY ZEDEKIAH FISK (Joseph, Zedekiah, Daniel, John, John, John, Nathaniel, William, Robert, Simon, Simon, William, Symond). b. Wendell, Mass., Jan. 15, 1849; m. in Brattleboro, Vt., Mar. 17, 1874, Ella Susan Marvell, b. Jan. 1, 1855. He is a farmer; res. No. Leverett, Mass.

   5082. i.   LEORA ELMA, b. July 10, 1875.
   5083. ii.   LUCY ELLA, b. Apr. 4, 1878.

3542. DR. HENRY JAMES FISK (James W., Daniel, Daniel, John, John, John, Nathaniel, William, Robert, Simon, Simon, William, Symond), b. Heath, Mass., June 30, 1848; m. May 13, 1871. Ida Alice Clark, b. Apr. 25, 1854. He is a practicing physician; res. Hartford, Conn., 223 Asylum St.

   5084. i.   LOUIS HENRY, b. Oct. 15, 1872; m. June 19, 1894; res. H.

3544. DR. WILLIAM WILLARD FISK (James W., Daniel, Daniel, John, John, John, Nathaniel, William, Robert, Simon, Simon, William, Symond), b. Heath, Mass., Sept. 1, 1856; m. Sept. 1. 1887, Lizzie G. Siebecker, b. Oct. 16, 1861. He is a practicing physician; res. No. Leverett, Mass.

   5085. i.   EDITH ELLA, b. July 26, 1889.

3552. MARCUS MORTON FISK (Dexter, Daniel, Daniel, John, John, John, Nathaniel, William, Robert, Simon, Simon, William, Symond), b. Erving, Mass., Aug. 31, 1840; m. in Halifax. Vt., Aug. 4, 1865, Sarah A. White, b. May, 1846; d. Feb. 7, 1880; m. 2d, Nov. 30, 1882, Laura M. Eaton. He is a mechanic; res. Springfield, Mass., 42 John St.

   5086. i.   CHARLES G., b. Dec. 12, 18—; m. Clara Howard.

3558. REV. NOBLE FISK (Daniel P., Daniel, John, John, John, Nathaniel, William, Robert, Simon, Simon, William, Symond), b. Heath. Mass., June 4, 1842; m. May 1, 1867, Lucy A. Pelton, b. May 15, 1842, Shelburne Falls. Mass. He was but 13 years of age when his father went west, and he went to work to support his mother and earn his own living, and do what he could to obtain an education.

After the war broke out he enlisted in the Forty-third Regiment Massachusetts Volunteers; was in the service about one year, and saw some hard marching and fighting, and came home broken down in health. Having saved his bounty, $125, and a part of his wages, he went to Wesleyan Academy, Wilbraham, Mass., and feeling it to be his duty to enter the ministry, he began study in preparation for that work. After spending two years at the academy, he went to the Methodist General Biblical Institute, at Concord, N. H., where he received two years in theological training. Soon after which he joined the New Hampshire Conference of the Methodist Episcopal Church, and has continued in the work of the ministry from that time to the present, with about the average success; res. Londonderry, N. H.

    5087. i.   LULU CHRISTINE, b. Feb. 28, 1870.
    5088. ii.   LELIA MARIA, b. May 27, 1873; m. Oct. 23, 1890, Arthur H. Cross; res. L.
    5089. iii. MARY ALBERTINE, b. Feb. 23, 1875.
    5090. iv. SARAH GRACE JOSEPHINE, b. Sept. 16, 1879; m. Nov. 30, 1895, Theron D. McGrath; res. W. Derry, N. H.

    3582. WILLIAM AUGUSTIN FISK (Ezra, Amariah, David, John, John, Nathaniel, William, Robert, Simon, Simon, William, Symond), b. Chaplin, Conn., Jan. 8, 1802; m. at Mansfield, Conn., Sept. 24, 1822, Selyma Storrs Whittemore, b. June 15, 1802; d. at Ashford, Conn., Apr. 16, 1883. He was a merchant. He d. in Malden, Ill., Oct. 16, 1871; res. Mansfield, Conn., and Malden, Ill.

    5091. i.   MARY A., b. Nov. 2, 1824; m. Jan. 16, 1849, ——— Richards, and d. Feb. 18, 1858. Ch.: Charles; res. Malden, Ill.
    5092. ii.   DAVID A., b. Sept. 19, 1826; d. Aug. 31. 1828.
    5093. iii. SALLY H., b. June 6, 1828; m. Dec. 25, 1845, Leander McWright; res. W. Ashford, Conn. He was b. June 14, 1819; d. Aug. 15, 1887. Was a farmer. Ch.: 1. Sarah S., b. Mar. 2, 1847; m. Apr. 5, 1868, Nathaniel Lyon Knowlton, West Ashford. Conn. 2, Roscoe H., b. Mar. 1, 1849; m. June 18, 1873, Annie E. Sykes, Warrenville, Conn. 3, Hobart L., b. July 17, 1851; m. Feb. 15, 1894, Isabell L. Bracket, Boston, Mass. 4. Carlton A., b. June 12, 1853; m. Dec. 25, 1875, Lizzie Hoffman, Princeton, Ill. 5, Willie Fisk, b. Feb. 7, 1856; m. Feb. 14, 1882, Annie Webb, St. Paul, Minn. 6, David A., b. Aug. 24, 1858; d. Apr. 24, 1859. 7, Clifton H., b. Feb. 25, 1861; m. Dec. 18, 1890, Ada C. Whitaker, West Ashford, Conn. 8, Clark Lee, b. June 28, 1864; unm.; Hartford, Conn. 9. Minnie L., b. Mar. 13, 1866; m. Dec. 30, 1892, Dr. C. W. S. Frost, Waterbury, Conn. 10, Fred M., b. Jan. 29, 1870; unm.; West Ashford, Conn.
    5094. iv. LUCY F., b. Apr. 7, 1830; m. June 4, 1850, Elias W. Watson; res. Malden, Ill. He was b. Mar. 25, 1823. Ch.: Ida Leonora Watson, b. Aug. 11, 1857; m. Sept. 16, 1879, to F. M. Johnson, Princeton, Ill. Carrie Fidelia Watson, b. May 26, 1860; Malden. Charles Augustus Watson, b. Apr. 30, 1863; m. Nov. 27, 1890, Princeton, Ill. William Tecumseh Sherman Watson, b. Mar. 7, 1866; Malden, Ill. Jane Melissa Watson, b. Apr. 5, 1868; m. Sept. 26, 1895, to F. S. Wright, Wyanet, Ill.
    5095. v.   ANDREW J., b. Aug. 13, 1833; m. Mary Hill.
    5096. vi. ELLEN A., b. Oct. 13, 1835; m. Mortimer Bartley; res. Malden, Ill.
    5097. vii. WM. H., b. Feb. 5, 1841; d. Nov. 15, 1858.

    3583. DR. CHARLES LEE FISK (Ezra, Amariah, David, David, John, John, Nathaniel, William, Robert, Simon, Simon, William, Symond), b. Dec. 26, 1805, Hampton, Conn.; m. Jan. 17, 1838, Emeline Moulton, b. Sept. 5, 1809; d. May 2, 1890. Charles Lee Fisk, M. D., was born at Hampton, Conn., Dec. 25, 1804, and is therefore in his 92d year in moderate health, except nearly total loss of eyesight. He studied medicine and taught school in Pittsburg, Pa., in his younger days; practiced for some years in Killingly, Conn., and for the past forty-three years in Greenfield, Mass., where he now resides. He has led a very active life and has always had a large and successful medical practice up to his 80th year. He was an early abolitionist and a contemporary of Garrison, Phillips and others. He is an independent free thinker and fully believes in nature's laws and that cause and effect govern and control the universe. The old doctor was made a Freemason in Pittsburg the night he was 21 years of age; he was loyal all through the turbulent times of Morgan and has long been a Knight Templar and a 33d degree Mason. There have been but few men of his pluck and nerve and strength of blood, strong perceptions, reasoning powers, readiness in debate, conversational gifts and extemporaneous speech. When he departs from this existence he will be long remembered as a man of remarkable personal character and ability, of a tender and sensitive nature, a lover of science and art, poetry, music, and all that is grand and glorious in life; res. Greenfield, Mass.

    5098. i.   CHARLES LEE, b. June 19, 1831; m. Mary E. Lamphear.
    5099. ii.   CAROLINE, b. Sept. 30, 1834; res. G.

    3586. DR. DANIEL DANFORTH FISK (Ezra, Amariah, David, David, John, John, Nathaniel, William, Robert, Simon, Simon, William, Symond), b. July 25, 1813, Chaplin, Conn.; m. Martha Hutton; m. 2d, Mary Jane Johnson. He was a practicing physician all his life; was graduated in Pittsburg, Pa.; was in practice in Danielsonville, Conn., the last twenty years of his life; was in Greenfield, Mass.; was a very skillful doctor. He d. Feb. 29, 1864; res. Greenfield, Mass.

    5100. i.   WILBUR A., b. Oct. 4, 1843; m. Clara F. Barrett and Flora J.
                 Capron.
    5101. ii.   MARTHA CORA, b. ———; m. ——— Henry; res. Manchester,
                 N. H.

    3592. JOSEPH DEWEY FISK (Elba, Jonathan, Jonathan, David, John, John, Nathaniel, William, Robert, Simon, Simon, William, Symond), b. Jan. 20, 1822, New York State; m. Aug. 4, 1841, Jane Maria Eaton; d. May 9, 1891. He was a woolen cloth manufacturer. He d. Oct. 23, 1854; res. Lyons, Wis.

    5101¼.i. SARAH BEATTIE, b. Oct. 12, 1849; m. Oct., 1869, M. Buttenber; res. Lake Geneva, Wis.
    5101½.ii. CLINTON Q., b. May 29, 1842; m. Helen Merriam.

    3599. ORVIN VERPLANK FISK (Elba, Jonathan, Jonathan, David, John, John, Nathaniel, William, Robert, Simon, Simon, William, Symond), b. Hardwick, N. Y., June 11, 1820; m. Aug. 23, 1841, Emily H. Moore, b. Feb. 15, 1824; d. Jan. 1, 1890. He is a farmer; res. Earlville, N. Y.

    5102. i.   LOUISA N., b. Hamilton, N. Y., Oct. 15, 1842; m. Oct. 15, 1866, Alfred H. Weeks, b. May 18, 1841; res. Lestershire, N. Y. Ch.: Ada May, b. Aug. 12, 1885.
    5103. ii.   ADA F., b. Jan. 29, 1846; m. Jan. 1, 1865, Wm. James Collier, res. Lake City, Minn. He was b. Dec. 4, 1844. Ch.: 1, Gertrude Lodema, b. Mar. 22, 1867; d. Sept. 1, 1872. 2, Emily Winifred, b. Jan. 16, 1869; d. Sept. 13, 1875. 3, Marion Dolly, b. June 20, 1871; present name Marion D. Colton; res. 202 N. Main St., East Rockford, Ill. 4, Wm. Van Buren, b. Apr. 7, 1878. 5, Eva Blossom, b. June 2, 1883; add. Lake City, Wabasha County, Minn.
    5104. iii. HERBERT S., b. June 18, 1847; m. and res. at Otselic, N. Y.
    5105. iv. EVA J., b. Apr. 13, 1853; m. Oct. 14, 1869, Byron Brown. He d., and she m. 2d, Dever Bellinger; res. Earlville, N. Y. Ch.: Erwin Lamont Brown, b. Feb. 26, 1871; m. Mar., 1889; add. 53 East Railroad St., Oneida, N. Y. Cora D. Brown, b. Dec. 2, 1873; m. ——— Jelliff, July 3, 1893; add. Earlville, N. Y.
    5106. v.   DEMER, b. June 2, 1857; d. Jan., 1861.
    5107. vi. EMMA O., b. June 5, 1860; m. Dec. 24, 1890, ——— Van Deusen; res. E.
    5108. vii. ROZELL O., b. Sept. 22, 1865; m. Nellie D. Slaver.
    5109. viii. ERNEST H., b. Nov. 24, 1872; m. July 26, 1890, Lottie A. Ralph, b. Apr. 17, 1871. He is a farmer; res. s. p. Earlville, N. Y.

    3602. REV. ASA FISK (Asa, Jonathan, Jonathan, David, John, John, Nathaniel, William, Robert, Simon, Simon, William, Symond), b. Cooperstown, N.

Y., Dec. 16, 1813; m. May 25, 1831, Sally Blowers, b. Apr. 22, 1806; d. Feb. 7, 1872; m. 2d, Apr. 6, 1872, Caroline Cottrell, b. Apr. 26, 1846. Asa Fisk lived the early part of his life in Susquehanna County. For many years he followed the trade of miller, his father's occupation. For a number of years he was a Methodist circuit preacher, but the latter years of his life were spent in market gardening on a small piece of land a short distance from Binghamton. He was a miller. He d. Apr. 6, 1891; res. Franklin, Pa.

5110. i. JANE S., b. July 1, 1832; m. Jan. 16, 1857, Charles Howard; res. Montrose, Pa.

5111. ii. MARY L., b. July 26, 1836; m. Feb. 2, 1855, Isaac Hughes; res. Binghamton, N. Y.

5112. iii. JOHN W., b. Oct. 15, 1840; m. Dec. 31, 1864, Sarah E. Rudy; res. Rockford, Ill.

5113. iv. GERTRUDE R., b. June 8, 1843; m. Mar. 12, 1864, Franklin M. Cole. He was b. Dec. 8, 1836; d. Jan. 16, 1890; was a farmer. She d. Oct. 23, 1894. Ch.: Sadie Isabelle, b. May 28, 1865; m. Nov. 13, 1881, Thomas Miller, and July 22, 1887, Lucien A. Crawford, b. Oct. 3, 1855; ch.: Sidney R. Miller, b. Sept. 10, 1882; res. Council Grove, Kan. Second one, b. Mar. 10, 1867; m. Apr. 15, 1891, Council Grove, Kan. Third one, b. Apr. 1, 1872; m. May 16, 1894, Council Grove, Kan. Fourth one, b. July 9, 1874, Council Grove, Kan.

5114. v. GEO. M., b. July 22, 1845; m. Martha Van Hoten.

5115. vi. ASA S., b. Nov. 15, 1835; m. Caroline L. Farr.

3603. JONATHAN FISK (Asa, Jonathan, Jonathan, David, John, John, Nathaniel, William, Robert, Simon, Simon, William, Symond), b. Dec., 1818, in Springville, Pa.; m. Sept. 20, 1834, Sally Clapp, b. Jan. 29, 1804; d. Mar. 22, 1872. He was a farmer; res. Wyoming, Ia.

5116. i. JONATHAN D., b. Aug. 8, 1835; d. Dec. 9, 1880.

5117. ii. LUCY ASHCROFT, b. Feb. 27, 1837.

5118. iii. SUEL T., b. Apr. 3, 1841.

5119. iv. CORNELIA L., b. Apr. 20, 1843; m. ——— Preston.

5120. v. RUFUS, b. Mar. 3, 1847; m. ———; d. Mar. 27, 1889.

3611. SAMUEL SHELLEY FISK (Asa, Jonathan, Jonathan, David, John, John, Nathaniel, William, Robert, Simon, Simon, William, Symond), b. Dunmock, Pa., Apr. 11, 1810; m. Martha Wylie. She d. in 1842; m. 2d, Apr. 16, 1843, Hannah Brown, b. Nov. 14, 1823. He was a builder and millwright. He d. in Sugar Run, Pa., Mar. 8, 1895; res. Skinner's Eddy, Pa.

5121. i. ANNA ELIZA, b. Feb. 9, 1860; m. Feb. 25, 1873, Joseph F. Mildrick; res. Hornets Ferry, Pa. He was b. Dec. 29, 1849; is a farmer. Ch.: Sammie, b. Jan. 12, 1886; Susie, b. Aug. 20, 1888; Will, b. May 25, 1890; Louie, b. Apr. 27, 1892; Joseph, b. Oct. 11, 1894; Katie, b. Feb. 1, 1875; m. Mar. 10, 1894, ——— Carrier; res. Lovelton, Pa. Ettie, b. Sept. 18, 1876; m. Apr. 20, 1895, ——— Waite; res. Sayre, Pa. Weltha, b. Mar. 14, 1879; m. Mar. 18, 1895, ——— Soaper; res. Luthers Mills, Bradford County, Pa.

5122. ii. WM. H., b. Sept. 9, 1842; m. Sarah Jane Wylie.

5123. iii. CHARLES W., b. ———; res. Shelton, Wash.

5124. iv. NANCY, b. ———; m. A. G. Gregory; res. Messhappen, Pa.

5125. v. LUCY, b. ———; m. Lewis Carpenter; res. Sugar Run, Pa. She d. ———.

5126. vi. MAUD, b. ———; d. 1844.

5127. vii. ARTHUR, b. ———; d. 1845.

5128. viii. MARTHA L., b. Dec. 22, 1846; m. Aug. 25, 1866, Mathias C. Oliver; res. Sugar Run. He was b. Jan. 20, 1844; d. Jan. 7, 1894; was a farmer. Ch.: John W., b. June 2, 1867; d. Oct. 4, 1880. Samuel E., b. Nov. 19, 1869; d. Dec. 13, 1880. Lucretia M., b. May 20, 1873; m. ——— Gannon; res. Hollenback, Bradford County, Pa. Earl J., b. Feb. 23, 1879. Hannah A., b. Feb. 27, 1885. Myra M., b. Oct. 6, 1888.

5129. ix.   ESTHER, b. 1849; d. 1850.
5130. x.   BRADLEY W., b. Aug. 5, 1851; m. Clara P. Provost.
5131. xi.   SAMUEL T., b. 1853; res. Sugar Run.
5132. xii. EDWARD J., b. June 20, 1855; m. Mrs. Minnie A. H. Crocker.
5133. xiii. ELIJAH, b. June 20, 1857; m. Myrtie Slayter.
5134. xiv. HESTER, b. 1862; m. John Meeks; res. Wilmot, Pa.
5135. xv.   GEORGE L. H., b. Apr. 7, 1862; m. Inez Gazlay.
5136. xvi. WELTHA, b. 1867; d. 1878.

3614. GEORGE DANIEL FISKE (Daniel S., Asa, Asa, David, John, John, Nathaniel, William, Robert, Simon, Simon, William, Symond), b. July 5, 1854, Brookfield, Mass.; m. at East Woodstock, Conn., Sept. 22, 1876, Minnie L. Spear; m. 2d, Oct. 22, 1889, Flora M. Taylor, b. Apr. 30, 1869. He is a druggist; res. 48 Lexington Ave., Springfield, Mass.
    5137. i.   CHARLES DANIEL, b. Jan. 26, 1878; res. Hamden, Mass.
    5138. ii. MILTON LEROY, b. Apr. 2, 1882; d. Sept. 22, 1893.

3617. JOHN MOORE FISK (Eli, Hezekiah, Asa, David, John, John, Nathaniel, William, Robert, Simon, Simon, William, Symond), b. Indiana Co., Pa., Sept. 17, 1822; m. Feb. 27, 1845, Sarah Ann McRaynolds, b. July 24, 1824. He lives in Petersburg, Ill., having moved there this fall. Last winter his golden wedding took place near Cantrall, Ill. They enjoy their usual good health. They lived on a farm one and a half miles east of his father's farm until 1865, when he sold out and purchased a farm in Fancy Creek township, Sangamon Co., Ill., and it has been their home until a few weeks ago (Nov., 1895), when he rented it and purchased a home in Petersburg, where he now lives. Their children are all married, except the youngest, and have flown from the parental nest; res. Petersburg, Ill.
    5139. i.   MATTHEW WILBUR WHEELER, b. Oct. 9, 1848; d. unm. Aug. 19, 1875.
    5140. ii. WARREN CHAUNCEY, b. Sept. 26, 1853; m. June 10, 1893, Margaret Chambers; res. Petersburg, Ill.
    5141. iii. WILLIS ELBERT, b. Aug. 15, 1858; m. Lilley Perkins; res. Huntingburg, Ind.
    5142. iv. ELMER McREYNOLDS, b. Jan. 26, 1867; unm.; res. St. Louis, Mo. He is cashier of the Equitable Life Insurance Co., of New York, at St. Louis, Mo.
    5143. v.   FRANCES LUCINDA, b. Feb. 5, 1846; m. Apr. 19, 1866, A. M. Canterbury; res. Peoria, Ill. He is engaged in the stockyards business under the firm name of A. M. Canterbury & Co.
    5144. vi. MARGARET JANE, b. June 30, 1850; m. Oct. 3, 1883, Thomas H. Bentley; res. Irving, So. Dak. One son.
    5145. vii. ESTHER ELIZABETH, b. June 10, 1860; m. Mar. 27, 1884, John H. Canterbury. Two ch.; res. Cantrall, Ill.

3618. REV. ELI COOLEY FISK (Eli, Hezekiah, Asa, David, John, John, Nathaniel, William, Robert, Simon, Simon, William, Symond), b. Cincinnati, O., Aug. 22, 1825; m. June 23, 1867, Rosanna Wagoner, b. Oct. 19, 1840. He attended with his brother the free schools at Cincinnati, and with his mother, in 1834, went east and visited relatives. While there the house was burned in Cincinnati. When they returned home in the fall they were three weeks coming down the Ohio River from Wheeling, W. Va. to Cincinnati, on a canal boat, for the river was so low that the steamboats could not run. They all came to Illinois in 1835, arriving at Havana, Aug. 7, being delayed by Eli C. having the small-pox. His father brought a steam engine to put up a saw mill, but not having the necessary capital, he sold out, but put up the mill for them; then moved on the farm in Aug., 1837, Eli C. now lives on. In Oct., 1842, a team ran away with him and harrowed him under; he has been a cripple, and walks with a cane, ever since. He attended school two or three quarters while living in Havana, and three while on the farm. In 1847 he entered the preparatory department of Illinois College. Graduated in 1852. He colported for the American Tract Society one vacation, and another for the American Sunday School Union. His labors were in Mason Co., Ill., and organized Sunday schools in nearly every schoolhouse in the county. He read theology with Rev. A. Hale, of Springfield, Ill. He preached his first sermon Oct. 12, 1856. Ordained Feb. 20, 1858 as pastor of the Mason Congregational Church, which he was the means of forming. He resigned Dec., 1859; preached for more than two years after, and supported himself. Finally the disloyal element became so defiant that he held many meetings throughout Mason and other counties in favor of the Union. He has been persecuted by that disloyal element ever since. In order to meet them, he studied law, so that the legal principles involved could be used by him in the controversy. He was admitted to the bar in Mar., 1868. He rarely practices, for he would rather have a clear conscience than the best legal reputation in the State. He has followed farming ever since he resigned the pastorate of the church, continuing on the old homestead. His marriage has been crowned with seven children, four daughters and three sons He has continued on the farm, and by successful crossing and interbreeding, produced the "Fisk" corn, both white and yellow. He is and has been the president of the Mason and Fulton Counties' Old Settlers' Society for nearly two years; been school treasurer quite a number of years, until he resigned; eight years notary public; got the Mason County Farmers' Institute on its feet, then resigned its secretaryship. He has been engaged in quite a number of other things, but never joined a secret society; res. Havana, Ill.

5146.   i.   MARTHA MARGARET, b. June 28, 1868; m. June 21, 1891, James W. Edlin, Jr.; res. Union, Ill.
5147.   ii.   LUCY ADDA OLIVE, b. Feb. 17, 1870; res. at home.
5148.   iii.   ELI CASPER, b. July 22, 1871; m. Adda L. Crater.
5149.   iv.   JOHN MOORE WAGONER, b. Oct. 5, 1873; res. at home.
5150.   v.   FRANK FRED'K, b. June 9, 1875; res. at home.
5151.   vi.   ROSE MARY ESTHER, b. Apr. 5, 1877; school teacher Mason City, Ill.
5152.   vii.   BERTHA ELENOR, b. July 26, 1880.

3621.   REV. WARREN COOLEY FISKE (Stephen, Hezekiah, Asa, David, John, John, Nathaniel, William, Robert, Simon, Simon, William, Symond), b. Wales, Mass., Sept. 21, 1816; m. May 19, 1847, Harriett Mindwell Parsons, b. East Haddam, Conn., Apr. 12, 1823. She now res. in Southington, Conn.; is a dau. of Rev. Isaac and Sarah (Budd) Parsons. He was born in Wales, Mass., formerly a part of Brimfield. His father was a farmer and he passed his early years in the customary round of duties pertaining to the life of a farmer's boy. When he was 12 years old he was converted and very soon formed the plan of getting an education. His father gave him his time and he went to Northampton where he was employed in a mill until he was able to enter Monson Academy. From there he went to Amherst College, from which he graduated in 1840. After teaching for two years at Salem, N. J., he entered the Theological Institute of Connecticut, then at East Windsor, from which he graduated in 1845. While pursuing a postgraduate course he was called to assist in evangelistic meetings at East Haddam, where he met and won for his wife, Miss Harriet M. Parsons, the daughter of the honored and beloved pastor of the East Haddam church for forty years, Rev. Isaac Parsons. There he was ordained May 19, 1847, and there, upon the same day he was married, the wedding ceremony following the ordination exercises. He immediately went to Wisconsin, as a home missionary, under the Connecticut Home Missionary Society. There his first child was born, and there too, in those western wilds, it was buried. His wife's health failed and he returned to the east and was installed pastor of the church in Marlborough, Nov. 8, 1850. Here he remained seven years. From this place he went to Canton, where he was installed Feb. 2, 1858. While at Canton the excitement over the anti-slavery controversy reached its height and preferring not to remain where the church seemed likely to be somewhat broken up by it he resigned and removed with his family to East Haddam. His wife's aged parents were still living and greatly needed his care. There he remained several years, but removed to Colchester where he taught in Bacon Academy There he had a severe attack of pneumonia. His health improved somewhat, and he again entered upon pastoral work, first at Barkhamsted, for nine months, and then at Wolcott, for three years. But the labor of a pastor's life proved too great for his failing health, and having purchased a farm at Charlton, Mass., he removed to that place, where he lived very quietly for twelve years. At the end of that period his health had so far declined that he was unable to even superintend the small farm which he owned. He sold it and removed to Southington, where his oldest son is a physician. There he lived for three years, slowly yielding to consumption; and there he fell asleep at the ripe age of 70. So ended a quiet, unobtrusive, successful life. Mr. Fiske's most prominent characteristic, perhaps, was faithfulness. Possessed of none of those elements which the world calls brilliant, never attracting attention by anything in any degree sensational, his ministry was successful because it was faithful. Mr. Fiske was a conservative man, emphatically a man of the "old school." He was interested in all the questions of the day, and had very decided convictions upon them all. He kept track in his sick room of all the current themes of the pulpit and the press, and talked with intelligence upon them. But he clung with ardent devotion to the belief and customs of the fathers. His convictions were the result of honest and earnest thought and he did not yield them to any one. He d. Apr. 17, 1887; res. Marlboro, Conn.

5153.   i.   HENRY MARTYN, b. Mar. 18, 1848; d. Mar. 5, 1850.
5154.   ii.   ISAAC PARSONS, b. Sept. 16, 1852; m. Clara E. Haven, Sarah
              E. Hayes, and Mrs. Mary (Stanton) Farr.
5155.   iii. SARA LYON, b. Nov. 4, 1854; unm.; res. at home.
5156.   iv.   WM. WARREN, b. June 26, 1857; m. Lida R. Seymour.

3622. ASA FISKE (Stephen, Hezekiah, Asa, David, John, John, Nathaniel, William, Robert, Simon, Simon, William, Symond), b. Wales, Mass., Dec. 20, 1818; m. in Deerfield, Aug. 26, 1845, Mary L. Graves, b. Aug. 20, 1825, dau. of Zedediah. He was a farmer. He d. Apr. 26, 1888; res. Greenfield, Mass.

5157.   i.   GEORGE E., b. July 22, 1858; m. May 6, 1878, in Whitehall,
              N. Y., Ella E. Watts, b. Nov. 16, 1857. Ch.: Harrie D., b. Jan.
              11, 1879. Irving W., b. July 20, 1881. Charles A., b. Jan. 21,
              1884. Flossie M., b. Mar. 11, 1887. He is a farmer and shoe
              cutter; res. Greenfield, Mass.
5158.   ii.   CARRIE M., b. ———.
5159.   iii. IRVING DEXTER, b. Aug. 1, 1850; m. Nov. 30, 1871, Josephine
              A. Johnson, b. June 17, 1851; d. Dec. 9, 1875, in Brattleboro,
              Vt. Ch.: 1, Herbert Newton, b. Oct. 8, 1875; res. Leominster,
              Mass. 2, Edward Irving, b. Sept. 8, 1873; d. Oct. 28, 1873. 3,
              Herman Walter, b. Oct. 8, 1875; d. Aug. 12, 1876.
5160.   iv.   CLARA ANNETTE, b. Mar. 10, 1856; res. 639 Lexington Ave.,
              New York City.
5161.   v.   WM. W., b. Aug. 3, 1868; killed Jan. 6, 1892.
5162.   vi.   DAU., b. ———; d. Aug. 8, 1849.
5163.   vii. NETTIE A., b. ———; m. Jan. 11, 1877, George L. Burt; res.
              Deerfield.

3624. ALFRED E. FISKE (Stephen, Hezekiah, Asa, David, John, John, Nathaniel, William, Robert, Simon, Simon, William, Symond), b. Wales, Mass., Mar. 18, 1824; m. Apr. 12, 1853, ——— ———. He d. Feb. 18, 1892.

5164.   i.   GEO. E., b. ———; res. Worcester, 18, So. Russell St.

3625. DR. LYMAN A. FISK (Stephen, Hezekiah, Asa, David, John, John, Nathaniel, William, Robert, Simon, Simon, William, Symond), b. Wales, Mass., Feb. 27, 1827; m. May 1, 1849, Cordelia Smith, b. July 5, 1829, dau. of John and Margaret Smith. He was born in Wales, and worked on his father's farm until he was 21 years of age, he then learned the carpenter's trade, and followed it several years. He then went into the livery business, and followed that eleven years. Then went to work as superintendent of a woolen mill, followed that several years. He is now situated on a farm in Wilbraham, nine miles from Springfield. He has real estate in Springfield and with that and his profession as a veterinary surgeon, his time is nearly all occupied; res. Wales and Springfield, Mass., and Wilbraham.

5165.   i.   EUGENE E., b. Wilbraham, Oct. 22, 1860; m. Jan. 22, 1885,
              Carrie Spaulding, of Brimfield, Mass.; res. W., s. p.
5166.   ii.   ADELBERT L., b. July 5, 1852; m. Mar., 1874, Clara Blakeley,
              of West Springfield, Mass. One child, b. Dec. 8, 1876; res.
              Brooklyn, N. Y.

3627. ELI BUEL FISKE (Stephen, Hezekiah, Asa, David, John, John, Nathaniel, William, Robert, Simon, Simon, William, Symond), b. Wales, Mass., Nov. 27, 1831; m. at Brimfield, Mass., Apr. 24, 1856, Martha Flint, of Charlton, b. Sept. 21, 1836. Eli B. Fiske was born in Wales, attended the schools in the place and worked on the farm with his father till 26 years of age, then he went to the woolen mill owned by R. P. Wales & Co., where he stayed eleven years, doing repairs; then removed to Springfield, Mass., where he now resides. He is a carpenter and builder, and many of the fine residences and business blocks there were built under his supervision; res. Springfield, Mass., 23 Morgan St.

    5167. i.   FRANK BUEL, b. July 28, 1858; m. June 4, 1879, Narcissa A. McClentic, of West Springfield, Mass.: res. Hartford, Conn., s. p. He is finisher in a book bindery.

    5168. ii. CHARLES STEPHEN, b. Apr. 25, 1861; m. Etta N. Haley.

    5169. iii. WM. ALFRED, b. Aug. 14, 1865; d. Nov. 18, 1873.

3631. ORRIN WALES FISKE (William H., Hezekiah, Asa, David, John, John, Nathaniel, William, Robert, Simon, Simon, William, Symond), b. Wales, Mass., Mar. 25, 1814; m. in Lunenburg, Mass., Nov. 22, 1835, Hannah Marilla Tucker, b. Jan. 20, 1818; res. Lexington, Mass.

    5170. i.   HENRY ALONZO, b. June 18, 1838; d. Oct. 8, 1861.

    5171. ii. JOSEPHINE AUGUSTA, b. June 30, 1844; d. Mar. 6, 1880.

    5172. iii. ISABEL TUCKER, b. June 9, 1851; m. June 7, 1870, Charles H. Rankin: res. Lex.

    5173. iv. HERBERT WINTHROP, b. Jan. 7, 1857; m. in Springfield, Mass., June 3, 1890, Alice G. Clary, b. Apr. 28, 1853. He is a hotel keeper; keeps the "Santa Monica;" res. 170 Huntington Ave., Boston, Mass., s. p.

    5174. v. WALTER JAMES, b. Dec. 8, 1854; d. Dec. 17, 1856.

3633. LOREN WALES FISK (William H., Hezekiah, Asa, David, John, John, Nathaniel, William, Robert, Simon, Simon, William, Symond), b. Wales, Mass., Oct. 25, 1817; m. Nov. 21, 1844, Eunice Barnes, b. Enfield, Conn., May 26, 1824. He was a farmer. He d. Mar. 31, 1886; res. Agawam, Mass.

    5175. iii. EDWARD SHUBEL, b. Aug. 2, 1854: res. Cleveland, O.

    5176. ii. WILLIAM LOREN, b. Apr. 8, 1852; res. A.

    5177. i.   GEO. DANFORTH, b. Aug. 19, 1845; m. in Springfield, Mar. 1, 1881, Eliza Brooks, b. Portland, Conn., July 2, 1843, s. p. He is a farmer; res. Agawam.

    5178. iv. EMMA LOUISA, b. Oct. 2, 1866: d. Mar. 31, 1867.

3635. DAVID H. FISKE (William H., Hezekiah, Asa, David, John, John, Nathaniel, William, Robert, Simon, Simon, William, Symond), b. Ludlow, Mass., Dec. 23, 1821; m. at Springfield, Oct. 17, 1848, Eunice M. Roberts, b. June 9, 1825. He d. Mar. 11, 1873; res. Greenfield, Mass., and Brownsville, Ark.

    5179. i.   EMMA THERESA, b. July 18, 1849: m. at Little Rock, Ark., Nov. 9, 1873, David H. Throope, b. Jan. 24, 1844. He is a merchant; res. 18 Salem St., Springfield, Mass. Ch.: 1, Edna E., b. Aug. 30, 1874.

    5180. ii. WM. ROBERTS, b. Mar. 8, 1853; d. unm., Nov. 30, 1888.

    5181. iii. KATIE DAVIS, b. Jan. 23, 1861; m. in Dennison, Tex., Eugene A. Sessions; res. 215 Bancroft St., Portland, Ore. Three ch.

3636. GORDON MILLER FISKE (William H., Hezekiah, Asa, David, John, John, Nathaniel, William, Robert, Simon, Simon, William, Symond), b. Ludlow, Mass., May 9, 1824; m. Sarah A. Putnam, b. June 4, 1824; d. Oct. 2, 1887. He d. July 25, 1879; res. Enfield and Palmer, Mass.

    5182. i.   CHARLES B., b. Feb. 13, 1845; m. Frances M. Calkins and Esther W. Chandler.

3638. LYMAN E. FISK (William H., Hezekiah, Asa, David, John, John, Nathaniel, William, Robert, Simon, Simon, William, Symond), b. Ludlow, Mass., Jan. 1, 1830; m. in Springfield, Dec. 10, 1851, Jane Maria Durfee, b. Jan. 11, 1831. Lyman Fisk was born in Ludlow, Mass.; removed to Agawam, Mass., and married Jane M. Durfee, at Springfield, Mass. He died in New York City. At the age of 18 he engaged in the hotel business at the Massasoit House, Springfield, Mass. From there he came to New York, in 1856, at the Girard House, and later and until after the War of the Rebellion he was proprietor of the Stevens House. In 1864 he retired from business. In 1869 he bought Taylor's Hotel, in Jersey City, and remained in active business there until 1880, when failing health compelled him to retire finally. He d. Dec. 12, 1889; res. New York, N. Y.

    5183. i.   WILLARD C., b. Mar. 26, 1856; m. Ida Earle.
    5184. ii.   HARRISON GREY, b. July 30, 1861; m. Minnie Maddern.
    5185. iii.   LYMAN OTIS, b. Apr. 15, 1868; m. Feb. 8, 1896, Lillie H. Palmer. He is associated with his brother, Harrison G. She is the daughter of Mr. and Mrs. A. M. Palmer.
    5186. iv.   JENNIE LOUISE, b. Sept. 8, 1857; d. Feb. 15, 1858.

    3641. DR. DANIEL SHAW FISKE (Asa, Hezekiah, Asa, David, John, John, Nathaniel, William, Robert, Simon, Simon, William, Symond), b. Wales, Mass., Nov. 13, 1820; m. in Sturbridge, June 19, 1849, Lovisa Elizabeth Glazier, b. Mar. 19, 1830. Daniel Shaw Fiske, born Wales, Mass., Nov. 13, 1820; received an academic education at Munson, Mass., and Southbridge, Mass. About the year 1839 he began the study of medicine with Dr. Calvin P. Fiske, of Sturbridge, Mass., graduating from Castleton Medical College, Castleton, Vt., in the spring of 1846, ranking third in a class of fifty-five. He began the practice of his profession at Brookfield, Mar., 1847, where he resided until he was compelled to cease his labor on account of sickness, Bright's disease, which resulted in his death. He married Lovisa E. Glazier, by whom three children were born. He served the town for fifteen years as a member of its school board, acting as chairman a part of that time. He d. Apr. 29, 1878; res. Brookfield, Mass.

    5187. i.   KATHERINE L., b. Oct. 8, 1850; m. Oct. 12, 1871, Harris A. Harmon; res. Franklin, Mass. He is a music teacher; s. p.
    5188. ii.   CAROLINE OLIVIA, b. Sept. 4, 1852; d. Sept. 26, 1853.
    5189. iii.   GEORGE D., b. July 5, 1854; m. Minnie L. Spear and Flora M. Taylor.

    3651. JOHN LESLIE FISK (James L., Hezekiah, Asa, David, John, John, Nathaniel, William, Robert, Simon, Simon, William, Symond), b. Jan. 3, 1832, Dryden, N. Y.; m. Dec. 19, 1855, in Oshkosh, Wis., Adaline D. Houston, b. Sept. 24, 1838. He is a farmer and mechanic; res. Omro, Wis.

    5190. i.   GEORGE W., b. Apr. 21, 1858; d. May 22, 1863.
    5191. ii.   CHARLES A., b. Mar. 9, 1860; m. Jan. 8, 1883; d. s. p. Aug. 23, 1893.
    5192. iii.   FRED O., b. Apr. 14, 1866; m. Nellie Litchfield.
    5193. iv.   J. ELMER, b. Jan. 21, 1868; res. 32 Wash. Ave., So. Minneapolis, Minn.

    3652. AUSTIN C. FISK (James L., Hezekiah, Asa, David, John, John, Nathaniel, William, Robert, Simon, Simon, William, Symond), b. Wellington, Conn., Sept. 3, 1822; m. at Oshkosh, Wis., June 17, 1849, Lucy Hollester, b. Mar. 12, 1823; d. Jan. 4, 1891. He is in the gardening and fruit growing business; res. Bloomer, Wis.

    5194. i.   ELIZA J., b. Aug. 20, 1850; m. —— Grady; res. Chippewa Falls, Wis.
    5195. i.   FLORENCE A., b. Sept. 7, 1851; m. —— Cole; res. Kaukauna, Wis.
    5196. iii.   EUGENE, b. Nov. 16, 1852; res. No. Yakima, Wash.

    3669. EVERETT YOUNG FISK (Calvin, Elisha, Asa, David, John, John, Nathaniel, William, Robert, Simon, Simon, William, Symond), b. Stafford, Conn., Jan. 16, 1834; m. June 9, 1863, Louisa Bartlett, b. June 29, 1837; res. Stafford, Conn.

    5197. i.   ANNA LOUISA, b. Apr. 1, 1865; m. Apr. 1, 1890, John F. Richardson, b. Sept. 5, 1859. He is a merchant; res. Preston, Conn. Ch.: Ruth Ann, b. Sept. 12, 1893.
    5198. ii.   JOHN EVERETT, b. Feb. 19, 1869; res. Rockville, Conn. John Everett Fisk is one of Rockville's well known professional men. He was born at Stafford, Conn., Feb. 19, 1869, and was educated at the Stafford High School, and the Hitchcock

School, of Brimfield, Mass. He is a lineal descendant of Sir Godfrey Fisk, who came from England, and was one of the first settlers of Medford, Mass. He is also a lineal descendant of Roger De Coigweria, who went from Normandy to England with William the Conqueror, about the year 1060. Mr. Fisk studied law with Hon. J. H. Reed, State's Attorney for Tolland Co., Conn., and was admitted to the bar in 1890, and within a short time located in Rockville, where he has succeeded in building a very remunerative and extensive practice. He has gained the reputation of being careful and conscientious and a person of deep judicial learning. Mr. Fisk has never married. In politics he is a consistent Republican.

5199.   iii. HENRY CONVERSE, b. Dec. 19, 1871; res. S.
5200.   iv.   MARY ELIZA, b. Nov. 17, 1876; res. S.

3670. JAMES HAYDEN FISK (Calvin, Elisha, Asa, David, John, John, Nathaniel, William, Robert, Simon, Simon, William, Symond), b. Stafford, Conn., Apr. 3, 1836; m. there May 9, 1859. Sophronia Rhoda Hiscox, b. June 28, 1837. He is a farmer; res. Woodstock Valley, Conn.

5201.   i.   JAMES CALVIN, b. Aug. 17, 1864; d. Aug. 30, 1864.
5202.   ii. CLARA SOPHRONIA, b. Dec. 7, 1865; m. in Worcester, Mass., Jan. 28, 1891, Ben Milton Chamberlain, b. Aug. 9, 1892. 2, is a market gardener. Ch.: 1, Rena Glee, b. Aug. 9, 1892. 2, Sumner Fisk, b. Mar. 12, 1895; res. Holden, Mass.

3673. FRANCIS E. FISKE (Calvin, Elisha, Asa, David, John, John, Nathaniel, William, Robert, Simon, Simon, William, Symond), b. Stafford, Conn., Feb. 14, 1846; m. there. Sept. 28, 1870, Charlotte C. Cutter, b. Dec. 17, 1849. He is a civil engineer; res. Westfield, Mass., 15 So. Broad St.

5203.   i.   MYRTA ELSA, b. June 28, 1871.
5204.   ii. MYRA ELVA, b. Dec. 7, 1875.

3674. GEORGE T. FISKE (Calvin, Elisha, Asa, David, John, John, Nathaniel, William, Robert, Simon, Simon, William, Symond), b. Stafford, Conn., Sept. 10, 1849; m. there, Oct. 26, 1870, Abbie Sophia Tyler, b. Stafford. He is in the woolen business; res. Staffordville, Conn.

5205.   i.   MAY ADA, b. June 13, 1872; m. Nov. 15, 1895, William S. Clayton, of Waltham, Mass.; res. S.
5206.   ii. BELLE ABBIE, b. Jan. 15, 1874; is a telegraph operator at Palmer, Mass.; res. S.

3682. MARCUS MORTON FISKE (Horatio N., Abraham, David, Thomas, William, John, Nathaniel, William, Simon, Simon, William, Symond), b. Weston, Feb. 2, 1840; m. Nov. 23, 1865, Abbie A. Cooper, b. Aug. 4, 1839. He was a farmer; res. Cochituate, Mass.

5207.   i.   FRANCES, b. June 6, 1872 (adopted); m. Sept. 22, 1891, Moses Murphy; res. 141 Lincoln Ave., Syracuse, N. Y.
5208.   ii. FREDERIC M., b. Dec. 2, 1877 (adopted).

3692. COL. FRANCIS SKINNER FISKE (Phinehas, Phinehas, Jonathan, Thomas, William, John, Nathaniel, William, Robert, Simon, Simon, William, Symond), b. Keene, N. H., Nov. 9, 1825; m. there Dec. 14, 1858, Annie Farnsworth Wilson, dau. of Gen. Jonas Wilson, b. Sept. 23, 1832. He was born in Keene, N. H.; educated at the public schools there and fitted for college; entered Dartmouth where he was graduated in 1843; entered the Dane law school of Harvard College and graduated in 1846; practiced law in Keene, N. H. When the war broke out he went to the front, in 1861, as Lieutenant-Colonel of the Second Regiment, New Hampshire Volunteers, and later was of the Twenty-sixth Regiment, Pennsylvania Volunteers. He was breveted Colonel and later Brigadier-General for meritorious services. He has been an officer of the United States courts in Boston since May, 1872. Since 1892 as United States Commissioner, he has held the preliminary trials of offenses charged to have been committed against the United States.

A recent issue of the Boston Traveler says: "Colonel Francis S. Fiske, the United States Commissioner, is one of the most familiar figures in Milton. Everyone, almost, seems to know him and he has a kind and cheerful word for all. For a man of his age, he is a great pedestrian, and on a pleasant morning he likes nothing better than to walk from his home on Milton Hill to the electric car and enjoy the ride into the city. Colonel Fiske is a good type of the gentleman of the old school, courteous and affable to all, with a special aptitude of bringing out a bright bon mot at the appropriate time. He has a dry, humorous way of speech which many of the younger generation have encountered in an attempt to appear bright at his expense; res. Keene, N. H., Boston and Milton, Mass.

5209. i. MARY WILSON, b. Nov. 15, 1859; unm.
5210. ii. EDITH ANNIE, b. Nov. 25, 1860; unm.
5211. iii. REDINGTON, b. July 11, 1863; res. Chicago, Ill.; unm.; assistant manager Central Union Telephone Company.
5212. iv. ROBERT FRANCIS, b. Dec. 19, 1864. He is with the Bell Telephone Company in Boston.
5213. v. ELIZABETH LAWRENCE, b. Nov. 2, 1869.

3694. CHARLES DEXTER FISKE (Jonathan D., Jonathan, Jonathan, Thomas, William, John, Nathaniel, William, Robert, Simon, Simon, William, Symond), b. Waltham, Mass., Nov. 12, 1844; m. there Mar. 31, 1868, Ella F. Haynes, b. Mar. 16, 1847; res. Moody St., Waltham, Mass.

5214. i. EDNA MAY, b. Oct. 24, 1868; m. Edward Arthur Furbush, b. Sept. 12, 1865; res. W. Ch.: 1, Edward Arthur, b. Dec. 10, 1891; 2, Marion Louise, b. Apr. 29, 1894.
5215. ii. CARRIE LOUISE, b. Oct. 24, 1869; m. July 1, 1890, Walter Livingstone Wigmore, b. 1867. Ch.: 1, Raymond Fiske, b. Feb. 28, 1891.
5216. iii. WALTER DEXTER, b. 1870; d. Aug. 3, 1871.
5217. iv. WALTER CLARK, b. Jan. 3, 1873.
5218. v. ADDIE SMITH, b. July 22, 1874.
5219. vi. ALFRED WARREN, b. Sept. 23, 1877.
5220. vii. CHARLES DEXTER, b. June 10, 1880.

3702. JEROME HORTON FISKE (Moses, Thomas, Jonathan, Thomas, William, John, Nathaniel, William, Robert, Simon, Simon, William, Symond),

JEROME HORTON FISKE.

b. Dover, N. H., Apr. 7, 1841; m. at Chicopee, Mass., Mar. 22, 1865, Sarah Bemis, b. Apr. 3, 1841; m. 2d, at Dover, Sept. 23, 1895, Nellie G. Long, b. June 10, 1878. He was born in Dover, N. H.; educated in the common schools; went to Newberne, N. C., in Dec., 1862, as private in Company D, Forty-sixth Massachusetts Volunteers—a nine months' regiment—was in about one year; was in the battles of Whitehall, Goldsboro, Kingston and the attack on Newberne in 1863, and his regiment was present at the battle of Gettysburg, though not engaged actively. They were detailed to support battery that was not called upon. After his discharge he returned to Chicopee, Mass., and for a year was private secretary of Mayor Alexander, of Springfield, Mass.; went to Boston in 1864 and was in custom house, Boston, until 1870; began the study of law in Salem with his wife's uncle, Hon. Geo. Wheatland, and was admitted to the Massachusetts and United States courts in due time; opened an office in Boston in 1879, being associated with the late Judge H. G. Parker; was City Solicitor of Malden, Mass., from 1883 to 1888, resigning this office on account of his increasing private practice; was first married to Sarah D. Bemis, of Chicopee; no children; second marriage to Nellie G. Long, of Boston; res. s. p. Boston, Mass.; office 611 Sears Bldg.

3706. WALTER BALFOUR FISKE (Moses, Thomas, Jonathan, Thomas, William, John, Nathaniel, William, Robert, Simon, Simon, William, Symond), b. Dover, N. H., in 1834; m. in Holyoke, Mass., in 1854, Matilda Henrietta Bruen, b. Dec. 18, 1836; d. Dec. 21, 1879. Walter B. Fiske was a well known printer and died at his residence on Pleasant View, near Pawtucket, R. I., in his 41st year. He was a native of Dover, N. H., where he learned his trade. For a score and more of years he worked in Springfield, Mass., Worcester, Mass., and Providence, R. I. He was employed several years in the book department of the Providence Press Company and as proofreader for Messrs. Hammond, Angell & Co., of Providence. He had musical talent and was literary in his tastes, frequently writing in verse. He was patriotic and loved his country, not being able to fight on account of poor health which terminated in consumption from which he died. He was beloved and respected, and was a brother of the well known actor, Moses W. Fiske. He d. May 4, 1874; res. Holyoke, Mass., and Pawtucket, R. I.

    5221. i.   WALTER EDMUND, b. Nov. 8, 1855; m. Bertha Lewis.
    5222. ii.   SUSIE JANE, b. Apr. 4, 1858; m. May 5, 1880, Fred A. Bradford; res. Melrose, Mass.

3707. CAPT. WALTER LESLIE FISKE (Jacob, Thomas, Jonathan, Thomas, William, John, Nathaniel, William, Robert, Simon, Simon, William, Symond), b. Belvidere, Ill., Jan. 8, 1855; m. Apr. 29, 1884, Mary Almeda Briggs, b. 1860; d. Mar. 9, 1885. He was born in Belvidere, Ill., where he was educated at the public schools and at Waverly, Ia. Later he taught school and worked in a drug store. In the Iowa Congressional District, represented by Hon. D. B. Henderson, young Fiske passed a successful competitive examination, both mental and physical, and was appointed to a West Point cadetship in 1873. While at school he was studious and at his graduation was number two in the large class. Captain Fisk is an officer of large experience, having been in charge of a number of important government works in various parts of the country. He graduated at the United States military school in June, 1877, and was assigned to the corps of engineers. He was on duty at the United States engineer school at Willets Point, N. Y., until September, 1880, when he was detailed as assistant to Gen. Q. A. Gilmore, and, under him, had local charge of United States river and harbor improvements in Florida until Feb., 1882. He started during that time the jetties both at Cumberland Sound, Georgia and Florida, and at the mouth of the St. John's River, Florida. These are important works, one of the jetties at the St. John's River being 9,400 feet in length, and the other 6,800. They are now doing good work, and have materially benefited the navigation of the river, up which deep-draught steamers ascend about 100 miles. Captain Fisk was assistant to Major S. M. Mansfield, corps of engineers, at Galveston, Tex., from Feb., 1882, to Oct., 1884, on United States river and harbor improvements in Texas, assisting during that time in making various hydrographic surveys of different harbors. From Oct., 1884, to Aug., 1885, he acted as secretary and disbursing officer of the Missouri River Commission, with immediate charge of the surveys of the Missouri River from Fort Benton, Mont., to its mouth. From Aug., 1885, to Aug., 1887, he was assistant professor of civil and military engineering at the United States Military Academy, and during September and November acted as assistant in the office of the chief of engineers, United States Army, at Washington, D. C. From Nov., 1877, to Feb., 1891, he was at New Orleans, in charge of United States river and harbor improvements in Louisiana, south of Red River, except the Mississippi River above the head of the passes and the upper end of the Atchafalaya. He had charge of the construction of about three miles of jetties at Sabine Pass, and reported upon "the depth and width of a channel secured and maintained by jetties at the mouth of the Mississippi River," upon which payments were made to the Eads estate, and as engineer of the seventh and eighth lighthouse districts had charge of the erection of eight lighthouses. From Feb., 1891, to Oct., 1892, Captain Fisk was stationed at Duluth, Minn., in charge of United States river and harbor improvements on Lake Superior, except the Portage lake and Lake Superior ship canals, having charge of important harbor improvements at Duluth, Superior, Marquette, Ashland and elsewhere. From Oct., 1892, to Nov., 1895, he was at the United States engineer school, Willet's Point, N. Y.. in command of Company A, Battalion of Engineers, United States Army, and instructor in electricity and torpedo service, or, technically, of "submarine mining." Since going from Willet's Point to Portland, Ore., Captain Fisk has had charge of all river and harbor improvements in Oregon, Washington and Idaho, and is also engineer of the thirteenth lighthouse district; res. Willet's Point, N. Y., and Portland, Ore.

    5223. i.   MARION WALTER, b. Feb. 21, 1885; res. with aunt at Elizabeth, N. J.

    3708. HENRY CUSHMAN FISK (Jacob, Thomas. Jonathan, Thomas, William, John, Nathaniel, William, Robert, Simon, Simon, William, Symond), b. July 16, 1844, Belvidere, Ill.; m. there Sept. 6, 1870, Elizabeth Ray, b. Apr. 26, 1851. He is a druggist; res. Waverly, Ia.

    5224. i.   SARAH LOUISE, b. July 16, 1871; m. June 4, 1890, Charles E. Ward; res. 11236 Indiana Ave., Chicago, Ill., Station T.
    5224. ii.   LESLIE CUSHMAN, b. Sept. 24, 1882.
    5225. iii.   LA ELLA CLARE, b. July 25, 1887.
    5226. iv.   CHAS. WILLARD, b. Jan. 3, 1891.

    3712. JOHN THORNTON KIRTLAND FISKE (Luke, Elijah, Samuel, Samuel, William, John, Nathaniel, William, Robert, Simon, Simon, William, Symond), b. Waltham, Mass., May 1, 1819; m. Nov. 28, 1841, Lydia Ann Stone, b. Aug. 6, 1824; d. Dec. 16, 1869. He was a farmer. He d. Jan. 22, 1860; res. Waltham, Mass.

    5227. i.   LYDIA ELIZABETH, b. Sept. 14, 1842; m. June 23, 1864, Henry Wm. Crafts; res. West Newton, Mass. Ch.: Harry Fiske, b. Jan. 10, 1874.

    3725. GEORGE ALFRED FISKE, JR. (George A.. William, Samuel, Samuel, William. John, Nathaniel, William, Robert, Simon, Simon, William, Symond), b. Boston, Aug. 14, 1841; m. there Dec. 14, 1870, Kate Washburn, b. Mar. 19, 1848. He was born in the good old city of Boston and has clung very fondly to it ever since his birth. His school days, preparatory to his college life. were passed at that well known Boston institution named Chauncy Hall school, where he was fitted for college, entering Harvard in the year 1858, without condition and graduating in the class of 1862; was a member of the famous Hasty Pudding Club. On Sept. 29, 1862, he enlisted as a private in the Forty-first Regiment, Massachusetts Volunteers, commanded by Col. Thomas Chickering, of piano fame. He was with the Forty-first as Commissary Sergeant until its departure to the Department of the Gulf, and just on the day of its departure received a commission as Second Lieutenant in that regiment, and was ordered to report for staff duty to Brigadier-General George L. Andrews, then in command of the remainder of the Banks expedition, with headquarters in New York City. With the last regiment composing the expedition, he sailed with General Andrews and staff for New Orleans early in 1863; was present during the whole of the memorable siege of Port Hudson, La., and with General Andrews was one of the first to enter that desolated place on the morning of its surrender; was placed in charge of General Gardner, one of its bravest defenders, and assisted in the parole of its other defenders. After its evacuation he remained at Port Hudson on garrison duty. He visited Vicksburg after its surrender, carrying dispatches to General McPherson, then in command at that point. He narrowly escaped capture as bearer of dispatches to General Smith at the beginning of the Red River campaign, ascending the river in a small steamer within a few miles of Fort De Russey before the expedition had made its start up the river, meeting General Smith the following morning with his command at the entrance to the river. On Oct. 27, 1863, he was commissioned First Lieutenant in the Forty-first Massachusetts Volunteers. and in Apr., 1864, visited the north with General Andrews, who was on sick leave. On July 12, 1864, was commissioned by President Lincoln as Paymaster of United States Army and ordered back to the Department of the Gulf with headquarters at New Orleans. On Oct. 1, 1864, he resigned his commission as Paymaster owing to ill health, and returned north; but owing to severe malaria contracted in the service, was obliged in Feb., 1866, to visit the Azores, and remained at Fayal, and St. Michaels at the Hot Springs until June, when he returned home. On his return he entered the employ of the Merchants' Union Express Company and during the last thirty years has remained in the same business, now the American Express Company, having had for several years during that period charge of Wells, Fargo & Co.'s banking business until they withdrew that part of their business from Boston. He is at the present time, and has been for many years, a member of the Massachusetts Commandery of the Military Order of the Loyal Legion, and for several years past has been treasurer of the Parish of All Saints, Dorchester (Boston); res. Lombard St., Dorchester, Mass.

5228.   i.   GEORGE CONVERSE, b. Feb. 28, 1872.
5229.   ii.   HENRY METCALF, b. Oct. 15, 1874. He is a student in Harvard College (1896).
5230.   iii.   MARY ELLIOTT, b. Aug. 31, 1879.

3736.   ARTHUR DENNY FISKE (Elijah, Nathan, Samuel, Samuel, William, John, Nathaniel, William, Robert, Simon, Simon, William, Symond), b. Cambridge, Mass., Aug. 21, 1843; m. Apr. 8, 1869, Caroline Williams Whitney, b. Jan. 15, 1848, dau. of George Jay, of Rochester, N. Y. (see Whitney genealogy by Fred C. Pierce); is a grain broker at 502 Produce Exchange, New York City; res. Morristown, N. J.

5231.   i.   JOSIAH MASON, b. Mar. 11, 1870; unm.; is in the banking and brokerage business at 66 Broadway, N. Y.
5232.   ii.   GEO. WHITNEY, b. Jan. 8, 1884.
5233.   iii.   ENDICOTT, b. Jan. 23, 1885.
5234.   iv.   PAULINE, b. Aug. 8, 1887.

3740.   DR. ROBERT TREAT PAINE FISKE (Oliver, Nathan, Nathan, Nathan, Nathan, Nathaniel, William, Robert, Simon, Simon, William, Symond), b. Worcester, Mass., Jan. 1, 1799; m. at Hingham, May 9, 1825, Mary Otis Gay, dau. of Ebenezer, Esq., and Mary A. (Otis) Gay, b. Barnstable, 1801; d. in H., Aug. 8, 1852; m. 2d, Oct. 16, 1854, Anna L. Baker, dau. of John and Sally L. (Loring) Baker, b. Boston, Nov. 28, 1814. "Dr. Fiske was the son of the late Dr. Oliver Fiske, and was born in Worcester. He graduated at Harvard University in 1818, and after pursuing his studies for the practice of medicine, removed to the town of Hingham. His father will be remembered as the founder and proprietor of the first, and for many years the only, nursery of fruit and ornamental trees in the country, and to whom in the first instance, this city is indebted for so much of the rural beauty which distinguishes it. Dr. Fiske inherited his father's taste and passionate love of nature. Before leaving permanently his native place, he originated and helped to execute a work, for which present and future generations of our citizens will bless his memory, although few perhaps may know even the name of their benefactor. Those beautiful rows of shade trees which line and adorn our Main, Front and Park Streets, were chiefly planted by an association of young men, then pursuing their legal and medical studies in the town, among whom Dr. Fiske was the most active. Frequently in later years has he pointed out to the writer of this notice an elm or ash or maple which his own hands had planted, that others might enjoy the shade thereof. In his adopted home, the same refined taste and public spirit have ever characterized him. The conversion of the old neglected town burial ground, which had been used for more than 200 years, into a beautiful, romantic, well kept rural cemetery, a task so difficult of accomplishment that it has scarcely in any other instance been undertaken, the embellishment of his own home, furnishing motive and incentive to like efforts by others, the educational and other institutions of the town, the blessings of the poor to whom he ministered, and the respect of all, are proof of the good works, and monuments to the memory of the 'Good Physician.'" He d. May 8, 1866; res. Hingham, Mass.

5235.   i.   MARY ALLYNE, b. May 30, 1826; unm.; res. H.
5236.   ii.   SARAH DUNCAN, b. Nov. 20, 1827; unm.; res. H.
5237.   iii.   OLIVER, b. Dec. 21, 1829; m. Margaret E. Thomas.

3942.   MAJOR WILLIAM EDWIN FISKE (William, Nathan, Nathan, Nathan, Nathan, Nathaniel, William, Robert, Simon, Simon, William, Symond), b. Brookfield, Mass., June 15, 1796; m. at Sullivan, N. Y., Jan. 4, 1824, Eliza M. Olcott, b. Nov. 8, 1802; d. May 8, 1876. Wm. E. Fiske about the time of the building of the Erie Canal came to Lenox, Madison County, N. Y., to get into what was then called the west. He went without a penny and walked the last thirteen miles on a snowy, slushy day. He brought grain by wagon load down to Albany, traded for groceries and other commodities and sold them in Lenox to the Indians and settlers. Later he established a store, finally two stores, one at Oneida Lake. He formed a partnership with a Mr. Howland (Howland & Fiske), burned the woods in that section to procure the ashes to manufacture potash. He did a successful business for fifty years, and was known as Major Fiske, one of the Inspector-Generals of the State of New York. He was elected to several political offices, but the latter years of his life he was a private banker and broker, under the firm name of William E. Fiske & Son. He died at Canastota. William E. Fiske was a man of character and ability, of the strictest integrity; while delicate and modest he never failed to stand by his opinion. He was a strong anti-slavery man; his house was a station on the underground railroad. He was also a strong temperance man and organized the first temperance society in his county. He wrote and lectured for the cause, and his writings and lectures were pronounced fine. He died beloved and respected by all those who knew him. He d. Nov. 23, 1873; res. Lenox and Canastota, N. Y.

5238. i. FRED CURTIS, b. Feb. 24, 1842; m. Agnes T. Clark.
5239. ii. WILLIAM BUCKMINSTER, b. Jan. 25, 1825; m. Frances Josephine Roberts.
5240. iii. FRANCES ELIZA, b. Oct. 22, 1829; m. Isaac Newton Messinger at Canastota, N. Y., Sept. 6, 1849. He was b. Feb. 28, 1821. Frances Eliza Messinger d. May 18, 1893. Isaac Newton Messinger d. Mar. 11, 1895. Ch.: Mary Elizabeth Trotwood Messinger, John Fiske Messinger, Frances Newton Messinger and Edna Fredrica Messinger.

M. Elizabeth T. Messinger, dau. of Frances Fiske Messinger, b. Feb. 26, 1851; m. Alfred Lindley Goodrich at Oneida, N. Y., Dec. 23, 1880. He was b. at Ithaca, N. Y., Oct. 1, 1854. M. Elizabeth T. Goodrich d. Jan. 4, 1890.

John Fiske Messinger, son of Frances Fiske Messinger, b. Nov. 14, 1853; d. Sept. 13, 1854.

Frances Newton Messinger, dau. of Frances Fiske Messinger, b. Nov. 12, 1858, m. Theodore Coles at Oneida, N. Y., Dec. 7, 1882. He was b. Oct. 6, 1845. Ch.: William Fiske Coles, b. Dec. 1, 1883; Frederic Messinger Coles, b. May 7, 1893; Francis Newton Coles, b. May 4, 1894. All died in infancy; res. Oneida.

Edna Fredrica Messinger, dau. of Frances Fiske Messinger, b. Mar. 7, 1870, m. at Oneida, N. Y., Alfred Lindley Goodrich, Dec. 15, 1892. Ch.: Margaret Frances Goodrich, b. July 26, 1893; d. in infancy.

3747. CAPT. SEWALL FISKE (Nathan, Jonathan, Nathan, Nathan, Nathan, Nathaniel, William, Robert, Simon, Simon, William, Symond), b. Weston, Sept. 8, 1792; m. Apr. 8, 1818, Martha Stearns, b. Oct. 19, 1787, dau. of Isaac, of Ashburnham; d. Oct. 2, 1868. Sewall Fiske was born on the old farm at Weston, and lived and died there. The old English custom has been observed by our ancestors from the first settlement at Weston of passing the land from father to son, and there has been no intervention. He was a farmer all his life, and in addition conducted upon the farm a store with a partner and employes, he buying all goods for the same. That was before the days of railroads, and they made a great deal of business by buying out countrymen who were on their way to Boston loaded down with poultry, turkeys, geese, ducks, chickens, etc. They came in droves in the winter time, utilizing the sleighing, and as the great highway through Massachusetts from Vermont and New Hampshire passed through the farm it gave many opportunities for speculation. In the fall he would remain in Boston from Monday morning to Saturday night engaged in disposing of this produce thus purchased from the northern farmers.

He commanded, in 1812, a company of infantry that, in connection with one other company, "The Ancient and Honorable Artillery of Boston," was called out by the State of Massachusetts to defend the arsenal at Watertown. The Boston company is still in existence. They both received their charter from George III. when Massachusetts was an English colony. He was a strong Whig. He was a delegate to the National Convention in Baltimore when Henry Clay was nominated. He and his wife were Congregationalists, members of the church in Lincoln, two and one-half miles from home. Every Sabbath two teams were employed in carrying the family to church, where the day was spent, and the long sermons of forenoon and afternoon listened to.

He was for many years prominent among his townsmen, and was many times elected as Selectman, Assessor and Tax Collector, as well as other town duties. He d. Mar. 1, 1872; res. Ashburnham, Mass.

5241. i.   ALONZO SEWALL, b. Oct. 4, 1818; m. Susan M. Colburn.
5242. ii. GUSTAVUS HENRY, b. July 18, 1820; d. Feb. 22, 1821.
5243. iii. MARY MALVINA, b. June 3, 1822; m. Sept. 12, 1843, Jeremiah Stratton Russel, of Worcester, who d. Nov. 2, 1844, leaving a son, Jeremiah Stratton, b. Oct. 31, 1844.
5244. iv. MARTHA ELVIRA, b. Mar. 1, 1824; m. Jan., 1855, Mr. Breneman, of Canton, Ia. She d., s. p., 1856.
5245. v.   MARIA HENRIETTA, b. Oct. 11, 1825; d. Feb. 9, 1833.
5246. vi. HENRY GUSTAVUS, b. Apr. 13, 1827; m. Elizabeth Wynkoop.
5247. vii. EDMUND SYLVESTER, b. June 11, 1829. He d. in California in 1860, leaving wife and one child, Ida; res. in Biddeford, Me.
5248. viii. ABIGAIL WARREN, b. June 9, 1831; m. Sept., 1853, J. Q. Adams, of Peterboro, N. H. Had three sons and one dau., Helen F.; res. Peterboro.

3748. REV. NATHAN WELBY FISKE (Nathan, Jonathan, Nathan, Nathan, Nathan, Nathaniel, William, Robert, Simon, Simon, William, Symond), b. Apr. 17, 1798; m. Nov. 4, 1828, Deborah Waterman Vinal, dau. of David, of Boston.

REV. NATHAN WELBY FISKE.

She d. Feb. 19, 1844. Rev. Nathan Welby Fiske was born in Weston, Mass., and died in Jerusalem, Palestine. He was graduated at Dartmouth in 1817, and had charge of an academy in Newcastle, Me., for a year. He was chosen tutor at Dartmouth in 1818, which post he held two years, and was graduated at Andover Theological Seminary in 1823. In November of that year he was ordained as an evangelist, and went to Savannah, Ga., to preach among the seamen and others not belonging to any church. In April, 1824, while yet in Savannah, he declined an invitation to supply the pastorate in Concord, N. H., during the session of the Legislature, and on the same day he declined the solicitation to represent the American Foreign Mission Board as a missionary to Palestine or to China. He was also offered the professorship of mathematics and natural philosophy in Middlebury College, Vt., but declined it, and became professor of Latin and Greek in Amherst in 1824, adding to his duties as instructor the department of belles-lettres from 1825 till 1833, and from 1833 till 1836 was professor of languages (including the modern) at Amherst. He was transferred to the chair of intellectual and moral philosophy, and held it from 1836 till the time of his death. In 1846, on account of failing health, he visited Palestine, where he died, and was buried in Jerusalem on Mount Zion. He was the father of the author Helen Hunt Jackson (q. v.) He published a "Manual of Classical Literature," based upon the German work of J. J. Eschenburg, with additions and a supplemental volume of plates (Philadelphia, 1836; 4th ed., 1843); "Sermons" (1850); "Young Peter's Tour Around the World," and "Story of Aleck; or, The History of Pitcairn's Island." His biography was published, with selections from his sermons and other writings, by Herman Humphrey, D. D. (Amherst, 1850). He d. May 27, 1847; res. Amherst, Mass.

32

5249. i. DAVID VINAL, b. Sept. 11, 1829; d. Oct. 4, 1829.

5250. ii. HELEN MARIA, b. Oct. 15, 1830. She died in San Francisco, Cal., Aug. 12, 1885. She was the daughter of Prof. Nathan W. Fiske, of Amherest, and was educated at the Ipswich, Mass., female seminary. In October, 1852, she married Capt. Edward B. Hunt. She had become known as a contributor to periodical literature, under the signature of "H. H.," when in October, 1875, she married William S. Jackson, and thereafter spent much of her time in Colorado Springs, where her husband was a banker. She became actively interested in the treatment of the Indians by the U. S. Government in 1879, and strove to better the condition of that race. In 1883 she was appointed special commissioner to examine into the condition of the Mission Indians of California, and while thus engaged she studied the history of the early Spanish missions. From her death-bed she wrote to the President a pathetic appeal with reference to "righting the wrongs of the Indian race." Her published works include "Verses" (Boston, 1870; enlarged ed., 1874); "Bits of Travel" (1872); "Bits of Talk About Home Matters" (1873); "Bits of Talk for Young People" (1876); "Bits of Travel at Home" (1878); "Nelly's Silver Mine" (1878); "The Story of Boon" (1879); "Letters from a Cat" (1880); "A Century of Dishonor," referring to the Indians (New York, 1881); "Mammy Tittleback and Her Family" (1881); "The Training of Children" (1882); "The Hunter Cats of Connorloa" (1884); "Ramona" (1884); "Zeph" (1886); "Glimpses of Three Coasts" (1886); "Sonnets and Lyrics" (1886); "Between Whiles" (1887); also "Mercy Philbrick's Choice" (1876) and "Hetty's Strange History" (1877), contributed to the "No-Name Series." The stories published under the penname of Saxe Holm have been attributed to her. She had two ch.: 1, Murray, d. young. 2, Warren H., b. Dec., 1855; d. Apr. 13, 1865.

5251. iii. HUMPHREY WASHBURNE, b. Oct. 16, 1832; d. Sept. 19, 1833.

5252. iv. ANN SCHOLFIELD, b. Dec. 25, 1834; m. Oct., 1854, Everett C. Banfield, of Charlestown. Ch.: 1, Richard, b. Nov. 15, 1855. 2, Anne F., b. July, 1857. 3, Helen F., b. May 22, 1859. 4, Nathan F., b. Nov. 15, 1860. 5, Mary C., b. July, 1865. 6, Abbie, b. ———. Res. Washington, D. C.

3750. HORATIO HANCOCK FISKE (Thaddeus, Jonathan, Nathan, Nathan, Nathan, Nathaniel, William, Robert, Simon, Simon, William, Symond), b. June 22, 1790; m. Mar. 29, 1818, Letitia Whittemore, dau. of Amos, of West Cambridge, inventor of the celebrated machine for making cards. Horatio H. and Letitia, his wife, owned the covenant in Arlington, Nov. 20, 1823, the same date Elmira, his daughter, was baptized. Horatio Hancock, son of Rev. Thaddeus, was bap. June 27, 1790. Horatio Hancock Fiske, b. June 22, 1790, "served an apprenticeship in the mercantile house of Munson & Barnard, Boston, from 1805 to 1813. He then commenced mercantile business in the co-partnership and under the firm name of Stanton, Fiske & Nichols, Boston, who were very enterprising, reputable, and successful merchants." He d. ae. 39, leaving a wife and two daus., Elmira and Caroline. An obituary notice in the Sentinel, Sept. 16, 1829, speaks of him as the only son of the Rev. Dr. Fiske, of West Cambridge, and as one of "our most active, correct and enterprising merchants. * * * Whatever was required of him was sure to be done punctually, faithfully, and to be to the best of his power * * * few perhaps live so short a period in whose character are combined more good qualities than in his, or fill up the measure of their days better than he." His daus. both m. George B. Neal, of Charlestown. He d. Sept. 13, 1829; res. Boston, Mass.

5253. i. ELMIRA, b. ———; m. George B. Neal, of Charlestown. Ch.: Caroline F., b. Feb. 23, 1852.

5254. ii. CAROLINE, b. ———; m. George B. Neal, of Charlestown.

3763. GEORGE FISKE (Jonathan, Jonathan, Nathan, Nathan, Nathan, Nathaniel, William, Robert, Simon, Simon, William, Symond), b. Medfield, Mass., Apr. 20, 1803; m. there, Mar. 29, 1829, Amy Plympton Mann, b. Mar. 25, 1805; d. Apr., 1881. For a number of years he carried on the business of tanning quite successfully, afterwards was a farmer. He was a man respected and honored in the community, holding the office of Selectman, Overseer of the Poor, and various other offices in town and church. He d. Sept. 2, 1878; res. Medfield, Mass.

5255. i.   ANNA MANN, b. Sept. 21, 1831; d. July 29, 1837.
5256. ii. ELIAS MANN, b. Mar. 22, 1834; d. Aug. 10, 1837.
5257. iii. SARAH BRADFORD, b. Aug. 31, 1836; m. May 19, 1864, Rev. James A. Laurie; res. Anacortes, Wash. He was b. Mar. 4, 1835. Is a Presbyterian clergyman. Ch.: 1, Amy Kirk, b. Aug. 7, 1866; d. Nov. 13, 1867. 2, Sarah Ellis, b. Oct. 25, 1868; d. Feb. 12, 1879. 3, James Anderson, b. Apr. 30, 1871; present add. 700 Park Ave., New York. 4, John Abbott, b. Sept. 25, 1875; Anacortes, Wash. 5, George Mann Fiske, b. Jan. 12, 1879; d. Apr. 14, 1882. 6, Annie, b. Apr. 23, 1881; Anacortes, Wash.
5258. iv. GEORGE, b. Jan. 25, 1839; d. Jan. 26, 1839.
5259. v.   CLARRISA, b. Dec. 27, 1839; m. July 16, 1863, Granville T. Fletcher; res. Worthington, Mass. He was b. Dec. 3, 1833; is an educator. Ch.: 1, Annie Fiske, b. at Castine, Me., June 17, 1870; P. O. add. Northampton, Mass. 2, Grenville Hewitt, b. at Castine, Me., Aug. 20, 1875; P. O. add. Northampton, Mass.
5260. vi. GEORGE M., b. May 2, 1842; m. Sarah W. Wilder.
5261. vii. CHARLES F., b. Aug. 20, 1848; m. Mary Nye.
5262. viii. ABIGAIL SMITH, b. Jan. 7, 1830; m. Mar. 31, 1860, Francis W. Goodale, of Marlboro, Mass. She d. Jan. 15, 1862, leaving a dau., Abbie F., who is unm. and res. in Duluth, Minn., where she is engaged in teaching.

3764. HON. AMOS FLAGG FISKE (Jonathan, Jonathan, Nathan, Nathan, Nathan, Nathaniel, William, Robert, Simon, Simon, William, Symond), b. Medfield, Mass., Aug. 1, 1805; m. in Marlow, Oct. 30, 1830, Eliza Stone, of Marlow, N. H., b. Oct. 21, 1809; d. May 15, 1891. Hon. Amos F. Fiske, late of Marlow, N. H., was born in Medfield, Mass. In early manhood he settled in Marlow, and opened a country store at what is known as Marlow Hill, where he conducted a thriving and prosperous business, until what is now Marlow Village became the principal place in that town; his store and family were then removed to that village. There he continued to thrive and became the foremost citizen of that town, both in wealth and position. He married Eliza Stone, of that town, who was a most estimable lady. They had five children, Harriett, Arthur W., Henry, Catherine and Eliza. Mr. Fiske and his wife were both members of the Methodist Church in Marlow, and very active in its support. By his will he endowed this church, and after his decease his widow contributed largely to its support. Mr. Fiske held various town, county and State offices, the principal of which was State Senator, to which office he was twice elected, from 1863 to 1866. He was a man of strong character and sterling integrity. He died in Marlow, respected by all who knew him. He d. Jan. 6, 1873; res. Marlow, N. H.

5263. i.   HARRIETT ADELAIDE, b. Apr. 8, 1834; m. Dec. 30, 1852, Dr. Marshall Perkins; res. Marlow. He was b. May 13, 1823. Is a practicing physician. Ch.: 1, James Marshall, b. Sept. 11, 1853; res. Marlow, N. H. 2, Annie Elisabeth, b. Nov. 27, 1856; m. —— Upton; res. Manchester, N. H. 3, Hattie Fiske, b. Feb. 20, 1859; m. —— Mitchell; res. Epping, N. H. 4, Henry Waldo, b. Mar. 9, 1862; P. O. add. Marlow, N. H. 5, Martha, b. Sept. 18, 1864; d. Mar. 30, 1866. 6, Daniel Herbert, b. Sept. 27, 1866; d. Sept. 6, 1875. 7, Kate Louise, b. July 23, 1869; P. O. add. Marlow. 8, Charles Amos, b. Apr. 24, 1872; add. Manchester. 9, Jessie May, b. May 9, 1878; add. Marlow.
5264. ii. ARTHUR W., b. Nov. 4, 1837; m. Emma E. Burr.
5265. iii. ELIZA, b. Mar. 23, 1844; m. Nov. 29, 1869, Alfred F. Howard. He is secretary of the Granite State Fire Insurance Co. Alfred

F. Howard was born in Marlow, N. H., Feb. 16, 1842. Was educated in the common schools of that town, at the Marlow Academy and New Hampshire Conference Seminary, at Tilton, N. H. Taught school at various places in this State.` Read law in the office of the late Judge William H. H. Allen, at Newport, N. H. Was admitted to the Sullivan County, N. H., bar in 1868, and commenced the practice of law in Portsmouth, N. H., the same year, where he filled the office of City Solicitor for two terms. In 1872 he was appointed Deputy Collector of Customs for the port of Portsmouth, by the late Collector Hon. John H. Bailey. Soon after Collector Bailey resigned, and Mr. Howard was promoted to fill the vacancy. This office he held until 1885, when he resigned to accept the position of secretary and manager of the Granite State Fire Insurance Company, of Portsmouth, which was organized that year by the Hon. Frank Jones. This position he still holds. Mr. Howard has also been Superintendent of Schools in his native town of Marlow, and the town of Newport, N. H. He was also a member from Portsmouth of the Constitutional Convention in 1876. Mr. Howard is now president of the New Hampshire Board of Underwriters, an organization which controls the rates and rules for fire underwriting in New Hampshire. Ch.: 1, Arthur Fiske, b. June 9, 1873; gr. at Amherst College, and is now student at Massachusetts Institute of Technology; res. Portsmouth, N. H. Arthur F. Howard was born in the city of Portsmouth, N. H. Was educated in the public schools of that city; graduated from the high school in 1889 and was awarded the first medal each year of the course. He then took a post-graduate course at this school for one year. Entered Amherst College in 1891, where he graduated in 1895, being one of fifteen men in his class who were elected members of the Phi Beta Kappa. In Sept., 1895, he entered the Massachusetts Institute of Technology, to take the course of electrical engineering. 2, Eliza, b. ———; d. Aug. 27, 1878.

5266. iv. CATHERINE, b. Feb. 6, 1840; m. Nov. 11, 1860, Perley E. Fox, b. Dec. 17, 1833; res. Marlow, N. H. Ch.: 1, Charles Henry, b. Jan. 8, 1865; d. Jan. 1, 1866.

5267. v. HENRY, b. Mar. 21, 1842; d. Feb. 12, 1876.

5268. vi. ELIZA, b. Apr. 22, 1833; d. Apr. 23, 1833.

5269. vii. CHARLES HENRY, b. Sept. 23, 1835; d. May, 1836.

3767. CHARLES AUGUSTUS FISKE (Jonathan, Jonathan, Nathan, Nathan, Nathan, Nathaniel, William, Robert, Simon, Simon, William, Symond), b. Medfield, Mass., Mar. 7, 1816; m. Apr. 3, 1845, Abby Waldron, b. in 1820; d. Jan. 14, 1856; m. 2d, Dec. 2, 1857, Ellen Boyd, of Medway, Mass. He was a commission merchant in Boston and passed an uneventful life. He d. May 1, 1879; res. No. Cambridge, Mass., Langdon St.

5270. i. ANNA LOUISA, b. Aug. 7, 1846; m. Nov. 9, 1871, Edwin Russell Hoag; res. 38 John St., Chelsea. Ch.: 1, Charles Russell, b. June 17, 1873. 2, Edwin Fiske, b. Dec. 7, 1874; d. Nov. 30, 1876. 3, Abbie Waldron, b. Nov. 14, 1878; d. July 23, 1879.

5271. ii. CHAS. AUGUSTUS, b. Oct. 28, 1850; m. Laura J. Ellis.

5272. iii. WM. BOYD, b. Nov. 17, 1858; d. unm., May 8, 1892.

5273. iv. CORNELIA BOYD, b. Nov. 1, 1861; res. unm., 39 Langdon St, No. Cambridge, Mass.

3769. AUGUSTUS HENRY FISKE (Isaac, Jonathan, Nathan, Nathan, Nathan, Nathaniel, William, Robert, Simon, Simon, William, Symond), b. Weston, Mass., Sept. 19, 1805; m. May 22, 1830, Hannah Rogers Bradford, b. July 7, 1810; d. Oct. 29, 1880. Augustus H. Fiske was born in Weston, Mass. His father was Isaac Fiske, and his mother Sukey (Hobbs) Fiske. He was educated at the Framingham Academy, and graduated from Harvard in 1825. He practiced law in Boston all his life. He lived in Boston until about 1848, when he moved back to Weston, still retaining his office in Boston. He was one of the leaders of the bar of his time. His wife was Hannah Rogers Bradford, a daughter of the late Capt. Gamaliel Bradford, of Boston, formerly of Duxbury, Mass. Mr. Fiske's learning as a lawyer was large and always ready for use, his judgment was prompt and sound, his instincts rarely at fault. His industry was untiring, and his executive talent so great that he despatched without aid and without apparent effort an amount of business detail which would seem incredible to any one who had not witnessed it. His sagacity in matters of business as well as in what pertained directly to his profession was remarkable. There are few of our merchants and business men who have not had occasion to appreciate and profit by it. With these qualities, and with a genial temper, a hearty manner, and a devotion to the interests of his clients, which even on his deathbed never let him spare himself, it is not surprising that he reached a position in his profession to which there are few parallels, and enjoyed more of the substantial fruits of success than has perhaps ever fallen to the lot of any other member of the Boston bar. He d. Mar. 22, 1864; res. Weston, Mass.

    5274. i.   ANDREW, b. June 4, 1854; m. Gertrude H. Horsford.
    5275. ii.   EDWARD, b. Sept. 2, 1832; m. Adelaide P. Frost.
    5276. iii.   MARGARET, b. Nov. 25, 1837; m. William Watson. She d. s. p. Mar. 31, 1886.
    5277. iv.   SARAH RIPLEY, b. Feb. 15, 1839; m. 1862, Major Sidney Willard. He was Major of the Thirty-fifth Massachusetts Volunteers, and was killed at Fredericksburg, Dec., 1862. She m. 2d, Jan., 1874, Rev. Chandler Robbins, of Boston, pastor of the Second Church. He d. 1881. Ch.: 1, Wm. B., b. ———. 2, Thomas II., b. ———. 3, Chandler, b. ———.
    5278. v.   CHARLES H., b. Oct. 26, 1840; m. Cornelia F. Robbins.
    5279. vi.   LUCY ANN, b. June 25, 1843; m. 1865, Frank Morrison. She d. s. p. May 2, 1866.
    5280. vii.   MARY ELIZABETH, b. May 10, 1841; m. June 5, 1866, Brenton H. Dickson. Two ch.: one son, Brenton H., Jr., add. 71 Kilby St., Boston.
    5281. viii.   GEORGE, b. Dec. 28, 1850; m. Mary Rood.
    5282. ix.   SUSAN ANN, b. Mar. 22, 1831; d. Jan. 16, 1838.

    3779. DEA. HENRY FISK (Samuel, Samuel, Nathan, Nathan, Nathan, Nathaniel, William, Robert, Simon, Simon, William, Symond), b. Aug. 17, 1808, Southbridge, Mass.; m. there Nov. 29, 1832, Sarah Belknap, b. Feb. 11, 1811. He d. May 9, 1881; res. Globe Village, Mass.

    5283. i.   SARAH LOUISA, b. Sept. 3, 1834; m. Sept. 16, 1869, Gayton Ballard; res. 51 Jefferson Ave., Brooklyn, N. Y. He was b. July 8, 1821. Is a manufacturer.
    5284. ii.   CAROLINE AUGUSTA, b. Sept., 1836; m. Nov. 3, 1858, Joseph Hodges. She d. Feb. 12, 1883. Ch.: Bertha L. Hodges; m. Geo. C. Stout; res. Brooklyn, N. Y., 51 Jefferson Ave.

    3784. JOSIAH FISKE (Josiah, Josiah, Josiah, Nathan, Nathan, Nathaniel, William, Robert, Simon, Simon, William, Symond), b. Pepperell, Mass., Nov. 14, 1781; m. Betsey Kimball, of Temple. He was accidentally drowned at Medford, Mass. He d. July 19, 1817; res. Temple, N. H.

    5284a. i.   ELIZA, b. Nov. 2, 1802, in Temple, N. H.; m. Benj. Franklin Stevens, of Mason, N. H., where they had five children; then removed to Osage, Mitchell Co., Ia.
    5284b. ii.   MARY, b. July 20, 1804, in Temple; m. Simon Farrar, of Temple; removed to New York City. Three children.
    5284c. iii.   JEREMIAH, b. Temple, Jan. 4, 1807; d. unm.
    5284d. iv.   PRESCOTT, b. Dec. 22, 1808, at Andover, Vt.; m. Elizabeth F. Vickery, of Hebron, N. H. Two children, b. in Boston: 1, Elizabeth Lowell Fiske, b. Nov. 2, 1836. 2. Edward Prescott Fiske, b. in Boston, Sept. 24, 1841; was with the Old Eleventh, at Baltimore, on Apr. 19, 1861.
    5284e. v.   ALONZO, b. in Andover, Vt., June 24, 1811; m. Rebecca Locke, of Boston. Two children.
    5284f. vi.   GEO. KIMBALL, b. Aug. 28, 1813, in N. Ipswich, N. H.; d. unm.

5284g. vii. ABIGAIL RAYMOND, b. in N. Ipswich, N. H., July 21, 1816; m. Isaac D. Brower, of New York City, where she now resides. Four children.

3788. JEREMIAH FISKE (Josiah, Josiah, Josiah, Nathan, Nathan, Nathaniel, William, Robert. Simon, Simon, William, Symond), b. Temple, N. H., Aug. 17, 1790; m. Sarah Heald, b. 1798; d. Mar. 23, 1858; m. 2d, Mrs. Cemina Munro, d. Nov., 1895. He was born in Temple, N. H., and was one of the largest farmers in the county. Of his eleven children, six were teachers in the public schools at one time. He resided on the old homestead. He d. Oct. 9, 1882; res. Temple, N. H.

5285. i. JAMES, b. Mar. 16, 1816. He d. in 1878, on the old homestead, unm.

5286. ii. SARAH ANN, b. Jan. 20, 1817; m. Dec. 1, 1842, Capt. Charles Walton; res. New Ipswich, N. H. She d. at Temple, 1885, having had six children, four of whom survived her.

5287. iii. LOIS, b. Mar. 21, 1819; d. July 29, 1836.

5288. iv. JOSIAH, b. Nov. 6, 1820; m. Rebecca Flint and Mary Flint.

5289. v. CHARLOTTE, b. July 9, 1822; m. May 14, 1846, Dr. Thomas Palmer, of Fitchburg, Mass. He is one of the most expert dental surgeons in the country. Had three children, one son and two daughters.

5290. vi. JEREMIAH, b. Feb. 10, 1824; m. Caroline Bailey.

5291. vii. ALVAH, b. Nov. 4, 1825. He d. of typhoid fever while on a visit to Indianapolis, Ind., Jan. 31, 1854. He was a young man of commanding talent, and died greatly lamented.

5292. viii. MARTIN H., b. May 10, 1827; m. Henrietta F. Breed.

5293. ix. EMILY, b. May 8, 1820; m. June 2, 1856, Daniel Lampson, of East Weymouth, Mass. He was killed in the battle of Fredericksburg, Dec., 1862. He left a son and daughter.

5294. x. REBECCA DAVIS, b. Feb. 20, 1831; m. Mar., 1865, Thomas Fessenden; res. Los Angeles, Cal. He d. leaving a son.

5295. xi. CHARLES F., b. Dec. 2, 1832; m. Emma Bailey.

3789. ARTEMAS FISKE (Josiah, Josiah, Josiah, Nathan, Nathan, Nathaniel, William, Robert. Simon. Simon, William, Symond), b. Temple, N. H., Sept. 11, 1792; m. Apr. 6, 1819, Lucy Jones, of Templeton, Mass., b. there June 29, 1799; d. Hayfield, Pa., Jan. 20, 1884. He was born in New Hampshire and resided on his father's farm until his marriage, when he moved to his own property. This was located about four miles from the old homestead at the foot of Kidder Mountain, where he died. He d. Mar. 26, 1829; res. New Ipswich, N. H.

5296. i. CHARLES A., b. Oct. 29, 1820; m. Sylvia C. Fuller.

5297. ii. LUCY, b. June 15, 1822; d. Nov., 1831; m. Oct. 19, 1843, James A. Tyler, of Connautville, Pa. She d. Nov. 24, 1889, in Kinsman, O. Ch.: 1, James Vernon, b. ———; res. Lima, O. 2, Dellia Wight, b. ———; res. Columbus, O.

3791. DAVID FISKE (Josiah, Josiah, Josiah, Nathan, Nathan, Nathaniel, William, Robert. Simon. Simon, William, Symond), b. Temple, N. H., Jan. 17, 1797; m. there Milly Sheldon, b. Jan. 5, 1798; d. Mar. 10, 1884. He was a farmer. He d. Nov. 26, 1880; res. Oxford, Chenango Co., N. Y.

5298. i. HORACE, b. Oxford, Chenango Co., N. Y., July 23, 1829; m. Martha Padgett.

5299. ii. EMILY, b. Feb. 25, 1833; m. Dec. 31, 1857, Joseph Esterbrook; res. Oxford. He was b. June 29, 1833; is a blacksmith. Ch.: 1, Anna A., b. Dec. 15, 1858; m. 1879, Charles W. Sherwood; add. Oxford, N. Y. 2, Abby A., b. Mar. 20, 1860; m. Jesse Fiske; add. No. Norwich, Chenango Co., N. Y. 3, Seymour H., b. Feb. 6, 1863; m. 1883; add. Norwich, N. Y. 4, William D., b. July 5, 1864; m. in 1883; add. Norwich, N. Y. 5, Ida B., b. Sept. 6, 1869; m. in 1891, Rev. E. Lee Berry; Altoona, Pa., 412 Howard Ave.

5300. iii. LUCY ANN, b. Feb. 3, 1823; m. June 29, 1853, Charles E. Peacock; res. Norwich, N. Y. He was b. May 21, 1842; d. Feb. 19, 1889; was on the police force. Ch.: 1. Mary, b. June 27,

1854; res. Holliston, Mass. 2, Etta, b. Mar. 2, 1869; res. Norwich, N. Y. 3, William, b. Dec. 4, 1871; res. St. Louis, 1833 Bleeker St.

5301. iv. LYDIA P., b. in Oxford, in 1827; m. Dec., 1854, Chauncey H. Barstow, b. July 3, 1829. She d. Feb. 12, 1868. Ch.: 1, Jerry Fiske, b. Sept. 10, 1866; res. Lincklaen, Chenango Co., N. Y.; m. July 12, 1893, Mary A. Newell; ch.: Ethel Maude, b. Oct. 28, 1894. 2, Florence A., b. Dec. 19, 1855; d. Oct. 16, 1871. 3, Emma J., b. Nov. 16, 1858; m. Nov. 25, 1890, C. H. Edgerton; add. Lincklaen, N. Y. 4, Barbara S., b. Aug. 5, 1864; m. Oct. 11, 1882, J. W. Burlison; add. Oxford, N. Y. 5, Sarah J., b. May 30, 1870; m. Mar. 17, 1886, R. Hoskins; add. West Bainbridge, Chen. Co., N. Y.

3792. SETH H. FISKE (Josiah, Josiah, Josiah, Nathan, Nathan, Nathaniel, William, Robert, Simon, Simon, William, Symond), b. Temple, N. H., Sept. 20, 1800; m. Lydia Putnam, of Marblehead, Mass., b. 1807; d. at Leroy, N. Y., Jan. 17, 1828; m. 2d, Hannah J. Miles, of Oxford, N. Y. He d. 1878; res. Temple, N. H.
5302. i. DAU., b. ———.

3792-1. JOHN FISK (David, Josiah, Josiah, Nathan, Nathan, Nathaniel, William, Robert, Simon, Simon, William, Symond), b. Hope, Me., Oct. 23, 1777; m. there Mar. 5, 1806, Cynthia Howe, b. 1784; d. Dec. 14, 1850. He was a native of Hope, Me., where he resided until his removal to Readfield, where he engaged in business with his son, Perley H. He was in partnership with him at the time of his death. He d. Mar. 19, 1838; res. Readfield, Me.
5302-1. i. CHARLES, b. Mar. 5, 1807; m. Lucy Ann Sprague.
5302-2. ii. GALEN B., b. Oct. 5, 1808; m. Sarah B. Robbins.
5302-3. iii. PERLEY HOWE, b. Aug. 16, 1815; m. Sarah Emeline Fogg.
5302-4. iv. JOEL H., b. Nov. 14, 1817; m. Mrs. Louisa Turner Weeks.
5302-5. v. ANN MARIA, b. Oct. 3, 1820; m. May 14, 1840, Daniel K. Frolock, of Smithfield, Me. She d. Sept. 14, 1847. Ch.: 1, Emma Ophelia, b. Apr. 15, 1845; m. in Portland, Me., Dec. 23, 1875, Henry E. Underwood, b. June 3, 1830; ch.: 1, Louis F., b. Jan. 18, 1878; res. Oxford St., Portland, Me. 2, Perley Fisk.
5302-6. vi. DAVID, b. July 4, 1823.

3792-2. BENJAMIN FISK (David, Josiah, Josiah, Nathan, Nathan, Nathaniel, William, Robert, Simon, Simon, William, Symond), b. Waltham, Mass., Mar., 1780; m. at Gen. Knox's home in Thomaston, Me., Roxanna Harrington, b. Nov., 1784; she d. in S. Hope, Me., Mar. 17, 1873. He was a farmer. He d. at Rockville, Sept., 1865; res. Camden, Me.
5302-7. i. MOSES H., b. May 3, 1816; m. Harriett S. Ingraham.
5302-8. ii. BENJAMIN, b. 1812; m. Mary E. Studley.
5302-9. iii. AMOS, b. ———; m. Irena Tolman; res. Rockville, Me.
5302-10. iv. ARATHUSA D., b. ———; m. Alvin Howard; res. West Rockport, Me.
5302-11. v. CAROLINE M., b. Mar. 6, 1827; m. Jan. 16, 1848, Jesse M. Crabtree; res. S. Hope, Me. He was b. Feb. 12, 1823; d. Jan. 25, 1893. He was a farmer. Ch.: Clara G., b. May 12, 1849; m. Aug. 7, 1869, ——— Nash; res. 75 Clark St., Lynn, Mass. Laura A., b. Aug. 15, 1851; d. Sept. 17, 1851. Frank A., b. Aug. 19, 1853; m. Nov. 4, 1878; res. So. Hope. Mary E., b. Sept. 3, 1855; m. July 17, 1875, ——— Annis; res. 42 Coburn St., Lynn, Mass. Cynthia R., b. Jan. 20, 1858; m. Nov. 8, 1879, ——— Perry; res. 36 Mudge St., Lynn, Mass. Martha L., b. Sept. 25, 1860; d. May 5, 1863. Hattie F., b. May 19, 1865; m. Oct. 16, 1889, ——— Reed; res. 9 Beach Ave., Lynn, Mass.
5302-12. vi. MARY ANN, b. ———; m. Charles Studley; res. Rockville, Me.; a dau. is Adelia L. Smith, of Rockville.
5302-13. vii. OLIVER, b. ———. He left home when 18 years of age and has never been heard from since; was supposed to have been lost at sea, and d. s. p.
5302-14. viii. BETSEY, b. ———; m. Joseph Carter. She d., and he m. her sister (see); a descendant is Betsey Young, of Warren, Me.

5302-15. ix.   LOLA, b. ———; m. Joseph Carter. He was b. Readfield, Me., Feb. 22, 1801; d. So. Hope, Me., Sept., 1887; was a carpenter. Ch.: 1, Betsey E., b. Aug., 1828; m., 1846, ——— Young, Pleasantville, Me. 2, Jos. O., b. Oct. 27, 1831; m. Oct. 7, 1856, Rosanna Burrows, b. Mar. 24, 1831; res. So. Hope, Me.; is a carpenter; ch.: Lola E., b. Aug. 1, 1857; m. ——— Fitch, South Hope, Me.; d. Sept. 29, 1881. John C., b. Apr. 2, 1859; d. Nov. 18, 1890. Geo. A., b. Sept. 23, 1860; m. ———, Rockland, Highlands, Me.; d. Jan. 1, 1892. Augustus S., b. Apr. 9, 1862; m. ———, Rockland Highlands, Me.; d. Nov., 1887. Myles L., b. July 12, 1864; m. ———, Danbury, Conn.; d. June 30, 1892. Maud C., b. Mar. 5, 1871; d. Aug. 30, 1892. 3, Benj. F., b. Apr., 1833; m. in 1858, South Hope, Me. 4. Adelia H., b. Mar., 1835; m., 1856, ——— Mariner; res. 31 Franklin St., Lynn, Mass. 5, Philander I., b. 1837; deceased. 6, Alvin A., b. Apr., 1839; m. in 1870; res. South Hope, Me. 7, Roscoe M., b. 1841; m. in 1863; res. W. Rockport, Me. Mr. Jesse Young, Pleasantville, Me. Mr. Frank Carter, Cleveland, Ohio. Mrs. L. A. Greene, 29 Rockaway St., Lynn, Mass. Miss Myrtle E. Carter, S. Hope, Me. Miss Evie M. Carter, W. Rockport, Me.

5302-16. x.   LOUISA, b. ———; m. James Darling.

5302-17. xi.   ROXANNA, b. ———; m. John Cleveland; a dau. is Louisa Sherer, of Rockland, Me.

3792-3.   DAVID FISK (David, Josiah, Josiah, Nathan, Nathan, Nathaniel, William, Robert, Simon, Simon, William, Symond), b. ———, Mass.; m. at Thomaston, Me., ——— Becket. She was b. in Thomaston and d. in Indiana, ae. 92. He was born in Mass. and moved to Kentucky in 1817. He went by water to Boston, Mass., and from there overland in a "C" spring coach. He was a man of means when he left Boston, but in exchange for $40,000 in gold—quite a fortune in those days—he took bills on a Detroit, Mich., bank. On his arrival in Cincinnati, Ohio, he learned that the Michigan bank had burst and he was without much ready cash. His daughter Hannah had the bills in her possession for a long time. While residing in Maine he owned what was known in those days as the "Owls Head," a celebrated point on the coast of Maine. He resided at Camden and Thomaston, Me. He was a Mason in high standing and on his removal to Kentucky organized a blue lodge. He died of "milk sickness," a disease not known much nowadays. He was a very large man and weighed 260 pounds. He purchased 1,000 acres of land which was left to the family on his death. He d. about 1835; res. Camden, Me., Readfield, Ohio, and ———, Ky.

5302-18. i.   WM. BECKET, b. Mar. 25, 1803; m. Cynthia Stevens.

5302-19. ii.   HANNAH, b. ———.

5302-20. iii.   SOLOMON, b. ———. He was instantly killed while an infant in his cradle by a pair of heavy tongs falling on his head and crushing his skull.

5302-21.	iv.	JOHN D., b. 1794; m. Margaret Simonton.			
5302-22.	v.	DAVID.	5302-27.	x.	PEGIE.
5302-23.	vi.	JONATHAN.	5302-28.	xi.	SUSAN.
5302-24.	vii.	GEORGE.	5302-29.	xii.	POLLY.
5302-25.	viii.	ALEXANDER.	5302-30.	xiii.	ANN.
5302-26.	ix.	AMOS.	5302-31.	xiv.	KITTIE.

3793.   DANIEL FISKE (Nathan, Daniel, Josiah, Nathan, Nathan, Nathaniel, William, Robert, Simon, Simon, William, Symond), b. Landgrove, Vt., Mar. 12, 1803; m. in Weston, Vt., in 1831, Florella Wyman, b. Sept. 4, 1809; d. Nov. 26, 1872. He was a farmer. He d. Sept. 23, 1881; res. Landgrove, Vt.

5303. i.   DANIEL D., b. Landgrove, Mar. 12, 1834; m. in Boston, Nov. 5, 1862, Maria Caldwell, b. Dec. 31, 1836; res., s. p., 44 Bedford St., Boston; is a restauranteur.

5304. ii.   HANNAH L., b. June 1, 1836; m. Nov., 1858, R. Clayton; res. 305 Stuyvesant Ave., Brooklyn, N. Y.

5305. iii.   BETSEY A., b. Oct. 17, 1838; unm.; res. 217 Larmartine St., Jamaica Plains, Mass.

5306. iv.   CHARLES C., b. Aug. 15, 1841; d. June 28, 1872.

5307. v. J. FRANK, b. Aug. 27, 1843; d. Dec. 28, 1865.
5308. vi. ROLLIN ABEL, b. Jan. 30, 1851; m. Annie E. Smith.
5309. vii. JULIA H., b. Mar. 24, 1856; unm.; res. 217 Lamartine St., Jamaica Plains, Mass.
5310. viii. WINSLOW C., b. Aug. 2, 1853; m. Frances B. White.

3798. JOHN DALE FISK (Nathan, Daniel, Josiah, Nathan, Nathan, Nathaniel, William, Robert, Simon, Simon, William, Symond), b. Landgrove, Vt., Feb. 10, 1812; m. May 22, 1840, Emily Olin, b. May 29, 1820; d. Feb. 21, 1874. He was a blacksmith. He d. Apr. 5, 1882; res. Bennington, Vt.

5311. i. MARY ANN, b. Aug. 19, 1841; d. May 3, 1842.
5312. ii. CAROLINE E., b. Sept. 5, 1843; m. Oct. 25, 1864, Dr. Silas Rollin Wilcox. He was b. July 20, 1839; is a physician; res. 635 Main St., Bennington, Vt. Ch.: Emma M., b. Nov. 28, 1866. John Fisk, b. Mar. 29, 1868; d. Jan. 10, 1872. Alfred Dexter, b. June 28, 1870; d. Jan. 6, 1872. Julia Fisk, b. Dec. 24, 1874. Susan Mary, b. Aug. 21, 1878. Caroline Louise, b. July 11, 1884, Bennington, Vt.
5313. iii. ALBERT, b. Mar. 12, 1846; d. June 27, 1865.
5314. iv. JULIA SAGE, b. Aug. 20, 1848.
5315. v. HENRY SAGE, b. Mar. 31, 1852; m. Apr., 1874, and res. Bennington, Vt.

3800. WALTER FISKE (Walter, Daniel, Josiah, Nathan, Nathan, Nathaniel, William, Robert, Simon, Simon, William, Symond), b. Wilton, N. H., May 26, 1796; m. in Providence, R. I., Mar. 8, 1812, Abigail Dickson, b. Sept., 1793; d. Aug. 24, 1846. He resided in Pepperell where he was born and his family was an unusually happy one. In 1837 he moved to Cambridge, Mass., and later to Weld, Me., finally settling in Dedham, Mass., where she died. He d. May 27, 1886; res. Pepperell and Dedham, Mass.

5316. i. MARY ANN, b. June, 1813; m. John E. Billings, b. July 10, 1810; d. Feb. 18, 1857. Ch.: 1, Chas. Edgar, b. Nov. 12, 1834; m. Aug. 7, 1861, Mary Murdock: res. Newton, Mass.; prominent citizen: three children. 2, Edward T., b. Dec. 17, 1838; m. Sept. 1, 1870, Abbie Holland Ewings; res. Newton; apothecary; one child. 3, Ellen Fiske, b. May 24, 1843; m. May 19, 1868, James Albert Sullivan; res. Watertown; apothecary; one child. 4, Emily Lovett, b. Sept. 17, 1845. 5, Henry Dunster, b. July 16, 1849; res. Boston.
5317. ii. HANNAH MARIA, b. May 5, 1822; unm.; res. Wellesley, Mass.
5318. iii. BENJ. N., b. Feb. 29, 1815; m. Eliza P. Warren.
5319. iv. SARAH NOSTLING, b. Mar. 31, 1817; m. May 4, 1843, Isaac Pierce Blood. He was b. in Hollis, N. H., Feb. 17, 1803. She d. Apr. 2, 1865; res. Hollis, N. H. Ch.: 1, Harriett Maria, b. July 17, 1844. 2, Geo. Henry, b. Jan. 7, 1848; m. Apr. 8, 1875, Harriett A. Hills. 3, Mary Ann, b. June 20, 1851; graduated State Normal School at So. Framingham, Mass.; res. Chicago, Ill. 4, Abbie Louisa, b. July 7, 1853. 5, Charles Walter, b. July 13, 1857.
5320. v. ACHSAH, b. Feb. 8, 1819; m. July 4, 1839, Charles Bell Merrill. She d. in Boston, Aug. 23, 1842. Ch.: 1, Charles Henry. He was in the war and was wounded in battle: died in the hospital at Washington, D. C., in May, 1864; unm. 2, Achsah Maria, m. Jabez Merrill.
5321. vi. HENRY WALTER, b. June 18, 1827; m. Harriett Waite and Sarah Elizabeth Green.

3801. DR. BENJAMIN NUTTING FISK (Walter, Daniel, Josiah, Nathan, Nathan, Nathaniel, William, Robert, Simon, Simon, William, Symond), b. Pepperell, Mass., Jan. 22, 1798; m. in Readfield, Me., Susannah G. Shedd, b. Mar. 15, 1797; d. Aug. 3, 1854. He was in the War of 1812 against Great Britain, and was 16 years old at that time. After the war he went to Maine and married Susannah Shedd, of Readfield; moved to Weld; moved from there to Sangerville; from there to Bangor, where he built a brick block: went from there to Mattawamkeag,

Penobscot County, and built a hotel there. His occupations were farming, lumbering, teaching school, and hotel business. He died at Mattawamkeag about forty-two years ago at the age of 56 years. He d. Apr. 5, 1855; res. Weld and Mattawamkeag, Me.

5322. i. BENJAMIN ABOTT, b. Sept. 21, 1822; m. Margaret E. Archer.
5323. ii. WALTER WARREN, b. Jan. 12, 1824; m. Rebecca Kimball and Florentine Gowen.
5324. iii. SUSANNA E., b. Aug. 9, 1825; d. Sept. 18, 1826.
5325. iv. HIRAM H., b. Dec. 6, 1827; d. ———.
5326. v. MARY ANN, b. Nov. 6, 1832.
5327. vi. JOSIAH F., b. Mar. 9, 1834; d. Aug. 3, 1854.
5328. vii. JEREMIAH H., b. Aug. 18, 1835; m. Jemima W. Gowen.
5329. viii. GEORGE W., b. Oct. 15, 1837; m.; a dau., Nellie, res. Bangor, Me.
5330. ix. DANIEL, REV., b. ———; is a clergyman; res. Florenceville, N. B.
5331. x. JOHN GREENLEAF, b. Mar. 31, 1831; m. at Jacksontown, N. B., Apr. 9, 1864, Harriet I. De Grass, b. May 29, 1849; res. s. p. in Medway, Me.; is hotel proprietor.

3802. JEREMIAH FISKE (Walter, Daniel, Josiah, Nathan, Nathan, Nathaniel, William; Robert, Simon, Simon, William, Symond), b. Wilton, N. H., Jan. 3, 1800; m. there Oct. 28, 1824, Peggy Burton; res. Wilton, N. H.

3803. GEO. W. H. FISKE (Josiah, Daniel, Josiah, Nathan, Nathan, Nathaniel, William, Robert, Simon, Simon, William, Symond), b. May 10, 1809; m. Oct. 8, 1835, Mary Chadwick. He d. Mar. 24, 1838.

5332. i. DAUGHTER, b. ———; m. W. Macomber; res. Sanquoit, N. Y.

3808. ARNOLD HUTCHINSON FISK (Varnum, Daniel, Josiah, Nathan, Nathan, Nathaniel, William, Robert, Simon, Simon, William, Symond), b. Wilton, N. H., June 4, 1814; m. in Norfolk, N. Y., May 1, 1838, Martha M. Van House, b. Sept. 16, 1816. He was a farmer. He d. May 16, 1863; res. Norfolk, N. Y., and Dennison, Mich.

5333. i. JULIA EMELINE, b. Aug. 5, 1841; m. Feb. 6, 1862, Lucien A. Cole. He was b. Nov. 20, 1834; is a farmer; res. Berlin, Mich. Ch.: Elmer E., b. Nov. 12, 1862; d. Feb. 16, 1886. Minnie O., b. Nov. 25, 1864; m. Oct. 3, 1890, Ethan A. Streeter; add. 559 N. Front St., Grand Rapids, Mich. Ira Arnold, b. Sept. 12, 1866; add. 559 N. Front St., Grand Rapids, Mich. Wm. B., b. July 28, 1872; add. Berlin, Ottawa County, Mich. Franklin B., b. Aug. 20, 1874; add. Berlin, Ottawa County, Mich. Edwin F., b. Sept. 15, 1877; add. Berlin, Ottawa County, Mich. Susie Mae, b. May 16, 1882; add. Berlin, Ottawa County, Mich.
5334. ii. SARAH C., b. Feb. 3, 1844; m., 1861, Daniel Zimmerman; res. 416 So. Division St., Grand Rapids, Mich.
5335. iii. CLIFTON EAMES, b. Jan. 31, 1847; d. in the Civil War June 10, 1865.
5336. iv. HELEN M., b. July 28, 1851; m. Oct. 7, 1871, James N. Cloud; res. So. Royalton, Vt. He was b. in 1846; is a jeweler. Ch.: Rubie E., b. May 8, 1875. Rufus B., b. Mar. 24, 1877. Harrie D., b. Oct. 3, 1880; add. of all South Royalton, Vt.
5337. v. GEO. W., b. June 26, 1839; m. Julia E. Cadwell.

3825. HENRY A. FISK (Abel, Abel, Josiah, Nathan, Nathan, Nathaniel, William, Robert, Simon, Simon, William, Symond), b. Wilton, N. H., May 22, 1833; m. Jan. 8, 1855, Sophronia Kidder, d. May 28, 1865; m. 2d, Nov. 18, 1867, Ella L. Prince, d. Oct. 28, 1881; m. 3d, July 10, 1882, Theo. E. Tower; res. Wilton, N. H.

5338. i. FRED T., b. Feb. 5, 1865; d. Aug. 27, 1865.
5339. ii. CORA L., b. No. Chelmsford, Mass.; m. Nov. 27, 1895, Will O. Dodge, of New Boston, N. H.
5340. iii. LULU, b. Apr. 1, 1883.

3828. SAMUEL CHEEVER FISKE (Joshua, Henry, Henry, Nathan, Nathan, Nathan, Nathaniel, William, Robert, Simon, Simon, William, Symond), b. Sturbridge. Mass., Apr. 12, 1804; m. Celestine Winslow Bottom, b. Aug. 25, 1805; d. 1873. He abandoned the old homestead farm to read law in the office of F. W. Bottom in Southbridge, and finally married his daughter. He gave that up to engage in cotton spinning in Southbridge, having made improvements in the water privilege on Quinebaug River, but he sought new fields and went to New York City and Brooklyn. For many years he was the only Fiske in the New York directory where he lived, until he engaged in the iron business in Pennsylvania. He finally settled in New York about 1849, and remained until he moved to New Jersey, where he died as I have recorded. He was a man of wonderful constitution and energy and succumbed at last to Bright's disease, from which he suffered for some years. He d. Plainfield, N. J., in 1874; res. Sturbridge, Mass., and Plainfield. N. J.

  5341. i. FREDERICK B., b. Aug. 25, 1830; m. Mary E. Wilson.
  5342. ii. ALEXANDER P., b. Nov. 6, 1833; unm.; res. New York City, N. Y., Gilsey House. He joined Fifty-seventh New York Volunteers as adjutant; was wounded at Fair Oaks and disqualified for field service. He was then on General Sumner's staff. Subsequently he was on the staff of General Dix, General Hooker and some others. He has been in business in New York since leaving the service, living at Gilsey House, N. Y., for twenty-five years consecutively; never married.
  5343. iii. EDWARD HENRY, b. 1837; d. 1838.
  5344. iv. ISABELLA CELESTINE, b. 1844; d. 1847.

  3830. CARLISLE ALANCENT FISK (Elias, Simeon, Henry, Nathan, Nathan, Nathan, Nathaniel, William, Robert, Simon, Simon, William, Symond), b. Providence, R. I., Feb. 7, 1808; m. at No. Providence, R. I., May 24, 1829. Eliza Ann Davis, b. Jan. 28, 1806; d. Dec. 18, 1848; m. 2d, 1851, Caroline M. Ely, d. ———. He was born in Rhode Island, but while a young man was employed in Globe Village in the Fisk mills there. He was employed in various places in Massachusetts and Connecticut and while living in Long Meadow formed a partnership with his brother-in-law, under the firm name of Fisk & Royce, and engaged in the manufacture of repeating rifles, about the first ever made. The partnership was dissolved soon after and Mr. Fisk removed to Pleasant Valley, Conn., where with his wife he joined the Methodist Episcopal Church. He followed his trade and for some time was engaged in Colt's Armory. Soon after the death of his wife in 1848 he moved to Springfield, Mass., and was employed in the United States Armory. He ever after resided in Springfield. He was a very industrious and temperate man all his life; well educated; honest and upright in his dealings, and kept well posted on all matters of the day, especially mechanics; he being a good natural mechanic from the start was therefore a good workman and toolmaker, and held some responsible positions. He had a large job on barrels at Colt's Armory; was foreman of Springfield Arms Company; superintendent of Young & Leavitt's Pistol Works, and other positions. He was a remarkably hearty and healthy man, never sick to be laid up only at his last sickness. He d. Sept. 16, 1865; res. Pleasant Valley, Conn., and Springfield, Mass.

  5345. i. ALONZO W., b. Mar. 16, 1831; m. Almira A. Stoddard and Isabelle Stires.
  5346. ii. MELISSA WILDER, b. Feb. 25, 1834; m. Philo S. Fuller; d. May 14, 1894, leaving three daughters.
  5347. iii. ELLEN MARIAH, b. Jan. 14, 1838; m. C. W. Newton. They have one son, C. P., who is m., and res. New York City. The parents res. 1202 W. Fayette St., Baltimore, Md.
  5348. iv. WILBUR D., b. June 7, 1841; m. Agnes H. Andrews.
  5349. v. EMILY ROYCE, b. Oct. 14, 1843; m. C. W. Taylor and R. B. Andrews. She had one son; res. 1202 W. Fayette St., Baltimore, Md.
  5350. vi. NETTIE E., b. Aug. 16, 1852; m. Mar. 17, 1881, Thos. T. Palsgrove, Ogden, Utah. Ch.: Harry, Mary and Mabel. He was b. Oct. 19, 1853.

  3834. DR. HENRY MORTIMER FISKE (Henry, David, Henry, Nathan, Nathan, Nathan, Nathaniel, William, Robert, Simon, Simon, William, Symond), b.

Dec. 10, 1823, Boston, Mass.; m. Nov. 30, 1845, Rosette Smith, b. Jan. 6, 1828. Dr. and Mrs. Fiske were married in Illinois in 1845, and six years later removed to California, where they have since resided, the past twenty-five years having been spent in San Francisco. He settled at Sutter Creek, where he was engaged in mining, and was elected State Senator from that district. From there he went to Woodland. He was instrumental in the erection of the Hesperian College there. The last twenty years he has resided in San Francisco, in which place he commanded the respect and esteem of every one familiar with his eventful career, being a member of the board of health and school director. The doctor began the practice of medicine when he was 18 years of age. For a long time he was employed by the Southern Pacific Railroad Company in that capacity. The couple recently celebrated their golden wedding. He d. in 1896; res. San Francisco, Cal., 2100 Bush St.

5351. i.   WILLIAM H., b. Apr. 20, 1860; m. Lydia May Warden.
5352. ii. SOPHIA E., b. Nov. 26, 1846; m. Benjamin Peart; res. Woodland, Cal. Ch.: Roscoe; Lloyd; Hartly; Norman; Rymond; Madaline; Sterling.
5353. iii. HELEN SUSAN, b. Jan. 6, 1850; m. John A. Faull; res. St. Helena, Cal. He is a miner. Ch.: Mary A.; John A.; Rose and Sophia, twins; Henry Fiske.

3836. FRANCIS LYMAN FISKE (Henry, David, Henry, Nathan, Nathan, Nathan, Nathaniel, William, Robert, Simon, Simon, William, Symond), b. Norwich, Conn., Aug. 8, 1832; m. Feb. 18, 1861, Eliza Ann Freeman, b. Mar. 25, 1833. He was born in Norwich, Conn., and when four years of age moved with his parents to Jackson, Mich. Later he returned east and for some time was in Wrentham and Sturbridge, and afterward at Kingston, Mass. At each of these places he learned something of the business methods which, in a few years, were to prove so beneficial to him in his business career. Finding but few chances open to him in the east, he decided to go west again. For a few years he was in Madison, Ind., later at Aurora, Ill., finally locating in Ottawa, in the same State, in 1856. There he has resided for nearly half a century, honored and respected by the entire community. He has been in the manufacturing business; also merchant tailor. In 1889 he visited California, and with his family traveled over the Continent of Europe, sojourned at Rome, Naples, Alexandria and Cairo. Took a trip up the Suez Canal. In 1892, with his family, he took a trip around the world, spending some time in the Sandwich Islands, in Japan, Yokohama, Canton, St. Petersburg, Spain, and other countries. He has never held public office but once, which he considers amply sufficient; res. Ottawa, Ill.

5354. i.   ALICE MARY, b. Jan. 30, 1862.
5355. ii. SARAH HELEN, b. Apr. 11, 1864.

3839. GEORGE DIXON FISKE (Henry, David, Henry, Nathan, Nathan, Nathan, Nathaniel, William, Robert, Simon, Simon, William, Symond), b. Fiskdale, Mass., July 31, 1827; m. in Boston, July 26, 1851, Elizabeth Chadbourne Loring, b. at No. Yarmouth, Me., July 12, 1826; d. Apr. 13, 1890. He is in the real estate business; res. Woodland, Cal.

5356. i.   HARRY W., b. May 28, 1852; m. Frances E. Warden.
5357. ii. GEO. D., b. Mar. 25, 1855; m. Oct. 8, 1884, Sophia Hazelton; res. Sanger, Cal.

3850. GEORGE JENKS FISKE (Josiah J., David, Henry, Nathan, Nathan, Nathan, Nathaniel, William, Robert, Simon, Simon, William, Symond), b. Wrentham, Mass., Aug. 4, 1829; m. in Boston, Aug. 15, 1866, Frances L. Beebe, dau. of James M., of Boston. She d. there, Feb. 25, 1890. He went into business early in life and later was well known as a member of the Boston firm of James M. Beebe & Co., contributing largely, by his skill and energy, in the management of the business, to the great success of that firm. George died at Nice, in France, in 1868, leaving a widow, Frances Lathrop, who was the daughter of James M. Beebe, Boston. He combined great business ability with the strictest integrity and a kindly disposition, which greatly endeared him to those who knew him. He d. in Nice, France, Dec. 4, 1868; res. Boston, Mass.

5358. i.   GEORGE S., b. Paris, France, May 19, 1867; res. 261 Clarendon St., Boston.

5359. ii. ESTHER L., b. Nice, France, Apr. 18, 1868; m. at Falmouth, Mass., Gardiner G. Hammond, b. Sept. 28, 1859. Ch.: 1, Frances L., b. Apr. 18, 1894. 2, Gardiner G. (3rd.), Apr. 15, 1895.

3860. LIBERTY BATES FISKE (Silas, Daniel, Daniel, Nathan, Nathan, Nathaniel, William, Robert, Simon, Simon, William, Symond), b. Sullivan, N. Y., Mar. 14, 1818; m. Mar. 6, 1848, Amy Ann Foster, b. Aug. 20, 1831; d. Apr. 11, 1861;

LIBERTY BATES FISKE.

m. 2d, Jan. 4, 1864, Nancy B. Foster, b. Sept. 25, 1833; d. June 14, 1874. He is a farmer. He has a cow bell stamped "D. Fiske, 1743." He was brought up on a farm of thirty acres, in New York, till he was 20 years of age, then left for Wisconsin; worked there three years by the month; bought a yoke of oxen; took a pre-emption on 160 acres of land for one year, and hired the money to pay for it at 25 per cent. Added sixty-three acres to it, built two large barns and one on it yet. Kept bachelor's hall for three years. Married a young wife; raised three children, two boys and a girl. The two boys are living each on a farm, one on the homestead; the other has 163 acres in Richland Co., Wis. His daughter and youngest boy were playing around a burning stump, when she was 6 years old; she stooped down to pick up some brush with her back to the fire, her clothes caught fire and she ran about five rods before her father reached her. He threw her on the ground, spread his coat over her, and extinguished the fire; she lived thirteen hours, and died, having suffered considerably; res, Burlington, Wis.

5360. i. GEORGE W., b. Dec. 10, 1848; m. Nov. 18, 1875; res. Burlington, Wis.
5361. ii. MELVILLE F., b. Jan. 25, 1851; m. Nellie A. Pratt.
5362. iii. MARIETTA, b. June 6, 1853; d. Nov. 4, 1859.
5363. iv. JOHN ELLSWORTH, b. ———; d. in infancy.

3861. LUCIUS WRIGHT FISKE (Silas, Daniel, Daniel, Nathan, Nathan, Nathan, Nathaniel, William, Robert, Simon, Simon, William, Symond), b. Sullivan, N. Y., July 29, 1816; m. Nov. 30, 1847, Mary Alling, b. Jan. 8, 1821. He was a farmer. He d. Aug. 11, 1890; res. Smyrna, N. Y., and Darien, Wis.
5364. i. GEO. ALLING, b. Oct. 16, 1848; m. Elizabeth E. DeWolf.
5365. ii. SARAH ELIZA, b. Mar. 12, 1850; unm.; res. D.
5366. iii. SILAS WRIGHT, b. Mar. 9, 1852; m. Sarah Jane Seaver.
5367. iv. HENRY NEWELL, b. Mar. 10, 1854; m. Georgia T. Matteson.
5368. v. EDGAR DANIEL, b. Oct. 5, 1856; m. Mary H. Hunter.
5369. vi. CHARLES CLARENCE, b. Jan. 16, 1859; m. Carrie Rinck.
5370. vii. STELLA ANDERSON, b. Oct. 24, 1862; unm.; res. Beaver Dam, Wis.

3874. JOHN P. FISKE (John, Daniel, Daniel, Nathan, Nathan, Nathan, Nathaniel, William, Robert, Simon, Simon, William, Symond), b. Cazenovia, N. Y., Sept. 2, 1830; m. at Detroit, June 16, 1858, Lucy A. Fuller, b. July 15, 1836. He is a merchant; res. Detroit, Mich., 112 Adelaide St., s. p.

3875. EDWIN D. FISKE (John, Daniel, Daniel, Nathan, Nathan, Nathan, Nathaniel, William, Robert, Simon, Simon, William, Symond), b. Nov. 8, 1835; m. ——— ———. He d. June 7, 1873.
5371. i. JULIA F., b. Oct. 7, 1867; m. ——— Fox; res. Canandaigua, N. Y.

LOUIS SAMUEL FISKE.

3882. LOUIS SAMUEL FISKE (Samuel L., Samuel, Daniel, Nathan, Nathan, Nathan, Nathaniel, William, Robert, Simon, Simon, William, Symond), b. Southbridge, Mass., Feb. 15, 1844; m. Apr. 24, 1883, Mary Dobson, b. Dec. 22, 1855; d. Feb. 28, 1886; m. 2d, May 10, 1894, Katherine Holmes Tucker. Louis Samuel Fiske was son of Samuel Lyon Fiske and Maria Louise Hodges Fiske. Was fitted for Harvard College, but deciding that he would not pursue a professional life, determined upon a practical textile education and learned woolen manufacturing. A desire for travel and adventure led him to associate himself with the wool trade in Philadelphia, which offered opportunity for satisfying these inclinations. Developing a talent for the business, he formed, together with John Dobson and Frank H. Keen, the wool house of Louis S. Fiske & Co., which is a most prominent, successful and progressive firm. Is a member of prominent associations, including Board of Trade, Trades League, Union League, New England Society and Radnor Hunt. A lover of outdoor sports and horses. Republican to the backbone. Never had but one ambition, and that was to be a merchant in the highest sense of the word, and establish an honorable reputation and name the world over, and he has succeeded; res. Philadelphia, Pa; office add. 34 So. Front St.

    5372. i. SARAH DOBSON, b. Feb. 11, 1886.

3883. SAMUEL FISK (William, William, William, William, Nathan, Nathaniel, William, Robert, Simon, Simon, William, Symond), b. Cayuga Co., N. Y., Sept. 4, 1806; m. July 16, 1834, Elvira Campbell, b. Feb. 17, 1815; d. Sept. 30, 1845. He was a farmer. He d. Apr. 1, 1892; res. Patriot, Ind.

    5373. i. MARY FRANCES, b. May 1, 1835; d. Aug. 13, 1841.
    5374. ii. ALONZO, b. Aug. 11, 1836; m. Clara T. Baker.
    5375. iii. ALETHIA, b. Sept. 22, 1838; m. Sept. 2, 1858, —— Hickman; res. P.

3884. NELSON FISK (William, William, William, William, Nathan, Nathaniel, William, Robert, Simon, Simon, William, Symond), b. Cayuga Co., N. Y., Oct. 19, 1814; m. May 10, 1839, Francina Baker, b. 1820; d. 1855; m. 2d, Mar. 10, 1862, Julia A. Hannah, b. Oct. 2, 1829. He is a farmer; res. Rising Sun, Ind.

    5376. i. SAMUEL, b. ——; m. and res. R. S. Two ch.
    5377. ii. BROWER, b. ——; m. and res. Madison Co., Ind. One son.
    5378. iii. MAHLON D., b. ——; m. and res. Aurora, Ind.
    5379. iv. CORDELIA, b. ——; d. young.
    5380. v. SILAS B., b. ——; m. and res. Oklahoma: has six children.
    5381. vi. LAURA B., b. ——; m. D. L. Wade; two daus. res. R. S.
    5382. vii. WILLIAM, b. ——; d. young.
    5383. viii. NELSON, b. Dec. 17, 1862; d. young.
    5384. ix. MALVIN W., b. July 14, 1864; res. R. S.
    5385. x. LIBBIE A., b. Aug. 28, 1867; res. R. S.
    5386. xi. ARTHUR M., b. Jan. 7, 1870; res. R. S.

3885. HIRAM FISK (William, William, William, William, Nathan, Nathaniel, William, Robert, Simon, Simon, William, Symond), b. Cayuga Co., N. Y., Oct. 8, 1816; m. Feb. 23, 1843, Cynthia Griswold, b. Jan. 31, 1825. He is a farmer; res. Rising Sun, Ind.

    5387. i. WILLIAM, b. ——.   5390. iv. THOMAS, b. ——.
    5388. ii. ALICE, b. ——.   5391. v. LUELLA, b. ——.
    5389. iii. IDA, b. ——.   5392. vi. CHARLES, b. ——.

3886. NATHANIEL FISK (William, William, William, William, Nathan, Nathaniel, William, Robert, Simon, Simon, William, Symond), b. Genoa, Cayuga Co., N. Y., June 30, 1810; m. in Florence, Ind., 1855, Icephena Morris, b. June 18, 1831; d. 1889. He was a farmer; res. Madison, Ind., 507 E. Main St.

    5393. i. LUCY MYRTLE, b. Jan. 7, 1874.
    5394. ii. CHRISTENY, b. June 8, 1857.
    5395. iii. SARAH ELLEN, b. July 14, 1859.
    5396. iv. DANIEL, b. Oct. 27, 1861; d. Aug. 24, 1868.
    5397. v. EMILY, b. Jan. 13, 1863; d. Aug. 13, 1868.
    5398. vi. INFANT, b. Aug. 26, 1865; d. same day.
    5399. vii. INFANT, b. Oct. 10, 1866; d. same day.

5400. viii. NELSON, b. Jan. 10, 1868.
5401. ix. BENJ. F., b. Jan. 4, 1870.

3887. DAVID FISK (William, William, William, William, Nathan, Nathaniel, William, Robert, Simon, Simon, William, Symond), b. Cayuga County, N. Y., Aug. 5, 1804; m. Prilla Humphrey.
 5402. i. HULDAH, b. ———; m. ——— Bonnell; res. Patriot, Ind.
 5403. ii. PAULINA, b. ———.
 5404. iii. ONE OTHER CHILD.

3894-2. ALFRED WINTER FISK (Sylvanus, William, William, William, Nathan, Nathan, Nathaniel, William, Robert, Simon, Simon, William, Symond), b. Brownsville, N. Y., Apr. 25, 1802; m. Oct. 3, 1823, Sally Gillett, b. Dec. 30, 1803; d. Feb. 9, 1836; m. 2d, Apr. 3, 1836, Abigail Randall. A. W. Fisk was born in Brownsville, Jefferson County, N. Y. He was the second son in a list of eight brothers. At an early age he went with his father, Sylvanus Fisk, to Genesee County, N. Y. While a boy he learned the carpenter and joiner's trade but did not work at it more than a small portion of his early manhood. At the age of 19 he settled on a portion of what was known as the Poultney heirs' tract of land in the town of Stafford; married at 21 and lived on it or another tract adjoining which he came in possession of later, all his remaining days. Early he made an agreement—articled—for his holdings at $5 per acre, and for more than twenty years he labored under that article, paying six per cent. compound interest. In the meantime he had cleared it and so improved it that it would readily sell at about $100 per acre; besides he had cared well for his family and indulged his hospitality and generosity largely. He refused $100 per acre for his farm by telling the man who offered it, "If it is worth that to you it is to me. I made it to live on and die on," and he did, at the age of 86 years. He d. in 1888; res. Stafford, N. Y.
 5404-1. i. WALLACE, b. ———; res. So. Byron, N. Y.
 5404-2. ii. LOVELL W., b. May 17, 1829; m. Julia K. Simonds.
 5404-3. iii. FRANKLIN, b. ———; served as Lieutenant in company of sappers and miners from Michigan three years and was honorably discharged.
 5404-4. iv. MURRAY, b. ———. He served in the federal army two years in a company of cavalry and received an honorable discharge.

3894-3. HENRY ALVA FISKE (Sylvanus, William, William, William, Nathan, Nathan, Nathaniel, William, Robert, Simon, Simon, William, Symond), b. Watertown, N. Y., Sept. 5, 1803; m. Nov. 23, 1825, Eliza Parker, b. Dec. 10, 1810; d. Jan. 20, 1874. He was a farmer. He d. Sept. 22, 1860; res. Stafford, N. Y.
 5404-5. i. SAMANTHA, b. Sept. 5, 1831.
 5404-6. ii. SYLVANUS W., b. Oct. 8, 1829; m. Genette Beswick.
 5404-7. iii. HENRIETTA, b. July 21, 1834; d. Feb. 25, 1845.
 5404-8. iv. EARLE I., b. Nov. 19, 1839; m. C——— C. Strong.
 5404-9. v. WILBER, b. May 5, 1843; d. Feb. 24, 1846.
 5404-10. vi. WILLIS, b. May 25, 1850; m. Maggie Lapp; res. 60 Fourth St., Rochester, N. Y.

3894-4. JESSE HARTWELL FISKE (Sylvanus, William, William, William, Nathan, Nathan, Nathaniel, William, Robert, Simon, Simon, William, Symond), b. Watertown, N. Y., Apr. 20, 1804; m. Jan. 10, 1829, Amanda Parker, b Apr. 17, 1813; she res. 317 No. Emporia Ave., Wichita, Kan. He was a farmer and d. in Spring Valley, Wis. He d. July, 1871; res. Stafford, N. Y.
 5404-11. i. AMANDA MALVINA, b. Nov. 29, 1830.
 5404-12. ii. ANN JANE, b. Apr. 3, 1832.
 5404-13. iii. HARRIETT ELIZABETH, b. June 13, 1834.
 5404-14. iv. ADELINE ELIZA, b. Mar. 3, 1837.
 5404-15. v. JESSE HARMON, b. Aug. 1, 1839.
 5404-16. vi. WYMAN PARKER, b. Feb. 23, 1842; m. Amy B. Stafford and Cora M. Bachelder.
 5404-17. vii. HELEN MARIA, b. Sept. 23, 1845.

3894-7. AMOS HOW FISK (Sylvanus, William, William, William, Nathan, Nathan, Nathaniel, William, Robert, Simon, Simon, William, Symond), b. Batavia,

N. Y., in 1812; m. there Nancy A. Gillett. He was a successful farmer. He d. Sept. 5, 1866; res. Batavia, N. Y., and Sturgis, Mich.

5404-18. ii. CHAUNCEY E., b. Jan. 21, 1847; m. Agnes Akey.

5404-19. i. ORLANDO P., b. ———. He was a lawyer in New York City.

5404-20. iii. THREE OTHER SONS.

3899. JOHN FISK (Rufus, Rufus, Stephen, William, Nathan, Nathan, Nathaniel, William, Robert, Simon, Simon, William, Symond), b. New Bethel, Conn., Feb. 9, 1799; m. in Connecticut, Mar. 14, 1820, Anna Osborn Stillman, b. Nov. 3, 1809; d. Mar. 31, 1864. John Fisk was in his youth a comb maker by trade, and he often mentioned the fact that he was a playfellow of P. T. Barnum, probably at New Bethel, where there is a comb factory still. He came west and settled in Manchester Township, Washtenaw County, in Michigan, probably about 1830, and engaged in farming. He had a large family of children. Although a mechanic and farmer, was a man of extended information, due to extensive reading; he was of irreproachable character, and although without means was highly respected in his neighborhood. He d. July 25, 1884; res. Manchester, Mich.

5405. i. HENRY C., b. 1823; m. Sarah J. Graves.

5406. ii. ELI, b. May 19, 1836; m. Jane Dorr.

5407. iii. GEORGE L., b. ———.

5408. iv. SUSAN, b. in 1823; m. Oct. 24, 1843, Jasper Davenport; res. Vassar, Mich. He was b. May 28, 1824; d. Oct. 2, 1890. Ch.: Annette, daughter of Jasper and Susan Davenport, b. Sept. 30, 1845; m. Stephen C. Wilcox, Oct. 21, 1867; d. Oct. 22, 1878. Cassius M. Davenport, son of Susan and Jasper Davenport, b. June 2, 1847.

5409. v. ALMIRA, b. ———; res. Clinton, Mich.

5410. vi. RUSSELL, b. Murphy's Center, Mich.

3907. JAMES M. FISKE (Rufus, Rufus, Stephen, William, Nathan, Nathan, Nathaniel, William, Robert, Simon, Simon, William, Symond), b. July 15, 1815, in Willington, Conn.; m. there July 19, 1835, Mary Ann Hinman, b. Aug. 6, 1818. He d. Dec. 7, 1843; res. Stafford Springs, Conn.

5411. i. MARCUS B., b. Apr. 4, 1838; m. Emma F. Howland.

5412. ii. HARRIET E., b. Nov. 18, 1841; d. Oct. 7, 1858.

3908. DR. MARCUS LYON FISKE (Rufus, Rufus, Stephen, William, Nathan, Nathan, Nathaniel, William, Robert, Simon, Simon, William, Symond), b. Willington, Conn., Dec. 16, 1817; m. Dec. 5, 1845, Frances Ann Tinker, of Vernon, Conn., b. Mar. 27, 1815; d. Oct. 20, 1853; m. 2d, May 14, 1856, Mrs. Emeline Lucretia Frazier, b. Aug. 1, 1824, dau. of Jos. and Eliza (Meigs) Frazier, of Norwich, Conn.; no issue. Dr. Fiske was born in Willington, Conn.; was educated in the public schools, the old fashioned New England "academies," and by private tuition; studied medicine at the Berkshire Medical College, Pittsfield, Mass., and at the Pennsylvania Medical College, Philadelphia, from which he received the degree of M. D., in 1842. He was a private student of Dr. George McClellan (founder of both the Jefferson and Pennsylvania Medical Colleges, Philadelphia, who was the father of Gen. G. B. McClellan). He settled in East Windsor, Conn., where he died Apr. 2, 1883. He received the honorary degree of M. A. from Trinity College, Hartford, in 1867. He was for many years, until his death, a zealous and devoted member of "that portion of the Catholic Church known in law as the Protestant Episcopal Church in the United States of America." Dr. Fiske was one who in a laborious and useful life reflected honor upon the family to which he belonged. He d. Apr. 2, 1883; res. East Windsor, Conn.

5413. i. LEBBEUS TINKER, b. Feb. 19, 1847; d. in Hartford, Conn., Mar. 11, 1864; sophomore in Trinity.

5414. ii. GEO. McC., b. Oct. 21, 1850; m. Mary G. Walker.

5415. iii. ANNA FRANCES, b. May, 1852; res. Warehouse Point, Conn.

3924. SOLON FISK (Leonard, Stephen, Stephen, William, Nathan, Nathan, Nathaniel, William, Robert, Simon, Simon, William, Symond), b. Jan. 12, 1826, Albany. Vt.; m. Apr. 18, 1848, Josephine K. Griffin, b. Apr. 18, 1826; d. 1876; m.

33

SOLON FISK.

2d, Apr. 10, 1878, Ellen M. Frink, b. Apr. 12, 1850, in Urbana, Ohio. Solon Fisk was born in Albany, Orleans County, Vt. The first twenty years were spent in Vermont, living in Albany, Brookfield, Bethel (with his grandfather), Montpelier, Berlin, Royalton, Hancock and Castleton; taught school four successive winters, beginning with the winter of 1842-43. At the close of his fourth school, in the spring of 1846, he went to Massachusetts, learned trade of machinist, working in Lowell, Boston, Annam and Charlestown, mostly on locomotive engines. In 1849 he removed to Concord, N. H., working as machinist for Northern Railroad Company. In 1850 he became a locomotive engineer, and as such helped to build the Vermont & Canada Railroad, living in Milton and St. Albans, on the line of that road. In 1851 and 1852 he lived in Burlington, Vt., engineer of all passenger trains between Burlington and Essex Junction, six miles out. In 1853 he was employed on new locomotive engines by the Amoskeag Manufacturing Company, in Manchester, N. H. In 1854 went to Zanesville, Ohio, and was employed there for four years in various capacities on Central Ohio Railroad, Columbus to Bellaire, as assistant master of machinery (at Bellaire), conductor, engineer, and finally contractor, to furnish this Central Ohio Railroad with wood, at that time used exclusively as fuel for locomotives, which contract he held for two years (and more). Then quitting railroading forever, as he thought, he read law, and was admitted to practice at Newark, Ohio, but belonged to the bar of Zanesville; followed this and the mining of coal, in which he was interested, through the war, but having a hankering for running a locomotive again, took a position offered him in 1865 on the Chicago & Alton Railroad, living for two years in Alton, the rest of the time in Bloomington. He continued at this business much longer than he designed to. In Nov., 1876, he quit it and has since then lived retired, in Bloomington; res. Bloomington, Ill.

    5416. i.   JOHN LEONARD, b. Feb. 18, 1879.
    5417. ii.   ROBERT SOLON, b. Dec. 31, 1881.
    5418. iii. HERMAN CHARLES, b. Oct. 23, 1882.
    5419. iv. HELEN AMELIA, b. Oct. 4, 1885.
    5420. v.   ANOTHER SON died in infancy.

    3930. EDGAR H. FISKE (Thomas J., Stephen, Stephen, William, Nathan, Nathan, Nathaniel, William, Robert, Simon, Simon, William, Symond), b. Bethel, Vt., Aug. 30, 1838; m. Aug. 31, 1862, Dannie L. Gage, b. Apr. 30, 1844. He is a blacksmith by trade and a farmer; res. Weybridge, Vt.

    5421. i.   INEZ D., b. Nov. 30, 1871; res. Vergennes, Vt.
    5422. ii. CLYDE E., b. Jan. 16, 1881; res. W.

    3937. JOHN COLT FISK (James, Stephen, Stephen, William, Nathan, Nathan, Nathaniel, William, Robert, Simon, Simon, William, Symond), b. Brookfield, Vt., Sept. 13, 1825; m. Jan. 19, 1853, Sarah M. Hubbard, of No. Charlestown, N. H. He d. Feb. 12, 1895; res. Stewart's Point, Cal

    5423. i.   CHARLES, b. ———; res. Stewart's Point, Cal.
    5423¼. ii. GEORGE.
    5423⅓.iii. EUGENE.
    5423½. iv. FRED.
    5423¾. v. WALTER.

3939. ANDREW JEFFERSON FISK (James, Stephen, Stephen, William, Nathan, Nathan, Nathaniel, William, Robert, Simon, Simon, William, Symond), b. Brookfield, Vt., Mar. 8, 1832; m. 1871. He d. Aug. 4, 1874; res. Stewart's Point, Cal.

5430. i. FRANK, b. ———.

3940. JAMES H. FISK (James, Stephen, Stephen, William, Nathan, Nathan, Nathaniel, William, Robert, Simon, Simon, William, Symond), b. Brookfield, Vt., Apr. 12, 1834; m. at Hancock, Vt., Mar. 26, 1868, Mary Jane Darling, of Hancock, b. Apr. 10, 1835. James H. Fisk, son of James and Eliza Colt Fisk, was born at Brookfield, Vt. His early education was received at the common schools and later at Bell's Commercial College, Chicago, Ill. In 1853 he went to California, where for three years he was engaged in gold mining. In 1856 located in Chicago, remaining here until 1860; from this time on until 1866 he was manufacturing lumber in Colorado and in Montana. Returning to Chicago, he engaged in the sporting goods business and has continued in this line ever since, a period of over thirty years, down to the present, 1896; res. 2977 South Park Ave., Chicago, Ill.

JAMES H. FISK.

5431. i. NELLIE DARLING, b. Jan. 18, 1869.
5432. ii. BERTHA ISABELLE, b. Oct. 31, 1873.
5433. iii. FRED DARLING, b. Mar. 20, 1875.

3950. MOSES FISK (Moses, Josiah, Nathan, William, Nathan, Nathan, Nathaniel, William, Robert, Simon, Simon, William, Symond), b. West Chesterfield, Mass., Nov. 11, 1804; m. Oct. 6, 1829, Lucretia S. Prentice, b. Oct. 10, 1806; d. Sept. 2, 1836; m. 2d, Apr. 27, 1837, Lornithia Pearl, of Chesterfield, Mass., b. Feb., 1809; d. Feb., 1864; m. 3d, Mrs. Stanton, who d. s. p. He was a hatter by trade and worked in West Chesterfield, Mass., married and went to live on his father's farm in Worthington where three of his children were born. His wife was a very large woman, weighed over 200 pounds; she was taken ill one day and died the next. A few days later Mr. Fisk had the misfortune to lose the sight of one of his eyes. He married a second time and moved to Chesterfield on his father's farm in 1851, having purchased the property of the other heirs. Later he moved to Williamsburg, married a third wife, and moved to near Thompsonville, Conn., where he died. He d. in Suffield, Conn., in Dec., 1875; res. Chesterfield and Worthington, Mass., and Thompsonville, Conn.

5434. i. FRANKLIN COLLINS, b. Sept. 22, 1830; m. Amelia Pierce.
5435. ii. MILTON MOSES, b. May 1, 1833; m. Maretta M. Miles.
5436. iii. LUCRETIA TERZAH, b. Oct. 16, 1835; m. Nov. 18, 1858, Lewis Guilford; res. Williamsburg, Mass. He was b. May 28, 1835; is a farmer. Ch.: Nellie Ann, b. May 21, 1863; m. June 18, 1879, Thomas Culver; add. Williamsburg, Mass. Freddie Lewis, b. Mar. 2, 1867; m. Aug. 27, 1893, Harriet Frost, b. Apr. 28, 1867; add. Williamsburg, Mass.
5437. iv. JAMES JOSIAH, b. Jan. 17, 1839; m. Fanny S. Harris.
5438. v. HARRIET AMANDA, b. Jan., 1841; m. Apr. 20, 1859, Andrew Guilford. She d. Sept., 1893, leaving four children.

3954. BUSHROD WASHINGTON FISK (Josiah, Josiah, Nathan, William, Nathan, Nathan, Nathaniel, William, Robert, Simon, Simon, William, Symond), b. Pottsdam, N. Y., Apr. 7, 1807; m. Mar. 30, 1831, at Great Barrington, Mass., Relief Holmes, b. Oct. 4, 1813. He was a farmer. He d. Jan. 31, 1890; res. Huntington, Mass.

5439. i.　HARRIETT O., b. Feb. 28, 1837; m. Nov. 18, 1861, Amos S. Cone; res. North Chester, Mass. He was b. Aug. 25, 1826; is a stone mason and farmer. She d. Feb. 22, 1896. Ch.: 1, Julia Nellie Powers, b. Sept. 27, 1862; m. Mar. 8, 1882; add. Worcester, Mass. 2, Clara Fidelia Hamilton, b. Sept. 10, 1865; m. Oct. 23, 1883; add. North Chester, Mass. 3, James William, b. Oct. 24, 1867; m. Feb. 22, 1891; add. West Worthington, Mass. 4, Frank Elvin, b. Feb. 17, 1870; unm.; add. Huntington, Mass. 5, George Marshall, b. Jan. 7, 1873; unm.; add. North Chester, Mass. 6, Willard Clayton, b. Aug. 10, 1874; d. Apr. 20, 1880. 7, Leroy Clifford, b. Feb. 1, 1877; unm.; add. North Chester, Mass.

5440. ii.　MARSHALL O., b. Feb. 9, 1839; m. Sarah F. Sizer and Laura A. Stevens.

5441. iii.　SARAH M., b. June 9, 1840; m. Feb. 5, 1866, Emerson Torrey; res. Chesterfield, Mass; b. Jan. 28, 1834; d. Feb. 15, 1895. He was a farmer. Ch.: 1, George Torrey, b. May 14, 1866; m. Nov. 20, 1889. 2, Anna, b. Nov. 30, 1870. 3, Francis, b. Aug. 17, 1873. 4, Ellen, b. Oct. 26, 1875; d. Feb. 22, 1894. 5, Mrs. Ida Rhoades, b. Sept. 3, 1878; m. Nov. 20, 1895. All res. in Chesterfield, except Anna, who lives in Florence, Mass.

5442. iv.　NATHAN A., b. July 28, 1849; m. and res. Russell, Mass.

5443. v.　CLINTON E., b. Feb. 14, 1852; m. Ida M. Trask.

5444. vi.　LYDIA E., b. Sept. 19, 1855; m. ——— Fowler; res. Springfield, Mass.

5445. vii.　ISAAC H., b. Feb. 17, 1858; m. Fannie G. Reed.

5446. viii.　NOBLE B., b. Apr. 17, 1842; n. c. m.

5447. ix.　MARTHA E., b. Jan. 19, 1848; n. c. m.

5448. x.　JULIA P., b. Nov. 12, 1865.

5449. xi.　RUFUS H., b. May 31, 1844; m. Helen A. Bicknell.

5450. xii.　ANNE M., b. Apr. 8, 1846; d. May 13, 1849.

3956. RODNEY FISK (Josiah, Josiah, Nathan, William, Nathan, Nathan, Nathaniel, William, Robert, Simon, Simon, William, Symond), b. Canton, N. Y., Mar. 11, 1809; m. in Huntington, Mass., May 21, 1839, Mary C. Cady, b. Jan. 8, 1809; d. Dec. 2, 1872. Rodney Fisk was a man of considerable talent, with a large brain, strong will power, ambitious. Was able to accumulate quite a little property, which probably amounted to about fifteen or twenty thousand dollars. He was drowned when he was 64, about five or six months after his wife's death. She died of typhoid fever. He d. May 10, 1873; res. Huntington, Mass.

5451. i.　EDSON H., b. Jan. 31, 1841; m. 1857; res. Park House, Springfield, Mass.

5452. ii.　JASON H., b. Nov. 25, 1842; m. Julia A. Hunter and Augusta Elder.

5453. iii.　MONROE J., b. July 31, 1848; m., and d. s. p. Aug. 28, 1877. His wid. m. D. M. Place; res. Chicago, Ill.

5454. iv.　ELLEN M., b. Sept. 3, 1844; m. Feb. 24, 1866, Judson S. Sizer; res. Kearney, Neb. He was b. Mar. 7, 1842. Is a coal dealer. Ch.: 1, Lucy P., b. May 3, 1868; m. Howard J. Hull, 1884, Kearney, Neb. 2, Fred J., b. Mar. 10, 1871; m. Nov. 20, 1895, Ella Knapp, Kearney, Neb. 3, Maud E., b. Jan. 2, 1876; m. June 20, 1895, James M. Savage, Alliance, Neb. 4, Clarence, b. July 21, 1881, Kearney, Neb. 5, Myrtis E., b. Oct. 9, 1882, Kearney, Neb.

5455. v.　HARLO A., b. Nov. 19, 1850; m. Ella M. Higgins.

5456. vi.　ELIZA J., b. Mar. 27, 1853; m. Feb. 19, 1874, Dwight M. Smith; m. 2d, Feb. 2, 1882, John Parks; m. 3d, Oct. 7, 1882, J. C. Cooper; res. Chester, Mass.

5457. vii.　MYRON R., b. Sept. 8, 1846; m. Addie S. Elder.

3957. RALPH HALE FISK (Josiah, Josiah, Nathan, William, Nathan, Nathan, Nathaniel, William, Robert, Simon, Simon, William, Symond), b. ———; m. ——— ———; res. Mass.

    5458. i. LAURA, b. ———; m. ——— Pierce; res. Littleville, Mass.
    5459. ii. ARTHUR, b. ———.
    5460. iii. RALPH, b. ———; res. Littleville, Mass.

3959. REV. JOSIAH FISK (Nathan, Josiah, Nathan, William, Nathan, Nathan, Nathaniel, William, Robert, Simon, Simon, William, Symond), b. Penfield, N. Y., Nov. 12, 1812; m. at Austin, Tex., Aug. 10, 1848, Narcissa L. White; d. Mar. 30, 1858; m. 2d, Oct. 10, 1860, Vashti Harkness, b. Mar. 4, 1821. He was born in Penfield, N. Y., and worked on the farm until his father's death in 1826. After doing various kinds of farm work and attending the district school, he went to Massachusetts to live with his father's brother. He attended the Cummington Academy, and later taught school in Yates, N. Y. One of his brothers was attending Hanover College in Indiana, and desiring a better education availed himself of an invitation to go there to school. At the commencement exercises he was chosen one of the speakers. After graduation he taught school in Gallatin Co., Ky., for a year and also began the study of law. Going to Jacksonville, Ill., he studied law with Hon. Stephen A. Douglas, and was later admitted to the bar and to practice in all the courts of the State. He opened an office in Hillsboro in 1835 and was at once elected Justice of the Peace, and in 1838 he was elected Representative to the Legislature, serving in the last session ever held in the old State House in Vandalia and the first in the new State House in Springfield, the present capital. Usher F. Linder, the Attorney-General of Illinois, was indicted for assault with intent to commit murder and suspended from office, and he acted as Attorney-General until Linder was tried and acquitted and resumed the office. In the fall of 1845 he removed to Texas. In 1846 he enlisted and served as Corporal in the war against Mexico. At the close of the war he engaged in the practice of law and in locating and buying and selling land. He owned 2,000 acres of land in Austin, Tex. When the Civil War broke out he was opposed to secession, and was obliged to flee to save his life. His property, which was quite valuable, was confiscated, and his adventures which he experienced while escaping to the south were very thrilling. On arriving in New Orleans he began the practice of law and acted as District Attorney of Jefferson Parish.

He has always believed in the Methodist Church since he can remember. He was licensed as an exorter, then as a local preacher and next admitted into the Louisiana Conference with an understanding that his appointment should be only nominal, and that he should be allowed to continue the practice of law and preach wherever called upon without any expense to the church. When the Constitutional Convention met and elected their officers the question came up for electing a chaplain. Several of the most eminent preachers of the United States were in the city. The members were divided in their choice. Mr. Wickliff, a delegate, arose and moved that Mr. Fisk be elected chaplain, for he could make the best prayer of any preacher in the city. One delegate arose and said: "Mr. President, the gentleman has made a very bold assertion. I would like for him to prove it." Mr. Wickliff arose and stated "Mr. Fisk can make the shortest prayer of any of the preachers here." That settled the question, and he was unanimously elected. He had not named the office to any person. He continued to practice law during the week and to preach Sundays until 1881, when he removed to Council Bluffs, Ia.

A Chicago paper recently published this:

"Council Bluffs, Ia., March 5, 1896.—Josiah Fisk today received notification that his claim against the city of New Orleans had been settled, and he will receive about $4,000.

"Fisk was a law student in the office of Abraham Lincoln. President Grant appointed him District Attorney for one of the branches of the city of New Orleans in 1868, and he served through the trying days of reconstruction. He was in office ten years. The Ku-Klux-Klan was active in that locality, and Fisk was equally active in running it down. He was finally advised to leave town, but declined.

"Soon after a man who resembled Fisk in appearance was killed by the Kuklux, and Fisk had to leave. He subsequently sued the city for his salary. Every effort was made to evade payment. Fisk got judgment for $9,500, and finally settled for $4,000."

Res. 147 Benton St., Council Bluffs, Ia.

5461. i. GIDEON GREENLEAF, b. July 29, 1849; d. Mar. 10, 1874.
5462. ii. JOSIAH NATHANIEL, b. Dec. 2, 1852; d. June 26, 1872.
5463. iii. BURR, b. July 17, 1853; d. June 8, 1854.
5464. iv. MARY W., b. Mar. 28, 1854; d. Dec. 15, 1858.
5465. v. NARCISSA, b. Mar. 30, 1858; m. —— Derby; res. New Orleans.
5466. vi. WILBUR, b. Nov. 10, 1861; m. Caroline E. Gilmore.
5467. vii. IRENE REBECCA, b. Jan. 24, 1851; d. Aug. 27, 1854.

3960. JOSEPH FISK (Nathan, Josiah, Nathan, William, Nathan, Nathan, Nathaniel, William, Robert, Simon, Simon, William, Symond), b. Oct. 13. 1818, Penfield, N. Y.; m. May 26, 1853, Elizabeth H. Sibley, b. Nov. 20, 1833. He was a farmer. He d. July 11, 1895; res. Honeoye Falls, N. Y.

5468. i. FRANK S., b. Jan. 11, 1858; m. Elizabeth J. Dennis.
5469. ii. JENNIE C., b. Nov. 9, 1862; m. Mar. 31, 1881, Benton, Townsend; res. H. F. Ch.: 1, Fisk Augustus, b. Oct. 19, 1881.
5470. iii. DELLA A., b. Sept. 7, 1864; m. Jan. 28, 1882, Charles Pratt; res. W. Bloomfield. N. Y. Ch.: 1, Jennie H., b. Mar. 5, 1883. 2, Joseph D., b. June 12, 1884. 3, Lulu D., b. Dec. 27, 1885. 4, Harrie C., b. Feb. 15, 1887. 5, Ruth A., b. Jan. 27, 1895.

3961. JUDGE GREENLEAF FISK (Nathan, Josiah, Nathan, William, Nathan, Nathan, Nathaniel, William, Robert, Simon, Simon, William, Symond), b. Albany, N. Y., May 19, 1807; m. at Bastrop, Tex., Mary A. Manlove, dau. of Col. Manlove; m. 2d, at Bastrop, Mrs. Mary (Piper) Hawkins, b. Feb. 25, 1833. Judge Greenleaf Fisk was born in New York State. At the age of 20 he professed Christ and united with the Presbyterian Church, and began to study for the ministry. He pursued his studies so far as to take one year in Lanes Theological Seminary, at Cincinnati. Leaving there, he studied a short time at Hanover College, Ind. After a time he and a companion embarked in a skiff on the Ohio River, and started for the west. He came to Texas while it was under Mexican rule. He married at Bastrop, Mary A., daughter of Col. Manlove. When the war of Texas Independence broke out, he enlisted and served through the entire war. He was present at the battle of San Jacinto, Apr. 21, 1836. Returning to his home, he found that his wife had been compelled by the Mexicans to seek safety in eastern Texas. He at length found her, having a child nearly a year old, which he had never seen. He was a member of Congress under the Republic of Texas. He afterwards moved to Williamson county, where his wife died, and he married Mrs. Mary Hawkins. From 1838 and onward, he made several trips to Brown county, in the capacity of surveyor, on one of which trips he was captured by the Indians, but afterwards released. He located most of the land since owned by him, in Brown county. In 1860 he moved to Brown county, and camped on the site of his rock residence in town. When the county was organized, in 1861, he was elected County Judge, and subsequently filled the office of District Clerk; County Clerk, County Treasurer, and Justice of the Peace. Since that time he has been closely identified with all the interests of Brown county. In Dec., 1886, he united with the Presbyterian Church. By failing strength, he was compelled to take his bed, and after five months of confinement, he passed peacefully away. The funeral services were conducted at the Presbyterian Church. In accordance with proclamation of the Mayor, all business houses in town were closed, and the church was packed to its uttermost capacity. Seldom has been expressed such a general sense of bereavement as well as sympathy for the afflicted family. The deceased had seven children by his first wife, two of whom still live. He had eight children by his second wife, all of whom live. He lived to see three great-grandchildren. Thus has passed away another of the old land marks. He d. Jan. 26, 1888; res. Brownwood, Tex.

5471. i. WM. AUGUSTUS, b. Apr. 20, 1836; d. ——.
5472. ii. JAMES BARTHOLOMEW, b. Aug. 16, 1838; d. ——.
5473. iii. ANN ELIZABETH, b. Dec. 1, 1840; d. ——.
5474. iv. JOSIAH, b. Dec. 20, 1842; res. Liberty Hill, Tex.
5475. v. MARGARET JANE, b. Oct. 16, 1840; d. ——.

5476. vi. SARAH ANN, b. Dec. 25, 1848; d. ———.
5477. vii. MARY ELMIRA, b. Apr. 11, 1851; d. ———.
5478. viii. GREENLEAF, b. Feb. 14, 1858: m. Nannie Grogan.
5479. ix. CICERO, b. Feb. 3, 1861; d. Nov. 13, 1894.
5480. x. EMMA, b. Feb. 3, 1861; m. June 6, 1877, R. B. Willson. He was
b. Sept. 20, 1841; d. July 20, 1892; was an extensive stock
raiser, prominent citizen and ex-Sheriff of Brown county;
res. Brownwood, Tex. Ch.: 1, Irene, b. July 22, 1878. 2, Ger-
tie, b. May 4, 1880. 3, Calvin Suggs, b. Feb. 22, 1882. 4,
Greenleaf Fisk, b. Mar. 17, 1885. 5, Emma Mozelle, b. Feb.
26, 1887. 6, Robert B., b. June 1, 1889. 7, Mattie W., b.
Sept. 20, 1892.
5481. xi. HOSEA, b. Mar. 18, 1863.
5482. xii. NAOMI, b. May 11, 1865; m. Nov. 4, 1884.
5483. xiii. MATTIE, b. July 24, 1867; m. Aug. 4, 1886, William Hodd, b.
June 18, 1859. He is a contractor and builder; res. Brownwood, Tex. Ch.: 1, Jessie, b. Sept. 16, 1887; d. Oct. 17, 1892.
2, John, b. Mar. 30, 1889; d. Nov. 6, 1892. 3, Gertrude, b.
Dec. 9, 1891. 4, Ruth, b. Dec. 11, 1895.
5484. xiv. PHOEBE, b. Oct. 9, 1869; m. Nov. 17, 1890, George Miller, b.
July 29, 1852; res. Brownwood, Tex. Ch.: 1, Mary Greenleaf,
b. Sept. 1, 1891. 2, Lorena Mosell, b. July 15, 1895; Brownwood, Brown Co., Tex.
5485. xv. MILTON. b. Feb. 25, 1874; m. Sept. 15, 1895, Millie Godwin, b.
June 3, 1874. Is a farmer; res. Brownwood, Tex., s. p.

3962. ABRAM CANFIELD FISK (Nathan, Josiah, Nathan, William, Nathan, Nathan, Nathaniel, William, Robert, Simon, Simon, William, Symond), b.
Feb. 19, 1816, New York State: m. Catherine Smith, b. 1818; d. July 11. 1881; m.
2d, May 29, 1883, Eleanor J. Fisk (see). A. C. Fisk is a native of the State of New
York, born near Rochester; came to Branch Co., Mich., in 1835; settled in
Coldwater, and purchased part of his present farm in the same year. He has
devoted most of his time to stock raising, being the oldest horseman in the west,
and to him is due the honor of first introducing the fine horses that the State of
Michigan now boasts of. He is the owner of the celebrated Maple Park breeding
stable; res. Coldwater, Mich.
5486. i. SMITH WILBUR, b. Apr. 4, 1839; m. Mary W. Andrus.
5487. ii. FRANK A., b. Apr. 17, 1844; m. May 24, 1874, ——— ———;
res. Coldwater, Mich. Ch.: 1, Frank, b. Feb. 16, 1875. 2,
Fred, b. July 28, 1876. 3, Delora A. C., b. ———.
5488. iii. WILLIAM B., b. Aug. 3, 1853; m. Feb. 1, 1876, Alice J. Gregory;
res. Coldwater.
5489. iv. ABRAHAM C., b. Sept. 24, 1855; res. Chicago, Ill., No. Clark
St., unm.

3967. JOEL FISK (Nathan, Josiah, Nathan, William, Nathan, Nathan, Nathaniel, William, Robert, Simon, Simon, William, Symond), b. Oct. 7, 1805; m.
Sarah Crippen. He d. 1880: res. Coldwater, Mich.
5490. i. CANFIELD, b. ———; res. C.

3968. PHILANDER FISK (Nathan, Josiah, Nathan, William, Nathan, Nathan, Nathaniel, William, Robert, Simon, Simon, William, Symond), b. Jan. 15,
1809, in Penfield, N. Y.; m. there 1832, Sarah Van Scouton, b. 1811; d. Apr. 7,
1843. He was a farmer. He d. in 1849; res. Penfield, N. Y.
5491 i. JOSIAH GREENLEAF, b Apr. 12, 1840; m. June 22, 1864,
Sophia J. Burns, b. Jan. 3, 1840; is constable; res. Penfield, N.
Y., s. p.
5492. ii. RUTH, b. in 1833; d. 1848.
5493. iii. WM. L., b. 1835. He d. in 1873, and left one son, who died
in Sept., 1890.
5494. iv. JAMES BURR. b. 1837. He enlisted in the Civil War, and was
killed in battle.

3979. HENRY FISKE (Asa, Aaron, Asa, Nathaniel, Nathaniel, Nathan, Nathaniel, William, Robert, Simon, Simon, William, Symond), b. Chesterfield, N. H., Feb. 27, 1802; m. Mar. 4, 1830, Lucinda Keyes, b. Apr. 24, 1806; d. Feb. 3, 1848; m. 2d, May 4, 1848, Mrs. Dorothy B. (Keyes) Fiske, b. Oct. 23, 1815; d. July 13, 1870, in Peterboro, N. H. He was born in New Hampshire, on a farm, and always was a farmer, though he taught school for a time in his youth; he always thought he has disobeyed a "call" in not going into the ministry. His life was uneventful and hard. He was a stern Calvinistic Methodist, more religious than practical, always in poverty and debt, and brought up his family with too rigid strictness. Most of his native life was spent on the rocky farm in the White Mountain region. He d. Apr. 2, 1858; res. Whitefield, N. H.

    5495. vi.   AMOS KIDDER, b. May 12, 1842; m. Caroline Child.
    5496. i.   JENNETTE, b. Sept. 31, 1821; m. Jonathan Metcalf, Nov. 11, 1855, who d. New Orleans, Mar. 7, 1864. Ch.: 1, Esmeralda Lucinda, b. Sept. 12, 1858. 2, Leslie Henry, b. May 7, 1861. 3, Herman, b. Sept. 13, 1863; d. Sept. 22, 1865. She m. 2d, William Metcalf, Whitefield, Nov. 21, 1868; res. Fitchburg, Mass.
    5497. ii.   WILLIAM HENRY, b. Jan. 22, 1833; unm.; res. Oakland, Cal., 1860 William St.
    5498. iii.   WILBUR F., b. Sept. 10, 1834; m. Sarah M. Townsend.
    5499. iii½. LOUIS ANN, b. June 29, 1837; d. July 5, 1837.
    5500. iv.   JULIETTE L., b. June 22, 1838; m. Charles E. Henry; res. Cal.
    5501. v.   JOHN H., b. Sept. 12, 1840; d. unm., May 10, 18—.
    5502. vii. FRANCIS W., b. May 12, 1849; m. Mary Jane Yardly.
    5503. viii. LLEWELLYN EUGENE, b. Dec. 26, 1852; n. f. k.
    5504. ix.   LUCINDA L., b. Jan. 24, 1848; d. Mar. 31, 1848.

3981. HON. RALPH FISKE (Asa, Aaron, Asa, Nathaniel, Nathaniel, Nathan, Nathaniel, William, Robert, Simon, Simon, William, Symond), b. May 7, 1804; m. Apr. 8, 1832, Polly Abbott Walker; d. Mar. 5, 1862; m. 2d, June 5, 1872, Esther Ann (Turner) Hall, s. p. Ralph Fiske spent all his life after coming to manhood, in the village of Whitefield, and all the active part of it in trade. For many years he kept the only store in the place, and when railroads and the lumber business stimulated its growth, he continued for some time to be one of its leading men of business, and accumulated considerable property. He often acted as executor, administrator or trustee, and was prominent in the public affairs of the town, serving it several times in local office and the State Legislature. Generally known as the "Squire," he was held in high esteem for his practical capacity and unswerving integrity. He was prominently connected with the Methodist Church. The last ten or fifteen years of his life were spent in quiet leisure. Mr. Fiske ever took a lively interest in the progress of the town, and had the confidence of his fellow citizens to a marked degree, so in the conduct of public affairs his judgment always, and his services often, were sought and obtained when the political party with which he was conscientiously allied was in the majority, and from 1836, the date of the first election to public service, for twenty-five years no name appears oftener in the civil list of the town than Ralph Fiske. He was of very positive nature; had his own ideas of right and justice, and never swerved from his own conceptions of duty. For fifty years he was an earnest, consistent member of the Methodist Church, and to his interest and encouragement does that society in Whitefield largely owe its present prosperity. His faith was not of that stern, unrelenting kind which we might expect, knowing that his early religious training was from a venerated mother, whose Calvinism was of the unmitigated sort. He d. Dec. 26, 1893; res. Whitefield, N. H.

    5505. i.   HAZEN WILLARD, b. Mar. 3, 1833; m. Martha Ann Chase.

3983. ERASTUS FISK (Asa, Aaron, Asa, Nathaniel, Nathaniel, Nathan, Nathaniel, William, Robert, Simon, Simon, William, Symond), b. Apr. 4, 1807, in Lunenburg, Vt.; m. Apr. 1, 1830, Sarah Cleveland, and six other times. Erastus resided in Grafton county, N. H., first in the town of Bath, then at Lisbon, and finally at Lyme, where he died. Generally he lived on a farm, but in his earlier years he had worked at the trade of mason and bricklayer, and often took jobs of that kind in later life. He was married seven times and succeeded in leaving a widow, who is still living at Lyme. Like all others of that generation, he was held in high respect by all who knew him, and was of a rather more genial disposition than most of the family, which was rather given to austerity. He d. June 4. 1891; res. Bath and Lyme, N. H.

 5506. vi.   SARAH CLEVELAND, b. Sept. 12, 1840; m. Sept. 26, 1864, David Hibbard; res. Canton, Mo. He is a farmer; was b. Oct. 20, 1840. Ch.: 1, Edward, b. Sept. 24, 1865; d. Sept. 12, 1867. 2, Cleon Melville, b. July 20, 1868; doctor; res. Boston, connected with Boston City Hospital. 3, George Fiske, b. Dec. 10, 1871. 4, Josephine Louise, b. Apr. 26, 1875. 5, Fred Cleveland, b. June 15, 1881.

 5507. i.   CHESTER CARLTON, b. Jan. 13, 1832; m.; d. Mar. 16, 1883.
 5508. iv.   DONNER CLEVELAND, b. Nov. 28, 1836; d. Oct. 1, 1838.
 5509. ii.   BETSEY CLEVELAND, b. May 12, 1833; d. Feb. 13, 1853.
 5510. iii.   AARON HIBBARD, b. Apr. 5, 1835; d. Apr. 30, 1837.
 5511. v.   HARRIETT FERRY, b. May 30, 1838; d. July 15, 1842.
 5512. vii.   ABBRO RAY, b. Sept. 28, 1843; m.; d. Feb. 22, 1878. His only child was Archer.

 3984. FREDERICK FISK (Asa, Aaron, Asa, Nathaniel, Nathaniel, Nathan, Nathaniel, William, Robert, Simon, Simon, William, Symond), b. Sept. 3, 1808; m. at Whitefield, N. H., Nov. 19, 1829, Sarah Clark. Frederick spent all his active life in the village of Lancaster, and for many years kept a hotel there known as the American House. It was a strictly temperance tavern, and at one time the leading hostelry of the place, and a resort of White Mountain travel in its earlier and simpler days. Selling the hotel property he engaged in the business of putting in drainage and water works in the growing village, partly by contract for the town and partly as a private undertaking. He was still engaged in this enterprise at the time of his death. He d. Jan. 4, 1873; res. Whitefield, and Lancaster, N. H.

 5513. i.   DIANTHA, b. Mar. 19, 1830; m. Feb. 13, 1856, Alvin Rosebrooks. She d. in Lancaster Feb. 21, 1865.
 5514. ii.   MOSES, b. Jan. 23, 1831; d. Dec. 4, 1834.
 5515. iii.   EDWARD P., b. Jan. 19, 1832; d. Oct. 19, 1853.
 5516. iv.   WILLIAM C., b. Mar. 14, 1833; m. Lydia Rowell and Hannah Gardner.
 5517. v.   ALICE, b. Apr. 15, 1840; m. Jan. 29, 1865, Albert E. Stevans; res. 527 Armstrong St., Columbus, O.
 5518. vi.   GEORGE, b. Oct. 5, 1841; d. Mar. 29, 1860.

 3986. FRANCIS FISK (Asa, Aaron, Asa, Nathaniel, Nathaniel, Nathan, Nathaniel, William, Robert, Simon, Simon, William, Symond), b. Mar. 8, 1811; m. Dec. 4, 1833, Dorothy B. Keyes. Francis died from cancer in the stomach at a comparatively early age. He owned and operated a saw mill in Whitefield on the Johns River, where it ran through an almost unbroken pine forest of primeval growth. He never lived elsewhere or was ever engaged in any other business. He d. Nov. 21, 1845; res. Whitefield, N. H.

 5519. i.   CHARLES HENRY, b. Aug. 30, 1835; d. July 13, 1850.
 5520. ii.   MARY MARIA, b. Jan. 22, 1837; m. May 22, 1856, Harvey Hadley; res. Lowell, Mass. Has two girls and one boy.
 5521. iii.   MARTHA ANN, b. Oct. 8, 1840; d. Oct. 25, 1841.

 3987. CHARLES FISK (Asa, Aaron, Asa, Nathaniel, Nathaniel, Nathan, Nathaniel, William, Robert, Simon, Simon, William, Symond), b. Guildhall, Vt., Feb. 17, 1814; m. in Oldtown, Me., Mar. 14, 1839, Mary Ann Eaton, b. Oct. 12, 1817; d. May 6, 1893. Charles had a store at Oldtown, Me., and he spent all his early manhood there, but he was taken with the early California "gold fever," and after some hesitation he sold out his business in Maine and emigrated to the Pacific coast about 1850 or soon after. He and his brother Royal freighted a vessel with sawed lumber and sent it "'round the Horn," and when it got to San Francisco the cargo was worth less in the market there than it cost on the New England coast. He had less predilection for city life than his brother Royal and went into the mountains and mining regions. He finally seems to have become permanent at Murphy's Ranche, now known as "Murphy's," where he was still living at last accounts. Res. Murphy's, Cal.

 5522. i.   MARY JANE, b. May 14, 1841; m. Geo. Mauk; res. Phoenix, Ariz.

5523. ii. CHARLES EATON, b. Apr. 2, 1843; res. unm. Hoboken, **Cal.**

5524. iii. JAMES NEWTON, b. Apr. 2, 1843; d. Apr. 7, 1843.

5525. iv. HESTER MARIA, b. Sept. 18, 1845; d. May 7, 1846.

5526. v. EMILY MARIA, b. Feb. 4, 1847; m. Frank H. Smith; res. 1215 L St., Sacramento, Cal.

5527. vi. EMMELINE EMANDA, b. Feb. 4, 1847; d. Feb. 25, 1847.

5528. vii. EUNICE ANN, b. Apr. 19, 1849; d. June 19, 1855.

5529. viii. FREDERICK EATON, b. Feb. 5, 1851; m. Lizzie Bassie; add. R. 417 Stamson Bldg., Los Angeles, Cal.

5530. ix. ROYAL F., b. June 19, 1853; d. Sept. 14, 1854.

5531. x. EFFIE ELDORA, b. Feb. 2, 1855; m. Nov. 9, 1872, Thos. H. Fowler; d. Dec. 6, 1873.

5532. xi. FRANK WILLIS, b. Mar. 20, 1857; m. July 17, 1879, Pamelia Shearer; res. Murphy's, Cal.

3989. PASCHAL FISK (Asa, Aaron, Asa, Nathaniel, Nathaniel, Nathan, Nathaniel, William, Robert, Simon, Simon, William, Symond), b. Aug. 26, 1819; m. ——— ———. Paschal went in early life from northern New Hampshire to Boston with Royal and engaged in business there. For many years he had a brokerage business and lived in Charlestown, then a separate municipality. He was a victim of dyspepsia, and on account of impaired health sought a country life near the sea shore. He bought a small farm, first at North Beverly and afterward at East Salisbury, where he passed his last years very quietly. He was a very religious man and like most of his brothers attached to the Methodist Church. He d. June 24, 1890; res. East Salisbury, Mass.

5533. i. CAROLINE, b. ———; m. ——— Lieber; res. East Salisbury.

3993. ANSON FISKE (Aaron, Aaron, Asa, Nathaniel, Nathaniel, Nathan, Nathaniel, William, Robert, Simon, Simon, William, Symond), b. Chesterfield, N. H., Sept. 28, 1801; m. Prudence How. He is a farmer; res. Guildhall, Vt., and Haverhill, N. H.

3995. WILLIAM FISKE (Aaron, Aaron, Asa, Nathaniel, Nathaniel, Nathan, Nathaniel, William, Robert, Simon, Simon, William, Symond), b. July 25, 1806, Lunenburg. Vt.; m. Nov. 16, 1830, Catherine H. Hudson, b. Mar. 4, 1805; d. May 13, 1885. He was a carpenter by trade and at one time a member of the firm of Fiske & Co., of Lowell, dealers in lumber. He d. Jan. 15, 1887; res. Lowell, Mass.

5534. i. WILLIAM OSCAR, b. June 4, 1836; m. Mary Augusta Fielding and Mrs. ——— Fox.

5535. ii. EDWARD AMBROSE, b. Nov. 22, 1838; m. Lizzie C. Dana.

5536. iii. HELEN CATHERINE, b. Aug. 8, 1842; unm.; res. 172 So. Broadway, Saratoga, N. Y.

5537. iv. GEORGE CLINTON, b. Oct. 27, 1831; d. unm. July 1, 1853.

3998. GEORGE WASHINGTON FISK (Aaron, Aaron, Asa, Nathaniel, Nathaniel, Nathan, Nathaniel, William, Robert, Simon, Simon, William, Symond), b. Mar. 3, 1812, Guildhall, Vt.; m. West Medway, Mass., Oct. 18, 1838, Eliza Brewer Cutler, b. May 17, 1815. He was at one time, in company with his brother William, boxmaking in Lowell, Mass., under the firm name of Fisk & Co. In 1864 he was head mechanic on the government works at Portsmouth, Va. Res. Lowell, Mass.

5538. i. HENRY B., b. Dec. 29, 1842; m. Lizzie Hollinger.

5539. ii. SARAH CUTLER, b. Feb. 22, 1845; res. Lowell.

5540. iii. EMMA, b. Oct. 14, 1848; m. Oct. 22, 1868, ——— Storer. She d. Mar. 16, 1874.

5541. iv. WARREN EUGENE, b. Aug. 10, 1839; d. Oct. 20, 1840.

4005. LARNED PHILLIPS FISKE (Abel, Aaron, Asa, Nathaniel, Nathaniel, Nathan, Nathaniel, William, Robert, Simon, Simon, William, Symond), b. Chesterfield, N. H., Aug. 31, 1808; m. in Granby Feb. 2, 1832, Sarah Maria White, b. Dec. 7, 1814; d. June 20, 1886. When he was about 1 year of age his father removed to northern Vermont, settling at or near St. Albans. At the beginning of the war of 1812 the family returned to Chesterfield. Here his boyhood was spent. His educational advantages were limited to the district schools of that day with a term or two at the Chesterfield Academy. When about 20 years of age he accompanied the family in its removal to Skip-Muck, now Chicopee Falls, Mass. Here he found employment. He removed to Constantia, now West Monroe, Oneida Co., N. Y. After a residence of two years and a half here he returned to Massachusetts and again located at Chicopee Falls, being employed in the mills at that place. From this time (1835) until 1849 he was employed in the cotton mills a greater part of the time. In the spring of 1849 on account of ill health he removed to Granby, Mass., and began farming, which occupation he followed as long as his physical powers permitted. He suffered from deafness for many years, which increased with age. In June, 1886, his wife died, and during the remainder of his life he made his home with his youngest son (A. W. Fiske). His death was due to old age. He d. Oct. 12, 1895; res. Granby, Mass.

> 5542. i. HOMER WHITE, b. Mar. 21, 1833; d. Oct. 18, 1847.
> 5543. ii. ARMORY DOOLITTLE, b. Nov. 16, 1835; d. Aug. 5, 1837.
> 5544. iii. HARTWELL, b. Sept. 25, 1837; d. Sept. 29, 1859.
> 5545. iv. ELLEN MARIA, b. July 4, 1840; m., 1861, Algernon S. Bartlett, b. Apr. 28, 1840; d. Jan. 27, 1865; m. 2d, Wm. A. Fiske; res. New London, Conn (see elsewhere).
> 5546. v. ELLIOTT HOBART, b. Dec. 29, 1848; m., Granby, Maria J. Church.
> 5547. vi. HOMER PRESTON, b. June 13, 1852; m. Chicopee, Glendora L. Roberts.
> 5548. vii. ARTHUR WILMOT, b. Apr. 15, 1855; m. Granby, Abbie W. Taylor.

4008. ABNER FISK Abel, Aaron, Asa, Nathaniel, Nathaniel, Nathan, Nathaniel, William, Robert, Simon, Simon, William, Symond), b. Apr. 17, 1813, in Chesterfield, N. H.; m. in Palmer, Mass., Aug. 25, 1836, Mary L. Smith, b. May 21, 1818; d. Feb. 4, 1895. He is a contractor and builder. Res. Keene, N. H.

> 5549. i. SARAH M., b. Oct. 17, 1837; m. Aug. 14, 1862, William A. Garfield. res. Keene, N. H. He was b. Apr. 5, 1839; d. Dec. 18, 1894. Ch.: 1, Sarphraney, M. E., b. Sept. 19, 1863; d. May 1, 1874. 2, Mary A., b. July 23, 1865. 3, Frank A., b. July 19, 1868. 4, Eliza S., b. Mar. 16, 1872; d. 1874.
> 5550. ii. WM. A., b. Nov. 2, 1839; m. Mrs. Ellen M. (Fiske) Bartlett.
> 5551. iii. MARY E., b. Sept. 17, 1844; d. Feb. 2, 1856.
> 5552. iv. GEO. W., b. Mar. 9, 1849; d. July 14, 1849.
> 5553. v. ANN J., June 5, 1852; d. Sept. 15, 1852.

4015. JOHN LANGDON FISK (Abel, Aaron, Asa, Nathaniel, Nathaniel, Nathan, Nathaniel, William, Robert, Simon, Simon, William, Symond), b. Feb. 7, 1828, Chesterfield, N. H.; m. at New Haven, Conn., Sept. 27, 1852, Cornelia H. Woodruff, b. Dec. 25, 1831. He is a mechinist. Res. 537 Washington, St., New Haven, Conn.

> 5554. i. MINNIE EULALIA SIMES, b. Feb. 25, 1855; m. Apr. 13, 1886; res. 167 Putnam St., New Haven, Conn.
> 5555. ii. ALICE FLORENCE CANDEE, b. Apr. 23, 1858; m. Jan. 1, 1882; res. 357 Washington St., New Haven Conn.
> 5556. iii. SAMUEL ELMER, b. Oct. 31, 1861; m. Emma M. Ford.
> 5557. iv. MARTHA BELLE, b. Feb. 3, 1864; d. Apr. 10, 1867.
> 5558. v. JOHN G. NORTH, b. Sept. 8, 1866; d. Apr. 15, 1867.

4017. JAMES ORAMEL FISK (Abel, Aaron, Asa, Nathaniel, Nathaniel, Nathan, Nathaniel, William, Robert, Simon, Simon, William, Symond). b. Chicopee, Mass., Apr. 25, 1841; m. at Springfield, July 9, 1865, Annie M. Parsons, b. Oct. 16, 1846. He is a carpenter by trade, but of late has represented the Glens Falls and other insurance companies in his city. Res. Woodland, Cal.

> 5559. ii. BURDETTE O., b. Jan. 25, 1877.
> 5560. i. GERTRUDE A., b. Oct. 12, 1873.

4023. FOSTER ALEXANDER FISK (Levi, Aaron, Asa, Nathaniel, Nathaniel, Nathan, Nathaniel, William, Robert, Simon, Simon, William, Symond),

b. Martinsburg, N. Y., Oct. 4, 1821; m. at Manchester, N. Y., July 3, 1846, Harriett Emaline Bliss, b. Delphi, N. Y., May 27, 1826. He is a cabinetmaker. **Res.** Ellisville, Ill.

5561. i. FRANK ELMER, b. Feb. 23, 1860; m. Ella A. Humphrey.
5562. ii. GEORGE L., b. Mar. 10, 1863; m. Martha J. Weaver.
5563. iii. ADELBERT C., b. Sept. 24, 1849; d. May 7, 1885; **m.** twice, Oct. 18, 1877, and Feb. 22, 1879.
5564. iv. EMMA R., b. Dec. 21, 1855; m. John Mott; res. E.
5565. v. EDWIN D., b. Dec. 14, 1857; m. Oct. 10, 1883; res. Prairie City, Ill.
5566. vi. BERT E., b. Mar. 4, 1868; m. May 4, 1893; res. Sparta, Ill.

4034. JONES FISKE (Aaron, Asa, Asa, Nathaniel, Nathaniel, Nathan, Nathaniel, William, Robert, Simon, Simon, William, Symond), b. Holliston, Mass., ———; m. Aseneth Thompson: res. Holliston, Mass.

5567. i. DORINDA, b. ———.
5568. ii. LOUISA b. ———.
5569. iii. JOSEPH, b. ———.
5570. iv. ALICE R., b. ———.

4036. FRANCIS FISK (Asa, Asa, Asa. Nathaniel, Nathaniel, Nathan, Nathaniel, Jeffrey, Robert, Simon, Simon, William, Symond), b. Holliston, Mass., Feb. 26, 1807; m. Oct. 29, 1833, Mercy Caroline Cooper. of Northbridge; m. 2d, Northbridge, Mass., Jan. 1, 1845, Anna Amy Aldrich, b. Nov. 22, 1813; d. in Westmoreland, N. H., Feb. 1, 1896. Francis Fisk, son of Asa and Susanna (Partridge) Fisk, was born in Holliston, Mass., Feb. 26, 1807. At an early age he left the paternal farm, deciding, as he used to say, that "if the earth would let him alone he would never scratch her face any more." He went to Boston, and after many discouragements, found employment in the retail grocery business. He gradually rose until he became proprietor of the business, but at about the age of 35 he lost the sight of one eye, after an unsuccessful operation for cataract. The sight of the other gradually failing he was obliged to retire from business. In 1857 he removed to Charlestown, Mass., where he spent the remainder of his days. He married for his first wife, Mercy C. Cooper. Of this union no descendants survive. He married second, Anna, Amy Aldrich, youngest daughter of Lyman and Anna (Bennett) Aldrich, of Northbridge, Mass. Of the five children by this marriage, all but two died young. The survivors are Lyman Beecher Fisk, of Cambridge, Mass., and Emma Augusta (Fisk) Green, of Westmoreland, N. H. Though a great sufferer from his eyes for more than half of his life, he bore it all with heroic fortitude until he passed away, beloved by his family and relatives, honored and respected by all who knew him. He d. Nov. 29, 1891; res. Boston and Charlestown, Mass.

5571. i. CHRISTOPHER C., b. Feb. 7, 1836; d. unm. Jan. 25, 1871.
5572. ii. CAROLINE C., b. June 29, 1841; m. Oct. 15, 1861, Samuel B. Thing, of Boston. She d. May 29, 1867.
5573. iii. FRANCIS, b. Oct. 14, 1846; d. Dec. 25, 1848.
5574. iv. FRANCIS B., b. Nov. 16, 1848; d. July 31, 1850.
5575. v. LYMAN BEECHER, b. Dec. 26, 1850; unm.; res. Cambridge, Mass.; is auditor of the Harvard Dining Association, Harvard College; add. Memorial Hall. He was born at Boston, Mass. At the age of six years he removed with his parents to Charlestown, Mass., where he completed the course of study in the primary, grammar and high schools, and in the last named was prepared for college. He entered Harvard College in 1869, and was graduated in 1873, with the degree A. B. cum laude. With the intention of finally entering the medical profession, he gave a few years to teaching, but while holding the position of principal of the high school at Keene, N. H., in 1876, his health failed so completely that he was obliged to resign, and for a number of years was unfitted to engage in active business of any kind. In 1882 he received from the corporation of Harvard University, an appointment as auditor of the Harvard Dining Association, and still holds (Dec., 1895) that position.
5576. vi. FRANKLIN P., b. Mar. 27, 1853; d. Sept. 15, 1856.

5577. vii. EMMA A., b. Feb. 22, 1857; m. Dec. 17, 1885, Robert H. Green, of Westmoreland,.N. H. Ch.: Earl Fisk, b. Aug. 8, 1888.

4040. ASA FISKE (Asa, Asa, Asa, Nathaniel, Nathaniel, Nathan, Nathaniel, Jeffrey, Robert, Simon, Simon, William, Symond), b. Holliston, Mass., Dec. 25, 1817; m. Pamelia Hollis. He is a banker in San F. Res. Boston, Mass., and 700 Hayes St., San Francisco, Cal.

    5578. i.   ELIZA, b. 1845.
    5579. ii.   PAMELIA, b. 1847.
    5580. iii. SON, b. 1849.

4041. CHARLES ELLIS FISKE (Samuel, Moses, Moses, Nathaniel, Nathaniel, Nathan, Nathaniel, William, Robert, Simon, Simon, William, Symond), b. Natick, Mass., Oct. 12, 1807; m. Aug. 9, 1835, Harriett Haven, of Dedham; d. Nov. 13, 1870. He d. Sept. 13, 1870; res. Natick, Mass.

    5581. i.   CHARLES P., b. Sept. 19, 1837; m. Jan. 2, 1867, Arniz Bacon; res. N., s. p.
    5582. ii.   JOHN ELIOT, b. Apr. 6, 1841; m. Mary Brigham.

4043. HON. EMERY FISKE (Moses, Moses, Moses, Nathaniel, Nathaniel, Nathan, Nathaniel, William, Robert, Simon, Simon, William, Symond), b. Framingham, Mass., Feb. 27, 1803; m. Apr. 16, 1829, Eunice Morse, of Natick; d. Sept. 6, 1886. Emery Fisk (as he wrote his name) was born in Framingham, Mass. He lived in Dedham five years. He then purchased a farm of 200 acres in Needham (now Wellesley), on which he remained till his death, in 1868 (May 17). His place was purchased of his second cousin, Isaiah Fiske, and still remains (in part) in the family. He was of account in the public affairs of his town and neighborhood. He was selectman of the town soon after his removal to it and was in request on committees of building and the like. He was a Representative in the Massachusetts Legislature two years, 1840 and 1841. He was also a member of the convention for revising the constitution of Massachusetts, 1853, in which were Choate, Sumner, Wilson, Banks, Boutwell, Morton, and all the prominent men of Massachusetts. He had eight children, all of whom but two died in infancy. He d. May 17, 1868; res. Needham, Mass.

    5583. vii. JOSEPH EMERY, b. Oct. 23, 1839; m. Ellen M. Ware and Abby S. Hastings.
    5584. i.   EMERY, b. Aug. 9, 1829; d. Sept. 7, 1829.
    5585. ii.   EUNICE LORITTA, b. June 15, 1831: d. Oct. 8, 1831.
    5586. iii. EMERY ADAMS, b. Apr. 5, 1833; d. Oct. 29, 1833.
    5587. iv. ABIGAIL BURGGES, b. Aug. 22, 1834; m. 1859, Augustus Eaton. They had four children, two are now living, Charles M., who graduated at Harvard College in 1890, and H. Harris.
    5588. v.   GEORGE HENRY, b. Sept. 28, 1836; d. June 22, 1837.
    5589. vi. SARAH ELIZABETH, b. June 16, 1838; d. Oct. 15, 1838.

4044. MOSES FISKE (Moses, Moses, Moses, Nathaniel, Nathaniel, Nathan, Nathaniel, William, Robert, Simon, Simon, William, Symond), b. Natick, Mass., Nov. 29, 1804; m. Apr. 28, 1833, Abigail T. Bryant; d. July 20, 1842; m. 2d, in Sherborne, Dec. 21, 1842, Aurelia Wight, of Dover. He was a steward and trustee in the Methodist Church. Was a a farmer. He d. Feb. 9, 1880; res. Framingham and Natick, Mass.

    5590. i.   JOHN WESLEY, b. Feb. 3, 1834; m. Apr. 13, 1857, Louisa A. Holbrook, and had two children. One is Amos Howard, b. Oct. 17, 1858. The father was a shoemaker.
    5591. ii.   MOSES LEROY, b. Nov. 17, 1839.
    5592. iii. WILLIAM FRANKLIN, b. Jan. 25, 1836; m. Dec., 1863, Isabel Laws.
    5593. iv. CHARLES MERRILL, b. Apr. 10, 1838.

4045. AARON FISKE (Moses, Moses, Moses, Nathaniel, Nathaniel, Nathan, Nathaniel, William, Robert, Simon, Simon, William, Symond), b. Natick, Mass., Nov. 29, 1804; m. May 24, 1831, Sally M. Mallery, of Natick, b. June 15, 1805. He was a farmer. Was a steward and trustee in the M. E. Church. He d. Aug. 10, 1881; res. Natick, Mass.

5594. i. WILBUR FILLMORE, b. May 24, 1832; d. Oct. 11, 1853. He was a very promising young man and had fitted for college.

5595. ii. LUCY SIBBELLA, b. Aug. 4, 1836; m. Apr. 11, 1858, Isaac A. Flagg. She d. Apr. 22, 1861.

5596. iii. MARY STONE, b. Sept. 19, 1839; m. Sept. 19, 1858, Wm. M. Bruce; res. N. He was b. Feb. 4, 1831. Is a box manufacturer. Ch.: 1, Frances A., b. Oct. 7, 1859, in Natick; m. July 10, 1889, to Frank H. Babcock, North Natick. 2, Wilbur F., b. Sept. 5, 1863; in Watertown, Mass.; m. Sept. 1, 1883; P. O. Natick, Mass. 3, Charles A., b. Dec. 9, 1867, in Natick, Mass.; m. Mar. 16, 1891; P. O. Natick, Mass. 4, Harvey E., b. Sept. 8, 1871; P. O. Poultney, Vt. 5, Adelbert M., b. Jan. 30, 1876, in Natick; P. O. add. Natick, Mass.

5597. iv. JOHN M., b. Mar. 26, 1845; m. Mary Tyet.

4048. ELBRIDGE FISKE (Moses, Moses, Moses, Nathaniel, Nathaniel, Nathan, Nathaniel, Jeffrey, Robert, Simon, Simon, William, Symond), b. Sept. 22, 1811; m. June 2, 1839, Mary Thornton, b. Duxbury, Mass., dau. of Capt. Wm. and Deborah (Turner) Thornton; d. May 11, 1885. He was born in Framingham, Mass., but resided most of the time until his marriage in Natick, Mass. After his marriage he resided in Boston. He was a mason by trade, made cement floors and did inside work. He was always a strong, healthy man, but during the latter part of his life his health failed rapidly; res. Roxbury, Mass., 20 Highland St.

5598. i. MARY ELIZABETH, b. Oct. 24, 1840; m. Dec. 6, 1860, John Edwin Clark, b. Portland, Me., Dec. 17, 1825; res. 20 Highland St., Roxbury, Mass. Ch.: 1, Bertram Fisk, b. Nov. 25, 1863; gr. Harvard College, 1887; m. Oct. 28, 1891, Helen Curtis Dale, of Malden, Mass., s. p.; res. Chicago, Ill., add. 211 Wabash Ave. 2, Evelyn Miles, b. Aug. 27, 1865; m. June 2, 1887, Jonathan Kersey Voshell, of Del.; ch.: Bertram Clark, b. Apr. 24, 1889; Allen Fiske, b. Oct. 28, 1893; res. Brooklyn, N. Y., care New York Life Insurance Company.

4049. REV. FRANKLIN FISKE (Moses, Moses, Moses, Nathaniel, Nathaniel, Nathan, Nathaniel, Jeffrey, Robert, Simon, Simon, William, Symond), b. Framingham, Mass., June 21, 1814; m. Mansfield, Mass., June 26, 1839, Chloe Catherine Stone, b. Feb. 20, 1817, Norton, Mass., d. Sept. 17, 1893. Their golden wedding was celebrated in Wilbraham, in June, 1889. Rev. Franklin Fisk, son of Moses Fisk and Sibella Jennison, was born in Framingham, Mass. He is next to the youngest of eight children, six brothers and two sisters, all of whom lived to be more than 64 years old. He was educated in the public schools of Natick, Mass., and at the Wesleyan Academy, Wilbraham, Mass., which he attended in 1832-3-4. During the years 1832-6 he taught several terms of school in various parts of Massachusetts, with great success. In 1836 he joined the New England Conference of the Methodist Episcopal Church, taking appointments in almost all parts of Massachusetts, and some in Connecticut, continuing in the active ministry for more than thirty years. He married Chloe Catharine Stone, who was a student with him at Wilbraham. To them were born eight children, four sons and four daughters, five of whom are still living. In 1867 he suffered a stroke of paralysis, which compelled him to leave the active work of the ministry. He settled at Wilbraham and became one of the well known residents. His beloved wife was taken from him by heart failure in 1893, after a happy union of fifty-four years. He has since resided with his children, under the shadows of Northwestern and Denver Universities, and Bates College. "Father" Fisk has been a famous character in connection with New England Methodism. Genial and social in temperament, keenly interested in all the affairs of the church, remarkably energetic in attendance upon camp meetings and religious assemblies far and near, he is very widely known and universally beloved. He and his wife were teachers. All his surviving children and all their wives and husbands have been teachers. The best known are Prof. Herbert F. Fisk, D. D., of Northwestern University, Evanston, Ill., and Everett O. Fisk, A. M., a prominent layman of Boston. Res. Auburndale, Mass.

5599. i. HERBERT F., b. Sept. 25, 1840; m. Anna Green.

5600. iv. EVERETT OLIN, b. Aug. 1, 1850; m. Helen C. Steele.

5601. ii. VESTA OLIVIA, b. Mar. 9, 1845; d. Nov., 1862.
5602. iii. JENNIE PORTER, b. Sept. 4, 1847; res. Auburndale.
5603. v. LUCIE ARABEL, b. June 4, 1852; m. Aug. 23, 1879, Wm. B. Herrick; res. Auburndale. He was b. Apr. 5, 1855, in Hartland, Conn. Is agent for the Fisk Teachers' Agency, in Boston. Ch.: 1, Olin Fisk, b. July 8, 1881. 2, Marion Lucy, b. Sept. 18, 1886. 3, Florence May, b. Oct. 4, 1888. 4, William Franklin, b. July 31, 1890.
5604. vi. SARAH ADELAIDE, b. Sept. 26, 1855; m. in 1879, Prof. W. C. Strong; res. Lewiston, Me.; now professor in Bates College. Prof. William Cyrus Strong, A. M., born in Andover, Conn., July 12, 1853, son of Wm. W. Strong, and Harriett M. Chappell; educated in the public schools of Andover, the Wesleyan Academy, Wilbraham, Mass.; the Wesleyan University, Middletown, Conn.; A. B. in 1879; A. M. in course; studied at Harvard University; taught in public schools during school and college courses; teacher of natural sciences at N. H. Conference Seminary, Tilton, N. H., 1879-81; same of Maine Wesleyan Seminary and Female College, 1881-91; same at high school, Westfield, Mass., 1891-2; professor of natural science, University of Denver, Denver, Colo., 1892-5; professor of physics, Bates College, Lewiston, Me., 1895; member of the Colorado Scientific Society; investigated the sanitary chemical character of the city waters of Denver; published pamphlet on "The Sanitary Chemical Character of the Artesian Waters of Denver." Patents for three inventions in the United States.
5605. vii. MAHLON, b. 1854; d. in infancy.
5606. viii. CHILIOS, b. 1854; d. in infancy.

4052. WILLIAM PATESHALL FISK (William, Moses, Moses, Nathaniel, Nathaniel, Nathan, Nathaniel, Jeffrey, Robert, Simon, Simon, William, Symond), b. Dec. 23, 1813, Cambridge, Mass.; m. at Exeter, N. H., Oct. 10, 1839, Lucy Folsom, b. July 25, 1813. He was a merchant. He d. June 19, 1869; res. Quincy, Ill., 712 Broadway.
5607. iv. JANE F., b. July 21, 1854; unm.; res. Q.
5608. i. WILLIAM HENRY, b. Nov. 3, 1840; d. Dec. 29, 1884.
5609. ii. HOWARD FOLSOM, b. Apr. 1, 1847; d. Sept. 6, 1847.
5610. iii. MARY EMMA, b. Sept. 18, 1849; m. Sept. 10, 1878, Gen. Elisha B. Hamilton. He is a prominent attorney and politician, and for a number of years was Inspector General on the Governor's staff; res. Quincy, Ill. Ch.: 1, Elisha Bentley, b. Aug. 23, 1879. 2, Lucy A., b. Aug. 19, 1880.

4058. JAMES CHAPLIN FISK (William, Moses, Moses, Nathaniel, Nathaniel, Nathan, Nathaniel, Jeffrey, Robert, Simon, Simon, William, Symond), b. Aug. 2, 1825, in Cambridge, Mass.; m. Oct. 29, 1861, Mary Grant Daniell, b. Jan. 27, 1833. He d. Dec. 15, 1885; res. Cambridge, Mass.
5611. i. JAMES LYMAN, b. June 24, 1862; d. unm., July 17, 1893.
5612. ii. OTIS DANIELL, b. Apr. 29, 1870; unm.; 32 Quincy St., Cambridge, Mass.
5613. iii. FREDERIC DANIELL, b. Aug. 12, 1864; unm.; 87 Milk St., Boston.
5614. iv. MARY WARREN, b. Aug. 13, 1871; d. Apr. 4, 1872.
5615. v. ELINOR KEITH, b. Mar. 13, 1873; d. Mar. 13, 1873.

4055. ROBERT FARRIS FISK (William, Moses, Moses, Nathaniel, Nathaniel, Nathan, Nathaniel, Jeffrey, Robert, Simon, Simon, William, Symond), b. May 5, 1819, Cambridge, Mass.; m. at New Haven, Conn., June 16, 1847, Narcissa Perry Whittemore, b. Mar. 20, 1824; d. Nov. 4, 1867. He was an attorney. He d. Dec. 16, 1843; res. Boston, Mass.
5616. iii. EDWARD P., b. Jan. 25, 1852; m. Josephine Wilson.
5617. i. SON, b. Apr. 10, 1848; d. Apr. 26, 1848.

5618. ii.   ROBERT FARRIS, b. June 3, 1850; unm.; 38 Hancock St., Boston, Mass.

5619. iv.   SAMUEL AUGUSTUS, b. Feb. 9, 1856; unm.; 37 Eighteenth Ave., Denver, Colo.; physician; was named after his paternal uncle, Dr. Samuel Augustus Fisk, of Northampton, Mass. In 1857 his parents moved to St. Paul, Minn., where they lived until the fall of 1863, returning at that time to live again in Cambridge, Mass. In November, 1867, his parents having both died, he went with his sister to live with his uncle, Dr. Samuel Augustus Fisk, in Northampton, Mass. This uncle legally adopted his sister, and was his guardian. He was fitted for college at the Round Hill School, in Northampton, and, later on, under the Rev. Josiah Clark, LL. D., he was prepared to enter college in 1872, but it was deemed best, on account of his youth, to keep him out for another year, and in 1873 he went to Yale,

DR. SAMUEL AUGUSTUS FISK.

and was graduated in 1877, receiving the degree of A. B. In the fall of 1877 he went to Harvard Medical School, and was graduated, receiving the degree of M. D. in 1880. He received, in the spring of 1880, an appointment, as house officer, to the Massachusetts General Hospital, in Boston, but was obliged to forego his appointment in consequence of having contracted an acute pulmonary tuberculosis, which sent him to Colorado in the fall of that year. From that time until the spring of 1883, he knocked about Colorado in search of health, living a part of the time at Poncha Springs, on the very frontier, and practicing medicine in a desultory manner. In May, 1883, he located in Denver, and was stricken down in the fall of the same year with a severe attack of rheumatic fever, accompanied with diabetes insipidus, from the effects of which latter trouble he has since suffered continuously. In the spring of 1884 he was elected to a chair in the medical department of the University of Denver, and has occupied in succession the chairs of anatomy, nervous diseases, and the practice of medicine, in that university, which latter chair, as professor of the practice of medicine, he still holds. In 1884 he was made secretary of the faculty, and held that position until the spring of 1895, when they elected him dean. In June, 1884, his alma mater, Yale, gave him the degree of Master of Arts. In June, 1887, he joined the American Climatological Association; in 1888 he was elected president of the Colorado State Medical Society; in 1890 he was elected a member of the Association of American Physi-

cians, and in 1894 a member of the American Public Health
Association. He is also a member of the American Academy
of Medicine, and belongs to the local medical societies. He
was one of the founders of the Colorado State Meteorological
Society, and he has interested himself to a considerable extent in the State Weather Bureau, and meteorological matters within the State. He is attending physician to the County
and St. Luke's hospitals, and was on the staff of the Deacon-
esses' Home, in Denver, during its existence. He has published articles in the Popular Science Monthly, science and
medical journals, bearing upon the climate of Colorado, with
reference, especially, to its influence in pulmonary diseases,
and has written on medical topics, principally typhoid fever,
in medical journals. He belongs to the Chamber of Commerce, in Denver, and several clubs. He has been president
of the Colorado Yale Alumni Association, and endeavors to
interest himself in local matters. He is also the vice-president of the Alumni Association of the Harvard Medical
School.

5620. v. ARTHUR LYMAN, b. May 15, 1860; unm.; is a physician;
res. 13 West Fiftieth St., New York, N. Y. Arthur Lyman
Fisk, M. D., born in St. Paul, Minn., May 15, 1860. Lived
there until the autumn of 1863. In Nov., 1863, the family
returned to Cambridge, Mass. Lived there until the autumn
of 1869, attending private and public schools. From Sept.,
1869, to June, 1876, at Greylock Institute, So. Williamstown,
Mass. From Sept., 1876, to June, 1879, at Williston Seminary,
Easthampton, Mass.; during this time his home was with his
uncle, Dr. Samuel A. Fiske, of Northampton. Entered Yale
University, Sept., 1879; graduated in June, 1883. From the
autumn of 1883 until Sept., 1885, he was in Colorado, engaged in ranching and business. In Sept., 1885, he commenced the study of medicine, at the Harvard Medical School,
in Boston, completing his studies in June, 1888. In Aug.,
1888, entered Massachusetts General Hospital, Boston, as a
member of the house staff; finished his service Feb., 1890.
Mar., 1890, he commenced the practice of medicine in New
York City, being associated with Dr. Robert Wobe. He
holds the following positions: Attending surgeon to Trinity
Hospital; assistant surgeon to the New York Cancer Hos-
pital; surgeon to the out-door department of the New York
Hospital, and lecturer of clinical surgery in the New York
Post-Graduate School and Hospital. He is a member of
New York Academy of Medicine; New York County Society;
Massachusetts Medical Society; Harvard Medical Association;
Harvard Medical Society of New York City; Hospital Gradu-
ates' Club. Social Clubs: Reform Club; Harvard Club of
New York City.

5621. vi. NIVA PERRY, b. Nov. 27, 1862; m. June 7, 1892, Francis
Ulshoeffer Paris; res. New York City, 144 E. Thirty-sixth St.

4066. JOSEPH FISKE (Calvin, Joshua, Moses, Nathaniel, Nathaniel, Nathan, Nathaniel, Jeffrey, Robert, Simon, Simon, William, Symond), b. Newton,
Upper Falls, Mass., Dec. 3, 1817; m. in Medway, Mary Allen, b. 1819; d. Jan. 19,
1860; m. 2d, Sept. 16, 1862, Nancy A. Darling, b. Sept. 16, 1832. He is a shoemaker and farmer; res. Bellingham, Mass.

5622. i. JOSEPH, b. 1839; d. unm., Feb. 20, 1860.
5623. ii. ELIZABETH, b. Jan. 23, 1842; m. George Thayer, and d. Oct.
28, 1875.
5624. iii. ORRIN F., b. Aug. 18, 1849; m. Lizabeth Bliss.
5625. iv. CHARLES, b. 1852; d. unm., in 1877.
5626. v. ELLENOR, b. ———; m. Charles Rockwood.
5627. vi. WILLARD, b. 1856; d. unm., in 1873.
34

5628. vii. HENRY S., b. May 1, 1867; unm.
5629. viii. MARY D., b. Aug. 2, 1869; unm.
5630. ix. IRENE, b. Jan. 22. 1875: m. Edmond Hodgkins.

4080. HON. JOHN NEWTON FISKE (John, Elijah, Moses, Nathaniel, Nathaniel, Nathan, Nathaniel, William, Robert, Simon, Simon, William, Symond), b. at East Washington, N. H., Nov. 27. 1821; m. at Fredericksburg, Va., Sept. 23. 1853, Margerite Matilda Mense, of Fredericksburg, Va., b. July 13, 1834. John N. Fiske was born at East Washington. N. H.. Nov. 27, 1821. He moved to New Hampton, N. H., with his father's family when quite small. When he was about 14 years old he left home and went to Boston, Mass., and made his home there until he was 21 years old: then he went to Fredericksburg, Va., and lived and married there Margerite M. Mense. In Apr., 1855, he went to Lancaster, S. C., and lived there two years; then went to Columbia, S. C.; lived there three years; then came to Augusta, Ga., bringing his wife and two children with him. He lived there until about eighteen years ago, when he went to Grovetown, Ga., where he died. At his decease he was in the fancy painting and decorating business in Augusta. Ga. He was a very intellectual and able man. For some time he was a member of the Grovetown Council, and Mayor for one term. He d. May 31, 1894; res. Fredericksburg, Va., and Grovetown, Ga.
  5631. i. WILLIAM M., b. Sept. 3, 1854; m. Carrie M. Savage.
  5632. ii. CATHERINE CRAIG, b. Apr. 3, 1857; unm.; res. G.
  5633. iii. JULIAN FRIEND. b. Mar. 3, 1860; m. Minnie E. Edwards.
  5634. iv. MAGGIE WALTENAH, b. Mar. 3, 1865; m. Feb. 12, 1890, Otis P. Florence; res. G.
  5635. v. MARY EDWARDS, b. May 26, 1878; d. June 22, 1878.
  5636. vi. JOHN ALFRED, b. May 26, 1878; d. June 22, 1878.

4084. FRIEND FULLER FISKE (John, Elijah, Moses. Nathaniel, Nathaniel. Nathan, Nathaniel, William, Robert, Simon, Simon, William, Symond), b. Washington, N. H., Apr. 6, 1828; m. in Hanson, Mass., Oct. 8, 1872, Jane B. Smith, b. Aug. 17, 1834. He is a farmer. During the Civil War he was in the service of the Christian commission; res. Webster and Mast Yard, N. H.
  5637. i. WILLIAM F., b. Mar. 10, 1876.

4088. REUBEN EAMES FISKE (David, David, John, John, Nathaniel, Nathan. Nathaniel. William. Robert. Simon, Simon, William, Symond). b. Holliston, Mass.. Feb. 28, 1809; m. Oct. 24. 1850, Betsey L. Plympton, of Medfield, dau. of Warren, b. Mar. 15, 1823; d. Jan. 26, 1888. He was a farmer. He d. June 5, 1879: res. Holliston, Mass.
  5638. i. ALPHONSO P., b. Jan. 7, 1852.
  5639. ii. MARY L., b. Jan. 9, 1854; m. Geo. W. Oliver; res. H. She d. leaving one child, Lena J.
  5640. iii. ALBERT I., b. May 18, 1857; m. in Sherborn, Mrs. Elizabeth F. Rockwood, b. Feb. 20. 1857; is a farmer; res. s. p. Holliston, Mass.
  5641. iv. HATTIE M., b. Aug. 3. 1861; m. June 15, 1890, Albert S. Pickering: res. Careyville, Mass. He was b. Jan. 28, 1847. Ch.: Louise E., b. Oct. 22, 1891.

4089. WILLIAM FISKE (David. David, John, John, Nathaniel, Nathan, Nathaniel, William, Robert, Simon. Simon. William, Symond), b. Holliston, Mass., Nov. 6, 1813; m. 1836, Rhoda Pike. He was accidentally killed by the kick of a horse; res. Holliston. Mass.
  5642. i. HENRY E., b. 1839.
  5643. ii. HERBERT W.. b. 1847. He is a dealer in horse blankets and harness at 1274 Washington St., Boston, Mass.

4090. TIMOTHY FISK (David, David, John, John, Nathaniel, Nathan, Nathaniel, William, Robert, Simon, Simon, William, Symond), b. Holliston, Mass., June 20, 1804; m. there Oct. 19, 1828. Lucretia Batchelder, dau. of Odlin Batchelder, of New Hampshire, b. Dec. 1, 1806: d. July, 1887. He is a farmer and is now living, in his 92d year. Timothy Fisk, son of David, Jr., and father of Hannah Eames, was born June 20, 1804, on a farm where he lived many years. His father died when he was only 12 years of age, he being the eldest son of five children, and he was kept at home to assist his widowed mother in carrying on the farm while the other children were placed elsewhere. He was a well-to-do, enterprising, hard-working farmer, and made himself famous as the knight of the sickle and scythe, and in later years quite a grower and dealer in cranberries; also in winter in the manufacture of ship pins, having quite a large trade with the shipbuilders of fifty years ago. By honest, industrious and temperate habits he accumulated a fair fortune to care for himself in his old age, now past 91 years. He is now living with his son, D. W. Fisk, in South Coventry, Conn., in very good health, and able to read the daily paper without glasses, and can write a very fair letter; res. Holliston, Mass., and South Coventry, Conn.

5644. i. DAVID W., b. Aug. 18, 1830; m. Angeline Tillinghast.
5645. ii. GEORGE, b. Apr. 1, 1832; d. 1832.
5646. iii. GEO. BATCHELDER, b. May 20, 1834; m. Adeliza M. Perry.
5647. iv. SOPHRONIA B., b. Aug. 12, 1838; m. Oct. 19, 1856, Rev. Daniel Jones; res. Stoneham, Mass.; d. Oct. 21, 1893. Ch.: 1. Alice C. b. Oct. 24, 1860; graduated a B. A., Wellesley College, 1883; principal of high school eight years, Abington, Mass. 2. Eva G., b. Sept. 17, 1864; a well known teacher.
5648. v. CATHERINE PALMER, b. Aug. 5, 1840; d. 1842.

4093. LOVETT FISKE (John, David, John, John, Nathaniel, Nathan, Nathaniel, William, Robert, Simon, Simon, William, Symond), b. Holliston, Mass., June 13, 1814; m. there Dec. 3, 1835, Alma Remington Greenhalgh, b. Nov. 23, 1815. For many years he was in the grocery business but of late has led a quiet, retired life; res. Holliston, Mass., and Portland, Conn.

5649. iii. ARTHUR IRVING, b. Aug. 19, 1848; m. Harriett Mowry.
5650. i. MARION JOSEPHINE, b. Apr. 1, 1837; d. Jan. 10, 1841.
5651. ii. ALMA GERTRUDE, b. June 15, 1842; d. Dec. 31, 1846.
5652. iv. ELLA AGNES, b. Oct. 19, 1857; m. May 14, 1890, Dr. Frank Potter; res. P. Ch.: Anna, Margaret and Arthur Fiske.

4094. HORACE FISKE (John, David, John, John, Nathaniel, Nathan, Nathaniel, William, Robert, Simon, Simon, William, Symond), b. Holliston, Mass., Sept. 2, 1800; m. Apr. 29, 1834, Melissa Newton; d. July 2, 1873. He d. in 1879; res. Holliston, Mass.

5653. i. SUSAN VICTORIA, b. Mar. 25, 1838; m. Jan., 1872, Samuel K. Littletrate, of Vermont, and d. s. p.
5654. ii. SARAH ELLEN, b. June 14, 1840; m. July 3, 1867, Wallace J. Maynard, of Shrewsbury, Mass.; s. p.

4095. ANER FISKE (John, David, John, John, Nathaniel, Nathan, Nathaniel, William, Robert, Simon, Simon, William, Symond), b. Holliston, Mass., Feb. 16, 1804; m. there Betsey Dix, of Holliston, b. Sept. 14, 1807; d. Apr. 26, 1882. He was a shoemaker. He d. Aug. 4, 1855; res. Holliston, Mass.

5655. i. CHANDLER, b. ———; d. young.
5656. ii. WILBER, b. June 20, 1834; m. Annie Bailey.
5657. iii. ABBIE, b. Oct. 16, 1838; m. Oct. 16, 1870, Levi Higgins; res. s. p. at Onset Bay, Mass. He was b. Nov. 10, 1837. They have an adopted child, Geo. W., b. July 24, 1872.
5658. iv. MARY ANN D., b. May 28, 1841; m. Wm. Christie, of Boston. Ch.: Ethel; res. 1368 Greenup St., Covington, Ky.

4096. JOHN FISKE (John, David, John, John, Nathaniel, Nathan, Nathaniel, William, Robert, Simon, Simon, William, Symond), b. Holliston, Mass., July 25, 1806; m. Mary Rockwood, of Holliston. He d. Oct. 10, 1867; res. Holliston, Mass.

5659. i. ELBRIDGE, b. ———; d. July, 1843.

4097. ABNER FISKE (John, David, John, John, Nathaniel, Nathan, Nathaniel, William, Robert, Simon, Simon, William, Symond), b. Holliston, Mass., Aug. 5, 1808; m. there 1832 Lorinda Bellows, b. 1810; d. Mar. 19, 1890. He was a painter. He d. June 17, 1888; res. Holliston, Mass.

5660. i. J. MILTON, b. Feb. 20, 1835; m. Ellen S. Worthington.

5661. ii.   MELVILLE, b. ——; m. Josephine Laurence, Nov. 10, 1834.
5662. iii. MELVINA, b. ——; m. Mar. 3, 1856, Freeman Battelle, b.
             June 14, 1836; res. Worcester, Mass. Ch.: Frank E., b. Dec.
             23, 1857; d. Dec. 18, 1871.
5663. iv.   ELWYN, b. ——; d. ae. two years.

4102. HORATIO FISKE (Nathan, David, John, John, Nathaniel, Nathan,
Nathaniel, William, Robert, Simon, Simon, William, Symond), b. Holliston,
Mass., 1794; m. Ellen Learned; m. 2d, Sally Learned; m. 3d, Elizabeth Adams;
res. Holliston, Mass.
5664. i.   SARAH, b. 1837; m. Ellis C. Turner; res. Chicago.
5665. ii.   MYRA, b. ——; m. Geo. Shaw; res. E. Weymouth, Mass.

4105. MARTIN FISK (Levi, David, John, John, Nathaniel, Nathan, Nathaniel, William, Robert, Simon, Simon, William, Symond), b. Oct., 1796; m. July
4, 1839, Sophia Howe, dau. of Samuel of Cumberland, R. I; res. Cumberland, R. I.
5665½.i.   SARAH, b. ——; m. —— Scott; res. Woonsocket, R. I.

4108. AMOS FISKE (Levi, David, John, John, Nathaniel, Nathan, Nathaniel, William, Robert, Simon, Simon, William, Symond), b. Holliston, Mass.,
Jan. 19, 1801; m. at Coventry, R. I., Feb. 26, 1826, Sarah Waterman, b. Aug. 29,
1806; d. Sept. 29, 1894. He was born in Holliston, Mass., moved to Providence,
R. I., and during his life was a very successful wholesale grocer in that city. He
d. Apr. 12, 1891; res. Providence, R. I.
5666. i.   EMELINE, b. Feb. 15, 1827; m. —— Walker. She d. Jan. 9,
             1861, leaving Adeline Frances, who m. a Risley, who res. s. p.
             at 26 Oak St., Providence, R. I.
5667. ii.   MARY ANNA, b. Nov. 13, 1829; m. —— Walker; res. Cran-
             ston, R. I.; has several children.
5668. iii. ALBERT LEWIS, b. July 27, 1832; m. and res. 26 Oak St., Prov-
             idence, R. I.; has three children.
5669. iv.   EDWARD WATERMAN, b. Oct. 5, 1834; m. in Coventry, R.
             I., May 28, 1854, Jane E. Ballou, b. Jan. 10, 1836; d. Dec. 25,
             1893. He is a wholesale grocer in Providence, R. I. Ch.:
             Amos, b. in Providence, R. I., Mar. 25, 1856; d. Oct. 28, 1860.
             Sarah W., b. in Providence, R. I., Jan. 12, 1858; m. Albert E.
             Angell; res. Washington, D. C.; clerk in War Department;
             three children. Annie U., b. in Coventry, R. I., Sept. 25, 1860;
             m. Dexter B. Clark; res. Woonsocket, R. I.; two children.
             Charles Ballou, b. in Providence, R. I., Aug. 9, 1862; d. Dec.
             10, 1893, leaving Eddie A. and Harrold, both res. Ashton, R. I.
             Walter Edward, b. in Providence, R. I., Nov. 19, 1866; m. Feb.,
             1891, Minnie A. Mowrey, b. Oct. 3, 1871; res. Cumberland
             Hill, R. I. Emma G., b. in Cumberland, R. I., Oct. 19, 1877;
             res. C.
5670. v.   WM. AUGUSTUS, b. Apr. 18, 1837; m. Susan W. Waterman

——. WILLIAM AUGUSTUS FISKE (Amos, Levi, David, John, John,
Nathaniel, Nathan, Nathaniel, William, Robert, Simon, Simon, William, Symond),
b. Warwick, R. I., Apr. 18, 1837; m. in Coventry, Jan. 24, 1861, Susan Wyman
Waterman, b. Feb. 16, 1841. Wholesale grocer; res. s. p. 65 Atlantic Ave., Providence, R. I.

4114. FERDINAND FISKE (Timothy, David, John, John, Nathaniel, Nathan, Nathaniel, William, Robert, Simon, Simon, William, Symond), b. Holliston,
Mass., Oct. 20, 1806; m. Apr. 15, 1840, Sarah A. Clark, b. Jan. 31, 1809; d. Apr. 5,
1893. He d. Oct. 14, 1883; res. Holliston, Mass.
5671. i.   JAMES FERDINAND, b. Aug. 1, 1841; m. Sarah M. Craig.
5672. ii.   RHODA EVELINE, b. Dec. 4, 1843; d. Apr. 19, 1853.
5673. iii. TIMOTHY JOSEPH, b. June 23, 1848; d. Apr. 30, 1853.

4123. THOMAS TROWBRIDGE FISK (Thomas, John, Isaac, John, Na-
thaniel, Nathan, Nathaniel, William, Robert, Simon, Simon, William, Symond), b.
Chesterfield, N. H., Nov. 27, 1806; m. May 6, 1827, Emily H. Hildreth, dau. of
Elijah. She d. in Hinsdale, N. H., Jan. 6, 1849; m. 2d, May 13, 1849, Mrs Adeline

Goodnow, b. Sept. 4, 1812; d. Aug. 24, 1861. He resided in New Hampshire all his life; was born in Chesterfield, and resided in Hinsdale. He was a farmer and conducted an express and trucking business. Later he began the manufacture of soaps in a small way with his son, Lucius I., which business has since grown to mammoth proportions and is now located at Springfield, Mass. He d. June 17, 1861; res. Hinsdale, N. H.

5674. i.   GEORGE C., b. Mar. 4, 1831; m. Maria E. Ripley.
5675. ii.   LUCIUS I., b. Oct. 18, 1833; m. Eveline E. Raymond.
5676. iii. NOYES W., b. May 15, 1839; m. Emeline G. Adams.
5677. iv. ADDIE E., b. Sept. 27, 1853; m. Henry Fanning; res. Springfield, Ohio.

4126. JOHN BOYLE FISK (Thomas, John, Isaac, John, Nathaniel, Nathan, Nathaniel, William, Robert, Simon, Simon, William, Symond), b. Chesterfield, N. H., Apr. 10, 1816; m. there in 1838 Arabell Robertson, dau. of Ebenezer, b. Apr. 12, 1815; d. Oct. 3, 1876; m. 2d, Nov. 21, 1877, Elizabeth A. (Chandler) Pierce, widow of John H. Pierce, of Chesterfield. He has been a farmer most of his life. In the early part of his life taught school nine years; has been superintendent of schools and selectman of the town; justice of peace of State forty-four years, and acted as trial justice twenty-five years; has settled a good many estates, and on the whole is a prominent man in the town and has always borne a good reputation; res. Chesterfield, N. H.

5678. i.   HARRISON F., b. May 15, 1840; m. Mary G. Wyman and Annie E. Frank.
5679. ii.   MARTHA DAVIS, b. Sept. 9, 1843; m. Henry Cleves Walker, of Portsmouth, N. H.; d. Jan. 7, 1876; m. 2d, Edward Stebbins, of Hinsdale. She d. Nov. 1, 1893. Ch.: 1, Horton D. Walker, m. Mabel Kenny; one dau., Martha Fisk, res. Greenfield, Mass. 2, Mary Ellen Cleves Walker, res. Hinsdale, N. H.
5680. iii. FRANK D., b. Feb. 17, 1846; m. Celina E. Aldrich.

4136. DANIEL HAVEN FISKE (William T., Daniel, Isaac, John, Nathaniel, Nathan, Nathaniel, William, Robert, Simon, Simon, William, Symond), b. Oxford, Mass., Aug. 13, 1802; m. Feb. 10, 1827, Caroline Willard, of Middletown, Vt. He was born in Massachusetts, and soon after marriage settled in Ellisburgh, N. Y., residing subsequently in Pulaski, Syracuse and Ithaca, N. Y. For many years he was in poor health. Was a merchant. He d. Feb. 3, 1884; res. Ellisburgh, N. Y.

5681. i.   CAROLINE, b. 1827; d. 1830.
5682. ii.   DANIEL W., b. Nov. 11, 1831; m. Jennie McGraw.
5683. iii. WILLIAM O., b. Jan. 23, 1835; m. Mary E. McGee.

4143. WILBUR HENRY FISKE (William T., Daniel, Isaac, John, Nathaniel, Nathan, Nathaniel, William, Robert, Simon, Simon, William, Symond), b. July 31, 1832, New York State; m. Nov., 1855, at Maquoketa, Ia., Myra Shaw. He d. Oct., 1862.

5684. i.   FERDINAND C., b. ——; m. and res. St. Louis, Mo.; add. 801 Union Trust Bldg. Ch.: Helen, b. ——.
5685. ii.   CHARLES WILBUR, b. Feb. 23, 1862; m. Nov. 22, 1894, Thekla Von Schraeder, b. Mar. 4, 1862; res. Eau Claire, Wis. He was born Feb. 23, 1862, at Maquoketa, Ia. Was educated at public schools and at the State University of Wisconsin, at Madison, belonging to class of 1884. Took a law course at Union College of Law, Chicago. Located at Eau Claire in 1886. Is a lawyer. Ch.: Dorothy, b. Sept. 2, 1895.

4144. MOSES MADISON FISKE (Isaac, Moses, Isaac, John, Nathaniel, Nathan, Nathaniel, William, Robert, Simon, Simon, William, Symond), b. in Barren, Co., Ky., Aug. 30, 1807; m. Mar. 31, 1831, Harriett Herring, b. Jan. 21, 1807; d. May 10, 1893. He was a farmer and newspaper agent. He d. Feb. 5, 1888; res. Framingham, Mass.

5686. i.   GEO. H., b. Feb. 26, 1832; m. Delia M. Moore and Angie W. Annett.

5687. ii.   WINSLOW JOHNSON, b. June 18, 1834; m. Susan Bigelow and
              Abbie F. Holcomb.
5688. iii.   HARRIET AUGUSTA, b. May 29, 1836; m. Nov. 3, 1852, Ho-
              ratio W. Gardner, of Sherborn.
5689. iv.   JOHN MURRAY, b. Sept. 28, 1838; m. Carrie E. Morgan.
5690. v.   MARIE ANTOINETTE, b. Aug. 20, 1840; m. Aug. 12, 1863,
              James Freeman, b. Apr. 4, 1836; d. Aug. 27, 1867; m. 2d, Sept.
              5, 1894, Willard Howe, b. Aug. 19, 1829; res. So. Framing-
              ham, Mass. Ch.: 1, James Everett Freeman, b. Dec. 31, 1864;
              m. Jan. 6, 1886; P. O. add. Everett, Mass. 2, Elizabeth E. Free-
              man, b. Mar. 28, 1867; d. Sept. 25, 1870. 3, Josie Ellen Free-
              man (adopted), b. Apr. 20, 1875; d. Aug. 9, 1886.
5691. vi.   ELLEN LOUISA, b. May 6, 1843; d. June 6, 1868.
5692. vii.   ANDREW JACKSON, b. June 8, 1845; m. Lizzie Clough.
5693. viii. SETH HERRING, b. Apr. 11, 1848; d. Dec. 5, 1870.

4145. REV. OLIVER J. FISKE (Isaac, Moses, Isaac, John, Nathaniel,
Nathan, Nathaniel, William, Robert, Simon, Simon, William, Symond), b. Nashville, Tenn., Jan. 24, 1809; m. Cumberland, R. I., May 26, 1839, Louisa Brown, of
Lime Rock, b. Cumberland, R. I., Mar. 11, 1816. Oliver Johnson Fiske was born
in the city of Nashville, Tenn., on the 24th day of January, 1809, and died in
Crawfordsville, Ind., Jan. 8, 1886. He was the son of Isaac and Elizabeth (Johnson) Fiske, both of whom were from New England. Soon after the birth of Oliver
they returned to Massachusetts and lived upon a farm in the town of Framingham
in that State. The subject of our sketch was the second of five brothers. The
common school education which he received in that village only gave him a keener
appetite for acquiring a more extensive knowledge. To go away to attend school
was out of the question, as his parents were poor. He determined, however, to
overcome all obstacles and not allow the prize which he so much desired to slip away,
from him. Acting under the advice of some friend he arranged a course of study.
Every moment when not at work on the farm he was mastering Latin and Greek.
While his companions were at play he was at study, and oftentimes sitting up until
after midnight pursuing the course he had marked out. During this time there
was a revival of religion at the Baptist Church at Framingham. He attended the
meetings and was converted. Soon after he became impressed with the desire to
preach the gospel. At last a way was opened for him to attend school at South Reading, Mass., after which he went to the theological school at Newton, remaining there
one year. He made up his mind that he would obtain a full collegiate education
and entered Brown University in the junior class and graduated in the class of
1837. In 1838 he was duly ordained at the Baptist Church at Lime Rock, Smithfield, R. I., and became pastor of that church. His labors here were successful;
many were added to the church and the older members were revived, and when he
resigned his pastorate the church was in a strong, healthy condition. He accepted a position as principal of a young ladies' seminary at Stewart's Creek,
County of Rutherford, Tenn. In 1839, before leaving Lime Rock, he married
Miss Maria Louisa Brown, of Cumberland, R. I. She was a great help to him in
his work as a teacher. Here he remained for about two years, and owing to the
unhealthfulness of the place where the seminary was situated he was obliged to
give up his school, and he accepted a situation to become principal of a boys' school
in Robertson County, Tenn. So successful was he here as a teacher that he had
many flattering inducements to go elsewhere to teach in different parts of the
south. He accepted an offer to become principal of an academy at Nashville,
Tenn. Here he prepared young men for college. He received many letters from
the members of faculties and presidents of colleges complimenting him on the
thorough manner in which his students were prepared to enter on their college
course. In 1850 he was called to the presidency of Enon College, at Gallatin,
Tenn., which position he accepted. Being connected with this institution brought
him in touch with the denomination he so much loved. Almost every Sabbath he
preached, sometimes going several hundred miles to preach at associations and
large churches. Many of his sermons were printed in the Tennessee Baptist and
other religious papers. In 1855, on account of his wife's health and desirous of
bringing up his family in a free State, he removed to Bloomington, Ill., where for
twenty years he was engaged in pastoral work and holding evangelistic meetings,

He did not keep a record of the number of persons converted under his preaching, but it would amount to hundreds. When completely worn out by hard work and failing health he went to live with his son Charles H. Fiske, at Crawfordsville, Ind. His last illness was a brief one, but it found him cheerful and bright and in a hope full of immortality. It was the peaceful end of a man whose whole life had been one of self-sacrificing devotion to the promotion of the interests of education and religion. Mr. Fiske had three children, Edwin B. Fiske, of Rochester, N. Y., lawyer; Oliver Edgar Fiske, who died of typhoid fever when 17 years of age, and Charles H. Fiske, who resides now in the city of Indianapolis, Ind. His wife is still living, though in feeble health. He d. Jan. 8, 1886; res. Nashville, Tenn., and Crawfordsville, Ind.

    5694. i.   EDWIN B., b. Dec. 16, 1841; m. Frances M. Price and Priscilla M. Westlake.

    5695. ii.   OLIVER EDGAR, b. ——; d. aged 17.

    5696. iii. CHARLES H., b. Jan. 8, 1849; m. Anna Rockwell.

    4148. EBENEZER W. FISKE (Isaac, Moses, Isaac, John, Nathaniel, Nathan, Nathaniel, William, Robert, Simon, Simon, William, Symond), b. Framingham, Mass., Oct. 22, 1819; m. at Waltham, Dec. 28, 1843, Caroline Matilda Smith, b. Feb. 7, 1822. He was born in Framingham, and learned the trade of harness maker. At the age of 21 he went to Waltham and engaged in business, when he was appointed deputy sheriff under Sheriff Hildreth, serving under both sheriffs, Keys and Kimball, and at the death of the latter, being senior deputy, he became acting sheriff. At the end of the year he was elected sheriff for three years, and his term would have expired the first of Jan., 1884. At the time of his succession to the office of high sheriff he had served as deputy thirty consecutive years. Mr. Fiske was always popular, running ahead of his ticket at elections. The members of the bar recognized in him a man who was eminently qualified for his office. He was often chosen moderator of the town meetings in Waltham, for a long time acted as coroner, had been justice of the peace, deputy collector of internal revenue, and assistant internal revenue assessor. He was a member of the board of water commissioners for Waltham one term of three years and declined re-election. He was an active Republican, always taking a lively interest in elections, and was an old member of the Middlesex Club. He d. Aug. 27, 1883; res. Waltham, Mass.

    5697. i.   GEORGE S., b. ——. He was on the editorial staff of Boston Herald, and d. Oct. 27, 1894.

    5698. ii.   FLORENCE, b. ——; m. Charles A. Houghton; res. 1220 Webster St., Oakland, Cal. Ch.: Shirley, b. 1882, and Ruth, b. 1885.

    5699. iii. EBEN W., b. May 22, 1860; m. Sarah F. Gibbs.

    5700. iv. ARTHUR H., b. Nov. 10, 1862; m. Apr. 11, 1894, Gertrude Louisa Wadleigh, b. Feb. 28, 1870; res. Waltham, Mass.; s. p. He is in the shoe and leather business.

    4151. FRANK P. FISK (Levi W., Parker, Asa, Bezaleel, Jonathan, David, David, David, Jeffrey, Robert, Simon, Simon, William, Symond), b. Dublin, N. H., May 31, 1858; m. in Peterboro, May 6, 1882, Hannah M. Spofford, b. July 8, 1865. He is a farmer; res. E. Harrisville, N. H.

    5701. i.   CHARLES P., b. Oct. 25, 1883.

    4167. EDWARD SUMNER FISKE (Edward R., Bezaleel, Nahum, Bezaleel, Jonathan, David, David, David, Jeffrey, Robert, Simon, Simon, William, Symond), b. Worcester, Mass., Sept. 23, 1845; m. Logansport, Ind., Oct. 10, 1883, Nellie Gray Smock, b. Oct. 19, 1861. He is a bookkeeper; res. s. p. 416 Main St., Worcester, Mass.

    4171. CHARLES WALDO FISKE (Edward R., Bezaleel, Nahum, Bezaleel, Jonathan, David, David, David, Jeffrey, Robert, Simon, Simon, William, Symond), b. Worcester, Mass., Jan. 23, 1859; m. at Providence, R. I., Oct 3, 1883, Martha Louise Gunderson, b. Aug. 10, 1859. He is a clerk; res. Boston, Mass.; add. 271 Albany St.

    5702. i.   OLIVE LOUISE, b. Nov. 14, 1884.

    5703. ii.   ANNA ELIZABETH, b. Feb. 7, 1886.

    5704. iii. MARY SUMNER, b. Dec. 22, 1889.

4177. ALONZO W. FISK (Alonzo W., Samuel, Samuel, Jonathan, David, David, David. Jaffery. Robert, Simon, Simon. William. Symond), b. Brooklyn, N. Y., Apr. 30, 1866; m. May 25, 1888. Mamie I. Smith, b. Oct. 14, 1868. He was born in Brooklyn; was educated in public schools of Brooklyn; first started out in business life with Wm. Henry Smith & Co., wholesale dry goods, New York City; then went with Watson & Stillman, machine business; then with John I. Hayes, machine business, of Brooklyn, and is now treasurer of the John I. Hayes Machine Company, 108 to 118 West St., Brooklyn: res. 114 West St., Brooklyn, N. Y.

    5705. i.   ELMER ALONZO, b. May 6, 1889; res. 1143 Lafayette Ave., Brooklyn.
    5706. ii.   ALBERT SOULARD, b. Oct. 19, 1890; res. 1143 Lafayette Ave., Brooklyn.
    5707. iii. EMMA FLORENCE, b. Oct. 27, 1894; res. 1143 Lafayette Ave., Brooklyn.

4187. DR. FRANCIS HOSEA FISK (Robert W., Abraham, Robert, Robert, Robert, David, David, Jeffrey, Robert, Simon, Simon, William, Symond), b. Cincinnati, Ohio, Jan. 15, 1836; m. in Omega, Tex., May 9, 1866, Mrs. Lizzie E. (Heasht) Witcher, b. Oct. 25, 1841. For many years he was a practicing physician. He is now editor and manager of "The Messenger." an A. O. U. W. paper; res. Nashville, Tenn.

    5708. i.   JAMES WILSON, b. Mar. 14, 1871; d. Jan. 4, 1886.
    5709. ii.   MARY E., b. May 17, 1874.
    5710. iii. KATHERYNE, b. July 26, 1876.

4193. JAMES WILLIAM FISK (James, Henry A., Robert, Robert, Robert, David, David, Jeffrey, Robert, Simon, Simon, William, Symond), b Putnam County, Ind., July 10, 1834; m. in Melrose, Ill., Jan. 25, 1858, Sarah J. Dodd, b. Apr. 2, 1843, in Melrose, Ill. He is a retired farmer; res. Ridge Farm, Ill.

    5711. i.   ROBERT W., b. Nov. 7, 1858; m. Belle Brown.
    5712. ii.   ALBERT S., b. Sept. 10, 1860; d. Oct. 24, 1880.
    5713. iii. JAMES E., b. Sept. 21, 1863; m. Maggie E. Horner and Laura E. Driskell.
    5714. iv. UNA R., b. Apr. 21, 1866; d. same day.

4195. RICHARD SIMPSON FISK (James, Henry A., Robert, Robert, Robert, David, David, Jeffrey, Robert. Simon, Simon, William, Symond), b. Greencastle, Ind., Sept. 12, 1841; m. there Dec. 31, 1861. Mary M. Wood, b. Apr. 13, 1845. He is a farmer; res. Altoona, Kan.

    5715. i.   MARY ALBERTINE, b. Nov. 14, 1867; m. —— Wolf; add. Altoona, Kan.
    5716. ii.   RICHARD L., b. Mar. 1, 1869; add. Altoona, Kan.
    5717. iii. VANORA A., b. Sept. 24, 1870; m. —— Kherrer; add. Altoona, Kan.
    5718. iv. ELDORA C., b. Dec. 31, 1872; m. —— Powell; add. Edmand, Oklahoma.
    5719. v.   EMA C., b. Jan. 25, 1875; m. —— Crainor; add. Havana, Montgomery County, Kan.
    5720. vi. BENJAMIN W., b. Mar. 14, 1877; add. Altoona, Kan.
    5721. vii. ALMA G., b. Jan. 9, 1880; add. Altoona, Kan.
    5722. viii. CRISTLE, b. Mar. 4, 1882; add. Altoona, Kan.
    5723. ix. SEPHRONA H., b. Feb. 23, 1884; add. Altoona, Kan.

4203. FRANCIS MARION FISK (James, Henry A., Robert, Robert, Robert, David, David, Jeffrey, Robert, Simon, Simon, William, Symond), b. Greencastle, Ind., Mar. 30, 1843; m. there Mary Candis Matkin, b. May 4, 1850. He is a farmer; res. Kiowa, Kan.

    5724. i.   CELESTA, b. June 7, 1869; m. —— Roach; res. Altoona, Kan.
    5725. ii.   LILLIAN, b. June 30, 1872; m. —— Haskett; res. K.
    5726. iii. LULU, b. Mar. 27, 1874; d. Oct. 4, 1883.
    5727. iv. ATHELBERT AMOS, b. Oct. 17, 1876.
    5728. v.   EFFIE, b. Dec. 25, 1879; d. Sept. 21, 1883.
    5729. vi. WALTER D., b. Mar. 25, 1881.
    5730. vii. ZENA, b. July 27, 1883.

5731. viii. ALICE, b. Aug. 10, 1885; d. Sept. 19, 1886.
5732. ix. HENRY CLAY, b. Aug. 8, 1887.
5733. x. OTHO G., b. Dec. 22, 1889.
5734. xi. SYLVA, b. Aug. 23, 1892.

4213. JOHN ROBERT FISK (Wiley B., Henry A., Robert, Robert, Robert, David, David, Jeffrey, Robert, Simon, Simon, William, Symond), b. McLain County, Ill., Sept. 15, 1839; m. Aug. 2, 1859, Emily Walters, d. Nov. 14, 1868; m. 2d, Mar. 21, 1869, Julia A. Colliver, b. Mar. 29, 1844. He is a farmer and extensive dealer in grain and stock; also in real estate and loan business; res. Caldwell, Kan.
5735. i. MARY E., b. ———.
5736. ii. DAVID W., b. ———.
5737. iii. WILEY R., b. ———.
5738. iv. LULIE C., b. ———.
5739. v. FRANK LESLIE, b. Dec. 30, 1873, in Carroll County, Mo.; is a school teacher in Caldwell, Kan.
5740. vi. JAMES E., b. ———.
5741. vii. ELLIOT M., b. ———.
5742. viii. MINERVA J., b. ———.
5743. ix. WILLIAM, b. ———.
5744. x. JOHN R., b. ———.
5745. xi. HATTIE, b. ———..
5746. xii. FRED L., b. ———.

4221. FRANK B. FISK (Wiley B., Henry A., Robert, Robert, Robert, David, David, Jeffrey, Robert, Simon, Simon, William, Symond), b. Kentucky, Oct. 24, 1862; m. in Mound City, Kan., Sept. 11, 1884, Caroline Lasswell, b. Feb. 27, 1864. He is a school teacher; res. Caldwell, Kan.
5747. i. BESSIE L., b. Feb. 26, 1889.
5748. ii. LIZZIE, b. Feb. 28, 1892.

4225. MARCUS M. FISK (Elijah P., John, David, Robert, Robert, David, David, Jeffrey, Robert, Simon, Simon, William, Symond), b. Boston, Mass., Apr. 1, 1842; m. ——— ———; res. 39 Bowdoin St., Boston, Mass.
5749. i. BLANCHE, b. May 15, 1870.
5750. ii. FRANK, b. July 24, 1872.
5751. iii. ARTHUR, b. Oct. 30, 1874.
5752. iv. PHILIP, b. Feb. 24, 1876.

4248. CHARLES HENRY FISK (John F., David, Ebenezer, Ebenezer, Ebenezer, David, David, David, Jeffrey, Robert, Simon, Simon, William, Symond), b. Fiskburg, Ky., Aug. 31, 1843; m. at Lexington, Oct. 23, 1866, Margaret A. Emmal, b. Feb. 3, 1848. Charles H. Fisk was born Aug. 31, 1843, at Fiskburg, Kenton County, Ky.; moved to Covington, Ky., in Oct., 1848; son of Hon. John F. and Elizabeth S. Fisk. His father was Lieutenant-Governor of Kentucky, and a strong union man during the War of the Rebellion. Chas. H. attended the public schools and graduated from the high school in 1858, but pursued his studies thereafter in that school in special classes; entered Miami University in Feb., 1860; graduated 1863. While in the university he was very popular with the great majority of the students, faculty and residents of Oxford. He became a member of Kappa Chapter of D. K. E. shortly after he entered college and was an ardent and devoted member of that fraternity. He was for a time the presiding officer in that chapter. He entered Miami Union Literary Society during his freshman year and became thoroughly identified with all the interests of that body. He was ambitious and successful in all of his efforts, and received at the hands of his fellow students and of the faculty more honors than were ever allotted to any other student at the university. He was chosen junior orator by his class; represented his college on celebration of Washington's birthday; was elected president of the Miami Union Literary Society in the last half of the junior year; chosen to deliver the address at the winter exhibition of Miami Union Literary Society in the first half of his senior year; was given the first honor in his class and delivered the valedictory on July 2, 1863. He was noted as the best foot ball kicker ever in the university. He was much inclined to mischief and in consequence was often in consultation with the faculty at the Friday afternoon meetings. After his graduation at Miami, Mr. Fisk entered the law office of his father and began seriously the study of the law. The father's partner died about six weeks later and Mr. Fisk began at once to assist his father in all matters. He attended the Cincinnati Law School and graduated therefrom with credit in the spring of 1864. He received his law license a few months before reaching his majority, but could not enter upon active practice until the fall of 1864. He practiced with his father till Feb., 1865, when he formed a partnership with Hon. John M. Scott and went to Lexington, Ky., to practice before the military courts and commissions. He was there during the remainder of 1865, in which brief period he defended thirty-three persons accused of murder with success and ability. In 1866 he returned to Covington and resumed the practice there with his father with whom he formed a partnership on Jan. 1, 1868, and the firm of John F. & Chas. H. Fisk has since continued. The senior, however, retired from active business in the spring of 1890. Mr. Fisk is an avowed Republican, but has not taken to political life as a business. He has devoted himself with untiring energy to the profession of his choice, and has been eminently successful. His clients have ever been among the best citizens and corporations in his vicinity. While in Lexington he became acquainted with the woman of his choice, and on Oct. 23, 1866, he was united in marriage to Miss Maggie Emmal, of that city. Three children have blessed this union, but the eldest child, a bright boy, was called hence in Jan., 1881, at the age of 13 years and 4 months. The second son, Otis H., graduated with honor from Yale University in 1892, and has been in Germany pursuing his studies since that time. He will remain there for a four years' course. The third child is Miss Elizabeth S., her grandmother's namesake, now (1894) in her 10th year. The subject of this sketch has been highly honored by the Masonic fraternity with which he has been intimately identified since 1877. He has been Grand Master of the Grand Lodge, Grand T. I. Master of the Grand Council, Grand High Priest of the Grand Chapter and Grand Commander of the Grand Commandery of Kentucky. He is a member of the Christian Church and prominent in all matters connected therewith. For about twenty-four years he has been superintendent of the Sunday school. In 1884 Mr. Fisk delivered a Masonic address on St. John's day in the college campus by invitation of the Masons of Oxford and vicinity. In 1890 he delivered the address to the alumni of Miami. He has filled two terms as president of the Miami University Association; res. 1017 Russell Ave., Covington, Ky.

5753.   i.   EMMAL, b. Sept. 3, 1867; d. Jan. 14, 1881. Emmal Fisk, the elder son of Mr. and Mrs. Chas. H. Fisk, was a bright boy and perhaps the best known and most popular boy of his age ever in that city. He was unusually strong and active for his years, but was called away from his family and friends by that terrible disease peritonitis at the age of 13 years and 4 months. The esteem in which he was held was shown by the fact that his funeral was attended by the largest number of people ever present at the funeral of any young person in the city.

5754.   ii. OTIS HARRISON, b. Mar. 5, 1870. He attended the public schools in Covington for some years, then spent two years in the school of Prof. Babbin in Cincinnati, and thereafter was with Professor Wyckoff at Walnut Hills, where he was prepared for Yale College, in which he entered the freshman class in 1888. At the end of that year he accompanied his father on an extended trip to the old country, and visited points of interest in England, Scotland, France and Germany, and very thoroughly explored Belgium, Italy and Ireland. He graduated with "honor" in the class of 1892 at Yale. In the fall of that year he went to Germany for the purpose of studying law in the universities there and of becoming proficient in the German language, of which he had at all times been a student. He entered at Leipsic where he spent one year. The next semester was passed at Berlin. He then went to Heidelberg, where he expected to remain one year. While there, however, he conceived the idea of surprising his parents by taking, as he says, a degree for his father. He remained six months longer than he intended, and on Aug. 2, 1895, received at the hands of the celebrated university at Heidelberg the degree of

"Doctor of Philosophy," "magnum cum laude." The essay submitted by him prior to his oral examination met with great favor, and two of the professors, Jellineck and Meyer, perhaps the most celebrated in their departments in Europe, who are issuing a series of Philosophical Works as part of the Heidelberg University Library series, have asked permission, which, of course, was granted, to publish the essay of Dr. Fisk as a portion of the first volume of said series. The laurel wreath with which he was crowned, and the "Dr's hat" from his "cake," he sent to his sister, by his father, who visited him last summer for the second time. He has returned to Leipsic, where he expects to receive the degree of Dr. de jura in 1896. He has traveled extensively on the continent during his vacations. He speaks and writes the German like a native. He proposes to practice law upon his return to his native land, but has not yet determined upon his location. He has just returned (1896) to Heide'berg for further degree.

5755. iii. ELIZABETH SARAH, b. June 27, 1884.

4251. JUDGE ROBERT BROWN FISK (John F., David, Ebenezer, Ebenezer, Ebenezer, David, David, David, Jeffrey, Robert, Simon, Simon, William, Symond), b. Covington, Ky., Mar. 2. 1852; m. at Logansport, Ind., Oct. 30, 1883, Julia Comly (Green) Ross, b. June 16, 1852. Robert Brown Fisk, son of John Flavell and Elizabeth Sarah Fisk, was born at Covington, Kenton County, Ky., on March 2, 1852, at the brick building, still standing, on the southeast corner of Scott Street, and the alley between Fifth and Sixth Streets. He was the fourth of seven children, there being a boy and two girls on each side of Robert. He attended the public schools in his native town, ultimately graduating from the high school there, after taking the first three years of a collegiate course, at the high school, under the able tutorship of Prof. John Wortham Hall, whose father, Dr. J. W. Hall, was for many years president of Miami University at Oxford, Ohio. At the high school he met Miss Julia Comly Green, sister-in-law of Professor Hall, who, subsequently, became Robert's wife, their engagement having been broken off, and, when Miss Green became a widow, renewed and their marriage resulting. Graduating with honors from this school, Robert immediately applied himself to the study of law, in the office of his father and brother, constituting the firm of J. F. & C. H. Fisk, in Covington. Robert was admitted to the practice of the law when not quite 20 years of age, and for several years continued in the office where he had studied, but never became a member of the firm. In 1880 he associated with himself Mr. William D. Brent, at that time a clerk in the office of J. F. & C. H. Fisk, and under the style of Fisk & Brent these two opened an office as attorneys, in the old Greer block, on Lower Market and Scott Street, Covington, Ky. Mr. Brent having been appointed city clerk to fill a vacancy, the partnership of Fisk & Brent was dissolved and Mr. Fisk after practicing in Covington for a time by himself, finally, in 1884, left his native city and located at Pierre in the then territory of Dakota, but now the capital of South Dakota. While living at Pierre, in 1885, Mr. Fisk was appointed by Hon. Gilbert A. Pierce, then Governor of the territory, as supervisor of the census taken of the territory in that year. The territory was divided, in this work, by an imaginary line, running about on the present line between North and South Dakota, Mr. Fisk having the supervision of the southern portion. This was a larger territory than ever before or since supervised by one person, it requiring a force of about four hundred enumerators to do the actual canvassing for returns, there being about 263,000 people in the district Mr. Fisk, however, was possessed of ambition to do well and an almost inexhaustible ability for work. He completed his work, returned his schedules, and for the first (and perhaps the only) time these returns were recognized and paid for by the National Government, in the proportion provided by law. The total expenses of the census for Mr. Fisk's district were about $27,000, and every cent of it was properly accounted for. While acting as supervisor of this census, Mr. Fisk was a witness before the sub-committee of the Senatorial Committee, appointed to inquire into the condition of the settlers on the Crow Creek Indian reservation, opened to settlement by proclamation of President Arthur, at about the close of his term of office, and "closed," by proclamation of President Cleveland, shortly after his ascension to the Presidency. Mr. Fisk's testimony, before this commit-tee, coupled with a very full exposition of the matter. tabulated, by Mr. Fisk, from his census schedules, had much to do with the subsequent action of Congress in recognizing the rights of these settlers and the congressional relief afforded them. This sub-committee was composed of Benjamin Harrison, of Indiana. John J. Ingalls of Kansas and Senator Jones of Arkansas. Just before leaving Covington, and just after going to Pierre, Mr. Fisk compiled, for the city of Covington, the statute laws of Kentucky, the ordinances of the city, and the decisions of the Court of Appeals of Kentucky, touching questions of importance to cities, a work which has received very high commendation from the bar of Kentucky. In 1884 Mr. Fisk made homestead filing on the S. W. ¼ of Section 6, Township 117, Range 75, in Potter County (now). South Dakota. and moved to that place. In 1890 he moved his residence to Gettysburg, the county seat of Potter County, where he had opened a law office in 1886, and where he still resides, engaged in the practice of law. In 1892 Mr. Fisk was secretary of the Volunteer World's Fair Com-mission of South Dakota, having been a delegate, sent by the Business Men's Association of Gettysburg, to the convention, at which that commission was formed. This commission afterward gave way to that appointed by the Governor of the State, with which Mr. Fisk was not connected. His wife is the great-granddaughter of Samuel Meredith, the first treasurer of the United States and a warm personal friend of Washington. Her father, Richard Green, was a native of Huddersfield, Yorkshire, England. He married Margaret Meredith, at Wilkes Barre, Pa.,· and was for many years a leading merchant of Dayton, Ohio, from which place he moved to near Logansport, Ind., where he died. Mrs. Fisk's mother is still living at the advanced age of 88 years, in the full possession of all her faculties, and having the appearance of a woman of not over 60. Mrs. Fisk is a woman of queenly form and face, a lady of rare accomplishments and noted for her domestic virtues. Mr. Fisk is counted a good lawyer and is ranked among the most eloquent and forcible speakers of South Dakota. He is a Republican in politics, a member of the Christian Church, and is now the County Judge of Pot-ter County. His home is a model of combined southern and western hospitality; his married life has been unusually felicitous and happy; res. Gettysburg, So. Dak.

    5756. i.   OLIN MEREDITH (adopted), b. Oct. 2, 1875.

    4253. JOHN FLAVEL FISK, JR. (John F., David, Ebenezer, Ebenezer, Ebenezer, David, David, David, Jeffrey, Robert, Simon, Simon, William, Symond), b. Covington, Ky., Nov. 27, 1858; m. at Milford, Ohio, Dec. 26, 1882, Grace Gatch, b. July 18, 1863; add. 429 Walnut St., Cincinnati, Ohio.

    5757. i.   GATCH FLAVEL, b. Sept. 19, 1887; d. July 14. 1888.
    5758. ii.   JOHN FLAVEL, b. June 21, 1890.

    4260. ALBERT GALLATIN FISK (Ebenezer, David, Ebenezer, Ebenezer, Ebenezer, David, David, David, Jeffrey, Robert, Simon, Simon. William, Symond), b. Fiskburg, Ky., May 4, 1844; m. in Florence, Ky.. Dec. 31, 1871, Mary A. Conner, b. Oct. 15, 1851. He is a farmer; res. Florence, Ky.

    5759. i.   HARRISON CONNER, b. May 26, 1873.

    4305. JOHN MINOT FISKE (Benjamin M., John M., Benjamin, Ebenezer, David, David. David. Jeffrey, Robert, Simon. Simon, William, Symond), b. Dec. 31, 1853. Chelmsford. Mass.; m. June 6, 1876, Katie S. Westervelt, b. Feb. 20, 1857. He is in the ornamental iron business. Res. New York City; P. O. box 983.

    5760. i.   KATE MARION, b. Mar. 20. 1877.
    5761. ii.   ANNA ADELLE, b. Aug. 24, 1879; d. Feb. 20, 1882.
    5762. iii. LILLIAN. b. Jan. 12, 1885; d. Feb. 20, 1885.
    5763. iv. ETHEL, b. Jan. 17, 1888.

    4306. JOSEPH WINN FISKE (Benjamin M., John M., Benjamin. Eben-ezer, David, David, David, Jeffrey, Robert, Simon, Simon, William, Symond), b. Mar. 5, 1857, Chelmsford, Mass.: m. at Somerville, Mass., June 3, 1885, Mary S. Harrington, b. Nov. 13, 1864. He is in the ornamental iron business. Res. Passaic, N. J.; add. P. O. box 983, New York City.

    5764. i.   WARREN RUSSELL, b. July 8, 1886.
    5765. ii.   HOWARD BENJAMIN, b. July 9, 1890.

4307. FREDERICK A. P. FISKE (Benjamin M., John M., Benjamin, Ebenezer, David, David, David, Jeffrey, Robert, Simon, Simon, William, Symond), b. Chelmsford, Mass., Oct. 4, 1859; m. at Winchester, July 2, 1890, Harriet Lydia Locke, b. Mar. 25, 1862. He is a graduate of Harvard College, 1881, and of the Harvard Law School, 1884, and is a member of the Suffolk bar, and is practicing with office at 10 Tremont St., room 32, Boston. Res. Somerville, Mass.; Boston add. 10 Tremont St.

    5766. i.   HELEN LOCKE, b. Oct. 6, 1892.

4317. WILLIAM B. FISKE (William B., Charles, Benjamin, Ebenezer, David, David David, Jeffrey, Robert, Simon, Simon, William, Symond), b. Boston, Mass., Jan. 28, 1857; m. there Mar. 2, 1895, Claire Earnestine Acorn, b. Jan. 1, 1865. Res. Chicago, Ill.; add. 42 River St., R. 216.

4360. WARREN NELSON FISK (Royal, Benoni, Benjamin, Benjamin, Benjamin, John, John, Phinehas, Thomas, Robert, Simon, Simon, William, Symond), b. Danby, Vt., Feb. 11, 1834; m. at Collins, N. Y., Apr. 15, 1855, Cordelia Rebecca Harris, b. May 12, 1835. He has been somewhat changeable in business pursuits, having tried farming, teaching, clerking in a general store, bookkeeping, commercial traveling, photography, etc. He has not made a large fortune out of all these, but having commenced with very little besides good health has "held his own" pretty well. He has a comfortable home. Res. North Freedom, Wis.

    5767. i.   ALBERT WALLACE, b. Oct. 21, 1857; m. Clara M. Perry.
    5768. ii.   BOY, b. Feb. 24, 1862; d. Feb. 26, 1862.
    5769. iii.   MARION EDWIN, b. Sept. 3, 1869; m. Anna O. Ware.

4362. ALBERT MEAD FISK (Royal, Benoni, Benjamin, Benjamin, Benjamin, John, John, Phinehas, Thomas, Robert, Simon, Simon, William, Symond), b. Danby, Vt., July 7, 1838; m. Nov. 29, 1868, Myra Elizabeth Douglas, b. June 26, 1845. Res. North Freedom, Wis.

    5770. i.   MERRITT WILBUR, b. Freedom, Wis., Nov. 2, 1869; d. Sept. 25, 1871.
    5771. ii.   BERT JAMES, b. Freedom, Wis., Aug. 31, 1873.
    5772. iii.   ELVA EUNICE, b. Freedom, Wis., Nov. 17, 1878.

4366. CHARLES WILBUR FISK (Royal, Benoni, Benjamin, Benjamin, Benjamin, John, John, Phinehas, Thomas, Robert, Simon, Simon, William, Symond), b. Collins, N. Y., Nov. 9, 1853; m. in Reedsburg, Wis., July 20, 1876, Lillian Eliza Dearborn, b. Jan. 11, 1857. Res. North Freedom, Wis.

    5773. i.   NELLIE LORENE, b. in Freedom, Wis., Aug. 14, 1877; m. Dec. 20, 1894, Joseph F. Hackett, b. 1869; res. North Freedom. Ch.: 1, Hazel, b. Oct. 20, 1895.
    5774. ii.   WILBUR EDWIN, b. Freedom, Wis., May 3, 1884.
    5775. iii.   BESSIE LILLIAN, b. Freedom, Wis., July 3, 1888.
    5776. iv.   ROYAL EARL, b. Freedom, Wis., Apr. 7, 1893.

4371. CAPT. HIRAM FISK (Hiram P., Benjamin, Benjamin, Benjamin, Benjamin, John, John, Phinehas, Thomas, Robert, Simon, Simon, William, Symond), b. Danby, Vt., Apr. 1, 1846; m. Dec. 11, 1864, Helen Forbes. Res. Danby Four Corners, Vt.

    5777. i.   LUTA, b. ———.
    5778. ii.   CHAS. BENJ., b. Dec. 15, 1870; res. with his uncle, Benj. A.

4372. BENJAMIN A. FISK (Hiram P., Benjamin, Benjamin, Benjamin, Benjamin, John, John, Phinehas, Thomas, Robert, Simon, Simon, William, Symond), b. Danby, Vt., Feb. 17, 1831; m. there Nov. 16, 1859, Mary Jane Green, b. Feb. 27, 1839. His occupation has been varied. His tastes are mechanical, more than farming, although he has followed the latter most of his life. He moved from Danby to Manchester in 1886 and owns the "Summit House." Res. Manchester, Vt.

    5779. i.   MARIETTA LOIS, b. Apr. 26, 1861; m. Nov. 16, 1882, Julius Hill; res. Sunderland, Vt. Ch.: 1, Jerome Fisk, b. Jan. 16, 1891. 2, Benj. Julius, b. Dec. 3, 1895.
    5780. ii.   ALICE ROSINA, b. July 27, 1870; res. M.
    5781. iii.   CHAS. BENJ., b. Dec. 15, 1870 (adopted); res. M.

4378. NOAH FISK (Lyman R., Benjamin, Benjamin, Benjamin, Benjamin, John, John, Phinehas, Thomas, Robert, Simon, Simon, William, Symond), b. Danby, Vt., May 26, 1827; m. Nov. 10, 1852, at Wallingford, Olive Ridlow, b. Apr. 1, 1831. He was brought up on his father's farm, and learned the trade of carpenter of his father, with whom he worked until 21 years of age. He then went to work for the Rutland & Burlington Railroad, on bridges and railroad buildings, and kept up the work for different railroad companies, until he was married. He then bought a place in Clarendon, Vt., where he now lives, and has always lived there, ever since, with the exception of one year, when he moved to Middletown, Vt., Apr., 1859, where he worked in a carpenter shop. With the exception of that one year he has worked at building and joiner work; res. Clarendon, Vt.

    5782. i.   ELLA, b. Mar. 17, 1854; m. Jan. 1, 1879, R. H. Tower. They res. C. Ch.: 1, David N., b. Dec. 23, 1879. 2, Fannie, b. Jan. 11, 1882. 3, Mollie S., b. June 6, 1885. 4, Ella, b. June 16, 1895.

    5783. ii.   OLLIE, b. Apr. 12, 1856; m. July 2, 1894, A. Thompson; res. C., s. p.

    5784. iii. ROLLA N., b. Apr. 5, 1858; m. Rebecca S. Colvin.

    5785. iv. GEO. W., b. May 16, 1861; unm.

    5786. v.   BURT E., b. Jan. 5, 1864; m. Sept. 18, 1894, Ida Cleveland, res. C., s. p.

    5787. vi. BELLE F., b. Oct. 28, 1870; m. Dec. 24, 1892, Geo. Edmonds; res. C., s. p.

4389. CALEB P. FISK (Oliver, Benjamin, Benjamin, Benjamin, Benjamin, John, John, Phinehas, Thomas, Robert, Simon, Simon, William, Symond), b. Danby, Vt., ——; m. Olive Ann Hulett. He enlisted Aug. 27, 1862, in Company B., Fourteenth Regiment Vermont Volunteers, for nine months. He died of disease at Wolf Run Shoals, Va., and his remains were sent home for interment. He d. June 20, 1863; res. Danby, Vt.

4393. NATHAN FISK (Reuben, Reuben, Benjamin, Benjamin, Benjamin, John, John, Phinehas, Thomas, Robert, Simon, Simon, William, Symond), b. Danby, Vt., Oct. 29, 1830; m. in Brant, N. Y., Nov. 30, 1853, Rhoda Fuller, b. May 31, 1834. He is a farmer; res. Wonewoc, Wis.

    5788. i.   THEODORE, b. June 14, 1859.

4395. REUBEN FISK (Reuben, Reuben, Benjamin, Benjamin, Benjamin, John, John, Phinehas, Thomas, Robert, Simon, Simon, William, Symond), b. Danby, Vt., Feb. 7, 1833; m. Mar. 4, 1855, —— ——; res. Wonewoc, Wis.

    5789. i.   JULIUS B., b. ——.

4398. AARON WILLIAM FISK (Fitz William, Rufus, Nathaniel, Benjamin, Benjamin, John, John, Phinehas, Thomas, Robert, Simon, Simon, William, Symond), b. Moira, N. Y., July 24, 1831; m. in New York State, Jan. 1, 1857, Hannah Sweet Phillips, b. May 16, 1831; d. Feb. 5, 1883. He is a farmer; res. Moline, Ill.

    5790. i.   PERRY BARNEY, b. May 15, 1852; m. Apr. 2, 1884; res. Moline.

4410. ALANSON FISKE (Alanson, Bateman, Nathaniel, Benjamin, Benjamin, John, John, Phinehas, Thomas, Robert, Simon, Simon, William, Symond), b. Georgetown, N. Y., ——; m. Abigail Lewis; d. in 1883. He was a boot and shoe maker. He d. ——; res. Plainfield and West Exeter, N. Y.

    5791. i.   EZRA J., b. 1833; m. Sophia E. Jaycox and Margrette Maguire.

4414. LEVI JACKSON FISK (Levi, Eber, Nathaniel, Benjamin, Benjamin, John, John, Phinehas, Thomas, Robert, Simon, Simon, William, Symond), b. Schroon, N. Y., Apr. 25, 1836; m. in Whitehall, N. Y., Marie Antoinette Wolcott, b. May 8, 1844. He was born in Essex county, N. Y., in 1836, son of a lumberman, and his early years gave him a practical training in all that pertained to the life of a lumberman. When still young, being possessed of a desire to seek his fortune with the great throng then hurrying west, shortly after the discovery of gold in California, he crossed the plains long before a locomotive whistle was there heard, and then it was at the risk of one's life that such a venture was made. He arrived at Salt Lake City shortly after the famous Mountain Meadow massacre, and, as it soon became manifest to him that a man who did not intend to become a Mormon, and did not want to adopt polygamy, had little chance of success there, he hastened on to Nevada. Eleven years of the most eventful char- acter were spent afterward, prospecting on the mountains of Nevada, Colorado, California, Idaho and Montana. At the outbreak of the Civil War, he joined a company of Rangers in Nevada, and they, starting east for the scene of hostili- ties, were recalled by the Governor to suppress an uprising in that State, and thereafter the Rangers were retained in Virginia City for the protection of property from Indians and outlaws. After the close of the war, Mr. Fisk returned east and decided to settle and enter into the lumber business in New York State. A few years of the quiet monotony of business life again brought on a desire for the rush and activity of the west, and he returned to Montana where he spent ten years in the lumber business and in railroad contracting. During this period he was one of the constructors of a branch of the Union Pacific Railroad, and he also built an hundred miles of the Northern Pacific Railroad. On the completion of the latter road, while on a visit east, circumstances brought him to Berkshire, and being pleased with the people and surroundings, he decided to retire from active busi- ness and enjoy the quiet of his present home, "Brookside," in Cheshire, which had been the home of his ancestors since the settlement of the Hoosac Valley. Mr. Fisk's education has been for the most part practical, having entered his father's mills after a few years' study in the public schools, though he later studied a year at Dickinson Academy, in Pennsylvania. Nevertheless the lessons taught him in the rough school of experience have served him best, and have made him one of those free, easy men of the western stamp who see the broad side of life, and overlook the petty differences so prevalent in the east. As a business man he has had experience enough to qualify him for most any position, and, coupled with this knowledge, has a keen insight of men and affairs that especially fits him as a legislator. With his home in the heart of a farming community, he is especially interested in all that concerns the farmer, and will no doubt prove of valuable service at the next session of the Legislature in the consideration of tuberculosis and bounty to farmers for cows killed. His large experience covers most any point on which he is liable to be sounded, and his residence here, coupled with his interest in his district, all make him the man for the place. There can be no doubt but Mr. Fisk will make us a most efficient and servicable Representa- tive. He is not a politician, though he has always identified himself with the Republican party; res. Cheshire, Mass.

5792. i. WILLIAM WOLCOTT, b. Oct. 25, 1870; res. C.

4420. DR. ANSEL JASON FISK (Lyman J., Eber, Nathaniel, Benjamin. Benjamin, John, John. Phinehas, Thomas, Robert, Simon, Simon, William, Sy- mond), b. June 16, 1829; m. Feb. 10, 1850, in Tioga, Pa., Jane E. Spencer. Ansel J. Fisk, M. D., son of Lyman and Betsey Fisk, was born at Schroon, Essex county, N. Y. At the age of 16 he came with his father to Tioga, Pa., where they engaged actively in lumbering, the young man attending to the financial part of the busi- ness, and keeping all the books and accounts. His school days were limited, his literary training meager, but he learned to be methodical in affairs, which was best evidenced in his career as a physician. Moved to Bellenart, Canada, in 1854, and by close attention to the manufacture of lumber, he soon acquired a fine compe- tence. Returning to Tioga, in 1861, he purchased large tracts of forest land, and building mills, continued the lumbering business for some years. In 1873 he com- menced the study of medicine with Dr. R. B. Smith, of Tioga, Pa. He attended his first course of lectures at Bellevue and graduated at Detroit Medical College, in 1876. He immediately entered upon practice at Farmington, Pa., and continued actively engaged in the duties of the profession until his health became so impaired that he could no longer labor in his chosen field. His boyhood days were spent amidst the scenes of the Great North woods, and the mountain ranges of the Adi- rondacks, where he became familiar with gun and rod and in mature years he ever enjoyed the recreation of hunting and fishing. Mr. Fisk was a born doctor and had a natural tendency toward medicine and surgery. At his lumber works in Canada, situated a long drive from a physician, he provided himself with a case of medi- cines and surgical instruments, and prescribed for his workmen, sewed up their cuts and dressed their injuries with excellent success. He had an intuitive faculty of diagnosis, and a quick perception at the bedside of fitting his medicine to the case in hand. Optimistic, of a hopeful temperament, cheerful and cheery in nature, he inspired his patients with confidence. Fertile in resources and of unlimited courage he never relaxed his efforts to save his patient. He was heroic in treatment and gave the maximum dose. The writer remembers prescribing 15 grains of potassium bromide, when Dr. Fisk, who was present, quietly remarked: "You are shooting bear with bird shot, give him 60," and Fisk was right. There was not a particle of jealousy in his nature, professional or otherwise. He was never known to utter a word in disparagement of a fellow physician, or to criticise the treatment of a case. He believed that there was room for all, and that the best interests of the profession could be attained by working in harmony. He soon after graduating became a member of this society and attended the meetings while his health permitted. In politics he was a Republican. After a painful illness of three years, during which time he made the same gallant fight for his own life, which he had always made for his patients, he died of Bright's disease on the 56th anniversary of his birth. He d. June 16, 1885; res. Tioga. Pa.

5793. i. WILLIAM J., b. Apr. 18, 1854; d. Apr. 13, 1874.
5794. ii. HENRY S., b. Jan. 26, 1859; m. Ella Eggleston.

4421. WILLIAM JACKSON FISK (Lyman, Eber, Nathaniel, Benjamin, Benjamin, John, John, Phinehas, Thomas, Robert, Simon, Simon, William, Symond), b. Essex Co., N. Y., Jan. 2, 1833; m. Tioga, Pa., Harriet H. Hammer, b. 1832. He is a filer; res. So. Williamsport, Pa.

5795. i. LYMAN J., b. Jan. 24, 1855.
5796. ii. CHAS. MUSINA, b. Aug. 20, 1859; m. Feb. 15, 1893, Harriett Ann Hammer, b. Oct. 30, 1865. He is a musician; res. 180 E. Ohio St., Chicago, Ill., s. p.
5797. iii. GEO., b. May 20, 1864.
5798. iv. LEWIS L., b. Apr. 3, 1866.
5799. v. LILLIE MAE, b. Apr. 6, 1872; m. —— Dougherty; res. Hughsville, Pa.

4437. JAMES F. FISK (John, Nathaniel, Nathaniel, Benjamin, Benjamin, John, John, Phinehas, Thomas, Robert, Simon, Simon, William, Symond), b. Brandon, Vt., June 2, 1835; m. at Sudbury, Feb. 8, 1860, Lois R. Clark, b. June 12, 1840. He is a farmer; res. Brandon, Vt.

5800. i. MINNIE A., b. Feb. 16, 1864; m. Feb. 9, 1887, Willard R. Stickney; res. Leicester.
5801. ii. WM. J., b. Nov. 14, 1865; m. Mar. 26, 1892; res. B.
5802. iii. DORA J., b. May 19, 1872; m. Apr. 5, 1892, Dana W. Ayer; res. B.
5803. iv. BESSIE A., b. Dec. 23, 1873; m. Sept. 28, 1893, Frank C. Ayer; res. 37 Jay St., West Somerville, Mass.
5804. v. CARRIE L., b. Dec. 17, 1878.
5805. vi. JAMIE F., b. Oct. 7, 1879.

4439. LORENZO CHAPIN FISKE (Gideon M., David, Nathaniel, Benjamin, Benjamin, John, John, Phinehas, Thomas, Robert, Simon, Simon, William, Symond), b. New Haven, Vt., Aug. 29, 1824; m. at Troy, N. Y., Aug. 7, 1856, Sarah Louise Young, b. Dec. 27, 1829; d. Dec. 30, 1892. At the age of 10 years he went to live with a dry goods merchant in Burlington, Vt., Sion Earl Howard by name; remained with him until he was 21, then went to Troy, N. Y., and entered the wholesale dry goods store of Van Schoonhoven & Proudfit, 227 River St. He was soon made a partner in the store, and remained there till 1882, when the firm dissolved, and he retired to private life. He was a man of much force of character, and all who knew him respected him. He died from apoplexy. He d. Nov. 27, 1893; res. Troy, N. Y.

5806. i. JAMES YOUNG, b. Oct. 31, 1861; is a bookkeeper; res. unm. Troy, N. Y., 184 First St.
5807. ii. MARY GARDNER, b. July 12, 1863; m. Oct. 17, 1888, —— Walkley; res. Brooklyn, N. Y., 51 MacDonough St.
5808. iii. BESSIE LOUISE, b. Oct. 14, 1869; unm.; res. Troy.

4440. GEORGE WALLACE FISKE (Gideon M., David, Nathaniel, Benjamin, Benjamin, John, John, Phinehas, Thomas, Robert, Simon, Simon, William, Symond), b. Williston, Vt., Dec. 29, 1827; m. at Essex, N. Y., Jan. 9, 1850, Jane

A. Reynolds, of Essex, N. Y., b. Westport, Oct. 10, 1826; d. Mar. 7, 1862; m. 2d,. at Burlington, Vt., Apr., 1880, Cornelia Rowe. He learned the printer's trade,. which he followed all his life, with the exception of a few years in New York City, he has worked on the Burlington Free Press. Of late years his eyes failed. him and he has been in poor health; res. Burlington, Vt.

    5809. i.   CHARLES REYNOLDS, b. Aug. 25, 1850; m. at Jersey City,. N. J., Nov. 21, 1880, Isabella Latcher Hinkley, b. Nov. 2, 1857. He is a stationary engineer; res. Johnstown, N. Y., s. p.

    5810. ii. THEODORE LORENZO, b. June 18, 1852; m. Sept., 1881; res. Fultonville, N. Y.

    5811. iii. GEORGE WALLACE, b. Dec. 29, 1859; res. 100 E. Twenty-seventh St., New York City.

    4441. ISAAC ALPIN FISKE (Gideon M., David, Nathaniel, Benjamin,. Benjamin, John, John, Phinehas, Thomas, Robert, Simon, Simon, William, Sy-mond), b. Burlington, Vt., Dec. 27, 1831; m. Marion Fruto, of Glen Ellyn. She: d. Sept. 5, 1871, in Lemont, Ill.; m. 2d, 1873, Libbie E. ———; res. Evanston, Ill.. Isaac was of a restless disposition, and left home in 1854; went to Illinois; stopped: a few days in Chicago, but it was during the cholera epidemic; went to Wheaton: and from there to Danby (Glen Ellyn) and went into a shop with Mr. Fruto. and learned the tinner's trade. Later he moved to Lemont, and opened an agri-cultural implement salesroom in connection with his hardware store. His wife died, he married again, and was soon after killed by the cars. He d. Sept. 4, 1874; res. Lemont, Ill.

    5812. i.   GEORGE WILLIAM, b. Apr. 18, 1857; m. Nellie E. Towner.

    5813. ii. FANNIE MAY, b. July 30, 1863; m. Dec. 11, 1883, William Ber-ry. She d. Jan. 6, 1892; res. Roundhouse, Ill. Ch.: 1, Nellie: Marion; b. ———; d. Dec., 1892. 2, George Le Roy.

    4446. ELIJAH DOTY FISK (William, David, Nathaniel, Benjamin, Benja-min, John, John, Phinehas, Thomas, Robert, Simon, Simon, William, Symond), b. Jan. 8, 1827, Jay, N. Y.; m. at Providence, N. Y., Dec. 25, 1851, Phebe Briggs, b. Nov. 20, 1828. He is a paper maker; res. Sandy Hill, N. Y.

    5814. i.   WILLIAM M., b. Nov. 24, 1852; d. Feb. 27, 1871.

    4448. DEA. JOSHUA P. FISKE (William, David, Nathaniel, Benjamin,. Benjamin, John, John, Phinehas, Thomas, Robert, Simon, Simon, William, Sy-mond), b. Peru, N. Y., May 3, 1835; m. at Jay, N. Y., May 31, 1865, Pamelia C. Somers, b. June 16, 1835. He was born in the town of Peru, Clinton Co., N. Y. Spent the first eight years of his life in Pierpont, St. Lawrence Co., N. Y. At which time his parents moved to Jay, Essex Co., N. Y. At 17 years of age he taught school in one of the districts of the town. Was a clerk in one of the stores of the town, after which he settled on a farm near Bridport, Vt. Was mar-ried; came west from Vermont, and settled on a farm near Emington, Livingston Co., Ill., in the year 1868. Raised two daughters; both are still living. Moved in 1881, to Streator, La Salle Co., Ill., where he is still living. He is working as an agent for the Metropolitan Life Insurance Company. He is a Republican, and in religion a Baptist; is deacon of the Baptist Church, and has been for several years; res. Streator, Ill., 315 W. Grant St.

    5815. i.   KATIE A., b. Oct. 24, 1867.

    5816. ii. ANNIE MAE, b. Sept. 12, 1872.

    4449. JAMES H. FISK (William, David, Nathaniel, Benjamin, Benjamin. John, John, Phinehas, Thomas, Robert, Simon, Simon, William, Symond), b. Pierpont, N. Y., Sept. 18, 1841; m. at Jay, Dec. 7, 1865, Mary A. Smith; d. Jan. 24, 1868; m. 2d, Dec. 31, 1871, Margaret Simpson. He is a carpenter; res. Jay, N. Y.

    5817. i.   WILBUR J., b. Sept. 18, 1867; m. Carrie E. Conger.

    5818. ii. JOHN HENRY, b. Oct. 26, 1872.

    5819. iii. HARTWELL E., b. Jan. 11, 1876.

    5820. iv. DAVID SIMPSON, b. Oct. 23, 1878.

    5821. v.   SARAH ISABELLE, b. Jan. 3, 1874.

    5822. vi. LULU MARGRET, b. June 23, 1881.

    5823. vii. LILLIAN A., b. Sept. 23, 1879; d. Jan. 29, 1881.

35

4454. HON. CHARLES FISKE (Elijah D., David, Nathaniel, Benjamin, Benjamin, John, John, Phinehas, Thomas, Robert, Simon, Simon, William, Symond), b. Orwell, Vt., Jan. 28, 1832; m. Apr. 27, 1857, Frances Julina Colburn, b. June 1, 1835. For the first ten years of his life he lived on a farm in Orwell, Vt. In 1842 he removed with his parents to Brandon, Vt. Was educated in the district schools and the seminary in that town. Was engaged in farming till 1863-4, when he entered the sheep business, making several trips to Ohio to introduce there the celebrated Vermont Merino sheep. Moved to a farm in Leicester, Vt., in Mar., 1865, where he lives at present. Has held at various times the offices of highway surveyor, school committee and collector, and auditor. Was lister (assessor) in 1883-4, and again in 1887-8. Has been several times elected a Justice of the Peace, which office he holds at present, and represented the town in the Legislature of 1892; res. Leicester, Vt.

 5824. i. BURTON COLBURN, b. May 1, 1863; m. Adelle A. Robinson.
 5825. ii. JOHN C., b. Mar. 30, 1866; m. at Brandon, Feb. 24, 1887, Alice R. Jennings; res. Leicester, Vt.

4461. STEPHEN BURLINGAME FISKE (Daniel, Stephen K, Daniel, Daniel, Benjamin, John, John, Phinehas, Thomas, Robert, Simon, Simon, William, Symond), b. Oct. 30, 1849, in Brookfield, Mass.; m. North Brookfield, Mass., Mar. 3, 1873, Alice N. Stebbins, b. July 23, 1852 He is a druggist and magistrate; res. East Jaffrey, N. H., and Upton, Mass.

 5826. i. CHARLES NORMAN, b. Apr. 22, 1876. He is a student in Harvard College and in the Harvard Medical School and will graduate in 1898.
 5827. ii. HARRY AUSTEN, b. June 12, 1880; res. U.
 5828. iii. WALTER HEYWOOD, b. Jan. 3, 1882; res. U.

4463. CHARLES DANIEL FISKE (Daniel, Stephen K., Daniel, Daniel, Benjamin, John, John, Phinehas, Thomas, Robert, Simon, Simon, William, Symond), b. Mar. 13, 1856; m. Feb. 26, 1887, Melinda Brooks; res. 720 Main St., Worcester, Mass.

4465. STEPHEN KNIGHT FISKE (Stephen, Stephen K., Daniel, Daniel, Benjamin, John, John, Phinehas, Thomas, Robert, Simon, Simon, William, Symond), b. Scituate, R. I., Aug. 28, 1842; m. Mar. 30, 1877, Hannah Maria Carr, b. July 6, 1856. He is a farmer; res. Hope, R. I.

 5829. i. EFFIE FRANCES, b. July 1, 1881.
 5830. ii. HARDIN ISAAC, b. Feb. 5, 1895.

4469. NATHAN FISKE (Ebenezer, Stephen K., Daniel, Daniel, Benjamin, John, John, Phinehas, Thomas, Robert, Simon, Simon, William, Symond), b. Coventry, R. I., Dec. 6, 1841; m. at Scituate, 1867, Melissa Emma Matteson, b. Apr. 11, 1845. He is a machinist and surveyor; res. Hope, R. I.

 5831. i. PERNELLA MERCY, b. June 20, 1870; m. 1887 ——— Hawkins; res. Hope.

4480. GEORGE RAY FISKE (Albert D., Isaac, Daniel, Benjamin, John, John, Phinehas, Thomas, Robert, Simon, Simon, William, Symond), b. Coventry, R. I., Oct. 27, 1866; m. June 14, 1887, Harriett E. Knight, b. July 14, 1866; d. Sept. 10, 1889; m. 2d, May 17, 1891, Mary A. E. Johnson, b. Aug. 19, 1873. He is a farmer; res. Summit, R. I.

 5832. i. EDITH MABEL, b. Feb. 12, 1893.
 5833. ii. RENA EVELYN, b. Jan. 3, 1895.

4490. CHARLES WAYLAND FISKE (Egbert H., Arnold, Daniel, Daniel, Benjamin, John, John, Phinehas, Thomas, Robert, Simon, Simon, William, Symond), b. Apr. 23, 1865, East Greenwich, R. I.; m. June 11, 1885, at Pascoag, Lizzie May Hawkes, b. Apr. 11, 1865. He is a locomotive engineer; res. 30 Hudson St., Providence, R. I.

 5834. i. WAYLAND EGBERT, b. July 5, 1886.
 5835. ii. EDITH LENORA, b. Feb. 24, 1889.

4493. CHARLES ABRAM FISKE (Abram, Abram, Jonathan, John, Benjamin, John, John, Phinehas, Thomas, Robert, Simon, Simon, William, Symond),

b. Rochester, N. Y., July 8, 1826; m. at Boardman, Ohio, Oct. 29, 1873, Lucile J. Detchon, b. Aug. 1, 1847. He is a farmer; res. Girard, Pa.

 5836. i. ELLA LUCILE, b. Apr. 3, 1875; attending college in Erie; well educated in music.

 5837. ii. CARL W., b. June 24, 1877; attending college in Cleveland, Ohio.

 4494. BRYANT HENRY FISKE (Abram, Abram, Jonathan, John, Benjamin, John, John, Phinehas, Thomas, Robert, Simon, Simon, William, Symond), b. Apr. 18, 1836; m. Oct. 25, 1863, Alice S. Barrett, b. Sept. 13, 1845. He was book-keeper. He d. Mar. 13, 1882; res. South Erie, Pa.

 5838. i. ELMER B., b. Sept. 9, 1864; m. Agnes L. Beam.

 5839. ii. VINCENT BARRETT, b. Oct. 14, 1868; res. unm. Lewisburg, Pa.

 4495. LYMAN THOMAS FISKE (Abram, Abram, Jonathan, John, Benjamin, John, John, Phinehas, Thomas, Robert, Simon, Simon, William, Symond), b. Sept. 14, 1830, Houndsfield, N. Y.; m. Mar. 10, 1866, Sallie A. Clark; m. 2d, Oct., 1867, Hannah Clark. He was a school teacher. He d. Aug. 25, 1887; res. New York. ·

 5840. i. HARRY, b. ———.

 5841. ii. ARTHUR, b. ———; d. ———.

 5842. iii. ADA, b. ———; d. ———.

 5843. iv. ESTHER, b. ———; d. ———.

 5844. v. LINTER, b. ———.

 4497. DANIEL D. FISKE (Abram, Abram, Jonathan, John, Benjamin, John, John, Phinehas, Thomas, Robert, Simon, Simon, William, Symond), b. Aug. 24, 1833, Niagara County, N. Y.; m. at Waterloo, N. Y., Apr. 29, 1861, Fannie J. Van Dorn, b. New York City, Sept. 27, 1846; d. Jan. 9, 1884. He is a carriage and coach trimmer; res. Miles Grove, Pa.

 5845. i. EDWARD D., b. July 28, 1862; d. July 14, 1884.

 5846. ii. WM. G., b. July 8, 1864; d. June 8, 1865.

 5847. iii. FRANK D., b. Aug. 24, 1872; d. Aug. 16, 1892.

 5848. iv. DANIEL JESSE, b. May 1, 1875.

 5849. v. GERTRUDE E., b. Jan. 5, 1877.

 5850. vi. GRACE M., b. Aug. 12, 1878.

 4498. LEONARD PAUL FISKE (Abraham, Abraham, Jonathan, John, Benjamin, John, John, Phinehas, Thomas, Robert, Simon, Simon, William, Symond), b. Greece, N. Y., Feb. 7, 1828; m. Feb. 25, 1858, Bulah Ann Wells, b. Spring, Pa., Dec. 9, 1831. He is a farmer; res. Kingsville, Ohio.

 5851. i. GERTRUDE (adopted), m. John Croft, Mar. 4, 1893; res. Cleveland, Ohio.

 4500. MATTHEW DIMOCK FISKE (Abram, Abram, Jonathan, John, Benjamin, John, John, Phinehas, Thomas, Robert, Simon, Simon, William, Symond), b. Aug. 20, 1823; m. 1844, Lucy A. Mitchell. He was killed. He d. Nov. 19, 1851; res. Kingsville, Ohio.

 5852. i. EDWIN SILAS, b. May 12, 1847; m. Emma L. Zinker.

 4503. FRANKLIN NORMAN FISKE (Abram, Abram, Jonathan, John, Benjamin, John, John, Phinehas, Thomas, Robert, Simon, Simon, William, Symond), b. Aug. 12, 1841; m. Ida S. Craig. He d. Nov. 22, 1876; res. Erie, Pa.

 5853. i. GERTRUDE, b. ———; adopted by her uncle, Leonard P. Fiske (see).

 5854. ii. IDA, b. ———.

 5855. iii. JOHN, b. ———.

 4506. ALFRED FISK (John, Abram, Jonathan, John, Benjamin, John, John, Phinehas, Thomas, Robert, Simon, Simon, William, Symond), b. Watertown, N. Y., Sept. 2, 1814; m. in Portage, Ohio, in Nov., 1839, Sarah Miller, b. Sept. 2, 1819; d. Oct. 14, 1885. He was a farmer. The obituary notice of him says: "His first conscientious duty was the education of his family. Whether as a public officer, or a private citizen, no one had ought to say against his honor and integrity, and no grander eulogy attaches to his name than that he lived and died an honest man." He d. May 11, 1876; res. Old Portage, Ohio, and Belmond, Ia.

5856. i.   ISADORE, b. Nov. 19, 1840; m. May 27, 1857, George W. Rogers, b. Feb. 16, 1834; d. Oct. 21, 1884; m. 2d, Jan. 11, 1894, John Notestine; res. Hardy, Iowa. Ch.: Celia Rogers, b. Sept. 7, 1858; d. Dec. 26, 1862. James A. Rogers, b. Aug. 3, 1869; m. Celia A. Ward, Mar. 20, 1884; d. Aug. 27, 1890. Luman H. Rogers, b. May 7, 1874; d. Aug. 15, 1891. Jessie M. Rogers, b. Nov. 15, 1871; m. Frank L. Nerman, Oct. 26, 1890; add. Alva, Wood County, Oklahoma. In 1856 Isadore went to Iowa with her parents; and at the age of 15 was employed as a teacher. In the following May she was married to George Rogers. When she was 18 her first story was published, none but her closest friends surmising her literary aspirations. This story was accepted by none other than Datus E. Coon, afterward Minister to Cuba. She signed herself "Eugenia." In 1884 her husband's health became so poor that they concluded to settle up their affairs in Belmond and go to southern Kansas, hoping the climate would be beneficial. But he grew weaker and weaker, until he passed away, a few months later. Soon after her husband's death, her children were prostrated with malarial fever. There was no voice to soothe, no heart to sympathize. It was late in January before health was restored, and to use her own expression: "To retrieve my broken fortunes, I resolved to take a claim, and make a home for my children." She heard of a piece of land out thirty-five miles from Harper, that had once been taken, and then abandoned, by a Missourian. According to the law, a piece of land must be entered, then lived upon, and improved six months, before Uncle Sam would receive payment. She went by wagon to Wichita, a distance of ninety-five miles, in the dead of winter, and presented her claim under the pre-emption law. She sent out lumber for a shanty to be built, and followed in February with the children. The winter was bleak, desolate, and forbidding—with snow and freezing winds. Home-sickness and despondency weighed crushingly upon her; and the loneliness at Harper seemed to pale beside the utter loneliness here in this shanty. When night spread her pall over them, there was no sound save the moaning dirge of the wind and the howling of the hungry coyotes for company. Unexpectedly the Missourian's son returned and illegally filed upon the land. The father had plowed eighteen furrows, and had boarded up a shanty without door, floor or window. This was done to keep others away, but the fraud was so apparent, he had not dared to return, since actual settlers had come, and must discover his trickery. The Carlisle Cattle Company owned land adjoining, and these men took advantage of the prejudice against the company, to circulate a report to the effect that Mrs. Rogers was proving up land in their favor. This made her much trouble. There were six men against one woman, and when she made final proof, they contested her right. She secured a prominent lawyer from Wichita, and fought them. After four months' delay, decision was made in her favor by the registrar and receiver. The Missourians appealed, and after six months, the case went against her, the land commissioner deciding that she was in intrigue with the Cattle Company. It was now that she realized the truth of an assertion of Brick Pomeroy's, in a private letter to her: "If we work from principle, we must not expect—

> To be carried through this world
> On flowery beds of ease;
> But we must ever limp along,
> As though we walked on peas."

The matter was taken to Washington, D. C., and L. Q. C. Lamar, the Secretary of the Interior, decided in her favor after many months of delay. She sold her land for $1,400, and went to Colorado with her elder son, who was suffering with consumption. The time came when she had to lay her sons, side by side, in a beautiful valley, with only the towering mountains to guard their resting place. She was married to Mr. Notestine in Hardy, Ia., an early settler, a member of the M. E. Church, and an influential citizen of Humboldt County. He was a soldier in the War of the Rebellion, and it was exactly thirty years from the time he was taken captive, and placed in Libby Prison, that he was again taken captive—this time by a woman. As Mrs. Notestine sits in her comfortable home, and looks back over the past, she sees a golden thread, reaching through the warp of her life, which has kept its place midst the rougher woof, forming beautiful figures in life's tapestry—and this thread is her literary aspirations. She has had many flattering words from editors, but none she values more than those which came from T. S. Arthur, for whom she has written more than for all others: "Your articles sound womanly." Her years have been more or less overcast with clouds, but as she nears the afternoon of life, her skies appear very auspicious. May the morrow be a fair day for her.

5857. ii. FRANCES, b. Aug. 13, 1842; m. Apr. 13, 1861, W. La Fayette Thacher, b. Oct. 8, 1835; d. Aug. 1, 1881. She was a school teacher and he was a carpenter; res. Chelsea, Mich. Ch.: Ralph Willmont, b. July 21, 1863, in Belmond, Ia. Helena Jane, b. May 6, 1869, in Scranton, Pa.; d. Sept. 2, 1870, in Scranton, Pa., aged 1 year and 4 months. Oren Alfred, b. Dec. 5, 1875, in Chelsea, Mich.

5858. iii. ELIZABETH JANE, b. Sept. 12, 1846; m. May 25, 1863, Charles M. Church; res. Goodell, Ia. He was b. Feb. 12, 1837; was a farmer. Ch.: Wendell P., b. Dec. 4, 1865; m. Oct. 26, 1887. Frank G., b. June 13, 1868. Helena C., b. Aug. 23, 1870; m. Dec. 28, 1894. Ione C., b. June 6, 1872; d. Dec. 17, 1873. Audrey, b. Sept. 14, 1877. Arden F., b. July 6, 1881. John M., b. Jan. 20, 1885. Gayle, b. Oct. 22, 1886.

5859. iv. MELVEN CHARLES, b. Apr. 28, 1850; unm. He began teaching at the age of 18, and taught most of the time for twenty years. He is at present keeping livery stables in Irene, So. Dak. To him is descended the traditional hammer recovered from the dead body of his ancestor in which it had been placed by the Indians in Rhode Island after the savages had scalped the defenseless settler.

4512. ANSON A. FISK (Ephraim J., Abram, Jonathan, John, Benjamin, John, John, Phinehas, Thomas, Robert, Simon, Simon, William, Symond), b. Watertown, N. Y., Feb. 24, 1832; m. Feb. 21, 1851, Rachel Jane Brought, b. Feb. 28, 1834; d. Dec. 1, 1894. He was a brick and stone mason. He d. in Coldwater, Feb. 20, 1865; res. Delaware County, Ohio, and Lakeview, Mich.

5860. i. ALBERT A., b. Feb. 23, 1848; m. Hattie E. Gale.

5861. ii. GEORGE WASHINGTON, b. Apr. 11, 1853; res. Bay City, Mich.

5862. iii. EDWIN PERRY, b. Mar. 31, 1863; res. Coldwater.

5863. iv. JULIA ADDIE, b. July 12, 1850; m. Nov. 13, 1876, Charles W. Sweet; res. Inland, Mich. He was b. Nov. 20, 1851; is a farmer. Ch.: Anna May, b. June 8, 1888.

5864. v. VIENIA ORCELIA, b. Apr. 25, 1864; m. in Traverse City, Mich., James H. Andrus; res. Bendon, Mich. He was b. June 18, 1858; is a farmer. Ch.: 1, Juttie, b. Jan. 5, 1880. 2, Minnie, b. Nov. 27, 1883. 3, Celie, b. Jan. 27, 1885.

5865. vi. ANSON, b. ——; d. ——.

5866. vii. KATIE, b. ——; d. ——.

5867. ix. EDWIN PERRY CLINTON, b. Mar. 31, 1862; m. Sarah Crouch, b. Aug. 21, 1872; d. Oct. 6, 1893; res. s. p. Lakeview, Mich.

4515. ORVILLE FISK (Ephraim J., Abram, Jonathan, John, Benjamin, John, John, Phinehas, Thomas, Robert, Simon, Simon, William, Symond), b. Watertown, N. Y., Aug. 2, 1819; m. in Erie, Pa., May 15, 1840, Esther Ann Vandyke, b. Apr. 15, 1824; d. Aug. 29, 1859; m. 2d, 1862, Mrs. Anna E. Ovitt. He is a turner by trade; res. Altoona, Mich.

5868. i. ALEXANDER, b. July 17, 1847; d. unm. in Andersonville Prison, in 1864.
5869. ii. EMELINE, b. Jan. 6, 1850; m. Nov., 1867, Samuel Allen; res. A. Ch.: 1, Mary M., b. Apr. 26, 1868; m. Apr. 3, 1889, ——— Strang. 2, Augusta, b. June 4, 1871; m. July 3, 1890, ——— Streeter.
5870. iii. GEO. EDWARD, b. Nov. 30, 1852; d. Jan. 6, 1853.
5871. iv. MARTHA ELIZABETH, b. Sept. 27, 1854; d. Oct. 22, 1854.
5872. v. H. J., b. Feb. 8, 1867; unm.; res. A.
5873. vi. WILLIAM, b. Jan. 6, 1870; m. Hattie Slater.
5874. vii. CLINTON B., b. June 13, 1873; m. Anna Woolworth.
5875. viii. MARY LORETTIE, b. Feb. 13, 1863; d. May 22, 1866.
5876. ix. OLIVE MAY, b. Sept. 5, 1876; d. Mar. 29, 1882.
5877. x. ELLA IRENA, b. Sept. 5, 1880; d. Apr. 1882.

4523. MAJOR GEORGE AUGUSTUS FISK (Daniel, Abraham, Jonathan, John, Benjamin, John, John, Phinehas, Thomas, Robert, Simon, Simon, William, Symond), b. Springfield, O., Aug. 5, 1831; m. Sparta, Wis., Jan. 1, 1857, Catherine E. Walrath, b. ———. She res. Sparta.

MAJOR GEORGE AUGUSTUS FISK.

George Augustus Fisk was the third son of Daniel Fisk, born in Springfield, O., Aug. 5, 1831; he moved with his parents to Sparta, Wis., in the spring of 1852; was married to Catherine Eliza Walrath, Jan. 1, 1857. George Augustus Fisk was an affectionate husband and father, a true friend, and sometimes forgiving his foes; a Democrat of the old school, not like the present time; brave as a lion, always ready to help those in distress. At the breaking out of the war all the slumbering heroism of his ancestors broke out in him. He used to say: "I am going to help whip the rebels," "I want to see fair play." In 1861 he raised a company of volunteers, and was appointed Captain of Company D, Eighteenth Wisconsin Regiment; was taken prisoner at the battle of Shiloh, Apr. 6; was a prisoner of war eight months, suffering everything but death. After his release he rejoined his regiment; was with it until after the surrender of Vicksburg, then his health failed, and he was sent home to die. He was honorably discharged. After a severe illness of three months he recovered. Nothing daunted he raised another company, which was joined to the Thirty-sixth Regiment, Wisconsin Volunteers, Company C; was appointed Captain; was in all the battles, including the battles of Cold Harbor, Hatcher's Run, with the regiment. The following letter from Brigadier-General T. W. Egan is submitted:

"Headquarters Second Division, Second Army Corps, Nov. 1, 1865.

"His Excellency, James T. Lewis, Governor of the State of Wisconsin. Your

Excellency: At this first opportunity since the recent reconnoissance in force, I address you in approval of the performance of the Thirty-sixth Wisconsin Volunteers, during that movement; they being commanded through it all by Captain George A. Fisk. As your excellency knows, this regiment came here new. They were rushed into the breach untried, in a campaign which has been fiercer and more bloody than Napoleon's. The Thirty-sixth made its debut in a battle, of which the London Times says that England could not levy or lose one-tenth of number placed hors de combat. It was a contest of veteran Americans, and the comparison with them of inexperienced Americans is most unequal. On reaching the field the Thirty-sixth took up their positions as firmly and steadily as the oldest. In all operations in mass, they were undistinguishable for compactness and celerity, from the best, but soon they were given an opportunity for individual action. After several charges and countercharges, in which the advantage remained with us, I determined to take the enemy's position across Hatcher's Run. The order to charge had just been given, when the enemy opened heavily upon my right and rear, and advanced upon my main line in heavy masses. His forces enclosed three sides, and with worse troops, the situation would have been menacing. To crown all, a heavy body of rebels was thrown upon my rear (the fourth side), and occupied the Boydton road, making a complete surround. A swift face by the rear rank, and wheeling charge by the New Jersey bridge, cleared my right flank, but from the threatening body in my rear, it remained with the Thirty-sixth Wisconsin to relieve me. Captain Fisk threw them into line, and dashed at the enemy. It was a short fight; that rebel brigade was instantaneously crumbled and destroyed, being mostly captured, with arms, colors and officers, to a total number three times greater than the Thirty-sixth. Having cleared my rear, the regiment returned to its place in line, and behaved equally well until it returned to camp. If Napoleon's regiment faltered once, so did they conquer themselves and take place with his bravest, and so in this more bitter contest, if the Thirty-sixth had anything to redeem, do I now depend upon them with my veterans   I am your excellency's obedient servant,

"T. W. Eagan, Brigadier-General Commanding Division."

He was commissioned as Major of the Thirty-sixth Regiment, Mar. 7, 1865. At the end of the war was offered a position in the United States Army as an officer, but instead came home, and in the fall of 1866 was elected Sheriff of Monroe county.

"Death of Major Fisk.—Still another of the old residents of Sparta has joined the silent majority. Major Geo. A. Fisk, who for two years past has been confined to his house, from a complication of ailments, breathed his last Friday morning, Aug. 13, 1886, at his residence in this city. Capt. Fisk was one of the very earliest residents of this vicinity, removing here with his father's family, in the spring of 1852. He was born in Springfield, O., Aug. 5, 1831, his age at death therefore being 56 years and nine days. His early residence in Sparta was marked by the usual incidents and vicissitudes of the Spartans in those days of the infant city, and he witnessed its growth from a hamlet in the wilderness, up to a thriving village. He had an active, courageous spirit, and at the breaking out of the war, was one of the first to spring to the front in his country's defense. He raised a company of volunteers, and was appointed Captain of Company D, Eighteenth Regiment, in 1861. He was captured by the enemy at Shiloh, Apr. 6, 1862, and was released Oct. 14, 1862. In 1864 he raised another company, which was joined to the Thirty-sixth Wisconsin Regiment as Company C, and of which he was appointed the Captain. This regiment was assigned to the First Brigade, Second Division, of the Second Army Corps, with which it served till the close of the war, seeing the severe service of the advance on Petersburg, and the siege of that place, from June 14, to Aug. 12, when it was removed down the James River, afterwards returning and participating in the fight at Reams' Station, on the 25th. Capt. Fisk took command of the regiment about this time. The Thirty-sixth and Capt. Fisk won especial praise for gallantry at the battle of Hatcher's Run, Oct. 27, where the Thirty-sixth was formed in line of battle, with the Second and Third Brigades on the right, and the Third Division in the rear. At 3 o'clock the enemy, in heavy force, charged the Third Division, causing it to break, thus cutting off all communication with the rear. Seeing the perilous condition, Captain Fisk ordered the regiment to face by the rear rank, fix bayonets and charge, which was handsomely executed, striking the rebels on the flank, doubling up their line, causing them to break and run, and capturing a large number of prisoners, with one stand of colors. In this engagement the casualties of the regiment were fifteen wounded and no missing. Brigadier-General Egan, commanding the Second Division, in his official report, speaks of the regiment in the highest terms, saying that 'it captured a larger number of prisoners than it had men engaged,' and refers especially to the gallant conduct and cool daring of Captain Fisk, commanding the regiment. Captain received an appointment as Major, Mar. 7, 1865. The regiment was mustered out July 12, 1865, and was disbanded at Madison on the 24th. Major Fisk served one term as Sheriff of the county, in 1866-68, subsequently engaging in selling farm machinery, in which he continued as long as his health permitted. His wife, Catherine E. Walrath, to whom he was married in 1857, survives him. The funeral took place Sunday afternoon from his residence, the Masonic fraternity conducting the obsequies, and John W. Lynn Post, G. A. R. and Spartan Lodge K. of P., of which he was also a member, escorting the remains. The interment took place in Woodlawn Cemetery." He d. Aug. 13, 1886; res. Sparta, Wis.

5878. iv. DANIEL AUGUSTUS, b. July 27, 1874. He is a student in Beloit College, and will graduate in June, 1897, an M. D. Daniel A. Fisk is a young man of quiet character. He completed the modern classical course in the Sparta High School, with the class of 1893. As a student he was patient and painstaking. Beneath his modest demeanor could be seen marks of strong character. He had a hearty admiration for the heroes of history, and took for the subject of his graduating oration, "The Men Who Never Die." At present Daniel is making a clean and creditable record in Beloit College.

5879. i. ELIZABETH MAY, b. Aug. 23, 1859; m. Aug. 29, 1883, Charles J. French. Ch.: 1, Joseph Sidney, b. Aug. 28, 1885. 2, Katherine, b. May 13, 1888. 3, Isora Hoffman, b. Feb. 4, 1895: res. 1559 Dudley St., Cincinnati, O.

5880. ii. JOSEPHINE, b. Nov. 10, 1861; m. Mar. 31, 1886, Wm. R. Jones. Ch.: 1, Carl Fiske, b. Jan. 26, 1889. 2, Earl H., b. Oct. 19, 1891; res. Sparta, Wis.

5881. iii. LENORA. b. Oct. 19, 1868; res. 1559 Dudley St., Cincinnati, O.

5882. v. GEORGIA, b. Aug. 4, 1866; res. Sparta; unm.

4534. DUANE THOMAS FISK (Abram, Jonathan, John, Benjamin, John, John, Phinehas, Thomas, Robert, Simon, Simon, William, Symond), b. June 8, 1833, Watertown, N. Y.; m. Dec. 24, 1856, Adelaide F. Heath, b. Aug., 1836. He d. May 24, 1862; res. Watertown, N. Y.

5883. i. ALICE LORINDA, b. June 14, 1858; m. 1879, Frank Hart. She d. s. p., Jan. 20, 1881.

5884. ii. CARRIE A., b. Oct. 12, 1860: m. Dec. 24, 1875, Isaac Horning. Ch.: 1, Minnie May, b. Oct. 25, 1876; m. Nov. 5, 1894. 2, John Horning, b. Jan., 1880; d. 1885. She m. 2d, Nov., 1885, Jay Cook, s. p.; res. Watertown, N. Y.

5885. iii. MARTHA MARY, b. Aug. 5, 1862: m. Fred N. Cook. Ch.: 1, Mabel, b. Feb. 19, 1884. 2, Glenn Duane, b. Feb. 9, 1886: res. Watertown, N. Y.

4547-1. STILLMAN KNIGHT FISK (Samuel K., Jonathan, K., Jonathan, John, Benjamin, John. John, Phinehas, Thomas, Robert, Simon. Simon, William, Symond), b. Scituate, R. I., Nov. 19, 1849; m. at Bristol, Mar. 28, 1881, Mrs. Belle H. White, b. Dec. 18, 1852; d. May 14, 1892. He is a railroad foreman. Res. Chicago, Ill, 6151 Stewart Ave., s. p.

4547-4. DR. ELMER SCOTT FISKE (Jeremiah, Jonathan K., Jonathan, John, Benjamin. John, John, Phinehas, Thomas, Robert, Simon, Simon, William, Symond), b. Manchester, N. H., Apr. 19, 1861: m. at No. Scituate. R. I., June 10, 1884, Mary C. Smith; m. 2d, Nov. 21, 1894, Mrs. Lina Florence (Orr) Thompson, b. Leeds, P. Q., Nov. 10, 1863. He was educated in the public schools at his native place, and at Smithville Seminary, North Scituate, R. I.; entered Yale in 1880, but did not finish the course, began the study of medicine with Dr. Walter

J. Smith, at North Scituate, R. I., in 1881; attended the University of the City of New York (medical department), and graduated from that institution in Mar., 1884. He began practice at Clayville, R. I., at once; removed to Providence, R. I., to practice, in Sept., 1884; was associated with Dr. E. B. Eddy, in Providence (Olneyville) for two years, after which he opened an office for himself. In 1884 was appointed and commissioned by the Governor as medical examiner for the first district, Providence county, R. I., for a term of six years. Was attending physician to the Providence Dispensary for two years, and attending physician to the Grace Memorial Home, Providence, R. I. Was superintendent of health for the town of Johnston, R. I., for three years; examiner for several fraternal organizations and life insurance companies. Removed to Willow City, N. Dak., in Mar., 1893. In 1894 was appointed county superintendent of health and secretary of the county board of health of Bottineau Co., N. Dak. Fellow of the Rhode Island Medical Society, American Medical Association and North Dakota Medical Association. He is a Mason, Knight of Pythias and member of several beneficial fraternal societies. In the two former has held various offices and is a member of grand lodges of both. Taught school for parts of two years in North Scituate, R. I., at the beginning of his medical studies. Has at times done some literary work. In 1889, because of poor health and overwork, was obliged to give up practice for a time; took a trip to Europe and the Azores, and resumed practice at Providence (Olneyville), R. I., in 1890; res. Willow City, N. Dak., s. p.

4547-5. CHARLES HERBERT FISKE (Jeremiah, Jonathan K., Jonathan, John, Benjamin, John, John, Phinehas, Thomas, Robert, Simon, Simon, William, Symond), b. No. Scituate, R. I., Nov. 1, 1851; m. at Manchester, N. H., Oct. 26, 1870, Mary Ayer Goodhue, b. Oct. 17, 1850. He is a commercial traveler; res. Providence, R. I., 32 Carleton St.

    5885-1. i.   ANNETTIE CONSTANCE, b. Mar. 23, 1872; d. June 1, 1877.
    5885-2. ii.   IDA MAY, b. May 18, 1874; unm.; res. at home.
    5885-3. iii.   STELLA, b. Dec. 31, 1875; d. Jan. 30, 1876.
    5885-4. iv.   MARY ELMA, b. Mar. 7, 1877; d. Oct. 1, 1879.

4547-7. WILLIS WARREN FISKE (Jeremiah, Jonathan, K., Jonathan, John, Benjamin, John, John, Phinehas, Thomas, Robert, Simon, Simon, William, Symond), b. Providence, R. I., Feb. 23, 1857; m. at No. Scituate, R. I., May 4, 1881, Minnie Lura Bowen, b. Apr. 17, 1859. His business is manufacture and mills supplies. He is chief of the Johnston, R. I., fire department; res. Olneyville, R. I.

    5885-5. i.   BESSIE LURA, b. Mar. 23, 1884.
    5885-6. ii.   HARRY ELDRID, b. Feb. 17, 1890.

4554. CHARLES AUGUSTUS FISKE (Peleg, Peleg, Peleg, John, Benjamin, John, John, Phinehas, Thomas, Robert, Simon, Simon, William, Symond), b. Pawtucket, R. I., Aug. 10, 1828; m. at New Albany, Ind., May 1, 1857, Rose Paul. He is a blacksmith and engineer; res. St. Mathews, Ky.

    5886. i.   ADDIA ELIZABETH, b. Feb. 13, 1857; m. Feb. 21, 1881, Dr. John W. Bradburn; res. St. M.
    5887. ii.   CHARLES ALEXANDER, b. June 19, 1860; m. Feb. 12, 1889, Lida Waters; res. St. M.
    5888. iii.   GEORGE WALTER, b. Dec. 11, 1866. He is unm.; res. Louisville, Ky. Is a member of the firm of Geiger, Fiske & Co., machine, boiler and sheet iron works, 715 East Main St.

4560. PELEG FISKE (Peleg, Peleg, Peleg, John, Benjamin, John, John, Phinehas, Thomas, Robert, Simon, Simon, William, Symond), b. New Albany, Ind., Mar. 27, 1847; m. there Feb. 8, 1877, Kate Stephens, b. Cleveland, O., July 28, 1853. He is a machinist and engineer. Res. New Albany, Ind.

    5889. i.   WM. PELEG, b. Mar. 22, 1878.
    5890. ii.   MARY BUCKLEY, b. Nov. 14, 1881.
 - 5891. iii.   FILINDA ADA, b. Aug. 12, 1885.
    5892. iv.   LOUIS HITE, b. Feb. 13, 1893.

4567. ALBERT HENRY FISKE (Philip, Peleg, Peleg, John, Benjamin, John, John, Phinehas, Thomas, Robert, Simon, Simon, William, Symond), b. Providence, R. I., June 26, 1834; m. at Pekin, Ill., Apr. 2, 1863, Mary J. Brawner, b. Dec. 11, 1833. He is a mechanical engineer. Res. Delavan, Ill.

    5893. i.   GEORGE EDWARD, b. May 31, 1866; res. Pensacola, Fla.

5894. ii. ANNA ELIZABETH, b. Jan. 22, 1870; res. D.
5895. iii. HARRY PHILIP, b. Nov. 26, 1871; res. D.
5896. iv. CHAS. ALEXANDER, b. Mar. 9, 1875; res. Winchester, Ill.

4574. JOHN THOMAS FISKE, JR. (John T., Philip M., Caleb, John, Benjamin, John, John, Phinehas, Thomas, Robert, Simon, Simon, William, Symond), b. Gloucester R. I., May 21, 1847; m. Sept. 1, 1875, Kate Evelyn Arnold, b. 1850. He is a manufacturer. Res. Pascoag, R. I.

5897. i. ABBY EDDY, b. Jan. 6, 1880.

4575. FRANK FISKE (John T., Philip M., Caleb, John, Benjamin, John, John, Phinehas, Thomas, Robert, Simon, Simon, William, Symond), b. Gloucester, R. I., Sept. 30, 1850; m. Sept. 11, 1890, Maranda Barnes, b. July 12, 1863. He is a bookkeeper. Res. Pascoag, R. I.

5898. i. FRANK, b. June 13, 1891.
5899. ii. RICHARD, b. May 8, 1894.

4585. HON. LEANDER W. FISKE (John M., Jeremiah, Job, Job, Benjamin, John, John, Phinehas, Thomas, Robert, Simon, Simon, William, Symond), b. Boonville, N. W., Sept. 30, 1835; m. there May 24, 1864, Margaret M. Ward, b. Jan. 10, 1837. He was born in Boonville; educated at the common schools, at Fairfield Academy and at a commercial college. He studied for the law; was admitted to the bar in 1860; opened an office in Boonville in 1861; enlisted in 1862, and was discharged in 1863 for deafness. He was elected to vote for Roscoe Conklin for Senator in 1866, he did so. He was a member of the Legislature of New York. Was nominated for Congress, but was beaten. He has been Judge Advocate of the G. A. R., Department New York, trustee of the Soldiers' Home of his State, county committee Republican party his county, and is now librarian of the Erwin Library and Institute of Boonville. Res. Boonville, N. Y., s. p.

HON. LEANDER W. FISKE.

4588. EDGAR L. FISK (John M., Jeremiah, Job, Job, Benjamin, John, John, Phinehas, Thomas, Robert, Simon, Simon, William, Symond), b. Sept. 3, 1848, Boonville, N. Y.; m. at Wasco, Minn., June 1, 1880, Marie C. Knudson, b. July 6, 1858. He is manager of the Montana Manufacturing Company. Res. Helena, Mont.

5900. i. LAWRENCE M., b. July 14, 1881.
5901. ii. EDITH M., b. July 10, 1883; d. Dec. 4, 1889.
5902. iii. LEANDER W., b. Sept. 23, 1886; d. Dec. 17, 1889.
5903. iv. FLORENCE V., b. July 11, 1889.
5904. v. LA-NETA, b. July 1, 1891.

4589. EUGENE WALLACE FISKE (John M., Jeremiah, Job, Job, Benjamin, John, John, Phinehas, Thomas, Robert, Simon, Simon, William, Symond), b. Boonville, N. Y., Mar. 8, 1851; m. Dec. 21, 1880, Kate I. Bailey, b. June 3, 1859. He is a general contractor and builder; res. Helena, Mont.

5905. i. AVIS, b. Mar. 22, 1882.
5906. ii. KENNETH B., b. Aug. 31, 1883.
5907. iii. GERTRUDE M., b. Feb. 22, 1888.
5908. iv. B. C., b. Jan. 29, 1891.

4594. WILSON FISKE (Isaac, Jeremiah, Job, Job, Benjamin, John, John, Phinehas, Thomas, Robert, Simon, Simon, William, Symond), b. Boonville, N.

Y., Feb. 11, 1836; m. Jan. 2, 1879, Harriet Seckerson, b. July 7, 1847. He is an artist; res. 763 Amsterdam Ave., New York City.

    5909. i.   JOHN W., b. Apr. 10, 1880.
    5910. ii.   CLINTON M., b. Sept. 6, 1887.

    4606. REV. RICHMOND FISK, D. D. (Richmond, Jeremiah, Jeremiah. Job, Benjamin, John, John, Phinehas, Thomas. Robert, Simon, Simon, William, Symond), b. Bennington, Vt., Feb. 23, 1836; m. at Newark, N. Y., May 8, 1861, Adelaide Bartle, b. May 30, 1840. Richmond Fisk, Jr., was born at Bennington Centre, Vt. Was fitted for college at Ball Seminary, Hoosick Falls, N. Y. Entered Williams College in 1854, spending two years there, and then two years at Union College, where he graduated in 1858. During three winters of his college course he taught school. On graduating he entered the law office of Hon. Stephen L. Magoun, of Hudson, N. Y., and had not a little experience in collecting rents on large estates of which Mr. Magoun was agent or administrator. Though a good and interested student of the law, his aptitude as developed by his favorite college studies of philosophy turned his mind more to the ministry than to the law as a calling. He entered the study of Rev. A. D. Mayo, then pastor of the Unitarian Church, Albany, N. Y., in 1859, and was ordained in 1861 as minister of the Universalist Church in Newark, Wayne County, N. Y. Was married to Adelaide Bartle, daughter of Col. James P. Bartle, of Newark. N. Y. Dr. Fisk has had settlements in Newark, N. Y., three years; Lockport, N. Y., three years, where he resigned, intending to accept a call to the professorship of Biblical languages in the Theological School of St. Lawrence University, Canton, N. Y., but was induced to take a pastorate at Auburn, N. Y., a large and important church, from which place, however, after three years, he was called to the presidency of the College of Science and Letters of St. Lawrence University. Here four years were spent in fostering the financial and educational interests of the college, his time divided between the duties of the professor's chair of mental and moral philosophy and the field seeking money and students. After nearly four years he accepted a call to Grand Rapids, and thence in three years to Sycamore, N. Y., where for ten years, from 1874 to 1884, he engaged, in connection with his church cares, in the charities of the city. He was instrumental in founding the Bureau of Labor and Charities of that city, and was its general secretary for seven years. He also established in connection with the bureau branches of the societies for the prevention of cruelty to children and to animals; also the Red Cross Society, of Miss Clara Barton, by which latter society thousands of dollars in clothing and money were sent to the flood sufferers of the South. He was also secretary of the Civil Service Society of Syracuse. He was obliged by over work to give up his manifold work in Syracuse, and, in 1884, accepted a call to Watertown, N. Y., where for eight years his ministry was prospered as in all his previous settlements, while for seven years of the time he was president of the Watertown Bureau of Charities, which he had aided in organizing while he was general secretary of the Syracuse Bureau. While located in Watertown, N. Y., he was appointed by Gov. Flower a trustee of the Asylum for Feeble Minded Women, at Newark, N. Y. He was one of the founders of the Jefferson County, N. Y., Historical Society, and its secretary for six years. In 1892 Dr. Fisk accepted a call to the Church of Our Father (Unitarian), of Boston (East), a large church and Sunday school, where his reputation as a charity worker preceding him has brought him actively in the great field of Boston charity work. He is vice-president of the Unitarian Sunday School Society, and of the East Boston Charity Organization Society, founder of the Starr King Unitarian Club, and is a member of the University Club of Boston. He has written much for the daily press in the cities where he has lived and contributed often to the magazines and papers of his church. He visited Europe in 1887, and spent three months with his daughter on the Continent and in England and Scotland and Ireland. He received the degree of D. D. from Taft's College in 1871. Dr. Fisk is a Mason, and is now prelate of William Parkman Commandery, of Boston; res. 251 Lexington St., East Boston, Mass.

    5911. i.   ALICE LOUISE, b. July 11, 1862; m. at Watertown, N. Y., June 25, 1889, Dr. Edwin Bynner Butterfield; res. Ayer, Mass. Ch.: 1, Hortense Elizabeth, b. May 15, 1893.

    4607. RUSSELL FISK (Richmond, Jeremiah, Jeremiah, Job, Benjamin, John, John, Phinehas, Thomas, Robert, Simon, Simon, William, Symond), b. Mar. 22,

1827, in Shaftsbury, Vt.; m. May 30, 1865, Martha C. Ranney, b. Sept. 13, 1842.
A Colorado paper says, New England is not very largely represented among the
citizens of Larimer County, Colo. Among the sons of the Green Mountain
State who are residing there may be mentioned our esteemed townsman, Russell
Fisk. Mr. Fisk came to Colorado twenty-three years ago, in May, 1870. For
many years he resided at Livermore, where he conducted a hotel and a large general store, and was at the same time engaged in the stock business. Mr. Fisk is
67 years of age, having been born Mar. 22, 1827, at Shaftsbury, Vt. He was married at West Townsend, in that State, May 30, 1865, to Martha C. Ranney. Mr.
Fisk is a veteran of the war of the Rebellion, and saw nearly four years of active
service in the Vermont Brigade, Second Division, Sixth Army Corps. He is a
member of the G. A. R. He always has been a most ardent and consistent Republican, and has always taken an active part in promoting the welfare of his party.
Of late years Mr. Fisk has been engaged in the commission business on Jefferson
Street in Fort Collins. He is a successful business man, and enjoys a wide reputation as a successful man in whatever enterprise he may undertake; res. Fort
Collins, Colo.

    5912.   i.   STELLA E., b. in New York, Apr. 2, 1868; m. A. C. Forrester in
                  June, 1894, in Denver, Colo.; add. 2355 Larimer St., Denver,
                  Colo.
    5913.   ii.   JAMES RUSSELL, b. in New York, Aug. 2, 1870; m. in June,
                  1894; present add. Hillsboro, N. M.
    5914.   iii.   ALFRED ARTHUR, b. in Greeley, Colo., Oct. 10, 1871; d. in
                  Livermore, Colo., June 5, 1875.
    5915.   iv.   JOSEPHINE IONA, b. in Livermore, Colo., July 15, 1877.
    5916.   v.   RAYMOND RANNEY, b. in Livermore, Mar. 6, 1880; present
                  add. Fort Collins, Colo.

    4610. GEORGE W. FISK (Richmond, Jeremiah, Jeremiah, Job, Benjamin,
John, John, Phinehas, Thomas, Robert, Simon, Simon, William, Symond), b. Bennington, Vt., May 30, 1838; m. at Cambridge, N. Y., Jan. 23, 1861, Lucy Elizabeth

Ames, b. Dec. 25, 1842; d. June 21, 1886;
m. 2d, at Hoosick Falls, N. Y., Dec. 28,
1887, Katherine Lois Moody, b. Aug.
28, 1862. George Warren Fisk was born
in Bennington, Vt., May 30, 1838. His
early boyhood was uneventful, being
spent on a farm; moved with his parents
to Hoosick Falls, Rensselaer County,
N. Y., in 1848. He attended school
there at Ball Seminary until his 17th
year; taught in district schools the five
following winters. It was said of him
that he was a good teacher; was married
Jan. 23, 1861, to Lucy Elizabeth Ames,
daughter of Lorenzo Ames, of Hudson,
Mich. In May, 1861, he enlisted for
three years, under Franklin M. Crossett,
in the Band of the Second Regiment,
Vermont Volunteers; was present at the
first Bull Run battle, July 21, 1861, as
well as at several other engagements of
less note; discharged from service with
the band Dec. 19, 1861; worked a number of years as pattern maker with "The
Walter A. Wood Mowing & Reaping
Machine Co.," of Hoosick Falls, N. Y.
In the spring of 1870 he joined the famous Union Colony of Colorado, as one
of the original members, which founded

GEORGE W. FISK.

the city of Greeley, Colo. He was called home that summer because of an almost
fatal accident to his wife; resumed work as a pattern maker. In the spring of 1876
returned to Greeley, Colo., which has been his home since, and the place where

his reputation as an artistic violin maker has been earned. His work in this line has received the unstinted commendation of such celebrated violinists as August Wilhelmj, Edouard Remenyi, George Lehmann, Ferdinand Stark, and many others of note, who unhesitatingly tell him that he has no living superior in the world, as a maker of fine violins, and very few equals. Edouard Remenyi, the great violin virtuoso, says in the Denver Daily Tribune, Aug. 31, 1883. * * * * "Among the thousand of 'fiddle makers' in Europe and America, Mr. Geo. W. Fisk, of Greeley, Colo., is one out of only four real violin makers that I have found in my travels over the world. His workmanship is well nigh perfect. * * * The violin he made for me is a beauty, and has a grand, mellow, magnificent tone. Mr. Fisk will back up all I have stated of him." Mr. Fisk was married the second time, Dec. 28, 1887, to Katherine Lois Moody. daughter of Dr. Nathan J. Moody, of Madison, Wis. One child, Eugene Moody Fisk, was born to them Aug. 10, 1891; res. Greeley, Colo.

    5917. i.   EUGENE MOODY, b. Aug. 10, 1891.

    4612. JEREMIAH M. FISK (Richmond, Jeremiah, Jeremiah, Job, Benjamin, John, John, Phinehas, Thomas, Robert, Simon, Simon, William, Symond), b. Shaftsbury, Vt., Mar. 6, 1845; m. at Troy, N. Y., Aug. 20, 1866, Abbie J. Wilson, b. Dec. 22, 1845; d. Aug. 13, 1888. He was a farmer for seventeen years but of late has worked at his trade; res. Hoosick Falls, N. Y.

    5918. i.   LURANA V., b. Aug. 13, 1867; m. David Lord; res. Denver, Colo.
    5919. ii.   ROSA J., b. Feb. 13, 1869; m. R. J. Houseman; res. Grand Junction, Colo.
    5920. iii.   RICHMOND A., b. Mar. 22, 1870; res. Shushan, Washington County, N. Y.
    5921. iv.   LUCY E., b. Sept. 27, 1876.
    5922. v.   ALONZO W., b. Aug. 15, 1880.
    5923. vi.   CORA A., b. July 19, 1883.
    5924. vii.   BURIED six children, four girls and two boys.

    4613. ARTHUR W. FISKE (Richmond, Jeremiah, Jeremiah, Job, Benjamin, John, John, Phinehas, Thomas, Robert, Simon, Simon, William, Symond), b. Dec. 19, 1848; m. Eloise Ingalls; she m. 2d, William Cooper; res. Denver, Colo; was a lawyer; educated at St. Lawrence University, Canton, N. Y., and died in 1876. He left a son, Arthur. He d. in 1876; res. ———.

    5925. i.   ARTHUR, b. in Chicago; res. Chicago, Ill.

    4614. LESTER MIAL FISK (Mial, Jeremiah, Jeremiah, Job, Benjamin, John, John, Phinehas, Thomas, Robert, Simon, Simon, William, Symond), b. Bennington, Vt., Sept. 2, 1836; m. there Sarah Jane Bradley, b. 1844; d. 1868; m. 2d, at Hoosick Falls, N. Y., Alvina Surdam. He is a pattern maker; res. Hoosick Falls, N. Y.

    5926. i.   JENNY, b. 1868; m. 1887; res. Lansingburg.
    5927. ii.   IRVING L., b. 1873; res. 40 Kirkland St., Cambridge, Mass.
    5928. iii.   LUCY R., b. 1879; res. H. F.

    4621. HIRAM HICKS FISK (Mial, Jeremiah, Jeremiah, Job, Benjamin, John, John, Phinehas, Thomas, Robert, Simon, Simon, William, Symond), b. Aug. 29, 1845; m. ———, Mary Rice. He d. ———; res. Rutland, Vt.

    4629. HORATIO P. FISK (Truman, Jeremiah, Jeremiah, Job, Benjamin, John, John, Phinehas, Thomas, Robert, Simon, Simon, William, Symond), b. Shaftsbury, Vt., Mar. 11, 1835; m. at Castile, N. Y., Jan. 1, 1862, Iris A. Chapin, b. Nov. 17, 1839. He was a farmer but is now retired; res. 61 Gibbs St., Rochester, N. Y.

    5929. i.   BARTON C., b. Aug. 9, 1864; d. May 10, 1865.
    5930. ii.   MAUD C., b. May 26, 1866; res. at home.
    5931. iii.   MARY A., b. Apr. 10, 1868; res. at home.

    4630. WARREN J. FISK (Truman, Jeremiah, Jeremiah, Job, Benjamin, John, John, Phinehas, Thomas. Robert. Simon, Simon, William, Symond), b. Castile, N. Y., Jan. 21, 1846; m. Sept. 8, 1875, Jane S. Kelsey, b. Sept. 5, 1851. He is a farmer; res. Perry, N. Y.

5932. i.   MYRTLE CLARE, b. Aug. 3, 1876.
5933. ii.   CARLA MAYE, b. Jan. 19, 1881.
5934. iii. HERVE KELSEY, b. Mar. 25, 1884.

4630-1. JOHN L. FISKE (John, Mial, Jeremiah, Job, Benjamin, John, John, Phinehas, Thomas, Robert, Simon, Simon, William, Symond), b. ——; m. —— ——. He d. in Texas; res. San Antonio, Tex.

  5934-1. i.   JAMES R., b. ——; m. ——.

4630-2. ALFRED L. FISK (Charles, Mial, Jeremiah, Job, Benjamin, John, John, Phinehas, Thomas, Robert, Simon, Simon, William, Symond), b. Scituate, R. I., Dec. 14, 1807; m. at Phenix, Oct. 25, 1832, Abby Ann Locke, b. Jan. 12, 1812; d. Apr. 25, 1895. He was a miller. He d. May 25, 1879; res. Pawtucket, R. I.

  5934-2. i.   PHEBE, b. Aug. 29, 1839; d. young.
  5934-3. ii.   MARIAH M., b. Nov. 1, 1840; d. young.
  5934-4. iii. ABBY FRANCIS, b. Jan. 7, 1842; d. young.
  5934-5. iv.   THOS. W., b. Aug. 5, 1845; d. young.
  5934-6. v.   MARY E., b. Apr. 13, 1847; m. Apr. 13, 1864, Joseph E. Hood, b. Oct. 7, 1840; res. 35 Laurel St., Pawtucket, R. I. Ch.: 1, Joseph Alfred, b. Oct. 8, 1847; d. Dec. 25, 1847. 2, Charles Edward, b. Nov. 8, 1872; m. Nov. 17, 1892; res. 204 East St., Pawtucket, R. I.
  5934-7. vi.   EDWARD, b. Apr. 17, 1849. He served in the War of the Rebellion for four years and died in the service.
  5934-8. vii. JEREMIAH L., b. Dec. 24, 1850; m. Apr. 27, 1879, Mary Louis Smith, b. Dec. 14, 1848. He is a miller; res. 375 Public St., Providence, R. I.

4630-3. CHARLES FISKE (Charles, Mial, Jeremiah, Job, Benjamin, John, John, Phinehas, Thomas, Robert, Simon, Simon, William, Symond), b. ——; m. —— ——; res. Pawtucket, R. I.

  5934-9. i.   CHARLES, b. ——; res. Pawtucket, R. I.
  5934-10. ii. EZERIAH, b. ——; res. Pawtucket, R. I.
  5934-11. iii. HENRIETTA, b ——; m. Thomas Westcott; res. Pawtucket.

4630-4. STERRY FISKE (Charles Mial, Jeremiah, Job, Benjamin, John, John, Phinehas, Thomas, Robert, Simon, Simon, William, Symond), b. Scituate, R. I., Sept. 16, 1801; m. Mary P. Spencer; res. Providence, R. I.

  5934-12. i.   SALLIE A., b. Mar. 25, 1830; m. Nov. 24, 1853, Daniel G. Hunt, b. July 1, 1831; d. Apr. 24, 1887. He was a jeweler. She res. 26 West Friendship St., Providence, R. I. Ch.: 1, Emma M. Hunt, b. June 29, 1855; d. Dec. 17, 1873. 2, Thomas G. Hunt, b. May 8, 1857, Providence, R. I.; m. Apr. 15, 1896. 3, Frederick D. Hunt, b. Apr. 18, 1860; m.; res. Chartley, Mass. 4, Geo. I. Hunt, b. May 4, 1866, Providence, R. I. 5, Wilhelmina Hunt, b. Mar. 8, 1871, Providence, R. I.
  5934-13. ii.   ALFRED, b. Mar. 31, 1832; m. Sept. 7, 1862.
  5934-14. iii. LEWIS P., b. Sept 6, 1834; m. ——.
  5934-15. iv.   PHEBE E., b. Jan. 27, 1836; d. ——.
  5934-16. v.   MARY E., b. May 4, 1839; m. Nov. 26, 1857.
  5934-17. vi.   BENJ. S., b. Aug. 18, 1841; m. ——.
  5934-18. vii. LYDIA M., b. Oct. 8, 1843; m. ——.
  5934-19. viii. GEO. A., b. Nov. 8, 1845; m. ——.
  5934-20. ix.   STERRY F., b. July 9, 1848; m. ——.

4630-8. EMORY FISKE (Job W., Moses, Jeremiah, Job, Benjamin, John, John, Phinehas, Thomas, Robert, Simon, Simon, William, Symond), b. Scituate, R. I., Feb. 26, 1807; m. in Johnson in 1829, Sophia A. Waterman, b. 1810; d. 1878. He was a machinist. He d. 1852; res. East Greenwich and Smithfield, R. I.

  5934-21. i.   SOPHIA ANN, b. Sept. 15, 1831; m. Aug. 22, 1851, William Green Stone; res. Providence, R. I. He was b. May 18, 1831. Is a jeweler. Ch.: 1, John Emery Stone, b. Jan. 27, 1853; res. unm. Providence, R. I. 2, William Eugene Stone, b. May 11, 1860; m. Dec. 25, 1883, Katherine Joyce; P. O. add. Worcester, Mass.

3, Eleanor Sophia Stone, b. Apr. 19, 1862; m. Jan. 19, 1887, Frank W. Rockwell; P. O. add. Providence, R. I. 4, Lilian Mary Stone, b. Aug. 16, 1868; res. unm. Providence, R. I.

5934-22. ii.   WILLIAM ALBERT, b. 1836; lost at sea.

5934-23. iii.   JAMES EMORY, b. Mar. 12, 1834; d. unm. Jan. 12, 1893.

5934-24. iv.   MARY ELIZABETH, b. Oct. 1, 1840; m. Oct. 1, 1857, Gilbert F. White; res. Pawtucket, R. I.

5934-25. v.   EDNA FRANCIS, b. Apr. 29, 1846; m. May 24, 1865, George Smith, res. Greenville, R. I. He was b. Nov., 1837. Is a painter. Ch.: 1, George Smith, b. Greenville, R. I., Sept. 2, 1868; m. 1892. 2, Carrie Chilson Smith, b. Greenville, R. I., Oct. 29, 1872. 3, Harold Fiske Smith, b. Greenville, R. I., Oct. 12, 1876. 4, Edna Frances Smith, b. Greenville, R. I., June 27, 1884. 5, Emily Greene Smith, b. Greenville, R. I., Feb. 16, 1886.

5934-26. vi.   LUCY ELLEN, b. May 5, 1849; m. Dec. 26, 1870, George Mabbett, b. May 20, 1849; res. Plymouth, Mass. He is a woolen manufacturer. Ch.: 1, Herbert Earle, Dec. 30, 1872. 2, Edith Louise, b. July 4, 1877. 3, George Emery, b. Oct., 1879. 4, James Fiske, b. Jan. 30, 1883 5, Harry Irving, b. Mar. 1, 1886.

5934-27. vii.   HARRIETT, b. ———; d. unm.

5934-28. viii. CARRIE ESTELLE, b. Apr. 30, 1852; m. in Providence, Apr. 23, 1874, Henry J. Bailey; res. Danville, R. I. He was b. Apr., 1851. Ch.: 1, Mary Louise, b. Aug. 31, 1875. 2, Emma Estelle, b. Jan. 27, 1879.

4630-9. HARLEY FISK (Job W., Moses, Jeremiah, Job, Benjamin, John, John, Phinehas, Thomas, Robert, Simon, Simon, William, Symond), b. North Scituate, R. I., Dec. 12, 1809; m. there Nov. 8, 1829, Susan Brickley Greene, b. July 5, 1810; d. Dec. 26, 1891. He d. Nov., 1873; res. North Scituate and Providence, R. I.

5934-29. i.   HENRY GREENE, b. Aug. 28, 1832; m. Oct. 9, 1859; add. 5 Washington Place, New York City, of the firm of Fisk, Clark & Flagg.

5934-30. ii.   STEPHEN WILBUR, b. Feb. 10, 1835; m. Sept., 1878, Josephine Washburn. He d. s. p. July 14, 1893. She res. 201 W. 55th St., New York City.

5934-31. iii.   HARLEY AUGUSTUS, b. Apr. 9, 1839; m. Helen M. Rouse.

5934-32. iv.   GILBERT EDWIN, b. Sept. 7, 1841; d. Dec. 18, 1894.

5934-33. v.   SUSAN ELEANOR, b. June 11, 1846; m. Sept. 2, 1871, William H. Butters. Res. 510 Washington Ave., St. Louis, Mo. He was b. June 20, 1839, in Boston; son of Wm. A. and Elizabeth Naylor Gray Butters, of Boston. Ch.: 1, Elizabeth Naylor, b. Dec. 29, 1873. 2, Marguerite Beatrice, b. June 4, 1875. He came to Chicago when a young man and became one of the partners in the auction and commission house of W. A. Butters & Co. In 1879 he withdrew, and after two years with Fisk & Hatch went to St. Louis, where he still resides.

5934-34. vi.   LAURA ANN, b. Aug. 23, 1830; m. June 16, 1850, Henry Averill Proctor, b. May 2, 1818; d. Apr. 26, 1869. He was a porkpacker; res. 1326 Westminster St., Providence, R. I. Ch.: 1, Forrest Leland Proctor, b. July 20, 1855; res. 1428 Tremont St., Denver, Colo. 2, Laura Greene Proctor, b. Mar. 31, 1861; res. 1326 Westminster St., Providence, R. I.

4630-10. ALBERT FISK (Job W., Moses, Jeremiah, Job, Benjamin, John, John, Phinehas, Thomas, Robert, Simon, Simon, William, Symond), b. ———; m. at Gloucester, R. I., Apr. 18, 1841, Jennett Burlingame, dau. of Sanford, of Gloucester. She d. in Scituate, R. I., in 1856. He d. July 21, 1847; res. Scituate, R. I.

5934-35. i.   WILLIAM H., b. June 11, 1842; m. Mary E. Paulk.

4631. NOAH FISKE (Caleb, Noah, Noah, Noah, Benjamin, John, John, Phinehas, Thomas, Robert, Simon, Simon, William, Symond), b. Oct. 5, 1820, in South Scituate, R. I.; m. Scituate, July 26, 1852, Huldah Bennett, b. Apr. 11, 1827; d. Dec. 15, 1894. He was a farmer and died in Washington, R. I. He d. Apr. 11, 1892; res. Anthony, R. I.

    5935. i.   BRADFORD M., b. Apr. 18, 1867; m. Phebe A. Corp.
    5936. ii.   HERBERT A., b. July 30, 1858; m. Paulina R. Salisbury.
    5937. iii. CHARLES CALEB, b. May 9, 1855; m. Dec. 11, 1879, Mary Isabella Crawford, b. Apr. 22, 1854. He is an express agent. Res. s. p. Groton, Conn.

4632. DANIEL BAKER FISK (Caleb, Noah, Noah, Noah, Benjamin, John, John, Phinehas, Thomas, Robert, Simon, Simon, William, Symond), b. Kent, R. I., Dec. 14, 1822; m. there Dec. 28, 1848, Mercelia Barbara Salisbury, b. Apr. 6, 1830. He is a farmer; res. Oak Lawn, R. I.

    5938. i.   JOSEPH WARREN, b. Aug. 8, 1860; m. Sept. 29, 1888, at Centerville, R. I., Jessie Wilson Lyon, b. Aug. 14, 1849. He is an engineer. Res. s. p. 149 Sutton St., Providence, R. I.
    5939. ii.   MARIA, b. Dec. 31, 1849; m.; res. Scituate.
    5940. iii. ANNICE ELIZA, b. July 2, 1851; unm.
    5941. iv. GEORGE THOMAS, b. Dec. 11, 1854; m. Maggie Kelley; res. Cranston, R. I.
    5942. v.   MARY FRANCES, b. Mar. 9, 1856.
    5943. vi. MANFORD EUGENE, b. Mar. 26, 1859; d. 1870.
    5944. vii. WILLIAM H., b. July 5, 1864; m. Marietta W. Tew.

4638. STEPHEN FRANCIS FISK (Stephen P., Stephen, Moses, Noah, Benjamin, John, John, Phinehas, Thomas, Robert, Simon, Simon, William, Symond), b. Pawtucket, R. I., Dec. 13, 1843; m. at Providence, Jan. 13, 1875, Susan J. Sheldon, b. Feb. 25, 1853. He has lived in Pawtucket most of the time since his birth. Served during the war in the Ninth Rhode Island Regiment, being one of its youngest members. Is a charter member of Tower Post G. A. R., and has taken an active part in the Masonic order, being a past master of Union Lodge, No. 10; a Knight Templar and a Shriner. He has taken an active part in military, and served five years as aid de camp on the staff of Major-General Walker in the State militia. Has carried on the drug business there for the past twenty years. Res. Pawtucket, R. I.

    5945. i.   HOPE SHELDON, b. July 15, 1882.

4639. HON. WILLIAM JUSTAN FISK (Joel S., Solomon, Ichabod E., Ebenezer, Ebenezer, John, John, Phinehas, Thomas, Robert, Simon, Simon, William, Symond), b. Brunswick, O., June 25, 1833; m. at Fond du Lac, Wis., Jan. 8, 1855, Mary J. Driggs, b. Dec. 6, 1834. The boyhood days of the subject of this memoir were passed in the manner of other boys. Attended such schools as the community afforded until he was 14 years of age, and from that time on through life he has earned his own living. His first work was performed in the land office in Green Bay in 1848, and while thus engaged he made the maps for the reservation of lands for the improvement of the Fox and Wisconsin Rivers. While an employe of the land office John Fitzgerald urged him to save his money and invest his savings in land. So thoroughly did Mr. Fitzgerald impress the matter upon his mind that the principle of economy was thoroughly ingrafted into him. Out of his first savings he purchased 120 acres of land, and thus became a property owner before he was 16. In 1849 he became an employe of a jeweler and watchmaker; the following year he obtained a position as clerk with a Fort Howard merchant at a salary of twenty-five dollars per month. At the end of two years, having saved some money and being desirous of improving his education, he attended the institute at Appleton, Wis., paying from his savings for his tuition and board. At the age of 20 years he returned to Fort Howard and at once began trading in the products brought into the town. Early in his boyhood days he had displayed his self-reliance, and his father encouraged him in the direction in which he had started by leaving him to his own resources. During his first year he entered into a contract with Chancy Lamb, of Clinton, Ia., to furnish him 400,000 shingles, at two dollars and a half a thousand. Mr. Lamb took a deep interest in the

young man and encouraged him a great deal. He paid him in advance $1,000 in cash for the shingles; and Mr. Fisk now says that that was the largest amount of money he had ever seen at one time, and made him feel wealthier than he has ever felt since. In the fall of 1853 Mr. Fisk entered the mercantile business in Fort Howard, and in 1855 erected a shingle mill, being the second man to manufacture sawed shingles in the west. His business was prosperous and he was successful in outside trading, and felt that he was on the high road to permanent prosperity when the panic of 1857 paralyzed the industries of the country and badly crippled Mr. Fisk's financial operations, although he remained perfectly solvent. Among his possessions were 2,000,000 shingles; but there was no market for them. He therefore suggested to E. A. Goodrich, now the controlling spirit of the Goodrich Transportation Company, to carry them to Chicago, where they should await a sale. This was done, but it required two years' time before the shingles were finally sold. In 1862 Mr. Fisk sold out his mercantile establishment, and in that year canvassed the county in the interest of voting bonds for the construction of a railroad. Being well known throughout the county he assisted most materially in having the necessary aid voted. Some of his experiences were interesting and humorous. Few persons, indeed, knew what a railroad was, and some of their ideas, drawn entirely from imagination, displayed dense ignorance. One man said he would favor it if it were only a canal; others thought the company would get the money and not build the road; others, that the road would not be used after it was built; another man, from "York State," who owned forty acres of land, had seen railroads and knew all about them, said that if the company would run across the corner of his land and give him a side-track and buy all the wood it needed of him he would vote in favor of the bonds! After the bonds were voted Mr. Fisk took a contract to furnish the timber and ties used in constructing the road between Appleton and Fort Howard, and also for building the railroad company's docks and elevator. Since then he has been operating continually with the Northwestern Railroad, furnishing a large amount of timber and ties for the use of the various divisions of that road. In 1871 he furnished the material for the construction of the road to Marinette, and in the following year did the same for the extension from Menominee to Escanaba. After his elder sons had grown to manhood he admitted them into the business, and now the firm is known as W. D. Fisk & Co., composed of himself and W. D. and Harry W. Fisk, two of his sons. For nearly thirty years Mr. Fisk has been connected with the banking interests of Green Bay. In 1865 he became a stockholder and director in the First National Bank, of Green Bay; in 1870 he became president of the City National Bank, and in 1874, when that institution was succeeded by the Kellogg National Bank, he became vice-president of the last named institution. In 1891 Mr. Kellogg died, and Mr. Fisk was induced to accept the presidency, and this position he now occupies. As a financier he enjoys a high reputation, and as a conservative, far-seeing banker he enjoys the confidence of all classes in the community. He has been engaged in a great number of enterprises during his business life in Green Bay, all of which have been benefited by his business ability. Before the advent of the railroads, communication with the outside world was carried on by boats in summer and by stages in winter. One company was known as the Green Bay & Menominee Navigation Company, and he was largely interested in this corporation, acting as its superintendent during its existence. Mr. Fisk owned large tracts of timber lands, and at the time of the Peshtigo fire in 1871, some 10,000 acres of valuable timber belonging to him were devoured by the flames; and he also lost heavily in the Chicago fire at the same time. This was a severe blow to him, but, undiscouraged, he went manfully to work and soon retrieved his fortunes. Politically Mr. Fisk is of Democratic antecedents, but is now strongly Republican. In 1860 he voted for Abraham Lincoln, and ever since then he has been a firm believer in the doctrines of Republicanism. In the early years of his business life he was Alderman of the city, and at one time filled the position of City Treasurer; and from 1862 to 1865 he was also Postmaster. In 1875 he was elected a member of the State Legislature, and was re-elected in 1876 and 1877. He was active, in a quiet way, in opposition to the "Granger" legislation against railroads, and was chairman of the committee on railroads when the famous Potter railroad law was repealed. He has never sought political positions, and has no desire for honors of that kind. He is a member of the Masonic fraternity, being now a Knight Templar. Mr. Fisk's career illustrates forcibly the power of steady application and

36

grit. Very early in life he displayed a degree of self-reliance and business ability which alone would assure success to any boy. He has overcome all obstacles and earned for himself the title of "self-made" man in the fullest sense of that often misused term. He has led an honorable, straightforward life, aiding all feasible enterprises that would materially benefit the cities of Green Bay and Fort Howard, and giving from his store to religious and charitable institutions. He is a member of no church, but believes in the power of religion for good, and the Young Men's Christian Association has found in him a warm friend and a generous patron. His career should serve as an inspiration to the younger and convince them that steady application, energetic grit and honest and upright conduct are the principles on which true success is founded. Personally Mr. Fisk is courteous and a pleasant, social companion. All his acts show him to be a retiring, unostentatious gentleman, and he commands the honor and respect of the entire community; res. Green Bay, Wis.

     5946.   i.   WILBUR D., b. Sept. 10, 1856; m. Eva Cornell.
     5947.   ii.   FRANK S., b. Aug. 24, 1858; accidentally shot in Chicago Jan. 20, 1881.
     5948.   iii.   HARRY W., b. Mar. 9, 1866; m. Amy Howland.
     5949.   iv.   G. WALLACE, b. Mar. 8, 1868; m. Maggie Doty.

    4641.   DR. MALANCTON HOGEBOOM FISK (Joel S., Solomon, Ichabod E., Ebenezer, Ebenezer, John, John, Phinehas, Thomas, Robert, Simon, Simon, William, Symond), b. May 28, 1843, in De Pere, Wis.; m. there, Oct. 19, 1868, Mary J. Lawton, b. Apr. 15, 1844. The name Lawton was originally spelled Layton. One John Layton, who was born in 1630, in 1652 went with some twenty-seven others, mostly from Connecticut and other portions of New England colonies, settled in Newtown, Long Island, N. Y., and purchased farms direct from the Indian owners, although also purchasing titles from the government of New Netherlands, of which Peter Stuyvesant was then governor; and it is worthy of record that this purchase from the Indians was the only one of that kind made, excepting a similar transaction effected by William Penn, in Pennsylvania. During John Layton's residence in New Netherlands, that colony fell into the hands of the Duke of York, and on account of the active and prominent part he took against Governor Stuyvesant, Layton made many enemies among the Dutch colonists. Consequently he moved with his family to Suffield, Conn., where he died Sept., 1690, and was buried in the Presbyterian graveyard by the side of his wife, Benedicta. Their gravestones are still (1894) extant, and the name inscribed thereon is plainly "Lawton," so that the change of the spelling of the name presumably must have taken place some time in the latter part of the seventeenth century. John Layton married, Sept. 21, 1659, Johanna Williams, by whom he had one daughter, Mary. He married, 2d, at Portsmouth, R. I., in 1665, Benedicta, and had three or more children, one of them, James, b. Apr. 5, 1673; m. Nov. 9, 1693, Abigail Lamb—two children; both d. young; she d. Nov. 14, 1696. He m., 2d, Faith Newell—five children; eldest was Christopher Jacob, b. July 20, 1701; m. 1731, Abigail Kellogg, b. in Leicester, Mass., in 1702; d. 1734, leaving one child, Pliny, b. 1732, in Suffield, Conn.; m. 1750, Lucretia Sargent; children except one died young, William, b. Apr. 9, 1759; m. 1784, at Flushing, L. I., Abigail Farrington, who d. about 1800—four children; eldest was Charles, b. 1787, at Leicester, Mass.; m. Jan. 17, 1809, Miss Sophia Dobson Willson, in New York City. In 1827 he moved to Ogdensburg, N. Y.; 1830 to Pottsville, Pa. He d. there July 21, 1858; his wife d. Apr. 19, 1844. They had fourteen children, the fifth of whom was Charles, b. Apr. 27, 1817; m. Apr. 7, 1842, Elizabeth Evans Ridgeway, and he d. Apr. 17, 1891, in De Pere, Wis. Mary Joy, b. Apr. 15, 1845, at St. Clair, Pa.; m. Oct. 19, 1868, Malancthon H. Fisk. He was born in Wisconsin, and has always resided in that State. After receiving an excellent education he studied medicine, and is now practicing in Wauwatosa. He was Mayor of De Pere, Brown County, Wis., for the first three years of its existence as a city. He is a Mason of the 32d degree; is now nominated as the first Worshipful Master of the Wauwatosa Lodge, now making application for a charter. Politically he has held no office, though like his father, Joel S. Fisk, he is a pronounced Democrat. He has been a resident of Mil. County for eight years and now serves on the consulting staff of the Mil. County Hospital, the County Hospital for Insane, and is president of the board of visiting physicians for the Chronic Insane Asylum; res. Wauwatosa, Wis.

5950. i.   RAYMON DOUSMAN, b. July 12, 1875.
5951. ii. ESTHER L., b. Apr. 13, 1884; d. Apr. 16, 1884.

4646. HARVEY NEWELL FISKE (Solomon N., Solomon, Ichabod E., Ebenezer, Ebenezer, John, John, Phinehas, Thomas, Robert, Simon, Simon, William, Symond), b. Chazy, N. Y., Aug. 2, 1854; m. at Brooklyn, Oct. 20, 1891, Florence Dean, b. Dec. 5, 1868. At 12 years of age he went to Newburg to attend school at Prof. Sigler's Academy. From there he went to New York City in 1873, where he has been ever since. His first five years' business experience was in the heavy hardware and ship chandlery line. For about a year and a half he went back to Chazy, then went into the roasted coffee business with the firm of Arbuckle Bros., of New York. For the last eight years he has been connected with and interested in the business of the Knapp Company, 52 to 58 Park Place, formerly Major & Knapp, lithographers, where he is still located. As to his success in life he has been fairly fortunate, having been blessed with a large portion of the good things of this life, social, financial, religious, and has a happy and comfortable home; res. 80 Rodney St., Brooklyn, N. Y.
    5952. i.   NEWELL RODNEY, b. Aug. 11, 1894.

4647. DR. WILLIAM M. L. FISKE (Almond D., Solomon, Ichabod E., Ebenezer, Ebenezer, John, John, Phinehas, Thomas, Robert, Simon, Simon, William, Symond), b. May 10, 1841, in New York City; m. in Rochester, Oct. 11, 1865, Julia Pancost Sage, b. June 14, 1845. There are many men whose professional ability is considerable; and with that their usefulness and interest to other people end. While, as a surgeon, Dr. Wm. M. L. Fiske stands among the few leading homeopathic physicians of New York which he lives. For more than twenty-five years Dr. Fiske has been in active practice in Brooklyn, N. Y., and in that time he has been president of the New York State Homeopathic Medical Society and the Kings County Homeopathic Medical Society. He was one of the founders and organizers of the Brooklyn Homeopathic Hospital and the Brooklyn (E. D.) Homeopathic Dispensary, and he is ex-medical director of the former and consulting surgeon and trustee of the latter, and consulting surgeon to the Memorial Hospital, besides being connected with a large number of benevolent institutions of the city.
    Dr. Fiske was born in New York City in 1841. His father was Almond D. Fiske, a well known inventor and manufacturer. He was a member of an old New England family, and through him Dr. Fiske is a direct descendant of Phineas Fiske, who came to America in one of the first four ships that brought the New England colonists, and settled Wenham, Mass. His ancestor, Symond Fiske, was Lord of the Manor of Shadhaugh, Suffolk, up to the time of the Wars of the Roses. Edward, second son of Dr. John, son of Phineas Fiske, the direct ancestor of Dr. Fiske, lived at the old homestead at Wenham, and died there in 1748. It is a fact worth notice that the first four graduates of Yale were descended from this Dr. John Fiske. His grandson and Dr. W. M. L. Fiske's great-grandfather, Ichabod Ebenezer Fiske, graduated from Yale in 1770, and became a preacher and scholar of some note. Dr. Fiske's mother was Phoebe Ann Raymond, daughter of Harvey Raymond, who moved to New York from Albany in 1830.
    Dr. Fiske prepared for college at Champlain Academy, New York, and graduated from the Bellevue Medical College in 1863. Owing to a promise that he would investigate homeopathy, he afterward attended the New York Homeopathic Medical College, and thus he twice received the degree of M. D. He has also received the degree from the New York Board of Regents, which was until recently conferred annually upon one prominent member of the State Medical Society.
    Soon after the war Dr. Fiske undertook the practice of medicine at Aurora, Ill., and later at Rochester, N. Y. He entered into partnership in 1870 with his old preceptor, Dr. Albert Wright, and after the latter's death continued the increasing practice. Dr. Fiske is the author of a number of monographs on Surgery, published in the "Transactions of the State and County Medical Societies." He has given much attention to the study of heredity, not only in diseases but in mental traits, and his semi-annual address as president of the State Society, in which he advocated the enforced celibacy of confirmed criminals, aroused marked attention

DR. WILLIAM M. L. FISKE.

and keen discussion. It is to be regretted that his medical practice prevents more active advocacy of his advanced ideas on this important subject.

Dr. Fiske is a Republican and a member of the Union League, Crescent, West Hampton Country, Lake Champlain Yacht, Hanover and New Manhattan Clubs.

In 1865 he married Miss Julia P. Sage, of Rochester. Of his three sons, two are graduates of Columbia and the second is about to become the fifth of the family to represent his generation in the profession of medicine. In spite of his incessant work Dr. Fiske knows how to thoroughly enjoy the comforts of life, and his hospitable home is filled with objects of art that he has collected. His only vacation this summer was a flying trip to Europe to attend a patient there.

In 1862 he enlisted in Company A, of the Forty-seventh Regiment New York State Militia, as a private soldier. After a month's service in the ranks he was appointed by General Morris as steward in the convalescent hospital, at Fort McHenry, and a few weeks later was promoted to acting assistant post surgeon, in charge of the post hospital, and served in that capacity until the expiration of the regiment's service; he then returned to Brooklyn, continued his studies at Bellevue Medical College, and was graduated in 1863. After a few months in private practice he again entered the service as acting assistant surgeon and remained until the close of the war. Res. 484 Bedford Ave., Brooklyn, N. Y.

5953. i. WM. RAYMOND, b. July 26, 1866; d. Nov. 7, 1872.

5954. ii. JOHN SAGE, b. July 4, 1870, in the city of Rochester, New York. Early removing to Brooklyn, he followed his studies at the Polytechnic Institute of that city and entered Columbia College in 1886. He graduated from the latter institution in 1890. During his course he was active in the general work of the college, ranking high in his studies throughout all four years, receiving several honors, including the scholarship in Greek. He was president of the Barnard Literary Society, the leading organization of its kind in the university, and an editor of the Columbiad, the junior publication, besides holding several offices in his class. He was a leading member of the D. K. E. fraternity and, when graduated, became a member of I. B. K. After graduation he traveled in Europe for further study and recreation, and on his return in 1891 entered the banking and commission house of J. M. Ceballos & Co., New York City, with which firm he is still connected. A member of the Presbyterian Church, he is identified with Y. M. C. A. work in Brooklyn, being at present one of the board of managers of the Eastern District Branch of this organization. In social life he takes an active interest and is a member of the Crescent Athletic Club of Brooklyn and the Circulo Colon Cervantes, the Spanish Club of New York.

5955. iii. EDWIN RODNEY, b. July 9, 1873. He studied at the Polytechnic Institute; graduated from that institution in 1888 and entered Columbia College. Throughout his course he received many honors because of high scholarship, notably in winning the prize in physics. He was president of the Barnard Literary Society, an editor of the Columbiad, held several positions of class distinction, and on graduation was made a member of I. B. K. He was also prominently connected with the D. K. E. fraternity. In 1892 he entered the New York Homeopathic Medical College, graduating in 1895, securing at that time the faculty prize for leading scholarship of his class during his three years' course and the alumni prize for the foremost student of the senior year. He was also valedictorian, the commencement orator and senior president of his class. Among class organizations he was prominent in the A. E. and Hahnemann societies. He also served in the New York (Chambers Street) and Lying-in Hospitals and Brooklyn Homeopathic Dispensary, and has taken the post-graduate course at the New York Ophthalmic College and Hospital. He is associated with his father in the practice of medicine in Brooklyn, and is a member of the American Institute of

Homeopathy and various city, county and state medical societies.

5956. iv. WM. M. L., JR., b. June 12, 1879.

4675. ARTHUR POTTER FISKE (Ira W., Ira, Ichabod E., Ebenezer, Ebenezer, John, John, Phinehas, Thomas, Robert, Simon, Simon, William, Symond), b. Kalamazoo, Mich., Apr. 23, 1865; m. there in 1887, Constance M. Parker. He was born in Kalamazoo and always resided there. His death was quite sudden and a great shock to his many friends. He was junior partner of the firm of Tyler & Fiske, lumber dealers and jobbers. His character was of the very highest type. He d. Nov. 26, 1889; res. Kalamazoo, Mich.

5957. i. ARTHUR, b. Oct. 26, 1889.

4695. BERTRAND EDGAR FISKE (James H., Solomon, Solomon, Ebenezer, Ebenezer, John, John, Phinehas, Thomas, Robert, Simon, Simon, William, Symond), b. Milwaukee, Ore., May 24, 1869; m. Portland, Feb. 15, 1893, Laura V. Beard, b. Oct. 21, 1869. He is connected with the postoffice department; res. Portland, Ore.

5958. i. NORMAN EDGAR, b. Dec. 7, 1893.

4703. JOHN FISKE (John, John, John, John, John, John, Phinehas, Thomas, Robert, Simon, Simon, William, Symond), b. Dec. 6, 1840, in Lebanon, N. Y.; m. Mar. 13, 1862, Nettie A. Morrow, b. Aug. 31, 1840, of Augusta, N. Y. His early education was received in the district schools. He was thoroughly grounded in the principles of agriculture by his father who cultivated vast farms. To complete John's education a short time was spent at Cazenovia Seminary, which plan the father did not approve, as he believed all knowledge could be gained by observation and practice, and as he wanted his son to be a farmer, time at school was thrown away. At the age of 21 John married. One of the numerous farms was settled upon John at his marriage. The old Ford house on the Ford farm became the home of John and his lovely wife. After the father's death in Mar., 1866, John came into possession of the old Fiske homestead where he now resides and the Blair farm. John has been a very successful farmer; he has expended vast sums of money in his buildings. He rebuilt the old house, tore down the old barns and built a very large modern barn instead, with accommodations for fifty head of cattle as well as eight horses. Two large hop kilns were built with accommodation for curing fifty thousand pounds of hops. John has made a thorough study of the cultivation of small fruits. One year he marketed one hundred bushels of strawberries. He has also gone into grape culture. He has a fine vineyard containing over seven hundred vines. This present year he will market three thousand pounds of grapes. He has a fine cherry and pear orchard started. The subject of our sketch is an active member of the Congregational Church. He is a member of the Grangers' Lodge, of the Equitable Aid Union and of the Free Mason's Lodge. He is regarded by all who know him well a model of strict integrity; res. Lebanon, N. Y.

5959. i. CAROLINE, b. Aug. 1, 1863; d. Sept. 17, 1864.
5960. ii. CORA ETTA, b. Oct. 26, 1865; res. Weehawken, N. J.; b. in Lebanon, N. Y.; attended the district school until she was 14 years old; studied music in the meantime; entered Cazenovia Seminary; pursued the Latin scientific course of study for two years which she dropped to pursue the course of study in the Albany Normal School. She graduated from Albany Jan. 23, 1885, with honors. She was chosen one of the essayists at the final exercises in one of the literary societies. President Cleveland conferred the diplomas at the commencement exercises which were held in the ——— Opera House. Since her graduations she has been actively engaged in the profession of teaching. She has taught in the intermediate department at the Fairport Union School, in the intermediate department of the Skaneateles Union School, at the Flushing High School, and at the present has charge of the first year work in the high school in the town of Union, N. J., which position she has held for six years. Miss Fiske is a member of the Protestant Episcopal Church. She has taught in Sunday school for the past six

years, has been a member of the Altar Society, church guild, Parish Aid Society, and young people's society. Miss Fiske is also interested in a working girls' club of which she is president. She was one of the followers of Miss Grace Dodge in the movement and one of the organizers of the club in the town of Union. The said club is now five years old. It has a membership of fifty girls between the ages of 12 and 30. It is an acknowledged fact that the club has done a vast amount of good. The subject of this sketch is also interested in a boys' club, whose object is the same as the girls, i. e., the greatest possible development of character. She helped organize the club and directed the drawing up of the by-laws. She is also a member of an association whose aim is to found a home for old people. She is interested in all legitimate sports with the exception of riding a "wheel," which she does not approve for ladies.

5961. iii. ADA LOUISE, b. July 19, 1867; m. Mar. 28, 1888, William Frederick Eldredge. She d. Feb. 15, 1891.
5962. iv. WM. JOHN, b. Nov. 6, 1874; res. L.

4708. LUMAN FISKE (John, John, John. John, John, John, Phinehas, Thomas, Robert, Simon, Simon, William, Symond), b. July 16, 1829, in Lebanon, N. Y.; m. in Smyrna in 1849, Angeline R Close, b. May, 1827; d. Apr. 14. 1881. Luman Fisk, a former resident of Lebanon, was found dead in a piece of timber land on which he had settled in the State of Washington. His death was evidently the result of heart trouble. The body was taken to the home of his son, P. R. Fisk, where the funeral was held under Masonic auspices, after which the remains were taken to Lebanon for interment. He d. Jan. 11, 1895; res. Lebanon, N. Y., and Chehabi, Wash.

5963. i. PERLEE R., b. May 15, 1852; m. Hattie N. Billings.
5964. ii. ISAAC L., b. July 3, 1855; m. Addie M. La Sells.
5965. iii. EPHRAIM J., b. Dec. 4, 1860; m. Eugenie Randall.

4711-2. PROF. HORACE SPENCER FISKE (John B., Horace, John, Benjamin, John, John, John, Phinehas, Thomas, Robert, Simon, Simon, William, Symond), b. Dexter, Mich., Nov. 4, 1859; m. June 22, 1889, Ida M. Nettleton at Lancaster N. H., b. Oct. 16, 1854 Horace Spencer Fiske was born at Dexter, Mich.; graduated in 1882 from Beloit College, where he was editor-in-chief of the Beloit College "Round Table," representative of Wisconsin in the Inter-state Oratorical Contest, and valedictorian of his class. A. B., Beloit College, 1882; A. M., University of Michigan, 1885; A. M., Beloit College, 1885; Instructor, Beloit College Academy, 1886-7; Chair, Political Economy and Civics, Wisconsin State Normal School, 1887-93; elected to Fellowship in English at University of Wisconsin, 1892; student at universities of Oxford and Cambridge, and Trinity College, Dublin, 1893-4; lecturer in English, University of Chicago, 1894;contributor to Christ's College Magazine, Cambridge, Eng., 1894; to the Oxford Magazine, 1894, and to the Century Magazine, Sept., 1892, and Mar., 1896; lecturer on Thought and Imagination in Shakespeare, University of Chicago, 1894-5; res. s. p. 5663 Washington Ave., Chicago, Ill.

4729. JAMES MONROE FISK (John P., Samuel B., Squire, John, Josiah, Samuel, William, William, John, William, Robert, Simon, Simon, William, Symond), b. Massachusetts, Aug., 1832; m. 1859, Anna Haynes, d. Feb., 1887. He d. Dec. 9, 1894; res. Lawrence, Mich.

5966. i. CORA, b. ———; m. Charles Conwell; res. L.
5967. ii. JOHN P., b. ———; unm.; res. L.
5968. iii. LOTTIE, b. ———; d. ———.
5969. iv. JAMES, b. ———; unm.; res. Central Lake, Mich.
5970. v. FREDERICK, b. ———; m. ———; res. Central Lake, Mich.
5971. vi. LOUIE, b. ———; d. ———.
5972. vii. JOSEPH, b. ———; unm.; res. L.

4730. CHARLES WESLEY FISK (John P., Samuel B., Squire, John, Josiah, Samuel, William, William, John, William, Robert, Simon, Simon, William,

Symond), b. Massachusetts, Mar. 17, 1834; m. Apr. 18, 1858, Adaline A. Norton. He was born in Williamstown, Mass.: went to Michigan with his parents when 9 years of age and resided there until 1879, when he moved to Chicago where he has resided ever since. He is a stock broker; res. 3601 Vincennes Ave., Chicago, Ill.

    5973. i.   IDA C., b. June 10, 1860; m. Nov. 6, 1882, James Joseph Carroll, b. Apr. 29, 1858; res. Marquette, Mich.

    5974. ii.   MAMIE RICHMOND, b. Nov. 30, 1867; m. Joseph C. Sassette; res. 79 Henry St., Brooklyn, N. Y.

    5975. iii.   JOSEPHINE, b. June, 1863; d. Oct. 19, 1865.

    4732. GEORGE WHITEFIELD FISK (John P., Samuel B., Squire, John, Josiah, Samuel, William, William, John, William, Robert, Simon, Simon, William, Symond), b. 1841; m. Kittie Smith; after his death she m. a Simpson. He was born in Williamstown, Mass., where he always resided. When the war broke out he enlisted in the Fourth Michigan Cavalry and died from the effects of exposure in College Hospital, Nashville, Tenn. He d. Dec. 28, 1862; res. Lawrence, Mich.

    5976. i.   GEORGE, b. 1862; unm.; res. Geneva, Mich.

    4735. JAMES FISK, JR. (James, Samuel B., Squire, John, Josiah, Samuel, William, William, John, William, Robert, Simon, Simon, William, Symond), b. Pownal, Vt., Apr. 1, 1835; m. in Nov., 1855, Lucy D. Moore, of Springfield, Mass., b. 1833. She res. 5 3 E. 8th St., South Boston, Mass. He was born near Battleboro, Vt.; was well educated; fitted for college, and it was his father's wish that he should enter "Williams," but all his tastes were for business, and after traveling with his father a year he went to Jordan & Marsh (Mr. Jordan being a friend of his father's) as a clerk. The second year he did so well and had so many original ideas that he was taken into the firm as an equal partner. Later he went to New York City, and for a time was the leading financier in that city, being largely interested with Jay Gould in the Erie Railway, until he was murdered by Stokes in 1872.

COL. JAMES FISKE, JR.

A person who knew him intimately writes as follows: "He never drank. On the contrary, he was elegant in manner, gentle and courtly, and had the most generous, unselfish heart of any person I ever knew. He was very fond of dress and display, but never of the vulgar sort; he had no low tastes and (like his father) was always temperate. I have often heard him say: 'Well, you may drink the wine if it pleases you, but give me my little cup of tea.' He was very fond of tea, and when he had any great 'deal' (as he was wont to call it) on the tapis, he would drink quantities of tea. He was the man who planned a great deal of the business for himself and Jay Gould when they were together. Mr. Gould was delicate and small while Mr. Fisk was the perfection of manly health and beauty. I have often heard him tell Mr. Gould to 'jump over in the sugar bowl and take a nap and let me do the hard work.' Every one who knew him loved him; he had the happiest, sweetest, and most unsuspicious disposition God ever

gave to any living man. The day he was murdered by Stokes a friend went to him
and said, ' Fisk, you will gain your suit today (he had a suit against Stokes for
$60,000, money he had loaned him), but do I pray you look out for Stokes for he
is a bad one.' Fisk replied: ' Oh! no, you are mistaken; he would no more harm
me than I would him.' After Fisk's death his father was ill for a year; in fact
insane, made so by the shock of his death. He (his father) was walking up Broadway and heard the news from boys crying it in the street. He fell unconscious
and remained so twenty-four hours. He never saw his dearly loved boy again;
he recovered his mind but his health never." He d. s. p. Jan. 7, 1872; res. New
York, N. Y.

4737. STEPHEN WINSLOW FISK (Samuel B., Samuel B., Squire, John,
Josiah, Samuel, William, William, John, William, Robert, Simon, Simon, William,
Symond), b. Aug. 15, 1831, in Monroe, Vt.; m. in Michigan, Emma Dyer; res.
Fisk, Mo.

    5977. i.   BERTHA V., b. ———; d. ———.
    5978. ii.   GRACE, b. ———; m. ———.
    5979. iii. ROY B., b. ———.
    5980. iv. WINNIE, b. ———.

4740. WILLIAM HENRY FISKE (William H., Haley, Squire, John, Josiah, Samuel, William, William, John, William, Robert, Simon, Simon, William,
Symond), b. New Brunswick, N. J., May 13, 1845; m. there Mar. 5, 1865, Mary
Elizabeth Houghton, b. Mar. 5, 1843. W. H. Fisk, Jr., was educated in private
and public schools in New Brunswick, N. J., and after clerking in New York for
half a dozen years returned home and took a position in a wholesale liquor house
as bookkeeper and head salesman. In 1884 he became reporter and afterward
assistant editor of the Times, the leading Democratic paper in Middlesex County,
N. J., and for a year or more—while Mr. A. E. Gordon, the proprietor, was United
States Marshal, and afterward when he had a paralytic stroke—wrote all the
editorials and did all the local work besides, sometimes working twenty hours a
day and seldom less than fourteen. On one occasion he went sixty hours with
only a couple of hours' sleep, and covered a report of a trip to Trenton and Bucks
County, Pennsylvania, and an excursion of a local order to Keyport, getting up
the editorials and most of the local matter besides. Singularly the work seemed
to do him good, as he felt no fatigue and did not miss the loss of sleep. On one
occasion, in 1887, he reported the proceedings of the State convention of the
Knights of Pythias, there being over nine hundred delegates present and wrote the
matter out in full while doing so in order to gain time to do other work. On his
return home he found the report had been lost, but, nothing daunted, sat down and
rewrote the matter while it was fresh in his memory. He was highly congratu-
lated by many of the Knights who knew of the loss of the papers. In 1889 he
started the first and only Sunday paper in New Brunswick or the county, or rather
purchased the plant after it had run six months and was about to be discontinued.
He ran this paper until the summer of 1895, when he stopped its publication, owing
to a variety of causes, principally of a political nature. It was an independent
paper but with Democratic tendencies; res. New Brunswick, N. J.

    5981. iii. CHARLES, b. Mar. 16, 1868. He was born in New Brunswick,
                N. J., and received his preliminary education in the public
                schools, graduating in 1884, with high honors from the high
                school. While in the latter school he did some newspaper
                work on The Times, and continued it for some time as city
                editor, until he went to study law in the office of Arnoux, Ritch
                & Woodford, in New York City. He was also in Judge
                Cowenhoven's office. The study of law did not suit him and
                he returned to his first love and became city editor on the
                Home News. In 1889 he entered St. Stephen's College at An-
                nandale, N. Y., taking a special course with the idea of entering
                the Episcopal ministry, and during the three years' course took
                all the first prizes and was congratulated publicly by one of the
                most eminent preachers in the country. In 1893 he entered
                the General Theological Seminary in New York City, and
                took the prize for an essay, two hundred college students com-

peting. He also gained a scholarship but did not accept it, and has stood at the head of all the classes he has entered. During the second and third years of his course he acted as lay reader, and by special permission wrote his own sermons and had charge of a church in Rahway, N. J., in 1895. This he gave up in the fall and took charge of a Sunday school in New York City in the morning and another in Brooklyn, N. Y. He graduate in June, 1896, and his friends predict a brilliant future for him. His law and newspaper work has been of great benefit to him in his new sphere. He is a ready writer and a good speaker, is very affable in manners and makes friends easily.

5982.   iv.   CLARA E., b. June 18, 1877; unm.
5983.   i.   DELIA M., b. Aug. 22, 1866; d. June 16, 1867.
5984.   ii.   MARY, b. May 6, 1870; d. Nov. 18, 1876.

4741. HALEY FISKE (William, Haley, Squire, John, Josiah, Samuel, William, William, John, William, Robert, Simon, Simon, William, Symond), b. Mar. 18, 1852, New Brunswick, N. J.; m. Jan. 10, 1878, Mary Garrettena Mulford, b. Sept. 5, 1856; d. Feb. 3, 1886; m. 2d, Apr. 27, 1887, Marione Cowles Cushman, b. Oct. 18, 1866.

Old Rutgers College has sent but few of her sons to the metropolis, but the proportion of those who have mapped out their life work and attained success there is very large in comparison with that of other colleges. Haley Fiske's rise in reputation and prosperity has been a continuous one since the day of his graduation at Rutgers in 1871. He was born in New Brunswick, N. J., Mar. 18, 1852. His parents, Wm. H. and Sarah H. Fiske, were born in Yonkers and New York City respectively, and settled for a time in New Brunswick, where Mr. Fiske was prepared for college in the school of Henry Waters, afterward well known as the Poughkeepsie school master. While in college Mr. Fiske was a member of the Philoclean Literary Society and the fraternity of Delta Phi. After leaving college he tried journalism for a year or two and then studied law with the firm of Arnoux, Ritch & Woodford, in which firm he subsequently became a partner. He remained such until his election as vice-president of the Metropolitan Life Insurance Company, in Oct., 1891. He had previously for many years had special charge of the legal business of that corporation. During his career as a lawyer he was engaged in many notable cases, the last of which, just before his retirement, being the Fayerweather Will contest. He was largely concerned in the settlement of the probate contest, culminating in the deed of gift by which so many colleges throughout the country were benefited. In the present suits over this settlement, in which five colleges appear as plaintiffs, Mr. Fiske represents Yale University and Rutgers College, defending the will and the settlement. Mr. Fiske is a director in and counsel for the Duluth Manufacturing Company, the Iron Car Equipment Company, treasurer of the church of St. Mary the Virgin, in West 45th Street, now become a wealthy corporation, and is vice-president of the Metropolitan Life Insurance Company. This company stood second among the great companies in the successful pursuit of business during the last fiscal year, and is now housed in its new building at 23d Street and Madison Avenue, a model of simplicity and elegance, built at a cost of nearly $2,000,000 by Napoleon Le Brun, the architect. He is a member of the Players', Grolier, Church and Delta Phi clubs and of the Bar Association. In politics he is allied to the Democratic party. It would be difficult to find in the whole range of the New York College Alumni Associations a more genial, delightful companion of equal ability. He is endowed by nature with those traits that make leaders among men; res. 1 Madison Ave., New York, N. Y.

5985.   i.   HELEN, b. June 26, 1884.
5986.   ii.   ARCHIBALD FALCONER CUSHMAN, b. Mar. 11, 1888.

4749. FREDERIC B. FISKE (John A., Nathan, John, John, Josiah, Samuel, William, William, John, William, Robert, Simon, Simon, William, Symond), b. Brooklyn, N. Y., Dec. 13, 1857; m. in Prov., R. I., Apr. 22, 1885, Louise Palmer, b. July 22, 1858; res. New York, N. Y., add. 59 Water St.

HALEY FISKE.

5987. i. FREDERIC PALMER, b. June 4, 1889.
5988. ii. LOUISE PERRY, b. June 12, 1892.

4751. WILBUR L. FISK (Stephen, Nathaniel, Jonathan, Jonathan, Josiah, Samuel, William, William John, William, Robert, Simon, Simon, William, Symond), b. July 17, 1844, at Blountville, Tenn.; m. in Kentucky Florence Van Peet, Oct. 7, 1851. He is a furniture, carriage and harness dealer; res. Vevay, Ind.
5989. i. ROBERT W., b. Dec. 8, 1874; m. ———.
5990. ii. FLORENCE NORMAN, b. Aug. 3, 1879.

4758. CHARLES PLINEY FISKE, JR. (Charles P., Nathaniel, Jonathan, Jonathan, Josiah. Samuel, William, William, John, William, Robert, Simon, Simon, William, Symond), b. Mayfield, N. Y., July 1, 1867; m. Dec. 15, 1892, Minerva Steele, b. Nov. 29, 1867. Chas. Fiske, Jr., was born at Mayfield, N. Y. His parents located in Gloversville, N. Y., in Dec., 1875, where he attended school until 1885. Taught a district school at West Bush, N. Y., from 1885 to 1886. Entered Union College at Schenectady, N. Y., in fall of 1887, from whence he graduated in June, 1891, receiving the degree of C. E. Was Assistant City Engineer of city of Gloversville from Apr., 1892, until Jan. 1, 1896, when he was appointed City Engineer for the year 1896; res. 39 E. State St., Gloversville, N. Y.
5991. i. KATHERINE S., b. Oct. 15, 1893.

4763. EDWARD C. FISK (Cornelius E., Edward, Jonathan D., David, Jonathan, Josiah, Samuel, William, John, William, Robert, Simon, Simon, William, Symond), b. Titusville, Pa., June 12, 1872; m. Feb. 3, 1892, Mary F. Fisk, dau. of Willis P., b. Dec. 2, 1870. He is editor and publisher of the Mayville Sentinel, and Chautauqua Era; res. Mayville, N. Y.
5992. i. EVERETT L., b. 1892.
5993. ii. KENNETH H., b. 1894.

4774. ALLEN GURDON FISK (Marcus R., James G., David, Jonathan, Josiah, Samuel, William, John, William, Robert, Simon, Simon, William, Symond), b. Somerset, N. Y., Feb. 5, 1845; m. in Iowa Feb., 1865, Julia Etta Spencer, b. Aug. 9, 1846. He is a locomotive engineer; res. 1420 3d St. W., Cedar Rapids, Ia.
5994. i. NEWTON R., b. Aug. 7, 1868.
5995. ii. ELLEN S., b. July 15, 1874.
5996. iii. ELVER O., b. Sept. 17, 1872.
5997. iv. LULU E., b. Feb. 18, 1879.
5998. v. MABEL P., b. Apr. 14, 1881.

4804. DE WITT HENRY FISK (Samuel W., Lewis M., David, Jonathan, Josiah, Samuel, William, John, William, Robert, Simon, Simon, William, Symond), b. Bradford, Pa., June 27, 1851; m. Red Wing, Minn., Feb. 16, 1879, Adda C. Ashelman, b. Jan. 4, 1860. De Witt Henry Fisk was born June 27, 1851, at or near Bradford, McKean Co., Pa. Lived with his parents in McKean Co., Pa., Cattaraugus Co., N. Y., and in Erie Co., Pa., until almost 12 years of age, when he came to Wisconsin with his parents and located at New Richmond, St. Croix Co., Wis. While his parents resided there in 1871 he went to Northfield, Minn., and attended Northfield and Carlton College up to 1876, when he went to Red Wing, Minn. Remained there almost two years, and married there Miss Adda C. Ashelman on Feb. 16, 1879. Then went to New Richmond with his wife to reside, and study law with Frank P. Chapman. Resided there until June, 1880. Moved to Ada, Norman Co., Minn. Remained there practicing law up to Oct. 6, 1888, and left there for Cheney, Spokane Co., Wash., where he has resided since engaged at practice of law. His family now consists of his wife and four children; res. Cheney, Wash.
5999. i. CHARLES DE WITT, b. Nov. 3, 1880.
6000. ii. ALLIE A., b. Jan. 30, 1882.
6001. iii. HENRY F., b. Mar. 19, 1885.
6002. iv. CLARA E., b. Oct. 1, 1888.

4812. CHARLES HUNTOON FISK (John S. C., John H., Ezra, Jonathan, Josiah, Samuel, William, William, John, William, Robert, Simon, Simon, William, Symond), b. Newark, N. Y., Nov. 24, 1863; m. Sept. 14, 1887, Edna F. Beal, b. June 1, 1866. He is a traveling salesman; res. Elmira, N. Y.

6003. i.   LESLIE BEAL, b. Feb. 27, 1891.
6004. ii.   CHAS. HUNTOON, b. Aug. 20, 1895.

4843. WILMOT FISK (Joseph W., Joseph, Joseph, Joseph, Mark, Joseph, William, William, John, William, Robert, Simon, Simon, William, Symond), b. Springville, Pa., Sept. 9, 1850; m. at Morrison, Ill., May 13, 1873, Sarah E. Humphrey, b. Dec. 25, 1848. He is a farmer; res. Morrison, Ill.
6005. i.   CLIFFORD J., b. Aug. 18, 1877.
6006. ii.   MAY, b. Aug. 8, 1879.
6007. iii. FRANK G., b. Apr. 21, 1881.
6008. iv.   MABLE, b. Oct. 9, 1884.
6009. v.   VERNA, b. Jan. 17, 1892.

4844. THERON S. FISK (Joseph W., Joseph, Joseph, Joseph, Mark, Joseph, William, William, John, William, Robert, Simon, Simon, William, Symond), b. Fisk Corners, Pa., July 20, 1860; m. at Valparaiso, Ind., May 27, 1886, Ella Capron, b. May 18, 1864. Theron S. Fisk, B. A., L.L. B., was born in Susquehanna Co., Pa. Removed with his father's family to Whiteside Co., Ill., in 1865, where he was raised on a farm, attending school winters. Began teaching at 19, after which he spent seven years working his way through college, graduating in the scientific, classical, elocutionary and law departments. Resides at Fairmont, Minn., and has an extensive law practice. He is an agnostic and Populist, and was a delegate to the Omaha National Convention of the P. P. in 1892. Hon. Ignatius Donnelly says: "Colonel Fisk is a physical as well as an intellectual giant, and I regard him as one of the finest orators in the entire northwest;" res. Fairmont, Minn.

THERON S. FISK.

6010. i.   HAROLD M., b. Sept. 19, 1887.
6011. ii.   DON R., b. Jan. 17, 1889.
6012. iii. RUTH, b. May 11, 1892.

4845. MELVIN FISK (Joseph W., Joseph, Joseph, Joseph, Mark, Joseph, William, William, John, William, Robert, Simon, Simon, William, Symond), b. Springville, Pa., Dec. 12, 1851; m. at Morrison, Dec. 16, 1874, Jennie E. Brumagin, b. Oct. 9, 1852. He is a grain and live stock dealer and proprietor of the Fisk House; res. Curlew, Ia.
6013. i.   ORVILLE B., b. Apr. 8, 1876.
6014. ii.   VALENTINE, b. Apr. 20, 1881.
6015. iii. ALICE, b. May 5, 1885.
6016. iv.   JENNIE A., b. Dec. 28, 1890.
6017. v.   MELVIN, b. Feb. 25, 1894.

4846. DR. CALVIN R. FISK (Joseph W., Joseph, Joseph, Joseph, Mark, Joseph, William, William, John, William, Robert, Simon, Simon, William, Symond), b. Susquehanna Co., Pa., Jan. 2, 1853; m. at Morrison, Ill., Mar. 1, 1880, Stella A. Martindale, b. Sept. 24, 1858. Calvin R. Fisk, M. D., son of Joseph W. and Rhoda E. (Strickland) Fisk, was born in Springville Township, Susquehanna Co., Pa. He is the fourth son of a family of twelve children. His eldest brother died in early infancy. There are still living six brothers and one sister of this large family, two sisters and three brothers with the parents having passed on to that unknown life, of which we hear so much and know so little. At about the close of the Civil War, in 1865, his parents moved from Pennsylvania to Illinois and located on a farm in Whiteside Co. Here the young doctor had the benefit of a country school in the winter and worked on the farm in the summer. In some mysterious manner he managed to get education enough so that he passed an examination and obtained a teacher's certificate and began teaching school in 1875. The following summer he visited his old home in Pennsylvania, and went on to Philadelphia to the Centennial Exposition, where he remained about two weeks. From there he went to Washington and visited the White House. Returning from Washington to Sterling, Ill., he attended the teachers' normal school and received his degree in the form of a first grade certificate for teaching school in Illinois, which vocation he followed for a short time. In the spring of 1878 he went west and spent a part of two years in Kansas and Nebraska. He was united in marriage to Stella A. Martindale in Morrison, Whiteside Co., Ill., soon after locating in Iowa. In 1882 he moved to Keokuk, Ia., and attended lectures at the College of Physicians and Surgeons and received the degree of M. D. on Feb. 26, 1884. Politically he has always voted with the reform movement on national questions, casting his first presidential vote for Peter Cooper. He was selected as a delegate-at-large to the National Convention held in

DR. CALVIN R. FISK.

MRS. CALVIN R. FISK.

St. Louis, July 22, 1896, by the People's party. Believing in reforms in all lines he is at the present time collecting data for a work entitled "The Art of Life," which will treat largely of physiology, psychology, and the laws of health and disease. His wife is author of that little work on political economy entitled, "The Condition and Remedy." Dr. Fisk has five brothers and one sister living, viz.: Wilmot Fisk, Morrison, Ill.; Melvin Fisk, Curlew, Ia.; W. E. Fisk, Lily, S. D.; Theron S. Fisk, Fairmont, Minn.; Alfred L. Fisk, Chicago, Ill.; Mrs. Harriet E. Emery, Lovewell, Kan. The doctor's family consists of wife and one son, Joseph E. Fisk, a fine boy, 12 years of age; res. Keokuk, Ia.

6017¼.i.   EDITH, b. Dec. 29, 1880; d. Apr. 3, 1891.
6017½.ii.   JOSEPH E., b. Mar. 27, 1884.
6017¾.iii.   ROLF P., b. Nov. 23, 1889; d. Apr. 10, 1891.

4851. CHARLES JOSEPH FISK (Clark S., Joseph, Joseph, Joseph, Mark, Joseph, William, William, John, William, Robert, Simon, Simon, William, Symond), b. Morrison, Ill., Mar. 11, 1862; m. Oct. 20, 1886, Ida M. Myers, b. Jan. 21, 1869, Sterling, Ill. Was born in Whiteside Co., Ill., in a car-roofed shanty. His parents were poor, and at the age of 11 years he commenced to earn his own livelihood by working out at farm work until he arrived at the age of 17, attending the common school winters. At the age of 17 he entered Northern Illinois College and Griffith's School of Oratory at Fulton, Ill., and at the end of the first year succeeded in procuring a teacher's certificate and thereafter taught school during the winters and atteded college during vacations, also reading law as occasion permitted, until the spring of 1885, when he entered the law offices of Woodruff & Andrews, at Morrison, Ill., and read law until the following spring, at which time he went to Larimore, N. Dak., and continued the study of law in the office of Wm. H. Fellows, a former college classmate, and in the fall of 1886 was admitted to practice, and has been in active practice ever since. In 1889 he removed to Grand Forks and entered into partnership with Tracy R. Bangs, under the firm name of Bangs & Fisk, and their law business has been steadily increasing until their practice is now one of the largest in the State. Two years ago he was appointed as a member of a commission to revise, codify and compile the laws of this State into seven codes. The work has recently been completed and is considered a credit to the young State of North Dakota. He has served in several offices, among which is Assistant United States Attorney for the district of North Dakota, and Assistant State's Attorney; also City Attorney of Larimore, Grand Forks and East Grand Forks. He voted for Cleveland in 1884, and has been a Democrat ever since, but Democrats are scarce in this community. He ran for member of the Legislature last fall and was beaten by both the Republicans and Pops; res. Grand Forks, N. Dak.

    6018. i.   M. HELENE, b. Aug. 19, 1893.
    6019. ii.   RUTH PAULINE, b. Aug. 11, 1891; d. Apr. 3, 1892.
    6020. iii. NELLIE M., b. Oct. 11, 1888; d. Oct. 27, 1888.

    4864. JOSEPH H. FISK (Joseph W., Joseph, Mark, Joseph, Mark, Joseph, William, John, William, Robert, Simon, Simon, William, Symond), b. July 23, 1870, in Raymond, N. H.; m. there Feb., 1893, Belle L. Patten. They have one daughter. He is a respected and exemplary citizen. He is also associated with his father in farming; res. Raymond, N. H.

    6021. i.   BLANCHE M., b. May 22, 1894.

    4866. MARK FISK (Joseph W., Joseph, Mark, Joseph, Mark, Joseph, William, John, William, Robert, Simon, Simon, William, Symond), b. Apr. 6, 1867, in Raymond, N. H.; m. Mar. 14, 1893, Nellie F. Mahon. Two children came to them, a daughter and a son. He enjoys the esteem of his townsmen in a marked degree. He is associated with his father in farming; res. Raymond, N. H.

    6022. i.   GLADYS, b. Jan. 29, 1894.
    6023. ii.   MARK E., b. Aug. 9, 1895.

    4868. REV. HENRY SAFFORD FISKE (Albert R., Abraham H., Benjamin, Nathaniel, Theophilus, Theophilus, William, William, John, William, Robert, Simon, Simon, William, Symond), b. South Danvers, Mass., Mar. 27, 1849; m. at Lynn, June 2, 1872, Annie F. Longfellow, b. Pittston, Me., Nov. 6, 1853, a relative of the poet, Longfellow. He was educated in the South Danvers schools, and adopted the profession of an artist; was teacher for a few years in the Salem (Mass.) Free Hand Evening Drawing School; studied painting in landscape with G. H. Southward, of Salem, and with Samuel L. Gerry in Boston; m. at Lynn, Mass., at the age of 24; went to Concord, N. H., the same year, and while there studied for the ministry with Rev. E. L. Conger, pastor of the Universalist Church; preached at Croydon during preparation for the ministry, and was settled first at West Rumney, N. H., where he was ordained; moved from there to Henniker in the same State, where he built a church and remained four years. From there moved to South Newmarket (now Newfields), where he remained about the same length of time, and where two children (twins) were born; was settled in Pittsfield, Me., two years, where one child died, at the age of three years and two months. From there was called to Rutland. Vt., where by four years' hard labor was instrumental in raising a heavy debt on the Universalist Church there, of something over $7,000; removed to Methuen, Mass., Nov. 1, 1894; res. Methuen, Mass.

    6024. i.   ALBERT R., b. Dec. 25, 1885.
    6025. ii.   AUGUSTINE LONGFELLOW, b. Dec. 25, 1885; d. 1888.

    4984. FREDERICK GEORGE FISK (Theodore, Orin M., Abraham. Samuel, Ephraim, Joseph, Samuel, Joseph, William, John, William, Robert, Simon, Simon, William, Symond), b. June 14, 1859; m. Dec. 17, 1885, Adelaide S. Hill; res. Osage, Ia.

    6026. i.   PEARL FLORENCE, b. Nov. 4, 1888.
    6027. ii.   NELLIE LOIS, b. Dec. 21, 1891.

    4993. MEEDHAM FISKE (Lafayette, Nathan P., Joseph, Isaac, Joseph, Samuel, Joseph, William, John, William, Robert, Simon, Simon, William, Symond), b. Feb. 4, 1863; m. June 9, 1891, Amelia O. Kapelski, b. Prussia, Sept. 22, 1862. He is a baggageman on the Big Four Railroad; res. Mattoon, Ill.

    6028. i.   HERBERT W., b. Apr. 23, 1892.
    6029. ii.   AMELIA MILDRED, b. Oct. 30, 1893.

    5012. CHARLES C. FISK (Dennison, David, John, John, John, John, John, Nathaniel, William, Robert, Simon, Simon, William, Symond), b. Brookfield, N. Y., Sept. 13, 1844; m. Sept. 13, 1865, Loretta E. Collins, b. May 20, 1847. He was a farmer; res. North Brookfield, N. Y.

    6030. i.   CORA L., b. Sept. 16, 1866; m. Ingham Birdsall, Mar. 16, 1887.
                 Ch.: Harry D., b. Sept. 21, 1888; add. North Brookfield.
    6031. ii.   CLARA J., b. Nov. 18, 1878; add. North Brookfield, N. Y.

    5015. DAVID L. FISK (Dennison, David, John, John, John, John, John, Nathaniel, William, Robert, Simon, Simon, William, Symond), b. Brookfield, N. Y., Jan. 1, 1829; m. at Garrison, Feb. 24, 1880, Frances E. Green, b. June 2, 1836.

D. L. Fisk, president of the State Hop Growers' Association, was born in North Brookfield, Jan. 1, 1829. Mr. Fisk has always lived in his town with the exception of one year when he resided in Hamilton. By occupation Mr. Fisk is a farmer and since boyhood has been connected with the hop growing industry. In politics he is a Republican and in 1871 was elected member of Assembly, and served as Justice of Sessions in 1886. He has also filled the office of coroner for a number of years and has been Justice of the Peace for twenty years. Mr. Fisk has been honored with the office of president of the Hop Growers' Association for a number of years, and has filled the position with credit to himself and the association. He is held in the highest esteem by his neighbors and many friends in his native town, and especially by the hop growers throughout central New York; res. s. p. North Brookfield, N. Y.

    5021. DAVID H. FISK (Friend L., David, John, John, John, John, John, Nathaniel, William, Robert, Simon, Simon, William, Symond), b. Ellington, N. Y., Apr. 25, 1831; m. there Saloma Johnson, b. Nov. 12, 1833. He is a farmer; res. Ellington, N. Y.

HON. DAVID L. FISK.

    6032. i.   WILBUR F., b. Mar. 20, 1855; m. Mattie Davis.
    6033. ii.   MAY E., b. Aug. 17, 1863; m. Jan. 15, 1881, Chauncey Hess; res. E. Ch.: Chas. Arthur, b. Apr. 13, 1886.
    6034. iii. FRANK L., b. Sept. 11, 1871; m. Feb. 15, 1893, Minnie Beach; res. E.
    6035. iv. FLORENCE B., b. Sept. 11, 1871; m. Apr. 15, 1890, Orrin Fairbanks; res. E. Ch.: Earl, b. Jan. 29, 1894.
    6036. v.   ELLA V., b. Mar. 2, 1858; d. Jan. 5, 1867.

    5026. JOHN H. FISK (James B., John, John, John, John, John, John, Nathaniel, William, Robert, Simon, Simon, William, Symond), b. July 7, 1831, in Royalton, N. Y.; m. in Chautauqua County, N. Y., Oct. 7, 1856, Mary Eliza Hamlin, b. Mar. 1, 1834. John H. Fisk was born in New York where he was schooled, married and followed the life of farmer, at Spring Hill, Fulton Co., Ohio; removed with family to Montana in the seventies and has since been a farmer and cattle grower. He has held the office of Justice of the Peace for twenty years; res. Bedford and Townsend, Mont.

6037. i. ESTELLE ISADORE, b. Nov. 5, 1857; d. Aug. 18, 1859.
6038. ii. EMMA NETTIE, b. Sept. 29, 1859; d. June 1, 1875.
6039. iii. MARVIN EMMETT, b. July 4, 1864; m. Oct. 22, 1890, ———
———; res. Helena, Mont.
6040. iv. ELMER ULYSSES, b. Nov. 21, 1868; res. Helena.

5028. CAPT. JAMES LIBERTY FISK (James B., John, John, John, John, John, John, Nathaniel, William, Robert, Simon, Simon, William, Symond), b. Royalton, N. Y., in 1835; m. Lydia Brerson, d. 1878. James L. Fisk was born in New. In early manhood emigrated to Minnesota and married; enlisted in Sixty-first; called from front to Washington and appointed by President Lincoln Captain and Assistant Quartermaster, and ordered to special duty, leading overland expeditions and planting colonies in Rocky Mountains in 1863-4-5-6, for development of gold and other metals. At present (1895) exploring Cannon Ball country, western Dakota; res. Mandan, No. Dak.
6041. i. DELL, b. ———; m. Geo. H. Frisbee and has three children.

5029. CAPT. ROBERT EMMET FISK (James B., John, John, John, John, John, John, Nathaniel, William, Robert, Simon, Simon, William, Symond), b. Pierpont, Ohio, Aug. 9, 1837; m. at Vernon Centre, Conn., Mar. 21, 1867, Elizabeth Chester, b. Feb. 18, 1846. Robert E. Fisk was born in Ohio, schooled in Pennsylvania and at Wabash College, Ind.; learned printer's trade; served from New York City through the war, 1861-65, in all grades, from private to captain; emigrated to Montana in 1866; established at Helena Daily and Weekly Herald, and for twenty-nine years has been its editor and joint proprietor; delegate in State and National Republican Conventions; served on National Republican Committee; ex-Postmaster of Helena; at present Department Commander Montana G. A. R. (1895); res. Helena, Mont.
6042. i. GRACE CHESTER, b. May 21, 1869; m. Oct. 1, 1890, Hardy Bryan.
6043. ii. ROBERT LOVELAND, b. Nov. 28, 1872.
6044. iii. RUFUS CLARKE, b. May 15, 1875.
6045. iv. ASA FRANCIS, b. Nov. 11, 1877.
6046. v. FLORENCE RUMLEY, b. Apr. 24, 1882.
6047. vi. JAMES KENNETT, b. Apr. 24, 1882.
Add. of all Helena, Mont.

5030. CAPT. DANIEL W. FISK (James B., John, John, John, John, John, John, Nathaniel, William, Robert, Simon, Simon William, Symond), b. Conneaut, Ohio, Apr. 5, 1839; m. Oct. 3, 1878, Julia F. Walker, dau. of Major Robert C. Walker, U. S. A., and niece of the late Hon. Jas. G. Blaine. Daniel W. Fisk was born in Ohio; followed commercial pursuits; served in late war from New York City, with rank of Captain; resident of Montana since 1867; for quarter century joint proprietor and business manager Daily Herald; res. s. p. Helena, Mont.

5031. VAN HYDEN FISK (James B., John, John, John, John, John, John, Nathaniel, William, Robert, Simon, Simon, William, Symond), b. Conneaut, Ohio, in 1841; m. at Helena, Mont. in 1876, Ellie Reed. Van H. Fisk was born in Ohio; served in the late war in First Minnesota Volunteers; emigrated to Montana in 1866; stock grower and newspaper publisher. He d. in 1890; res. Helena, Mont.
6048. i. CHARLES, b. ———.
6049. ii. EFFIE MAY, b. ———.
6050. iii. HAYDEN, b. ———.

5032. ANDREW J. FISK (James B., John, John, John, John, John, John, Nathaniel, William, Robert, Simon, Simon, William, Symond), b. La Grange, N. Y., Jan. 8, 1849; m. July 26, 1873, Clara A. Wilcox, b. Oct. 30, 1858. Andrew J. Fisk was born in New York; schooled in Indiana and Minnesota; served in late war in Second Minnesota Cavalry; resident of Montana since 1866; Post Grand Master Masonic Order, Montana. For twenty-five years joint proprietor Daily Herald, Helena; secretary Herald Pub. Co. (1895); res. Helena, Mont.
6051. i. LAURA L., b. in 1880.
6052. ii. ANDREW J., b. 1883.
37

5054. WILLIAM VAUGHN FISKE (George A., James, William, William, John, John, John, John, Nathaniel, William, Robert, Simon, Simon, William, Symond), b. Newton, Mass., Mar. 10, 1863; m. in Worcester, Sept. 24, 1892, Bertha M. Ball, b. Sept. 2, 1872. He is a locomotive engineer; res. 21 High St., Northampton, Mass.

 6053. i. ARVILLA R., b. June 23, 1894.

5056. FRED M. FISK (Daniel, Jabez, Daniel, Jonathan, John, John, Nathaniel, William, Robert, Simon, Simon, William, Symond), b. Adrian, Mich., Oct. 27, 1855; m. Oct. 25, 1879, Lillie M. Blair, of Morenci, Mich. He is a manufacturing chemist; res. 451 Oxford St., London, Eng.; s. p.

5086. CHARLES GREENLEAF FISK (Marcus M., Dexter, Daniel, Daniel, John, John, John, Nathaniel, William, Robert, Simon, Simon, William, Symond), b. Colerain, Mass., Dec. 12, 1866; m. July 24, 1887, Clara Howard, b. Nov. 16, 1866. He is a machinist; res. 86 North St., Springfield, Mass.

 6053a. i. MARGARET HOWARD, b. Nov. 3, 1888.
 6053b. ii. MARCUS HENRY, b. Feb. 21, 1891.
 6053c. iii. HELEN DEANS, b. Feb. 22, 1896.

5095. ANDREW JACKSON FISK (William A., Ezra, Amariah, David, John, John, Nathaniel, William, Robert, Simon, Simon, William, Symond), b. Mansfield, Conn., Aug. 13, 1833; m. at Ottawa, Ill., Sept. 15, 1856, Mary Hill, b. May 18, 1836. He is a farmer; res. Mendota, Ill.

 6054. i. MARY ALEDA, b. Dec. 24, 1857; d. Dec. 8, 1860.
 6055. ii. NORA HENRIETTA, b. Sept. 15, 1859; m. Dec. 16, 1885, David Reeser, res. Harvey, Ill.
 6056. iii. ANDREW HAMLIN, b. Mar. 4, 1861; m. Teresa Brosch.
 6057. iv. LAVINA MAY, b. Sept. 4, 1862; m. Jan. 1, 1885, Frank C. Ferbush; res. Earl, Ill.
 6058. v. A. NATHALIA, b. Mar. 11, 1864; m. Nov. 23, 1885, Lorin Butterfield; res. Earl, Ill.
 6059. vi. JOHN WM., b. Apr. 16, 1866; d. July 28, 1879.
 6060. vii. GALOND DOLPH, b. Nov. 14, 1867; m. Cora Mosvell.
 6061. viii. KARL D. C. V. F., b. Nov. 3, 1869; m. L. E. Farr.
 6062. ix. GEO. WASHINGTON, b. Dec. 20, 1875; res. Yale, Ia.
 6063. x. LUTIE EDNA, b. June 5, 1871; m. May 16, 1894, W. Stroch; res. Yale, Ia.
 6064. xi. HATTIE M., b. Mar. 20, 1874; d. May 10, 1877.
 6065. xii. EDDIE ROY, b. Dec. 23, 1878.
 6066. xiii. LEROY LEWIS, b. Oct. 24, 1880.

5098. DR. CHARLES LEE FISK, JR. (Charles L., Ezra, Amariah, David, David, John, John, Nathaniel, William, Robert, Simon, Simon, William, Symond), b. Chaplin, Conn., June 19, 1831; m. at Greenfield, Mass., Mar. 11, 1876, Mary E. Lamphear, b. Sept. 2, 1852. He was liberally educated and graduated, and studied medicine away from home in Hartford, Cincinnati, New York and Philadelphia under very eminent and able teachers and professors, and graduated in medicine both in Cincinnati and New York. He was a pupil of the great surgeon Carnochan of New York for several years, and saw surgical service with McClellan in the peninsular campaign. He has been in practice at Greenfield, Mass., for forty years, where he now resides, and has performed with great success all of the operations in surgery both in civil and military life. He is an old member of the Massachusetts Medical Society; has been United States Pension Surgeon of large experience; is now town physician, hospital surgeon and chairman of the Board of Health. Dr. Fisk came from medical stock, his father and uncle, Dr. Daniel D. Fisk, having been eminent physicians in Greenfield. He has numbered among his friends and acquaintances the most eminent men in medical, military, legal and political life in this country, from the days of Webster and Clay to the present time, and has been a power to elevate men to high office and position, but has never himself sought for or held political office. Dr. Fisk has a family consisting of a wife, three sons and a daughter, all living under his roof; res. Greenfield, Mass.

 6067. i. ALBA, b. Mar. 6, 1877.

6068. ii.   EZRA, b. May 16, 1881.
6069. iii. WENDELL PHILLIPS, b. Sept. 27, 1884.
6070. iv.   ELEANOR STOUGHTON, b. Dec. 1, 1886.

5100. WILBUR AUGUSTUS FISK (Daniel D., Ezra, Amariah, David, David, John, John, Nathaniel, William, Robert, Simon, Simon, William, Symond), b. Bethel, Vt., Oct. 4, 1843; m. Oct. 30, 1873, Clara F. Barrett, b. Aug. 2, 1850; d. Apr. 17, 1893; m. 2d, June 26, 1895, Flora Judith Capron, b. Feb. 10, 1870. He started his business career at 18 in the jewelry business in Greenfield, Mass.; served a four years' apprenticeship but went to war during the time for four months. Then went to New York; was traveling salesman for a large manufacturing jewelry house for seven years. During this time, in 1873, he married the only daughter of William E. Barrett, of Providence, R. I. One year after this marriage he went to Providence, and went into the seed and agricultural business with the firm of W. E. Barrett & Co.; became a partner in 1880. His life is now and always has been a strictly commercial one; res. s. p. Providence, R. I.; add. 65 Canal St.

5101½. CLINTON QUINCY FISK (Joseph D., Elba, Jonathan, Jonathan, David, John, John, Nathaniel, William, Robert, Simon, Simon, William, Symond), b. Weatherfield, N. Y., May 29, 1842; m. at Lake Geneva, Wis., Dec. 20, 1866, Helen Merriam, b. July 5, 1843. He is a farmer; res. East Delavan, Wis.
6071. i.   HARVEY DEWEY, b. Bloomfield, Wis., Aug. 26, 1868; m. in Pecatonica, Ill., June 12, 1895, Mabel Meyers, b. May 14, 1871; res. s. p. Pecatonica, Ill.
6072. ii. EDWIN BRUCE, b. Jan. 25, 1875; res. Chicago, Ill.
6073. iii. LEON ARTHUR, b. Dec. 16, 1884; res. L. G.

5108. ROZELL O. FISK (Orrin V., Elba, Jonathan, Jonathan, David, John, John, Nathaniel, William, Robert, Simon, Simon, William, Symond), b. Sept. 21, 1865, Otselic Centre, N. Y.; m. July 4, 1885, Nellie D. Slaver, b. Feb. 7, 1869. He is a farmer; res. Ingall's Crossing, N. Y.
6074. i.   LORA E., b. Aug. 24, 1888.
6075. ii. HERBIE O., b. Oct. 24, 1893.

5114. GEORGE M. FISK (Asa, Asa, Jonathan, Jonathan, David, John, John, Nathaniel, William, Robert, Simon, Simon, William, Symond), b. July 22, 1845, in Sciota, Pa.; m. in Liberty, Pa., July 22, 1872, Martha Van Hoten, b. Mar. 14, 1849. He is a gardener; res. Binghamton, N. Y.
6076. i.   ARBA R., b. ———; m. Carrie Covey.
6077. ii. OCIE OLIE, b. ———.
6078. iii. LORA MERTIE, b. ———.
6079. iv. BERTHA, b. ———.
6080. v.   HERMAN, b. ———.
6081. vi. WILLIE, b. ———.

5115. ASA SATON FISK (Asa, Asa, Jonathan, Jonathan, David, John, John, Nathaniel, William, Robert, Simon, Simon, William, Symond), b. Franklin, Pa., Nov. 15, 1835; m. Jan. 2, 1855, in Jenningsville, Pa., Caroline L. Farr, b. Apr. 10, 1837. Asa S. Fisk was also a miller. He followed that trade until 1859, when he was caught in the machinery of the grist mill at Potterville, Bradford County, Pa., and so badly injured that he never recovered from the effects of it. From that time on he has spent most of his time on a farm in Pennsylvania. In 1885 he moved to Binghamton, N. Y., and for the last ten years has raised small fruits and vegetables for the market; res. 143 Conklin Ave., Binghamton, N. Y.
6082. i.   WALLACE V., b. Apr. 4, 1856; m. Mrs. Jennie Rosencrance.
6083. ii. FRANK O., b. Feb. 4, 1859; m. Theresa M. Mosley.
6084. iii. IDA S., b. Aug. 6, 1877; res. at home.

5122. WILLIAM HENRY FISK (Samuel S., Asa, Jonathan, Jonathan, David, John, John, Nathaniel, William, Robert, Simon, Simon, William, Symond), b. Skinner's Eddy, Pa., Sept. 9, 1842; m. Coudersport, Pa., June 12, 1863, Sarah Jane Wylie, b. Oct. 2, 1838. He is a farmer; res. Orting, Wash.
6085. i.   HATTIE L., b. Aug. 29, 1864; d. ———.
6086. ii. WILLIAM WYLIE, b. Aug. 26, 1865; d. 1866.

6087. iii. MINNIE E., b. Nov. 23, 1866; d. 1882.
6088. iv. ALLIE S., b. Nov. 17, 1868.
6089. v. CHARLIE A., b. July 1, 1871.
6090. vi. LEWIS CASS, b. Aug. 9, 1873; d. 1874.
6091. vii. MARTHA R., b. Jan. 28, 1875.
6092. viii. LUCIE J., b. Mar. 11, 1877.

5130. BRADLEY WAKEMAN FISK (Samuel S., Asa, Jonathan, Jonathan, David, John, John, Nathaniel, William, Robert, Simon, Simon, William, Symond), b. Browntown, Pa., Aug. 5, 1851; m. in Seattle, Wash., Sept. 5, 1877, Clara P. Provost, b. Dec. 29, 1859. He is a lumberman; res. Sedro, Skagit County, Wash.
6093. i. LILLIE B., b. Aug. 30, 1878.
6094. ii. CHAS. W., b. July 25, 1880.
6095. iii. ALEXANDER P., b. Mar. 18, 1884.
6096. iv. HATTIE L., b. July 30, 1887; d. Sept. 22, 1887.
6097. v. CLARA I., b. Nov. 9, 1888.
6098. vi. GEO. L., b. Mar. 15, 1890; d. Mar. 16, 1890.
6099. vii. CLARENCE B., b. Nov. 12, 1892.

5132. EDWARD JONATHAN FISK (Samuel S., Asa, Jonathan, Jonathan, David, John, John, Nathaniel, William, Robert, Simon, Simon, William, Symond), b. Browntown, Pa., June 20, 1855; m. June 3, 1879, Mrs. Minnie Alice (Harding) Crocker, b. Aug. 13, 1855. He is a locomotive engineer; res. Boone, Ia.
6100. i. RAY BLISS, b. Jan. 9, 1880.
6101. ii. ROBERT THEODORE, b. Apr. 29, 1883.
6102. iii. WALTER BURRELL, b. Aug. 21, 1885.
6103. iv. HOWARD MILLER, b. —— 14, 1888.
6104. v. CLIDE ALLEN, b. Mar. 29, 1891.
6105. vi. LLOYD MERLIND TERRILL, b. June 7, 1894.

5133. ELIJAH FISK (Samuel S., Asa, Jonathan, Jonathan, David, John, John, Nathaniel, William, Robert, Simon, Simon, William, Symond), b. Browntown, Pa., July 20, 1857; m. in New Albany, Pa., July 3, 1886, Myrtie Sluyter, b. Sept. 2, 1869. He is a farmer; res. Sugar Run, Pa.
6106. i. WALTER CAMP, b. July 7, 1889.

5135. GEORGE L. H. FISK (Samuel S., Asa, Jonathan, Jonathan, David, John, John, Nathaniel, William, Robert, Simon, Simon, William, Symond), b. Skinner's Eddy, Pa., Apr. 7, 1862; m. in Albion, N. Y., June 7, 1887, Inez Gazlay, b. Pultneyville, N. Y., Nov. 17, 1862. He is conductor on a passenger train on the Michigan Central Railroad; res. West Bay City, Mich.
6107. i. JOSEPH LANDON, b. Sept. 17, 1891.

5148. ELI CASPER FISK (Eli C., Eli, Hezekiah, Asa, David, John, John, Nathaniel, William, Robert, Simon, Simon, William, Symond), b. Havana, Ill., July 22, 1871; m. Apr. 5, 1893, Adda L. Crater. He is a farmer; res. Forest City, Ill.
6108. i. SON, d. ae. 3 days.
6109. ii. SON, b. June, 1895.

5154. DR. ISAAC PARSONS FISKE (Warren C., Stephen, Hezekiah, Asa, David, John, John, Nathaniel, William, Robert, Simon, Simon, William, Symond), b. Marlboro, Conn., Sept. 16, 1852; m. June 2, 1875, Clara Elizabeth Haven, b. July 30, 1849; d. Feb. 1, 1882; m. 2d, June 13, 1883, Sarah Elizabeth Hayes, b. May, 1857; d. June 24, 1890; m. 3d, Feb. 9, 1891, Mrs. Mary (Stanton) Farr, b. May, 1865; res. 218 No. Main St., Waterbury, Conn.
6110. i. FRED'K WM., b. Oct. 7, 1880; d. same day.
6111. ii. FRANK WARREN, b. July 29, 1885.
6112. iii. FRED'K DANA, b. Jan. 26, 1887; d. Sept. 24, 1887.
6113. iv. RAYMOND STANTON, b. July 6, 1892; d. Aug. 8, 1895.
6114. v. CLARENCE STANTON, b. Aug. 26, 1895.

5156. WILLIAM WARREN FISKE (Warren C., Stephen, Hezekiah, Asa, David, John, John, Nathaniel, William, Robert, Simon, Simon, William, Symond),

b. Marlboro, Conn., June 6, 1857; m. Charlton, Mass., Nov. 25, 1880, Lida R. Seymour, b. Mar. 26, 1856. William was born in Marlboro, Conn., June 26, 1857, the youngest of four children. His father was a Congregational minister, and his mother daughter of a Congregational minister. He was therefore carefully reared and instructed in the Bible and catechism, and was peculiarly sensitive to and receptive of religious impressions. Failing health led his father six years later to a farm in East Haddam, Conn., where William was taught at home by his mother. For reading the Bible through in course when eight years old he was given his first Bible by his mother. The following year he united with the Congregational Church in Colchester, Conn., whither the family moved to educate the children at Bacon Academy. In 1869 he went to Wolcott, Conn., for three years, going to school winters and working on a farm summers. In 1872 the family removed to Charlton, Mass., when he went to Wilbraham to prepare at Wesleyan Academy to enter the senior class of the scientific course in Williston Seminary, Easthampton, Mass., graduating second in the class June 16, 1875. His first venture in business life was rewarded with fine success as general agent for New England of a firm in Bogota, South America. He represented the same firm at the Centennial in Philadelphia, 1876, and there first met the young lady from Ohio, who subsequently became his wife. Visiting Baltimore in 1877, he became acquainted with Mr. Henry W. Eastman, an inventor and a resident of Baltimore. With him he entered into partnership for the general introduction throughout the country of Eastman's Alterable Church Registers, a convenient directory of church services for hotels and public buildings. On Nov. 25, 1880, at Charlton, Mass., he married Miss Lida Robertson Seymour, of Oberlin, Ohio. Their first settlement and experience in housekeeping was in Cleveland, Ohio, during the summer of 1881. Finding the location unsuited to the best interests of the national character of the firm's business, Mr. Fiske decided, after visiting Washington, Baltimore, New York and Philadelphia to locate permanently in Philadelphia, which he did in Jan., 1882. The following May his first child, a son, was born who died the following November and was laid to rest in the family lot in Southington, Conn., on Thanksgiving day. In 1883 he bought out the interest of Mr. Eastman, of Baltimore, in the firm of Eastman & Fiske and continued the business and manufacture of hotel church directories under his own name as publisher. Mr. and Mrs. Fiske on making their home in Philadelphia at once identified themselves with the Northminster Presbyterian Church, of which Mr. Fiske was chosen a ruling elder in 1887, and has held this office for the past nine years; res 3319 Hamilton St., Philadelphia, Pa.

    6115. i.   MALCOLM DORR, b. May 25, 1882; d. Nov. 26, 1882.
    6116. ii.   ROBERT SEYMOUR, b. Mar. 6, 1885.
    6117. iii. FLEDA, b. July 29, 1888.
    6118. iv. DONALD ROBERTSON. b. Oct. 15, 1891.
    6119. v.   SEYMOUR, b. Aug. 23, 1895.

    5168. CHARLES STEPHEN FISKE (Eli B., Stephen, Hezekiah, Asa, David, John, John, Nathaniel, William, Robert, Simon, Simon, William, Symond), b. Wales, Mass., Apr. 25, 1861; m. in Boston, June 28, 1893, Etta Noyes Haley, b. Nov. 5, 1867. He is a commercial traveler; res. 122 Pembroke St., Boston, Mass.

    6120. i.   DONOLD RAE, b. Feb. 7, 1895.

    5182. CHARLES BYRON FISKE (Gordon M., William H., Hezekiah, Asa, David, John, John, Nathaniel, William, Robert, Simon, Simon, William, Symond), b. Enfield, Mass., Feb. 13, 1845; m. at Palmer, Oct. 9, 1866, Frances M. Calkins, b. Mar. 28, 1847; d. June 5, 1877; m. 2d, at Rockford, Ill., Oct. 14, 1878, Esther N. Chandler, b. Sept. 12, 1838; d. Sept. 11, 1893. He is a prominent citizen there; res. Palmer, Mass.

    6121. i.   MAY, b. Sept. 29, 1880.
    6122. ii.   RUTH, b. Nov. 24, 1883.

    5183. CAPT. WILLARD CLINTON FISK (Lyman E., William H., Hezekiah, Asa, David, John, John, Nathaniel, William, Robert, Simon, Simon, William, Symond), b. New York City, Mar. 26, 1858; m. there Oct. 12, 1880, Ida C. Earle, b. Nov. 28, 1855. Willard Clinton Fisk was born in New York City; removed with his parents to Jersey City in 1869, where he has since resided; graduated from New York University in June, 1876, and from Columbia Law School in 1878; studied law in the office of Gov. Leon Abbett, of New Jersey, and was admitted to the

New Jersey bar in June, 1878; was associated in practice with Governor Abbett until his election as Governor of New Jersey in 1884; was appointed private secretary to the Governor in 1884, and served three years; formed partnership in 1884 in the practice of law with Randolph Parmly and John Olendorf, under the firm name of Parmly, Olendorf & Fisk, with offices in Jersey City; continued in the firm until Jan. 1, 1896; formed partnership Jan. 1, 1896, with Allan L. McDermott, under the firm name of McDermott & Fisk; has been a member of the Board of Riparian Commissioners of New Jersey since 1890; a member of the Seventh Regiment, New York, since 1874, and has held in that organization commissions as a Second Lieutenant, First Lieutenant, Adjutant and Captain, which rank is now held, being in command of Company "D;" is a member of the New York Society Sons of the Revolution. He married Ida C. Earle, of Jersey City; had two children; res. 243 Washington St., Jersey City, N. J.

    6123. i.   CLINTON EARLE, b. Apr. 13, 1882.

    6124. ii. HARRISON OTIS, b. Dec. 6, 1886; d. Sept. 21, 1895. He met his death by drowning at Manasquan, N. J. The party which included Mrs. Willard Fiske and two sons set out for the beach late in the afternoon to enjoy their daily bath. The bathing grounds are near the Manasquan Inlet, and the tides create a current that at times is exceedingly dangerous. After disrobing at the bath houses the party walked down to the surf, and Mrs. Fisk and her two sons, Harrison Otis and Clinton, entered the water. The others of the party came in a few minutes later. All were bathing, as they thought, at a safe distance from the beach, and all went well, when a cry was heard for help. It was noticed that Harrison had ventured out beyond his depth and was struggling in the water. The little fellow's cries seemed to create a panic among the bathers. The elder son, Clinton, rushed to his brother's rescue, and it seemed that he, too, had gone beyond his depth and was in danger. At this instant all the ladies in the party seemed to realize the danger to the boys and all appeared to rush headlong into the foamy billows. In the excitement there were noticed two or three heavy cross seas racing up and down and a whirl in the foam that told the startled onlookers that the party was in the midst of a deadly whirlpool. Mrs. Fisk was seen floundering about in the water, and the young women made an attempt to reach her, but they were engulfed in the swiftly flowing tide and drowned. Some strollers on the beach made an effort to rescue the drowing women, but they only succeeded in bringing Mrs. Fisk to shore. She was unconscious, and was resuscitated with difficulty. The bodies of the other two women were recovered, but young Fisk's body was carried out to sea.

    5184. HARRISON GREY FISKE (Lyman E., William H., Hezekiah, Asa, David, John, John, Nathaniel, William, Robert, Simon, Simon, William, Symond), b. New York City, July 30, 1861; m. Mar. 19, 1890, Minnie Maddern. Mrs. Fiske began to star at 15. If ever the American stage had a veritable enfant de la balle in its history that child was Minnie Maddern. Born of professional parents —for her mother, Lizzie Maddern, was an actress, and her father, Tom Davies, the pioneer circuit manager of the west—she was literally cradled in the theater, reared in the glare of the footlights, inoculated from her birth with the atmosphere of the theater and a mistress of the secrets of the playhouse even while her baby tongue could not yet distinctly speak her native language. By parentage she is English. Her maternal grandmother was a girl of good family, who, while still in her teens, eloped with her music master, a proceeding frowned upon by the family, who at once cast her off. Being very much enamored of her music lover, this did not trouble her at all, and the young people proceeded to be happy on nothing a year and to raise a large family. When the children were seven they thought of America as more roomy than England for a family that increased so rapidly, and they emigrated. All the children were musical, so the father formed a concert company, in which each of the youngsters played some instrument, and Lizzie Maddern (afterward the mother of Minnie), in a high comb and queer pantalettes, at the age of 12, was the first cornet of the strolling band. it is a tradition in the family that Lizzie Maddern at that age could score the music for the orchestra, and did it. The Maddern family produced quite a number of respectable actors and actresses, while Tom Davies, who married Lizzie Maddern, is well remembered by those posted on theatrical affairs. He was a small, red-haired man of a temper as violent as his mind was erratic, and his escapades and his eccentricities were in his time the topic of many a strolling tale. Minnie Maddern inherited her father's red hair and something of his temperament. She began her professional career at the age of 3. At the age of 14 she had drifted into comic opera. At the age of 15 she became the star of a lurid melodrama. At the time the writer first saw her she was a slight girl, with the daintiest of hands and feet, and as sweet a voice as ever spoke across the footlights. She was a creature of suggestions, an unearthly sort of a girl, with her tousled red hair, her white face. her thin, nervous lips and her deep gray eyes. But she was only a girl, more remarkable for what she might become

HARRISON G. FISKE.

than for what she was. Her youth, her red hair, her dainty, girlish figure had suggested to a manager that here might be another mintmaker—another Lotta. Now, the antipodes are not wider apart than Minnie Maddern and Lotta, but the mistake was made and she was started wrong in her career. In her undeveloped mind were only dim ideas of her future, and so she drifted on the way

Minnie Maddern Fiske

that others marked out for her, doing the work allotted for her, indifferently going from one trifling play to another, perhaps dimly conscious of the mistake that had been made, possibly as dimly conscious that time alone would remedy the blunder, A brief review of Mrs. Fiske's more important associations will interest even the casual friend of the stage. She played the round of child's parts with Barry Sullivan, and later with Lucille Western. She was the original Little Fritz in J. K. Emmet's first productions at Wallack's and Niblo's; she appeared with Laura Keene in "Hunted Down" during the New York run of that play; she appeared as Prince Arthur in the notable revival of "King John" at Booth's Theater, with John McCullough, J. B. Booth and Agnes Booth; as Paul in "The Octoroon;" as Franko in "Guy Mannering," with Mrs. Waller; Sibyl in "A Wolf in Sheep's Clothing," with Charlotte le Clerq; Little Mary Morgan in "Ten Nights in a Barroom," with Yankee Locke; the child in "Across the Continent," with Oliver Dowd Byron; the child's parts with E. L. Davenport;

Heinrich and Meenie in "Rip Van Winkle;" Adrienne in Daly's "Monsieur Alphonse," the boy's part in "The Bosom Friend;" Georgie in "Frou-Frou," with Mrs. Scott Siddons; Hilda in Emmet's "Karl and Hilda;" Ralph Rackstraw in Hooley's Juvenile Pinafore Company, and Clip in "A Messenger from Jarvis Section." At 10 years of age she acted the Sun God in David Bidwell's production of "The Ice Witch," and she also appeared in "Aladdin," "The White Fawn," and other spectacular pieces. Mrs. Fiske is a woman of intensely active intellectuality and her five years of comparative seclusion have been fruitful in more ways than one.

Harrison Grey Fiske, the editor and proprietor of The Mirror, was born in Harrison, Westchester County, N. Y. He attended private schools in New York, studied music and the languages for several years, acquired a knowledge of elocution and rhetoric from the late George Vandenhoff, when abroad, was prepared for college by a tutor, and finally entered the New York University. His tastes were essentially literary and artistic, and during his stay at college he wrote many sketches and short stories for the newspapers, and sent New York letters regularly to several southern and western dailies. He held his first staff position on the Jersey City Argus, writing editorials and dramatic criticisms. In July, 1879, he became attached to The Mirror, as a special contributor, and in the fall of the same year bought an interest in the stock company that then owned it. The following winter Mr. Fiske was selected by the company to take editorial charge. He was 18 years of age at the time, the youngest editor in the country. In spite of his youth he conceived and adopted a sagacious, independent and vigorous policy which speedily put The Mirror in the van of stage journals, bringing it influence, prosperity and the largest circulation ever achieved by any dramatic paper in the world. Five years ago Mr. Fiske obtained a controlling interest in The Mirror, but from the day he took charge of its destinies he had enjoyed sole power, acting upon such advice as commended itself to his judgment, but brooking no interference from stockholders or others in respect to the lines of his own journalistic policy. Last May he purchased the outstanding shares of stock and became the sole and responsible proprietor. Mr. Fiske does a vast amount of work and yet is accessible to a large number of visitors. He writes the editorials, the principal dramatic criticisms, "The Usher," special articles, paragraphs—in fact, his busy pen contributes to almost every department of the paper. On an average he turns out between ten and twelve columns during the working hours of the early days of the week. In addition to this he supervises every portion of the paper and keeps a strict watch on every line that goes into it. This latter duty is somewhat unusual among editors, but Mr. Fiske realizes the importance and never neglects it. He prefers to share personal knowledge of everything that he publishes with personal responsibility for it. And he likes work. For the past nine years he has never been absent from his post but once. On that occasion illness confined him to his home for a week. Even then, however, he had the "revises" brought to him and with the aid of a blue pencil transformed the sick chamber into a sanctum. At different times Mr. Fiske has been the dramatic critic of two New York daily papers and written editorials for another. But he relinquished outside work of every description two years ago in order to devote his whole time and energies to The Mirror. He is a member of the New York Press Club, the Fellowcraft Club, a yachting association, and several other social and literary institutions, but the only organization in which he takes an active personal interest is the Actor's Fund of America, of which he has been the secretary for several years. Res. s. p. New York, N. Y.; add. 1432 Broadway.

5192. FRED OTTO FISKE (John L., James L., Hezekiah, Asa, David, John, John, Nathaniel, William, Robert, Simon, Simon, William, Symond), b. Apr. 12, 1866, in Omro, Wis.; m. in Minneapolis, Jan. 8, 1895, Nellie Litchfield, b. Feb. 9, 1870. He is in the jewelry business in Minneapolis and at Waterville, Minn.; res. s. p. 32 Washington Ave. So., Minneapolis, Minn.

5221. WALTER EDWARD FISKE (Walter B., Moses, Thomas, Jonathan, Thomas, William, John, Nathaniel, William, Robert, Simon, Simon, William, Symond), b. Holyoke, Mass., Nov. 8, 1855; m. in Providence, R. I., May 23, 1888, Bertha Lewis, b. Nov. 18, 1860. Walter Edward Fiske, son of Walter B. and Matilda H. Fiske, was born in Holyoke, Mass., Nov. 8, 1855. He grew up very much like other children where one's parents are in moderate circumstances. He was given a good common school education and graduated from Cady's Academy, in the town of Barrington, R. I. He entered Brown University in the fall of 1875. Owing to severe illness, on completing his freshman year he was compelled to leave the university. He engaged as clerk for two years with the Boston & Philadelphia S. S. Co. In Jan., 1879, he accepted a position with the Howard Sterling Company, silversmiths. He commenced at the lowest rung of the ladder. On Dec. 31, 1891, he was promoted as secretary of the company above mentioned, which position he occupies. While in Brown University he was first tenor in the Glee Club, and since then he has identified himself with several musical organizations in Providence. He has taken the role of the "Captain" in Pinafore, the "Major General" in the Pirates of Penzance, and the "Marquis" in Chimes of Normandy, with pronounced success in the Opera House of this city. He is a Congregationalist and has always taken an active part in church work. He has a pleasant home on Waterman Street, where with wife and two children he is enjoying the sunny side of life; res. Providence, R. I.

6125. i.   DWIGHT LEWIS, b. Aug. 25, 1891.
6126. ii.   KATHARINE BRADFORD, b. July 12, 1893.

5237. HON. OLIVER FISKE (Robert T. P., Oliver, Nathan, Nathan, Nathan, Nathan, Nathaniel, William, Robert, Simon, Simon, William, Symond), b. Hingham, Mass., Dec. 21, 1829; m. June 2, 1858, Margaret E. Thomas, b. Apr. 1, 1841. After he became of age and married, he went out west to Iowa, where he remained until 1865, and meantime made quite a little fortune in the grain warehousing business and other ventures. He was then induced to come east and to go into the stock market, which resulted rather badly. Gradually he, being a stanch Republican, became more or less prominent in political life, and held important governmental positions and always with great credit. Under President Grant, he was United States Marshal for the Southern District of New York, succeeding Gen. Geo. H. Sharpe. His methods and office were examined by a Democratic State Committee and the result was a testimonial to his capability, etc., from the committee. Some years after this he was sent to the State Legislature as member of Assembly from Richmond County, which is noteworthy, as the county was then ordinarily Democratic, by twelve hundred to sixteen hundred majority. He has now retired from active life, and is in good health; res. New Brighton, N. Y.

6127. i.   MARY OTIS, b. Apr. 14, 1859; d. June 3, 1861.
6128. ii.   ROBERT T. P., b. Apr. 24, 1860; m. Miriam W. Miller.
6129. iii. CATHERINE, b. Iowa City, July 4, 1862; d. in Hingham, Sept. 22, 1863.
6130. iv.   OLIVER THOMAS, b. May 28, 1865; m.; s. p.
6131. v.   MARGARET, b. Dec. 24, 1867; d. Nov. 15, 1876.
6132. vi.   FRANCIS SHAW, b. May 28, 1869.
6133. vii. LYDIA GAY, b. Aug. 29, 1872.
6134. viii. DUNCAN, b. Aug. 27, 1877.

5238. FREDERICK CURTIS FISKE (William E., William, Nathan, Nathan, Nathan, Nathan, Nathaniel, William, Robert, Simon, Simon, William, Symond), b. Canastota, N. Y., Feb. 24, 1842; m. June 24, 1863, Agnes T. Clark, b. May 23, 1842. He received his education in the common schools, Fort Edward Institute and Cazenovia Seminary. He commenced the study of medicine and surgery with Dr. V. W. Mason and finished the course at the College of Physicians and Surgeons in New York City. Then went into the drug and general store business; was president of Canastota village two terms; was supervisor of his town five terms; member of assembly from Madison County; organized the Canastota Knife Company, and has been its president for twenty years; was a member of the firm of Wm. E. Fiske & Son, bankers and brokers; was superintendent of the purchase of right of way from New York to Buffalo, for West Shore Railroad Company, and for the last seven years has been real estate agent for the New York and New Haven & Hartford Railroad Company, and has spent seven million dollars for their right of way; res. s. p. 36 W. 27th St., New York, N. Y.

5239. WILLIAM BUCKMINSTER FISKE (William E., William, Nathan, Nathan, Nathan, Nathan, Nathaniel, William, Robert, Simon, Simon, William, Symond), b. New York, Jan. 25, 1825; m. there June 27, 1849, Frances Josephine Roberts, b. July 27, 1825. William Buckminster Fiske, son of William Edwin Fiske, was born in Sullivan, Madison Co., N. Y.; received his education in the common schools and Syracuse University; went into the general store business under firm name Fiske & Messinger; after a few years sold his interest and went with the Syracuse & Oswego Railroad Company, and assisted in the building of that road, after which he went into the clothing trade; was a successful merchant, and a respected man. He d. Dec. 2, 1860; res. Syracuse, N. Y.

6135. i. WM. ADDISON, b. Feb. 17, 1853; d. at Coldwater, Mich., July 7, 1878; unm.

5241. HON. ALONZO SEWALL FISKE (Sewall, Nathan, Jonathan, Nathan, Nathan, Nathaniel, William, Robert, Simon, Simon, William, Symond), b. in Weston, Oct. 4, 1818; m. in Lincoln, Sept. 12, 1843, Susan Maria Colburn, b. Aug. 31, 1824, dau. of Wm. and Nabby, of Lincoln. Alonzo was for many years in charge of most of the town business of Weston. He was Assessor and Tax Collector, Selectman and Justice of the Peace. He represented Weston in the Legislature, and attended to all the business of raising and equipping Weston's quota of troops in the Civil War. He d. Aug. 27, 1893; res. Waltham, Mass.

6136. i. MARIA ANTOINETTE, b. Feb. 17, 1845; d. Mar. 15, 1872.
6137. ii. HELEN AMELIA, b. June 11, 1849; m. Oct. 17, 1871, Edson P. Warren; res. Falmouth, Mass.
6138. iii. MARTHA E., b. Sept. 4, 1852; m. Jan. 31, 1874, Louis H. Whitney, of Boston; res. Lincoln. He was b. July 20, 1845 (Charles H., Nathan, Abijah, Joseph, Benjamin, Joseph, John, John). Ch.: 1, Edith Fiske, b. Nov. 30, 1875. 2, Louis Lincoln, b. Dec. 15, 1876. 3, Clifford Brigham, b. Sept. 5, 1880.
6139. iv. NATHAN SEWALL, b. Aug. 9, 1854; unm.; a farmer; res. Kendall Green, Mass.
6140. v. SUSAN FRANCIS, b. Feb. 7, 1857; d. June 5, 1860.
6141. vi. ABIGAIL COLBURN, b. Feb. 3, 1862; m. Dec. 22, 1885, Dana March Dustin; res. Marion, Mass. He is a teacher; was b. June 14, 1859. Ch.: 1, Helen Colburn, b. Aug. 14, 1888.
6142. vii. HATTIE L., b. Feb. 15, 1862; d. Mar. 29, 1879.

5246. HENRY GUSTAVUS FISK (Sewall, Nathan, Jonathan, Nathan, Nathan, Nathan, Nathaniel, William, Robert, Simon, Simon, William, Symond), b. Weston, Mass., Apr. 13, 1827; m. California, Apr. 15, 1860, Elizabeth Wynekoop, b. Aug. 24, 1834. He was born in Weston, Apr. 13, 1827. Like all New England farmers' boys he worked on the farm in spring and summer and attended the district school in winter; also attended the high school in Weston. He lived two and one-half miles from the high school in Weston Centre, consequently it was too far to walk, and with three or four sisters, older than himself, rode to school, keeping horse and carriage until night to take them home. He afterward attended Phillips Academy in Andover. He has a vivid recollection of going from there to attend the Whig celebration at Bunker Hill in 1844; of meeting there his father and brother and many friends. At the age of 18 he left home and went to the city of Worcester to learn a trade, that of working in sheet metals. He spent two years there, then one year in the city of Nashua, N. H.; after that one year in Clintonville, and the balance of the time, until going to California, in Boston, Waltham and Grafton. In 1851 his brother Edward and himself made arrangements to go to California. They had the usual experience of the California bound in those early days. That is, they were taken up the Chargees River in boats rowed by the natives, spent one night at Gorgona, and then mounted mules and rode to Panama. Here they found no boat to take them on the Pacific side. They remained in Panama nearly two months and took the first passage that could be obtained to San Francisco, where they arrived in good health and spirits. His brother Edward went up to the mines for a short time and he stopped in Sacramento. After a few months Edward came to Sacramento and they both went to San Francisco, where they succeeded in finding employment at their trade, which they followed diligently for nearly a year, then commenced business on their own account. This business was continued up to 1891. In 1856 he visited his old home. That was about the time the Free Soil party was started. Colonel Fremont was at that time in San Francisco, and they became acquainted with him and Mrs. Fremont through business relations. A few years after his return to San Francisco he chartered a large schooner, filled her with goods and shipped them to Mexico. He spent nearly a year in Mazatland, Tepic, San Blas and other places in Mexico, while his brother attended to the business in San Francisco. He returned to San Francisco about the time of the breaking out of the Civil War, and shortly thereafter went to Virginia City, in Nevada. That was not long after the Comstock mines were discovered. He remained there twenty-one months, removed his family there and built a house for them. They sent over half a dozen of their best men and did a large roofing business as the town grew up. Spent much time also in mining operations, and lost a large amount of money also by them. Shortly after his return to San Francisco his brother died, and from that time to the present his home has been in San Francisco. He has done an extensive business on that coast, extending to the neighboring States and territories and employing many men. The season that the Palace Hotel was built they had in their employ over 175 men. about half that number employed on that building. Res. 710 Central Ave., San Francisco, Cal.

6143. i. HENRY G., JR., b. Jan. 24, 1861; m. Oct. 29, 1885, Annie Redell. He d. in San Francisco, s. p., Mar. 16, 1889.

6144. ii. MARTHA ELIZABETH, b. Feb. 26, 1862; d. Jan. 15, 1876.

6145. iii. ELEANOR, b. Dec. 5, 1864;m. May 2, 1885, Clarence K. Harmon, b. ———, Baltimore Md. They have one child, Stella Harmon, b. Aug. 5, 1886, in San Francisco; res. 710 Central Ave., San Francisco.

6146. iv. ESTELLE, b. June 17, 1868; res. San Francisco.

6147. v. ALICE, b. Nov. 21, 1870; m. May 19, 1892, Wm. P. Todd. of New Rochelle, N. Y. Ch.: 1, Stedman Fiske Todd, b. Apr. 19, 1893. 2, Theodsia Todd, b. Oct. 11, 1895.

6148. vi. LILLIAN, b. Oct. 25, 1872; m. May 17, 1894, Hallet K. Mitchell. b. Haverhill, Mass. They have one child, Dwight Kimball Mitchell, b. Mar. 25, 1895; res. 710 Central Ave., San Francisco.

5260. GEORGE MANN FISKE (George, Jonathan, Jonathan, Nathan, Nathan, Nathan, Nathaniel, William, Robert, Simon, Simon, William, Symond), b. Medfield, Mass., May 2, 1842; m. there Sept. 25, 1865, Sarah Whitney Wilder, b. June 8, 1844. He was born in Medfield. Mass. Received his education in the schools of that town. Enlisted in Company D, Forty-second Regiment, Massachusetts Volunteers, in Aug., 1862, serving in Texas and Louisiana under General Banks. Returning from the war engaged in farming with his father till 1871, when he went to Boston and became connected with James Edmond & Co. in the manufacture of fire brick, clay retorts, and the importation of sewer pipe, fire brick, etc. In 1877 the firm of Fiske, Coleman & Co. was formed in the same line of business. In 1880 the business was merged into a corporation, the Boston Fire Brick Company. The Boston Terra Cotta Company was also organized. Mr. Fiske taking the treasurership of the latter, and his firm the management of both corporations. In the rapid and remarkable development of the manufacture of architectural terra cotta, and of buff, mottled and other fancy colored building bricks, Mr. Fiske has been in the foremost ranks, and has become well known all over the country as a leader in his line of business: res. Auburndale, Mass.

6150. i. JONATHAN PARKER, b. Oct. 8, 1866; m. Oct. 20, 1890, Lucy Adams Johnson; res. Schenectady, N. Y.

6151. ii. ELIAS MANN, b. Dec. 8, 1879; d. same day.

6152. iii. AMY PLYMPTON, b. Mar. 13, 1882 (adopted).

5261. CHARLES FRANCIS FISKE (George, Jonathan, Jonathan, Nathan, Nathan, Nathan, Nathaniel, William, Robert. Simon, Simon, William, Symond), b. Medfield, Mass., Aug. 20, 1848; m. Oct. 2, 1871, at Boston, Mary Nye, b. Sept. 10, 1847. He was brought up on a farm; received a common school education, and left home at the age of 18. He went to work in a book store in Boston and continued as boy, clerk, and salesman until 1880, when he went into the book and publishing business for himself under the firm name of De Wolfe. Fiske & Co. He has built up a large business in that line; res. Hyde Park, Mass.; Boston add. 361 Washington St.

6153. i. GEORGE FRANCIS. b. June 11, 1872. He graduated at Amherst College in 1893. Teaching at Manchester. Vt.

6154. ii. RICHARD FELT. b. Dec. 16, 1876; d. Sept. 16, 1878.

6155. iii. CHARLES ARTHUR, b. July 12, 1879, Hyde Park, Mass.

6156. iv. ROBERT CHESTER, b. Aug. 1, 1882, Hyde Park, Mass.

6157. v. MARGARET HELEN, b. June 16, 1884, Hyde Park, Mass.
6158. vi. MARY ELIZABETH, b. Jan. 1, 1886, Hyde Park, Mass.

5264. ARTHUR W. FISKE (Amos F., Jonathan, Jonathan, Nathan, Nathan, Nathan, Nathaniel, William, Robert, Simon, Simon, William, Symond), b. Marlow, N. H., Nov. 4, 1837; m. in Hartford, Conn., Sept. 5, 1867, Emma E. Burr. He d. in 1886; res. Washington, D. C.
6159. i. CHARLES A., b. in 1868; res. 1521 Columbia St., Washington, D. C.
6160. ii. FRED'K WM., b. in 1869; d. in Washington, D. C., in 1889.

5271. CHARLES AUGUSTUS FISK (Charles A., Jonathan, Jonathan, Nathan, Nathan, Nathan, Nathaniel, William, Robert, Simon, Simon, William, Symond), b. Cambridge, Mass., Oct. 28, 1850; m. Sept., 1876, Laura J. Ellis, b. Aug., 1859; res. Norwood St., Marlboro, Mass.
6161. i. WALTER ELLIS, b. Feb. 16, 1880.
6162. ii. MINNIE, b. Apr. 27, 1887.
6163. iii. HARVEY ELLIS, b. Mar. 6, 1890.

5274. ANDREW FISKE (Augustus H., Isaac, Jonathan, Nathan, Nathan, Nathan, Nathaniel, William, Robert, Simon, Simon, William, Symond) b. Weston. Mass. Sept. 19, 1854; m. June 22, 1878, Gertrude H. Horsford, b. July 9, 1852. He was born in Weston, Mass. His father was Augustus H. Fiske and his mother Hannah Rogers (Bradford) Fiske. He attended school in Boston until he was 15 years old, when he went to Phillips Exeter Academy and remained there two years, graduating in 1871. He entered Harvard and graduated from there in 1875. After a year of travel he entered the Harvard Law School, graduating in 1878. He then entered the office of Hon. E. Rockwood Hoar in Boston and was admitted to the bar in Suffolk Co. (Boston), Mass., in Feb., 1880. He has since practiced law in Boston, having his residence in Weston. He married Gertrude H. Horsford, daughter of Prof. E. N. Horsford, of Cambridge; res. Weston, Mass.
6164. i. GERTRUDE HORSFORD, b. Apr. 16, 1879.
6165. ii. AUGUSTUS HENRY, b. May 28, 1880.
6166. iii. EBEN NORTON HORSFORD, b. May 4, 1883.
6167. iv. GARDINER HORSFORD, b. Sept. 14, 1892.
6168. v. CORNELIA HORSFORD, b. Aug. 20, 1895.

5275. EDWARD FISKE (Augustus H., Isaac, Jonathan, Nathan, Nathan, Nathan, Nathaniel, William, Robert, Simon, Simon, William, Symond), b. Sept. 2, 1832, in Concord, Mass.; m. at Milo, Me., Oct. 13, 1863, Adelaide P. Frost, b. Mar. 15, 1840. He was fitted for college at the Boston Latin School; was graduated from Harvard in 1853. He studied law with his father, Augustus H. Fiske, Esq., and practiced law in his father's office in Boston till his health broke down. He lived in Weston, Mass., the latter part of his life, and died of consumption Jan. 30, 1870; res. Weston, Mass.
6169. i. EDWARD, b. Sullivan, Me., July 8, 1864; m. at Waltham, d. Nov. 6, 1893; his res. Weston. He was born at Sullivan, Mass., Apr. 30, 1893, Ethel Warren Kidder, b. Oct. 14, 1867; d. Nov. 6, 1893; he res. Weston. He was born at Sullivan, Me. Son of Edward Fiske and Adelaide P. (Frost) Fiske. About 1866 his parents moved to Weston, Mass., where he has lived ever since. His mother is still living. He attended the public schools in Weston from about 1872 to 1879. Studied a year with Geo. L. Mayberry, Esq., and then, in 1880, entered Hopkinson's School in Boston to fit for college. He entered Harvard in 1883, and was graduated in 1887. In 1887 he entered the Harvard Law School, took the regular course, and received the degree of LL. B. in 1890; was admitted to the Suffolk bar in July, 1890, and has since had an office in Boston. In politics he is an independent—sometimes described as mugwump—and in religion a Unitarian. He has never held any public office.
6170. ii. SUSAN H., b. Jan. 30, 1868; res. Weston.

5278. CHARLES HERVEY FISKE (Augustus H., Isaac, Jonathan, Nathan, Nathan, Nathan, Nathaniel, William, Robert, Simon, Simon, William, Symond),

b. Oct. 26, 1840, Boston, Mass.; m. June 4, 1868, Cornelia Frothingham Robbins, b. Aug. 29, 1840; d. Feb. 29, 1872. He fitted for Harvard College at the private Latin School of Epes S. Dinwell, Esq., in Boston, and graduated at Harvard College in the class of 1860. He studied law in his father's office, admitted to the bar in Suffolk County, Dec., 1894, and practiced there until his death, since which time he has practiced law alone; res. Boston, Mass.; add. R. 660 Congress St.

    6171. i. CHARLES HERVEY, b. Feb. 18, 1872; m. June 20, 1895, Mary D. Thorndike at Cambridge, Mass. He fitted for college at school of J. P. Hopkinson, Esq., successor of E. S. Dinwell. He graduated at Harvard College, class of 1893; is now studying law at the Law School of Harvard University; res. 405 Marlboro St., Boston.

    5281. GEORGE FISKE (Augustus H., Isaac, Jonathan, Nathan, Nathan, Nathan, Nathaniel, William, Robert, Simon, Simon, William, Symond), b. Dec. 28, 1850, in Boston, Mass.; m. at Lynn, Dec. 13, 1888, Mary E. Rood, b. July 25, 1855. He was born in Boston, Mass. Was educated in private schools in Boston, and fitted for Harvard University under a private tutor. Graduated from Harvard in 1872, taking the B. A. degree. After graduation he lived for about three years in Europe. Married Mary Elizabeth Rood, of Picton, Nova Scotia. Their only child, a boy, died very soon after birth. He lives at present in Concord, Mass., which is his legal residence. Has never engaged in active business; res. Concord, Mass., and Boston, Mass.; add. is room 60 Congress St.

    6172. i. ONE CHILD, b. and d. 1891.

    5288. JOSIAH FISKE (Jeremiah, Josiah, Josiah, Josiah, Nathan, Nathan, Nathaniel, William, Robert, Simon, Simon, William, Symond), b. Temple, N. H., Nov. 6, 1820; m. in Lowell, Mass., Mar. 5, 1848, Rebecca Flint, of Waltham, Mass., b. Jan. 15, 1827; d. Dec. 16, 1852; m. 2d, Mar. 25, 1865, Mary Flint, of Nashua, N. H. He is a farmer; res. Temple, N. H.

    6173. i. ORLO J., b. Dec. 11. 1848; m. Francena M. Fogg.

    5290. DR. JEREMIAH FISKE (Jeremiah, Josiah, Josiah, Josiah, Nathan, Nathan, Nathaniel, William, Robert, Simon. Simon, William, Symond), b. Temple, N. H., Feb 10, 1824; m. in Lowell, Mass., Feb. 17, 1853, Caroline Bailey, of Green field, N. H., b. Feb. 19, 1830. Dr. Jeremiah Fisk, born in Temple, Feb. 10, 1824. Attended Appleton Academy, New Ipswich, N. H., for a time, and finished his education at Hancock Academy. Afterwards studied dentistry with Dr. T. Palmer, his brother-in-law, at Fitchburg, Mass. Settled in Clinton, in 1849, where he had a very successful practice for several years. Several prominent New England dentists studied with him. He has gradually relinquished his profession, in order to look after his real estate; res. Clinton, Mass., 30. Walnut St.

ELLA A. FISKE.

    6174. i. ELLA ATHELIA, b. Dec. 15, 1853; unm.

    6175. ii. CARRIE NOVELLA, b. July 5, 1860; m. Oct. 28, 1891, Willard Forrest Hallett; res. 280 Lafayette St., Bridgeport, Conn.

    5292. PROF MARTIN H. FISK, D. D. (Jeremiah, Josiah, Josiah, Josiah, Nathan, Nathan, Nathaniel, William, Robert, Simon, Simon, William, Symond), b. Temple, N. H., May 10, 1827; m. June 20, 1865, Henrietta F. Breed, of Peterboro, N. H., b. Sept. 27, 1827. Martin Hold Fiske was born in Temple, N. H. Spent his early life farming. Fitted for college at New Ipswich. Appleton Academy, and entered Dartmouth College, N. H., where he graduated in 1852, ranking the third in his class. He was employed as civil engineer on the Baltimore & Ohio Railroad for a time; left that position to assume the presidency of Paducah College, Ky., and remained there until the institution was broken up by the Civil War.. He was employed as professor in high schools and colleges until 1891, when failing health compelled him to retire from the profession. Since that time he has lived on the old homestead where he was born; res. Paris, Tenn., and Temple, N. H.

    6176. i.   HENRY MARTIN, b. Nov. 22, 1866; d. Oct. 27, 1874.
    6177. ii.   ETTA MARIA, b. June 9, 1869; d. Oct. 28, 1874.
    6178. iii. TWO OTHER CHILDREN, b. ———; d. in infancy.
    6179. iv. MABELLE E., b. July 20, 1875 (adopted); at Cushing Academy, Ashburnham, Mass.

5295. DR. CHARLES FREEMAN FISK (Jeremiah, Josiah, Josiah, Josiah, Nathan Nathan, Nathaniel, William, Robert, Simon, Simon, William, Symond), b. Dec. 2, 1832, Temple, N. H.; m. in Cambridge, Nov. 23, 1863, Emma Bailey, of Greenfield, N. H., b. Oct., 1836. She d. Dec. 2, 1894. He is a dentist; res. Greenfield, Mass., and Milford, N. H.

    6180. i.   SARAH JOSEPHINE, b. July 3, 1867.
    6181. ii.   HENRY MARTIN, b. Aug. 26, 1875.

5296. CHARLES ADAMS FISK (Artemas, Josiah, Josiah. Josiah, Nathan, Nathan, Nathaniel, William, Robert, Simon, Simon, William, Symond), b. New Ipswich, N. H., Oct. 29, 1820; m. Dec. 30, 1841, Sylvia C. Fuller, of Summit, Pa., d. Apr. 5, 1891. He was born in New Hampshire, at the foot of Kidder Mountain. After the death of his father he resided for some time in Templeton, Mass., until the removal of his mother to Pike, N. Y., when he went there. In the spring of 1837 his uncle moved to Summerhill, Crawford Co., Pa., and he went with him, leaving his mother and sister. He remained with him until he was 21 years of age. He then married and his mother and sister went to live with him and remained until his sister was married. His mother died at his home. He is a carpenter by trade, but has followed farming most of his life.; res. Hayfield, Pa.

    6182. i.   CHARLES ANTHONY, b. Oct. 1, 1849; m. Ella A. Morse.
    6183. ii.   ROYAL ALONZO, b. Sept. 7, 1851; m. Ida Satterlee.
    6184. iii. BENJ. WOOSTER, b. Aug. 5, 1853; m. Oris McGalrey.

5298. HORACE FISKE (David, Josiah, Josiah, Josiah, Nathan, Nathan, Nathaniel, William, Robert, Simon, Simon, William, Symond), b. Oxford, N. Y., July 23, 1829; m. Oct. 30, 1850, Martha, Padgett, b. 1831; d. May 15, 1872. He is a farmer; res. Oxford, N. Y.

    6185. i.   SHELDON W., b. Dec. 6, 1851; m. Sarah R. Jones.
    6186. ii.   CHARLES H., b. May 30, 1853; m. Alice Sweet.
    6187. iii. JAMES V. B., b. Dec. 16, 1855; d. Sept. 14, 1879.

5302-1. CHARLES FISK (John, David, Josiah, Josiah, Nathan, Nathan, Nathaniel, William, Robert, Simon, Simon, William, Symond), b. Hope, Me., Mar. 5, 1807; m. there May 9, 1831, Lucy Ann Sprague. He d. Feb. 5, 1835; res. in Maine.

    6187-1.i.   JOHN, b. ———.
    6187-2.ii. CLYNTHIA, b. ———.

5302-2. GALEN BULLEN FISK (John, David, Josiah, Josiah, Nathan, Nathan, Nathaniel, William, Robert, Simon, Simon, William, Symond), b. Camden, Me., Oct. 16, 1810; m. in Hope, Aug. 10, 1830, Sarah B. Robbins, of Hope, b. July 17, 1812. She res. So. T. He was a farmer and drover. He d. Sept. 22, 1859; res. So. Thomaston, Me.

    6187-3. i.   CHARLES, b. 1836; m. Feb., 1859, Sarah McKellar; res. So. Thomastown.
    6187-4. ii. AMOS, b. Jan. 20, 1838; m. Julia D. Hayden; res. R.
    6187-5. iii. LEWIS S., b. 1840.
    6187-6. iv. IRENE R., b. 1842; m. Apr. 23, 1862, Capt. O. R. Perry; res. So. T.

6187-7. v. OLIVE ANN, b. Apr. 20, 1844; m. Nov. 7, 1863, John F. Perry; res. 2745 Aldrich Ave. S., Minneapolis, Minn. He was b. Feb. 4, 1839. Ch.: 1, Edwin C., b. Dec. 30, 1864; m. May 5, 1886; P. O. add. 28 Irving Ave., Minneapolis, Minn. 2, Alethea Hix, b. Aug. 15, 1866; m. June 21, 1893, —— Soosawa; res. 3320 Harriett Ave., Minneapolis. 3, Minnie Olive, b. July 17, 1868; unm.; res. 2745 Aldrich Ave. So., Minneapolis, Minn. 4, Clinton Morrison, b. Aug. 22, 1871; res. New Ulm, Minn. 5, Guy Arthur, b. Nov. 5, 1877; res. 2745 Aldrich Ave. So., Minneapolis, Minn.

6187-8. vi. GEO. FRANKLIN, b. 1846; m. Bertha E. Cox.

6187-9. vii. JOEL MERRILL, b. Jan. 27, 1849; m. in Rockland, Me., Mary E. Robinson, b. June 4, 1849; d. May 6, 1874. He is a farmer; res. Rockland, Me., s. p.

6187-10. viii. LAURETTA, b. 1852.

6187-11. ix. ERNOGINE C., b. 1859; res. Savannah, Ga.

6187-12. x. LUCENIA, b. ——; m. ——; d. ——, s. p.

6187-13. xi. ALETHEA M., b. 1856.

5302-3. PERLEY HOWE FISK (John, David, Josiah, Josiah, Nathan, Nathan, Nathaniel, William, Robert, Simon, Simon, William, Symond), b. Readfield, Me., Aug. 16, 1815; m. Sept. 25, 1841, Sarah Emeline Fogg, b. June 30, 1821; d. in Brooklyn, N. Y., Nov. 20, 1895. He was in business with his father and was quite successful. During the last few years of his life, when his health failed, he speculated. He d. Mar. 27, 1876; res. Readfield, Me.

6187-14. i. ANN JUDSON, b. Oct. 2, 1842; d. Nov. 24, 1845.

6187-15. ii. EMMA FRANCES, b. Dec. 22, 1843; m. Mar. 12, 1872, Timothy H. Roberts, in Whitneys Point, N. Y. He was b. there Mar. 21, 1846. He is a lawyer, at 47 John St., New York City. Ch.: 1, Arthur Perley, b. at W. P., Feb. 25, 1873; d. Apr. 12, 1889, at Parkville, N. Y.; res. 212 Tulip St., Brooklyn, N. Y.

6187-16. iii. NELLIE MARIA, b. Aug. 5, 1846; m. Oct. 11, 1870, Arthur J. Porter, in Readfield, Me. He was b. Nov. 24, 1846; res. Strong, Me. Ch.: 1, Emma Hunter, b. July 2, 1871; m. Sept. 1, 1895, Fred V. Gilman; res. Madison, Me. 2, Fred Perley Jeremy, b. Sept. 10, 1874. 3, James Arthur Roberts, b. Apr. 16, 1879. 4, George Davis, b. May 27, 1882.

6187-17. iv. MELLIE LOVINA, b. Nov. 22, 1851; d. Oct. 19, 1854.

5302-4. JOEL HOWE FISK (John, David, Josiah, Josiah, Nathan, Nathan, Nathaniel, William, Robert, Simon, Simon William, Symond), b. Nov. 14, 1817, Hope, Me.; m. in No. Whitefield, Me., June 24, 1845, Mrs. Louisa Turner Weeks, b. Nov. 28, 1814; d. Feb. 26, 1878. He was a grocer. He d. Mar. 17, 1861; res. No. Whitefield, Me.

6187-18. i. GEORGE H., b. Feb. 11, 1847; m. Mary R. Stemper.

6187-19. ii. CHARLES TURNER, b. Aug. 3, 1849; m. Ella O. Hersey

6187-20. iii. BRIGGS TURNER, b. Mar. 12, 1857; m. Feb. 25, 1883, Ellen Brown, at Oshkosh, Wis.; d. at East Machias, Me., May 14, 1884, s. p.

5302-7. CAPT. MOSES HARRINGTON FISK (Benjamin, David, Josiah, Josiah, Nathan, Nathan, Nathaniel, William, Robert, Simon, Simon, William, Symond), b. Camden, Me., May 3, 1816; m. Jan. 23, 1848, Harriett S. Ingraham, b. May 30, 1829, dau. of Joseph. He is a retired sea captain; commanded the bark "George Thomas."; res. Rockland, Me., 69 No. Main St.

6187-21. i. ALVAN BLACKINTON, b. June 10, 1849; d. Aug., 1849.

6187-22. ii. WILLIAM H., b. Feb. 20, 1851; m. Ellen Geddes.

6187-23. iii. EVA H., b. Sept. 28, 1853; m. May 6, 1873, —— Crockett; res. R.

6187-24. v. MARY IMOGENE, b. Feb. 25, 1856; m. May 30, 18—, G. Chamberlain; res. Green's Landing, Me.

6187-25. iv. CARRIE S., b. July 31, 1857; m. Sept. 6, 1882, A. H. Jones; res. R.

6187-26.vi. THORNIA D.. b. Mar. 20, 1860; m. Sept. 6, 1883, G. K. Mayo; res. R.

5302-8. BENJAMIN FISKE (Benjamin, David, Josiah, Josiah, Nathan, Nathan, Nathaniel, William, Robert, Simon, Simon, William, Symond), b. Camden, Me., 1812; m. there, 1831, Mary Emily Studley, b. Apr. 9, 1816; d. Apr. 18, 1878. He was a farmer. He d. 1852; res. Camden, Me.

6187-27.i. CHARLES H., b. July 3, 1840; m. Mary E. Spofford.
6187-28.ii. JAMES D., b. ———; res. 64 Mechanic St., Rockland, Me.
6187-29.iii. JOHN A., b. ———; res. Norwood. Mass.
6187-30.iv. SARAH FRANCES, b. Oct. 4, 1850; m. Jan. 27, 1876, Frederick C. Pohlmann; res. Coulterville, Cal. Ch.: 1, Marietta, b. Jan. 9, 1877.
6187-31.v. OLIVER, b. ———: res. Coulterville, Cal. He d. s. p.
6187-32.vi. FRANKLIN M., b. ———; d. ———.
6187-33.vii. MARGARET A., b. ———; d. ———. A dau. is Nora E. Carroll, Rockville, Me.
6187-34.viii. NETTIE, b. ———; d. ———.
6187-35.ix. EMILY ORVILLE, b. Apr. 9, 1842; m. Oct. 12, 1858, Benjamin F. Brewster. He was b. Mar. 4, 1832. Is a joiner; res. Rockville, Me. Ch.: 1, Fiske E., b. Nov. 8, 1860; m. 1890; res. Mystic, Conn. 2, Etta E., b. Sept., 186—: m. Dec. 18, 1886, Augustus S. Rankin; res. 78 Cedar St., Rockland, Me.
6187-36.x. ROXANNA, b. ———; d. ———.
6187-37.xi. BENJIETTA, b. ———.

5302-8. WILLIAM BECKET FISK (David, David, Josiah, Josiah, Nathan, Nathan, Nathaniel, William, Robert, Simon, Simon, William, Symond), b. Camden, Me., Mar. 25, 1803; m. Kenton, Ky., 1831, Cynthia Stevens, b. 1813; d. Aug. 20, 1844. He was born in Maine and moved to Kenton Co., Ky., when 14 years of age, in 1817. On the death of his father he took charge of the farm, with his mother's advice, and when the estate was settled was given 203 acres of land as his share. This he lost through the manipulations of his father-in-law. He d. in Cowley Co., Kan., 1876; res. Kenton Co., Ky.

6187-39.i. HIRAM A., b. Jan. 10, 1833; m. Clara Louise Ward and Martha Francis Ward.
6187-40.ii. CHARLES, b. May, 1835; m. Semy Elliott.
6187-40.iii. SUSAN, b. Jan. 29, 1837; m. ——— Bailey; res. Wichita, Kan.
6187-41.iv. FRANCIS MARION, b. Dec. 12, 1838; res. Mt. Zion, Ill.

5302-21. JOHN D. FISKE (David, David, Josiah, Josiah, Nathan, Nathan, Nathaniel. William, Robert, Simon, Simon, William, Symond), b. Thomaston, Me., 1794; m. Feb. 11, 1816, Margaret Simonton, b. 1795; d. Apr. 1, 1874. He d. June 3, 1823; res. Campbell Co., Ky.

6187-42.i. HIRAM, b. Mar. 28, 1818; m. Mary E. Bowley.
6187-43.ii. CHARLOTTE, b. Mar. 31, 1820; m. Nov. 19, 1835, Henry Munroe; res. Lincolnville Beach, Me. He was b. Aug. 21, 1811. Is a sailor. Ch.: 1, Ellen Munroe, b. July 24, 1838; m. ——— Kidder; add. Camden, Me. 2, Margaret C. I., b. Oct. 14, 1839; m. Josiah French; d. Jan. 22, 1893. 3, Olive A., b. Sept. 5, 1841; d. Feb. 14, 1849. 4, John H., b. Aug. 23, 1843; m. Emerly Drinkwater; add. Lincolnville Beach, Me. 5, Laura, b. Sept. 5, 1845; m. Geo. Collins, of Camden; add. Cabool, Mo. 6. Hiram F., b. May 9, 1848; m. Mary Thomas; add. Camden, Me. 7, Hudson H., b. Apr. 20, 1850; seaman. 8, Louisa A. B., b. Nov. 24, 1852; d. Mar. 29, 1863.
6187-44.iii. ALPHA, b. Aug. 21, 1821; m. ——— Ames. She d. 1875. Had a daughter, Margaret.
6187-45.iv. LOUISA, b. Mar. 10, 1824; m. ——— Manning. She d. Feb., 1885. A son, George, res. Rockland, Me.
6187-46.v. WM. H. H., b. 1840; res. Decatur, Ill.
6187-47.vi. HENRY CLAY, b. Oct. 7, 1841; m. Sarah Guard.
6187-48.vii. JOSEPHINE, b. 1844; d. ae. six months.

5308. ROLLIN ABEL FISKE (Daniel, Nathan, Daniel, Josiah, Nathan, Nathan, Nathaniel, William, Robert, Simon, Simon, William, Symond), b. Landgrove, Vt., Jan. 30, 1851; m. in Boston, July 30, 1879, Annie E. Smith, b. Nov. 26, 1860. He is a real estate agent; res. Jamaica Plain, Mass., 217 Larmartine St.

    6188. i.   LENA M., b. June 17, 1880.
    6189. ii.   RAYMOND T., b. Aug. 3, 1885.
    6190. iii. CORA L., b. Nov. 17, 1890.
    6191. iv. BABY, b. July 9, 1895.

5310. WINSLOW C. FISK (Daniel, Nathan, Daniel, Josiah, Nathan, Nathan, Nathaniel, William, Robert, Simon, Simon, William, Symond), b. Sandgrove, Vt., Aug. 2, 1853; m. Dec. 9, 1874, Frances Bryant White, of Weston, Vt. She d. in Boston, Nov. 9, 1888; res. Topeka, Kan., 300 W. Sixth St.

    6192. i.   ERNEST LLOYD, b. in Boston, Aug. 19, 1876.

5318. BENJAMIN NUTTING FISKE (Walter, Walter, Daniel, Josiah, Nathan, Nathan, Nathaniel, William, Robert, Simon, Simon, William, Symond), b. Pepperell, Mass., Feb. 29, 1815; m. in Boston, July 1, 1846, Eliza Pierce Warren, d. June 19, 1893. He resided in Pepperell until 1837, when he moved to Boston, and later to Medway; res. Boston, Mass., and Medway, Me.

    6193. i.   EMILY DICKINSON, b. Sept. 12, 1847; m. Apr. 7, 1877, Charles F. Moore; res. Medway, Me. Ch.: 1, Rachel Emily. 2, Anne. 3, Bertha.
    6194. ii.   THEODORE VARNUM, b. Feb. 13, 1849; m. Augusta Hathaway. Has two children.
    6195. iii. HENRY DUNSTER, b. May 6, 1851; unm.

5321. HENRY WALTER FISKE (Walter, Walter, Daniel, Josiah, Nathan, Nathan, Nathaniel, William, Robert, Simon, Simon, William, Symond), b. Pepperell, Mass., June 18, 1827; m. Feb. 15, 1852, Harriett Waite, of Medway, Me.; d. ————; m. 2d, Dec. 31, 1863, Sarah Elizabeth Green. He moved to Canada and resided there until 1867. Removed to Cambridgeport, Vt., and later to Mattewamkeag; res. Canada and Mattewamkeag, Me.

    6196. i.   ABIGAIL DICKSON, b. ————.
    6197. ii.   HARRIETT ELLEN, b. ————.
    6198. iii. LAURA, b. ————; d. in infancy.
    6199. iv. CHARLES EDGAR, b. ————; res. Turtle Lake, Wis.

5322. BENJAMIN A. FISKE (Benjamin N., Walter, Daniel, Josiah, Nathan, Nathan, Nathaniel, William, Robert, Simon, Simon, William, Symond), b. Weld, Me., Sept. 21, 1822; m. in Cherryfield, Me., Margaret E. Archer, b. Oct. 15, 1825; d. Jan. 12, 1884. He is a trader in provisions and groceries; res. Bangor, Me., 211 Harlow St.

    6200. i.   CHARLES ABBOTT, b. Mar. 5, 1850; m. in Hope, Ark., Mattie Wood. She d. Dec. 17, 1884. Ch.: 1, Lillian Gertrude, b. Sept. 21, 1882; res. Hannibal, Mo.
    6201. ii.   WILLARD H., b. Mar. 2, 1851; unm.; res. B.
    6202. iii. FRED J., b. Mar. 12, 1854; m. Ada M. Pond.
    6203. iv. LILLIAN G., b. Mar. 15, 1862; m. Ed Plummer; res. Bath, Me.

5323. WALTER W. FISK (Benjamin N., Walter, Daniel, Josiah, Nathan, Nathan, Nathaniel, William, Robert, Simon, Simon, William, Symond), b. Weld, Me., Jan. 12, 1824; m. in Lincoln, Me., 1855, Rebecca Kimball, b. Aug. 10, 1844; d. 1862; m. 2d, July 30, 1864, Florentine Gowen. On reaching his majority he engaged in the lumber business, and for thirty-three years followed that and keeping hotel on the Penobscot River. In 1875 he moved to Wisconsin and engaged in the hotel business, being proprietor of the Fisk House, at Turtle Lake; res. Turtle Lake, Wis.

    6204. i.   ELLEN MAY, b. July 6, 1856; d. July 26, 1883.
    6205. ii.   HERBERT W., b. Oct. 29, 1858.
    6206. iii. FRANK E., b. Oct. 31, 1865; m. Maud Taylor.
    6207. iv. CARRIE MABEL, b. Oct. 16, 1867; m. John Hogan; res. Heath, Minn., s. p.
    6208. v.   MARY AUGUSTA, b. Jan. 12, 1869; m. Ed Digman; res. Sault Ste. Marie, Mich.
    6209. vi. EUGENE W., b. Apr. 25, 1884; res. T. L.

38

5328. JEREMIAH H. FISKE (Benjamin N., Walter, Daniel, Josiah, Nathan, Nathan, Nathaniel, William, Robert, Simon, Simon, William, Symond), b. Lincoln, Me., Aug. 18, 1835; m. Feb. 7, 1868, Jemima W. Gowen, b. Mar. 17, 1849. He is a merchant; res. Lincoln, Me.

    6210. i.   ANNA GERTRUDE, b. Dec. 26, 1869.
    6211. ii.   RAYMOND H., b. Mar. 18, 1889.

    5337. GEORGE W. FISK (Arnold H., Varnum, Daniel, Josiah, Nathan, Nathan, Nathaniel, William, Robert, Simon, Simon, William, Symond), b. Norfolk, N. Y., June 26, 1839; m. Feb. 23, 1861, Julia E. Cadwell, b. June 28, 1841. He is a wagonmaker; res. Summerland, Cal.

    6212. i.   E. CLIFTON, b. May 3, 1862; m. June 29, 1884, Lillian E. Hadden, b. June 19, 1864; d. Dec. 21, 1884, s. p. He is a printer; res. Summerland, Cal.
    6213. ii.   ESSIE M., b. June 14, 1865; d. Aug. 20, 1886.
    6214. iii. ELROY E., b. July 12, 1867; d. July 18, 1869.
    6215. iv. CYREN E., b. June 12, 1869; is with the Herald, at Los Angeles, Cal.
    6216. v.   CYRUS E., b. June 12, 1869; res. 860 Sand St., Los A.
    6217. vi. STEWART ANSON, b. Coopersville, Mich., May 22, 1875; m. Sept. 22, 1895, Nellie A. Eberle, b. Sept. 22, 1877. He is a printer; res. s. p. Downey, Cal.
    6218. vii. CARROLL A., b. ———; res. Summerland.

    5341. FREDERICK BOTTOM FISKE (Samuel C., Joshua, Henry, Henry, Nathan, Nathan, Nathan, Nathaniel, William, Robert, Simon, Simon, William, Symond), b. Southbridge, Mass., Aug. 25, 1830; m. in New York, June 15, 1852, Mary Elizabeth Wilson, b. Jan. 29, 1832. He was educated partly in Southbridge, and afterwards in Connecticut, leaving school, however, at 16, and entering business life in New York, where he has ever since lived and done business. He was the first secretary of the Elevated Railroad in New York, and in younger days was member of clubs there. Was a commercial traveler in the United States for many years, and has been abroad for health and pleasure; res. New York, N. Y., add. 15 Beekman St.; res. 100 W. Sixty-seventh St.

    6220. i.   WILSON, b. May 20, 1855; m. Annie T. Southard.
    6221. ii.   ALEXANDER MOTT, b. Aug. 1, 1862; res. at home.
    6222. iii. LAURA CELESTINE, b. Apr. 12, 1857; m. 2d, Dec. 20, 1888, James H. McKinley, b. Feb. 25, 1860, s. p.
    6223. iv. FERD'K V., b. June 20, 1860; d. Dec. 3, 1863.

    5345. ALONZO WILBUR FISK (Carlisle A., Elias, Simeon, Henry, Nathan, Nathan, Nathan, Nathaniel, William, Robert, Simon, Simon, William, Symond), b. Mar. 16, 1831, Springfield, Mass.; m. in Abingdon, Ill., Sept. 12, 1858, Almira A. Stoddard, b. Gouverneur, N. Y., June 22, 1836; burned to death in Avon, Ill., Dec. 2, 1859; m. 2d, Feb. 12, 1865, Isabelle Stires. He passed his boyhood days in Springfield and Pleasant Valley, Conn. Attended district school and afterwards Prof. Herrick's high school. He worked for his father in Colt's Armory, in Hartford, Conn., and in the United States Armory, in Springfield, where he learned the trade of gunsmith. He followed the advice of Horace Greeley, went west, and resided in Chicago, Rochelle, and Avon, Ill. At the breaking out of the Civil War he assisted in organizing the Avon Guards, and was made First Sergeant. Gov. Yates refused to accept the company, as the quota was full. He returned east and was employed for four years in the United States Armory making guns. At the close of the war he went back west and located in Bushnell, where he has since resided. After traveling for seven years he studied apiculture and engaged quite extensively in the bee and honey business. Has been president of McDonough County Beekeepers' Association; res. Bushnell, Ill.

    6224. i.   EMMA R., b. Sept. 4, 1859; d. Sept. 23, 1866.
    6225. ii.   MYRA ANN, b. Jan. 12, 1866; m. Albert F. Pearce; res. Bushnell. Have three children.
    6226. iii. NELLY AGNES, b. Apr. 7, 1868; d. Jan. 19, 1869.
    6227. iv. DORA BELL, b. Dec. 29, 1869; d. Dec. 21, 1875.
    6228. v.   ERNEST WILBUR, b. Mar. 22, 1873.
    6229. vi. EDGAR ALONZO, b. Apr. 30, 1875.
    6230. vii. JAMES EARL, b. July 10, 1879.

5348. MAJOR WILBUR DAVIS FISKE (Carlisle A., Elias, Simeon, Henry, Nathan, Nathan, Nathan, Nathaniel, William, Robert, Simon, Simon, William, Symond), b. Pleasant Valley, Conn., June 7, 1841; m. Feb. 1, 1866, Agnes Hosmer Andrews, b. Nov. 9, 1843. Wilbur Davis Fiske, born in Barkhampsted, Conn., June 7, 1841, and lived there, and at Pleasant Valley, Conn., until he was 7 years old, when his mother died, and his father took him to live with a man in Pleasant Valley, named Moses. Then, about one year after that, he took him to Springfield, Mass., and in a short time to Stafford, Conn. to live with his aunt, Mary E. Cushman. Some time after this his father married again, and resided at Springfield. Wilbur did not stay long, but went back to his Aunt Mary's. He stayed there a year or two, and worked for a neighbor, Mr. Cummings. Went back to Springfield on a visit, and went to work there for Edmund Bigelow, Esq., and was with him three or four years. He sent him to school winters at his home in Bennington, Vt., and he lived with his father, Dr. William Bigelow, one of God's noblemen. In the fall of 1857, his time at Springfield had expired with Edmund Bigelow, and he made arrangements with a doctor in Pittsfield, Mass., to go there and study medicine under him, but on account of the panic of 1857 did not go, but went to New Britain, Conn., with Buckley & Newton, to learn the machinist trade, and steam and hydraulic engineering. They built the gas works and water works for New Britain, and did work all about that section of country. The war broke out; he was then first assistant engineer of the New Britain fire department; he enlisted and helped raise a company for the Fourteenth Regiment Connecticut Volunteers. He was just then coming to be 21 years old, and before he left the State, was made a Freemason in the lodge at New Britain; went to war with the Fourteenth Regiment, Company F, and was attached to the Second Corps, Army of the Potomac. Antietam was his first real battle. At the battle of Fredericksburg, Va., he was in command of the company, and was dangerously wounded, Dec. 13, 1862. Doctors said he could not live but five or six hours; shot through the stomach. He went home, got better, went back, and was just on time to go through the Chancellorsville battle, under Gen. Joe Hooker; then he was soon off for Gettysburg campaign, and the battle of Gettysburg. The boys did themselves proud on that field. They helped stop Pickett's charge, and were just at the right of the bloody angle, and captured six stands of rebel colors in that charge, more than any other regiment got on that day. It was the grandest day he had ever seen in his whole life. When the fight was over that night, it was estimated that he weighed a little over 200 tons. On Oct. 14, 1863, he was wounded again, at the battle of Bristoe Station; then after that, had a beautiful typhoid fever that mustered him out of the service, and he has never seen a well day since; went home to Springfield, Mass., and worked for Mr. E. Bigelow again about six months, then engaged with Geo. Dwight, Jr., & Co., in steam and hydraulic engineering business, and the manufacture of steam pumps. They soon sent him to Boston. Mass., to open a warehouse there for them. He stayed there about one and a half years, and the company was changed to the Norwalk Iron Works. He then left them, and went to work for Knowles & Sibley, manufacturers of the Knowles steam pumps, with his headquarters in New York, and established a warehouse in New York for them. For nine or ten years, with headquarters in New York, he traveled all over the United States, sold pumping machinery for all purposes, and established agencies all over the country and Canada, and the company finally became the Knowles Steam Pump Works. After the great Boston fire he came to Boston to establish business on a better plan for the New England and Canadian trade, and opened a warehouse in Boston for this purpose, and in about six years thereafter the Knowles Steam Pump Works was sold to the Geo. F. Blake Manufacturing Company, who now run both concerns separately. Since that time he has been the general agent of both concerns for the New England States, and sometimes has been called out of the New England States, and has taken charge of all water works contracts in this territory, and the erection of the pumping machinery, and attended to the selling department in all of its multiform variety for pumping air, gas, water, or any other liquids known, and to be actuated by steam, electricity, belt, or geared power for all purposes, and is still in this same concern and business with headquarters in Boston, Mass. He lives in Melrose, Mass., and belongs to the Wyoming Lodge, Waverly Chapter, Hugh de Payens Commandery, U. S. Grant Post No. 4 G. A. R., a member of the First Congregational Church, and in politics a black Republican. He has filled several town offices; was on the board of water commissioners about twelve years, and chairman five years, and is a member of the Association of the Fourteenth Regiment Connecticut Volunteers, and the Association of the Army of the Potomac. He enlisted as a private and obtained every position in the company up to a captaincy; res. Melrose, Mass.; Boston add. 185 Devonshire St.

6231. i. HOWARD CARLYLE, b. June 16, 1867; m. Dec. 28, 1893, Maude Darricott Fenno, at Brookline, b. Mar. 23, 1867; add. 185 Devonshire St. He is a mechanical engineer.

6232. ii. CARROLL ANDREWS, b. Sept. 18, 1874; res. Melrose.

5351. WILLIAM HENRY FISKE (Henry M., Henry, David, Henry, Nathan, Nathan, Nathan, Nathaniel, William, Robert, Simon, Simon, William, Symond), b. Woodland, Cal., Apr. 20, 1860; m. at San Luis Obispo, Sept. 12, 1883, Lydia May Warden, b. Aug. 5, 1865. He was born in Woodland, Cal., where his father was a practicing physician. He received an excellent education; was married at San Luis Obispo. For some time he has been the resident manager at Portland, Ore., for F. Chevalier & Co., whisky merchants and liquor dealers of San Francisco, Cal. He has four girls; res. Portland, Ore.; P. O. box 303.

6233. i. HELEN, b. Oct. 10, 1884; d. Dec. 1, 1884.

6234. ii. LESLIE, b. Jan. 15, 1887.

6235. iii. WILMA, b. Mar. 15, 1891.

6236. iv. SHIRLEY, b. Aug. 22, 1894.

5356. HARRY WATERMAN FISKE (George D., Henry, David, Henry, Nathan, Nathan, Nathan, Nathaniel, William, Robert, Simon, Simon, William, Symond), b. McDowell Hill, Cal., May 28, 1852; m., 1880, Frances E. Warden, of San Louis Obispo. He d. July 31, 1887; res. Santa Barbara Co., Cal.

5361. MELVILLE FRANKLIN FISKE (Liberty B., Silas, David, David, Nathan, Nathan, Nathaniel, William, Robert, Simon, Simon, William, Symond), b. Burlington, Wis., Jan. 25, 1851; m. May 15, 1875, Nellie A. Pratt, b. Nov. 25, 1853. He is a farmer; res. Twin Bluffs, Wis.

6237. i. JENNIE MAY, b. Apr. 22, 1876; m. Sept. 20, 1895, Geo. Keene; res. Twin Bluffs, Wis.

6238. ii. FRANK E., b. Sept. 28, 1877.

6239. iii. GEO. WALLACE, b. June 18, 1879.

5364. GEORGE ALLING FISKE (Lucius W., Silas, Daniel, Daniel, Nathan, Nathan, Nathan, Nathaniel, William, Robert, Simon, Simon, William, Symond), b. Sullivan, N. Y., Oct. 16, 1848; m. Feb. 18, 1891, Elizabeth E. De Wolf, b. Oct. 28, 1849. He is a farmer; res. Delavan, Wis., s. p.

5366. SILAS WRIGHT FISKE (Lucius W., Silas, Daniel, Daniel, Nathan, Nathan, Nathan, Nathaniel, William, Robert, Simon, Simon, William, Symond), b. Sullivan, N. Y., Mar. 9, 1852; m. at Darien, Wis., Nov. 12, 1874, Sarah Jane Seaver, b. Oct. 4, 1854. He is a farmer; res. Darien, Wis.

6240. i. MINNIE ALLING, b. Sept. 14, 1875.

6241. ii. ROLLIN HERBERT, b. Apr. 3, 1880.

6242. iii. MABEL MARTHA, b. Jan. 28, 1886.

5367. HENRY NEWELL FISKE (Lucius W., Silas, Daniel, Daniel, Nathan, Nathan, Nathan, Nathaniel, William, Simon, Simon, William, Symond), b. Mar. 10, 1854; m. Feb. 13, 1883, Georgia I. Matteson, b. Oct. 20, 1860; res. Delavan, Wis.

6243. i. RALPH M., b. May 10, 1884.

6244. ii. BERT, b. Dec. 13, 1886; d. Feb. 28, 1887.

6245. iii. LEON E., b. May 22, 1888.

6246. iv. STELLA R., b. Oct. 26, 1890.

6247. v. LAURA, b. Sept. 27, 1895.

5368. EDGAR DANIEL FISKE (Lucius W., Silas, Daniel, Daniel, Nathan, Nathan, Nathan, Nathaniel, William, Robert, Simon, Simon, William, Symond), b. O., 1855; m. Aug. 5, 1885, Mary H. Hunter, of Ripon, Wis., b. June 14, 1852; res. lands, Colo., s. p.; P. O. box 211.

5369. CHARLES CLARENCE FISKE (Lucius W., Silas, Daniel, Daniel, Nathan, Nathan, Nathan, Nathaniel, William, Robert, Simon, Simon, William, Symond), b. Jan. 16, 1859, Darien, Wis.; m. there Mar. 28, 1894, Carrie Rinck, b. Feb. 16, 1866; res. Darien, Wis.

6248. i. EVELYN, b. Mar. 14, 1895.

5374. ALONZO FISK (Samuel, William, William, William, William, Nathan, Nathaniel, William, Robert, Simon, Simon, William,, Symond), b. Patriot, Ind., Aug. 14, 1836; m. at Rising Sun, Apr. 7, 1861, Clara T. Baker, b. Oct. 2, 1840. He is a farmer; res. Patriot, Ind.

6249. i. WILLIAM A., b. Jan. 15, 1862; d. Nov. 15, 1884.
6250. ii. ANNA B., b. Jan. 17, 1866.
6251. iii. EMMA G., b. Apr. 2, 1868.
6252. iv. GEO. B., b. Jan. 16, 1865; d. Feb. 17, 1865.

5404-2. LOVELL W. FISK (Alfred W., Sylvanus, William, William, William, Nathan, Nathan, Nathaniel, William, Robert, Simon, Simon, William, Symond), b. Stafford. N. Y., May 17, 1829; m. Oct. 25, 1852, Julia K. Simonds, b. Oct. 25, 1832. L. W. Fisk was born in the town of Stafford, Genesee County, N. Y.; lived with his father until of age; made the most of a limited common school education; taught school winter seasons from the age of nineteen to 24 in and adjoining his native township, except one term in Wisconsin. He always followed farming; res. Chewelah, Wash.

6253. i. ALFRED J., b. Dec. 17, 1853; d. May 29, 1876.
6254. ii. JULIUS M., b. Feb. 17, 1856; m. Clara Ellison.
6255. iii. CLEMENT L., b. Oct. 15, 1857; m. Charlotte Gilbert.
6256. iv. MARY AMELIA, b. Jan. 17, 1861; d. Feb. 12, 1865.
6257. v. B. C., b. May 19, 1863; d. Mar. 18, 1866.
6258. vi. EVA M., b. Aug. 25, 1871; res. C.
6259. vii. SABRA L., b. Apr. 13, 1875; d. Jan. 24, 1879.
6260. viii. HOWARD L., b. Sept. 17, 1878; res. C.

5404-6. SYLVANUS W. FISKE (Henry A., Sylvanus, William, William, William, Nathan, Nathan, Nathaniel, William, Robert, Simon, Simon, William, Symond), b. Stafford, N. Y., Oct. 8, 1829; m. Nov. 4, 1851, Genette Beswick, b. Dec. 4, 1831; d. Mar. 20, 1880. He is a farmer; res. Morganville, N. Y.

6261. i. HENRY LEE, b. Nov. 29, 1861; d. Feb. 19, 1879.

5404-16. WYMAN PARKER FISK (Jesse H., Sylvanus, William, William, William, Nathan, Nathan, Nathaniel, William, Robert, Simon, Simon, William, Symond), b. Stafford, N. Y., Feb. 21, 1842; m. Nov., 1861, Amy Booth Stafford, b. May, 1842; d. Oct., 1863; m. 2d, Jan., 1867, Cora Bachelder, b. July, 1850. He is a farmer; res. Fall River, Wis.

6262. i. ALLIE, b. Sept., 1863; m. Sept., 1886, Meridy Pansphilon.
6263. ii. MAUD, b. Jan. 8, 1868; m. Sept. 18, 1888, C. H. Marshall; res. Marion, Ia.
6264. iii. LOTTIE A., b. Mar. 27, 1871.
6265. iv. ANNA L., b. Oct. 3, 1875.
6266. v. HELEN M., b. Apr. 23, 1878.

5404-18. CHAUNCEY E. FISK (Amos H., Sylvanus, William, William, William, Nathan, Nathan, Nathaniel, William, Robert, Simon, Simon, William, Symond), b. Batavia, N. Y., Jan. 21, 1847; m. in Mendon, Mich., Agnes Akey, b. Lima, Ohio. Conductor C. E. Fisk, who for several years was in charge of the Santa Fe lake train, but was transferred to the Howard branch when the Terminal people took charge of the run, has moved his family to Emporia, Kan.; res. Emporia, Kan.

6267. i. GERTRUDE B., b. Sept. 8, 1869, in Mendon, St. Joseph Co., Mich.; add. Emporia, Kan.
6268. ii. CLAUD E., b. May 5, 1871, in Bloomington, Ill.; add. Kansas City, Mo.

5405. HENRY C. FISK (John, Rufus, Rufus, Stephen, William, Nathan, Nathan, Nathaniel, William, Robert, Simon, Simon, William, Symond), b. Manchester, Mich., in 1823; m. in 1846, Sarah Jane Graves, b. Dec. 22, 1825; d. Aug. 24, 1892.

He was born in Manchester Township about the time his parents came to Michigan. Most of his father's children died in childhood. He inherited his father's disposition and character to a large degree. He was a carpenter by trade and many of the houses in the neighborhood where he lived, still standing, were built by him. He enlisted in the Seventeenth Michigan Infantry in Aug., 1862, and served with that regiment in its many battles, until Nov. 16, 1863, when he was killed at Campbell's Station, Tenn. He d. Nov. 16, 1863; res. Manchester, Mich.

      6269. i.   OPHELIA, b. 1848; d. May, 1878.
      6270. ii.   EMORY, b. 1850; d. May, 1866.
      6271. iii. CASSIUS C., b. Dec. 22, 1860.
      6272. iv. CHARLES H., b. June 19, 1858; m. Ida J. Dorr.

    5406. ELI FISK (John, Rufus, Rufus, Stephen, William, Nathan, Nathan, Nathaniel, William, Robert, Simon, Simon, William, Symond), b. Manchester, Mich., May 19, 1836; m. there Jane Dorr, b. Dec., 1835. He is a farmer; res. Tompkins Centre, Mich.

      6273. i.   LOLA IRENE, b. May 6, 1861; m. Oct. 4, 1885, Edward Fenn.
      6274. ii.   EFFIE J., b. Nov. 27, 1862.
      6275. iii. JOHN R., b. Apr. 3, 1867; m. Jennie Tompkins.
      6276. iv. ANNIE L., b. Aug. 27, 1870.
      6277. v.   MILLIE, b. Sept. 1, 1872; d. Aug. 24, 1874.
      6278. vi. MARCUS S., b. Oct. 19, 1874; d. July 19, 1876.

    5411. DR. MARCUS B. FISK (James M., Rufus, Rufus, Stephen, William, Nathan, Nathan, Nathaniel, William, Robert, Simon, Simon, William, Symond), b. Willington, Conn., Apr. 4, 1838; m. Stafford Springs, Dec. 22, 1864, Emma F. Howland, b. Oct. 12, 1847. He was born in

Willington, Conn., and was graduated at Yale Medical Institution in 1863. Not wishing to make a mortuary record, he engaged in business life from which he has acquired a varied and valuable experience. He says: "Our family have never been money grabbers as a rule, Integrity being the motto. 'Iter ad astra per virtute,' or 'Virtute ad astra,' is claimed to have been the legend on the coat of arms. Some outcrying exceptions have arisen of course." He has been Judge of Probate, Town Clerk and Town Treasurer; res. Stafford Springs, Conn.

      6279. i.   MARY E., b. Sept. 7, 1869; d. July 11, 1870.
      6280. ii.   ROBERT H., b. Jan. 1, 1873; res. Worcester, Mass.; care of Worcester Coal Co., Southbridge St.
      6281. iii. RICHARD M., b. Nov. 14, 1876; res. S. S.

DR. MARCUS B. FISK.

    5414. REV. GEORGE McCLELLAN FISKE (Marcus L., Rufus, Rufus, Stephen, William, Nathan, Nathan, Nathaniel, William, Robert, Simon, Simon, William, Symond), b. East Windsor, Conn., Oct. 21, 1850; m. June 4, 1874, Mary Greenough Walker, dau. of Rev. William Sydney Walker, D. D., of Burlington, N. J., and his wife Eliza (Greenough), b. Ithaca, N. Y., Sept. 15, 1849. He was graduated from Trinity College, Hartford, in the class of 1870, and from the Berkeley Divinity School, Middletown, Conn., in 1874; priest of the Episcopal Church; rector at present of St. Stephen's Church, Providence, R. I. In 1888 elected bishop of the diocese of Fond du Lac, but declined; received the honorary degree of D. D. from Trinity College, Hartford. Conn., in 1888; res. 86 George St., Providence, R. I.

6282. i. DE LANCEY WALKER, b. at Burlington, N. J., Mar. 16, 1875.
6283. ii. MARY GREENOUGH WALKER, b. at Burlington, N. J., May 10, 1876.
6284. iii. REGINALD, b. at Burlington, N. J., Aug. 14, 1877.
6285. iv. ELIZA GREENOUGH, b. at Burlington, N. J., Oct. 7, 1878.
6286. v. GEORGIA FRANCES. b. at Burlington, N. J., Mar. 20, 1880.
6287. vi. CAROLINE BARD, b. in Philadelphia, Pa., July 19, 1881; d. at Burlington, N. J., Sept. 13, 1881.
6288. vii. WILLIAM SYDNEY WALKER, b. at Burlington, N. J., Sept. 15, 1882.
6289. viii. ERNEST, b. Peekskill, N. Y., May 24, 1884.

5434. FRANKLIN COLLINS FISK (Moses, Moses, Josiah, Nathan, William, Nathan, Nathan, Nathaniel, William, Robert, Simon, Simon, William, Symond), b. Sept. 22, 1830, West Chesterfield, Mass.; m. in Windsor, Mass., Mar. 1, 1854, Amelia J. Pierce, b. Aug. 25, 1831; d. Dec. 19, 1889. He was in the mercantile business. He d. in Northampton, Mar. 12, 1887; res. Williamsburg, Mass.

6290. i. CORA IRENE, b. July 27, 1856; d. Apr., 1864.
6291. ii. NELLIE JOANNA, b. July 29, 1858; d. Apr., 1864.
6292. iii. EFFA LUCRETIA, b. Aug. 23, 1860; m. Dec. 12, 1889, J. Dane Proctor. He was b. Nov., 1860; res. s. p. in Williamsburg; is a druggist.
6293. iv. CLAYTON FRANKLIN, b. July 3, 1868; d. Jan. 13, 1885.

5435. MILTON MOSES FISK (Moses, Moses, Josiah, Nathan, William, Nathan, Nathan, Nathaniel, William, Robert, Simon, Simon, William, Symond), b. Worthington, Mass., May 1, 1834; m. in Conway, Jan. 17, 1865, Maretta M. Miles. b. Mar. 17, 1840. He was brought up on a farm in Worthington, went to school when four years of age, and did work about his father's place. When he was 17 his father moved to Chesterfield. When he was 18 years of age he had a severe sickness and a piece of bone six inches long came out of one of his limbs. He was lame for several years. Later engaged in the retail grocery trade, and after that, about twenty years ago, went into the produce business in Northampton, in which he has been very successful; res. Northampton, Mass.

6294. i. IDA E., b. Jan. 3, 1870; res. at home.
6295. ii. BESSIE S., b. Jan. 27, 1872. She was graduated at Smith College from the musical department.
6296. iii. CHARLES K., b. Apr. 14, 1874; res. at home.
6297. iv. MARVIN MOSES, b. ———; d. in infancy.

5437. JAMES JOSIAH FISKE (Moses, Moses, Josiah, Nathan, William, Nathan, Nathan, Nathaniel, William, Robert, Simon, Simon, William, Symond), b. Worthington, Mass., Jan. 17, 1839; m. at Charlemont, Jan. 15, 1863, Fanny S. Harris, b. Dec. 15, 1838. He is in the express business; res. 13 Union St., Northampton, Mass.

6298. i. GEO. WILBUR, b. June 1, 1868; res. N.
6299. ii. MINNIE LORA, b. June 18, 1872.

5440. MARSHALL O. FISK (Bushrod W., Josiah, Josiah, Nathan. William, Nathan, Nathan, Nathaniel, William, Robert. Simon, Simon, William, Symond), b. Huntington, Mass., Feb. 9, 1839; m. at Blandford, Nov., 1858, Sarah Fidelia Sizer; m. 2d, at Springfield, May 30, 1886, Laura A. Stevens, b. Aug. 15, 1853. He is employed in the United States Armory; res. 219 Tyler St., Springfield, Mass.

6300. i. EMMA F., b. June 23, 1862; m. June 9, 1892, ——— Smith; res. 120 Westminster St., Providence, R. I.

5443. CLINTON E. FISK (Bushrod W., Josiah, Josiah, Nathan, William, Nathan, Nathan, Nathaniel, William, Robert. Simon. Simon, William, Symond), b. Feb. 14, 1852, Huntington, Mass.; m. Dec. 30, 1880, at West Chesterfield, Ida M. Trask, b. May 9, 1863. He is a farmer; res. West Chesterfield, Mass.

6301. i. ROSE IDELLA, b. Apr. 16, 1882, West Chesterfield, Mass.; unm.
6302. ii. WILMER C., b. June 18, 1890, West Chesterfield, Mass.

5445. ISAAC HINCKLY FISK (Bushrod W., Josiah, Josiah, Nathan, William, Nathan, Nathan, Nathaniel, William, Robert, Simon, Simon, William, Symond), b. Huntington, Mass., Feb. 17, 1858; m. Hamptonburg, N. J., Feb. 17, 1880, Fannie Gale Reed, b. July 30, 1859. He is a locomotive fireman on the Boston & Albany Railroad; res. Merrick, Mass.

    6303. i.   EDWIN REED, b. Mar. 28, 1881.
    6304. ii.   LILLIAN AMY, b. Feb. 16, 1883.
    6305. iii.   WALTER MARSHALL, b. Aug. 31, 1885.
    6306. iv.   EDITH LAURA, b. Sept. 12, 1892.
           Add. Merrick, Mass.; living with their parents.

5449. RUFUS H. FISK (Bushrod W., Josiah, Josiah, Nathan, William, Nathan, Nathan, Nathaniel, William, Robert, Simon, Simon, William, Symond), b. May 31, 1844, Huntington, Mass.; m. at Chesterfield, Mass., Mar. 5, 1868, Helen Angeline Bicknell, b. June 30, 1850. He was a millwright. During the late war he served in the Forty-sixth Regiment Massachusetts Volunteer Infantry. He d. Apr. 19, 1896; res. Chesterfield, Mass.

    6307. i.   LEROY EARNEST, b. Oct. 15, 1876. He is a watchmaker's apprentice; res. Keene, N. H.
    6308. ii.   HELEN EVA, b. Mar. 28, 1882; res. C.

5452. JASON H. FISK (Rodney, Josiah, Josiah, Nathan, William, Nathan, Nathaniel, William, Robert, Simon, Simon, William, Symond), b. Nov. 25, 1842, in Huntington, Mass.; m. in Blandford, in 1861, Julia A. Hunter, b. 1841; d. Apr. 1, 1884; m. 2d, July 3, 1884, Augusta Elder, b. Aug. 18, 1856. Jason H. Fisk was one of the prominent business men of Huntington, and died in Northampton. He was born in Huntington and served in the Civil War to the credit of his native town, and was at one time commander of the Grand Army post. He lived several years on a farm in Chester, and while there served three years as selectman, assessor and overseer of the poor, and upon his return to Huntington served several years in the same capacity, also being deputy sheriff of Hampshire and Hampden Counties. He was a large land owner and was engaged in lumbering, owning over one thousand acres and carrying on a steam mill. He was a Democrat in politics and was twice that party's candidate for Representative, and in a district overwhelmingly Republican, polled far more than the party vote. He d. Apr. 10, 1896; res. Chester and Northampton, Mass.

    6309. i.   OTHO H., b. Aug. 29, 1866; m. Julia E. Case.
    6310. ii.   HARLOW J., b. July 5, 1875; res. H.
    6311. iii.   FRED M., b. Jan. 10, 1881; res. H.
    6312. iv.   JASON H., JR., b. Sept. 22, 1882; res. H.
    6313. v.   MARY LUCY, b. July 3, 1865; m. Aug. 18, 1886, Fred Hondish, and died in California Jan. 13, 1891.
    6314. vi.   GUY A., b. Dec. 15, 1885.
    6315. vii.   GRACE A., b. Apr. 18, 1887.
    6316. viii.   RAYMOND H., b. Aug. 18, 1889.
    6317. ix.   WILLIAM KIMBALL, b. May 21, 1892.

5455. DR. HARLO ADONIRAM FISK (Rodney, Josiah, Josiah, Nathan, William, Nathan, Nathan, Nathaniel, William, Robert, Simon, Simon, William, Symond), b. Huntington, Mass., Nov. 19, 1850; m. Nov. 5, 1878, Ella Mara Higgins, b. Sept. 10, 1853. He attended the public schools in Huntington, and two terms at Wilbraham Academy. He studied medicine with Dr. C. C. Cady, of Sennett, N. Y., and in 1877 was graduated in New York City from the College of Physicians and Surgeons, and at once began practice in Chester, Mass., and later located in East Longmeadow, where he has since resided. He is well liked by the citizens and has a most successful practice in that section; res. East Longmeadow, Mass.

    6318. i.   HOWARD H., b. Apr. 18, 1880.
    6319. ii.   MARY G., b. Mar. 15, 1882.
    6320. iii.   HAROLD M., b. Oct. 24, 1884.
    6321. iv.   GRACE E., b. Mar. 10, 1888.

5457. MYRON RODNEY FISKE (Rodney, Josiah, Josiah, Nathan, William, Nathan, Nathan, Nathaniel, William, Robert, Simon, Simon, William, Symond), b. Huntington, Mass., Sept. 8, 1846; m. Chester, Mass., Jan. 29, 1879, Addie Samantha Elder, b. Jan. 29, 1860. He is a lumber dealer and contractor; res. Huntington, Mass.

6322.   i.   ADDIE BEATRICE, b. Dec. 10, 1879.
6323.   ii.   HELEN AUGUSTA, b. Sept. 11, 1881; d. Mar. 4, 1882.
6324.   iii.   FANNY HOWE, b. Feb. 23, 1883.
6325.   iv.   MYRON SPENCER, b. May 25, 1885.
6326.   v.   FAITH LOUISE, b. Aug. 17, 1889.

5466. REV. WILBUR FISK (Josiah, Nathan, Josiah, Nathan, William, Nathan, Nathan, Nathaniel, William, Robert, Simon, Simon, William, Symond), b. Fiskville, Tex., Nov. 10, 1861; m. Oct. 9, 1890, Caroline Elliott Gilmore, b. July 12, 1870. Wilbur Fisk was born in Travis County, Texas. Went with his parents to New Orleans in 1866 and remained there attending school and clerking in a grocery store until the spring of 1881, when he went to Council Bluffs, Pottawattamie County, State of Iowa. There he attended school until the spring of 1882, when he was licensed as a local preacher. In 1883 he joined the Des Moines Methodist Conference and was appointed to take charge of the Council Bluffs circuit until he was permitted to join the Garret Biblical Institute, where he remained until he graduated. He was then transferred from the Des Moines Conference to the Rock River Conference, Illinois. He was appointed to the Yorkville station, which position he filled for five years. At the fall session of that conference he was appointed to take charge of the Hinckley station, in said Rock River Conference, Illinois, at which point he now resides and is giving general satisfaction; res. Hinckley, Ill.

6327.   i.   FLOYD GILMORE, b. Sept. 29, 1891.
6328.   ii.   WENDELL, b. Dec. 13, 1893; d. Sept. 16, 1895.
6329.   iii.   LOUISE, b. Feb. 2, 1895.

5468. FRANK SIBLEY FISK (Joseph, Nathan, Josiah, Nathan, William, Nathan, Nathan, Nathaniel, William, Robert, Simon, Simon, William, Symond), b. Honeoye Falls, N. Y., Jan. 11, 1858; m. Oct. 13, 1880, Elizabeth Jane Dennis, b. Dec. 5, 1861; res. Miller's Corners, Ontario Co., N. Y.

6330.   i.   ALLIE E., b. Sept. 14, 1881.
6331   ii.   EMMA T., b. Mar. 19, 1887.
6332.   iii.   EDITH, b. June 21, 1890; d. Aug. 25, 1890.
6333.   iv.   NETTIE C., b. Dec. 7, 1893.

5478. GREENLEAF FISK (Greenleaf, Nathan, Josiah, Nathan, William, Nathan, Nathan, Nathaniel, William, Robert, Simon, Simon, William, Symond), b. Feb. 14, 1858, Brown Co., Texas; m. there Jan. 10, 1879, Nannie Grogan, b. Aug. 2, 1860. He is a farmer; res. Brownwood, Tex.

6334.   i.   PHILANDER, b. Jan. 11, 1880.
6335.   ii.   W. AUGUSTUS, b. Feb. 21, 1883.
6336.   iii.   M. ETHEL, b. Nov. 27, 1885.
6337.   iv.   FRANK GROGAN, b. Aug. 21, 1888.
6338.   v.   HELEN M., b. Sept. 20, 1890.

5486. CAPT. SMITH WILBUR FISKE (Abram C., Nathan, Josiah, Nathan, William, Nathan, Nathan, Nathaniel, William, Robert, Simon, Simon, William, Symond), b. Coldwater, Mich., Apr. 4, 1839; m. there May 7, 1863, Mary Northan Androus, b. Ann Arbor, Mich., Sept. 27, 1842. He was born in Coldwater, Mich., where he was raised on a farm until he was 18 years old. At that age he went to Albion, Mich., to college to finish his education, after which he was employed in the Coldwater postoffice and bank for several years, in 1859-60. In 1861 came the firing upon Fort Sumter, the tocsin of a "wicked and gigantic rebellion." The loyal young men of Michigan sprang to arms. Mr. Fiske was among the first to join the Coldwater cadets, a militia company already organized. Within a few hours after that eventful 12th of April, the cadets were drilling daily in the public square, cheered and encouraged by the admiring eyes of hundreds who gathered around them. The cadets were soon accepted and became Company C of the First Michigan Infantry. After a short stop in Detroit they were hurried on to Washington, which they reached May 16, where they were welcomed by the cheers of hundreds, as they were the first western regiment to reach the capitol. They made the first advance across the Long Bridge, driving in the rebel pickets,

CAPT. SMITH WILBUR FISKE.

taking possesion of Alexandria May 24, the ill-fated Ellsworth reaching it by stream at about the same hour. After the shooting of Ellsworth, the Michigan men helped the enraged zouaves in despoiling the Marshall House, where the tragic affair occurred, and Mr. Fiske has still in his possession a piece of gilded frame of a mirror, which he carried away as a memento of the affair. July found the Michigan boys still at the front; and Mr. Fiske writes to the home folks from Little Rocky Run, Va., under date of July 20, "that they are only six miles from Manassas Junction, within two and a half miles from the enemy's strongest fortification, that they are expecting orders to move at any moment, and all are in readiness. They would probably go forward that night, and the supposition was that a great battle would soon take place." He was right. They did move that night, and when daylight came, it was the morning of that terrible Sunday, July 21, when our newly united troops fought the great battle of Manassas, or Bull Run, which ended in a complete panic and rout of the Union forces and a retreat on Washington. The First Michigan was in the thickest of the fight and lost heavily. Many of the Coldwater boys were killed or missing. Clinton B. Fisk, afterward a well known General, wrote from Washington, on July 23, of saved and missing, and mentioned Smith Fiske as having a slight injury to one knee. Mr. Fiske became First Lieutenant in the Nineteenth Michigan Infantry early in 1862, but was obliged to resign June, 1863, on account of severe illness. But two months later we find him recruiting for the Ninth Michigan Cavalry, which was organized at Coldwater, Mich., and he became First Lieutenant of Company K. He left for Kentucky with his regiment May 20, having been married to Miss Mary N. Androus May 7. He left his bride with the promise that if possible he would send for her. They remained in camp near Hickman Bridge for three weeks, Mrs. Fiske reaching there a few hours before they broke camp. She saw him again for a few moments July 4 at Stamford. Then the regiment disappeared and their friends knew nothing of their whereabouts for nearly three weeks, except that they were in chase of General Morgan and his southern guerrillas, who were carrying terror into the homes of Kentucky, Indiana and Ohio. Mrs. Fiske not being able to hear from her husband, finally went on to Cincinnati, hoping that there she might gain news of his whereabouts. All was confusion, marshal law having been proclaimed, and many troops massed around the city. On July 24 the Ninth Regiment cavalry reached Covington and camped in pleasant quarters, and on that same Friday afternoon Mrs. Fiske found a boarding place within a short walk of camp, and they hoped now to be together for a few days at least. At 4 a. m., July 25, the regiment again departed, Lieutenant Fiske being in command of Company K, supposing they were going out on picket duty around Cincinnati. And that was the last Mrs. Fiske knew of their movements, until Sunday at 8 p. m. she received the following telegram from Surgeon Nash at Salineville, O.: "Lieutenant Smith Fiske is dangerously wounded. Come at once." Taking a train at Cincinnati that same evening at 10 Mrs. Fiske reached her husband's side on Monday at 6 p. m.. But to go back to the regiment: When they left camp Saturday morning they were hurried into box cars and taken as rapidly as possible to northeast Ohio to cut off Morgan's retreat. Morgan, being tracked, was soon overtaken, when skirmishing commenced and continued until dark, with some loss in wounded, driving the enemy during the entire night. On the morning of the 26th, Morgan being flanked and hard pressed, was forced into an engagement, which resulted, after a severe fight of an hour and a half, in the complete rout of his forces, with a loss of 23 killed, 44 wounded and 305 prisoners, while the detachment of the Ninth lost in wounded Lieutenant Fiske and 7 men. The pursuit was continued, Morgan flying in confusion, until, meeting with the forces under General Shackelford a few hours later, he surrendered. Lieutenant Fiske was shot in the breast about 8 a. m., the bullet going through the body, stopping just below the skin, where it was cut out. It missed his heart by half an inch, passing through the lower part of the lung. He was soon carried to a neighboring farm house, and the wound dressed by the Surgeon, he being the only officer injured in the skirmish. Surgeon Nash met Mrs. Fiske Monday evening at the station and took her out to Mr. Sharp's farm. As they reached the locality of the fight it seemed like a gala day, as hundreds had come from near and far to see what was to be seen. As one of them said, he never had a chance to see a wounded man before—and he an officer. There were at least two or three hundred men, women and children crowded around the house, pressing into doors and windows. It was a terribly hot July day. The Lieutenant was lying in the wing of a log house, the room and yard full. The bed itself was surrounded by a number of young girls busy fanning and waiting upon him, while he was gasping for want of air. Six long weeks they remained in that log house. The hot, dusty August days were very trying, with no blinds or shades to the widows, and the walls and bedstead filled with bed bugs. It was not until six weeks that Lieutenant Fiske began to improve, in spite of the doctors, who insisted that he would not live, and the middle of September found him strong enough to be put on a bed and carried to the town, four miles away, where he was gladly welcomed to the best house in the village, the home of Mr. Nickerson. They gave up the parlor for their use, and showered upon them kindnesses of all kinds. Mrs. Fiske says she will never forget how good that first supper tasted, the first good meal she had had in many weeks. When Mr. Fiske was able to talk he had many visitors from the surrounding farms, all anxious to see and hear him tell of his experiences. He vividly remembers one man who spent an hour or two in telling him how he appreciated his bravery, and finally, on his leaving, presenting him with a silver half dollar as a token of his regard. Bread and cake were brought from twenty and thirty miles, and at one time Mrs. Fiske said she had the bureau drawer full of such tokens. The days passed swiftly, and late in September they were able to reach Cleveland and take the boat for Detroit, from whence by rail to Coldwater, which they reached early in October. In November, 1863, on account of disability he resigned, and was then appointed postmaster in Coldwater, Mich., which he held until the Democratic administration took charge, after which he was a merchant in the boot and shoe business until 1877 at Coldwater, Mich., when he sold out and afterward went into the wholesale boot and shoe business at Sherman, Tex., remaining there two years, selling out in 1879. In 1880 he moved to Minneapolis, Minn., with his family, where he connected himself with the W. S. Nott Company, wholesale rubber boot, shoe, belting and clothing business, remaining up to the present time; res. Minneapolis, Minn.

6339. i. HARRY TAFT, b. Feb. 14, 1865; res. Chicago, Ill. He was born at Coldwater, Mich., where he attended the public schools until 1885, in the spring of which year he removed to California, and there remained in business until 1889, when he went to Minneapolis, Minn., and was in the employ of Bradstreet, Thurber & Co., general house furnishers and decorators, which is his business—decorating and draperies. He is at the present time in Chicago following that vocation.

6340. ii. DOUGLASS A., b. Feb. 2, 1867; m. Alice V. Torrance.

6341. iii. WILBUR CANFIELD, b. June 16, 1871; m. Nov., 1894, Florence Leopold. He was born in Coldwater, Mich. He attended the public schools at Coldwater, Mich., until the family moved to Minneapolis in the spring of 1885. He attended the high school at that city, from which he graduated with honors in the year 1890. After that he entered the University of Minnesota and completed his sophomore year. Since that time he has been in the employ of the W. S. Nott Company as cashier, a wholesale jobbing house of Minneapolis.

5495. AMOS KIDDER FISKE (Henry, Asa, Aaron, Asa, Nathaniel, Nathaniel, Nathan, Nathaniel, William, Robert, Simon, Simon, William, Symond), b. Whitefield, N. H., May 12, 1842; m. Oct. 27, 1870, Caroline Child, of Cambridge,

AMOS KIDDER FISKE.

Mass. Amos Kidder Fiske was born in Whitefield, N. H., May 12, 1842. His early years were spent partly on a rough farm in Whitefield and partly in the factory village of Peterboro, N. H., in poverty and hard work. At the age of 16 he found himself without parents or guardian and without a dollar, but with much ambition and little education. He worked in a cotton mill in Peterboro in order to earn money to go to school, and in the spring of 1860 went to Appleton Academy, New Ipswich, N. H. By dint of hard work and study, and extreme energy, earning most of his expenses, was prepared for college in two years; entered Harvard in 1862, borrowing $50 to go to Cambridge, and get a foothold; got through with help of scholarships and other aids with a little borrowing, and was graduated in 1866 summa cum laude, being also class poet of the year. In the autumn of 1866 came to New York, with borrowed money and letters of introduction, including one from George Ticknor to George Ticknor Curtis. Spent first year mostly in private tutoring and got even with the world; then entered law office of Sargent T. Fay, with which Mr. Curtis

was connected as counsel; was admitted to the bar in a year, in the meantime and for a year afterward assisting Mr. Curtis in the preparation of his life of Daniel Webster; did all the collecting, sifting and arranging of material, and preparing it to the hand of the author, etc.; also became contributor the same year (1867) to the Annual Cyclopaedia, and kept it up for fifteen years or so. In 1869 abandoned law for journalism and entered the office of the New York Times in September, during brief reign of John Bigelow, after the death of Raymond. He was married, Oct. 27, 1870, to Caroline Child, of Cambridge, Mass., youngest sister of Prof. Francis J. Child. At the beginning of 1872 he went to the Evening Mail as associate editor, under the late J. M. Bundy, and in the spring of 1874 to Boston, as leading editorial writer on the Daily Globe. In 1878 he returned to New York and joined the staff of the Times, where he has been ever since, writing editorials. He has contributed occasionally to Harper's Weekly, and had two or three articles in the Forum, one on the "Remedies of Municipal Misgovernment." He has also written two books. "Midnight Talks at the Club" (Fords, Howard & Hulbert, 1890), and "Beyond the Bourne" (same publishers, 1891). His children were educated in private schools in New York City until 1888, when his son, Philip Sidney, b. Sept. 7, 1872, was ready for college. The family then went to Cambridge to live. The girls entered "Cambridge school," a private institution in charge of Arthur Gilmer, and devoted to preparing students for the "Harvard Annex," now Radcliffe College. His son's health broke down in the fall of 1891, and he took him on a three months' trip to the south, Cuba, Mexico, and the Pacific coast, after which he served an apprenticeship in journalism, as a reporter in the Times office until the summer of 1893, when he returned to college, and completed his course in June, 1894. For the year past has been working on newspapers in Boston, but is not definitely settled. His daughter, Annette, born Oct. 13, 1873, entered the "Annex" (society for the collegiate instruction of women, which became Radcliffe College in 1893-4) in 1890, graduated 1894, magna cum laude, but continued there as a graduate student and intends to remain another year. His daughter Marguerite, born Jan. 28, 1876, entered "Annex" as "special student" in 1892, devoting herself chiefly to modern languages, and will continue another year on same footing. Special students do not take regular degree. Res. New York, N. Y., care The Century, 7 W. 43d St.

6342. i.   PHILIP SIDNEY, b. Sept. 7, 1872. He is connected with the Youth's Companion, in the business department in Boston, Mass.

6343. ii.   ANNETTE, b. Oct. 13, 1873.

6344. iii. MARGUERITE, b. Jan. 28, 1876.

5498. WILBUR F. FISK (Henry, Asa, Aaron, Asa, Nathaniel, Nathaniel, Nathan, Nathaniel, William, Robert, Simon, Simon, William, Symond), b. Lunenburg, Vt., Sept. 10, 1834; m. May 9, 1867, Sarah M. Townsend, b. Sept. 9, 1847. He was born in Lunenburg, Vt., and christened and named for the celebrated Methodist preacher, Wilbur Fisk. When five years of age he moved with parents to Whitefield, N. H., and remained there until his removal to the west village in Peterboro in Dec., 1851. Returning to Vermont he remained a short time, and in the spring of 1857 started west and located in Minnesota. In 1865, in February, he enlisted in the First Minnesota Heavy Artillery, and went to Chattanooga, Tenn., where he was stationed; was mustered out of the service at Nashville the last of September the same year, and was discharged at Fort Snelling Oct. 9, 1865. He located a claim near Stillwater, Minn., when he first went west, and on his return from the war went back on his farm where he has since resided. Both his daughters are advance course graduates of the Minnesota State Normal School at St. Cloud. They stood very high in their classes and are both now engaged in teaching; res. Clear Water, Minn.

6345. i.   L. ESTELLA, b. Oct. 18, 1868.

6346. ii.   S. EMILY, b. July 29, 1871.

5502. FRANCIS WINSLOW FISK (Henry, Asa, Aaron, Asa, Nathaniel, Nathaniel, Nathan, Nathaniel, William, Robert, Simon, Simon, William, Symond), b. Whitefield, N. H., May 12, 1849; m. May 31, 1875, at Bellows Falls, Vt., Mary Jane Yardly, of Harrisville, N. H., b. June 10, 1851. Francis Winslow Fisk was born at Whitefield, N. H.; moved to West Peterboro, N. H., in 1858, residing there until 1863; removed to Harrisville, formerly Nelson, N. H., residing there until Sept., 1868; attended Appleton Academy, New Ipswich, one term in the fall of 1867; entered Phillips Exeter Academy, Sept., 1869, taking the regular course, which at that time was completed in three years; graduated in June, 1871, the class being known as the class of P. E. A., '71. In Sept., 1871, entered Amherst College, Amherst, Mass., being a member of the class known as the class of '75; attended this college until Feb. 9, 1875; entered the employ of Ginn Bros., publishers, of Boston, Mass.; married in the Immanuel Church of Bellows Falls, Vt.; removed to Springfield, Mass., and in Oct., 1877, removed to Westfield, Mass.; studied law in the office of H. W. Ely, of Westfield, Mass.; was admitted to the Hampden County bar in June, 1881; practiced law in Westfield, Mass., until Oct., 1883, at which time a trip was taken to Bismarck, N. D., returning to Minneapolis, Minn., in June, 1884; removed family to Minneapolis in July, 1884, where he still resides.

6347. i.   FLORENCE ETHELYNE, b. Feb. 26, 1876.

6348. ii.   NINA MAE, b. May 1, 1878.

6349. iii. EDITH BELLE, b. Nov. 9, 1880.

6350. iv. MAUD ESTELLA, b. Feb. 13, 1883.

6351. v.   HENRY NELSON, b. Apr. 12, 1885.

6352. vi. BLANCHE GERTRUDE, b. May 12, 1889.

5505. HAZEN W. FISKE (Ralph, Asa, Aaron, Asa, Nathaniel, Nathaniel, Nathan, Nathaniel, William, Robert, Simon, Simon, William, Symond), b. Dalton, N. H., Mar. 3, 1833; m. June 15, 1862, Martha Ann Chase; res. Whitefield, N. H.

6353. i.   MARY LOUISE, b. Mar. 29, 1870; m. Oct. 15, 1891, Fred W. Aldrich.

5516. WILLIAM C. FISK (Frederick, Asa, Aaron, Asa, Nathaniel, Nathaniel, Nathan, Nathaniel, William, Robert, Simon, Simon, William, Symond), b. Whitefield, N. H., Mar. 14, 1833; m. Feb. 20, 1855, Lydia Rowell; d. Apr., 1874; m. 2d, Sept. 17, 1876, Hannah Gardner; res. Groveton, N. H.

6354. i.   NELLIE F., b. Apr. 15, 1856; d. Sept. 20, 1877.
6355. ii.   EDWARD W., b. Aug. 28, 1863; m. Maggie Brown; one child, res. Lancaster, N. H.

5534. GEN. WILLIAM OSCAR FISKE (William, Aaron, Aaron, Asa, Nathaniel, Nathaniel, Nathan, Nathaniel, William, Robert, Simon, Simon, William, Symond), b. Lowell, Mass., June 4, 1836; m. Nov., 1871, Mary Augusta Fielding, b. May 8, 1848; d. Apr. 19, 1876; m. 2d, June, 1882, Mrs. Fox; res. Saratoga, N. Y. William Oscar Fiske was son of William Fiske. The brick house in which he was born was built by his father and is still standing at the corner of Andover and Fayette Streets. He was educated in the Lowell schools and at the Merrimack Normal Institute at Reeds Ferry, N. H. His first business experience was with the produce firm of A. L. Waite & Co., of which he became a member. Subsequently he engaged in similar business in Boston, and it was in this pursuit that the Civil War found him in 1861. He entered the service as First Lieutenant on the 16th of April of that year, on the staff of Gen. B. F. Butler, and served during the three months' campaign in the vicinity of Fortress Monroe, and took part in the engagements at Big Bethel and Hatteras Inlet. The unfortunate differences between Governor Andrew and General Butler during the war will be well remembered by all who were not in their infancy in those days. The Governor refused to recognize General Butler's appointments and consequently the commission of First Lieutenant of a company, which the deceased was then given by General Butler was not recognized by the State; and in the official report of the affair at Hatteras Inlet, where Captain Fiske swam ashore from the vessel to carry a despatch from General Butler to the commander of the land forces, he is mentioned with approbation as "Mr. Fiske of Massachusetts." A contemporary edition of Harper's Weekly contained an account, with illustration, of this exploit, and the young hero was thenceforth famous. The papers of that time mention him as the most distinguished of the Massachusetts men, save Gen. Butler. Returning to Massachusetts with General Butler, he was appointed Assistant Quartermaster-General, for the department of New England, with headquarters at Camp Chase (fair grounds, Lowell). While at home he was presented with a regulation sword, belt and saddle by his grateful fellow-citizens. Here he remained till the command was ordered south to the Department of the Gulf. At Ship Island he was transferred to the command of Gen. George F. Shepley, as Commissary of Subsistence with the rank of Captain, which was his first recognized commission, after having served nine months without pay. In this capacity he acted a portion of the time while General Shepley was Military Governor of Louisiana. During his official career he was under a West Point officer, who was noted rather for querulousness than ability, and Captain Fiske, with other officers of the department, was subject to an investigation, which, in his case, resulted in bringing him very high commendation instead of censure. When General Butler received authority to recruit and raise troops in Louisiana, Captain Fiske was assigned to the United States barracks, in New Orleans, as Quartermaster and Commissary for that post, which was the recruiting station of the department. He was subsequently commissioned as Major of the First Louisiana Regiment, which was the first Union white regiment raised in any of the Confederate States. The regiment took an active part in most of the engagements in that department. Donaldsonville, Irish Bend, Port Hudson, Cox's Plantation, Mansura, Francesville, and the battlefields of the Red River campaign—all were crimsoned with their blood. He was wounded in the leg while engaged in forcing a landing in the engagement at Irish Bend, Grand Lake, near Bayou Teche, during the first advance on Port Hudson under General Banks. Against the advice of the surgeon he left the hospital and went on to the field. Almost the first thing that met his eye was the dead body of Colonel Holcomb, of Connecticut, his own commanding officer, who had been killed while leading his troops in the brave and famous attempt that was made to storm the enemy's works that day. Colonel Fiske's brother, Maj. E. A. Fiske, of Lawrence, took part in same engagement. After this (June 15, 1863) the Lowell boy was commissioned Colonel, and during the Red River campaign, he commanded the Second Brigade, Nineteenth Army Corps, a part of the time. An act of special importance and bravery was his recapture of guns from Gen. Dick Taylor. During his long service he was absent from duty but thirty days. March 13, 1865, he was breveted Brigadier-General of volunteers for gallant and meritorious conduct.

In all these years of military service his bearing was such as to command the love of his soldiers and respect of all officers. When he returned to New Orleans on business after the close of the war he was tendered a banquet at the St. Charles Hotel, with every mark of respect due to a distinguished person. When he was mustered out he returned to Lowell and as soon as the congratulations of his rejoicing friends would allow him, he engaged in business, his first venture being the southern lumber business, in which the late Josiah B. Fielding was his partner. The firm name was "Fielding & Fiske." This, however, was short-lived, for in June, 1871, Mr. Fielding having died, the old firm of J. B. Fielding & Co. was succeeded by the present well-known house of Fiske & Spalding. General Fiske was a very public-spirited man, though the only civil office he ever held was that of Councilman in 1869 and 1870. His first rate executive ability made him always in demand whenever any charitable or social enterprise or public demonstration of any magnitude was proposed. Besides being a member of Kilwinning Lodge, F. & A. M., and Pilgrim Commandery, K. T., and of the Loyal Legion, he was one of the charter members of B. F. Butler Post, No. 42, G. A. R., and was commander of the post. In 1870 he was junior vice-commander of the department of Massachusetts, G. A. R. He was appointed Assistant Quartermaster-General on the staff of Governor Talbot in 1879, and aide-de-camp to Governor Long in 1880, each time with the rank of Colonel. In society he was a favorite, where his modesty, urbanity, good fellowship and probity were appreciated. Even the above meager account of his military exploits proves that his was not an ordinary career. He was born a soldier, and gave ample evidence of all those qualities which go to make up a successful commander. He won every title that was bestowed upon him, and that of Brigadier-General is no meaningless compliment. Those who were in the war will remember with what frequency his name appeared in print in those days. In his private life he was upright and honorable, and in business he has been blessed with the same success which characterized his operations upon the field of battle. He d. Feb. 2, 1886; res. Lowell, Mass.

6356. i. JULIA HUDSON, b. Aug. 9, 1873; res. 172 So. Broadway, Saratoga Springs, N. Y.

6357. ii. JOSIAH FIELDING, b. July 30, 1875; res. L.

5535. MAJOR EDWARD AMBROSE FISKE (William, Aaron, Aaron, Asa, Nathaniel, Nathaniel, Nathan, Nathaniel, William, Robert, Simon, Simon, William, Symond), b. Lowell, Mass., Nov. 22, 1838; m. at Lawrence, June 20, 1883, Lizzie Crosby Dana, b. Jan. 11, 1855. Major Fiske was born in Lowell and there spent his early days. He was the son of William Fiske, of that city, and a brother of Gen. W. O. Fiske. When the Civil War broke out deceased was 23 years old, and was exploring timber lands in Canada, one hundred miles north of Montreal. Hearing that his country's flag had been assailed by traitor's hands, he set out at once for home and arriving in Lowell at noon time of a September day, 1861, he made his way at once to the recruiting office. Here he was rejected, as he was below the required height. That night he sought out a shoemaker and ordered two thicknesses of leather to be placed on his shoes. Returning next day to the recruiting office, he was again rejected, but seemed so anxious to go to the front that after a while he was passed and sent to Camp Chase with the nucleus of a regiment. Company B, to which Private Fiske was attached, had been recruited by Captain Blanchard. On Sept. 5, 1861, the company was mustered in. Deceased was elected Second Lieutenant Nov. 27, 1861, and advanced to First Lieutenant Aug. 21, 1862. The company was made a part of the Thirtieth Massachusetts Regiment and was dispatched with that regiment for service on the Gulf. On Oct. 21, 1862, Lieutenant Fiske was promoted to Captain and with his company engaged in service at New Orleans, and subsequently was ordered up the river to Baton Rouge. During the siege of Vicksburg his regiment did duty on the river. The rebel gunboat Arkansas was near by and doing a great deal of damage. Two Union gunboats were ordered in pursuit and Captain Fiske had charge of one. A conflict resulted and raged for six hours. During that time the Captain, pistol in hand, stood by the pilot house, directing the movement of the gunboat. Men were falling on all sides, but he bravely held his position until the battle closed. Later his regiment was ordered up the Red River to join Gen. Banks' expedition. He was placed in charge of the commissary department but as he was anxious to get to the front he was placed on General Berge's staff. During the campaign two horses were shot from beneath him. On the last occasion his horse fell upon his sword and pinned down, he was compelled to cut his straps and flee for his life. Being sent to Washington on business, he was granted a furlough home and was presented by friends with two beautiful swords. Returning to his regiment he took an active part in the closing engagements of the war, and on Feb. 17, 1865, was breveted Major for gallant services on the field. His term of services lasted four years and four months. At the close of the war the Major leased a plantation in South Carolina, investing several thousand dollars. Sectional hatred was rampant in that locality, and before the first crop was harvested he sought more peaceful quarters in the north, being threatened with death if he persisted in remaining. He left for Pennsylvania and in 1868 came to Lawrence, where he engaged in the business, which he conducted in person until disease, which has now caused his death, fastened upon him two years before. He was a member of the Loyal Legion of Massachusetts, of Bethany Commandery Knights Templar, and Tuscan Lodge of Masons. He was commander of Needham Post, Grand Army, in 1870, and was instrumental, more than any other man, in raising funds for and erecting the beautiful soldiers' monument on the common. No braver soldier, more discreet and capable officer went from Massachusetts into the service of the country; no truer comrade of the Grand Army, with deeper, more constant devotion to the interests of all who had defended the flag, ever lived in that city; no more generous hearted, open handed, public spirited citizen, has blessed any community; a more unselfish, steadfast, self-sacrificing friend, has not been born or lived in this generation than Major Edward A. Fiske. He d. Dec. 28, 1887; res. s. p. 7 East Haverhill St., Lawrence, Mass.

5538. HENRY BREWER FISKE (George W., Aaron, Aaron, Asa, Nathaniel, Nathaniel, Nathan, Nathaniel, William, Robert, Simon, Simon, William, Symond), b. Lowell, Mass., Dec. 29, 1842; m. at Washington, D. C., June 17, 1884, Lizzie Hollinger, b. July 6, 1850. He is a lumber merchant and his Boston office is at 27 Kilby Street; res. Winthrop, Mass.
    6358. i.   STARR HOLLINGER, b. Oct. 31, 1885.

5546. ELLIOTT HOBART FISKE (Larned P., Abel, Aaron, Asa, Nathaniel, Nathaniel, Nathan, Nathaniel, William, Robert, Simon, Simon, William, Symond), b. Chicopee, Mass., Dec. 29, 1848; m. at Granby, Mass., Mar. 30, 1871, Mary J. Church, b. Dec. 13, 1845. He is a farmer; res. Granby, Mass.
    6359. i.   ARTHUR W., b. Mar. 13, 1872; m. June 6, 1893; res. Granby.

5547. HOMER PRESTON FISKE (Larned P., Abel, Aaron, Asa, Nathaniel, Nathaniel, Nathan, Nathaniel, William, Robert, Simon, Simon, William, Symond), b. Granby, Mass., June 13, 1852; m. at Chicopee, May 12, 1875, Glendora Louisa Roberts, b. Aug. 23, 1853. His early life was spent in his native town. He received his limited education in the district schools, with two terms at the grammar school and one term at Burnett's Classical Institute, Springfield, Mass. He worked in his native town at farming until 1884, when he removed to Chicopee, Mass., where he learned the trade of case hardening, at which he worked until Dec. 21, 1888, when he was scalded by the explosion of a soda kettle by which he was laid up for twenty months, and nearly lost the use of his right arm, after which he went to work for C. H. Morton, as manager of the Scrap Iron and Metals Yard at Holyoke, Mass. In 1894 he bought out the business at Holyoke, Mass.; res. Chicopee, Mass.
    6360. i.   HUBERT HARTWELL, b. June 4, 1876.
    6361. ii.   RALPH FINLEY, b. Feb. 1, 1880.

5548. ARTHUR W. FISKE (Larned P., Abel, Aaron, Asa, Nathaniel, Nathaniel, Nathan, Nathaniel, William, Robert, Simon, Simon, William, Symond), b. Granby, Mass., Apr. 15, 1855; m. at Amherst, Aug. 27, 1884, Abbie Warren Taylor, b. May 2, 1854. His early life was spent in his native town receiving the education obtained in the public schools. In the fall of 1874 he entered Monson Academy, Monson, Mass., where he graduated in 1876; entered Williams College in fall of 1876. In fall of 1877 transferred his college relations to Amherst College, Amherst, Mass., where he was graduated in 1880. For the next five years he spent most of the time employed in teaching. Since that time he has spent his time farming in his native town, doing some work as a private tutor; res. Granby, Mass.
    6362. i.   WILMOT TAYLOR, b. June 6, 1888.
    6363. ii.   WINIFRED WHITE, b. June 6, 1888.

5550. WILLIAM A. FISKE (Abner, Abel, Aaron, Asa, Nathaniel, Nathaniel, Nathan, Nathaniel, William, Robert, Simon, Simon, William, Symond), b. Chicopee, Mass., Nov. 2, 1839; m. at Chicopee, Apr. 4, 1866, Mrs. Ellen M. (Fiske) Bartlett, b. July 4, 1840. He is a carpenter and builder; res. New London, Conn.

    6364. i.   ADDIE C. BARTLETT, b. Dec. 18, 1861; res. N. L.
    6365. ii. AGNES C., b. Feb. 5, 1868; d. Aug. 28, 1868.
    6366. iii. CARRIE E., b. July 10, 1872; d. June 27, 1874.
    6367. iv. CLIFFORD C., b. Aug. 9, 1876.

5555. SAMUEL ELMER FISK (John L., Abel, Aaron, Asa, Nathaniel, Nathaniel, Nathan, Nathaniel, William, Robert, Simon, Simon, William, Symond), b. Oct. 31, 1861, Jacksonville, Ill.; m. in New York City, Apr. 1, 1886, Emma M. Ford, b. Jan. 23, 1859. He is a cycle manufacturer; res. New York, N. Y., 194 Lewis St., s. p.

5561. FRANK ELMER FISK (Foster A., Levi, Aaron, Asa, Nathaniel, Nathaniel, Nathan, Nathaniel, William, Robert, Simon, Simon, William, Symond), b. Ellisville, Ill., Feb. 23, 1860; m. in Shenandoah, Ia., Sept. 12, 1882, Ella A. Humphrey, b. Nov. 16, 1862. He is a druggist; was graduated at a regular school of pharmacy, and owns a drug store at 750 West Harrison St.; res. Chicago, Ill., 324 Hermitage Ave.

    6368. i.   FRANK BYRON, b. June 27, 1883.
    6369. ii. ZOE ELLA, b. Aug. 18, 1886.
    6370. iii. EULAH MAUD, b. Feb. 6, 1890.
    6371. iv. RALPH WALDO, b. May 15, 1892; d. May 17, 1892.

5562. GEORGE LAWRENCE FISK (Foster A., Levi, Aaron, Asa, Nathaniel, Nathaniel, Nathan, Nathaniel, William, Robert, Simon, Simon, William, Symond), b. Ellisville, Ill., Mar. 10, 1863; m. at Deerfield, Ill., Sept. 9, 1885, Martha J. Weaver, b. Apr. 12, 1861. He is a tinner and hardware merchant; res. Prairie City, Ill.

    6372. i. ALVAH COURT, b. Jan. 3, 1887.
    6373. ii. ERROL CARL, b. Feb. 20, 1892.

5582. JOHN ELIOT FISKE (Charles E., Samuel, Moses, Nathaniel, Nathaniel, Nathan, Nathaniel, William, Robert, Simon, Simon, William, Symond), b. Natick, Mass., Apr. 6. 1841; m. June 17, 1865, Mary Brigham; res. Los Angeles, Cal.

    6374. i.   SAMUEL, b. June 15, 1866.
    6375. ii. DANA, b. Oct. 14, 1867.
    6376. iii. AGNES, b. Jan. 24, 1872.

5583. HON. JOSEPH EMERY FISKE (Emery, Moses, Moses, Moses, Nathaniel, Nathaniel, Nathan, Nathaniel, Jeffrey, Robert, Simon, Simon, William, Symond), b. Needham, Mass., Oct. 23, 1839; m. June 1, 1869, Ellen M. Ware, dau. of Dexter and Mary C. (Smith) Ware, b. 1841; d. Jan. 17, 1871; m. 2d, June 5, 1872, Abby Sawyer Hastings, of Sterling. His wife, after a loving short twenty-two years, died Mar. 16, 1894, greatly loved and respected by her neighbors and townspeople. Joseph Emery Fiske, son of Emery, was born in Wellesley (then Needham, Mass.), where he still resides in the house in which he was born. He went to district school till 1852, then for two terms to school in Falmouth, fitting finally for college at school of N. T. Allen, West Newton, 1855-7. He entered Harvard University, 1857, graduating 1861. He entered Andover Theological Seminary, 1861, remaining one year, then entered the Forty-third Regiment Massachusetts Volunteers, serving as orderly sergeant till May, 1862, when he received commission of Second Lieutenant in Second Regiment Massachusetts Artillery, then Aug., First Lieutenant, Oct., Captain. Served in Virginia and North Carolina; captured at Plymouth, N. C., 1864, by rebel ram Albemarle; was in prison at Andersonville, Macon, Savannah, Charleston, Columbia, till Feb. 16, 1865, when he escaped. He served on the staff of Gen. F. P. Blair, commanding the Seventeenth Army Corps. Was mustered out May 15, 1865, at the close of the war. He returned to Andover, and finished the course, graduating in 1867, but did not follow the profession. He remained with his father till his death, after a

89

HON. JOSEPH EMERY FISKE.

prolonged illness. His business has been confined to real estate transactions. He was Selectman of Needham from 1873 to 1877. On the board of school committee of Needham and Wellesley, 1876-1894. On water board, Wellesley, 1893-1895, and in various other town offices. He was Representative in the lower branch of Massachusetts Legislature, in 1874, serving on general important committees. He was a member of the Senate of Massachusetts for the two years of 1876 and 1877. In 1890 he, with his wife and daughters, spent the summer in Europe, and 1892 all spent the summer in England visiting the birthplace of the Fiske family, in Suffolk, where many of the family still live; res. Wellesley Farms, Mass.

 6377. i. ELLEN WARE, b. Jan. 14, 1871. She was graduated at Wellesley College, in 1892.

 6378. ii. ISABELLA HOWE, b. Apr. 29, 1874. She is now, 1895, in the senior class at Wellesley College.

 6379. iii. ABBY HASTINGS, b. Apr. 29, 1874; d. Oct. 12, 1874.

 5597. JOHN MALLORY FISKE (Aaron, Moses, Moses, Moses, Nathaniel, Nathaniel, Nathan, Nathaniel, Jeffrey, Robert, Simon, Simon, William, Symond), b. Natick, Mass., Mar. 26, 1845; m. at Andover, Sept. 25, 1867, Mary Tyer, b. Aug. 24, 1838. He is a hardware merchant; res. Natick, Mass.

 6380. i. ELLEN LOUISA, b. June 13, 1869.

 6381. ii. HENRY GEORGE, b. Bangor, Me., June 25, 1872; unm.; is a rubber merchant in Bangor, Me.

 6382. iii. FRANK, b. Aug. 12, 1874; d. Jan. 20, 1879.

 5599. REV. HERBERT FRANKLIN FISK, D. D. (Franklin, Moses, Moses, Moses, Nathaniel, Nathaniel, Nathan, Nathaniel, Jeffrey, Robert, Simon, Simon, William, Symond), b. in Stoughton, Mass., Sept. 25, 1840; m. July 11, 1866, Anna Green, of Portageville. Herbert F. Fisk was born in Stoughton, Mass.; prepared for college at Wesleyan Academy, Wilbraham, Mass.; entered Wesleyan University, Middletown, Conn., 1856, and was graduated, A. B., in 1860; received from Wesleyan University A. M., in 1863, and D. D. in 1888. In 1860-61 teacher of Latin and Mathematics, Delaware Literary Institute, Franklin, Delaware Co., N. Y.; 1861-63, principal of Shelburne Academy, Vermont; 1863-67, teacher of Latin and Greek, Cazenovia Seminary, N. Y.; 1867-68, teacher of Latin and Greek, Wesleyan Academy, Wilbraham, Mass.; 1868-73, principal of Genesee Wesleyan Seminary, Lima, N. Y.; 1873-88, principal of the Academy of Northwestern University, Evanston, Ill.; since 1888, professor of Pedagogics in Northwestern University, and principal of the Academy; res. Evanston, Ill.

REV. HERBERT FRANKLIN FISK.

 6383. i. AURORA THOMPSON, b. Wilbraham, Mass., Feb. 4, 1868; gr. A. B., Northwestern University, 1890; m. June 18, 1892, Charles Zeublin, now assistant professor in the University of Chicago.

 6384. ii. ELLEN GREEN, b. Apr. 24, 1875; res. Evanston, Ill.

 5600. EVERETT OLIN FISK, A. M. (Franklin, Moses, Moses, Moses, Nathaniel, Nathaniel, Nathan, Nathaniel, Jeffrey, Robert, Simon, Simon, William,

Symond), b. Marlboro, Mass., Aug. 1, 1850; m. Sept. 12, 1882, Helen Chase Steele, b. Sept. 1, 1855. Everett O. Fisk, president of the Fisk Teachers' Agency, now holds an almost pre-eminent position among those who are advancing the interests of education. In the two years following his graduation from the Wesleyan University, Mr. Fisk taught in Connecticut, after which he became New England agent of the publishing firm of Ginn & Co., a position in which he gained an enviable reputation for conscientious work. The Fisk Teachers' Agency was established in Boston, in 1885, and subsequently offices were located in New York, Chicago, Washington, Los Angeles, Minneapolis, and Toronto. Through his capacity as president of this organization, Mr. Fisk has become well known as an educator and has visited every large city in the United States and Canada, and many important cities in Europe. Mr. Fisk also holds a very prominent place as a promoter of public welfare in almost all of its departments. He is president of the Boston Missionary and Church Extension Society, and also of the Boston Methodist Social Union. He is vice-president of the Evangelistic Association of New England, and is connected in an official capacity with the Municipal League of Boston, the Boston Y. M. C. A., and the American Peace Society. Mr. Fisk was a delegate to the general conference of the Methodist Episcopal Church, in 1892. He is a member of the Boston Art Club, the University Club of Boston, and the Twentieth Century Club. From the position which Mr. Fisk holds he has a large field for usefulness. He is a man who has made the best of his opportunities, and one whom Wesleyan is proud to own as her son; res. 4 Ashburton Pl., Boston, Mass.

    6385. i.   HARRIETTE STORER, b. Oct. 14, 1884.

    5616. EDWARD PERRY FISKE (Robert F., William, Moses, Moses, Nathaniel, Nathaniel, Nathan, Nathaniel, Jeffrey, Robert, Simon, Simon, William, Symond), b. Boston, Mass., Jan. 25, 1852; m. there, June 25, 1890, Josephine Wilson, b. Milford, Mass., Sept. 5, 1857. He is clerk of the Metropolitan Sewerage Commission of Mass.; res. 76 Bartlett St., Roxbury, s. p.; bus. add., Boston, Mass., 110 Boylston St.

    5631. WILLIAM MAYER FISKE (John N., John, Elijah, Moses, Nathaniel, Nathaniel, Nathan, Nathaniel, William, Robert, Simon, Simon, William, Symond), b. Sept. 3, 1854, Fredericksburg, Va.; m. May 26, 1887, Carrie M. Savage. He was born in Virginia, and with his parents moved to Grovetown, Ga. He was a farmer until two years ago, when, in company with his brother, he began the manufacture of stone ware and pottery; res. Grovetown, Ga., s. p.

    5633. JULIAN FRIEND FISKE (John N., John, Elijah, Moses, Nathaniel, Nathaniel, Nathan, Nathaniel, William, Robert, Simon, Simon, William, Symond), b. Augusta, Ga., Mar. 3, 1860; m. at Athens, Sept. 25, 1888, Minnie Evans Edwards, b. Oct. 14, 1866, at Antioch, Ga. He was born in Augusta, Ga., and followed agricultural pursuits until two years ago, when, in company with his brother, he began the manufacture of pottery and stone ware, in which he has been quite successful. His wife is the daughter of ex-Senator E. F. Edwards, of Covington, Ga.; res. Grovetown, Ga.

    6386. i.   NEWTON FLURNOY, b. Oct. 8, 1889.
    6387. ii. JENNIE MAY, b. Mar. 10, 1892.
    6388. iii. JOHN WILLIE, b. July 25, 1895.

    5644. DAVID WARREN FISKE (Timothy, David, David, John, John, Nathaniel, Nathan, Nathaniel, William, Robert, Simon, Simon, William, Symond), b. Holliston, Mass., Aug. 18, 1830; m. at Griswold, Conn., Apr. 4, 1860, Angeline Tillinghast, b. Jan., 1836. He was for some time in the boot and shoe business, later lumbering, and now farming; res. So. Coventry, Conn.

    6389. i.   GEO. WALDO, b. Nov. 5, 1862; m. Mary Bascom.
    6390. ii. EDWARD EVERETT, b. June 30, 1865; m. Luella Doan.
    6391. iii. CARRIE ETTA, b. Sept. 22, 1867; d. 1869.
    6392. iv. BERTIE GRANT, b. Jan. 3, 1878; res. So. C.

    5646. DEA. GEORGE BATCHELDER FISKE (Timothy, David, David, John, John, Nathaniel, Nathan, Nathaniel, William, Robert, Simon, Simon, William, Symond), b. Holliston, Mass., May 20, 1834; m. there, Nov. 14, 1856, Adeliza

M. Perry, b. May 17, 1836, dau. of Abel H. Dea. Geo. Batchelder Fiske, the third son of Timothy and Lucretia Batchelder, born in Holliston, Mass. His early life was spent on the farm, with the usual benefits of the public schools, and by his personal efforts was enabled to pursue a higher education at Mt. Hollis Seminary, thus fitting himself for active mercantile life, which he commenced at the age of 18, with good success. In 1856 he married Ada M. Perry, a successful teacher in the public schools, and had two sons and two daughters. Mr. Fiske pursued the study of engraving and printing of bank notes, and being skilled in the art, he was engaged in teaching and instructing the bankers and business men of the cities and towns of New England in the art of detecting counterfeit and altered bank notes at sight. Mr. Fiske has been a member of the Congregational Church for many years, and served on all of its official boards with satisfaction and esteem. In politics Mr. Fiske has always been a Republican, and deeply interested in good government in all things. Early in life was a strong advocate of the largest liberty of speech and action to promote the best results. A strong friend

DEA. GEORGE BATCHELDER FISKE.

and admirer of Abraham Lincoln for President; he was appointed as postmaster, and served two terms, and was elected by the town as treasurer and collector, serving seven years, with a grand record. As his town recognized good abilities, they elected him as town clerk, and he served them as such for fifteen years, many times receiving a unanimous vote. Mr. Fiske was elected a Representative from this district to the general court, 1880, redeeming the district from his political opponents, and was re-elected the next year by an increased majority, when he served both years as clerk of important committees, also using his knowledge of the business of insurance (which he had acquired from many years of actual practice) in improving the insurance laws of the State and enacting and establishing a long needed uniform policy of insurance for all companies doing business in this State. Mr. Fiske has been a member of the school board for many years, and served as clerk. Also a member of the Holliston, Medway and Millis School Union for the employment and supervision of it; superintendent of the schools in said towns, he having been one of the promoters of this excellent plan of providing a better system of graded schools for the small towns. During the spare hours of Mr. Fiske's busy life he introduced the business of knitting by machinery in a small way, which grew to large proportions, employing at times sixty hands in manufacturing seamless hosiery (the first in this State), knitted goods, and a specialty of infants' underwear, all of which found ready and profitable sales. Holliston being an enterprising and progressive town, concluded to advocate and encourage the building of an electric railway to its larger neighbors, and thus called a town meeting and elected a committee to proceed for the best interests of the town, and Mr. Fiske was chosen on the committee and elected as its clerk, on whom fell the responsible duties of formulating a contract for the town, also supervising the survey and location of the railway tracks, locating and building car houses, and whatever was of interest to his town. Mr. Fiske being of a genial social bearing, a promoter of the good and true, assisted in encouraging the institution of Mt. Hollis Masonic Lodge, and in 1865 was the first regularly raised Mason in that lodge, and also proceeded until he became a Sir Knight in the Milford Commandery, of Massachusetts. Mr. Fiske is a member of the Holliston Lodge of the Knights of Honor, and a firm believer in great good that has been done and is being accomplished by this noble order to the widows and families of its members. Mr. and Mrs. Fiske being firm believers in a higher education for those who deserve it, that the better the education the better citizen, that the educated man or woman can obtain a higher position in society and a more lucrative situation in the business world, and acting on that line, have educated their children accordingly. Mr. Fiske was this year (1896) elected chairman of the school board by a full vote; res. Holliston, Mass.

6393. i. EUSTACE LINCOLN, b. Nov. 26, 1860; m. June 20, 1894, Jennie E. Lawson; res. Fitchburg, Mass., s. p. He was born at Holliston, Middlesex Co., Mass., of George B. and Adaliza M. (Perry) Fiske; was educated in public and high schools of that place. For six years was in business with his father, manufacturing knit goods, and in insurance (fire) business. In 1883 entered Harvard Medical School, of Harvard University, from which he obtained his degree of M. D., in 1886. The summer of that year was appointed assistant resident physician of Adams Asylum, at Jamaica Plain, Mass., which position he occupied two years. He then began active general practice of medicine and surgery in Fitchburg, Mass., and still remains there. He is a member of Massachusetts Medical Society; treasurer of Worcester North District Medical Society, and has held the same position in Fitchburg Society for Medical Improvement. Is prominent in secret societies, being a member of all the grand lodges in Odd Fellowship, in Massachusetts; a Knight Templar, and has membership in many smaller organizations. Is a popular and prosperous physician in his adopted city. Held no political office, as he is not in politics. Is a Republican.

6394. ii. MINNIE FLORENCE, b. Sept. 2, 1864; unm., B. A., Wellesley College, 1888.

6395. iii. EFFIE L., b. Aug. 29, 1862; m. Nov. 14, 1884, Edward C. Rawson. He was b. Dec. 11, 1860; res. Holliston, Mass. Ch.: 1, Geo. Edward, b. Dec. 6, 1886. 2, Florence Hemenway, b. June 13, 1890.

6396. iv. GEO. WALTER, b. June 3, 1872; A. B., Amherst College, in 1895. He is now, 1896, a student at the Hartford Theological Seminary, at Hartford, Conn. Fitted for college in native town schools; entered Amherst College, 1890; graduated from same, June, 1894; member of Phi Delta Theta Society; was active in securing the society's present house on the college grounds; wears the key significant of his high scholarship; received numerous prizes on Biblical literature at Amherst College. Entered Hartford Theological Seminary, Hartford, Conn., Oct., 1895, and at present studying for ministry; not married; is a Republican in politics.

5649. PROF. ARTHUR IRVING FISKE (Lovett, John, David, John, John, Nathaniel, Nathan, Nathaniel, William, Robert, Simon, Simon, William, Symond), b. Holliston, Mass., Aug. 19, 1848; m. Dec. 25, 1879, Harriett Mowry, b. Aug. 26, 1858. He was born in Holliston; was educated at Exeter Academy, and was graduated at Harvard University in the class of 1869. He was appointed tutor in Greek soon after his graduation and remained a member of the Harvard faculty until July 1, 1873. He was then elected Greek master in the Boston Latin School, and has continued there for the past twenty-two years; res. 17 Montrose St., Roxbury, Mass.

6397. i. AGNES MOWRY, b. Nov. 4, 1881.
6398. ii. BERTHA GREENHALGH, b. Mar. 19, 1884.

5656. WILBER FISKE (Abner, John, David, John, John, Nathaniel, Nathan, Nathaniel, William, Robert, Simon, Simon, William, Symond), b. Holliston, Mass., June 20, 1834; m. Annie Bailey; res. Boston, Mass.

6399. i. NINA, b. ——; m. H. Lincoln; res. New Orleans, La.

5660. J. MILTON FISKE (Aner, John, David, John, John, Nathaniel, Nathan, Nathaniel, William, Robert. Simon, Simon, William, Symond), b. Holliston, Mass., Feb. 20, 1835; m. May 4, 1859, at Savannah, Ga., Ellen Sophia Worthington, b. Feb. 1, 1841. He was a painter, teacher and merchant in Georgia, enlisted in the War of the Rebellion. He was 54 years old at his death, and served in the War of the Rebellion as a member of Company F, First Massachusetts Cavalry. Was engaged in twelve battles, in one of which he received a wound from a shell which rendered him senseless; and this wound, together with injuries received from a fall, caused his long sickness and final death. He joined the Baptist Church in Savannah, Ga., in 1859, but in late years, before his illness, he attended the Methodist Church. He was very fond of music. He suffered intensely, bearing pain without a murmur, and always received tender and constant care from his wife and children. He was a sincere and earnest christian man, a true soldier of the cross, as well as for the government. He d. Oct. 23, 1889; res. Holliston, Mass.

    6400. i.   ALICE IMOGENE, b. Feb. 29, 1860; m. Mar. 30, 1879, E. W. Loring; res. Holliston. Ch.: 1, Harvey Wells, b. Nov. 28, 1879; res. Boston.

    6401. ii.   HARVEY WM., b. Nov. 18, 1861; res. Holliston; unm.

    6402. iii. WALTER H., b. Apr. 27, 1864; m. Ada M. Gifford.

    6403. iv. LOUIS WORTHINGTON, b. Apr. 6, 1887.

    6404. v.   ALICE MARION, b. Oct. 26, 1888.

    6405. vi. WALTER RAYMOND, b. Oct. 15, 1890.

5661. MELVILLE FISKE (Abner, John, David, John, John, Nathaniel, Nathan, Nathaniel, William, Robert, Simon, Simon, William, Symond), b. Holliston, Mass., Nov. 10, 1834; m. there Josephine Lawrence, b. Medway. He d. Apr., 1893; res. Medway, Mass.

    6406. i.   MYRTIE, b. ———; res. Medway.

5671. JAMES FERDINAND FISKE (Ferdinand, Timothy, David, John, John, Nathaniel, Nathan, Nathaniel, William, Robert, Simon, Simon, William, Symond), b. Holliston, Mass., Aug. 1, 1841; m. Leicester. June 4, 1865, Sarah Maria Craig, b. July 4, 1844. He is Postmaster and Town Treasurer; res. Holliston, Mass.

    6407. i.   ANNIE LOUISE, b. May 25, 1866.

    6408. ii.   CHARLES AUGUSTUS, b. Nov. 28, 1867; d. Mar. , 1870.

    6409. iii. STELLA GERTRUDE, b. Dec. 5, 1868; m. Oct. 26 .892, A. F. Wilder; res. 1000 Ellis St., Brunswick, Ga.

    6410. iv. LESLIE CLARK, b. Apr. 7, 1873.

    6411. v.   LOTTIE WARREN, b. Dec. 8, 1874; d. Aug. 19, 1875.

5674. GEORGE C. FISK (Thomas T., Thomas, John, Isaac. John, Nathaniel, Nathan, Nathaniel, William, Robert, Simon, Simon, William, Symond), b. Mar. 4, 1831, Hinsdale, N. H.; m. June 7, 1853, Maria E. Ripley, b. Sept. 6, 1835, at Winchester, N. H.. The president and superintendent of the Wason Manufacturing Company, George C. Fisk, exemplifies in his career the possibilities of every young man who sets out early in life to accomplish whatever he undertakes and to pursue that which has in it something worth striving for. Mr. Fisk was born in Hinsdale, N. H., and he began work in a country store at Hinsdale, kept by E. W. Hunt and by Amidon & Holland. But selling dry goods and drawing molasses did not suit his taste as well as working in a shop, so he concluded to try his fortune elsewhere. At 20 years of age, in 1851, he left Hinsdale for Springfield, carrying with him $15 as his total cash capital with which to buffet what might prove to be "the shafts of outrageous fortune." Not meeting with just what he first desired to engage in, he entered here a dry goods store, but left that, and tried for a time work in a grocery store. That did not promise to be any more congenial than what he had experienced at Hinsdale, and not many months afterward he went west. At Cleveland, O., he stopped to renew the acquaintance of a friend. He had some rather indefinite promises as to work, but as it was not forthcoming he turned book agent, and commenced selling Mrs. Stowe's "Uncle Tom's Cabin." That venture flourished until a crabbed old fellow threatened to kick him out of his house if he ever caught him selling any more books to his family, and that suggested to him the propriety of still going farther west. He went to Beloit, Wis., and looked about the town; but the slipshod way of conducting business, then characteristic of all new towns in the west, turned his thoughts backward to New England. He found that to succeed in the west capital was just as necessary as in the east, and the next thing he did was to return to Springfield. Eleazer Ripley was about to begin the manufacture of locomotives, and he wanted a bookkeeper. While the machinery was being put in he went home to Hinsdale to make a desk. Two weeks later Mr. Ripley sent for him to return. Mr. Wason was about to go west on a business trip, and he wanted Mr. Fisk to act temporarily as bookkeeper for him in his absence. Mr. Ripley consented, and what was intended only as a temporary engagement resulted in permanent employment. It may be interesting to know that he commenced with Mr. Wason on a salary of $1 a day. From his first employment he rose to paymaster as well as bookkeeper, and in 1854 to a partnership interest. When the company was incorporated, he was made treasurer, and later still vice-president, and president and general manager on the death of Mr. Wason, which positions he continues to hold. Few

GEORGE C. FISK.

men have shown such tireless energy in the pursuit of business, from the early beginning of the company up to its complete triumph, and have seen so much coming back in return. Through summer and winter for many years Mr. Fisk was the first man at the shop, fully knowing that the eye of the master inspired close attention to the work in hand. If there was a contract to be had, he was off for it, and back again as quickly as possible, to see that the work was speedily finished. Wherever he went he carried a tabulated form of cost of work with him, and if any one wanted an estimate in the middle of the night, he could give it to him at once. It was this promptness, and giving each what he agreed to give in the way of finished work, that brought him many thousands of dollars when some other concerns were running short time. After the shops were located at Brightwood—a name given to the locality in honor of Dr. Holland's "Brightwood," which is perched upon the eminence to the east of it—Mr. Fisk bought "Brightwood" itself of Dr. Holland, who had gone to New York to edit Scribner's Monthly, now the Century—a home that the genial doctor left with many regrets, and which Mr. Fisk succeeded to with as lively feelings of personal satisfaction. It was near his work, and it has a charming outlook among the trees—conspicuous, and often noticed by travelers up and down the Connecticut valley—in its bright and tasteful colors, harmonizing so completely with the deep green of surrounding foliage of summer months. To give a summary in chronological order of Mr. Fisk's connection and promotion with the Wason Company it would read: Entered the office of T. W. Wason, Sept. 8, 1852, at $1 a day; admitted to the firm, Dec., 1854; elected treasurer, Jan. 17. 1862; elected vice-president, Apr. 14, 1869; elected president, Feb. 6, 1871. Mr. Fisk has been a hard worker in every sense, but of late years he has found more time for recreation, though always keeping a close watch on his large and increasing business. He has given some attention to the rearing of Holstein stock, and is interested in other kinds of manufacturing, holding an interest in the Fisk Soap Works, the Springfield Power Company, and is the owner of a mill for the manufacture of paper at Hinsdale. Some years since he conceived the plan of building a place for entertainment in Brightwood, and Fisk's Casino is the result. It was dedicated in 1885, and has since furnished a place for amateur theatricals, conducted entirely by home talent. It was built entirely by Mr. Fisk, and it is, indeed, a charming place, and which is highly appreciated. The

Brightwood Dramatic Club has often given representations worthy those older in experience, and added much to the rational enjoyment of the neighborhood. The Casino stands at the corner of Main street and Wason avenue, and is sixty-six by thirty-seven feet. The interior is finished in hard wood and pleasingly ornamented by tasteful decorations; res. Springfield, Mass.

6412. i.   CHARLES A., b. Aug. 15, 1853; m. Jennie Graves and Helena J. Young.
6413. ii.   ELENA M., b. July 26, 1856; d. Sept. 2, 1864.
6414. iii. GEO. C., JR., b. Dec. 31, 1867; d. Apr. 15, 1879.
6415. iv.   BELLE R., b. Oct. 9, 1862; m. June 21, 1888, Oliver H. Dickinson, of Springfield. He was b. Mar. 10, 1863. Res. Detroit, Mich. Ch.: 1, George Fisk, b. July 5, 1890. 2, Julia, b. Oct. 23, 1891. 3, Minerva, b. Oct. 23, 1891.
6416. v.   ROBERT HENRY, b. May 10, 1879; d. Aug. 6, 1879.

5675. LUCIUS I. FISK (Thomas T., Thomas, John, Isaac, John, Nathaniel, Nathan, Nathaniel, William, Robert, Simon, Simon, William, Symond), b. Oct. 18, 1833, in Hinsdale, N. H.; m. Oct. 25, 1860, Eveline E. Raymond, b. June 17, 1835. He was a member of the firm of L. I. Fisk & Co., manufacturers of soaps. He d. s. p. Aug. 17, 1880; res. Springfield, Mass.

5676. NOYES W. FISK (Thomas T., Thomas, John, Isaac, John, Nathaniel, Nathan, Nathaniel, William, Robert, Simon, Simon, William, Symond), b. May 15, 1839; m. Aug. 27, 1862, Emeline G. Adams, b. May 10, 1842. He was born in Hinsdale, N. H., and while a small boy assisted his father in the manufacture of soaps. Later he clerked in a country store in his native town. He remained there four years, and went to Northampton and kept books for Thayer & Sargent. While in Northampton he was taken sick and obliged to go home and remain about a year. In the meantime his eldest brother, George C. Fisk, now president of the Wason Manufacturing Company, had come to Springfield and was a member of the car manufacturing firm of Thomas W. Wason & Co., and as soon as Noyes W. was able he came to Springfield and entered the office of Wason & Co. as bookkeeper. After a year or so his place there was taken by Henry S. Hyde, now treasurer of the Wason Manufacturing Company, and he became bookkeeper for E. B. Haskell & Sons, grocers, and remained with them until he enlisted, in 1862, in Company A, of the Forty-sixth regiment. When he had served out the term as a private, he returned to Springfield and started for himself in the grocery and provision business. In 1867 he sold out and went into the manufacture of lamp black on the corner of Chestnut and Ringgold streets. He had hardly got well started in his new venture, when he woke up one morning in Feb., 1868, to find that all his buildings, except one had been burned and he then sold out what remained of his business, and May 15, 1868, went into the soap business. This was started in Hinsdale, in 1857, by Mr. Fisk's father and brother. In 1861, the senior Mr. Fisk died and William Smith bought his interest in the business. The removal of the business was then determined upon, and in the spring of 1861, the business was established. A year or two after the removal Mr. Smith died. The principal markets for the Fisk Manufacturing Company's goods are in New England, New York, New Jersey, Pennsylvania and Ohio, and steady and gratifying growth of the business is the best possible evidence of the estimation in which the company's goods are held. Mr. Fisk was for seven years a member of the common council and has for eleven years been a member of the water commissioners and the only man connected with the water department who has no salary. He is a director in the Chicopee National Bank, the Springfield Woodworking Company, the Hampden Paint Works, and the Masonic Mutual Insurance Company, and is a trustee of the School for Christian Workers, the Winthrop Club, and Springfield Commandery of Knights Templar. These positions of public and financial trust show the estimation in which Mr. Fisk is held by the general and business community. Mr. and Mrs. Fisk are members of Memorial Church, but since their removal to Ward Five have attended the First Church, where they are valued workers; res. Springfield, Mass.

6417. i.   HARRY G., b. 1873.

5678. HARRY FREDERICK FISK (John B., Thomas T., Thomas, John, Isaac, John, Nathaniel, Nathan, Nathaniel, William, Robert, Simon, Simon, Will-

iam, Symond), b. May 15, 1840, in Chesterfield, N. H.; m. Oct. 19, 1865, Mary G.
Wyman, b. Aug. 6, 1845, dau. of Timothy, of Chester, Vt.; m. 2d, Feb. 2, 1892,
Annie E. Frank, of Springfield, Ill., b. Apr., 1866. He was born in Chesterfield,
N. H., and soon after his majority engaged in business in Hinsdale, N. H. Later
he moved to Springfield, Mass., and was in business there. During the war he
served as private in the Sixth New Hampshire Regiment, in Company E, and was
in the struggle for two years. While in Massachusetts he engaged in the whip
business, and is now traveling salesman for the Ohio Whip Company, of Osborn,
O.; res. Hinsdale, N. H., and Springfield, Ill., 909 So. Fifth St.

    6418.   i.   FRED N., b. Aug. 3, 1867; m. Carrie A. Ware.

    5680. FRANK DELOS FISK (John B., Thomas T., Thomas, John, Isaac,
John, Nathaniel, Nathan, Nathaniel, William, Robert, Simon, Simon, William,
Symond), b. Feb. 17, 1846, Chesterfield, N. H.; m. at Hinsdale, Jan. 5, 1870, Celinia
Emily Aldrich, dau. of Alfred, of Westmoreland, N. H. He left home when he
was 16, worked as clerk in a country store three years; two years in dry goods
business in Boston. At 21 he went in business for himself in Hinsdale, N. H.
Was in Hinsdale eighteen years. Was postmaster of Hinsdale twelve years. Re-
ceived his first appointment from Grant; second, Hayes; third, Garfield, and fourth,
Arthur. Resigned soon after he received his fourth appointment, in 1885, and
bought half interest in the hardware business of C. F. Thompson & Co., of Brattleboro, Vt. After four years sold out; since then has been traveling salesman for
Charles Millar & Son, of Utica, N. Y.; res. Brattleboro, Vt.

    6419.   i.   INFANT SON, b. July 2, 1874; d. Aug. 15, 1874.
    6420.   ii.   PAULINE, b. July 13, 1875.
    6421. iii.   MARION, b. Mar. 30, 1877.
    6422.   iv.   FLORENCE, b. Oct. 18, 1878.

    5682. PROF. DANIEL WILLARD FISKE (Daniel H., William T., Daniel,
Isaac, John, Nathaniel, Nathan, Nathaniel, William, Robert, Simon, Simon, William, Symond), b. Ellisburgh, N. Y., Nov. 11, 1831; m. July 14, 1880, Jennie McGraw,
d. Sept. 30, 1881, s. p. When very young he disclosed an uncommon aptitude for
the acquisition of languages, and a precocious interest in both literature and
politics. He pursued his school education at Cazenovia Seminary and at Hamilton College, but left that institution in his sophomore year to go abroad and
study the Scandinavian languages. At Copenhagen he enjoyed the friendship of
Prof. Rafu, the distinguished Danish archaeologist. With little aid except some
occasional correspondence with the New York Tribune, he sustained himself
during 1849-52, passing two years in the University of Upsala, giving lessons in
English and lecturing on American literature, and speaking Swedish so well that
he commonly passed with the students for a Swede. In 1852 he returned to New
York and took a place in the Astor Library, where he remained as assistant
until 1859, still pursuing his studies in languages, and in making a collection of
Icelandic books, which soon became the most considerable in this country. So
enthusiastically had he directed his attention to that enlightened island that it
was said that few natives were more familiar with its geography, history, politics,
and literature than he. In 1859-60 he was general secretary of the American
Geographical Society. In 1861-2 he was again abroad, and attached to the American legation at Vienna, under Minister John Lothrop Motley. Returning, he was
editor of the Daily Journal, of Syracuse, N. Y., in 1864-6, and through 1867 had
charge of the Hartford (Conn.) Courant, from which he was called in 1868, after
another extensive tour abroad, which embraced Egypt and Palestine, to the professorship of the north European languages, and the place of chief librarian, at
Cornell University. In his unremitting labors for years in the classroom, as librarian, and as director of the university press, no inconsiderable degree of the success
of the institution is due. During this time he took a deep interest in the reform
of the civil service, and was a most influential writer and lecturer in its behalf. In
1879 he was again abroad for five months, and visited Iceland. He had been a principal promoter in this country of the contribution of a library on the celebration of
the national millennium, and upon his arrival he was the guest of the nation and
accorded honors seldom, if ever, given before by one nation to a private citizen
of another. His health failing from his severe application to college duties, he
went abroad again in 1880. In that year, in Berlin, he married Miss Jennie Mc-

Graw, of Ithaca, N. Y., who died in Sept., 1881. In 1881 he resigned his offices at Cornell and took up his permanent residence in Florence, Italy. Although his chief work had been that of a scholar and bibliopole, he has been a voluminous contributor to various Swedish, Icelandic and German journals, and to the American press. He was one of the famous chess tournament of 1857, and in conjunction with Paul Morphy, edited the "American Chess Monthly" in 1857-60, and compiled the "Book of the American Chess Congress" (New York, 1859). He has edited various university publications, such as the "Ten-Year Book of Cornell," the "Register," etc., and many bibliographical publications, such as the "University Library Bulletin," the "Bibliographia Psiupsilonica," etc. He was one of the chief promoters of the chapter-house system in the Greek letters societies. He is now engaged in completing his two private book collections, one relating to Petrarch, the other to Icelandic history and literature—the most considerable collections in existence relating to those subjects—and is printing privately a series of "Bibliographical Notices" illustrating his collections. Prof. Fiske has received the degree of A. M. from Hamilton and that of Ph. D. from Cornell; res. San Domenico, Villa Lauder, Florence, Italy.

5683. PROF. WILLIAM ORVILLE FIŞKE (Daniel H., William T., Daniel, Isaac, John, Nathaniel, Nathan, Nathaniel, William, Robert, Simon, Simon, William, Symond), b. Ellisburgh, N. Y., Jan. 23, 1835; m. Dec. 24, 1866, Mary E. McGee; d. June, 1891. He is a professor of music; res. Syracuse, N. Y., 127 Madison St.

    6423. i.   JAMES WILLARD, b. Dec. 12, 1870; m. Margaret D. McCarthy.
    6424. ii.   WILLIAM ORVILLE, b. ———.
    6425. iii. CARRIE IRENE, b. ———.
    6426. iv. FLORENCE CECELIA, b. ———.
    6427. v.   ALICE VIDA, b. ———.

5686. GEORGE H. FISK (Moses M., Isaac, Moses, Isaac, John, Nathaniel, Nathan, Nathaniel, William, Robert, Simon, Simon, William, Symond), b. Feb. 26, 1832, Framingham, Mass.; m. at Natick, Apr. 12, 1855, Delia M. Moore; m. 2d, Mar., 1859, Angie W. Annett. She res. W. Newton, Mass. He d. Dec. 5, 1895; res. Newton, Mass.

    6428. i.   S. WILBUR, b. May 1, 1872. He is a plumber; res. W. Newton, Mass.
    6429. ii.   EFFIE, b. Jan. 25, 1861; m. July 10, 1884, Arthur H. Laurence, 326 Fourth St., Marietta, O. He was b. Nov. 24, 1856; res. Marietta, O. Ch.: 1, Etta May, b. Dec. 23, 1885. 2, William Arthur, b. Apr. 26, 1887. 3, Edith Willena, b. July 2, 1890. 4, Edward Wells, b. June 17, 1892. 5, Harold Fiske, b. Jan. 21, 1894.

5687. WINSLOW JOHNSON FISKE (Moses M., Isaac, Moses, Isaac, John, Nathaniel, Nathan, Nathaniel, William, Robert, Simon, Simon, William, Symond), b. June 18, 1834, Framingham, Mass.; m. Susan Bigelow. She d. s. p.; m. 2d, Abbie F. Holcomb, b. July 21, 1849. He d. Jan. 14, 1894; res. West Newton, Mass.

    6431. i.   HERFORD ARTHUR, b. Aug. 29, 1880; unm.; res. W. N., P. O. box 531.
    6432. ii.   WALTER, b. Dec. 28, 1871; m. May 14, 1894; res. W. N.
    6433. iii. SUSAN GREENWOOD, b. Sept. 16, 1884.

5689. CAPT. JOHN MURRAY FISK (Moses M., Isaac, Moses, Isaac, John, Nathaniel, Nathan, Nathaniel, William, Robert, Simon, Simon, William, Symond), b. Framingham, Mass., Sept. 28, 1838; m. at West Dedham, Oct. 22, 1861, Carrie E. Morgan, b. Aug. 25, 1837. John M. Fisk was born in Framingham, and was the son of Moses M. and Harriet H. Fisk of that town. He was one of a family of eight children. But two of these survive him—Mrs. Horatio Gardner, of East Holliston, and Mrs. Willard Howe, of South Framingham. As a boy Capt. Fisk was a hard worker. He graduated from the Framingham high school, and in 1860 went to work for William H. Brackett, at Newton, Mass., in the provision business. Soon after he was elected constable of the town. He was the only policeman in Newton at that time, and was the first man to hold

CAPT. JOHN MURRAY FISK

such a position there. He lived in Newton twenty-four years. In 1872 he was appointed deputy sheriff, which position he held for twelve years. In May, 1884 he was appointed special sheriff for High Sheriff Cushing, and placed in charge of the Middlesex .county house of correction, East Cambridge, which position he held until his death. Capt. Fisk married Caroline E. Morgan, daughter of John Morgan, of West Dedham. She survives him. One child was born to them. She is Mrs. George D. Ford, wife of Capt. Fisk's able assistant. Capt. Fisk was a thirty-second degree Mason, and a member of many secret societies, among them Newton Blue Lodge, Royal Arch, Cambridge Commandery, Royal Arcanum, Ancient and Honorable Artillery and Mystic Shrine. He was also a member of the Colonial Club. By his death Middlesex county loses one of the most efficient officers it has ever had and the prisoners who have come under his charge will miss a good friend. The sentiment of the whole community is expressed in the tribute paid Capt. Fisk recently by Representative John H. Ponce, who said to a Globe reporter: "As a deputy sheriff Capt. Fisk was a universal favorite with the lawyers of Middlesex county. He was prompt and reliable in the service of the processes of the courts, and was looked upon as authority on many mooted questions. He was especially kind and helpful to young attorneys. Since he has been master of the house of correction there has been no word of complaint as to the management of the institution or the treatment of prisoners. While keeping them in the closest custody, he has been most humane in his treatment of them. He was highly respected by the judges of the county. His acts of private charity among the poor in East Cambridge were numerous, and his death is spoken of with great sorrow by the people in his district." He d. May 3, 1896; res. East Cambridge, Mass.

6434. i.   LILLIAN FRANCES, m. Nov. 28, 1882, Geo. D. Ford, deputy warden of the Middlesex Co., house of correction, East Cambridge, Mass.

5692. ANDREW JACKSON FISK (Moses M., Isaac, Moses, Isaac, John, Nathaniel, Nathan, Nathaniel, William, Robert, Simon, Simon, William, Symond), b. June 8, 1845; m. Mar. 20, 1868, Lizzie Clough. He d. Mar. 5, 1895; res. Newton, Mass.

6435. i.   ANDREW FREEMAN, b. West Newton, Mass.

5694. EDWIN BROWN FISKE (Oliver J., Isaac, Moses, Isaac, John, Nathaniel, Nathan, Nathaniel, William, Robert, Simon, Simon, William, Symond), b. Rutherford County, Tenn., Dec. 16, 1841; m. May 8, 1867, in Avon, N. Y., Frances M. Price, d. Mar. 18, 1873; m. 2d, Dec. 8, 1875, Priscilla M. Westlake, b. May 14, 1850. Edwin B. Fiske, the eldest of three children born to Oliver J. Fiske and Maria L. (Brown) Fiske. The subject of our sketch was born in Rutherford County and in the State of Tennessee. At the age of 14 his parents removed to Bloomington, Ill. He worked on his father's farm during the summer and in the winter went to school. When the State Normal University was located at Bloomington he was one of the first to enroll his name as a student in that institution. Before graduating he made up his mind that he would obtain a collegiate education and went to Providence, R. I., and entered the high school in that city, from which he graduated. He then entered Brown University; while there the War of the Rebellion broke out and he enlisted in Company B, Tenth Regiment Rhode Island Volunteers. His health broke down and he was honorably discharged and entered college again, but owing to ill health contracted while in the army he was not able to continue his studies and went to Chicago, where he found a position in the employ of William B. Keen & Co., as a commercial traveler. On the restoration of his health he entered the Law School at Albany, N. Y., and graduated from that school in May, 1865. He then commenced the practice of law in the city of Syracuse, N. Y., in partnership with Irving G. Vann, who is now a Judge of the Court of Appeals in that State. While in that city he married Frances J. Price, of Avon, N. Y. His practice in the law was quite lucrative, but owing to close application to business his health became once more impaired and he removed to Perry, N. Y. His practice here was not so lucrative as it was in the city, but it was far more beneficial to his health. While in Perry his wife died (Mar. 19, 1873). In the following fall he removed to Rochester, N. Y., where he now resides. In 1875 he married Priscilla M. Westlake, of Perry, N. Y. He has one son by his second wife. Edwin Westlake Fiske, born on the 19th day of Dec., 1876, and who is now attending Rochester University. Mr. Fiske has always taken quite an interest in politics, though not a politician in the strict sense of the word. An ardent Republican and in every presidential campaign takes the stump for the nominees of that party. He is a member of the Baptist Church and held quite a number of offices in that church Superintendent of the Sunday school; deacon and trustee—the last two he now holds in the Lyell Avenue Baptist Church at Rochester. He is interested in quite a number of enterprises of a local character and also in mining operations in British Columbia; res. Rochester, N. Y.; add. 32 Smith's Arcade.

    6436. i.   EDWIN WESTLAKE, b. Dec. 19, 1876; is now (1896) in the University of Rochester.

5696. CHARLES H. FISKE (Oliver J., Isaac, Moses, Isaac, John, Nathaniel, Nathan, Nathaniel, William, Robert, Simon, Simon, William, Symond), b. Nashville, Tenn., Jan. 8, 1849; m. at Indianapolis, Ind., Apr. 10, 1871, Anna Rockwell, b. Aug. 11, 1856; res. Indianapolis, Ind.

    6437. i.   EMMA LOUISE, b. June 27, 1878.
    6438. ii.   FLORENCE GRACE, b. Aug. 1, 1880.
    6439. iii.   ELIZABETH, b. June 9, 1889.

5699. EBEN WINSLOW FISKE, JR. (Eben W., Ebenezer W., Isaac, Moses, Isaac, John, Nathaniel, Nathan, Nathaniel, William, Robert, Simon, Simon, William, Symond), b. Waltham, Mass., May 22, 1860; m. May 8, 1884, Sarah Frances Gibbs, b. Dec. 19, 1857. Eben Winslow is assistant secretary of a large stove and furnace company, and is president of the board of Aldermen; res. Lyman St., Waltham, Mass.

    6440. i.   EBEN WINSLOW, b. Jan. 5, 1886.

5711. ROBERT W. FISK (James W., James, Henry A., Robert, Robert, Robert, David, David, Jeffrey, Robert, Simon, Simon, William, Symond), b. Melrose, Ill., Nov. 7, 1858; m. in Danville, Ill., Dec. 24, 1889, Belle Brown, b. Dec. 16, 1869. He is an attorney at law; res. Ridge Farm, Ill.

    6441. i.   UNA D., b. May 17, 1891.

5713. JAMES E. FISK (James W., James, Henry A., Robert, Robert, Robert, David, David, Jeffrey, Robert, Simon, Simon, William, Symond), b. Melrose, Ill., Sept. 21, 1863; m. June 21, 1884, Maggie E. Horner; m. 2d, May 22, 1892, Laura E. Driskell.

    6442. i.   EARL A., b. Nov. 26, 1885.
    6443. ii.   WM. E., b. Aug. 22, 1893.

5767. ALBERT WALLACE FISK (Warren N., Royal, Benoni, Benjamin, Benjamin, Benjamin, John, John, Phinehas, Thomas, Robert, Simon, Simon, William, Symond), b. Reedsburg, Wis., Oct. 21, 1857; m. at De Kalb, Ill., Feb. 21,

ALBERT WALLACE FISK.

1883, Clara M. Perry, b. Apr. 27, 1861. He was first employed as stenographer and later bookkeeper at Ellwood Works in De Kalb. He is now superintendent of the celebrated Ellwood stock farm; res. De Kalb, Ill.

6444. i. KATHERINE LOUISE, b. Jan. 10, 1884.
6445. ii. PERRY WARREN, b. Aug. 5, 1886.
6446. iii. ALVAN WALLACE, b. Aug. 23, 1892.
6447. iv. HARRIS DOWNER, b. Mar. 8, 1894.

5769. MARION EDWIN FISK (Warren N., Royal, Benoni, Benjamin, Benjamin, Benjamin, John, John, Phinehas, Thomas, Robert, Simon, Simon, William, Symond), b. —— Sept. 3, 1869; m. June 3, 1893, in Prairie du Sac, Wis., Anna Othelia Ware, b. Nov. 3, 1868; res. Loganville, Wis.
6448. i. DAUGHTER, b. Sept. 27, 1893; d. Oct. 31, 1893.

5784. ROLLA N. FISK (Noah, Lyman R., Benjamin, Benjamin, Benjamin, Benjamin, John, John, Phinehas, Thomas, Robert, Simon, Simon, William, Symond), b. Apr. 4, 1858; m. Jan. 24, 1881, Rebecca S. Colvin; res. Chippenhook, Vt.

6449. i. LEE C., b. Jan. 6, 1882.
6450. ii. EARL A., b. Oct. 19, 1883.
6451. iii. NOAH L., b. Feb. 22, 1887.
6452. iv. NORA R., b. Jan. 26, 1889.

5791. EZRA JAMES FISKE (Alanson, Alanson, Bateman, Nathaniel, Benjamin, Benjamin, John, John, Phinehas, Thomas, Robert, Simon, Simon, William, Symond), b. Plainfield, N. Y., in 1833; m. in 1858 Sophia Elizabeth Jaycox, b. in 1843; d. in 1860; m. 2d, 1860, in Oxford, N. Y., Margarette Maguire, b. in 1841. He is a blacksmith; res. West Coventry, N. Y., P. O. box 104.
6453. i. SOPHIA ELIZABETH, b. Sept. 13, 1859; m. George Hamilton; res. West Coventry.
6454. ii. MARY KATE, b. Dec. 23, 1860; unm.

5794. HENRY SPENCER FISK (Ansel J., Lyman J., Eber, Nathaniel, Benjamin, Benjamin, John, John, Phinehas, Thomas, Robert, Simon, Simon, William, Symond), b. Jan. 26, 1859, in Tioga, Pa.; m. there Dec. 29, 1889, Ella Eggleston; res. Tioga, Pa.
6455. i. JENNIE E., b. July 23, 1880.
6456. ii. HARRY J., b. Feb. 19, 1887.

5812. GEORGE WILLIAM FISKE (Isaac A., Gideon M., David, Nathaniel, Benjamin, Benjamin, John, John, Phinehas, Thomas, Robert, Simon, Simon, William, Symond), b. Glen Ellyn, Ill., Apr. 18, 1857; m. in Springfield, Ill., Apr. 27, 1881, Nellie Elizabeth Towner, b. Oct. 10, 1861, dau. of William H. When he became of age he went into the hardware business in Roundhouse, Ill. Later he disposed of his business and for a while was express messenger. Later he was employed by the Singer Stone Company, at Springfield, and is now with the Phoenix Stone Company of Chicago. He is a faithful and competent young man; res. at 714 So. Eighth St., Springfield, and Chicago, Ill.
6457. i. FANNIE ELIZABETH, b. Feb. 7, 1885.
6458. ii. MARION CAROLINE, b. June 23, 1889.
6459. iii. GEORGE TOWNER, b. Dec. 18, 1891.
6460. iv. LAVINIA, b. Jan. 16, 1894; d. Feb. 12, 1895.

5817. WILBER JAMES FISK (James H., William, David, Nathaniel, Benjamin, Benjamin, John, John, Phinehas, Thomas, Robert, Simon, Simon, William, Symond), b. Jay, N. Y., Sept. 18, 1867; m. there Oct. 28, 1891, Carrie E. Conger, b. Jan. 10, 1860. He is a teacher; res. Saranac Lake, N. Y.

6461. i. FLORENCE VIVIAN, b. Sept. 16, 1892.
6462. ii. MABEL SARA, b. Mar. 19, 1894.

5824. BURTON COLBURN FISKE (Charles, Elijah D., David, Nathaniel, Benjamin, Benjamin, John, John, Phinehas, Thomas, Robert, Simon, Simon, William, Symond), b. May 1, 1863, Brandon, Vt.; m. at Westford, Dec. 24, 1889, Adelle A. Robinson, of Westford, Vt., b. Sept. 9, 1863. He was raised on a farm; received his education in the district schools in Leicester, Vt., and the graded school at Brandon, Vt.; taught school during the winter of 1879, and again in 1881; had charge of the graded school in East Brainerd, Minn., in 1882 and 1883; returned to Vermont in 1883, and the following spring entered the employ of the Vermont Marble Company at Proctor, Vt., where he remained till Jan., 1888; went to Worcester, Mass., in Aug., 1888, to enter the employ of Cutting & Bishop, building contractors; remained with them until the dissolution of that firm, May 1, 1893, when he became a member of the present firm of Cutting, Bradwell & Co.; add. 11 Foster St., Worcester, Mass.

6463. i. FANNY ROBINSON, b. Jan. 15, 1892.

5838. ELMER BRYANT FISK (Bryant H., Abram, Abram, Jonathan, John, Benjamin, John, John, Phinehas, Thomas, Robert, Simon, Simon, William, Symond), b. Sept. 9, 1864, Linesville, Pa.; m. at Jamestown, N. Y., Oct. 2, 1890, Agnes Leon Beam, b. Feb. 3, 1873. He is engaged in railroad office work; res. 2707 Holland St., Erie, Pa.

6464. i. HERBERT E., b. Sept. 30, 1891.

5852. EDWIN S. FISK (Matthew D., Abram, Abram, Jonathan, John, Benjamin, John, John, Phinehas, Thomas, Robert, Simon, Simon, William, Symond), b. Kingsville, Ohio, May 12, 1847; m. there Emma L. Zinker, b. Mar. 12, 1849. He is a carpenter; res. Conneaut, Ohio.

6465. i. JUDD W., b. in Kingsville, July 26, 1870; m. Ida Macdonald.
6466. ii. MARY L., b. in Monroe, Ashtabula County, Ohio, Apr. 16, 1872.
6467. iii. ROY S., b. in Kingsville, Feb. 20, 1887.

5866. ALBERT A. FISK (Anson A., Ephraim J., Abram, Jonathan, John, Benjamin, John, John, Phinehas, Thomas, Robert, Simon, Simon, William, Symond), b. Mount Gilead, Ohio, Feb. 22, 1852; m. Feb. 16, 1876, Hattie E. Gale, b. July 6, 1859. He is a lumberman; res. Bear Lake, Mich.

6468. i. CLARA JANE, b. June 6, 1887.
6469. ii. JAMES A., b. Oct. 24, 1891; d. Sept. 16, 1893.
6470. iii. ETTA MAY, b. Mar. 24, 1893.
6471. iv. JOHN A., b. July 18, 1895.

5873. WILLIAM FISK (Orville, Ephraim, Abram, Jonathan, John, Benjamin, John, John, Phinehas, Thomas, Robert, Simon, Simon, William, Symond), b. Jan. 6, 1870, Austin, Mich.; m. Sept. 15, 1893, Hattie Slater, b. Fowlerville, Mich., Nov. 18, 1868. He is a miller; res. s. p. Altoona, Mich.

5874. CLINTON B. FISK (Orville, Ephraim, Abram, Jonathan, John, Benjamin, John, John, Phinehas, Thomas, Robert, Simon, Simon, William, Symond), b. June 13, 1873, Austin, Mich.; m. Jan. 11, 1896, Anna Woolworth, b. Deerfield, Mich., June 26, 1876. He is a shingle weaver; res. s. p. Altoona, Mich.

5934-1. JAMES R. FISKE (John L., John, Mial, Jeremiah, Job, Benjamin, John, John, Phinehas, Thomas, Robert, Simon, Simon, William, Symond), b. ———; m. ——— ———. James R. Fiske, son of John L. Fiske, a cousin of Philander, served in the Confederate Army. He lived at San Antonio, Tex., and was conscripted. He was with Lee's famous army of northern Virginia which confronted the Army of the Potomac in so many desperate and bloody engagements; res. San Antonio, Tex.

5934-31. HARLEY AUGUSTUS FISK (Harley, Job W., Moses, Jeremiah, Job, Benjamin, John, John, Phinehas, Thomas, Robert, Simon, Simon, William, Symond), b. No. Scituate, R. I., Apr. 9, 1839; m. in Providence, Sept. 10, 1860, Helen Maria Rouse, b. Feb. 18, 1842; res. 143 Broad St., Providence, R. I.

    6471-1. i.   JOSEPHINE, b. Apr. 30, 1862; m. Oct. 24, 1882, Edgar Avery Smith.

5934-35. WILLIAM HARRISON FISK (Albert, Job, Moses, Jeremiah, Job, Benjamin, John, John, Phinehas, Thomas, Robert, Simon, Simon, William, Symond), b. Scituate, R. I., June 11, 1842; m. at Webster, Mass., in Apr., 1867, Mary E. Pavlk; res. 113½ Beacon Ave., Providence, R. I.

    6471-2. i.   ALBERT C., b. Oct. 17, 1871; m. May 22, 1895; res. Windsor Locks, Conn.

5935. BRADFORD MELVIN FISKE (Noah, Caleb, Noah, Noah, Noah, Benjamin, John, John, Phinehas, Thomas, Robert, Simon, Simon, William, Symond), b. Coventry, R. I., Apr. 18, 1867; m. there Dec. 10, 1889, Phebe A. Corp. b. Foster, R. I., Sept. 14, 1876. He is a mechanic; res. Coventry Centre, R. I.

    6472. i.   BYRON R., b. Jan. 22, 1891.
    6473. ii.   WALTER A., b. Aug. 28, 1892; d. June 6, 1895.

5936. HERBERT ALLEN FISKE (Noah, Caleb, Noah, Noah, Noah, Benjamin, John, John, Phinehas, Thomas, Robert, Simon, Simon, William, Symond), b. Foster, R. I., July 30, 1858; m. in Centerville, Oct. 11, 1877, Paulina Read Salisbury, b. Feb. 17, 1859. He was a carpenter; res. Anthony, R. I.

    6474. i.   JENNIE MELISSA, b. May 20, 1878; res. A.

5944. WILLIAM HENRY FISKE (Daniel B., Caleb, Noah, Noah, Noah, Benjamin, John, John, Phinehas, Thomas, Robert, Simon, Simon, William, Symond), b. Cranston, Harrisville, R. I., July 5, 1864; m. Oct. 26, 1891, Marietta Willard Tew, b. Feb. 26, 1861. He is a farmer. His postoffice address is Athol, Mass.; res. Royalston, Mass.

    6475. i.   VERA ANNA, b. Jan. 21, 1895.

5946. WILBUR DRIGGS FISK (William J., Joel S., Solomon, Ichabod E., Ebenezer, Ebenezer, John, John, Phinehas, Thomas, Robert, Simon, Simon, William, Symond), b. Fort Howard, Wis., Sept. 10, 1856; m. at Valentine, Neb., Jan. 8, 1885, Eva Cornell, b. Feb. 28, 1857. After having completed his education at Lawrence University, he entered the business of his father at Green Bay, the firm being known as W. D. Fisk & Co., contractors of telegraph poles, ties and timber supplies to railroads, and has been continuously engaged in this business to the present time. Politically he is a Republican, and has held various city and county offices. He is a Freemason, having attained the Knight Templar degree; res. Green Bay, Wis.

    6476. i.   HIRAM C., b. Oct. 19, 1885.
    6477. ii.   MARY, b. July 6, 1887.

5948. HARRY W. FISK (William J., Joel S., Solomon, Ichabod E., Ebenezer, Ebenezer, John, John, Phinehas, Thomas, Robert, Simon, Simon, William, Symond), b. Mar. 9, 1866, Fort Howard, Wis.; m. July 22, 1890, Amy Howland, of Chico, Cal. He received his education in the high school of Green Bay, and on attaining his majority became a member of the firm of W. D. Fisk & Co., contractors of railway supplies, ties, timber and woods at Green Bay, and has continued in that business since. He is an active worker in the Republican party; res. Green Bay, Wis.

    6478. i.   ELSIE, b. ———.
    6479. ii.   HARRY H., b. ———.

5949. GEORGE WALLACE FISK (William J., Joel S., Solomon, Ichabod E., Ebenezer, Ebenezer, John, John, Phinehas, Thomas, Robert, Simon, Simon, William, Symond), b. Mar. 8, 1868; m. July 22, 1889, Maggie Doty, b. Jan. 2, 1871; res. Green Bay, Wis.

    6480. i.   EARL ELLSWORTH, b. Feb. 27, 1892.
    6481. ii.   RUTH, b. Sept. 9, 1894.

5963. PERLEE ROLLIN FISK (Luman, John, John, John, John, John, John, Phinehas, Thomas, Robert, Simon, Simon, William, Symond), b. Lebanon, N. Y., May 15, 1852; m. there Sept. 24, 1872, Hattie A. Billings, b. May 21, 1854. He is a farmer; res. Hamilton, N. Y.

    6482. i.   GRACE BILLINGS, b. July 22, 1877.
    6483. ii. MILLIE ANGELINE, b. Feb. 8, 1880.
    6484. iii. MATTIE MAY, b. June 26, 1883.

5964. ISAAC LUMAN FISKE (Luman, John, John, John, John, John, John, Phinehas, Thomas, Robert, Simon, Simon, William, Symond), b. Lebanon, N. Y., July 3, 1855; m. there May 26, 1875, Addie M. La Sells, b. Aug. 8, 1855. He is a traveling salesman; res. 709 N. 12th St., Beatrice, Neb.

    6485. i. HAROLD L., b. 1889.
    6486. ii. FLORENCE, b. 1884.

5965. EPHRAIM J. FISK (Luman, John, John, John, John, John, John, Phinehas, Thomas, Robert, Simon, Simon, William, Symond), b. Lebanon, N. Y., Dec. 4, 1860; m. Oct. 7, 1884, Eugenie Randall, b. Apr. 22, 1861. He is a lawyer; res. Fairport, N. Y.

    6487. i. MILDRED, b. Nov. 7, 1888.
    6488. ii. HAZEL, b. Aug. 17, 1890.

6032. WILBUR F. FISK (David H., Friend L., David, John, John, John, John, John, Nathaniel, William, Robert, Simon, Simon, William, Symond), b. Ellington, N. Y., Mar. 20, 1855; m. July 4, 1874, Mattie Davis; res. Ellington, N. Y.

    6489. i. MERL W., b. June 26, 1876.
    6490. ii. BERTHA E., b. June 9, 1879; m. Nov. 14, 1894, Jay Milspaw; res. Ellington.
    6491. iii. TEDDY L., b. July 17, 1886.
    6492. iv. CHAS. H., b. Nov. 16, 1888.
    6493. v. HOYT VICTOR, b. Dec. 26, 1892; d. Sept. 2, 1893.

6056. PROF. ANDREW HAMLIN FISK (Andrew J., William A., Ezra, Amariah, David, John, John, Nathaniel, William, Robert, Simon, Simon, William, Symond), b. Mar. 4, 1861, Malden, Ill.; m. in Keokuk, Ia., Nov. 6, 1890, Teresa Anna Brosch, b. Nov. 7, 1872. He is an expert optician; res. s. p. 221 W. South St., Galesburg, Ill.

6060. GOLOND DOLPH FISK (Andrew J., William A., Ezra, Amariah, David, John, John, Nathaniel, William, Robert. Simon, Simon, William, Symond), b. Nov. 14, 1867, Mendota, Ill.; m. Oct. 28, 1892, Cora E. Maxwell, b. Nov. 15, 1867. He is a painter; res. 850 Polk St., Chicago, Ill.

    6494. i. CORINNE, b. Sept. 6, 1893.
    6495. ii. MARY, b. Feb. 4, 1895; d. May 1, 1895.

6061. PROF. KARL D. C. V. FISK (Andrew J., William A., Ezra, Amariah, David, John, John, Nathaniel, William, Robert, Simon, Simon, William, Symond), b. Nov. 3, 1869, at Meriden, Ill.; m. at West Union, Ia., Oct. 12, 1892, Lorena E. Farr, b. Mar. 10, 1868. He is a scientific optician; res. s. p. West Union, Iowa.

6082. WALLACE V. FISK (Asa S., Asa, Asa, Jonathan, Jonathan, David, John, John, Nathaniel, William, Robert, Simon, Simon, William, Symond), b. Apr. 4, 1856, in Bradford, Pa.; m. Dec. 30, 1880, Mrs. Jennie Rosencrance, b. Apr. 2, 1861; res. 14 Second St., Binghamton, N. Y.

    6496. i   EARNEST I., b. Apr. 16, 1882.
    6497. ii ALTRON C., b. Aug. 20, 1889.

6083. FRANK OTHNIEL FISK (Asa S., Asa, Asa, Jonathan, Jonathan, David, John, John, Nathaniel, William, Robert, Simon, Simon, William, Symond), b. Potterville, Pa., Feb. 4, 1859; m. in Harrisburgh, Oct. 4, 1889, Teresa M. Morley, b. Feb. 25, 1861. He is a carpenter; res. 247 Conklin Ave., Binghamton, N. Y.

    6498. i. EDNA C., b. Nov. 9, 1883.

6128. ROBERT TRENT PAINE FISKE (Oliver, Robert T. P., Oliver, Nathan, Nathan, Nathan, Nathan, Nathaniel, William, Robert, Simon, Simon, William, Symond), b. Iowa City, Ia., Apr. 24, 1860; m. at New Brighton, N. Y., Miriam Walley Miller, b. Mar. 11, 1873. He has never meddled in politics or other

40

public affairs, until during the last year, 1895. He is a Democrat, and was appointed Postmaster at the Tompkinsville office by President Cleveland, on Oct. 1, 1895; graduated from the Columbia College Law School, and was admitted to the bar at Poughkeepsie, N. Y., in the year 1881; res. New Brighton, N. Y.; New York office, 102 Wall St.

6499. i. MIRIAM, b. July 24, 1894.

6173. ORLO J. FISKE (Josiah, Jeremiah, Josiah, Josiah, Josiah, Nathan, Nathan, Nathaniel, William, Robert, Simon, Simon, William, Symond), b. Temple, N. H., Dec. 11, 1848; m. at Manchester, N. H., Dec. 25, 1878, Francena M. Fogg, b. in Boston, Apr. 22, 1854; d. June 10, 1891. He was a hardware merchant and died in Boston. He d. June 3, 1894; res. Temple, N. H., and Boston, Mass.

6500. i. ORLO J., b. Nov. 1, 1879.
6501. ii. MAUDE M., b. Aug. 20, 1881.
6502. iii. HARRY M., b. Oct. 12, 1885.

6182. CHARLES ANTHONY FISK (Charles A., Artemas, Josiah, Josiah, Josiah, Nathan, Nathan, Nathaniel, William, Robert, Simon, Simon, William, Symond), b. Oct. 1, 1849, in Hayfield, Pa.; m. Aug. 1, 1875, Ella A. Morse, b. Oct. 23, 1856. He was born in Hayfield, worked for his father summers, and attended school winters until he was 21 years of age. He taught school for a short time, but since his marriage he has been engaged in farming; res. Hayfield, Pa.

6503. i. ADA ADELL, b. Jan. 3, 1877.
6504. ii. FLORA, b. Oct. 12, 1882.
6505. iii. SYLVIA, b. July 6, 1893.

6183. ROYAL ALONZO FISK (Charles A., Artemas, Josiah, Josiah, Josiah, Nathan, Nathan, Nathaniel, William, Robert, Simon, Simon, William, Symond). b. Hayfield, Pa., Sept. 7, 1851; m. Apr. 22, 1877, Ida Satterlee, b. Mar. 2, 1852. Royal, like his elder brother, spent his early days on a farm and attending school each winter. After he was 21 years of age he spent a few years running a shingle factory and planing mill, then settled on a farm where he now resides; res. Hayfield, Pa.

6506. i. MYRTLE, b. Feb. 9, 1881.
6507. ii. GRACE, b. Nov. 11, 1883.
6508. iii. LILLIAN, b. May 4, 1888; d. Oct. 28, 1890.

6184. BENJAMIN WOOSTER FISK (Charles A., Artemas, Josiah, Josiah, Josiah, Nathan, Nathan, Nathaniel, William, Robert, Simon, Simon, William, Symond), b. Hayfield, Pa., Aug. 5, 1853; m. Mar. 23, 1887, Ovis McGalsey. His early days, like those of his brothers', were spent on a farm and attending school. After he was 21 years of age he went to Kinsman, Ohio, and embarked in the small fruit and market gardening business and teaching school winters. He subsequently married and settled on a farm where he is now engaged in the same business; res. Vernon, Ohio.

6509. i. They had one child, but it only lived three days.

6185. SHELDON W. FISKE (Horace, David, Josiah, Josiah, Josiah, Nathan, Nathan, Nathaniel, William, Robert, Simon, Simon, William, Symond). b. Oxford, N. Y., Dec. 6, 1851; m. Feb. 22, 1877, Sarah R. Jones; res. Oxford and De Ruyter, N. Y.

6510. i. GRACE S., b. May 26, 1883; d. Oct. 21, 1894.

6186. CHARLES H. FISKE (Horace, David, Josiah, Josiah, Josiah, Nathan, Nathan, Nathaniel, William, Robert, Simon, Simon, William, Symond), b. Oxford, N. Y., May 30, 1853; m. Nov. 10, 1874, Alice Sweet, d. Jan. 14, 1877; res. Oxford, N. Y.

6511. i. CHARLES H., b. May 4, 1876.

6187-4. AMOS FISKE (Galon B., John, David, Josiah, Josiah, Nathan, Nathan, Nathaniel, William, Robert, Simon, Simon, William, Symond), b. Readfield, Me., Jan. 20, 1838; m. Oct. 6, 1866, Julia D. Hayden, b. So. Thomaston, Me., Feb. 25, 1839. During the war he was a member of the First Maine Cavalry; is a carpenter by trade; res. Rockland, Me.

6511-1. i. FRED'K O., b. Mar. 18, 1868; m. Oct. 26, 1892, Minnie L. Mitchell.
6511-2. ii. CHAS. A., b. Jan. 23, 1872; d. Apr. 12, 1880.

6511-2½. iii. JENNIE C., b. Oct. 6, 1876.
6511-3. iv. IRENE H., b. Dec. 24, 1880.

6187-8. GEORGE FRANKLIN FISK (Galon, John, David, Josiah, Josiah, Nathan, Nathan, Nathaniel, William, Robert, Simon, Simon, William, Symond), b. Readfield, Me., 1846; m. in Chillicothe, Mo., in 1872, Berthena E. Cox, b. 1846. He is a farmer; res. Chillicothe, Mo.

6511-4. i. CHAS. WALTER, b. Sept. 23, 1873.
6511-5. ii. MARCY OLIVE, b. Apr. 26, 1875; m. Joseph Couch; res. C.

6187-18. GEORGE HENRY FISK (Joel H., John, David, Josiah, Josiah, Nathan, Nathan, Nathaniel, William, Robert, Simon, Simon, William, Symond), b. Readfield, Me., Feb. 11, 1847; m. Nov. 13, 1881, at Chicago, Mary R. Stemper, b. Feb. 4, 1863. He is a carpenter; res. Chicago Lawn, Ill.

6511-6. i. GEO. EDWIN, b. Feb. 8, 1883.
6511-7. ii. MARY LOUISA, b. Dec. 10, 1884.
6511-8. iii. NELLIE LORETTA, b. June 24, 1888; d. Aug. 1, 1889.

6187-19. DR. CHARLES TURNER FISK (Joel H., John, David, Josiah, Josiah, Nathan, Nathan, Nathaniel, William, Robert, Simon, Simon, William, Symond), b. East Boston, Mass., Aug. 3, 1849; m. at Hollowell, Me., Mar. 23, 1874, Ella O. Hersey, b. Jan. 19, 1848. He was born at East Boston. When quite young his parents moved to Readfield, Me., and afterward to North Whitefield, Me. His life up to the age of 13 was as usual to boys brought up in the country. When 13 years of age he went to work for a hardware firm in Gardiner, Me., and remained with them several years. At the age of 17 he went to California, crossing the Isthmus, twenty-six days en route; remained four years and six months in California; returned to his mother's home in Searsmont, Me., in 1871. During the year he went into the wholesale hay business at Gardiner, Me., remaining until 1872, when he went to Lewiston, Me., and bought a drug store; continued the business until 1875, when the fever for traveling (and seeing new lands) got possession of him. He sold his drug business and started for the west in 1876, landing in Minneapolis, Minn., in midsummer; followed various vocations for a year or more, when he finally took up his present specialty, the treatment of rectal diseases, in 1877. He remained there one year, under instructions of one Dr. Steele, one of Minneapolis' best physicians. He practiced for a while in Kalamazoo, Mich.; finally returned to Maine in 1878; located in Auburn and remained in practice there until 1889, when he finally moved to his present location, Lewiston, Me. He has visited the city of Portland regularly every Saturday for the past twelve years; has had a lucrative practice there during that time, and has built up a practice throughout the entire state that is very gratifying to him; res. 332 Main St., Lewiston, Me.

6511-9. i. AGNES MAY, b. Apr. 26, 1876; d. Apr. 29, 1876.
6511-10. i. EDWIN COOPER, b. June 7, 1881.
6511-11. ii. ETHEL LOUISA, b. Feb. 17, 1884.

6187-22. CAPT. WILLIAM HENRY FISK (Moses H., Benjamin, David, Josiah, Josiah, Nathan, Nathan, Nathaniel, William, Robert, Simon, Simon, William, Symond), b. Feb. 20, 1851, in Rockland, Me.; m. in Gardiner, Ellen Geddes, b. in England. He is a sea captain; res. Sumner St., Rockland, Me.

6511-12. i. LOUISE GEDDES, b. 1890.
6511-13. ii. KATHLEEN HARRIET, b. 1893.

6187-27. HON. CHARLES HENRY FISKE (Benjamin, Benjamin, David, Josiah, Josiah, Nathan, Nathan, Nathaniel, William, Robert. Simon, Simon, William, Symond), b. Camden, Me., July 3, 1840; m. Nov. 27, 1865, Mary E. Spofford, b. Mar. 16, 1846. Hon. C. H. Fiske, of Old Orchard, was the able representative in the Legislature from Old Orchard (the first from that town) in 1889. He has been in the summer hotel business for twenty years, and has been eminently successful in that line of work. Hotel Fiske at Old Orchard is noted far and wide for its excellent accommodations and has an immense patronage. Mr. Fiske has added to his house the present year. It is three stories high. He never has been able to accommodate all those who have applied for rooms and the addition will be well received by the general public. Mr. Fiske cannot be supassed in the business in which he is engaged; res. Old Orchard, Me.

6511-14. i. AUSTIN H., b. Dec. 20, 1871.

6511-15. ii.   FREDDIE, b. Oct. 25, 1876; d. Nov. 12, 1876.
6511-16. iii. EVA MAY, b. Jan. 21, 1878; d. Jan. 22, 1878.
6511-17. iv.   FLORENCE W., b. Dec. 6, 1880.

6187-39. HIRAM ABIFF FISK (William B., David, David, Josiah, Josiah, Nathan, Nathan, Nathaniel, William, Robert, Simon, Simon, William, Symond), b. Jan. 10, 1833; m. Apr. 13, 1858, Clara Louise Ward, b. Jan. 25, 1840; d. Sept. 9, 1859; m. 2d, Nov. 14, 1860, Martha Francis Ward; res. Indianapolis, Ind., and Ottawa, Kan.

6511-18. i.   WILLIAM WARD, b. Mar. 27, 1862; m. Sept. 21, 1884, Ida M. Leake.
6511-19. ii. HENRY MORTON, b. July 27, 1864; m. Nellie A. France.
6511-20. iii. CLARA MAY, b. Aug. 17, 1866; d. Oct. 12, 1885.
6511-21. iv. ARTHUR WARD, b. Oct. 3, 1868.
6511-22. v.   ROBERT, b. Oct. 17, 1870; d. Aug. 4, 1871.
6511-23. vi. MABEL, b. Nov. 24, 1873.
6511-24. vii. EDITH EUGENIA, b. Feb. 25, 1876.
6511-25. viii. ROSA IRENA, b. Apr. 1, 1879; d. Aug. 13, 1880.
6511-26. ix. EARL RUSSELL, b. Nov. 24, 1881.
6511-27. x.   RALPH, b. July 23, 1884; d. Feb. 2, 1885.

6187-40. CHARLES FISK (William B., David, David, Josiah, Josiah, Nathan, Nathan, Nathaniel, William, Robert, Simon, Simon, William, Symond), b. Fiskburg, Kenton County, Ky., May 25, 1834; m. at Aurora, Ind., Semy Elliott, b. May, 1840. He is a street contractor; res. Aurora, Ind.

6511-28. i.   JAMES H., b. 1861; res. Cincinnati, Ohio.
6511-29. ii. NELLY, b. 1863; res. Chattanooga, Tenn.
6511-30. iii. ALVA, b. ———.
6511-31. iv. CHARLES, b. ———.
6511-32. v.   EVA, b. ———.

6187-42. HIRAM FISKE (John D., David, David, Josiah, Josiah, Nathan, Nathan, Nathaniel, William, Robert, Simon, Simon, William, Symond), b. Campbell County, Ky., Mar. 28, 1818; m. at So. Hope, Me., Mary E. Bowley, b. Apr. 14, 1822. He is a carpenter; res. So. Hope, Me.

6511-35a. i. EDITH F., b. Mar. 13, 1847; m. Sept. 22, 1872, ——— Dunbar; res. So. Hope.
6511-35b. ii. CLARA L., b. Dec. 29, 1850; res. So. Hope.
6511-35c. iii. VALEDA C., b. Feb. 5, 1853; m. Jan. 1, 1873, ———Titus; res. 1196 Dorchester Ave., Dorchester, Mass.
6511-35d. iv. DECATUR E., b. Sept. 15, 1855; m. Carrie E. Linnekin.
6511-35e. v. CHARLIE L., b. Nov. 8, 1862; d. Aug. 5, 1864.
6511-35f. vi. NORA A., b. Nov. 9, 1864; res. So. Hope.

6187-43. HENRY CLAY FISKE (William B., David, David, Josiah, Josiah, Nathan, Nathan, Nathaniel, William, Robert, Simon, Simon, William, Symond), b. Cincinnati, Ohio, Oct. 7, 1841; m. in Elizabethtown, Ohio, Sarah Guard, b. Feb. 11, 1846. He is a carriage manufacturer; res. Aurora and Indianapolis, Ind.

6511-35. i.   WM. E., b. 1868; m. ———; res. Indiana.
6511-36. ii. CARRIE EDNA, b. 1873; d. 1891.
6511-37. iii. SHERMAN CARROL, b. 1882; res. Indianapolis.
6511-38. iv. JAMES GUARD, b. Feb. 11, 1870, M. D.; res. unm. Fort Dodge, Ia.

6194. THEODORE VARNUM FISKE (Benjamin N., Walter, Walter, Daniel, Josiah, Nathan, Nathan, Nathaniel, William, Robert, Simon, Simon, William, Symond), b. Medway, Me., Feb. 13, 1849; m. there Augusta Hathaway. He d. June 12, 1880; res. Medway, Me.

6512. i.   THEODORE EDGAR, b. 1873.
6513. ii.   HARRIE, b. 1876.
6514. iii. GILBERT DIXON, b. 1881.

6202. FRED J. FISKE (Benjamin A., Benjamin N., Walter, Daniel, Josiah, Nathan, Nathan, Nathaniel, William, Robert, Simon, Simon, William, Symond), b. Mar. 12, 1854, Mattawamkeag, Me.; m. May 24, 1878, Ada M. Pond, b. Oct. 2, 1851. He is a surveyor; res. 105 Date St., Bangor, Me.

6515. i. MAUDE LUELLA, b. Nov. 21, 1878.
6516. ii. GRACE MAY, b. July 27, 1880.

6220. WILSON FISKE (Frederick B., Samuel C., Joshua, Henry, Henry, Nathan, Nathan, Nathan, Nathaniel, William, Robert, Simon, Simon, William, Symond), b. New York City, May 20, 1855; m. Sept. 12, 1883, Annie Trescott Southard, b. So. Boston, Nov. 3, 1854, dau. of Zibeon and Helen Maria (Trescott) Southard, d. Feb. 19, 1894; res. New York City, N. Y.; add. 15 Beekman St.
6517. i. PAUL SOUTHARD, b. Aug. 30, 1884.
6518. ii. MILDRED, b. Dec. 23, 1893.

6254. JULIUS M. FISK (Lovell W., Alfred W., Sylvanus, William, William, William, Nathan, Nathan, Nathaniel, William, Robert, Simon, Simon, William, Symond), b. Feb. 17, 1856; m. Dec. 19, 1881, Clara Ellison; res. Chewelah, Wash.
6519. i. RAYMOND, b. Oct. 19, 1882; d. Oct. 27, 1889.
6520. ii. ALICE E., b. May 16, 1885.

6255. CLEMENT L. FISK (Lovell W., Alfred W., Sylvanus, William, William, William, Nathan, Nathan, Nathaniel, William, Robert, Simon, Simon, William, Symond), b. Oct. 15, 1857; m. Oct. 24, 1885, Charlotte Gilbert; res. 644 Selby Ave., St. Paul, Minn.
6521. i. EARL G., b. Apr. 17, 1891.

6272. HON. CHARLES H. FISK (Henry C., John, Rufus, Rufus, Stephen, William, Nathan, Nathan, Nathaniel, William, Robert, Simon, Simon, William, Symond), b. Manchester, Mich., June 19, 1858; m. at Clinton, Oct. 3, 1882, Ida J. Dorr, b. Nov. 20, 1858. His mother was a daughter of Job Graves, a native of Deerfield, Franklin County, Mass., and a descendant of the early settlers in the colonies. Therefore his ancestors were strictly of New England descent and of the oldest families of New England, and his grandfathers both partook of the characteristics of the New England people. He has often made the statement that of all the men he has ever known, he has not known of better men than his grandfathers. After his father was killed in the army, with his mother and younger brother he removed to Franklin Township, Lenawee County, Mich., where he attended country schools. These, supplemented by two years in the village schools at Clinton, in the same county, and one year at Adrian College, in the same county, completed his preparatory education. He taught country schools for three years, and afterward, at the age of 20, entered the law office of Alfred Russell, of Detroit, Mich. After eighteen months' study he was admitted to the bar and practiced common law for five years, after which he took up the study and later the practice of patent law, of which he now makes a specialty. In the fall of 1894 he was nominated by the Republican party in Detroit as one of ten Representatives from the city at large in the State Legislature; he was recognized as one of the leaders of the House, and his services to his constituents is indicated in the newspaper notices of the day. He is about five feet ten inches in height, and weighs about 250 pounds. He has always been a Republican in politics, as were his father and grandfather before him. His grandfather had liberal ideas in religious matters. His father was a member of the Congregational Church, but he has never affiliated with any church, and has been considered liberal in his views. One of the Detroit papers in referring to the Representatives in the Legislature said of Hon. Chas. H. Fisk: "Fisk bore himself all through as the opponent of such methods as those which led to the eternal disgrace of that body, and he took the side of the people as against that of the corporations. In all things he acted well, but he was only a drop in an ocean most of the time. A really strong man, an honest man, a man of good information and some undoubted ambition to occupy higher political station, he was the one member of the delegation from Detroit who can be said to have made the most favorable impression at the capital." Res. Detroit, Mich.; add. 42 Hodges Block.
6522. i. ISABELL M., b. June 30, 1883.
6523. ii. HENRY C., b. Mar. 12, 1887; d. Feb. 19, 1891.

6275. JOHN RUSSELL FISK (Eli, John, Rufus, Rufus, Stephen, William, Nathan, Nathan, Nathaniel, William, Robert, Simon, Simon, William, Symond), b. Tompkins, Mich., Apr. 3, 1867; m. there May 8, 1890, Jennie Tompkins; res. Tompkins, Mich.
6524. i. EDITH, b. Mar. 28, 1891.

6309. OTHO H. FISK (Jason H., Rodney, Josiah, Josiah, Nathan, William, Nathan, Nathaniel, William, Robert, Simon, Simon, William, Symond), b. Chester, Mass., Aug. 29, 1866; m. Dec. 10, 1890, Julia E. Case, b. July 28, 1878. The earlier part of his life while a boy was spent on old homestead, four miles from Huntington, in Chester. He left home when about 15 years old; went to Springfield, engaged to work one year at meat business and 'here continued for one year. At the end of year the proprietor sold out and he engaged next store in bakery business; had been there only three months when sickness compelled him to retire from this business, and he was unable to do much for a year. Then worked at the lumber and grain business with his father at Huntington, continuing until Nov., 1888, when he began for himself in same business. In 1889 he sold out and went to Kearney City, Neb., where he remained four months; when he returned and began a year of study at Childs Business College, finishing in July, 1890. He then engaged with F. W. Tucker as Fisk & Tucker, to carry on meat business on State Street, Springfield, but sold out in about three months to Mr. Tucker, as business was very dull. He next went to Huntington, where he was married Dec. 10, 1890, and again began with his father in the lumber and feed business, which he continued until Sept. 1891, when he began in the meat business, which he has since carried on together with apples and fruit of all kinds. In 1895 he shipped about forty car loads of apples. In 1894 he bought a small place three-fourths of a mile from Huntington, where he and family live. He has two children, a boy and a girl; res. Huntington, Mass.

    6525. i.   RUTH MAE, b. Sept. 15, 1891.
    6526. ii.   PAUL EDWARD, b. Jan. 13, 1893.

6340. DOUGLAS ANDRUS FISKE (Smith W., Abram C., Nathan, Josiah, Nathan, William, Nathan, Nathan, Nathaniel, William, Robert, Simon, Simon, William, Symond), b. Coldwater, Mich., Feb. 2, 1867; m. at Minneapolis, Minn., Sept. 22, 1891, Alice V. Torrance, b. Mar. 8, 1870. He was born in Coldwater, Mich., where he resided until he was 17 years of age, attending the public schools of that city. In 1885, together with his parents and brothers, he moved to Minneapolis and entered the high school at that place and graduated therefrom in the year 1886 with second honors. He attended the University of Minnesota during the fall of 1886 and 1887, when he was compelled, on account of health, to go to California, where he remained for a year and a half, residing at various places from San Francisco down to San Diego; spent a year at Los Angeles in the real estate business, having purchased one-third of 5,000 acres, and his company platted a town, which they called Carleton, situated twenty-six miles from Los Angeles. He returned to Minneapolis in the summer of 1888 and again attended the University of Minnesota for another year, when he entered the law department in 1889 and graduated therefrom in 1891. He was married to Miss Alice Torrance, of that city, and ever since that time has been actually engaged in the practice of law; res. 4626 Fremont Ave. S., Minneapolis, Minn.

DOUGLAS ANDRUS FISKE.

    6527. i.   TORRANCE, b. Sept. 30, 1892.
    6528. ii.   LOIS, b. Apr. 20, 1894.

6389. GEORGE WALDO FISKE (David W., Timothy, David, David, John, John, Nathaniel, Nathan, Nathaniel, William, Robert, Simon, Simon, William, Symond), b. Nov. 5, 1862; m. at Columbia, Conn., 1889, Mary Bascom; res. Rockville, Conn.

6529. i.　LEON B., b. 1893.

6390.　EDWARD EVERETT FISKE (David W., Timothy, David, David, John, John, Nathaniel, Nathan, Nathaniel, William, Robert, Simon, Simon, William, Symond), b. June 30, 1865; m. at Vernon, Conn., Oct. 19, 1891, Luella Doan; res. Vernon, Conn.

6530. i.　RAYMOND D., b. Aug., 1892.

6402.　WALTER HENRY FISKE (J. Milton, Abner, John, David, John, John, Nathaniel, Nathan, Nathaniel, William, Robert, Simon, Simon, William, Symond), b. Holliston, Mass., Apr. 27, 1864; m. in Boston, Feb. 14, 1886, Ada M. Gifford, of West Brookfield. He d. May 6, 1893; res. Holliston, Mass.

6531. i.　LEWIS WORTHINGTON, b. Apr. 6, 1887.
6532. ii.　MARION ALICE, b. Oct. 26, 1888.
6533. iii.　WALTER RAYMOND, b. Oct. 15, 1890.

6412.　CHARLES A. FISK (George C., Thomas T., Thomas, John, Isaac, John, Nathaniel, Nathan, Nathaniel, William, Robert, Simon, Simon, William, Symond), b. Springfield, Mass., Aug. 15, 1853; m. Oct. 17, 1887, Jennie Graves, of Springfield, Mass., b. Feb. 18, 1855; d. June 9, 1889; m. 2d, Oct. 23, 1894, Helena J. Young, b. Nov. 5, 1868. He was born in Springfield, Mass., and has always resided there; was educated at the public schools, and after completing his education has been in the employ of the Wason Manufacturing Company as cashier; res. Springfield, Mass.

6534. i.　LENA, b. June 29, 1879; d. Aug. 9, 1879.
6535. ii.　MATTIE, b. June 2, 1881.

6418.　FRED NATHANIEL FISK (Harrison F., John B., Thomas T., Thomas, John, Isaac, John, Nathaniel, Nathan, Nathaniel, William, Robert, Simon, Simon, William, Symond), b. Hinsdale, N. H., Aug. 3, 1867; m. Oct. 11, 1894, Carrie A. Ware, of Southbridge, Mass., b. there Sept. 14, 1868. He is connected with the freight department of New York, New Haven and Hartford Railroad; res. s. p. 256 Portsea St., New Haven, Conn.

6423.　JAMES WILLARD FISKE (William O., Daniel H., William T., Daniel, Isaac, John, Nathaniel, Nathan, Nathaniel, William, Robert, Simon, Simon, William, Symond), b. Oswego, N. Y., Dec. 12, 1870; m. July 12, 1891, Margaret D. McCarthy, b. Dec. 14, 1873. He is a clerk and is connected with the Washburn & Moen Manufacturing Company; res. Worcester, Mass.

6536. i.　MAY C., b. May, 1895.

6511-1.　FREDERICK O. FISKE (Amos, Galon B., John, David, Josiah, Josiah, Nathan, Nathan, Nathaniel, William, Robert, Simon, Simon, William, Symond), b. Rockland, Me., Mar. 18, 1868; m. Oct. 26, 1892, Minnie L. Mitchell; res. Bangor, Me.

6537. i.　LEROY SANGSTER, b. Sept. 3, 1894.

6511-19.　HENRY MORTON FISK (Hiram A., William B., David, David, Josiah, Josiah, Nathan, Nathan, Nathaniel, William, Robert, Simon, Simon, William, Symond), b. July 27, 1864; m. at Lyndon, Kan., July 21, 1886, Nellie Amelia France, b. Komo, Ill., Apr. 29, 1867; res. Chicago, Ill.

6538. i.　LEON WALTER, b. Oct. 11, 1887.
6539. ii.　GLEN EIMEN, b. Dec. 19, 1889.
6540. iii.　ROLLIN, b. Mar. 11, 1892.
6541. iv.　WINNIFRED HESTER, b. June 29, 1895.

6511-35d.　DECATUR E. FISKE (Hiram, John D., David, David, Josiah, Josiah, Nathan, Nathan, Nathaniel, William, Robert, Simon, Simon, William, Symond), b. South Hope, Me., Sept. 15, 1855; m. at Union, Mar. 4, 1882, Carrie E. Linnekin, b. Mar. 24, 1858. He is proprietor of the Fiske House at South Hope; res. South Hope, Me.

6542. i.　ETTA LOUISE, b. Nov. 18, 1883.
6543. ii.　MYRTLE BLANCHE, b. June 29, 1890.

FISKE INDEX.

Christian Names of Fiskes and Fisks.

INDEX TO OTHER NAMES.

✝